Foundations of Business Law and Legal Environment

Seventh Edition

PHILLIP J. SCALETTA, JR.
Krannert Graduate School of Management
Purdue University

GEORGE D. CAMERON III
Ross School of Business
The University of Michigan

Foundations of Business Law and Legal Environment, Seventh Edition

Phillip J. Scaletta, Jr., Krannert Graduate School of Management, Purdue University

George D. Cameron III, Ross School of Business, The University of Michigan

Executive Editors: Michele Baird, Maureen Staudt, and Michael Stranz

Marketing Manager: Lydia Lester

Managing Editor: Greg Albert

Sr. Marketing Coordinators: Lindsay Annett and Sara Mercurio

Production/Manufacturing Manager: Donna M. Brown

Premedia Supervisor: Becki Walker

Rights and Permissions Specialist: Kalina Ingham Hintz

Production Editor: K.A. Espy

Cover Image: © 2007 Getty

Composition House: Cadmus/KGL

For product information and technology assistance, contact us at
Cengage Learning Customer & Sales Support, 1-800-354-9706

Library of Congress Control Number: 2008931020
Student Edition ISBN 13: 978-1-426-63118-4
Student Edition ISBN 10: 1-426-63118-9

Cengage Learning
5191 Natorp Boulevard
Mason, OH 45040
USA

Cengage Learning products are represented in Canada by
Nelson Education, Ltd.

For your course and learning solutions, visit **academic.cengage.com**
Purchase any of our products at your local college store or at our preferred online store **www.ichapters.com**

Printed in the United States of America
1 2 3 4 5 6 7 12 11 10 09 08

To Helen, on our 63rd
—Phil

To Julie, on our 43rd
—George

And to each other,
on a successful
33-year-collaboration

PREFACE

This seventh edition of **Foundations of Business Law and Legal Environment** continues the basic organization we established in our last revision. We have grouped the legal topics covered in the typical two-term or three-quarter law courses into five "parts"—Legal Environment, Contracts, Property, Finance, and Organizations. Within each part, we cover both case law and statutes, and both private law and regulatory law. Our objective is to provide a unified treatment of the applicable rules on each topic. Our chapter on formation of the contract, for instance, integrates the common law rules on offer and acceptance with the UCC rules for the formation of sales of goods contracts. Similarly, "Property" includes a chapter covering land use and environmental regulation, and "Organizations" includes a chapter covering employment nondiscrimination rules and other employment regulations.

We have continued our full chapter coverage of intellectual Property (with several new cases), in recognition of the importance of this area of the law to the global information-based economy. To maintain the symmetry of this part, we had previously combined leases/bailments of goods and leases of land into one chapter. The UCC's rules on performance and remedies for sales of goods contracts remain in Chapter 14, which covers the general contract rules on these points.

Part I (Legal Environment) was almost completely restructured in our sixth edition, and we have retained that sequencing in this seventh edition. To emphasize the importance of comparative and international law to global business operations, that material appears as Chapter 2. Given the potential application of antitrust law and trade practices law to almost any aspect of business operations, we feel that those materials should probably be covered in our introductory Part I. As a result, this part may look a bit different than others' sequencing.

We continue to believe that students of the law need to read real cases, not just editorial summaries. We want them to read what the court actually said, not just what Phil and George say the court said. Reading the court's actual words is the only way to get the full flavor of the law, and the only way to give the students a chance to analyze and criticize the court's reasoning. We are committed to finding the best teaching cases we can—current, relevant, interesting illustrations. We have thus included some 70 new cases—nearly half of the total, and nearly all from the 2000s—in this edition. Nearly all the chapters have at least one new case; several chapters have three or four new cases. Many of the old, classic favorites that we replaced have been converted into end-of-chapter problems.

We continue to believe that accuracy and completeness are not incompatible with readability. We believe that the legal topics have been covered with a reasonable completeness and a high degree of accuracy. We have tried to present the technical legal concepts in non-technical language and to explain technical terms where they must be used. We urge our colleagues and their students to contact us with any suggestions for improvement. We welcome your input.

April 2008

Phillip J. Scaletta, Jr.

George D. Cameron III

BRIEF CONTENTS

TABLE OF CONTENTS

Part Two
Contract Law

Part Five
Law of Organizations

PART 1

Legal Environment

Part One is designed to introduce you to the law and to provide a basic foundation as you continue through the various specialized parts of this text. For example, Part Two, Contract Law, is a study of contracts and presumes the student has acquired the foundation of Part One.

Part One presents an introduction to the legal environment of business. It covers the definition of law and provides a comparison of law in the United States to that of foreign countries; the civil procedure followed in national and state court systems; the regulation of business by administrative agencies and the constitutional limitations on such regulation; the international legal implications a business person must be aware of when involved in trade outside the United States; the problems of antitrust and trade regulation; criminal law and tort law; and accountants' liability.

All of these general areas comprise an important part of the environment in which a business operates on a day-to-day basis.

CHAPTER 1

Ethics and the Common Law

Chapter Objectives

This chapter will:

- Define the term law.
- Discuss the sources of law in the United States.
- Outline the classifications of law.
- Explain the use of uniform laws in the U.S. legal system.
- Introduce the Restatements of the Law and their role in the legal system.
- Introduce the doctrine of precedent.
- Introduce ethics and the law.
- Explain the history of equity law.

This chapter discusses society's need for rules of human conduct and the relationship between ethical "rules" and legal rules. Our main focus is on the workings of a common law system, using the U.S. legal system as our primary example. We show how the three main distinguishing features of the common law system try to promote the ethical values of truthfulness and fairness in human relationships. We also identify the sources of law in the United States and define the major categories of legal rules.

Society's Rules of Conduct

Nearly all of us live and work in close proximity to others and interact with them daily. For most of us, most of the time, these relationships are probably positive—or at least not negative enough to lead us to demand sanctions against the person guilty of the offensive conduct. Many of the problems that do arise between people are resolved through informal discussions, with a little good will and understanding on both sides. Rarely does a neighbor's loud playing of radios and televisions reach a level that we feel forced to go to court for a remedy, but the courts are there for those exceptional cases.

There are, in other words, informal rules (and sanctions) in addition to society's formal rules and sanctions found in its legal system. Simpler, smaller, more homogeneous societies can function quite well without many formal legal rules. Acceptable conduct is learned by observing others, especially the society's elder members. Customs for the sharing of land, water, and other resources are established through a history of usage. At some point, however, social relationships become so complex and diverse that customary, informal rules no longer provide the needed guidance. Nations trying to function effectively in the terribly complex world of the second millennium will surely need sophisticated legal systems to provide rules and sanctions for today's much more complicated social relationships.

Ethics

How *should* we treat each other? What duties do we owe one another? What is the proper relationship between the citizen and the nation? What is "justice"? These are the kinds of questions usually discussed under the heading of "ethics." Philosophers have pondered over these questions since earliest historical times. Indeed, some of the best studies of these issues were done by the ancient Chinese scholar Confucius and by the early Greek writers Plato and Aristotle. In the intervening centuries, many others—Thomas Aquinas, Immanuel Kant, and John Locke—made important contributions to the discussion. In modern times, authors such as Morris Cohen and John Rawls have continued to expand our understanding of these difficult and profound problems.

Law

When a society reaches that developmental stage in which the informal, customary rules evolve into mandatory forms of behavior, with governmental sanctions for noncompliance, it is appropriate to say that "law" has arrived. Private revenge ("an eye for an eye") is replaced by a criminal prosecution, with the government prosecuting the offender, and often also by a private lawsuit, in which a victim of the offense asks for monetary compensation for the harm caused.

In the broadest sense, the difference between law and ethics is the difference between *must* and *ought*. Law tells us what we must do and provides governmentally imposed sanctions if we fail to do it. Ethics tells us what we should do, but there are no sanctions for purely ethical violations—other than our own consciences, and public disapproval if our unethical conduct comes to light.

Law is a rough synonym for the noun *rule*. A law is a rule of conduct. In the physical sciences, one studies the law of gravity and other similar rules regarding the behavior of physical objects. In this book, we are concerned with the rules for human and organizational conduct for which governmental sanctions are provided. As defined by the famous English jurist William Blackstone, law is the expression of the nation's sovereign, "commanding what is right and prohibiting what is wrong."[1]

In the United States, law is promulgated by the sovereign people, acting through our selected representatives. The people as a whole, through these constitutionally chosen agents, prescribe the rules of conduct for individuals and organizations.

Writing in the late 1800s, the great jurist Oliver Wendell Holmes, Jr., provided another famous definition of law: "The prophecies of what the courts will do in fact, and nothing more pretentious, are what I mean by the law."[2]

At the time, the courts were clearly the dominant legal institution in this country. Congress and the state legislatures were generally not inclined to interfere in individuals' private conduct or business affairs, and there were few regulatory agencies. Today, by contrast, the legal scene has changed a great deal. Our legislatures have created hundreds of national, state, and local regulatory agencies that have the power to issue regulations, to decide disputes on matters falling under their jurisdiction, or to do both. Our legislatures continue to pass increasing number of laws to tax and regulate businesses and individuals. Clearly the courts are only one source of law today, although they still do set the ground rules for the operation of our legal system as a whole.

Justice—The Intersection of Law and Ethics

There is, of course, considerable (but not complete) overlap between ethics and law. In their operations, legal systems generally try to achieve justice, which is itself an ethical concept. Some criminal laws prohibit actions that would be seen by most, if not all, people as wrongful in an ethical or moral sense—murder, rape, libel, and arson. These crimes are often referred to as *malum in se,* that is, wrong in and of themselves. Other criminal statutes create offenses simply because society needs to have everyone operating under the same set of assumptions, such as which side of the road is the proper place for driving one's motor vehicle. In some nations it is the right-hand side of the road; in others, the left-hand side. There is no ethical or moral superiority in either rule, but each nation must have a set of such automobile operation rules, if chaos is to be avoided.

Out of the many ethical principles developed over the centuries, two—truthfulness and fairness—seem particularly relevant to legal relationships. Both are also principles of long standing, dating back at least to Aristotle's great work, *Nicomachean Ethics.*

Truthfulness is required in all commercial transactions, and indeed in all human interactions, because we communicate with each other. We exchange information and then act, at least in part, on the basis of that information. Lying to the other party in the hopes of gaining a commercial advantage would generally be defined as unethical conduct. For Aristotle, the truth teller was "worthy of praise."

> *[T]he man who loves truth, and is truthful where nothing is at stake, will be more truthful where something is at stake; he will avoid falsehood as something base, seeing that he avoided it even for its own sake; and such a man is worthy of praise.*[3]

Fairness in the context of commercial transactions implies an exchange of values of approximate equality. At least as of the time of the exchange, each party believes he or she is receiving value for value given. However, it is often true that our expectations are not fulfilled. Some of the things we receive turn out not to be as useful or as pleasurable as we imagined they would be. To a great extent, that is simply the nature of things. We often desire something intensely, only to be severely disappointed by the post-acquisition actuality. Fairness in the ethical sense does not imply the "complete satisfaction," which is used in so many advertisements. Fairness does mean that each party receives the thing bargained for and that the thing has a real value. Aristotle also discussed fairness, in the context of what is just:

> *Both the lawless man and the grasping and unfair man are thought to be unjust, so that evidently both the law-abiding and the fair man will be just. The just, then, is the lawful and the fair, the unjust, the unlawful and the unfair.*[4]

The idea of dealing fairly and justly with other people is "the greatest of virtues." "It is complete [virtue] because he who possesses it can exercise his virtue not only in himself but towards his neighbor also; for many men can exercise virtue in their own affairs, but not in their relations to their neighbor."[5]

How, then, does our modern legal system try to implement these two great ethical principles? There are three distinguishing features of an **Anglo-American legal system:** the separate court of equity, the doctrine of precedent, and the trial by jury. Each of the three operates to help ensure truthfulness and fairness in our legal system.

Anglo-American Common Law

Equity

Appropriately enough it is also Aristotle who best explains a legal system's need for **equity.** Equity's flexibility is required to supplement the rigidity of the general legal rules, that is, to provide for the exceptional case.

> *Our next subject is equity and the equitable, . . . and their respective relations to justice and the just. . . .*
>
> *What creates the problem is that the equitable is just, but not the legally just but a correction of legal justice. The reason is that all law is universal but about some things it is not possible to make a universal statement which shall be correct. In those cases, then, in which it is necessary to speak universally, but not possible to do so correctly, the law takes the usual case, though it is not ignorant of the possibility of error. . . . When the law speaks universally, then, and a case arises on it which is not covered by the universal statement, then it is right, where the legislator fails us and has erred by over-simplicity, to correct the omission—to say what the legislator himself would have said had he been present, and would have put into his law if he had known.*[6]

The English legal system responded to its need for equity by developing a second set of courts, using different judges (the chancellors) to administer these supplementary principles. According to Plucknett, however, "many rules which have since become distinctive of chancery make their first appearance in the common law courts" (Theodore F. T. Plucknett, *A Concise History of the Common Law*, 5th ed., Boston: Little, Brown & Company, 1956, p. 677). Further, he says, "[t]here was, therefore, no fundamental inconsistency between equity and common law; the one was not alien to the other." The new Chancery Court "did not originate English Equity, for it simply carried on the work of the older courts by developing in greater fullness and with a different machinery the equity inherent in royal justice" (Plucknett, p. 679).

There was no logical necessity for using different courts to administer the principles of equity. Plucknett remarks on "the abandonment by the common law judges of their ancient powers of discretion." Why this happened remains somewhat unclear. Political factors—fear of giving too much power and independence to the common law judges—probably played a part. Philosophically, most common law lawyers and judges preferred the law's certainty to equity's flexibility. Plucknett notes that "the common law was essentially the law of land." Land titles and land transactions required certainty, not creativity. "The [common law] lawyers had a maxim that they would tolerate a 'mischief' (a failure of substantial justice in a particular case) rather than an 'inconvenience' (a breach of legal principle)" (Plucknett, p. 680).

The chancellors, acting in the king's name, developed a set of equitable remedies for situations in which the normal remedies of the **common law** did not provide complete justice. The **injunction** was the equity remedy to prevent a continuing wrong. The equity court ordered the offender to cease and desist, in the king's name. Failure to comply with the court order could result in a fine or imprisonment. Specific performance was the remedy to require performance of a contract for land or for unique goods. Money damages, the usual common law remedy, would not provide adequate relief in such cases because the plaintiff would still not have the thing bargained for. The chancellors also developed an assortment of other remedies to deal with special situations, including reformation, rescission, restitution, and redemption. They recognized rights created by assignments and trusts. In sum, it was the Chancery Courts, applying the principles of equity, which provided the rules required by a developing English society.

Many aspects of the English legal system were transplanted to the American colonies. Blackstone's *Commentaries on the Laws of England*, first published in 1765, were widely read and widely used in America. "The Commentaries had a tremendous sale there, for not only did they contain some very useful matter on public law, but also served as the principal means of the colonists' information as to the state of English law in general" (Plucknett, p. 287).

After independence, guarantees of the right to trial by jury were written into the U.S. Constitution and the constitutions of most, if not all, states. The Seventh Amendment to the U.S. Constitution preserves the right to a trial by jury in civil cases at common law involving $20 or more. The key phrase *at common law* thus excludes equity cases and freezes the law/equity distinction into the Constitution. Later, when most states and the national courts combined legal procedure with equity procedure, these constitutional provisions meant that the statutory combination could not be complete. The law/equity distinction still has to be made to determine whether the parties are entitled to a trial by jury.

England reunited law and equity, by statute, in 1875. Similar recombination has taken place in the U.S. courts and in most states. Judges in these "combined" courts have all the powers of the common law judges and all the powers of the equity chancellors. A few states still maintain separate equity courts, most notably Delaware, where many corporate litigations are heard by the Chancery Court.

Whether administered by a separate court or not, the function of equity remains essentially what has been for centuries, that is, providing special remedies to do more complete justice between the parties. In this sense, then, equity continues to serve as "the keepers of the King's [Queen's] conscience." The "maxims" of equity developed by the chancellors retain their force and utility: "Equity acts on the conscience"; "Equity looks to the intent rather than to the form"; "He who seeks equity must do equity." Perhaps the greatest and most basic equitable principle of all is stated as: "Equity will not suffer a wrong to be without a remedy." Even though no longer separate and independent, equity operates within our modern legal system as a built-in guarantor of the ethical principle of fairness.

The *Great West Life* case shows that the distinction between law and equity is alive and well in the new millennium and not just as to the constitutional right to a trial by jury.

Doctrine of Precedent

The **doctrine of precedent** is the second distinguishing feature of an Anglo-American system, or "common-law," system. The key to a common-law system is the courts' decisions in actual cases that have been litigated in the past. Current cases are decided on the basis of the rules announced in prior ones. To produce fairness and predictability, the rule used yesterday to decide the case between Jones and Smith should also be used to decide the similar case that is now before the court between Green and Harris. The working presumption of the system is summed up in the Latin phrase *stare decisis:* "Let the decision stand."

Exhibit 1.1: English Legal System (1350–1873)

Criminal Law	Civil Law				
	Common Law Writs (forms of action)				Equity
	Assumpsit contract dollar damages	Trespass tort dollar damages	Replevin return of personal property	Ejectment return of real property	
JURY	*JURY*				*NO JURY*

CASE 1

Great West Life & Annuity v. Knudson
534 U.S. 204 (2002)

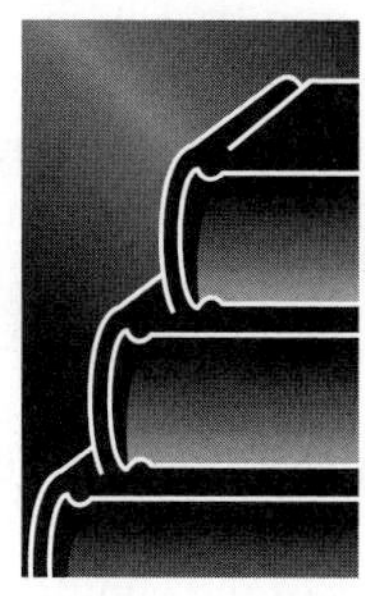

Facts: Janette Knudson was rendered quadriplegic by a car accident in June 1992. She was covered under the medical plan of her husband's employer, Earth Systems, Inc. The plan paid $411,157.11 of her medical expenses, all but $75,000 of which came from Great West insurance company. The plan provides that it can recover for benefits paid by the plan that the beneficiary is entitled to recover from a third party. When Janette and her husband Eric agreed to settle their 1993 state court lawsuit against Hyundai Motor and other defendants for $650,000, Great West objected to the proposed payment to it of only $13,828.70. (A total of $256,745.30 was to go a trust for Janette's future medical expenses; $373,426 for lawyers' fees; and $5,000 to reimburse California Medicaid.)

Great West first tried to have the Knudsons' state lawsuit removed to a U.S. District Court, which ruled that it would not take the case. Great West then filed its own lawsuit in the same U.S. District Court, asking for an injunction—pursuant to section 502(a)(3) of the Employment Retirement Income Security Act (ERISA)—ordering the Knudsons to reimburse the full $411,157.11, from their lawsuit settlement. The U.S. District Court granted summary judgment in favor of the Knudsons, and the U.S. Court of Appeals affirmed. The U.S. Supreme Court granted Great West's petition for certiorari (agreeing to review the decision.)

Issue: Are the plaintiffs requesting an *equitable* remedy?

Decision: No. Judgment affirmed.

Opinion by Justice Scalia: "We have observed repeatedly that ERISA is a 'comprehensive and reticulated statute,' the product of a decade of congressional study of the Nation's private employee benefit system.... We have therefore been especially 'reluctant to tamper with [the] enforcement scheme' embodied in the statute by extending remedies not specifically authorized by its text.... Indeed, we have noted that ERISA's 'carefully crafted and detailed enforcement scheme provides strong evidence that Congress did not intend to authorize other remedies that it simply forgot to incorporate expressly.

"Section 502(a)(3) authorizes a civil action: 'by a participant, beneficiary, or fiduciary (A) to enjoin any act or practice which violates ... the terms of the plan, or (B) to obtain other appropriate equitable relief (i) to redress such violations or (ii) to enforce any provisions of ... the terms of the plan.'...

"As we explained in *Mertens*, 'equitable' relief must mean something less than all relief.' [W]e held that the term 'equitable relief' in S.502(a)(3) must refer to 'those categories of relief that were typically available in equity.'...

"Here, petitioners seek, in essence, to impose personal liability on [the Knudsons] for a contractual obligation to pay money—available in equity....

"First petitioners argue that they are entitled to relief under S.502(a)(3)(A) because they seek 'to enjoin an act or practice'—[the Knudsons'] failure to reimburse the plan—'which violates ... the terms of the plan.' But an injunction to compel the payment of money past due under a contract, or specific performance of a past due monetary obligation, was not typically available in equity....

"Second, petitioners argue that their suit is authorized by S.502(a)(3)(B) because they seek restitution, which they characterize as a form of equitable relief. However, not all relief falling under the rubric of restitution is available in equity. In the days of the divided bench, restitution was available in certain cases at law, and in certain others in equity. *See*, e.g., ... Muir, ERISA Remedies: Chimera or Congressional Compromise?, 81 Iowa L. Rev. 1, 36-37 (1995).... Thus, 'restitution is a legal remedy when ordered in a case at law and an equitable remedy ... when ordered in an equity case,' and whether it is legal or equitable depends on 'the basis for [the plaintiff's] claim' and the nature of the underlying remedies sought....

"[A] plaintiff could seek restitution in equity, ordinarily in the form of a constructive trust or an equitable lien, where money or property identified as belonging in good conscience to the plaintiff could clearly be traced to particular funds or property in the defendant's possession....

"Here, the funds to which petitioners claim an entitlement under the Plan's reimbursement provision—the proceeds from the settlement of [the Knudsons'] tort action—are not in [the Knudsons'] possession.... The kind of restitution that the petitioners seek, therefore, is not equitable—the imposition of a constructive trust or equitable lien on particular property—but legal—the imposition of personal liability for the benefits that they conferred on [the Knudsons].

"Admittedly, our cases have not previously drawn this fine distinction between restitution at law and restitution in equity, but neither have they involved an issue to which the distinction was relevant.... Thus, as courts and commentators have noted, 'all the [Supreme] Court meant [in *Mertens* and other cases] was that restitution, in contrast to damages, is a remedy commonly ordered in equity cases and therefore an equitable remedy in a sense in which damages, though occasionally awarded in equity cases, are not.'... *See*, Muir, 81 Iowa L. Rev., at 36 (analyzing *Mertens* and explaining that 'only equitable restitution will be available under Section 502(a)(3)')....

"It is easy to disparage the law-equity distinction as 'an ancient classification,'... and an 'obsolete distinction.'... Like it or not, however, that classification and distinction has been specified in the statute, and there is no way to give the specification meaning—indeed, there is no way to render the unmistakable limitation of the statute a limitation at all—except by adverting to the differences between law and equity to which the statute refers. The dissents greatly exaggerate, moreover, the difficulty of that task. Congress felt comfortable referring to equitable relief in this statute—as it has in many others [the Court notes 77 other statutes]—precisely because the basic contours of this term are well known.... What will introduce a high degree of confusion into congressional use (and lawyers' understanding) of the statutory term 'equity' is the rolling revision of its content contemplated by the dissents....

"Because petitioners are seeking legal relief—the imposition of personal liability on [the Knudsons] for a contractual obligation to pay money—S.502(a)(3) does not authorize this action. Accordingly, we affirm the judgment of the Court of Appeals."

Once a particular rule has been announced for a particular kind of case, that rule should generally be followed in future cases involving the same problem, unless there are compelling reasons for changing the rule. Confronted with a new problem that demands a solution, the judges try to reason by analogy from the older rules to develop the new rule for the new situation.

The doctrine of precedent operates in three different ways, or at three different levels: the effect of the decisions of a higher court on lower courts within the same system, the effect of prior decisions of the same court on a current case, and the effect of prior decisions in other states or countries on a current case. Where there is a clearly applicable precedent case, a lower court in the same jurisdiction should follow the precedent and apply the rule it establishes. In practice, the rule is not quite that simple because trial judges may try to avoid the precedent if they disagree with the result it produces in the case at hand. When that happens, the trial court will, of course, be reversed on appeal, unless the higher court wishes to change its mind and reverse or modify its own precedent.

Typically, when judges, lawyers, and commentators speak of the doctrine of precedent they are referring to its second level of operation, that is, the relationship between prior decisions of the same court and the case that is to be decided now. What impact should these prior decisions in similar cases have on the case at hand? Most courts will follow their established precedent cases most of the time, particularly in the commercial law areas emphasized in this book. Societal changes since the precedent-setting decision may determine whether or not the court will follow a particular precedent. In 1954, in *Brown v. Board of Education*, the U.S. Supreme Court was unanimous in overruling the clearly incorrect precedent established in the 1896 *Plessy v. Ferguson* case, which permitted racially segregated public facilities. On the other hand, the Supreme Court has repeatedly refused to overrule its 1922 baseball precedent, as seen in the *Flood* case.

The *Flood* decision has at long last been partially corrected by Congress. On October 27, 1998, President Clinton signed the "Curt Flood Act of 1998," which removes baseball's unique antitrust exemption as to employment matters. Only baseball's employment decisions are now subject to the Sherman Act, however; organized baseball's decisions as to team relocation, league expansion, and the like, remain exempt. After 76 years, Justice Oliver Wendell Holmes, Jr., has been partially overruled.

The *Crist* case shows that the "business of baseball" is still exempt from both national and state antitrust laws!

Courts are generally more willing to reexamine points of constitutional, criminal, and tort law than they are to upset established rules in contract and commercial law in which parties have based business relationships on existing rules. In many cases, a court may not want to reverse its previous decision, as in the *Brown* case, because doing so might upset many other contracts and relationships; however, the court still may not want to follow its precedent. In such cases, a court may use one of several devices to avoid the precedent. Occasionally, a court will simply ignore one of its own precedents, although this is hard to do if one of the lawyers has cited the precedent case in his or her legal brief or argument. The most common avoidance tactic is called **distinguishing the precedent on the facts,** meaning that the court shows how the precedent case really involved facts that were sufficiently different to justify a different decision. That process was at work in the 1957 *Radovich* case in which the Supreme Court "distinguished" football from baseball. In the years since *Radovich*, as noted in the *Flood* case, the Court has continued to uphold the baseball

CASE 2

Flood v. Kuhn
522 U.S. 3 (1997)

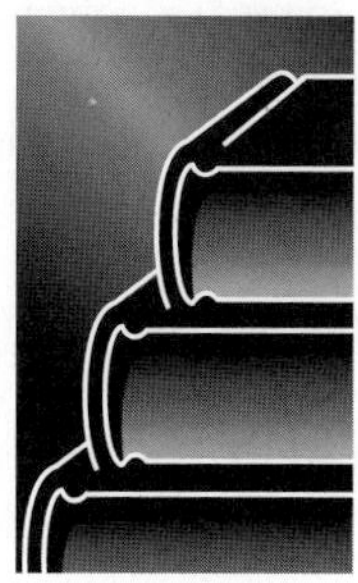

Facts: Curtis C. Flood began his major league career in 1956 when he signed a contract with the Cincinnati Reds. He had no attorney or agent to advise him on that occasion. He was traded to the St. Louis Cardinals before the 1958 season. Flood rose to fame as a center fielder with the Cardinals during the years 1958 to 1969.

In October 1969, Flood was traded to the Philadelphia Phillies of the National League in a multi-player transaction. He was not consulted about the trade. He was informed by telephone and received formal notice only after the deal had been consummated. In December, his request to the commissioner of baseball to be made a free agent was denied.

Flood then instituted his antitrust suit in U.S. District Court. The complaint charged violations of the U.S. antitrust laws and civil rights statutes, violation of state statutes and the common law, and the imposition of a form of peonage and involuntary service contrary to the Thirteenth Amendment. Flood sought declaratory and injunctive relief and treble damages.

The District Court judge denied the request for an injunction. Trial was held in 1970. The judge held that the cases of *Federal Baseball Club v. National League*, 259 U.S. 200 (1922), and *Toolson v. New York Yankees, Inc.* 346 U.S. 356 (1953), were controlling. Judgment was entered for the defendants.

The U.S. Second Circuit Court of Appeals affirmed the District Court opinion. The case was accepted for review by the U.S. Supreme Court.

Issue: Should the baseball precedents be followed?

Decision: Yes. Judgment affirmed.

Opinion by Justice Blackmun: "For the third time in fifty years the Court is asked specifically to rule that professional baseball's reserve system is within the reach of the federal antitrust laws. Collateral issues of state law and of federal labor policy are also advanced....

"*Federal Baseball Club v. National League* ... was a suit for treble damages instituted by a member of the Federal League (Baltimore) against the National and American Leagues and others....

"Mr. Justice Holmes, in speaking succinctly for a unanimous Court said:

> *The business is giving exhibitions of baseball, which are purely state affairs.... But the fact that in order to give the exhibitions, the Leagues must induce free persons to cross state lines and must arrange and pay for their doing so is not enough to change the character of the business.... The transport is a mere incident, not the essential thing. That to which it is incident, the exhibition, although made for money would not be called a trade or commerce in the commonly accepted use of those words. As it is put by the defendant, personal effort, not related to production, is not a subject of commerce. That which in its consummation is not commerce does not become commerce among the states because the transportation that we have mentioned takes place....*

"In the years that followed, baseball continued to be subject to intermittent antitrust attack. The courts, however, rejected these challenges on the authority of *Federal Baseball.* In some cases, stress was laid, although unsuccessfully, on new factors such as the development of radio and television with their substantial additional revenues to baseball. For the most part, however, the Holmes opinion was generally and necessarily accepted as controlling authority....

"The Court ... in the *Toolson*, *Kowalski*, and *Corbett* cases ... affirmed the judgments of the respective courts of appeals in those three cases.... *Federal Baseball* was cited as holding that the 'business of providing public baseball games for profit between clubs of professional baseball players was not within the scope of the federal antitrust laws,' and:

> *Congress has had the ruling under consideration but has not seen fit to bring such business under these laws by legislation having prospective effect. The business has thus been left for thirty years to develop, on the understanding that it was not subject to existing antitrust legislation. The present cases ask us to overrule the prior decision, and with retrospective effect, hold the legislation applicable. We think that if there are evils in this field which now warrant application to it of the antitrust laws it should be by legislation. Without reexamination of the underlying issues, the judgments below are affirmed on the authority of* Federal Baseball Club of Baltimore v. National League of Professional Baseball Clubs, *supra, so far as that decision determines that Congress had no intention of including the business of baseball within the scope of the federal antitrust laws....*

"This series of decisions understandably spawned extensive commentary, some of it mildly critical and much of it not; nearly all of it looked to Congress for any remedy that might be deemed essential.

"Legislative proposals have been numerous and persistent. Since *Toolson*, more than fifty bills have been introduced in Congress relative to the applicability or nonapplicability of the antitrust laws to baseball....

"In view of all this, it seems appropriate now to say that:

1. Professional baseball is a business and it is engaged in interstate commerce.

2. With its reserve system enjoying exemption from the antitrust laws, baseball is, in a very distinct sense, an exception and an anomaly. *Federal Baseball* and *Toolson* have become an aberration confined to baseball.

3. Even though others might regard this as 'unrealistic, inconsistent, or illogical,' see *Radovich*, ... the aberration is an established one, and one that has been recognized not only in *Federal Baseball* and *Toolson* but in *Shubert*, *International Boxing*, and *Radovich*, as well, a total of five consecutive cases in this Court. It is an aberration that has been with us now for half a century, one heretofore deemed fully entitled to the benefit of *stare decisis*, and one that has survived the Court's expanding concept of interstate commerce. It rests on a recognition and an acceptance of baseball's unique characteristics and needs.

4. Other professional sports operating interstate—football, boxing, basketball, and presumably hockey and golf—are not so exempt.

5. The advent of radio and television, with their consequent increased coverage and additional revenues, has not occasioned an overruling of *Federal Baseball* and *Toolson*.

6. The Court has emphasized that since 1922 baseball, with full and continuing congressional awareness, has been allowed to develop and to expand unhindered by federal legislative action. Remedial legislation has been introduced repeatedly in Congress, but none has ever been enacted. The Court, accordingly, has concluded that Congress as yet has had no intention to subject baseball's reserve system to the reach of the antitrust statutes. This, obviously, has been deemed to be something other than mere congressional silence and passivity....

7. The Court has expressed concern about the confusion and the retroactivity problems that inevitably would result with a judicial overturning of *Federal Baseball*. It has voiced a preference that if any change is made, it comes by legislative action that, by its nature, is only prospective in operation....

"This emphasis and this concern are still with us. We continue to be loathe, fifty years after *Federal Baseball* and almost two decades after *Toolson*, to overturn those cases judicially when Congress, by its positive inaction, has allowed those decisions to stand for so long and far beyond mere inference and implication, has clearly evinced a desire not to disapprove them legislatively.

"Accordingly, we adhere once again to *Federal Baseball* and *Toolson* and to their application to professional baseball. We adhere also to *International Boxing* and *Radovich* and to their respective applications to professional boxing and professional football. If there is any inconsistency or illogic in all this, it is an inconsistency and illogic of long standing that is to be remedied by the Congress and not by this Court. If we were to act otherwise, we would be withdrawing from the conclusion as to congressional intent made in *Toolson* and from the concerns as to retrospectivity therein expressed. Under these circumstances, there is merit in consistency even though some might claim that beneath that consistency is a layer of inconsistency....

"[W]hat the court said in *Federal Baseball* in 1922 and what is said in *Toolson* in 1953, we say again here in 1972; the remedy, if any is indicated, is for congressional, and not judicial, action."

exemption from antitrust, while at the same time subjecting other professional sports to antitrust regulation.

Another mechanism for avoiding an undesirable precedent is to **distinguish the precedent on the law.** The precedent is a precedent only for the rule of law that was actually necessary to the decision in the case. The judge writing the opinion of the court may have said a lot of things, but not everything in the opinion is necessarily a binding rule for future cases. These nonbinding "extra" statements in opinions are called *obiter dicta*, or just *dicta* meaning that the court is saying things that are not actually necessary to decide the case. Perhaps the most famous example of such dicta is Chief Justice John Marshall's 1803 opinion in *Marbury v. Madison*. None of his comments on the validity of *Marbury's* claim are "the law" because the Supreme Court actually decided it could not, constitutionally, hear the case.

In the more recent *State Oil* case, the Supreme Court not only overruled an antitrust precedent, but it also distinguished *Flood* and *Toolson*, the baseball precedents.

Finally, the doctrine of precedent operates in a third way. Suppose that the case that has to be decided today is unprecedented; that is, no decided cases in the state have ever dealt with the problem. The court can respond in two ways. One approach is simply to dismiss the complaint for failure to state a cause of action; this usually occurs when the plaintiff wants the court to recognize a new right or a new theory of liability. Where the underlying theory of liability has been recognized but there is simply no case applying it to the given situation, the courts will use precedents in a third way—by borrowing precedents

CASE 3

Major League Baseball v. Crist

331 F.3d 1177 (11 Cir. 2003)

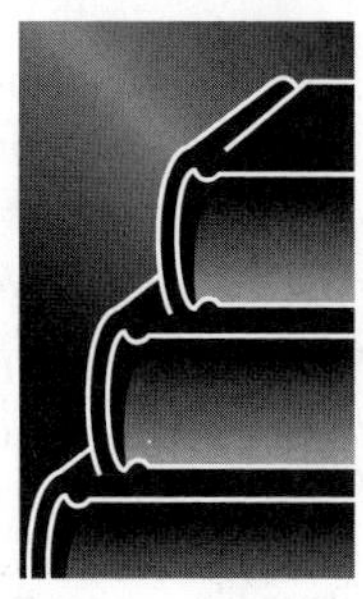

Facts: Major League Baseball (MLB) is an unincorporated association of 30 major league baseball clubs. On November 6, 2001, a supermajority of the clubs voted in favor of eliminating two teams from the league. The Florida Marlins and the Tampa Bay Devil Rays were the only clubs to oppose this move; they were both prime candidates for elimination. The then Attorney General of Florida, Robert Butterworth, was quoted as saying that he would do whatever he could "to keep [baseball] in Florida." Using his authority under Florida's antitrust statute, he issued several civil investigative demands (CIDs) to the two Florida teams, MLB, and MLB Commissioner Allan Selig. The CIDs asked questions and required production of "voluminous documents." The targets of the CIDs filed this lawsuit in U.S. District Court, challenging the validity of the CIDs. The District Court ruled in the plaintiffs' favor, and the Florida Attorney General (by then Charlie Crist—who has since been elected Governor of Florida) appealed.

Issue: Does the judicially created "antitrust exemption" for professional baseball preempt state antitrust regulation?

Decision: Yes, it does. Judgment affirmed.

Opinion by Judge Tjoflat: "For better or worse, professional baseball has long enjoyed an exemption [from the antitrust laws]. The scope of this exemption—a judge-made rule premised upon dubious rationales and labeled an 'aberration' by the Supreme Court—has been the subject of extensive litigation over the years. In this case, we are called upon to address two key issues: (1) the effect of the federal rule upon state antitrust law and (2) whether the exemption extends beyond antitrust prosecutions into the realm of mere investigations. With regard to the first issue, we hold that the federal exemption preempts state antitrust law. As for the second issue, we hold that the Florida Attorney General cannot proceed with the investigation in this case. This holding is based upon the Fourth Amendment and state law rather than the antitrust exemption. In this vein, our analysis differs significantly from that of the district court, although we ultimately affirm its decision....

"The 'business of baseball' is exempt from the federal antitrust laws.... [T]he Attorney General argues that the exemption has limits. Specifically, the Attorney General contends that the exemption might not be triggered if the facts established by the impending investigation show that the plaintiffs engaged in non-exempt conduct.

"The Attorney General's position is no doubt correct, but what conduct could possibly be non-exempt? [T]he issue of contraction concerns a matter that is central to baseball's league structure—specifically, the number of clubs that may participate in league play.... As the district court stated, 'It is difficult to conceive of a decision more integral to the business of major league baseball than the number of clubs that will be allowed to compete.' ... When the applicability of baseball's exemption is so apparent, no factual development is necessary....

"Any discussion of whether Congress meant to immunize the business of baseball from all antitrust law (as opposed to federal antitrust law) is, of course, fanciful because Congress never conveyed its preference one way or the other. The exemption is entirely judge-made.... Our analysis must turn to the critical language utilized by the Supreme Court in *Flood:* '[The district court] rejected the state law claims because state antitrust regulation would conflict with federal policy and because "uniformity (is required) in any regulation of baseball and its reserve system." The Court of Appeals, in affirming, stated, "As the burden on interstate commerce outweighs the states' interests in regulating baseball's reserve system, the Commerce Clause precludes the application here of state antitrust law." As applied to organized baseball ... these statements adequately dispose of the state law claims.'

"[I]t is far from axiomatic that exemptions from prosecution necessarily entail a concomitant right to be free from investigation....

"It makes no sense, the plaintiffs contend, to allow an investigation into conduct that we know is perfectly legal before the investigation commences. We agree with this sentiment, although we find it more appropriate to locate the right to be free from baseless investigations (commonly referred to as 'fishing expeditions') in other sources of law rather than the antitrust exemption itself....

"The death of the business-of-baseball exemption would likely be met with considerable fanfare, save for the club owners who benefit from the rule. The exemption was founded upon a dubious premise, and it has been upheld in subsequent cases because of an equally dubious premise. Moreover, the welfare losses stemming from the potentially anticompetitive agreements among professional sports clubs have been well documented.... It is up to the Supreme Court or Congress to overrule Flood outright, or perhaps to devise a more cabined exemption. As an intermediate appellate court, we have no choice but to hold that the district court was correct in granting judgment in favor of the plaintiffs.

"AFFIRMED."

CASE 4

STATE OIL CO. v. KHAN
522 U.S. 3 (1997)

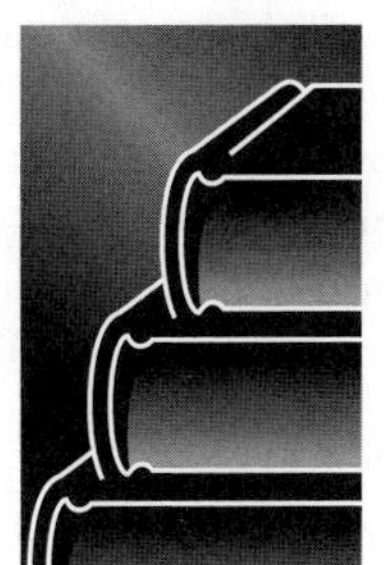

Facts: Barkat U. Khan (and his corporation) entered into an agreement with State Oil Company, to lease and operate a gas station and convenience store owned by State Oil. The agreement provided that Khan would obtain the station's gasoline supply from State Oil at a price equal to a suggested retail price set by State Oil, less a margin of 3.25 cents per gallon. Under the agreement, Khan could charge any amount for gasoline sold to the station's customers, but if the price charged was higher than State Oil's suggested retail price, the excess was to be rebated to State Oil. Khan could sell gasoline for less that State Oil's suggested retail price, but any such decrease would reduce his 3.25 cents-per-gallon margin.

About a year after Khan began operating the gas station, he fell behind in lease payments. State Oil then gave notice of its intent to terminate the agreement and sued in state court to evict Khan. At State Oil's request, the state court appointed a receiver to operate the gas station. The receiver operated the station for several months without being subject to the price restraints in Khan's agreement with State Oil. According to Khan, the receiver obtained an overall profit margin in excess of 3.25 cents per gallon by lowering the price of regular-grade gasoline and raising the price of premium grades.

Khan then sued State Oil in the U.S. District Court, alleging in part that State Oil had engaged in price fixing in violation of Section 1 of the Sherman Act, by preventing him from raising or lowering retail gas prices. The District Court found that the complaint did not state a per se violation and entered summary judgment for State Oil on respondents' Sherman Act claim. The Court of Appeals for the Seventh Circuit reversed, and State Oil petitioned for U.S. Supreme Court review.

Issue: Does the setting of *maximum* retail resale prices constitute a per se violation of the Sherman Act?

Decision: No. Judgment of the Court of Appeals is reversed, and case is remanded.

Opinion by Justice O'Connor: "In *Albrecht v. Herald Co.*, . . . (1968), this Court held that vertical maximum price fixing is a *per se* violation. . . . In this case, we are asked to reconsider that decision of this Court. We conclude that *Albrecht* should be overruled. . . .

"Although the Sherman Act, by its terms, prohibits every agreement 'in restraint of trade,' this Court has long recognized that Congress intended to outlaw only unreasonable restraints. . . . As a consequence, most antitrust claims are analyzed under a 'rule of reason,' according to which the finder of fact must decide whether the questioned practice imposes an unreasonable restraint on competition, taking into account a variety of factors, including specific information about the relevant business, its condition before and after the restraint was imposed, and the restraint's history, nature, and effect. . . .

"Some types of restraints, however, have such predictable and pernicious anti-competitive effect, and such limited potential for procompetitive benefit, that they are deemed unlawful *per se*. . . . *Per se* treatment is appropriate '[o]nce experience with a particular kind of restraint enables the Court to predict with confidence that the rule of reason will condemn it.' . . . Thus, we have expressed reluctance to adopt *per se* rules with regard to 'restraints imposed in the context of business relationships where the economic impact of certain practices is not immediately obvious.'. . .

"*Albrecht* . . . involved a newspaper publisher who had granted exclusive territories to independent carriers subject to their adherence to a maximum price on re-sale of the newspapers to the public. Influenced by its [prior] decisions, . . . the Court concluded that it was *per se* unlawful for the publisher to fix the maximum resale price of its newspapers. . . . The Court acknowledged that '[m]aximum and minimum price fixing may have different consequences in many situations,' but nonetheless condemned maximum price fixing for 'substituting the perhaps erroneous judgment of a seller for the forces of the competitive market.' . . .

"*Albrecht* was animated in part by the fear that vertical maximum price fixing could allow suppliers to discriminate against certain dealers, restrict the services that dealers could afford to offer customers or disguise minimum price fixing schemes. . . . The Court rejected the notion (both on the record of that case and in the abstract) that, because the newspaper publisher 'granted exclusive territories, a price ceiling was necessary to protect the public from price gouging by dealers who had monopoly power in their own territories.' . . .

"After reconsidering *Albrecht's* rationale and the substantial criticism the decision has received, however, we conclude that there is insufficient economic justification for *per se* invalidation of vertical maximum price fixing. That is so not only because it is difficult to accept the assumptions underlying *Albrecht*, but also because *Albrecht* has little or no relevance to ongoing enforcement of the Sherman Act. . . . Moreover, neither the parties nor any of the *amici curiae* have called our attention to any cases in which enforcement efforts have been directed solely against the conduct encompassed by *Albrecht's per se* rule.

"Despite what Chief Judge Posner aptly described as *Albrecht's* 'infirmities, [and] its increasingly wobbly, moth-eaten foundation,' . . . there remains the question whether *Albrecht* deserves continuing respect under the doctrine of *stare decisis*. The Court of Appeals was correct in applying that principle despite disagreement with *Albrecht*, for it is this Court's prerogative alone to overrule one of its precedents.

"We approach the reconsideration of decisions of this Court with the utmost caution. *Stare decisis* reflects 'a policy judgment that "in most matters it is more important that the applicable rule of law be settled than that it be settled right".' ... It 'is the preferred course because it promotes the evenhanded, predictable, and consistent development of legal principles, fosters reliance on judicial decisions, and contributes to the actual and perceived integrity of the judicial process.' ... This Court has expressed its reluctance to overrule decisions involving statutory interpretation, ... and has acknowledged that *stare decisis* concerns are at their acme in cases involving property and contract rights.... Both of those concerns are arguably relevant in this case.

"But '*[s]tare decisis* is not an inexorable command.' ... In the area of antitrust law, there is a competing interest, well-represented in this Court's decisions, in recognizing and adapting to changed circumstances and the lessons of accumulated experience. Thus, the general presumption that legislative changes should be left to Congress has less force with respect to the Sherman Act in light of the accepted view that Congress 'expected the courts to give shape to the statute's broad mandate by drawing on common-law tradition.' ... As we have explained, the term 'restraint of trade,' as used in S.1, also 'invokes the common law itself, and not merely the static content that the common law had assigned to the term in 1890.' ... Accordingly, this Court has reconsidered its decisions construing the Sherman Act when the theoretical underpinnings of those decisions are called into serious question....

"Although the rule of *Albrecht* has been in effect for some time, the inquiry we must undertake requires considering 'the effect of the antitrust laws upon vertical distributional restraints in the American economy today.' ... Now that we confront *Albrecht* directly, we find its conceptual foundations gravely weakened.

"In overruling *Albrecht*, we of course do not hold that all vertical maximum price fixing is *per se* lawful. Instead, vertical maximum price fixing, like the majority of commercial arrangements subject to the antitrust laws, should be evaluated under the rule of reason. In our view, rule-of-reason analysis will effectively identify those situations in which vertical maximum price fixing amounts to anti-competitive conduct."

from other states, or even from other countries, particularly from countries with similar legal systems. However, it is important to note that one state's decisions are not binding rules in a second state unless and until courts in the second state accept them as precedents in cases decided there.

Trial by Jury

The **trial by jury** is a third distinguishing feature of an Anglo-American legal system. Whereas early Greek law used a vote of all assembled freemen to decide some trials (you may recall that Socrates was condemned to drink poisonous hemlock) and whereas other systems have used and do use some form of the jury, it has a special place in the historical development and the current operation of the Anglo-American legal system.

Historically, the jury developed as an important check against the arbitrary exercise of governmental power, both in England and in the United States. Particularly in criminal cases, this function continues to be exercised by the jury today. In civil cases, the jury injects into the legal system the "conscience of the community" on such matters as the standard of care expected of an ordinary reasonable person.

In no other legal system does the jury have the power to hear such a wide range of cases. All but the most minor criminal violations are triable to a jury. Many regulatory violations are also subject to trial by jury. It is true that a litigant seeking a special equitable remedy will not have the right to a jury in most states, but that exception still leaves most ordinary civil cases subject to a trial by jury. The ordinary civil lawsuit for money damages for tort or for breach of contract is required to be tried to a jury if either litigant demands one. (Many states, however, do not use a jury in their small claims courts, where only a limited dollar recovery is permitted, usually $1,000 or less.)

Likewise, in no other system is the jury given as much discretion in arriving at its verdict, or is the verdict given the same finality, as in an Anglo-American system. If the plaintiff alleges facts that state a valid legal claim, and then at the trial introduces some minimal evidence in support of those allegations, the result in that civil case is up to the jury. The trial judge will instruct jurors as to what the law is and what their options are, and in some states may even comment on the weight of the evidence presented, but the jury will decide the outcome. There are some procedural safeguards against obviously incorrect verdicts, but in the vast majority of cases, the judgment will be entered based on the verdict of the trial jury.

The *DeJesus* case examines the constitutionality of peremptory challenges to jurors on the basis of their religious affiliation.

CASE 5

United States of America v. DeJesus
347 F.3d 500 (3 Cir. 2003)

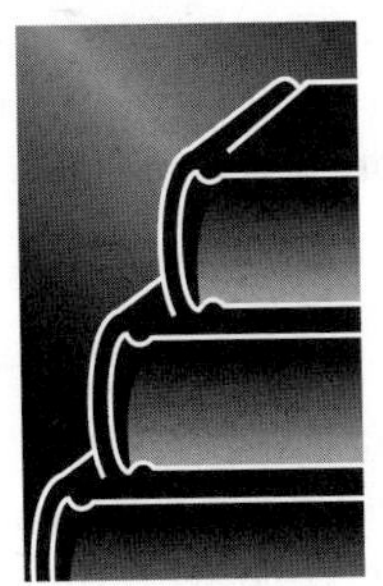

Facts: Following a report of a stolen car and a high-speed chase, Jerry DeJesus was arrested and searched. He had a gun and two ammunition clips in his jacket pocket. Due to his prior felony conviction, he was charged with "illegal possession of a firearm by a convicted felon." At his first trial, the jury was unable to reach a verdict. After a 3-day second trial, he was found guilty. His appeal is based on the prosecution's peremptory challenges to two religiously active prospective jurors, Ronald McBride and James Bates.

During the selection process, McBride disclosed that a cousin had been murdered but that he (McBride) had learned to forgive the murderer. McBride stated on the juror questionnaire that he was active in his church, read religious literature, sang in church choirs, and held several religious degrees. Bates also engaged in church activities, was a church officer and trustee, and read the Bible and related literature. The prosecution stated that its challenges were not based on religion, as such, but on McBride's possible reluctance to convict, and on Bates' refusal to make eye contact during the selection process.

Both McBride and Bates were African American, but the prosecution also used a peremptory to excuse George Pressey, a white man who was likewise active in his church. The final jury had seven women and six men; one juror was Hispanic, three were African Americans, and nine were white. The prosecution did not use three of its six peremptories; the defense still had three of its ten.

Issue: Were the peremptory challenges based on religion?

Decision: No. Judgment affirmed.

Opinion by Judge Fuentes: "Peremptory challenges are a part of our common law heritage and play a crucial part in empanel[l]ing fair and impartial juries. The decision to exercise a peremptory strike need not be supported by any reason. It is usually based on educated guesses about probabilities based on the limited information available to an attorney about prospective jurors. The challenge is intended for those situations in which an attorney cannot articulate a specific conflict, but has some reason to believe a juror may be less desirable than other jurors who may be called.... Nonetheless, the Supreme Court established in *Batson* that ... the Equal Protection Clause must prevent prosecutors from using peremptory strikes to remove jurors on the basis of race.... The Supreme Court extended that logic to peremptory strikes based on gender in *J.E.B. v. Alabama*.... But it remains the rule that peremptory strikes are presumptively valid until it is shown that they were exercised on an unconstitutional basis, such as race or gender....

"In *Hernandez* ... the Court summarized the process to be followed in a criminal case when defense counsel challenges the government's peremptory challenge: 'In *Batson*, we outlined a three-step process.... First, the defendant must make a prima facie showing that the prosecutor has exercised peremptory challenges on the basis of race. Second ... the burden shifts to the prosecutor to articulate a race-neutral explanation.... Finally, the trial court must determine whether the defendant has carried his burden of proving purposeful discrimination.' ...

"At the second prong of the *Batson* analysis, we examine the government's explanation to determine if it was facially race-neutral. The second step 'does not demand an explanation that is persuasive, or even plausible.'... 'Unless a discriminatory intent is inherent in the prosecutor's explanation, the reason offered will be deemed race-neutral.' ...

"With respect to the third prong, the District Court found that 'the mix of reasons articulated by the prosecution team, and confirmed in several instances by counsel's contemporaneous notes of the jurors' characteristics, represent the true and sincere reasons.' ...

"Whether the government has engaged in impermissible discrimination during jury selection is a matter that is uniquely within the province of the trial judge.... 'There will seldom be much evidence bearing on that issue, and the best evidence often will be the demeanor of the attorney who exercises the challenge. As with the state of mind of a juror, evaluation of the prosecutor's state of mind based on demeanor and credibility lies "peculiarly within a trial judge's province".' ...

"For the aforementioned reasons, we affirm DeJesus' conviction and sentence."

Judicial Review

There are, of course, differences from country to country within the Anglo American legal family. Again, England no longer uses the distinction between law and equity. It also rarely uses the trial by jury for civil cases, in contrast to the United States. Perhaps the most significant difference, however, is that Great Britain does not recognize **judicial review:** the power of the courts to declare legislative acts unconstitutional. As in most parliamentary systems, the legislature is the final source of political power (other than the people as a whole); the courts are subordinate to the legislature.

Under the separation of powers doctrine, U.S. courts have the power to invalidate legislative as well as administrative acts found to be in conflict with the Constitution. State courts have similar power under their state constitutions. Moreover, the issue of constitutionality may be raised by any litigant in any sort of case. A debtor whose car is repossessed because monthly payments were not being made may ask a state or national court to declare that the repossession procedure provided by state law violates the due process clause of the U.S. Constitution, for example. Although a few countries have so-called constitutional courts, their jurisdiction can be invoked only in a special, limited procedure. Judicial review as it is practiced in the United States is still a unique institution.

Classification of Law

Public versus Private Law

Most legal systems recognize two broad categories of legal rules: public law and private law. **Private law** is concerned with the legal relationships between individuals. The role of the government is limited to setting and enforcing the ground rules of the game; the decision on whether to "play" or not, with whom, about what, and on what terms, is left to the individuals and organizations involved. For example, no one (as yet) orders you to buy a new TV: If you think you might want one, you decide on the make and model and then negotiate with one or more retailers to try to get the best price and terms. The role of the government in this private law transaction is limited to specifying the requirements for an enforceable contract and the remedies available in the event of a breach by one of the parties.

Public law areas, by contrast, involve the government acting in its sovereign capacity in some way—either as a contending party or by forcing action or inaction or by specifying the terms of a relationship. Criminal law, constitutional law, and administrative law are major public law areas. Criminal law involves the government as the prosecutor, claiming that a wrong has been done against society as a whole. **Constitutional law** provides the basic framework for the functioning of the government, as well as guarantees of rights and prohibitions against certain government actions. **Administrative law** covers all the areas of governmental regulation through administrative agencies. In the field of labor law, for example, the National Labor Relations Board (NLRB) polices union-management relations and the Equal Employment Opportunity Commission (EEOC) tries to prevent discrimination in employment. Although commercial law was (and perhaps still is) primarily a private law topic, there are now many important public law aspects in this field. We will examine most of these, as well as the more traditional public law areas, such as labor law, antitrust law, and securities law. These public law rules are sometimes called the "legal environment" of business.

Criminal Law and Civil Law

Criminal law encompasses national and state statutes that make the commission or omission of certain acts punishable by fine or imprisonment. In criminal cases, the state or national government prosecutes the person who disobeyed the criminal law.

For example, Harry Horrible mugged a woman, took her pocketbook, and ran. The police arrested him, and he was prosecuted for assault and battery and theft, found guilty, and sentenced to jail. The woman lost her purse and several dollars, missed several days of work at her job, and still has unpaid doctor and hospital bills because of her injuries. The criminal law does not give her the right to have her bills paid, to be compensated for her pain and suffering, or to be reimbursed for the cost of a new purse. Criminal law only attempts to fine or imprison the wrongdoer. The wrong being punished is a wrong against society.

Civil law provides for compensation for personal injury, loss of property, and breach of contract. This is the body of statutory and **case law** that sets out the rights and duties between individuals in society. For example, in the previous situation, the state may put Harry Horrible in jail under criminal law, but who is going to pay the bills and reimburse the victim for her loss? Under civil law, more specifically tort law, the woman could sue Harry Horrible for monetary damages. This would be a separate lawsuit.

Substantive and Procedural Law

Law is also classified as substantive law and procedural law. **Substantive law** defines the rights and duties of individuals and institutions in their mutual relationships. In a jury trial, for example, after the jurors have heard the evidence, the judge instructs them on the law. The judge is giving them the substantive law of the case. In the same trial, **procedural law** governs the admission of evidence, the sequence of the lawsuit, and possible appeal. Procedural law can be defined as the law that governs the enforcement of substantive law. It is essentially concerned with the rules of the game, not necessarily the outcome. Procedural law will be discussed further in Chapter 4 when we review the court system and its procedure.

National Law and State Law

A final generalized distinction needs to be made—between national law and state law. As we will discuss in more detail in Chapter 3, ours is a federal system of government, meaning that we have both a national government and the several state governments. Both levels of government have lawmaking powers. Most of the topics that we cover in this book are private law topics, within the states' jurisdiction. There are, however, many significant national regulations that have an impact on business operations (and our personal activities). In addition, it is the national Supreme Court that is the final "umpire" within the system, at least until a constitutional amendment is passed that changes the Supreme Court's interpretation of the Constitution.

Sources of U.S. Law

It is often said that the source of U.S. law is English law. True, the early settlers of our country were primarily of English origin, and their legal traditions influenced the U.S. legal system. Our legal system is not entirely independent of its English counterpart. However, the framers of the U.S. Constitution had lived under the English legal system and had fought and won a revolution to free themselves of some of its features. Thus the U.S. legal system differs from the English legal system in many ways.

Constitution of the United States

The **Constitution** of the United States is the **"supreme law of the land."** This means no statute enacted by the U.S. Congress or a state legislative body, no decision of any court, and no state constitution can be contrary to the U.S. Constitution. Any enactment or decision found to be contrary to the Constitution will be declared null and void by the courts.

The Constitution provides for additional sources of law in Articles I, II, and III. Article I establishes Congress as the legislative branch of government and specifies congressional powers and the limitations on those powers. Article II establishes the office of the President and the executive branch of government and defines the scope of the executive's power. Article III provides that the judicial power of the United States shall be vested in one supreme court and such other courts as the Congress may establish.

Thus, these three articles of the Constitution established the three branches of our national government—the legislative branch to create law, the executive branch to administer and enforce the law, and the judicial branch to interpret the law and to act as guardian of the Constitution.

Treaties

Article II, Section 2, of the Constitution, also gave the President the power to make **treaties;** however, all treaties must be made with the advice and consent of the Senate of the United States. This source of law is increasingly important in our relationships with foreign nations because treaties affect both military matters and our trade relationships with the other nations of the world. With today's satellite communication and computer networks interwoven across the globe, we need new international legal agreement on rules for conducting international business. Treaty power is an important way to meet those needs.

The treaty power of the United States is a source of law not only for international affairs but also for internal affairs. A treaty, once approved by the Senate, has the same force and effect as laws enacted by the U.S. Congress. Thus, a treaty concerning U.S. internal affairs is superior to any state law or any state constitution.

Statutes

Congress creates new law and changes prior law by passing legislation, often referred to as "Acts of Congress" or **statutes.** Each House of Congress must pass the same bill, and the President must sign it, before it becomes a law. If the President refuses to sign a bill, Congress can override the veto by repassing the bill by a two-thirds vote in each House.

Administrative Agencies

Another large body of law is created by the various regulations and pronouncements of administrative agencies, both national and state. On the national level we have agencies such as the National Labor Relations Board (NLRB), the Federal Trade Commission (FTC), and the Equal Employment Opportunity Commission (EEOC). On the state level, we have agencies such as the Public Utilities Commission, the Workers' Compensation Board, and various consumer commissions.

Administrative agencies are created by national or state legislatures, which delegate specific tasks and functions to the agency. The legislature may later limit the agency's authority or dispose of the agency entirely. We will discuss constitutional law and administrative agencies in more detail in Chapter 3.

State Legal Systems

The Tenth Amendment to the Constitution provides that the powers not delegated to the United States by the Constitution or prohibited by it to the states are reserved to the states, respectively, or to the people. This amendment is often called the states' rights amendment. It allows the states to govern themselves in all areas where the Constitution does not specify national regulation.

Each state thus has its own constitution, governor, legislature, and courts. State court systems will be discussed in Chapter 4.

Uniform Laws and Restatements

Because a good deal of business is done across state lines, there is a need to minimize conflicts among state laws. The National Conference of Commissioners on Uniform State Laws was created in 1891. Representatives from each of the states, the District of Columbia, and Puerto Rico gathered to promote uniformity in state laws. The conferees reviewed the various state laws and judicial decisions and, in cooperation with the American Law Institute, drafted model statutes governing various areas. They then suggested that the states adopt these new model laws and repeal their previous laws. The ultimate goal was uniform state business laws throughout the country. The most notable accomplishment of the Commissioners is the Uniform Commercial Code, which has been adopted in 49 states. Louisiana is the only state that has not adopted the entire Uniform Commercial Code. Other **uniform laws** deal with such topics as partnerships and decedents' estates.

The task of systematizing case law has been undertaken by a private agency, the American Law Institute. The ALI is a group of law professors and practitioners. It has published treatises called Restatements of the Law covering many business-related areas, such as torts, property, trusts, and agency. The ALI's writers have attempted to review the vast volume of case law and to set out in organized, encyclopedia-like form the generally accepted rules of law on specific topics. These **Restatements** are not like the statutes of a state. They are only for reference and are periodically revised and updated. They serve a very useful purpose by allowing lawyers and judges to quickly see what the generally accepted rule of law is on a specific legal point. Judges often adopt the rules set out in the Restatements, thus making those rules part of the actual law.

Significance of This Chapter

Before beginning to study and learn specific rules of law, a student must first establish a general foundation upon which to build further blocks of knowledge. In establishing such a foundation it is necessary for the student to be able to define law, to understand the need for law in our society, to know the sources of our law, and to have a general understanding of how our legal system operates.

IMPORTANT TERMS AND CONCEPTS

administrative agencies
administrative law
Anglo-American legal system
case law
civil law
common law
Constitution
constitutional law
criminal law
distinguish the precedent on the law.
distinguishing the precedent on the facts
doctrine of precedent
injection
judicial review
private law
procedural law
public law
Restatements
statutes
Substantive law
supreme law of the land
treaties
trial by jury
uniform laws

QUESTIONS AND PROBLEMS FOR DISCUSSION

1. What are the distinguishing features of a common law system?

2. What is the difference between substantive law and procedural law? Give an example of each.

3. How does a court distinguish a precedent case on the facts?

4. Why was the court of equity developed?

5. Alumsports, Inc., a manufacturer of baseball bats, sued Batoff Company for alleged patent infringement. Alumsports said that it had the patent on a certain design for aluminum baseball bats and that Batoff was making the same product. Batoff argues that the patent is invalid because baseball is not commerce and Congress lacks the power to regulate it. Thus the congressionally established patent system cannot be applied to baseball equipment.

   What is the result and why?

6. Hap Hapless, the former owner of a now-bankrupt minor league baseball team, sues the commissioner of major league baseball and all the major league club owners for damages sustained to his franchise when a major league team moved into the same geographic area. Hap alleges that the fans went to see the major league games, rather than coming to see his minor league team play. He says that the loss in revenues that resulted from this forced him to go out of business. He claims damages for unfair competition under the appropriate sections of the antitrust laws. The commissioner and the owners argue that the case should be dismissed, under the authority of *Federal Baseball*.

   How should the court rule, and why?

7. Bropp was convicted of possession of burglar tools after police had stopped his car, searched it without a warrant, and found the burglar tools. He was convicted in 1990. At that time, a state could permit the use of improperly seized evidence in a criminal trial if it wished to do so. In 1991, the U.S. Supreme Court reversed its prior precedent case and held that a state could not use any illegally seized evidence in a criminal trial. Bropp now appeals his conviction on the basis of the new ruling by the U.S. Supreme Court.

   How should the state appeals court rule? Explain.

8. Harold owns and operates a traveling dog and pony show. He gives exhibitions in several states. The U.S. Secretary of Agriculture attempted to impose regulations on Harold as to the care and feeding of his animals, pursuant to authority granted under the Animal Welfare Act. Harold says that his exhibitions are not interstate commerce and that he is, therefore, not subject to congressional regulation under the authority of the Federal Baseball case.

   How should the court rule, and why? Would there be a different result if Harold had a permanent location and gave exhibitions only in that one place?

9. The Crow Indian Tribe is established on a large reservation in the state of Montana. Valuable coal deposits underlie a large part of the reservation. In 1975, the tribe leased coal mining rights to Moreland Resources, which quickly began operations. In 1985, Montana enacted a coal mining tax, imposed at the rate of 30 percent of market value, on all coal producers in the state. Between 1985 and 1998, Moreland paid over $60,000,000 in coal taxes to

Montana. In 1998, the Crow Indian Tribe enacted its own coal tax of 25 percent. Moreland does not want to pay both coal taxes.

What arguments can it make in a lawsuit?

10. Richard Alan Rothchild became engaged to be married to Carol Sue Cohen. Both were over 21 years of age. Richard gave Carol a diamond engagement ring which was valued at $1,000. Shortly before the wedding date, Richard was killed in an automobile accident, and Carol sued to have the court confirm her right to the ring.

The state has no statute or court decision that provides a rule for this sort of case. The court must decide this case because one way or another, someone will end up with the ring.

How should the trial court judge proceed in making his or her decision? Explain.

NOTES

1. Sir William Blackstone, Commentaries on the Laws of England, I, at 44—quoted in Morris R. Cohen and Felix S. Cohen, Readings on Jurisprudence and Legal Philosophy, NY: Prentice-Hall, Inc. 1951, p. 384.

2. Oliver Wendell Holmes, Jr., The Path of the Law [from Collected Legal Papers, NY: Harcourt, Brace & Co., 1920]—quoted in Cohen & Cohen, op. cit., supra, p. 417.

3. Robert Maynard Hutchins, ed., Great Books of the Western World, Chicago: Encyclopedia Brittanica, Inc. 1952, vol. 9 , Aristotle II, W. D. Ross, tr., p. 374.

4. Robert Maynard Hutchins, ed., Great Books of the Western World, Chicago: Encyclopedia Brittanica, Inc. 1952, vol. 9 , Aristotle II, W. D. Ross, tr., p. 376.

5. Robert Maynard Hutchins, ed., Great Books of the Western World, Chicago: Encyclopedia Brittanica, Inc. 1952, vol. 9 , Aristotle II, W. D. Ross, tr., p. 377.

6. Robert Maynard Hutchins, ed., Great Books of the Western World, Chicago: Encyclopedia Brittanica, Inc. 1952, vol. 9 , Aristotle II, W. D. Ross, tr., pp. 385–386.

CHAPTER 2

Comparative Law and International Law

Chapter Objectives

This chapter will:

- Outline the world's major types of legal systems.
- Introduce international law and identify its sources.
- Describe the International Court of Justice and its purpose.
- Explain why U.S. courts have jurisdiction to hear international law disputes in some cases.
- Discuss why international arbitration is preferable to going to court in many international law cases.
- Define the scope of the United Nations Convention on Contracts for the International Sale of Goods.
- Introduce letters of credit and the ways they are used in international trade.
- Compare the doctrines of Sovereign Immunity and Act of State.

Today most large U.S. corporations and many smaller U.S. firms are engaged in international trade. Nearly all U.S. businesses and workers are subject to foreign competition and to the effects of international financial and economic operations. Many large U.S. companies derive over half of their income from overseas operations; in that sense, they are truly **"multinationals."** Nearly all of the largest corporations in the United States fall into this latter category. Many smaller firms and individuals are now also doing business on the World Wide Web. Many of us thus need to have an appreciation of the laws of other nations, and of international law, to operate effectively in the global economy.

Thus, the international stakes are very high. Although our economy is not yet as dependent on foreign trade as many other countries, we are not immune from international economic trends. The global economy is not fully integrated, but there are substantial connections—enough so that serious problems in one nation do tend to spread to others. If nothing else, a particular nation's economic problems will surely have an impact on U.S. companies' operations in that nation. Doing business in other nations therefore requires an understanding of those nations' economic, political, *and* legal systems. Because the doing of business *by definition* involves the establishing of legal relations, international managers simply must be aware of the possibility that different legal rules will apply to their international transactions.

Added legal complications arise in different ways when business is transacted across national borders. Nearly always, questions may be raised about which nation's law applies to the cross-border transaction. These "conflicts-of-laws" are similar to those that arise within the United States in many interstate transactions, but in the international context are much more complex due to the much greater differences between the legal systems involved. We thus begin this chapter with a brief overview of the major types of national legal systems and compare them to our own common law system.

There is also a separate body of international law that may be applicable to particular commercial transactions. There is now a treaty that provides many of the legal rules for international sales of goods, for example. International law rules are also very important in commercial dealings with other governments as buyers of goods and services and in protecting investors in other nations. International law also plays a role in sorting out where lawsuits can occur and which nation's law applies to international disputes.

Most recently, regional groupings of nations, most especially the European Union (EU), have created supranational legal institutions. There are EU courts and administrative agencies that have the power to create and administer binding legal rules for the nations who are EU members and for businesses operating within the EU. Because the EU is the world's largest trading unit, these rules are very important to all the world's businesses.

Comparative Law

There are several other types of legal systems existing today, in addition to the common law system used by the United States, the United Kingdom, Canada, Australia, New Zealand, and other nations. Of course, even within this common law "family," there are differences from nation to nation. Most countries in this group do not permit their courts to declare acts of the national legislature "unconstitutional," as the United States does. Some have unified, written constitutional documents; others do not. In some, jury trials are generally available, even in ordinary civil cases; other nations use the trial jury much more sparingly. All, however, recognize the doctrine of precedent, as discussed in Chapter 1. "The law" is in the cases: Prior judicial decisions are the sources of rules that are used to decide present cases. There is no comprehensive legislatively produced "code"; rather, statutes tend to be specific solutions for specific problems. It is the reliance on case law that primarily distinguishes the common law nations from those using the various other types of systems.

Civil Law Systems

The major alternative system that developed under Western civilization is called the civil law system, or the code law system. There is some ambiguity in either term. All legal systems hear and decide civil law cases, in the sense of disputes between individuals, and many countries refer to their statutes dealing with particular topics as "codes." A civil law or code law system, however, is one in which the body of the legal rules is contained in one or a few comprehensive legislative enactments. All the law is brought together at one time in a systematized statement of the applicable legal rules. In France, for example, the process occurred in the early 1800s, under Napoleon's reign. National legal codes for the whole of France were adopted, covering civil law, civil procedure, criminal law, criminal procedure, and commercial law. This civil code is still the basic law in France today; the same rules would be applied to work out much the same results in ordinary cases of tort and contract.

Court cases in such a system are not considered to be an authoritative source of the legal rules, as they are in an Anglo-American system. The fact that a particular court interpreted a particular provision of the civil code in a particular way does not mean that future courts are bound to interpret that provision in the same way. They may or may not do so. The law is in the code, not in the cases. Where several cases all have interpreted a provision in a particular way, the French courts may feel bound to reach the same result in future cases, under the doctrine of *jurisprudence constante*. The major agency for growth and change, however, is the legislature, not the courts.

Civil law systems are used by most of the countries of Europe and Central and South America. Many of the countries of Asia and Africa adopted civil and commercial codes patterned on those of Europe to facilitate business transactions and commercial development. Many countries that were colonies have residues of the codes that were imposed on them during their colonial period.

Roman-Dutch Systems

As the result of another historical combination of circumstances, a very few countries today operate under what is called a Roman-Dutch System. These are former Dutch colonies, which were under Dutch rule at a time when the Netherlands had not yet adopted its modern civil code; it did so in 1823. The Dutch system at the time was based on the Roman law, as explained and developed by Dutch commentators. Several centuries of Roman legal developments had been summarized and systematized under the emperor Justinian in the *Corpus Juris Civilis*, published from 529 to 534 AD. The Dutch scholars then wrote comments explaining how the various Roman law rules applied in their country. Under this system, the "lawgiver" is the professor, not the judge and not the legislator. The judges should be guided by the authoritative textbook statements as to what the law is and how it is to be applied. The legislature, of course, has the power to change the law by enacting statutes, but until it does so, the law is in the textbooks.

This rather strange system exists, at least in residual form, in the former Dutch colonies of South Africa and Sri Lanka (formerly, Ceylon) and, perhaps, in Guyana.

Communist (Soviet) Legal Systems

Although Communist theory initially emphasized a future society in which there would be no need for law and the other organs of state power, the reality of governing a large and diverse empire forced some rather dramatic doctrinal and operational changes. Prior to the Bolshevik Revolution in 1917, Russia had been slowly developing as a civil law system. Tsarist Russia was an autocracy of the most extreme sort for most of its history, but some substantial progress toward the development of an independent bench and bar had been made with the reforms in 1861 and 1864. Presumably, further progress along these lines would have been made under the non-Bolshevik revolutionaries.

During most of its history, the Bolshevik regime had wavered between the ideological purity expressed in the idea that the law would "wither away" after the revolution, and the practical necessities involved in ruling the Soviet Union. Stalin decided in the 1930s that he needed a stronger state apparatus, rather than a "withered" one, and the concept of "socialist legality" was emphasized. Communist law was to be developed as law of a "new type," not based on the exploitation of one class by another, as were all "bourgeois" legal systems. This new legal system was to function in the interim period between the revolution and the achievement of the stage of full communism. Officially, the law was still supposed to wither away at some future date, but the time frame became rather indefinite. The practicalities of governance prevailed over ideological purity.

How, then, does Communist law differ from other systems? First, of course, its theoretical underpinnings are quite different. Justice is a bourgeois abstraction. Soviet judges were to be guided instead by their revolutionary legal consciousness. Second, all governmental agencies and institutions are really sources of legal rules; the decree or order of a lower level agency stands as the rule to be obeyed, unless and until it is superseded by a rule from a higher authority. Third, and perhaps most significant, the government and the party are above the law, rather than the other way around. One would find it hard to imagine, for instance, that any Soviet court could have ordered Gorbachev to produce documents that he wished to keep secret, as happened to President Nixon. Fourth, as a corollary, the bench and bar in the Soviet Union were not fully independent of governmental and political control. Although Soviet lawyers had some considerable latitude in handling ordinary contract, tort, and property cases, they could not function as the fearless champions of civil rights. As a result, there is a fifth dissimilarity from Western systems: Civil rights were granted or withheld by a Soviet-style regime to suit its own political and economic purposes; they may be exercised only in accordance with the wishes of the regime.

The Soviet-type system does have codes that have been adopted by the legislative bodies (although they may not be organized in quite so comprehensive a fashion as those in most civil law countries). It does have courts, judges, and lawyers. In recent years, the regime seemed to give the legal experts more freedom to operate. None of these surface similarities, however, should be allowed to obscure the fundamental differences that remained. The Soviet Union itself, of course, no longer exists. Remnants of this system survive in China, North Korea, Vietnam, and Cuba.

Religious and Customary Systems

For hundreds of millions of people, a religious or customary legal system provides the rules for their personal rights and behavior. Such topics as parent-child and husband-wife relationships, inheritance and other property rights, charitable transfers, and an individual's relationship with a religious organization are likely to be covered under these systems. A religious or customary system typically does not cover the legal topics involved in modern commerce and industry—business organizations, commercial contracts, patents and copyrights, and the like.

Customary tribal law still governs the personal lives of many Africans. In the Muslim countries of North Africa, the Middle East, and the rest of Asia, the Koran provides an authoritative source of legal rules for the topics that it covers. In India, Hindu law applies to the vast majority of the population. Jewish law contains provisions for marriage, divorce, and charitable giving that many of that faith feel are binding legal rules. Tribal law is still applied in many cases involving the personal or property rights of American Indians.

In the following case, the defendant is attempting to argue that Jewish law rather than the law of the state of Michigan is the controlling law concerning the transaction between the parties.

Mixed Systems

Because of the worldwide dispersal of legal, political, economic, and social ideas, many countries today have what might be best described as a "mixed" legal system. After the Dutch had imposed their Roman-Dutch legal system on the island of Ceylon, for example, the island became an English colony. English commercial statutes like the sales of goods act were adopted for Ceylon by the new colonial power. Both of these colonial legal systems continued to coexist with several earlier customary systems that predated the Dutch. The English commercial statutes were also adopted for India during its colonial period; since independence, India has patterned many of its constitutional law concepts on those of the U.S. Supreme Court. Iraq patterned its commercial code after that of France. And so it goes.

One of the most interesting legal "mixtures" ever was created on July 1, 1997, when the British Crown Colony of Hong Kong was returned to the People's Republic of China (PRC), as a "Special Administrative Region" (SAR). Under the United Kingdom/PRC

CASE 1

Congregation B'nai Sholom v. Martin
173 N.W.2d 504 (MI 1969)

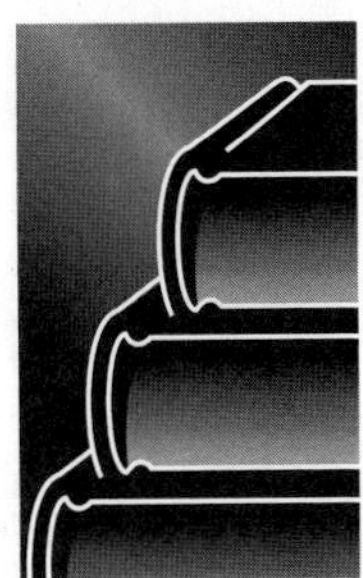

Facts: In January 1959, defendant Morris Martin became chairman of the Synagogue Building Committee. On April 22, 1959, plaintiff contracted Ira J. Miller, a professional fund-raiser, to assist in raising funds to build a new synagogue. On or about June 1, 1959, Morris Martin delivered to plaintiff's campaign office four pledge cards. The first three were signed, respectively, by Irving Martin, Jack Martin, and Morris Martin. The fourth was signed by Morris Martin in the name of Bessie Martin Steinberg. The four pledge cards were not filled out as to amount. Morris Martin wrote the words, "Total Donation $25,000.00" on an attached scrap of paper. Later in 1959, disputes arose between Morris Martin and other members of the congregation. On October 29, 1959, and again on November 8, 1959, Morris Martin attempted to withdraw the pledge.

On December 20, 1962, plaintiff, a nonprofit corporation, brought suit against Morris Martin, Irving Martin, Jack Martin, and Bessie Martin Steinberg. On November 17, 1965, the defendants filed a motion to amend their answer, which the trial judge denied. On August 24, 1966, the trial judge issued an opinion in which he granted judgment in favor of plaintiff against defendant Morris Martin for the sum of $25,000, plus interest at 5 percent from June 30, 1964; Morris Martin was granted the right within 30 days to introduce a third party action for contribution from defendants Jack Martin and Irving Martin. Appeal was taken from the judgment in favor of plaintiff and against Morris Martin to the Court of Appeals, which affirmed the trial judge. The case was then appealed to the Michigan Supreme Court.

Issue: Should the defendants have been permitted to amend their answer so as to raise the application of Jewish law as a defense?

Decision: Yes. Judgment reversed, and case remanded for further proceedings.

Opinion by Justice Adams: "The trial judge erred in denying defendants' motions for leave to amend for the reason that the affidavit of Dr. Rabbi Bernard B. Perlow raised a question of fact as to Jewish custom which may be controlling upon the parties. . . .

"The defendants' motions to amend were supported by the affidavit of a Dr. Rabbi Bernard D. Perlow, a rabbi and a scholar. After stating his qualifications as an expert witness, he included the following points in his opinion:

5. That the religious customs, practices, and laws binding on all Jews are codified in the work known as the *Shulchan Aruch;* that this code is generally regarded as binding as a matter of religious faith by both Orthodox and Conservative Jews. . . .

6. That in the opinion of this deponent, the *Shulchan Aruch*, as well as the custom and tradition for more than a thousand years, prohibits the bringing of a suit in the civil courts of any state by a synagogue against any of its members or vice versa and is contrary to Jewish law and is prohibited; that any such civil controversy must be first brought before the Jewish religious court known as the Beth Din (a Jewish rabbinical court); that under Jewish law, matters of charity to the synagogue go to the heart of the Jewish religion; that a charitable contribution to a synagogue is considered a religious matter by and between the synagogue and the member; that for a synagogue to file a suit against one of its members upon an alleged charitable contribution without submitting it to a Beth Din is what is known in Jewish law as a "Chillul Hashem" which is a profanation of God's name and such action is such a grave sin in Jewish law, that it warrants excommunication. . . .

7. That it is expressly stated in Hyman E. Goldin's translation of Rabbi Solomon Ganzfried's Code of Jewish Law, Kidzur Schulchan Aruch, published in New York City by the Hebrew Publishing Company in 1961, volume 4, page 67, that it is forbidden to bring a suit in the civil courts even if their decision would be in accordance with the law of Israel; that even if the two litigants are willing to try the case before such a court, it is forbidden; that even if they make an oral or a written agreement to that effect, it is of no avail; that whoever takes a case against another Jew involving religious matters, is a Godless person and he has violated and defiled the law of Moses. . . .

"Nothing appears in the record before us in this case to warrant the trial judge's denial of the motion. When the rights of the parties are being tested on motions for summary judgment filed, not at the election of the parties themselves but at the behest of the trial judge, a defendant should most certainly be allowed to amend to assert any defense he may have before the court has ruled."

CASE 2

Hong Kong SAR v. Ma Wai Kwan & Ors

1997-2 HKC 315 (H.K. Court of Appeal, 1997)

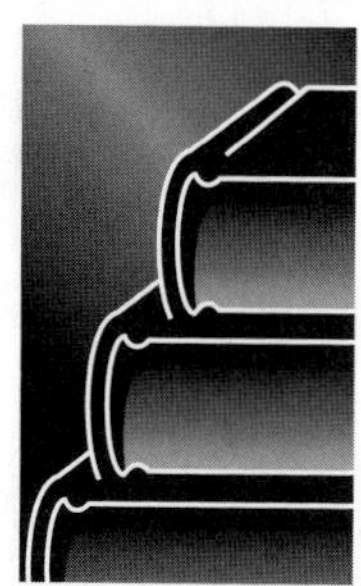

Facts: Three people were on trial in Hong Kong for the crime of "conspiracy to pervert the course of public justice," when the United Kingdom returned the colony to the PRC on July 1, 1997. On July 3, the defendants suggested to the trial court that the common law (i.e., non-statutory) crime with which they were charged was no longer part of the law in the Hong Kong SAR. For an authoritative interpretation of that legal issue, the prosecution asked the Court of Appeal for a ruling. A three-judge panel (Chan, Nazareth, and Mortimer) heard the arguments and made the ruling.

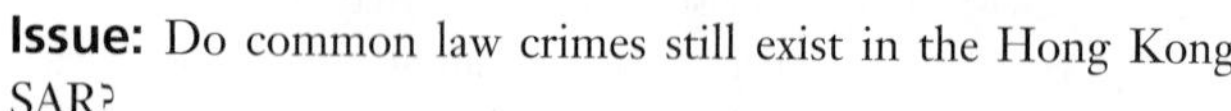

Issue: Do common law crimes still exist in the Hong Kong SAR?

Decision: Yes. Case remanded for trial.

Opinion by Chief Judge Chan: "On 19 December 1984, the Joint Declaration was signed between the Government of the People's Republic of China (PRC) and the Government of the United Kingdom. By this Joint Declaration, Hong Kong was to be restored to China with effect from 1 July 1997. Under art. 3 of the Joint Declaration, China declared certain basic policies regarding Hong Kong. There was to be established the HKSAR, which would enjoy a high degree of autonomy. Under art. 3(12), these basic policies would be stipulated in a Basic Law to be promulgated by the NPC [National People's Congress], and would remain unchanged for fifty years from 1 July 1997. These policies were further elaborated in Annex I to the Joint Declaration. The Basic Law for the HKSAR was drafted by the Drafting Committee of the Basic Laws, which consisted of members from China and Hong Kong. It took many years to complete. It was promulgated on 4 April 1990, and was to take effect from 1 July 1997.

"The Basic Law is not only a brainchild of an international treaty, the Joint Declaration. It is also a national law of the PRC and the constitution of the HKSAR. It translates the basic policies enshrined in the Joint Declaration into more practical terms. The essence of these policies is that the current social, economic, and legal systems in Hong Kong will remain unchanged for fifty years. The purpose of the Basic Law is to ensure that these basic policies are implemented and that there can be continued stability and prosperity for the HKSAR. Continuity after the change of sovereignty is therefore of vital importance. . . .

"The Basic Law is a unique document. It reflects a treaty made between two nations. It deals with the relationship between the Sovereign and an autonomous region which practices a different system. It stipulates the organizations and functions of the different branches of government. It sets out the rights and obligations of the citizens. Hence, it has at least three dimensions: international, domestic and constitutional. It must also be borne in mind that it was not drafted by common law lawyers. It was drafted in the Chinese language with an official English version, but the Chinese version takes precedence in case of discrepancies. That being the background and features of the Basic Law, it is obvious that there will be difficulties in the interpretation of the various provisions. . . . In my view, the generous and purposive approach may not be applicable in interpreting every article of the Basic Law. However, in the context of the present case which involves the constitutional aspects of the Basic Law, I agree that this approach is more appropriate. . . .

"In my view, the intent of the Basic Law is clear. There is to be no change in our laws and legal system (except those which contravene the Basic Law). These are the very fabric of our society. Continuity is the key to stability. Any disruption will be disastrous. Even one moment of legal vacuum may lead to chaos. Everything relating to the laws and the legal system except those provisions which contravene the Basic Law has to continue to be in force. The existing system must already be in place on 1 July 1997. That must be the intent of the Basic Law. . . .

> "The wording is equally clear. The Basic Law is the constitution of the HKSAR. It is the most important piece of law in the land. It states clearly what the position is as from 1 July 1997. In my view, the word 'shall' in these provisions can only be used in the mandatory and declaratory sense. The meaning of these provisions is this. On 1 July 1997, when the HKSAR comes into existence and the Basic Law comes into effect, these are to be the laws and legal system in force and the principles applicable in place. There is no express or implied requirement in any of these provisions that the laws previously in force or the legal system previously in place need to be formally adopted before they can continue to be applicable after the change of sovereignty. On the contrary, the use of the terms 'shall be maintained,' 'shall continue' and 'shall be' leaves absolutely no doubt in my mind that there can be no question of any need for an act of adoption. These terms are totally inconsistent with such a requirement. . . .
>
> "The respondents' argument is based mainly on Article 160, which uses the words 'shall be adopted.' It is suggested that 'shall' in this term is used in the future tense. In my view, that provision cannot be read in isolation but must be considered in the light of the rest of the Basic Law, including in particular the articles to which I have referred above. It cannot be construed to have a meaning which is inconsistent with the other articles relating to the adoption of the existing laws and legal system. . . .

"For the reasons which I have set out above, I have come to the conclusion that upon a true construction and interpretation of the relevant provisions of the Basic Law, the laws previously in force in Hong Kong, including the common law, have been adopted and became the laws of HKSAR on 1 July 1997, the judicial system together with the principles applicable to court proceedings have continued, and indictments and pending court proceedings have continued to be valid.

"The answers to the questions reserved for this court are that the common law has survived the change of sovereignty, and the three respondents are liable to answer to and be tried under the amended indictment."

Although this first major decision on Hong Kong's new status is thus very encouraging, the jury is still out as to how long this special situation will be able to exist. The serious financial crisis that spread through much of Asia in late 1997 and early 1998 may force some painful adjustments in Hong Kong's unique economic and financial arrangements. Whatever occurs, the SAR's economic importance within the world trading system will make developments there closely watched by global businesses.

treaty providing for this change of sovereignty, and under the PRC's "Basic Law" for the Hong Kong SAR, Hong Kong was to retain its British-derived common law (except where it conflicted with the Basic Law) for 50 years after the transfer. This attempt to maintain a "common law" island in a "communist sea" raises any number of very interesting questions, which the courts are only beginning to decide. The above case is one early interpretation of how these unmatched pieces are going to be fitted together.

International Law

History

International trade is of course nothing new. Neither are international relations or treaties between sovereign states. Almost from earliest recorded times, **customs** developed for the proper handling of international affairs and the problems that inevitably arose. Much of early international law was concerned with the law of the sea—freedom of passage, rights of ships in foreign ports, salvage and fishing rights, and the like—and with the rules covering foreign diplomatic personnel. City-states and nations that were important commercial and trading centers often published collections of the customs that governed international trade. There is evidence that the Egyptians had such international law practices as early as 1400 BC. Rhodes, the largest of the Dodecanese Islands, in the Aegean Sea, had a "code" of international law by 700 BC. The Greek city-states also adopted certain practices for dealing with diplomatic personnel and trading disputes. Roman law developed the ***ius gentium***, which dealt with relations between noncitizens, as an alternative to the ***ius civile***, which applied only to citizens. Because of its adoption of more universally applicable legal principles, the ius gentium eventually came to dominate the great Roman legal system. Important collections of international legal practices were published by Visby, Sweden, one of the most important members of the Hanseatic League in the 11th century, and by Louis IX of France (the Code of Oleron) in the mid-13th century. Legal historians generally date modern international law from the adoption of the Treaty of Westphalia in 1648.

These rules were originally labelled the "Law of Nations," indicating that they were applicable primarily (or exclusively) to the relations between nations. With the increasing recognition of the international rights of public and private organizations—and of individuals, the phrase *international law* came into general use. The terms *supranational law* and *transnational law* are also applied to these rules that transcend national boundaries.

Sources

International law is drawn from the widest variety of sources; custom, treaties, judicial precedents, and textbooks have all played a part in its development. Hugo Grotius, a Dutch lawyer, is usually called "the father of international law" because of his great work, *De Jure Bellis ac Pacis*, published in 1625. In it, he spoke of international law as being based on **natural law**, which was common to all nations—the "dictate of right reason." This was in marked contrast to the "positivists," who derived international law from the customs of nations in their dealings with each other. In fact, both of these elements have played a part, along with specific treaties governing the international relations of two or more countries, and decisions of arbitrators and national and international courts.

The Covenant of the League of Nations established the World Court in the Hague after World War I. A similar body, the **International Court of Justice (ICJ),** functions there today under the United Nations (UN) charter. Not all nations have fully accepted the jurisdiction of the ICJ in all matters, and many very important matters remain to be resolved by specific treaties. One of the major unresolved international law problems relates to the use of the seabed of the world's oceans and the right to the enormous quantities of mineral nodules that are to be found there. The Communist nations and the "have-nots" generally favor some sort of world ownership, through the UN. The United States and most of the developed countries favor an arrangement that will leave substantial room for free enterprise mining of the ocean floor. The economic and political stakes in this one question are enormous.

By definition, customs take time to develop. This is especially true in the international arena, with the many different forms of political, economic, and social arrangements in some 200 sovereign nations. The relationships that are occurring in our modern world at lightning speed will not wait for "custom" to develop over decades or centuries. International sales, financing, investment, communication, franchising, and other transactions are happening, whether the legal rules are there or not. Increasingly, to meet the demands of modern trade and commerce, nations have turned to treaties. The UN Convention on **Contracts for the International Sale of Goods (CISG)** is perhaps the most notable example of this sort of international legislation. There are many other examples, such as the international carriage of goods, the use of letters of credit and negotiable instruments, and the taking of evidence in other countries. Within the EU, massive new bodies of laws and regulations are being generated by the legal institutions set up under the 1957 Treaty of Rome.

Treaties also take time to draft and to adopt, but much less time than the development of customs. Once properly adopted by a nation, according to its constitutional procedures, the treaty becomes law for that nation. There is generally no question as to when and how this happens. The treaty will still need to be interpreted and applied by the various courts to specific situations, but there is usually no argument over what the law "is"—it is the treaty, as written.

The *Aquino* case shows that both U.S. state courts and national courts have the power to interpret and apply treaties.

CASE 3

Aquino v. Asiana Airlines, Inc.

105 Cal.App.4th 1272 (CA 2003)

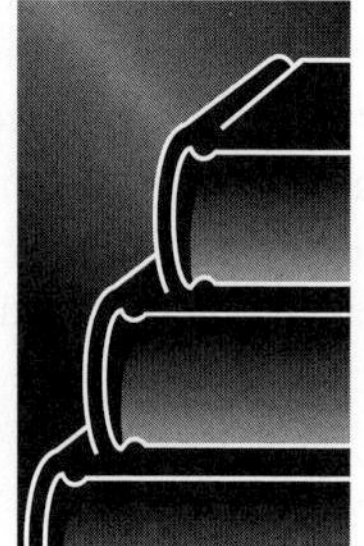

Facts: Modesta Aquino and her husband David (now deceased) had round-trip tickets for an Asiana flight on November 29, 1999, from San Francisco to the Philippines. When they attempted to check in, their daughter was asked how old they were. When told they were 90, an Asiana manager said they would need a doctor's certificate indicating it was safe for them to fly. They walked to the airport medical clinic, were not given a medical certificate, and then walked back to Asiana. When their daughter insisted they should be permitted on the plane, the manager threatened to call the police, who did arrive shortly. The Aquinos left the airport and later took another airline to the Philippines, where David died on February 5, 2000.

Modesta sued for herself and on behalf of David, alleging various tort and contract claims under state law. The trial court granted Asiana's motion for summary judgment. Aquino appealed.

Issue: Were the plaintiffs engaged in "embarking or disembarking" at the time of the defendants' alleged wrongful conduct? Are plaintiffs' claims preempted by the national Airline Deregulation Act of 1978?

Decision: No. Judgment reversed as to all claims other than "intentional infliction of emotional distress."

Opinion by Judge Rivera: "Where it is applicable, the Warsaw Convention provides the exclusive remedy for personal injuries. . . .

"However, in order for the Warsaw Convention to govern a claim, the incident giving rise to the claim must take place 'on board the aircraft or in the course of any of the operations of embarking or disembarking.' . . .

"The question of whether a passenger is involved in any of the operations of embarking is a question of law to be decided based on the facts of each case. . . . In making this determination, courts focus on several factors, in particular '(1) activity of the passengers at the time of the accident; (2) the restrictions, if any, on their movements; (3) the imminence of actual boarding; [and] (4) the physical proximity of the passengers to the gate.' . . .

"Courts have found the Warsaw Convention inapplicable . . . where passengers were still in common areas, were not under the control of airline personnel, or were not physically near the departure gate. . . .

"Based on the record presented, we conclude the Aquinos were not engaged in the operations of embarking. At the time of the events giving rise to this action, they were in a common passenger area, attempting to check in. They had not checked their luggage or received their boarding passes. They had not progressed through security to an area restricted to passengers. Indeed, their claim is that they were not allowed to begin the operations of embarkation. The record does not show that they ever became engaged in those operations. Asiana does not direct us to any case extending the reach of the Warsaw Convention to the stage of attempting to check in, and our independent research does not disclose any. . . .

"Asiana argues that even if the Warsaw Convention does not preempt this action, the Airline Deregulation Act of 1978 does. . . .

"The scope of this preemption, particularly as it relates to 'service,' has been the subject of considerable dispute, although it is clear that the Act does not preempt all state law based actions related to an airline's conduct. . . .

"The federal circuit courts have not devised a uniform test for determining whether a state law action is related to an airline's 'service.' . . .

"We agree with both the [U.S.] Ninth Circuit Court of Appeals and the [California] Second District Court of Appeals that the Act does not preempt state law personal injury and discrimination claims that have only a peripheral effect on deregulation. . . .

"The Aquinos have also alleged a cause of action for breach of contract. The United States Supreme Court has concluded that the Act does not preempt routine breach of contract claims. . . .

"Accordingly, we conclude the Act does not preempt any of the Aquinos' claims. . . .

"We affirm the judgment of the superior court to the extent it granted summary judgment on the cause of action for intentional infliction of emotional distress. In all other respects, we reverse the judgment and remand for further proceedings consistent with this opinion."

International Courts

Because nations have been very reluctant to give up any of their ultimate sovereign power to international bodies, the use of truly international courts has, historically, been quite limited. National governments do not want to have their own decisions reviewed by a multinational body that may represent very different political and ideological views than their own. As a result, most cases involving international law are in fact litigated in national courts, including, in the United States, the state courts. The *Aquino* case above illustrates this point, as do many other examples. Two international courts are worth noting. Additionally, **arbitration** has been a popular method of resolving international disputes, both those arising between private parties and those involving governments or their agencies.

International Court of Justice

The ICJ was established as the successor to the Permanent Court of International Justice to hear disputes between nations. The ICJ was authorized by Chapter XIV of the UN charter and an annexed statute. This statute is a comprehensive statement of the ICJ's organization, jurisdiction, and procedure.

The statute provides that the ICJ shall consist of 15 judges and that no more than two of them shall be citizens of the same nation. They must be people of high moral character, and they must have the same qualifications as would be required in their respective countries for appointment to the highest judicial offices in those countries, or they must be **jurisconsults** of recognized competence in international law. The judges are elected by the UN General Assembly and by the UN Security Council from a list of nominations submitted by nominating bodies from the various member nations. Their term of office is 9 years, with five members of the court being reelected or replaced every 3 years.

The General Assembly and the Security Council must hold their elections independently of each other. If a person's name appears on the list of successful candidates of both the General Assembly and the Security Council, that person is elected. If there are no successful candidates after the first meeting and ballot, then two more meetings may be held and ballots cast. If there is still no agreement, then a deadlock procedure must be followed. Three members of the Security Council and three members of the General Assembly will then meet and make the final selection of the people to fill the vacancies.

The ICJ was not set up to hear disputes between private citizens concerning international contract or property disputes. Because only nations may be parties in cases that are brought before the ICJ, the court's decisions are of less significance to international business operations than are the decisions of national courts that apply international law.

European Union Courts. As noted previously, the EU has a number of legal bodies that are empowered to establish rules binding across national borders. Originally, there was only one court—the European Court of Justice. To help with the greatly increased workload of interpreting all the many new EU regulations, the Court of First Instance was set up in 1987.

These courts hear cases involving EU law and regulations, which supersede national laws to the extent of any conflict. Each nation's courts are supposed to follow EU law, but if one party feels they did not, an appeal can be taken to the EU courts. Although these EU court decisions are binding only with the EU, they may be used as evidence of customary international law. As a result of the activity of these EU courts, therefore, international law is growing rapidly.

Thus far, no other regional economic grouping has set up a supranational court system of this kind.

NAFTA Trade Dispute Panels. The North American Free Trade Agreement (NAFTA; Canada, Mexico, United States) did not set up any court comparable to those in the EU. It does, however, establish a procedure for nonbinding arbitration of trade disputes among the members.

NAFTA provides a right of consultation when one member feels that another is violating the rules. If not settled through consultation within 45 days, NAFTA's Trade Commission (representatives from the three nations, who oversee the implementation of the agreement) tries to mediate the dispute. Failing that, the complaining nation can choose to have the dispute heard by a World Trade Organization (WTO) panel or a NAFTA panel. The complainant's choice is normally final, but for disputes involving the respondent's rules on health and safety, environment, or conservation, that nation can insist on a NAFTA arbitration. The NAFTA panel's final report is sent to the Trade Commission. The parties to the dispute then have 30 days to finalize a settlement (usually, by adopting the panel's recommendations). If there is no final resolution by the parties, the complaining nation (assuming it has won the arbitration) can revoke benefits equivalent to those it has been denied.

Special procedures are also available for such matters as investment disputes, alleged dumping of goods, and others. (See the *New York Times*, March 11, 2001, Section 3.)

World Trade Organization Trade Dispute Panels. The WTO, established as a result of the 1994 renegotiation of the General Agreement on Tariffs and Trade (GATT), also provides a mechanism for the resolution of trade disputes among its members. The WTO procedure is similar to that under NAFTA—consultation between the parties; investigation and report of the panel; appellate review; adoption of the panel (or appellate) decision; and implementation of the decision.

If a WTO member complains about the action of another, the complainant may demand consultation on the issue. The respondent has 10 days to reply and must agree to start discussions within 30 days. Failing such agreement, the complaining member can ask for the immediate establishment of an investigatory panel. The parties have 60 days to discuss and settle their dispute between themselves.

If there is no settlement, the complainant can ask that a panel be established. The panel reviews the parties' documents and arguments and can also gather evidence independently. It is required to submit both an interim and a final report.

Either party can request a review of the legal questions involved, by the WTO's Appellate Body. It is composed of seven members, appointed for 4-year terms. (They may be reappointed once.)

The Appellate Body's decisions are sent to the WTO's Dispute Settlement Body (DSB), which is a special assembly with representatives from all WTO members. Panel decisions also go to the DSB. All decisions must be approved by the DSB, unless its members *unanimously* reject the decision.

At the implementation stage, an offending nation is first given a reasonable time (normally 15 months) to bring its rules into line with WTO requirements. Failing that, the parties try to negotiate a fair compensation (some special trade benefit) for the violation. If there is still no agreement, the complainant asks the DSB for permission to retaliate against the offending nation, for example, by revoking some of its WTO privileges in trading with the complainant.

WTO procedures also permit binding arbitration as an alternative to the panel/appeal/DSB steps.

International Arbitration

It is very common for international business contracts to contain an arbitration clause whereby the parties agree to submit any controversy relating to the contract to an arbitrator or an arbitration panel, rather than to go to court. In any business contract dispute, arbitration will almost certainly save time and legal expense, and the parties can select an arbitrator with expertise in the substantive area involved. These same advantages hold at the international level, but there are additional procedural reasons for including such a clause in the international contract. With an international dispute, there are always potential questions as to which court in what country would have jurisdiction, how service of process can be effected across international boundaries, and which country's law applies. These problems can be minimized with an arbitration clause that specifies the law to be applied, the method of selecting the arbitrator, the procedures to be followed, and the allocation of expenses between the parties. Although it is true that arbitrators' awards are sometimes not paid voluntarily, they will generally be enforced by the courts of most nations if a lawsuit is necessary.

Conflicts of Laws

Much of private international law (the rules covering international disputes between private parties) has to do with the conflicts that inevitably arise as to which nation's law should apply. This is also described as the "choice-of-law" problem. Much the same set of problems, albeit on a smaller scale, exists between state legal systems within the United States.

Whose Law Should Apply?

An elaborate set of rules, or at least presumptions, has been worked out for international disputes. Questions as to the validity of a contract are generally decided according to the law of the nation where the contract was made. Issues arising out of the performance of a contract are usually resolved by the law of the nation where performance occurs. If there are questions as to the internal management or organization of a business, those are decided according to the law of the nation where the firm was organized. For tort cases, the court may use the law of the place where the tort was committed or the law of the nation that has the greatest interest in the case, all facts considered. Each of these rather simplistic "rules" is of course subject to interpretation and to various exceptions.

There is also a clear rule that the court hearing the case uses its own procedure. However, there may still be sharp differences in interpretation as to what is "procedure" and what is "substantive law."

Due to the uncertainties surrounding this choice-of-law problem, the parties to an international contract may very well want to include their own "choice" clause in their contract. Within limits, courts will generally recognize and enforce such contract clauses.

Where Can the Case Be Tried?

An equally difficult problem arises in choosing the place where the case is to be heard. Usually, a defendant will want the trial in its home nation, where it has a kind of "home-court advantage," due to logistics and its familiarity with the system. The plaintiff will have to weigh the costs of travel and local counsel into the equation in deciding whether to pursue the case in another nation that could be some distance away. The plaintiff's lawyer will try to find a forum where there is a good chance of winning the case and a good chance of recovering substantial damages.

Where Can a Company Be Taxed?

Equally important to the bottom line (or perhaps even more so) is the question of where a company can be taxed—and for what. In general, the rules for international taxation are similar to those applicable among the states, within the United States.

A company's sales can be taxed by the nation in which those sales are made. This rule may cause litigation over sales made on the Internet, but the probable interpretation is that the "net" sale is made in the country where the customer's order is accepted by the seller. If such out-of-nation sales are exempt from sales tax there, the customer company may have to pay a so-called "use" tax to its government for the privilege of using the goods in that nation. In many nations, property owners are required to pay annual taxes. This is a simple enough calculation for real estate, which by definition is immovable. For personal property, however, there can be very complex apportionment issues when the property is used in more than one nation. Which country gets to tax how much of an airline's airplane fleet that is being used in many nations over the course of a year? The problem is complicated by the fact that nations are not required to use the same formula to do the apportioning, and by the fact that there is no international court to set the ground rules, as there is in the United States. A company owes an income tax (if there is one) to any nation in which it is earning income. For multinationals, some income may in fact be taxed twice, if nations are using different apportionment formulas for calculating their appropriate taxable shares of the multinational's income. The company will of course have to pay fees and charges to its home nation for the privilege of organizing as a firm and may have to pay annual fees for the privilege of doing business as such in any nation in which it has operations.

In addition to the complexities involved in the aforementioned rules, there are some additional constitutional problems in the United States, with respect to the taxation of international business operations. State and local governments may not be able to impose personal property taxes on planes and ships that are being fully taxed by their home country. The **U.S. Constitution** prohibits states from imposing tariffs on exports or imports and the national government from taxing exports. Various national government programs also limit taxation in "duty-free" zones and locations. Similar restrictions doubtless exist in most nations, so that the job of keeping a multinational company in tax compliance, in all its locations, is probably having a significant impact on the bottom line.

Extraterritoriality

Conflict of laws is virtually inevitable any time one nationattempts to enforce its laws with respect to persons and things outside its geographic territory. Although there is a general presumption against the validity of such extraterritorial enforcement, nations are increasingly trying to justify it under one theory or another. The United States has been one of the most aggressive "legal imperialists," to the point of causing the serious alienation of some of its strongest allies.

Antitrust law is the oldest and perhaps still the most controversial area in which the United States applies its law to activities overseas. In the 1945 *Alcoa* case, the U.S. Second Circuit ruled that acts in other nations that were intended to have, and in fact did have, significant "effects" within the U.S. market could be prosecuted under the **Sherman Antitrust Act**. Since that time, a considerable body of international law has developed in support of this "effects" doctrine. Other nations have also used this argument as a basis for applying their laws to conduct outside their geographic borders.

In response to discovery orders from U.S. courts directed against their businesses, the United Kingdom and several other nations have passed so-called "blocking" statutes. These laws order the nation's businesses *not* to comply with the U.S. courts' discovery orders. In addition, the United Kingdom also has "clawback" statutes that permit its businesses to sue U.S. companies (that are subject to the UK courts' jurisdiction), to recover the punitive parts of treble damages awarded in U.S. antitrust cases. Nation-to-nation negotiations have thus far been unable to resolve these serious conflicts of laws issues.

If antitrust is the most controversial area of international application of national laws, the U.S. **Foreign Corrupt Practices Act of 1977 (FCPA)** is surely a close second. The FCPA prohibits payments by U.S. companies to foreign government officials to influence their decisions on purchases of goods and services for the government. The FCPA applies even if such payments are customary, and expected, in that other nation. Such payments are permitted by the FCPA only if they are expressly permitted by statute in the other nation. The FCPA does permit the reimbursement of a foreign official's reasonable expenses incurred during contract negotiations. It also allows payments of small sums to minor officials as a kind of "tip" ("grease payment") for doing their (nondiscretionary) duties swiftly and effectively. It would thus be illegal to make a payment to a foreign official to get him or her to decide to buy your goods rather than a competitor's, but it would be permissible to pay a few dollars to the local customs inspector to have him or her expedite the processing of your incoming goods. What is illegal is bribery of an official to influence that person's discretionary decision.

Serious criminal penalties are provided for illegal bribes. Individuals are subject to up to 5 years in prison, plus fines up to $100,000, for each willful violation of the FCPA. Companies may be fined up to $2 million for each offense. Companies are not permitted to reimburse their employees for fines paid for such violations.

Other nations have accused the United States of "cultural imperialism" in applying its business standards to transactions in their country. The jurisdictional justification for the FCPA is that that United States is merely regulating the conduct of *their* businesses, including their conduct overseas. They are not attempting to tell French firms what they can do in France, only telling U.S. firms what they can do in France. Nonetheless, there is certainly an extraterritoriality problem with the FCPA. More recently, the United States has led efforts to get some international standards for trade practices, especially through such organizations as the Organization for Economic Cooperation and Development (OECD). The OECD nations include most of Western Europe, Japan, Australia, New Zealand, and Canada, in addition to the United States. Adoption of a multinational standard by most of the world's developed nations would go a long way toward easing the conflicts of laws related to business practices.

The OECD has also been very active in developing rules to protect the environment. Here, too, such multinational agreement would minimize the potential conflicts among the very different national environmental standards. Multination treaties on this subject have also been proposed. In the absence of international standards, companies clearly have a legal duty to comply with the environmental rules where their facilities are located. The more difficult questions relate to whether they also have a duty to consider the rules in other nations, where their operations may inflict environmental damage. Cutting down the Brazilian rain forest has worldwide environmental (and other) implications. Is it sufficient merely to comply with Brazil's environmental laws? If there is such a further obligation, by whose standards is it to be judged? Who protects the "global commons"—space, the oceans, Antarctica? In a 1993 case, the U.S. Court of Appeals for the District of Columbia Circuit decided that the activities of U.S. agencies in Antarctica were subject to U.S. environmental laws. Because the agency that had made the decision was located in D.C. and directing its own personnel in Antarctica, the decision required the filing of an environmental impact statement, in accordance with U.S. law.

Sovereign Immunity and Act of State Doctrines

Two recognized rules of international law limit the ability of courts in one nation to review the acts of other nations' governments. The **sovereign immunity doctrine** says that a government cannot be sued without its consent—not only in its own courts, but also in the courts of other nations. Some nations claim this immunity extends to all governmental activities, of whatever nature, including the actions of a government as the operator of nationalized/socialized industries. Other nations (including the United States) limit the sovereign's immunity from suit to more traditional governmental operations and do not extend it to a government's "business" activities. The U.S. Foreign Sovereign Immunities Act of 1976 codifies this more limited immunity rule, for lawsuits in U.S. courts.

CASE 4

Doe v. Unocal
110 F.Supp.2d 1294 (C.D. CA 2000)

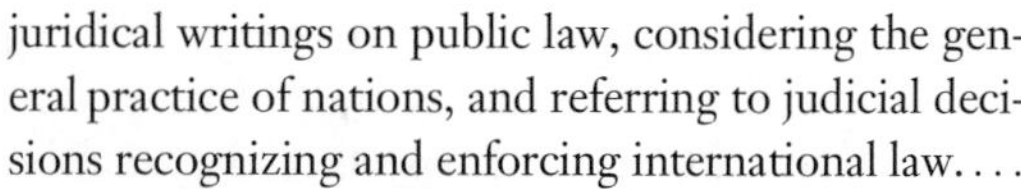

Facts: Unocal entered into a joint venture with Total S.A.—a French oil company—and the Burma (present-day Myanmar) government, to extract natural gas from oil fields off the coast and to transport the gas in a new pipeline to the border of Thailand. Fifteen Burmese villagers from the Tenasserim region filed these two lawsuits, alleging international law violations including torture, rape, murder, forced labor, and forced relocation. They further allege California state torts, including false imprisonment, assault, intentional infliction of emotional distress, and negligence. These wrongs were allegedly committed by the Burmese military while engaged in building roads and providing security for the pipeline.

Unocal has moved for a directed verdict.

Issue: Is Unocal liable under international law for wrongful actions by agents of the Burmese Government?

Decision: No. Summary judgment for Unocal.

Opinion by Judge Lew: "The Alien Tort Claims Act ('ATCA') states: 'The district courts shall have original jurisdiction of any civil action by an alien for a tort only, committed in violation of the law of nations or a treaty of the United States.' . . .

"Actionable violations of international law must be of a norm that is specific, universal, and obligatory. . . . When ascertaining the content of the law of nations, the Court must interpret international law not as it was in 1789 (the year the ATCA was enacted), but as it has evolved and exists among the nations of the world today. . . . The norms of the law of nations are found by consulting juridical writings on public law, considering the general practice of nations, and referring to judicial decisions recognizing and enforcing international law. . . .

"The parties dispute whether only those violations that rise to the level of a jus cogen violation are actionable under [the ATCA]. . . . Customary international law rests on the consent of the states. . . . Those states that refuse to agree to a norm of customary international law are not bound by it. . . . In contrast, jus cogens norms, norms derived from values taken to be fundamental by the international community, enjoy the highest status within customary international law and are binding on all nations. . . . It is well accepted that torture, murder, genocide and slavery all constitute violations of jus cogens norms. . . .

"Here, Plaintiffs present evidence that before joining the Project, Unocal knew that the military had a record of committing human rights abuses; that the Project hired the military to provide security for the Project, a military that forced villagers to work and entire villages to relocate for the benefit of the Project; that the military, while forcing villagers to work and relocate, committed numerous acts of violence; and that Unocal knew, or should have known that the military did commit, was committing, and would continue to commit these tortuous acts. . . . Unocal and [the Government] shared the goal of a profitable project. However, this shared goal does not establish joint action. Plaintiffs present no evidence that Unocal 'participated or influenced' the military's unlawful conduct; nor do Plaintiffs present evidence that Unocal 'conspired' with the military to commit the challenged conduct. . . .

"For the reasons set forth above, Unocal's motion for summary judgment as to Plaintiffs' federal claims is GRANTED and Plaintiffs' state law claims are dismissed without prejudice."

Although only a government may claim "sovereign immunity," the **act of state doctrine** may be raised by private litigants as well as governments. This rule says that the validity of the actions of a government within its own nation cannot be reviewed by the courts of other nations. Thus, in the famous *Sabbatino* case, the U.S. Supreme Court decided that U.S. courts could not judge the legality of Cuba's nationalization of certain business assets. And despite the very unfriendly relations between the United States and Cuba, the State Department actually filed an amicus curiae brief in support of the Cuban government's position!

The *Unocal* case illustrates a significant current problem: the extent to which a company can be held liable for the wrongful acts of its governmental business partner.

International Sales of Goods

One of the most recent important developments in the area of international commercial law is the adoption by 50 or more nations of the UN CISG. According to its terms, CISG applies when the parties to the sale of goods are doing the deal through offices that are located in two nations, each of which has ratified the CISG. It also applies if only one party's relevant office is located in a CISG nation, but the normal international choice-of-law rules favor the application of that nation's laws. However, when the United States ratified CISG, they specified that it would apply only where both parties were doing business through offices located in CISG nations. For businesses working out of U.S. offices, then, CISG will apply only if the trading partner is working through an office in another CISG nation. Even if CISG does (potentially) apply under these rules, it permits the parties to choose another body of law if they wish or to modify in their agreement any of the CISG rules.

CISG applies only to commercial (business to business) sales of goods, not to consumer transactions. It does not cover liability for personal injuries allegedly caused by the goods, even if the sale of the goods was made to a business. (Potential liability for on-the-job employee injuries will continue to be covered by the law of the buyer's or the seller's nation.) Although CISG does cover the passing of risk of loss of the goods (see Chapter 17), it does not cover title issues. Ownership of the goods, and the rights of third parties against the goods, will also be covered by local law, not the CISG. Likewise, "validity" questions arising because of alleged fraud or illegality are left to local law.

CISG's rules on contract formation are discussed in Chapters 8, 9, and 10. The risk of loss rules are covered in Chapter 17. Sellers' quality obligations are summarized and compared in Chapter 18. Selected sections of CISG, covering these major issues, appear as Appendix D.

Letters of Credit

The **letter of credit** is a very common and very useful financial arrangement in international trade. Of course, it may also be used for business transactions occurring wholly within one country or even as a means of establishing one's credit for nonbusiness purposes, but its main use is in international business transactions.

The basic idea of a letter of credit is simple enough. As defined in the Uniform Commercial Code (UCC) 5-103, a letter of credit means "an engagement by a bank or other person made at the request of a customer ... that the issuer will honor drafts or other demands for payment upon compliance with the condition specified in the credit." A letter of credit may be either revocable or irrevocable. In many cases the draft or demand for payment must be accompanied by the presentation of certain required documents, such as a bill of lading indicating that goods have been shipped. Typically the "customer" referred to in the preceding definition is a foreign buyer of goods. The letter of credit is being used as the payment mechanism for the goods. The buyer goes to its bank, where it has established credit, and requests that the bank issue a letter of credit in favor of the overseas seller, which is the "beneficiary" of the credit. The credit will indicate the maximum amount of money that the seller is authorized to draw and will specify what documents the seller will have to present to the bank to get the money. Quite frequently, the arrangement will provide for the buyer's bank to transmit the letter to a bank in the seller's country, for convenience. When the seller ships goods according to the terms of the sales contract, it presents the shipping documents to the bank and gets the contract price for them.

Within the United States, **UCC, Article 5** governs letters of credit. In international transactions, the parties should specify which country's law controls the transaction. In the absence of such a provision in the parties' contract, the general rules of private international law (choice-of-law rules) would determine which country's law should be applied to the dispute. As to disputes between the customer and its bank relating to the issuance and validity of the letter of credit, the law of the country of issuance would probably be applied. As to the responsibilities of the correspondent bank in the seller's country for handling the credit and verifying the documents presented, that country's law should be applied. Once again, it is best to anticipate such problems and make provisions in the contract for handling them when and if they arise.

Significance of This Chapter

As business operations have become increasingly global, it has become increasingly more important for managers to have some appreciation of other nations' legal systems. Dealing across national boundaries inevitably involves questions of whose law will apply to the transaction. To the extent that contracting parties have some choice in deciding this question for themselves, it is important for them to know something about what the choices are and how particular choices may affect the transaction. Hence, comparative law and international law have become essential parts of the modern manager's tool package.

IMPORTANT TERMS AND CONCEPTS

act of state doctrine
arbitration
Contracts for the International Sale of Goods (CISG)
customs
ius civile
ius gentium
Foreign Corrupt Practices Act of 1977 (FCPA)
multinationals
International Court of Justice (ICJ)
jurisconsults
letter of credit
natural law
Sherman Antitrust Act
sovereign immunity doctrine
UCC, Article 5
U.S. Constitution

QUESTIONS AND PROBLEMS FOR DISCUSSION

1. A major U.S. corporation had a contract with a foreign government to supply certain goods and services. The foreign government accepts the goods and services and then refuses to pay. Can the U.S. corporation sue the foreign government in the ICJ? Why or why not? If not, where can they bring suit?

2. What is the difference between the act of state doctrine and the sovereign immunity doctrine?

3. Why are letters of credit used in foreign commerce? Why doesn't the buyer just send its check in payment for the goods?

4. Are decisions of national courts that apply to international legal situations as significant to the management of international business as the decisions of the ICJ? Why?

5. Mitsubishi Motors made an agreement to distribute automobiles manufactured by Mitsubishi to Chrysler dealers outside the United States. Soler Chrysler-Plymouth is such a dealer in Puerto Rico. The sales agreement provided for arbitration of all disputes arising out of the agreement or a breach of the agreement. There were disputes, and the parties could not work them out, so Mitsubishi filed a suit in U.S. District Court to compel arbitration of the disputes. Soler Chrysler-Plymouth responded with allegations of antitrust violations. The district court ordered arbitration of the disputes, including the antitrust issues. The appellate court reversed the trial court insofar as the arbitration of the antitrust issues because it felt antitrust matters should be decided by courts, not arbitrators. The case was later heard by the U.S. Supreme Court.

   Should the parties' mutual agreement to arbitrate all disputes be restricted to only non-antitrust disputes? Why or why not?

6. Sumitomo Shoji America, Inc., is a New York corporation and wholly owned subsidiary of Sumitomo Shoji Kabushiki Kaisha, a Japanese general trading company. Plaintiffs are past and present female secretarial employees of Sumitomo. All but one of the plaintiffs are U.S. citizens; that one exception is a Japanese citizen living in the United States. Plaintiffs brought this suit as a class action claiming that Sumitomo's alleged practice of hiring only male Japanese citizens to fill executive, managerial, and sales positions violated Title VII of the Civil Rights Act of 1964. Respondents sought both injunctive relief and damages.

   Sumitomo asked the court to dismiss the complaint because it was exempt from coverage of the civil rights laws as a result of the Friendship, Commerce, and Navigation (FCN) Treaty between the United States and Japan. The FCN Treaty permits companies of each country to follow that country's rules in selecting executives and managers. The District Court refused to dismiss. The Court of Appeals reversed, saying Sumitomo was exempt under the provisions of the treaty.

   On review, how should the U.S. Supreme Court rule, and why?

7. Edwin Cohen, chairman of General Atlantic Corp., attended an antiques fair in London, England. While there, he spoke with a manager of Spink Ltd., a U.K. company, about the possibility of his company's buying six of the exhibited art pieces. He denies he ever agreed to buy them. He did not take possession of them or sign any written agreement. (English law currently does not require a written agreement for such sales, but New York's UCC does.)

   After Cohen returned to New York, he received an invoice for $33,968 for his alleged purchase of the six art pieces. When neither Cohen nor General Atlantic paid the invoice, Spink Ltd. sued both of them in New York. The defendants asked the New York court to dismiss the case because application of the English law would be "repugnant" to the policy of the New York UCC.

   Should the English law be applied? Explain.

8. The International Association of Machinists (IAM), a U.S.-based labor union, was disturbed by the high price of oil and petroleum-derived products in the United States. They believed the actions of the Organization of the Petroleum Exporting Countries, popularly known as OPEC, were the cause of this burden on the U.S. public. Accordingly, IAM sued OPEC and its member nations, alleging that their price-setting activities violated U.S. antitrust laws. IAM sought injunctive relief and damages. The District Court entered a final judgment in favor of the defendants, holding that it lacked jurisdiction and that IAM had no valid antitrust claim.

   The OPEC nations produce and export oil either through government-owned companies or through government participation in private companies. Prior to the formation of OPEC, these diverse and sometimes antagonistic countries were plagued with fluctuating oil prices. Without coordination among them, oil was often in oversupply on the world market, resulting in low prices.

   OPEC achieves its goals by a system of production limits and royalties that its members unanimously adopt. There is no enforcement arm of OPEC. The force behind OPEC decrees is the collective self-interest of the 11 nations.

   After formation of OPEC, it is alleged, the price of crude oil increased 10-fold and more.

   How should this lawsuit be decided?

9. Domingo Castro Alfaro worked for Standard Fruit Company on its banana plantation in Costa Rica. He and 81 other employees claim they suffered personal injuries, including sterility, from being exposed to a pesticide that was manufactured by Dow and by Shell Oil and then sold by those companies to Standard Fruit. The 82 employees and their wives filed a lawsuit against Dow and Shell in Houston, Texas, in state court. Both defendants are incorporated in Delaware. However, Shell has its corporate world headquarters in Houston, and Dow operates the largest chemical plant in the United States, in Freeport, Texas, about 60 miles from Houston.

   Dow and Shell asked the Texas court to dismiss the case as being brought in an "inconvenient" location because the injuries occurred in Costa Rica, to Costa Rica citizens. (The legal doctrine that permits courts to dismiss lawsuits on such grounds is called *forum non conveniens*). A Texas statute says that personal injury actions "may be enforced" in Texas courts even though the injury occurred in another country. The pesticide at issue, dibromochloropropane (DBCP), was banned for use in the United States in 1977. Dow and Shell, both before and after the U.S. ban, shipped hundreds of thousands of gallons of DBCP to Standard Fruit in Costa Rica for use there. The estimated maximum recovery per worker for the injuries claimed in the United States would be $1,080 in Costa Rica.

   The Texas trial court did dismiss the case, on the basis of forum non conveniens. The Texas Court of Appeals reversed that decision and sent the case back to the trial court for a trial on the merits of the plaintiffs' claims. Dow and Shell then filed a further appeal with the Texas Supreme Court.

   How should the state supreme court decide this case, and why?

10. Dawn Stovall and her mother Esther Shaleen bought roundtrip air tickets from Minneapolis, Minnesota, to London, England. Both going and coming, they had to change planes in Boston, Massachusetts. On the flight back, they landed in Boston, were processed through immigration and customs, and given vouchers for a bus ride on the Massachusetts Port Authority bus from the international terminal to the domestic terminal, where they would get on the plane for Minneapolis. The bus was crowded, but they got on anyway. As the bus rounded a corner, both women fell out. Dawn was hurt; her mother was killed. Their lawsuit against Northwest Airlines claimed that the Warsaw Convention applied, because they "were in the process of embarking or disembarking" when the accident happened. (They had boarding cards for the domestic flight, and Northwest still had their luggage and arranged for the bus ride.)

    Northwest asked the court for a summary judgment because more than 1 hour had passed since they got off the international flight, over 2 hours remained until they were to board the domestic flight, they were not inside either terminal, they did not have to take the bus but could travel between terminals any way they wished, and the bus accident was not the kind of incident intended to be covered by the Warsaw Convention.

    How should the court rule here, and why?

CHAPTER 3

Constitutional Law and Administrative Law

Chapter Objectives

This chapter will:

- Explore constitutional limitations on government regulation of business.
- Examine the protection found in the First Amendment.
- Explain the power the commerce clause gives Congress.
- Describe how the contract clause limits state regulation of business.
- Introduce the privileges and immunities clause and the equal protection clause found in the Fourteenth Amendment.
- Discuss administrative agencies and their power to adjudicate disputes.

The U.S. Constitution provides the framework within which the three branches of the national government, the state governments, and all of society must operate. It provides the legal rules for deciding disputes between government agencies and between government agencies and private persons, including business organizations. We previously referenced this constitutional structure in Chapter 1. Constitutional issues will appear in various contexts throughout the rest of the book because our system permits private litigants to raise constitutional arguments in any ordinary lawsuit. Because it is so frequently involved in our example cases, the Constitution is reprinted in full in Appendix A.

In this chapter, we will discuss the primary constitutional limitations on the regulation of business. Protection exists against improper actions by both national and state governments. Similar protections are found in state constitutions against arbitrary or unfair actions by the states and their agencies. A business affected by such arbitrary state action may thus challenge such action under applicable provisions of that state's constitution, as well as under the appropriate clauses of the **U.S. Constitution**.

Because much business regulation results from action taken by national and state administrative agencies, this chapter also outlines their origin, functions, and procedures.

U.S. Constitutional Framework

Most readers of this text are probably already familiar with the basic provisions of the U.S. Constitution, but these legal concepts are so important that they are worth restating briefly. The two basic structural rules are **separation of powers** and **federalism**. Each of these basic rules has significant consequences for business regulation by the national and state governments.

Separation of Powers

The Founding Fathers were well aware of the dangers involved when governmental powers were concentrated in one person or one agency. They had been subjected to various acts of tyranny during the colonial period and had fought a 5-year revolution to establish an independent nation. They did not want to replace "a foreign tyrant with a domestic one."

They did see the need for a national government, but it had to be controllable. The answer was to divide governmental authority among three branches—legislative, executive, and judicial. Each would have only *some* powers and authority, and each would operate to check the others. This is known as the system of "checks and balances." To take just one example, the Supreme Court decides what actions by the other two branches (and by the states) are constitutional. But their decision can be overridden by a constitutional amendment. Likewise, the Court's decision on the meaning of an act of Congress can be overridden by Congress's passing of an amendment or a whole new statute. (The Curt Flood Act of 1998 did this to the 1922 baseball precedent, as noted in Chapter 1.)

This "separation" is reinforced by having each of the three branches selected by a different method. The President is elected by popular vote, state by state, with the plurality vote getter in each state receiving all of that state's electoral votes. The candidate receiving a majority of the electoral votes nationally is elected for a 4-year term. Senators are elected by popular vote, on a statewide basis, for 6-year terms, but only one-third of them are elected each 2 years. Members of the House of Representatives are elected for 2-year terms, from local districts within a state; each state has at least one member, with additional members being apportioned on the basis of population. Justices of the Supreme Court are appointed for life ("on good behavior"), after nomination by the president and confirmation by the Senate. Thus, each part of the government has a different constituency and a different term of office.

Federalism

The second structural device by which the Constitution limits government power is federalism, that is, a system in which there are two levels of government, with each level operating independently within its own sphere of authority. (This contrasts with the unitary system of government found in France, Japan, the United Kingdom, and other nations. Other federal systems include Canada, Australia, Germany, and Switzerland.)

The Constitution delegates certain powers to the national government; all other powers are reserved to the states or to the people. These grants of national power are very broad, but not unlimited. If any branch or agency of the national government acts outside its delegated powers, that action can be challenged in court and declared unconstitutional. There are several examples of such challenges in this chapter and throughout the book.

Preemption

Where the national government is acting within its proper scope of authority under the Constitution, its valid actions supersede any inconsistent state government actions. This concept is called **preemption**. We have already seen preemption at work in the *Flood* case in Chapter 1. Curt Flood could not claim that organized baseball's "player reserve" system violated state antitrust law because the U.S. Supreme Court decided that such claims would conflict with the national (Court-created) exemption from national antitrust law. These national versus state policy conflicts arise quite frequently, as seen in the *White Buffalo* case.

CASE 1

White Buffalo Ventures, L.L.C. v. University of Texas at Austin

420 F.3d 366 (5 Cir. 2005)

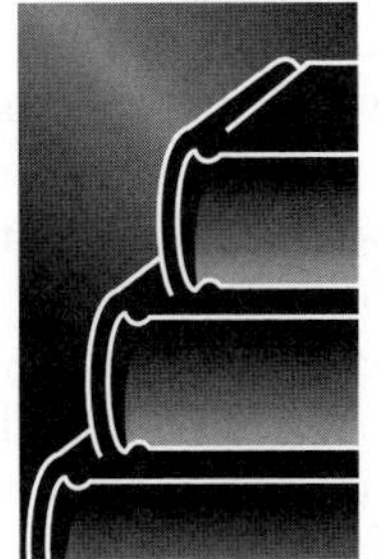

Facts: White Buffalo operates several online dating services, including longhornsingles.com, which targets students at the University of Texas (UT) at Austin. Pursuant to its internal antisolicitation policy, UT blocked White Buffalo's attempts to send unsolicited bulk commercial e-mails. White Buffalo sued in U.S. District Court, asking for an injunction against UT to prevent it from interfering with these e-mails. The court denied the injunction, and White Buffalo appealed.

In 2003, the national government adopted the Controlling the Assault of Non-Solicited Pornography and Marketings Act (CAN-SPAM), but this act contains a provision that permits Internet service providers to employ protection measures.

Issues: Does the national CAN-SPAM Act preempt the university's antispam policy? Does the university's antispam policy violate First Amendment protection for freedom of speech, as made applicable to the states by the due process clause of the Fourteenth Amendment?

Decision: No. No. Judgment affirmed.

Opinion by Judge Smith: "The doctrine of preemption stems from the Supremacy Clause ['This Constitution, and the laws of the United States which shall be made in pursuance thereof, ... shall be the supreme Law of the Land. ...' U.S. Constitution, Article VI clause 2], which gives federal law precedence over a conflicting state law. ...

"Although a court should begin with the expression provided by Congress, it must also 'identify the domain expressly preempted.'... The fact that Congress has expressly preempted certain activity is plain, but the scope of that express preemption is not. The power to supplant state law is 'an extraordinary power in a federalist system.'... Preemption radically alters the balance of state and federal authority, so the Supreme Court has historically refused to impose that alteration interstitially. ... The Court has expressed this principle as a presumption against preemption. ... Supremacy Clause analysis is a classic 'tie goes to the state' jurisprudence, and the existence of an express preemption provision does not always plainly demarcate what the federal law expressly preempts. ...

"[I]n addition to setting forth the preemption clause, S. 7707 carves out a set of entities to be exempt from any possible preemptive effect. It states that 'nothing in this chapter shall be construed to have any effect on the lawfulness or unlawfulness ... of the adoption, implementation, or enforcement by a provider of Internet access service of a policy of declining to transmit, route, relay, handle, or store certain types of electronic mail messages.'...

"As a result of Congress's apparent failure to contemplate this question, we must not infer preemption. The textual ambiguity triggers the strong presumption against such a finding, and we cannot be sure whether UT's regulations fall within the ambit of the express preemption clause. UT may therefore implement the Regents' Rules without violating the Supremacy Clause. ...

"Whether UT has violated While Buffalo's First Amendment rights turns on the resolution of the four-part commercial speech test in *Central Hudson Gas & Electric*. ...

"Under the first Central Hudson prong, we must determine whether the speech is unlawful or misleading. ... Both parties agree that White Buffalo's commercial solicitations are legal and that they contain factually accurate information. ...

"Under the second Central Hudson prong we must assess the 'substantiality' of the government's proffered interests. ... UT advances two primary interests: (1) safeguarding the time and interests of those with UT email accounts ('user efficiency') and (2) protecting the efficiency of its networks and servers ('server efficiency'). ...

"For purposes of evaluating the summary judgment, we acknowledge as substantial the government's gatekeeping interest in protecting users of its email network from the hassle associated with unwanted spam. ...

"Pursuant to the third ... prong, we must next determine whether the UT policy directly advances both proffered substantial interests. ... Again, there can be no serious dispute that UT's anti-spam policy, which blocks specific incoming commercial spam after account-holders have complained about it, directly advances both interests. ...

"Having resolved the first three ... questions in UT's favor, we must finally conduct the most difficult inquiry—whether the ITC policy is no more extensive than necessary to achieve at least one of the two substantial state interests. ...

"A governmental entity may assert that a statute serves multiple interests, and only one of those need be substantial. ... The ITC policy survives First Amendment scrutiny despite its failure to justify that policy in relationship to the server efficiency interest. We therefore decide that the UT's anti-spam policy is constitutionally permissible under Central Hudson. Because we so decide, we need not address what type of First Amendment forum a public university email network constitutes.

"The summary judgment is AFFIRMED."

U.S. Constitutional Limitations

Limits on National Government Regulations

The general prohibition against unfair or arbitrary action by the national government and its agencies is the **Fifth Amendment due process of law** clause: "nor shall any person ... be deprived of life, liberty, or property, without due process of law." This clause is one of the greatest legal statements ever made, an important step in the development of Anglo-American common law. The clause has both procedural and substantive content. Procedurally, it means that actions of the national government that affect specific individuals can only be taken by following certain required steps, and that, overall, the government's decision must be reached through a process that is "fundamentally fair" to those affected. Fairness in the constitutional sense usually requires a **hearing** before an impartial decision maker, adequate **notice** of the proposed action, the right to be represented by counsel, the right to confront and cross-examine adverse witnesses, the right to present one's own witnesses and arguments, and the right to court review of the initial decision.

Substantively, the due process clause means that there are some things that the government simply may not do, even if it follows an established procedure. This clause is thus an important protection against the possible tyranny of a majority. Even if a bill is passed by Congress and signed by the President, the statute may still be challenged as being unconstitutional. It may be ruled unconstitutional because it violates one of the specific provisions of the Constitution, such as freedom of speech, or because it violates the division of power established between national and state governments or among the three branches of the national government. Statutes may also be invalidated when they attempt to regulate matters that are none of the government's concern. In 1970, for example, the U.S. Supreme Court overturned a state law prohibiting the distribution of birth control information to married adults *(Griswold v. Connecticut)*. Presumably, a similar national statute would also be unconstitutional. There is a constitutional "right to privacy" even though it is not expressly stated anywhere in the Constitution. The Ninth Amendment specifically states that the list of rights in the other amendments is not exclusive.

Violations of Specific Bill of Rights Sections

Even though proper legislative procedure was followed in passing a statute, and even though the enforcement agency is proceeding in accordance with the statute's provisions, such action by the government cannot violate any of the specific protections found in the **Bill of Rights**. These include all the specific criminal procedures requirements that will be discussed in Chapter 6; the First Amendment freedoms of speech, press, assembly, and religion; the prohibition against taking private property unless just compensation is paid; the protection against warrantless searches and seizures provided by the **Fourth Amendment**; and others. Not all of these provisions have always been vigorously enforced, especially when businesses are being affected rather than individuals. The privilege against being forced to testify against oneself in a criminal case is generally not applicable to corporations.

Outer Limits of the Commerce Clause

Congress is given full power to regulate interstate commerce, foreign trade, and commerce with the American Indian tribes. On these topics, the Supreme Court has said several times that the power of Congress is as complete as if there were only a national government and is subject only to the restrictions contained in other sections of the Constitution. Congress clearly has the power under the **commerce clause** to pass Occupational Safety and Health Administration (OSHA), for example, but it could not provide for warrantless searches of private property.

So long as it acts within constitutional limits, however, Congress has a free hand as to the extent and type of regulation it places on interstate commerce. It may outlaw practices that are harmful to the public, and it may restrict or prohibit interstate shipments of dangerous products. It may itself specify illegalities in some detail, or it may choose to legislate only broad guidelines and to delegate to an administrative agency the power to make the detailed rules of practice. It may adopt national legislation that preempts state laws, or it may delegate most of its power to regulate a particular area to the states.

If it wishes, Congress may also regulate intrastate commerce that has an impact on interstate commerce. The rationale for this auxiliary power is that it is necessary, or may be necessary, to effectually regulate interstate commerce. In the famous case of *Wickard v. Filburn* (1942), the Supreme Court upheld, under the commerce clause, regulations of agricultural production that reached all the way to a farmer who was growing grain for use on his own farm. If that analysis is valid, it is hard to imagine very many activities that could not be subjected to the commerce power if Congress wished to do so. Of course, if a particular statute says that it applies only to those activities *in* commerce, rather than to any that *affect* commerce, Congress is indicating that the statute is not to apply to purely intrastate matters.

CASE 2

United States v. Lopez
514 U.S. 549 (1995)

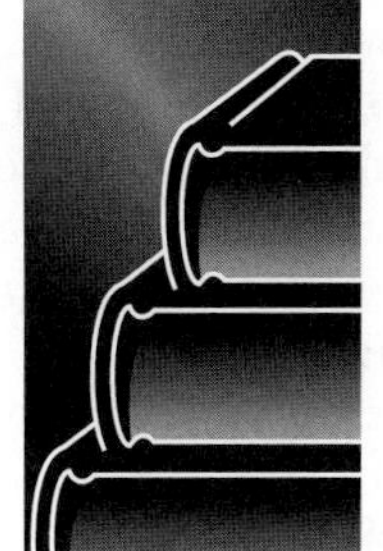

Facts: On March 10, 1992, Lopez—a 12th grade student—arrived at Edison High School in San Antonio, Texas, carrying a concealed .38 caliber handgun and five bullets. Acting on an anonymous tip, the school authorities confronted him. Lopez admitted he had the gun, and he was arrested and charged with a violation of Texas state law. The next day, the Texas charges were dropped, and federal agents charged Lopez with a criminal violation of the national Gun Free School Zones Act of 1990 (GFSZ). He was indicted, tried (in U.S. District Court), convicted, and sentenced to 6 months in prison and 2 years' supervised release. His conviction was reversed by the U.S. Fifth Circuit, which held the GFSZ Act unconstitutional. The U.S. government requested certiorari.

Issue: Does the commerce clause provide a basis for enacting the GFSZ Act?

Decision: No. Judgment of the Court of Appeals is affirmed.

Opinion by Chief Justice Rehnquist: "We start with first principles. The Constitution creates a Federal Government of enumerated powers. . . . As James Madison wrote, 'the powers delegated by the proposed Constitution to the federal government are few and defined. Those which are to remain in the state governments are numerous and indefinite.'. . . This constitutionally mandated division of authority 'was adopted by the Framers to ensure protection of our fundamental liberties.'. . . 'Just as the separation and independence of the coordinate branches of the Federal Government serve to prevent the accumulation of excessive power in any one branch, a healthy balance of power between the States and the Federal Government will reduce the risk of tyranny and abuse from either front.'. . .

"The Constitution delegates to Congress the power 'to regulate Commerce with Foreign Nations, and among the several States, and with the Indian Tribes.'. . . The Court, through Chief Justice Marshall, first defined the nature of Congress' commerce power in *Gibbons v. Ogden* . . .: 'It is not intended to say that these words comprehend that commerce, which is completely internal, which is carried on between man and man in a State, or between different parts of the same State, and which does not extend to or affect other States. Such a power would be inconvenient, and is certainly unnecessary.'. . .

"For nearly a century thereafter, the Court's Commerce Clause decisions dealt but rarely with the extent of Congress' power, and almost entirely with the Commerce Clause as a limit on state legislation that discriminated against interstate commerce. . . .

"In 1887, Congress enacted the Interstate Commerce Act, . . . and in 1890, Congress enacted the Sherman Antitrust Act. . . . These laws ushered in a new era of federal regulation under the commerce power. When cases involving these laws first reached this Court, we [took] the approach that Congress could not regulate activities such as 'production,' 'manufacturing,' and 'mining.'. . .

"In . . . *Schechter Poultry Corp.*, . . . the Court struck down [national] regulations that fixed the hours and wages of individuals employed by an intrastate business because the activity being regulated related to interstate commerce only indirectly. In doing so, the Court characterized the distinction between direct and indirect effects of intrastate commerce upon interstate commerce as 'a fundamental one, essential to the maintenance of our constitutional system.'. . .

"[E]ven [the] modern era precedents which have expanded congressional power under the Commerce Clause confirm that this power is subject to outer limits. . . . Since that time, Congress has heeded that warning and undertaken to decide whether a rational basis existed for concluding that a regulated activity sufficiently affected interstate commerce. . . .

"Even *Wickard*, which is perhaps the most far reaching example of Commerce Clause authority over intrastate activity, involved economic activity in a way that the possession of a gun in a school zone does not. . . .

"Admittedly, a determination whether an intrastate activity is commercial or noncommercial may in some cases result in legal uncertainty. But, so long as Congress' authority is limited to those powers enumerated in the Constitution, and so long as those enumerated powers are interpreted as having judicially enforceable outer limits, congressional legislation under the Commerce Clause will always engender 'legal uncertainty.'. . .

"The possession of a gun in a local school zone is in no sense an economic activity that might, through repetition elsewhere, substantially affect any sort of interstate commerce. . . .

"To uphold the Government's contentions here, we would have to pile inference upon inference in a manner that would bid fair to convert congressional authority under the Commerce Clause to a general police power of the sort retained by the States. . . . This we are unwilling to do."

Limits on State Government Regulation

As units of government that are sovereign within their own area, the states retain, under the U.S. Constitution, their "police power." The **police power** of a government is its power to regulate activities under its jurisdiction to promote the public health, safety, and welfare. The states' powers in this regard are limited, however, by general and specific provisions in the Constitution. Some of these limitations are prohibitions against particular types of state action, such as the contracts clause. Article I, Section 10 reads in part as follows: "No State shall pass . . . any . . . Law impairing the obligation of Contracts. . . ." Originally, the provision was intended to prevent state legislatures from passing laws that would prevent the enforcement of valid contracts and the collection of debts. For a period of some 50 years after the Civil War, the **contracts clause** was one of the major legal arguments used to invalidate government regulations of business. Rejected as an argument in 1934 in the *Blaisdell* case, the contracts clause fell into disuse until 1978, when it was revived in the *Allied Structural* case.

Privileges and Immunities

Because a corporation is not considered a "citizen" for the purposes of the **Fourteenth Amendment privileges and immunities** clause, it need not be given any of the privileges and immunities of citizenship. Individual citizens conducting their businesses, however, would be protected by that clause. Even corporations might benefit indirectly, if a state's regulation of individual employees were held unconstitutional. When Alaska passed a statute requiring that its residents be hired in preference to new arrivals for work on oil and gas projects, employer corporations could not challenge the statute on this basis. But the act was ruled unconstitutional when it was challenged by five newly arrived workers who had been denied jobs in favor of Alaska residents (*Hicklin v. Orbeck*, 1978). The corporations operating these projects in Alaska were thus free to hire anyone who applied for the job and was qualified, Alaska resident or not.

Equal Protection

Because the word used in this section of the Fourteenth Amendment is "person," and corporations are persons, neither they nor individuals can be denied equal protection by a state. This clause does not mean that a state cannot draw distinctions and treat different persons differently. It does mean, however, that any distinctions must be based on reasonable and rational criteria. There can be no arbitrary or invidious discrimination.

The courts use two tests when violations of this clause are alleged. The **strict scrutiny test** is used where the regulation has an impact on a fundamental right, such as freedom of speech, or where it adversely affects a "suspect class" of people. A suspect class is one that has been subjected to past acts of discrimination or that may have special disadvantages. Such groups might include racial, religious, or nationality minorities. Such state regulations will pass the test only if necessary to achieve a "compelling state interest," and if drawn as narrowly as possible to achieve it.

The alternative, and easier, test is the **"rational basis" test**. With no fundamental rights or suspect classes involved, a state classification would be presumed valid if there were any rational basis for it. The state's differential treatment must be related to the regulatory objective sought by the state, but if it is, it is presumed valid. The fact that other methods might be used to achieve the same result is not enough to invalidate a state's choice under this test. Many state regulations would be invalid under the first test; very few would be under this one. Most business regulations will probably be tested under this second, more generous standard.

The affirmative action admissions policy of the University of Michigan Law School is being challenged in the *Grutter* case.

CASE 3

GRUTTER V. BOLLINGER
539 U.S. 306 (2003)

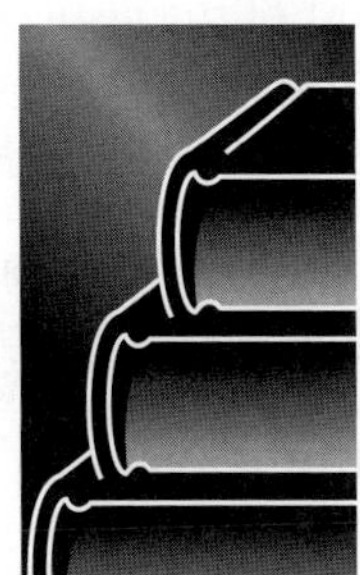

Facts: Barbara Grutter, a white resident of Michigan, applied for admission to the University of Michigan Law School in 1996. She had a 3.8 undergraduate grade average and a score of 161 on the Law School Admission Test. Although both of these factors are heavily weighted in the admissions process, the law school also considers race and ethnicity, to try to ensure a "critical mass" of each of three "historically underrepresented minorities"—African Americans, Hispanics, and American Indians. Grutter was originally put on a "wait list," but was ultimately rejected for admission.

Grutter sued in U.S. District Court, alleging that she was discriminated against on the basis of her race, in violation of the equal protection clause of the Fourteenth Amendment, Title VI of the 1964 Civil Rights Act, and 42 U.S. Code s. 1981. After an extensive trial, the court ruled in her favor. The U.S. Sixth Circuit reversed (by one vote, with all judges participating). Grutter then petitioned for U.S. Supreme Court review. The Supreme Court agreed to hear the case and voted 5 to 4 to affirm the Sixth Circuit.

Issue: Does the University of Michigan Law School's admission procedure violate the equal protection clause of the Fourteenth Amendment?

Decision: No. Judgment affirmed.

Opinion by Justice O'Connor: "Although all governmental uses of race are subject to strict scrutiny, not all are invalidated by it. . . . When race-based action is necessary to further a compelling governmental interest, such action does not violate the constitutional guarantee of equal protection so long as the narrow-tailoring requirement is also satisfied.

"[T]he Law School asks us to recognize, in the context of higher education, a compelling state interest in student body diversity. . . .

"The Law School's educational judgment that such diversity is essential to its educational mission is one to which we defer. . . . Our scrutiny of the interest asserted by the Law School is no less strict for taking into account complex educational judgments in an area that lies primarily within the expertise of the university. Our holding today is in keeping with our tradition of giving a degree of deference to a university's academic decisions, within constitutionally prescribed limits. . . .

"In addition to the expert studies and reports entered into evidence at trial, numerous studies show that student body diversity promotes learning outcomes, and 'better prepares students for an increasingly diverse workforce and society, and better prepares them as professionals.'. . .

"These benefits are not theoretical but real, as major American businesses have made clear that the skills needed in today's increasingly global marketplace can only be developed through exposure to widely diverse people, cultures, ideas, and viewpoints. . . .

"In order to cultivate a set of leaders with legitimacy in the eyes of the citizenry, it is necessary that the path to leadership be visibly open to talented and qualified individuals of every race and ethnicity. . . .

"Universities can . . . consider race or ethnicity . . . as a 'plus' factor in the context of individualized consideration of each and every applicant. . . .

"The Law School affords this individualized consideration to applicants of all races. . . .

"[T]he Law School's race-conscious admissions program adequately ensures that all factors that may contribute to student body diversity are meaningfully considered alongside race in admissions decisions. . . .

"The Law School frequently accepts nonminority applicants with grades and test scores lower than underrepresented minority applicants (and other nonminority applicants) who are rejected. . . .

"The judgment of Court of Appeals for the Sixth Circuit . . . is affirmed."

Due Process

As was true under the Fifth Amendment, due process has both a substantive and a procedural content. Procedurally, no state can deny any person (including corporate persons) life, liberty, or property without following a fair procedure. Because the Fourteenth Amendment does not itself spell out all the details of required criminal procedure found in the Bill of Rights, the courts have allowed some flexibility to the states in that area. For example, the Fifth Amendment requires indictment by a grand jury in serious crimes, but the states are permitted to use an alternative procedure called an **information**. The information drafted by the prosecutor/district attorney serves the same function as an indictment in informing the court and the defendant what the charges are, what facts are alleged, and what possible penalties are involved. Although the details may vary from state to state and from regulation to regulation, the overall procedure must be basically fair to the affected parties.

The substantive meaning of the **Fourteenth Amendment due process of law** clause is similar to that of the Fifth Amendment. Even if a fair procedure is provided, the courts may rule that the content of the regulation makes it invalid. Such invalidity may be found because the regulation violates a specific prohibition of the Constitution or because it infringes on one of the protected rights.

Since the 1930s, most of the justices have been more willing to defer to the state legislatures' judgments as to regulations of property and contract rights than to those that infringe on personal freedoms, such as speech, press, and assembly. Some justices and text writers continue to believe that commercial speech is less deserving of protection than noncommercial speech and may use that distinction to validate one regulation while invalidating another. Not all justices make these distinctions or apply them in the same way, so that the court is badly divided in many such cases. A majority may agree on the result in a case, but for quite different reasons, and there may be one or more dissenting opinions. As a result, it is often difficult to extract any rules or guidelines for future business conduct.

The *Kasky* case shows some of the difficulties in reconciling freedom of speech and various types of government regulations.

Commerce Clause

Another very significant limitation on the regulatory power of state governments stems from the power granted to Congress under the commerce clause. Because one of the major purposes of the Constitution was to create a national marketplace for our people's goods and services, the states cannot unduly or unfairly interfere with interstate commerce. Similarly, the commerce clause limits the states' power to tax interstate business.

To be valid, state regulations cannot discriminate against interstate commerce in favor of local businesses. Interstate businesses must be given a fair chance of competition in local markets. Second, a state regulation cannot unduly burden interstate commerce. In one famous case, an Illinois statute required curved mud flaps over the rear tires of all large trucks. The flat mud flaps that were used to comply with the laws of all other states would not comply with the Illinois law. Nor would the curved mud flaps comply with the other states' laws. As a result, an interstate trucker would have to drive around Illinois, stop at the state borders to change mud flaps, or drive through and risk a ticket. The U.S.

CASE 4

Kasky v. Nike, Inc.
45 P.3d 243 (CA 2002)

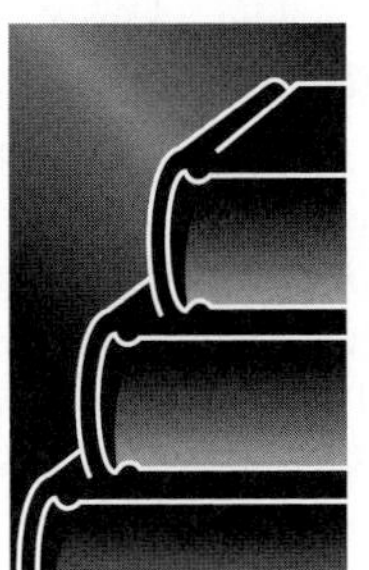

Facts: Marc Kasky is a California resident, suing on behalf of the general public of the state, for alleged false and misleading statements by Nike about its contractors' labor practices in overseas factories. Nike is an Oregon corporation, with its principal place of business in that state. It is authorized to do business in California, and does promote and distribute its products there. Most of its products are manufactured by subcontractors in China, Vietnam, and Indonesia. Most of the workers in these factories are women under the age of 24. In response to a TV and newspaper campaign, which alleged that these workers were being physically and economically abused, Nike published rebuttal statements. Kasky alleges some of these statements were false and misleading, in violation of state law. He asks that the court order Nike to disgorge all revenue produced by false and misleading statements; to correct any misstatements; and to cease misrepresenting factory working conditions.

The trial court dismissed the complaint on the basis of freedom of speech. The court of appeal affirmed. The state Supreme Court agreed to review the case.

Issue: Are Nike's statements "commercial" speech?

Decision: Yes. Judgment reversed; case remanded.

Opinion by Judge Kennard: " 'The [U.S.] Constitution accords less protection to commercial speech than to other constitutionally safeguarded forms of expression.'...

"For noncommercial speech entitled to full First Amendment protection, a content based regulation is valid under the First Amendment only if it can withstand strict scrutiny, which requires that the regulation be narrowly tailored (that is, the least restrictive means) to promote a compelling government interest....

" 'By contrast, regulation of commercial speech based on content is less problematic.'... To determine the validity of a content based regulation of commercial speech, the United States Supreme Court has articulated an intermediate scrutiny test.... 'At the outset, we must determine whether the expression is protected by the First Amendment. For commercial speech to come within that protection, it at least must concern lawful activity and not be misleading. Next, we ask whether the asserted governmental interest is substantial. If both inquiries yield positive answers, we must determine whether the regulation directly advances the governmental interest asserted, and whether it is not more extensive than is necessary to serve that interest.'... The court has clarified that the last part of the test—determining whether the regulation is not more extensive than 'necessary'—does not require the government to adopt the least restrictive means, but instead requires only a 'reasonable fit' between the government's purpose and the means chosen to achieve it....

" 'There is no constitutional value in false statements of fact. Neither the intentional lie nor the careless error materially advances society's interest in "uninhibited, robust, and wide open debate on public issues".'... For this reason, 'untruthful speech, commercial or otherwise, has never been protected for its own sake.'...

"Nevertheless, in some instances the First Amendment imposes restraints on lawsuits seeking damages for injurious falsehoods. It does so 'to eliminate the risk of undue self censorship and the suppression of truthful material'... and thereby to give freedom of expression the 'breathing space' it needs to survive.... Thus, 'some false and misleading statements are entitled to First Amendment protection in the political realm.'...

"The United States Supreme Court has stated that the category of commercial speech consists at its core of ' "speech proposing a commercial transaction".'... Although in one case the court said that this description was 'the test for identifying commercial speech'... in other decisions the court has indicated that the category of commercial speech is not limited to this core argument....

"Thus, although the court [has] identified three factors—advertising format, product references, and commercial motivation—that in combination supported a characterization of commercial speech, ... the court has not only rejected the notion that any of these factors is sufficient by itself, but it also declined to hold that all of these factors in combination, or any one of them individually, is necessary to support a commercial speech characterization....

"The [U.S.] Supreme Court has not adopted an all purpose test to distinguish commercial from non commercial speech under the First Amendment, nor has this court adopted such a test under the state Constitution, nor do we propose to do so here. A close reading of the high court's commercial speech decisions suggests, however, that it is possible to formulate a limited purpose test. We conclude, therefore, that when a court must decide whether particular speech may be subjected to laws aimed at preventing false advertising or other forms of commercial deception, categorizing a particular statement as commercial or non-commercial speech requires consideration of three elements: the speaker, the intended audience, and the content of the message....

"Here, the first element—a commercial speaker—is satisfied because the speakers—Nike and its officers and directors—are engaged in commerce. Specifically, they manufacture, import, distribute, and sell consumer goods in the form of athletic shoes and apparel.

"The second element—an intended commercial audience—is also satisfied. Nike's letters to university presidents and directors of athletic departments were addressed directly to actual and potential purchasers of Nike's products, because college and university athletic departments are major purchasers of athletic shoes and apparel. . . . Nike's press releases and letters to newspaper editors, although addressed to the public generally, were also intended to reach and influence actual and potential purchasers of Nike products. . . .

"The third element—representations of fact of a commercial nature—is also present. In describing its own labor policies, and the practices and working conditions in factories where its products are made, Nike was making factual representations about its own business operations. In speaking to consumers about working conditions and labor practices in the factories where its products are made, Nike addressed matters within its own knowledge. . . . Thus, Nike was in a position to readily verify the truth of any factual assertions it made on these topics. . . .

"Finally, governmental regulation of Nike's speech about working conditions in factories where Nike products are made is consistent with traditional government authority to regulate commercial transactions for the protection of consumers by preventing false and misleading commercial practices. . . .

"Because in the statements at issue here Nike was acting as a commercial speaker, because its intended audience was primarily the buyers of its products, and because the statements consisted of factual representations about its own business operations, we conclude that the statements were commercial speech for purposes of applying state laws designed to prevent false advertising and other forms of commercial deception. . . .

"The judgment of the Court of Appeal is reversed, and the matter is remanded to that court for further proceedings consistent with this opinion."

Supreme Court decided that this state law unduly burdened the interstate truckers and held it unconstitutional.

Finally, a state regulation is not valid where Congress, under the commerce clause, has preempted the particular subject area. The *Flood v. Kuhn* case (1972), involving baseball, is one such example; Congress preempted the regulation of professional sports. Frequently, Congress does not specify whether it wishes to preclude state action on a particular subject, so the courts are forced to imply a congressional intent from the legislative history of the national statute and from the degree of comprehensiveness of the national regulations.

Justice Clarence Thomas's opinion in the *Oregon Waste Systems* case, which follows, discusses these "negative" implications of the commerce clause.

CASE 5

Oregon Waste Systems, Inc. v. Department of Environmental Quality

511 U.S. 93 (1994)

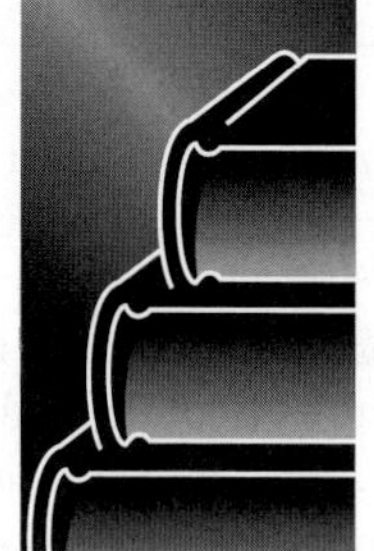

Facts: In 1989, the state of Oregon—which already levied a wide range of fees on landfill operations to fund the state's comprehensive regulation of solid waste disposal—imposed a surcharge on the disposal within the state of solid waste generated out of state. The statute imposing the surcharge provided that the amount of the surcharge had to be based on the costs to the state and its political subdivisions of disposing of such out-of-state waste that was not otherwise paid for under specified statutes. A state agency set the surcharge, by rule, at $2.25 per ton. In conjunction with the surcharge, the state imposed a fee, capped at $0.85 per ton, on the in-state disposal of waste generated within the state. The operator of a solid waste landfill, and a company which transported solid waste from another state to a landfill in Oregon, alleged that the surcharge and its enabling statutes violated the federal Constitution's commerce clause. The Court of Appeals, however, upheld the statutes and rule. The Supreme Court of Oregon affirmed.

Issue: Does the Oregon tax violate the commerce clause?

Decision: Yes. Judgment reversed, and cases remanded.

Opinion by Justice Thomas: "The Commerce Clause provides that 'the Congress shall have Power . . . to regulate Commerce . . . among the several States.' Though phrased as a grant of regulatory power to Congress, . . . the Clause has long been understood to have a 'negative' aspect that denies the States the power unjustifiably to discriminate against or burden the interstate flow of articles of commerce. . . . As we use the term here, 'discrimination' simply means differential treatment of in-state and out-of-state economic interests that benefits the former and burdens the latter. If a restriction on commerce is discriminatory, it is virtually per se invalid. . . . By contrast, nondiscriminatory regulations that have only incidental effects on interstate commerce are valid 'unless the burden imposed on such commerce is clearly excessive in relation to the putative local benefits.'. . . We deem it . . . obvious here that Oregon's $2.25 per ton surcharge is discriminatory on its face. The surcharge subjects waste from other States to a fee almost three times greater than the $0.85 per ton charge imposed on solid in-state waste. The statutory determinant for which fee applies to any particular shipment of solid waste to an Oregon landfill is whether or not the waste was 'generated out-of-state.'... It is well established, however, that a law is discriminatory if it 'tax[es] a transaction or incident more heavily when it crosses state lines than when it occurs entirely within the State.'...

Because the Oregon surcharge is discriminatory, the virtually per se rule of invalidity provides the proper legal standard here, not the ... balancing test. As a result, the surcharge must be invalidated unless respondents can 'show that it advances a legitimate local purpose that cannot be adequately served by reasonable nondiscriminatory alternatives.'... Our cases require that justifications for discriminatory restrictions on commerce pass the 'strictest scrutiny.' The State's burden of justification is so heavy that 'facial discrimination by itself may be a fatal defect.'...

"Respondents' principal defense of the higher surcharge on out-of-state waste is that it is a 'compensatory tax' necessary to make shippers of such waste pay their 'fair share' of the costs imposed on Oregon by the disposal of their waste in the State. ...

"Although it is often no mean feat to determine whether a challenged tax is a compensatory tax, we have little difficulty concluding that the Oregon surcharge is not such a tax. Oregon does not impose a specific charge of at least $2.25 per ton on shippers of waste generated in Oregon, for which the out-of-state surcharge might be considered compensatory. In fact, the only analogous charge on the disposal of Oregon waste is $0.85 per ton, approximately one-third of the amount imposed on waste from other States. ... Respondents' failure to identify a specific charge on intrastate commerce equal to or exceeding the surcharge is fatal to their claim. ...

"We recognize that the States have broad discretion to configure their systems of taxation as they deem appropriate. ... All we intimate here is that their discretion in this regard, as in all others, is bounded by any relevant limitations of the Federal Constitution, in these cases the negative Commerce Clause. Because respondents have offered no legitimate reason to subject waste generated in other States to a discriminatory surcharge approximately three times as high as that imposed on waste generated in Oregon, the surcharge is facially invalid under the negative Commerce Clause. Accordingly, the judgment of the Oregon Supreme Court is reversed, and the cases are remanded for further proceedings not inconsistent with this opinion."

Administrative Agencies

Origins and Functions

Often referred to as the "headless fourth branch of government," **administrative agencies** originated as a means to deal with the complex problems of a modern urban society. Judges and juries lack the technical expertise to solve problems in such areas as telecommunications, transportation, investment securities, and labor relations. Furthermore, court procedures tend to be technical and subject to lengthy delays.

The original idea of the independent regulatory agency was to provide a body of technical experts who could render faster decisions based on the realities of the field and free of the legal technicalities of the courtroom. Congress also wanted these agencies free of direct control by the President, so that they would be better able to implement the policy standards established by Congress in the statutes creating the agencies and defining their powers. The idea was for Congress to set out the basic objectives and standards, and the agencies then to implement those policies with detailed rules and individual decisions.

Originally, there was considerable concern over the extent to which Congress could lawfully delegate the legislative power given to it in Article I to these other bodies. One of the centerpieces of Franklin D. Roosevelt's New Deal, the National Industrial Recovery Act (NIRA) of 1933, was invalidated on these grounds in the famous "sick chicken" case, *Schechter Poultry Corp. v. United States*, 295 U.S. 495 (1935). The NIRA authorized industry groups to draw up "codes of fair competition," which could then be approved by the President. Schechter had been prosecuted for violating such a code. The Supreme Court said that Congress could not lawfully give such groups a blank check for whatever regulations they thought wise. The NIRA was declared unconstitutional. Subsequently, almost as broad grants of discretion to administrative agencies have been upheld, so that the *Schechter* rule is of little value today.

Problems

Gradually, as administrative agencies' procedures became more formalized, they were subject to many of the same criticisms that had previously been leveled against the courts.

Delays and technicalities existed in agency proceedings, too. Not all agency members were experts; some were political cronies, lacking experience in the areas they were supposed to be regulating. Many staffers drifted back and forth between agencies and private employment, creating the appearance at least of serious conflicts of interest. Questions were raised by scholars and affected parties about the fairness of a hearing where the same body was investigator, prosecutor, and judge and was charged by Congress with implementing specific policy results.

Our national economy is strong and vibrant enough to tolerate some tinkering of this sort, but there are limits. The New Deal created agencies like a computer doing permutations of the alphabet. The 1960s and 1970s were almost as bad, and in some ways, even worse. Entire industries were subjected to bureaucratic controls—banking, transportation, communication, power. Key aspects of nearly all industries were subjected to agency control—labor relations, issuance of securities, trade practices, mergers. Nearly all businesses are subject to environmental and safety controls. Such controls are not totally evil or counterproductive; in many cases, they were adopted because of gross abuses. The total impact of such regulations, however, can be devastating. At some point, a straw breaks the camel's back; one additional regulation becomes a cost that makes the business unprofitable. The real miracle of American business is that it has persevered and prospered, despite these massive additional costs.

Reform and Deregulation

In the late 1970s, people finally began to talk seriously about deregulating significant sectors of the economy. In part, this discussion was due to a resurgence of free market economics, but it also occurred because the regulated economy was not performing satisfactorily.

Innovation was occurring, and new jobs were being created in white collar, unregulated industries, such as computers. Steel, autos, and transportation—burdened with stifling regulations and conflict-oriented labor relations—were in trouble. The Japanese model of labor management cooperation was promoted as the wave of the future. Administrative rules were seen as barriers to new methods and new relationships. The nuclear power industry, for example, has been prevented from building new plants in the United States, while it flourishes in such countries as France and Japan.

Significant deregulation has already occurred in the power, banking, and transportation industries. In other areas, agencies, such as OSHA, have a more realistic view of their function. Instead of requiring the rehanging of fire extinguishers that were an inch or two out of line with the OSHA standards, the agency has now concentrated on more serious health hazards in the workplace. At the state level, "sunset" laws are being considered, which would terminate an agency after a certain number of years unless specific legislative renewal of the agency was enacted.

No one wants to return to the days of robber barons and polluted air and water. The challenge for both business and government as we begin the 21st century is to develop administrative regulations only where necessary and to make them rational and cost effective.

Administrative Procedure

The following discussion focuses on the constitutional and statutory requirements for administrative action.

Requirement of a Hearing

When an agency is acting in its legislative capacity, adopting rules, it need not hold a trial-type hearing. If it does hold hearings prior to the adoption of such a rule, it is not bound by the evidence produced at the hearing, any more than Congress is in its legislative capacity. When an agency acts as a court, however, and adjudicates an individual matter, it usually can do so only after a trial-type hearing. In this capacity, it is bound by the evidence in the record, just as a court would be. Its decision must be based on that evidence and stem from that evidence. Although the agency is given considerable discretion in setting the details of that hearing, it must be basically fair to those affected.

Requirement of Notice

If there is to be a trial-type hearing, the party affected must be given adequate notice to prepare for it. In practice, however, the courts have interpreted this requirement quite loosely. The evidence introduced may vary from the charges alleged, unless the variation would be unfair to the affected party.

Notice usually is sent through the mail to directly affected parties. Where a general agency decision is involved, notice is usually given through the *Federal Register*, the official bulletin for agency action.

Requirement of Confrontation

Our legal system does not favor secret accusers. Personal prejudice and envy may be motivating factors in the accusation. We want the accusers to come forward and to be available for cross-examination. We feel that truth and justice can only be served when the accusers and the accused confront each other. Otherwise, as Justice Douglas once stated, "So far as we or the Board know, the accusers may be psychopaths or venal people, . . . who revel in being informers. They may bear old grudges. Under crossexamination their stories might disappear like bubbles. Their whispered confidences might turn out to be yarns conceived by twisted minds or by people who, though sincere, have poor faculties of observation and memory."[1]

Once again, however, these general rules requiring confrontation are subject to modification under particular circumstances through the agency's administrative discretion. The U.S. Supreme Court ruled in 1960 that the people who had accused state voter registrars of violations of national voting laws did not have to appear and confront the registrars. The Court felt that anonymity had to be preserved in that situation. This case (*Hannah v. Larche*, 363 U.S. 420) is clearly an exception to the general rule.

Right to Counsel

As is true in criminal proceedings, the person accused in an administrative proceeding is entitled to be represented by counsel. This requirement is also a deeply imbedded element of our common law heritage. The right to counsel may be limited, however, where the agency is conducting an investigation rather than adjudicating a disputed matter. In one famous case, *In re Groban*, 352 U.S. 330 (1957), the U.S. Supreme Court decided that a state fire marshal conducting an arson investigation did not have to give witnesses the right to counsel, even though they had been compelled to appear and to testify. The witnesses were not directly accused—yet. The court felt that this sort of investigation was analogous to a grand jury investigation of possible crimes, where the right to counsel has traditionally been limited.

Right to an Impartial Hearing Officer

One of the traditional concerns with administrative agencies is their alleged lack of impartiality because they are charged with the enforcement of the statutes so as to produce the desired policy results. Part of this concern is also due to the fact that staff members may move back and forth between an agency and the industry it is trying to regulate; the fear is that such people may become promoters rather than regulators. Legislative directions to the agency are sometimes not clear: Congress directed the original Atomic Energy Commission to promote and regulate the atomic power industry. These sorts of problems are an inevitable part of the agency regulatory process and are tolerated as part of the price of using the agency method.

Where the administrator has a direct, personal stake in the outcome of a proceeding, however, the possibility of bias is so great that the procedure, or the administrator, or both, must be changed. In one classic example, the mayors of Ohio cities were given the power to hear alleged violations of the prohibition laws. The mayor would be paid court costs only if the accused was found guilty. In *Tumey v. Ohio*, 273 U.S. 510 (1927), the U.S.

Supreme Court held that this procedural arrangement violated the accused person's right to an impartial decision on the charges.

To try to separate their investigation and prosecution functions from their trial and adjudication functions, many agencies have a separate staff of hearing examiners, now called **administrative law judges** (ALJs). The prosecution staff decides whether to issue a complaint. If they do, there is a hearing before an ALJ, who must render a decision on the facts presented during the hearing.

Right to Review

Part of the agreement on using the administrative agency system, with all its ambiguities and conflicting loyalties, was an understanding that court review of these decisions would be available. Some possibility of unfairness could be tolerated, if court review were available to correct the most obvious abuses.

In many of the important agencies, such as the National Labor Relations Board (NLRB), the Federal Communications Commission (FCC), and the Federal Trade Commission (FTC), the agency itself—the board or commission—may review the findings and order of its ALJ prior to a court appeal. This internal agency review procedure varies somewhat from agency to agency. In some instances, the review is a limited one, "on the record:" Did the ALJ follow the statute, and is his or her order supported by evidence in the trial record? If so, the agency affirms the decision, much as an appellate court would. In other agencies, the board or commission may itself use the hearing record for making its own decision in the matter, just as if it had heard the case itself—a **de novo review**.

Although courts are quite willing to reverse an agency's interpretation of its statute, they generally defer to the agency's findings of fact and its orders, if based on evidence in the hearing record. The agency is the expert, and its policy decisions should stand, unless they are arbitrary or biased. For the most part, courts do not have an effective check on agency decisions because few decisions will be unsupported in the hearing record.

The next case shows, however, that courts are willing to review agency actions to make sure that the agency is not violating constitutional rights. (It also shows that an alligator is "more like a mushroom than a peach"!)

CASE 6

Pelts & Skins, L.L.C. v. Jenkins

259 F.Supp.2d 482 (M.D. LA 2003)

Facts: The state of Louisiana requires alligator farmers to pay "license fees" and "tag fees" to the state's Department of Wildlife and Fisheries (DWF). A portion of these funds is then used by the DWF to finance generic marketing of alligator products, with state representatives visiting trade shows and fashion houses and developing various promotional materials. The plaintiff objects to being required to pay for advertising with which it "vehemently" disagrees and sues for an injunction to prevent the DWF from continuing these expenditures. (James Jenkins is the Secretary of the DWF.)

Issue: Does the state agency regulation violate the free speech clause of the First Amendment, as made applicable to the states through the Fourteenth Amendment due process clause?

Decision: Yes. Judgment for Plaintiff.

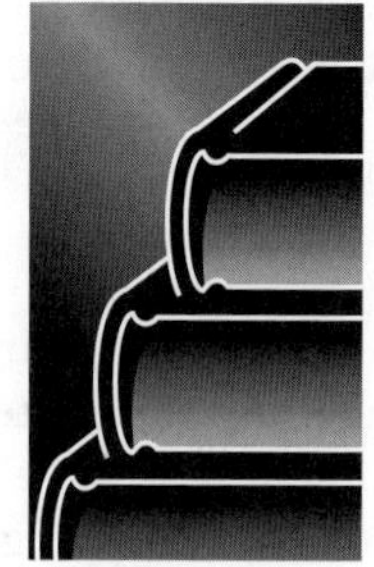

Opinion by Judge Parker: "The [U.S.] Supreme Court has held that the Constitution prohibits the government from compelling the producers of mushrooms to pay for generic advertising to which they object, but allows the government to compel producers of peaches to pay for such advertising. Resolution of this case requires the court to determine whether Louisiana alligator producers are more like mushroom producers than like peach producers. The answer to that riddle determines whether a Louisiana statute compelling farmers of alligators to fund generic advertising treads upon the First Amendment rights of plaintiff....

"The essence of government speech is when the government speaks in favor of a public policy....

"Several cases have considered the degree of the government's involvement in the workings of whatever Board or Council manages mandatory assessments. These cases generally maintain that the greater degree of involvement, the greater chance that the government speech doctrine will be invoked. Here, however, while the Secretary does appoint nine of the Alligator Council's eleven members, he himself does not sit on the Council. Moreover, those he appoints do not represent him; rather, the statute requires that they represent a cross section of alligator trappers, hunters, farmers, and coastal landowners from across the state. . . .

"Because the generic advertising here involved is not government speech, plaintiff is free to challenge such advertising on First Amendment grounds. . . .

"The Louisiana statutory scheme at issue here is different from *Glickman* in a number of ways. . . . The court . . . cannot characterize the statutory scheme as a 'broad collective enterprise' which constrains an alligator producer's freedom to act. Similarly, the statutory scheme cannot be characterized as one of economic regulation such that mandated participation in an advertising program may be viewed merely as one of any number of cooperative acts or forced association. The alligator industry is also not exempt from the antitrust law of the United States. In short, the Louisiana alligator industry, while regulated, is not heavily regulated (at least not as heavily regulated as the peach industry in *Glickman*). . . .

"The undersigned admits to a certain degree of difficulty in maintaining an appropriately straight judicial face while attempting to apply the Supreme Court precepts that explain the simple language of the First Amendment to the alligator advertising program at issue here.

"When important constitutional issues must be resolved by a determination of whether an alligator is more like a mushroom than a peach, then in the words of Justice Thomas: 'Surely we have lost our way.'. . .

"Accordingly, judgment shall be entered in favor of plaintiff, Pelts & Skins, L.L.C."

Quasi-Judicial Procedures in Administrative Agencies

The NLRB, the FTC, the Environmental Protection Agency (EPA), OSHA, and many other national and state administrative agencies daily hear disputes concerning violations of their rules and regulations. Typically, the businessperson will have more contact with administrative agencies than with the court system. The procedure for the determination of disputes in the administrative agency system is termed *quasi-judicial* because it does not have the full authority of a court and because the party being tried does not have the right to trial by jury. Nearly all decisions of administrative bodies are subject to judicial review by an appellate court.

To give the student an understanding of a typical administrative agency quasi-judicial procedure, we will follow a NLRB case from beginning to end.

National Labor Relations Board Procedure in Unfair Labor Practices Cases

Charge

An NLRB regional office is notified that an employer or a union is engaged in one or more unfair labor practices. This means that the employer or the union has violated the statutory rules by which both labor unions and management must conduct themselves. The complaining party is then asked to complete a **charge**, which is simply a form specifying what unfair labor practice has been committed and by whom. Once a charge is filed, a field examiner conducts an investigation. This is done to determine whether there is sufficient evidence of a violation to proceed to a formal hearing. If the field examiner does not find evidence sufficient to support further activity in the case, then the charge will be dismissed.

Formal Complaint

If the evidence found was sufficient to justify pursuing the case, then a **formal complaint** will be filed by the NLRB's Office of General Counsel. This complaint contains the specific allegations of wrongdoing. The employer or the labor union alleged to be in violation will be given a copy of the charges and an opportunity to answer them.

Answer

The answer filed in this case is similar to the answer filed in a civil case. The answer may deny some allegations and admit others. Typically, allegations concerning violation of the National Labor Relations Act will be denied, and allegations concerning time and place will be admitted.

Hearing

A hearing is then scheduled at which an ALJ hears testimony. Witnesses are presented by both parties in a manner similar to the procedure followed in a trial of a civil lawsuit. At the end of the testimony, the parties are allowed to make summarization statements.

Findings of Fact and Conclusions of Law

The ALJ will prepare a written decision titled "Findings of Fact and Conclusions of Law." After the ALJ has rendered a decision, either of the parties may request an appeal. This must be done within 20 days after the decision. If an appeal is not requested, the decision of the ALJ becomes final. If a request for an appeal is made, then the parties will file legal briefs to support their positions. They may request oral arguments before the five-member NLRB in Washington, D.C.

Board Review

The NLRB will review the briefs of the parties, hear oral arguments, and render a decision and order. The NLRB itself has no legal power to enforce its order. If the finding is against the employer or the union and that party refuses to comply with its order, then the NLRB must ask the U.S. Court of Appeals for a judgment to enforce its order. Or if the employer or the union feels that the NLRB decision is incorrect or unfair, it may appeal the decision to the U.S. Court of Appeals.

Review by the U.S. Court of Appeals

The U.S. Court of Appeals will review the decision of the NLRB upon the petition of any interested party or upon request of the NLRB if enforcement of an order is requested. The review by the court is concerned with two questions: first, was the decision of the NLRB supported by substantial evidence; and second, did the NLRB follow the correct substantive law? If the court agrees with the NLRB's decision, it will order compliance. If the court disagrees with the NLRB, it can reverse the NLRB's decision and dismiss the case or send the case back for a rehearing.

Review by the Supreme Court

Either party may petition the U.S. Supreme Court for a writ of certiorari to review the decision of the U.S. Court of Appeals. If the writ of certiorari is granted, a review will be had, and the parties will have to comply with the final judgment of the Supreme Court. If the Supreme Court refuses to issue a writ of certiorari, then the judgment of the U.S. Court of Appeals is final. The failure of a party to obey a court order can be punishable as either civil or criminal contempt of court.

The procedure of the NLRB is typical of the procedure used by most of the administrative agencies that have quasi-judicial authority. In other words, an investigation will be conducted and an initial hearing will be held before an ALJ, with the right of an appeal to a quasi-judicial board and with the right of a later appeal to an appellate court. The legal justification for not giving the right to trial by jury in these cases is that they are not legal trials and that the decision rendered is not a civil judgment for money. They are more like an equity injunction—an order to comply with the law, an order to pay back wages, or an order to rehire.

The following flowchart outlines the procedures for an unfair labor practice case before the NLRB.

Significance of This Chapter

Government regulation of business is one of the most important legal areas for the modern business manager. Many business decisions are subject to detailed, and often confusing, regulations. Likewise, entire industries may operate under an administrative agency as the watchdog of the public interest. In this context, it is important to remember that even the government must play by the rules, and that court review is available when an agency oversteps its boundaries or acts in an arbitrary and unfair manner.

Exhibit 3.1: Quasi-Judicial Procedure in an Administrative Agency—the NLRB

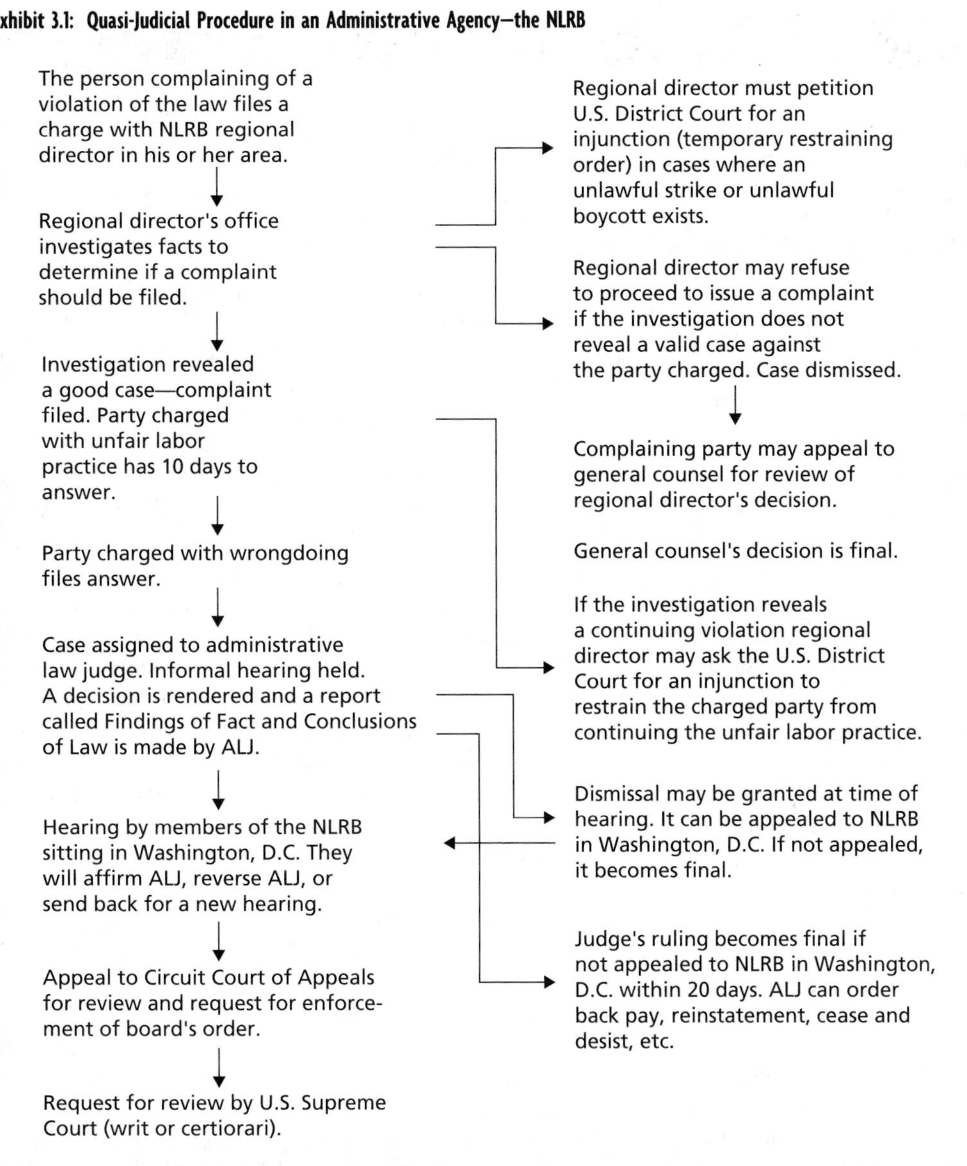

This chapter outlined the basic framework for government regulation of business. Other specific constitutional issues will be raised in other chapters. Questions about the constitutionality of a particular government action may be raised by the affected party, so each of us needs to know the basic constitutional rules.

IMPORTANT TERMS AND CONCEPTS

administrative agencies
administrative law judges
Bill of Rights
charge
commerce clause
contracts clause
de novo review
federalism
Fifth Amendment due process of law
formal complaint
Fourteenth Amendment due process of law
Fourteenth Amendment privileges and immunities
Fourth Amendment
hearing
"rational basis" test
information
notice
police power
preemption
separation of powers
strict scrutiny test
U.S. Constitution

QUESTIONS AND PROBLEMS FOR DISCUSSION

1. What is the purpose of the "equal protection" clause of the U.S. Constitution? Who is it meant to protect? Must a state always treat all people and corporations equally? Explain.

2. What is the purpose of the supremacy clause of the Constitution?

3. What is the *Federal Register?* What purpose does it serve?

4. Is there a constitutional right of privacy? If so, where is it stated in the Constitution? Discuss.

5. The Gray Panthers is an organization formed to promote the rights of the elderly. The national Medicaid program provides funds to states that pay for medical treatment for the poor. An individual's benefits depend on the financial resources "available" to him or her. Some states assume ("deem") that part of a spouse's income is available to an applicant for Medicaid. As a result, some people do not qualify for benefits at all or qualify for reduced benefits. The Gray Panthers challenged the U.S. regulations that permit the states to deem a spouse's income to the Medicaid applicant without examining the facts of the individual case. Both the U.S. District Court and the Court of Appeals for the District of Columbia held the regulations invalid.

   Are these regulations valid? Discuss.

6. Dow Chemical Co. operates a 2,000-acre facility manufacturing chemicals in Midland, Michigan. The facility consists of numerous covered buildings, with manufacturing equipment and piping conduits located between the various buildings exposed to visual observation from the air. At all times, Dow has maintained elaborate security around the perimeter of the complex, barring ground-level public views of these areas. It also investigates any low-level flights by aircraft over the facility. Dow has not undertaken, however, to conceal all manufacturing equipment within the complex from aerial views. Dow maintains that the cost of covering its exposed equipment would be prohibitive.

   Enforcement officials of EPA, with Dow's consent, made an on-site inspection of two power plants in this complex. A subsequent EPA request for a second inspection, however, was denied, and the EPA did not thereafter seek an administrative search warrant. Instead, the EPA employed a commercial aerial photographer, using a standard floor-mounted, precision aerial mapping camera, to take photographs of the facility from altitudes of 12,000, 3,000, and 1,200 feet. At all times the aircraft was lawfully within navigable airspace.

   The EPA did not inform Dow of this aerial photography, but when Dow became aware of it, Dow brought suit in the District Court, alleging that the EPA's action violated the Fourth Amendment and was beyond the EPA's statutory investigative authority. The District Court granted Dow's motion for summary judgment on the ground that the EPA had no authority to take aerial photographs and that doing so was a search violating the Fourth Amendment. The EPA was permanently enjoined from taking aerial photographs of Dow's premises and from disseminating, releasing, or copying the photographs already taken.

   The Court of Appeals reversed, and the case was appealed to the U.S. Supreme Court.

   Have Dow's rights been violated? Why or why not?

7. Plaintiff filed a civil antitrust action, seeking an injunction and treble damages, on behalf of himself and all other purchasers of residential real estate in the prior 4 years in the greater New Orleans area who had used the services of one of the defendant real estate brokers. Plaintiff alleged a conspiracy to fix commission rates and real estate prices. Defendants moved to dismiss alleging: (1) that their activities were only local in nature, (2) that there was no legal requirement that a broker be employed in the sale of real estate, and (3) that they did not usually procure financing or insurance, nor did they examine the validity of the sellers' titles. The U.S. District Court dismissed the complaint, and the Court of Appeals affirmed.

   How should the U.S. Supreme Court rule, and why?

8. The Minnesota legislature enacted a statute banning the retail sale of milk in plastic nonreturnable, nonrefillable containers, but permitting such sale in other nonreturnable, nonrefillable containers, such as paperboard milk cartons. Clover Leaf Creamery Co. brought this action challenging the statute and contends that the statute violates the equal protection and commerce clauses of the Constitution.

   The parties agree that the standard of review applicable to this case under the equal protection clause is the familiar "rational basis" test. Moreover, they agree that the purposes of the act cited by the legislature—promoting resource conservation, easing solid waste disposal problems, and conserving energy—are legitimate state purposes. Thus, the controversy in this case centers on the narrow issue of whether the legislative classification between plastic and nonplastic nonreturnable milk containers is rationally related to achievement of the statutory purposes. The Minnesota District Court, the trial court, found the statute invalid. The Minnesota Supreme Court also found the statute invalid, and the State of Minnesota appealed to the U.S. Supreme Court.

   Does the statute violate the Constitution? Explain.

9. Senator Arlen Specter and others filed this action under the Administrative Procedure Act of 1946 (APA) and the Defense Base Closure and Realignment Act of 1990 seeking to enjoin Secretary of the Navy John Dalton from carrying

out the president's decision, pursuant to the 1990 act, to close the Philadelphia Naval Shipyard. The District Court dismissed the complaint on the alternative grounds that the 1990 act itself precluded judicial review and that the political question doctrine foreclosed judicial intervention. In affirming in part and reversing in part, the Court of Appeals held that judicial review of the closure decision was available to ensure that the Secretary of Defense and the Defense Base Closure and Realignment Commission, as participants in the selection process, had complied with the procedural mandates specified by Congress. Dalton asked for review.

How should the Court rule, and why?

NOTE

1. Peters v. Hobby, 349 U.S. 331 (1955), at p. 350.

CHAPTER 4

Court Systems and Civil Procedure

Chapter Objectives

This chapter will:

- Introduce the courts and levels of appeal in the U.S. state and national court systems.
- Discuss the jurisdiction of state and national courts.
- Explain the general rules that apply when conflicts of law arise.
- Introduce the procedure followed in civil lawsuits.
- Examine methods of enforcing court judgments.
- Explain class action suits.
- Compare arbitration and mediation as means of resolving disputes.

Legal principles are meaningless without effective mechanisms for resolving disputes and enforcing the law. In Chapter 1, we noted the two major classifications of law—**procedural law** and substantive law. This chapter focuses on procedural law—how courts hear cases. (Nearly all of the rest of the book discusses the various substantive law rules.) Our purpose in this chapter is not to equip you to litigate your own case. Rather, you should know what is involved in the litigation process, so that you can make a more informed decision as to when you want to litigate a dispute.

We will first examine our dual court system, then review the major steps in a civil litigation, and conclude with a brief look at two alternative methods of dispute resolution.

Court Systems

We noted in Chapter 3 that the United States has a federal system of government, meaning that there is a national government and 50 state governments. In most nations with federal systems, there is only one national court—a supreme court, which resolves inconsistencies and disputes between the several states or regions. The United States is unique, in that we have a complete set of national courts, as well as the court systems in our 50 states.

Managers (and citizens) need to be aware of both systems because cases involving business issues (and personal rights) may occur in either system. Although most substantive law pertaining to business is state law, there are many national regulations that may apply, as we saw in the last chapter. In addition, there are some cases that may be filed in either system, as will be discussed in the next sections.

National Court System

The Constitution establishes only the Supreme Court, but then gives Congress the power to set up other national courts as the need arises. The national court system now also includes courts of appeal, district courts, and several specialty courts, in addition to the administrative agencies that were discussed in Chapter 3. Trials are held in the district courts or the specialty courts. Appeals go to the courts of appeal for the various geographic areas or to one of the specialty appeals courts. A final level of appeal to the Supreme Court is now nearly always at the Court's discretion.

The power of a court to hear particular kinds of case is called its **subject-matter jurisdiction. U.S. District Courts** have both civil and criminal subject-matter jurisdiction. They hear criminal cases in which the crime charged is a violation of national law. (State crimes are tried in the appropriate state courts.) U.S. District Courts also hear civil cases that involve national substantive law or certain classes of persons. Civil cases involving the Constitution, treaties, and national statutes, such as those dealing with patents and copyrights, are heard in the district courts. So are cases arising under maritime or admiralty law. Cases involving the United States as a party, the representatives to foreign governments, or one of our states against another state or its citizens or foreign persons can also be tried in district court. However, since passage of the Eleventh Amendment, no claim against a state by persons from another state or from another nation can be heard in national courts.

For businesses, the most important basis for using the district courts is **diversity of citizenship.** If all plaintiffs are citizens of states different than those of all defendants (that is, no state is represented on both sides of the case), and if at least $75,000 is "at issue" in the case, the district court can hear the case, even though it involves no substantive national law at all. The district court is an alternative place for trial, in addition to the appropriate state court or courts. If the plaintiff files such a case in the U.S. District Court, it will be tried there. If the plaintiff files in an appropriate state court, but the defendant wishes to have the case heard in district court, the defendant can file a petition to have the case removed from the state court to a district court in that state. If the defendant does not have the case removed, it will stay in the state court, be tried there, and appealed (if at all) through the state's appellate levels. If there is no national substantive law involved, and no diversity with $75,000 at stake, the civil case will be tried in a state court.

Because there is no national substantive law involved in a diversity case, the district court will have to decide which state's law should be applied. It will do this by applying the

choice of law rules of the state in which it is located. In general, questions as to the validity of a contract are decided according to the law of the place where the contract was made. Questions relating to the performance of the contract are decided according to the law of the place of performance. For torts, a court may apply the law of the place the tort was committed or the law of the state having the greatest "grouping of contacts" with the tort. For procedural issues, the district court will follow the federal rules of civil procedure.

The *JPMorgan* case involves a question of diversity of citizenship jurisdiction.

CASE 1

JPMorgan Chase Bank v. Traffic Stream (BVI)

536 U.S. 88 (2002)

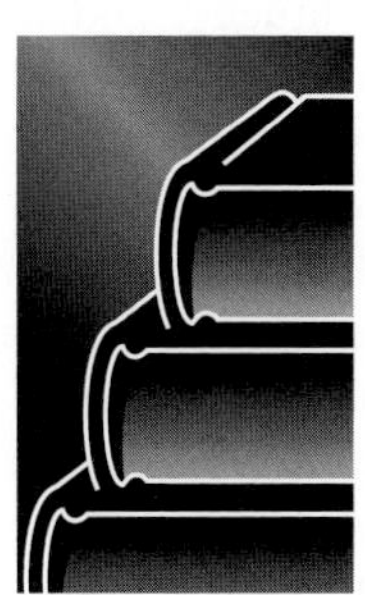

Facts: Traffic Stream is a corporation organized under the laws of the British Virgin Islands (BVI), an overseas territory of the United Kingdom. In 1998, Chase Manhattan Bank (now JPMorgan Chase) agreed to finance some ventures that Traffic Stream had organized to build and operate toll roads in China. The contract provided that it would be governed by the laws of New York and that Traffic Stream agreed to be subject to the jurisdiction of the federal courts there.

Chase sued Traffic Stream for breach of contract in the U.S. District Court in New York. The court granted Chase's motion for summary judgment, but on appeal the Second Circuit ordered that the case be dismissed. Because Traffic Stream was not the citizen or subject of an independent foreign nation, the national courts did not have subject-matter jurisdiction. The Supreme Court granted Chase's petition for certiorari.

Issue: Is a corporation of the BVI a "citizen or subject of a foreign state" for purposes of diversity of citizenship?

Decision: Yes. Judgment reversed.

Opinion by Justice Souter: "Title 28 U.S.C. s.1332(a)(2) provides district courts with 'original jurisdiction of all civil actions where the matter in controversy exceeds the sum or value of $75,000 ... and is between ... citizens of a State and citizens or subjects of a foreign state.' A 'corporation of a foreign state is, for purposes of jurisdiction in the courts of the United States, to be deemed, constructively, a citizen or subject of such State.' ... 'For purposes of international law, a corporation has the nationality of the state under the laws of which the corporation is organized.' ...

"The argument that the status of the BVI renders the statute inapplicable begins by assuming that Traffic Stream, organized under BVI law, must be a citizen or subject of the BVI alone. Since the BVI is a British Overseas territory, unrecognized by the United States Executive Branch as an independent foreign state, it is supposed to follow that for purposes of alienage jurisdiction Traffic Stream is not a citizen or subject of a 'foreign state' within the meaning of S.1332(a)(2).

"Even on the assumption, however, that a foreign state must be diplomatically recognized by our own Government to qualify as such under the jurisdictional statute, ... we have never held that the requisite status as citizen or subject must be held directly from a formally recognized state, as distinct from such a state's legal dependency. On the contrary, a consideration of the relationships of the BVI and the recognized state of the United Kingdom convinces us that any such distinction would be entirely beside the point of the statute providing alienage jurisdiction....

"The relationship between the BVI's powers over corporations and the sources of these powers in Crown and Parliament places the United Kingdom well within the range of concern addressed by Article III and S.1332(a)(2). The United Kingdom exercises ultimate authority over the BVI's statutory law, including its corporate law and the law of corporate charter, and it exercises responsibility for the BVI's external relations. These exercises of power and responsibility point to just the kind of relationship that the Framers believed would bind sovereigns 'by inclination, as well as duty, to redress the wrongs' against their nationals....

"Traffic Stream's alternative argument is that BVI corporations are not 'citizens or subjects' of the United Kingdom. Traffic Stream begins with the old fiction that a corporation is just an association of shareholders, presumed to reside in the place of incorporation ... with the result that, for jurisdictional purposes, a suit against the corporation should be understood as a suit against the shareholders.... Traffic Stream proceeds to read the British Nationality Act, 1981, as a declaration by the United Kingdom that BVI residents are not its citizens or subjects, but mere 'nationals,' without the rights and privileges of citizens or subjects.... Traffic Stream insists that because it is legally nothing more than a collection of noncitizen individuals, the corporation itself cannot be treated as deserving of access to the courts of the United States under a statute that opens them to foreign citizens and subjects.

"The less important flaw in the argument is its reliance on the outdated legal construct of corporations as collections of shareholders linked by contract, ... a view long since replaced by the corporations as independent legal entities.... Thus, Traffic Stream's whole notion of corporate citizenship derived from natural persons is irrelevant to jurisdictional inquiry in the United States today....

"But the argument's more significant weakness is its failure to recognize that jurisdictional analysis under the law of the United States is not ultimately governed by the law of the United Kingdom, whatever that may be.... [O]ur jurisdictional concern here is with the meaning of 'citizen' and 'subject' as those terms are used in S.1332(a)(2)....

"Traffic Stream concedes that BVI are at least 'nationals' of the United Kingdom.... Given the object of the alienage statute, ... there is no serious question that 'nationals' were meant to be amenable to the jurisdiction if the federal courts, leaving it immaterial for our purposes that the law of the United Kingdom may provide different rights of abode for individuals in the territories.

"[T]he United Kingdom's retention and exercise of authority over the BVI renders BVI citizens, both natural and juridic, 'citizens or subjects' of the United Kingdom under 28 U.S.C. S.1332(a). We therefore reverse the judgment of the Court of Appeals."

U.S. Circuit Courts of Appeal hear appeals from U.S. District Courts in their "Circuits," that is, groups of states. The U.S. Sixth Circuit, for example, consists of the states of Ohio, Michigan, Kentucky, and Tennessee. The Sixth Circuit Court of Appeals is located in Cincinnati, Ohio, and hears appeals from the U.S. District Courts in those four states. The District of Columbia Circuit Court of Appeals reviews decisions by the lower federal courts there and also decisions by the many federal agencies located in Washington, D.C. The court of appeals for the federal circuit hears appeals from the national specialty courts, such as the Court of International Trade and the Claims Court and also from certain agencies, such as the Patent and Trademark Office.

The courts of appeal have no power to try cases, only to hear appeals from lower U.S. courts and agencies.

The **U.S. Supreme Court** does have some "original jurisdiction" (to try cases that have not been heard by lower courts), but it is very limited. Article III of the Constitution states that the Supreme Court can try cases involving diplomatic personnel from another nation, and cases in which one of our states is a party. In all other cases that can be heard by the national courts, the Supreme Court has only appellate jurisdiction as defined by Congress. In the famous *Marbury v. Madison* case (1803), the Court decided that Congress could not, by statute, increase the Court's original jurisdiction. The Supreme Court rarely uses this original jurisdiction because the district courts can also hear such cases.

As noted previously, most cases come to the Supreme Court via a discretionary review. The party wishing review files a petition for the **writ of certiorari** with the Court. This party is called the petitioner and is listed first in the title of the Supreme Court case—no matter who was the original plaintiff. The party opposing the petition for review is called the respondent and is listed as the second party in the title of the case (the party after the *v*). If four of the nine justices vote in favor of hearing the case, the petition for certiorari is granted, and the case will have a full review by the Court. If fewer than four vote to hear the case, the petition is not granted, and the decision of the lower court stands as the final judgment in the case. Failure to grant the petition does not mean that the Supreme Court necessarily agrees with the result reached by the lower court in the case. There may be any number of reasons why the Supreme Court Justices think that the case does not deserve their review.

State Court Systems

Each state has designed its own state court system to fit its own needs. No uniform pattern applies to all states; however, most follow a general pattern with a four-tier judicial system.

The first tier, or lowest level, of the typical state judicial system consists of specialty courts of limited jurisdiction. The justice of the peace court is perhaps the oldest of these specialty courts. Normally, this court has jurisdiction over civil cases involving small amounts of money, nonfelony criminal matters, and traffic cases in which the accused person is willing to plead guilty. Usually, there is no provision for a jury trial in this court.

The judge in most instances serves part-time and is often not a lawyer. Court may be held in the judge's home or place of business. Many states have abolished the justice of the peace court and replaced it with a county court or a small claims court, with a full-time judge who must meet certain educational requirements. Still, these courts usually do not provide for trial by jury.

In this first tier, we also find police magistrate courts and municipal courts. Police magistrate courts are usually created to handle traffic offenses and minor criminal matters. Depending on the state, municipal courts may handle minor civil and criminal matters. Municipal courts often allow trial by jury, whereas police magistrate courts normally do not. Both courts' proceedings are usually quick and inexpensive. Most people who come before them are not represented by lawyers. They do, of course, have a right to appeal the courts' decisions.

Generally, municipal and police magistrate courts do not record all testimony and proceedings, and the appeal is made to the trial court of general jurisdiction (which is in the second tier of the state judicial system). There the case is tried **de novo,** which means that a new trial is held, rather than just a review of the record. In some states, however, a record of proceedings is kept, and the appeal is directed to an appellate court for review, rather than for a retrial.

Also found in the first tier of state judicial systems are domestic relations courts. These courts generally handle cases involving marital relations and child custody. Probate courts, also known as surrogate courts, generally administer decedents' estates, the guardianship of minor children and people declared incompetent to handle their own affairs, and matters involving juveniles. Some states use a separate court to hear juvenile cases. Typically there is no provision for trial by jury in domestic relations, probate, and juvenile cases. These courts usually answer to the trial court of general jurisdiction, but again some states permit appeals directly to an appellate court.

In the second of four tiers of the typical state court system, we find the trial court with general jurisdiction. This court may be called a district court, a superior court, a common pleas court, or (in New York) the supreme court. In most states, each county has one or more trial courts with general jurisdiction. In all states, these are courts of record, meaning proceedings are recorded. Usually there is no limit on the monetary amounts involved in cases in these courts. They handle criminal, civil, and equity matters.

The third tier in this four-tier structure is an intermediate appellate court. This court hears appeals from the courts below it. The appellate court is a reviewing court; no new evidence is presented to it. The court reviews the trial transcript, the testimony, and the decision of the lower court. The attorneys for each side submit written briefs of the law that they contend applies, and the court, in some cases, listens to oral arguments of the

Exhibit 4.1: Supreme Court

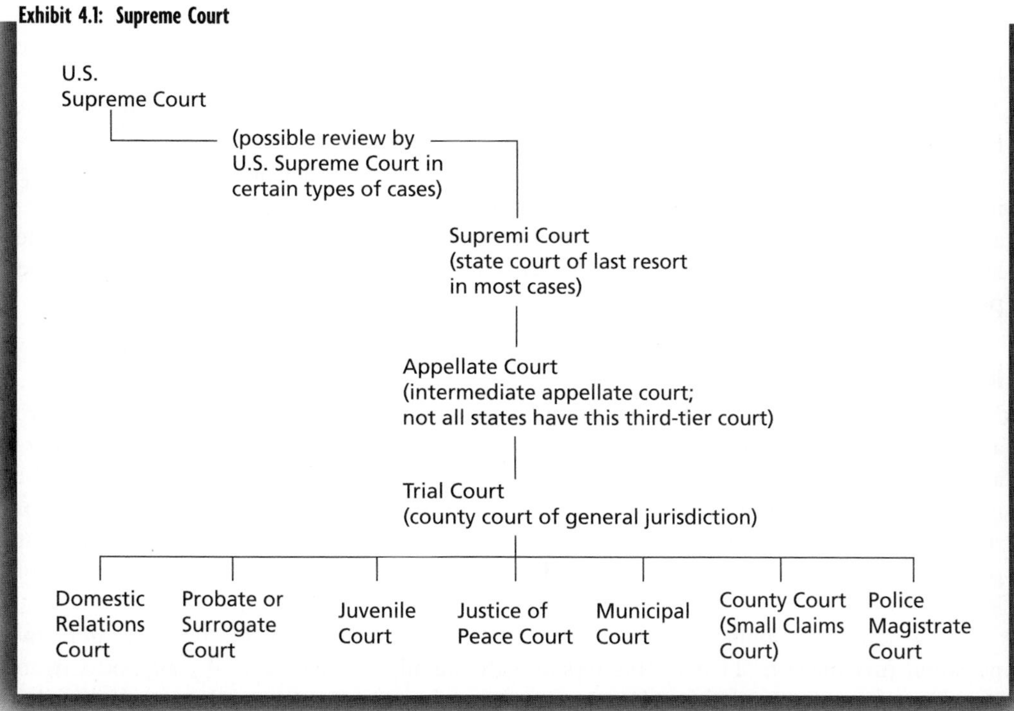

attorneys of each side. Then this court renders one of three types of decisions: to affirm the lower court's decision, to reverse the lower court's decision and give judgment to the appealing party, or to reverse the lower court's decision and remand (send) the case back to the trial court for a new trial or other proceedings in accordance with the court's opinion.

The party wishing to appeal a lower court's judgment (called the **appellant**) must allege error in the trial. For example, perhaps the trial judge allowed the jury to hear inadmissible evidence or gave the jury incorrect instructions on the law.

In some states, the title of the appellate case may be reversed from the title of the case in the lower court. For example, Smith sued Jones in the lower court. The case is titled *Smith v. Jones.* Smith won; Jones appeals. Some states now list the case as *Jones v. Smith*, with the appellant's name first.

This third tier, the intermediate appellate court, is not found in all states. It is usually needed in states with large populations and a large volume of cases.

The fourth tier of state judicial systems is the state's court of last resort. This court may be called the supreme court of errors and appeals, the supreme judicial court, the court of appeals, or simply the supreme court. Like the intermediate appellate court, this is a reviewing court; it holds no new trials. The procedure for review in this court is similar to the procedure for review at the intermediate appellate court level. This court, however, is the party's last resort for appeal in the great majority of the cases that originate in the state court system.

The decisions of a state's highest court may be reviewed by the U.S. Supreme Court if they involve questions of national law. One party's claim that the state's procedures violated due process of law, as required by the Fourteenth Amendment, would be such a case. So would a case in which the state courts had interpreted the meaning of a treaty or an act of Congress. The party making such a national law **("federal question")** claim files a petition for writ of certiorari with the U.S. Supreme Court, as discussed earlier in this chapter. The Supreme Court then decides whether it should review the state case.

Civil Procedure

Each court system has its own procedure for hearing cases. The court where the case is actually tried will use that state's rules of civil procedure. The national courts use the *Federal Rules of Civil Procedure.* Thus, holding the trial in one location or another can change any procedural rule. Questions such as whether the case can be tried before a jury, how many people there are on the jury, how many of them the plaintiff needs to convince to get a verdict, what evidence is admissible, what privileges against testifying exist, and a whole host of similar issues may all have different answers from one court system to another. Although the overall civil procedure systems may be quite similar, very often "the devil is in the details."

For these reasons, and also for the tactical advantages that may be involved in litigating in one location rather than another, the plaintiff's lawyer will try to select the most favorable place to hold the trial. Likewise, the defendant's lawyer will try to resist having the lawsuit in an unfavorable location. The key to these choices is **jurisdiction over the person.**

Jurisdiction over the Person

No court has jurisdiction to hear cases involving anyone and everyone in the world; there are limits to a court's power to force people to appear and defend lawsuits. A person generally must have had some sort of connection with the state (or nation) in which the lawsuit is filed, or with persons or things in that state, to justify holding the lawsuit there. Some of these connections are so significant that they permit any type of lawsuit to be filed in that place against the person. Other, so-called "minimum contacts" permit the filing only of lawsuits that arise out of or relate to the "contact" itself.

The significant connections in the first group are referred to as the bases for **general personal jurisdiction**. That is, the person is "generally" suable here—by anybody, from anywhere, for any sort of claim. Our system recognizes three such connections: **domicile,** consent, and presence. A person can be sued for any sort of claim where he or she has permanent residence—the person's "home state" (or country). This rule applies whether or not the person is actually physically present when the lawsuit is filed. For individuals, the location of domicile is a matter of having a residence that is considered "permanent." (See the *Keck* case problem at the end of the chapter.) For corporations, the state (or nation) of incorporation is the company's domicile. However, it is also possible for a company to acquire a second, "commercial domicile," where it has its principal place of business—its home office or major facility.

The second basis of general personal jurisdiction is **consent** by the litigant to have the case tried in a particular location. The plaintiff consents to have the case heard there by filing the lawsuit with the particular court. But jurisdiction over one party does not also give the court jurisdiction over the other. The problem is the defendant. The defendant may not want to consent to the plaintiff's chosen location unless there are possible benefits to *both* parties from having the case tried there. In many commercial contracts, there may be a forum selection clause, which means that the parties have agreed in advance on the location for any potential lawsuit arising from the contract. (See the *Shute* case problem at the end of the chapter.)

The third basis of general personal jurisdiction is **presence**. An individual can be sued anywhere he or she can be personally served with process from the court. If a plaintiff discovers that you are going to Hawaii for a vacation or a conference, files a lawsuit there, and properly serves you with the court papers while you are there, you are subject to the jurisdiction of the Hawaii courts. The Hawaii courts might decide not to hear the case, on the basis of the location being inconvenient, but if they want to hear the case, they have the jurisdiction over you to do so. Because a corporation has no physical being at all, it is deemed "present" for jurisdiction purposes anywhere it is doing a "systematic and regular part of its general business." That means that many large companies can be sued in a number of locations, even though the claim, which is the basis of the lawsuit, did not arise in those places.

Limited Personal Jurisdiction

Most states in this country, and many other nations, also provide for court jurisdiction over persons who are not domiciled or present there and have not consented to be sued there. These rules are often referred to as **"long-arm" statutes.** For our states, the U.S. Supreme Court requires that such state laws be based on certain minimum contacts and that allowing the lawsuit in that location will not offend traditional notions of fair play and due process.

Among the minimum contacts that have been used by various states are: making a contract there, committing a tort there, owning real property or tangible personal property there, insuring a risk there, making a contract elsewhere to deliver goods or perform services there, and serving as an officer or a director in a company formed there or having its principal place of business there. Of course, not all states have the same standards or interpret them the same way even if they are similarly worded. These jurisdictional complexities are another reason why the parties may want to include a choice of forum clause in their commercial contract.

The *CMMC* case shows the Texas courts struggling with the application of these rules to an international seller of business equipment.

U.S. District Courts hearing diversity of citizenship cases have the same long-arm personal jurisdiction over nonresidents as the general trial courts in the state where they are located. If a state court could force the out-of-stater to appear and defend the lawsuit, so can a U.S. District Court in a diversity case. The U.S. courts' "arms" are as long as, but no longer than, those of a **state trial court.** The *Clune* case illustrates that rule.

Venue

Jurisdiction, as defined previously, means the authority or power to hear a case. Technically, all courts of general jurisdiction in a state might have jurisdiction to hear a specific type of case. The question then arises, which one of those many courts that had jurisdiction *should* hear the case? **Venue** rules decide that question. Most state venue statutes provide that a lawsuit against a defendant be commenced in the defendant's county of residence or

CASE 2

CMMC v. Salinas

929 S.W.2d 435 (TX 1996)

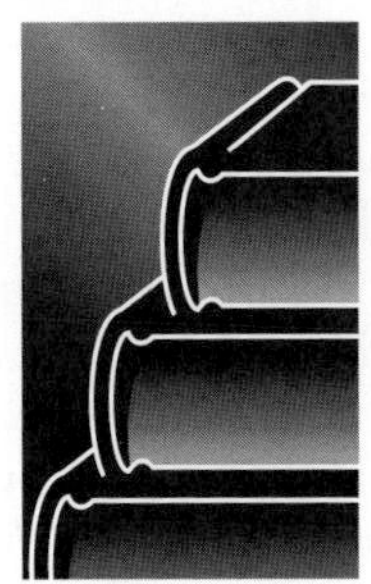

Facts: Hill Country Cellars, a small winery located in Cedar Park, Texas, ordered a winepress from KLR Machines, an independent distributor of wine and juice equipment. KLR ordered the winepress from CMMC, a French manufacturer. KLR told CMMC to wire the winepress for electrical use in the United States and to make shipping arrangements to get the machine from Challones, France, to Houston, Texas.

CMMC sells its products primarily in Europe. It does not directly market in the United States but does provide KLR with promotional materials. Buyers can deal through KLR or directly with CMMC. CMMC has no operations in Texas but did make one prior sale to another Texas customer. Hill Country Cellars never had any direct contact with CMMC but did see a CMMC product ad authored by KLR. KLR has no operations in Texas but has made three or four equipment sales there in the preceding 10 years.

Ambrocio Salinas, an employee of Hill Country Cellars, was cleaning the winepress when he injured his arm. Claiming the machine was defective, Salinas filed a product liability lawsuit in Texas state court. The trial court dismissed the case based on lack of personal jurisdiction over CMMC. The appeals court reversed, and CMMC appealed.

Issue: Can a state court constitutionally assert personal jurisdiction over a nonresident seller merely because the seller knew that its product would be shipped to that state?

Decision: No. Judgment of the court of appeals is reversed; trial court's dismissal is affirmed.

Opinion by Justice Hecht: "Salinas argues, and the court of appeals agreed, that CMMC's release of its winepress into the steam of commerce with knowledge of the intended destination is sufficient to subject it to personal jurisdiction under our decisions. . . .

"In World-Wide Volkswagen, the United States Supreme Court stated a basis for personal jurisdiction that has come to be referred to a the stream-of-commerce doctrine. . . . Applying this rule, the Court held that a car distributor and retail dealer, both doing business in New York, did not have minimum contacts with Oklahoma simply because cars they sold ended up in that state.

"Seven years later, the Court was unable to agree on the scope of the rule. . . . In Asahi, a motorcyclist filed suit in a California court to recover damages for personal injury. Settlements among the parties left pending only a cross-claim . . . for indemnity by a Taiwanese tire tube manufacturer, Cheng Shin Rubber Industrial Company, against a Japanese manufacturer of the tube's valve assembly, Asahi Metal Industry Company. . . .

"Justice O'Connor . . . concluded that Asahi did not have sufficient contacts with California to be subject to personal jurisdiction in state court. Asahi's mere awareness that its products might end up in California was not enough to show that it purposely availed itself of the market in the forum state. . . . [She] explained: 'Some courts have understood the Due Process Clause, as interpreted in World-Wide Volkswagen, to allow an exercise of personal jurisdiction to be based on no more than the defendant's act of placing the product in the stream of commerce. Other courts . . . require the action of the defendant to be more purposefully directed at the forum State than the mere act of placing a product in the stream of commerce. . . . We now find this latter position to be consonant with the requirements of due process. . . . The placement of a product into the stream of commerce, without more, is not an action of the defendant purposefully directed toward the forum State. . . . [A] defendant's awareness that the steam of commerce may or will sweep the product into the forum State does not convert the mere act of placing the product into the stream into an act purposefully directed toward the forum State.' . . .

"Even if a defendant has substantial contacts with a state, the state court cannot exercise personal jurisdiction over the defendant if to do so would offend traditional notions of fairness. In Asahi, the Supreme Court was unanimous in holding that it was unfair to subject Asahi to the jurisdiction of a California court.

"For now, we need not take sides in the Asahi debate over the stream-of-commerce doctrine because of the difference in the factual circumstances of that case and the one now before us. Asahi's products were regularly sold in California, although not by Asahi. CMMC's wine-producing equipment did not regularly find its way to Texas. . . . CMMC's mere knowledge that its winepress was to be sold and used in Texas and its wiring the machine for use in the United States were not sufficient to subject CMMC to the jurisdiction of Texas courts. . . . Even Justice Brennan's view of the stream-of-commerce doctrine would not allow jurisdiction absent a 'regular and anticipated flow of products from manufacture to distribution to retail sale.' . . . There is no flow of products from CMMC to Texas; there is scarcely a dribble. . . .

"Accordingly, the judgment of the court of appeals is reversed and the judgment of the district court dismissing [the case against] CMMC is affirmed."

CASE 3

Clune v. Alimak AB & Industrivarden Service AB

233 F.3d 538 (8 Cir. 2000)

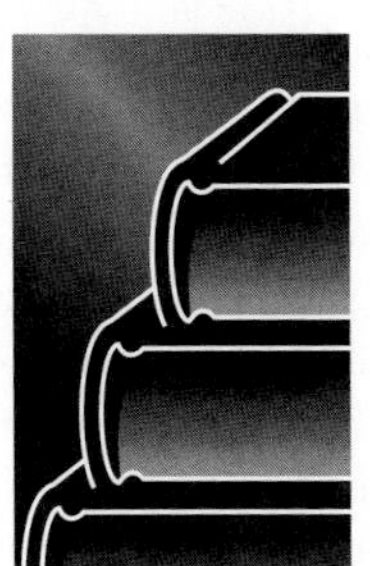

Facts: In February 1996, Joseph Clune was working at a construction site in Kansas City, Missouri, when he fell to his death from a construction hoist. The hoist was manufactured in Sweden by Alimak AB, a Swedish corporation (also known at various times as Linden-Alimak AB). Industrivarden is one of two successor corporations to Alimak; it exists solely to handle Alimak's liabilities.

The hoist was sold by F.O.B. Swedish port to Esco Corporation, one of Alimak's two U.S. distributors, in 1972. Alimak later bought its other U.S. distributor, renamed it Alimak, Inc., and made it the exclusive U.S. distributor. Although the two companies were separate entities, they did have some common directors, and subsidiary personnel went to Sweden for product discussions and service training. Some 700 construction hoists were sold in the United States, about 20 to 40 of which ended up in Missouri.

Joseph's wife and two children filed a wrongful death lawsuit in U.S. District Court in Missouri. The case was dismissed for lack of personal jurisdiction over the defendant.

Issue: Can U.S. courts in Missouri exercise jurisdiction over the defendant?

Decision: Yes. Judgment reversed; case remanded.

Opinion by Judge Lay: "We apply a two-part test to the jurisdictional issue. First, whether the state's long-arm statute is satisfied, and second, whether the exercise of jurisdiction comports with due process....

"The Missouri long-arm statute confers jurisdiction over nonresidents who commit tortious acts within the state.... Missouri courts have interpreted the statute broadly to cover those cases where the Due Process Clause permits the assertion of personal jurisdiction.... Thus, the critical factor in our analysis is whether the exercise of personal jurisdiction in this case comports with due process.

"The Due Process Clause establishes the parameters of a state's power to assert personal jurisdiction over a nonresident defendant.... Due process requires that the defendant 'have certain minimum contacts' with the forum state 'such that the maintenance of the suit does not offend traditional notions of fair play and substantial justice.' ... The Supreme Court has rejected 'talismanic' formulas to personal jurisdiction.... Rather, we must carefully consider the facts of each case to assess the nature of the contacts between the defendant and the forum state.... The factors we weigh include: the burden on the defendant, the interests of the forum state in adjudicating the dispute, the plaintiff's interest in obtaining convenient and effective relief, the interstate judicial system's interest in obtaining the most efficient resolution of controversies, and the shared interest of the several states in furthering fundamental substantive social policies....

"The baseline for minimum contacts is 'some act by which the defendant purposefully avails itself of the privilege of conducting activities in the forum state, thus invoking the benefits and protections of its laws.' ... The defendant's conduct must be such that he or she 'should reasonably anticipate being haled into court there.' ... In other words, personal jurisdiction may be exercised consonant with due process 'over a corporation that delivers its products into the stream of commerce with the expectation that they will be purchased by consumers in the forum state.' ...

"In the present case, Alimak did more than simply set a product adrift in the international stream of commerce. The record shows ... Alimak AB created the distribution system that brought the hoist to Missouri....

"Alimak AB designed its construction hoists for the United State market. The company had exclusive distribution agreements with United States distributors. The Swedish parent's logo was displayed on products that were sold in the United States.... Alimak AB also conducted training seminars in the United States for technicians employed by Alimak, Inc. who serviced hoists that were sold by the subsidiary. Of the 700 construction hoists that were sold in the United States by the company's distributors, between twenty and forty ended up in Missouri. This fact alone makes it difficult for us to characterize the hoist's location in Missouri as random, attenuated or fortuitous.... Additionally, the Swedish parent provided sales brochures and instruction manuals to its distributors for use in promoting and servicing its products in the United States. Members of the Swedish parent's board of directors also served as directors of the subsidiary. Any of these facts, taken alone, might fall short of purposeful availment, however, when taken together they show that ... Alimak AB engaged in a series of activities that were designed to generate profits to the parent from its subsidiar[y's] sales across the United States....

"The Supreme Court has noted that 'the unique burdens placed upon one who must defend oneself in a foreign legal system should have significant weight in assessing the reasonableness of stretching the long arm of personal jurisdiction over national borders.' ... As we have noted, Industrivarden is a shell corporation that has no employees or products to sell. Essentially, the company exists through its insurance company. The overwhelming majority of the evidence in this case will be found in Missouri or the surrounding area, such as the construction hoist, eyewitnesses, medical records and documents material to the incident. As a result, Industrivarden would have to come to Missouri to investigate and gather evidence no matter where a trial were to take place. With the help of modern technology and transportation, Industrivarden easily will be able to collect any relevant documents that are in Sweden and transport them to the United States. For these reasons, any burden Industrivarden might undertake in defending itself in Missouri will be minimal.

"It is readily apparent that Missouri has the strongest interest of any forum in adjudicating this dispute. The accident that gave rise to the case occurred in Missouri. Joseph Clune was an employee of the Missouri company, he worked and paid taxes in that state, and his death occurred there as a result of a product sold in that forum. No other state has a more compelling connection to this case.

"The Clunes' interest in obtaining convenient and effective relief is best satisfied by adjudicating this dispute in Missouri. Although they are residents of Kansas, Kansas is not a viable venue for this case and Missouri is the closest choice. In any event, Missouri is abundantly more convenient for the Clunes than if this case were to be tried in Sweden. Our decision today in no way guarantees the Clunes['] success in this suit. However, it likely would be impossible for this family of three who ha[ve] lost their husband and father to travel abroad to seek restitution for his death.

"Trying this case in Missouri federal court also satisfies the judicial system's interest in obtaining the most efficient resolution of this controversy. We exercise caution when subjecting a foreign corporation to jurisdiction in the United States, but are satisfied that . . . Alimak AB affirmatively took on the risk of liabilities here.

"Finally, the adjudication of this dispute in Missouri ensures the fundamental social policy of safety in goods that enter our marketplace. As commercial borders are dismantled in the increasingly global marketplace, more products are available to consumers in the United States. It is essential that our laws designed to protect the health and safety of human beings not be lost in this flurry of commerce.

"The judgment of dismissal by the district court is vacated and the cause is remanded for further proceedings."

in the county in which the cause of action arose. For example, if a plaintiff in an automobile accident case filed suit in a county other than the county where the accident occurred or where the defendant resided, then the defendant could have the venue changed to one of those locations.

Venue also may be changed when the possibility of selecting a fair and impartial jury in the county where the lawsuit was filed is in question. In that case, the defendant could request a change of venue to an adjoining county. This might occur in a case involving local residents who assumed that all college students drink beer and drive at high rates of speed. In that case, it would be better to change the venue to an adjoining county where the residents are not in constant contact with college students and might not be prejudiced against students.

Pleading Stage

The first step in filing a lawsuit is the preparation of a **complaint,** sometimes called a petition or a declaration. The complaint will state the names of the parties involved. The party bringing the action is called the **plaintiff,** and the party being sued is called the **defendant.** The complaint will state the plaintiff's version of what happened, where it happened, when it happened, how it happened, and why it happened, and it will allege that it happened as the result of the defendant's wrongful acts. Then it will state what the injuries or damages were, and it will conclude with a request for an amount of money.

The attorney for the plaintiff will file this complaint with the clerk of an appropriate court. The court will issue a **summons,** which will be served on the defendant, to give notification of the lawsuit and to inform defendant when and where an appearance must be made if the defendant wishes to defend. Usually a copy of the complaint is served along with the summons so that the defendant will know the particulars of the lawsuit.

The rules for serving a summons vary for different types of lawsuits and from state to state. The most common method is service to the defendant in person by a sheriff or another authorized official. Service may also be made by registered or certified mail with a return receipt. In some jurisdictions, a summons may be legally served if it is handed to a member of the defendant's household; however, there are restrictions as to the age of the party receiving the summons. Handing the summons to the defendant's husband or wife would be proper service, but handing it to the defendant's 8-year-old child would not.

In many cases, the defendant will be a resident of another state. Under the long-arm statutes discussed earlier, service can be made by sending a copy of the summons and the complaint by certified letter to the defendant's last known address and to the secretary of state in the state where the suit was filed.

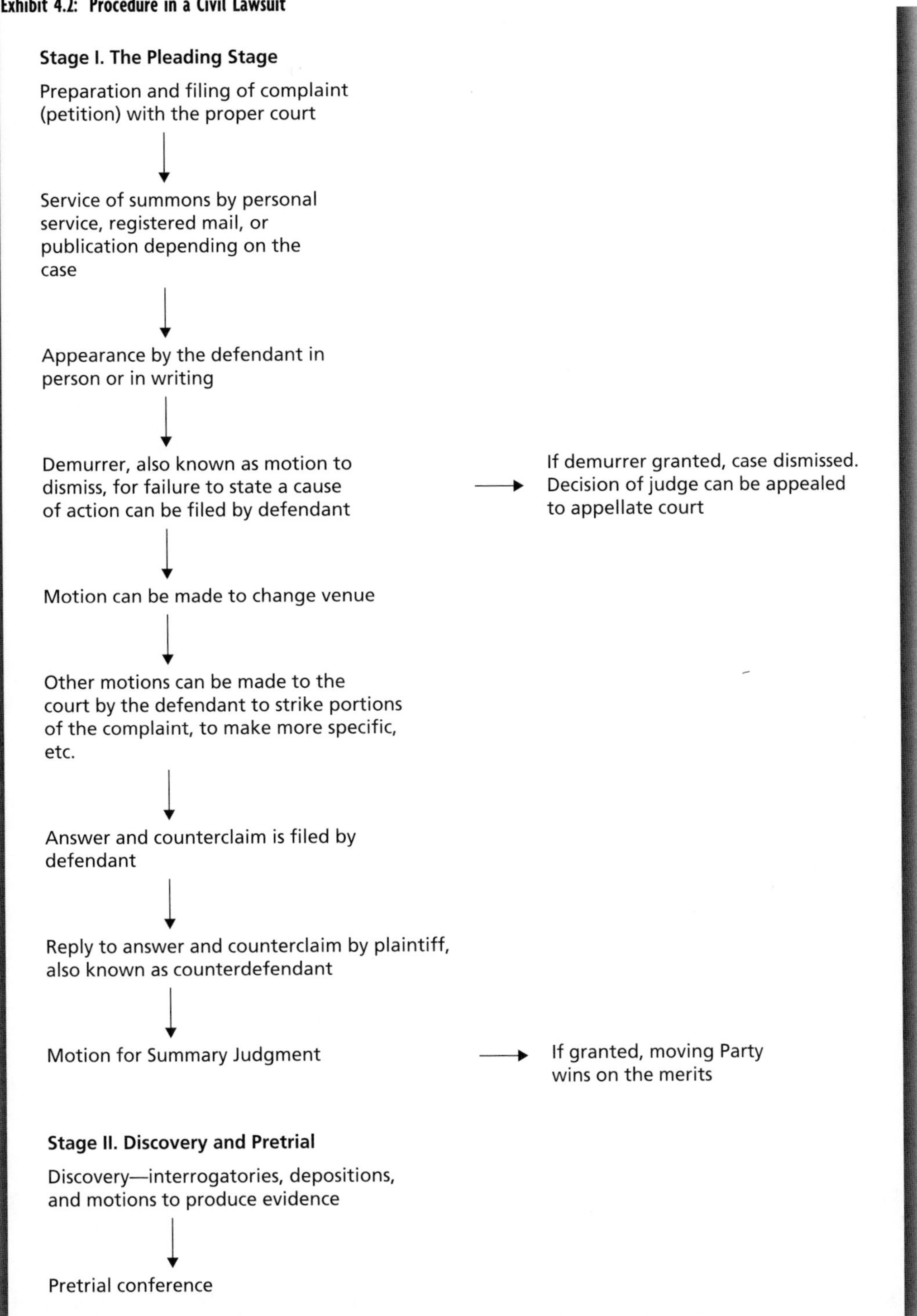
Exhibit 4.2: Procedure in a Civil Lawsuit

Stage I. The Pleading Stage
Preparation and filing of complaint (petition) with the proper court
Service of summons by personal service, registered mail, or publication depending on the case
Appearance by the defendant in person or in writing
Demurrer, also known as motion to dismiss, for failure to state a cause of action can be filed by defendant
If demurrer granted, case dismissed. Decision of judge can be appealed to appellate court
Motion can be made to change venue
Other motions can be made to the court by the defendant to strike portions of the complaint, to make more specific, etc.
Answer and counterclaim is filed by defendant
Reply to answer and counterclaim by plaintiff, also known as counterdefendant
Motion for Summary Judgment
If granted, moving Party wins on the merits
Stage II. Discovery and Pretrial
Discovery—interrogatories, depositions, and motions to produce evidence
Pretrial conference

Notice of some types of cases can be published in a local newspaper a required number of times when the whereabouts of the defendant is unknown. An example would be an adoption case in which one of the natural parents could not be located. Publication would be acceptable because the circumstances prevent service on that parent personally or by certified mail.

Once the complaint has been filed and the summons has been properly served on the defendant, the defendant must appear in court within a specified time, such as 20 days within receipt of the summons. Failure to appear either in person or by an attorney within that time will be treated as an admission of guilt, and the court will enter a **default judgment** against

Exhibit 4.2a:

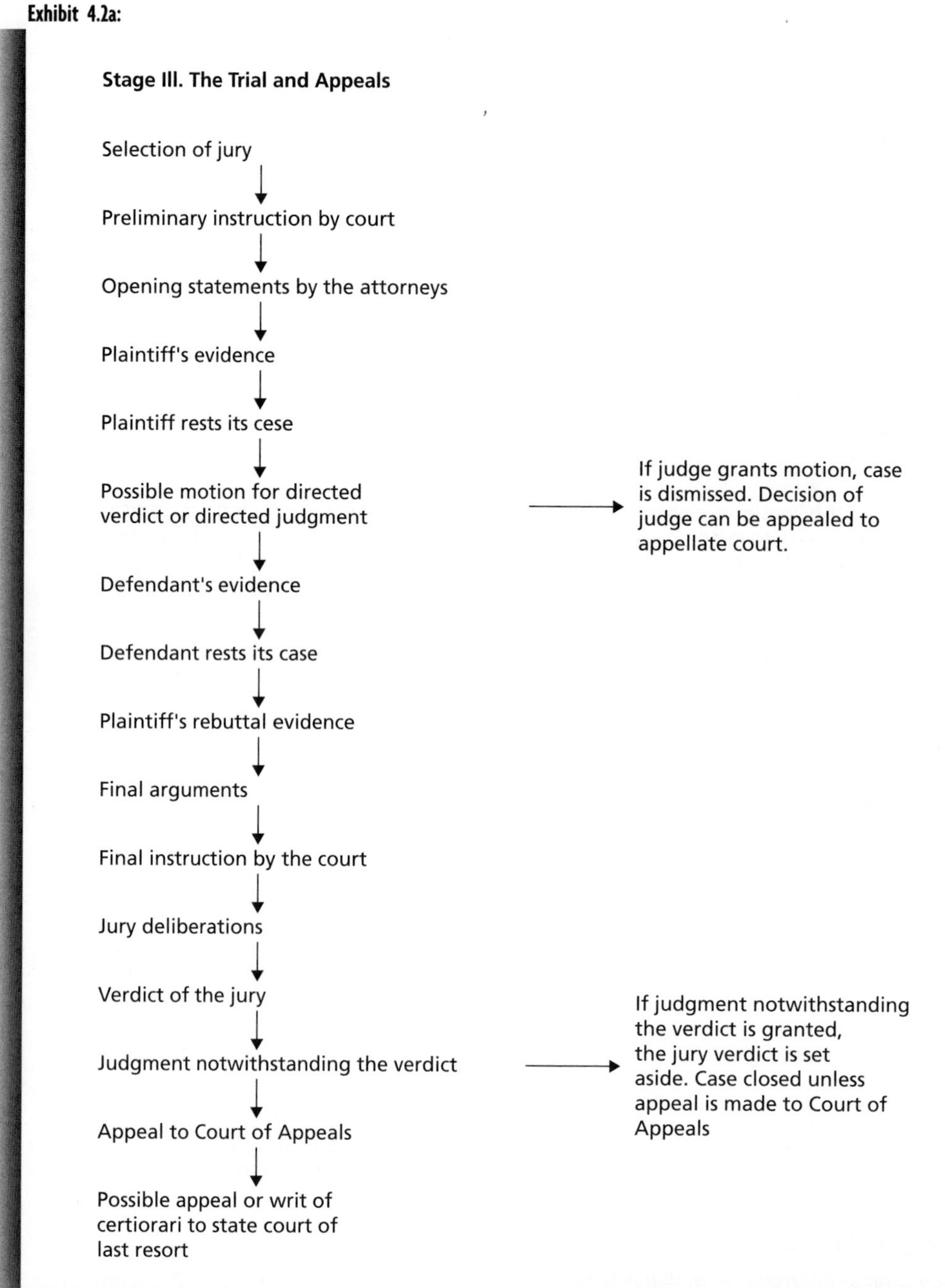

the defendant. Under certain circumstances, the defendant may have this default judgment set aside. An example occurs when the defendant can prove service of the summons was improper.

Assuming the defendant does appear as summoned, the first question he or she may raise is whether the lawsuit was filed within the proper statutory period. This period is set by the state's **statute of limitations.** For a tort action, the period will normally vary from 1 to 5 years after the date of the occurrence, depending on the law of the state where the occurrence took place. In a breach of contract case, the period may vary from 5 to 10 years. Special provisions apply if the defendant is a governmental body. Notice of intent to sue may be required within 3 to 6 months after the occurrence, depending on applicable law.

The defendant may challenge the sufficiency of the complaint by filing a **demurrer,** or **motion to dismiss,** or attack the complaint with motions concerning jurisdiction or venue. To be legally sufficient, a complaint must state a **cause of action.** That is, the complaint filed by the plaintiff must state that the plaintiff had a specific legal right, that the defendant had a legal duty and breached it, and that the plaintiff was injured as a proximate result of the breach. This is the first of four safety valves in the trial of a civil lawsuit. If the judge finds the plaintiff did not have a specific legal right or if the defendant owed no legal duty to the plaintiff, the demurrer will be granted and the lawsuit is dismissed.

The *Parex Bank* case rules on a motion to dismiss based on forum *non conveniens* (location of the court [the forum Plaintiff has chosen] is inconvenient).

The next important pleading is the **answer,** in which the defendant must affirm or deny the allegations the plaintiff made in the complaint. The defendant may very well admit some facts, such as the time and place of the occurrence. The defendant would, however, deny allegations regarding his or her negligence. In addition to answering the plaintiff's claims, the defendant may make a claim for damages by filing a **counterclaim.** This is also called a **cross complaint** in some states. In this pleading, the defendant will allege that the plaintiff was negligent and will state a claim for damages. The plaintiff must now answer the cross complaint or counterclaim in a pleading called a **reply.**

A second safety valve is a motion for **summary judgment,** or judgment on the pleadings. If there are no significant fact issues in the case, as described in the pleadings, one or both parties may ask the court to enter an immediate judgment without a trial. For instance, the defendant has a receipt or a cancelled check showing that the claim on which the plaintiff filed suit has in fact been paid. Or the defendant can demonstrate that he or she did not owe the claim in the first place; it was someone else, with a similar name. In these clear-cut cases, the court should enter a summary judgment, which is a decision on the merits of the case. Unlike the motion to dismiss (where the claim can be re-filed), the summary judgment ends the case between the parties (subject to appeal, of course).

Pretrial Stage

During the second stage of a trial, called the **pretrial** stage, the parties and their lawyers prepare the case for trial. Most major metropolitan areas have a long backlog of cases, so a case filed today may not come to trial for several years. This presents several problems. **Witnesses** tend to forget facts about the case as time goes by. They may die or move out of the jurisdiction, which means they cannot legally be brought back for trial.

Three general methods of discovery are used. First, each party may file interrogatories to be answered by the other. **Interrogatories** are lists of questions that probe for information about the person, the incident, and the damages. The questions must be relevant to the case, but interrogatories tend to be "fishing expeditions." They are usually not admissible as evidence in court.

Interrogatories normally are followed by depositions. A **deposition** is sworn testimony that is subject to cross-examination and is admissible as evidence. Depositions may be taken from the parties and from witnesses, both witnesses to the incident and expert witnesses, such as doctors, engineers, and economists.

Depositions basically serve two purposes. First, they discover the testimony. A party who has testified under oath will be guilty of perjury if he or she materially changes the testimony later. Second, depositions preserve the testimony in case the witness dies or moves and cannot be located. Doctors and other experts testifying in a case may not be able to appear at the trial, but their depositions can be used.

Traditionally, depositions have been taken in the presence of a court reporter, who types a record of the testimony. If the deposition has to be used at the trial, it is simply read in court. Today many courts are experimenting with videotape depositions that can be played in the courtroom. This technique can speed up trials when scheduling problems occur. Some attorneys would ask to postpone a trial rather than enter testimony read from a deposition, but they will be less hesitant to present videotaped depositions when witnesses are not available.

A third **discovery** procedure is a motion by one party to have the other party produce certain items of evidence for review. For example, the defendant may ask the plaintiff for copies of medical reports, bills, photographs, and other material that the plaintiff intends to submit at the trial.

Courts may not compel testimony or production of documents in violation of a recognized privilege of confidentiality. Such privileges may exist under a state's general common law rules of evidence or under a specific statute. As will be more fully discussed in Chapter 6,

CASE 4

Parex Bank v. Russian Savings Bank

116 F.Supp.2d 415 (S.D. NY 2000)

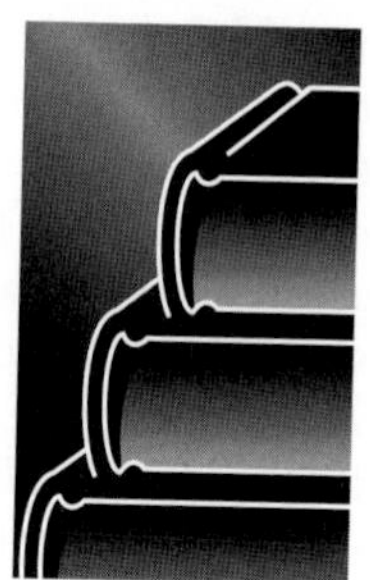

Facts: Parex Bank, organized in Latvia, sued for breach of contract and for deceptive business practices, under New York law. Defendant is a Russian open joint-stock company known by various names, but usually referred to by Sberbank. The dispute stems from Sberbank's failure to honor a Nondeliverable Forward Exchange (NFE) contract. NFE contracts enabled foreign investors to hedge their investments in ruble-denominated Russian securities. A bank would contract to convert rubles into dollars at a specified rate, on a specified date. When the Russian financial system collapsed in 1998, and the ruble was substantially devalued, Parex demanded payment of \$3,755,642.01 to satisfy the terms of its settlement. Parex then sued in New York state court. Sberbank removed the case to the U.S. District Court. Sberbank now moves to dismiss the case for lack of personal jurisdiction, forum non conveniens, and failure to state a claim.

Issue: Is Russia an "adequate alternate forum"?

Decision: No. Motion to dismiss is denied.

Opinion by Judge Sweet: "Sberbank's actions surrounding this currency transaction were sufficient to establish the constitutionally requisite minimum contacts to support the exercise of personal jurisdiction. Sberbank consented to make payment in dollars to Parex's Bank of New York account in the event that the exchange rate changed unfavorably, and to receive payment into its New York account if the rate changed favorably. In addition, Sberbank accepted Parex's security deposit into its own Bank of New York account as security for the repayment of the NDF contract when it was due.... Sberbank 'routinely conducts exchange deals through and in New York state.'...

"In combination, Sberbank's use of accounts at Bank of New York for this particular transaction and its practice of conducting other similar transactions using New York banks establishes Sberbank's 'minimum contacts' with this jurisdiction....

"The equitable doctrine of forum non conveniens allows a court to dismiss even if the court is a permissible venue and has proper jurisdiction over the claim.... This inquiry involves two steps (1) determining whether there is an adequate alternate forum for the dispute, ... and (2) balancing the public and private interest factors the Supreme Court described in Gilbert....

"The first step of the forum non conveniens inquiry requires the Court to determine whether Russia would be an adequate alternative forum in which to adjudicate the dispute. A foreign forum is not inadequate merely because its justice system differs from that of the United States.... [C]omity requires that this Court abstain from adversely judging the quality of Russia's justice system unless Parex makes a showing of inadequate procedural safeguards.... Absent such a showing, it is 'rare' that courts find ... an alternative forum to be inadequate....

"Russia is an adequate alternative forum if (1) Sberbank is subject to service of process there, and (2) the forum permits a satisfactory remedy.... Both parties agree that Sberbank is subject to service of process in Russia....

"The question thus becomes whether the Moscow City Arbitration Court permits a satisfactory remedy.... [W]hile an alternate forum's less favorable substantive law should ordinarily not weigh heavily against dismissal, this factor increases in significance when 'the remedy provided by the alternative forum is so clearly inadequate or unsatisfactory that it is no remedy at all.'...

"Even if Russia employs different procedures than the United States courts, Sberbank has met its burden of proving that Russia's judicial system affords adequate procedural protections upon the face of its statutory provisions....

"Parex argues that Russia is not an adequate alternate forum because ... Russian law does not recognize NDF contracts as [per a]recent decision from the highest arbitration court in Russia, the Supreme Arbitrazh Court....

"Sberbank's motion to dismiss for forum non conveniens is denied at this time for lack of proof that Russia will permit any litigation of the NDF contract....

"Parex has made no showing that the currency exchange between the party banks in this case is 'consumer-oriented' under [New York law]....

"For the foregoing reasons, the motions to dismiss for lack of personal jurisdiction and forum non conveniens are denied, and the motion to dismiss Count II is granted."

people cannot be required to testify as to matters that might subject them to criminal prosecution. Attorneys cannot testify about matters their clients communicated to them in confidence. Other widely recognized privileges exist for communications to the clergy, physicians, and spouses. In some states, statutes may provide privileges against disclosure for the records of teachers, newspaper reporters, accountants, and others. Generally, a privilege against disclosure can be waived by the person in whose favor it operates. A client, for instance, could waive his or her privilege and permit an attorney to testify as to matters that otherwise could not be disclosed.

After both sides have completed discovery, the court will schedule a **pretrial conference.** The purpose of the pretrial hearing is twofold. First, it enables the judge to get the attorneys representing the plaintiff and the defendant together and to determine whether or not there can be an amicable settlement. Here the judge acts more as a mediator than as a judge. When possible, the judge will encourage the parties to negotiate a settlement so the case can be dismissed before trial. If, on the other hand, a settlement appears impossible, the judge will try to determine whether any items of evidence can be admitted without objection to save time at the trial. In some jurisdictions, the judge will have the parties exchange lists of the witnesses they are going to have testify. The theory is that the trial should present no surprises and that each party should have an opportunity to know the other party's evidence. If it appears that the case will have to be tried, a trial date will be set.

Trial Stage

The actual trial of the lawsuit is a series of events that we will review in the order of their occurrence. The flowcharts on pages 69 and 70 outline the overall sequence in a civil case.

Selection of a Jury

Unless the judge is to hear a case without a jury, the first step in a trial is the selection of a jury. (Generally, there is no right to trial by jury in equity cases. Even if the parties have the right to a jury trial, they may waive it.) Traditionally, a jury was composed of 12 people, but many jurisdictions have reduced that number to six for some cases. Selecting the jury is a very important phase of the trial. To have a fair trial, jurors must be unbiased, fair, and impartial.

A list of prospective jurors is selected at random from the eligible voters in the county where a state court lawsuit is to be tried or in the court district where a U.S. District Court suit is to be tried. Prospective jurors are called to the courtroom, where attorneys for the plaintiff and the defendant question them to uncover biases or other reasons they could not serve as fair and impartial jurors. For example, the prospective jurors may be asked whether they are related to any of the parties in the lawsuit or any of the attorneys, whether they have had business dealings with the parties, or whether they know the parties socially. They may also be asked whether they have read about the cause of action in the newspapers and whether they have already formed an opinion about the guilt or innocence of the parties. This examination is called **voir dire.**

If a prospective juror admits prejudice, or if a prejudice is implied by a relationship to someone associated with the case, the prospective juror may be challenged for cause. If the court agrees that the prospective juror is prejudiced or cannot be a fair and impartial juror, the prospective juror will be dismissed. In addition to the **challenges for cause,** each side in the lawsuit will be given a certain number of **peremptory challenges.** No cause need be stated for making a peremptory challenge. The purpose of the peremptory challenge is to give each side an opportunity to dismiss certain jurors who, for one reason or another, the attorney feels may be prejudiced against his or her client. Peremptory challenges may or may not be used.

Preliminary Instructions by the Court

After the jury has been selected and seated in the jury box, the judge will give jurors **preliminary instructions** concerning the trial. The judge will outline the issue for trial and explain the burden of proof, the credibility of witnesses, and the manner in which the jurors should weigh the testimony they are about to hear.

Opening Statements by the Attorneys

The **opening statement** is not evidence; it is only a preview of coming attractions. As the complaining party, the plaintiff has the burden of proof and thus has first opening statement. In the opening statement the plaintiff's attorney tells jurors what type of case they are to hear and briefly explains what the plaintiff intends to prove. The defendant's attorney then makes an opening statement, telling the jury what the defendant expects to prove. Now the jury has an overview of the case and is ready to hear the evidence.

Plaintiff's Evidence

The plaintiff, having the burden of proof, is first to present evidence. The plaintiff's attorney calls a witness to the stand and asks this person questions; this is called direct examination. After this questioning, the defendant's attorney can **cross-examine** the witness to test the accuracy of the witness's statements. After the cross-examination, the plaintiff's attorney can conduct redirect examination to try to reestablish points challenged on cross-examination. Exhibits such as photographs, charts, documents, and articles of clothing may be submitted as evidence. This process continues until all of the plaintiff's witnesses have testified. The plaintiff will then rest his or her case.

Motion for Directed Verdict or Directed Judgment

We have now reached the third "safety valve" in the litigation. You will recall that after the complaint was filed and the summons was served, the defendant had an opportunity to file a demurrer (a motion to dismiss for failure to state a cause of action) and to have the case dismissed if in fact there was no legal right or legal duty. Now, after the plaintiff has presented evidence and rested his or her case, the defendant may make a motion for a **directed verdict,** if there is a jury. If the judge feels that no issue of fact is to be decided by the jury, then the judge will direct a verdict in favor of the defendant. If there is no jury, a motion can be made for a directed judgment in favor of the defendant. If an issue of fact has been raised for the jury to decide, then the trial must go on.

Defendant's Evidence

The defendant's attorney will now call the defense witnesses, and the same process of questioning will occur. The defendant's attorney will ask questions under direct examination; the plaintiff's attorney will cross-examine; and the defendant's attorney will have an opportunity for redirect examination of the witnesses. The defendant may submit exhibits of evidentiary material for the defense. Then the defendant rests.

Plaintiff's Rebuttal Evidence

The plaintiff has the right to recall witnesses or to call additional witnesses for the sole purposes of rebutting the defendant's evidence.

Final Arguments

Because the plaintiff has the burden of proving the case against the defendant, the plaintiff is entitled to present the first closing argument. This is also called a summation. Here, the plaintiff's attorney reviews all the testimony and tries to convince the jurors that the plaintiff's evidence is stronger than the defendant's evidence and that the plaintiff should win. In a civil case, the jury decides not only who is right but also the amount of the verdict. Thus, the plaintiff's attorney also argues the value of the plaintiff's claim. The defendant's attorney then argues the opposite side of the case. Then the plaintiff is entitled to a final rebuttal or closing argument.

Final Instructions by the Judge

The jurors now need to know what substantive law applies to the case. The judge reads prepared instructions on the law to the jury. In most jurisdictions, the attorneys for each side prepare proposed instructions, and the judge selects those appropriate for the case. The judge may also add instructions not submitted by either attorney.

Jury Deliberations

After hearing the judge's instructions on the law, jurors are taken to the jury room. Their first order of business is to select a foreman. Then they commence deliberations.

The jury must be convinced that the plaintiff has proved his or her case by a preponderance of the evidence to find for the plaintiff. In some civil cases, such a claim that fraud has been committed, the person alleging fraud is required to prove it by "clear and convincing" evidence. Either of these standards of proof is far short of the criminal standard: "beyond any reasonable doubt."

Verdict

When the jurors have reached agreement they return to the courtroom and the foreman reads their verdict. The verdict must be unanimous in most jurisdictions, although some states require agreement of only 10 of 12 or 5 of 6 jurors. Because civil juries decide both questions of fact and the dollar amount of the verdict, they seldom become a hung jury, which is a jury that has become deadlocked in trying to reach a unanimous verdict.

Judgment Notwithstanding the Verdict

Here we have the fourth safety valve in the system, **judgment notwithstanding the verdict.** The judge has veto power over the jury in the rare situations where the jury has obviously failed to follow the instructions on the law. At such times, the judge can disregard the verdict and enter a judgment contrary to it. In the vast majority of cases, however, the judge enters a judgment on the basis of the jury's verdict.

The trial judge also has some discretionary control over the amount of the jury's verdict. If a plaintiff's evidence clearly shows damages beyond those awarded by the jury, the trial judge may suggest an increase in the amount of the award, as an alternative to granting the plaintiff's motion for an entire new trial. If the defendant agrees with this suggestion, the award is raised. If not, a new trial is ordered. This procedure is called additur. Likewise, a similar suggestion can be made as to a grossly excessive award. The defendant's motion for a new trial is denied on condition that the plaintiff agrees to a reduction in the damages award. This process is called remittitur.

Civil Appellate Procedure

After the verdict has been rendered and the judgment entered, the losing party has a right to an appeal. The procedural requirements of the court system must be followed. Notice of intent to appeal must be given within a specified time after the judgment is rendered. The procedure before the appellate court has been discussed earlier in this chapter. After all appeal procedures have been exhausted, a final judgment will be rendered, provided the court judgment has been affirmed. Of course, if there was a reversal, then we are faced with a new trial or other action in accordance with the appellate court's instructions.

In the great majority of cases, no appeal is filed, and at the end of the time allotted for filing an appeal, the judgment becomes final. Thus we come to the next step in the trial of a civil case, enforcement of the judgment.

Enforcement of Judgments

A judgment rendered against a party is worthless without a procedure to enforce and collect that judgment. In years past, people were put in debtor's prison for failing to pay their bills, but no such procedure exists today. Now, if a person obtains a judgment for money against another person, there are basically three ways to collect that judgment. One way is for the party on whose behalf the judgment was rendered to levy execution on the property of the party against whom the judgment was rendered. The debtor's property that is not exempt from execution under state or national law may be seized by a law officer with a court order. It is then sold at a public sale, and the proceeds are applied against the judgment.

A second way to collect is to have the wages of the person against whom the judgment was rendered garnished, subject to the state and national laws concerning **garnishment.** There are exemptions under the national and state laws that do not allow the owner of a judgment to secure the total wages of the debtor. The judgment debtor's bank accounts may also be garnished.

The third way to collect is to secure a lien against property owned by the debtor. For example, a lien may be placed against real estate owned by the debtor. The debtor cannot sell and give clear title to the real estate without first paying the lien. In some cases, the property may be sold through a further court process to enforce the lien.

In the following case, the defendants did not appear in the Idaho court to argue the case, so the court entered a default judgment in favor of the plaintiff. The defendants then filed a "special appearance" with the Idaho court to claim that the judgment was void for lack of personal jurisdiction. When the Idaho district court ruled that it had had proper jurisdiction to hear the case against them, the defendants then appealed to the Idaho Supreme Court. The case raises interesting issues about jurisdiction over Internet buyers and sellers.

CASE 5

Blimka v. My Web Wholesaler, LLC

152 P.2d 594 (ID 2007)

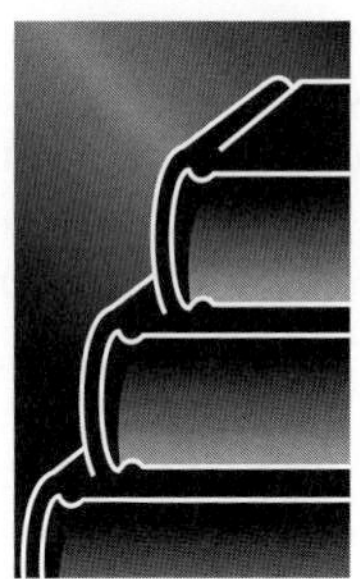

Facts: My Web is a Maine limited liability company, with its sole place of business in Athens, Maine. It maintains a Web site, through which it wholesales salvaged and distressed merchandise. Mike Blimka subscribed to its listserv, through which he received an e-mail offer to sell jeans in bulk. He spoke with several My Web employees by telephone, including the manager—Lisa DePalma, and agreed to buy 26,500 pairs at $0.79 each. He sent the money, and the jeans were shipped to him. When they arrived, he claimed that they had been misrepresented as to quality, value, and wrapping. Blimka sued, claiming fraud and breach of warranties.

My Web and DePalma were properly served with notice of the lawsuit but did not appear in the Idaho court to defend the case. The Idaho district court entered a default judgment in favor of Blimka. Defendants asked the district court to declare that the judgment was void because they were not subject to its jurisdiction. The district court refused to do so, and defendants appealed to the state supreme court.

Issue: Was the default judgment in the district court void because the court lacked personal jurisdiction over the defendants?

Decision: No. Judgment affirmed.

Opinion by Justice Jones: "The proper exercise of personal jurisdiction over non-resident defendants by an Idaho court involves satisfying two criteria.... First, the court must determine that the non-resident defendant's actions fall within the scope of Idaho's long-arm statute.... Second, the court must determine that exercising jurisdiction over the non-resident defendant comports with the constitutional standards of the Due Process Clause of the U.S. Constitution....

"Since we conclude that jurisdiction existed on the fraud claim, both with respect to My Web and DePalma, and because that claim supports all relief granted in the judgment, we need not address the issue of jurisdiction over the contract claims.

"Idaho's long-arm statute extends jurisdiction to 'the commission of a tortious act within this state.' ... This court has held that 'an allegation that an injury has occurred in Idaho in a tortious manner is sufficient.' ... This is remedial legislation designed to provide a forum for Idaho residents and should be liberally construed to effectuate that purpose....

"In this case, the allegedly fraudulent representations were directed at an Idaho resident and the injury occurred in this state. Thus, we hold that Blimka's allegation of fraud was sufficient to invoke the tortious acts language of Idaho Code S. 5-514(b) with respect to both defendants.

"Next, the defendants contend that their contacts with Idaho were insufficient under the Due Process Clause of the U.S. Constitution to permit personal jurisdiction in this case. The Fourteenth Amendment to the U.S. Constitution permits a state to exercise personal jurisdiction over a non-resident defendant when that defendant has certain minimum contacts with the state such that the maintenance of the suit does not offend 'traditional notions of fair play and substantial justice.' ...

"Blimka's complaint alleged that the defendants committed the intentional tort of fraud. In the Calder case, the U.S. Supreme Court distinguished 'untargeted negligence' from intentional, and allegedly tortious, acts expressly aimed at the forum, and adopted an 'effects' test to address what contacts are necessary to satisfy minimum contacts in the context of an intentional tort expressly aimed at the forum state.... The Court held that minimum contacts were satisfied where the defendants allegedly committed the intentional tort of libel outside of the forum state, but the effects of the tort were directed to, and suffered in, the forum state....

"Like the defendants in Calder, the defendants in this case were not charged with mere 'untargeted negligence.' Rather, they were charged with the commission of a fraud in Idaho. Blimka alleged that the defendants intentionally misrepresented facts regarding the quality, value, and packaging of the jeans during telephonic and electronic communications. At all times during the communications, the defendants knew that

Blimka was residing in Idaho. Therefore, . . . 'their intentional, and allegedly tortious actions were expressly aimed' at Idaho, and they realized that the brunt of the damage resulting from these actions would occur in Idaho. . . . Where an Idaho resident alleges that a defendant in Maine intentionally directed false representations to, and caused injury in Idaho, that resident need not travel to Maine to pursue his or her claim against the perpetrator of the fraud. . . . The defendants' actions satisfy minimum contacts with respect to the fraud allegations.

"Additionally, because the defendants purposefully directed their allegedly false representations into Idaho, the exercise of personal jurisdiction is presumed not to offend traditional notions of fair play and substantial justice. . . . Idaho has an ever-increasing interest in protecting its residents from fraud committed on them from afar by electronic means. Given the fact, the defendants should have reasonably anticipated being haled into Idaho courts. . . .

"In sum, neither the Idaho long-arm statute nor the Due Process Clause precluded the district court from exercising personal jurisdiction over the defendants and entering a binding judgment against them in this case. As a result, the district court's decision to deny the defendants' motion for relief from judgment was not an abuse of that court's discretion and will not be disturbed by this court. . . .

"The decision of the district court is affirmed. Blimka is awarded attorney fees and costs on appeal."

Full Faith and Credit

In some cases, the judgment debtor may not have enough property in the state that issued the judgment to satisfy it. If the debtor owns property in other states, it may be necessary to take the judgment from the state where the judgment was rendered to those other states and to ask for its enforcement there. When this happens, the "**Full Faith and Credit Clause**" in Article IV of the U.S. Constitution comes into play. This clause requires each state to give "full faith and credit" to the public acts, records, and judicial proceedings of other states. The successful judgment creditor cannot be forced to relitigate the whole case in other states to enforce the claim. Other states can, however, examine the judgment to make sure that the court that issued it had jurisdiction. If the court in the state where the judgment was rendered had jurisdiction, the other states have no choice; they must enforce the judgment just as they would one of their own. The ultimate decision as to what are adequate jurisdictional bases is made by the U.S. Supreme Court because a matter of constitutional interpretation is at issue.

Class Actions

Traditionally, plaintiffs have pursued their claims on an individual basis. However, courts have occasionally permitted plaintiffs to represent a large class of claimants in which the claims of all the parties are similar and arise out of the same occurrence. This is called a **class action.** The most common example of a class action is one shareholder bringing an action against a corporation for some alleged mismanagement and resulting loss. That one shareholder represents all other similar stockholders who allege similar damage. Obviously the court can hear one case more expeditiously and at less expense than hundreds or thousands of similar cases. Class actions also help overcome inequality of means. The big corporation can afford litigation more than a single plaintiff can. However, if many plaintiffs join forces, the expense is far less for each individual.

Under the current Federal Rules of Civil Procedure, four prerequisites must all be met before a class action may be maintained in the U.S. District Court:

1. The class is so numerous that joinder of all its members is impractical.
2. The class members have common questions of law or fact.
3. The claim or defense of the class representative is typical of that of the absent class members.
4. The representative will fairly and adequately protect the interests of the class.

The rules also provide that one of the following conditions must exist:

1. The prosecution of separate actions might result in inconsistent or varying judgments.
2. The prosecution of separate actions might in practice dispose of the interests of other members or impede their ability to protect those interests.

3. The defendant has acted or refused to act on grounds generally applicable to all members of the class, so that injunctive or declaratory relief for the whole class is appropriate.
4. The court finds that a class action is the best method to adjudicate the controversy.

If a class action based on diversity of citizenship is filed in U.S. District Court, the amount per claim must be at least $75,000. However, the U.S. Supreme Court has ruled recently that at least some class actions may be heard if there is a main claimant with at least $75,000 at stake; other persons' closely related claims for less than that amount can still be members of the class, based on the district courts' supplemental jurisdiction. The individual states also have rules for class actions, many of which are similar to the Federal Rules, with one notable exception. State courts require no minimum amount per claim. Also, many states have passed specific environmental and consumer laws authorizing class actions under certain circumstances.

Arbitration and Mediation as Methods of Dispute Resolution

Arbitration

When thinking of **arbitration,** one normally thinks of labor law and the arbitration of grievances and the arbitration clauses in labor contracts. Arbitration, of course, has been used extensively as a method of settling grievance disputes in labor-management relations. However, arbitration has also been used as a method of deciding other types of disputes.

In the public bargaining sector, public employees are not allowed to strike. Thus, it is common for agreements between labor and management to be reached by submitting the offers of both parties to one or more arbitrators for a final decision as to the contract terms. This procedure is being more extensively used as unionization spreads among public employees.

Another type of arbitration has also been growing in popularity. This is the commercial arbitration of business disputes that would normally be handled in civil lawsuits, such as disputes involving a breach of contract. If such a case were filed in a civil court, there would be considerable expense for court costs and legal fees for both parties and, usually, considerable delay in getting the case to trial. Also, the typical judge does not have expertise in all fields. In commercial arbitration, the arbitrator selected often has special expertise in the area that the dispute involves. For example, the parties have a dispute concerning their obligations under a contract to build a multimillion-dollar building. Time is of the essence. The parties cannot wait 6 or 7 years for this case to come up before a court. If the case is submitted to arbitration, they can get a decision within a very short time and then proceed in accordance with the arbitrator's decision.

In arbitration there is no set procedure, such as one would find in a court of law or even in an administrative agency. There is, however, one prerequisite to arbitration; namely, that both parties agree to submit the dispute to arbitration. This can be done by inserting an arbitration clause into the original document, such as a contract. If there is no such clause, the parties may still agree at a later date to submit a dispute to arbitration. For example, they may agree to have the case heard by a single arbitrator or by a panel of three arbitrators. If they agree to use three arbitrators, they may decide that each party will select an arbitrator of its choice and that the two arbitrators they select will choose the third arbitrator.

By agreeing to submit a dispute to arbitration, a party also agrees to abide by the arbitrator's ruling. The only exceptions would be if someone could prove that the arbitrator had a financial or personal interest in the matter that prejudiced the decision, that fraud or perjury was involved in the testimony, or that the arbitrator mistakenly failed to follow the law on a material issue. Otherwise, the arbitrator's decision is final. If one of these exceptions can be proved, a court will set aside the arbitrator's decision.

There is only one solution to the problem of enforcement. If the loser refuses to abide by the arbitrator's decision, the winner's only recourse is to go to court to have the arbitrator's decision enforced.

Arbitration is a fast, inexpensive method for resolving commercial disputes. However, its effectiveness depends greatly on the attitude of the parties. Most businesses today want their legal disputes settled out of court and as cheaply and quickly as possible. Arbitration can be the answer.

Mediation

A mediator does not decide the dispute between the parties, but rather tries to help them reach a negotiated settlement. The mediator can suggest compromises and trade-offs to the parties. Having a neutral third party be the first to suggest a compromise can be very useful in solving the dispute, especially when neither side wants to be the first to "give in." The **mediation** process is totally under the control of the parties, and the solution can be whatever they agree to.

Private Judges

A newer procedure, which holds great promise for solving business disputes, involves the hiring of a private judge, with the parties paying a fee for this service. These people are usually retired judges who have expertise in a particular area of the law. Their decisions are binding on the parties, and they are bound to follow the normal court rules on evidence. Unlike a regular court, however, the trial can be held in private, at the parties' convenience. In many states, no official transcript is required, although the decision can be appealed to the regular appellate courts. The advantages to this procedure are speed, convenience, privacy, and expertise.

Mini-Trials

Another very promising new procedure is the mini-trial. Each side prepares a presentation of the essential parts of its side of the dispute. The presentation is made before a neutral advisor who has no power to decide the dispute. The presentation is brief, no more than 1 or 2 days—in contrast to weeks or months for a complex case in the regular courts. The presenter for each side does have the authority to settle the dispute on the spot. If they fail to settle, the neutral advisor—an expert in the area—may indicate which way the case would probably be decided in court. The parties may then negotiate further. This system is similar to mediation in that any settlement must be accepted by both sides. It otherwise has the same advantages as the private judge system.

Significance of This Chapter

Every executive in business must realize the possibility of legal disputes and involvement in the legal process. This chapter introduced both the state and national court systems. It described the procedure of a civil lawsuit from the filing of the suit to the final appeal and enforcement of the judgment, including a discussion of the formal legal system. This chapter also reviewed dispute resolution by private arbitration, which saves time and legal expenses and is used in a large number of commercial contracts.

A basic understanding of these processes is useful in working with a lawyer to prepare a case and in deciding whether to settle or to litigate.

IMPORTANT TERMS AND CONCEPTS

answer
appellant
arbitration
cause of action
challenges for cause
choice of law
class action
complaint
consent
counterclaim
cross complaint
cross-examine
de novo
default judgment
defendant
demurrer
deposition
directed verdict
discovery
diversity of citizenship
domicile
Full Faith and Credit Clause
garnishment
general personal jurisdiction
federal question
"long-arm" statutes
interrogatories
judgment notwithstanding the verdict
jurisdiction over the person
mediation

motion to dismiss
opening statement
peremptory challenges
plaintiff
presence
pretrial
pretrial conference
preliminary instructions
procedural law
reply
state trial court
statute of limitations
subject-matter jurisdiction
summary judgment
summons
U.S. Circuit Courts of Appeal
U.S. District Courts
U.S. Supreme Court
venue
voir dire
witnesses
writ of certiorari

QUESTIONS AND PROBLEMS FOR DISCUSSION

1. What are long-arm statutes, and what purposes do they serve? Give an example in which a long-arm statute would be used.

2. What substantive law must a U.S. District Court apply in a trial of a tort case? What procedural law will the court follow?

3. How does jurisdiction differ from venue? Define and discuss each term.

4. What is a demurrer? Where in the trial stage could it be used?

5. Floyd Wiles, a resident of Cook County, Illinois, sued defendant Morita Iron Works Co. Ltd., a Japanese corporation that designed and manufactured the machine that allegedly caused plaintiff's injuries. Plaintiff's employer, Astro Packaging Co., is a corporation that operates plants in Hawthorne, New Jersey, and Alsip, Illinois. Astro purchased four machines from defendant. Two were shipped to the New Jersey plant, and two were shipped to the Illinois plant. Plaintiff was employed at Astro's Alsip, Illinois plant. One of the machines allegedly caused personal injuries to plaintiff, for which plaintiff seeks damages from defendant.

   Morita, which has no facilities or personnel in Illinois, moves to dismiss the case.

   How should the courts rule on this motion? Discuss.

6. James E. Keck filed a divorce petition in Cook County, Illinois. Dolores Keck answered the complaint and asked for separate maintenance. While the Illinois case was still pending, James moved to Nevada and received a divorce through the Nevada courts. He then moved back to Illinois. The trial court upheld Dolores's claim that the Nevada decree was invalid, but the appeals court reversed, saying that the Nevada decree must be given full faith and credit.

   James lived in Nevada only 2 months; he returned immediately upon obtaining his decree; he retained his apartment in Chicago and returned there; he retained his job in Chicago and returned to it; he retained his Chicago bank accounts and his Illinois driver's license. Within 1 or 2 days after arriving in Nevada, he contacted a lawyer about getting a divorce.

   How should the Illinois Supreme Court decide this case? Explain.

7. Eulala Shute and her husband bought tickets for a cruise on the Tropicale, a ship operated by Carnival. The Shutes lived in the state of Washington and bought the tickets through a travel agent located there. The travel agent sent their payment to Carnival at its headquarters in Miami, Florida. Carnival prepared the tickets and sent them back to the Shutes. On the face of each ticket was a statement indicating that it was subject to the conditions on the back. Statements on the back of the ticket said that the customers accepted all printed terms by accepting the ticket and that any disputes "shall be litigated, if at all, in and before a Court located in the State of Florida, USA, to the exclusion of the Courts of any other state or country."

   The Shutes boarded the ship in Los Angeles for the cruise to Puerto Vallarta, Mexico. While the ship was in international waters off the Mexican Coast, Eulala was injured when she slipped on a deck mat during a tour of the ship's galley. The Shutes filed a lawsuit in the U.S. District Court in the state of Washington. Carnival asked the court for summary judgment on the basis of the forum selection clause on the tickets.

   Is the "choice" clause enforceable? Why or why not?

8. On June 8, Nancy Moran, then 17 years old, visited the home of Mr. and Mrs. Grigsby to meet with a number of friends, including Randy Williams, a young lady of 15 years, who was residing with Grigsbys at the time. The group congregated in the basement, which was being used as a family room and laundry room.

   Everyone left the basement, except Nancy and Randy. Apparently these two girls were at a loss for entertainment as eventually they centered their attention on a lit Christmas tree-shaped candle on a shelf behind the couch. The girls began to discuss whether the candle was scented. After agreeing that it was not, Randy, while remarking "Well, let's make it scented," impulsively grabbed a "drip bottle" of Faberge's Tigress cologne, which had been placed by Mrs. Grigsby in the basement for use as a laundry deodorant, and began to pour its contents onto the lower portion of the candle somewhat below the flame. Instantaneously, a burst of fire sprang out and burned Nancy's neck and breasts as she stood nearby watching but not fully aware of what her friend was doing.

   Ms. Moran brought suit against Faberge, Inc. The jury gave a verdict in favor of Ms. Moran. However, the judge granted judgment notwithstanding the verdict in favor of defendant Faberge, Inc. Plaintiff appealed.

   Did the trial judge decide correctly? Why or why not?

CHAPTER 5

Antitrust Law and Trade Practices Law

Chapter Objectives

This chapter will:

- Introduce antitrust laws, including the Sherman Act, the Clayton Act, the Robinson-Patman Act, and the Federal Trade Commission Act.
- Review several major decisions applying and interpreting the antitrust statutes.
- Summarize major changes in government policy toward mergers.
- Indicate the Federal Trade Commission's major areas of jurisdiction.

The word *antitrust* is used to describe laws that were passed by Congress to protect the public from monopolies. Actually we should refer to these laws as antimonopoly laws. They were called antitrust laws because during the late 1800s, companies in many industries transferred control of their companies to a voting trust. The trustee could be a separate corporation, an individual, or group of individuals, who now had control of manufacture, sale, distribution, and pricing of a large share of the products of the particular industry. The result was the elimination of competition among the sellers in the industry. Thus, a monopoly was created and the public suffered, because without competition, the public must pay the price dictated by the monopoly, not the price that would be set by a competitive market. Antitrust or antimonopoly law consists not only of the famous **Sherman Act** but also other legislation, Supreme Court cases, and Justice Department guidelines. Over the last decade antitrust law has again become front-page news, as the Justice Department has prosecuted Microsoft Corporation.

The Sherman Act

It is hard to say whether Senator John Sherman of Ohio would be pleased with the growth of his century-old offspring. The Sherman Antitrust Act was passed in 1890 as the first attempt by the national government to deal with the perceived abuses of market power by the giant industrial corporations that had sprung up after the Civil War.

In the broadest possible language, the Sherman Act stated: "Every contract, combination in the form of trust or otherwise, or conspiracy, in restraint of trade or commerce among the several States, or with foreign nations, is hereby declared to be illegal." Section 2 of the act defined another broad category of offenses: "Every person who shall monopolize, or attempt to monopolize, or combine or conspire with any other person or persons, to monopolize any part of the trade or commerce among the several States, or with foreign nations, shall be deemed guilty of a misdemeanor." The act was clearly aimed at the giant concentrations of economic power that existed in many industries—the "trusts." Firms that should have been competing against each other were working together and were in many cases tied together organizationally through voting trusts. Quite clearly, the act was intended to reach such anticompetitive schemes as price-fixing, bid-rigging, and market splitting.

The continuing dilemma of antitrust interpretation is whether or not the act was intended to go beyond those obvious, specific practices to prohibit "bigness" as such. If one company competes aggressively, builds a better product at lower cost, and succeeds in getting nearly all the potential customers to deal with it, has it violated the antitrust laws? Stated most simply, is market success illegal? This is where opinions diverge.

Two Conflicting Interpretations

There are two opposing schools of thought on the basic meaning and purpose of the Sherman Act and the other antitrust laws; for want of better terminology, the **legal school** and the **economic school.** The dispute is not quite as simple as the terms suggest because some economists support the legal view, and many lawyers and judges take the economic view.

The legal approach starts with the premise that size alone is not made illegal by the Sherman Act; there is specific support for this approach in the 1890 debates in Congress. To be guilty of an antitrust violation, a company must be shown to have actually abused its position of market power. What counts are the methods used and the intent of those using them. Free and fair competition will result in winners *and* losers in the marketplace; the winners should not be penalized if they have won "fair and square." This view of antitrust emphasizes protecting the *process* of competition rather than trying to ensure the survival of specific *competitors.* If customers want to deal with GM and IBM, should the government step in to "preserve" other car makers and computer manufacturers? Supporters of the legal approach would answer no.

The economic approach starts from the premise that large concentrations of economic power are bad per se, that our democratic society is endangered by such power blocs, and that Congress intended the antitrust laws as a vehicle for preserving an economic structure that embraces a number of smaller, independent economic units. In this view, economic efficiencies may at times have to be sacrificed to preserve this sort of market structure. The Robinson-Patman Act of 1936 (sometimes referred to as the "anti-chain store act" and discussed later in this chapter) clearly points in this direction. What counts in this approach is the market structure; large size and market dominance are inherently bad. There is an antitrust violation if a company has the *potential* power to abuse, whether or not it has actually been guilty of any specific abuse. This view of antitrust is clearly most concerned with protecting competitors, even to the point of insulating them from the rigors of effective competition.

Unfortunately for students, teachers, lawyers, and most of all for businesses, the antitrust laws have been interpreted *both* ways by various courts with various combinations of judges. Depending in large part on the basic policy view taken by a majority of the justices on the U.S. Supreme Court, a given course of business conduct may or may not be deemed to violate the antitrust laws. If some of the case opinions in this chapter seem to conflict, that is because they probably do conflict.

Penalties for Violation

These basic questions of interpretation are of more than academic interest to the business community because of the broad reach of the antitrust statutes and the serious penalties that may be imposed for violations. The three basic enforcement mechanisms are criminal prosecution, civil suit by the U.S. government (the Justice Department or the Federal Trade Commission), and civil suit by private parties.

Criminal cases are usually pursued by the Justice Department only for conduct that is deemed to be illegal per se, without any test of "reasonableness." **Price-fixing** is one such example. If convicted, a corporation now faces a fine of up to $1 million. For individuals, criminal penalties include a fine of up to $100,000 and/or a maximum of 3 years in jail. Historically, jail sentences were rarely imposed, but the courts' attitude has been changing. Executives served more time in jail for price-fixing in 1978 than in the entire preceding 87 years of the Sherman Act's existence. The Justice Department was also able to establish in the electrical industry price-fixing cases in the 1960s that it does not have to accept a nolo contendere plea to the criminal charges. **Nolo contendere** means no contest. The ruling against automatic acceptance of nolo pleas is important because a plea of guilty can be used by a civil plaintiff to help prove a case for damages; a nolo plea is not an admission of guilt and cannot be used by a civil plaintiff to prove his or her case.

Because of the much higher standard of proof required in a criminal case (beyond any reasonable doubt) and the general reluctance of juries to subject someone to the chance of prison for nonviolent, business-related conduct, the Justice Department and the Federal Trade Commission (FTC) prefer to file civil actions in many cases. Anticompetitive conduct may be enjoined; divestiture (separation) may be ordered when an illegal **merger** between businesses has taken place; and other civil remedies may be involved. In 1974, for instance, the FTC agreed to a settlement of its complaint against Xerox, by the terms of which Xerox was required to make its entire portfolio of about 2,000 patents available to any other firm that wanted to enter the copier market. Much of the fear of antitrust lawsuits stems from the fact that private parties can recover **treble damages** (three times the actual injury shown) plus reasonable attorney fees. This measure of damages is a very real incentive to litigate, and thus a significant deterrent to antitrust violations.

Monopoly Power in One Company

The first big case under the Sherman Act was against the Sugar Trust, which controlled about 98 percent of U.S. sugar production. The Sugar Trust escaped liability when the Supreme Court held that manufacturing was not "commerce" and was therefore not covered by the act. This interpretation was soon overruled, and in the famous *Standard Oil* case of 1911 a majority of five justices voted to apply a **rule of reason** in antitrust cases. The Standard Oil majority correctly concluded that a literal reading of the act ("every contract") would produce absurd results because every business contract "restrains" trade in the sense of denying a particular business opportunity to others. In other words, if you contract to buy Smith's used car, Smith has "foreclosed" others from selling you a used car, unless you need more than one. Likewise, you have "foreclosed" Smith's opportunities to sell his used car to other buyers.

Clearly, the act must have been aimed at something other than those normal business contracts with their normal business consequences. Although the majority adopted a reasonableness test, they did not really apply it to the facts of the *Standard Oil* case and ordered the combination split up without much investigation of actual economic performance.

In the landmark *Alcoa* case in 1945, Circuit Judge Hand stated that monopoly power was illegal per se, regardless of how it had been attained and regardless of whether or not it had been abused. The case had been started in 1937 in U.S. District Court, where Judge Caffey heard 155 witnesses, viewed 1,803 exhibits, and produced a trial record of 58,000 pages. After 4 years the court decided that Alcoa was not guilty on any of the 140 criminal counts. Judge Hand and the Second Circuit Court of Appeals reversed Judge Caffey on *one* count and took that as the opportunity to radically reinterpret the Sherman Act. The appeals court found a monopoly by a very restrictive definition of the **relevant market,** which excluded aluminum made from reprocessed scrap and aluminum produced abroad. Although the *Alcoa* decision was not reviewed by the Supreme Court, the principle stated there was generally accepted in the Supreme Court's 1946 decision in the *American Tobacco* case. A court's determination of the dimensions of the "relevant market" may thus be decisive in deciding whether or not there is a "monopoly."

In the famous "cellophane" case (*U.S. v. Du Pont,* 351 U.S. 377), the U.S. Supreme Court decided that the relevant market was all flexible packaging materials, not just cellophane. Although Du Pont produced almost 75 percent of the cellophane made in the United States, its share of the much larger packaging market was less than 20 percent. With that larger market definition, Du Pont was held not guilty of the monopolization charge.

In the 1960s and 1970s, the government filed monopolization charges against such industrial giants as IBM and AT&T and threatened several times to try to break up GM. In the early 1970s, the late Senator Philip Hart of Michigan sponsored an "Industrial Reorganization Act" that would have created a new government agency with the power to restructure industries where an oligopoly existed. An oligopoly was defined as four or fewer firms controlling over 50 percent of a market. In the late 1970s, as the energy crisis worsened, several states passed laws prohibiting oil companies (the large refiners) from also owning retail gas stations. Also, the FTC's long-pending case against the four large cereal makers, charging a "shared monopoly" in violation of the Sherman Act, was finally dismissed. Such a theory would have opened many firms to prosecution. Under the Reagan administration's more liberal view of "bigness," the *IBM* case was finally dropped and the *AT&T* case was settled. AT&T agreed to give up its local telephone businesses in return for the right to compete in computers and other high-tech fields.

The following case, filed by the U.S. Department of Justice in 1998, charged that Microsoft was abusing its monopoly position in personal computer operating systems. Because Microsoft was at the time (and still is) one of the largest and most profitable companies in the world, and a major component of the "new economy," the case has been well covered in the media. (See, for example, *New York Times,* September 7, 2001, pp. A1, A5, C5.) The Justice Department and the plaintiff states finally did agree to a settlement of the case. On remand from the U.S. Court of Appeals, the U.S. District Court decided not to order the breakup of the company, but only to prohibit it from engaging in certain illegal practices. Even though the U.S. case had been settled, Microsoft suffered several more years of uncertainty while it tried to work out a settlement of antitrust charges brought by the European Union's competition regulators.

Attempts to Monopolize

Section 2 of the Sherman Act also prohibits attempts to monopolize. Courts have disagreed as to what must be proved to show a violation of this section. Generally, it is necessary to show a specific intent to monopolize, but it is not necessary to show that the defendant already has monopoly power. The charge is that the defendant is *attempting* to achieve monopoly power. Disagreement exists over whether a "dangerous probability" of success in acquiring monopoly power must also be shown. Some courts have required this

CASE 1

United States of America v. Microsoft Corporation
253 F.3d 34 (D.C. Cir. 2001)

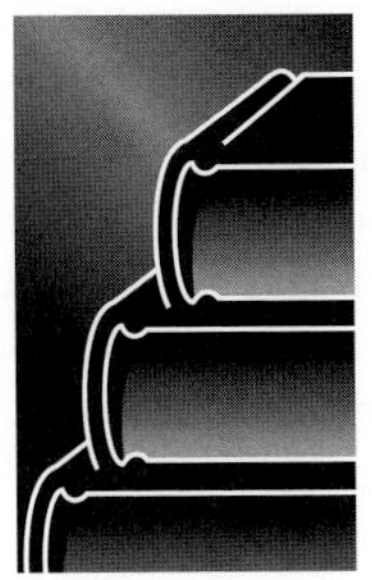

Facts: In 1994, the U.S. Justice Department filed a lawsuit that charged Microsoft with unlawfully maintaining a monopoly in computer operating systems. That case was settled by a consent decree. Three years later, the Justice Department filed a civil contempt action, claiming the company was violating the terms of the consent decree. The U.S. District Court granted a preliminary injunction against Microsoft. Just before the D.C. Circuit decided the appeal of that case in favor of Microsoft, the Justice Department filed a new case, alleging other violations of the Sherman Act, Sections 1 and 2. Eighteen states also filed lawsuits, which were consolidated with the new U.S. case.

After a 76-day bench trial, the U.S. District Court found that Microsoft had violated Section 2 of the Sherman Act by maintaining a monopoly in the market for Intel-compatible PC operating systems, and by attempting to gain a monopoly in the market for Internet browsers and had violated Section 1 by tying together Windows and its Internet Explorer. Judge Jackson ordered Microsoft to submit a plan for breaking the company into two parts—an operating systems business and an applications business. Microsoft appealed. The appeal was heard by a special seven-judge panel of the D.C. Circuit. The panel reached a unanimous decision.

Issue: Did Microsoft violate the antitrust statutes?

Decision: Yes. Judgment affirmed as to liability, but remanded for a re-hearing as to appropriate remedies.

Opinion by the Court *(Per Curiam)*: "Before turning to the merits of Microsoft's various arguments, we pause to reflect briefly on two matters of note, one practical and one theoretical.

"The practical matter relates to the temporal dimension of this case. The litigation timeline in this case is hardly problematic. Indeed, it is noteworthy that a case of this magnitude and complexity has proceeded from the filing of complaints through trial to appellate decision in a mere three years....

"What is somewhat problematic, however, is that just over six years have passed since Microsoft engaged in the first conduct plaintiffs allege to be anticompetitive. As the record in this case indicates, six years seems like an eternity in the computer industry. By the time a court can assess liability, firms, products, and the marketplace are likely to have changed dramatically. This, in turn, threatens enormous practical difficulties for courts considering the appropriate measure of relief in equitable enforcement actions, both in crafting injunctive remedies in the first instance and reviewing those remedies in the second. Conduct remedies may be unavailing in such cases, because innovation to a large degree has already rendered the anticompetitive conduct obsolete (although by no means harmless). And broader structural remedies present their own set of problems, including how a court goes about restoring competition to a dramatically changed, and constantly changing, marketplace. That is just one reason why we find the District Court's refusal in the present case to hold an evidentiary hearing on remedies—to update and flesh out the available information before seriously entertaining the possibility of dramatic structural relief so problematic....

"We do not mean to say that enforcement actions will no longer play an important role in curbing infringements of the antitrust laws in technologically dynamic markets, nor do we assume this in assessing the merits of this case. Even in those cases where forward-looking remedies appear limited, the Government will continue to have an interest in defining the contours of the antitrust laws so that law-abiding firms will have a clear sense of what is permissible and what is not. And the threat of private damage actions will remain to deter those firms inclined to test the limits of the law.

"The second matter of note is more theoretical in nature. We decide this case against a backdrop of significant debate amongst academics and practitioners over the extent to which 'old economy' S.2 monopolization doctrines should apply to firms competing in dynamic technological markets characterized by network effects. In markets characterized by network effects, one product or standard tends towards dominance, because 'the utility that a user derives from consumption of the good increases with the number of other agents consuming the good.' ... Once a product or standard achieves wide acceptance, it becomes more or less entrenched. Competition in such industries is 'for the field' rather than 'within the field.' ...

"In technologically dynamic markets, however, such entrenchment may be temporary, because innovation may alter the field altogether.... Rapid technological change leads to markets in which 'firms compete through innovation for temporary market dominance, from which they may be displaced by the next wave of product advancements.'... Microsoft argues that the operating system market is just such a market.

"Whether or not Microsoft's characterization of the operating system market is correct does not appreciably alter our mission in assessing the alleged antitrust violations in the present case. As an initial matter, we note that there is no consensus among commentators on the question of whether, and to what extent, current monopolization doctrine should be amended to account for competition in technologically dynamic markets characterized by network effects.... Indeed, there is some suggestion that that the economic consequences of network effects and technological dynamism act to offset one another, thereby making it difficult to formulate categorical antitrust rules absent a particularized analysis of a given market....

"The District Court ... found that Microsoft possesses monopoly power in the market for Intel-compatible PC operating systems. Focusing primarily on Microsoft's efforts to suppress Netscape Navigator's threat to its operating system monopoly, the court also found that Microsoft maintained its power not through competition on the merits, but through unlawful means. Microsoft challenges both conclusions. . . .

"We begin by considering whether Microsoft possesses monopoly power ... and finding that it does, we turn to the question whether it maintained this power through anticompetitive means. Agreeing with the District Court that the company behaved anticompetitively ... and that these actions contributed to the maintenance of its monopoly power ... we affirm the court's finding of liability for monopolization. . . .

"In this case, after concluding that Microsoft had monopoly power, the District Court held that Microsoft had violated S.2 by engaging in a variety of exclusionary acts ... to maintain its monopoly by preventing the effective distribution and use of products that might threaten that monopoly. Specifically, the District Court held Microsoft liable for: (1) the way in which it integrated IE into Windows; (2) its various dealings with Original Equipment Manufacturers ('OEMs'), Internet Access Providers ('IAPs'), Internet Content Providers ('ICPs'), Independent Software Vendors ('ISVs'), and Apple Computer; (3) its efforts to contain and to subvert Java technologies; and (4) its course of conduct as a whole. . . .

"Microsoft's efforts to gain market share in one market (browsers) served to meet the threat to Microsoft's monopoly in another market (operating systems) by keeping rival browsers from gaining the critical mass of users necessary to attract developer attention away from Windows as the platform for software development. . . .

"In evaluating the restrictions in Microsoft's agreements licensing Windows to OEMs, we first consider whether plaintiffs have made out a prima facie case by demonstrating that the restrictions have an anticompetitive effect. . . . [W]e conclude that plaintiffs have met this burden as to all the restrictions. We then consider Microsoft's proffered justifications for the restrictions and, for the most part, hold those justifications insufficient. . . .

"[T]he District Court found that 'Microsoft's executives believed ... its contractual restrictions placed on OEMs would not be sufficient in themselves to reverse the direction of Navigator's usage share. Consequently, in late 1995 or early 1996, Microsoft set out to bind [IE] more tightly to Windows 98 as a technical matter.' ...

"As a general rule, courts are properly very skeptical about claims that competition has been harmed by a dominant firm's product design changes. . . . Judicial deference to product innovation, however, does not mean that a monopolist's product design decisions are per se lawful. . . .

"Microsoft had included IE in the Add/Remove Programs utility in Windows 95, ... but when it modified Windows 95 to produce Windows 98, it took IE out of the Add/Remove Programs utility. This change reduces the usage share of rival browsers not by making Microsoft's own browser more attractive to consumers but, rather, by discouraging OEMs from distributing rival products. . . . Because Microsoft's conduct, through something other than competition on the merits, has the effect of significantly reducing usage of rivals' products and hence protecting its own operating system monopoly, it is anticompetitive. . . .

"Microsoft designed Windows 98 'so that using Navigator on Windows 98 would have unpleasant consequences for users' by, in some circumstances, overriding the user's choice of a browser other than IE as his or her default browser. . . .

"[W]e hold that Microsoft's exclusion of IE from the Add/Remove Programs utility and its commingling of browser and operating system code constitute exclusionary conduct, in violation of S.2. . . .

"[W]e affirm the District Court's decision holding that Microsoft's exclusive contracts with IAPs are exclusionary devices, in violation of S.2 of the Sherman Act. . . .

"[W]e affirm the conclusion that Microsoft's threats to Intel were exclusionary, in violation of S.2 of the Sherman Act. . . .

"We conclude, however, that the District Court's remedies decree must be vacated for three independent reasons: (1) the court failed to hold a remedies-specific evidentiary hearing when there were disputed facts; (2) the court failed to provide adequate reasons for its decreed remedies; and (3) this Court has revised the scope of Microsoft's liability and it is impossible to determine to what extent that should effect the remedies provisions. . . .

"The judgment of the District Court is affirmed in part, reversed in part, and remanded in part. We vacate in full the Final Judgment embodying the remedial order, and remand the case to the District Court for reassignment to a different trial judge for further proceedings consistent with this order."

element; others have not. This other group of courts has found violations in which the intent was coupled with an attempt to acquire a monopoly. Sometimes, in the second group of cases, the courts did not even seem too worried about establishing the relevant market.

Concerted Activities among Competitors

When competing companies get together to fix prices, limit output, or divide markets, the antitrust violation is clear. These practices are so inherently anticompetitive that they are classified as **per se violations;** that is, no "rule of reason" defense is available. In the 1927 *Trenton Potteries* case, the U.S. Supreme Court held that the defendants' good motives and the reasonableness of the prices they set were both irrelevant; the power to fix reasonable prices was also the power to fix unreasonable prices at some future time. In 1940, in the *Socony-Vacuum Oil* case, the Court said that the government did not have to prove that the defendants had been successful in raising prices, only that they had conspired with the intent to do so. In a 1933 decision that stands virtually alone, the Supreme Court did rule in favor of coal producers who had entered into a "reasonable" price and output agreement; in the midst of a terrible depression, reasonable cooperation in the industry was permitted.

One of the most troublesome conspiracy areas involves the cooperative activities of trade associations, especially the collection and reporting of price information. The government's problem in these cases is to prevent the trade association from being used as a price-fixing mechanism while permitting legitimate cooperative activities. In cases dealing with manufacturers of sugar, lumber, and linseed oil, the Supreme Court has indicated that "reporting" of specific prices charged to specific customers is probably evidence of an agreement to charge everyone the same prices. In a case involving cement manufacturers, the Court permitted such reporting, in which there was a history of some firms delivering extra, "free" cement, billing the customer, and splitting the extra profits with the contractor.

Another difficult problem relates to the proof necessary to substantiate the conspiracy charge. Price uniformity, in and of itself, does not necessarily indicate the existence of a conspiracy, especially where similar increases can be shown to have stemmed from uniformly increased costs of production and delivery. On the other hand, specific instances of joint price increases and reductions, when new firms entered the market, were held to show a conspiracy based on **conscious parallelism** in the 1946 *American Tobacco* case. This doctrine was limited by the 1954 *Theatre Enterprises* decision, which stated that parallel business behavior was not itself illegal nor was it conclusive proof of an illegal conspiracy. In most such cases the existence of a conspiracy is for the jury to decide.

Just as "it takes two to tango," it takes two to make up a conspiracy. There is no such legal animal as a "solo" conspiracy; two or more persons must be involved. Can a parent corporation and its wholly owned subsidiary be the two "persons" in an antitrust conspiracy? In an important 1984 decision (*Copperweld Corp. v. Independence Tube Corp.*, 467 U.S. 752), the Supreme Court said "no" to that question.

Resale Price Maintenance and Refusals to Deal

For many years the manufacturers of some products have attempted to control the prices at which retailers sell the products, usually by establishing a minimum retail price. Most states passed so-called **fair trade laws** by 1940. Fair trade laws are laws that allow the manufacturer to set a retail price for which the product must be sold. The retailer can sell the product for more, but not for less than the set price. Congress passed the Miller Tydings Amendment to the Sherman Act in 1937 to exempt such state laws from antitrust, and then passed the McGuire Amendment to the FTC Act in 1952, so that **nonsigner plans** were also exempt from antitrust. In a nonsigner plan, if one retailer in a state agreed to the minimum prices, all retailers in that state were bound to adhere to them. Even with this legislative support, manufacturers found it very difficult to "police" their minimum prices and they could not prevent an interstate shipment of goods at a lower price from a non-fair-trade state. In 1975, Congress brought the fair-trade movement to an end by repealing the 1937 and 1952 amendments; nearly any fair-trade arrangement would now be an antitrust violation.

What about refusals to deal as possible antitrust violations? Except for certain businesses that are bound to deal with all members of the public on an equal basis, such as innkeepers and common carriers, it is generally assumed that a business is free to decide with whom it will deal and on what terms. In the 1960 *Parke Davis* case, however, the Court said that where the manufacturer entwined its wholesalers and retailers in a policing arrangement it had created an illegal conspiracy under the Sherman Act. In Chapter 1, in the *State Oil* case, we saw the Supreme Court reverse a precedent that had applied a per se illegality rule to agreements setting a maximum resale price. More recently, the Supreme Court has taken a much bolder step—reversing a precedent nearly 100 years old that applied a per se approach to agreements setting a minimum resale price.

CASE 2

Leegin Creative Leather Pdts v. PSKS, Inc., dba Kay's Kloset

127 S.Ct. 2705 (2007)

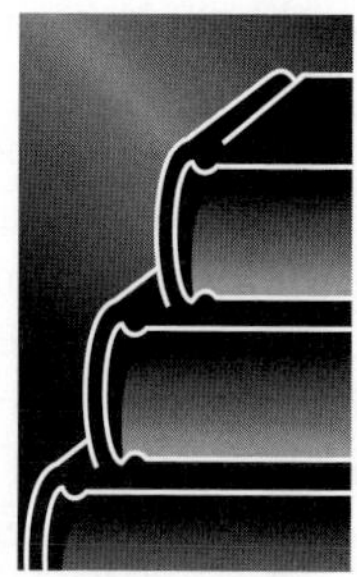

Facts: Leegin established a pricing policy that required retail dealers handling its "high-end designer" products to maintain a minimum resale price. When PSKS began discounting Leegin products, Leegin refused further inventory to PSKS. PSKS sued, alleging violation of section 1 of the Sherman Act. The trial judge refused to admit Leegin's offer of expert testimony as to the beneficial effects of such minimum pricing arrangements. The jury found a violation and assessed $1.2 million damages, which the trial court automatically tripled. With attorney fees and court costs, a judgment was entered against Leegin for $3,975,000.80. Leegin appealed, but the U.S. Fifth Circuit said that it was bound by the 1911 Supreme Court precedent in Dr. Miles and could not consider the "reasonableness" of the arrangement. The Supreme Court agreed to review the case.

Issue: Should vertical agreements to set minimum retail prices be judged per se illegal?

Decision: No. Judgment reversed, and case remanded.

Opinion by Justice Kennedy: "The rule of reason is the accepted standard for testing whether a practice restrains trade in violation of S.1. . . .

"Resort to per se rules is confined to restraints . . . 'that would always or almost always tend to restrict competition an decrease output.' . . .

"The Court in Dr. Miles relied on a treatise published in 1628, but failed to discuss in detail the business reasons that would motivate a manufacturer situated in 1911 to make use of vertical price restraints. . . . The general restraint on alienation . . . tended to evoke policy concerns extraneous to the question that controls here. Usually associated with land, not chattels, the rule arose from restrictions removing real property from the stream of commerce for generations. The Court should be cautious about putting dispositive weight on doctrines from antiquity but of slight relevance. We reaffirm that 'the state of the common law 400 or even 100 years ago is irrelevant to the issue before us: the effect of the antitrust laws upon vertical distributional restraints in the American economy today.' . . .

"Our recent cases formulate antitrust principles in accordance with the appreciated differences in economic effect between vertical and horizontal agreements, differences the Dr. Miles Court failed to consider. . . .

"Absent vertical price restraints, the retail services that enhance interbrand competition might be underprovided. This is because discounting retailers can free ride on retailers who furnish services and then capture some of the increased demand those services generate. . . .

"Resale price maintenance, in addition, can increase interbrand competition by facilitating market entry for new firms and brands. . . .

"Resale price maintenance can also increase interbrand competition by encouraging retailer services that would not be provided even absent free riding. . . .

"Notwithstanding the risks of unlawful conduct, it cannot be stated with any degree of confidence that resale price maintenance 'always or almost always tends to restrict competition and decrease output.' . . . Vertical agreements establishing minimum resale prices can have either procompetitive or anticompetitive effects, depending upon the circumstances in which they are formed. And although the empirical evidence on the topic is limited, it does not suggest efficient uses of the agreements are infrequent or hypothetical. . . . As the [per se] rule would proscribe a significant amount of procompetitive conduct, these agreements appear ill suited for per se condemnation. . . .

"Resale price maintenance, it is true, does have economic dangers. If the rule of reason were to apply to vertical price restraints, courts would have to be diligent in eliminating their anticompetitive uses from the market. . . .

"Stare decisis . . . does not compel our continued adherence to the per se rule against vertical price restraints. As discussed earlier, respected authorities in the economics literature suggest the per se rule is inappropriate, and there is now widespread agreement that resale price maintenance can have procompetitive effects. . . . It is also significant that both the Department of Justice and the Federal Trade Commission—the antitrust enforcement agencies with the ability to assess the long-term impacts of resale price maintenance—have recommended that this Court replace the per se rule with the traditional rule of reason. . . . In the antitrust context the fact that a decision has been 'called into serious question' justifies our reevaluation of it. . . .

"In more recent cases the Court, following a common-law approach, has continued to temper, limit, or overrule once strict prohibitions on vertical restraints. In 1977, the Court overturned the per se rule for vertical nonprice restraints, adopting the rule of reason in its stead. . . .

"Continuing in that direction, in two cases in the 1980's the Court defined legal rules to limit the reach of Dr. Miles and to accommodate the doctrines enunciated in GTE Sylvania and Colgate. . . .

"Most recently, in 1997, after examining the issue of vertical maximum price-fixing agreements in light of commentary and real experience, the Court overruled a 29-year-old precedent treating those agreements as per se illegal. . . . It held instead that they should be evaluated under the traditional rule of reason . . . Our continued limiting of the reach of the decision in Dr. Miles and our recent treatment of other vertical restraints justify the conclusion that Dr. Miles should not be retained.

"The Dr. Miles rule is also inconsistent with a principled framework, for it makes little economic sense when analyzed with our other cases on vertical restraints. If we were to decide the procompetitive effects of resale price maintenance were insufficient to overrule Dr. Miles, then cases such as Colgate and GTE Sylvania themselves would be called into question....

"For these reasons, the Court's decision in Dr. Miles Medical ... is now overruled. Vertical price restraints are to be judged according to the rule of reason....

"The judgment of the Court of Appeals is reversed, and the case is remanded for proceedings consistent with this opinion.

"It is so ordered."

Territorial and Other Distribution Restrictions

Manufacturers may wish to restrict resales by their wholesalers or retailers. The manufacturer may get its distributor to agree not to resell the product outside a particular geographic area or not to resell to a particular class of customers. For example, the manufacturer may want to handle all sales of the product to the government or to institutional buyers, such as schools and hospitals. Where the manufacturer has granted exclusive sales territories to its several distributors, it does not want them stepping on each other's toes. Rather than having its distributors compete with each other for the same set of customers, it wants each of them to compete with other suppliers' products—within their assigned area. These restrictions are designed to increase **interbrand competition,** at the expense of **intrabrand competition.**

The Clayton Act

Section 1 of the Sherman Act of 1890 had stated: "Every contract, combination in the form of a trust or otherwise, or conspiracy, in restraint of trade or commerce among the several states, or with foreign nations, is hereby declared to be illegal." The *Standard Oil* case added the rule of reason when judging these contracts and combinations. Still, courts lacked a real definition or classification of what was illegal and what was legal. This need for specific classifications of contracts or combinations that may be illegal brought about the passage of the **Clayton Act** in 1914. The important sections of the Clayton Act that affect antitrust are Sections 2, 3, 7, and 8.

Section 2 of the Clayton Act prohibits price discrimination, subject to certain exclusions and exceptions. **Price discrimination** is simply selling products of the same kind and quality to different customers for different prices. This topic will be discussed later in this chapter.

Tying Contracts and Exclusive Dealing Agreements

Section 3 prohibits tying contracts and exclusive dealing agreements. A **tying contract** is an arrangement whereby the customer is required to buy a product or service it may not

Exhibit 5.1: Product Distribution Patterns

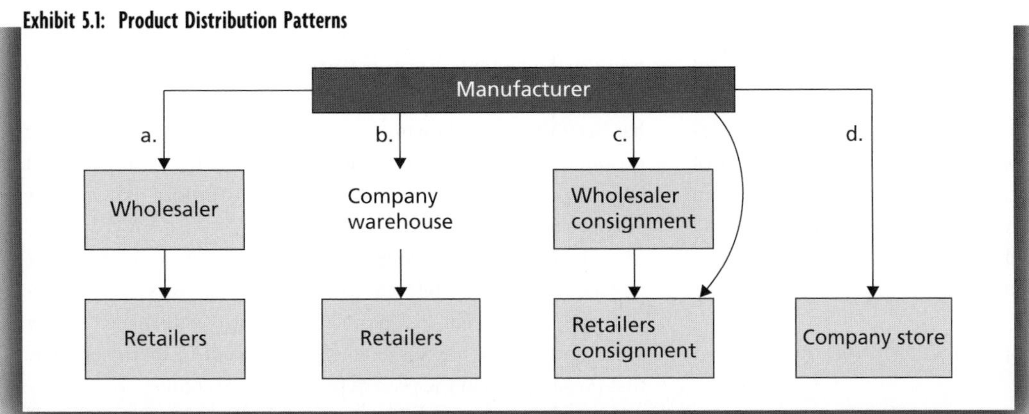

want to buy the product it does want; in the retail trade, this is sometimes referred to as **full-line forcing**. Tying contracts, said the Supreme Court in the 1958 *Northern Pacific Railway* case, are presumed to be illegal "because of their pernicious effect on competition and lack of any redeeming virtue." Unless some very special facts are present, tying contracts are hard to justify.

Exclusive dealing agreements should be analyzed quite differently from tying contracts because in many situations both the seller and the buyer benefit from such commitments. The buyer has an assured supply and protection against price fluctuations; the seller has an assured market and can plan production more realistically. Such agreements therefore must be tested on a case-by-case basis, under the rule of reason. The motives of the parties are important, and so is the impact of the particular agreement on the relevant market.

The *Illinois Tool Works* case shows that the Supreme Court is willing to reconsider some of its earlier antitrust rulings in the light of recent economic research and market experience. The alleged "tie" is being used by a patent holder to require co-purchase of unpatented goods.

CASE 3

Illinois Tool Works, Inc., v. Independent Ink, Inc.

547 U.S. 28 (2006)

Facts: Trident, Inc. and its parent corporation Illinois Tool Works manufacture printing systems that include three relevant components—a patented electric impulse ink jet printhead, a patented ink container (a bottle with a valved cap) that attaches to the printhead, and specially designed (but unpatented) ink. They sell these systems to original equipment manufacturers (OEMs) who are licensed to incorporate the printheads and containers into printers that are in turn sold to companies for use in printing barcodes on cartons and packaging materials. The OEMs agree that they will purchase their ink exclusively from Trident and Illinois Tool, and that neither the OEMs nor their customers will refill the patented containers with any other kind of ink.

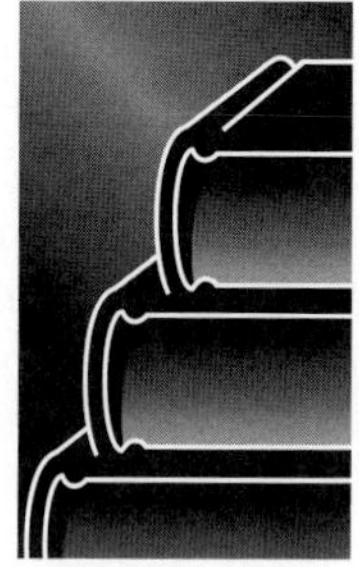

Independent Ink developed an ink with the same chemical composition as that sold by Trident and Illinois Tool. Their patent infringement against Independent was dismissed, and Independent then filed its own suit challenging the validity of Trident's patents. Independent later added claims of illegal tying and monopolization, in violation of sections 1 and 2 of the Sherman Act. The U.S. District Court issued a summary judgment for defendants on the antitrust claims because Independent had provided no evidence of the relevant market or of defendants' power in a defined market. Relying on certain Supreme Court precedents, the U.S. Court of Appeals for the Federal Circuit reversed, holding that there was a "presumption" of market power when the tying product was patented.

Issue: Is there a presumption of market power in a "patent misuse" case?

Decision: No. Judgment reversed, and case remanded for trial.

Opinion by Justice Stevens: "[F]our different rules of law have supported challenges to tying arrangements. They have been condemned as improper extensions of the patent monopoly under the patent misuse doctrine, as unfair methods of competition under S.5 of the Federal Trade Commission Act, ... as contracts tending to create a monopoly under S.3 of the Clayton Act.... and as contracts in restraint of trade under S.1 of the Sherman Act.... In all of those instances, the justification for the challenge rested on either an assumption or a showing that the defendant's position of power in the market for the tying product was being used to restrain competition in the market for the tied product.... 'Our cases have concluded that the essential characteristic of an invalid tying arrangement lies in the seller's exploitation of its control over the tying product to force the buyer into the purchase of a tied product that the buyer either did not want at all, or might have preferred to purchase elsewhere on different terms.'...

"Over the years, however, this Court's disapproval of tying arrangements has substantially diminished. Rather than relying on assumptions, in its more recent opinions the Court has required a showing of market power in the tying product.... Our early opinions consistently assumed that '[t]ying arrangements serve hardly any purpose beyond the suppression of competition.'...

"Congress' most recent narrowing of the patent misuse defense ... is directly relevant to this case. Four years after our decision in Jefferson Parish repeated the patent-equals-market-power presumption ... Congress amended the Patent Code to eliminate that presumption in the present patent misuse context....

"After considering the congressional judgment reflected in the 1988 amendment, we conclude that tying arrangements involving patented products should be evaluated under the standards applied in cases like Fortner II and Jefferson Parish rather than under the per se rule applied in Morton Salt and Loew's. While some such arrangements are still unlawful, such as those that are the product of a true monopoly or a market-wide conspiracy, ... that conclusion must be supported by proof of power in the relevant market rather than by a mere presumption thereof....

"[T]he vast majority of academic literature recognizes that a patent does not necessarily confer market power. Similarly, while price discrimination may provide evidence of market power, particularly if buttressed by evidence that the patentee has charged an above-market price for the tied package ... it is generally recognized that it also occurs in fully competitive markets.... We are not persuaded that the combination of these two factors should give rise to a presumption of market power when neither is sufficient to do so standing alone. Rather, the lesson to be learned from International Salt and the academic community is the same: Many tying arrangements, even those involving patents and requirements ties, are fully consistent with a free, competitive market.

"Congress, the antitrust enforcement agencies, and most economists have all reached the conclusion that a patent does not necessarily confer market power upon the patentee. Today, we reach the same conclusion, and therefore hold that, in all cases involving a tying arrangement, the plaintiff must prove that the defendant has market power in the tying product.

"When the case returns to the District Court, [Independent Ink] should ... be given a fair opportunity to develop and introduce evidence on that issue, as well as any other issues remaining to its S.1 claims. Accordingly, the judgment of the Court of Appeals is vacated, and the case remanded for further proceedings consistent with this opinion.

"It is so ordered."

Mergers

Section 7 of the Clayton Act prohibits certain mergers where the effect of the merger may be to substantially lessen competition.

Mergers may be divided into three basic classifications: (1) horizontal mergers, (2) vertical mergers, and (3) conglomerate mergers. A **horizontal merger** occurs when two competing firms merge. For example, one retail grocery chain merges with another retail grocery chain, both of which compete in the same geographic area. A **vertical merger** is one in which a manufacturer merges with a wholesale distributor or a retail chain, which does business in the same product market as the manufacturer. For example, a manufacturer of shoes owns no retail outlets so it merges with a company that runs a chain of retail stores selling shoes. A **conglomerate merger** is a merger in which the acquiring firm is not in the same line of commerce as the firm being acquired, and thus the acquired firm was neither a competitor nor a supplier nor a former customer. An example of a conglomerate merger would be a firm that manufactures bicycles buying a company that makes water beds. The key question in all three of these types of mergers is whether or not the merger may substantially lessen competition.

Section 7 of the Clayton Act of 1914 was largely ineffective during its first 40 years on the statute books, due to restrictive Supreme Court interpretations and a lack of enforcement vigor. Section 7, in its original version, established a kind of per se rule that prohibited any acquisition by a company of a controlling stock interest in a competitor. In several cases in the 1920s and 1930s, the Supreme Court held that an acquisition of a competitor's *assets* was not prohibited. The *Du Pont/GM* case, filed in 1949, resulted in a drastic reinterpretation of the original Section 7, but it really set no precedent because Congress had in the meantime passed the 1950 Celler-Kefauver Amendment, which substantially reworked Section 7.

The amended Section 7 covered one corporation's acquisition of the stock or the assets of another "where in any line of commerce in any section of the country, the effect of such acquisition may be substantially to lessen competition, or to tend to create a monopoly." This new version clearly established an incipiency test; the acquisition was illegal if there was a reasonable probability that it would have future anticompetitive effects.

Using the revised Section 7, the government was able to stop the proposed merger of Bethlehem Steel and Youngstown Sheet & Tube in 1958 (but Youngstown was subsequently merged into Lykes and Lykes into LTV). The first case to come to the Supreme Court under the new Section 7 was the Brown Shoe acquisition of Kinney Shoes, a merger that had both vertical and horizontal aspects because both companies were manufacturers and retailers. Using a very restrictive definition of the market that excluded shoe retailers such as Sears, Montgomery Ward, and JC Penney, and ignoring the fact that Kinney stores bought more shoes from independent manufacturers after the merger than it had before, the Supreme Court found the merger illegal.

Merger Guidelines. To resolve some of the uncertainty as to which mergers would be challenged, the Justice Department in 1968 issued its **merger guidelines.** These guidelines did little more than summarize the existing case law; horizontal mergers between competitors in a highly concentrated market would be challenged when each firm had as little as 4 percent of the market; vertical mergers would be challenged when the supplier had 10 percent of the sales and the purchaser firm bought at least 6 percent of the goods involved; conglomerate mergers would be brought to court when the acquiring firm was a "potential entrant" into the market through internal expansion, when the merger created a danger of reciprocal buying, or when the acquiring firm's resources were so extensive as to give the acquired firm an unfair advantage over its smaller competitors.

In 1982, the FTC issued their revised horizontal merger guidelines, and in 1984 the Justice Department issued their revised horizontal merger guidelines. On April 2, 1992, the U.S. Department of Justice and the FTC jointly issued new and revised horizontal merger guidelines. These new guidelines jointly issued by the Justice Department and the FTC outline the present enforcement policy of both the Justice Department and the FTC concerning horizontal acquisitions and mergers subject to Section 7 of the Clayton Act, as amended. These new guidelines described the specific standards and the analytical process that will be used to determine whether to challenge a horizontal merger. One of the key factors in the decision-making process is to determine what the post-merger market concentration will be and the anticipated increase in market concentration that might result from such a merger. These guidelines use a mathematical formula—the **Herfindahl-Hirschman Index (HHI)** to describe the approximate level of concentration already existing in an industry. If the level is too high, the proposed merger will probably be challenged. The market share of each existing competitor is squared and these figures are totaled. If the total is 1,000 or less, indicating a relatively unconcentrated market, the proposed merger will probably not be challenged. If the total is over 1,800, the Justice Department or the FTC would probably object. Between these figures, the agency involved will evaluate the amount of concentration the proposed merger would add to the industry. The market shares of the proposed merger partners will be added together and squared, and totaled with the other firms' squared market shares. The original total will be subtracted from this new total to see how many points have been added. If more than 100 points would be added to the HHI, the merger will probably be challenged; under 50, probably not. Between these extremes, the agency will weigh other industry factors and then decide whether to permit the merger or to challenge it. Vertical and conglomerate mergers are generally not viewed as posing serious marketplace threats by the Justice Department and the FTC.

The *Heinz* case involves the pre-merger notification requirement and the use of the HHI to evaluate the probable effect of the proposed merger.

Interlocking Directors

Section 8 of the Clayton Act prohibits certain interlocking directorates. An interlocking directorate exists when a person is a director in any two or more competing corporations. Section 8 would prohibit an interlocking directorate if any one of the corporations has capital, surplus, and undivided profits aggregating more than $1 million, and if the companies are engaged in commerce, and if they are not banks, banking associations, trust companies, or common carriers.

Similar to the history of Section 7, there were very few proceedings against **interlocking directors** for the first 40 years after the Clayton Act was passed. Cases against W.T. Grant and Sears, Roebuck & Co. were decided in 1953, and Section 8 of the Clayton Act was revived. A District Court forced the common director of Sears and B.F. Goodrich to resign from the Sears board, and 5 years later the same District Court held that its decree would be violated if the same person served on the Goodrich board and as a director of Sears' Savings and Profit Sharing Pension Fund. There was renewed emphasis on enforcement of this section in the 1970s, and a common director of Chrysler and General Electric

CASE 4

Federal Trade Commission v. H.J. Heinz Co.

246 F.3d 708 (D.C. Cir. 2001)

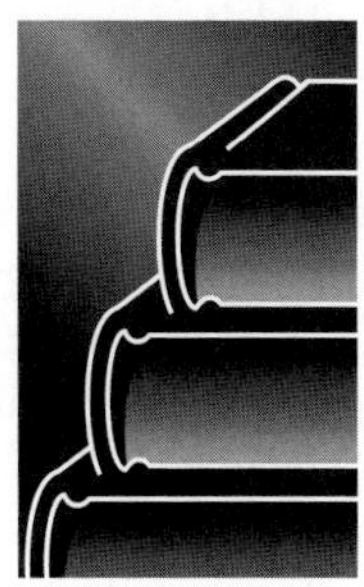

Facts: On February 28, 2000, H.J. Heinz Company and Milnot Holding Corporation (Beech-Nut brands) entered into a merger agreement. Claiming that the merger would violate Section 7 of the Clayton Act, the FTC asked the U.S. District Court for a preliminary injunction, to delay the merger pending the outcome of an FTC administrative investigation. The District Court denied the inunction, and the FTC appealed.

Four million infants in the U.S. consume 80 million cases of baby food annually, a domestic market of about $1 billion. Gerber (65 percent), Heinz (17.4 percent), and Beech-Nut (15.4 percent) dominate the market. Gerber brands are found in 80 percent of the nation's supermarkets, and it has a brand loyalty greater than any other product in the country. Heinz is sold in about 40 percent of all supermarkets; it is marketed nationwide, but its U.S. sales are concentrated in northern New England, the Midwest, and the South and Southeast. (Internationally, however, it is the industry leader, with $1 billion in annual sales.) Beech-Nut is sold in about 45 percent of U.S. stores; its market is mainly in New York, New Jersey, Florida, and California.

Issue: Should a preliminary injunction be granted?

Decision: Yes. Judgment reversed; case remanded.

Opinion by Judge Henderson: "'Whenever the Commission has reason to believe that a corporation is violating, or is about to violate, Section 7 of the Clayton Act, the FTC may seek a preliminary injunction to prevent a merger pending the Commission's administrative adjudication of the merger's legality.' ... Section 13(b) [of the FTC Act] provides for the grant of a preliminary injunction where such action would be in the public interest—as determined by a weighing of the equities and a consideration of the Commission's likelihood of success on the merits....

"To determine likelihood of success on the merits we measure the probability that, after an administrative hearing on the merits, the Commission will succeed in proving that the effect of the Heinz/Beech-Nut merger 'may be substantially to lessen competition, or to tend to create a monopoly' in violation of Section 7 of the Clayton Act....

"First the government must show that the merger would produce 'a firm controlling an undue percentage share of the relevant market, and [would result] in a significant increase in the concentration of firms in that market.' ... Such a showing establishes a 'presumption' that the merger will substantially lessen competition.... To rebut the presumption, the defendants must produce evidence that 'shows that the market share statistics [give] an inaccurate account of the merger's probable effects on competition' in the relevant market....

"Merger law 'rests upon the theory that, where rivals are few, firms will be able to coordinate their behavior, either by overt collusion or implicit understanding, in order to restrict output and achieve profits above competitive levels.' ... Increases in concentration above certain levels are thought to 'rais[e] a likelihood of "interdependent anticompetitive conduct".' ... Market concentration, or the lack thereof, is often measured by the Herfindahl-Hirschman Index (HHI)....

"Sufficiently large HHI figures establish the FTC's prima facie case that a merger is anti-competitive.... The district court found that the pre-merger HHI 'score for the baby food industry is 4775—indicative of a highly concentrated industry.... The merger of Heinz and Beech-Nut will increase the HHI by 510 points. This creates, by a wide margin, a presumption that the merger will lessen competition in the domestic jarred baby food market.... Here, the FTC's market concentration statistics are bolstered by the indisputable fact that the merger will eliminate competition between the two merging partners at the wholesale level, where they are currently the only competitors for what the district court described as the 'second position on the supermarket shelves.' ... Heinz's own documents recognize the wholesale competition and anticipate that the merger will end it.... Indeed, those documents disclose that Heinz considered three options to end the vigorous wholesale competition with Beech-Nut: two involved innovative measures while the third entailed the acquisition of Beech-Nut.... Heinz chose the third, and least pro-competitive, of the options....

"Finally, the anticompetitive effect of the merger is further enhanced by high barriers to market entry. The district court found that there had been no significant entries in the baby food market in decades and that new entry was 'difficult and improbable.' ... This finding largely eliminates the possibility that the reduced competition caused by the merger will be ameliorated by new competition from outsiders and further strengthens the FTC's case....

"As far as we can determine, no court has ever approved a merger to duopoly under similar circumstances....

"[T]he high market concentration levels present in this case require, in rebuttal, proof of extraordinary efficiencies, which the appellees failed to supply....

"Although the FTC's showing of likelihood of success creates a presumption in favor of preliminary injunctive relief, we must still weigh the equities in order to decide whether enjoining the merger would be in the public interest.... The principal public equity weighing in favor of issuance of preliminary injunctive relief is the public interest in effective enforcement of the antitrust laws.... The Congress specifically had this public equity consideration in mind when it enacted section 13(b).... The district court found, and there is no dispute, that if the merger were allowed to proceed, subsequent administrative and judicial proceedings on the merits 'will not matter' because Beech-Nut's manufacturing facility 'will be closed, the Beech-Nut distribution channels will be closed, the new label and recipes will be in place, and it will be impossible as a practical matter to undo the transaction.' ... Hence, if the merger were ultimately found to violate the Clayton Act, it would be impossible to recreate pre-merger competition.... Section 13(b) itself embodies congressional recognition of the fact that divestiture is an inadequate and unsatisfactory remedy in a merger case ...

"On the other side of the ledger, the appellees claim that the injunction would deny consumers the procompetitive advantages of the merger.... If the merger makes economic sense now, the appellees have offered no reason why it would not do so later. Moreover, Beech-Nut's principal assets of value to Heinz are, assertedly, its recipes and brand name. Nothing in the record leads us to believe that both will not still exist when the FTC completes its work. It may be that Beech-Nut will have to sell its recipes to Heinz at a lower price than the price of today's merger. But that is at best a 'private' equity which does not affect our analysis of the impact on the market of the two options now before us and which has not in any event been urged by appellees....

"It is important to emphasize the posture of this case. We do not decide whether the FTC will ultimately prove its case or whether the defendants' claimed efficiencies will carry the day. Our task is to review the district court's order to determine whether, under Section 13(b), preliminary injunctive relief would be in the public interest. We have considered the FTC's likelihood of success on the merits. We have weighed the equities. We conclude that the FTC has raised serious and substantial questions. We also conclude that the public equities weigh in favor of preliminary injunctive relief and therefore that a preliminary injunction would be in the public interest. Accordingly, we reverse the district court's denial of preliminary injunctive relief and remand the case for entry of a preliminary injunction pursuant to Section 13(b) of the Federal Trade Commission Act."

was forced to resign from the GE board because both companies made air conditioners. Potentially, there is a considerable area of antitrust violation under this section.

It is important to note that the Sherman Act is an "after the fact" law, which means you cannot be prosecuted until you have committed a violation. The Clayton Act is a "before the fact" law, meaning that its purpose is not to punish someone for having done a wrongful act, but to prevent damage to competition in the marketplace. For example, under Section 7 of the Clayton Act a proposed merger may be stopped before it is consummated if the merger might tend to substantially lessen competition. If the merger has already been consummated, as in the case of *U.S. v. E.I. du Pont Nemours & Co.*, and if a substantial lessening of competition appears possible, even though there is no evidence of wrongdoing, the court will order divestiture.

This before the fact purpose of the Clayton Act is also evident in Section 2 and Section 3 cases because it is not necessary to show actual damage has occurred, only that such competitive damage may occur if the specific actions are not discontinued. Section 8 also does not require showing that a director who happens to be on the board of directors of two competing companies is actually a bad person who is doing something wrong. The director may be removed before the opportunity to do anything wrong arises.

Robinson-Patman Act

One of the most difficult antitrust problems occurs when a seller charges different prices to two or more buyers for the same type of goods. As mentioned earlier, this is price discrimination. The original Section 2 of the Clayton Act of 1914 did contain a provision aimed at the seller who cuts prices in competitive locations and maintained higher prices everywhere else. The early cases, however, interpreted this section to prohibit only discrimination between *competing* buyers, and thus there were few prosecutions under it. By the mid-1930s, grocery store chains had become very powerful buyers and were demanding and getting quantity discounts. As the Supreme Court noted in the *Morton Salt* case, volume discounts of the large chains enabled them to sell Morton Salt at retail for less than the price at which independent wholesalers could sell it to their retail store customers. In 1936, under intense pressure from small independent retailers and wholesalers, Congress passed the **Robinson-Patman Act** to amend Section 2 of the Clayton Act.

The Offense

The Robinson-Patman Act basically states that it is unlawful for any seller to discriminate in price between different purchasers, if the sale involves goods and not services, if the sales constitute interstate rather than intrastate commerce, if the goods are of **like kind and quality,** and provided the effect of such discrimination may be to substantially lessen competition or tend to create a monopoly in any line of commerce. The responsibility for prosecuting Robinson-Patman violations rests with the FTC. As is true for other antitrust violations, any private parties who are injured by the illegal price discrimination may also bring their own case for damages.

A common practice among large manufacturers and food processors is to package products under their own brand name and also produce and package the product for certain volume customers under the customer's private label. The question arises: Must the manufacturers charge the same price for the private label goods as they do for their own brand name goods? In the 1966 case of *F.T.C. v. Borden Company,* the Supreme Court found the two products to be of like kind and quality regardless of the difference in the label.

Nonprofit Institutions Exemption

Only 2 years after passage of Robinson-Patman, Congress adopted the **Nonprofit-Institutions Act (NIA)** as an amendment. The NIA exempts from the application of Robinson-Patman "purchases of their supplies for their own use by schools, . . . hospitals, and charitable institutions not operated for profit." Manufacturers and other suppliers can thus provide special prices to these kinds of nonprofit agencies without violating Robinson-Patman.

Even here there have been definitional problems. The agencies themselves are usually easy enough to categorize. (There may be some question about some of the self-defined "nonprofit" agencies that solicit funds on television and elsewhere.) But there are some tough issues involved in deciding what is an agency's "own use." Can professors get the special discount, as well as the school itself? How about students? How about participants in a one-day seminar at the school? How about librarians at the school? Noninstructional staff? Spouses? Significant others? Alumni? Some difficult decisions may have to be made when these various groups also demand the special pricing.

The "Meeting Competition" Defense

Recognizing that in many cases a seller firm must cut its price to meet a lower price quoted by a competitor, Congress specifically provided for such a defense. A seller relying on the **meeting competition defense** must be acting in good faith; knowledge that the competitor's lower price is itself illegal would probably prevent a finding of good faith.

The "Cost Justification" Defense

In an important proviso to Section 2(a), Congress indicated that it did not wish to outlaw price differentials that could be justified by cost savings. If genuine cost savings could be realized on larger orders, a seller ought to be able to pass them on to the buyer. The theory of the **cost justification defense** is that if a price differential can be justified to the customer, it is lawful to pass that savings along to the customer.

For example, Company X wants to purchase 100,000 items that you produce and ship without separate wrapping and packaging. Company Y orders 5,000 of the identical item and wants each item individually packaged. Obviously, your cost per item for Company Y's order is going to be far greater than your cost per item to fill Company X's order. If you can prove a cost savings, you can charge Company X less per item than you charge Company Y. However, be sure you have good records as to costs because if a case of price discrimination is brought against you, you have the burden of proving the cost justification and its exact amount.

The "Obsolete or Perishable Goods" Defense

This defense is a rather obvious one. A seller who has obsolete or perishable goods needs to get rid of them for the best price. Also, because the quantity of these goods is limited, they present little likelihood of any substantial lessening of competition in the market.

Predatory Pricing

Another potentially significant limitation on a business's pricing decisions exists under Section 2 of the Sherman Act, which outlaws attempts to monopolize, as well as an accomplished monopolization. The courts have generally recognized that a violation of this section has occurred when a business has a specific intent to control prices or destroy competition, has engaged in predatory or anticompetitive conduct designed to accomplish that unlawful purpose, and has a "dangerous probability" of success. These elements are often difficult to define in a particular situation. Intent may be inferred from conduct, and market power is certainly one factor in deciding whether there is a likelihood of successful monopolization, but the courts have also been careful not to make these inferences too quickly or too easily.

One indication the courts have used in such cases is the practice of pricing a product below its cost, usually described as **predatory pricing.** The idea is that a large firm can stand such losses on one of its products longer than a small firm, which may be selling only the targeted product line. Traditionally, the courts used a concept of total costs—both variable costs for labor and materials and fixed costs for such things as buildings and research. In 1975, Harvard law professors Phillip Areeda and Donald Turner suggested that the legal test for predatory pricing should be based only on variable costs. The fixed costs would be incurred anyway, and a business could very well decide to sell additional units at a price that covered variable costs for perfectly legitimate reasons. The company would probably wish to keep its workers employed, and to maintain or increase its market share, by making additional sales at a price that covered the variable costs. A number of U.S. Courts of Appeals have adopted the Areeda-Turner analysis. In those circuits it has become more difficult to prove a charge of predatory pricing.

Federal Trade Commission Act

In 1914 Congress not only passed the Clayton Act but also the **Federal Trade Commission Act.** This act created a new administrative agency with very broad powers in the area of trade regulation. The FTC has the responsibility of investigating alleged violations of Sections 2, 3, 7, and 8 of the Clayton Act and has the authority to issue **cease-and-desist orders** to stop certain illegal practices and activities. Failure to comply with a cease-and-desist order from the FTC can result in fines of up to $10,000 for each day the violation continues.

The Federal Trade Commission and False Advertising

Section 5 of the Federal Trade Commission Act of 1914 prohibited unfair methods of competition and unfair or deceptive acts or practices. The FTC's original enforcement emphasis was against deceptive advertising. Many of the states had statutes that outlawed deceptive advertising, but enforcement varied from state to state. This sort of violation obviously injured both competitors and consumers, so it was probably a good place to start. Although the FTC's approach to unfair methods of competition has become much broader over the years, especially since the 1970s, it continues to be alert for false and deceptive advertising.

False Advertising under the Lanham Act

As will be discussed in Chapter 16, the **Lanham Act** of 1946 is the basic U.S. statute protecting trademarks, service marks, and "trade dress" (the "look and feel" of a product). However, the Lanham Act also covers **false advertising** or ads that are misleading, in that they misrepresent either the advertiser's product or service, or a competitor's product or service. Pizza Hut is attempting to enforce this kind of civil liability in the next case.

The Federal Trade Commission and Unfair Trade Practices

As it moved beyond false advertising cases, the FTC's basic difficulty became one of definition. Just what did its statute mean? What exactly are **unfair methods of competition?**

CASE 5

PIZZA HUT, INC. v. PAPA JOHN'S INT'L., INC.
227 F.3d 489 (5 Cir. 2000)

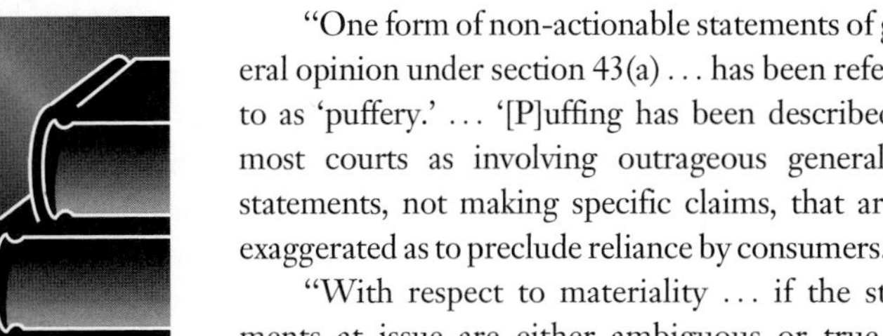

Facts: With over 7,000 stores, Pizza Hut is the largest pizza chain in the United States Papa John's is third largest, with over 2,000 locations. In 1996, Papa John's received trademark registration for its new slogan, "Better Ingredients. Better Pizza." In 1997, Pizza Hut's new ad campaign claimed "better taste," and "dared" anyone to find a "better pizza." Papa John's responded with a series of ads comparing their "fresh-pack" tomato sauce with Pizza Hut's reprocessed sauce, and their dough made using "clear filtered water" with the "biggest chain" using "whatever comes out of the tap." The tag line on these comparative ads was the trademarked slogan.

Pizza Hut sued, alleging Lanham Act violations. The jury found that the slogan was misleading when used in the comparative ads because there were no discernable differences in the respective sauces and doughs. The trial court issued an injunction against the use of Papa John's trademarked slogan and against any ad claim that its ingredients are superior to Pizza Hut's, and they awarded Pizza Hut $467,619.75 damages. Papa John's appealed.

Issue: Were Papa John's ad statements false or misleading?

Decision: No. Judgment reversed, and case remanded.

Opinion by Judge Jolly: "The law governing false advertising claims under section 43(a) of the Lanham Act is well settled. In order to obtain monetary damages of equitable relief in the form of an injunction, 'a plaintiff must demonstrate that the commercial advertisement or promotion is either literally false or that ... it is likely to mislead and confuse consumers.' ... If the statement is shown to be misleading, the plaintiff must also introduce evidence of the statement's impact on consumers, referred to as materiality. ...

"Essential to any claim under section 43(a) ... is a determination of whether the challenged statement is one of fact—actionable under section 43(a)—or one of general opinion—not actionable under section 43(a). Bald assertions of superiority or general statements of opinion cannot form the basis of Lanham Act liability. ... Rather the statements at issue must be a 'specific and measurable claim, capable of being proved true or false or of being reasonably interpreted as a statement of objective fact.'. ...

"One form of non-actionable statements of general opinion under section 43(a) ... has been referred to as 'puffery.' ... '[P]uffing has been described by most courts as involving outrageous generalized statements, not making specific claims, that are so exaggerated as to preclude reliance by consumers.' ...

"With respect to materiality ... if the statements at issue are either ambiguous or true but misleading, the plaintiff must produce evidence of actual deception. ...

"The type of evidence needed to prove materiality ... varies depending on what type of recovery the plaintiff seeks. Plaintiffs looking to recover monetary damages for false or misleading advertising that is not literally false must prove actual deception. ... Plaintiffs attempting to prove actual deception have to produce evidence of actual consumer reaction to the challenged advertising or surveys showing that a substantial number of consumers were actually misled by the advertisements. ...

"Plaintiffs seeking injunctive relief must prove that defendant's representations 'have a tendency to deceive consumers.' ...

"Bisecting the slogan 'Better Ingredients. Better Pizza.,' it is clear that the assertion by Papa John's that it makes a 'Better Pizza' is a general statement of opinion regarding the superiority of its product over all others. This simple statement, 'Better Pizza.,' epitomizes the exaggerated advertising, blustering, and boasting by a manufacturer upon which no consumer would reasonably rely. ...

"Concluding that when the slogan was used as the tag line in the sauce and dough ads it became misleading, we must now determine whether reasonable consumers would have a tendency to rely on this misleading statement of fact in making their purchasing decisions. We conclude that Pizza Hut has failed to adduce evidence establishing that the misleading statement of fact conveyed was material to the consumers to which the slogan was directed. Consequently, because such evidence of materiality is necessary to establish liability under the Lanham Act, the district court erred in denying Papa John's motion for judgment as a matter of law. ...

"Therefore, the judgment of the district court denying Papa John's motion for judgment as a matter of law is REVERSED; the final judgment of the district court is VACATED; and the case is REMANDED for entry of judgment for Papa John's."

To some people, "all's fair in love and war"—and business. The drafters of the statute had clearly left the phrase vague and flexible, so that the FTC would be able to deal with new unfair devices as they were developed. If only specific practices had been prohibited, business firms and their lawyers could quickly circumvent the act by restructuring their operations. Although the uncertainty was intentional, it has nevertheless caused problems.

Unfair methods clearly include violations of the Sherman Act and the Clayton Act (including Robinson-

Patman) and incipient Sherman Act violations. The Supreme Court has also held that methods that violate the "basic policy" of the Sherman and Clayton Acts, even though not specifically listed in the acts, can be reached under Section 5. Practices that injure customers can be prosecuted without necessarily showing that any competitor has been injured. All types of behavior that might be classified as "bad business morals" can also be reached under Section 5, including such things as tampering with a competitor's goods, deceptive packaging, and delivering unordered goods. In 1972 the Supreme Court decided that the FTC had general rule-making power; that is, the FTC did not have to proceed on a case-by-case basis but could promulgate rules of behavior, just like the National Labor Relations Board (NLRB), the Securities and Exchange Commission (SEC), and other agencies. Since then, the FTC has been quite aggressive in adopting rules for competitive conduct. Most recently, there have been attempts in Congress to curb the FTC's growing power over commercial practices.

Other Federal Trade Commission Jurisdiction

The FTC was also given the responsibility for enforcing a series of labeling acts passed in the 1940s and 1950s: the Wool Products Act (1941), the Fur Products Act (1952), the Textile Fibre Act (1958), and the Flammable Fabrics Act (1954). The enforcement mechanisms include both cease-and-desist orders and criminal penalties. The FTC also enforces the 1975 Magnuson-Moss Warranty Act, discussed in Chapter 18.

As part of the consumerism movement of the 1960s and 1970s, the FTC was given increased enforcement jurisdiction under several new statutes. The Truth in Lending Act, which requires disclosure of the true annual percentage rate of interest and other information to the consumer or farmer borrower, places primary enforcement in the Federal Reserve Board. The Fair Credit Reporting Act creates new debtor rights against credit bureaus, as does the Fair Credit Billing Act in disputes with creditors. Congress also limited debt collection practices with the Fair Debt Collection Practices Act. Many of these new statutes provide the possibility of private damage suits and administrative agency action. The FTC was given joint jurisdiction with the Department of Health and Welfare (now Department of Health and Human Services) to enforce the new Fair Packaging Act, which requires label disclosures and limits sellers' claims.

Probably because Congress felt that more specific engineering and technical expertise was needed to deal with the problem, the FTC was not given enforcement responsibility under the 1972 Consumer Product Safety Act. A new Consumer Product Safety Commission (CPSC) and a new Advisory Council were created by the act. The CPSC collects and distributes data on product safety and product-related injuries. Injured consumers can bring suits in the U.S. courts if the alleged damages are $10,000 or more, and the further distribution of the "unsafe" product may be enjoined. The manufacturer may also be fined $2,000 for each violation, but the total fine for a single product cannot exceed $500,000.

Significance of This Chapter

The antitrust laws are significant because to maintain a competitive marketplace we must prevent anticompetitive schemes, such as price-fixing, market splitting, resale price maintenance, and tying contracts. The antitrust laws try to prevent actions that may restrain competition.

Pricing decisions are at the heart of the competitive process and are the essence of the free enterprise system. Our national laws nonetheless impose significant restrictions on a business's freedom to make such decisions. Even though the Robinson-Patman Act seems outdated and incompatible with a free marketplace, it lurks in the statute books, waiting to trap the unwary marketer. People responsible for pricing and other marketing decisions need to be aware of these basic rules of the game.

Likewise, although the FTC Act does not provide a complete list of "unfair methods of competition," a marketing executive can get a good idea of the outer boundaries by reading some of the landmark cases. This chapter is designed to provide a sensitivity for these legal boundaries on competition.

IMPORTANT TERMS AND CONCEPTS

cease-and-desist orders
Clayton Act
conglomerate merger
conscious parallelism
cost justification defense
economic school
exclusive dealing agreements
fair trade laws
false advertising
Federal Trade Commission Act.
full-line forcing
Herfindahl-Hirschman Index (HHI)
horizontal merger
interbrand competition
interlocking directors
intrabrand competition
Lanham Act
legal school
like kind and quality
meeting competition defense
merger
merger guidelines
nolo contendere
Nonprofit-Institutions Act (NIA)
nonsigner plans
per se violations
predatory pricing
price discrimination
price-fixing
relevant market
Robinson-Patman Act
rule of reason
Sherman Act
treble damages
tying contract
unfair methods of competition?
vertical merger

QUESTIONS AND PROBLEMS FOR DISCUSSION

1. Why is resale price maintenance a violation of the antitrust law? What is the difference between resale price maintenance and refusal to deal?

2. Why should the government regulate corporate mergers? Is any merger good, or are they all bad? Where should we draw the line? What are the merger guidelines?

3. What is the role of the FTC with regard to antitrust laws? What specific laws does the FTC have authority to enforce?

4. It is often said that the Sherman Act is an after the fact law, whereas the Clayton Act is a before the fact law. Explain what this means.

5. In preparation for the 1995 Georgia Bar Examination, Jay Palmer and other law students contracted to take a bar review course offered by respondent BRG of Georgia, Inc. (BRG). In this litigation, they contend that the price of BRG's course was enhanced by reason of an unlawful agreement between BRG and respondent Harcourt Brace Jovanovich Legal and Professional Publications (HBJ), the nation's largest provider of bar review materials and lecture services.

   HBJ began offering a Georgia bar review course on a limited basis in 1976 and was in direct, and often intense, competition with BRG during the period from 1977 to 1979. BRG and HBJ were the two main providers of bar review courses in Georgia during this time period. In early 1980, they entered into an agreement that gave BRG an exclusive license to market HBJ's material in Georgia and to use its trade name "Bar/Bri." The parties agreed that HBJ would not compete with BRG in Georgia and that BRG would not compete with HBJ outside of Georgia. Under the agreement, HBJ received $100 per student enrolled by BRG and 40 percent of all revenues over $350. Immediately after the 1980 agreement, the price of BRG's course was increased from $150 to over $400.

   Did this agreement violate the antitrust laws?

6. Ted Bates & Company, Inc., an advertising agency, prepared for Colgate three 1-minute commercials designed to show that Rapid Shave could soften even the toughness of sandpaper. Each of the commercials contained the same "sandpaper test." The announcer informed the audience that, "To prove RAPID SHAVE'S super-moisturizing power, we put it right from the can on this tough, dry sandpaper. It was apply [pause] soak [pause] and off in a stroke." While the announcer was speaking, Rapid Shave was applied to a substance that appeared to be sandpaper, and immediately thereafter a razor was shown shaving the substance clean.

   The FTC issued a complaint against Colgate and Bates charging that the commercials were false and deceptive. The evidence before the hearing examiner disclosed that sandpaper of the type depicted in the commercials could not be shaved immediately following the application of Rapid Shave but required a substantial soaking period of approximately 80 minutes. The evidence also showed that the substance resembling sandpaper was in fact a simulated prop, or "mock-up," made of plexiglass to which sand had been applied. However, the examiner found that Rapid Shave could shave sandpaper, even though not in the short time represented by the commercials, and that if real sandpaper had been used in the commercials the inadequacies of television transmission would have made it appear to viewers to be nothing more than plain, colored paper.

   How should this case be decided? Discuss.

7. Monfort of Colorado, Inc., the plaintiff, owns and operates three integrated beef-packing plants, that is,

plants for both the slaughter of cattle and the fabrication of beef. Monfort operates in both the market for fed cattle (the input market) and the market for fabricated beef (the output market). These markets are highly competitive, and the profit margins of the major beef packers are low. The current markets are a product of two decades of intense competition, during which time packers with modern integrated plants have gradually displaced packers with separate slaughter and fabrication plants.

Monfort is the country's fifth-largest beef packer. Excel Corporation is the second-largest packer. Excel operates five integrated plants and one fabrication plant. It is a wholly owned subsidiary of Cargill, Inc., a large privately owned corporation with more than 150 subsidiaries in at least 35 countries.

Excel signed an agreement to acquire the third-largest packer in the market, Spencer Beef, a division of the Land O'Lakes agricultural cooperative. Spencer Beef owned two integrated plants and one slaughtering plant. After the acquisition, Excel would still be the second-largest packer but would command a market share almost equal to that of the largest packer, IBP, Inc. Monfort brought an action under Section 16 of the Clayton Act to enjoin the prospective merger.

Should this merger be enjoined? Why or why not?

8. Marner-Silas Co. has been selling Blisteine, a mouthwash, for nearly 40 years. The formula for the product has not changed during this period, but at various times, Marner-Silas has advertised that Blisteine relieves colds and sore throats. The FTC has solid medical evidence that these claims are not true.

   How should the FTC proceed, and what remedy should it require of Marner-Silas? Explain.

9. Leon Rippof advertised eyeglasses for sale at his store, "from $7.50 complete, including lenses, frames, and case." Some of his ads mentioned a "modest examination fee"; others did not. Of the 1,400 pairs of eyeglasses he sold during the prior year, only nine were sold at $7.50; most cost considerably more than that.

   Has Rippof committed false advertising? Discuss.

10. Atlantic Richfield Co. (ARCO), a large integrated oil company, operates company-owned retail stations and franchises stations to dealers. ARCO urged its dealers to match the retail prices of independents like USA. ARCO gave its dealers temporary allowances and also reduced their costs by eliminating credit card sales. As a result, ARCO and its dealers increased market share to the detriment of USA and similar independents. USA sued, alleging a conspiracy to set maximum retail prices, a per se violation of Section 1 of the Sherman Act. The District Court granted summary judgment for ARCO, but the Ninth Circuit reversed.

    How should the U.S. Supreme Court decide this case? Explain.

11. Texaco is a large integrated oil company. Between 1972 and 1981, it sold gasoline at its retail tank wagon prices to Hasbrouck and 11 other independent Texaco retailers, but gave large discounts to Gull and Dompier. Gull resold the gas under its own name. Dompier resold the gas to retailers as Texaco gas. Both distributors picked up the gasoline from Texaco and delivered it to their retail outlets; neither had any large storage facilities. Texaco also paid Dompier for delivering the gasoline to retailers. Texaco had refused a request by two of the plaintiffs to pick up their own gasoline. The shares of Gull and Dompier in the Spokane market increased dramatically, while the plaintiffs' shares declined. Plaintiffs sued in 1976, alleging violations of the Robinson-Patman Act. Texaco argued that because Gull and Dompier were performing some wholesaler functions, they could be given a "wholesaler discount." The trial court, after a jury trial, awarded treble damages of $449,900, and the Court of Appeals affirmed.

    Will this decision be affirmed by the U.S. Supreme Court? Why or why not?

CHAPTER 6

Criminal Law and Criminal Procedure

Chapter Objectives

This chapter will:

- Define *crime.*
- Compare and contrast civil and criminal proceedings.
- Explain why a corporate executive could be found guilty of a crime for acts committed in the name of the corporation.
- Review the rights a person accused of a crime has under criminal law.

Traditionally the business manager has been less concerned about criminal law than about contract law, tort law, corporation law, and other mainstream business law subjects. This is changing. Criminal law, particularly as it applies to **white-collar crimes,** is becoming an area of considerable concern. Managers need to be aware of a number of business crimes, including one of the newest types of crime: computer theft. Computer theft encompasses embezzlement of funds, theft of programs, and theft of confidential business information and records—all through the use and manipulation of computers and other electronic devices.

In addition to having to concern themselves with white-collar or business crimes, corporate officers and directors need to know what kinds of circumstances can make them subject to both civil lawsuits and criminal charges.

Definition of Crime

A **crime** can be defined as a public wrong. To maintain an orderly society, the government must set standards of conduct that the members of society must observe. Failure to observe these standards must be enforced by some form of societal pressure, such as fines or imprisonment. A crime may involve either the commission of a specific act or the omission or failure to act under certain circumstances. For the commission or omission of an act to be classified as a crime, the legislature, either national or state, must have passed a statute declaring the commission or omission of that act to be a crime. Usually, it is also necessary to prove that the act was done with wrongful intent.

Many of the acts or omissions that have been defined as crimes may also be torts. A tort, as defined in Chapter 7, is a private wrong for which the wronged person may recover monetary damages. If someone is mugged on the street, the mugger may be punished in a criminal court by a fine or imprisonment. The person who has been mugged, as the victim of a private wrong, has a legal right to bring a civil action at his or her own expense to recover monetary damages from the mugger.

Classifications of Crime

Crimes are usually classified as felonies or misdemeanors. Traditionally **felonies** have been serious crimes, such as murder, rape, robbery, burglary, arson, theft, and larceny. A crime is not a felony, however, unless a statute designates it as such. Felonies are normally punishable by jail sentences of at least 1 year, plus possible fines.

Misdemeanors are criminal offenses other than felonies. Typically, misdemeanors are punished by small fines or jail sentences not exceeding 1 year, or both a fine and imprisonment. Normally the person who has been convicted of a misdemeanor is confined in a county jail rather than the state penitentiary. The fines imposed for misdemeanors are normally smaller than the fines imposed for felonies. No standard is common to all states; different states have different crime classifications and different levels of punishment. Each state is responsible for creating its own criminal law, but state criminal law cannot conflict with any applicable national law, including the U.S. Constitution.

Business Crimes

Because this textbook focuses on business-related legal matters, the major focus here will be on crimes that are relevant to the operation of a business. The following are some typical business crimes.

Larceny

Larceny, or theft as it is commonly called, is simply the unlawful taking of another person's personal property with the intent of depriving the owner of the property. Shoplifting is an example of larceny with which the businessperson has to be concerned. Larceny is also committed by employees who carry off goods and merchandise.

Robbery

Robbery, like larceny, involves the unlawful taking of personal property. However, the unlawful taking in a robbery involves the use of force, putting other people in fear of injury. Thus, robbery is a more serious crime than larceny because it has the potential of physical harm to individuals.

Embezzlement

With **embezzlement,** a person who had lawful possession of someone else's money or property used the property or money for his or her own purposes. A typical case here would be a bank employee who was in charge of certain funds and used some of the funds for personal purposes. Many embezzlers borrow money with the intent of paying it back later. In most jurisdictions the person who takes money with the intent of returning it is still guilty of embezzlement.

Arson

Arson is willfully setting fire to and burning someone else's building. In old English common law, arson referred primarily to the burning of someone else's dwelling house. Under most state statutes, arson now covers the burning of business buildings as well as dwellings.

Defrauding Consumers by Use of the Mails

Using the mails to solicit money for fraudulent purposes is a crime. This could include schemes to sell phony corporate stocks and bonds, false statements about products that when received are not as advertised, and numerous other situations in which people use the mails to convey false information for the purpose of committing fraud. National laws also make it a crime to send pornographic materials through the mails.

Defrauding Consumers by Using False Labels, Measures, and Weights

In recent years a number of national and state laws have been passed concerning false weights, measures, and labels. Again, intention is a key factor in this crime. A simple mistake in weight or measurement is not a crime. There must be an intent to defraud or cheat the consumer.

Forgery

Forgery is the false or fraudulent making, or the material alteration with the intent to defraud, of any writing which, if genuine, would be of legal effect and create legal liability.

Credit Card Fraud

Illegal and fraudulent use of stolen credit cards has become a major concern to credit card companies. In 1971, Congress passed a law that limited an individual's liability to $50 per stolen credit card. Although an individual cannot be liable for more than $50 per stolen card, the loss of credit card companies is not limited.

Computer Crime

Computer crime is the newest and perhaps the most important area of criminal law of concern to business managers. Computer-related crimes range from the theft of a computer program worth thousands of dollars to the use of computers to embezzle millions of dollars.

Criminal Liability of Accountants

This is also a new area of criminal law. Traditionally, professionals such as accountants, lawyers, and doctors were found liable for civil damages for malpractice but were not prosecuted criminally for acts of mere negligence. In recent years a number of criminal cases have been brought against accountants, particularly in connection with their failure to discover and report fraud by corporate officers or employees.

The Securities Act of 1933 makes an accountant criminally liable if the accountant willfully makes a false statement regarding a material fact or willfully omits a material fact in a registration statement. The penalty can be a fine of up to $10,000, 5 years in prison, or both.

Section 32(a) of the 1934 Act makes an accountant criminally liable if the accountant willfully makes a false or misleading statement regarding a material fact in a report required to be filed under the 1934 Act, such as the 10-K reports. The penalty can be a fine of up to $10,000, 5 years in prison, or both.

The 2001 multibillion meltdown of Enron, at the time one of the 10 largest companies in the United States, led to the next case. Although many accounting irregularities—by both Enron's internal accounting staff and their independent auditors (Arthur Andersen LLP)—were alleged, the crime charged arose from Andersen's document shredding of Enron-related materials. The firm was convicted for one offense of "knowingly . . . corruptly persuad[ing] another person . . . with intent to . . . cause" that person to "withhold" documents from or "alter" documents for use in, an "official proceeding." By the time the U.S. Supreme Court heard this case on appeal, the Andersen firm had been destroyed by the massive negative publicity surrounding the criminal conviction.

CASE 1

ARTHUR ANDERSEN, LLP v. UNTIED STATES

544 U.S. 695 (2005)

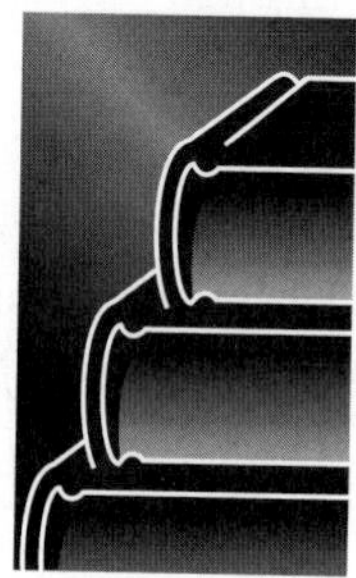

Facts: In the 1990s, Enron Corporation morphed from an operator of natural gas pipelines into an energy conglomerate and adopted "aggressive" accounting practices. The Andersen firm audited its books and certified its official reports filed with the Securities and Exchange Commission (SEC). David Duncan headed the firm's "engagement team" for Enron, with Michael Odom as his supervisor. In 2000, Enron's financial performance began to decline, and the problems grew worse in 2001. On August 14, Enron CEO Jeffrey Skilling resigned, and Enron's founder Kenneth Lay was reappointed CEO. Sherron Watkins, a senior accountant at Enron, told Lay (and Duncan and Odom) that Enron "could implode in a wave of accounting scandals." A story about possible "improprieties" at Enron appeared in the August 28 *Wall Street Journal*, and the SEC opened an informal investigation.

On October 10, Odom spoke at a general training meeting attended by 89 Andersen employees, including 10 from the Enron engagement team. He urged them to follow Andersen's document retention policy, which called for a single central engagement file that "should contain only that information which is relevant to supporting our work." Subsequently, Enron-related documents were destroyed. On October 30, the SEC opened a formal investigation and sent Enron a letter requesting accounting documents. Andersen was served with an SEC subpoena for Enron records on November 8. On November 9, Duncan's secretary sent an e-mail that stated: "Per Dave—no more shredding. . . . We have been officially served for our documents."

In March 2002, Arthur Andersen LLP was indicted in U.S. District Court in Texas on one count (charged with *one* wrongful act) of violating U.S. Code s.1512(b). After initially announcing it was deadlocked, a jury finally did convict Andersen. The conviction was affirmed by the U.S. Court of Appeals, and Andersen petitioned for certiorari.

Issue: Did the trial court judge correctly instruct the jury on the law?

Decision: No. Judgment reversed, and case remanded.

Opinion by Chief Justice Rehnquist: "Chapter 73 of Title 18 of the United States Code provides criminal sanctions for those who obstruct justice. . . .

"In this case our attention is focused on what it means to 'knowingly . . . corruptly persuade' another person 'with intent to . . . cause' that person to 'withhold' documents from, or 'alter' documents for use in, an 'official proceeding.' . . .

" 'We have traditionally exercised restraint in assessing the reach of a federal criminal statute, both out of deference to Congress . . . and out of concern that a "fair warning should be given to the world in language that the common world will understand, of what the law intends to do if a certain line is passed".' . . .

"Such restraint is particularly appropriate here, where the act underlying the conviction—'persuasion'—is by itself innocuous. Indeed, 'persuading' a person 'with intent to . . . cause' that person to 'withhold' testimony or documents from a Government proceeding or Government official is not inherently malign. . . .

"'Document retention policies,' which are created in part to keep certain information from getting into the hands of others, including the Government, are common in business. . . . It is, of course, not wrongful for a manager to instruct his employees to comply with a valid document retention policy under ordinary circumstances.

"Acknowledging this point, the parties have largely focused their attention on the word 'corruptly' as the key to what may or may not lawfully be done in the situation presented here. Section 1512(b) punishes not just 'corruptly persuading' another, but 'knowingly . . . corruptly persuading' another. . . . The Government suggests that 'knowingly' does not modify 'corruptly persuades,' but that is not how the statute naturally reads. It provides the mens rea—'knowingly'—and then a list of acts—'uses intimidation or physical force, threatens, or corruptly persuades.' . . .

"Joining these meanings together here makes sense both linguistically and in the statutory scheme. Only persons conscious of their wrongdoing can be said to 'knowingly . . . corruptly persuade.' And limiting criminality to persuaders conscious of their wrongdoing sensibly allows S.1512(b) to reach only those with the level of 'culpability . . . we usually require in order to impose criminal liability.' . . .

"[I]t is striking how little culpability the instructions required. For example, the jury was told that, 'even if [petitioner] honestly and sincerely believed that its conduct was lawful, you may find [petitioner] guilty.' . . . The instructions also dilute the meaning of 'corruptly' so that it covered innocent conduct. . . .

"The instructions were also infirm for another reason. They led the jury to believe that it did not have to find any nexus between the 'persuasion' to destroy documents and any particular proceeding. . . . A 'knowingly . . . corrupt persuader' cannot be someone who persuades others to shred documents under a document retention policy when he does not have in contemplation any particular official proceeding in which those documents might be material. . . .

"For these reasons, the jury instructions here were flawed in important respects. The judgment of the Court of Appeals is reversed, and the case is remanded for further proceedings consistent with this opinion."

Mail Fraud Statute

The mail fraud statute imposes criminal liability upon persons who either send false financial statements in the U.S. mails or conspire to send false financial statements in the U.S. mail.

In the case of the *United States v. Simon*, often referred to as the *Continental Vending* case, decided by the U.S. Second Circuit in 1969, accountants were found criminally liable. That case involved violations of Section 32(a) of the 1934 act as well as the mail fraud statute.

Foreign Corrupt Practices Act

As noted in Chapter 2, the Foreign Corrupt Practices Act (FCPA) was passed by the U.S. Congress in 1977 to discourage payment of bribes by U.S. corporations to foreign officials for favors in business dealings.

This act prohibits both businesses registered under the provisions of the 1934 Securities Exchange Act and U.S. businesses not so registered from offering or giving anything of value to a foreign official to obtain a new business relationship or to retain a business relationship previously established. A willful violation of the provisions of this act can result in a criminal conviction with penalties of up to $10,000 and/or 5 years in prison for the individual or individuals involved and fines to the corporation of up to $2 million.

Internal Revenue Code

The Internal Revenue Code provides for criminal penalties including fines and imprisonment for accountants (tax preparers) who willfully prepare false tax returns or willfully assist a client to evade taxes.

Commercial Bribery

Over the past two decades the press has exposed many cases of **commercial bribery,** payoffs to politicians, and illegal campaign contributions. A problem in many of these cases is that a corporation made the illegal contribution or paid the bribe. You can fine a corporation, but you cannot put one in jail. Should the executive who made the decision to have the corporation disobey the law also be criminally liable? Such activities by U.S. corporations in other countries were the major reason behind passage of the FCPA, discussed previously.

Antitrust Violations

As noted in Chapter 5, some antitrust violations may be prosecuted as crimes by the U.S. Department of Justice. Price-fixing conspiracies by competitors are particularly susceptible to criminal prosecution. As seen in the following case, even Mr. Taubman's advanced age, ill health, social status, wealth, and extensive charitable contributions did not save him from a prison sentence.

CASE 2

United States of America v. Taubman
297 F.3d 161 (2 Cir. 2002)

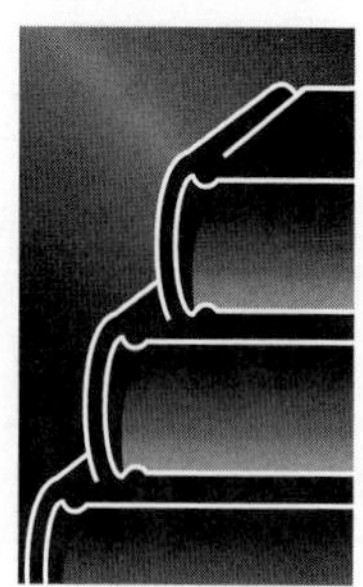

Facts: A. Alfred Taubman appeals from the denial of his motion for a new trial and from a judgment of conviction after a jury trial. He was convicted of conspiracy to fix prices, in violation of Section 1 of the Sherman Antitrust Act, while he was chairman of the board of Sotheby's Holdings, Inc. He also asked to be released from jail, pending appeal.

Taubman claims that his meetings with Anthony J. Tennant, the chairman of UK-based Christie's International, plc, were not about price-fixing; and that the price-fixing was done by the two companies' CEOs—Diana Brooks of Sotheby's and Christopher Davidge of Christie's. Taubman says that the District Court's rulings prevented him from presenting his defense effectively, by: (1) not requiring testimony from Lord Peter Carrington, Tennant's predecessor; (2) excluding testimony from Taubman's administrative assistant about Taubman's statements after a meeting with Tennant; (3) excluding notes in Tennant's handwriting about his relationship with Lord Thomas Camoys, a senior official at Sotheby's; (4) refusing to tell ["charge"] the jury that competitors may meet for perfectly legal reasons; (5) permitting the prosecution to quote Adam Smith to the jury: "People in the same trade seldom meet together even for merriment or diversion, but the conversation ends in a conspiracy against the public and in some contrivance to raise prices."

Issue: Did the district court's rulings deny Taubman a fair trial?

Decision: No. Conviction affirmed.

Opinion by the Court *(Per Curiam)*: "We understood Taubman's counsel to concede at oral argument that, viewed in the light most favorable to the Government, ... th[e] evidence was sufficient to support Taubman's conviction for the charged crime. Taubman argues, however, that the District Court's errors deprived him of a fair trial.

"We turn first to the District Court's evidentiary rulings, which we review for abuse of discretion.... In doing so, we bear in mind that 'a judge has not abused [his] discretion simply because [he] has made a different decision than we would have made in the first instance.' ...

"With respect to [Carrington], the District Court held that Taubman failed to demonstrate the materiality of Carrington's testimony at trial. Carrington had previously testified in a December 2000 deposition in a related civil action—a deposition taken by one of Taubman's attorneys—that he had met Taubman once, and then only to 'shake [Taubman's] hand,' and otherwise had never spoken with Taubman.

"With respect to Taubman's statement to his administrative assistant, the District Court excluded it as hearsay. The District Court held that Taubman did not establish that the testimony was admissible ... to show Taubman's state of mind when he went to the relevant meeting, because it was not made contemporaneously with that meeting....

"With respect to the notes of the alleged April 1995 meeting between Tennant and Camoys, the District Court also excluded them as hearsay ... because Tennant was under no obligation to make them and because Taubman had not established that the document was created under circumstances indicative of trustworthiness....

"We have carefully examined each of these rulings and all of Taubman's arguments regarding them and hold that the District Court did not abuse its discretion.... With respect to the notes, we observe that district courts have 'broad latitude' in excluding evidence ... 'even where the exclusion of evidence affects the defense case.' ...

"In any event, any error in the District Court's evidentiary rulings was, in the particular circumstances presented, harmless. Taubman's knowledge of and participation in the conspiracy to fix prices was not established by circumstantial evidence, it was established by direct evidence—the testimony of Brooks and Davidge....

"Any error to give the requested charge [to the jury] was also harmless. The Government's case did not depend upon (and, indeed, the Court's charge, read as a whole, did not permit ...) the jury's inferring Taubman's knowledge of or participation in the conspiracy from the mere fact of his numerous meetings with Tennant....

"The Adam Smith quotation is more problematic....

"In the instant case, however, the Government relied on overwhelming direct evidence of Taubman's knowledge of and participation in the conspiracy, as noted above. Accordingly, we conclude that ... the Government's inclusion of the Adam Smith quotation in the Government's summation was harmless....

"[W]e affirm the judgment of the District Court.

"[I]n light of our decision, we deny the motion for release pending appeal."

Criminal Liability of Corporate Executives

In stockholder actions against managers, corporate directors, and corporate officers, corporate executives have always been individually accountable in civil court for their acts of negligence in the operation of the business. If criminal charges were filed, however, typically the corporation was charged with the crime. Because a corporation cannot be jailed, the corporation simply paid the fine and the case was closed. For many years a protective shield seemed to exist between the manager, corporate directors, and corporate officers, and the criminal prosecutor. This corporate shield was first pierced in the electrical industry price-fixing conspiracy case in 1960. In that case, several corporate executives were sent to jail. The corporate shield has been disintegrating ever since.

Criminal Procedure

Procedural Protections for Criminal Defendants

Your rights under criminal law are considerably different from your rights under civil law. Under civil law, if you are sued for breach of contract or for the commission of a tort, the usual remedy is monetary damages. None of us wants to lose money. However, if we are unfortunate enough to have a very large judgment assessed against us and we do not have the funds to satisfy it, we have the opportunity to file for bankruptcy. (Bankruptcy will be covered in Chapter 22.) A person who is adjudicated a bankrupt is free from most prior debts and is, in effect, born again, as far as his or her financial life is concerned.

On the other hand, a person who is convicted of a crime may be jailed and/or fined. If the crime is a felony, the person also may lose certain civil rights. In some states convicted felons lose the right to vote, the right to serve on juries, and the right to hold public office. Also, professional practitioners convicted of a crime may lose their right to practice their profession. For instance, a lawyer may face disbarment if convicted. Thus, the consequences of a criminal conviction are more serious than those of a civil judgment for money. A person convicted of a crime will carry this record for life. In fact, if capital punishment is allowed, the person may lose his or her life. Thus, the guarantees the law must give to a person charged with a crime are much greater than the guarantees that must be given in a civil trial for monetary damages.

Following are some of the guarantees that are essential in a criminal trial, but need not be provided in a civil trial.

Prohibition against Unreasonable Search and Seizure

The Fourth Amendment to the U.S. Constitution prohibits unreasonable searches and "seizures" of evidence in private homes and businesses. This same restriction has also been been applied to evidence-gathering by state officials, as part of constitutionally required "due process" under the Fourteenth Amendment. The improperly seized evidence is usually excluded from the criminal trial, even if it provides strong evidence of the accused person's guilt.

The *Kyllo* case shows the impact of advanced technology on these rules.

Right to a Speedy, Public Trial by Jury

The **Sixth Amendment** to the U.S. Constitution guarantees a speedy public **trial by jury** in criminal cases. In civil cases in large metropolitan areas, the trial may be delayed several years after the time the lawsuit was filed. A person charged with a crime should have his or her day in court promptly, and it must be public. The trial must be before a jury, unless the defendant waives the right to a jury trial.

In addition to having the right to a speedy, public trial by jury, an accused in a criminal case also has the right to be judged by a fair and impartial jury, one not subjected to the pressures and prejudices of the newspaper and television media during the trial.

Presumption of Innocence

The judge must instruct the jury in a criminal trial that the defendant is innocent until proven guilty, that is, there is a **presumption of innocence**. The jury is instructed that the

CASE 3

KYLLO V. UNITED STATES OF AMERICA
533 U.S 27 (2001)

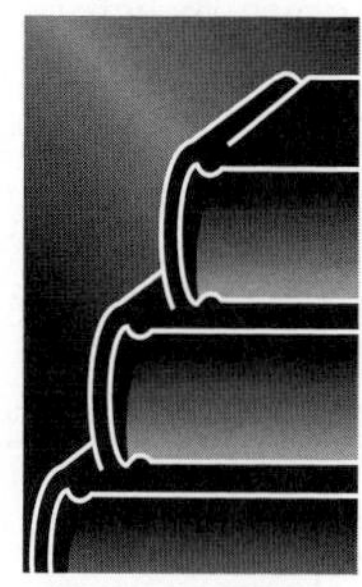

Facts: William Elliott, an agent of the U.S. Department of the Interior, suspected that Danny Kyllo was growing marijuana inside his home in Florence, Oregon. Such indoor cultivation is usually done with high-intensity heat lamps. At 3:20 am on January 16, 1992, agents Elliott and Dan Haas used a thermal imaging device to scan the outside of the triplex apartment building that included Kyllo's residence. (They were in a parked car across the street from the building.) The device converts heat radiation into images based on relative warmth: black for cool, white for hot, and shades of gray showing relative differences. The images showed that the garage roof and one side of Kyllo's apartment were hotter than the rest of the building. Based on tips from informants, Kyllo's utility bills, and the thermal images, a U.S. magistrate judge issued a search warrant. The agents found more than 100 growing marijuana plants.

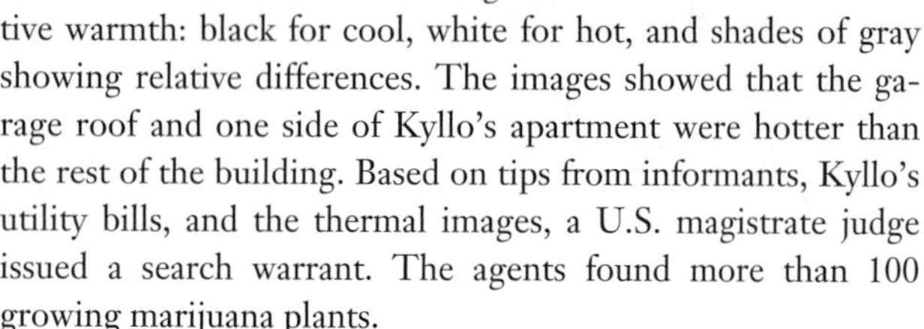

Kyllo was indicted on one count of manufacturing marijuana. When his motion to suppress the evidence found in his home was overruled, he entered a conditional guilty plea. On appeal, the Ninth Circuit remanded the case for an evidentiary hearing on the intrusiveness of the thermal imaging process. Based on its findings, the U.S. District Court upheld the validity of the search warrant, and the Ninth Circuit ultimately affirmed that ruling. The Supreme Court granted certiorari.

Issue: Is the use of a thermal-imaging device, aimed at a private home from a public street to detect relative amounts of heat within the home, a "search" within the meaning of the Fourth Amendment?

Decision: Yes. Judgment reversed; case remanded.

Opinion by Justice Scalia: "'At the very core' of the Fourth Amendment 'stands the right of a man to retreat into his own home and there to be free from unreasonable governmental intrusion.' ... With few exceptions, the question whether a warrantless search of a house is reasonable and hence constitutional must be answered no....

"On the other hand, the antecedent question of whether or not a Fourth Amendment 'search' has occurred is not so simple under our precedent[s]. The permissibility of ordinary visual surveillance of a home used to be clear because, well into the 20th century, our Fourth Amendment jurisprudence was tied to common-law trespass.... We have since decoupled violation of a person's Fourth Amendment rights from trespassory violation of his property....

"One might think that the new validating rationale would be that examining the portion of a house that is in plain public view, while it is a 'search' despite the absence of trespass, is not an 'unreasonable' one under the Fourth Amendment.... But in fact we have held that visual observation is no 'search' at all—perhaps in order to preserve somewhat more intact our doctrine that warrantless searches are presumptively unconstitutional.... We have subsequently ... [held] that a Fourth Amendment search does not occur—even when the explicitly protected location of a house is concerned—unless 'the individual manifested a subjective expectation of privacy in the object of the challenged search' and 'society [is] willing to recognize that expectation as reasonable.' ...

"It would be foolish to contend that the degree of privacy secured to citizens by the Fourth Amendment has been entirely unaffected by the advance of technology.... The question we confront today is what limits there are upon this power of technology to shrink the realm of guaranteed privacy....

"[I]n the case of the search of the interior of homes ... there is a ready criterion, with deep roots in the common law, of the minimal expectation of privacy that exists, and that is acknowledged to be reasonable. To withdraw protection of this minimum expectation would be to permit police technology to erode the privacy guaranteed by the Fourth Amendment. We think that obtaining by sense-enhancing technology any information regarding the interior of the home that could not otherwise have been obtained without physical 'intrusion into a constitutionally protected area' ... constitutes a search—at least where (as here) the technology in question is not in general public use. This assures preservation of that degree of privacy against government that existed when the Fourth Amendment was adopted. On the basis of this criterion, the information obtained by the thermal imager in this case was the product of a search....

"Since we hold the Thermovision imaging to have been an unlawful search, it will remain for the District Court to determine whether, without the evidence it provided, the search warrant issued in this case was supported by probable cause—and if not, whether there is any other basis for supporting admission of the evidence that the search pursuant to the warrant produced."

Dissent by Justice Stevens: "There is, in my judgment, a distinction of constitutional magnitude between 'through-the-wall surveillance' that gives the observer or listener direct access to information in a private area, on the one hand, and the thought processes used to draw inferences from information in the public domain, on the other hand. The Court has created a rule that purports to deal with direct observations of the inside of the home, but the case before us merely involves indirect deductions from 'off-the-wall' surveillance, that is, observations of the exterior of the home. Those observations were made with a fairly primitive thermal imager that gathered data exposed on the outside of petitioner's home but did not invade any constitutionally protected interest in privacy. Moreover, I believe that the supposedly 'bright-line' rule the Court has created in response to its concerns about future technological developments is unnecessary, unwise, and inconsistent with the Fourth Amendment. . . .

"To be sure, the homeowner has a reasonable expectation of privacy concerning what takes place within his home, and the Fourth Amendment's protection against physical invasions of the home should apply to their functional equivalent. But the equipment in this case did not penetrate the walls of petitioner's home, and while it did pick up 'details of the home' that were exposed to the public, . . . it did not obtain 'any information regarding the interior of the home.' . . . In the Court's own words, based on what the thermal imager 'showed' regarding the outside of petitioner's home, the officers 'concluded' that petitioner was engaging in illegal activity inside the home. . . . It would be quite absurd to characterize their thought processes as 'searches,' regardless of whether they inferred (rightly) that petitioner was growing marijuana in his house, or (wrongly) that 'the lady of the house [was taking] her daily sauna and bath.' . . .

"I respectfully dissent."

case against the defendant must be proved beyond a reasonable doubt, unlike a civil case where the plaintiff must simply prove the case by a preponderance of the evidence. This means that the jury must simply believe the plaintiff's story more than it believes the defendant's story. In a criminal case, the jury in most jurisdictions has only one thing to decide, and that is guilt or innocence. The jury's verdict must be unanimous. Punishment is normally decided by the judge or at a second deliberation of the jury. In civil cases, the jury not only decides whether the plaintiff gets a verdict or the defendant gets a verdict, it may also decide how much money the plaintiff will be awarded.

Privilege against Self-Incrimination

In a criminal case the person charged with a crime cannot be forced to testify against himself or herself. This, of course, is the **privilege against self-incrimination** that is provided by the Fifth Amendment of the U.S. Constitution. In an ordinary civil trial, a defendant may be required to testify or be found in civil contempt of court.

Right to Counsel

The Sixth Amendment to the U.S. Constitution provides that the accused in a criminal trial shall have the **right to counsel.** If the accused cannot afford an attorney, an attorney will be appointed for the accused by the court at the expense of the state. In most civil cases, no attorney is appointed for a defendant. The defendant must personally hire an attorney or act as his or her own counsel. Many metropolitan areas and many university towns now have legal aid societies that furnish free legal counsel to people who cannot afford the services of an attorney.

Right to a Miranda-Type Warning

The famous case of *Miranda v. Arizona*, 384 U.S. 436 (1966) initiated the so-called **Miranda-type warning** that now must be given to an accused at the time of arrest. Briefly, the accused must be told that he or she has the right to remain silent, that any statements made can be used in court by the prosecution, that he or she has the right to have an attorney present when being questioned, and that an attorney will be appointed by the court if the defendant cannot afford one.

Prohibition against Double Jeopardy

In criminal trials there is also the Fifth Amendment guarantee against **double jeopardy.** If a person charged with a crime has been found innocent, even though later evidence may prove that the person was in fact guilty of the crime, the person may not be tried again. The state may not appeal a verdict of not guilty. Once a person has been tried and found innocent, that is the end of the case. In a civil case, either party may appeal a decision.

Requirement of Mens Rea

In a criminal case, a person may not be found guilty of a crime unless the person had a mental intent to commit the crime. We often hear about the defense of temporary insanity

CASE 4

DAVIS V. U.S.

512 U.S. 452 (1994)

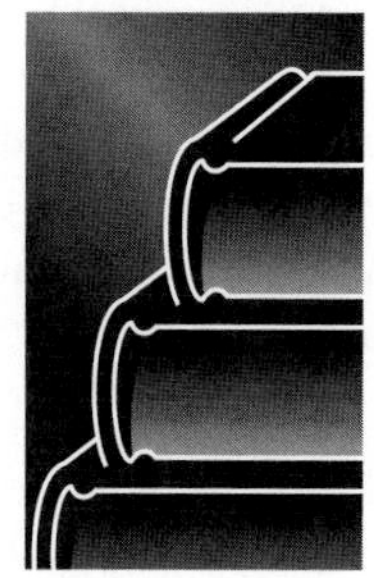

Facts: Pool brought trouble—not to River City, but to the Charleston Naval Base. Robert Davis, a member of the United States Navy, spent the evening of October 2, 1988, shooting pool at a club on the base. Another sailor, Keith Shackleford, lost a game and a $30 wager to Davis, but Shackleford refused to pay. After the club closed, Shackleford was beaten to death with a pool cue on a loading dock behind the commissary. The body was found early the next morning.

The investigation by the Naval Investigative Service (NIS) gradually focused on Davis. Investigative agents determined that he was at the club that evening and that he was absent without authorization from his duty station the next morning. The agents also learned that only privately owned pool cues could be removed from the club premises and that Davis owned two cues—one of which had a bloodstain on it. The agents were told by various people that petitioner either had admitted committing the crime or had recounted details that clearly indicated his involvement in the killing.

On November 4, 1988, Davis was interviewed at the NIS office. As required by military law, the agents advised petitioner that he was a suspect in the killing, that he was not required to make a statement, that any statement could be used against him at a trial by court-martial, and that he was entitled to speak with an attorney and have an attorney present during questioning. Davis waived his rights to remain silent and to counsel, both orally and in writing.

About an hour and a half into the interview, Davis said, "Maybe I should talk to a lawyer." According to the uncontradicted testimony of one of the interviewing agents, the interview than proceeded as follows:

> "*[We] made it very clear that we're not here to violate his rights, that if he wants a lawyer, then we will stop any kind of questioning with him, that we weren't going to pursue the matter unless we have it clarified is he asking for a lawyer or is he just making a comment about a lawyer, and he said, ['] No, I'm not asking for a lawyer,' and then he continued on, and said, 'No, I don't want a lawyer.'*"

After a short break, the agents reminded Davis of his rights to remain silent and to counsel. The interview then continued for another hour, until Davis said, "I think I want a lawyer before I say anything else." At that point, questioning ceased.

At his general court-martial, Davis moved to suppress statements made during the November 4 interview. The military judge denied the motion. Davis was convicted on one specification of unpremeditated murder. He was sentenced to confinement for life, dishonorable discharge, forfeiture of all pay and allowances, and a reduction in rank to the lowest pay grade. The convening authority approved the finding and sentence. The Navy-Marine Corps Court of Military Review affirmed. The United States Court of Military Appeals granted discretionary review and affirmed.

Issue: Was Davis' first statement a request for counsel?

Decision: No. Judgment affirmed.

Opinion by Justice O'Connor: "The applicability of the 'rigid' prophylactic rule of *Edwards* requires courts to 'determine whether the accused *actually invoked* his right to counsel.... ' To avoid difficulties of proof and to provide guidance to officers conducting interrogations, this is an objective inquiry.... Invocation of the *Miranda* right to counsel 'requires, at a minimum, some statement that can reasonably be construed to be an expression of a desire for the assistance of an attorney.... ' But if a suspect makes a reference to an attorney that is ambiguous or equivocal in that a reasonable officer in light of the circumstances would have understood only that the suspect *might* be invoking the right to counsel, our precedents do not require the cessation of questioning....

"Rather, the suspect must unambiguously request counsel. As we have observed, 'a statement either is such an assertion of the right to counsel or it is not.... ' Although a suspect need not 'speak with the discrimination of an Oxford don,' ... he must articulate his desire to have counsel present sufficiently clearly that a reasonable police officer in the circumstances would understand the statement to be a request for an attorney. If the statement fails to meet the requisite level of clarity, *Edwards* does not require that the officers stop questioning the suspect....

"We recognize that requiring a clear assertion of the right to counsel might disadvantage some suspects who—because of fear, intimidation, lack of linguistic skills, or a variety of other reasons—will not clearly articulate their right to counsel although they actually want to have a lawyer present. But the primary protection afforded suspects subject to custodial interrogation is the *Miranda* warnings themselves. '[F]ull comprehension of the rights to remain silent and request an attorney [is] sufficient to dispel whatever coercion is inherent in the interrogation process' ... A suspect who knowingly and voluntarily waives his right to counsel after having that right explained to him has indicated his willingness to deal with the police unassisted. Although *Edwards* provides an additional protection—if a suspect subsequently requests an attorney, questioning must cease—it is one that must be affirmatively invoked by the suspect.

"In considering how a suspect must invoke the right to counsel, we must consider the other side of the *Miranda* equation: the need for effective law enforcement. Although the courts ensure compliance with the *Miranda* requirements through the exclusionary rule, it is police officers who must actually decide whether or not they can question a suspect. The *Edwards* rule—questioning must cease if the suspect asks for a lawyer—provides a bright line that can be applied by officers in the real world of investigation and interrogation without unduly hampering the gathering of information. But if we were to require questioning to cease if a suspect makes a statement that might be a request for an attorney, this clarity and ease of application would be lost. Police officers would be forced to make difficult judgment calls about whether the suspect in fact wants a lawyer even though he hasn't said so, with the threat of suppression if they guess wrong. We therefore hold that, after a knowing and voluntary waiver of the *Miranda* rights, law enforcement officers may continue questioning until and unless the suspect clearly requests an attorney. . . .

"To recapitulate: We held in *Miranda* that a suspect is entitled to the assistance of counsel during custodial interrogation even though the Constitution does not provide for such assistance. We held in *Edwards* that if the suspect invokes the right to counsel at any time, the police must immediately cease questioning him until an attorney is present. But we are unwilling to create a third layer of prophylaxis to prevent police questioning when the suspect *might* want a lawyer. Unless the suspect actually requests an attorney, questioning may continue.

"The courts below found that petitioner's remark to the NIS agents—'Maybe I should talk to a lawyer'—was not a request for counsel, and we see no reason to disturb that conclusion. The NIS agents therefore were not required to stop questioning petitioner, though it was entirely proper for them to clarify whether petitioner in fact wanted a lawyer. Because there is no ground for suppression of petitioner's statements, the judgment of the Court of Military Appeals is Affirmed."

in criminal cases. If a person charged with the commission of a crime did not know what he or she was doing, then the person is not guilty of the crime because there was no mental intent to commit it. Some states have a doctrine called irresistible impulse. In those states, a person who can convince a jury he or she had an irresistible impulse to commit the criminal act is not guilty. The typical case here would be a husband or wife finding the spouse in bed with another person and striking or shooting them in a fit of rage.

A person who is intoxicated or under the influence of drugs may not be guilty of acts committed while in that condition. However, in such cases the question arises as to whether the person became intoxicated or fell under the influence of drugs voluntarily or involuntarily, and whether the person was incapable of having a mental intent. If the person became intoxicated or fell under the influence of drugs voluntarily and was still capable of a mental intent, then the majority of courts would find the person guilty. For example, Sam Soak went to a party, voluntarily imbibed too much liquor, got into his car to drive home, and while swerving down the street, hit and killed a pedestrian. Sam may very well be found guilty of manslaughter.

If the person who committed a crime was a child under the age of reason, then the child would not legally have sufficient **mens rea,** or mental intent, to be guilty of the crime. In most states, a child under 7 years of age is presumed to be incapable of the mental intent to commit a crime. Over the age of 7 years the individual child's capacity of mental intent becomes an open question. Here again, state laws differ.

Definiteness Requirement

To be constitutionally valid, a criminal statute must be definite enough to give the public fair warning of the types of conduct that are being subjected to criminal penalties. Even if all the required procedural steps have been followed, a criminal defendant can challenge the statute itself, as being too vague in defining just what is "illegal." The next case illustrates this point.

Stages in Criminal Cases

The procedure in a criminal trial differs considerably from the procedure in a civil trial, which we reviewed in Chapter 4.

In a civil case, the injured party simply chooses a lawyer and proceeds to file a civil lawsuit at his or her own expense. That party can control the lawsuit; that is, the injured party, the plaintiff, can settle the case out of court, pursue the case through trial, or dismiss the case entirely at any point during the proceedings. In a criminal case, the injured party simply reports the commission of a crime to the proper authority, and the state or national government takes over. The injured individual has no further control over the case.

CASE 5

CITY OF SUMNER V. WALSH

61 P.3d 1111 (WA 2003)

Facts: The city of Sumner, Washington adopted a juvenile curfew ordinance that made it unlawful for minors to be in public places during certain late night hours and for their parents to permit them to be there. Exceptions are made for minors who are going to or from work, adult-supervised events, or school-sponsored activities; who are engaged in interstate commerce; or who are on "errands" for their parents. Errands are not defined in the ordinance.

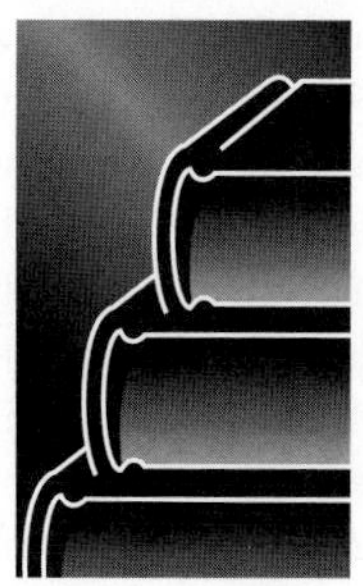

Justin Walsh, age 14, was stopped by police twice on July 25, 1999, at about 1:45 am and 2:30 am, and again on July 30, at about 2 am. Justin's father (Thomas Walsh), when contacted by the police, said that Justin was on errands. The police issued citations for ordinance violations for both days. The municipal court dismissed the charges against Justin because the court did not have jurisdiction to try juvenile cases, but it did fine Thomas Walsh $50 for each offense. On appeal, the superior court upheld the convictions. Thomas Walsh filed a further appeal with the court of appeals, and that court transferred the case to the state supreme court.

Issue: Is the statute clear enough to be understood and enforced fairly?

Decision: No. Judgment reversed.

Opinion by Chief Justice Alexander: "We must ... determine if ... Sumner's curfew ordinance 'is unconstitutional because it violates fundamental rights of juveniles and their parents, and is also void for vagueness.' ...

"The void-for-vagueness doctrine is rooted in principles of due process.... 'To avoid unconstitutional vagueness, an ordinance must (1) define the offense with sufficient definiteness that ordinary people can understand what conduct is prohibited; and (2) establish standards to permit police to enforce the law in a non-arbitrary, non-discriminatory manner.' ...

"Since the city has limited the meaning of the term 'remain' ... to 'linger or stay,' we must determine if the latter words are sufficiently precise so that ordinary people can understand what conduct is prohibited and police officers will know how to enforce the law in a nonarbitrary, nondiscriminatory manner.... These terms are not, in our judgment, sufficiently precise so that a person of ordinary intelligence is accorded fair notice of what conduct is prohibited. Neither do these terms provide sufficient guidance to officers endeavoring to determine if a juvenile's conduct is exempt from the ordinance....

"In sum, an ordinance which affords a police officer broad discretion to determine if a juvenile is in violation when tying his or her shoe or pumping gas does not withstand a vagueness challenge.

"Considering the discretion that police officers are accorded under the ordinance, one is left to wonder whether the practical effect of the ordinance is to simply make it unlawful for a juvenile to be present in a public place during curfew hours....

"[W]e believe that the term 'errand' is also vague in that it fails to provide sufficient notice of what conduct is prohibited or standards for police officers to enforce that conduct....

"Thus, we reverse Walsh's convictions for being in violation of the ordinance."

The first step in the procedure of a criminal case is the report of the crime and the investigation. If the investigators are unable to find evidence sufficient to prosecute, then no arrest is made. Many cases will fall into the unsolved category. If the investigation does produce evidence that would support prosecution of the case, then an arrest is made. At the time of the arrest, the arresting officer must inform the suspect of the rights in the *Miranda* warning. After having been arrested, the person will be booked. This process involves photographing and fingerprinting the subject and making up a record containing the subject's name, address, age, weight, height, and other pertinent information. The person now has a "police record."

The accused then is entitled to an appearance before a judge and will be informed that he or she has the right to have counsel present. At this hearing, the judge must determine whether the person shall be released on bail or without bail or returned to jail. If the person is to be released on bail, then the judge must set the amount. Bail must be paid or pledged to the court before the defendant is released, although in many minor cases the judge will release the person without bail.

The next step in the criminal process is to determine whether or not there is sufficient evidence to try the person for the crime charged. In serious crimes, a **grand jury** may be

Exhibit 6.1: Procedure in a Criminal Trial

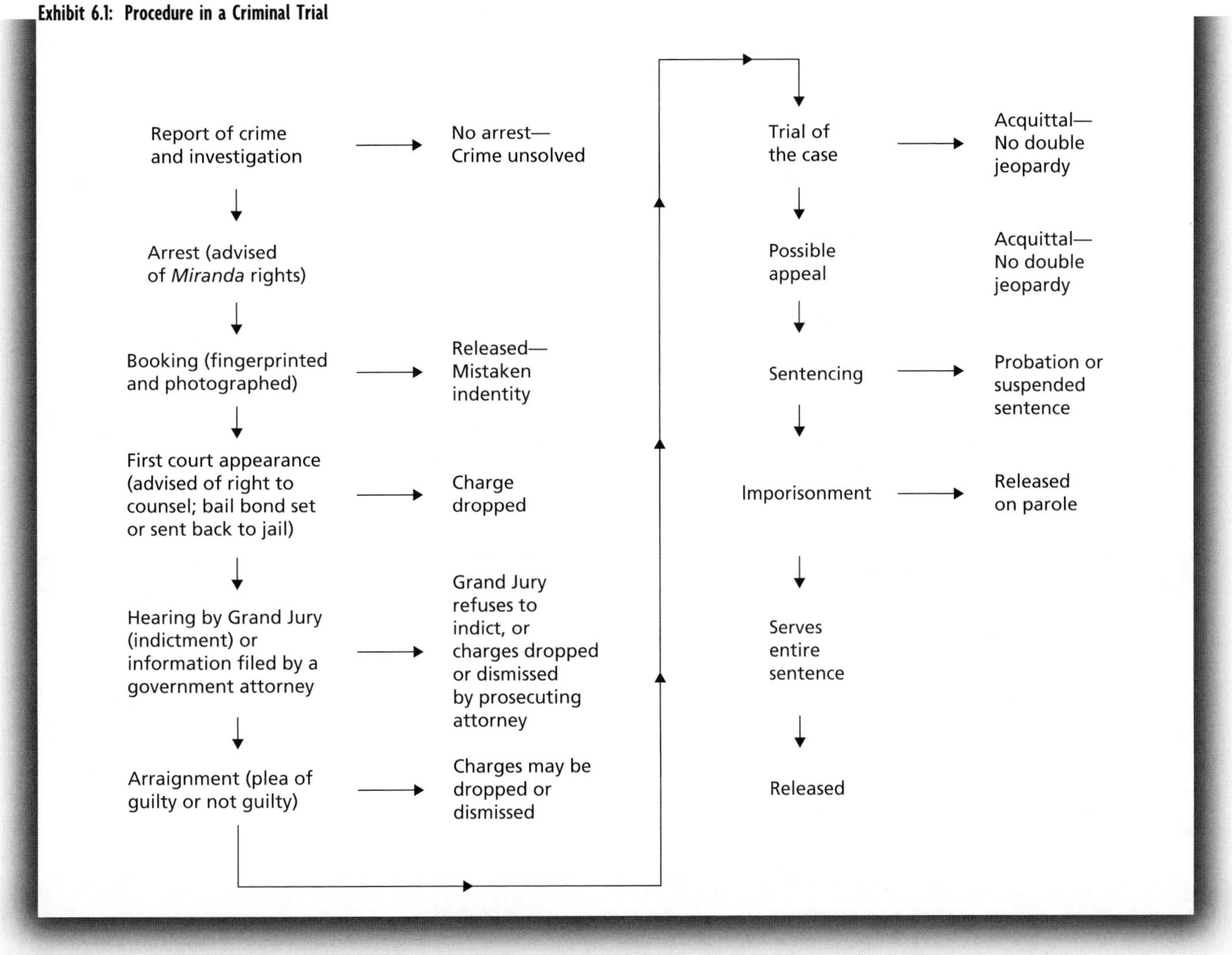

Step	Alternative outcome
Report of crime and investigation	No arrest— Crime unsolved
Arrest (advised of *Miranda* rights)	
Booking (fingerprinted and photographed)	Released— Mistaken indentity
First court appearance (advised of right to counsel; bail bond set or sent back to jail)	Charge dropped
Hearing by Grand Jury (indictment) or information filed by a government attorney	Grand Jury refuses to indict, or charges dropped or dismissed by prosecuting attorney
Arraignment (plea of guilty or not guilty)	Charges may be dropped or dismissed
Trial of the case	Acquittal— No double jeopardy
Possible appeal	Acquittal— No double jeopardy
Sentencing	Probation or suspended sentence
Imporisonment	Released on parole
Serves entire sentence	
Released	

impaneled to hear evidence to determine whether or not there is sufficient cause to proceed to a regular trial. If the grand jury finds sufficient evidence, it will issue an **indictment.** In other cases, the prosecuting attorney will file an **information,** or formal statement of the charges, which will allow the case to proceed to a regular trial.

At this stage of the proceeding the prosecutor must decide what crime the accused should be prosecuted for. Probably the prosecution and the defense will engage in the process called **plea bargaining**. A very typical example of plea bargaining would take place when a person was arrested for drunken driving—normally punishable by a fine, possible imprisonment, and suspension of driving privileges. If the blood alcohol test or the breath analyzer test was borderline or just slightly over the legal limit, the prosecuting attorney will often agree to reduce the charge to speeding or reckless driving, which are lesser offenses, if the accused will plead guilty. The prosecutor realizes that the case is not too strong and a conviction for a lesser offense is better than a possible "not guilty" verdict on the drunken driving charge.

The next step is the **arraignment** hearing. Here the accused party must plead to the charges—either not guilty or guilty. If the party pleads guilty, then, of course, the next step is **sentencing**. If, on the other hand, the party pleads not guilty, a trial must be scheduled. The accused person has a right to a jury trial and a right to a speedy trial. After the trial the party is either acquitted and released, or, if the jury found the party guilty, there is the possibility of appeal. The appellate court may affirm the conviction, or it may reverse and order a retrial. If the appellate procedure has been exhausted and the party has not been acquitted or released, then the party is sentenced to a jail term and/or fine. At this point the judge may decide to put the person on **probation,** to suspend the sentence, or to send the person to jail. If the person goes to jail, he or she can be paroled within a stated period of time or serve out the entire sentence before being released to go back into society.

Although increases in the crime rate are often blamed on weak judges and a weak criminal law system, a system can to be only as good as the people who operate it. We must remember that under our system of law, a person charged with a crime is presumed innocent until proven guilty beyond a reasonable doubt. In most of the cases that go to trial, the crucial decision of guilty or not guilty is made, not by the judge, but by a jury of people selected at random from the community.

Significance of This Chapter

The study of criminal law was not traditionally a subject of concern for the businessperson. However, with the increase in the volume and types of white-collar crimes, businesspeople need to be aware of situations that invite prosecution under criminal law. This chapter reviews the various types of business-related crime and the steps and requirements of criminal procedure.

IMPORTANT TERMS AND CONCEPTS

arraignment
commercial bribery
crime
double jeopardy
embezzlement
felonies
grand jury
indictment
information
mens rea
Miranda-type warning
misdemeanors
plea bargaining
presumption of innocence
privilege against self-incrimination
probation
right to counsel
sentencing
Sixth Amendment
trial by jury
white-collar crimes

QUESTIONS AND PROBLEMS FOR DISCUSSION

1. How can a business manager prevent being held criminally liable for company actions? Discuss.

2. What is the Miranda-type warning? To whom is this warning given and when?

3. Should we continue to allow plea bargaining in the criminal justice system? What are the pros and cons of this process?

4. What is the purpose of the grand jury hearing?

5. Winans was co-author of a *Wall Street Journal* investment advice column, which, because of its perceived quality and integrity, had an impact on the market prices of the stocks it discussed. Although he was familiar with the *Journal's* rule that the column's contents were the *Journal's* confidential information prior to publication, Winans entered into a scheme with petitioner Felis and another stockbroker who, in exchange for advance information from Winans as to the timing and contents of the column, bought and sold stocks based on the column's probable impact on the market and shared their profits with Winans. On the basis of this scheme, Winans and Felis were convicted of violations of the federal securities laws and of the federal mail and wire fraud statutes, which prohibit the use of the mails or of electronic transmissions to execute "any scheme or artifice to defraud, or for obtaining money or property by means of false or fraudulent pretenses, representations, or promises." David Carpenter, Winans' roommate, was convicted for aiding and abetting the scheme. The Court of Appeals affirmed. Carpenter and Winans asked for Supreme Court review.

   Do the national criminal statutes against mail and wire fraud apply to an employee's misappropriation of business information?

6. Sheppard was arrested, tried, and convicted of murdering his wife. The trial was held in the common pleas court of Cuyahoga County, Ohio. Sheppard's conviction was affirmed by the Supreme Court of Ohio. Sheppard filed a petition for habeas corpus in U.S. District Court against the prison warden, seeking release from custody. His contention was that he was denied a fair trial because the trial judge failed to protect him from inherently prejudicial publicity that saturated the community and also because the judge allowed extensive newspaper, radio, and television coverage of his trial in the courtroom itself. The District Court ruled in favor of the petition for habeas corpus; the U.S. Court of Appeals reversed; and the Supreme Court of the United States granted certiorari.

   How should the Supreme Court rule, and why?

7. Mr. Park was the president of Acme Markets Inc., a large retail food chain, with 12 warehouses, 874 stores, and 36,000 employees. The Food and Drug Administration (FDA) advised the company and its president of unsanitary conditions in its warehouses and requested that the conditions be cleaned up. Some cleanup was done, but the warehouses still did not meet minimum standards. The U.S. government then filed a criminal action against both the company and Park for the continued violation. The company pleaded guilty, and Park pleaded not guilty. He did not feel personally responsible for the failure of other employees in the company. The trial court still found him guilty. The appeals court reversed, and the U.S. Supreme Court granted certiorari.

    Is Park guilty of a crime? Explain.

8. Nicholas Katsafanas and Edward Plevel worked out a scheme to enrich themselves by the means of the computer-run state lottery. They first decided that the winning number combination (always one with three numerals) for the draw of April 24, would consist of only the numerals 4 and 6. There are eight possible three digit number combinations using only 4 or 6.

    They purchased lottery tickets for all the possible number combinations from retail ticket vendors at various locations. The rigging, or "fix," took place in the studio of WTAE in Pittsburgh, Allegheny County, by means of placing counterfeit balls in the machines used in the drawing. When the winning number combination, 666, was drawn, Plevel telephoned Michael Keyser, an administrative officer in the Lottery Bureau in Harrisburg, Dauphin County. Keyser programmed 666 into the computer, and the conspirators or their agents subsequently cashed in their winning tickets.

    Katsafanas and Plevel were convicted of conspiracy, theft by deception, criminal mischief, rigging a publicly exhibited contest, and perjury. They moved for a new trial. Defendants claim that they were erroneously brought to trial in Dauphin County (the locus of the computer) because none of the manipulation of the lottery equipment used to select the winning numbers took place in Dauphin County. The trial judge denied their motion and they appealed.

    Have they been tried in the wrong place? Explain.

9. National Student Marketing Corporation ("Marketing") was formed in 1966. It charged fees to businesses for marketing their products and services directly to students in an "attractive package" of merchandise. Marketing's stock went public in 1968 at $6 a share; 5 months later it was selling at $80 a share.

    Peat, Marwick, Mitchell & Co. (PMM) became Marketing's auditors in August 1968. Anthony Natelli was the engagement partner for the account and the manager of PMM's office in Washington, D.C. Joseph Scansaroli was the audit supervisor for the account.

    Many of Marketing's fee arrangements were only oral commitments. Using their estimates of the completion of its services on the accounts, the CPAs made a 1968 year-end adjustment for "unbilled accounts receivable" of $1.7 million and turned a loss into a profit twice that of the previous year. About $1 million of the oral commitments were written off by May 1969. Marketing's 1968 income thereby went down more than $200,000 but Scansaroli and Natelli covered this by "reversing" a deferred tax credit for about the same amount. The financial statements that were filed with a proxy statement proposing a merger with six other firms did not show any adjustment in Marketing's profit figure for 1968. A $12 million commitment from Pontiac (GM) was backdated so as to be included in the period through May 31, 1969. When Natelli questioned this practice, he was told that there was a commitment from Eastern Airlines for a similar amount that could be included, so he let it pass. The financial statements did not show that Marketing had written off $1 million of its 1968 sales and more than $2 million of the unbilled sales for 1968 and 1969. Marketing should have showed no profit for 1969, but instead, the financial statement prepared by Natelli and Scansaroli and filed with a proxy statement that was relied upon by other companies in a proposed merger showed tremendous profits and was in fact false and misleading. Natelli and Scansaroli were criminally prosecuted under Section 32(a) of the 1934 Securities Exchange Act for willfully and knowingly making false and misleading statements in a corporation's proxy statement. Both were convicted in U.S. District Court, which imposed a 1-year sentence and a $10,000 fine on Natelli, suspending all but 60 days of imprisonment, and a 1-year sentence and a $2,500 fine on Scansaroli suspending all but 10 days of the imprisonment. Both appealed.

    Should their convictions be affirmed? Why or why not?

CHAPTER 7

Tort Law and Professionals' Liability

Chapter Objectives

This chapter will:

- Define *tort.*
- Explain the four general categories of torts.
- Discuss what types of acts or omissions constitute negligence.
- Review possible defenses against a tort lawsuit.
- Introduce the theory of strict liability.
- Explain workers' compensation laws and the no-fault system of automobile tort compensation.
- Define *professional negligence.*
- Discuss the states' disagreements on the scope of an accountant's duty.
- Discuss certified public accountant liability under the Securities Acts.

Although business managers may face legal problems resulting from crimes, they are also fair game for a civil lawsuit. Customers may sue for injuries received if they slip or fall on the premises; they may sue for injuries resulting from defective products. Competitors may sue for alleged slander or libel, and this list could go on and on. We live in a litigious society, and if we are to survive, we must know our rights as well as our duties regarding potential lawsuits. This chapter discusses the various types of torts and the defenses that may be raised against various claims.

Definition and Classifications

A **tort** is a civil wrong committed when one individual, having a legal duty not to invade the legal rights of another individual, breaches that legal duty, causing damage to the person, property, or reputation of that other individual. The person whose rights have been invaded and who has suffered damage may then bring action in a civil court to recover monetary damages suffered because of the invasion of rights. These rights and duties may be derived from statutory or common law. When we speak of an individual, we mean a legal individual, such as a corporation, or a natural individual, a human being.

A tort may also be a crime. For example, a drunken driver runs a red light and hits your car in the intersection. You have a cause of action in tort against that person for your property damage and personal injury. The drunken driver may also be prosecuted criminally for driving a motor vehicle under the influence of intoxicating beverages. Most nonintentional torts, however, are not crimes.

Also, a tortious civil wrong must be distinguished from a contractual civil wrong, in which the rights and duties arise out of a specific contractual agreement. In a tort, the rights and duties are imposed by general laws that apply to others under similar circumstances, such as traffic laws and general laws of negligence.

Torts can be classified into four general categories. First, there are **intentional torts.** These are wrongs that the wrongdoers intended to commit. Second, there are **negligent torts.** These are wrongs that the wrongdoers did not mean to commit. They simply failed to act as ordinary, prudent, reasonable persons would have acted under similar circumstances. For example, in the typical automobile accident, the driver of the automobile does not mean to strike another automobile and damage it or to damage his or her own automobile. He or she was simply not careful and was not acting as a reasonable and prudent person. Third, there are **strict liability torts.** This classification comprises situations in which the law finds that the person or persons committing the torts are "strictly liable," meaning that there is no need for the plaintiff to prove negligence on the part of the defendant. The defendant is simply liable, as a matter of law, for the harmful results caused. The fourth major tort category is **vicarious liability**—one person is held liable for the torts of another, based on some relationship between them, such as employer/employee or principal/agent.

Intentional Torts

An intentional tort is an intentional breach of one's legal duty to another person that invades that person's rights and causes physical or mental damage to that person or damage to that person's reputation or property.

Intentional torts can be subdivided into three categories: torts against the physical person, torts against the reputation of the person, and torts against the property of the person. Following are some of the common torts against the physical person.

Torts against the Physical Person

Assault. An assault is an intentional act by one person that causes another person to be in immediate apprehension for his or her safety. Apprehension does not necessarily mean fear because fear is a very subjective term. Some people may be in apprehension for their safety without actually being frightened, whereas other people may be frightened without justifiable cause. Courts have held that mere words are not sufficient to prove a case of assault, even if the words are provoking or insulting. Also, threats of future injury are not the basis for assault. To prove a case of assault, it must be shown that the defendant committed a specific act or acts that put the plaintiff in apprehension for his or her immediate safety, not simply future safety. Although the tort of assault is classified as an intentional tort, it is not necessary to prove that the defendant actually intended to harm the plaintiff. It is sufficient to show that a reasonable person under the circumstances would have been in apprehension for his or her safety. Assault can also be a crime as well as a tort. For example, using a gun to commit the assault would be the crime of assault with a deadly weapon.

Battery. Battery is the intentional contact or touching of another person without that person's permission and without legal justification. The contact or touching must cause injury. It is not necessary that there be a specific intent to cause harm. Nor is it necessary that the contact be directly with the person. For example, the tort of battery is committed if one person puts in motion an object that strikes another person, say, by shooting a gun or throwing a knife, or if one person strikes another person with an object in hand.

In battery cases, it is important to know that you "take the plaintiff as you find him or her." This means that you are responsible for the results of your actions even though you could not have foreseen the final result. For example, there was a case where a person struck another person on the head with an umbrella. Normally this would have resulted in a minor lump on the head, but the victim had a metal plate in his head and the blow dislodged the metal plate, forcing it into the brain, killing the victim.

Not all touching or contact is considered battery. For example, people are often bumped, pushed, and jostled when they walk through the crowded aisles of department stores or walk out of crowded sports stadiums. Here there is physical contact and touching by other people that may cause discomfort and that may be offensive. From a legal standpoint, however, these are not considered batteries because there is an implied consent to such "touching."

Technical Battery. When we defined the tort of battery, we stated that it was the intentional contact or touching of another person without that person's permission. A technical battery occurs when the person gives consent to physical contact of one sort and then a different kind of contact occurs or the terms of the consent are exceeded. Damages may be claimed under this theory against a surgeon who performs "extra" surgical procedures while the patient is under anesthesia. In the absence of some sort of emergency, the surgeon's act is tortious and the patient could recover damages. This is a very different kind of liability than that in a malpractice action, in which the claim is that the physician did not perform the agreed treatment or procedure in accordance with reasonable professional standards.

Intentional Infliction of Mental Distress. Courts in the various states are now recognizing the intentional infliction of emotional or mental distress as a tort, without the necessity of showing either physical injury or a threat of physical contact, such as one would find in the torts of assault and battery. The tort of intentional infliction of emotional or mental distress is an entirely separate tort from the torts of assault and battery. This tort may be defined as an act or the use of words by a person with the intent of causing another person to experience anxiety, fright, terror, or some other form of emotional and mental distress.

Historically, the courts have discouraged and denied claims for emotional and mental distress unless the person had also suffered some accompanying physical injury. They thought that allowing claims for mental or emotional distress would encourage fictitious claims. Physical injury can be verified by X-ray and visual appearance. Emotional and mental distress is a very subjective claim, and until recently such injuries often could not be objectively verified. However, advances in medical science have given us more accurate methods of measuring and verifying such injuries.

The courts are still concerned about the potential for misuse of this particular tort. Generally, courts have held that to have recovery, it must be shown that the mental distress or disturbance is real and not simply an annoyance or hurt feelings or something of that nature. Actual mental injury must be shown. The courts also require that before one can recover for this tort, it must be shown that the conduct of the defendant has been outrageous in character and generally of a type that is intolerable in a civilized community.

False Imprisonment. **False imprisonment** can be defined as the intentional detention of a person without that person's permission. It is not necessary that there be actual physical detention. However, the courts have required that the detained person be detained by at least a threat of force, either expressed or implied. Also, the detention must be for more than a reasonable amount of time.

False Arrest. False arrest is similar to false imprisonment in that it is the intentional detention of an individual without that person's permission. In the case of false arrest, the detention is imposed under an asserted legal authority. If, in fact, the person making the arrest does not have proper legal authority to do so, then we would have the tort of false arrest. In the case of false arrest, as in the case of false imprisonment, it is not necessary that the person detaining the suspect use force. For example, a person dressed in a police uniform with a badge indicating authority states to you: "You are under arrest. I am taking you to the police station." Most people would go along peacefully rather than resist arrest. If, in fact, there was no reasonable ground, no probable cause, to believe that you had committed a specific crime, then you were wrongfully deprived of your freedom, and you would have an action for false arrest and false imprisonment.

Torts against the Reputation of the Person

Next we come to intentional torts that injure the person's reputation. These are often called **defamation** of character.

Libel and Slander. Libel and slander are both torts involving intentional defamation of character by the tort-feasor. **Libel** is defamation of character that can be read or seen, and **slander** is defamation of character that can be heard. In both libel and slander cases, it must be proven that a defamatory statement or defamatory material was published. In the case of libel, this means that the defamatory material was published in a book, magazine, or newspaper or in the form of a movie, pictures, a statue, or some other physical form whereby the material was seen by a person or persons other than the person about whom the material was published. If you write a personal letter to an individual and make defamatory statements about the individual in that letter, this does not constitute publication because no one other than the individual to whom you are writing is intended to see the letter. In the case of slander, publication means that the statement was heard by someone other than the person about whom the defamatory statement was made. Thus, the simple test in slander and libel cases is: Did anyone other than the subject of the defamatory statement or material hear, read, or see the statement or material? If no third person heard, read, or saw the statement or material, then there is no slander or libel. If a third party did hear the defamatory statement or read or see the defamatory material, then we have a potential lawsuit for defamation of character.

The next issue is the truth of the defamatory statement or material. Generally speaking, truth is a defense to slander or libel. The exception is a situation in which the party publishing the defamatory statement or material is doing so with a malicious intent to injure the other party. This is called a technical tort. An example of this would be the publication of the fact that a person now well established in society committed a crime while a teenager. Let us say that as a teenager the person stole an automobile and took it for a joyride, was arrested and convicted, and paid his or her debt to society. Then, some years later, after the person had established a good reputation in society, someone found out about this skeleton in the closet and published the information with the sole purpose of maligning the person's character. Here, even though the statement is true, it was obviously made for malicious purposes, and thus there would be a right of action for this defamation of character.

There are also cases in which defamatory statements may be either absolutely **privileged** or **conditionally privileged.** Lawyers and judges may not be sued for slander for the statements made by them during the trial of a lawsuit. Also, if a member of Congress makes a defamatory statement on the floor of Congress, the legislator may not be held liable for the statement. There is also a different standard with regard to slander and libel when the statement is made about a public official or a public figure, rather than a private individual.

The amount of the verdict in slander and libel cases is often a matter of concern. For example, the famous movie and television comedian Carol Burnett was libeled by an article published in the *National Enquirer*. She brought a suit for libel against the *National Enquirer* in California Superior Court and the jury awarded a verdict of $300,000 for general damages and $1,300,000 for punitive damages. Although Burnett suffered emotional distress, she admitted she never had to have psychiatric treatment or counseling. Also, she suffered no lost income due to the libelous statements. The trial judge, responding to a motion for judgment notwithstanding the verdict, reduced the general damages to $50,000, and the California State Court of Appeals reduced the punitive damages to $150,000. There really is not any formula for damages in slander and libel cases. The slander and libel victim typically will not have medical bills or lost wages claims, such as a person who was injured in an automobile accident might have. Also, it is usually impossible to calculate in a dollar amount the damage caused to the victim's reputation. Thus, each case is going to have to be judged on its own set of facts.

Invasion of Privacy. The area of individual privacy has been very highly publicized in recent years, and several state and national statutes have been passed concerning the individual's right to privacy. These new laws are primarily concerned with the **invasion of privacy** by the computer with regard to credit records and bank records that contain sensitive information about individuals. New statutes also protect employment records and school records.

In addition to the current concern about invasion of privacy by the computer and various electronic data processing procedures, there has been a concern about many more traditional invasions of the individual's privacy. One of the most common of these invasions of privacy is eavesdropping by wiretapping or other electronic devices. Such eavesdropping is a national crime as well as a tort, and it is prohibited except in the rare cases in which it has been authorized by national statutory law. Another invasion of privacy is the use of a person's photograph under objectionable circumstances. Simply turning the television camera and taking pictures of the people in the bleachers at a baseball game is not an invasion of privacy. However, if someone takes an embarrassing picture of you and uses it without your permission, you may have an action for invasion of privacy.

As with libel and slander, we again have a conflict with the constitutional protection of freedom of speech and freedom of the press. Thus, if you are involved in a matter of public interest, your rights of privacy are affected accordingly. For example, if you are involved in an automobile accident, newspaper photographers may be snapping photographs of you at the scene of the accident; or if you are arrested, the TV cameras may be directed toward you. Here you are news; thus your right of privacy must be secondary to the freedom of the press to publish the news. For similar reasons, a public figure does not have the same right of privacy as an ordinary citizen.

The *John Doe/Tony Twist* case illustrates some of these points.

Torts against the Person's Property

Trespass to Real Property. The general rule of law with regard to **trespass** to real property is that the owner of real property has the right not only to exclusive possession of a specific piece of ground and the buildings and other things on that ground, but also to exclusive possession of the airspace above the ground and the area below the ground. The old common law rule was that the owner of the land owned all of the airspace above the land and the area below the land all the way to the middle of the earth. This rule had to be modified when we started to use airspace for airplane travel. Now the landowner still owns the airspace above the land, subject, however, to the right of airplanes to fly through that airspace. With regard to the space below the land, the possessor of the land surface also possesses the soil and space below the surface to the extent that he or she can effectively use that soil or space, either now or in the future. When we talk about space below the land, we are talking about the ownership of the oil, gas, coal, water, and other valuable minerals and resources that may be present under the surface.

To have the tort of trespass to your land, it is not necessary that there be actual damage to your land. In all of the other torts previously mentioned, damage had to be proven

CASE 1

JOHN DOE AKA TONY TWIST V. TCI CABLEVISION

110 S.W.3d 363 (MO 2003)

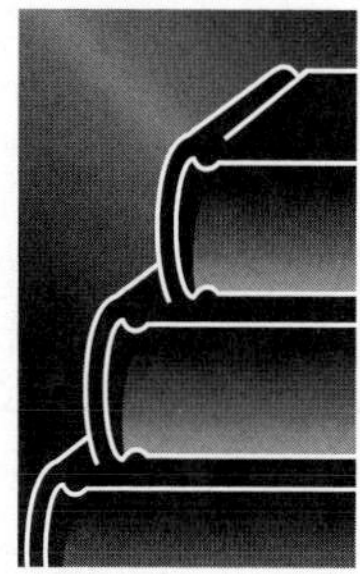

Facts: Tony Twist played in the National Hockey League from 1988 to 1999 for the St. Louis Blues and the Quebec Nordiques. His main role was as an on-ice "enforcer," protecting his team from excessive physical contact by opponents and physically punishing them. He was very popular with the fans, especially in St. Louis. He hosted a TV talk show, endorsed products, and was involved with children's charities.

In 1992, Todd McFarlane created the comic book *Spawn*, described as "a dark and surreal fantasy," whose lead character has made a pact with the devil and commits violent and sexual acts on the devil's behalf. In 1993, a very nasty Mafia don, Anthony "Tony Twist" Twistelli, was added to the story line. The magazine indicated that the "don" was based on the real Tony Twist, and *Spawn* fans asked Twist and his mother for autographs. *Spawn's* publishers targeted hockey fans, and Twist lost at least one product endorsement as a result of this name association. Twist sued for misappropriation of name, and the jury awarded $24,500,000. The trial judge gave defendants a judgment not withstanding the jury verdict (JNOV), or alternatively, an order for a new trial. Twist appealed.

Issue: Did defendants violate Twist's "right of publicity"?

Decision: Yes. JNOV is reversed, and a new trial is ordered.

Opinion by Judge Limbaugh: "The tort of misappropriation of name is one of four recognized torts falling under the general heading of invasion of privacy.... The interest protected by the misappropriation of name tort 'is the interest of the individual in the exclusive use of his own identity, in so far as it is represented by his name or likeness, and in so far as the use may be of benefit to him or others.' ... Recently, development of the misappropriation of name tort has given rise to a separate yet similar tort termed the 'right of publicity,' which is said to 'protect a person from losing the benefit of their [sic] work in creating a publicly recognizable persona.' ... Though facially similar, the protections afforded by each tort are slightly different: 'the [misappropriation of name] tort protects against intrusion upon an individual's private self-esteem and dignity, while the right of publicity protects against commercial loss caused by appropriation of an individual's [identity] for commercial exploitation.' ... ('In contrast to the [misappropriation of name tort], the right of publicity is not intended to protect the person's feelings....')

"Because the two torts differ in the type of protection that each seeks to provide, there are corresponding differences between the types of damages that may be recovered. In a misappropriation of name action, a plaintiff may recover damages not only for pecuniary loss, but also for mental or emotional distress and suffering.... By contrast, in a right of publicity action, 'the measure of damages properly focuses on the pecuniary loss to the plaintiff or the unjust pecuniary gain to the defendant.' ...

"Here, all parties agree that the 'Tony Twist' character is not 'about' him, in that the character does not physically resemble Twist nor does the Spawn story line attempt to track Twist's real life....

"[T]he grant of JNOV was based on the commercial advantage element of the cause of action....

"Twist contends, and this Court agrees, that the evidence admitted at trial was sufficient to establish [defendants'] intent to gain a commercial advantage by using Twist's name to attract consumer attention to Spawn comic books and related products.... At a minimum, [defendants'] statements and actions reveal their intent to create the impression that Twist was somehow associated with the Spawn comic book, and this alone is sufficient to establish the commercial advantage element in a right of publicity action....

"Having determined that Twist made a submissible case at trial, we next address whether the right of publicity claim is nevertheless prohibited by the First Amendment. Courts throughout the country have struggled with this issue.... Of course, not all speech is protected under the First Amendment, and in cases like this, courts often will weigh the state's interest in protecting a plaintiff's property right to the commercial value of his or her name and identity against the defendant's right to free speech....

"'If a product is being sold that predominantly exploits the commercial value of an individual's identity, that product should be held to violate the right of publicity and not be protected by the First Amendment, even if there is some "expressive" content in it that might qualify as "speech" in other circumstances. If, on the other hand, the predominant purpose of the product is to make an expressive comment on or about a celebrity, the expressive values could be given greater weight.' ...

"For the foregoing reasons, the circuit court's judgment notwithstanding the verdict is reversed, the judgment granting a new trial is affirmed, the judgment denying injunctive relief is affirmed, and the case is remanded."

before a recovery could be made. In the tort of trespass to land, you can sue the trespasser even though there was no actual damage and the court will award nominal damages, perhaps $1 and costs.

Trespass to Personal Property. This tort allows the owner of personal property to bring an action against a person or persons who interfere with his or her exclusive possession of an item of personal property. Unlike the plaintiff in a case involving trespass to real property, the plaintiff in a case involving trespass to personal property must show and prove monetary damage to get a verdict against the trespasser.

Conversion. The tort of **conversion** is the unlawful taking and use of personal property owned by another person. In other words, it is the conversion of another person's property to your own use. This sounds like theft. However, you will recall that to have theft, one has to have a mens rea, or mental intent, to steal. In the tort of conversion, the person converting the property to his or her own use does not necessarily have the intent to steal. The person may feel that he or she has the right to use the property. A good example of conversion would be a case where the branches of your neighbor's apple tree hang over the lot line so that the apples are over your property. You honestly feel that you have a right to these apples; after all, they are over your property in your airspace. After you pick the apples, your neighbor tells you that the apples belong to him and that you should give them to him. If you fail to give your neighbor the apples, you are guilty of the tort of conversion. The apples and the branches that hung over the lot line are in effect trespassing on your airspace; however, you do not have the right of ownership to them. You may, however, cut off the branches at the lot line and put them on your neighbor's land. You cannot keep them.

Deceit-Fraud. The tort of **deceit,** also called fraud, involves a situation where one or more parties, fraudulently and with the intent to deceive, misrepresent certain facts, either through oral or written statement or through an artifice or device of some type, and another party relies on the misrepresentation and is damaged. Fraud in connection with the making of a contract is discussed more fully in Chapter 11.

Abuse of Civil Process. This tort involves an intentional use of the civil legal process for a purpose that is wrongful and for which the process was not designed. A person may bring a civil action against you simply to harass you and cause you the expense of defending the lawsuit, when in fact the person has no legitimate claim against you. You may sue him or her for damages as a result of this wrongful use of the civil process.

Malicious Prosecution. The tort of malicious prosecution is similar to the tort of abuse of civil process. However, it involves the criminal process. An example would be a case in which the police and the court system take action against you because a person has maliciously and without probable cause sworn out a criminal complaint against you. You can sue that person for malicious prosecution and recover damages.

Interference with Economic Relations. This tort concerns your right to conduct your business free from malicious and intentional interference that might destroy the business. The free enterprise system is based on the competitive marketplace. However, competition must be kept within reasonable bounds. It is certainly permissible for one business to lower its price in an effort to competitively secure a market advantage. However, when a person or a business intentionally uses economic resources to injure another person or business for reasons other than the legal reasons for competition, the tort of **interference with economic relations** has been committed.

The tort of interference with economic relations also encompasses interference with contractual relations. If Johnny Rich, a nightclub owner, induces a famous entertainer to breach a contract with another nightclub to come to work for him, the employer who had a contract with the entertainer can sue Johnny Rich for interference with his contractual relations.

Negligent Torts

Each person in society is bound to take reasonable care not to injure the person, the reputation, or the property of those persons likely to be affected by his or her behavior. Any act or omission in breach of that duty that causes damage to others may cause a person to be liable for damages to the person or persons affected by that act or omission. In the negligent tort case, the question is not, as it was with the intentional tort, whether the person intended to cause the injury or damage. The question is simply, did the person act in a negligent manner?

To win a **negligence** case, the plaintiff must prove (1) the existence of a duty of care owed by defendant; (2) breach of that duty by defendant; (3) causation of plaintiff's injuries by defendant's breach; and (4) damages to plaintiff.

The *Remsburg* case focuses on the existence of a duty.

CASE 2

Remsburg v. Montgomery

831 A.2d 18 (MD 2003)

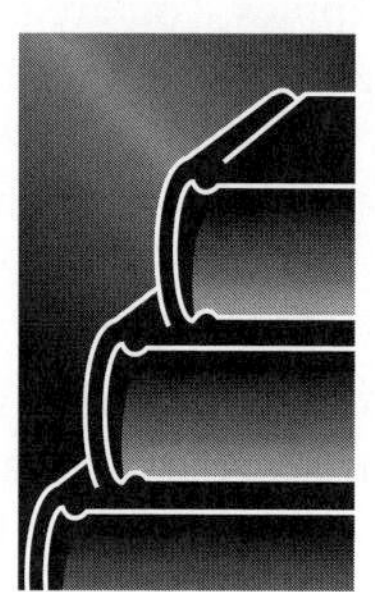

Facts: While deer hunting on November 28, 1999, James Remsburg Jr. accidentally shot Charles and Brian Montgomery.

The Remsburg hunting party had been organized by James Jr.'s father, James Sr. James Sr. had paid the Mongomerys for several years for permission to hunt on their land, but had not made any specific arrangements for the 1999 season. All the members of the Remsburg party were on adjoining land, except for James Jr., who was in a tree stand that he had built several years before on Montgomery property. Charles Montgomery and his son Brian were hunting on their land, but their presence was not known by the Remsburg group. Although he was an experienced hunter (27 years old), James Jr. did not properly identify his target before he fired his shotgun. The slug grazed Brian's neck, severed an artery in Charles' right arm, and lodged in Charles' torso. The Montgomerys sued both Remsburgs, but settled their claim against James Jr. James Sr. moved for summary judgment, which was granted by the trial court. The court of special appeals agreed that there was no claim against James Sr. for trespass but held that he might be liable under a negligence theory. James Remsburg Sr. appealed.

Issue: As organizer of the hunting party, did Remsburg Sr. owe a duty of care to third parties?

Decision: No. Judgment reversed, as to possible negligence.

Opinion by Judge Harrell: "[This] case ... presents a matter of first impression in this Court. The essential question is whether ... a hunter who organizes a hunting party may be held liable for injuries caused to others as a result of the negligent acts of another member of his or her hunting party....

"As first established in Maryland nearly a century ago: 'there can be no negligence where there is no duty that is due; for negligence is the breach of some duty that one person owes to another.' ... Thus, our analysis of a negligence cause of action usually begins with the question of whether a legally cognizable duty existed....

"In determining the existence of a duty, we consider, among other things: 'the foreseeability of harm to the plaintiff, the degree of certainty that the plaintiff suffered the injury, the closeness of the connection between the defendant's conduct and the injury suffered, the moral blame attached to the defendant's conduct, the policy of preventing future harm, the extent of the burden to the defendant and consequences to the community of imposing a duty to exercise care with resulting liability for breach, and the availability, cost and prevalence of insurance for the risk involved.' ... While foreseeability is often considered among the most important of these factors, its existence alone does not suffice to establish a duty under Maryland law.... '[T]here is no general duty to control a third person's conduct so as to prevent personal harm to another, unless a "special relationship" exists either between the actor and the third person or between the actor and the person injured.' ...

"[S]uch a 'special duty' to protect another from the acts of a third party may be established '(1) by statute or rule; (2) by contractual or other private relationship; or (3) indirectly or impliedly by virtue of the relationship between the tortfeasor and a third party.' ...

"We first examine whether Maryland statutes or regulations regarding hunting create a duty in tort upon Remsburg Sr. to protect the Montgomerys....

"Absent from these statutes and regulations is any specific mention of a duty placed upon a leader of a hunting party, by virtue of his or her position as such, to protect all other hunters or landowners from the negligent acts of members of his or her hunting party....

"It is undisputed that no contract existed between Remsburg Sr. and Remsburg Jr. The Montgomerys repeatedly deny that any contractual agreement existed between Remsburg Sr. and Charles Montgomery that would include the land where the accident occurred. . . .

"[T]he creation of a 'special duty' by virtue of a 'special relationship' between the parties can be established by either (1) the inherent nature of the relationship between the parties; or (2) by one party undertaking to protect or assist the other party, and thus inducing reliance upon the conduct of the acting party. We conclude that the Montgomerys did not establish a triable issue as to the existence of a special relationship by either of these methods. . . .

"We conclude that Remsburg Sr. did not owe a duty to the Montgomerys to protect them from the negligent acts of Remsburg Jr. . . .

"Without a duty there can be no actionable negligence and, as such, the trial court's grant of summary judgment in favor of Remsburg Sr. was proper."

Reasonable Care. The standard used to determine the absence or presence of negligence is a very simple one. The standard is, simply, did the person act in a manner similar to that in which a reasonable and prudent person would have acted under the same or similar circumstances? Would the reasonable and prudent person have foreseen the dangers of his or her action, and was the damage or injury proximately caused by the action or the failure to act of the individual being charged with the tort? The question then arises: Who is this reasonable and prudent person? The reasonable and prudent person is an imaginary person, and when deciding a case involving a negligent tort, jurors are instructed not to use themselves as examples of the reasonable and prudent person. The jurors must determine not what they individually would have done in the same or a similar situation but what that imaginary person called the reasonable and prudent person would have done. Obviously, this standard is not very precise, and it is certainly subject to great variations. The standard, however, has operated very successfully over the years because it does take into consideration changes in technology and changes in societal mores that the jury will impute to the reasonable and prudent person. Also, it would be impossible to have a specific statutory code that would cover every possible act or omission that could be considered negligent. Thus, negligence continues to be decided on a case-by-case basis.

Proximate Cause. A person may commit a negligent act or may negligently fail to act under certain circumstances. However, that person will not be liable to any person who is damaged or injured as a result of such act or omission unless it can be shown that the damage or injury was proximately caused by the negligent act or omission. For a negligent act or omission to be a **proximate cause** of damage or injury, it must be a cause that in a natural and continuous sequence, unbroken by any intervening cause, produced the injury, and it must be a cause without which the injury would not have occurred. An example would be a motorist who was driving at a high rate of speed, hit a chuckhole, lost control of the vehicle, struck a water hydrant, breaking off the hydrant and causing the street to flood and water to flow into the basement of a house near the hydrant. The driver would be liable not only for the damage to the water hydrant, but also for the damage to the house because that damage was proximately caused by the driver's negligence.

If, while the street was flooded, a city bus came down the street and stopped and let off an elderly lady who stepped into the water and slipped, fell, and broke her hip, would the driver of the vehicle that struck the water hydrant be responsible for her injuries? Were her injuries proximately caused by his negligence? The answer would be no. The lady was not injured as a result of a natural and continuous chain of events commencing with the motorist's negligent driving. There was an intervening cause—the negligence of the bus driver entering a dangerously flooded area and the negligence of the elderly lady stepping off the bus into the flooded street.

There are situations in which the actions or omissions of more than one person are a proximate cause of damage or injury to a person or property. If two cars collide in an intersection and one of the cars strikes a legally parked car, it may be found that the negligence of both of the drivers in the collision proximately caused the damage to the parked car. Thus, it is not necessary that any one act or omission be the sole proximate cause of damage or injury.

Foreseeability. For a defendant to be liable to a plaintiff for a tortious act or omission to act, not only must the act or omission be a proximate cause of the damage or injury, but the ultimate damage or injury must also be foreseeable by the reasonable and prudent person.

The jury must be instructed by the trial judge to find each of these essential parts of the plaintiff's case, if there is to be a verdict for the plaintiff.

Strict Liability

Strict liability is liability without fault. In a strict liability case, the defendant will be liable for injuries caused by his or her actions, even though the defendant was not negligent in any way and the defendant did not intentionally injure the plaintiff. This concept of liability without fault is comparatively new in our legal system. The traditional theories of tort involve intentional wrongful acts, negligent acts, or omissions in which the person did not intend to injure the other party wrongfully, but through his or her carelessness or negligence the other party was injured and thus should have a right to recover. In developing the theory of no-fault or liability without fault, the courts and the legislatures are not really looking at right or wrong, but at who can best bear the cost of the loss. In other words, if you are going to engage in certain types of activities, then you must realize that persons might be injured by your activities even though you do nothing legally wrong and do not intend to hurt anyone. When you enter into certain activities you must simply be prepared to pay for the consequences of your actions, regardless of any legal fault on your part.

Whether strict liability should be applied to Pyrodyne is the issue in the next case.

CASE 3

Klein v. Pyrodyne Corp.

810 P.2d 917 (WA 1991)

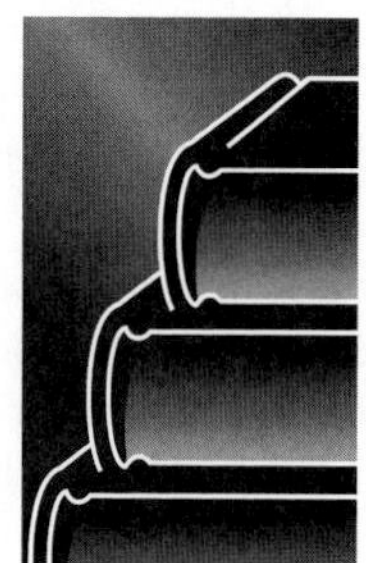

Facts: Defendant Pyrodyne Corporation (Pyrodyne) is a general contractor for aerial fireworks at public fireworks displays. Pyrodyne contracted to procure fireworks, to provide pyrotechnic operators, and to display the fireworks at the Western Washington State Fairgrounds in Puyallup, Washington on July 4, 1987. All operators of the fireworks display were Pyrodyne employees acting within the scope of their employment duties.

During the fireworks display, one of the 5-inch mortars was knocked into a horizontal position. From this position a rocket inside was ignited and discharged. The rocket flew 500 feet in a trajectory parallel to the earth and exploded near the crowd of onlookers. Plaintiffs Danny and Marion Klein were injured by the explosion. Mr. Klein's clothing was set on fire, and he suffered facial burns and serious injury to his eyes.

The Kleins brought suit against Pyrodyne under theories of products liability and strict liability. Pyrodyne filed a motion for summary judgment, which the trial court granted as to the products liability claim. The trial court denied Pyrodyne's summary judgment motion regarding the Kleins' strict liability claim, holding that Pyrodyne was strictly liable without fault and ordering summary judgment in favor of the Kleins on the issue of liability. Pyrodyne appealed.

Issue: Is the operator of a fireworks display subject to strict liability?

Decision: Yes. Judgment affirmed.

Opinion by Justice Guy: "The modern doctrine of strict liability for abnormally dangerous activities derives from . . . *Rylands v. Fletcher*, 3 L.R.-H.L. 330, [1868] All E.R. 1, 12, in which the defendant's reservoir flooded mine shafts on the plaintiff's adjoining land. *Rylands v. Fletcher* has come to stand for the rule that 'the defendant will be liable when he damages another by a thing or activity unduly dangerous and inappropriate to the place where it is maintained in the light of the character of that place and its surroundings. . . .'

"The basic principle of *Rylands v. Fletcher* has been accepted by the Restatement (Second) of Torts (1977). . . . Section 519 of the Restatement provides that any party carrying on an 'abnormally dangerous activity' is strictly liable for ensuing damages. The test for what constitutes such an activity is stated in Section 520 of the Restatement. Both Restatement sections have been adopted by this court, and determination of whether an activity is an 'abnormally dangerous activity' is a question of law. . . .

"Section 520 of the Restatement lists six factors that are to be considered in determining whether an activity is 'abnormally dangerous.' The factors are as follows:

(a) existence of a high degree of risk of some harm to the person, land, or chattels of others.

(b) likelihood that the harm that results from it will be great.

(c) inability to eliminate the risk by the exercise of reasonable care.

(d) extent to which the activity is not a matter of common usage.

(e) inappropriateness of the activity to the place where it is carried on.

(f) extent to which its value to the community is outweighed by its dangerous attributes.. . .

"The comments to Section 520 explain how these factors should be evaluated:

> *Any one of them is not necessarily sufficient of itself in a particular case, and ordinarily several of them will be required for strict liability. On the other hand, it is not necessary that each of them be present, especially if others weigh heavily. Because of the interplay of these various factors, it is not possible to reduce abnormally dangerous activities to any definition. The essential question is whether the risk created is so unusual, either because of its magnitude or because of the circumstances surrounding it, as to justify the imposition of strict liability for the harm that results from it, even though it is carried on with all reasonable care.. . .*

"We find that the factors stated in clauses (a), (b), and (c) are all present in the case of fireworks displays. Any time a person ignites rockets with the intention of sending them aloft to explode in the presence of large crowds of people, a high risk of serious personal injury or property damage is created. That risk arises because of the possibility that a rocket will malfunction or be misdirected. Furthermore, no matter how much care pyrotechnicians exercise, they cannot entirely eliminate the high risk inherent in setting off powerful explosives such as fireworks near crowds. . . .

"In sum, we find that setting off public fireworks displays satisfies four of the six conditions under the Restatement test; that is, it is an activity that is not 'of common usage' and that presents an ineliminably high risk of serious bodily injury or property damage. We therefore hold that conducting public fireworks displays is an abnormally dangerous activity justifying the imposition of strict liability. . . .

"Pyrodyne argues that even if there is strict liability for fireworks, its liability under the facts of this case is cut off by the manufacturer's negligence, the existence of which we assume for purposes of evaluating the propriety of the trial court's summary judgment. According to Pyrodyne, a rocket detonated without leaving the mortar box because it was negligently manufactured. This detonation, Pyrodyne asserts, was what caused the misfire of the second rocket, which in turn resulted in the Kleins' injuries. Pyrodyne reasons that the manufacturer's negligence acted as an intervening or outside force that cuts off Pyrodyne's liability. . . .

"In the present case, negligence on the part of the fireworks manufacturer is readily foreseeable in relation to the extraordinary risk created by conducting a public fireworks display. Therefore, even if such negligence may properly be regarded as an intervening cause, an issue we need not decide, it cannot function to relieve Pyrodyne from liability. This is not to say, however, that in a proper case a defendant in a strict liability action could not pursue a claim against a third party and enforce a right of contribution to an extent proportionate to that party's fault.

"We hold that Pyrodyne Corporation is strictly liable for all damages suffered as a result of the July 1987 fireworks display. Detonating fireworks displays constitutes an abnormally dangerous activity warranting strict liability. Public policy also supports this conclusion. Furthermore, RCW 70.77.285 mandates the payment of all damages caused by fireworks displays, regardless of whether those damages were due to the pyrotechnicians' negligence. This establishes the standard of strict liability for pyrotechnicians. Therefore, we affirm the decision of the trial court."

Strict liability has been imposed on owners or possessors of wild animals. If you keep a wild animal on your premises, you are going to be strictly liable for any damages that the animal does to other people or to the property of other persons. The owner or possessor of hard-hooved animals, such as cattle, horses, and donkeys, may also be held strictly liable for injuries caused by those animals. The owner or possessor of a dog or a cat would not normally be liable unless he or she knows the animal to be dangerous. The common law rule was that a dog is entitled to its first bite. This, of course, meant that until the dog has bitten someone it is not known to be dangerous. This would be true with regard to a small dog. However, if a person kept a large Doberman that was constantly growling and baring its teeth at anyone who came near to it, obviously this dog appears to have dangerous propensities, and its owner would be strictly liable for any injury or damage caused by it.

Strict liability has also been imposed on persons who are responsible for activities, the production of products, or conditions on their property that are unreasonably dangerous and that might cause injury to other persons. An example would be a construction contractor blasting out stumps or blasting hard rock in excavating for a building. If the blasting caused structural damage to nearby buildings or homes or if personal property within the buildings or homes were damaged by the concussion of the explosions, then the contractor would be strictly liable.

A third area of strict liability involves products liability. Traditionally, we had the theory of *caveat emptor*, which meant "let the buyer beware." The theory was that the buyer had a duty to inspect the goods when delivered, and unless there was intentional fraud or deceit, the buyer was simply stuck with them if defects later appeared. This area of law has changed radically over the past 40 years. Product liability is discussed in depth in Chapter 18.

Vicarious Liability

One person may be liable for the torts of another on the basis of some relationship between them. This doctrine provides that the boss will pay. You might also call this the "deep pocket" doctrine. Under the doctrine of ***respondeat superior***, a principal may be liable for the tortious acts of an agent, provided the agent was acting in the scope of employment for the principal. Also, in the case of a simple employer-employee relationship, if the employee is acting in the scope of employment (i.e., doing the employer's job) and commits a negligent or intentional act, then the employer will be liable under the doctrine of respondeat superior. It is important to note here that the employee is still liable for his or her own actions. In other words, both employee and employer or both agent and principal could be liable in tort. This rule is discussed further in the chapter on agency.

Family members are not usually liable for each other's torts. One spouse generally cannot be held liable for the other's wrongful conduct. Parents may be held liable for the torts of their children if the parent entrusts the child with a dangerous mechanism or fails to properly supervise a child known to be violent. A parent is also liable for directing or sanctioning a child's wrong and for torts committed while the child is acting as the parent's agent. Some states have special statutes on this point.

States disagree on the liability of social hosts for injuries caused by their guests, as seen in the *Reeder* case.

CASE 4

Reeder v. Daniel

61 S.W.3d 359 (TX 2001)

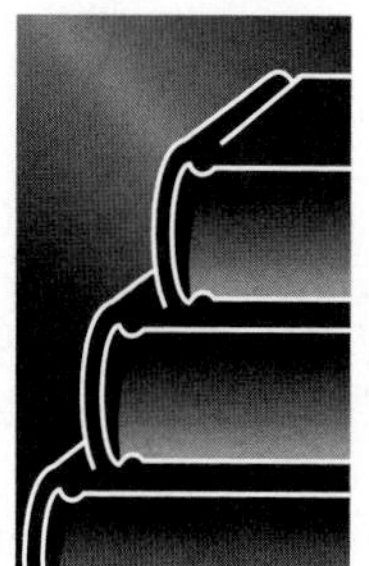

Facts: Seventeen-year-old Jeff Lawson struck and injured Andrew Daniel after drinking "at least 12" beers at a party hosted by Tyler Reeder, the teenage son of Tom and Pam Reeder. Tom and Pam were out of town. There is no evidence that Tyler himself bought any alcohol, but Lawson admitted that he and another underage friend bought several cases of beer and brought them to the Reeder home. Tyler did help to load the beer into the refrigerator and several coolers. Daniel came to the party uninvited and apparently had an ongoing feud with Lawson. Daniel ignored Tyler's request that he leave, and Lawson then struck Daniel.

Daniel sued Lawson, Tyler Reeder, and Tom and Pam Reeder. Daniel settled his claim against Lawson. The trial court granted summary judgment in favor of all three Reeders, but the court of appeals held that Tyler Reeder could be held liable if a jury found that he had "made alcohol available" to a minor. Tyler Reeder appealed.

Issue: Can an injured third party recover against a social host for injuries sustained as a result of the host's serving of alcoholic beverages?

Decision: No. Judgment of the court of appeals is reversed; summary judgment for defendant (Tyler Reeder) is reinstated.

Opinion by Justice Enoch: "Negligence per se is a common-law doctrine that allows courts to rely on a penal statute to define a reasonably prudent person's standard of care. Here, Daniel asserts that Tyler's conduct was negligent per se because it violated ... section 106.06 ... , which makes it a criminal offense to make alcohol available to persons under twenty-one. But it is well established that criminal statutes do not always represent a standard for civil liability.... In determining whether a penal statute provides the basis for a civil cause of action, we must consider whether recognizing such an accompanying civil action would be inconsistent with legislative intent.

"In *Smith v. Merritt*, we held that, by enacting ... section 106.06, prohibiting making alcohol available to minors, the Legislature did not intend to provide for a negligence per se action against social hosts for serving alcohol to persons age eighteen to twenty.... At that time, we did not reach the question of whether a per se cause of action may exist for making alcohol available to persons under eighteen.

"Daniel now urges us to recognize such a cause of action. He asserts that the Dram Shop Act's exclusivity provision applies only to persons aged eighteen and older. . . .

"We disagree with Daniel's position. As we stated in Smith, the Legislature divided the Alcoholic Beverage Code into separate criminal and civil liability sections. The criminal statute at issue here, Section 106.06, appears in Title 4, entitled 'Regulatory and Penal Provisions. . . .' By contrast, the Dram Shop Act, establishing civil liability for serving alcohol, appears in Title I, 'General Provisions,' under Chapter 2, 'Civil Liabilities for Serving Beverages.' Thus, the Legislature established a bifurcated criminal and civil liability scheme.

"Moreover, in enacting the Dram Shop Act, the Legislature specifically considered and rejected providing for a civil cause of action against social hosts. The bill's earlier versions created civil causes of action against both commercial providers and social hosts. But the legislative conference committee eventually deleted social host liability from the bill's final version, imposing liability only on commercial providers.

"As well, we note that courts in other jurisdictions have been reluctant to recognize a social-host cause of action when the state legislature has been active in regulating alcoholic beverages. During the 1980s, in response to growing concerns over drunk driving, several jurisdictions recognized civil causes of action against alcohol providers for violating a criminal statute by serving alcohol to minors. But more recently other courts have been hesitant to recognize civil liability for social hosts when there is no statute specifically authorizing such liability. . . .

"Similarly, the Texas Legislature's enactments in this area caution us against recognizing a new common-law cause of action against social hosts. . . . Not only do the Legislature's actions demonstrate an intent to treat criminal liability separately from civil liability and an intent to treat commercial providers differently from social hosts, but the Legislature has been especially active in this area. . . .

"Accordingly, we will not disturb the Legislature's regulatory scheme by judicially recognizing a cause of action against social hosts who 'make alcohol available' to guests under age eighteen."

Other Theories of Liability for Tort

Res Ipsa Loquitur

The term ***res ipsa loquitur*** means "the thing speaks for itself." The plaintiff normally has the burden of proving that the defendant failed to act in a reasonable and prudent manner, that the accident was foreseeable, and that the damage or injury was a proximate cause of the defendant's action. Normally the plaintiff has available various types of evidence, such as skid marks and eyewitnesses.

In some cases, it is obvious that the accident would not have happened had it not been for negligence on the part of the defendant, but the plaintiff does not have access to information that would verify or prove such negligence. An example would be a situation in which a person was a passenger in an airplane and the airplane struck a mountain. The plane was demolished, and all its occupants died. In this case, the next of kin of the passengers will bring suit for the wrongful deaths. However, a plaintiff here lacks access to the physical evidence needed to prove this case. We know that airplanes normally do not run into mountains and that someone's negligence probably caused the accident. The cause may have been a malfunction or a breakdown in the aircraft itself; it may have been a manufacturing defect; or it may have been a failure on the part of the airline to properly service and inspect. It may also have been pilot error or error on the part of air traffic control. In such cases, the plaintiff pleads the theory of *res ipsa loquitur*, and the burden is shifted to the defendant to prove that they were not negligent.

Last Clear Chance Doctrine

Simply stated, the **last clear chance doctrine** provides that the liable party is the party who had the last clear chance to avoid damage or injury to the other party. This doctrine imposes a duty upon one party to exercise care in avoiding injury to another party who has negligently placed himself or herself in a situation of danger. For example, suppose that a motorist on a very cold day started up his or her automobile, drove up to an intersection while the motor was still cold, and proceeded to pull out into the intersection. The motor died, causing the car to stall crosswise in the intersection. Cars approaching the stalled vehicle would then have a duty to exercise reasonable care to try to avoid injury to the driver who had negligently placed himself or herself in a position of peril. Thus, if an oncoming motorist could swerve to the right or the left and go around this stalled car or could stop before hitting it, then the driver would have a duty to do so.

Liability of Owners and Occupiers of Land

Land owners and occupiers may be liable in tort under one or more of the aforementioned theories for injuries sustained by persons on the premises and by persons off the premises.

Liability to Persons Off the Premises

Torts that arise from the unreasonable or unlawful use by a person of his or her own property in such a manner as to interfere with the rights of other property owners, with resulting damage, are called **nuisance** torts.

Nuisance torts may be classified as private or public. An example of a private nuisance situation would be one in which your neighbor is an amateur inventor who produces various offensive odors and smoke that make it unpleasant for you to go outside your house. Another example would be a situation in which your neighbor has a dog that howls all night. The test with regard to a nuisance case is whether the interference with your enjoyment of your property is substantial and unreasonable and whether that interference would be offensive or inconvenient to a reasonable or prudent person. The victim may sue for money damages, an injunction, or both remedies together.

A public nuisance can be defined as the doing of something or the failure to do something as a result of which the safety, health, or morals of the public are injuriously affected. Public nuisances may be criminal as well as civil. Examples of public nuisances are the storing of explosives on a person's premises, allowing people to smoke marijuana on the premises, and nearly any other use of the premises that could adversely affect the safety, health, or morals of the community. The shooting of fireworks in the streets is also a public nuisance. Many public nuisances may also be private nuisances. A public nuisance is an offense against the state, and as such it is subject to criminal prosecution if it is a specifically criminal act, and it may be subject to abatement by governmental order. If the public nuisance also injures private parties, those private parties may have their own actions separate from the government because private parties are concerned with damages for their own injuries.

Liability to Persons on the Premises

As to liability for injuries to persons on the premises, most courts impose varying standards of care on the landowner based on the legal status of the injured person.

Employees. The employer owes each employee a duty to provide a reasonably safe place in which to work. Modern statutes have substantially changed the legal rules pertaining to this duty.

Historically, if an employee was injured on the job, the employees could sue the employer for medical bills incurred and for lost wages. However, the employer had three defenses: assumption of risk, contributory negligence, and the fellow servant rule. Thus, if the employee knew the machine being operated was faulty, continued to operate it, and was injured, the employer would not be liable. Also, if the employee removed a safety guard to clean out scrap, and then forgot to replace it, and the employee was injured, the employer could defend under the doctrine of contributory negligence. If a fellow employee negligently bumped another employee, causing the first employee to fall against a machine and be injured, the employer again could successfully defend the action. The net result of the use of the traditional tort system for claims for work-related injuries to employees was that most employees simply could not collect from the employer due to these defenses, and the cost of litigation often exceeded the claimed damages. Thus, the system of no-fault compensation for employees' injuries in the course of employment was developed. Every state now has a **workers' compensation** statute. Essentially these statutes provide that if an employee is killed or injured on the job, or becomes ill or disabled due to an occupational disease, the employer or its insurance carrier will have to pay all reasonable medical bills and a percentage of the lost wages during the period of disability. A settlement, or periodic payments, will be made if the employee suffered some permanent disability, such as the loss of an eye or the loss of a percentage of function of an arm or leg. Death benefits are payable to the deceased employee's dependents.

The key concept in workers' compensation is that it is no-fault. The employee may have negligently left the safety guard off the machine or continued to operate a machine the employee knew to be faulty, but the employee will still collect all the statutory benefits if the employee is accidentally injured.

If the employee intentionally and knowingly injures himself or herself then, normally, no benefits will be awarded.

Invitees. A similarly high duty of care is owed to business invitees—customers, clients, suppliers, and others who come onto the property with the owner's permission and for the owner's benefit. The storekeeper owes those customers a duty to provide a reasonably safe place in which to shop. The essence of this duty is based on negligence—would a reasonable store owner have been aware of the dangerous condition that caused the injury? There is thus a duty to the customer to take reasonable steps to inspect and to maintain the store or office to which customers are invited.

Licensees. A lesser duty of care is owed to persons who are on the premises with permission, but without providing any financial benefit to the landowner. Your social guests fall into this category. Your only duty to the guest is to warn of *known* dangers. If your guest is injured by a condition of which you were not aware, you are not liable. You do not, in other words, owe the guest a reasonably safe place in which to socialize. Of course you would be liable for any other negligence that caused injury to the guest, such as the careless handling of kerosene near an open barbecue grill.

Trespassers. The landowner's only duty toward trespassers is a negative one—not to *intentionally* cause them injury. These persons are on the property without the owner's permission, so the owner clearly owes them no affirmative duty of care. "I was hurt on your property while I was committing a tort against you, so you are liable to me!"—such a rule would seem to violate all standards of common sense and justice. One does occasionally read about decisions that seem to violate common sense and that award damages to trespassers. Some of them may be based on the landowner's having in effect intentionally injured the trespasser by setting traps or digging holes. Some of them may just be due to overly sympathetic judges.

In recent years, several states have passed statutes that grant landowners the right to use deadly force to repel intruders, even if there is no immediate threat to one's own life. The danger here is obvious: People who come to the wrong door by mistake or who are lost or otherwise seeking help, may be shot by a too-quick-on-the-trigger property owner.

There is a very different rule in most states for trespassing children—the theory of **attractive nuisance.** For example, if an old refrigerator and an old junk car are sitting on your premises, these are called attractive nuisances because they simply invite young children to come over and climb around on them. If these children are injured, you are strictly liable for injuries to them, even though you did not intentionally do anything wrong and, in fact, the children were trespassing on your property.

Other Tort Rules

Defenses to Negligent Torts

There are three basic defenses to negligent torts. They are: (1) contributory negligence, or comparative negligence, depending on the rule of law adopted by the particular state; (2) assumption of risk; and (3) act of God.

Contributory negligence on the part of the plaintiff is a complete bar to recovery by the plaintiff in a state that has adopted the contributory negligence doctrine. A simple example of contributory negligence would be a situation in which Mr. Leadfoot was northbound on a through highway at a speed of 75 miles per hour in a 30-mile-per-hour zone. Ms. Badsight was driving without her glasses, which she was required to wear when driving, and not seeing a stop sign, drove into the intersection into the side of Mr. Leadfoot's car. Obviously, Ms. Badsight was negligent for driving without prescription glasses and for failing to stop at the stop sign. Also, her negligence was a proximate cause of the accident because it directly contributed to the accident. On the other hand, Mr. Leadfoot was contributorily negligent because he was driving in excess of the speed limit and his speed was a contributing factor to the collision. Thus, in a contributory negligence state, neither one will recover from the other.

Historically, the great majority of the states followed the contributory negligence doctrine. If the plaintiff was guilty of negligence, no matter how slight, the plaintiff could recover nothing from the defendant. This admittedly was a very harsh rule, but it was accepted by the majority of states. In recent years, there has been a trend toward the doctrine of **comparative negligence,** also referred to as comparative fault. The justification of this doctrine is that it is not as harsh as the contributory negligence doctrine because we are not going to penalize a plaintiff and refuse to allow any recovery whatsoever simply because the plaintiff was, in the estimation of the jury, slightly negligent. Today nearly 80 percent of the states have some form of comparative fault law. Briefly, under a typical comparative fault law, a plaintiff will be entitled to recover against a defendant if the plaintiff's comparative fault is not greater than the comparative fault of the defendant or the combination of defendants. Thus, if the plaintiff's fault exceeds 50 percent, then the plaintiff will not recover at all. However, if the plaintiff's comparative fault is less than 50 percent, the plaintiff's recovery will be reduced by the percentage of the plaintiff's fault. Let's take a situation in which the plaintiff's damages are $100,000, the defendant's comparative fault is 50 percent, and the plaintiff's comparative fault is 50 percent. Under the old contributory negligence doctrine, the plaintiff could recover nothing. Under the comparative fault doctrine, the plaintiff would still recover $50,000, which would be 50 percent of the plaintiff's damages. If, however, the jury found that the plaintiff's comparative fault was in excess of 50 percent (i.e., 51% or 52%), the plaintiff would recover nothing. The problem, of course, is how do you determine the percentage of fault of each party? This is a question that has to be resolved in a case-by-case basis by the jury or by the judge if the case is being tried without a jury.

The defense of assumption of risk may be a complete defense to a plaintiff's negligent tort action. When a person is aware of the danger in a situation, yet continues to expose himself or herself to that danger and is then injured, that person cannot complain of the defendant's negligence.

The third defense is the defense of act of God. If lightning strikes a large tree in your yard, causing the tree to fall on and crush your neighbor's car, you would not be liable because the proximate cause of the damage was a so-called act of God. Similarly, if a tornado swept your tree into your neighbor's house, you would not be liable. If, however, you had a dead tree in your backyard that you intended to cut down because the tree was rotten and dangerous, and one day a strong wind toppled the tree onto your neighbor's car, then you would not be able to use the defense of act of God because you were aware of the condition of the tree and also should have been aware of the possibility that a windstorm would cause the tree to fall and do damage to others.

Immunity from Tort Action

Certain people, organizations, and governmental bodies have traditionally been immune from tort liability under certain circumstances.

At common law, a husband could not sue his wife and a wife could not sue her husband for personal torts. The theory of courts was that such litigation would destroy family unity. Also, traditionally, a child could not sue either parent. These common law intrafamily immunities are gradually being eroded because the reason for **immunity** is no longer as strong as it used to be. Today, we generally believe that injured parties should be able to sue wrongdoers, whoever they may be. In most cases, the spouse or the child is not actually suing the other spouse or the parent, but in effect is going after insurance proceeds. The spouse or the parent is a defendant in name only.

Charitable organizations traditionally were immune to tort liability. The theory was that to impose tort liability on the funds of the charitable organization would cripple its good work and would discourage donations to the organization. This immunity is also being eroded or completely eliminated in many states. Here again, the original reasons for the immunity are no longer valid. A charitable organization today can buy liability insurance, and the cost of this insurance can be part of its regular budget. Thus, the organization needs no more protection than any other business, and it should be liable for injury caused to innocent persons. An example would be the charitable hospital. A person negligently injured when a patient in a charitable hospital certainly should have the same rights of recovery in tort against the charitable hospital as he or she would have had if the injury had occurred in a profit-making hospital. In either case, the injury to the patient is the same, and the fault is the same.

The third traditional immunity is called **sovereign immunity;** simply stated, this means that the government may not be sued for its torts. The government can be defined as the U.S. government, state governments, municipal or county governments, or any governmental subdivision. The national government enacted the U.S. Tort Claims Act in 1946. This act established certain conditions for lawsuits and claims against the national government. Many states have also passed tort claims acts or other legislative acts, limiting the sovereign immunity of the state, cities, and other governmental units. Some states, however, have established dollar limits on claims that can be recovered from them. The general trend in sovereign immunity is toward its elimination. Here again, the state, city, or other governmental subdivision can purchase liability insurance and thus budget the cost on an annual basis.

No-Fault System of Automobile Tort Compensation

Traditionally, the negligent party whose negligence proximately caused injury to another person or to another person's property would be found liable in tort and would have judgment entered against him or her, provided the defendant did not have a valid defense, such as contributory negligence, assumption of risk, or act of God.

As indicated earlier in this chapter, the defense of contributory negligence as a complete defense was found to be harsh and unfair and unjust in many cases. The doctrine of comparative negligence has now replaced the traditional contributory negligence doctrine in most states.

This fault system works satisfactorily in the majority of tort cases. However, there is one specific class of tort claims—automobile accident cases—in which certain states by legislative enactment have replaced the fault system with a no-fault system of compensation. The proponents of the automobile no-fault system argue that it will cut insurance rates because it will save litigation expenses, such as attorney fees and court costs. The theory of a **no-fault auto insurance** system is simple. Each automobile owner-driver carries his or her own insurance. If that person has an accident, his or her own insurance company pays the doctor bills, lost wages, and car repair bills. The system sounds good: no attorney fees, no court costs. But what about pain and suffering or permanent impairment? A professional basketball player earning $500,000 per year is involved in an automobile accident and has to have his right arm amputated. What kind of settlement is he entitled to? Compare the basketball player's case to a case in which a schoolteacher is involved in a similar accident and had his right arm amputated. Should both men get the same amount because they both lost a right arm?

Critics of the no-fault system argue that no-fault statutes take away the injured person's day in court, the right to a trial by jury. To overcome this criticism, most no-fault laws allow claimants to sue in court if their injuries are serious or their damages exceed a certain dollar amount.

No-fault systems can reduce court congestion and can be an effective method for promptly resolving minor automobile property damage and nonserious injury claims.

Common Law Liability of Sellers of Services

Contract Law

The professional, whether an accountant, attorney, physician, or other professional, may be liable to the client for breach of contract if the professional fails to perform the contract with the client. An accountant or other professional sells services to clients. If the professional fails to perform the services as agreed, then the professional will be liable to the client under the theory of breach of contract. The client will be entitled to money damages sufficient to compensate the client for the out-of-pocket damages the client suffered as a result of the breach of contract by the professional. An example would be a situation in which the client had contracted with an accountant to furnish a financial statement to the client's bank by a certain date because the client had a loan commitment and guaranteed interest rate up to that date, which the accountant was aware of. If the accountant failed to deliver the financial report to the bank within the required time period, and as a result of the accountant's failure, the client's loan was turned down or the interest rate went up, then the client could sue the accountant for breach of contract and recover any out-of-pocket loss. The professional may not avoid this liability by delegating the duties to other persons. If an accountant delegates the duty of preparing your tax returns to a subordinate, the accountant will still be liable if a breach of contract occurs. Contract law will be reviewed and discussed in more detail in Part II, Contracts, which follows this chapter. The liability of accountants or other professionals to their clients under contract law is essentially the same as the liability of any party to a contract who fails to perform in accordance with the terms of the contract.

Negligence

An accountant or other professional owes a duty to the client to exercise **reasonable care** in the performance of the terms of the contract. Failure to exercise this reasonable care may be considered negligence on the part of the professional. The obvious question here is what constitutes reasonable care and what does not. Generally speaking, reasonable care has been defined as the exercise of the same degree or amount of skill and care that other similar professionals practicing in the same locality would exercise under the same or similar circumstances. The professional being judged may also be evaluated by general standards of the specific profession as well as the standard of skill and care of similar professionals in the locality. For example, individual states have enacted codes of ethics and/or rules of professional conduct for the practice of law, the medical profession has its ethical standards, certified professional engineers have ethical codes, and certified public accountants (CPAs) also have standards of care required by their profession. These standards are the **generally accepted accounting principles**, known as **GAAP,** and the **generally accepted auditing standards**, known as **GAAS.**

Examples of situations in which a professional would be liable to his or her client for negligence would be the case of an attorney who failed to file a lawsuit for the client within the statutory period, causing the client to lose the right to receive damages from the adverse party; a physician who prescribed the wrong medication, which injured the patient, or the CPA who miscalculated or made omissions or other errors in the tax report for the client, causing the client to have to pay tax penalties.

The flood of lawsuits stemming from the Enron debacle—the "disappearance" of the fifth largest corporation in the U.S.—is certain to add whole new chapters to the liability of accountants, officers, directors, and agents. Enron's accountant, the venerable and respected "Big Five" accounting firm of Arthur Andersen, was criminally prosecuted for shredding Enron documents. By the time the U.S. Supreme Court reversed the firm's conviction, the firm had been destroyed by the adverse publicity. (The case is presented in Chapter 6.) Most of its worldwide affiliates have jumped ship. Whether any of its core businesses can still be salvaged is unclear as of this writing.

Liability to Third Parties

It is in this category of liability that the CPA is often in a more precarious liability position than other professionals. CPAs are often found liable to third parties (nonclients) who foreseeably and justifiably relied on the CPA's report to its client. In the other professions, we do not find the same degree of liability to third parties. For example, if a surgeon performs an operation and sews up the incision leaving a sponge in the wound, the only person who can claim against the surgeon is the patient, or perhaps the patient's estate or his dependents if the patient died as a result of negligence in the surgical process. Similarly in the case of an attorney, the threat of a malpractice claim is from clients, not third parties. Thus CPAs find themselves in a unique situation with regard to third party liability.

Ultramares Doctrine

Accountants do more than simply make up tax returns for clients. One of the most common tasks the accountant performs for the client is the auditing and certification of the business organization's financial reports. Obviously the accountant would be liable to the client for a mistake in the auditing and preparation and certification of a financial report if the client suffered damages as a result of the mistake because the accountant and the client are "in privity of contract." This means they have a contractual arrangement, and therefore have responsibilities to each other.

The question arises, what happens if the client takes this audited and certified financial report to a bank to convince the bank that the client is solvent and has assets to repay the loan being requested? If the accountant negligently made a mistake in the audit and certification of the financial report and in fact the client's financial status is not as portrayed in the report, can the bank sue the accountant if they suffered damages as a result of their reliance on the report? In 1931, Chief Judge Benjamin Cardozo of the New York Court of Appeals, the highest court of the state of New York, addressed the problem of liability of accountants to third persons (nonclients) in *Ultramares Corp. v. Touche*, 174 N.E. 441 (1931). Judges in courts all over the United States followed the precedent set by that decision for many years. It was referred to as the ***Ultramares* doctrine.**

In the *Ultramares* case, Touche, the accounting firm, had audited the financial records of Fred Stern & Co. and prepared a financial statement as a result of the audit. Ultramares Corporation, relying on the financial statement prepared by Touche, loaned money to Fred Stern & Co. Later Fred Stern & Co. could not pay back the loans and declared bankruptcy. Actually Fred Stern & Co. was insolvent at the time the financial statement was made. Judge Cardozo in the *Ultramares* case stated that an accountant has a duty and responsibility not only to the client, but to all third parties who relied on their reports, if the accountant was guilty of fraud. However, if the mistake or misstatement was simply the result of negligence, then the accountant would not be liable to nonclients, that is, third persons, unless the nonclient was known by the accountant to be an intended user who would be relying on the accountant's reports. This case established the *primary beneficiary* test. That is, unless the third party (nonclient) was known by the accountant to be a primary beneficiary of the accountant's work product, then the accountant would not be liable to such third party for negligence.

The *Ultramares* doctrine gave accountants a special protection that is not available to all professionals. For example, take the case of the architect who designed a building in Minneapolis, Minnesota, and miscalculated the roof weight load factors. After the building was erected, the roof fell in following the first heavy snowfall, and hundreds of people were injured. Those injured people can sue and collect damages from the architect even though the error was not the result of fraud but simply negligence. In that case, the court would find it was foreseeable that people occupying the building would be injured if the roof collapsed. The architect was aware of this potential liability when the design was made and had a duty, not only to its clients but to all foreseeable users, to design the building to withstand natural and expected roof loads, such as a snowfall. Accountants under the *Ultramares* doctrine are not liable to any and all persons who might be damaged by relying on their work product.

In recent years, courts in many states have refused to follow the *Ultramares* doctrine. These courts have extended the liability of accountants beyond the client and the primary beneficiary nonclient to nonclients who were not known to the accountant but who were in a foreseen class of users of the accountant's work product. Some courts have extended liability to foreseeable users generally. The foreseen class of users doctrine has been adopted in the *Restatement (Second) of Torts.*

Restatement (Second) of Torts

The **Restatement (Second) of Torts** was published in 1977. The relevant section reads as follows:

§552. Information Negligently Supplied for the Guidance of Others

(1) One who, in the course of his business, profession, or employment, or in any other transaction in which he has a pecuniary interest, supplies false information

for the guidance of others in their business transactions, is subject to liability for pecuniary loss caused to them by their justifiable reliance upon the information, if he fails to exercise reasonable care or competence in obtaining or communicating the information.

(2) Except as stated in Subsection (3), the liability stated in Subsection (1) is limited to loss suffered

(a) by the person or one of a limited group of persons for whose benefit and guidance he intends to supply the information or knows that the recipient intends to supply it; and

(b) through reliance upon it in a transaction that he intends the information to influence or knows that the recipient so intends or in a substantially similar transaction.

(3) The liability of one who is under a public duty to give the information extends to loss suffered by any of the class of persons for whose benefit the duty is created, in any of the transactions in which it is intended to protect them.

The language of the *Restatement* expands the class of third party nonclients who can sue and recover from the accountant. The *Restatement* extends liability to certain *foreseen* beneficiaries but not to any and all *foreseeable* users of the accountant's work.

Foreseeable Users Doctrine

This doctrine is the most recent in origin and the most liberal in extending liability of the accountant. It holds that accountants may be held liable not only to nonclients who are **primary beneficiaries** (the *Ultramares* doctrine) or to reasonably foreseen beneficiaries (the *Restatement* concept) but also to foreseeable third parties. In 1983, the New Jersey Supreme Court found it was not in the public interest to give accountants the special protection against lawsuits by nonclients who were neither primary beneficiaries nor reasonably foreseen beneficiaries. Instead, the court felt accountants should be liable for their negligence to the foreseeable users of their work product, just as other professionals would be liable.

Ultramares Reaffirmed

The New York Court of Appeals in 1985 again addressed the question of liability of accountants to third persons (nonclients) in *Credit Alliance Corporation v. Arthur Andersen & Co.*, 483 N.E.2d 110. The court in that case essentially reaffirmed the original *Ultramares* doctrine and went on to list three requirements that must be met before a nonclient can hold an accountant liable for negligence. These requirements are: (1) the accountants must have been aware that their work product was to be used for a particular purpose, (2) in the furtherance of which a known party was intended to rely, and (3) some conduct on the part of the accountants linking them to that party must evidence the accountant's understanding of that party's reliance. Thus, we have a considerable difference in opinion among the various states as to the liability of accountants to third party nonclients. The accountant should be aware of which of the three legal concepts his or her state has adopted: the *Ultramares* doctrine, the *Restatement* concept, or the foreseeable users doctrine.

The *Presnell* case shows that Section 552 is also applicable to other professionals who supply false information to third parties.

Fraud

An accountant may be found liable to the client or third persons for "actual" fraud. Actual fraud occurs when the accountant intentionally misstates or omits material facts intending to mislead the client or third persons who will rely on the accountant's work product. Material facts are facts that would be considered to be important to decision making based on the accountant's work product. If the client or the third party justifiably relied on the misstatement or the omission and suffered damage, then the accountant will be liable for that person's out-of-pocket damages. Also, in some cases, the courts may allow punitive

CASE 5

Presnell Construction Mgrs., Inc. v. EH Construction, L.L.C.

134 S.W.3d 575 (KY 2004)

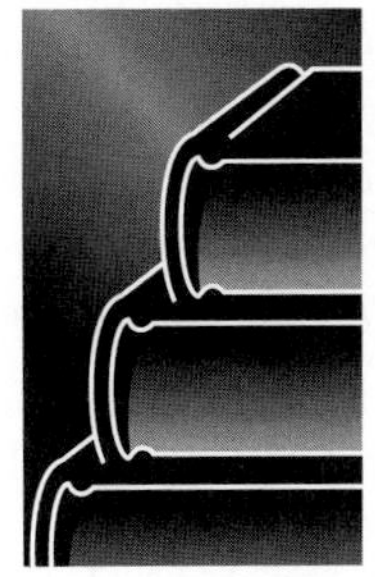

Facts: DeLor Design Group, the owner of a commercial building, hired Presnell to act as the construction manager for the building's renovation ("the Project"). DeLor also hired EH Construction to provide "general trades" work on the Project. EH claimed that Presnell's failure to properly supervise the Project and to provide EH with necessary information had caused EH to sustain economic losses in trying to do the construction work. The trial court dismissed EH's claims against Presnell for negligent supervision and negligent misrepresentation. The Court of Appeals reversed. Presnell appealed.

Issue: Did EH Construction allege a valid claim against Presnell under Section 552 of the *Restatement (Second) of Torts?*

Decision: Yes. Judgment (of the Court of Appeals) affirmed.

Opinion by The [Entire] Court: "Although privity [of contract] is no longer required to maintain a tort action, . . . 'one who is not a party to the contract or in privity thereto may not maintain an action for negligence which consists merely in the breach of the contract.' . . . Accordingly, unless Presnell breached some duty to EH apart from its duties to DeLor under the contract—i.e., an independent duty—EH, who was, at most, an incidental beneficiary of the contract between DeLor and Presnell, cannot maintain an action in negligence against Presnell. In order to determine whether such an independent duty exists, we next turn to the tort of negligent misrepresentation. . . .

"Although Kentucky appellate courts have long recognized the tort of fraudulent misrepresentation and delineated its elements, . . . we have neither adopted S. 552 nor explicitly recognized the tort of negligent misrepresentation as it relates to either economic loss or physical harm. . . . Nevertheless, Kentucky's appellate courts have cited S. 552 with approval, and have otherwise suggested that Kentucky recognizes a tort action for negligent misrepresentation. . . .

"Because we find S. 552 to be consistent with Kentucky case law, we join the majority of jurisdictions and hereby adopt S. 552's standards for negligent misrepresentation claims in this jurisdiction. . . .

"[P]rivity is not necessary to maintain a tort action, and, by adopting S. 552, we agree that the tort of negligent misrepresentation defines an independent duty for which recovery in tort for economic loss is available. Therefore, we agree with the Court of Appeals' conclusion that EH could maintain a tort action for negligent misrepresentation against Presnell under the pleadings in this case and the limited facts developed to this point. . . .

"[A]t this time, EH's complaint sufficiently states a claim against Presnell for negligent misrepresentation. However, EH's claim for negligent supervision of the Project does not articulate a claim that is independent of Presnell's contractual duties. Accordingly, the trial court did not err in dismissing that claim. . . .

"For the foregoing reasons, we affirm the Court of Appeals and vacate the trial court's summary judgment dismissing the complaint."

damages to be awarded against the accountant. **Punitive damages** are a method of punishing the fraudulent wrongdoer in addition to making the wrongdoer pay for the actual damage caused by the wrong.

There are other cases in which the accountant is not guilty of an intentional misstatement or omission of material facts and the accountant did not intend to mislead anyone, but the actions of the accountant were not simply negligent actions; they were grossly negligent. By this we mean the accountant was guilty of an uncaring and reckless disregard for the accuracy and possible consequences of the use of his or her work product. If there were misstatements or omission of material fact in the work product, the accountant could be found guilty of constructive fraud. Typically the plaintiff, who has justifiably relied on an erroneous financial report that was audited and certified by an independent accountant, when there is no evidence of actual fraud, will allege negligence, constructive fraud, and also breach of contract, thus covering all the bases.

Accountant's Statutory Liabilities

Securities Act of 1933

The **Securities Act of 1933** requires issuers of securities to file a registration statement. This **registration statement** must contain financial statements and other information relating to the security. The purpose of this registration statement is to give the prospective buyers an opportunity to learn about the security before making a purchase. The 1933 Securities Act is often referred to as "The Truth in Securities Law." Chapter 35 discusses the 1933 Securities Act in more detail.

Section 11 of the 1933 Securities Act makes an accountant who provides inaccurate financial information used in a securities registration statement liable to a purchaser of the securities. Section 11(a), which specifically refers to accountants' liability, reads in part as follows:

> *In case any part of the registration statement, when such part became effective, contained an untrue statement of a material fact or omitted to state a material fact required to be stated therein or necessary to make the statements therein not misleading, any person acquiring such security . . . may sue . . . every accountant . . . who has with his consent been named as having prepared or certified any part of the registration statement.*

The first question to be answered is what constitutes a **material fact.** Briefly, a material fact is a factual statement that would have been important to the purchaser in making the decision to purchase or not to purchase.

Once it has been determined that there has been a misstatement of a material fact or an omission of a material fact, the next question is whether the accountant exercised **due diligence** in the preparation of the material and whether the accountant made reasonable efforts to determine the accuracy of the factual statements prior to the time the registration statement was made available to purchasers.

Section 11 does not require the purchaser of securities issued based on a registration statement that contained misstatements of material fact or omissions of material fact to prove that the purchaser actually relied on the misstatements or omissions when purchasing the securities. Also, the purchaser does not have to prove the accountant/auditor was negligent. The burden is on the accountant to prove that he or she used due diligence in preparation and presentation of the material in the registration statement. Section 11 lawsuits against the accountant are also subject to a statute of limitations. The purchaser has only 1 year from the date the misstatement or omission is discovered, or in some cases, from the date the misstatement or omission should have been discovered. In no instance can a purchaser file suit against the accountant once a period of 3 years has elapsed after the securities were first offered to the public.

Securities Act of 1934

The **Securities Act of 1934** was passed to regulate the day-to-day trading of securities sold through the national stock exchanges. The 1934 Securities Act also set up the Securities and Exchange Commission (SEC). The companies regulated are typically those with more than $3,000,000 in assets and having over 500 stockholders. The 1934 act is also covered in more detail in Chapter 35.

Under the 1934 act, businesses whose securities are regulated are required to register their securities and to file quarterly and annual reports with the SEC. The quarterly report is called a **10-Q report** and the annual report is called a **10-K report.** These reports contain financial information that must be certified by an independent public accountant. These reports are available to the public.

Most suits brought against accountants under the 1934 act are based on Section 10(b), **SEC Rule 10b(5)** or Section 18 of the 1934 act. Section 10b reads as follows:

> *It shall be unlawful for any person, directly or indirectly, by the use of any means or instrumentality of interstate commerce or of the mails, or of any facility of any national securities exchange . . . (b) To use or employ, in connection with the purchase or sale of any security registered on a national securities exchange or any security not so registered, any manipulative or deceptive device or contrivance in contravention of such rules and regulations as the commission may prescribe as necessary or appropriate in the public interest or for the protection of investors.*

Section 10b allows the SEC to make further rules and regulations as necessary. Rule 10b(5) reads as follows:

> *It shall be unlawful for any person, directly or indirectly, by the use of any means or instrumentality of interstate commerce, or of the mails, or of any facility of any national*

securities exchange: (a) to employ any device, scheme, or artifice to defraud; (b) to make any untrue statement of a material fact or to omit to state a material fact necessary in order to make the statements made, in the light of the circumstances under which they were made, not misleading; or (c) to engage in any act, practice, or course of business which operates or would operate as a fraud or deceit upon any person, in connection with the purchase or sale of any security.

Section 10b and SEC Rule 10b(5) are very broad. They apply to any false statements or omissions made by the accountant, even though the statement was not made in an application document or report filed with the SEC. These provisions are primarily concerned with fraud.

Section 18 of the 1934 act is really a disclosure provision. It only applies to statements made in applications, reports, and documents filed with the SEC. Section 18 reads as follows:

Any person who shall make or cause to be made any statement in any application, report, or document filed . . . which . . . was . . . false or misleading with respect to any material fact, shall be liable to any person . . . who, in reliance upon such statement, shall have purchased or sold a security at a price which was affected by such statement, for damages caused by such reliance, unless the person sued shall prove that he acted in good faith and had no knowledge that such statement was false or misleading.

An accountant's liability under the 1934 act, Section 10b, or SEC Rule 10b(5) must be based on fraudulent conduct, not mere negligence. As you will recall, under the 1933 act, the accountant was liable if there was a false statement or omission in the registration statement even though the purchaser had not relied on such statement or omission. The accountant's only defense was due diligence. In other words, the accountant was guilty until he or she proved a defense of due diligence. The burden of proof is on the accountant under the 1933 act.

Under Section 10b and SEC Rule 10b(5), the accountant is not liable unless fraud is proved by the purchaser. The purchaser has the burden of proving reasonable reliance on the alleged false and material statement and a financial loss as a result of such reliance. Thus, the burden is entirely on the purchaser under Section 10b and SEC Rule 10b(5). Here the accountant is innocent until proven guilty.

Section 18 does not require the proof of fraudulent conduct on the part of the accountant before the accountant may be found liable. It simply provides that if there is a false or misleading statement made by the accountant in an application, document, or report filed with the SEC, the accountant could be found liable to a purchaser of the security involved, provided the purchaser reasonably relied on the false or misleading statement and suffered a loss due to the reliance. The accountant can escape such liability by proving a lack of knowledge that the statements were either false or misleading and that he or she acted in good faith. What constitutes good faith? This means the accountant made a reasonable effort to be truthful and did not intentionally put in false or misleading information. On the other hand, if the accountant did not actually know that the statements were false or misleading, but had been grossly negligent—he or she clearly did not follow standard procedures and was guilty of obvious misconduct in conducting the investigation then the court would no doubt find the accountant guilty. The accountant will not be held civilly liable for simple, honest mistakes, only for mistakes that result from gross inattention and misconduct.

There is also a statute of limitations that applies to actions filed under the provisions of the 1934 act. The same 1-year and 3-year limitations that apply to actions filed under the 1933 act apply to actions filed under the 1934 act.

Racketeer Influenced and Corrupt Organizations

In 1970, the U.S. Congress passed the Racketeer Influenced and Corrupt Organizations Act, known as RICO. The intent of this law was to control the influence of organized crime on legitimate businesses. The act has criminal penalties and civil provisions that allow the imposition of treble damages. Under this law stockholders can bring civil suits for treble damages and even get their attorney fees paid.

Originally the act was aimed at so-called organized crime, but when Congress defined the types of crimes it applied to, they included such crimes as mail fraud and fraud in the sale of securities, which were not previously considered to be the types of crimes in which so-called organized crime was involved. At any rate, this poorly and broadly worded law has been used to bring civil lawsuits against CPAs who may have been involved with a business that has been accused, but not necessarily convicted, of a pattern of racketeering activity. Almost any fraud committed by a business may be interpreted as being a violation of this act.

Procedural Issues

In Chapter 4 we discussed procedural issues, specifically the right of the court to compel testimony or production of documents. It was pointed out that there is a recognized privilege of confidentiality for certain professions. For example, attorneys cannot be forced to reveal matters communicated to them in confidence by their clients.

The question arose as to whether a similar privilege of confidentiality exists between the client and his or her accountant. Chief Justice Burger, speaking for the Supreme Court of the United States in the case of *U.S. v. Arthur Young & Company* in 1984, found there was no privilege of confidentiality concerning an accountant's work product.

As a consequence of this case, many clients who are concerned about the confidentiality of their records will engage an attorney to handle their specific problems. The attorney then hires an accountant to assist. Thus, the accountant's work is the attorney's work product and protected by the attorney-client privilege of confidentiality.

Accountant's Criminal Liability

We briefly introduced you to the problem of criminal liability of accountants in Chapter 5, and we will now cover this area in more detail.

Securities Acts

Section 24 of the 1933 act makes an accountant criminally liable if the accountant willfully makes a false statement regarding a material fact or willfully omits a material fact in a registration statement. The penalty can be a fine of up to $10,000, 5 years in prison, or both.

Section 32(a) of the 1934 act makes an accountant criminally liable if the accountant willfully makes a false or misleading statement regarding a material fact in a report required to be filed under the 1934 act such as the 10-K reports. The penalty can be a fine of up to $10,000, 5 years in prison, or both.

Mail Fraud Statute

This statute imposes criminal liability on persons who either send false financial statements in the U.S. mails or conspire to send false financial statements in the U.S. mail.

In the case of the *United States v. Simon*, often referred to as the *Continental Vending* case, decided by the U.S. Second Circuit in 1969, accountants were found criminally liable. That case involved violations of Section 32(a) of the 1934 act and the Mail Fraud Statute.

Foreign Corrupt Practices Act

This act was passed by the U.S. Congress in 1977 to discourage payment of bribes by U.S. corporations to foreign officials for favors in business dealings.

This act prohibits both businesses registered under the provisions of the 1934 Securities Exchange Act and U.S. businesses not so registered from offering or giving anything of value to a foreign official to obtain a new business relationship or to retain a business relationship previously established. A willful violation of the provisions of this act can result in a criminal conviction with penalties of up to $100,000 and/or 5 years in prison for the individual or individuals involved and fines to the corporation of up to $2 million.

Accountants are concerned with this law because it amended Section 13(b) of the Securities Exchange Act of 1934. The law now requires businesses that are registered with and report to the SEC to keep accurate and complete records of all transactions and disposition of assets. Also, the company must maintain a system of internal accounting to check on all cash payments and see that they are specifically authorized by management. The accountant is now charged with new responsibilities, which could result in severe criminal charges, if this law is violated. The SEC is the watchdog: They will investigate and then refer the case to the Justice Department for criminal prosecution if they find a violation.

Internal Revenue Code

The Internal Revenue Code provides for criminal penalties including fines and imprisonment for accountants (tax preparers) who willfully prepare false tax returns or willfully assist a client to evade taxes.

Significance of This Chapter

We live in a legalistic society, and the law of torts is a very important concern for individuals and businesspeople. Anything we do or say in our personal or business lives could subject us to liability. This chapter reviews the various types of torts that may occur, the main defenses that are available against such claims, and some of the recent developments in this area of the law.

Professional liability lawsuits have become a serious concern, with some professionals limiting the scope of the services they provide (e.g., medical doctors avoiding lawsuit-prone specialties) or even changing careers. In some areas, malpractice insurance is no longer available or has become too expensive to afford. Service providers must be prepared to show that they have exercised the appropriate level of professional care in performing their duties.

IMPORTANT TERMS AND CONCEPTS

10-K report
10-Q report
attractive nuisance
comparative negligence
conditionally privileged
conversion
deceit
defamation
due diligence
false imprisonment
generally accepted accounting principles (GAAP)
generally accepted auditing standards (GAAS)
immunity
intentional torts
interference with economic relations
invasion of privacy
last clear chance doctrine
libel
material fact
negligence
negligent torts
no-fault auto insurance
nuisance
primary beneficiaries
privileged
proximate cause
punitive damages
res ipsa loquitur
respondeat superior
reasonable care
registration statement
Restatement (Second) of Torts
SEC Rule 10b(5)
Securities Act of 1933
Securities Act of 1934
slander
sovereign immunity
strict liability torts
tort
trespass
Ultramares doctrine
vicarious liability
workers' compensation

QUESTIONS AND PROBLEMS FOR DISCUSSION

1. How does a tort differ from a crime? Explain how a person's action or failure to act can be both criminal and tortious.

2. If you were the manager of a retail store, what instructions would you give to your salespeople about apprehending shoplifting suspects?

3. Explain the rationale for prohibiting a public official from winning a libel or slander judgment unless the official proves that the defamation was made with malice.

4. What is the difference in the scope of the accountant's duty under the *Restatement* rule, as opposed to the *Ultramares* doctrine?

5. Bertha L. Briney inherited an 80-acre tract in southwest Mahaska County where her grandparents and parents had lived. No one occupied the house thereafter. Her husband, Edward, attempted to care for the land. He kept no farm machinery there. The outbuildings became dilapidated.

   For about 10 years, there occurred a series of trespassing and housebreaking events with loss of some household items, the breaking of windows, and "messing up of the property in general." The latest occurred June 8, prior to the event on July 16.

   The Brineys through the years boarded up the windows and doors in an attempt to stop the intrusions. They had posted "no trespass" signs on the land several years before. The nearest one was 35 feet from the house. On June 11, they set "a shotgun trap" in the north bedroom. After Mr. Briney cleaned and oiled his 20-gauge shotgun, defendants took it to the old house where they secured it to an iron bed with the barrel pointed at the bedroom door. It was rigged with wire from the doorknob to the gun's trigger so it would fire when the door was opened. Briney first pointed the gun so an intruder would be hit in the stomach but at Mrs. Briney's suggestion it was lowered to fit the legs. He admitted he did so "because I was mad and tired of being tormented" but "he did not intend to injure anyone." He gave no explanation of why he used a loaded shell and set it to hit a person already in the house. Tin was nailed over the bedroom window. The spring gun could not be seen from the outside. No warning of its presence was posted.

   Katko lived with his wife and worked regularly as a gasoline station attendant in Eddyville, 7 miles from the old house. He had observed it for several years while hunting in the area and considered it as being abandoned. Prior to July 16, Katko and McDonough had been to the premises and found several old bottles and fruit jars that they took and added to their collection of antiques. On that date about 9:30 pm, they made a second trip to the Briney property. They entered the old house by removing a board from a porch window that was without glass. As plaintiff started to open the north bedroom door, the shotgun went off, striking him in the right leg about the ankle bone. Much of his leg, including part of the tibia, was blown away. Only by McDonough's assistance was plaintiff able to get out of the house and after crawling some distance was put in his vehicle and rushed to a doctor and then to a hospital. He remained in the hospital 40 days. Katko sued.

   Have the Brineys committed a tort? Discuss.

6. Mrs. Garner entered Southwest Drugstore, found the bar of soap she wanted, took it to the cashier, paid for it, and received a sales ticket. The cashier put the soap in a small bag. Mrs. Garner walked out of the store, but before she got to her car, the manager of the store yelled out at her, telling her to stop, and accused her of stealing the bar of soap. She denied it, but he told her she would have to go back into the store with him to prove that she had not stolen the soap. There were a number of people in the parking lot who heard the manager's loud and rude accusations. When the manager and Mrs. Garner got back to the store, the cashier verified that Mrs. Garner had paid for the soap. Mrs. Garner was then released. She became ill and distressed as a result of the incident. She required medical treatment for her distress.

   A Mississippi statute allows a merchant to stop and question a person if the merchant has reasonable grounds to believe that the person is attempting to commit the crime of shoplifting. Mrs. Garner sued Southwest Drug Stores for false imprisonment and slander, and a verdict for $8,000 was rendered in her favor in the lower court. Southwest Drug Stores appealed.

   How should the appeals court rule, and why?

7. On August 11, 4-year-old Joel Goode drowned in a man-made waterway or moat at Walt Disney World. He was with his mother, Marietta Goode, who noticed that he was missing shortly after 11 PM. Approximately 3 hours later, Joel's body was found in 5 feet of water a short distance from where he had become separated from his mother. An autopsy found no evidence of foul play and established the cause of death as drowning. No one saw Joel enter the waterway.

   Joel's parents sued Walt Disney World for the wrongful death of their son. The jury returned a verdict of $1 million for Joel's father, Harry Goode, and $1 million for Joel's mother Marietta. The jury also determined that Disney and Joel's mother were each 50 percent negligent.

   What judgment should be given here? Explain.

8. Russo and Olive Dribble owned a large male goat, which they kept in a pen. One morning the Dribbles' two sons, aged 10 and 7, missed the school bus. Their parents had

already left for work, so the boys were home alone. They let the goat out of his pen to play with him. At this point, the goat was still within the Dribbles' fenced-in front yard. When the boys went across the street to visit their friend, Mr. Pappe, the goat jumped the fence and followed them. Pappe poked the goat in the side with his cane to try to get it off his property. The goat attacked Pappe and seriously injured him. Pappe was taken to the hospital, treated for a month, and then released. He was readmitted about 3 months later and died about a month after that. Pappe's estate sues the Dribbles.

Is there any basis for tort liability here? Discuss.

PART 2

Contract Law

Contract law affects every transaction in which an individual or a business may be involved. Every sale of goods or services to a customer is a contract. Investments made by stockholders are contracts. Purchases or rentals of land and equipment are contracts. Hiring agreements are contracts. Agreements with professional firms for advertising, accounting, and legal services are contracts. Contract law is important to you as a consumer and as a future business manager.

Contract law principles also form the basis for many other specialized bodies of law, such as sales of goods, secured transactions, insurance, suretyship, and commercial paper. Although each of these other topics is covered later in this text, it is important to understand contract law principles before studying those more specific topics. Contract law is the foundation; the particular rules and exceptions for each of these specialized topics are the rooms of the house.

For these reasons, contract law is given extensive coverage in Part Two. We first give you some basic definitions and terminology, then we examine the formation of the agreement and its enforceability. We then proceed to discuss the major defenses a party may assert against liability on a contract. We also explain and discuss the situations in which persons other than the two parties who made the agreement may have rights under it. We then review the various ways in which contract liability may be excused or discharged. Finally, we review the remedies available when one party breaches a contract. These chapters obviously cannot cover the subject in the same depth as a full year's work in law school. After studying them, however, you will have a very good overview of the major rules involved in the formation, performance, and enforcement of contracts.

CHAPTER 8

Agreements and Contracts

Chapter Objectives

This chapter will:

- Outline the elements of a valid contract.
- Emphasize the consensual nature of contracts.
- Indicate the essential elements of an offer.
- Explain when and how an offer terminates.
- Indicate the essential elements of an acceptance, and when it becomes effective.

Contract law is perhaps the most basic area of civil law. Every business transaction, be it oral or written, for the purchase or sale of goods, land, or intangible personal property, involves principles of contract law. Contract law is the foundation for many other areas of law.

For example, suppose that two persons want to establish a business. Whether they propose a partnership, a corporation, or any other type of organization, their venture involves principles of contract law. If employees are to be hired, any agreement between employer and employees involves contract law. The business must operate from physical premises and use machinery and equipment, and each of these necessities may be purchased or perhaps leased. Either way, principles of contract law apply.

When the organization begins transacting business, it must purchase raw materials, and those purchases involve contract law. After the raw materials are processed into products, the manufacturer's sales to wholesalers, wholesalers' subsequent sales to retailers, and retailers' sales to consumers are all controlled by principles of contract law.

Thus we must understand the principles of contract law before we study the laws governing sales, commercial paper, secured transactions, agency, business organizations, employer-employee relations, ownership of property, and the various other areas that affect the businessperson and the daily operation of the business entity.

Sources of Contract Law

Contract law stems from case law, the **Uniform Commercial Code (UCC)**, and other state statutes. As noted in Chapter 1, all states have adopted the UCC except Louisiana, which has enacted only those parts of the UCC that do not conflict with its version of the Napoleonic Code.

As you study contract law, remember that the common law governs some contract transactions, or parts of them, whereas the UCC governs others. If the contract involves the sale of land or the sale of services, traditional common law rules will normally apply unless some specific state statutory law pertains to that transaction. If the transaction involves the sale of personal property, then any applicable provisions of the UCC will supersede the common law rules (see Exhibit 8-1).

The sale of land or services in transactions not covered by any specific state statutory law normally will be covered by the general contract rules summarized by the **Restatement of Contracts**. As we noted in Chapter 1, the Restatements are treatises prepared by the American Law Institute (ALI). These Restatements are presented in an encyclopedia-like form and give the generally accepted rules of law on specific topics. The Restatements are not the actual law, only a reference to the generally applied rules.

When confronted with new or difficult questions, or when prior cases have reached differing results, courts frequently use textbooks and law review articles. Such sources are not themselves the law, but they can assist a court in seeing the issues involved. Two of the most widely cited contracts texts are those by Professor Williston and Professor Corbin.

Just what is a "contract"? In simplest terms, it is a private agreement that imposes legal duties on the parties that agree to it. Of course, there are many refinements and exceptions to this overall definition. That is why there are seven chapters on contracts in this book.

Definition of a Contract

For the commercial contracts that it covers, the UCC, in Section 1-201(11) defines a contract as the "total legal obligation which results from the parties' agreement as affected by this Act and any other applicable rules of law." Upon reviewing this definition, we find the term **agreement** is not defined. Is an agreement always legally binding on the parties? Do all agreements create a legal obligation? Must an agreement be in writing and signed by the parties to create legal obligations? Section 1-201(3) of the UCC defines agreement as "*the bargain of the parties in fact as found in their language or by implication from other circumstances including course of dealing or usage of trade or course of performance as provided in the Act. Whether an agreement has legal consequences is determined by the provisions of this Act if applicable, otherwise by the law of contracts.*"

Exhibit 8.1: Sources of Contract Law

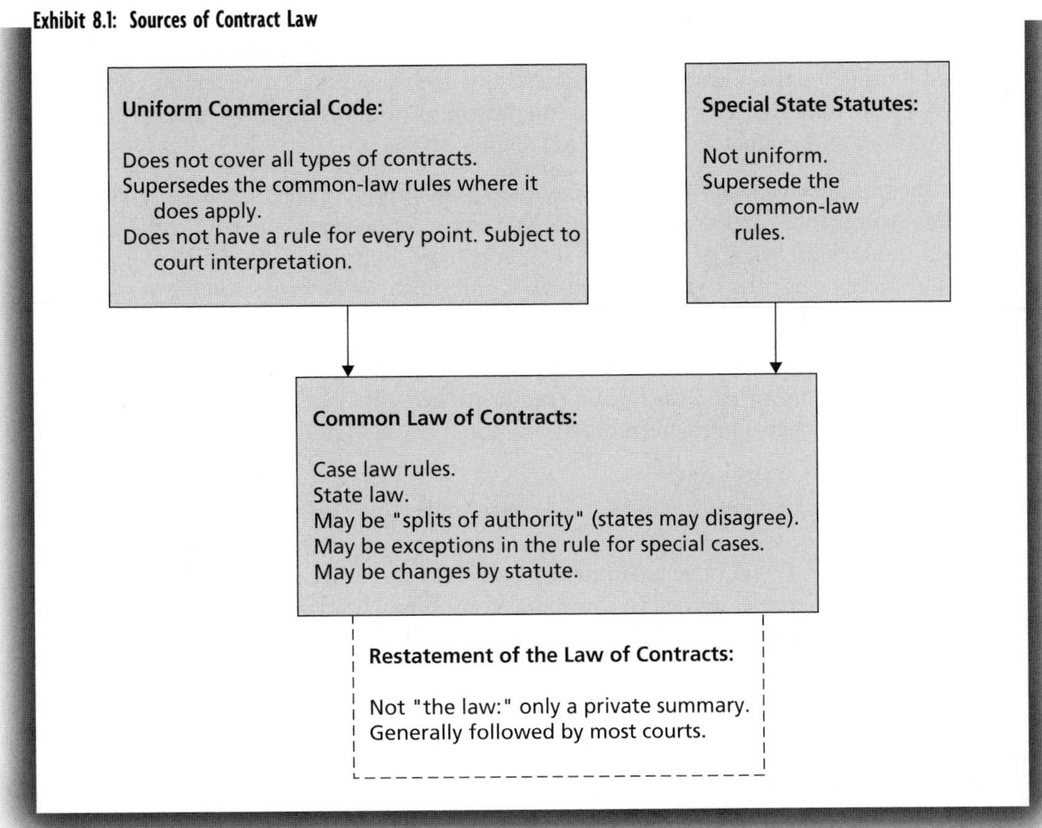

Uniform Commercial Code:
Does not cover all types of contracts.
Supersedes the common-law rules where it does apply.
Does not have a rule for every point. Subject to court interpretation.
Special State Statutes:
Not uniform.
Supersede the common-law rules.
Common Law of Contracts:
Case law rules.
State law.
May be "splits of authority" (states may disagree).
May be exceptions in the rule for special cases.
May be changes by statute.
Restatement of the Law of Contracts:
Not "the law:" only a private summary.
Generally followed by most courts.

The agreement is simply the bargain agreed upon by the parties. It may or may not create legal obligations against the parties, depending on the terms of the bargain and the applicable law. For example, a promise between two friends to meet and go to the movies constitutes an agreement because both parties agreed to meet at a certain time and place. However, the obligations created are only social and not legally enforceable as a contract.

Section 1-201(3) of the UCC makes it clear that an agreement need not be in writing and signed by the parties. It can be oral; it can even be implied from nonverbal actions of the parties. Oral contracts are fully enforceable, unless terms of the oral agreement conflict with the provisions of the Statute of Frauds. The Statute of Frauds, which requires that certain types of contracts be proved by a signed writing, will be discussed in Chapter 10.

Basic Requirements of a Valid Contract

Not all discussions, or even all agreements, are enforced as contracts. A contract requires two basic elements, but several other factors may affect its enforceability. These requirements are:

1. That an agreement be made between the parties. To have such an agreement, there must be an offer and an acceptance, each intended as such. The process of making the agreement is discussed in this chapter.

2. That the agreement indicates an exchange of values. The technical legal term here is **consideration**, which usually means that benefits and burdens are involved on both sides. A totally one-sided agreement, such as a promise of a gift, generally cannot be enforced as a contract. These technical rules are discussed in Chapter 9.

   The combination of elements 1 and 2 indicate a contractual agreement. In determining whether the contract is fully valid and enforceable, however, the courts may also consider several other matters. These are usually raised as defense arguments, when there is a lawsuit to enforce the alleged contract.

3. That the agreement be in the form required by the applicable law. Some types of contracts, such as those for land, are subject to the **Statute of Frauds**, which requires a signed writing for the contract to be enforceable. If this special statute applies, and there is no writing that meets its requirements, the contract is unenforceable in court. This writing requirement is discussed in Chapter 10.
4. That there is legal capacity to make a contract. **Capacity** here refers (normally) to mental competence. The law recognizes that minor children and mental incompetents should not be held liable, as a rule, for their contracts. Such people's contracts are usually voidable, at their option. These rules, and those for other persons with special legal status, are discussed in Chapter 11.
5. That the agreement be based on the real consent of the parties, without fraud, coercion, or mistake. When someone has been forced or tricked into making a contract, it is voidable at his or her option, and sometimes, totally void. These rules are also discussed in Chapter 11.
6. That the purpose and performance of the contract be legal. Where the agreement involves the commission of some criminal act, the courts will generally refuse to recognize it at all. It will be deemed totally null and void, as far as any civil case is concerned. If the parties agreed to a criminal conspiracy, however, they may be prosecuted under the criminal law. Various types of illegality that may occur in contracts are discussed in Chapter 12.

Classifications of Contracts

Contracts are classified with regard to their formation, the nature of the required acceptance, their enforceability, and the extent to which the terms of the contract have been performed. The same contract may thus be placed in four different categories, depending on which feature is being examined (see Exhibit 8-2).

Method of Formation

Express Contract. An **express contract** is a contract, either oral or written, in which the terms of the contract are clearly and openly stated, in words.

Implied Contract. An **implied contract** is a contract in which the agreement between the parties was not stated orally or in writing; however, the fact that a contract was intended can be implied from the circumstances or the conduct of the parties. This type of contract is very common. For example, suppose that you call the plumber to come repair a leaky faucet. You are at work, and you tell the plumber that the key is under the doormat. When you come home the key is back under the doormat, the door is locked, and the faucet is repaired. You owe the plumber a reasonable fee for the repair even though you gave no

Exhibit 8.2: Classifications of Contracts

Method of Formation	Nature of Acceptance	Extent of Performance	Enforceability
Express Contract	Bilateral	Executed	Valid
Implied Contract	Unilateral	Executory	Void
Quasi-Contract (implied in law)			Voidable
			Unenforceable

oral or written promise to pay. The fact that you called the plumber, who is in business for profit, is evidence of an implied promise to pay for services rendered.

Quasi-Contract or Implied in Law Contract. A **quasi-contract** is not really a contract at all because there has been no agreement between the parties. Quasi-contract is simply a remedy that the courts have developed to prevent **unjust enrichment**. It is an obligation implied by law rather than by the parties' conduct. In a quasi-contract situation one party receives a benefit that had been neither ordered nor requested. Still, the law will not allow one party to be unjustly enriched at the expense of the other party. Persons cannot use a quasi-contract lawsuit to recover for benefits that they voluntarily conferred on another party without that person's knowledge or consent, or for benefits conferred under conditions that justify the receiving party to believe that they were a gift. Any recovery made is based solely on the extent of the unjust enrichment to the receiving party and not necessarily the loss that the plaintiff suffered.

To recover on the basis of quasi-contract, the plaintiff not only must show that the defendant has been "enriched," but also that the retention of the benefit by the defendant without compensation to the plaintiff would be "unjust." This means that there must be proof that the defendant is guilty of some misconduct, fault, or undue advantage. Money paid by mistake must nearly always be returned because the defendant can easily do so without harm or damage. On the other hand, if someone mows your lawn by mistake when you were not at home to tell them not to do so you have probably received a free mowing job. You do not have to pay for this "benefit" because you were in no way to blame for the other party's mistake, had no chance to prevent the mowing, and because the mowing service cannot really be returned. (Try "un-mowing" a lawn sometime.)

Nature of Acceptance

Bilateral Contract. In a **bilateral contract**, one person promises to do something in exchange for a promise from another person. Simply stated, a bilateral contract is a promise for a promise. An example of a bilateral contract would be a situation in which Phil offers to sell his car to George for $10,000. George accepts the offer. Phil has promised to sell his car to George, and George has promised to buy the car for the agreed price. Thus, a promise to sell was exchanged for a promise to buy, and a bilateral contract was made.

Unilateral Contract. A **unilateral contract** is a contract in which a promise is made in exchange for an act or for refraining from an action. The promisor promises certain benefits if another person or persons will act in a certain way, or perhaps not do a certain act. At any rate, there is no contract until the requested act is performed or the forbearance occurs.

A good example of a unilateral contract would be the posting of a reward for a lost dog: "I will pay $50 to anyone who will return my lost dog." No contract exists until someone shows up with the dog in response to the offer. At that point, the offeror will have to give that person the promised amount in exchange for that person's handing over the dog.

An example of a unilateral contract in which the promise is made in exchange for refraining from action would be a situation in which Mr. Jones had expressed an interest in bidding on a certain item at an auction. Ms. Smith was aware of this and told Mr. Jones, "I will give you $100 if you refrain from bidding on that certain item." No promise was made by Mr. Jones. When the item came up for sale, Mr. Jones refrained from bidding. He accepted the offer of Ms. Smith by *not* bidding. This example also shows the important difference between unilateral and bilateral contracts. Because Mr. Jones made no *promise* not to bid, he was thus free to do so if he wished. Had he entered into a bilateral contract, he would have promised not to bid and would have been legally bound not to do so.

Extent of Performance

Executed Contract. An **executed contract** is one wherein the obligations created by the contract have been fulfilled by the parties and nothing is left to be done. In other words, the case is closed.

Executory Contract. In an **executory contract** something remains to be done. A contract can be wholly executory when there has been no performance at all yet, but each party has merely made a promise to the other. Or the contract can be partially executory when one party has performed partially or when one party has completely performed and the other has performed partially but still owes some additional performance.

Enforceability

Valid Contract. A contract that contains all the necessary requirements for formation and enforcement is a **valid contract**.

Void Contract. A void contract is not a legal contract. As the term void implies, the agreement that was bargained for is null and void without legal effect. A "contract" between a person and a hit man to murder someone for insurance benefits would be an example of a void "contract" because the law refuses to recognize and enforce a bargain requiring unlawful conduct.

Voidable Contract. A contract can be classified as a **voidable contract** when one or both of the parties has the legal right to terminate the obligation. If the promisor is a minor and decides to assert that minority to avoid the contract, then the minor's contract obligation will be avoided. If the party with the power to avoid liability chooses not to do so, then the contract will be enforceable.

Unenforceable Contract. A contract can be unenforceable even though its formation was valid because it does not meet some specific statutory requirement. For example, consider an oral contract for the sale of goods for $500 or more. Under the Statute of Frauds, such a contract must be in writing or it will not be enforced. This is not to say that oral contracts for the sale of goods for $500 or more are illegal or void. It simply says that in case a party to that oral contract challenges its existence, the courts will not grant a remedy unless the party against whom enforcement is sought has signed a writing.

Another example of an **unenforceable contract** could occur when one of the parties did not perform. The statute of limitations may preclude the other party's claim for breach of contract. The statute of limitations requires that a lawsuit be filed within a prescribed time after the breach of contract occurs. If the party alleging a breach by the other party does not file a lawsuit in the prescribed time, the court will not enforce the contract. Other regulatory statutes, such as the bankruptcy act, also could affect enforceability.

Formation of the Agreement

Our basic contract formula may be stated as follows: **Contract = Agreement + Consideration**. That is, for promises to have legal consequences as contracts, there must be an agreement between the parties that they will have such consequences, and that agreement must involve an exchange of legally sufficient considerations, or values.

We now examine the agreement part of the formula, which may be stated as a subformula: **Agreement = Offer + Acceptance**. To learn whether there was a contractual agreement, we will need to know the answers to three main questions: What is an "offer"? How long is an offer open for acceptance? What is an effective acceptance?

Definition of an Offer

Preliminary Negotiations Distinguished from Offers. Parties may engage in extended preliminary discussions before one of them finally makes a direct business proposition to the other. Buyers typically want to compare prices and payment terms, and therefore may request such information from several prospective sellers. Sellers may have only one or a limited number of items available, but they will contact a number of prospective buyers to see whether any of them is interested. Thus, a buyer who asks, "What will you take for your car?" is only seeking price information and is not making an offer to buy. Likewise, a would-be seller who responds, "$400," is only supplying the requested information and is not making an offer to sell at that price, to this buyer, or to anyone else.

The element that distinguishes an **offer** from such **preliminary negotiations**, the thing that makes it an offer, is a **promise** to do business. The promise may be stated expressly, in so many words ("I'll give you $400 for your car"), or it may be implied from the language used and the surrounding facts and circumstances. This promise gives the **offeree**, the person to whom the offer is made, the power to change the legal relationships between the parties by accepting the offer and forming a contract. Because, typically, price quotations and advertisements do not contain such promises, they are not considered to be offers. However, stores that advertise products for sale to the public are required by state **false advertising** statutes and by Federal Trade Commission (FTC) regulations to have "reasonable quantities" of the advertised items available or sale. They cannot, in other words, rely on the general contract law rule that "advertisements are not offers" without being liable for fines under the false advertising laws.

Identity of Offeree. Because, as a general rule, you have no legal duty to do business with anyone unless and until a contract is made, you can as an **offeror** specify the person or persons to whom your offer is made. You can make the offer to as many or as few persons as you wish, on whatever basis you wish. Today, however, an offeror's power to pick and choose the persons with whom to do business is subject to some important limitations by both state and national civil rights acts.

Not all types of contracts, or all potential offerors, or all possible bases of discrimination between offerees, are prohibited by these acts. Each such statute must be read carefully to see exactly what forms of discrimination are covered.

Usually it is illegal to discriminate on the basis of race, color, religion, sex, or national origin, for contracts involving employment, real estate purchase or rental, or places of "public accommodation." Employment discrimination is discussed further in Chapter 30.

Communication to Offeree. It is really no more than common sense to say that an offer has no legal effect as an offer until it has been communicated to the intended offeree or offerees. If I mail you a letter containing an offer, but then change my mind and get the letter back from the post office before it is delivered to you, no offer has been made. Even if you somehow learn what happened, there would be nothing for you to "accept." If the letter were on my desk waiting for my signature, and you or one of your agents happened to be in my office and read the letter without my having authorized you to do so, no offer would have been made to you. In other words, it is my offer, and it is not effective until I intend that it be effective.

Manner of Acceptance. Also, because it is my offer, I determine the **manner of acceptance**; I tell you what you have to do to accept it. The required **acceptance** can be as ridiculous, as stupid, or as difficult as I choose to make it; if you want to accept, you must do so on whatever terms I specify. Of course, you are not obligated to accept my terms; you can propose your own terms or ignore the offer completely. Your counterproposal, however, does not create a contract; it is a **counteroffer** that has the effect of rejecting (and thus terminating) my original offer.

When the offeror requests a return promise, that person has offered a bilateral contract—a promise in return for a promise. If the offeree accepts by making the requested return promise, each party is then both a **promisor** making a promise and a **promisee** receiving a promise from the other party. For a bilateral contract to exist, then, both parties must be bound to perform, or neither is bound. Most contracts are bilateral in form. My offer to sell you a used book is really my promise to transfer ownership of the book to you if you promise to pay me the requested contract price.

If instead the offeror requests the performance of some act, the offer is for a unilateral contract. A newspaper ad that states: "I offer $100 reward for the return of my lost poodle, Fifi" is offering a unilateral contract. To accept, one would have to perform the requested act—bring the lost dog back to the owner. Promising to look for the dog would not be an acceptance in this case because that is not what the offeror requested as the price of the promise. On the other hand, because no return promise has been made, no one is obliged to look for the dog, and there is no case for breach of contract if the dog is never returned.

(Reasonably) Definite Terms Necessary. Courts do not require that exact agreement be reached on all points for a contract to be enforceable. Obviously, the more specific and complete the terms are, the less chance there is for misunderstanding and possible lawsuit. However, the courts are aware that parties very often intend agreements but do not bother to spell out the terms completely.

At some point, however, the terms become so vague and indefinite that a court can only hold that there was no contract made because the parties never really agreed on anything. Confronted with an employee's claim that he had been promised "some share of the profits" of the business, a Wisconsin court had to say that there was no way for it to enforce such a "promise" because it could not know what share the parties might have had in mind.

CASE 1

Leonard v. Pepsico, Inc.

88 F.Supp.2d 116 (S.D. NY 1999)

Facts: John Leonard saw a TV commercial from Pepsi that indicated that customers could get "Pepsi stuff" by buying its products. Required "purchase points" were specified for different merchandise items. At the end of the ad, a high school student was shown landing a "Harrier" jet fighter at his school. The "points" price for the jet was 7,000,000. The ad also noted that extra points could be bought for 10 cents each. John raised the money, and sent Pepsi a check for $700,000. Pepsi refused to send a jet, and John sued for breach of contract.

Issue: Were the Pepsi stuff advertisements offers?

Decision: No. Summary judgment for Pepsi.

Opinion by Judge Wood: "The general rule is that an advertisement does not constitute an offer. . . .

"It is quite possible to make a definite and operative offer to buy or sell goods by advertisement, in a newspaper, by a handbill, a catalog or circular or on a placard in a store window. It is not customary to do this, however; and the presumption is the other way. . . . Such advertisements are understood to be mere requests to consider and examine and negotiate; and no one can reasonably regard them as otherwise unless the circumstances are exceptional and the words are very plain and clear. . . .

"An advertisement is not transformed into an enforceable offer merely by a potential offeree's expression of willingness to accept the offer through, among other means, completion of an order form. . . . Under these principles, plaintiff's letter of March 27, 1996, with the Order Form and the appropriate number of Pepsi Points, constituted the offer. There would be no enforceable contract until defendant accepted the Order Form and cashed the check. . . .

"The present case is distinguishable from *Lefkowitz*. First, the commercial cannot be regarded in itself as sufficiently definite, because it specifically reserved the details of the offer to a separate writing, the Catalog. . . . [T]he absence of any words of limitation such as 'first come, first served' renders the alleged offer sufficiently indefinite that no contract could be formed. . . .

"If it is clear that an offer was not serious, then no offer has been made. . . .

"[T]he number of Pepsi Points . . . required to 'purchase' the jet is 7,000,000. . . . The cost of a Harrier Jet is roughly $23,000,000, a fact of which the plaintiff was aware when he set out to gather the amount he believed necessary to accept the alleged offer. . . . Even if an objective, reasonable person were not aware of this fact, he would conclude that purchasing a fighter plane for $700,000 is a deal too good to be true. . . .

"The absence of any writing setting forth the alleged contract in this case provides an entirely separate reason for granting summary judgment."

UCC Special Rules for Goods. The UCC (Sections 2-204, 2-305, 2-306) has liberalized this requirement to some extent for sales of goods contracts, by permitting the parties to use "requirements" or "output" as quantity terms and to leave the price term open, that is, unspecified. Even here, however, there are limits. There must be a real promise, not just an illusory one, such as, "I promise to buy as much as I want to buy." To be enforceable, the promise must be definite enough to restrict the promisor's freedom of action if the offer is accepted.

Intent to Contract. In most cases where the parties have exchanged promises, there probably has been a real "meeting of the minds"; that is, each party intended a promise in the same way that it was understood by the other. Such a mutual understanding, that is, an **intent to contract**, obviously forms the contractual agreement.

There are cases, however, in which one of the parties claims that no contract was ever formed because he or she did not "intend" that the promise be taken seriously—that it

CASE 2

Conolly v. Clark

457 F.3d 872 (8 Cir. 2006)

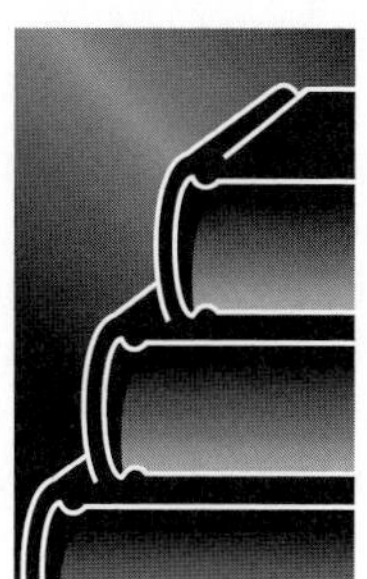

Facts: Kelly Conolly sued James Clark, claiming that Clark had breached an oral agreement to sell him Clark's majority stock interest in Clark Brothers Transfer, Inc. They had begun discussing a possible deal in early 2003. After signing a confidentiality agreement on October 17, Conolly was given company financial information, and Clark asked Conolly to send him a written offer within 10 to 14 days after October 28. Conolly sent an expressly nonbinding "letter of intent"—not including an offer—on November 12. The letter stated that the deal would include a purchase price to be agreed on, as well as specific provisions on his assumption of existing company liabilities and employment contracts, and an agreement by Clark not to compete with the company after the sale. On November 15, the parties orally agreed on a purchase price of $15.5 million for Clark's majority shares, and Clark asked for a final proposal. Conolly's lawyer sent Clark a nonbinding letter of intent that again indicated the employment contracts and no-compete agreement would be detailed later. An acceptance form was attached to this letter, but neither party ever signed it. On February 15, 2004, Clark sold his shares of Clark Brothers to someone else for $30.5 million.

Issue: Did the parties reach an agreement definite enough to enforce?

Decision: No. Judgment affirmed.

Opinion by Judge Hansen: "On appeal, Conolly argues that the district court erred by concluding as a matter of law that the parties' oral agreement of November 13, 2003, was not sufficiently definite to form a binding contract. 'In order to establish an express contract there must be a definite proposal and an unconditional and absolute acceptance thereof.' ... Additionally ... when considering whether the parties intended to be bound by a contract, the evidence 'is to be viewed objectively, not subjectively.' ... Except in the clearest of cases, the question of whether the parties intended to contract is a factual one to be resolved by the finder of fact.... However, 'when the provisions of an alleged contract being sued upon are so cursory, indefinite, and conditional as to fail as a matter of law to establish an objective intent on the parties to be bound thereby, no factual issues exist.' ...

"Conolly argues that judgment as [a] matter of law was not justified because the terms of the oral agreement were sufficiently definite to demonstrate an objective intent to be bound in contract. Conolly asserts that Clark agreed to the purchase price and agreed that both the structure of the deal and other details could be worked out, and Conolly states that he and Clark shook hands to confirm their intentions. We note that 'an "agreement to agree" is not enforceable...' and "[a] contract is not formed if the parties contemplate that something remains to be done to establish contractual arrangements or if elements are left for future arrangement." ...

"The undisputed documentary evidence of subsequent ongoing negotiations indicates that the terms of the oral agreement were not sufficiently definite to demonstrate an objective intent to be bound at the time of the November 13, 2003, shake of the hands. While a purchase price was reached orally, subsequent e-mail correspondence indicates that the proposals on how to structure the deal were preliminary and that certain material terms, such as the assumption of debt, were still negotiable. Conolly's January 6, 2004, 'non-binding letter of intent,' which neither party signed, sets out several specific terms which were, in the words of Conolly's attorney, how 'we believe the transaction would be structured.' ... The letter does not purport to be a mere memorialization of the terms orally agreed upon but clearly states the understanding that 'this is merely a non-binding letter of intent, subject to Buyer's satisfaction of its investigation of Seller and the assets, and the execution by you and Buyer of the definitive purchase agreement, and does not represent a binding commitment by either Seller or Buyer.' ... The objective evidence thus demonstrates that the parties continued to negotiate in non-binding terms after the alleged oral agreement. The district court did not err in concluding as a matter of law that the terms of the oral agreement were not sufficiently definite to indicate an objective intent to be bound....

"Accordingly, we affirm the judgment of the district court."

have contractual effect. In such cases a court will not require the other party to prove an actual meeting of the minds; it is enough if the trier of fact is convinced that a reasonable person would have believed that the promise was seriously intended. What counts, in other words, is not what the promisor really intended but the impression that those words and actions created in the mind of the other party. If the "joke" was convincing enough to fool a reasonable person and if the other party was not aware of the joke when accepting the offer, there is a contract.

Whether there was a "meeting of the minds" is also at issue in the *Conolly* case.

Another aspect of the intent to contract problem arises when one party claims that certain parts of a signed, written contract are not binding because he or she did not read the contract or did not understand it. Absent special facts, such as fraud or illiteracy, courts generally will not accept this argument. In general, the rule is that you are bound by what you sign—read or unread, understood or not understood.

Duration and Termination of Offers

Lapse of Time. Even though no specific termination date or length of time during which the offer will remain open is stated, the offer will not be open for acceptance forever. In such cases the offer will terminate at the expiration of a **reasonable time**. What constitutes a reasonable time depends on the facts of the particular case, and litigations will result because one party claims to have accepted in time and the other party claims that the acceptance was too late because a reasonable time had already elapsed. When an offer is made during a person-to-person conversation, either face-to-face or over the telephone, and nothing is stated about its being open for some period of time, the presumption is that the offer terminates when the conversation ends.

When an offer states that it will terminate on a specific date, as in "This offer will end August 14, 2003," the day named is the last day on which an acceptance can occur. Unless facts and circumstances indicate otherwise, an acceptance that took legal effect any time on that date would form a contract. When an offer was made by a retail store with regular business hours, it would normally have to be accepted during business hours, by the date specified in the offer. Actual communication of the acceptance to the retail store, within the specified time period, would also usually be necessary.

When an offer sent by letter indicates that it will be open for a period of time, as in "This offer is good for 30 days," the time period normally begins to run as of the date of the writing, even though the letter is not received through the mails for several days. But if the offer says that the offeree has a certain period of time within which "to consider" or "to accept" it, the time period does not commence until the letter is delivered.

Revocability of Offers. In most cases, even though the offeror has stated that the offer will remain open for a period of time, the offeror has both the power and the right to revoke it if such a revocation takes legal effect prior to an acceptance. Since these so-called **continuing offers** are not supported by any value given by the offeree to the offeror, the offeror is not bound by his or her promise to keep the offer open. Usually, therefore, to be sure to have the promised 30 days to investigate and consider the offer, an offeree must "buy" the 30 days by forming a preliminary **option contract** with the offeror. An offeror who has received the agreed money or other value in exchange for his or her "30-day" promise is no longer free to revoke the offer without being liable for breach of the option contract. (Note that there is still no contract on the main offer; the offeree may decide, after thinking about the main offer for the 30 days, that he or she does not wish to do business after all.)

For offers to buy or sell goods, the UCC (2-205) contains a special rule on revocability. If such an offer is made by a **merchant**, in a signed writing, and by its terms gives assurance that it will remain open for some period of time, it is not revocable, even though nothing has been paid to the merchant to keep it open. The merchant is bound to keep the **firm offer** open for the time period stated, or for a reasonable time if the offer gives such assurance, but does not state a specific cutoff date. In no case is the merchant bound for more than 3 months under this rule. As defined in the UCC, a merchant is a dealer or other expert with respect to the type of goods involved in the contract.

Implied Revocation. If an offer is revocable, it may be revoked expressly or impliedly. **Implied revocation** occurs when the court feels that underlying facts and circumstances have changed to such an extent that the agreement contemplated by the parties can no longer be made. The death or insanity of either the offeror or the offeree, for instance, impliedly revokes any outstanding offers because one of the intended parties no longer has the capacity to contract. Likewise, the destruction of the intended subject matter of the contract operates to terminate any unaccepted offers for its purchase or sale. A sale of the only item available does not, however, impliedly revoke an outstanding offer. In a situation in which a seller-offeror made an offer to Buyer 1 and then sells that item to a third party, the offeror's first offer to Buyer 1 is not terminated unless and until Buyer 1 learns of the sale. If, in the meantime, Buyer 1 has effectively accepted the offer, the seller is bound to two contracts for the same item and will be guilty of breaching one of the contracts unless one of the buyers will accept a substitute.

Express Revocation. With an **express revocation**, the offeror's intent is usually clear enough: "I revoke"; "The deal's off"; "My offer is hereby cancelled." The main problem in these cases is not whether the offeror meant to revoke but whether the offeror's revocation took legal effect before the offeree's acceptance. If a revocation takes legal effect before the intended acceptance, there is no contract, and the would-be acceptance is only a counteroffer. If an acceptance takes legal effect first, there is a contract, and the revocation is inoperative.

Communication of Revocation. When the parties are dealing face-to-face or over the telephone, the jury or judge must determine, as a matter of fact, which party spoke the "magic words" first. When the parties are communicating by letter or telegram, there is an additional complexity in the case because communications may cross each other in transit—a revocation and an acceptance may be in the mail at the same time. Many such problems are solved by applying two presumptions that courts have worked out as to when communications take legal effect: Generally, a revocation is not effective until it is received, whereas an acceptance letter takes legal effect as soon as it is mailed. In general, a letter is received when the post office finishes handling it; that is, when the letter is delivered at the place a party has designated for receipt of such communications. If you have a mailbox on your front porch and you have left a letter of acceptance of my offer in the mailbox for the mail carrier to pick up, the jury will then have to decide whether the mail carrier dropped my letter of revocation in the mailbox first and then took out your letter of acceptance, or vice versa. In the first case, there is no contract; in the second case, there is a contract.

The UCC establishes a special rule for **communications to an organization**, for all types of contracts that it covers, such as sales of goods, secured transactions, commercial paper, and investment securities. "Organization" includes businesses, such as partnerships and corporations, and also trusts, decedents' estates, and governmental agencies. Such organizations do not "receive" a notice or notification until it comes to the attention of the person who is conducting the transaction, or within the time when it would have come to that person's attention if the organization had a proper procedure for handling incoming communications. If you were negotiating a UCC contract with a large automobile company, for example, your notice would not be received when the post office delivered a sack of mail to the company. Your notice would be received when it actually reached the desk of the individual you were dealing with or when it should have reached that person if the company had a proper mail-handling system. This may not sound like a big difference, but it could be important. If that company executive mailed a letter accepting your offer to sell steel before your revocation letter got to the sender's desk, a contract would exist. Under prior law, and even now for non-UCC contracts, your letter of revocation would be presumed effective when received by the company, and your offer would terminate at that point.

Revocation of Offer of Unilateral Contract. There is one other conceptually difficult problem regarding revocations. This problem arises when the offeror has offered a unilateral contract. Suppose an offeree, intending to accept, has started to perform the requested act and is then notified by the offeror that the offer is revoked. There is no acceptance unless and until the offeree completes the performance requested, but shouldn't the offeree, in all fairness, be given the chance to finish? Courts disagree here; there are at least three rules. Some states, following the old common law, permit the offer to be withdrawn any time prior to complete performance of the requested act on the basis that every offeree should know that this can happen in a unilateral contract situation. Most courts use a rule that says that an offeree's commencement of performance makes the offer irrevocable for a reasonable period of time, which gives the offeree a chance to finish the performance. If the offeree does render complete performance as requested, then the offeror must perform as promised. A few states go one step further and say that when an offeree has made substantial preparations to perform, the offeree must be given a chance to do so.

Rejection or Counteroffer. A **rejection** by the offeree indicates that the offeree does not wish to do business at all. A counteroffer indicates that the offeree is willing to contract but on terms different from those stated in the original offer. Either of these responses by an offeree operates to terminate the original offer; each of them takes legal effect when it is received by the offeror. A counteroffer gives the original offeror the power to form a contract on the basis of the new terms, by accepting the counteroffer. If the offeree inquires about the possibility of alternative terms but does not indicate an unwillingness to accept the terms offered, such an inquiry is not considered a rejection.

Timing of an Effective Acceptance

When Effective. Like all other person-to-person communications, words of acceptance spoken during a conversation and heard at almost the same instant take legal effect immediately. As we have seen, most litigations arise when the parties have been negotiating by correspondence and their communications have crossed in transit.

As a convenient method of solving some of these problems, the courts have created the **mailbox rule**, which states that a letter of acceptance is effective when it is mailed. This has the effect of placing the risk of lost, delayed, or misdelivered communications on the offeror. The rule holds that there is a contract at the instant the letter is placed in the mailbox, even though the letter is delivered late or not delivered at all.

Exceptions to the Mailbox Rule. There are several situations in which a response intended as an acceptance is not effective when it is sent, but only if and when it is received; that is, there are exceptions to mailbox rule. Perhaps the most obvious of these is the situation in which the letter does not give the offeror's correct address or does not have sufficient postage to be delivered through regular postal procedures. Here the risk of misdelivery should be borne by the offeree, and the letter is an effective acceptance only when it is delivered (if it is delivered at all).

Section 40 of the *Restatement of Contracts, Second*, also indicates that there is no mailbox presumption in effect where the offeree first sends a rejection communication and then tries to accept. The second communication is only a counteroffer unless it overtakes the earlier rejection and is received by the offeror before the rejection is received.

A third exception occurs when an offer specifies that the offeror must receive the offeree's acceptance communication before the acceptance is effective. The mailbox rule is only a presumption; it applies unless the offeror says otherwise. For example, "We must have your acceptance in our main office by the close of business next Friday."

Fourth, there may be no mailbox rule when the offeree responds by using a communication means different from the means of communication that the offeror used for the offer. Generally, if the offeror did not specify the use of a particular means of communication, the offeree may use a different, but still reasonable means of communicating an acceptance and have the acceptance effective when sent (e.g., offer by letter, acceptance-response by telegram). However, if the offeree uses another means of communication that the court feels is "unreasonable" and therefore not "intended" by the offeror, the acceptance is effective only if and when it is delivered (e.g., offer by letter, acceptance-response by carrier pigeon). Finally, if the offeror has specified the one means by which the acceptance must be communicated, a response by any other means is not an acceptance, but only a counteroffer. When you make an offer, you can specify exactly when and how acceptance is to occur.

Nature of an Effective Acceptance

Three main problems arise regarding the nature of an effective acceptance. First, what happens when an offeree responds by saying that the offeree wants to do business but adds, deletes, or modifies one or more of the terms of the offer? Second, what happens when a seller-offeree responds to an order for goods by shipping "nonconforming" (different) goods? And third, when, if ever, does silence by an offeree constitute an effective acceptance?

Offeree Changes Terms. At common law, to be an effective acceptance, a response-communication must agree exactly with the terms of the offer; courts often say it must be a **mirror image** of the offer. This mirror image rule does not mean that the acceptance must literally restate all the terms of the offer, just that it must agree with all of them. Given the right set of facts, a response as simple as "OK" could be interpreted as an acceptance. What the rule does mean is that a response that changes one or more terms is most likely a counteroffer rather than an acceptance, so that no contract is formed when the response is sent. If, for example, an employer writes you a letter offering you a job starting June 1 and you reply, "I accept, but I can't start until June 20," at that point you do not have a job. You have simply made a counteroffer.

As applied by the courts, this rule meant that there was no contract on the buyer's terms in the very frequently occurring situation in which the buyer-offeror sends the seller an order for goods and the seller responds with an acknowledgment/invoice form that contains additional or different terms. If the seller ships the goods and the buyer receives and uses them, there is a contract on the seller's terms. The buyer's use is an acceptance of the seller's counteroffer. If the buyer refused to accept the goods on those terms (e.g., "There are no warranties, express or implied"), there is no contract, and the seller will have to absorb the shipping charges. Dissatisfaction with these results led to a specific UCC provision, 2-207, to deal with this problem in the sale of goods situation. The *Olefins* case discusses these issues.

CASE 3

Olefins Trading, Inc. v. Han Yang Chem. Corp.

9 F.3d 282 (3 Cir. 1993)

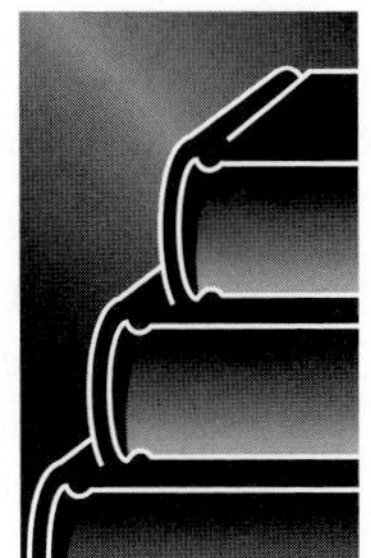

Facts: Olefins is a Connecticut corporation engaged in the trading and marketing of bulk chemicals and chemical products. Han Yang Corp. is a South Korean Corporation and is engaged in the manufacture of petrochemical products. Han Yang maintains an office in New Jersey for the purpose of "sourcing" chemicals for use in its petrochemical business.

On March 13, 1991, Y.I. Han of Olefins and Shin Lee of Han Yang exchanged written confirmation letters outlining the terms of an oral contract formed by the parties on that date. Under the term of the oral contract, Han Yang promised to purchase 4,500 metric tons ("mt") of bulk ethylene (+ 5% at Olefins' option) from Olefins at a price of $915/mt. Olefins promised to deliver the ethylene 1 month later to Han Yang's manufacturing facility in Yeosu, South Korea. Both parties agreed that payment was to be made via a letter of credit in the amount of $4,117,500. Although contested at trial, the jury found that Han Yang had promised to open this letter of credit by March 15, 1991. In addition, both parties agreed that Olefins' chemical supplier, Repsol Petroleum, would produce the ethylene and would ship it directly from Tarragona, Spain to Yeosu, South Korea.

On March 14, 1991, Olefins entered into a supply contract with Repsol for the purchase and sale of 4,500 mt of ethylene to satisfy its obligation to Han Yang. Olefins promised to pay Repsol $890/mt for the ethylene. That same day, Olefins nominated the ship *Teviot* as the cargo vessel that would transport the ethylene from Spain to South Korea. At trial, both Olefins and Han Yang stipulated that the *Teviot* could carry exactly 4,600 mt of ethylene.

Shortly after the contract was formed, however, the international market price of ethylene began to drop dramatically. By early April of 1991, the market price of ethylene was set at approximately $600/mt on a "cost, insurance, and freight" (CIF) basis to South Korea, almost $300/mt less than the international market price 2 weeks earlier. As of April 2, 1991, Han Yang still had not opened a letter of credit as originally agreed.

On April 4, 1991, both parties orally agreed to reduce the quantity of ethylene from 4,500 mt (+ 5%) to 4,200 mt (maximum) and to discount the price from $915/mt to $900/mt. Olefins asserts that both parties also orally agreed that Han Yang would issue Olefins a "commercial credit" in the amount of $238,125 by April 5, 1991; this sum was to be paid to Olefins in the next Olefins-Han Yang transaction. Han Yang vehemently denied having assented to this latter term.

After the parties' oral negotiations concluded, Han Yang sent Olefins a revised purchase confirmation recounting the terms of the modified ethylene contract. The confirmation contained the new quantity and discounted price for the modified ethylene contract, but it did not mention the commercial credit. Olefins responded by insisting that Han Yang concede the commercial credit in the amount of $238,125 "as per agreed on the phone." Han Yang did not respond.

On April 8, 1991, Olefins sent Han Yang a letter demanding that Han Yang open a letter of credit immediately "along with a letter confirming commercial settlement of [Olefins'] estimated losses equaling U.S. $238,125." Again, Han Yang did not accede to the commercial credit term, but on April 9, 1991, Han Yang opened a letter of credit in the modified contract amount of $3,780,000 (4,200 mt × $900/mt) naming Olefins as the beneficiary.

On April 19, 1991, Olefins extended an offer to Han Yang for another shipment of bulk ethylene to Yeosu, South Korea. Ostensibly, this offer was made by Olefins to enable it to recover the commercial credit from the April 4, 1991 transaction. Han Yang rejected this offer.

On April 23, 1991, the *Teviot* was loaded with 4,170 mt of ethylene, bound for South Korea. Olefins asserted that Han Yang caused it to suffer actual losses under the modified contract in the amount of $195,245.55. The jury found for Olefins, but the trial judge entered a judgment for Han Yang.

Issue: Was there an agreement for a "commercial credit" as part of the modified contract?

Decision: Yes. Judgment reversed; case remanded.

Opinion by Circuit Judge Mansmann: "The question of whether the parties have mutually assented to a term is peculiarly a question of fact and properly placed with the factfinder.... In returning a verdict in favor of Olefins, the jury specifically found that Han Yang had expressly agreed to issue the commercial credit to Olefins. Our task is not to disturb that finding; rather, we must enforce the verdict unless it is not supported by the evidence in the record or is otherwise contrary to the law.

"Han Yang argues that the jury verdict is contrary to the law because UCC § 2-207 prevents the commercial credit term from becoming a part of the Olefins-Han Yang contract. We disagree. We hold—consistent with the jury verdict—that because the commercial credit term was specifically agreed upon over the telephone before the parties exchanged confirmatory memoranda, UCC § 2-207 may not be utilized to exclude that term from the contract.

"Section 2-207 of the UCC is designed to prescribe by law, what non-negotiated terms are to be considered a part of a contract—not to exclude those terms specifically negotiated and agreed upon. One of the main purposes of UCC § 2-207 is to facilitate oral contracts that are usually negotiated over the telephone and only later reduced to a writing. In particular, UCC § 2-207 is designed to serve as a way of dealing with conflicting or additional terms that were never a part of the bargaining process.... In other words, terms governed by UCC § 2-207 are those terms that were never expressly agreed upon; rather, they appear only later as non-negotiated terms in confirmatory memoranda or other types of business forms purporting to 'confirm' what was previously discussed orally....

"This is not the situation before us. Here, Olefins and Han Yang expressly agreed to the commercial credit term. It is that agreement which must control....

"Having concluded that the jury's verdict was not contrary to the law, we must now consider whether it was supported by sufficient evidence in the record. Pursuant to Rule 50(a)(1) of the Federal Rules of Civil Procedure, the court may grant a renewed motion for judgment as a matter of law if 'there is no legally sufficient evidentiary basis for a reasonable jury to have found for the prevailing party....' The 'legally sufficient evidentiary basis' has also been characterized as a 'minimum quantum of evidence....' Accordingly, if there is minimally sufficient evidence to support the jury's finding that the commercial credit was an orally agreed upon term, then the court erred in granting Han Yang's Rule 50(b) motion.

"At trial, Y.I. Han of Olefins testified that during the telephone conversation of April 4, 1991, Han Yang's president expressly agreed to issue a commercial credit to Olefins....

"We find further support that there was an oral agreement on the commercial credit term in the testimony of Han Yang's president, Shin Lee. On cross examination, Mr. Lee was questioned abut certain notations he made on a telefax message that he had received from Olefins earlier that day....

"On the basis of this testimony and the telefax messages from Olefins and Han Yang, we conclude that there is sufficient evidence in the record to provide the 'legally sufficient evidentiary basis' necessary to sustain the jury's verdict.... Consequently, we find that the district court erred by granting Han Yang's renewed motion for judgment as a matter of law....

"We will vacate the order of the district court granting Han Yang's renewed motion for judgment as a matter of law. We will instruct the district court to consider Han Yang's motion for a new trial to the extent that allegations of misconduct and the erroneous introduction of evidence are asserted."

UCC 2-207 first says that a response from the seller that indicates that the seller wants to do business is an acceptance, not a counteroffer, even though it contains terms "additional to or different from" those in the offer. The only way for the offeree (seller) to avoid this result is to make the acceptance expressly "conditional on assent to the additional or different terms"—in other words, to clearly make it a counteroffer.

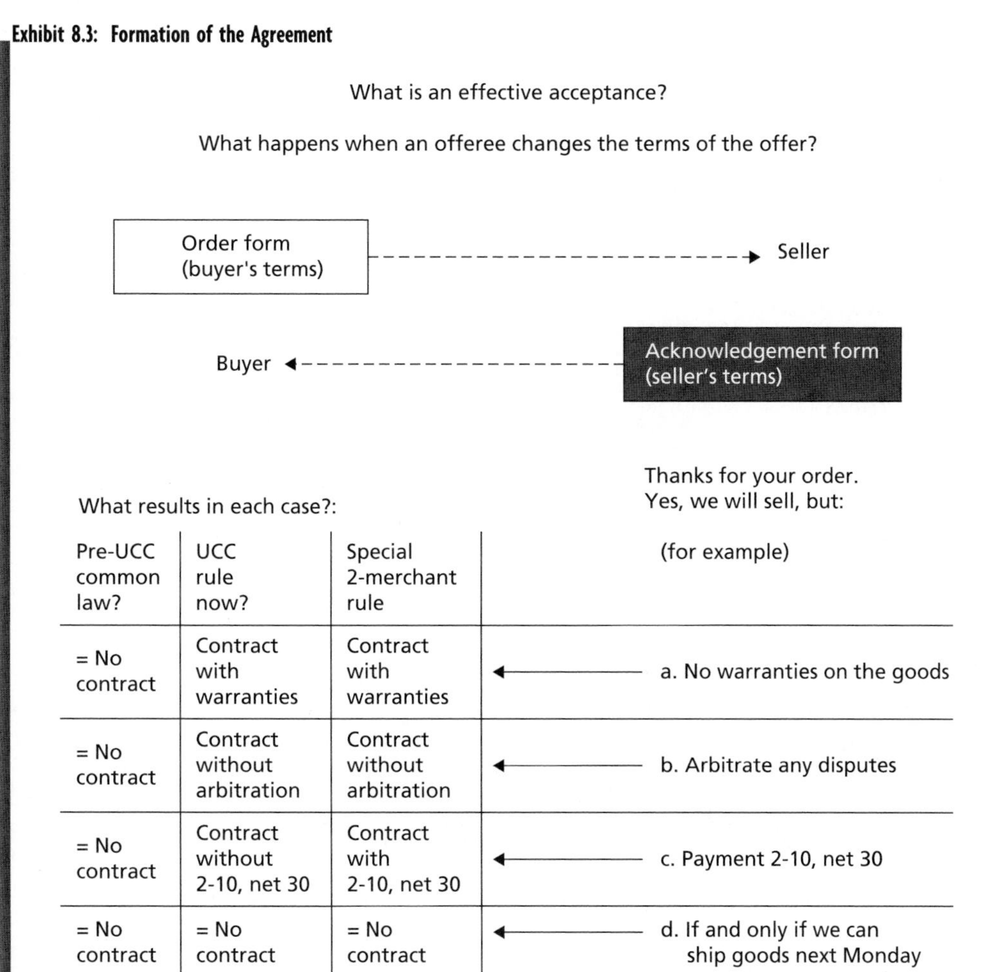
What is an effective acceptance?
What happens when an offeree changes the terms of the offer?
Order form
(buyer's terms)
Seller
Buyer
Acknowledgement form
(seller's terms)
Thanks for your order.
Yes, we will sell, but:
What results in each case?:

Pre-UCC common law?	UCC rule now?	Special 2-merchant rule	(for example)
= No contract	Contract with warranties	Contract with warranties	← a. No warranties on the goods
= No contract	Contract without arbitration	Contract without arbitration	← b. Arbitrate any disputes
= No contract	Contract without 2-10, net 30	Contract with 2-10, net 30	← c. Payment 2-10, net 30
= No contract	= No contract	= No contract	← d. If and only if we can ship goods next Monday

Exhibit 8.3: Formation of the Agreement

Having thus created a contract for the sale of goods, the UCC then proceeds to answer the question: On whose terms? The UCC states: "The additional terms are to be construed as proposals for addition to the contract." In other words, they are *not* part of the contract unless they are specifically agreed to by the offeror; otherwise, there is a contract on the terms of the original offer. When both parties are "merchants," the additional terms become part of the contract unless: (a) the original offer said otherwise, (b) they materially alter the original offer, or (c) the offeror objects to their inclusion within a reasonable time after the offeror has notice of them. When the offeree merchant has included such terms and the offeror-merchant has said nothing specific about their inclusion, the litigation will focus on whether or not the new terms "materially alter" the original offer (see Exhibit 8-3).

Seller Ships Nonconforming Goods. Exactly the same sort of problem, with exactly the same results under the common law rules, is presented by the seller who responds to an order by shipping goods that do not conform to the terms of the order. Buyers were frequently placed in a situation in which they either had to accept the nonconforming goods and make whatever use they could of them, paying for any modifications out of their own pocket or send the nonconforming goods back and sustain "shut-down-the-plant" losses. [Buyer orders blue widgets; seller ships green. If buyer uses green, buyer has accepted seller's counteroffer, and there is a contract for green (see Exhibit 8-4).]

The UCC also has a specific provision, 2-206(1)(b), to deal with this sale of goods problem. The new Code rule states that even a shipment of **nonconforming goods** by the seller, in response to an order, is to be interpreted as an acceptance rather than a counteroffer. (Under the UCC, in the preceding example, there is a contract for blue widgets and

Exhibit 8.4: Formation of the Agreement

OFFEREE CHANGES TERMS

Common Law: Mirror Image Rule	*UCC 2-207: Only for Sale of Goods*
Order ⟶ ⟵ Invoice (Shipment of goods) any changes in invoice = COUNTEROFFER Buyer receives and uses Goods = Acceptance of S's COUNTEROFFER ——— = CONTRACT ON SELLER'S TERMS If Buyer rejects Goods = NO CONTRACT	Order ⟶ ⟵ Invoice (Shipment of goods) = ACCEPTANCE, unless ... Buyer receives and uses Goods ——— = CONTRACT, UNLESS S. EXPRESSLY STATES THAT ITS ACCEPTANCE IS CONDITIONAL ON B's ASSENT TO NEW OR DIFFERENT TERMS. GENERAL RULE: NEW TERMS ARE ONLY PROPOSALS FOR ADDITION TO CONTRACT THAT HAS ALREADY BEEN MADE ON B's TERMS. IF BOTH PARTIES ARE MERCHANTS: NEW TERMS IN, UNLESS: Offeror notifies, or Original Offer specified no new terms, or New Terms materially change Offer.

SELLER SHIPS NONCONFORMING GOODS

Common Law	*UCC 2-206-l(b)*
Order (BLUE widgets) ⟶ ⟵ Ships GREEN = COUNTEROFFER: "GREEN" Buyer receives and uses Goods = ACCEPTANCE OF S' COUNTEROFFER ——— = CONTRACT FOR GREEN; SELLER HAS NOT BREACHED, BUYER GETS NO DAMAGES. or Buyer rejects Goods: no contract ever existed: no breach by Seller, Buyer gets no damages	Order (BLUE widgets) ⟶ ⟵ Ships GREEN = ACCEPTANCE: "BLUE," UNLESS ——— = CONTRACT FOR BLUE, WHICH SELLER HAS BREACHED, UNLESS S. NOTIFIES BUYER THAT GOODS OFFERED FOR ACCOMODATION

the seller has breached this contract and is liable for damages unless the seller sends blue widgets to the buyer within the time permitted by the contract.) The buyer is protected; whether the buyer uses the nonconforming goods or rejects them and buys elsewhere, the buyer can still collect whatever damages are sustained.

Silence as Acceptance. Because, normally, an offeree has no duty to respond to an offer, the offeree's failure to respond cannot be given any particular legal significance. The offeree's silence is therefore not effective as an acceptance in most cases. The common law did, however, recognize four exceptions to this general rule.

First, when an offeree has the opportunity to reject offered services but instead takes the benefit of them, the offeree's silence does imply an acceptance. By permitting the offeror to perform services that a reasonable person should have known were not being offered for nothing, the offeree has impliedly agreed to pay a fair market price for them.

Second, when the offeror has told the offeree that he or she can accept the offer by not saying or doing anything, just by remaining silent, and the offeree actually does intend his or her silence to have that effect, it does.

Third, when because of previous dealings, such as a standing order with a book or record club, the offeree has indicated to the offeror that nonnotification by the offeree means that the standing order should be continued, the offeree's silence has the effect of continuing the standing order.

Finally, when nonordered merchandise is sent to the offeree and the offeree exercises "dominion" over it, this dominion has the effect of an acceptance and an implied promise to pay the offered contract price. An example would be reading an unordered book or magazine or giving it to someone else.

The second and fourth rules have now been substantially changed because nearly all states have **unordered goods statutes**. These laws vary; the strongest ones make such unsolicited goods an absolute, out-and-out gift to the recipient, who has no obligation to return them, to pay for them, or to account for them in any way.

Special "Cancellation" Rules

At the point when the agreement had been formed by offer and acceptance (and assuming an exchange of legally sufficient considerations), the common law analysis would have said there was a binding contract. This result still occurs in the vast majority of contract situations. However, there is a growing trend under new statutes and regulations to give the consumer/buyer a "cancellation" privilege for at least a limited period of time, even after the contract has been entered into.

For example, FTC regulations and statutes in several states give the consumer a 3-day cancellation option when the contract is entered into in the consumer's home and is for more than a specified minimum amount. Each of these new laws is likely to contain some exceptions; life insurance sales and emergency home repairs may not be covered, for instance.

The U.S. Truth-in-Lending Act gives a similar 3-day rescission option in which the borrower's residence has been used as security for a loan, except for the first mortgage to finance the original purchase of the house. The National Interstate Land Sales Act gives a buyer 48 hours to revoke a purchase of land when the buyer has not been given the required "property report" on the land. Many of the states have separate laws covering these same general areas.

If the proposed Uniform Consumer Credit Code (UCCC) is widely adopted by the states, it will cover more transactions than any of the preceding examples; its 3-day cancellation privilege applies to any consumer transaction for goods or services, with no dollar minimum, when the sale is made in the buyer's home, or when the home is used as collateral (other than in the original purchase of the home). The UCCC has not yet been widely adopted.

For consumer transactions, at least, it appears that we will have to ask this fourth question about many agreements in the very near future.

Uniform Computer Information Transactions Act and United Nations Convention on Contracts for the International Sales of Goods Rules

Uniform Computer Information Transactions Act Rules for Offer and Acceptance

A ponderous new statute, the Uniform Computer Information Transactions Act (UCITA), has been proposed for adoption by the 50 states. According to its definitions, "computer information" is "information in electronic form which is obtained from or through the use of a computer or which is in a form capable of being processed by a computer." A "computer information transaction" is therefore an agreement "to create, modify, transfer, or license computer information or informational rights in computer information."

UCITA has its own version of the mirror image rule in Section 204. A purported acceptance is effective as such, even though it contains "terms that vary from the terms of the offer, unless the acceptance materially alters the offer." The non-material changes that conflict with the original offer are not part of the contract. Between merchants, non-material additional terms will become part of the contract unless objected to by the other merchant. If either party is not a merchant, the non-material additional terms do not become part of the contract unless agreed to by the other party. If there are material changes, there is no contract unless the other party agrees to them, or all the circumstances establish the existence of a contract.

United Nations Convention on Contracts for the International Sale of Goods Rules for Offer and Acceptance

By way of comparison to both the UCC and the UCITA, the U.N. Convention on Contracts for the International Sale of Goods (UNC/CISG), having adopted the mirror image rule, then goes on to state that an acceptance can contain non-material "additional or different terms," and still act as an acceptance, unless the offeror objects. If there is no objection, there is a contract—which includes these non-material changes. The implication is that if the offeror objects, there is no contract at all. Article 19-3 provides a list of material changes: those "relating, among other things, to the price, payment, quality and quantity of the goods, place and time of delivery, extent of one party's liability to the other or the settlement of disputes." An otherwise positive response that included one or more such changes would presumably be a counteroffer, even if not objected to by the offeror. Thus a California car dealer ordering parts from a German supplier would be subject to quite different rules (UNC/CISG) than those applicable if the electronic message were sent to a Michigan manufacturer (UCC), or if the order were for computer software (UCITA—perhaps).

The *Asante* case discusses the applicability of the CISG to an international sale of computer equipment parts.

CASE 4

Asante Technologies, Inc. v. PMC-Sierra, Inc.

164 F.Supp.2d 1142 (N.D. CA 2001)

Facts: Plaintiff Asante is a Delaware corporation, with its principal place of business in California. It produces network switches, an electronic component used to connect multiple computers to one another and to the Internet. It buys application-specific integrated circuits (ASICs) from PMC-Sierra. PMC is also a Delaware corporation, with its principal place of business in British Columbia, Canada. It also has an engineering office in Portland, Oregon. Its products are sold in California by an authorized distributor, Unique Technologies, located in California. Four of the five batches of ASICs involved here were purchased through Unique; the fifth purchase order was sent directly to PMC-Sierra in Canada. PMC-Sierra shipped the goods from Canada directly to Asante; payment was made through Unique. Asante's purchase orders specified that California law was applicable; PMC-Sierra's shipment documents specified British Columbia law and Canada Law applied.

Not mentioning the CISG, Asante filed its complaint in California state court. PMC-Sierra had the case removed to U.S. District Court, on the basis that a "federal question" (the interpretation of a treaty—CISG) was involved. Asante has now moved to have the case remanded to the state court.

Issue: Does the CISG apply to this contract, so that the case can be tried in U.S. District Court?

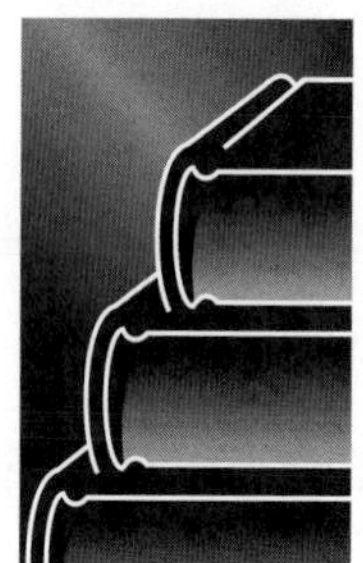

Decision: Yes. Plaintiff's motion to remand is denied.

Opinion by Judge Ware: "The Complaint asserts . . . two claims for breach of contract and a claim for breach of express warranty based on the failure of the delivered ASICs to conform to the agreed technical specifications. . . . In support of these claims, Plaintiff relies on multiple representations allegedly made by Defendant regarding the technical specifications of the ASICs products at issue. . . . It appears undisputed that each of these alleged representations . . . was issued from Defendant's headquarters in British Columbia, Canada. . . .

"Rather than challenge the Canadian source of these documents, Plaintiff shifts its emphasis to the purchase orders submitted by Plaintiff to Unique Technologies, a nonexclusive distributor of Defendant's products. Plaintiff asserts that Unique acted in the United States as an agent of Defendant, and that Plaintiff's contacts with Unique establish Defendant's place of business in the U.S. for the purposes of this contract.

"Plaintiff has failed to persuade the Court that Unique acted as the agent of Defendant. Plaintiff provides no legal support for this proposition. To the contrary, a distributor of goods for resale is normally not treated as an agent of the manufacturer. . . . 'One who receives goods from another for resale to a third person is not thereby the other's agent in the transaction.' ... Plaintiff has produced no evidence of consent by Defendant to be bound by the acts of Unique. To the contrary, Defendant cites the distributorship agreement with Unique, which expressly states that the contract does not 'allow Distributor to create or assume any obligation on behalf of [Defendant] for any purpose whatsoever.' ... Furthermore, while Unique may distribute Defendant's products, Plaintiff does not allege that Unique made any representations regarding technical specifications on behalf of Defendant. Indeed, Unique is not even mentioned in the Complaint. To the extent that representations were made regarding the technical specifications of the ASICs, and those specifications were not satisfied by the delivered goods, the relevant agreement is that between Plaintiff and Defendant. Accordingly, the Court finds that Unique is not an agent of Defendant in this dispute. Plaintiff's dealings with Unique do not establish Defendant's place of business in the United States.

"Plaintiff's claims concern breaches of representations made by Defendant from Canada. Moreover, the products in question are manufactured in Canada, and Plaintiff knew that Defendant was Canadian, having sent one purchase order directly to Defendant in Canada by fax.... Anthony Contos, Plaintiff's Vice President of Finance and Administration ... states that Plaintiff's primary contact with Defendant 'during the development and engineering of the ASICs at issue ... was with [Defendant's] facilities in Portland, Oregon.' ... The Court concludes that these contacts are not sufficient to override the fact that most if not all of Defendant's alleged misrepresentations regarding the technical specifications of the products emanated from Canada.... Moreover, Plaintiff directly corresponded with Defendant at Defendant's Canadian address.... In contrast, Plaintiff has not identified any specific representation or correspondence emanating from Defendant's Oregon branch. For these reasons, the Court finds that Defendant's place of business that has the closest relationship to the contract and its performance is British Columbia, Canada. Consequently, the contract at issue in this litigation is between parties from two different Contracting States, Canada and the United States....

"Plaintiff argues that, even if the Parties are from two nations that have adopted the CISG, the choice of law provisions in the 'Terms and Conditions' set forth by both Parties reflect the Parties' intent to 'opt out' of the application of the treaty.... Defendant asserts that merely choosing the law of a jurisdiction is insufficient to opt out of the CISG, absent express exclusion of the CISG. The Court finds that the particular choice of law provisions in the 'Terms and Conditions' of both parties are inadequate to effectuate an opt out of the CISG....

"Although the CISG is plainly limited in its scope, ... the CISG nevertheless can and does preempt state contract law to the extent that the state causes of action fall within the scope of the CISG....

"For the foregoing reasons, Plaintiff's Motion to Remand is DENIED."

Significance of This Chapter

Whenever a claim for breach of contract is asserted, the other party may argue that no agreement was ever reached and thus there was no duty to perform. As we have seen, this "no agreement" argument may be made as to the entire alleged contract or only as to particular terms. When this argument is presented, the claimant must prove that an offer had been made and that it was accepted while still open for acceptance. Failure to prove any of these points means that there was no contract and, therefore, no breach and no liability.

Typically, actual cases will involve other defense arguments along with "no agreement." For discussion purposes in the remaining contracts chapters, we will assume that an agreement did exist.

The next chapter will discuss the second part of our contract formula: the requirement that the parties' agreement provides for an exchange of values or that it involves one of the recognized alternative bases for enforcement.

IMPORTANT TERMS AND CONCEPTS

acceptance
agreement
Agreement = Offer + Acceptance
bilateral contract
capacity
communications to an organization
consideration
continuing offers
contract = Agreement + Consideration
contract law
counteroffer
executed contract
executory contract
express contract
express revocation
false advertising
firm offer
implied contract
implied revocation
intent to contract
mailbox rule
manner of acceptance
merchant
mirror image
nonconforming goods
offer
offeree
offeror
option contract
preliminary negotiations

promise
promisee
promisor
quasi-contract
reasonable time
rejection
Restatement of Contracts
Statute of Frauds
unenforceable contract
Uniform Commercial Code (UCC)
unilateral contract
unjust enrichment
unordered goods statutes
valid contract
voidable contract

QUESTIONS AND PROBLEMS FOR DISCUSSION

1. What is the meaning and significance of the mailbox rule?

2. What is the difference between a firm offer and a continuing offer?

3. What is the difference between an implied-in-fact contract and an implied-in-law contract?

4. What is the difference between a bilateral contract and a unilateral contract?

5. On February 27, 1967, Rudy Turilli, owner of the Jesse James Museum at Stanton, Missouri, appeared on Joe Pyne's late-evening TV "talk show." Rudy discussed his theory that Jesse James (the famous train and bank robber) had not really been shot in the back and killed by Robert Ford in 1882 but had lived into the 1950s and had actually stayed with Rudy at his museum. During the course of the discussion, Rudy said he believed his theory so strongly that he "would pay $10,000 to anyone, yourself, Mr. Pyne, Mr. Gruber, the audience, and the network audience, to anyone who could prove me wrong."

   Stella James (Jesse's daughter-in-law) and her two daughters claimed the $10,000 on the basis of several affidavits, from people in and acquainted with the James family, stating facts that tended to prove that Jesse was killed in 1882. Rudy refused to pay, and Stella James and her two daughters brought suit to collect the reward. Rudy appealed the judgment for the plaintiffs.

   Have the plaintiffs complied with the terms of the offer of the reward?

6. Compo, Inc., mailed out an advertising circular to a large number of businesses. The circular was mailed in August and was headlined "Christmas comes early at Compo." It described a list of premiums that could be selected, based on the size of an order. Deal 25E gave the customer a new LeCount convertible and fifty Dazzo cameras for only $1,000 extra with an order of $500,000 or more. The Piggie Bank ordered over $500,000 worth of computers and software and indicated that it wanted Deal 25E. Compo telephoned Piggie and told them that their order was refused. Piggie bought their computers elsewhere and now sues Compo for damages.

   What is the result, and why?

7. On April 6, the defendant published the following advertisement in a Minneapolis newspaper: "SATURDAY 9 am SHARP. 3 BRAND NEW FUR COATS. Worth to $100.00. First Come, First Served. $1 EACH."

   On April 13, the defendant published a similar advertisement: "SATURDAY 9 am 2 BRAND NEW PASTEL MINK 3-SKIN SCARFS. Selling for $89.50. Out they go Saturday. Each . . . $1.00, 1 BLACK LAPIN STOLE, Beautiful, Worth $139.50 . . . $1.00. First Come, First Served."

   On each Saturday the plaintiff was the first to present himself at the appropriate counter in the defendant's store. On the first Saturday, he demanded the advertised coat, and on the second Saturday, he demanded the advertised stole. On both occasions, he indicated his readiness to pay the sales price of $1, and on both occasions, the defendant refused to sell the merchandise to the plaintiff, stating at the time of the plaintiff's first visit that by a "house rule" the offer was intended for women only and sales would not be made to men, and at the time of the second visit that the plaintiff knew the defendant's house rules. The defendant appealed the trial court's award of $138.50 damages.

   How should the appeals court rule? Explain.

8. Marc Pevar asked several manufacturers for price quotes on the medium density overlay plywood that his company needed. Evans made the lowest quote, in a telephone conversation on October 12, 1995. Pevar claims that it called Evans back on October 14 and ordered the plywood. Evans admits getting the call but denies that it accepted that order. Pevar later sent Evans a written purchase order for the plywood. This written order specified the price, quantity, and shipping instructions but did not mention warranties or remedies for breach. On October 19, Evans sent Pevar a written acknowledgment of the order. Evans's form said that the contract was expressly conditional on Pevar's agreement to all its terms, including a disclaimer of most warranties and a limitation of remedies. Evans shipped the plywood, which was accepted and paid for by Pevar. Pevar later brought suit for breach of warranty; Evans claimed its acknowledgment form controlled the terms of the contract. Both parties moved for summary judgment.

   Who wins, and why?

9. Plaintiff was formerly a patrolman with the Nebraska State Patrol. He filed an action for overtime pay. The claim was denied. He then appealed to the district court for

Lancaster County, Nebraska, and the court also denied his claim. He states he was hired on the basis of a 50-hour week and paid a stated monthly salary. Plaintiff states he worked many hours overtime and if he determined his hourly rate by dividing his monthly salary on the basis of 50 hours per week then he is entitled to $2,142.53 in overtime pay. He states that he is entitled to overtime under the theory of implied contract. He appeals.

How should the court decide?

10. Chilewich International is a New York import/export company. In 2005, it contracted to sell footwear to Razno Export, a Russian company. Their contract specified that any disputes would be heard by arbitration in the Moscow Chamber of Commerce. To provide the boots, Chilewich contacted Filanto S.P.A., a large Italian manufacturer. Chilewich claims that a March 13, 2006 letter it sent to Filanto contains the essential terms of their contract; the letter indicated that the terms of the prior contract with Razno were "incorporated as far as practicable," and that all claims would be arbitrated in Moscow. Filanto signed and returned a copy of this letter, but attached its own letter that indicated that it agreed with only three terms of the prior Razno contract.

    Claiming they were defective, Chilewich rejected 90,000 boots. Filanto sued in U.S. District Court in New York. Chilewich moved to have the case heard in Moscow, "as agreed." The international Arbitration Convention requires arbitration if there is a contract clause to that effect, or a separate signed arbitration agreement or one "contained in an exchange of letters or telegrams." Filanto claimed it had never agreed to arbitrate.

    Where should this case be heard, and why?

CHAPTER 9

Consideration and Unconscionability

Chapter Objectives

This chapter will:

- Define the term *consideration.*
- Discuss the four methods of complying with the consideration requirement.
- Explain the various types of exchanges that do not provide a legally sufficient consideration.
- Discuss the doctrine of unconscionability.

This chapter is concerned with the second part of our contract "formula"—the requirement of consideration. Once again, we need to know the answers to three main questions: What does the law mean by consideration? What are the basic methods of complying with this requirement? What do the courts accept as legally sufficient consideration?

We will use Uncle Ned and his nephew Johnny to provide some factually simple hypothetical examples of how the consideration rules work.

Definition of the Consideration Requirement

Basic Definitions

In our legal system a promise is generally not enforceable as a contract, even if it is agreed to by the promisee, unless the promise is supported by legally sufficient **consideration**. In other words, a completely one-sided promise of benefits (a promise of "something for nothing") does not generally bind the **promisor** to performance or make the promisor liable in the event of nonperformance. If Uncle Ned promises to give Johnny $5,000 as a Christmas present and then changes his mind, Johnny cannot sue and collect the $5,000, even if the promise was written and signed or was made in front of witnesses. The consideration requirement, most simply stated, means that unless *something* is given in return for the promise, the promise is not legally enforceable.

Source and Recipient of Consideration

The required consideration may be supplied by the **promisee** or by a third person. Uncle Ned would be contractually obligated if he had promised Johnny the $5,000 in return for a house painting job and Johnny saw to it that the job was done, whether or not Johnny did the work. When Uncle Ned gets his house painted according to the terms of the agreement, he owes Johnny the $5,000 (see Exhibit 9-1).

Likewise, the benefits given in return for the promise may be given to the promisor or to a third person. If Uncle Ned promised the $5,000 to Johnny if Johnny would paint H.O. Moaner's house, he is bound to pay the money if Johnny does the job. Even if no one receives anything that most people would think of as a "benefit," there is legally sufficient

Exhibit 9.1: Consideration

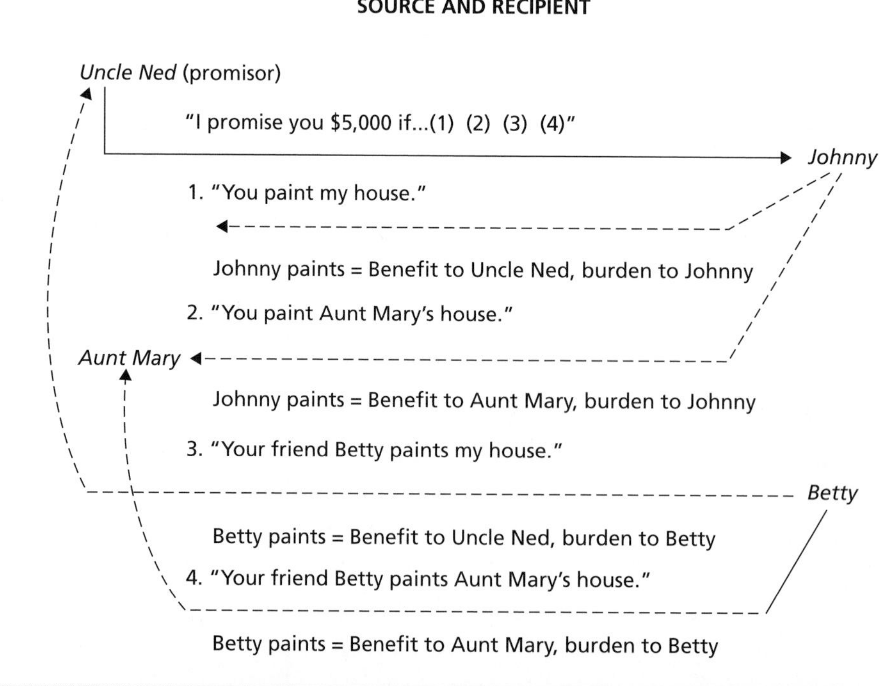

consideration if the promisee has assumed a burden, by doing something that he or she was not already legally bound to do. If Uncle Ned promises the $5,000 to Johnny if Johnny stops smoking until age 21, and Johnny does so, Uncle Ned is legally obligated to pay the money. In each of these last two examples, Uncle Ned has received a legal benefit, in the sense that he got the performance he bargained for as the price for his promise, and he has therefore received consideration.

Compliance with the Consideration Requirement

There are four ways in which the consideration requirement may be satisfied, so that the promisor is legally bound to perform his or her promise: (1) a **bargained-for exchange of values**, (2) a change of legal position by the promisee in reliance on the promise, (3) the seal, or (4) a statutory exception to the requirement. In each of the last three cases, the promise is enforced even though there was no exchange or bargain in the usual sense.

Bargained-for Exchange of Values

The basic meaning of the consideration requirement is that there must be a bargain for there to be a contract; promises to make gifts, with nothing given in return, are not legally enforceable. The usual method of complying with the consideration requirement, therefore, is to prove the existence of a bargain, to prove that something was given or promised in return. Because the law generally does not concern itself with whether the bargain was a good one or a bad one, but only with the question of whether there was in fact a bargain, the promisee should be able to enforce the promise by showing that there was an agreement for any sort of exchange of benefits.

In most cases the existence or nonexistence of a bargain can be seen pretty clearly, but the facts are somewhat ambiguous in a few situations. One of the most difficult distinctions to draw is that between a condition attached to the promise of a gift (no contract) and a burden undertaken as part of a bargain (contract).

Suppose that Uncle Ned says to Johnny, "Come over to the house Saturday night, and I'll fix you a steak dinner." Is Uncle Ned contractually obligated to provide a steak dinner

Exhibit 9.2: The Consideration Element in a Litigation

PLAINTIFF v. DEFENDANT

Sues to enforce an alleged contract →

1. We had an agreement.
2. It was supported by consideration.
3. I was ready to perform (or had performed).
4. You breached.
5. I am damaged as a result.

← I am not liable, because no consideration

Proof of consideration, or an alternate →

a. Bargained-for exchange of values (something for something)
b. Promissory estoppel
c. Seal (in some states)
d. Special statutory exception

when Johnny arrives as requested? No, he is not—for two reasons. First, Uncle Ned's promise is not intended by him, or reasonably understood by Johnny, as a contractual arrangement. Second, "coming over to the house" is neither intended nor understood as the price of the steak dinner.

What about the case where Uncle Ned tells Johnny, "When you get married, I'll give you $5,000," and Johnny does in fact get married? Whether Johnny's marriage supplies consideration for Uncle Ned's promise depends on the parties' intent, as derived by the court from the surrounding facts and circumstances. If Johnny already had his wedding planned and the date set and Uncle Ned was just making a promise of a cash wedding gift, there is probably no consideration for the promise and thus no contract. But if Uncle Ned is trying to induce Johnny away from life as a "swinging single," the initiative for the marriage comes from Uncle Ned rather than Johnny, and Johnny in response to the promise does as his uncle requests and gets married, Uncle Ned is contractually bound to pay the money. (Such a promise would probably have to be made in a signed writing to be enforceable.)

In the next case example, it appears that Mr. Pitts may have provided some benefits to the company but was unable to show any agreement for an exchange of benefits.

CASE 1

Pitts v. McGraw-Edison Company

329 F.2d 412 (6 Cir. 1964)

Facts: Plaintiff was a manufacturer's representative in Memphis, Tennessee, for a period of many years prior to July 1, 1955. For approximately 25 years preceding that date, he sold the products of the defendant, McGraw-Edison Company, on a commission basis in an assigned territory comprising several southern states. In his capacity as a manufacturer's representative, he was an independent businessman, hiring and firing his own employees, paying his own expenses and overhead, and managing his business as he saw fit. He had no written contract with the defendant, and the defendant had no obligation to him except to compensate him on a commission basis for sales made in the assigned territory. It was terminable at will, without notice, by either party at any time. The plaintiff was free to handle any other products he desired, including those of competitors of the defendant, and he did so until early in 1954, when on his own volition and without any requirement by the defendant, he discontinued his representation of other manufacturers.

In April 1955, when the plaintiff was approximately 67 years of age, he accompanied O. Dee Harrison, the sales manager for the defendant, to Little Rock, Arkansas, for a meeting with one Paul Thurman, who had formerly worked for the plaintiff but at the time was working in the State of Arkansas as a factory representative for the defendant and others. At that meeting, Mr. Harrison told the plaintiff that the defendant was making arrangements for the plaintiff to retire at a time shortly thereafter and for Thurman to take over the plaintiff's territory, with the plaintiff receiving an overwrite commission of 1 percent from the defendant on all sales made in the territory. Thereafter the plaintiff received a letter dated July 1, 1955, from O. Dee Harrison reading in part as follows:

> *Dear Lou:*
>
> *Whether you know it or not, you are on retirement effective July 1st. But to make the matter of retirement a little less distasteful, we are going ahead as you and I talked last time we were together by paying each month 1 percent of the ... sales from the Mississippi and Tennessee states. You will get your check each month just as you have been in the habit of getting our check on commissions. Let us hope that there is enough to help keep a few pork chops on the table and a few biscuits in the oven.*
>
> *We are going to keep you on the list for bulletins, Lou, so that you will know what is going on. I know that you will help Paul in every way that you can, and I know that your help will be greatly appreciated by Paul.*

A letter dated July 20 also said:

> *We will keep you on the mailing list and any time you can throw a little weight our way we will appreciate any effort you make, Lou. And any time you have any questions, don't be afraid to ask us about them.*

The plaintiff received a check from the defendant each month regularly from July 1955 through June 1960 covering the 1 percent commission on sales in the specified territory.

On July 23, 1960, the defendant sent a letter reading in part as follows:

> *Dear Mr. Pitts:*
>
> *I am enclosing our check #50064752 for $238.51 which, according to our records, completes the five-year series of payments to be paid after your retirement from the Company.*

Pitts sued for $15,000 damages. Following a trial to the court without a jury, the district judge held that the plaintiff was not entitled to recover any amount whatever and dismissed his complaint.

Issue: Had Pitts promised or provided any benefits to the company in exchange for the 1 percent commission?

Decision: No. Judgment affirmed.

Opinion *by* Circuit Judge Miller: "Plaintiff contends that the negotiations between the Company and him leading to his retirement were in substance an offer on the part of the Company that if he would retire as a manufacturer's representative on July 1, 1955, and turn over to his successor representative all of his customer account records containing valuable information on active and inactive accounts, which had been built up over a period of twenty years or more, the Company would pay him monthly thereafter a 1 percent overwrite commission on sales by the defendant in the territory which was at that time allotted to him; that after considering the offer, he accepted it and thereafter carried it out by retiring as a manufacturer's representative and turning over to his successor the stipulated records; and that the defendant breached the contract by refusing to make the payments after July 1, 1960.

"In considering these contentions, it must be kept in mind that the plaintiff was an independent businessman, not an employee of the defendant. His relationship with the defendant could be terminated by either party at any time without notice and without liability therefor. The plaintiff in his testimony concedes this, and it was so found as a fact by the District Judge. Unless the plaintiff is able to establish a valid contract obligating the defendant to pay the 'retirement' benefits claimed, he has no cause of action.

"Assuming, without so holding, that there was a promise by the defendant to pay the plaintiff the retirement benefits claimed, we are faced with the question of what consideration passed from the plaintiff to the defendant to make this promise enforceable.

"Plaintiff vigorously argues that although he did not *promise* to do anything or to refrain from doing anything, as plainly appears from the two letters, and so conceded by him, consideration nevertheless exists because of the action taken by him at the request of the defendant, namely, his retirement as a manufacturer's representative, including other manufacturers as well as the defendant, and his turning over to the defendant his personal records, pertaining to customers and sales over a period of years in the past. There would be merit in this contention if it was supported by the facts....

"However, these factual contentions of the plaintiff were disputed by the evidence of the defendant. The District Judge made findings of fact that the plaintiff was not required by the terms of the letters, or by any other statements on the part of the defendant, or its agents, to do anything whatsoever; that upon his retirement of July 1, 1955, the plaintiff was free to handle the products of any other manufacturer or competitor if he so desired, to seek other employment, or to do as he pleased; that nothing in the arrangement circumscribed the plaintiff's actions or rights in any manner; and that the plaintiff was not obligated to perform any duties on behalf of the defendant. These findings are fully supported by the evidence. In fact, they were substantially conceded by the plaintiff in the cross-examination of him as a witness in which he apparently contended that he did certain things for the defendant after his retirement although he was not required to do so."

Change of Position in Reliance

Most courts today accept the rule stated in Section 90 of the *Restatement of the Law of Contracts, Second:* "A promise which the promisor should reasonably expect to induce action or forbearance of a definite and substantial character on the part of the promisee or a third person, and which does induce such action or forbearance is binding if injustice can be avoided only by enforcement of the promise." In other words, when the promisee, reasonably relying on the promise of benefits, makes a substantial change in his or her legal position, a court will estop (prevent) the promisor from using the "no consideration" argument when he or she is sued on the promise. The courts usually refer to this concept as **promissory estoppel**.

If, after Uncle Ned makes his promise of a $5,000 gift, Jonny goes out and buys a new car, which he would not have bought except for his reliance on the promise, Uncle Ned may be estopped from asserting a no consideration defense when Johnny sues him for the money. Johnny would have to prove that his reliance was reasonable.

The *Jordan* case is a classic example of this doctrine.

The Seal

As an alternative method of holding people to promises made and accepted, the common law said that if the promise was made in writing and "sealed," there was a **conclusive presumption** that consideration had been given in return.

Promisors, in other words, were not able to make the no consideration argument against their signed and sealed written promises. The use of the word **seal** or the initials "L.S." before or after the promisor's signature was sufficient.

CASE 2

JORDAN v. MOUNT SINAI HOSPITAL OF GREATER MIAMI, INC.

276 So.2d 102 (FL App. 1973)

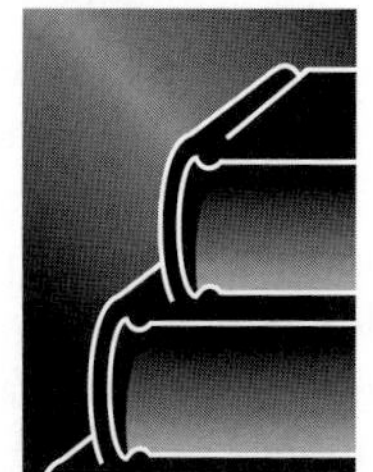

Facts: Harry M. Burt died November 18, 1968. Mount Sinai filed in the probate court its claim against his estate alleging a balance of $40,000 due on each of two pledges. The trial court ruled in favor of Mount Sinai, and Burt's estate appealed.

On February 23 and May 15, 1968, Harry M. Burt signed two pledges of $50,000 each. He made payments of $10,000 on each pledge. At the time of his death, $80,000 remained to be paid.

The subscription agreements were in the following form:

> "*MOUNT SINAI HOSPITAL DEVELOPMENT FUND*
>
> "*In consideration of and to induce the subscriptions of others, I (we) promise to pay to Mount Sinai Hospital of Greater Miami, Inc. or order the sum of Fifty Thousand and no/100 dollars, $5,000 payable herewith: Balance in nine equal annual installments commencing on.*
>
> "*Signature*
> "*Date*"

Issue: Were the pledges to Mount Sinai supported by consideration?

Decision: No. Judgment reversed. (Burt's estate wins.)

Opinion by Judge Crews: "The primary question is whether the consideration stated in the subscription is legally sufficient to make binding the promise of the subscriber so as to be enforceable by the promise. The briefs of able counsel failed to cite a Florida case in point, and our independent research has not disclosed one. It is not a question, however, that has not been answered by other authorities.

"A few jurisdictions have found and approved as consideration the mutual promise of subscribers. But as stated in 83 C.J.S. Subscriptions @ 5, subparagraph (3), there is definitely a conflict of authority on this point. . . .

"The connecting thread in most of these cases is that the agreement which was sought to be enforced (a voluntary promise on the part of the payor), either imposed upon the promisee some obligation which it assumed, or the requested performance of some service on the strength of the promise. When those conditions were met, there was sufficient legal consideration to uphold enforcement of the promise; for if money is promised to be paid upon the condition that the promisee will do some act or perform certain services, then the latter may, upon performance, compel payment.

"While the rule is frequently stated without exception, a factual exception or additional circumstances seems to be apparent in the majority of those cases; that circumstance being one of actual reliance upon the subscription by the charitable institution. . . .

"A goodly number of jurisdictions and certain learned text writers, notably Williston and Corbin, are of the opinion that mutual promises to subscribe lack sufficient consideration to allow enforcement of charitable pledges. . . . 'It is doubtless possible for two or more persons to make mutual promises that each will give a specified amount to a charity or other object, but in the case of ordinary charitable subscription, the promise of each subscriber is made directly to the charity, or its trustees, and it is frequently made without any reference to the subscription of others. If induced at all by previous or expected subscriptions, this inducement only affects the motive of the subscriber; it cannot be said that the previous subscriptions were given in exchange for the later one. Indeed the earlier subscriptions would be open to the objection of being past consideration so far as a later subscription was concerned.' . . .

"Additionally, it has been held that labor and expenses in obtaining other subscribers do not constitute a consideration to support a promise of charitable contribution . . . and subscriptions which are conditioned upon all subscriptions for a like purpose aggregating a certain amount of money by a certain date are deemed to lack legal consideration to make them enforceable. . . .

"A majority of courts which have enforced charitable subscriptions do so on the theory of a unilateral-bilateral contract, or by applying the doctrine of promissory estoppel. . . .

"In such states, neither a request in a unilateral contract nor a return promise in a bilateral contract need to be expressed, because implication will suffice. . . .

"For the doctrine of promissory estoppel to be applicable, the promisor must make a promise which he should reasonably expect to induce action or forbearance of a substantial character on the part of the promisee, and where injustice could only be avoided by the enforcement of the promise. . . . [T]he charity must perform acts or incur expenses in reliance upon the strength of the pledge . . .

"The pledges state only that they are made 'in consideration of and to induce the subscriptions of others.'

"We view this statement as a mere gratuitous promise to a future gift lacking consideration and hence, unenforceable as a nudum pactum. We would still adhere to this proposition even if there had been evidence, which there was not, that the decedent's pledges were used to induce others to subscribe. . . .

"The pledge cards made no specific reference as to the purpose of the gift except to indicate that it was to the 'Development Fund.' Appellee did not claim or assert below that the subscriber gave to some specific project or cause which was thereafter instituted in total or partial reliance on the promise of future contributions. Hence, there is no predicate upon which this court could adopt the unilateral-bilateral doctrine, to enforce a charitable pledge even if it were so inclined.

"Neither can the appellee find solace in the doctrine of promissory estoppel. The record is devoid of any evidence that the promisee was induced in reliance upon decedent's promise to take any substantial action, or to forego any material right, so that an injustice could only be avoided by applying this equitable doctrine. . . .

"Courts should act with restraint in respect to the public policy arguments endeavoring to sustain a mere charitable subscription. To ascribe consideration where there is none, or to adopt any other theory which affords charities a different legal rationale than other entities, is to approve fiction.

"The wisdom of such a policy, its possible detriment as well as its benefit to public bodies, may be the subject of legislative inquiry and decision.

"In the interim, educational, religious, fraternal, or other charitable institutions will have to depend upon the goodwill reposing in the heart of an educated, religious, fraternal, or charitable disposed donor for payment of a gratuitous promise."

Only a few states follow this rule today. In about half of the states, a seal on the signed writing supplies a **rebuttable presumption** of consideration, meaning that the promisor still has a chance to prove that no consideration was given for the promise. Similarly, in many states the presence of a corporate seal on a document creates a rebuttable presumption that the document was executed by someone who had authority to act for the corporation.

In about half of the states, the presence of a seal on a signed, written document creates no presumption at all as to consideration: The promisee must prove consideration by one of the other methods.

Uniform Commercial Code Rule on the Seal. This last, "no-effect-at-all" rule is adopted by the Uniform Commercial Code (UCC) (2-203) for the sale of goods, so that many states now have two rules on the seal—one for goods and one for other contracts. The problem of the seal is further complicated by the fact that many states allow a longer "statute of limitations" period in which to bring suit where the contract is "sealed."

Statutory Exceptions to the Consideration Requirement

A respectable body of legal opinion holds that the consideration requirement has caused more problems than it has prevented, and that people should be bound to perform whatever they promised to perform, at least when the promise was made in a signed writing, whether or not the person gets anything in return. These same ideas may have been the rationale for the common law rule on the seal; they find their modern expression in various statutes that provide that certain promises are enforceable even though no consideration was given in return. One such provision is the firm offer rule discussed in Chapter 8. If a merchant's signed, written offer to buy or sell goods says that the offer will remain open for acceptance, it is not revocable by the merchant (within certain time limits) even though the merchant has received no consideration for the promise to keep the offer open. Similarly, the Model Business Corporation Act, Section 17, provides that an offer to subscribe to shares of stock is not revocable for a period of 6 months unless otherwise agreed.

Uniform Commercial Code Waiver Rule. The UCC contains two other "no-consideration-required" sections that have very broad potential application (and are thus very important). UCC 1-107 permits a party to a contract to waive any claim the party may have for an alleged breach of the contract by means of a signed writing. No special form is required, and no consideration need be received by the person giving up the contract claim. Because this section is in Article 1 of the UCC, it applies to all of the types of contracts covered in any other section of the Code.

Uniform Commercial Code Modification of Sale of Goods. UCC 2-209(1) applies only to contracts for the sale of goods, but it is also a very significant exception to the consideration requirement. It provides that any agreement modifying a preexisting contract for the sale of goods needs no consideration to be binding. (Normally, any change in an existing contract must be a "two-way" change—each party must receive consideration.) Suppose that you contract to buy a new car, but decide after you have driven it for 2 days that you would like rear-seat stereo speakers for the radio. You call up the dealer and talk to your salesman, and the salesman promises to install the speakers for no additional charge if you bring the car in next Monday. If the jury believes your testimony that such a modification of the original car contract was agreed to, the dealer is now contractually bound to install the speakers. Without 2-209(1), the dealer would *not* be bound because the dealer received no new consideration for the speakers. (*Remember* that this Code rule applies *only* to goods contracts. If you want to modify other types of contracts, such as those for land or services, there must be consideration moving both ways.)

Special (No Consideration) Statutes. In addition to these Code provisions, special statutory provisions applying the no-consideration-required rule to other types of contracts have been adopted by some states. The following statute, adopted by Michigan in 1941, is an example: "Agreements to Modify or Discharge Contracts, Section 1. An agreement hereafter made to change or modify, or to discharge in whole or in part, any contract, obligation, or lease, or any mortgage or other security interest in personal or real property, shall not be invalid because of the absence of consideration: Provided, that the agreement changing, modifying, or discharging such contract, obligation, lease, mortgage or security interest shall not be valid or binding unless it shall be in writing and signed by the party against whom it is sought to enforce the change, modification, or discharge."

Contracts for the International Sale of Goods Rules. Following the civil law system, Contracts for the International Sale of Goods (CISG) does not require proof of consideration for there to be a valid contract. As noted in the last chapter, CISG does provide that contract offers must be kept open for acceptance if the offer so indicates, even if no consideration has been paid to the offeror. This is essentially the same position taken by the UCC.

The enforceability of agreed modifications of a prior goods contract is not completely clear, but most of them would presumably be valid, if the agreement can be proved.

Courts' Definitions of Legally Sufficient Consideration

Legal Sufficiency versus Adequacy

As noted previously, the courts do not generally concern themselves with whether the parties have made a "good deal" or a "bad deal"; they will enforce stupid and unreasonable contracts as well as wise and reasonable ones. To be legally sufficient, a consideration need not be "adequate," in the sense of being a reasonable estimate of a jury's idea of fair market value. Unless there are unusual circumstances, such as fraud, duress, or undue influence, it is enough that something of value was received in return as the price of the promise, even though that "something" does not seem very desirable to the judge or jury. Freedom of contract means that you have the power to make your own bargains and that you are generally bound by the bargains you make once you have agreed to them.

Courts continue to state these general rules, and yet they seem more and more willing to "remake" contracts so as to arrive at "fair" results. For one thing, the *gross* inadequacy of the consideration received by one party is some evidence to support that party's claim that he or she was defrauded or subjected to duress or undue influence. Also, where a court finds such gross inadequacy it will generally refuse to exercise its equity powers to order specific performance of the unfair contract because "He who seeks equity must do equity." A court may even refuse to award money damages in such a case, by using the concept of **unconscionability**, which means that the contract is so terribly unfair that it should not be enforced as written.

Traditionally, the emphasis of the common law has been on freedom of contract, or letting the parties make any sort of contractual arrangement they want so long as it is not illegal. Increasingly, however, recognizing that contracts in modern society do not always represent real bargaining between equals, courts have been rewriting contracts by refusing to enforce provisions that they regard as unduly harsh, oppressive, or unjust. Courts have been discovering that they have always had a common law power to refuse enforcement of such unconscionable provisions, even without Section 2-302 of the UCC.

For the purpose of calculating amounts due under the U.S. estate and gift taxes, the Internal Revenue Code requires examination of alleged "contracts" to make sure that each party has received "an adequate [and full] consideration in money and money's worth." For example, if Uncle Ned promises Johnny $50,000 for painting a picket fence, there may technically be a contract, but the IRS will view the transaction as a gift by Uncle Ned of the difference between $50,000 and the fair market value of the painting job.

As noted in Chapter 8, moreover, the courts do require that the promise given in return be definite enough to impose some restrictions on that party's freedom of action. An **illusory promise**, such as one to buy as many parts as one wanted to order, imposes no real obligation to do any business at all. It seems as if a promise is being made, but there is no real commitment. An illusory promise thus does not supply consideration for a promise made in return. There is no contract in this situation, and neither party is bound to any performance. Because the buyer provided no consideration to the seller, the seller would not be bound to sell any parts at the stated price, even if the buyer later had ordered some. The order would be an offer to buy, which the seller is absolutely free to reject because there was no contract originally.

The following pages discuss some of the other "returns" that the courts do not generally accept as supplying a legally sufficient consideration.

Nominal Consideration

Nominal means "in name only" or "very small." "**Nominal consideration**" usually refers to the recital of $1 as consideration. Nothing is inherently wrong with $1 or any other very small amount as consideration for a return promise, if that amount is in fact intended and agreed to as the price of the bargain. Most courts, however, do not accept the mere recital of a fictitious dollar bill as legally sufficient consideration.

Good Consideration

As it appears in most legal forms ("and other good and valuable consideration"), good seems to be used as a synonym for valuable (and thus legally sufficient) consideration. However, that is not the meaning given to the term by most authoritative legal texts, they generally define **good consideration** in terms of a promise to be a "good relative," and thus not legally sufficient. "Nice family feelings" do not provide a legally sufficient consideration. When Johnny promises to be a "good nephew" (kind, loyal, and loving) in return for Uncle Ned's promise of $5,000, there is no consideration for Uncle Ned's promise, and Uncle Ned is not contractually bound to pay the money.

Past Consideration

A promise of benefits is not changed from a gift into a contract by the fact that the promisee has given something to the promisor in a previous, separate transaction. Such so-called **past consideration** is no consideration for the new promise of benefits. It is this rule that requires that a modification of a preexisting contract must be supported by a new exchange of considerations to be enforceable, except for UCC 2-209(1). Likewise, this rule generally prevents a "good Samaritan" from enforcing a promise to repay the good Samaritan for benefits previously conferred on the promisor as a gift. Because no contract was entered into or intended at the time the benefits were originally provided, those benefits—a completed gift—constitute past consideration.

Moral Consideration

Generally, the courts treat the existence of a moral obligation in the same way that they treat past consideration. The fact that a person is morally obligated to provide certain benefits does not supply consideration for that person's promise to provide them. By most standards the person who received aid and comfort from the good Samaritan would be morally obligated to repay the good Samaritan when able to do so, but the courts do not regard this moral obligation as a legally sufficient consideration.

In three situations the courts will generally enforce a promise on the basis of some idea of moral obligation. Two of them are closely related—new promises to pay a debt barred by a discharge in **bankruptcy** or by the running of the **statute of limitations**. In each of these cases, the debtor has received the values the debtor contracted for but has not paid for them; in each case the debtor has a technical defense that would prevent a successful lawsuit to collect the debt. Nevertheless, when the debtor makes a new promise to pay the discharged debt in either of these cases, most courts will hold the debtor to the new promise, even though the debtor has received no new consideration, on the theory that "a person ought to pay his or her debts." In most states one or both of these new promises must be made in a signed writing to be enforceable.

The third situation relates to promises made to charitable organizations. **Charitable promises** are sometimes enforceable, though the courts do not always agree on why they are. Some courts imply mutual promises between and among the donors not to revoke their pledges to the charity. When the charity has "moved in reliance" on the promises, the doctrine of promissory estoppel can be applied. An example would be hiring an architect to design a new building or taking an option on land. Even without applying either of these ideas, some courts apparently enforce promises to charitable organizations on the basis of some underlying "moral obligation" to support good works.

Preexisting Duty Rule

A promise to do or the actual doing of something that one is already bound to do anyway does not supply consideration for a return promise. Thus, when a landowner promises an extra bonus to a builder if the builder will get a job done on time, in accordance with the terms of the original contract, the builder cannot collect this promised bonus even if the builder does get the job done on time. The builder was already legally obligated to do so and has promised nothing new in return for the bonus. Similarly, police officers usually cannot collect rewards offered for the capture of criminals when they make the arrest in their own jurisdiction, in the line of their official duties. The following case presents the application of this rule in a slightly different factual context.

CASE 3

Mundell v. Stellmon
825 P.2d 510 (ID App. 1992)

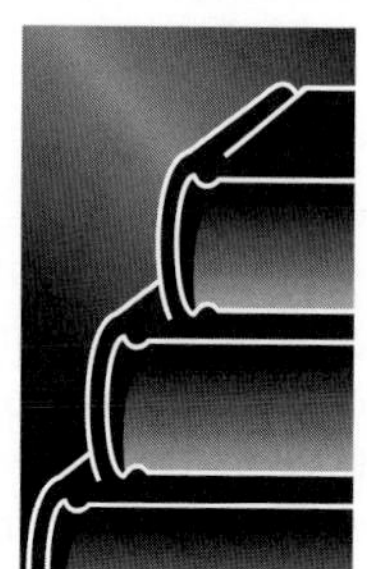

Facts: This action for declaratory judgment was brought by Eva Mundell, surviving spouse of Orie Mundell, to determine the ownership of 450 beehives that Orie had given to his son, James, prior to Orie's death. Eva claims that Orie's transfers of beehives to James were unauthorized gifts of the Mundells' community property, and thus invalid transfers. James claims the beehives were not gifts but were validly transferred to him as part of his compensation for working in the Mundells' beekeeping business. After a hearing, the district court determined that James had received the beehives as compensation for his labor in the Mundells' business, and thus, although the beehives had been community property, they were effectively transferred to James in consideration for his work that benefited the community business. Eva appealed this decision.

Orie and Eva Mundell owned and operated a beekeeping business consisting of approximately 1,000 beehives and the equipment to service those hives. During the years 1975 though 1978 the Mundells had difficulty retaining employees in their beekeeping business. Various negative conditions of working in the beekeeping business could explain why the Mundells had difficulty maintaining an experienced staff of workers. Work in the beekeeping business is seasonal, providing income for only about 6 months out of the year. The majority of the work, which requires a great deal of heavy lifting, is performed outdoors, during the hot summer months. The discomfort of performing arduous physical labor in summer heat is exacerbated by the fullbody protective clothing beekeepers must wear. Despite the protective clothing, workers are stung as many as five or more times a day while harvesting honey.

In 1978, James began working full-time in his father's and stepmother's beekeeping business. Because he had helped his father in the business throughout his youth, James had significant beekeeping experience that enabled him to provide valuable service to the Mundells' business. By the time of his father's death in July of 1988, James had worked continuously in the Mundells' beekeeping business for 10 years. Initially, James was paid a salary of $600 per month. In the early 1980s, James's salary was increased to $800 per month. In addition, James began receiving bonuses in the form of beehives. He received 25 to 50 beehives per year. Eventually, James was able to create new hives from his existing hives. He also purchased beehives from other beekeepers. Records submitted to the United States Agricultural Stabilization and Conservation Services (ASCS) indicated that James owned approximately 485 beehives in 1987.

The Mundells filed applications for loans from the ASCS, which requires that the honey producer certify the number of hives that produced the honey and the ownership of the hives.

ASCS records indicate the Orie and Eva Mundell claimed ownership of 1,300 hives in 1984 and 1985, 1,000 in 1986, and 1,010 in 1987. ASCS records indicate that James Mundell had 185 beehives in 1984, 225 beehives in 1985, 300 beehives in 1986, and 485 beehives in 1987.

Tax returns prepared by Eva Mundell indicate that, at the time of Orie's death, James owned 25 percent of the total honey crop. At trial, however, Eva asserted that the hives had been gifts to James from Orie's half of the community property and were not compensatory bonuses distributed from the business.

Issue: Did James provide consideration in exchange for the beehives?

Decision: Yes. Judgment for James is affirmed.

Opinion by Judge Silak: "As a preliminary matter, we will discuss the definition of the word 'bonus' as it applies to the analysis of this case. Both parties have cited the definitions listed in BLACK'S LAW DICTIONARY: 'A consideration or premium paid in addition to what is strictly due. A gratuity to which the recipient has no right to make a demand.... A premium or extra or irregular remuneration in consideration of offices performed or to encourage their performance.... An extra consideration given for what is received, or something given in addition to what is ordinarily received by, or strictly due, the recipient.... An addition to salary or wages normally paid for extraordinary work. An inducement to employees to procure efficient and faithful service.'... Some of the above definitions imply that a bonus may be a gift if it is a mere gratuity given without consideration. On the other hand, if there is consideration on the part of the employee such as extraordinary work, efficient and faithful service, or continuous service for a specific length of time, the bonus takes on the character of payments made in consideration of services rendered to the employer, and the employer may even become bound contractually to pay the bonus....

"James and Orie formed a contractual agreement that James would receive beehives as part os his compensation, and ... the beehives which were transferred to James were given to him as bonuses to supplement his monthly wages. Though the district court did not make a specific finding, it is evident from the record that the bonuses were given, at least in part, as payment for ongoing service in an arduous, low paying, seasonal job. This evidence adequately supports the district court's finding that James's continuous service benefited the beekeeping business. In turn, this fact supports the district court's conclusion that the beehives were given to James as bonuses which were part of his total compensation....

"Eva was fully aware that James was receiving the beehives over the years of his employment.... Eva personally prepared James's tax returns which reflected the fact that James was the owner of the beehives given to him by his father. In addition, the ASCS document prepared and certified by Orie and Eva, as well as James and his wife, recorded the number of beehive colonies owned by the respective parties. These records support a finding that Eva knew of and acquiesced in the transfer of the beehives to James."

Part Payment

One of the most common applications of the **preexisting duty rule** is in cases in which a debtor offers to pay part of the debt if the creditor will accept the part payment as full satisfaction of the debt. Obviously, in most cases, the creditor is willing to agree to anything to get some cash, especially if the debt is past due and the debtor is in questionable financial condition. Does such an agreement prevent the creditor from later suing to collect the unpaid balance of the original debt? At common law, the general rule was clear: No, the creditor is not prevented from collecting the balance because the debtor's part payment was nothing more (in fact less) than the debtor was already legally obligated to pay.

Only under special circumstances would the part payment legally discharge the debt in full. If the part payment of a debt was made and accepted by the creditor as payment in full before the debt was in fact due, the creditor would be bound by the acceptance of this "early payment." The creditor in this case did receive new consideration for the agreement to surrender the balance of the debt because the creditor had no right to receive any payment on the date that the payment was actually made. There is likewise consideration for the discharge of the entire debt if the part payment is accompanied by "some new item," received and accepted by the creditor, which the creditor was not previously legally entitled to receive. There is consideration (at least technically), and the debt is (probably) discharged, when a creditor agrees to accept a ballpoint pen and $600 in cash in full satisfaction of a $1,000 debt. Finally, when there is an honest, good faith dispute over the amount that is actually owed and the creditor agrees to take a lesser sum in full payment, the creditor is bound and the debt is discharged.

Uniform Commercial Code Rules on Part Payment

Some legal writers have suggested that under UCC 1-107, 2-209(1), and 3-408, the cashing of a part-payment check discharges the debt in full if the check so indicates, even if there is no dispute. Most of the cases decided since the adoption of the Code, however, continue to apply the common law rules discussed previously, without reference to any of these Code sections. It is thus not clear how a court would apply these sections if they were properly briefed and argued. It certainly appears that creditors would be much safer in sending such checks back and suing for the entire balance due. At the very least, a creditor should be aware that cashing such a check may cancel the right to sue for the balance of the debt, as seen in the next case.

Unconscionable Contracts

Courts have become increasingly willing to refuse enforcement of contract provisions that are not specifically illegal but which they simply do not like. Traditionally the emphasis of the common law has been on freedom of contract, or letting the parties make any sort of contractual arrangement they want so long as it is not illegal. Increasingly, however, recognizing that contracts in modern society do not always represent real bargaining between equals, courts have been rewriting contracts by refusing to enforce provisions that they regard as unduly harsh, oppressive, or unjust. Courts have discovered that they have always had a common law power to refuse enforcement of such "unconscionable" provisions, even without Section 2-302 of the UCC.

CASE 4

Myron Soik & Sons v. Stokely USA

498 N.W.2d 897 (WI App. 1993)

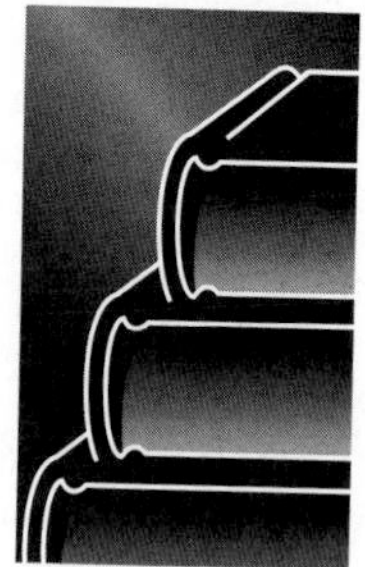

Facts: This is a class action by farmers growing corn under contract with Stokely USA, Inc., a vegetable canning company. The growers sued Stokely, claiming the company had failed to pay the amounts due them under the contracts.

The growers' claims center on a section of the 1990 corn contract providing a method of payment for "passed acreage"—corn grown by them but not taken by the company. Under the contracts, passed acreage payments were to be made from a fund set up with equal contributions from the growers and the company based on total tons harvested from all growers. Believing that the payments made by Stokely under these provisions were inadequate, the growers sued.

The plaintiff class included several growers who had retained and cashed the checks Stokely had sent to them for the 1990 crop, and the company moved for summary judgment dismissing these plaintiffs from the action. Stokely claimed that the checks had been properly calculated under the terms of the contract and that their acceptance and negotiation by the growers constituted an accord and satisfaction of the company's obligations under the contracts.

The trial court denied the motion, concluding as a matter of law that the defense of accord and satisfaction was unavailable to Stokely.

In early 1990, Stokely contracted with various Wisconsin corn growers to purchase sweet corn. The contracts were all identical and contained provisions for payment to the growers if some or all of their corn crop was "passed"—if it was fit for harvest but Stokely declined to take it. The passed acreage provisions of Stokely's 1990 Sweet Corn Contract provided as follows:

> *The [Growers'] compensation for the production of sweet corn suitable for processing and fit for harvesting but not harvested at the direction of the Company shall be computed as if it were harvested....*
>
> *The [Growers] and the Company agree to share the cost of payments made for nonharvested crops ... as follows: Total payments made for non-harvested sweet corn acreage will be divided by total tons of sweet corn produced ... to establish a per ton allocation of said cost. The [Growers] will be responsible for this cost up to a maximum of $2.00 per ton. In the event that the combined contribution of $4.00 per ton ... is not sufficient to meet total calculated non-harvested crop compensation, payment will be prorated to the extent of funds collected from the Company and [the Growers].* (Emphasis Added.)

During the 1990 harvest, Stokely "passed" some or all of the corn it had agreed to purchase from the growers. Then, after the season, Stokely notified the growers by letter that the money that had been paid into the crop compensation fund under the provisions of the contract was insufficient to pay them in full for their passed acreage crops and that, as a result, they would be receiving prorated payments:

> *This is to inform you that the non-harvested crop compensation fund is not sufficient this year to pay total calculated non-harvested crop compensation in full. This means your payment will be prorated to the extent the claims against the fund exceed its amount. The exact amount of the proration is now being calculated....*

Details as to the proration will accompany your check.

A few days later, Stokely mailed checks in reduced amounts to the growers, along with a letter stating:

> *Enclosed is your Stokely USA, Inc., 1990 Sweet Corn contract payment.*
>
> *Your payment has been calculated according to the formula set forth in the contract for non-harvested crops. . . .*
>
> *Unfortunately, the total fund of $1,029,375.05 is insufficient to pay claims against it in full, and as a consequence, your payment has been prorated. The proration is 53.49 percent.*
>
> *Please contact me if you have any questions.*

Issue: Were the growers' claims paid in full when they cashed the checks?

Decision: Yes. Judgment reversed. (Stokely wins.)

Opinion by Chief Judge Eich: "An accord and satisfaction is an agreement to discharge an existing disputed claim and constitutes a defense to an action to enforce the claim. . . . It is a rule 'resting not only on principles of contract law but on principles of sound public policy, that is, interests of resolving disputes informally without litigation and of fairness. . . .' In *Flambeau*, the supreme court discussed the principles underlying the rule and the protections it affords to the debtor.

"The interests of fairness dictate that a creditor who cashes a check offered in full payment should be bound by the terms of the offer. The debtor's intent is known, and allowing the creditor to keep the money disregarding the debtor's conditions seems unfair. . . . The doctrine of accord and satisfaction includes safeguards designed to protect a creditor from an overreaching debtor: there must be a good faith dispute about the debt [and] the creditor must have reasonable notice that the check is intended to be in full satisfaction of the debt. . . .

"We thus consider whether there was a dispute between Stokely and the growers at the time the checks were received and cashed, and whether the growers had reasonable notice that Stokely's checks were intended by the company in full satisfaction of its obligations under the 'passed acreage' provisions of the contracts. . . .

"Prior to receiving any communication from Stokely, the growers knew from the terms of their contracts that they were to be paid for 'passed' acreage in an amount calculated 'as if [that acreage] had been harvested,' and that these payments would come from a fund comprised of equal contributions from Stokely and themselves. They also knew that in the event these contributions were insufficient to allow Stokely to pay at the 'harvested crop' rate, they would receive only a prorata share of the amount of money actually in the fund.

"Then after the harvest, the growers were informed by Stokely's first letter that their payment 'this year' would have to be prorated under the contract. And in a second letter—the one enclosing the lower-than-expected checks—they were plainly advised that the amount being paid constitute 'your Stokely . . . 1990 Sweet Corn crop payment,' and the details of the prorata calculation were explained to them.

"The growers, obviously, had expected to receive a larger amount. But, armed with the above information, they nevertheless decided to cash the checks. Admittedly, the checks did not contain the words 'full payment,' as in Flambeau; but we do not believe such 'magic language' is essential to the debtor's ability to raise the defense of accord and satisfaction. The test, after, is one of reason: '[T]he creditor must have *reasonable notice* that the check is intended to be in full satisfaction of the debt. . . .'

"We conclude on this record that: (1) at the time the checks were received and cashed a 'dispute' within the meaning of the rule of accord and satisfaction existed between Stokely and the plaintiff growers, all of whom, obviously, disagreed with the company's application of the prorata clause; and (2) the correspondence preceding and accompanying the reduced payment gave the growers reasonable notice that the checks were intended as full payment under the contract. As a result, the growers' acts of accepting and cashing the checks must be considered acceptance of the tendered amount in full settlement of Stokely's obligations under the 1990 corn contracts."

Significance of This Chapter

Not all promises are contractually enforceable, even if proved to have been made and accepted. The basic idea of the consideration requirement is that a person ought not to be required to perform a promise made to another unless the promisor received something of value in return for the promise. Although it is inevitable that some promisors will be disappointed in what they have received in return, that in itself is no basis for not performing their promises. But it is also true that courts are increasingly willing to examine the agreement to make sure that a genuine exchange of values was promised, particularly where one of the parties lacks education and experience.

Fairness also underlies the concept of promissory estoppel as an alternative basis for enforcement. It is just not fair to let someone make the no consideration argument after a promise has been relied on by another party. Courts may also use the estoppel concept to prevent someone from using the Statute of Frauds to deny liability on an oral promise. The next chapter will discuss this point in more detail.

IMPORTANT TERMS AND CONCEPTS

bankruptcy
bargained-for exchange of values
charitable promises
conclusive presumption
consideration
good consideration
illusory promise
nominal consideration
past consideration
preexisting duty rule
promisee
promisor
promissory estoppel
rebuttable presumption
seal
statute of limitations
unconscionability

QUESTIONS AND PROBLEMS FOR DISCUSSION

1. When will a promisor be estopped from arguing that he or she is not bound to perform the promise because he or she received no consideration for it?

2. What is the effect of a promisor's placing a "seal" on a written promise?

3. What is the meaning and significance of past consideration?

4. When will part payment of a debt, if offered and accepted "in full payment," actually discharge the whole debt?

5. Relying on the representations of Lukowitz, a representative of Red Owl Stores, that the company would set him up in business in a franchised Red Owl grocery store for a capital investment of $18,000, Hoffman and his wife did the following: sold their existing bakery business and building; bought a small grocery store, ran it for several months "to get some experience," and then resold it; took an option on the proposed site for the Red Owl store and made a down payment on the lot; moved the family's home; and rented a house in the town where the new store was to be located. Red Owl kept increasing the capital requirements, and the deal for the new store fell through without the parties ever having agreed to a contract. Hoffman and his wife sued for the damages they sustained as a result of the aforementioned transaction. The trial court ordered judgment for the plaintiffs, based on the jury's verdict, but said a new trial would be required to determine the exact amount of the loss suffered by the sale of the small grocery store. Both parties appealed.

   Is this a case for the application of the doctrine of "promissory estoppel"?

6. Sam Leone worked as a foreman for Precision, which was a subcontractor on a construction project. Sam was covered under a collective bargaining contract between Precision and the construction workers' union. Sam and his wife Ella sued to enforce an alleged oral promise of a bonus of one-half of the difference between the estimated cost of the project and its actual cost. The jury found for Sam and Ella, for $17,789.28, and the trial judge refused Precision's request for a judgment notwithstanding the verdict. Precision appealed.

   Was Precision's promise to Sam supported by a legally sufficient consideration?

   Yes. Judgment affirmed.

7. During the period from 1987 to 1992 Ora Lee Williams purchased a number of household items from Walker-Thomas, for which payment was to be made in installments. The terms of each purchase were contained in a printed form contract that set forth the value of the purchased item and purported to lease the item to her for a stipulated monthly rent payment. The contract then provided, in substance, that title would remain in Walker-Thomas until the total of all the monthly payments equaled the stated value of the item, at which time Williams could take title. In the event of a default in the payment of any monthly installment, Walker-Thomas could repossess the item.

   The contract further provided that "the amount of each periodical installment payment to be made by [purchaser] to the Company under this present lease shall be inclusive of and not in addition to the amount of each installment payment to be made by [purchaser] under such prior leases, bills or accounts; and all payments now and hereafter made by [purchaser] shall be credited pro rata on all outstanding leases, bills, and accounts due the Company by [purchaser] at the time each such payment is made." Williams defaulted, and Walker-Thomas sued to repossess all items Williams bought.

   Should it be able to enforce this contract? Explain.

8. On December 8, the defendants owed the plaintiffs for goods sold between that date and the previous May at an agreed price, the sum of $7,714.37. On December 27, the defendants delivered to the plaintiffs three promissory notes amounting in the aggregate to $3,462.24 secured by a mortgage on the stock, fixtures, and other property of the defendants, located in East Saginaw, Michigan. These notes and the mortgage were received by plaintiffs under an agreement to accept them in full satisfaction and discharge

of the indebtedness. Plaintiffs then sued for the balance of the original amount due.

How should the court rule this claim?

9. Horatio began working for Steel Chain Company in 1961 as an order clerk. He subsequently became traffic manager, sales representative, president, and finally, chairman of the board of directors. In 1990, while he was chairman, the six other directors prepared a proposed agreement for his retirement. Horatio knew nothing about it until the agreement was presented to him at a board meeting. The agreement provided that the company would pay Horatio $20,000 for the current fiscal year and $15,000 a year for the rest of his life and that Horatio, in turn, would be available for consultation and would not compete with the company in its domestic or overseas markets. Horatio signed the agreement. In 1993, the company stopped making the promised annual payments to Horatio and asked him to accept smaller payments. He refused and sued for breach of contract.

   Does Horatio have a valid claim? Why or why not?

10. O'Neil seeks a declaratory judgement that he is the owner of a valuable painting, allegedly the work of Peter Paul Rubens and titled "Hunting of the Caledonian Boar." This painting was a part of the art collection acquired by the defendants during their marriage.

    On August 18, 1990, James Paul DeLaney purportedly sold the painting to plaintiff for $10 and "other good and valuable consideration." A written contract, embodying terms of the agreement, was prepared and signed by plaintiff and James Paul DeLaney. Jeannette DeLaney was not a party to that contract. The painting was then brought to plaintiff's apartment where it was hung on the wall.

    When asked what the contract term "other good and valuable consideration" meant to him, plaintiff stated:

    That to me and Mr. DeLaney means our friendship and favors that we have done; and as you put it earlier, the love and affection that one had for another. Mr. DeLaney didn't have any children, and I assume he looked upon me as a son.

    Under cross-examination, plaintiff was asked whether he gave James Paul DeLaney anything else other than $10 and love and affection in exchange for the painting. Plaintiff responded: "No, not really."

    At the time of the sale of the painting, plaintiff believed it was worth $100,000 if not authenticated as a Rubens original, and if authenticated, several hundred thousand dollars.

    Jeanette DeLaney claims an ownership interest in the painting. O'Neil says the sale to him ended her rights.

    Did O'Neil buy the painting? Discuss.

CHAPTER 10

Statute of Frauds and Parol Evidence Rule

Chapter Objectives

This chapter will:

- Explain the need for written proof of a contract.
- Indicate the major types of contracts that are subject to this requirement.
- Discuss the methods of complying with this requirement.
- Indicate the results if the Statute of Frauds applies to a contract and has not been satisfied.
- Explain the major exceptions to the unenforceability result if the statute has not been satisfied.
- Explain the operation of the parol evidence rule.
- Indicate the situations in which the rule does not apply.
- Indicate the major exceptions to the rule.

Although the parties have entered into an agreement and their agreement is supported by an exchange of legally sufficient considerations, courts, in many situations, will refuse to enforce some or all of the promises exchanged unless the alleged promises can be proved by something more than oral testimony. The **Statute of Frauds** requires that certain types of contractual promises be contained in a signed writing to be enforceable in court. The parol evidence rule prevents a party from contradicting the terms of a complete written contract, once signed, by the use of outside, or parol, evidence.

Statute of Frauds: Origins, Development, and Basic Purpose

One year after the United States celebrated its bicentennial, the Statute of Frauds celebrated its tricentennial. The English Parliament passed the original statute in 1677 to deal with what was perceived to be a serious legal problem: the possibility that a court would force a party to perform a contract that had never really been made, solely on the basis of perjured oral testimony. The solution to this problem seemed simple enough: require that a contract be proved by something more than oral testimony before you enforce it. Thus, the Statute of Frauds ("An Act for Prevention of Frauds and Perjuries") was adopted.

Parliament did not go as far as requiring that *all* contracts be evidenced by a signed writing to be enforceable in court. Rather, it confined this new requirement to what seemed to be "important" contracts and to other situations in which intentional perjury or mistaken testimony seemed likely. As a result, the following types of contracts had to be in writing to be enforceable in court: the sale of any interest in real estate; the sale of goods worth £10 or more; any contract that by its terms could not possibly be completed within 1 year from the date it was made; any promise to pay the debt of another party; any promise by the executor or administrator of a decedent's estate to pay the estate's debts out of his or her own funds; any promise made "in consideration of marriage." This list formed the basis for similar statutes in nearly all of our states.

To see how the Statute of Frauds works today, we need to know the answers to three questions: What contracts are now subject to the Statute of Frauds? How does one comply with the Statute of Frauds requirement? What results follow if the Statute of Frauds applies and has not been satisfied? We will now consider each of these questions in turn.

Contracts Subject to the Statute of Frauds

Pre-Uniform Commercial Code Holdovers

Three provisions of the 1677 statute that have general commercial significance have, on the whole, survived in their original form: the transfer of any interest in real estate, any promise to pay the debt of another, any contract which by its terms cannot be performed within 1 year. Prior to the Uniform Commercial Code (UCC), many states had also adopted a Statute of Frauds provision, which required all assignments, or transfers, of contract rights to be made in writing. (Assignments are discussed more fully in Chapter 13.)

Real Estate Transfers

"Any interest" in land means just that: every case in which one or more parties are voluntarily creating such an interest in another or divesting themselves of such an interest. Most courts agree that leases, mortgages, easements, and options on real estate are all subject to this requirement, although options might be excluded in some states. Also, most states do have a statutory exception for short-term leases; if the term of an oral lease is not more than 1 year, the lease is enforceable. Although real estate brokers do not have an "interest" in the real estate under this section of the Statute of Frauds, in most states real estate brokers are required by a separate statutory provision to have their commission arrangements in writing to make them enforceable.

Some definitional problems arise where the contract relates to things that are growing on, attached to, or contained in the land. Generally, these questions will be answered by reference to UCC 2-107. If the contract requires the seller to "sever" minerals or the like, or a structure or its materials, the contract is a sale of goods within Article 2. If the buyer is to do the severing, until the buyer does so, the contract would be assumed to deal with an "interest" in the land. When the subject matter of the contract is timber, growing crops, "or other things attached to realty and capable of severance without material harm thereto," but not covered under the first rule, the contract is a sale of goods, regardless of who does the severing. The significance of the distinction can be seen later, in the discussion of what is a sufficient compliance with the Statute of Frauds provision that applies to the contract.

Promises to Pay the Debt of Another

Parliament probably included this provision because both the principal debtor and the creditor have an incentive to commit perjury in this case. Here, too, there are definitional questions to be resolved. This section does not apply to direct, "original" promises to confer benefits on a third party—only to "secondary" or supplemental promises. This section of the Statute of Frauds does not apply where the promisor's main motive in making the promise is to benefit *himself* or *herself* rather than just to "backstop" the principal debtor's credit. Finally, the section does not apply when the secondary promise is made to the principal debtor rather than to the creditor (see Exhibit 10-1).

The *General Marketing Services* case deals with these issues.

Exhibit 10.1: Statute of Frauds: Debt of Another?

What is a promise to pay the debt "of another"?

Promisor: to Promisee:		Debt of Another
a. *Uncle Ned* *Johnny*		
You need the European experience. If you go, I will pay your first $3,000 in expenses.	=	No. (oral OK) Not made to third party creditor
b. *Uncle Ned* *Eaters Club*		
My nephew is going to Europe. Send him a set of the luggage you advertised, and bill me.	=	No. (oral OK) Promisor is making the purchase, even though goods are going to Johnny
c. *Uncle Ned* *Amex Credit*		
My nephew is going to Europe. He is authorized to use my Amex Credit card for the next two weeks.	=	No. (oral OK) Oral authorization of Johnny as agent; Johnny is making debts for Uncle Ned
d. *Uncle Ned* *Harolds Store*		
My nephew will probably need some new suits for his European trip. Go ahead and sell them to him. I will pay if he doesn't pay.	=	Yes. (writing required) Uncle Ned is promising to pay Johnny's debt if Johnny does not.

CASE 1

General Marketing Services v. American Motorsports, Inc., Innovation Management, Inc., and Zehr

393 F.Supp.2d 901 (D. MN 2005)

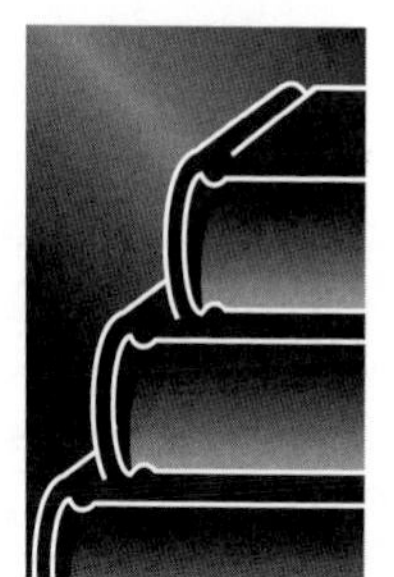

Facts: General Marketing Services (GMS), having provided database and customer-management services to American Motorsports, Inc. (AMI), sued to collect the claimed balance due on the account ($317,111.19). Joined as defendants were Innovation Management, Inc. (IMI; AMI's parent corporation) and David Zehr (an AMI employee who had allegedly guaranteed payment). Dissatisfied with the work, AMI refused to pay the balance. There is no evidence in the record that Zehr had ever been a shareholder or officer in AMI or IMI, or that either corporation has ever given him any bonus, commission, or incentive pay. Zehr has filed a motion for summary judgment on all claims against him.

Issue: Can the alleged oral promises made by Zehr be enforced against him?

Decision: No. Zehr's motion for summary judgment on all claims is granted.

Opinion by Judge Davis: "Zehr notes that even if he made [the] oral statements (which he denies), they would be collateral promises excluded by the statute of frauds.... ('A collateral promise is not enforceable under the Statute of Frauds unless there is a writing.') ... 'Whether a promise is original or collateral depends upon what the parties mutually understood the promise to be.' ... A collateral promise is 'one that provides no (direct) benefit to the promisor.' ... In contrast, original promises must directly or primarily benefit the promisor....

"Because Zehr would have received no benefit from the alleged promises, they were collateral promises that require a writing.... Without such writing, Plaintiff now seeks to 'torture mere words of encouragement into an absolute promise.' ...

"Plaintiff contends that even if Zehr's alleged statements were interpreted to be collateral promises, the statute of frauds does not apply because Plaintiff relied on those promises and fully performed as a result....

"Even viewing the facts in the light most favorable to Plaintiff, the record contains no documentation or other writing to substantiate Plaintiff's claim that Zehr made a personal guarantee, rather than speaking in his capacity as an agent. Because the statute of frauds requires a writing to substantiate personal guarantees, and because the record contains no such writing, summary judgment as to Plaintiff's breach-of-personal-guarantee claim is appropriate....

"Zehr next argues that even if the statute of frauds does not apply to the equitable claims of misrepresentation, promissory estoppel, and unjust enrichment, Plaintiff has nonetheless failed to provide evidence sufficient to support these claims. Because claims in equity do not require an enforceable contract, making the statute of frauds inapplicable to these claims, the following analysis is required....

"To support is claim of fraudulent misrepresentation, Plaintiff provides the text of only one alleged statement: 'I will not leave you to hang out to dry. I will always make this square.' This statement is insufficient to establish fraudulent misrepresentation as a matter of law....

"Here, even assuming that Zehr made the vague statements, ... Plaintiff provides no evidence to demonstrate that these statements were made as a personal guarantee, rather than in Zehr's capacity as an employee....

"Further, a claim for fraudulent misrepresentation must include a representation of a past or present event.... Here, each of Zehr's alleged statements involves a future promise.... Because these statements are forward-looking, they fail the ... requirement that the statement at issue involve a 'past or existing material fact susceptible of knowledge.' As such, Plaintiff's misrepresentation claim must fail....

"Plaintiff has presented no evidence to dispute that Zehr was, indeed, an AMI employee, and it is clear that Zehr's statements (assuming they were made) did not give rise to promissory estoppel but instead were unenforceable as collateral promises. Consequently, summary judgment on Plaintiff's promissory estoppel claim is appropriate as a matter of law....

"Zehr lastly argues that Plaintiff's unjust enrichment claim against him should be dismissed. To succeed in a claim of unjust enrichment, a claimant must show 'that another party knowingly received something of value to which he was not entitled, and that the circumstances are such that it would be unjust for that person to retain the benefit.' ...

"The record contains no evidence that Zehr received anything of value from his alleged statements to Plaintiff, and any conceivable benefit through his continued employment or AMI's continuing to be in business is tangential, at best. Further, AMI did not provide any benefits 'unknowingly or unwillingly,' as required by [the theory of unjust enrichment]. As such, summary judgment of Plaintiff's unjust enrichment claim, like its other claims against Zehr, is properly granted."

Contracts Impossible to Perform within One Year

The probable reason for inclusion of the **year clause** was the likelihood that the parties and witnesses would tend to forget the provisions of the contract, or would remember them differently, when the performances extended over a relatively long period of time. Thus, if on the day a contract is made, the parties can see that there is absolutely no way to perform it within 1 year from that date, the contract must be evidenced by a signed writing. As applied by the courts, the test is not how long the performances were likely to take or, with hindsight, how long they actually took. The test is whether there was any conceivable way that the contract *could* have been fully performed, according to its terms, within a year from the date it was made. If it could have been performed within a year, the oral contract is perfectly valid and perfectly enforceable in court (assuming that the jury believes the oral testimony).

Thus, an oral contract for lifetime employment, in which performance is to start within 1 year of the date the contract is made, is enforceable because the employee could conceivably die within the first year. But where the employee is hired for more than 1 year, or is not to start performing until some future date and then is to work for at least a year, the oral contract is not enforceable.

Uniform Commercial Code Statute of Frauds Provisions

The Code contains several specific Statute of Frauds provisions. Contracts for the sale of goods with a price of $500 or more, or intangible personal property over $5,000 in amount, and contracts creating a security interest or establishing a letter of credit must be evidenced by some sort of writing. In addition, "negotiable instruments" under Article 3 and "documents" under Article 7, by definition, involve signed writings with particular characteristics.

Sales of Goods for $500 or More

As defined in Section 2-105(1), *goods* means tangible, movable personal property, but it can also refer to things that are currently attached to land, as noted earlier in this chapter. There can be a contract for the sale of goods that do not exist yet, with the seller promising to produce them or get them from a third party prior to the delivery date specified in the contract.

In some cases, it is hard to decide whether the contract is a contract for the sale of goods or a contract for services. The distinction is very important here because there is no Statute of Frauds that is generally applicable to services contracts. If a services contract, such as a promise to construct a building on land already owned by the customer, can be performed within 1 year, it can be oral and still be enforceable, no matter how much money it involves. If a contract is for goods worth $500 or more, Section 2-201 applies. (In 2002, Michigan amended its UCC to increase this amount to $1,000. So far, this does not seem to be a trend among the states.)

A contract to buy a $600 color TV is clearly a contract for the sale of goods even if the seller also promises to deliver and set up the TV as part of the contract. Likewise, if you buy all the parts for a TV set in a kit, and then hire a TV technician to put the set together for you, your contract with the technician is clearly a services contract. Many contracts are more ambiguous, however, such as your contract for the purchase of a custom-made suit from a tailor, or your contract with an artist to have your portrait painted, or your contract to have your car fixed or your house aluminum-sided, all of which involve both labor and materials. (A court would most probably decide that the suit and portrait contracts are primarily for goods and that the car repair and aluminum siding contracts are primarily for services.)

Leases of Goods for $1,000 or More

As equipment and vehicle leasing became popular with businesses and consumers, a new "Article 2A: Leases" was added to the UCC. Much of its coverage parallels that of Article 2. The statute of frauds section for leases of goods requires a writing for leases with a total price of $1,000 or more, so that only very low-cost leases are enforceable if oral.

Sales of Investment Securities

Simply put, **investment securities** are stocks and bonds. Since its inception over 50 years ago, the UCC had contained a statute of frauds covering all contracts for the sale of investment securities—Section 8-319. Somehow, the U.S. securities markets had managed to survive (and indeed, flourish) with that universal writing requirement in place. As the new millennium approached, perhaps because of the great increase in electronically communicated contracts, that requirement has been abolished. The UCC no longer requires written evidence for enforcement of securities contracts. It is now our word against yours, in court, as to whether there was such a contract, and if so, what its terms were.

Sales of Intangible Personal Property for $5,000 or More

After eliminating goods, investment securities, and security agreements, Section 1-206 covers "personal property." Included here are the sales of **miscellaneous intangible property**, such as copyrights, patents, royalties, trademarks, and trade names, and tort claims for damages. If the contract amount of such items is $5,000 or more, there must be a signed writing.

The *Melstad* case helps define what things are covered under this UCC section.

Security Agreements

When a creditor ("secured party") wishes to use a piece of personal property as collateral for the payment of some obligation, the creditor must have a written security agreement that creates or provides for such a "security interest" and the writing must be signed by the debtor. Without such a writing the creditor has no rights against the specific collateral when the debtor goes into default unless the creditor actually has possession of the collateral. (**Secured transactions** are explained in Chapters 23 and 24.)

Letters of Credit

Letters of credit are widely used in international trade, when the credit standing of a buyer may not be known to the seller. Before leaving his or her country, the buyer arranges to have a bank honor drafts (orders for money) up to a certain amount. With such a written agreement from a recognized bank in the buyer's own country, the buyer can have ready access to funds from banks in a foreign country. Obviously, any such letter of credit, and any modification thereof, must be contained in a signed writing.

Modifications

Because of the common law requirement that a document must contain all the material terms to comply with the Statute of Frauds, subsequently agreed-to modifications of such contract must also be evidenced by a signed writing to be enforceable. Such changes can be written on the original document and initialed, or a new document covering the modifications can be prepared and signed by the parties. In a real estate transaction, for example, any later agreement to modify the signed writing by changing the total contract price, the monthly payments, the acreage involved, the interest rate, or even such things as the date of possession, almost certainly has to be written to be enforced in court.

Uniform Commercial Code Rule for Modification of Goods Contract

For sales of goods, however, the rules are quite different because of the wording of the applicable Code provisions. Because the signed writing here does not have to contain all the terms agreed on, or even all the material terms, oral modifications of a previous written contract for goods should be enforceable in nearly every case. The one thing that Section 2-201(1) does not permit is an oral modification that increases the quantity term stated in the signed writing. (For example, the parties enter into a written contract for 1,000 bushels of wheat at $3 per bushel. They can later orally agree to raise or lower the price, to change the delivery date, or to lower the quantity to 700 bushels. What they cannot do without a new writing is to increase the quantity to 1,200 bushels. The quantity term in the original

CASE 2

MELSTAD v. KOVAC AND RAIDER INDUSTRIES, INC.

723 N.W.2d 699 (SD 2006)

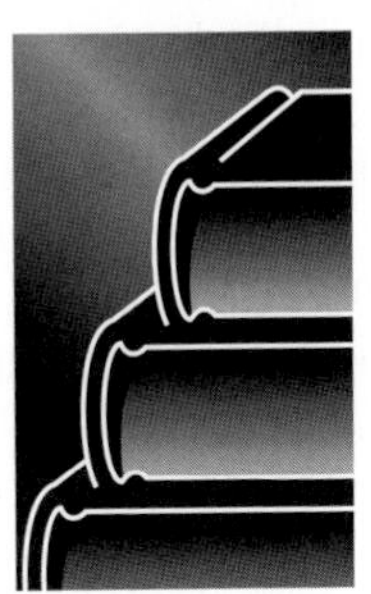

Facts: Katherine Melstad was seriously injured in a motor vehicle accident. She sued the driver and owner of the other vehicle (a "semi" truck), Harvey Kovac and Raider Industries. After her first lawyer resigned, Melstad hired Jack Der Hagopian to represent her for a contingent fee of one-third of any judgment or settlement. Jury trial was set for October 5, 2004. Pretrial mediation did not produce a settlement, but the parties continued to negotiate. Melstad reduced her original $1.5 million claim to $750,000, and the defendants increased their original $125,000 offer to $250,000. Der Hagopian claimed that on October 3 she had authorized him to lower her claim to $500,000, and his telephone records for that date show that he spoke to her at least three times, and his paralegal at least seven times. He communicated that figure to opposing counsel on the morning of October 4, and a fax of that date to Melstad references that amount. He says he then convinced her to lower the figure to $450,000, and that mount appears in an October 4 fax to him from opposing counsel, in which they offer to pay $300,000. He claims she then agreed to accept that amount, but asked him to make one final counteroffer at $325,000. The defendants agreed to pay $325,000 and filed a motion with the court to enforce the settlement agreement. Der Hagopian asked the court for a lien against those funds to enforce his fee agreement ($113,900.79, plus interest from October 4). The trial court granted both motions. Melstad appealed, claiming that she never authorized Der Hagopian to settle the claim, and that any such oral agreement was unenforceable under UCC 1-206(1).

Issue: Is a client's authorization of her attorney to settle her lawsuit a "sale of personal property" that is required to be in writing by UCC 1-206?

Decision: No. Judgment enforcing the settlement agreement is affirmed.

Opinion by Justice Meierhenry: "Melstad first argues that a provision of the Uniform Commercial Code . . . 1-206(1) governs the transaction and requires written authority for an attorney to settle a claim on behalf of a client. The statutory provision upon which she relies applies to the enforcement of a sale of personal property over $5000.00 in value. . . .

"Melstad argues that the transaction is analogous to a sale of personal property since a cause of action is something of value and can be owned. Thus, she argues, an attorney receiving the cause of action from a client is like a sale of personal property and would fall under . . . 1-206(1), which requires the contract to be in writing. Melstad has not cited nor are we aware of any jurisdiction that has adopted this analysis. A similar argument was made and rejected in [an Iowa case]. . . . The Iowa Appellate Court determined that 'the settlement of a personal injury lawsuit is not a contract for the sale of personal property, nor would it typically fall within any specific article of the commercial code.' . . . [W]e also decline to consider a personal injury settlement as a contract for a sale of personal property and find no merit in Melstad's assertion that a provision in the commercial code requires an attorney to obtain a client's written authority to settle a lawsuit on the client's behalf.

"Melstad next contends that because . . . the South Dakota Rules of Professional Conduct require contingent fee agreements to be in writing, an attorney's authority to settle must also be in writing. Melstad relies on SDCL 59-2-3, which provides 'authority to enter into a contract . . . required by law to be in writing, can only be given by an instrument in writing.' . . . Under the facts of this case, the underlying agreement is clearly the settlement agreement between Melstad and defendants Kovac and Raider. Since the law does not require personal injury settlements to be in writing, it necessarily follows that a lawyer's authority to settle on behalf of a client also need not be in writing. [C]onsequently, SDCL 59-2-3 does not apply. . . .

"While an attorney 'may negotiate for and advise settlement of [a] controversy,' the decision to settle belongs to the client. . . . The client must expressly give her attorney the authority to settle, and the law of agency determines whether the attorney has received such authority. . . . Authority to enter into a contract on behalf of the principal can be created by express authorization from the principal or by the acquiescence of the principal in the actions of the agent. . . . The question before the trial court was whether Melstad had expressly authorized her attorney to settle for the final amount. After considering all the evidence, the trial court determined that she had. The trial court specifically found that Melstad gave Der Hagopian express authorization to settle for $325,000 and 'only later did she change her mind and [attempt] to repudiate the settlement.' Melstad contends that the trial court erred when it made that finding. . . .

"A review of the record supports the trial court's determination that Melstad expressly authorized her attorney to settle for the final amount. . . .

"Whether the parties had a meeting of the minds is a question of fact. . . .

"[T]he trial court's finding of mutual assent to the material terms of the settlement was based on the words and conduct of the parties and was not clearly erroneous. . . .

"Affirmed."

writing cannot be increased orally, and 200 more bushels means $600 worth of goods, so this "modification" has to be evidenced by a new writing.) When there was originally an enforceable oral contract for under $500 and the agreed modification brings the price to over $500, the contract as modified must be evidenced by a writing, or else the modification cannot be enforced and the original terms stand. (For example, the parties orally agree to a contract for 150 bushels of wheat at $3 per bushel. Later they agree to raise the price per bushel to $3.50, for a total price of $525. This modification must be in writing to be enforced.)

Remember from the last chapter that such modifications need no new exchange of considerations in a sale of goods case; they can be completely one-sided and still be binding under Section 2-209(1). For other types of contracts, however, there has to be new consideration moving both ways for such modifications to be enforceable, even if the modifications are in writing.

Consideration Substitutes

Chapter 9 contained several examples of statutory provisions that made certain kinds of promises enforceable even without consideration. Typically, such promises will have to be contained in a signed writing to be enforceable. UCC 2-209(1) does not require modifications of a preexisting sale of goods contract to be in writing, nor, in some states, do the statutes that cover new promises to pay debts barred by the statute of limitations or by a bankruptcy discharge. (As always, of course, it is a good idea to have the promise in writing even though no statute requires it, simply because a signed, written promise is easier to prove in court.)

Compliance with the Statute of Frauds

General Common Law Rule

The method of compliance intended by the original 1677 statute was a signed writing. As interpreted by the courts, this requirement came to mean that the writing had to contain "all the material terms" and that a writing that did not clearly spell out all the important provisions of the contract was not sufficient to comply with the statute. In general, this **all-material-terms rule** continues to be used for those Statute of Frauds provisions described previously as common law "holdovers."

The all-material-terms rule can be seen operating most clearly in real estate transactions, in which most courts have used the **4-P's** interpretation. To comply with the statute for real estate, the signed writing has to at least contain the *p*arties, the *p*roperty, the *p*rice, and the *p*ayment terms. If the terms are simple, a very short memorandum conceivably could contain all these elements. More typically, however, payment for real estate is to be made over an extended period of time, interest must be calculated on the unpaid balance and paid periodically, and other special provisions are agreed to. In such cases the parties run a very real risk that a court may later find their document to be insufficient to comply with the statute.

Sales of Goods Compliance: Five Alternatives

The UCC, Section 2-201, provides five alternative methods of compliance: a signed writing, a writing in confirmation, special manufacture, **admission in court**, and part performance.

Unlike the common law rule, the **signed writing** for the sale of goods need not contain all the material terms: "a writing is not insufficient because it omits or incorrectly states a term agreed upon." The writing must indicate that a contract for sale has been made; it must be signed by the party against whom enforcement is sought or by that party's authorized agent; and it must contain the quantity term ("the contract is not enforceable under this paragraph beyond the quantity of goods stated"). Price, packaging, and delivery terms can all be omitted and then filled in by supplementary evidence. A very simple notation on the check given for the down payment would be sufficient, for example, "Down payment on one 1997 Buick." The buyer's signature on the check binds the buyer to the contract; the seller is also bound when the seller endorses the check so that the check can be cashed.

When both parties are merchants and there is no writing that evidences a contract because agreement has been reached over the telephone or in personal conversation, the Code provides a method of compliance called a **writing in confirmation**. This is a brand-new Code concept, unknown in prior law. It is a "bootstrap" method: Our contract becomes enforceable by me against you on the basis of a writing signed by me, not by you. If within a reasonable time after the oral contract has been made, one **merchant** sends the other a written confirmation of the contract and the confirmation is a sufficient writing against the sender-merchant, it also becomes a sufficient writing against the receiver-merchant unless the receiver-merchant sends back notice of objection to its contents within 10 days after receiving it. This Code rule is saying two things to merchants: First, to be on the safe side, always send written confirmation of the contract (preferably by registered mail) before you expend time and money in reliance on an oral agreement; and second, *read your mail!*

To protect the seller of goods against a potentially unfair result, UCC Section 2-201 provides a separate alternative for **specially manufactured goods**. When the buyer has a change of mind and tries to cancel an oral order for custom-made goods, the seller can enforce the oral contract by convincing the jury that the goods the seller is making are "for the buyer," that the seller has substantially started to produce the goods or has made commitments to get them from someone else, and that the goods cannot be readily resold in the ordinary course of the seller's business. This case thus raises several fact questions; basically, the jury has to be convinced that the seller will be stuck with the proverbial "white elephant" if the oral contract, actually made, is not enforced.

The oral contract is also enforceable against a party who admits its existence in pleadings, testimony, or otherwise in court. As with the writing alternatives, the contract is not enforceable under this provision beyond the **quantity of goods admitted**.

Finally, the **part performance** alternative has been substantially changed by the Code. Previously, either party could use the other's receipt and acceptance of a partial performance as evidence of a much larger contract. For example, a seller who could prove having delivered 50 bushels of wheat to a buyer who had accepted the goods might then allege that this was merely the first installment on an oral contract for 1,000 bushels of wheat; if the jury believed the seller, the seller could get the contract enforced on that basis. The drafters of the Code felt that this result circumvented the policy of the Statute of Frauds, so they provided that partial performance by one party makes the contract enforceable against the other party only to the same, pro rata extent. Thus, in the preceding example the seller can collect only the contract price for the 50 bushels of wheat delivered and accepted; the rest of the oral contract remains unenforceable. However, if the goods are an indivisible unit, such as a car or a Boeing 707, the buyer's payment of part of the contract price, received and accepted by the seller, does have the effect of making the entire contract enforceable.

Compliance Alternatives under Other Code Sections

The UCC permits the use of these same basic alternatives for lease of goods, except for the writing in confirmation between merchants. To be sufficient, a writing under this leases section (2A-201) must also contain the lease term (the time span of the lease) and the quantity of goods being leased. Other terms may of course be included in the signed writing, but are not absolutely required to enforce the contract.

For security agreements, there must be a writing by which the debtor grants the secured party a security interest in the described collateral, and only if the debtor signs the writing will the secured party have the right to repossess and resell the collateral if the debtor goes into default. The only instances in which such a writing is not required are in cases where the secured party has possession of the collateral, such as "pledge" or "pawn" transactions.

For sales of miscellaneous intangibles at a contract price of $5,000 or more, no alternative to the writing is provided. The signed writing must indicate that a contract has been made, must describe the subject matter of the contract, and must contain a price term.

Uniform Computer Information Transactions Act Writing Requirements

The Uniform Computer Information Transactions Act (UCITA) also contains a writing requirement in which the computer information transaction requires payment of a "contract fee" of $5,000 or more. However, if the agreement is a license for a period of 1 year or less (or terminable at will), no writing is required, even if the fee is $5,000 or more.

For computer information transactions, UCITA's writing requirement is worded a bit differently. Rather than a signed writing, UCITA specifies an "authenticated record." Similar alternatives based on part performance and admission in court are also provided. Interestingly, because one can surely imagine the development and sale of custom-designed computer information packages, there is no "special manufacture" alternative. The "writing [record] in confirmation" alternative is there, but only as between merchants (using essentially the same definition as the UCC). In UCITA, the merchant receiving the "record" in confirmation is given "a reasonable time" to object to it, rather than the 10 days specified in the UCC.

United Nations Convention on Contracts for the International Sale of Goods Writing Requirements

If the United Nations Convention on Contracts for the International Sale of Goods (UNC/CISG) applies to an international sale of goods, no writing is required to enforce the contract. It may be proved by oral and/or written evidence.

Results if the Statute of Frauds Applies and It Has Not Been Satisfied

Unenforceable in Court

In the vast majority of cases in which the Statute of Frauds applies and has not been complied with, the contract is unenforceable in court. This does not mean that the contract is illegal in any way or that the parties have violated any criminal law. Nor does it mean that if the parties perform the contract in full, one of the parties can later move to rescind the performances on the basis that the contract should have been evidenced by a writing and never was. **Unenforceable contract** as applied here simply means that there will be no court remedy for the enforcement of such a contract and that the court will not assist either party with its sanctions for nonperformance of the contract unless the contract can be proved by the required writing.

This result is not changed by the fact that one party has relied in good faith (but stupidly) on the existence of the unenforceable oral contract. Courts do not generally feel that they are permitted to work out a result forbidden by the Statute of Frauds just because a particular plaintiff presents an appealing set of facts.

Part Performance Exceptions

The UCC's exceptions in which part performance of an oral contract for goods or securities has taken place have already been discussed as alternatives. In addition, courts have worked out limited exceptions to the unenforceability result for contracts involving real estate or the year clause.

When one party has in good faith conferred benefits on the other under an oral contract that is unenforceable because of the year clause, a court will generally permit recovery in **quasi-contract** of the fair market value of the benefits so as to prevent **unjust enrichment**. An employee who worked for 3 months under a 2-year oral contract would thus be able to recover the fair market value of any services for which he or she had not been paid already. This exception would not, however, permit the recovery of moving expenses, bonuses, or other special compensation promised as part of the unenforceable oral agreement. The entire contract is enforceable, according to the **Restatement of Contracts, Second**, only where one party has *fully* performed his or her obligations; that party can then enforce the other party's full return performance.

For real estate contracts, the courts have developed a doctrine called **equitable estoppel**, which prevents a party from relying on the Statute of Frauds under certain limited circumstances and thus has the effect of making an oral contract enforceable. The courts have permitted either party to enforce an oral contract in which the buyer has taken possession of real estate with the seller's permission and has made substantial permanent physical improvements or (perhaps) in which the buyer has taken possession and has made a part payment on the contract price. This doctrine is generally not applicable in cases in which there has been only a part payment of the price or only a taking of possession by the buyer, or only "reliance" expenditures, such as preparation of documents by the seller or moving expenses by the buyer.

It is never advisable to rely on the slim chance that a court will salvage your situation by applying one of the exceptions to the Statute of Frauds. The only safe course is to get it in writing! (And make sure the other party signs the writing!)

Exhibit 10.2: Statute of Frauds: Compliance?

ALTERNATIVE METHODS OF COMPLIANCE WITH THE STATUTE OF FRAUDS

	Signed Writing	*Writing in Conformation*	*Admission in Court*	*Part Performance*	*Special Manufacture*
Real estate	All material terms, signed PTBC	NO	Split	Yes = Buyer possession + payment or improvements	N.A.
Year clause	All material terms, signed PTBC	NO	Split	Quasi-K for benefits conferred	N.A.
Debt of another	All material terms, signed PTBC	NO	Split	N.A.	N.A.
Goods $500 or more	Contract QUANTITY signed PAWEIS	To: PAWEIS(M) Contract QUANTITY signed SENDER M	Yes—up to QUANTITY admitted	Yes—for a pro rata part if divisible	Yes—if all elements proved
Investment securities	Oral O.K.	Oral O.K.	Oral O.K.	Oral O.K.	Oral O.K.
Secured transaction	SECURITY INTEREST DESCRIPTION signed DEBTOR	No	No	Yes—possession of collateral by Creditor	N.A.
Miscellaneous intangibles $5,000 or more	Contract PRICE SUBJECT MATTER signed PAWEIS	No	No	No	N.A.

Notice that only the signature of the "Party to be charged"/"Party against whom enforcement is sought" is required on the writing.

With a sale of real estate, for example:
(a) If only BUYER has signed a 4P's writing, the SELLER could sue for enforcement, but the BUYER could not.
(b) If only SELLER has signed a 4P's writing, the BUYER could sue for enforcement, but the SELLER could not.
(c) If NEITHER has signed a 4P's writing, NEITHER could sue for enforcement.
(d) If BOTH have signed a 4P's writing, EITHER could sue for enforcement.

CASE 3

Starry Const. Co., Inc. v. Murphy Oil USA

785 F.Supp. 1356 (D. MN 1992)

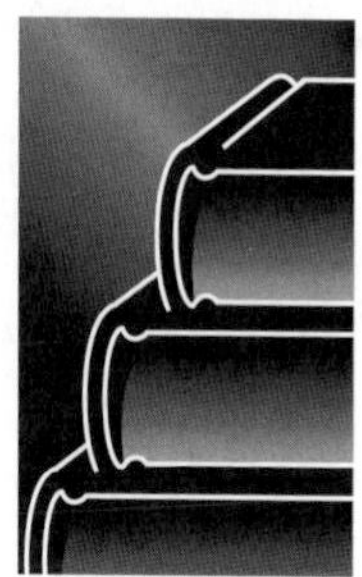

Facts: This case, arising in the context of the highway construction industry, involves the purported modification to a contract for the sale of asphalt cement oil. Plaintiff Starry Construction Co. (Starry) is a general contractor engaged in the business of asphalt road construction. Defendant Murphy Oil USA, Inc. (Murphy) is a supplier of asphalt cement oil, one of the materials required for installing asphalt pavement.

In March 1990, Robert Billingsley, one of Murphy's sales managers, orally agreed to sell Starry 20,000 tons of asphalt cement oil for $90 per ton, excluding taxes. Murphy sent Steven Minnerath, Starry's president, a sales acknowledgment form dated April 12, 1990. That form by its terms confirms the quantity and price of Starry's order, but also contains in particular the following clauses:

> *Fire, flood, strikes, differences with workmen, accidents to plants or machinery, failure of or unusual conditions surrounding the usual source of supplies of material, or other causes beyond the control of either party shall be a sufficient excuse for any delay or failure upon the part of either party to perform this order, provided, however, that such party shall notify the other with reasonable promptness as to the existence of such cause.*
>
> *If, by reason of any said causes, Murphy is unable to make deliveries to all its customers (whether under contract or not) its failure in whole or in part to make deliveries to purchaser, while delivering to others, shall not be a breach of this agreement and in such event Murphy may, but shall not be obligated to, prorate its available supply.*

Starry acknowledges receiving the form, but neither signed nor returned it to Murphy. According to Minnerath, the form included additional terms that were not a part of the oral agreement. Instead, Minnerath proceeded to bid work for Starry, allegedly under the assumption that Starry and Murphy had a valid oral contract that was limited to the terms specifically agreed upon.

Toward the end of April, Minnerath determined that Starry would need more oil. He contacted Billingsley and requested an additional 5,000 tons. Billingsley said that he would "check on it" and inform Starry in a day or so. Murphy did not contact Starry. Several days later, Minnerath called Billingsley, who allegedly indicated that Murphy would sell the additional oil on the same terms and conditions as those initially agreed to. Although Starry allegedly obtained additional work based on the increased figures, Minnerath neglected to send a confirmatory memorandum of this oral modification.

During the spring and summer of 1990, Minnerath periodically communicated with Billingsley regarding the delivery of asphalt cement oil. Minnerath allegedly told Billingsley that Starry had obtained enough work to use all of the asphalt cement oil, including the additional 5,000 tons, that Murphy had agreed to provide. Minnerath claims that Billingsley never contested the quantity under the contract in their discussions.

In August 1990, Iraq invaded Kuwait. Members of the media reported that prices for all oil-based products were likely to rise substantially. During September 1990, approximately 1 month before the end of the 1990 paving season, Murphy began experiencing an unprecedented demand for asphalt cement oil. Essentially, Murphy's customers began requesting the full amount of oil under their contracts after the War in the Persian Gulf began, whereas historically they requested only 90 to 95 percent of those amounts.

Tom O'Brien, Starry's comptroller, became concerned that Murphy would not supply the additional oil. He asked Minnerath to call Billingsley and obtain a written confirmation of the modification. Minnerath did so. Billingsley allegedly responded, "Don't worry about it. I'll take care of you. I've never cheated you in the past. You are a good customer, and I treat our good customers right."

Later, Minnerath learned that Murphy was promoting Billingsley and would be replacing him with Michael Palmgren. Minnerath allegedly called Billingsley once again and suggested the need to let his successor know about the agreement for 25,000 tons. Minnerath claims that Billingsley told him that he would leave a note on Palmgren's desk. Although Minnerath claims that after replacing Billingsley Palmgren acknowledged that he had seen such a note, Palmgren does not remember one.

In September 1990, Palmgren informed Starry that because of an oil crisis Murphy would be forced to allocate its supply. Consequently, Starry would not be receiving the additional 5,000 tons of oil, although Murphy did eventually supply an additional 107 tons. Believing that Murphy would inevitably provide the full 5,000 tons requested, Starry did not approach other suppliers to cover the shortfall until September 24, 1990. At that time, Starry agreed to purchase 1,000 tons of oil from Richards Asphalt Company for $117 per ton. In addition, Starry agreed to purchase another 3,000 tons from the Ashland Petroleum Company at $130 per ton on September 30, 1990.

On October 5, 1990, Minnerath, on advice of counsel, sent Palmgren a letter. That letter contained the following paragraph:

> *When we met on September 27, 1990, you indicated that you would get back to us with some kind of a schedule of the amount and timing for the ... [asphalt cement oil] you would give us so that we could, in turn, schedule our hot mix plants and make arrangements to purchase oil elsewhere if you would not supply us with the 25,000 ton called for by our Agreement.*

The letter further provides:

We now understand that you intend to provide us with approximately fifty-four ton of oil per day, but won't guarantee its availability.

Murphy now denies that the agreement was ever modified to include an additional 5,000 tons of oil.

Issue: Does the Statute of Frauds prevent proof of the alleged oral modification?

Decision: Yes. Summary judgment for Defendant.

Opinion by Judge MacLaughlin: "Starry claims that it has in fact satisfied the merchant exception. According to Starry, Section 336.2-201(2) is satisfied if within a reasonable time after the oral contract was made Starry sent a writing confirming the contract. Starry claims that Minnerath's letter of October 5, 1990 constitutes such a writing.

"This question thus boils down to whether the October 1990 letter satisfies the merchant exception. Although there is apparently no requirement that a letter confirming a contract be sent in the ordinary course of business, or that it take a particular form, the Court finds that under these circumstances a six-month delay in the sending of the letter was unreasonable as a matter of law. First, Starry candidly acknowledges that it has been able to find no case in which a period of more than four months was held to be reasonable under the merchant exception. The inordinate length of time alone in this case justifies holding the delay unreasonable. Moreover, the circumstances surrounding the relationship of the parties make a six-month delay unreasonable.... In this case, a writing in confirmation of the oral modification would lock the parties into a modified supply contract at a particular price. The volatility of the petroleum market, the radical fluctuations in price and supply, all counsel in favor of prompt confirmation....

"In any event, Starry could have protected itself. All it needed to do was to send a letter confirming the modification; Murphy did not even need to sign it. Minnerath candidly acknowledges that he simply neglected to send one.... Moreover, Murphy's repeated refusal to provide confirmation should have indicated to Starry that Murphy did not acknowledge the existence of the modification. Thus, the Court concludes that the merchant exception is not satisfied by the October 5, 1990 letter....

"Starry also argues that the statute is satisfied because there is evidence of a writing as required under Section 336.2-201(1). Starry correctly argues that as long as a quantity term is included, the form of the writing is unimportant. It 'may be written in lead pencil on a scratch pad....' In this case, Starry claims that a written note which Robert Billingsley left for Michael Palmgren, stating that Murphy had agreed to provide the additional 5,000 tons of asphalt cement oil, constitutes a writing within the meaning of the statute....

"To accept Starry's argument, the Court would have to rely solely upon the testimony of the proponent of the contract. This 'is exactly what the statute of frauds seeks to avoid....' The oral testimony of the plaintiff does not constitute a writing sufficient to satisfy the statute of frauds. Further, even if the Court were to accept Starry's argument that there was such a note, there is no evidence that the note contained the requisite quantity term. This alleged note therefore does not satisfy the statute....

"The final question in the statute of frauds analysis is whether some exception to the statute applies, making the alleged oral modification enforceable. Starry relies upon two. The first exception is contained in Section 336.2-201(3)(b).... A party against whom enforcement is sought need not actually admit that there was a contract; he only need admit the facts the legal consequence of which is a contract in order to be deprived of the statute of frauds defense....

"Starry claims that three admissions by Murphy in its testimony and pleadings satisfy the statute. First, in its memorandum in support of its motion, Murphy admits having supplied Starry with an additional 107 tons of asphalt cement oil.... Second, Starry claims that Billingsley's acknowledgement that the additional oil was discussed during March 1990, combined with the evidence that Starry had received enough work to be able to use the additional amount, establishes the plausibility of Starry's claim and satisfies the purposes underlying the statute of frauds. Finally, Starry argues that an adverse credibility determination may amount to an admission.... According to Starry, Palmgren's unlikely loss of memory regarding the existence of the note satisfies the admission exception....

"Starry's positions seem tenuous at best. There are at least two problems with respect to its argument that supplying 107 tons of oil constitutes an admission for statute of a contract for 5,000 tons. First, the Court cannot infer from the fact that Murphy supplied oil to Starry, a regular customer, that Murphy would not have done so without a contract because it would invalidate any allocation program. To the contrary, the statute expressly provides that the seller 'may include [in its allocation program] regular customers not then under contract as well as his own requirements for further manufacture....' The only requirement is that the allocation must be fair and reasonable.... Second, the admissions exception expressly provides that 'the contract is not enforceable ... beyond the quantity of goods admitted....' Assuming that there was an oral contract for an additional 5,000 tons of asphalt cement oil, that contract is enforceable only up to the 107 tons admitted.

"Starry's third argument seems the least persuasive. Credibility determinations are inappropriate when reviewing motions for summary judgment.... Regardless, Murphy's employees have denied under oath that the contract was modified. The admissions exception does not apply when the party against whom enforcement is sought denies under oath the existence of a modification....

"The second exception to the statute of frauds relied upon by Starry is the equitable estoppel exception. The Uniform Commercial Code provides that unless specifically displaced by Code provisions, the principles of law and equity, including estoppel, supplement its provisions.... Minnesota courts have long held that the doctrine of equitable estoppel may limit the application of the statute of frauds....

"Without addressing whether a party seeking refuge under equitable estoppel must show unconscionability, it is clear that misrepresentation of a material fact is an indispensable element. . . . The parties seem to acknowledge that there is no evidence of misrepresentation, either intentional or unintentional. Thus, the equitable estoppel exception does not undermine Murphy's statute of frauds defense.

"After analyzing the application of the statute of frauds under the three-part inquiry, the Court finds that the statute of frauds precludes Starry's claim of an oral modification beyond the 107 tons of additional oil. The statute of frauds clearly applies, given that the contract as purportedly modified involves the sale of goods for the price of $500 or more. The statute has not been satisfied, either through the merchant exception or the allegedly lost note. Finally, the admission exception permits enforcement only for the additional 107 tons, while the estoppel exception does not apply at all. The Court will therefore grant Murphy's motion for summary judgment."

Parol Evidence Rule

Nature and Operation of the Rule

Just as the operation of the Statute of Frauds can be summarized in the sentence "Get it in writing," so can the significance of the **parol evidence rule** be summarized by slightly modifying the sentence to read: "Get it *all* in writing!" The rule says that prior "outside" evidence cannot be used to change the terms of a complete, final written contract. It is a rule that limits the evidence a court can consider in interpreting the parties' agreement.

Although the application of the parol evidence rule may seem to produce harsh or unfair results in particular situations, the equities are not all on one side. There are sound, practical reasons for the rule's existence. It is, ultimately, another example of the courts' efforts to find and enforce the intent of the parties. The contracting parties may have engaged in extended negotiations before reaching their agreement. They may have exchanged numerous oral and written proposals and counterproposals, some accepted by the other side, some rejected. Then, at the end of this lengthy process, they signed a document that either expressly stated or implied that it was intended by them as the full, final, and complete written expression of their agreement.

At this point, the parol evidence rule comes into operation. Once a party has signed such a document, the rule prevents that party from unilaterally changing or modifying its terms by using parol, or outside, evidence. The document means what it says: "blue" means blue, not green; "10 tons" means 10 tons, not 100 tons or 10 pounds. If a term or a provision on a particular subject is not contained in the document, the presumption is that it was left out on purpose because the parties did not intend that it be included. In short, the rule operates against the "add-on-a-term" person, who is trying to say, "Yes, that's the contract I signed. Yes, that's the deal I made. But—there's something else that we agreed on that's not in the document." In general, the "add-on" person will (and should) lose this argument; parol evidence will not be admitted to change the terms of the written document.

In other words, the parol evidence rule operates to protect *both* parties, by guaranteeing the integrity of the document they both signed and intended as the contract. The rule is really not saying anything more "unfair" than that a person is, generally, bound by what he or she has signed. If the document is not "right," if it doesn't contain all the terms you have agreed on, *do not sign it*!

Situations Not Covered by the Rule

Because the purpose of the parol evidence rule is to make final a document that the parties intended to be final, the rule has no application in contract situations in which no such full, final, and complete document has ever been signed. In these cases, there is no "rule" that prohibits the court from looking at all relevant evidence. If the seller has simply given the buyer a sales receipt, or if the parties have merely exchanged letters, no such complete document exists, so all evidence is admissible to show what the parties intended to include as part of the contract. For sales of goods, a final writing may be "explained or supplemented," but not "contradicted," by "consistent additional terms," "unless the court finds the writing to have been intended also as a complete and exclusive statement of the terms of the agreement" (UCC, 2-202[b]). What this means in plain English is that a court may be a little more reluctant to apply the parol evidence rule in a sale of goods case in which the contract does not contain a specific, "This is it" statement.

Again remembering the basic purpose of the parol evidence rule, it obviously has no application in situations in which the alleged modification of the terms in the document occurred *after* the document was signed. The document is presumed final as of the time it was signed. The parties may decide to modify it later, and the parol evidence rule does not prevent either of them from trying to convince a jury that such modifications were in fact agreed to. (There may, however, be both consideration and Statute of Frauds problems as to such subsequent modifications, as noted previously.)

For sales of goods, the UCC permits the parties to agree that a written contract can only be modified by a subsequent written (and signed) agreement.

Third, and even more obviously, the rule has no application when there are two contracts, one evidenced by a complete writing, the other oral. The fact that one contract is written does not prevent a party from trying to prove that there was a second, oral contract. If you buy a used car from your next door neighbors for $900, and they also agree to let you park the car in their garage for the next 6 months for $10 a month, the fact that you have signed a complete written contract for the sale of the car will not prevent you from trying to prove the existence of the separate oral contract to rent the garage space.

Exceptions to the Operation of the Parol Evidence Rule

Like many of the other rules of evidence, the parol evidence rule is subject to some important exceptions. That is, the trier of fact can consider parol evidence in some situations, at least for some purposes, even though a complete written document exists and even though the evidentiary facts occurred before the document was signed.

Stated most simply, parol evidence is admissible when it is being offered to help the court interpret the terms of the written contract or to show the existence of a defense against the written contract, not to *change* the terms of the written contract. The line is not always easy to draw, although in some cases the correct result seems fairly obvious.

Ambiguities. The easiest cases to decide are those in which the writing makes no sense by itself, due to ambiguities, contradictory provisions, or coded "nonsense" terms. In these cases a court must use extrinsic evidence to discover what the parties "really meant." When both parties are engaged in a particular trade or business and certain words have acquired a customary meaning in that business, courts generally permit either party to prove that special meaning even though the words have a "plain English" meaning, too. Thus, an Oregon court permitted a seller to prove that "50 percent protein" really meant *49.50 percent* protein in the dog food business, and the seller could therefore collect the full contract price per ton for all shipments of dog food scraps with a protein content of at least 49.50 percent. For sales of goods, the UCC now permits the parties to explain or supplement a "final" writing by course of dealing, usage of trade, or course of performance.

Oral Conditions. Most courts will also allow a party to show that the written contract was intended to be subject to an orally agreed-upon condition precedent, that they intended no deal at all unless and until some special condition was satisfied. Similarly, if the writing states as a fact something that is just not so, a party can usually prove the truth. For instance, if your contract to buy a new TV set not only describes the set and states the price and the payment terms, but also goes on to say that the set "has been delivered," when in fact it has not been delivered, you can prove that you did not get the TV set as promised. (But the parol evidence rule will generally prevent you from changing "one TV" into two TVs, or "$600" into $450, or "TV" into stereo.)

Defenses. Courts are quite liberal in allowing proof of the existence of a defense against liability on the written contract. In most cases this is not really a contradiction of the writing because the writing does not usually contain such provisions as "This contract is legal"

CASE 4

Donahue et al. v. Artisan Entertainment, Inc.

2002 U.S. Dist. LEXIS 5930 (S.D. NY 2002)

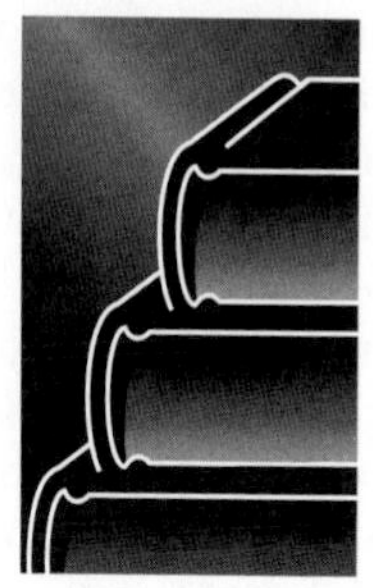

Facts: Heather Donahue, Michael Williams, and Joshua Leonard played the three main characters in the hit movie, "The Blair Witch Project" (worldwide gross receipts of about $240 million). They claim that the defendant has made unauthorized use of their names and likenesses from that film, and of other images of them. Artisan says that all its uses of names and pictures were authorized in the original acting contracts that were entered into with the picture's producer, Haxan Films, and then transferred by Haxan to Artisan. Artisan has since made a second film, "Blair Witch 2," and has been using names and pictures from the first film to help promote the second.

A New York statute says that commercial use of a person's name or picture, without consent, creates a tort claim against the user. Artisan moves for a summary judgment based on the wording of the Haxan contracts signed by the plaintiffs.

Issue: Is the defendant entitled to a summary judgment based on the wording of the contracts?

Decision: No. A trial is required.

Opinion by Judge Koeltl: "If a contract is unambiguous, a court is 'required to give effect to the contract as written and may not consider extrinsic evidence to alter or interpret its meaning.'... Contractual language 'whose meaning is otherwise plain is not ambiguous merely because the parties urge different interpretations in the litigation.'... Where the contractual language is subject to more than one reasonable meaning and where extrinsic evidence of the parties' intent exists, the question of the proper interpretation should be submitted to the trier of fact....

"In this case the parties agree that the interpretation of P.5 of the acting contracts is pivotal. It is true that ... the phrase 'all rights to the results and proceeds of [the plaintiff's] services' appears to contemplate an unlimited grant or retention of rights when read in isolation, and courts often refuse to read limitations into broad grants of rights.... However, the Court should 'examine the entire contract' in order to 'safeguard against adopting an interpretation that would render any individual provision superfluous.'... The 'all ... results and proceeds' clause in P.5 is immediately followed by three more specific sentences....

"The plaintiffs ... argue that the parties' inclusion of specific supplemental grants in the contract indicates that they did not intend the first sentence of P.5 to be a broad and unlimited grant. Since that contention is reasonable and the defendants' interpretation would render some language in the contract superfluous, the Court cannot determine as a matter of law that the defendants' interpretation of P.5 is correct for purposes of a motion for summary judgment. Furthermore, both sides have presented extrinsic evidence, although of varying probative value, that they claim would illuminate the intent of the parties. Thus, the proper interpretation of the contract is a question for the finder of fact that cannot be resolved on this motion....

"For the reasons explained above, the defendants' motion for summary judgment is denied."

or "There was no duress." The contract may, however, contain a representation that the party signing it is of full legal age, and there are some courts that prevent a minor from asserting lack of capacity if the minor has stated otherwise in writing. (The next chapter has a more complete discussion of this point, and other defenses are covered as well.)

The *Donahue* case interprets a contract for services.

United Nations Convention on Contracts for the International Sale of Goods and the Parol Evidence Rule. The language of Article 8 of the CISG seems clearly to repudiate the Parol Evidence Rule, although not specifically by name. Section 8(1) says that a party's statements and conduct are to be interpreted according to its intent, "where the other party knew of could not have been unaware what that intent was." Section 8(2) states that, if 8(1) is not applicable, such statements and conduct are to be interpreted according to the meaning a reasonable person would give them. And finally, section 8(3) provides that, in determining what a reasonable person would believe, "due consideration is to be given to all relevant circumstances of the case including the negotiations, any practices which the parties have established between themselves, usages and any subsequent conduct by the parties." At the very least, Article 8 permits a much more wide-ranging inquiry by the court into what the contract really means.

The *MCC-Marble* case explores these issues.

CASE 5

MCC-Marble Ceramic v. Ceramica Nuovo D'Agostino, S.p.A.

144 F.3d 1384 (11 Cir. 1998)

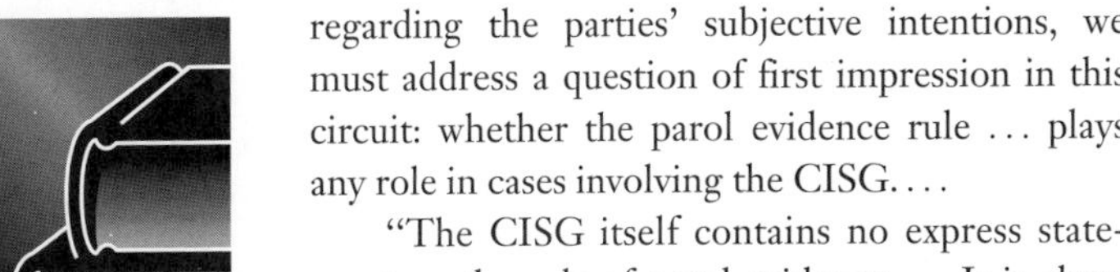

Facts: MCC is a Florida corporation that retails ceramic tiles. Ceramica is an Italian manufacturer of tiles. MCC's president, Juan Carlos Monzon, attended a trade fair in Bologna, Italy, and entered into a contract with Ceramica. Monzon did not read or speak Italian. He signed a pre-printed (in Italian) contract after negotiating with Gianni Silingardi, Ceramica's commercial director, using another Ceramica employee (Gianfranco Copelli) as translator. One of the terms on the back of the form gave Ceramica the right to suspend or cancel the contract if the buyer defaulted in paying for goods delivered.

When MCC sued for failure to deliver as promised, Ceramica cited the cancellation clause. MCC claimed that it had had no intent to be bound by the terms on the back of the form, and introduced affidavits to that effect from Monzon, Silingardi, and Copelli. Ceramica was granted summary judgment by the U.S. District Court, and MCC appealed.

Issue: Is parol evidence (the affidavits) admissible to contradict the terms of the written contract?

Decision: Yes. Judgment reversed, and case remanded.

Opinion by Judge Birch: "Contrary to what is familiar practice in United States courts, the CISG appears to permit a substantial inquiry into the parties' subjective intent, even if the parties did not engage in any objectively ascertainable means of registering this intent.... The plain language of the Convention ... requires an inquiry into a party's subjective intent as long as the other party to the contract was aware of that intent....

"Given our determination that the magistrate judge and the district court should have considered MCC's affidavits regarding the parties' subjective intentions, we must address a question of first impression in this circuit: whether the parol evidence rule ... plays any role in cases involving the CISG....

"The CISG itself contains no express statement on the role of parol evidence.... It is clear, however, that the drafters of the CISG were comfortable with the concept of permitting parties to rely on oral contracts because they eschewed any statutes of fraud provision and expressly provided for the enforcement of oral contracts.... Given article 8(1)'s directive to use the intent of the parties to interpret their statements and conduct, article 8(3) is a clear instruction to admit and consider parol evidence regarding the negotiations to the extent they reveal the parties' subjective intent....

"Our reading of article 8(3) as a rejection of the parol evidence rule ... is in accordance with the great weight of academic commentary on the issue....

"[MCC's] affidavits raise an issue of material fact regarding the parties' intent to incorporate the provisions on the reverse of the form contract. If the finder of fact determines that the parties did not intend to rely on those provisions, then the more general provisions of the CISG will govern the outcome of the dispute....

"[W]e conclude that the CISG ... precludes summary judgment in this case because MCC has raised an issue of material fact concerning the parties' subjective intent to be bound by the terms on the reverse side of the pre-printed contract. The CISG also precludes the application of the parol evidence rule.... Accordingly, we REVERSE the District Court's grant of summary judgment and REMAND this case for further proceedings consistent with this opinion."

Significance of This Chapter

Knowledge of the two major rules discussed in this chapter—the Statute of Frauds and the parol evidence rule—could save you and any organization you represent from many unnecessary lawsuits. This chapter contains the most significant legal "first-aid" rules in the entire book: *Get it in writing—and get it **all** in writing!* In some cases, you don't have any enforceable contract at all if you do not follow the rules. In other cases, you may wind up with a contract other than the one you intended if you do not follow the rules.

People tend to forget promises and guarantees once they have your contract price, or your goods, land, or services. Promises are harder to "forget" if you have them in a signed writing. Take a little extra time and write up the agreement, or rewrite it, if it does not state the terms correctly. If the written agreement is not clear and understandable, you should probably have your lawyer check it over for you. Once you sign it, you will be bound by it, so make sure you know what it says—and make sure the *other* party signs it too, and that you get a signed copy. An ounce of written prevention is worth several pounds of lawyers.

IMPORTANT TERMS AND CONCEPTS

4-P's
admission in court
all-material-terms rule
equitable estoppel
investment securities
letters of credit
merchant
miscellaneous intangible property
parol evidence rule
part performance
quantity of goods admitted
quasi-contract
Restatement of Contracts, Second
secured transactions
signed writing
specially manufactured goods
Statute of Frauds
unenforceable contract
unjust enrichment
writing in confirmation
year clause

QUESTIONS AND PROBLEMS FOR DISCUSSION

1. When is an oral contract enforceable in court?

2. What happens when the Statute of Frauds applies to a contract and only one party signs a writing that is sufficient to comply with its requirements?

3. When does the Statute of Frauds apply to an employment contract?

4. What must a writing include, under the UCC, to comply with the Statute of Frauds?

5. The plaintiffs were small independent oil dealers with their main operations in North Carolina. The defendant was a refiner, dependent almost entirely on producers for its supply of crude oil. It had for some years been selling its product to the plaintiffs. In anticipation of the oil shortage, which all parties in the industry apparently foresaw, discussions as to future supplies were held among the parties. It was contended by the plaintiffs that the defendant agreed to supply them with certain fixed quantities of gasoline. As the energy crisis deepened, the defendant's suppliers drastically reduced its supply of crude oil. The defendant accordingly proceeded to allocate on a lower percentage its deliveries to its contract customers and to notify customers such as the plaintiffs, whom it denominated noncontract customers, that it would make no further sales to them. Preliminary injunctive relief was granted in both instances. In each case the defendant appealed.

   How should the appeals court rule?

6. Gisaburo Kiyose taught in the Department of East Asian Languages on the Bloomington campus of Indiana University. From 1984 to 1986, he was a teaching associate; from 1986 to April 1993, a lecturer. He received his Ph.D. in 1993 and was appointed an assistant professor. He claims that he was promised lifetime employment, beginning with a 3-year appointment as assistant professor. He was notified in 1993 that he would not be reappointed for 1994–95. He further claims that he turned down five offers from other schools because of Indiana's promise. The trial court granted defendants' motion to dismiss.

   Was this ruling correct? Why or why not?

7. Kenneth Sierens and James Thompson sued Edwin Clausen for breach of two alleged oral agreements to sell them a total of 3,500 bushels of soybeans. They said they sent Clausen a written confirmation, in accordance with UCC 2-201(2). Clausen had been a farmer for 34 years, was then cultivating 180 acres of corn and 150 acres of soybeans, and had for the past 5 years sold his crops to grain elevators in both cash sales and futures contracts. The trial court held that Clausen was a farmer and not a "merchant" for the purposes of UCC 2-201(2). It dismissed the complaint, and the appellate court affirmed.

   Will the state supreme court affirm? Explain.

8. Between the approximate dates of July 26 and September 11, the plaintiff provided hospital care, laboratory facilities, and medication to the patient William H Rowe. Rowe's sons, M.H. Rowe and William W. Rowe, had asked the plaintiff, Dr. Peterson, to do so, and had promised to pay him. When Dr. Peterson sued the sons, the trial court gave him $2,739.25, the account balance. The sons appealed.

   The evidence discloses at least four conversations between the parties concerning payment for services to be furnished the patient. Appellants were at the hospital the day after William H. Rowe was admitted, and while there, discussed with appellee the matter of making financial arrangements. Appellee explained to appellants that the patient was very ill and would require extensive treatment. Appellants informed appellee that their father had no financial means; nevertheless, appellant M.H. Rowe stated that appellants themselves would pay for such service. His exact statement was: "You go right ahead and give him whatever is necessary to save his life and I will pay for it." Subsequently, on July 29, appellants, accompanied by their wives, came to the hospital, and again appellant M.H. Rowe stated to appellee: "Well, we want you to do everything you can to save his life, and we don't want you to spare any expense, because whatever he needs, doctor, you go ahead and get it and I will pay you." On July 31, the date of the operation, appellants were at the hospital, and again the question of payment of expenses was renewed. At that time, M.H. Rowe voluntarily authorized the services of special nurses, stating: "[B]ecause whatever he needs, I want him to have it and I will pay you for it." To which appellant William W. Rowe assented as follows: "That is correct, anything that—any expense. Do not spare any expense on my father, and I will pay you for it."

Did the trial court decide correctly?

CHAPTER 11

Contractual Capacity and Reality of Consent

Chapter Objectives

This chapter will:

- Discuss the effect of lack of capacity on a contract.
- Explain the main theories of liability that may be asserted against a minor who makes a contract.
- Discuss other groups of persons with special legal status or limited contractual capacity.
- Discuss the five elements needed to prove a fraud case.
- Differentiate innocent misrepresentation, undue influence, and duress.
- Indicate the different types of mistakes that may occur in a contracting situation and their impact on a contract's enforceability.

Even though parties have entered into a contract that appears complete, and the agreement is enforceable under the Statute of Frauds, they still may have defenses against liability on the contract. Depending on the defense proved, the contract may be voidable at the option of one or both parties, the whole contract may be unenforceable, or the entire agreement may be void.

We consider, first, defenses based on a party's lack of **capacity to contract.** Capacity questions may be raised with regard to minors, insane people, people under the influence of alcohol or other drugs, aliens, American Indians, convicts, married women, and private and governmental corporations. Rulings on these questions are usually made according to the law of the place where the contract is entered into, except where real estate is involved; for realty, the law of the state where the realty is located determines capacity questions.

Lack of Capacity

Minors or "Legal Infants"

It is sometimes said that "minors cannot make contracts." That is patently not so; **minors** (legal infants) can and do make millions of dollars' worth of contracts every day. What is distinctive about the minor's contract is that it is voidable at his or her option or that the minor can later elect not to be bound by it. But make no mistake; the other party, unless that party too lacks full contractual capacity, is bound to the agreement with the minor. The common law judges were concerned with the possibility that the "infant" might be taken advantage of, and so gave the minor the virtually absolute right of disaffirmance. Although minors today may be more sophisticated at an earlier age, this rule continues to be applied by the courts.

We need, then, to examine the scope of minors' power to disaffirm their contracts and to see when minors may be liable under five different legal bases for liability (see Exhibit 11-1).

Exhibit 11.1: Litigation Against the Minor: Five Theories of Liability

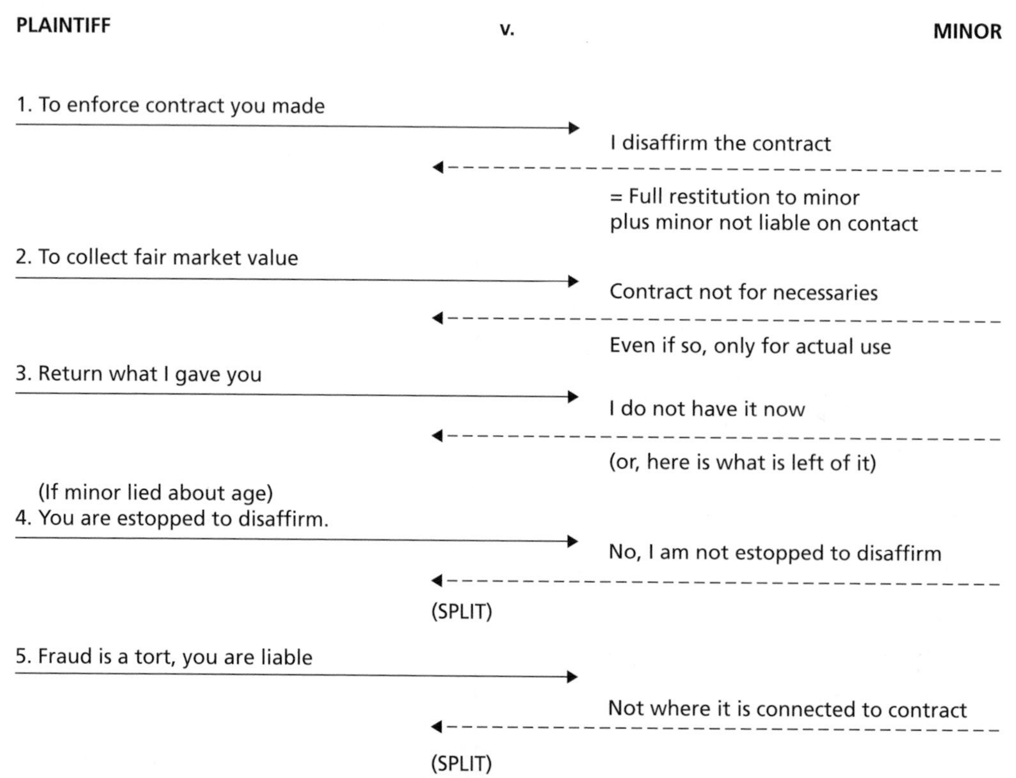

Scope of the Minor's Power to Disaffirm

The common law set the age of legal majority at 21, and until quite recently that was also the age used for full contractual capacity in nearly all states. The adoption of the Voting Rights Amendment, setting the voting age at 18, has led most states to similarly lower their age of majority to 18 (except perhaps for the age at which one can lawfully buy alcoholic beverages). Different ages, however, may still exist in some states for such matters as criminal responsibility, marriage without parental consent, and making a valid will. However, we are concerned here only with the legal capacity to make fully binding contracts.

Whatever age is established in a state, it refers strictly to chronological age. How old the minors "look," or how "experienced" they are, is completely irrelevant to minors' power to disaffirm their contracts. Equally irrelevant is the fact that the minors might be living away from their parents and are totally free of their control (i.e., emancipated). These facts would, however, be relevant in deciding whether an item was a "necessary," as will be discussed.

In general, minors have the power to disaffirm any contract they make while still a minor. In some states, certain contracts are made binding against the minor by special statutes (bank accounts and life insurance contracts are typical examples), but these are special, and very limited, exceptions.

In most states, minors can disaffirm a contract any time while they are still minors and for a reasonable time after arriving at the age of majority. For contracts involving real estate, most states say that minors cannot disaffirm until reaching the age of majority, and then they have a reasonable time to elect to affirm or disaffirm. What is a reasonable time within which to disaffirm is a question to be determined by the facts of each case, with the courts paying particular attention to whether the minor was aware of the right to disaffirm.

Any words or actions that indicate the minor's intent not to be bound by the contract are sufficient notice of disaffirmance. Asking for the money back or offering to return items bought while a minor would be clear indications of an intent to disaffirm. When the contract is completely "executory" (i.e., not performed by either side), even the minor's silence may amount to a disaffirmance. The minor's failure to confirm the unperformed contract after age 18 indicates an unwillingness to be bound by it, but the receipt and retention of benefits or the making of a payment on the contract by the former minor would probably be a ratification of the contract. Silence has the opposite implication when the minor has received the performance of the other party and has, in return, performed under the contract while still a minor, and then turns 18 but says nothing about wanting to disaffirm. In this case, silence beyond the reasonable time for disaffirmance equals ratification.

All states agree that **ratification** by the minor can occur only after the minor has arrived at the age of majority; otherwise, any ratification can be disaffirmed because it too occurred while the person was a minor. In addition to the silence case described previously, ratification can be made by express statements, such as "I'll keep the car," or it may be implied from the retention of benefits, or from payments made after the minor has reached age 18.

Effect of Minor's Disaffirmance on the Contract

Once a minor has effectively exercised the power to disaffirm a contract, the minor can no longer be held liable for any promises made therein; the minor's contract was voidable, and the minor has elected to avoid it. Thus, when a minor purchased an automobile and promised to make installment payments for the balance of the contract price, if the minor disaffirms, then the minor is no longer liable for the balance still due. Likewise, a minor who disaffirms such a **voidable contract** generally has the legal right to receive all benefits already transferred to the other party under the contract. For example, in the car purchase case, the minor is entitled to the return of all monies already paid to the seller of the car. A minor who gave the seller a trade-in car as part of the down payment is entitled to the return of that too, or of its fair market value if the seller no longer has it.

When the benefits given by the minor have been retransferred to third parties, the minor can generally sue such third parties and demand the return of such property. Thus a minor who sells real estate while a minor would be able to reclaim it even as against a good faith third party who bought the real estate from the minor's buyer. As exceptions to the general third-party rule, the Uniform Commercial Code (UCC) protects good faith purchaser third parties against such claims by minors in two situations: when the minor's goods have been resold by the initial buyer to a good faith purchaser or when a promissory note or other negotiable instrument executed by a minor has gotten into the hands of a **holder in due course (HDC),** which is basically, just another name for a good faith purchaser). This HDC rule is discussed in detail in Part Four, Law of Finance. In each of these two exception situations, the minor could not recover the instrument or the goods from the third party. The minor could, however, still use minority to avoid liability as the seller/transferor of the property.

Liability in Quasi-Contract for Necessaries

To prevent **unjust enrichment** and to provide a remedy for people who have transferred benefits but have no enforceable contract claim for their price, the common law courts developed the concept of **quasi-contract.** While acknowledging that there is no enforceable contract claim, this theory permits a plaintiff to collect the **reasonable market value** of benefits that the plaintiff has conferred, "as if" a contract existed.

A minor is liable in quasi-contract for the reasonable market value of **necessaries** actually furnished to the minor pursuant to the minor's now-disaffirmed contract. The other party has the burden of proving that whatever was furnished was actually a necessary to the *particular* minor whom the party dealt with; proof that general categories of necessaries, such as food, clothing, shelter, or medical services, were furnished to the minor is not sufficient to establish the seller's right to recovery. It must also be shown that the minor in question had no source of supply of these items and that the items were furnished to the minor in reasonable amounts. An apartment would not be a necessary, for example, for minors who could live with their parents; and even if an apartment were a necessary for the particular minor, a 10-room penthouse would probably not be. Although the courts today are somewhat more liberal in defining necessaries, sellers of such obvious "luxury" items as stereos, TVs, and vacations probably have no case under this theory. Even where an item is found to be a necessary, the proper measure of recovery is only its fair market value (a fact question), not its contract price, and that *only* for the benefits already conferred on and used by the minor. In the case of the apartment found to be a necessary, the landlord can collect only what a jury determines to be the fair market value and only for the period of time that the minor stayed in the apartment.

Minor's Duty to Make Restitution

Under the general rule, as applied in most states, a minor who wishes to disaffirm a contract has the duty to return to the other party whatever contract benefits are still in the minor's possession at the time of disaffirmance. In most states the minor has no duty to reimburse the other party for that portion of the consideration that the minor has lost, wasted, or disposed of during infancy. In the classic example, a 16-year-old boy buys a new Cadillac, drives it until he is almost 18, then "totals" it in an accident. In most states the minor's only duty of **restitution** is to return the wreck; the minor is not liable for the use value of the car while the minor had it or for the extensive "depreciation" in the value of the car. Similarly, if the minor had resold the car and spent the proceeds, the minor would have nothing at all to restore but could still disaffirm the original purchase contract and get back whatever payment the minor had made to the original seller. (In short, car dealers are repeatedly warned: "*Do not sell to minors!*") The same result—no restitution at all by the minor—occurs when the minor has received intangible benefits, such as a vacation or services.

The *Mitchell* case is a recent example of how these rules operate to protect minors.

Estoppel to Assert Minority

As applied in most states, the aforementioned rules are hard enough on the adult seller, but even harsher results occur when minors have misrepresented their age and thus have induced the other party to contract on the assumption that they were adults.

CASE 1

Mitchell v. Mitchell
963 S.W.2d 222 (KY App. 1998)

Facts: Sherri Mitchell was injured on October 14, 1995, while traveling as a passenger in an automobile owned by her father, Donnie Fee, and operated by her husband, the appellee, Michael J. Mitchell. On October 25, 1995, Sherri, age seventeen, executed a release settling her bodily injury claim for $2,500. No conservator [guardian] was appointed at the time the release was executed.

Sherri filed a motion for declaratory judgment alleging that her incapacity at the time the release was executed rendered it null and void. The appellees argued, and the trial court agreed, that Sherri's marriage emancipated her, removing any disability she had as a minor, including the capacity to contract.

Issue: Does marriage remove a minor's disability to contract?

Decision: No. Judgment reversed. (Sherri wins.)

Opinion by Judge Emberton: "Ky.Rev. Stat. (KRS) 387.010 defines minor as anyone under the age of eighteen. Ordinarily, a contract executed by a minor is enforceable by the minor but may be avoided by the minor if not affirmed by him after reaching adulthood. Although the minor has the legal capacity to contract, he has the privilege of avoiding the contract.... Although there are certain exceptions to this general rule, none is applicable to this case.

"A settlement agreement and release of a third-party tortfeasor has been held to be voidable by the infant.... A repudiation of the agreement requires that the minor return the consideration paid pursuant to that agreement....

"The privilege bestowed upon a minor to avoid contracts made during infancy is given for policy reasons. Infants, as with other classes of disabilities, are presumed to be insufficiently mature or experienced to effectively bargain with those who have attained legal age, and any transaction which may result in a financial loss to them or in a depletion of their estates is scrutinized with care....

"Marriage of the infant emancipates the minor; it does not, however, make the minor *sui juris*.... 'Although parental emancipation may free the infant from parental control, it does not remove all of the disabilities of infancy. It does not, for example, enlarge or affect the minor's capacity or incapacity to contract.' ...

"The rule may seem antiquated in view of the arguable maturity of today's youth. It may seem ironic that a minor can drive a car yet not be bound by the contract to purchase that car or be responsible for his torts and crimes yet unable to settle a dispute against a tortfeasor. The distinction to be made is that too frequently a contract involves negotiation and thought beyond the maturity of most people under the age of eighteen. For the same reason, we are unpersuaded by the cases cited by appellee dealing with the statute of limitations....

"We cannot adopt a rule that marriage by the minor somehow classifies him as more mature and intelligent than his unmarried counterpart. We ... find that logic and common sense would not encourage such a result since marriage by a minor too frequently may itself be indicative of a lack of wisdom and maturity....

"This case is reversed and remanded for an order avoiding the settlement and release executed by appellant."

Estoppel, remember, is the legal rule that prevents a party from denying the legal effectiveness of a previous statement, after another party has changed his or her position in reliance on the earlier statement. Shouldn't that rule be applied when the other party has made a contract in reliance on the minor's statement that the minor was of legal age to contract? Shouldn't the minor, in other words, be estopped from asserting minority in such a case? Some courts do apply estoppel against the minor here, but the majority do not. A special California statute provides a procedure for court approval of employment contracts for minor athletes and artists; the minor-employee is bound to the contract once the court approves it.

Tort Liability for Misrepresentation of Age

Minors are, as a general rule, liable for their own torts, and intentional misrepresentation is a tort—fraud. Should not the other party, having been damaged by reasonable reliance on the minor's **misrepresentation of age,** be able to sue the minor on a tort theory of liability even though the contract has been disaffirmed? Once again, the courts are split on this point. A slight majority still follows the older view that the minor cannot be sued in tort; doing so would amount to holding the minor liable on his or her contract. The policy protecting the minor against unnecessary contracts is more important to most courts than the policy of holding the minor liable for torts.

It probably should also be noted at this point that a minor's parents are not generally liable for the minor's torts or the minor's contracts, although they are legally obligated to support the minor with the necessities of life. Some states do have statutes that make parents liable for their minor children's intentional torts, up to a specific dollar amount of damages.

People Who Are Insane, Intoxicated, or Drugged

Contracts made by people who lack contractual capacity because their ability to make decisions has been impaired by mental disease or defect, or by alcohol or drugs, are treated in much the same way as contracts made by minors. As a general rule, when a person's mental faculties are so impaired that the person does not understand the nature and consequences of the transaction, that is, an insane person, the resulting contract is voidable at the person's option when the person recovers, or at the option of a subsequently appointed guardian. If any such person has previously been taken before a (probate) court, adjudged incompetent to manage his or her own affairs, and had a guardian appointed, then later contracts made by that person are not just voidable but totally void. The person need take no action to disaffirm the contracts; they simply will not be recognized by the courts.

Such people are generally liable in quasi-contract for the fair market value of necessaries furnished to them during their period of disability (assuming that these needs are not already being met by a guardian), under basically the same rules as those that apply to minors. Much more strictly than with the minor, the courts require the mentally disabled person to make full restitution in money or the equivalent to disaffirm contracts entered into in good faith by the other party.

Aliens

Aliens in the United States are not generally subject to any contractual disability unless they are in the country illegally or their country is at war with ours. In either case, they will usually not be able to use our courts to enforce contracts. Aside from these two exceptional cases, some states—and even the national government—have made efforts to reserve to citizens certain rights and privileges, such as real estate ownership, practice of such professions as law and medicine, and government employment.

Aliens do not have to be given the "privileges and immunities of citizenship" under the Fourteenth Amendment because they are obviously not citizens. But they are "persons," and thus they are protected by the due process of law clauses of the Fifth and Fourteenth Amendments and by the equal protection clause of the Fourteenth Amendment. The courts' problem, when such "citizens only" laws are challenged, is to try to decide which rights and privileges fall into which category. Voting in political elections and holding political office are obviously rights that do not have to be extended to aliens. The present tendency of the courts is to invalidate all other restrictions on aliens. A new U.S. statute does, however, require employers to verify the legal residency of all aliens who apply for employment.

Currently, because of the large number of illegal aliens residing in this country, a significant question persists: To what extent do such people qualify for government benefits, such as education, housing, and workers' compensation? Here again, the tendency is to require that such benefits be made available to illegal aliens, too. Even the traditional rule that denies illegal aliens access to our courts is being changed, as seen in several recent cases.

American Indians

It sounds very strange to say it, some 200 years after the birth of the United States, but it is nonetheless true: The original inhabitants of this country, the **American Indians,** may still be subject to different legal rules because of their national origin. This special legal status is not necessarily all bad; it may involve special privileges and immunities as well as disabilities. Albert B. LeBlanc, a full-blooded Chippewa Indian, did not have to get a commercial fishing license from the Michigan Department of Natural Resources, since an 1836 treaty with the U.S. government reserved such fishing rights to the Chippewa nation. Likewise, a Navajo woman, Rosalind McClanahan, could not be required to pay Arizona state income tax on income she earned on the Navajo reservation. Inheritance of property, particularly for American Indians living on reservations, may still be governed by tribal law rather than the general inheritance law of the particular state. Reservation businesses and the Bureau of Indian Affairs may engage in preferential hiring of American Indians without violating the 1964 Civil Rights Act.

Although the foregoing examples would probably be thought of as advantages enjoyed by American Indians because of their special status, members of particular American Indian tribes may still be subject to some residual contractual disabilities under old U.S. treaties and statutes.

Convicts

Upon conviction for certain crimes, a person may be sentenced to confinement in a U.S. or state prison. Such a sentence does not, however, mean that the **convict** loses the general capacity to contract and to own property. Likewise, even in prison the person is still protected by the U.S. and state constitutions. Even prisoners have the capacity to appoint agents and attorneys and through them to make contracts and manage their property and affairs; such contracts made on a prisoner's behalf are, generally, fully enforceable by and against the prisoner.

Conviction of crimes involving force or fraud may, however, carry certain other disabilities. A person who has been released after having served the required sentence may be prevented from holding political (or labor union) office for some period of time. The person may also be prevented from practicing a licensed profession, such as law or medicine. Spiro Agnew, for example, was disbarred as a lawyer after pleading "no contest" to tax evasion charges.

Married Women

At common law, husband and wife are regarded legally as one person. As applied in contract and tort situations, this doctrine of **coverture** meant that the wife lacked the capacity to manage even her separately owned property or separate income and that no tort liability could exist between the spouses. The contracts that a married woman attempted to make were totally void. The wife could, however, obligate her husband in quasi-contract for necessaries furnished to her for herself, their children, or their home.

In nearly all states these rules have been changed by statute or constitution, so that a married woman enjoys the same legal rights and powers as her husband. She can own, manage, and dispose of her own property and has joint control of the jointly owned property. She, not he, is legally entitled to receive her earnings from her job. State courts have also been permitting the spouses to sue each other in tort, at least in some cases. Also, under modern interpretations, a wife would be similarly obligated in quasi-contract for necessaries furnished to her husband when she had income or property and he did not.

Residues of the common law rules remain in a few states, where a married woman may not be able to convey real estate, to mortgage jointly owned property, or act as a guarantor of someone else's debt without the husband's consent. Until 1963, Texas continued to apply the basic rules of coverture, so that a married woman lacked the capacity to contract unless she went through a special court procedure that removed her disability. Michigan continued to apply the coverture rules into the 1970s, and it did so despite Article 10, Section 1 of its 1963 constitution, which says: "The disabilities of coverture as to property are abolished." A 1982 Michigan statute appears to make the married woman liable in most cases in which she has cosigned a contract with her husband.

The Equal Rights Amendment to the U.S. Constitution, if ever ratified, will almost certainly overturn any state laws that provide for different legal results based solely on sex.

Corporations

Private Corporations. Because corporations are "artificial" persons, existing only in the eyes of the law, they can have and exercise only those powers that the law gives them. In this sense, they have limited legal capacity; they can make contracts only in those areas of activity in which they have been authorized to be engaged. Modern corporation statutes are generally very liberal in granting corporate powers, and even if a corporation makes a contract that is outside its charter powers, most courts today do not permit either of the parties to the contract to raise that fact as a defense when sued on the contract. These matters are discussed more fully in Chapter 33.

Public (Municipal) Corporations. Like both profit and nonprofit **private corporations, public corporations** are creatures of limited legal authority, possessing only those powers given to them by constitutional or statutory provisions. The courts will normally not permit any enforcement of contracts made by a public corporation in excess of its powers, on the theory that to do so would injure the public through the illegal expenditures of public funds. Contracting procedures for public bodies are usually subject to very specific regulations, which must be complied with if one hopes to have an enforceable contract with them.

Other Defenses

A second group of defenses centers on the idea that one of the parties did not really consent to the terms of the contract that the other wishes to enforce. Although courts generally continue to require both parties to live up to the bargain they made, the problem in many cases is to discover exactly what they really did agree to. Included here are cases involving **fraud, innocent misrepresentation, duress, undue influence,** and **mistake.**

Fraud

Many types of fraud may be crimes, so that criminal charges can be filed against the wrongdoer. False advertising and other deceptive practices may also result in administrative proceedings before the Federal Trade Commission (FTC) or similar state bodies. We are concerned here, however, with the civil aspects of fraud, with its impact on the contract.

Civil fraud is of two kinds: fraud in the execution and fraud in the inducement. **Fraud in the execution** describes a situation in which one party is deceived as to the very nature of the transaction. The party is not aware that a contract is being made, or at least that he or she is making the one that the plaintiff now seeks to enforce. Elvis, for example, fighting his way toward the exit from a concert hall, in the midst of a screaming mass of fans, was signing autograph books as fast as he could. One clever person shoved a folded piece of paper at him, and Elvis signed, not knowing that the unseen part of the paper contained a contract to buy a new set of encyclopedias. On these facts, there is fraud in the execution, and the purported "contract" is totally void. Elvis was deceived as to the very nature of the "transaction" he was entering into, without having had a reasonable opportunity to discover the truth.

The far more common kind of civil fraud is **fraud in the inducement,** in which the defrauded party is aware of entering into a contract and intends to do so, but has been deceived about some aspect of the contract. Usually fraud in the inducement involves misrepresentation of what the defrauded party is to receive. A used car falsely represented as being in A-1 mechanical condition illustrates this concept.

Although different courts may use slightly different formulations, the typical fraud case requires proof of five elements: (1) misrepresentation of a material fact, (2) knowledge of falsity, (3) intent to deceive, (4) reasonable reliance by the other party, and (5) damage to the defrauded party. Because fraud is so easily alleged by anyone having second thoughts about a contract, courts typically require proof of fraud by independent evidence that is clear and convincing. The plaintiff's testimony, by itself, is not sufficient proof of the fraud case, unless admitted by the defendant (see Exhibit 11-2).

Misrepresentation of Material Fact. A statement must contain a factual assertion to provide the basis for a fraud case. Statements of opinion are therefore not generally treated as statements of

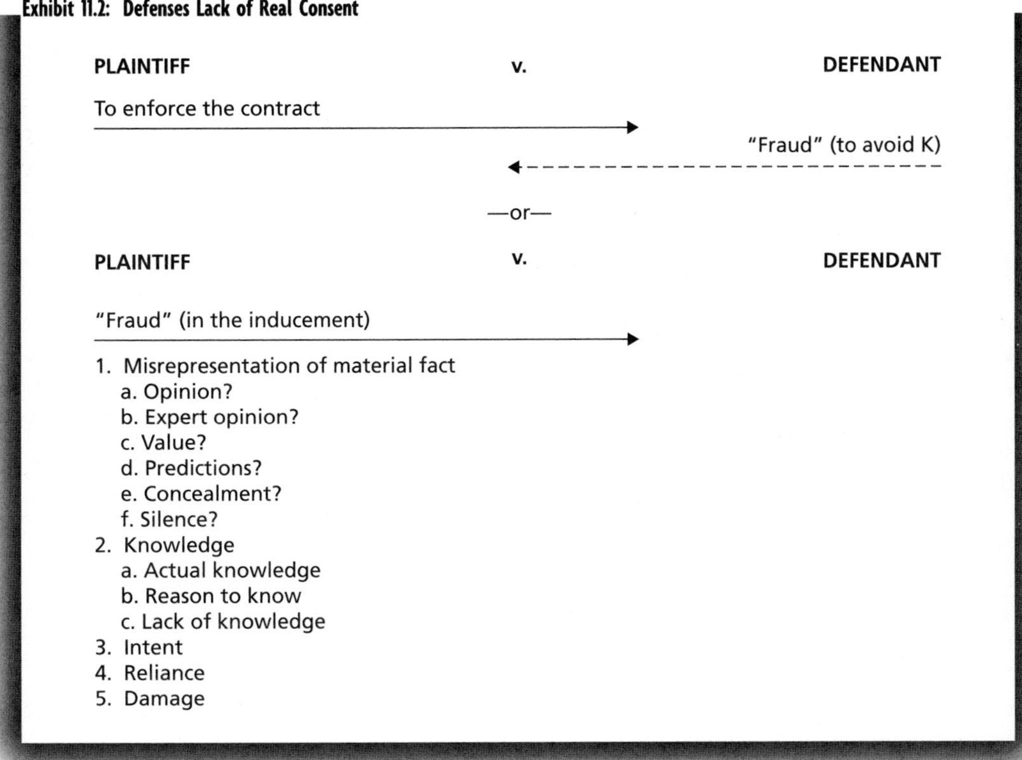

Exhibit 11.2: Defenses Lack of Real Consent

fact, so long as the statements do in fact represent the speaker's honestly held opinion. Sellers are also given some latitude in "puffing" their wares, so that such statements as, "It's the best car for the money," or, "It looks great on you," are not normally intended or understood as factual descriptions. Thus, a statement by an individual selling a used car that it is "in good shape mechanically" would not be fraudulent unless the buyer could show that the seller knew that there were mechanical defects in the car at the time of the statements. A car dealer making the same kind of statement, however, would be making a misrepresentation of fact because "expert opinions" are generally treated as statements of fact.

Predictions of future events over which the speaker has no control are generally not regarded as statements of fact. When the speaker's promises concern the speaker's own future behavior, however, a misrepresentation of fact can be proved by showing that the speaker had no such intention at the time of the statements. If a buyer promises to use a piece of land for residential purposes only, there is fraud where the seller can show that the buyer had already signed construction and lease contracts for a gasoline station at the time the "residential use" statement was made.

Although a party to an "arm's-length" transaction between equals generally has no affirmative duty to disclose every known fact, in several situations nondisclosure or silence can be interpreted as a fraudulent misrepresentation. The most obvious case requiring affirmative disclosure occurs when the party knowing the facts has created a mistaken belief in the mind of the other person through actions (concealment) or prior communications (which were true when spoken but have become false).

A second case requiring full disclosure occurs when the transaction is not arm's length but rather involves a fiduciary relationship, such as lawyer-client or guardian-ward. A lawyer who buys a piece of real estate from a client and has a resale deal with Wonder World already lined up, would have a duty to tell the client about the resale deal, whereas a buyer in an ordinary transaction would not.

A third group of cases is more difficult to define. Most courts today are increasingly willing to impose fraud remedies for nondisclosure when one party (usually the buyer) has had no reasonable opportunity to discover the truth and when the undisclosed fact is so significant that the contract might not have been made at all if the fact had been known.

Examples are the house with a serious termite infestation and the used car with dangerously defective brakes.

Knowledge of Falsity. There is no fraud unless it can be shown that the speaker made a misrepresentation with knowledge that it was false. However, there are three ways to prove this knowledge, or *scienter*, element. One way is to show that the speaker knew the statement was a lie at the time of the statement. The speaker knew the car was not in "A-1 mechanical shape" because the day before, the garage mechanic said to get rid of the car or be prepared to spend a lot of money because it needed a lot of work.

Even if the speaker did not actually know from personal inspection or from the mechanic that the car was in bad shape, there was knowledge if the speaker had reason to know that he or she was not telling the truth about the car's condition. Presumably, every reasonable car driver knows that a car in A-1 mechanical shape does not burn a quart of oil every 100 miles or require repeated pumping of the brake pedal to get the car to stop. A speaker who knew of these operating characteristics would certainly have reason to know that the car was not in A-1 shape.

Finally, knowledge can be proved by proving lack of knowledge. Assume that a car dealership has just taken a used car as a trade-in; no complete mechanical inspection of the car has been made. Nevertheless, when a buyer comes to the used-car lot and inquires about the car, the buyer is told that it is in "A-l shape" and buys it on that basis. If the car has serious defects, fraud has been committed in this case. The salesperson who made the "A-l" statement knew that he or she did not know anything at all about the car's real mechanical condition; thus the salesperson was lying and was aware of lying about the extent of information he or she had on the car.

Intent to Deceive. In most cases, knowledge of the lie and intent to deceive go so closely hand in hand that some courts do not even consider them separately. But what about the person who says, "Yes, I knew I was lying. But I didn't intend that the other party should be hurt by it. I thought things would come out all right in the end." For want of a better label, we might refer to this as the "Uncle Oscar" defense: "Yes, I lied, and I knew I was lying, but I did it for your own good." The few cases that have considered this argument have rejected it; the requirement is not proof of intent to injure or do harm, only of intent to deceive. Deception for any motive, good or bad, is fraud, assuming that the other four elements are also proved.

Reasonable Reliance. Even though the liar is the nastiest person imaginable, the liar has not committed fraud unless the other party can show that he or she reasonably relied on the misrepresentation. It is not enough to show that the person was in fact deceived; the person complaining must also convince the trier of fact that it was reasonable to rely on the misstatement. There is clearly no fraud if the other party knows the truth but goes ahead and makes the contract anyway. On the other hand, reliance is reasonable when an independent verification of the representation would require considerable time, money, and effort. When the truth is readily ascertainable, it is probably not reasonable to rely on the misstatement. If the used-car salesman tells you the car has only 25,000 miles and the odometer in the car shows the mileage is 48,000, most juries would probably decide that a reasonable person would have checked the odometer before relying on the salesperson's statement. Each case ultimately rests on its own facts.

Damage to the Defrauded Party. As a final essential part of a fraud case, the defrauded party must prove having sustained damage as a result of the misrepresentation. Suppose that a seller of land fraudulently represents that there is gold on it, and there is no gold, but there is oil. The land with oil is worth more than it would have been with gold, so the buyer probably does not have a case of fraud. (The buyer probably will not want to rescind anyway.) Even in the gold/oil case, however, the buyer has wound up with a contract different from the one the buyer intended to have, so in that sense the buyer may have suffered an "injury" that would permit the buyer to rescind if the buyer wanted to.

Generally, to justify **rescission** of the entire contract, the misrepresented fact must relate to an essential part of the bargain. If the defrauded party wishes to keep the contract in force and collect "make-it-right" or difference in value damages, the party must prove the amount of the dollar loss that the party has sustained because of the fraud. Because fraud is an intentional tort, punitive damages (over and above the actual loss) may also be collected in many of these cases.

The *Johnson* case shows that a fraud claim may also be used as a defense, when the liar sues to enforce the contract.

CASE 2

Johnson v. Honeywell Information Systems, Inc.

955 F.2d 409 (6 Cir. 1992)

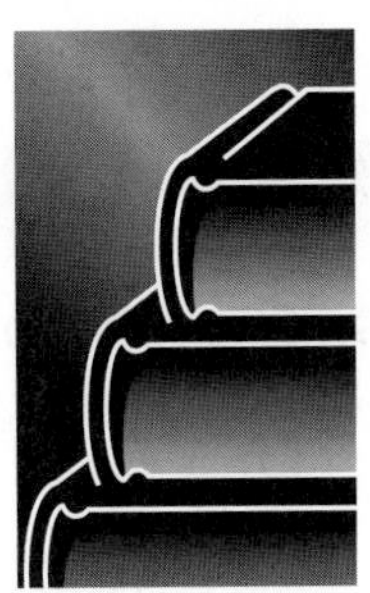

Facts: Honeywell placed a help-wanted ad for a person with a college degree and "four to six years combined personnel and industrial relations experience." Mildred Johnson applied for the job. On her application, she indicated that she had a Bachelor of Arts degree from the University of Detroit and the required minimum work experience. The application form she signed stated that the submission of any false information "may be cause for immediate discharge at any time thereafter should I be employed by Honeywell." She was hired in 1976 and performed satisfactorily until mid-1983. In 1983, she was criticized by her supervisors for ineffectiveness, uncooperativeness, and unavailability by telephone. When she refused to make the suggested improvements, she was fired in November 1984. She sued for breach of contract on the basis that she could be fired only for "just cause." Her lawsuit also claimed that she had been fired in retaliation for being too aggressive in meeting affirmative action goals. [Affirmative action requires employers to attempt to hire and promote minorities, so that their numbers in the work force approximate their numbers in the general population.] A discharge for this reason would violate the Michigan civil rights act. While gathering evidence for the trial, Honeywell discovered that Johnson had lied on her application.

The U.S. District Court denied Honeywell's motion for a summary judgment on each claim. The trial judge felt that "after-acquired" evidence could not be used to justify the firing decision because the evidence that Johnson had lied on her application was unknown when the decision was made. After a trial, the court did direct a verdict for Honeywell on the civil rights claim, but the jury was permitted to decide for Johnson on the breach of contract claim.

Issue: Can an employee's misrepresentations on a job application be used as a defense against a claim by the employee for breach of contract?

Decision: Yes, they can. Judgment reversed because the trial judge should have granted Honeywell's pretrial motions for summary judgment.

Opinion by Judge Ryan: "Johnson's most glaring misrepresentation involved her education. While she claimed in her employment application to have earned a Bachelor of Arts degree from the University of Detroit, Johnson actually completed only four courses at the University and audited two others.... Johnson similarly submitted false information regarding the nature and extent of her studies at Wayne State University, stating that she had studied Applied Management for one year. Wayne State had no record of her enrollment. Johnson also exaggerated some prior job descriptions and falsely claimed to have been managing some of her properties in the year between her prior job and her hiring at Honeywell....

"We believe the Michigan Supreme Court would hold that just cause for termination of employment may include facts unknown to an employer at the time of dismissal, though obviously such facts would be neither the actual nor inducing cause for the discharge.

"This result is principally grounded upon the holding of the Michigan Court of Appeals in *Bradley*, but it is also based on the general applicability of this rule, its common sense, and the dearth of Michigan Case Law to the contrary....

"In order to provide a defense to an employer in a wrongful discharge claim, the after-acquired evidence must establish valid and legitimate reasons for the termination of employment. As a general rule, in cases of resume fraud, summary judgment will be appropriate where the misrepresentation or omission was material, directly related to measuring a candidate for employment, and was relied upon by the employer in making the hiring decision....

"We do not hold that any or all misrepresentations on an employment application constitute just cause for dismissal or serve as a complete defense to a wrongful discharge action. We conclude, however, that Johnson's misrepresentations, by virtue of their nature and number, and when viewed in the context of Honeywell's express requirement of a college degree and its warning to applicants that misrepresentations may constitute cause for termination of employment, provide adequate and just cause for her dismissal as a matter of law even though they were unknown to Honeywell at the time of her discharge."

[The court also said that no remedy could be given on the civil rights claim. Someone who is hired as a doctor, but who has falsified credentials, could not later collect damages even though later fired because of race, sex, religion, or age.]

Innocent Misrepresentation

In some cases, speakers may have honestly and reasonably believed they were telling the truth and may have had no intent to mislead anyone. Still, if the speaker in fact misrepresented the truth, damages to the other party may be as bad as if there had been fraud. The net effect is the same, whether the misrepresentation was made fraudulently or "innocently." For this reason, where the fact innocently misstated has been proved to be a very important part of the contract, most courts will permit rescission by the other party. In most states, if the misrepresented fact is not material enough to justify rescission, the contract stands as is; no damages remedy is given. In a few states damages can be recovered even for an **innocent misrepresentation**, as an alternative remedy to rescission. Because there has been no intentional tort, punitive damages are not recoverable for innocent misrepresentation.

Both fraud and innocent representation were argued as possible theories of liability in the following case.

CASE 3

Bortz v. Noon

729 A.2d 555 (PA 1998)

Facts: Albert Bortz and his former wife signed an agreement to buy the home of Patrick and Virginia Noon. Coldwell Banker Real Estate, represented by Renee Valent, was the selling broker. Bortz applied to Coldwell Banker Residential Mortgage Services (CBRMS) for a mortgage loan; CBRMS required that the septic system for the home be tested to make sure it was working properly. The septic system failed the test, and a contractor (J. J. Nolte) was hired to repair it. At some point, a woman from the title insurance company (Suburban Settlement) told Valent that the septic system had been fixed and that the closing on the home could be scheduled. Valent passed this information along to Bortz, and the closing was scheduled. After the closing, Bortz learned that the septic system had failed the test again and that it could not be repaired. Bortz had to connect the house to the public sewer system at a cost of over $15,000.

Bortz sued Coldwell Banker Real Estate, Suburban Settlement, and the Noons—for money damages and rescission of the house sale. The Noons sued Nolte as a third-party defendant. The chancellor denied rescission of the sale, but awarded Bortz $15,300 damages against Coldwell Banker Real Estate. The appellate court agreed with the damages award, but held that Nolte and Suburban Settlement could also be liable to Bortz. Coldwell Banker Real Estate appealed the damages award against it.

Issue: Is the broker liable for the misstatement by its agent Renee Valent?

Decision: No. Judgment reversed.

Opinion by Justice Newman: "Generally, a misrepresentation may be actionable pursuant to three theories: Intentional Misrepresentation, Negligent Misrepresentation, and Innocent Misrepresentation. . . .

"Here, there is no evidence supporting a conclusion that [Valent] intentionally misrepresented any fact to [Bortz], nor intended to deceive [him] by failing to give him copies of the septic system report, which she herself did not have. While [Valent] made an affirmative representation that the dye test was clear, there is no finding that [she] made any representation with knowledge that it was false. Instead, [she] was giving information to [Bortz] that she received from the Title Company, an apparently reputable company, so that she could schedule the closing. [Valent] had no agency relationship with the Title Company or Nolte, and she had not selected Nolte to perform the septic tank repairs nor asked him to do the dye test. . . . Moreover, there was no evidence in the record that [Valent] intended to mislead [Bortz] in any way, a required element of intentional misrepresentation. . . .

"The elements of negligent misrepresentation differ from intentional misrepresentation in that the misrepresentation must concern a material fact and the speaker need not know his or her words are untrue, but must have failed to make a reasonable investigation of the truth of these words. . . . Moreover, like any action for negligence, there must be an existence of a duty owed by one party to another. . . .

"Here, neither the Chancellor nor the Superior Court specifically articulated the exact legal theory supporting their ultimate finding of liability. However, although not specifically labeled, it appears that both . . . found Coldwell Banker liable based upon either a negligent or [an] innocent misrepresentation, for [Valent's] statement to [Bortz] that the septic system had passed the dye test and for negligently failing to provide him with Nolte's written reports. . . .

"While we recognize that there is no reason to per se omit a real estate broker or its agent from liability for . . .

misrepresentations negligently made, a reasonable review of the record ... does not support the conclusion that [Valent] made a negligent misrepresentation, or negligently failed to disclose the Nolte report, because there is not an adequate record of evidence to support a conclusion that [she] had a duty to investigate the accuracy of the dye test, or that she had a duty to provide [Bortz] with ... Nolte's report.... The dye test was part of the requirement of the Lender's mortgage and it was the Title Company that on two occasions misrepresented facts to both [Valent] and [Bortz]....

"We believe that imposing [a] duty to investigate ... would place too high a burden on real estate agents. It would be an unreasonable burden on them because it would make it their responsibility to guarantee the accuracy of pre-closing tests done by persons with whom they have no relationship....

"A claim for an 'innocent' misrepresentation has been recognized in this Commonwealth in order to rescind a real estate transaction that is based upon a material misrepresentation, even if the misrepresentation was innocently made. However, we have found no cases in which this Court adopted this theory as a basis to award monetary damages for tort recovery....

"For the reasons set forth in this Opinion, we reverse the Superior Court's determination and hold that Coldwell Banker is not liable to [Bortz] for the affirmative misrepresentations of [Valent]."

Undue Influence

As noted in our discussion of fraud, when any sort of fiduciary relationship exists, as in lawyer-client, guardian-ward, or doctor-patient, one of the parties to the transaction may have misused the trust and confidence that the other has given to benefit at the other's expense. One party may rely on the advice of the trusted lawyer, doctor, or guardian as the basis for entering into a contract with that person. When such an underlying relationship exists between the contracting parties, the courts will examine their bargain very carefully to make sure that it represents the true intent of the "subordinate" party and that all the facts had been disclosed to that party.

Even without an underlying fiduciary relationship, it is possible to prove that a contract exists because of **undue influence** rather than by free choice, although this case is not nearly as easy to prove. Such cases might arise in the context of an emotional or romantic relationship between the parties to the contract. When proved, undue influence makes the contract voidable by the party of whom advantage was taken.

Duress

Closely related to the idea of undue influence is that of duress. **Duress** means something more than just pressure or "hard selling." The most obvious cases involve violence or threats of violence against the contracting party. Threats to commence a criminal prosecution unless money is paid or promised also constitute duress, but simply threatening to bring a civil suit for money allegedly owed is not duress. Although sales pressure or hard selling is not considered duress, threats of economic harm against the buyer by the seller, if the buyer does not accept seller's terms, is economic duress, and courts will recognize such threats as duress. A person can be injured by being struck by a baseball bat, but can also be injured by the misuse of economic power by an adversary. The violence-type duress makes the resulting contract totally void. Other duress makes the contract voidable by the party who was pressured into making it.

Mistake

The contracting parties can be "mistaken" about so many things that it is impossible to catalog all of the conceivable factual combinations. Mistakes may occur in the formation of the agreement, in writing up the deal, or in performance. Rather than a comprehensive list, what follows is a discussion of some of the most frequent kinds of mistakes: **mutual mistake in basic assumptions, material unilateral mistake, mistake in integration,** and **mistake in performance**.

Mutual Mistake in Basic Assumptions. When both parties enter into a contract assuming the existence of some particular fact or condition that later turns out not to have been so, there is no contract at all if the fact is "basic" (material) to the contract. Efrem Zimbalist, Sr., the famous concert violinist, bought two violins that both he and the seller assumed were a genuine Stradivarius and a genuine Guarnerius. In fact, both violins were merely good copies. When he discovered the truth, Zimbalist was entitled to get his money back; neither party intended a contract for fake violins.

Many "mutual mistake" cases arise from a latent ambiguity in the terms of the contract; that is, a word or phrase really describes more than one thing, and each party understands it to mean something different. In the classic example, a buyer and a seller contracted in England for "certain goods, to wit, 125 bales Surat cotton to arrive ex ship Peerless from Bombay." Unknown to either the buyer or the seller, there were two ships called *Peerless*, and both were in Bombay and both had some Surat cotton on board. To make the story complete, incredible though it may seem, they were both bound for

CASE 4

Akahoshi v. Southern Waste Services

181 F.Supp.2d 711 (E.D. MI 2001)

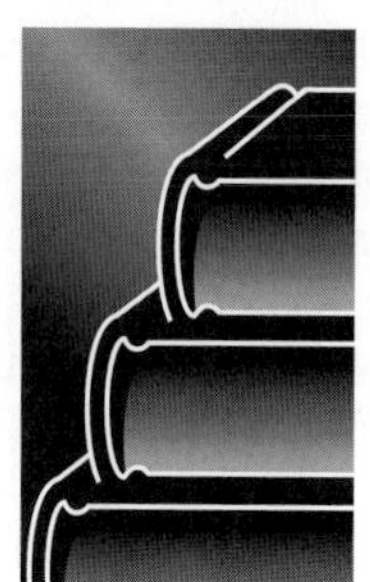

Facts: On October 1, 1998, Joey Akahoshi was injured by a backhoe while he was working on an environmental cleanup project at Elba, Alabama. He filed a negligence lawsuit against Southern Waste and Kevin Green on October 10, 2000. In August, 2001, Akahoshi and Southern Waste agreed to settle the claim for $50,000. He signed a release of liability agreement and sent it to Southern Waste on September 7, 2001. Defendant had liability insurance through Reliance Insurance, but its financial condition "went from bad to worse" between September 7, 2001 and October 3, 2001. Reliance Insurance was ordered to be liquidated by the state of Pennsylvania, so that Southern Waste would not be able to get any of the $50,000 from its insurance policy. Southern Waste says it entered into the settlement agreement assuming that the settlement payment would come from its liability insurance. The settlement agreement itself contained no such provision or condition.

Akahoshi has sued to enforce the settlement agreement.

Issue: Was there a mutual mistake in basic assumptions?

Decision: No. Judgment entered to enforce the settlement agreement.

Opinion by Judge Duggan: "Generally, [rescission] of a contract for mutual mistake is available where a mistake relates to a basic assumption about a fact in existence at the time of the execution of the contract upon [the basis of] which the contract is made and which materially affects the agreed performance.... 'The erroneous belief of one or both of the parties must relate to a fact in existence at the time the contract is executed.' ... 'That is to say, the belief which is found to be in error may not be, in substance, a prediction at to a future occurrence or non-occurrence.' ...

"Moreover, [rescission] of a contract for mutual mistake is not available where the party seeking [it] has assumed the risk of loss in connection with the mistake. 'A party bears the risk of a mistake when: (a) the risk is allocated to him by agreement of the parties, or (b) he is aware, at the time the contract is made, that he has only limited knowledge with respect to the facts to which the mistake relates[,] but treats his limited knowledge as sufficient, or (c) the risk is allocated to him by the court on the ground that it is reasonable in the circumstances to do so.' ...

"While it may be true that both parties 'expected' that the insurance carrier would pay the settlement, there is nothing in the settlement agreement that makes such 'expectations' a condition of the settlement. Such mistaken 'expectations' do not 'relate to a fact in existence at the time the [settlement] was reached.' Rather, the 'alleged mistake' is more akin to a 'prediction as to a future occurrence or non-occurrence.'

"The Court notes that the release, by its terms, mentions only the parties and makes absolutely no reference to the insurance carrier. The Court is aware that the usual procedure is not to include the name of the insurance carrier because the carrier is not a party to the action. However, in this case, defense counsel was aware of the insurance carrier's 'precarious financial condition' at the time the proposed settlement agreement was drafted. If it was defense counsel's intent that the settlement agreement was to be conditioned on the insurance carrier paying the settlement amount, such a provision should have been made an express condition of the settlement proposal, which Plaintiff could have accepted or rejected.

"Not only does the release not mention Defendants' current position that the settlement is conditioned on the insurance carrier's ability to pay the settlement proceeds, but the release drafted by Defendants' counsel specifically provides that:

> *'The undersigned further declares and represents that no promise, inducement or agreement not herein expressed has been made to the undersigned and that this Release contains the entire agreement between the parties hereto and that the terms of this Release are contractual and not a mere recital.'*

"Accordingly, Defendants have not persuaded the Court that the settlement agreement should be voided on the basis of a 'mutual mistake'."

London, one to arrive in October and one in December. The buyer knew only about the "October" *Peerless;* the seller knew only about the "December" *Peerless.* When the buyer's cotton was not delivered in October and the buyer sued for breach of contract, the English court correctly held that no damages were recoverable because no contract had ever really been made. The parties were talking about two different things and had never really agreed.

There is no mistake, and thus there is a binding contract, when both parties are aware that they lack knowledge about a particular fact of condition and take their mutual ignorance into account in setting the terms of the contract. In a Wisconsin case, the finder of a pretty stone in a field took the stone to a friend and asked the friend what he thought it was worth. The friend said he did not know either, but that he would pay the finder $1 for it. After the sale the stone was identified as an uncut diamond, worth $700. There was no mistake in this case, in the legal sense, because both parties were aware when they contracted that they did not know the true identity or worth of the stone.

Because much of modern commerce is based on differing estimates of the value of land, goods, and securities, most courts also adhere to a rule that says that mistake relief will not be given where the only error concerns the value of an item rather than its identity. The mistake in the *Zimbalist* case, for example, was not as to the value of fake violins but as to whether the violins were genuine or fake. This difference is probably easy enough to see in most instances, but some cases are a little harder to decide.

The *Akahoshi* case involves a claim of mutual mistake in basic assumptions. (Reading between the lines, one wonders if the events of September 1, 2001 had anything to do with the demise of the defendant's insurance company.)

Material Unilateral Mistake. Generally, the fact that one party to the contract has made a mistake of some sort affords no basis for relief, so long as the other party was unaware of the mistake and was acting in good faith. Most courts do, however, say that there is no contract where the mistake was so "gross" that the other party should have been aware of it. This situation arises most frequently when bids are being solicited for a certain job. Several bid offers are submitted, and one is way out of line. Courts usually will not permit the offeree to "snap up" what the offeree has good reason to know must be a mistaken bid, thus binding the honestly mistaken bidder to an unfair contract. Just how gross the mistake has to be to trigger this rule is a question of fact.

Mistake in Integration. Both the courts and the **Restatement** continue to state as the general rule that one is bound by what he or she signs. Yet, almost in the same breath, courts everywhere also continue to grant relief ("reformation") for what is commonly termed mistake in integration—an alleged mistake in writing up the terms agreed on. Much of the seeming conflict between the two rules can be explained by the difference between the specifically bargained-out terms and the printed terms in a form contract. Many printed contracts use fairly standardized terms—what lawyers refer to as "boilerplate." When you sign a form contract, you are bound by all this standardized language. On the other hand, when a specifically agreed-on term has been written up incorrectly, courts are willing to correct the error. In such a case one party alleges that a written document is incorrect, that it does not accurately state the terms actually agreed on. If there is evidence to support this claim, a court with equity powers can "reform" the document to make it agree with the actual intent of the parties, and then enforce the document as corrected. The document is rewritten, and then enforced.

Mistake in Performance. Perhaps the most difficult cases of all in which to work out a mutually fair result are those involving a mistake in performance. Someone performs for the wrong person, or at the wrong time, or in the wrong place, or when the party was not really contractually obligated to perform at all. When the performance involves money or a tangible object that can be easily returned, the solution is simple; the person who has received the money or other item by mistake must return it.

When construction or demolition takes place at the wrong site, however, the problem is not so easily resolved. What does one do for the owner of the apartment house that the wrecking crew tore down "by mistake"? Even if the owners are given the full fair market value of the old building, plus lost rentals, until a new one is built, they have still been the unwilling participants in a forced sale of the old building, with all sorts of possible adverse tax consequences. How about the landowners who get a new house put up on their lot "by mistake"? Should these people have to pay for the new house, and if so, how much? Or should they be able to force the removal of the house and the restoration of the pristine ecology? For these, as for many other "mistake" questions, there are no easy or universal answers.

Significance of This Chapter

The basic idea of a contract is that it is a relationship that we have entered into voluntarily because we wished to do so. It is not something that is imposed on us by someone else; it is a relationship that we have imposed on ourselves. When our consent to the contract has occurred because of factual misrepresentation by the other party, legal relief from the terms of the contract is available—either rescission or damages. If the misrepresentation was intentional, punitive damages should be available against the person who has committed an intentional wrong. When no agreement ever really occurred, either because the parties were talking about two different things and did not know that, or because they both assumed the existence of a material fact that was not so, no contract exists, and legal relief should be given. Even where only one party has made a serious mistake, there is no contract if the other is aware of the mistake. In all of these situations, what appears at first to be a contract may not be enforceable because one or both parties were unaware of the true facts.

Although it is certainly true that most minors do pay their debts and meet their other contractual obligations, it is important for the other contracting party to be aware of what can happen when a contract is made with a minor. Even though the age of majority has been lowered to 18 by most states, and even though more courts are willing to permit some recourse against a minor who makes an intentional misrepresentation of age, minors still enjoy a special legal status. Courts still will give them special protection when they act innocently. If you are contracting with minors, you need to know the possible results.

Similarly, although many courts and legislatures are moving to eliminate special restrictions on legal rights and privileges, some do still remain. You also need to be aware of these possibilities because again there can be serious legal consequences when your contract is declared void or voidable due to the other party's lack of capacity.

IMPORTANT TERMS AND CONCEPTS

aliens
American Indians
capacity to contract
convict
coverture
duress
estoppel
fraud in the execution
fraud in the inducement
holder in due course (HDC)
innocent misrepresentation
material unilateral mistake
minors
misrepresentation of age
mistake
mistake in integration
mistake in performance
mutual mistake in basic assumptions
necessaries
private corporations
public corporations
quasi-contract
ratification
reasonable market value
rescission
restatement
restitution
undue influence
unjust enrichment
voidable contract

QUESTIONS AND PROBLEMS FOR DISCUSSION

1. What happens when a minor disaffirms a contract for necessaries?

2. Why is a defrauded party permitted to rescind a contract?

3. Why is there generally no relief given when both parties were mistaken as to the value of the subject matter of the contract?

4. When can a contract be rescinded because of duress?

5. Defendant Charles Edward Smith, Jr., purchased an automobile from plaintiff on August 15, 1993. On that date, defendant was 17 years old and would have his 18th birthday on September 25, 1993. Defendant executed a purchase money security agreement to finance $2,362, the balance due on the purchase price of the automobile payable in thirty installments of $99.05 each. Plaintiff subsequently assigned the purchase money security agreement to First Union National Bank. After having made 11 monthly payments pursuant to the installment loan contract, 10 of which were made after his 18th birthday, defendant voluntarily returned the automobile to plaintiff and defaulted on his payment obligations. Upon default, First Union reassigned the purchase money security agreement to plaintiff, which proceeded to sell the automobile at public auction. At the time of sale, a balance was owing on the purchase money security agreement of $1,521.52. The car was sold for $700, leaving a deficiency of $821.52. From the judgment dismissing plaintiff's complaint, plaintiff appealed.

   What result on appeal, and why?

6. In December 1991, Harold M. Janinda was transferred by his employer from Denver, Colorado, to Mountain Home, Idaho. In looking for housing for his family and income-producing property, he consulted a local real estate agency. A Mr. Swearingen of that agency showed him several parcels of real estate, including Mrs. Lanning's rental and residence property consisting of duplex apartments, six trailer spaces, and three-bedroom house. This property was located a short distance outside the city limits of Mountain Home, within the county, and obtained its water supply from two shallow wells on the property.

   On January 24, 1992, Mrs. Lanning received information indicating that one of the wells was contaminated, but she did not disclose this fact to Mr. Swearingen when he asked about the water supply. About 2 weeks later, Janinda bought the property. Janinda now sues to rescind the contract.

   What result and why?

7. Kemper sued to rescind a bid it had submitted to do the piping work for a sewer project. The city requires that 10 percent of the bid price be posted as a bond, in favor of the city, guaranteeing that the bidder would do the job for the bid price if awarded the contract. Three of Kemper's employees worked until 2 AM of the day the bids were due in preparing Kemper's bid. Over 1,000 different items were involved in preparing these estimates. When the work of these three men was combined and the estimates were totalled, a $301,769 item was omitted. Kemper's bid came in at $780,305. The three competing bids were $1,049,592, $1,183,000, and $1,278,895. The mistake was discovered a few hours after the bids were opened. Kemper explained what had happened and withdrew its bid, but the city accepted the bid anyway. When Kemper refused to enter into a contract at the mistaken price, the city awarded the contract to the next lowest bidder and claimed that Kemper's 10 percent bond was forfeited to the city. The trial court held that Kemper was entitled to rescind its bid and its bond.

   Was this ruling correct? Explain.

8. A.N. Peddy contracted to buy certain real estate from Bessie Montgomery, a married woman. Title 34, § 73 of the Alabama Code denies a wife the power to convey or mortgage her lands without her husband's consent. If he does not join in signing the deed or mortgage, it is void. Bessie changed her mind about selling, and, because her husband had not cosigned the land contract, she relied on the statute as a defense. When Peddy sued for specific performance of the contract, the trial court gave Bessie a summary judgment.

   How should the appeals court rule?

CHAPTER 12

Illegality and Impossibility

Chapter Objectives

This chapter will:

- Explain the results that may occur when a contractual performance is illegal.
- Indicate the most frequently occurring types of illegality.
- Discuss those illegalities having special importance for business operations, including noncompliance with licensing laws, Sunday laws, and usury laws.
- Explain the possible results if a court decides that a contract is against public policy.
- Define impossibility as an excuse for nonperformance of a contract.

In the vast majority of cases, both the formation of the contract and the performances it requires are lawful. When a bargain transaction is illegal, either in its formation or in the performances required, the court attempts to do exactly the opposite of what it normally does; instead of enforcing the intent of the parties, the court tries to frustrate it. Because the bargain is illegal in some respect, the court will try to prevent the illegality from occurring and to discourage similar illegal bargains in the future. Specific results vary from case to case, yet this policy underlies all "illegality" cases.

This chapter discusses the results the courts work out in some of the most frequent illegality cases as well as several examples of courts refusing to enforce contract provisions that are not specifically illegal, but just against public policy (see Exhibit 12-1).

Exhibit 12.1: Illegality and Public Policy

Type of Illeqality	I.P.D.?	Results?
(A) Commission of crime or tort	*Yes*	Leave as is. (No court remedies)
(B) Gambling: Lottery	*Yes*	Repent and rescind.
(C) Licensing		
(1) Revenue	*No*	Get license, then sue. (or) sue without license.
(2) Regulatory	*No*	Collect no contract price. Collect no quasi-contract. Refund $ paid already. Liable for any damages.
(D) Usury: Split on definition	*No*	Collect no excess interest. (or) collect no interest. (or) forfeit some principal. (or) forfeit all principal.
(E) Sunday laws	*No*	Leave as is (or) permit weekday affirmance
(F) Restraint of trade:		
(1) Common law	*Yes/No*	O.K. if reasonable. Split if not reasonable.
(2) Statutes		
(a) National	*Yes/No*	Leave as is if I.P.D. If not, give remedies to innocent party.
(b) State	*Yes/No*	Leave as is if I.P.D. If not, give remedies to innocent party.
(G) Interference with governmental processes:		
(1) Lobbying = not illegal, so long as no improper methods		
(2) Bribery, etc.	*Yes/No*	Leave as is (same as A).
(H) Against public policy (or) unconscionable, but not illegal	*No*	U.C.C. 2-302 choices: 1. Void whole contract. 2. Void unconscionable clause, then enforce K. 3. Interpret unconscionable clause to avoid unconscionable results.

Illegal Bargains

Commission of Crime or Tort

The clearest case for the application of these illegality rules occurs when the would-be contract calls for a performance specifically defined as criminal under applicable state statutory law or involves the commission of an intentional tort against some third party. In popular jargon, the arrangement between the local Big Boss and Murder, Inc., which calls for the removal of the crosstown competition, is called a contract. Clearly, the courts should not (and will not) have any part in the enforcement of such a contract, regardless of the stage of performance or nonperformance in which it is brought to the attention of the court. Whether the hit man has taken the money and has refused to perform or has done the job in an unworkman-like way, or the Big Boss has refused to pay for the services rendered, the court should refuse to recognize any rights or duties flowing from such a contract and simply leave these equally guilty parties where it finds them, with no relief to either. Conspiracy to commit murder is itself a crime, so very few such contracts are brought to the attention of a court.

Gambling, Lotteries, and Games of Chance

Nearly all forms of **gambling** are illegal in most states, and the parties to an illegal bet are clearly **in pari delicto;** that is, they are equally guilty of violating the law, so that there should be no reason to prefer one over the other. Still, different legal rules are applied to

CASE 1

Dickerson v. Deno
770 So.2d 63 (AL 2001)

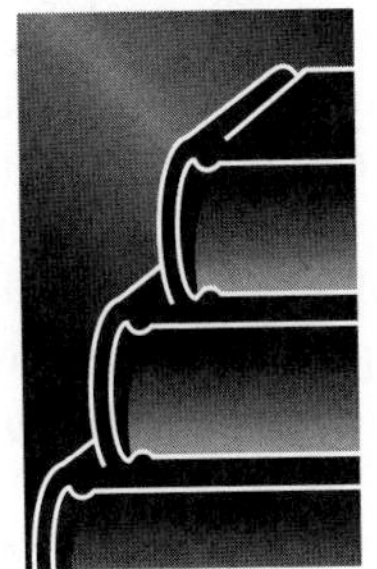

Facts: Edward Seward was a regular customer at the Waffle House in Grand Bay, Alabama. On several occasions, he gave Florida lottery tickets to friends and relatives, including Waffle House employees. For the March 6, 1999, Florida lottery drawing, he gave a ticket to each of five employees, in separate envelopes. Tonda Dickerson received a winning ticket, which entitled her to half of the $10 million prize. (There was one other person who also had the winning number.)

Sandra Deno and the other three Waffle House employees who had received tickets from Seward for this drawing claimed that the five employees had orally agreed to share equally whatever winnings any one of them received. When Tonda refused to share, Sandra and the other three sued her. After a trial, the judge ordered enforcement of the oral contract. Dickerson appealed.

Issue: Was this prize-sharing agreement illegal, and thus void?

Decision: Yes. Judgment reversed.

Opinion by Justice Maddox: "Dickerson argues on appeal that the alleged oral agreement . . . was unenforceable because it lacked the necessary elements of a valid and enforceable contract. She also argues that, assuming . . . that [it did], it was void as a gambling contract, because . . . it was an agreement made in Alabama and S. 8-1-150 specifically provides that 'all contracts founded in whole or in part on a gambling consideration are void.' . . .

"[W]e conclude that the parties presented sufficient evidence to support a finding that [they] did orally agree that if any one of them should win the lottery, then they all would divide the proceeds. . . .

"The plaintiffs . . . cite several cases they contend support their argument that the oral agreement in this case is not void because . . . 'an agreement to share proceeds from a winning lottery ticket is simply not a wager between the parties to the agreement in the State of Alabama.' . . .

"We agree with Dickerson . . . that there was no agreement to jointly purchase or to jointly hold the lottery tickets. Each ticket was purchased by Seward in Florida and was presented by him to one or another of the parties, separately. The alleged oral contract in this case was an exchange of promises to share winnings from the parties' individually owned lottery tickets upon the happening of the uncertain event that the numbers drawn in the Florida lottery matched the numbers on one of the tickets held by the five individuals. . . . Consequently, we conclude that the agreement at issue here was 'founded . . . on a gambling consideration,' within the meaning of that phrase in S. 8-1-150 and that it was, therefore, void.

"The judgment of the trial court is . . . reversed and a judgment rendered for defendant Dickerson."

the bet case. Because the illegal purpose of a bet is to pay money to the winner based on the outcome of a game, race, fight, or whatever, the courts attempt to frustrate that purpose by permitting the losers of the bets to "repent" and repudiate their bets (*and* get their money back) at any time before the money is actually paid to the winner. If you "see the light" only after your team has lost, you can still (legally) repudiate your bet and keep your money (or get it back from the stakeholder), as long as you indicate your intent to do so before the money is actually paid over to the winner. The same rule applies when you try unsuccessfully to fill an inside straight in poker: You can take your money back from the pot (though you may lose a lot of friends, and hands, in doing so).

Most state gambling statutes are broad enough to cover lotteries, license plate bingo, and similar games of chance; some states also have separate statutes to cover these other forms of gambling. States are also attempting to prohibit newer forms of risk taking, such as the so-called chain letter and pyramid forms of selling. All of these statutes are subject to judicial interpretation as to just what they prohibit and just what the courts should refuse to enforce.

The *Dickerson* case shows the Alabama Supreme Court distinguishing several precedents from other states that had held lottery-sharing contracts to be valid and enforceable.

Licensing Statutes

In a 1969 study the U.S. Labor Department estimated that over 500 different occupations required a license of some sort from at least one governmental body, including such jobs as beekeeper, rainmaker, tattoo artist, and fund-raiser. The "illegality" problem here occurs when an unlicensed person performs services for which a license is required. Should the client-customer be required to pay for the services received from the unlicensed practitioner?

Courts usually try to answer this question by first categorizing the **licensing statute** in question as either a **regulatory statute** or **revenue raising statute.** Of course, many statutes will include both legislative purposes, but what the court is trying to decide is whether the basic reason for the license is to protect persons from unqualified or unscrupulous practitioners or just to raise some money for the government. If the licensing statute contains educational and experiential requirements and specifies that a standardized test must be passed to get a license, it is pretty clearly regulatory in character. The fewer such standards it contains, the more it looks like just a revenue raiser.

Statutes licensing professionals, such as lawyers, accountants, dentists, and physicians, are clearly regulatory in nature. On the other hand, a statute that required one to have a license to keep bees, but which permitted anyone to be licensed by paying $200, is only designed to raise revenue.

If a statute is regulatory in nature, the results of not being properly licensed under it are serious. In addition to being liable for whatever punishments are provided for practicing without the required license and for any malpractice against the client, unlicensed practitioners will usually be denied any recovery for the service performed even if they later get licensed. On the other hand, if the statute is designed only to bring in money, the worst that will happen to unlicensed practitioners is being required to get licensed before being able to sue to recover for services already performed.

Sunday Laws

About half of the states have some sort of statute prohibiting the doing of business, or at least some types of business, on Sunday. Some of the more recently enacted statutes give the target merchants the option of closing either Sunday or Saturday. These statutes are an obvious outgrowth of the old colonial **Blue Laws,** which prohibited doing almost anything on Sunday except going to church. Although these laws clearly interfere with the "free exercise of religion" and clearly "establish" the Christian Sunday (in most cases) as *the* official day of rest, the U.S. Supreme Court upheld their constitutionality in 1961.

Merchants who wish to remain open on Sunday have fared better by challenging these laws in state courts, under the state's own constitution, either on the "religion" ground or on the ground that the legislation arbitrarily discriminates between products and businesses.

When there is a valid **Sunday law** in force, some rather surprising results may occur, as illustrated by an old New Hampshire case in which two cows were sold on a Sunday with the price to be paid later. When the buyer did not pay and the seller repossessed the cows, the seller was held liable for trespass because an absolute ownership of the cows had passed to the buyer. But when the seller sued for the contract price, the court permitted the buyer to use the illegality defense because the contract had been made on a Sunday! The court's main reason for this result was that the parties were equally guilty and should

CASE 2

Faraone d/b/a Five Star Video v. City of East Providence

935 F.Supp. 82 (D. RI 1996)

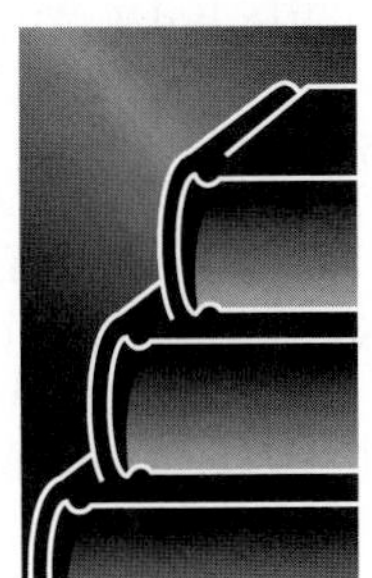

Facts: Plaintiff, Joseph Faraone, owns and operates a video rental and sale business on Willett Avenue in East Providence, Rhode Island. Plaintiff has operated his business for approximately 10 years and holds a state-issued retail license and a city-issued Sunday/holiday sales license. He rents and sells a wide range of videos, roughly 10 percent of which he estimates might be considered "adult oriented" or "X-rated." Plaintiff voluntarily segregates these videos from the remaining collection and places them in a designated area of his store.

This matter is before the court on plaintiff's motion for a preliminary injunction. He alleges that a license "stipulation" adopted by the East Providence City Council, which prohibits the sale or rental of "any adult oriented X-rated videos on Sundays or holidays," is preempted by state law and violates the First Amendment of the United States Constitution. The defendant, the city of East Providence, counters that the restriction placed on all Sunday/holiday sales licenses is permissible under state law and is a valid content-neutral regulation designed to serve a legitimate government interest.

Issue: Is the Sunday/holiday sales restriction unconstitutional?

Decision: Yes. The city is enjoined from enforcing this restriction.

Opinion by District Judge Lisi: "Having considered and rejected plaintiff's state law preemption argument, this court turns its attention to his First Amendment claim.

"Plaintiff contends that the stipulation attached to his Sunday/holiday sales license contravenes the First Amendment guarantee of freedom of speech because it is a content-based regulation of protected speech that does not serve any legitimate government interest. As such, plaintiff argues that the stipulation must be subjected to strict judicial scrutiny. The defendant avers that the stipulation is not aimed at the content of the banned videos; rather, that the restriction should be analyzed as a 'time, place, or manner regulation' aimed at the 'secondary effects' of the operation of plaintiff's business 'on the surrounding community.' Accordingly, the defendant contends that the stipulation should be subjected to intermediate scrutiny.

"In order to apply the proper level of scrutiny to the stipulation now before the court, it must first be determined whether the stipulation is 'content-based' or 'content-neutral.' 'The principal inquiry in determining content neutrality, in speech cases generally and in time, place, or manner cases in particular, is whether the government has adopted a regulation of speech because of disagreement with the message it conveys.' ... A municipality is not required to 'steer away from content at all costs, or else risk strict scrutiny. "A regulation that serves purposes unrelated to the content of expression is deemed neutral, even if it has an incidental effect on some speakers or messages but not others."' ...

"The defendant argues that the Sunday/holiday restriction is a permissible time, place, or manner regulation, and thus should be subject to the less exacting test of intermediate scrutiny, because it does not ban the sale or rental of these videos altogether, but rather provides that the sales or rentals may not take place on Sundays or holidays. In so doing, however, the defendant completely ignores the blatant content-based description of those items which are banned. The license stipulation here targets 'adult oriented X-rated videos.' The members of the East Providence City Council, the individuals responsible for monitoring compliance, and the plaintiff must refer to the message (i.e., the content) of the subject videos in order to discern whether their sale or rental on Sundays or holidays is prohibited. Clearly, the stipulation is aimed at regulating the content of the speech and, therefore, must be subjected to strict judicial scrutiny....

"In this case, the defendant has failed to rebut the presumption of invalidity. The defendant has offered no palpable justification for restricting the rental or sale of the videos on Sundays or holidays. Accordingly, I conclude that the stipulation constitutes an impermissible abrogation of the freedom of speech guaranteed by the First Amendment. Since this determination is dispositive, I need not reach plaintiff's claim that the stipulation is also impermissibly vague....

"For these reasons, plaintiff's Motion for Preliminary Injunction has been granted."

therefore have been left where they were when performance of the illegal bargain ceased—the buyer with the cows, the seller without the money. In many states today, a court would construct an "implied promise" to pay the contract price if the buyer retained the property and would say that this promise was legal because it was "made" on a weekday.

The *Faraone* case shows that a Sunday statute may also violate other constitutional provisions.

Usury

Usury is very easy to define: it is the charging of an illegally high rate of interest. This simple definition is not always so easy to apply to particular cases. Each state must decide two subsidiary questions: What is interest, and what is an illegally high rate? States do not agree on the answers to these questions.

Interest is generally defined as the charge for a loan of money or for the forbearance of a debt. Because the impact on the buyer-debtor is the same in either case, and because the seller-lender ought not to be able to evade the maximum rate by merely calling interest something else, most courts today would probably hold that a **time-price differential** charged in a credit sale is in fact interest, but there are cases reaching the opposite result. Monthly **service charges** on revolving charge accounts have been held to be interest by nearly every court to consider the problem since 1970. Some states have specific statutes regulating these special kinds of credit arrangements and permitting the creditor to charge a higher rate of interest than that permitted by the state's general usury law. Nearly all courts agree that bona fide charges for separate services, such as credit reports on the debtor, appraisals of collateral, and filing fees, are valid and are not to be calculated as part of the interest charge.

How high is too high? The general usury law in most states specifies a maximum annual interest rate of from 7 to 10 percent. In most states corporations are not protected by usury laws, and this same idea has been extended in several states to any loan to a business, incorporated or not. Small loan companies are typically governed by their own statute, which permits them to charge a much higher interest rate (usually 24 to 36 percent). Credit unions and other special lenders may also have their own special statutory rate. One of the main objectives of the proposed Uniform Consumer Credit Code (UCCC) is to simplify this hodgepodge of existing laws.

The states disagree not only on the definition of interest and the rate permitted but also on what the remedy should be when a lender tries to charge a usurious rate. At least four types of results have been worked out: (1) forfeiture of only the excessive amount of interest; (2) forfeiture of all interest; (3) forfeiture of double or triple the amount of interest charged; and (4) forfeiture of the entire debt, both principal and interest.

CASE 3

SWINDELL V. FEDERAL NATL. MORTGAGE ASS'N

409 S.E.2d 892 (NC 1994)

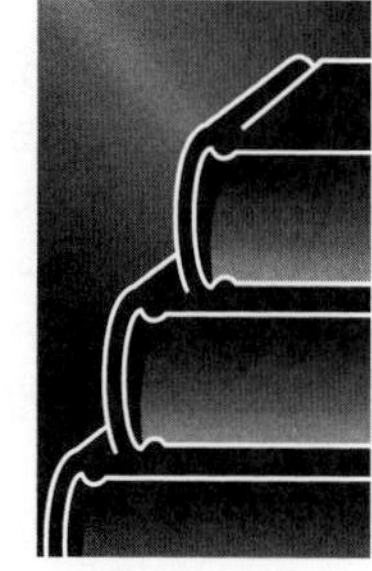

Facts: On March 22, 1985, plaintiffs executed an adjustable rate note secured by a deed of trust on a home for $112,500.00. The note was executed on a multistate Federal National Mortgage Association (FNMA) Uniform Instrument form, which included a provision for late payment charges. A late payment charge rate of 5 percent of the overdue payment of principal and interest was typed in a blank provided on the form.

The FNMA purchased the note from the lender, Epic Mortgage Inc., in March 1985. Skyline Mortgage Corporation succeeded Epic as servicer of the loan. On October 14, 1987, Skyline sent plaintiffs notice of uncollected late charges. When Skyline discovered that the late payment penalty rate on plaintiffs' note exceeded the legal maximum under North Carolina law, it offered to reduce the rate to 4 percent, pursuant to the "Loan Charges" paragraph in the note. Defendants never collected a late payment penalty from plaintiffs.

Plaintiffs filed a complaint and an amended complaint for declaratory judgment, averring the 5 percent late charge was assessed on a payment not yet due, the charge was usurious under N.C.G.S.

§ 24-10.1, and reduction of that rate to 4 percent was fraudulent and a material alteration discharging plaintiffs from their obligations under the note. Plaintiffs sought a judgment declaring the loan usurious, requiring defendant to forfeit all interest due under the note to FNMA or Skyline, or both, or, alternatively, discharging plaintiffs from the note pursuant to N.C.G.S. § 25-3-407. Plaintiffs further sought the court's application of N.C.G.S. § 24-2.1 and an award of all interest paid by them to any holder of the note from and after March 22, 1985 to the date of the court's order.

The trial court granted defendants' motion for summary judgment and denied that of plaintiffs. The Court of Appeals affirmed in part and reversed in part. The Court of Appeals imposed a penalty it considered consistent with the purpose of the usury statutes: defendants forfeited their right to collect late charges on the loan but did not forfeit their right to receive principal and interest.

Issue: If a late charge is usurious, must the lender forfeit all interest on the loan itself?

Decision: No. Judgment of Court of Appeals affirmed.

Opinion by Chief Justice Exum: "Chapter 24 of the General Statutes, entitled 'interest,' governs a number of lending transactions for which it either states maximum interest rates or excepts the transaction from such statutory constraints.... Among the 'transactions' governed by this chapter is a lender's charge for a borrower's late payment, for which the statute states a maximum rate:

(a) Subject to the limitations contained in subsection (b) of this section, any lender may charge a party to a loan or extension of credit governed by the provisions of G.S. 24-1.1, 24-1.2, or 24-1.1A a late payment charge as agreed upon by the parties in the loan contract.

(b) No lender may charge a late payment charge;

(1) In excess of 4 percent (4%) of the amount of the payment past due....

"The predecessor statute, N.C.G.S. § 24-10(e), in effect at the time plaintiffs signed their note, was essentially identical. The single statute in Chapter 24 stating penalties for charges exceeding the maximum rates stipulated in its provisions provides, in pertinent part:

The taking, receiving, reserving or charging a greater rate of interest than permitted by this chapter or other applicable law, either before or after the interest may accrue, when knowingly done, shall be a forfeiture of the entire interest which the note or other evidence of debt carries with it, or which has been agreed to be paid thereon....

"The forfeiture provisions of N.C.G.S. § 24-2 are 'in the nature of a penalty intended to induce an observance of the statute, and it is the duty of the courts so to expound and apply the law as to carry out the legislative intent....' We are convinced that the General Assembly, which specified a maximum legal rate for late payment fees in N.C.G.S. § 24-10.1, considered such fees 'interest' and intended to induce observance of that law through the penalty provisions of N.C.G.S. § 24-2....

"The note executed by plaintiffs in actuality contemplated interest for two separable monetary transactions. The more obvious transaction was the contract for a home loan exceeding $10,000, for which the parties were free to agree on any rate of interest.... The second transaction contemplated was the cost of money retained the delayed loan payment. A late payment fee has two purposes: to encourage the borrower to pay on time and to compensate the lender for the loss of use of the payment held for the period of the delay. In the latter case, the late payment charge is interest, for it is compensation fixed by the parties for the detention of money or for the lender's forbearance in collecting the late payment.

"The elements of usury are a loan or forbearance of the collection of money, an understanding that the money owed will be paid, payment or an agreement to pay interest at a rate greater than allowed by law, and the lender's corrupt intent to receive more in interest than the legal rate permits for use of the money loaned....

The corrupt intent required to constitute usury is simply the intentional charging of more for money lent than the law allows. Where the lender intentionally charges the borrower a greater rate of interest than the law allows and his purpose is clearly revealed on the face of the instrument, a corrupt intent to violate the usury law on the part of the lender is shown....

"These four elements are all present with regard to the late payment penalty provision in plaintiffs' note. First, there was a 'loan' consisting in this context of the amount of principal and interest thereon due in the allegedly overdue payment. The note's scheduled repayment of principal and interest thereon indicated the parties' expectation that each payment would eventually be made. The note provided that a payment delayed more than fifteen days would be assessed late charges at 5 percent of the payment amount, a rate that exceeded the legally permissible rate. Corrupt intent was shown simply in imposing the usurious rate. 'A profit, greater than the lawful rate of interest, intentionally exacted as a bonus for the loan of money, ... is a violation of the usury laws, it matters not what form or disguise it may assume....'

"The penalty for charging usurious interest, whether or not it is collected, is the 'forfeiture of the entire interest which the ... evidence of debt carries with it....' In the restricted context of a late charge on a delayed payment, 'forfeiture of ... interest' in no way implicates the interest on the principal. When late charges are usurious, 'the entire interest' can only signify any and all penalty fees for late payments. The penalty fee is 'interest.' It is compensation for the detention of money owed another, and all such compensation must be forfeited when its rate is usurious, as defined by the laws of this state....

"We conclude it was the intent of the General Assembly to enforce late charges violating N.C.G.S. § 24-10.1 by the penalty provisions of N.C.G.S. § 24-2, which, under the facts of this case, require the lender's forfeit of all late charges to which it would otherwise be entitled under the terms of the loan. We accordingly hold the decision of the Court of Appeals is modified and affirmed."

Common Law Restraint of Trade

Contracts that produce unreasonable restraints of trade were illegal under the common law, and they continue to be prohibited by many modern state and national statutes. However, the courts have long recognized that certain types of restraints serve a legitimate business function. In two situations in particular, the courts have recognized and enforced reasonable restraints of trade. When someone buys a business, that person is also buying goodwill. The courts permit the buyer to protect this goodwill by requiring the seller not to engage in a competing business within a reasonable geographic area for a reasonable period of time. If this restraint or **covenant not to compete** were not permitted, the seller could immediately regain most or all former customers by going back into business right across the street. Similarly, former employees, partners, or other business associates can be restrained from going to work for a competing firm, within reasonable area and time limits, if this is necessary to protect a former employer's goodwill, customer lists, or trade secrets.

When the area or time limitations are unreasonable, and therefore illegal, the courts do not agree on what should happen. Some courts throw out the restraint entirely, thus giving the restrained party a better bargain than was made originally. Other courts use a "blue pencil" and rewrite the limitations to make them reasonable. The problem with this approach is that it encourages the buyer or employer to write in unreasonable limitations because, if these are challenged in court, the worst outcome is that they will only be made reasonable.

The accompanying case illustrates the common use made of such restraints in professional organizations.

CASE 4

Wausau Medical Center, S.C. v. Asplund

514 N.W.2d 34 (WI App. 1994)

Facts: Dr. Asplund was twice employed as a general and vascular surgeon at Wausau Medical Center (WMC), a multispecialty clinic. His first employment was from August 1988 to the end of July 1989. Asplund was WMC's first vascular surgeon, and this was Asplund's first professional practice following his residency. With this employment, Asplund entered into a contract with WMC that contained a restrictive covenant. Asplund voluntarily terminated his employment and moved to Iowa to participate in a transplant program in July 1989. WMC did not have a vascular surgeon between July 1989 and August 1990.

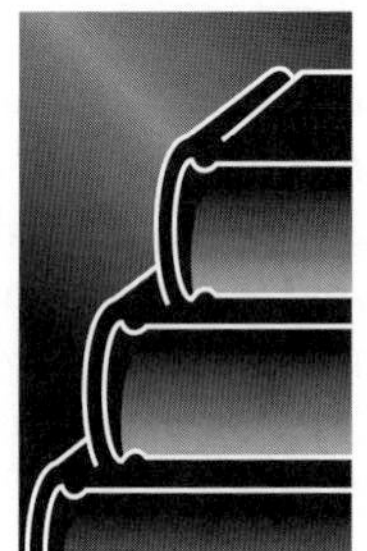

Within a year, Asplund decided that he wanted to return to Wausau. Asplund began negotiations with WMC. The negotiations broke off at one point because Asplund wanted the restrictive covenant stricken from the new contract, and WMC refused to do so. Nevertheless, Asplund commenced a second term of employment in August 1990 after signing an employment contract that contained a restrictive covenant. The covenant, which was identical to the one contained in his first contract, stated:

> *Covenant Not to Compete. The Employee agrees that if his employment with the Corporation is terminated for any reason, he will not engage in the practice of medicine or any phase or specialty thereof in competition with the Employer for a period of two (2) years from the date of termination of his employment within Marathon County, Wisconsin. The Employee hereby consents to an issuance of an injunction by a court of competent jurisdiction to enjoin the violation of the foregoing in addition to any other remedies available to the Corporation. In lieu of said injunction, the Corporation shall have the option to recover as liquidated damages from the Employee a sum equal to 20 percent (20%) of the total cumulative professional charges made by the Employee during the twelve-month period immediately preceding the termination date.*

In September 1990, 45 days after he started, Asplund gave WMC 60 days' notice of his employment termination. Asplund formed a service corporation, Mark Asplund, S.C., while still employed at WMC. After his employment at WMC was terminated, he began his surgery practice in Wausau as an employee of the service corporation.

Asplund originally commenced this action by seeking to have the restrictive covenant declared unenforceable. Initially, WMC obtained a 5-day temporary restraining order but was later denied a temporary injunction following a hearing. WMC filed a counterclaim and a third-party complaint against Asplund and his service corporation. Asplund voluntarily dismissed his claim, making WMC the plaintiff, and he then moved for summary judgment dismissing all WMC's claims against him and the service corporation. The trial court granted summary judgment in favor of Asplund, who sought costs, which were also granted. WMC appealed.

Issue: Is the restrictive covenant enforceable?

Decision: No. Judgment affirmed.

Opinion by Presiding Judge Cane: "The following canons of construction of restrictive covenants have been adopted: (1) These restrictions are prima facie suspect, (2) they must withstand close scrutiny to pass legal muster as being reasonable, (3) they will not be construed to extend beyond their proper import or further than the language of the contract absolutely requires, and (4) they are to be construed in favor of the employee.. . .

"Under § 103.465, STATS., a covenant not to compete within a specific time and a specific territory is lawful only if the restrictions imposed are reasonably necessary for the protection of the employer. Five inquiries are made in evaluating the enforceability of a covenant not to compete. The covenant must: (1) be necessary for the protection of the employer, (2) provide a reasonable time restriction, (3) provide a reasonable territorial limit, (4) be reasonable as to the employee, and (5) be reasonable as to the general public.. . .

"Our consideration of whether the covenant not to compete was necessary to protect WMC is two-fold. First, we must look to the facts as of the time the contract was entered into. At that point, it can be argued that WMC was anticipating the unfair competition that Asplund could provide in the event that his employment was terminated. WMC's apparent concern was that Asplund's association with WMC would enhance his reputation and thereby make him a formidable competitor (i.e., that his enhanced reputation would be a special circumstance which would render the restrictive covenant reasonably necessary for the protection of WMC's business).. . . WMC was also concerned that it would provide Asplund with a client and referral base, which he would later take with him, again making the covenant reasonably necessary to protect WMC's business.

"[W]e conclude that facts surrounding the employment itself are also to be considered. While WMC could reasonably anticipate a protectible interest, as of the signing of the contract, since Asplund was not yet provided with any clients, referrals or an enhanced reputation, WMC had not yet acquired a protectible interest. Therefore we must go on to determine whether the anticipated protectible interest was ever acquired. We conclude that it was not.. . .

"It is . . . undisputed that the amount of work Asplund did in his first forty-five days of employment was sparse, to the point of concern on the part of WMC. It is further undisputed that in the remaining sixty days of his employment, after he gave his termination notice, he received very few referrals from his colleagues.

"We conclude, as a matter of law, that the minimal referral contacts WMC provided Asplund with during his short tenure do not amount to a reasonable protectible interest. Further, we conclude that his short three-and-one-half-month tenure with WMC was insufficient to materially aid in his reputation. His brief employment with WMC was such that Asplund only provided 'legitimate and ordinary competition of the type that a stranger could give.. . .' Therefore, WMC did not acquire a protectible right against competition by Asplund through this brief employment on either of these bases.

"WMC next argues that it acquired a protectible interest because Asplund performed unique specialized services.. . .

"[I]n order to establish a protectible interest, WMC would have to establish that Asplund's unique skills were acquired at WMC. No one disputes that Asplund acquired his vascular surgery skills prior to his employment, that there was no other vascular surgeon at WMC from whom he could enhance these unique skills, and that Asplund's short tenure at WMC prevented him from significantly improving his skills. Thus, the evidence is undisputed that Asplund did not acquire his unique skills from his employment with WMC, and, consequently, WMC did not acquire a protectible interest.

"WMC's final argument regarding the restrictive covenant is that Asplund had access to competitive information at WMC and, as a result, the covenant is reasonably necessary to protect WMC. The key piece of competitive information was the patient lists.. . .

"In this case, although Asplund did not take any of this information with him, during his employment he had access to patient lists. However, Asplund, who was one of many physicians at WMC, did not have the type of control or influence over his patients so as to use this access for any competitive advantage. This was especially true in light of his surgery practice. Unlike, for example, a general practitioner, a patient's relationship with a surgeon is, hopefully, restricted to one encounter. Further, WMC did not put forth substantial efforts to acquire new patients for Asplund, and gave him very few referrals during his final sixty days there. Additionally, in his short tenure Asplund could not have established the type of 'special relationship' with his patients so as to have such influence. Therefore, WMC did not acquire a protectible right to reasonably prevent competition from Asplund by virtue of his access to the patient lists.. . .

"As mentioned, restrictive covenants are suspect and must be closely scrutinized to pass legal muster as being reasonable.. . . Because WMC failed to prove that the covenant not to compete is reasonably necessary for the protection of WMC, we conclude that the covenant is unenforceable.. . . Because our conclusion is dispositive with regard to the enforceability of the covenant, we need not address WMC's remaining arguments concerning the restrictive covenant."

Improper Interference with Governmental Processes

In the wake of Watergate, with the absolutely unprecedented loss through resignation of both a President and a Vice-President of the United States and with the disclosures of illegal political contributions by some of our largest national corporations, many people have been made much more aware of the possibilities for the corruption of governmental processes. Coercion or **bribery** of public officials is clearly illegal, and any "contract" involving such "services" would be void. **Lobbying,** on the other hand, is perfectly lawful and an essential part of the democratic process, and lobbying contracts that do not involve any improper means are valid and enforceable in court.

In most states mere failure to report a crime, called misprision, is no longer criminal; however, a person who actively aids in concealing a crime or agrees not to file criminal charges in return for a consideration is committing a criminal act. Perjury and jury tampering are both crimes. Although at one time maintenance (stirring up litigation) was a crime, this rule has been modified as a result of the activities of such organizations as the National Association for the Advancement of Colored People (NAACP), Legal Defense Fund, and Nader's Raiders. The old common law judges were so jealous of their prerogatives that they even held arbitration agreements to be illegal "obstructions of justice," but this view has been almost completely repudiated.

The Watergate scandal has left this entire area of the law somewhat unsettled, as new legislation has been adopted to limit private political contributions and new attempts are under way to permit political activities by employees of the U.S. government.

Illegality or Impossibility as an Excuse for Nonperformance

Subsequent Illegality

When the performances called for by the contract were legal when made but were subsequently made illegal by statute or administrative regulation, the now-illegal contract duties are discharged by operation of law. This is clearly the only fair result: Neither party normally assumes this kind of risk, and neither ought to be forced to perform if by doing so; he or she is breaking the law. The adoption of the Eighteenth Amendment and the Volstead Act, which made it illegal to manufacture, transport, or sell alcoholic beverages, provided one illustration of this rule in effect. More current examples might involve changes in the legal rules pertaining to foreign investments, currency exchange, ownership of gold by U.S. citizens, and sales of "strategic" materials to Communist countries.

Impossibility

When a contract specifies performance by one certain party or when the performance requires the existence of a particular thing, the death or disability of the party or the destruction of the thing will normally discharge the performance obligation through **objective impossibility.** That is, because the contract is so specific, no one at all can render the required performance. A promise to deliver "all of my tomato crop" is discharged if the tomato crop is destroyed without any fault on the part of the grower. A promise to deliver "1,000 tons of tomatoes" is probably not discharged when the grower's own crop fails because the grower could buy other tomatoes on the market and deliver them. Where no specific thing is identified, there is only "subjective impossibility," which does not operate to discharge contract obligations.

Commercial Impracticability and Frustration

Closely related to the idea of impossibility are the ideas of **impracticability** and **frustration.** A performance may not actually be impossible to render, but it may be financially impracticable to do it, in the sense that it is stupid or nonsensical to require the performance. If a trucking company has a contract to transport a racehorse to Churchill Downs for the Kentucky Derby, and the horse dies, it would clearly be commercially impracticable to require the owner to pay the trucking company for transporting the dead horse to Churchill Downs, although that performance is not impossible. The Uniform Commercial Code contains specific provisions, in Section 2-615, for dealing with this problem in sale of goods cases.

Frustration is closely related to impossibility. Again, the performance specified in the contract is not technically impossible, but the entire purpose or reason for making the contract no longer exists because of the happening of some unforeseeable event. The classic case of frustration involved the renting of rooms in London for exorbitant prices to enable the guests to see the coronation parade of King Edward VII. On the day designated in the "leases," there was no parade because the king had caught a cold and postponed it. Although there was nothing impossible about performance by either the landlord or the tenant, at least one English court agreed that the contract duty should be discharged.

Bargains against Public Policy

Among the kinds of provisions challengeable as **against public policy** are those attempting to insulate landlords, employers, and bailees from liability for their own negligence and those that purport to waive or give up specific statutory protections. Anyone who has ever rented a house or an apartment knows that landlords' lawyers are particularly adept at coming up with objectionable lease provisions: no pets, no motorcycles, no waterbeds, no alcohol; tenant waives right to trial by jury; landlord may inspect the premises at any hour of the day or night, with or without notice to the tenant. Although the landlord surely has a legitimate concern with what happens on the premises, some of the preceding seem to constitute an unwarranted intrusion into the tenant's affairs; this balance has not yet been fully and finally defined.

These are not closed categories. As society's values change, provisions that are readily accepted and enforced today may become against public policy and thus unenforceable. In any case where the results called for by the terms of the contract seem unduly harsh, this additional defense argument should be presented to the court. What can you lose?

The *Berryhill* case raises the question of parents' rights to agree to a different level of child support payments than that provided by state law.

CASE 5

Berryhill v. Rhodes

21 S.W.3d 188 (TN 2000)

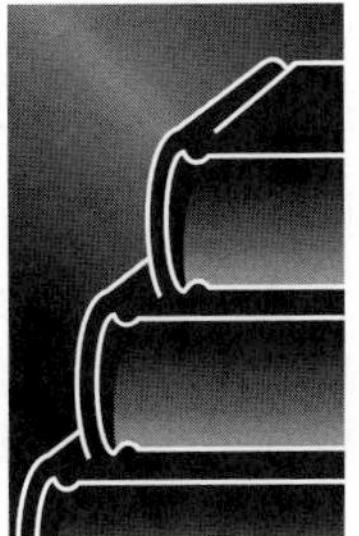

Facts: Betty Berryhill was a patient of Memphis psychiatrist Dr. Charles T. Rhodes in 1975 or 1976. Betty and Charles began a sexual relationship that resulted in the birth of a child, Anika Berryhill, on September 5, 1977. Charles paid the delivery-related medical bills not covered by insurance. He then began paying Betty $200 a month, increased to $300 a month 6 months later. He made these payments until Anika was 18 years old, but refused to give Betty additional amounts. In October 1995, Betty filed a lawsuit to recover additional child support based on the state's official child support guidelines. Charles claims that the parties had expressly or impliedly agreed to a lower support amount.

The juvenile court referee found that the agreed amount was "just and reasonable" and that it would be "unfair and unreasonable" to award additional support payments. The juvenile court affirmed. The court of appeals initially reversed, but ultimately affirmed the juvenile court's findings. Betty appealed.

Issue: Can the parties lawfully agree to a level of child support lower than that specified in the official state guidelines?

Decision: No. Judgment reversed; case remanded.

Opinion by Judge Holder: "Our paternity and child support statutes and the Child Support Guidelines evince a policy that children should be supported by their fathers. The paternity statutes provide a process by which the putative father can be identified. Once identified, the father is required to furnish support and education for the child.... The paternity statutes incorporate both the child support provisions pertaining to divorce decrees as well as the Child Support Guidelines.... The legal duty of support exists in all cases....

"Tennessee Code Annotated S.36-5-101(h), incorporated in the paternity statute, states that any agreement reached by parents regarding child support may be affirmed, ratified, and incorporated into a divorce decree. This subsection contemplates that the agreement: 1) will be in writing; 2) will be approved by a court; 3) will be incorporated into a court order; and 4) will contain the parties' acknowledgement that they may not alter the agreement without court approval. If the parties meet these requirements, they may enter into a valid agreement to set child support. In this case, the parties met none of the requirements of the statute. We fail to see how the enactment of S.36-5-101(h) evinces legislative intent to uphold private agreements that fail to comply with the statute in any respect. . . .

"Although this Court has not specifically addressed the issue of the validity of a private agreement for payment of child support, other states that have considered the issue have found such agreements violate public policy. . . .

"Courts in several jurisdictions have found that a child's right to support cannot be bargained away by a parent to the child's detriment. . . .

"We find the holdings and reasoning of these courts to be persuasive. Tennessee's statutory provisions for the establishment of paternity and support and the Child Support Guidelines evince a policy that fathers will support their children. Private agreements used to circumvent the obligations set forth in the statutes and guidelines contravene that policy. . . .

"We conclude that private agreements for the payment of child support violate public policy. We remand the case for an application of the Child Support Guidelines to determine the amount of child support that would be owed under the guidelines, and, if appropriate, for findings of fact justifying a conclusion that the application of the guidelines would be unjust or inappropriate."

Significance of This Chapter

As statutes and administrative regulations multiply, it becomes increasingly possible that contracting parties may on occasion agree to do some illegal act. Generally, for successful criminal prosecution, criminal intent must be proved. Intent is usually irrelevant, however, as far as the enforcement of an illegal bargain is concerned. Both parties are presumed to know the applicable criminal law; whether or not they do in fact is usually irrelevant—their purported contract is void or voidable. When a statute or regulation is designed to protect one of the parties to the transaction, the courts will try to work out results that achieve that objective. Otherwise, when both parties are equally guilty, the court's general approach will be to leave all parties as is. Because either of these rules can result in the forfeiture of substantial economic values, you need to be alert to the major types of illegality that may occur in contracting situations.

IMPORTANT TERMS AND CONCEPTS

against public policy
Blue Laws
bribery
covenant not to compete
frustration
gambling
impracticability
in pari delicto
licensing statute
lobbying
objective impossibility
regulatory statute
revenue raising statute
service charges
Sunday law
time-price differential
usury

QUESTIONS AND PROBLEMS FOR DISCUSSION

1. What results occur when a credit contract specifies an illegally high rate of interest on the debt?

2. When and how can the seller of a business be prevented from competing with it after selling it?

3. To what extent are Sunday contracts illegal?

4. What happens when a person contracts to perform services without having the required license to do so?

5. Gunstock Acres is a vacation, retirement home–type development in New Hampshire, and solicitations are made by mail and through the media for a free weekend to review the development. In response to such an invitation the buyer went to the development with friends on Friday, January 24, 1996. On Sunday morning, January 26, 1996, after discussions with a salesman, the buyer signed the contract dated January 25, 1996, and delivered a check for $100.

Subsequently, William Cameron made a down payment and paid 28 monthly installments, paying more than $3,800 toward the purchase price of $6,495. He made several visits to the property, the last in October 1998 and observed roads in rough condition. He had correspondence with the seller relating to delinquent payments and possible sale of the lot. In August 1997, he went to the seller's office in Fitchburg, Massachusetts, and was told that finding a buyer would be his responsibility. He was unsuccessful in finding a buyer.

Cameron filed a lawsuit, asking the court to declare the contract void because it was executed on Sunday. He lives in Massachusetts; both states have Sunday laws. The trial court dismissed the case. Cameron appealed.

Is this contract void because it violates a Sunday law that prohibits "actions which disturb others" on Sunday?

6. R.E. Fuse operates a garbage collection service in the towns of Cleen and Teidy. In June 1989, he made an oral agreement with Wesley Trashy to hire him as a garbage truck driver. In November, Fuse handed Wesley a written document that stated that, upon severance of employment, Trashy would not engage in garbage collection within 15 miles of Cleen and Teidy for a period of 5 years. Trashy, who knew that his signature on the document was a precondition for continued employment, signed the agreement. In September 1990, Wesley Trashy quit his job and immediately went into the garbage collection business for himself. Fuse now brings an action against Trashy for breach of contract.

   What decision? Why?

7. The parties executed a valid written contract by which Mr. and Mrs. Christy agreed to buy an apartment from Mrs. Pilkinton for $30,000. When the time came for performance, the purchasers, although not insolvent, were unable to raise enough money to carry out their contract. Mrs. Pilkinton, after having tendered a deed to the property, brought this suit. At the trial the defendants' evidence tended to show that, as a result of a decline in Christys' used car business, they do not possess, and cannot borrow the unpaid balance of $29,900.

   The Christys claim their obligation is discharged by impossibility. Is that a valid defense in this case? Explain.

8. A neurosurgeon named Fusillo engaged in discussions with the defendant Cohen in the summer and fall of 1991 that led to an oral understanding that the defendant would associate with Fusillo in the practice of neurology in Malden and vicinity, where Fusillo had been in practice since 1983. The association began on November 6, 1991. About a week later Fusillo asked the defendant to sign an "employment agreement," which stated that it represented the entire agreement of the parties and contained the restrictive covenant. The defendant expressed reluctance to sign it but did so after consulting with an attorney. Middlesex Corporation, of which Fusillo was president and sole stockholder, was chartered on December 3, 1991, and Fusillo assigned the employment agreement to it on December 7. Cohen left the corporation and began his own practice. Middlesex got an injunction from the trial court. Cohen appealed.

   Should the injunction be sustained on appeal? Why or why not?

9. Sinkin Beverage Company was licensed by Blitz [illegible] as a wholesale distributor in 1975. The written contract that the parties signed at that time provided that either one could cancel at any time, for any reason or for no reason at all. Sinkin was the exclusive distributor for Blitz products in Suffould County 1975 to 1994, and its Blitz sales constitute a large part of its wholesale business. In 1994, Blitz notified Sinkin that the contract would be terminated in 10 days. Sinkin sues for an injunction against the termination, claiming that the contract clause is unconscionable.

   Should this injunction be granted? Explain.

CHAPTER 13

Third-Party Beneficiaries and Assignment

Chapter Objectives

This chapter will:

- Indicate how persons other than the contracting parties may acquire rights under a contract.
- Explain third-party beneficiary contracts.
- Differentiate donee beneficiaries, creditor beneficiaries, and incidental beneficiaries.
- Explain the difference between assignment of rights and delegation of duties.
- Discuss the rules for assigning rights.
- Explain how a debtor's rights may be affected when a creditor assigns the right to receive the contract price.

The problems discussed in this chapter are quite different from any we have considered so far. Here our basic question is whether persons other than the parties who actually negotiated and agreed to the contract should be given the right to demand performance under it. The answer given by the early common law was simple: No! Today, however, courts do recognize the rights of these "strangers"—both assignees and third-party beneficiaries—at least in some situations and subject to many complicated and technical limitations.

Third-Party Beneficiary Contracts

Basic Concepts and Definitions

A **third-party beneficiary contract** is one in which at least one of the performances called for is intended for the direct benefit of a person or persons other than the parties who actually made the contract. **Donee beneficiaries** are persons who receive this benefit as a gift, without any prior duty on anyone's part to provide them with the benefit. In most cases, persons named as the beneficiaries in life insurance policies are donees. A **creditor beneficiary** is one to whom the benefit was already owed, as a result of a prior legal relationship. If creditors have sold or financed purchases of such items as cars, appliances, or real estate to buyers who resell the as-yet-unpaid-for items to purchasers who agree to take over the payments, the creditors are third-party creditor beneficiaries of the take-over-the-payments contracts. In these cases, the creditor beneficiary has two parties to look to for payment: the original debtor and the takeover buyer.

Exhibit 13.1: Assignment and Third-Party Beneficiary Contracts

THIRD PARTY BENEFICIARIES

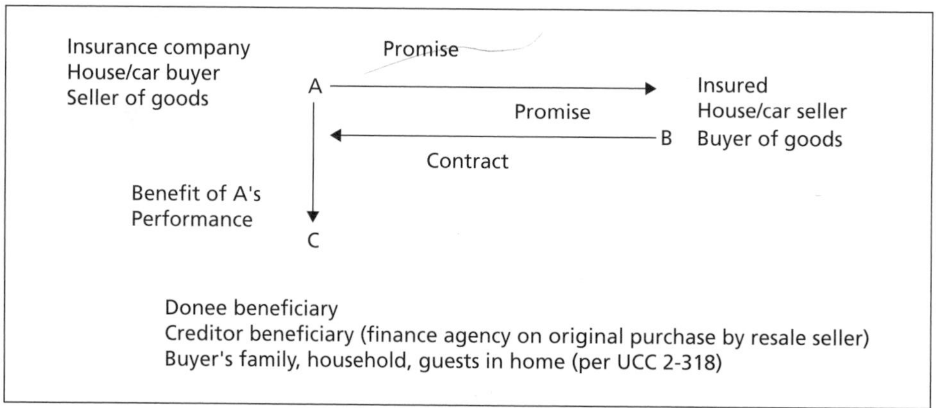

ASSIGNMENT

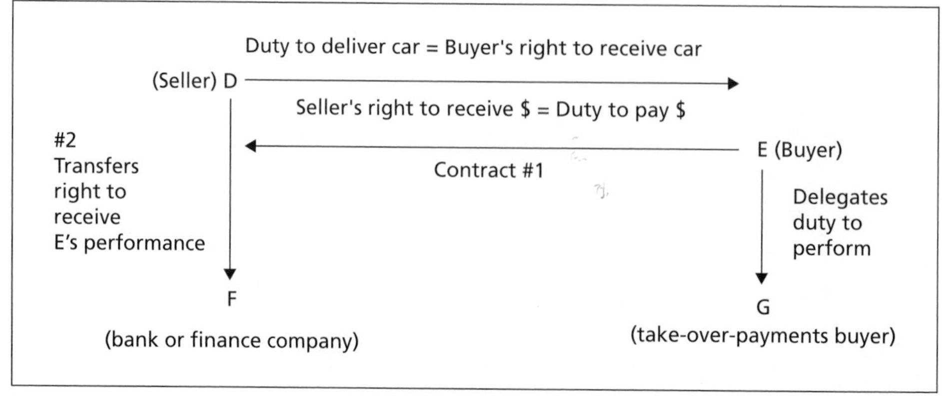

promised, the original buyer remains personally liable and can be sued by the original seller. When a right has been validly assigned, however, the assignee completely displaces the original owner of the right, to whom performance was due. However, the original debtor is free of liability for a **delegated duty** only if the original obligee (creditor) agrees to the substitution of the new obligor (debtor) in place of the original one and agrees to discharge the original one. This change of parties, called a novation, is discussed further in the next chapter. Without the obligee's consent, the performance of a duty cannot even be delegated to another person if the duty involves an individualized service or if there is a particular reason for dealing with one certain person.

Assignability of Contract Rights

To determine whether or not rights are assignable, we must consider contracts in three categories. First, there are contracts whose rights are not assignable unless the obligor specifically agrees to the assignment. This category includes contracts involving some personal element, such as the personal service of the obligor or the personal credit or requirements of the obligee, and contracts in which the performance of the duty could be materially changed if the assignment were recognized. The UCC adopts this same basic approach for sales of goods in Section 2-210(2).

Probably the vast majority of contracts fall into the second category, in which the rights are assignable unless there is a specific contract prohibition against assignment. In most cases, contract rights for such things as land, securities, or goods would be presumed to be transferable to others unless the parties had specifically agreed otherwise. Section 2-210(3) of the UCC says that to prohibit assignment of the right to receive goods, a contract clause must very clearly specify that result; a general prohibition of transfer of "the contract" is only effective to prohibit a delegation of duties.

Such contact prohibitions may raise particularly troublesome problems during corporate restructurings. Asset values that cannot legally be assigned without the consent of the other original contracting party will not be available to the proposed merger or buyout partner. The entire acquisition may have to be renegotiated (or abandoned). Merger and acquisition specialist Bruce Wasserman discusses these issues in his book, *Big Deal.* (See pages 535 to 542.)

The third group of contracts results from the UCC's effort to make sure that businesses will be able to use their accounts as financing collateral without having to get each account debtor's consent. Section 9-318(4) says that even if the contract specifically prohibits assignment of the right to receive payment for goods sold or leased or services performed, the creditor can go ahead and assign the account anyway, without the debtor's consent; the contract provision will not be enforced. For example, when you buy your new TV on time, even getting a specific clause written into your contract will not enable you to avoid dealing with a finance company if the dealer wants to assign your contract.

As a rule, present assignments of future rights are fully effective; that is, one can effectively transfer ownership now of the right, under an existing contract, to receive a performance at some future date. However, any purported assignment of rights under a contract that does not exist yet, but is merely anticipated, is totally void. An unemployed person has not made an effective assignment by signing a contract with an employment agency that purports to assign one-third of the first month's wages to the agency when it gets that person a new job. In addition, most states have specific regulatory statutes covering wage assignments and limiting the percentage share that can be assigned.

The validity and scope of an assignment were one set of issues in the *Tickanen* case.

Due on Sale Clauses in Real Estate Mortgages

A **due on sale clause** does not, technically, prohibit the resale of real estate before an existing mortgage is paid off. What it does say is that when such a resale occurs, the entire remaining mortgage balance becomes immediately due and payable. As a practical result, this means that no assignment of the existing mortgage to the resale purchaser can occur; the resale purchaser will have to qualify for new financing. As interest rates soared in the late 1970s and early 1980s, mortgage lenders did not want to be bound on the 20- and 30-year mortgages that they had written at 6 to 9 percent interest rates. The lenders began to enforce their due on sale clauses vigorously.

CASE 2

Tickanen v. Harris & Harris, Ltd.

461 F.Supp.2d 863 (E.D. WI 2006)

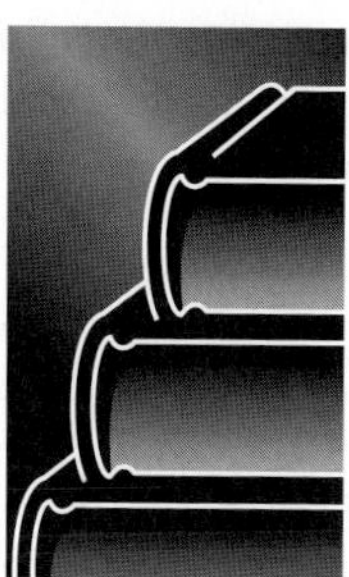

Facts: Helen Tickanen and John Theurich filed a lawsuit claiming that Harris & Harris had violated the national Fair Debt Collection Practices Act by sending them collection letters that incorrectly identified the "creditor." Barbara Schneider was later added as a plaintiff. Claiming that Tickanen and Schneider had agreed to an arbitration clause as part of their credit card contracts with Boston Store, Harris filed a Motion to Compel Arbitration as to their claims. Boston Store had sent notices to its credit card holders in 1999 that the arbitration clause was being added to their credit card agreements, and that any cardholder who objected to the addition should so notify the store. The notice also said that any future use of the cards would constitute an agreement to be bound by the arbitration provision. In 2003, National Bank of Great Lakes assigned Boston Store accounts to Household Bank, which later became HSBC Bank Nevada. HSBC then became the credit card issuer for Boston Store, and all existing cardholders were notified of the change. Under the new arrangement, HSBC could assign its rights without further notice the cardholders. Plaintiffs' accounts had been closed and assigned to Harris & Harris for collection. The collection letters identified "Boston Store" as the creditor.

Issue: Is the arbitration agreement effective between Harris and the plaintiffs?

Decision: Yes. Arbitration is ordered as to the claims of Tickanen and Schneider.

Opinion by Magistrate Judge Goodstein: "Plaintiffs allege any arbitration agreement was never effective as to them. Furthermore, plaintiffs allege Harris was a non-signatory to the arbitration agreement and therefore cannot claim rights under Boston Store's contract with plaintiffs.

" '[A]ssignee ... stands in the shoes of the assignors.' ... In the case at hand, Boston Store sent plaintiffs a notice indicating HSBC assumed all Boston Store's previous credit card accounts and HSBC reserved the right to assign the debt at any time, without notice. The notice also indicated if one did not agree with the terms, card holders should return a postcard indicating this; furthermore, any purchases made on their account after the effective date, October 15, 1999, would constitute acceptance of these changes. The court concludes that the plaintiffs consented to the terms of the agreement by their conduct in making purchases after this date....

"Furthermore, a non-signatory can compel arbitration by equitable estoppel....

"Here, plaintiffs are alleging Harris sent out debt collection letters with the wrong creditor listed, Boston Store, when in fact HSBC owned the debt at that time and Harris was debt collector. If this is true, plaintiffs are acknowledging the existence of a debt, which was assigned to Harris. Plaintiffs cannot acknowledge the debt and ignore the concomitant arbitration agreement. Plaintiffs are 'presuming the existence of the written agreement.' ... Therefore, plaintiffs should be estopped from denying part of the agreement and asserting only part of the agreement was assigned to Harris.

"The arbitration agreement properly applies to Harris as it does to plaintiffs....

"The arbitration provision included in plaintiffs' agreement gives the broadest meaning possible to 'claim.' ... Therefore, this provision indicates plaintiffs agreed to arbitrate any claims they had against the signatory and assignees. There is no reason to believe this agreement does not include violations under the FDCPA ...

"IT IS ... ORDERED that Harris's Motion to Compel Arbitration is granted. All proceedings against Helen Tickanen and Barbara Schneider are thus stayed pending completion of arbitration."

Although outright prohibitions on assignments by real estate buyers would generally be enforceable, some state courts refused to enforce due on sale clauses. For a time, there was a distinction based on whether the lender was state chartered or U.S. chartered. U.S. regulations specifically recognized the validity of the due on sale, but a state lending institution, competing for the same business, might not be able to enforce the clause. As a result of the 1982 Garn-St. Germain statute passed by Congress, due on sale clauses are now generally enforceable.

Warranties of Assignor to Assignee

When a contract right has been transferred for value, the Restatement says that the assignor makes three implied warranties to the assignee:

1. That the assignor will do nothing to defeat or impair the value of the assignment and that he or she has no knowledge of any fact that would do so.

2. That the right, as assigned, actually exists and is subject to no limitations or defenses good against the assignor, except those stated or apparent.

3. That any writing given or shown to the assignee as evidence of the right is genuine and what it purports to be.

In addition, the seller/assignor of the right can be sued for breach of warranty and/or fraud for any express statements made that are not true, such as a statement that a credit check had been made on the buyer/debtor, or that the buyer/debtor had a steady job. Note, however, that there is no implied guarantee that the buyer/debtor is solvent or will in fact perform as promised. In most cases in which accounts receivable are being assigned on a regular basis, as with a car dealer to a manufacturer's financing subsidiary, the assignment agreement itself will include a specific recourse provision. The assignor may have to buy back all uncollectible accounts, or none of them, or only some of them. The parties are free to work this out as they choose.

Delegation of Duty to Assignee

Courts are not agreed as to whether, in taking the assignment, an assignee is also impliedly agreeing to perform any remaining duties owed by his or her assignor to the other original party. Most of the older cases say that no such promise is implied; many of the newer ones have adopted a contrary rule. In any event, all of the surrounding facts and circumstances, and especially the language of the assignment itself, will be examined to see whether such a promise should be implied. The simplest solution to this problem is to specify the result desired in the assignment itself.

For the sale of goods, the UCC adopts the view of the newer cases, so that an acceptance by the assignee of a general assignment also constitutes the assignee's promise to perform all of the assignor's remaining duties, unless the language of the assignment or the circumstances indicate otherwise.

The significance of such a promise by the assignee is that nonperformance of the reciprocal duty gives (or may give) the other party an excuse for withholding the required return performance or even a basis for bringing a lawsuit against the assignee for breach of contract.

Notice to Obligor

All courts agree that, as between the assignor and the assignee, the assignment is effective when it is made, even though notice of the assignment has not been communicated to the obligor. However, notice (or its absence) does have some important legal consequences. Payment or other performance that the obligor gives to the assignor, before receiving notice that the obligation has been assigned and that the performance should now be made to the assignee, completely discharges that part of the original contract obligation. The assignee cannot sue the obligor and force a repeat performance but instead would have to sue the assignor. Similarly, the obligor can assert defenses or counterclaims against the assignee even on totally unrelated transactions between the obligor and the assignor if such claims arose before the obligor received notice of the assignment. For example: Dull buys a used car and a new car from Sharpie. Dull pays cash for the used car and finances the new car. Sharpie assigns the financing contract on the new car to the Bigger Bank. Until Dull gets notice of this assignment he can use as a defense against paying the balance due, not only any defects in the new car but also any defects in the used car. Once Dull gets notice of the assignment of his new car contract to Bigger Bank he can use only defects in the new car as his reason for nonpayment. After notice has been received, any additional problems with the used car will have to be taken up separately with Sharpie.

Notice is also significant in working out the problems encountered when the assignor has made more than one assignment of the same right. Although this should not occur, and the assignor is clearly liable for breach of implied warranties to both assignees, the situation does arise and rules have been developed to deal with it. To a retailer or a construction firm caught in a temporary cash flow squeeze, a "temporary" double assignment of the accounts receivable looks like a painless solution, with no one ever being the wiser. Too often, however, the optimism is not justified, and the double financing is discovered in a bankruptcy proceeding. The problem, then, is that there is only one sum of money to be paid, and there are two assignee-claimants. Which one should be paid first?

The states do not agree on the answer to this question. In the states that follow the **English rule** (probably still the minority), the assignee who first gives notice to the obligor is entitled to priority of payment. In the states that follow the **American rule,** the first assignment in point of time is given priority, but subject to several exceptions where notice has not been given. Under these exceptions, the first assignee loses if:

1. The first assignment was revocable or voidable by the assignor.
2. Payment has been made to the second assignee.
3. A judgment has been entered in favor of the second assignee.
4. A substitute contract has been negotiated by the second assignee and the debtor.
5. A specific writing representing the account, such as a savings account passbook, has been given to the second assignee.

Even in an American-rule state, therefore, it is important to give notice to the obligor immediately.

The Code will be of some help in dealing with this problem because **Article 9** covers most assignments for value as **secured transactions,** and generally requires the filing of a **public notice** that such financing arrangements are in force for them to be effective against third parties. When such a filing is required by Article 9 and has not yet occurred, a subsequent assignee of the accounts who gave value for them, had no knowledge of the first assignment, and filed its own public notice would be entitled to priority. It is, therefore, important for the first assignee to file the required public notice and to notify the obligor.

CASE 3

America First Credit Union v. First Security Bank of Utah, N.A.

930 P.2d 1198 (UT 1997)

Facts: American First Credit Union (AFCU) made a series of three loans to Renaissance, a supplier of food service to military bases under government contracts, to furnish Renaissance with working capital and to pay outstanding loans owing to AFCU and other lenders. At the time the first loan was made, Renaissance executed a security agreement with AFCU assigning as collateral a savings certificate it owned for $99,999 issued by First Security Bank. AFCU prepared a written notice of assignment, signed by Don Newsom, president and sole shareholder of Renaissance, and subsequently by an officer of First Security acknowledging receipt. The notice of assignment provided as follows:

> *"We are holding as collateral on a Line of Credit Savings Certificate No. 984993 in the amount of $99,999, in the name of Renaissance Exchange. Renaissance Exchange, Inc. is willing to pledge this certificate as collateral on their loan with America First Credit Union.*
>
> *"Renaissance Exchange, Inc.*
> *"[signed by Renaissance president]*
>
> *"American First Credit Union is holding the original certificate as collateral. We would appreciate your acknowledgment of the Assignment, also confirming the balance of $99,999. This Assignment will be in affect [sic] until you have received written notice of our release of the Assignment. Please acknowledge the Assignment and the balance by signing below. One copy should be retained in your files.*
>
> *"First Security Bank of Utah*
> *[signed by bank officer]"*

The savings certificate stated on its face that payment would be made to the registered owner "upon presentation and surrender of this certificate properly endorsed," and that otherwise upon maturity the account would automatically be renewed for a like period at the interest rate then offered.

At the time the second loan was made, AFCU prepared a second notice of assignment identical to the first. The certificate had previously matured and been renewed, and the new certificate number was hand-lettered by First Security on the notice of assignment to replace the original number and then signed by a First Security officer. Subsequently, First Security replaced the savings certificate with a special daytime certificate of deposit. This certificate did not state on its face that it had to be presented for payment. Consequently, to alert its personnel to the assignment, the bank placed a "flag" or "block" on the account in its computer system. When the certificate rolled over for the third time, First Security inadvertently removed the computer flag but did not notify AFCU of either the change in procedure or the removal of the flag.

AFCU held the certificate only as collateral on the Renaissance loan and therefore had no right to the proceeds except in the event of Renaissance's default. When the certificate matured for the third time, Newsom represented to First Security that the assignment had been released, and withdrew the proceeds of $99,999, although AFCU had not given First Security notice of release of the assignment. Newsom deposited the funds in Renaissance's AFCU checking account and subsequently paid them out. Seven months later, Renaissance defaulted with a balance of $551,529.31 owing on its third loan from AFCU, out of the original amount of $657,000. AFCU demanded payment of the certificate by First Security, but the bank refused payment. AFCU then brought this suit against First Security, which in turn asserted a third-party claim against Renaissance and Don Newsom for $99,999. In a separate action, AFCU sued Newsom and Renaissance for the total balance owing on the loan. The actions were consolidated.

The trial court ruled that AFCU had an enforceable security interest in the certificate and that First Security had breached its duty to honor that interest. The court imposed judgment against First Security and also awarded judgment in favor of AFCU against Newsom and Renaissance for the loan balance and in favor of First Security against Newsom and Renaissance for the certificate proceeds. First Security appealed to the court of appeals, which affirmed.

Issue: Did First Security receive adequate notice of the assignment?

Decision: Yes. Judgment for AFCU is affirmed.

Opinion by Justice Howe: "First Security contends that it did not breach any duty to AFCU by paying the proceeds to Renaissance because the notice of assignment was inadequate in that it did not direct First Security to pay AFCU, and when First Security paid the proceeds to Renaissance, AFCU had no present right to them.

"[UCC 9-318] imposes a two-pronged notice requirement. First, notice of the assignment must be given. Second, the notice must state that payments are to be made to the assignee. First Security admits receiving notice of the assignment but contends that because it did not receive notice that payment should be made to AFCU, it was entitled to pay Renaissance. AFCU responds that the second prong of . . . 9-318(3) is tailored to 'indirect collection' situations and therefore does not apply here. . . .

"[T]he plain language of the notice of assignment, which one of First Security's officers acknowledged receiving, informed the bank of the assignment, that it would continue in force until revoked in writing, and that AFCU was holding the certificate of deposit. Furthermore, First Security knew that the certificate itself required presentation and [i]ndorsement before payment could be made. Thus payment of the certificate proceeds to Renaissance should have been impossible by First Security's own policy as long as AFCU held the certificate. When that policy changed, the computer flag on the account replaced the certificate as notice to First Security that payment was to be made to AFCU rather than to Renaissance. First Security's generation of the computer flag demonstrates that it had notice of the change in payment. Its failure to notify AFCU that the actual certificate was no longer required for payment and its erroneous removal of the computer flag were unilateral actions taken after the notice was complete and had no impact upon the duties of either party. The statute should not be read as requiring more of AFCU than what it did to apprise First Security of its continuing interest in the certificate.

"We therefore hold that First Security received notice of the assignment and that payment was to be made to AFCU as required by . . . 9-318(3). Thus we affirm the finding of the trial court, upheld by the court of appeals, that First Security received 'reasonable notice.' By releasing the account proceeds to Renaissance while on notice of the unretracted assignment of the account as collateral for the AFCU loan, First Security breached its statutory duty to AFCU."

Availability of Defenses against Assignee

As it began to recognize the validity of assignments, the common law developed a rule that said that the assignee took the assigned contract right subject to all claims and defenses that the obligor could assert against the assignor. The assignee stepped into the assignor's legal shoes, and the shoes did not get any bigger just because someone else was wearing them. Although the assignee could at least cut off the obligor's claims on unrelated transactions by getting notice to that person, there was no way that the assignee could stand in any better enforcement position than assignor with respect to the assigned contract itself.

Obviously, a promise to pay money or render some other performance becomes much more uncertain and, therefore much less valuable, if it is subject to all sorts of unknown contingencies. To deal with this problem, the merchant community developed the **negotiable instrument,** which is basically just a written promise to pay money stated in a

Exhibit 13.2: Assignment and Third-Party Beneficiary Contracts

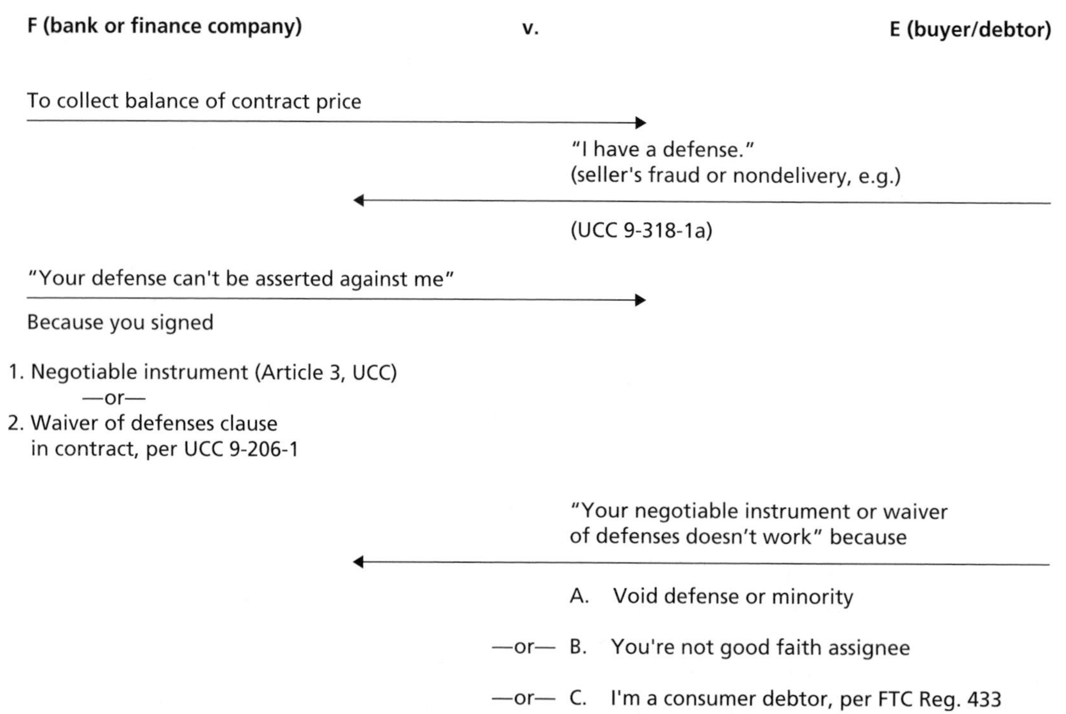
F (bank or finance company)
v.
E (buyer/debtor)
To collect balance of contract price
"I have a defense."
(seller's fraud or nondelivery, e.g.)
(UCC 9-318-1a)
"Your defense can't be asserted against me"
Because you signed
1. Negotiable instrument (Article 3, UCC)
—or—
2. Waiver of defenses clause
in contract, per UCC 9-206-1
"Your negotiable instrument or waiver
of defenses doesn't work" because
A. Void defense or minority
—or— B. You're not good faith assignee
—or— C. I'm a consumer debtor, per FTC Reg. 433

particular way. The law merchant said that if a promise to pay money was in negotiable form and was properly transferred to a good faith purchaser, then the debtor would not be able to assert most voidable-type defenses against the transferee. This was a "negotiation," not just an assignment. When the buyer-debtor had signed a negotiable promissory note for 100 bushels of wheat, which the seller had never delivered, the buyer would have to pay the amount of the note to the bank or finance company to which the note had been sold and then bring a lawsuit for breach of contract against the seller. Article 9 of the Code permitted the parties to work out this same basic result without using a negotiable instrument, by simply placing a provision to that effect, called a **waiver-of-defenses,** in the contract itself (see Exhibit 13-2).

These two "exceptions"—the negotiable instrument and the waiver-of-defenses clause—came into such widespread and common use that they all but swallowed up the general rule. The result was that many, many buyers had to pay for a "dead horse"—the undelivered wheat, the fraudulently represented car, the unperformed services. As a result of the consumer movement of the 1960s and 1970s, first some of the states and then the Federal Trade Commission (FTC) adopted rules that invalidated both of these devices in consumer contracts. As the law stands today, these devices are available only when the debtor is a business or other "nonconsumer." One important loophole does remain, however: When the consumer personally negotiates a direct loan from the financing agency, and *then* gives the cash to the seller, the dead horse result still occurs. The consumer who is referred to the financing agency by the seller is protected, however.

The *Woffard* case illustrates some of these problems.

Significance of This Chapter

Modern business operations require the free assignability of contract rights. Much business at all levels of production and distribution is done on credit, and sellers often do not have sufficient capital to do their own accounts receivable financing. The solution, of course, is to assign the accounts receivable to a bank or finance company, for cash, so that ongoing

CASE 4

First New England Financial Corp. v. Woffard
421 So.2d 590 (FL 1982)

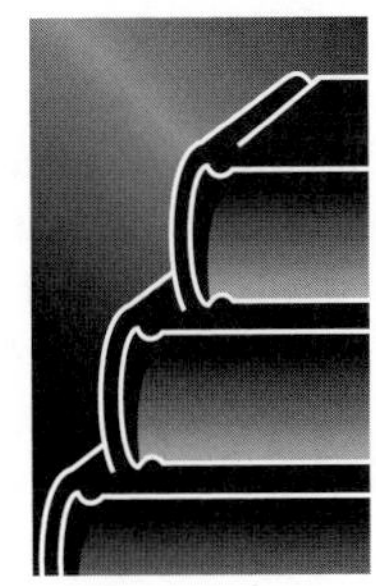

Facts: When Woffard decided to buy a 36-foot sailing yacht from a yacht broker, the broker suggested that he contact First New England Financial Corporation (FNEFC) to finance the deal. FNEFC represented out-of-state banks that were interested in making marine loans. FNEFC approved Woffard's credit, and he signed a printed retail installment contract to buy the yacht. By its terms, the contract was simultaneously assigned to FNEFC, which reassigned it the next day to City Trust, a Connecticut bank. City Trust's name, address, and telephone number were on the contract, under that of FNEFC. Woffard got a coupon payment book from City Trust several weeks later.

On Woffard's first sea voyage, he discovered several manufacturing defects in the yacht. He notified the broker, the manufacturer, FNEFC, and City Trust. He kept making his payments for eight months, but finally stopped when no one agreed to fix the defects. City Trust and FNEFC sued for the balance due, $42,054.25. Woffard counterclaimed for the return of his $12,349.56 down payment, his monthly payments, and costs for docking and maintenance.

Issue: Can Woffard assert his claims?

Decision: Yes. Judgment affirmed.

Opinion by Justice Dauksch: "The Contract in the present case, entitled 'Marine Security Agreement—Retail Installment Contract' contains the provision set forth in 16 CFR § 433.2:

NOTICE:

Any holder of this consumer credit contract is subject to all claims and defenses which the debtor could assert against the seller of goods or services obtained pursuant hereto or with the proceeds hereof. Recovery hereunder by the debtor shall not exceed amounts paid by the debtor hereunder.

"This provision allows a consumer to set up, against one who finances a purchase, those claims and defenses which could be asserted against the seller of goods. Immediately following that provision is:

NOTICE ABOVE DOES NOT APPLY IF:

a. *The amount financed . . . exceeds $25,000.00. In such case, holder, nevertheless, shall be subject to all defenses which Buyer may have against Seller under this contract pursuant to the applicable State Law since the Notice above is a Federal rule rather than a State rule and does not eliminate defenses under State law.*

or

b. *This Consumer Contract form is used for a boat purchased primarily for commercial or business use. In such case, Buyer agrees not to assert any claim or defense arising out of this sale against Seller as a defense, counterclaim, or setoff to any action by any assignee for the unpaid balance of the total of payments or for possession of the boat.*

"As the amount financed in this consumer transaction exceeds $25,000.00, we look to applicable state law to determine whether appellant is subject to appellee's claims/defenses. Under Section 679.206(1), an agreement by a buyer waiving any claims/defenses against the seller is enforceable by an assignee who takes his assignment for value, in good faith and without notice of any claim/defense. Such an agreement waiving claims/defenses often appears in the form of a waiver of defenses clause in a contract. There is no such clause in this contract. Section 679.206(1) also provides that a buyer who, as part of one transaction, signs both a negotiable instrument and a security agreement makes such an agreement waiving claims/defenses. The contract does not meet the requisites of negotiability and does not appear to be a negotiable instrument. Thus, Section 679.206(1) is inapplicable.

"The contract created a purchase money security interest to be retained by the seller or seller's assignee. Section 679.206(2) provides that 'when a seller retains a purchase money security interest in goods, the chapter on sales (Chapter 672) governs the sale and any disclaimer, limitation, or modification of the seller's warranties.' Before reaching the merits of appellee's counterclaim for breach of warranty, governed by Chapter 672, we must first see if any other state law prevents appellee's assertion of the claim against the assignee. . . .

"An assignee has traditionally been subject to defenses or set-offs existing before an account debtor is notified of the assignments. When the account debtor's defenses on an assigned claim arise from the contract between him and the assignor, it makes no difference whether the breach giving rise to the defense occurs before or after the account debtor is notified of the assignment. The account debtor may also have claims against the assignor which arise independently of that contract: an assignee is subject to all such claims which accrue before, and free of all those which accrue after, the account debtor is notified. The account debtor may waive his right to assert claims or defenses against the assignee to the extent provided in Section 679.206. . . . This is in accord with the general rule in sales transactions that the assignee takes his assignment subject to the purchaser's defenses, set-offs and counterclaims against the seller. . . .

"Just as an assignee is subject to defenses and claims accruing before the obligor receives notification, so a sub-assignee is subject to defenses and claims accruing between the assignee and obligor before the obligor receives notice of the sub-assignment. Defenses and claims arising from the terms of the contract creating the right are available to the obligor regardless of when they accrue....

"Appellee's claim of breach of warranty arose out of the terms of the contract and also accrued before receipt of notification of assignment. Testimony during trial proved that appellee told the seller that he specifically wanted to buy a sailing yacht that he could live aboard full time and also use for pleasure sailing. Appellee told the seller the yacht must be suitable for 'blue water' sailing (i.e., ocean sailing). Thus, if there was a breach of warranty, it arose out of the terms of the contract (as incorporating the sale agreement) and accrued before appellee received notification of assignment, in this case by receipt of the coupon payment books....

"To be effective, a seller's disclaimer of warranties in the sale of consumer goods must be part of the basis of the bargain between the parties.... The evidence indicates that appellee and seller entered into the sales agreement on the premise that the yacht was suitable for appellee's purposes. Circumstances indicate that seller's disclaimer of warranty of fitness for a particular purpose was not made a part of the bargain; to the contrary, seller's warranty of fitness for the particular purpose was an essential factor in the initial agreement between the parties."

business operations can continue. Even individuals—such as inventors and authors—need to be able to assign patents and copyrights for tax, estate, and other purposes. It is also true that there are situations in which performance by a substitute party is necessary or desirable. In all of these situations, the law is concerned with meeting the practical necessities of trade and commerce, while at the same time maintaining the basic terms of the original contract. For this reason, and also because many of these transactions are themselves quite involved, the legal rules for assignments are quite complex.

Modern law also needs to recognize that there are many situations in which promises are made for the benefit of third parties, and rules need to be provided for these cases, too.

Both of these concepts will almost certainly apply to transactions throughout your personal and professional activities.

IMPORTANT TERMS AND CONCEPTS

American rule
Article 9
assignment of contract rights
creditor beneficiary
delegated duty
donee beneficiaries
due on sale clause
English rule
incidental beneficiaries
negotiable instrument
obligee
obligor
public notice
Restatement of Contracts
secured transactions
third-party beneficiary contract
waiver-of-defenses

QUESTIONS AND PROBLEMS FOR DISCUSSION

1. What is an incidental beneficiary?
2. When can contract duties be delegated?
3. When can a debtor not assert defenses to the assigned contract obligation against the assignee of the contract?
4. When does an assignee have recourse against the assignor?
5. Ethel Wido sued Pipeline Oil Corporation and its franchised service station operator on the New York State Thruway, Carl Pump, for failure to provide road services to her husband. Their car developed a flat tire, and a passing state trooper ordered Carl Pump to come to the aid of the stranded motorists. Carl neglected to do so, and after waiting for over 2 hours, Ethel's husband, a stout accountant, tried to change the tire himself. The work exhausted him, so that he collapsed. He died shortly thereafter of a heart attack.

   What is the result, and why?
6. Air Metals was a subcontractor on a construction job for Tompkins-Beckwith Co., and was required to furnish a surety bond guaranteeing its proper performance of the job. American Fire & Casualty issued the bond for Air Metals, but required that Air Metals give them a conditional assignment of all moneys due under the construction contract "in the event of default" by Air Metals. Air Metals did so, but Tompkins-Beckwith was not notified. Air Metals

borrowed money from Boulevard National Bank and gave them an absolute assignment of all moneys due or to become due from Tompkins-Beckwith, who again was not notified. Then Air Metals defaulted on the construction contract. American Fire notified Tompkins-Beckwith of their assignment, and Tompkins-Beckwith agreed to pay them what was owed to Air Metals. Boulevard then notified Tompkins-Beckwith of their assignment, which was actually the "first" in time because the one to American Fire was to take effect only if and when Air Metals went into default. Boulevard lost in the trial court. Boulevard appealed from the judgment for American Fire.

How should the appeal be decided?

7. Plaintiff-appellants Pauline and George Brown appeal from a summary judgment in favor of the three defendants, National Super Markets, Sentry Security Agency, and T. G. Watkins, a security guard employed by Sentry.

   Pauline and George Brown brought a negligence action against the defendants after Pauline was shot and seriously injured by an unknown assailant in National's parking lot. The Browns allege that the defendants have a duty to protect National's patrons both in the store and in the parking lot and that they breached that duty. Defendants denied that they have such a duty and filed a motion for summary judgment. The trial court granted the motion.

   Appellants maintain that summary judgment should not have been granted because as a matter of law their petition properly stated a claim of actionable negligence. The petition claims that in the 2 years prior to Mrs. Brown's assault there were 16 incidents of reported robbery involving a firearm and seven incidents of reported strong-arm robberies as well as 136 other reported crimes on National's premises. Appellants maintain that this known criminal activity and conduct creates special facts and circumstances giving rise to a duty on behalf of the defendants to protect store patrons against assaults.

   Are the Browns correct? Explain.

8. Raymond and Connie Loftus sue for damages to their home, which they were trying to sell. Plaintiffs entered into an exclusive contract with American Realty, under which American Realty was given the exclusive right to offer plaintiff's home for sale. Plaintiffs moved out of the house, and shut off all of the appliances with the exception of the furnace.

   Under the contract, the realty company was to assume the responsibility for performing any tasks necessary for the closing of the transaction, including turning on utilities. An offer was made for plaintiffs' house, which offer was accepted by plaintiffs. Prior to the closing, American Realty hired Fitzpatrick to light the gas water heater. In opening the gas valve to the water heater, Fitzpatrick also opened an uncapped gas line. As a result, the house exploded and burned, resulting in damages totalling $22,500.

   Defendant Fitzpatrick was discharged in bankruptcy prior to trial in this matter.

   Do plaintiffs have a valid claim against American Realty? Explain.

9. When Cathy and Dennis Brown were divorced, Cathy was awarded the use of the family home until she ceased to use it as a principal residence, or she remarried, or their youngest child turned 18. When any of these events happened, the house was to be sold and Dennis was to receive $13,000 of the sale proceeds, plus interest from the date of the decree. The divorce decree also ordered Dennis to pay $37.50 per child per week, until each child turned 18. Three months later, Dennis transferred his interest in the house to Gary and Sheila Smith, for $5,000. The Smiths recorded their deed with the correct government office, and Cathy Brown knew about this transaction. At that time, Dennis was up to date with his child support payments, but he later stopped paying and owed Cathy $19,305.

   When the youngest child turned 18, the Smiths filed a lawsuit, asking the court to determine their rights against the house. Cathy claims that Dennis could not assign his interest in the house, and that even if he could do so, he owes her more than his claim is worth.

   Is she correct? Explain.

CHAPTER 14

Breach, Excuse, and Remedies

Chapter Objectives

This chapter will:

- Explain how contract duties may be excused or discharged.
- Differentiate conditions concurrent, conditions precedent, and conditions subsequent.
- Indicate how a breach by one party may affect the other party's performance obligations.
- Define the various types of new agreements that the parties may use to modify their prior contract.
- Explain how the court's judgment in a contract dispute supersedes all claims under the original contract.
- Discuss alternative remedies for breach of contract.
- Compare the special Uniform Commercial Code rules for goods contracts.

Although the vast majority of contracts are performed according to their terms, many are not. Not all nonperformances will produce liability for breach of contract, however; in some of these cases nonperforming parties will have legal excuses for their failure. These legal excuses, or discharges of liability, can be placed in five general groupings: (1) conditions, (2) breach by other party, (3) discharge by new agreement, (4) discharge by merger, and (5) discharge by operation of law. We now proceed to consider each of these groups.

Conditions

Basic Concepts and Definitions

A **condition** is an act, event, or set of facts to which the parties have attached some special legal significance. The parties have included it in their contract with the intent that its occurrence or nonoccurrence will operate to modify, suspend, or completely discharge a performance duty under the contract. Conditions may be expressly stated or implied from the facts and circumstances.

In terms of how they operate, conditions are classified as precedent, concurrent, and **conditions subsequent**. A **condition precedent** prevents a contract duty from arising until it occurs. If a tailor promises that you will be personally satisfied with your new custom-made suit, and you are not satisfied, you do not have to take the suit and pay for it—no "personal satisfaction" (the condition precedent)—no duty to take the suit. **Concurrent conditions,** which are usually implied by law, operate so that each party's duty to perform is conditioned on the other party's being ready, willing, and able to render the required return performance. The most typical example of concurrent conditions in action is the cash sale transaction, but they also may arise in other contexts, as in the *Pittman* case.

CASE 1

Pittman v. Canham
2 CA App.4th 556 (1992)

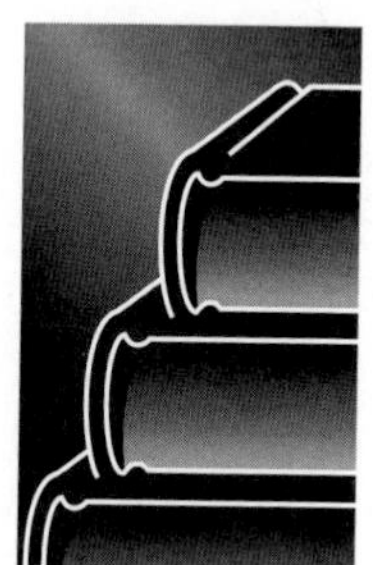

Facts: Jeffrey A. Pittman was a licensed real estate broker. In 1987, he contacted Lily V. Canham, then 85 years old, to purchase a parcel of property she owned in San Luis Obispo County. After many telephone calls to Canham between May and November 1987, she agreed to sell a 56-acre parcel to Pittman for $250,000.

Pittman drafted a contract dated November 24, 1987, and deposited $1,000 in escrow. The contract called for a further deposit of $24,000 in cash, with the balance of the purchase price to be paid by a note secured by a deed of trust on the property. Closing of escrow was to be within 30 days. The contract provided that "[t]ime is of the essence. All modifications or extensions shall be in writing signed by the parties."

The parties executed escrow instructions that provided: "Time is of the essence of these instructions. If this escrow is not in condition to close by the Time Limit Date of December 24, 1987, and written demand for cancellation is received by you from any principal to this escrow after said date, you shall act in accordance with [other provisions of the instructions]. . . . If no demand for cancellation is made, you will proceed to close this escrow when the principals have complied with the escrow instructions." Paragraph 2 of Section 4 of the instructions provided, however, that the instructions were not intended to amend, modify, or supersede the contract.

About the second week of December, Canham gave a signed copy of the escrow instructions to Pittman for delivery to escrow. With the instructions, Canham included a signed deed of the property. The escrow company pointed out, however, that the deed had not been notarized. When Pittman contacted Canham, she told him she would have it notarized at an escrow company near her home.

The December 24 closing date came and went. Canham had not tendered a notarized deed nor had Pittman tendered $24,000, a promissory note, or a deed of trust. By March 1988, Canham had been contacted by another broker who wanted to list the property. On March 21, she told Pittman she wanted $10,000 per acre. Pittman embarked on an effort to find out what a fair price for the property was. In May 1988, Canham told Pittman that she had entered into a contract with other purchasers to buy the property for $600,000. Pittman wrote a letter demanding that she perform on his contract, but she sold the property to the other buyers. Pittman sued Canham for breach of contract. At trial, he attributed the difference in the

$250,000 he offered Canham and the $600,000 sales price 6 months later to an escalating real estate market.

At the end of Pittman's case, the trial court granted Canham's motion for a judgment in her favor.

Issue: Was the contract discharged by non-occurrence of the concurrent conditions?

Decision: Yes. Judgment for Canham affirmed.

Opinion by Judge Gilbert: "When is a contract no longer a contract? When it contains concurrent conditions and neither party tenders timely performance. Unlike love or taxes, concurrent conditions do not last forever.

"We hold that where a contract creates concurrent conditions and neither party tenders timely performance, both parties are discharged. We affirm the judgment. . . .

"Pittman contends the trial court erred in finding he was in default for failing to tender the purchase money note and deed of trust. He concedes that the result reached by the trial court would be proper if his performance had been a condition precedent, but he points out that here the contract provision requiring Canham to deliver a recordable deed into escrow and the provision requiring him to deposit money, a note and a deed of trust are concurrent conditions. Pittman claims that unlike the failure to perform a condition precedent, the failure of both parties to perform concurrent conditions does not automatically terminate the contract, but that one party must tender performance before the other party is in default. . . .

"Concurrent conditions are conditions precedent which are mutually dependent, and the only important difference between a concurrent condition and a condition precedent is that the condition precedent must be performed before another duty arises, whereas a tender of performance is sufficient in the case of a concurrent condition. . . .

"Contrary to Pittman's assertion, the failure of both parties to perform concurrent conditions does not leave the contract open for an indefinite period so that either party can tender performance at his leisure. The failure of both parties to perform concurrent conditions during the time for performance results in a discharge of both parties' duty to perform. Thus, where the parties have made time the essence of the contract, at the expiration of time without tender by either party, both parties are discharged. . . . Here, because time was made the essence of the contract, the failure of both parties to tender performance by December 24, 1987, discharged both from performing. Neither party can hold the other in default and no cause of action to enforce the contract arises. . . .

"Pittman relies on the portion of the escrow instructions that states: 'Time is of the essence of these instructions. . . . If this escrow is not in condition to close by the Time Limit Date of December 24, 1987, and . . . [i]f no demand for cancellation is made, you will proceed to close this escrow when the principals have complied with the escrow instructions.' He claims this provision shows that time was not truly of the essence in this transaction.

"But it is difficult to see how a paragraph that begins with the words '[t]ime is of the essence' could reasonably be construed as meaning time is not truly of the essence. The provision relied on by Pittman merely instructs the escrow holder not to cancel escrow on its own initiative, but to close escrow should the parties voluntarily and notwithstanding discharge mutually decide to perform. As we read the paragraph, it does not purport to give a party the unilateral right to demand performance after the time for performance has passed. Such a construction would render meaningless the parties' agreement that time is of the essence.

"We appreciate the reluctance of a buyer to act first by placing money into escrow. But in a contract with concurrent conditions, the buyer and seller cannot keep saying to one another, 'No, you first.' Ultimately, in such a case, the buyer seeking enforcement comes in second; he loses."

Conditions Subsequent Discharge or Excuse an Existing Duty of Performance. An automobile liability insurance policy, for example, may provide that the insurance company's duty to defend liability claims under the policy is excused when the insured admits liability for the accident. Or a property insurance policy may specify that coverage lapses when a structure is unoccupied for more than a certain period of time. Whether a condition exists or has occurred is generally a question of fact, to be proved like any other.

Conditions of Approval or Satisfaction. Especially in large construction contracts, the parties may specify that a third party's approval is required before the final payment has to be made. In construction, this third party is typically the architect who drew the plans and specifications for the job. Until the builder can convince the architect that the job conforms to the plans, the landowner/customer does not have to make the final payment on the contract price. When the architect is withholding approval in bad faith, or as part of a fraudulent scheme against the builder, most courts would probably hold this condition to have been satisfied and require the landowner/customer to pay the balance due.

In some contracts, personal satisfaction of the buyer/customer is guaranteed: The parties' intent is that if they are not satisfied, they are not bound to pay the contract price. In trying to determine whether or not such a condition has been met, so that the seller can collect the contract price, the courts use two different tests: an individualized, or subjective, test and a reasonable person, or objective, test. The individualized test requires that the particular buyer be satisfied before payment is due, whereas the objective test says that if a reasonable person would be satisfied with the performance offered by the seller, the buyer must pay.

When the contract is for an item involving personal taste, such as a custom-tailored suit, a portrait, or a statue, personal satisfaction probably means just that: no deal unless the individual buyer indicates that he or she is satisfied. When the contract involves an item of everyday mechanical utility, such as a furnace, personal satisfaction is probably a jury question under the reasonable person test: Either the furnace is working properly, or it is not; if it is, the buyer ought to be satisfied with it.

Besides the nature of the item, the other main factor considered by the courts in determining which test to use is what happens to the item if the satisfaction condition is not met. The suit, portrait, or sculpture stays with the seller; there is no unjust enrichment of the buyer, though the seller may be stuck with an unmarketable item. With something like an aluminum siding job, however, the situation is quite different. Because it is somewhat uneconomical to remove aluminum siding from a house, the courts would almost certainly apply the reasonable person test to the job.

Timely Performance as a Condition Precedent. What happens when one party is late in performing or offering to perform contract obligations? Any provable damages resulting from the delay in performance should be collectible without question. The real question, however, is whether or not the other party can refuse to accept the offered late performance and use the failure to perform on time as a basis for rescinding the whole contract. Courts generally consider this problem in terms of whether or not "time is of the essence," meaning that the parties have either expressly or impliedly made timely performance a condition precedent.

In a few early cases, time was presumed to be of the essence in a sale of goods, but this does not seem to be the general rule, and it is clearly not the rule for real estate or construction contracts. When the parties have not clearly specified in the contract that time is of the essence, the court must determine, as a question of fact, whether or not such a condition precedent should be implied.

Doctrine of Substantial Performance

Courts are reluctant to excuse a party's contractual obligations completely just because the other party has committed a relatively minor breach. Although many cases involve the simple, one-shot performances completed exactly in accordance with the contract terms, many other cases, such as construction contracts, deal with more complex performances that extend over a considerable period of time. In construction contracts, jobs are rarely completed exactly in accordance with the agreed plans and specifications. Should minor deviations by the builder permit the buyer to rescind the whole contract?

The courts have answered this question in the negative, by applying the doctrine of **substantial performance.** What this doctrine says is that if the builder has acted in good faith and has done the job in substantial compliance with the contract, the builder can enforce the contract and collect the contract price. Any damages that result from any noncompliance, no matter how trivial, can be collected by the buyer or deducted from the amount of the contractor's recovery. Perfection is not required. The buyer of a new house would not be able to rescind the contract just because the kitchen was painted green instead of blue, but that buyer could force the builder to repaint or deduct the price of the paint job from the contract price if the builder refused.

The doctrine of substantial performance will not be applied when the builder has intentionally substituted inferior materials or used other production shortcuts in a fraudulent attempt to make extra money. Nor will it be applied when the builder has only partially, rather than substantially, performed. In such cases buyers can rescind the whole contract. If the partially built structure has been placed on land already owned by the buyers, they are probably liable in quasi-contract for the fair market value of the labor and materials, but even in this case they can probably deduct any provable damages they have sustained (see Exhibit 14-1).

Exhibit 14.1: Excuses for Nonperformance

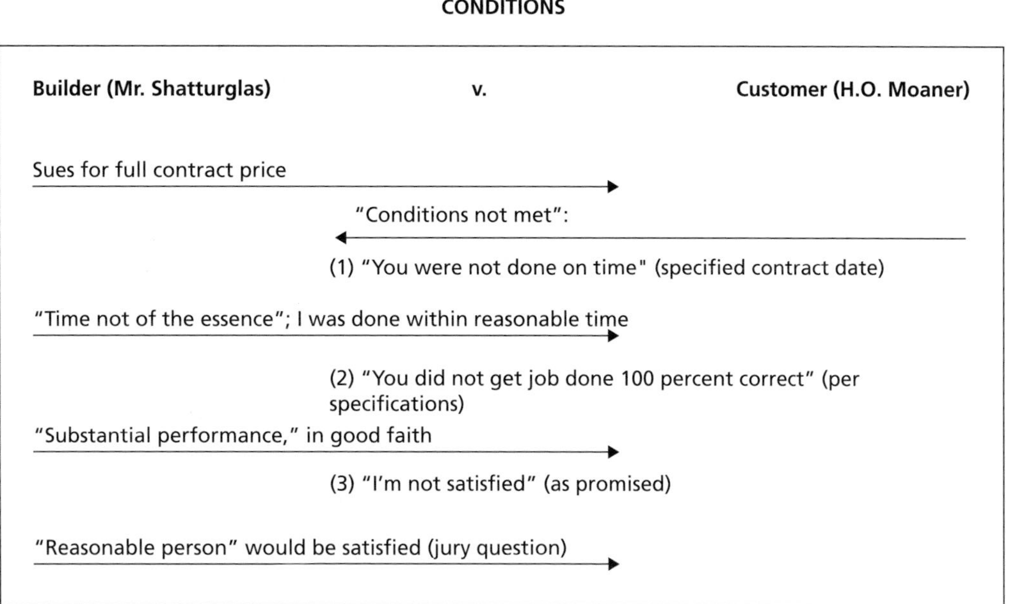

CONDITIONS
Builder (Mr. Shatturglas)
v.
Customer (H.O. Moaner)
Sues for full contract price
"Conditions not met":
(1) "You were not done on time" (specified contract date)
"Time not of the essence"; I was done within reasonable time
(2) "You did not get job done 100 percent correct" (per specifications)
"Substantial performance," in good faith
(3) "I'm not satisfied" (as promised)
"Reasonable person" would be satisfied (jury question)

Breach by Other Party

In General

When the plaintiff brings an action for breach of contract, a possible response by the defendant is the argument "You breached first." That is, the defendant argues that his or her own nonperformance was not a breach because the plaintiff's prior nonperformance justified the defendant's refusal to perform. Although in some cases the courts have treated the reciprocal performances as "independent," they generally accept this argument as a sufficient excuse when the prior breach by the plaintiff was a material one. It would, generally, be unfair to require the defendant to perform or hold the defendant liable for not performing if he or she has not received what the plaintiff promised in return. However, it would be equally unfair for the defendant to repudiate the whole contract and completely refuse to perform if the plaintiff has committed only a minor, relatively insignificant breach.

Breach of Installment Contract

It is even more difficult to work out a fair result when the contract calls for a series of performances by one or both parties, rather than a single exchange. What should be the measure of recovery when a party partially performs and then fails to deliver one or more of the installments still due?

The courts usually try to solve this problem by first determining whether the contract is divisible or indivisible. If the contract is held to be divisible into a series of pro rata exchanges, the court will usually permit the breaching party to recover the agreed reciprocal performance, less any damages the breach has caused to the other party. An employee who quits after having worked for 3 months under a 1-year contract would usually be able to collect the agreed contract salary for the 3 months worked, less any damages the employer sustains as a result of the breach. If the contract is held to be indivisible, or "entire," a party guilty of a material breach should collect only the fair market value of any benefits retained by the other party, less damages caused by the breach.

Anticipatory Repudiation

An **anticipatory repudiation** occurs when one party, by words or conduct, indicates unwillingness or inability to perform contract duties when the time for performance arrives. In other words, the party announces in advance that he or she is not going to perform as scheduled. In nearly all cases the courts treat such an unequivocal repudiation of the contract as a present breach, giving the injured party the right to make other arrangements immediately and sue for any damages caused, if in fact performance does not occur. The courts do not apply this rule to promises to pay money at a future date; a present statement of intention not to pay a future debt normally does not accelerate the due date of the debt unless there is a special provision to that effect. The courts also normally permit a party to retract a repudiation, provided the retraction is made before the other party has substantially changed legal position because of the repudiation.

Adequate Assurance

For the sale of goods, the Uniform Commercial Code's (UCC) rules for dealing with breach and repudiation problems are substantially the same as the common law principles discussed previously. The code does, however, give the injured party one very important new protection: the right to demand **adequate assurance** (2-609).

A breach by one of the parties to a goods contract may not be material enough in itself to justify rescission of the whole contract; for example, a 2- or 3-day delay in delivery of 1 month's shipment of goods on an installment contract. Still, such a breach may create a doubt in the mind of the other party as to whether or not the breaching party will be able and willing to continue to perform. The same is true when one party has repudiated and then retracted: Does this person mean it or not? When will this person do the same thing again?

A party who has reasonable grounds for feeling "insecure" may make a written demand that the other party furnish "adequate assurance of due performance." So long as the insecure party is being commercially reasonable, any performance for which the agreed return has not already been received may be withheld until receipt of such adequate assurance. When a proper demand for assurance has been made, the other party's failure to respond within a reasonable time (not over 30 days) is treated as a repudiation of the contract. At that point, the party who made the demand can go ahead and make other arrangements, without being guilty of a breach, and can sue for any damages sustained because of the other party's repudiation.

Buyer's Acceptance of Goods

Under the UCC, acceptance of the goods occurs when, having had a reasonable opportunity to inspect them, the buyer indicates that they do conform to the contract or that they are acceptable despite some nonconformity, or when the buyer simply fails to effectively reject them. Any act by the buyer that is inconsistent with the seller's ownership of the goods is likewise an acceptance, but if the act is wrongful as against the seller, it is an acceptance only if it is ratified by the seller. "Acceptance of a part of any commercial unit is acceptance of that entire unit."

Once the buyer has accepted the goods, they must be paid for at the contract rate. Further, the burden is now on the buyer to prove any alleged breach with respect to the accepted goods. The buyer must also prove that the seller was notified of the breach within a reasonable time after the buyer discovered it or should have discovered it. If the buyer has accepted the goods, it follows logically that they can no longer be rejected. Nor can an acceptance be revoked when the buyer knew of the nonconformity at the time of acceptance, unless the buyer accepted with the reasonable assumption that the nonconformity would be cured. Except for the foregoing provisions, acceptance does not prevent the buyer from pursuing any other remedy provided for nonconformity of the goods.

The buyer may revoke or withdraw an acceptance of any lot or commercial unit that is subsequently discovered to have a substantial nonconformity if the defect could not reasonably have been discovered before acceptance, or if the buyer was induced to accept the goods by the seller's assurance that a known defect would be cured, and the seller has not seasonably cured the defect. The buyer must revoke the acceptance within a reasonable time after he or she discovers, or should have discovered, the defect "and before any substantial change in condition of the goods which is not caused by their own defects" (2-608[2]). The buyer, after having notified the seller of such a proper revocation, has the same rights against the goods as if they had been rejected initially.

Buyer's Rejection of Goods

A buyer wishing to reject goods because of their nonconformity must do so within a reasonable time after delivery or tender and must "seasonably" notify the seller of the rejection. Once the buyer has rejected the goods, any exercise of ownership over them by the buyer is wrongful as against the seller. The buyer, unless entitled to retain possession under 2-711(3), is required to take reasonable care of the seller's rejected goods until the seller has had a reasonable chance to remove them. When the buyer is a merchant and the seller does not have an agent or a place of business nearby, the buyer must follow the seller's reasonable instructions with respect to the disposition of the rejected goods. If the goods are perishable or otherwise subject to a rapid decline in value, the buyer must make reasonable efforts to resell them even if the seller has not sent instructions. Under those circumstances, it would not be fair or reasonable to permit the buyer to watch the goods spoil without making some effort to salvage them.

Seller's Right to "Cure" Defects

UCC 2-508 gives the seller a "second chance" in two situations when the buyer rejects a delivery or tender of goods because of their nonconformity to the terms of the contract. If the contract time for performance has not yet expired, the seller can seasonably notify the buyer of its intent to cure the nonconformity, and then make a conforming delivery within the contract time. For example, if the buyer rejected a tender of 500 units because the contract called for 700 units, the seller could notify the buyer that it would deliver the full 700, and then do so within the contract period. The buyer would be required to take the second shipment of 700 units.

When the buyer rejects goods the seller had reasonable grounds to believe would be acceptable, the seller is allowed a reasonable time after the contract date to substitute a conforming delivery. The purpose of this rule is to avoid unfair, "surprise" rejections, for technical reasons, in which the goods are substantially conforming and would usually be accepted in the trade or business involved. As several cases have pointed out, however, the seller's right to cure is not unlimited. The seller must be acting honestly and reasonably, not trying to knowingly pass off inferior goods or to force the buyer into an acceptance.

The *Chancellor* case discusses these sale-of-goods performance rules.

CASE 2

Chancellor Development Company v. Brand v. Jacob Mobile Homes, Inc.

896 S.W.2d 672 (MO App. 1995)

Facts: Third-party plaintiffs, Louis and Debra Brand (hereinafter plaintiffs) brought this action against third-party defendant, Jacob Mobile Homes, Inc. (Jacob) in two counts seeking damages for breach of contract and negligence in the sale and delivery of a mobile home. The trial court granted Jacob's motion for summary judgment on both counts. Plaintiffs appealed, asserting that genuine issues of material fact precluded summary judgment.

In count one of their third-party petition, plaintiffs alleged that they had entered into a contract with Jacob to purchase a mobile home, that the mobile home was delivered in a nonconforming and damaged condition, and that plaintiffs notified Jacob of the nonconformity, rejected delivery, and tendered the home back to Jacob. As damages for this breach of contract, they sought return of their down payment, sales tax, and interest payments and reimbursement for installation and other expenses in the total amount of $13,000. In count two, plaintiffs reincorporated the allegations relating to their contract with Jacob and further alleged that Jacob or its agents negligently delivered the mobile home before the slab and driveway were prepared, resulting in damage to the mobile home.

Jacob denied the allegations and moved for summary judgment. As one of its grounds, it stated that it had repaired the damage to the home and that plaintiffs had accepted those repairs and their acceptance constituted full accord and satisfaction. In support of its motion, Jacob filed affidavits and exhibits.

Plaintiffs filed a memorandum in opposition supported by affidavits of the two plaintiffs and the subsequent purchaser of their mobile home. They assert that summary judgment was improper because substantial fact questions remained. The trial court granted the motion.

Issue: Did the Brands properly revoke their acceptance of the goods?

Decision: No. Judgment affirmed.

Opinion by Judge Crane: "Plaintiffs contend that in count one they stated a claim for relief for breach of contract based on a delivery of nonconforming goods, In response to Jacob's claim that plaintiffs accepted the mobile home after it was repaired, plaintiffs assert they accepted the mobile home under the reasonable assumption that the defects would be cured and that they revoked their acceptance under S.400.2-608 when the defects were not seasonably cured. . . .

"However, S.400.2-606(1)(c) RSMo 1994 provides that any act by a buyer inconsistent with seller's ownership will constitute acceptance of goods. Accordingly, if, after proper rejection, a buyer uses goods in a manner inconsistent with the seller's ownership that use nullifies the rescission and constitutes an acceptance of the goods. . . . Once a buyer accepts a tender, the seller acquires a right to its price on the contract terms. . . . A buyer's actions which are inconsistent with seller's ownership are 'many and varied' and include 'making payments, taking possession of the goods, use of the goods, repairing, working on them, attempts to resell them, and dealing with them in other varied ways.' . . . Thus a buyer's acts of pricing, displaying, advertising, and selling goods after giving notice or revocation were inconsistent with seller's ownership and constituted acceptance. . . .

"A buyer's revocation of acceptance under the Uniform Commercial Code (UCC) is necessarily the buyer's recognition that the property as to which acceptance is revoked belongs to the seller. . . . A buyer's act of dominion over goods, including sale of the goods, is inconsistent with a buyer's claim of revocation of acceptance. . . .

"In support of its motion for summary judgment, Jacob filed the affidavit of Jacob's treasurer, Randy Clark. Clark recited that plaintiffs had purchased a mobile home from Jacob pursuant to a Delivery Agreement and Contract on November 27, 1990. He asserted that on February 27, 1991, plaintiff Louis Brand asked him if Jacob would resell his home. Clark further averred: 'Defendant's Exhibit 10 is the original Contract signed by Louis Brand and me reflecting the agreement of Jacob Mobile Homes, Inc, to resell the home,' He also attached the contract dated February 27, 1991 to his affidavit. This agreement was written on a preprinted purchase agreement form. However, except for the mobile home description, Brand's name and address and the signatures of Clark and Louis Brand, the preprinted form provisions were not filled in or marked. Instead, the agreement contained the following handwritten provision: 'Jacob MH agrees to move home into our sales lot and attempt to sell it. Seller, Lou Brand, agrees to pay for the move and to make payments on home until sold. Jacob MH will collect sales commission from buyer of home.' Jacob also filed the affidavit of a repairman it had hired who stated that on January 4, 1991, he had made the repairs the Brands had requested.

"In their affidavits in opposition to the motion, plaintiffs described the damages and attested that they had notified Jacob of the damage and gave it an opportunity to repair and Jacob failed to do so. They averred that on February 27, 1991, plaintiff Louis Brand told Clark that they wanted to return the home and told Jacob the deficiencies with the home. However, neither plaintiff denied the existence or the contents of the February 27 agreement or that Louis Brand had signed it. In fact, they did not mention this agreement in their affidavits. Plaintiffs acknowledged that the trailer was subsequently moved to Jacob's premises at plaintiffs' expense.

"We view the record in the light most favorable to plaintiffs and therefore assume that: (1) there was damage to the home, (2) plaintiffs notified Jacob of the damage, (3) Jacob did not repair all of the damage, and (4) plaintiffs asked to return the trailer. However, Jacob is still entitled to summary judgment on the grounds of acceptance because 'any' act inconsistent with revocation of acceptance is enough to constitute acceptance under S.400.2-606(1)(c). It was undisputed that plaintiff Louis Brand signed an agreement in which Jacob agreed to move the home onto its lot and to attempt to sell it and in which plaintiff agreed to pay to move the home onto Jacob's lot and agreed to make payments on the home until it was sold. In so doing, plaintiff Brand acted as an owner desiring to sell property with the help of a broker. Louis Brand's action is consistent with ownership and inconsistent with plaintiffs' claim that plaintiffs revoked acceptance. Under S.400.2-606(1)(c) this act, which is inconsistent with seller's ownership, constitutes acceptance. . . .

"The trial court's judgment is affirmed."

Discharge by New Agreement

The parties themselves created their reciprocal rights and duties by making the agreement. It is their contract, and unless the rights of third parties are involved in some way, the parties can call off their agreement any time they both wish to do so, or they can substitute a new arrangement for the old one. There are many technical terms to describe the different types of new agreements, but they all come down to the same basic argument: "My nonperformance under the original contract was excused because we made a new deal." We now consider the main types of "new deals."

Mutual Rescission

As a rule, the parties can call off their existing contract any time they wish, as long as they both agree to do so. This case is called a **mutual rescission,** to distinguish it from the case in which the remedy of rescission is given to one party because of a material breach by the other. If the parties have mutually agreed to a rescission, neither can later claim that the other's nonperformance of the contract was a breach.

When partial performance has already occurred, the mutual rescission agreement should provide for part payment or restitution. If there is no such provision in the rescission agreement, any retained benefits would almost certainly have to be paid for at fair market value.

Novation

Although the derivation and common sense meaning of the term ***novation*** would seem to apply to any new agreement that the parties intend to substitute for their existing contract, the courts generally apply the term only to those new arrangements that involve a substitution of parties. That is, a new debtor is substituted for the original debtor, with the consent of the creditor, or the obligation is assigned to a new creditor for whom the debtor agrees to perform.

If, in the take-over-the-payments example used in the last chapter, the mortgagee/creditor agrees to accept the resale buyer as the sole obligor and to discharge the original mortgage/debtor, there has been a novation. Whether the new agreement is called a novation or simply a new contract, it must itself be a valid contract to have the effect of discharging the original one (see Exhibit 14-2).

Accord and Satisfaction

This term is usually applied to a situation in which the obligee/creditor has agreed to accept a substituted performance, in place of the original one. For example, Dan Debtor owes Carl Creditor $1,000. Dan does not have the cash, but he does own a used car, which he offers to convey to Carl in lieu of the $1,000. Carl, of course, does not have to take the car; he can sue Dan for the $1,000 if it is not paid when due. If Carl does agree to take the car, there is an accord. At that point, the $1,000 debt is not yet discharged; if Carl does not get the car, he can sue Dan either for $1,000 or for breach of the accord. When Dan delivers the car as agreed, however, the $1,000 debt has been discharged by an **accord and satisfaction.**

Unfortunately, from the standpoint of clarity, courts also use the term *accord and satisfaction* to refer to situations involving part payment of a debt, especially when the debt is in dispute. (See our earlier discussion of this problem in Chapter 9.) The creditor's cashing of the "in full" check is that person's agreement to the accord and satisfaction and acceptance of the substituted performance thereunder.

Waiver or Estoppel

A **waiver** is the intentional surrender of a known right or benefit; a person simply chooses not to demand that something that is due be given. Your apartment lease, for example, specifies that the rent must be paid in advance on the 1st of each month, but the landlord tells you that payment can be made by the 10th; this is a waiver of the right to insist on payment by the 1st. Ordinarily, this kind of waiver "before breach" can be retracted by proper notice to the other party, unless consideration was given for the waiver or unless the other party has made a substantial change of position in reliance on the waiver. Contrariwise, courts usually hold that a waiver of the right to sue for a breach that has already occurred does not require any new consideration to be binding. (See UCC 1-107, previously referred to in Chapter 9.) A waiver may also be inferred from a party's conduct.

Release

A **release** also involves the giving up of some right, but it is based on a written contract. Releases are commonly used in situations in which there is a contingent or disputed liability, as in auto accident cases or in employment termination agreements. The law generally favors compromises and settlements of disputes, particularly in light of the tremendous backlog of civil litigation that is clogging the courts. Traditionally, therefore, courts have been reluctant to permit parties to avoid the effect of a release they have previously given unless there is very strong evidence of fraud, undue influence, mistake, or other defense.

Exhibit 14.2: Excuses for Nonperformance

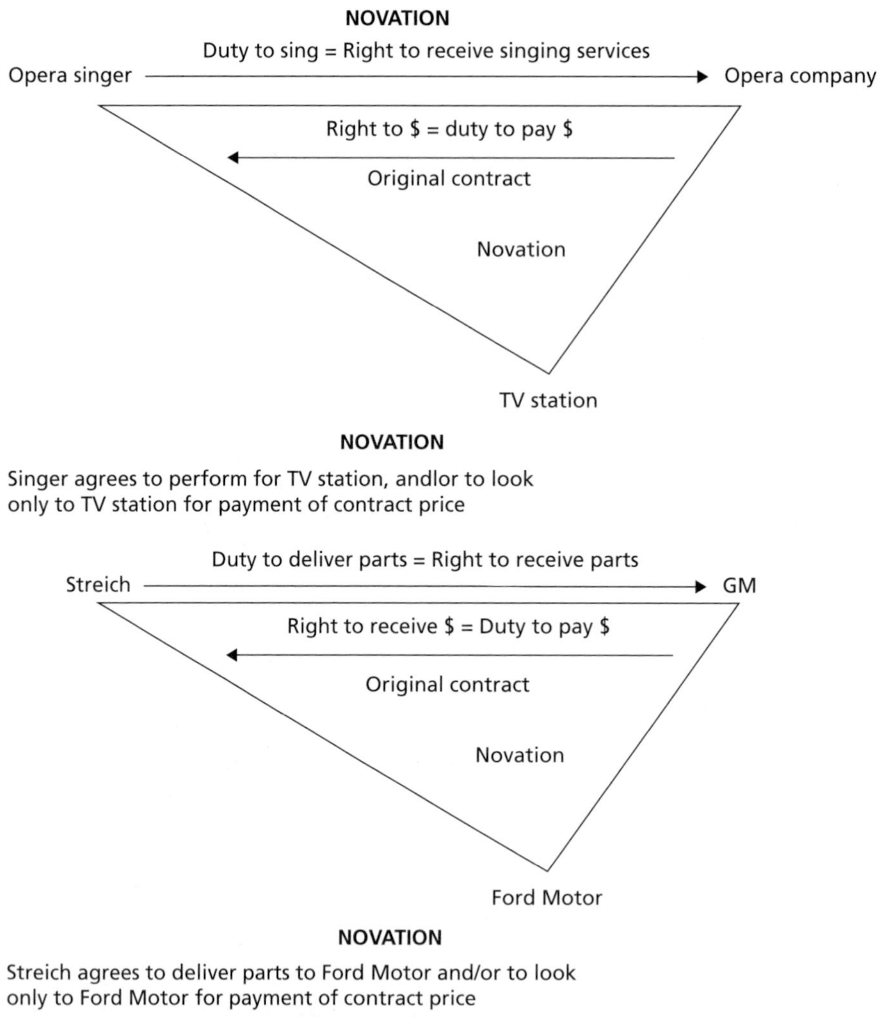
NOVATION
Duty to sing = Right to receive singing services
Opera singer
Opera company
Right to $ = duty to pay $
Original contract
Novation
TV station
NOVATION
Singer agrees to perform for TV station, andlor to look only to TV station for payment of contract price
Duty to deliver parts = Right to receive parts
Streich
GM
Right to receive $ = Duty to pay $
Original contract
Novation
Ford Motor
NOVATION
Streich agrees to deliver parts to Ford Motor and/or to look only to Ford Motor for payment of contract price

Although courts today are more and more willing to stretch a point in favor of the "little guy," the *Stetzel* case (see Problem 6) shows that they will still look for some evidence to support the claimed defense against the effect of a release.

Account Stated

The **account stated** is based on the same fundamental principle as accord and satisfaction: The law favors settlements. When, after a series of transactions between them, the parties have agreed on a final statement of the net amount due, there is an account stated. No further reliance can be placed on the earlier transactions; the amount that is now due and owing is that agreed to in the account stated. An account stated can arise when the creditor sends a summary statement of the account and the debtor retains the statement without objection beyond a reasonable time. In other words, the agreement to the account stated can be implied as well as expressed.

Discharge by Merger

In General

As used here, the doctrine of **merger** means that the prior obligation has been superseded by a "better" one, better in the sense of being easier to prove, to transfer, or to collect.

Merger may be effected by a new agreement between the parties or by **judgment.** The three most common examples of such better legal obligations (other than a judgment) are the sealed contract, the negotiable instrument, and the secured debt. Because many states have abolished by statute the common law effect of the seal on the presumption of consideration, there would be no merger effect in those states, if a sealed contract were given in satisfaction of an unsealed one. In a state where the seal makes the contract easier to prove in court, or (perhaps) even if the seal only has the effect of keeping the debt alive for a longer time, the acceptance of a sealed contract by the creditor in place of the unsealed one should have the merger effect.

A negotiable instrument is clearly a much better form of legal obligation than an ordinary "open-book account." For example, you owe your dentist, Dr. Paul Pullit, $300 for services rendered. If he sues to collect, he will have to produce office records, witnesses, and so forth, to prove that he in fact gave you this consideration and that you agreed to pay for it at his prices. Such a collection suit would involve substantial disruption of his regular office routine and a loss of time and money, even though he would ultimately win. If he accepts your offer of a 90-day negotiable promissory note for $250 as satisfaction of the account, he could in fact be net dollars ahead even if he is forced to sue on the note because the note carries a presumption of consideration that *you* would have to overcome with evidence. Because of this fact, the note is much more readily transferable than the account. If your dentist does not want to wait the 90 days and collect the interest, he or she will have a much easier time selling your note to a bank than he or she would have in assigning your account.

Finally, if the debt is made more certain of collection because the debtor gives the creditor a mortgage or other security interest against a specific piece of the debtor's property, that is clearly a better deal for the creditor. If your dentist agrees to take your new contract promise to pay $250, secured by your used car as collateral, in satisfaction of the $300 open-book amount, there has been a merger and the old account debt is discharged.

Judgment

The doctrine of **res judicata** says that once "the thing has been adjudicated," it cannot be relitigated. Whatever rights and duties may have been alleged as the result of the prior legal relationship have been superseded by the court's final judgment; the prior obligations have been merged into the judgment.

There is an important distinction between a **joint obligation,** in which all debtors must be sued at the same time if they are to be held liable, and a **joint and several obligation,** in which the creditor may get a judgment against one or more of the debtors and still retain the right to sue the others. The same result would follow if the creditor released one joint debtor; such action releases the entire debt against all the joint debtors.

Discharge by Operation of Law

Statute of Limitations

At least in most states, debts do not last forever. At some point, it becomes rather unfair for an alleged creditor to revive ancient history and begin a litigation over a matter that should have been long forgotten (and probably has been by nearly everyone else). Again, the law encourages the parties to settle their disputes and requires them to commence any necessary litigation before memories fade completely. At some point, if no action has been taken to enforce an alleged obligation, it is good public policy to declare that the debtor has a defense if that person does not wish to pay the ancient debt. This **statute of limitations** defense is a technical one, and it is not particularly favored by the courts, but where it does apply, it is a complete defense against a lawsuit based on the old debt or breach of contract claim. In most states, the limitations period for tort actions is considerably shorter than the one for contracts.

Bankruptcy; Composition with Creditors

A discharge in a bankruptcy proceeding also operates as a technical defense in favor of the debtor, as to all debts and claims provable under bankruptcy rules. This same result occurs whether the debtor has filed a "voluntary" petition with the bankruptcy court or has been forced into an "involuntary" bankruptcy by one or more creditors. Like the statute of limitations, a **bankruptcy discharge** is a technical defense that can be waived by the debtor when that person makes a new promise after bankruptcy to pay the old debt. When the debtor is a consumer, there are strict rules for such "new promises," as discussed in the bankruptcy chapter.

To avoid the administrative costs and (some of) the legal expenses incident to a bankruptcy proceeding, a person's creditors may, as a group, voluntarily agree to accept less than full payment in full satisfaction of their debts. A creditor cannot be forced to make such an agreement but may wish to do so to receive payment for a higher percentage of the claim paid than if the debtor were forced through bankruptcy. Such a **composition with creditors** operates like an accord and satisfaction.

The "subsequent illegality" and "impossibility" arguments discussed in Chapter 12 also fall in this fifth category.

General Principles for Remedies

A rational decision to litigate a claim must be based on economic, psychological, and legal factors. In many cases, a party can be a legal winner (that is, get a favorable judgment) and still be an economic loser, by not being compensated for all economic losses, to say nothing of the psychological strains endured during the litigation process. The potential litigant faces the distinct possibility of not recovering all out-of-pocket expenses for court costs and attorney fees. In addition, the person's "downtime" during litigation is not compensable; that is, the plaintiff may collect "lost revenue" resulting from a breach of contract but will not collect "lost revenue" resulting from having to be in court. Also, any mental stress resulting from the pressures of the litigation process is not compensable.

Court Costs and Attorney Fees

Court costs, which include filing fees, jury fees, witness fees, and transcripts, are usually assessed against the losing party. When a public question is involved, however, the court may decide to let the taxpayers, rather than one of the parties, bear the costs of the litigation. The trial judge generally has great discretion in determining which items of costs were really necessary to the litigation and should, therefore, be paid by the loser.

Almost alone among the legal systems of the civilized world, the common law system did not permit victorious litigants to recover their lawyers' charges as part of court costs. In large part, this rule resulted because each lawyer-client contract was created through a private agreement, with no official fee schedule limiting the amount that could be charged. Because there was no general court control over legal fees, it was felt that the court could not properly charge them against the losing party. Attorney fees are still not generally included as court costs. To assess them against the losing party, there must be a specific provision to that effect in the contract of the parties or in a statute covering the kind of claim being litigated.

All of these factors should be very carefully considered by anyone contemplating litigation. Even if you win legally, you may still lose financially.

Election of Remedies

The strict application of logical principles does not always produce justice in particular cases, and the early common law always tried to be logical. Common law rules of pleading, for example, required a plaintiff who had two alternative remedies for an alleged breach of contract to choose between them if they were "inconsistent." The two most clearly inconsistent remedies are specific performance and rescission and restitution. In the first, the plaintiff insists that the contract be performed as agreed, in the second, the plaintiff wants to call off the whole deal and put everything back where it was.

The plaintiff's main difficulty under these early rules was that the choice had to be made when the complaint was filed; that is, at a time when the plaintiff did not yet know whether or not a case for restitution could be proved. A court might find that the plaintiff had waited too long to rescind, for example, and deny the restitution remedy. But if the plaintiff then tried to sue for damages in a second case, the early civil procedure rules would prohibit the suit because a binding **"election of remedies"** had been made when the first lawsuit was filed. As a result, some plaintiffs received no remedy at all, just because they (or their lawyers) had guessed wrong initially.

Some of the injustice inherent in these rules has been removed by the adoption of civil procedure rules that permit the plaintiff to file a complaint asking for such inconsistent remedies in the alternative ("I want *either* rescission and restitution *or* damages"). Such alternative pleading is possible in a majority of states and in the U.S. District Courts. Even with this liberalization, however, the plaintiff must still make an election of remedies at some point in the litigation. Such an election might mean deciding whether or not to keep the house with the leaky basement and get damages for the wet furniture and for fixing the leak, or to ask for the money back and a rescission of the house deal. If rescission is granted, no dollar damages for the wet furniture will be awarded. Because of the potential harshness of these election rules, it becomes important to know which remedies are inconsistent and thus require an election.

The best possible rule for the plaintiff is found in the UCC rules for the sale of goods, which do not require the plaintiff to make any election at all. Buyers of goods who prove their case for rescission can get their money back and also can collect all provable damages that they have sustained while the goods were in their possession.

Damages

Underlying Factors

In determining the amount of damages that a plaintiff can collect for a breach of contract, the court will subject the claimed damages to four tests: **causation, certainty, foreseeability,** and **mitigation.** To be collectible, compensatory damages must meet each of these tests.

First, the plaintiff must prove that the alleged damages were caused by the breach and not by something else. Lost profits that result when a supplier fails to deliver may be recoverable, but if the plaintiff's lower sales are due to a general economic downturn, the breaching seller should not be liable because his or her breach did not cause the "injury."

Second, the plaintiff must be able to prove the amount of damages with *reasonable* certainty. Damages for lost profits and for mental stress are difficult to collect, in part, for this reason. Courts are reluctant to permit jury speculation and sympathy to substitute for solid evidence of amount of injury.

A third significant limitation on the amount of damages awarded is that the damages sustained must have been reasonably foreseeable at the time the contract was made. That is, a party is not held legally responsible for damages that result from a breach of contract unless the party ought to have known that damages of that sort would result from the nonperformance. Damages for lost profits that result from a "shut down the plant" situation are especially difficult to collect because of the application of this foreseeability principle. Obviously, your safeguard here is to make sure that your suppliers and contractors are fully informed as to your requirements and of the consequences of their failure to perform.

Finally, it is only common sense to require the injured party to take reasonable steps to mitigate, or hold down, losses. Even though one party has breached, it would not be fair to that party to allow the other party to simply sit back and watch the damages mount up, without making any effort to get an alternative performance from someone else. The law, therefore, generally requires injured parties to make reasonable efforts to mitigate their damages. If a car manufacturer did not get an expected shipment of needed parts from a supplier, the car maker would have to try to buy them from another source. The car maker could not just close the plant when they used up their existing inventory of the part, without making reasonable efforts to get more somewhere else.

Because a lease of real estate is a conveyance of an interest in the land as well as a contract, courts at one time did not apply the mitigation rule to landlords. Landlords could simply sue for the agreed rental price whether the tenant was using the premises or not. There is now a growing trend toward removing this exception, thereby forcing the landlord to mitigate by rerenting the premises before collecting damages against a tenant who has moved out prior to the expiration of the lease.

Compensatory Damages

The basic purpose of the damages remedy is to compensate the injured party for the loss sustained by the other party's breach; that is, to put the injured party, so far as possible, in the place he or she would have been if the contract had been properly and fully performed. The measure of **compensatory damages** is the difference between the performance promised and the performance given; thus general compensatory damages are sometimes called **difference-money damages.** For example, if a used car is represented to be in "A-1 shape," and it is not, compensatory damages would give the buyer the amount of money necessary to put the car into "A-1 shape."

Special compensatory damages, or **consequential damages**, are awarded for losses that are further down in the chain of causation, losses over and above the difference-money losses that are caused by the breach. For example, if the buyer of the aforementioned used car had to take a cab to work twice because the car would not start, special compensatory damages should be given to cover the cab fare. Again, there may be questions here of causation and of foreseeability.

Nominal Damages and Punitive Damages

When there has been a breach of contract, but the injured party is unable to show any actual losses as a result, the plaintiff will be awarded **nominal damages** (almost always $1) and court costs, provided the case is proved. Obviously, most such cases will not be litigated. But nominal damages play an important part in a case that contains the right combination of facts for **punitive damages** to be awarded. Once the injured party proves a case for breach of contract, an award of punitive damages can be added on, to punish the defendant who has been guilty of repeated, willful violations of the rights of others (again, even though no actual damages can be proved).

Cases involving fraudulent or other intentionally tortuous conduct are particularly appropriate for punitive damage awards, as seen in the *Mathias* case.

Liquidated Damages

The general policy of the law to favor settlements of claims after they arise also operates to validate remedy provisions agreed to in advance, as part of the original contract. The parties are generally free to specify in advance what steps can be taken if their contract is breached by one of them. However, because many contracts are entered into between parties with unequal bargaining power, and because in many cases form contracts drafted by one party are used, the courts examine such **liquidated damages** provisions very carefully. These clauses must be basically fair, and a substantial forfeiture of rights must not result from a relatively minor breach. When a valid liquidated damages provision exists, the amount specified can be collected for a breach without any proof of actual damages. If the court decides that an unreasonably large amount has been specified as a **penalty** for a breach of the contract, the clause will not be enforced.

Uniform Commercial Code Limitation of Remedies

In accordance with its general "freedom of contract" approach, the UCC permits parties to the sale of goods contract to specify what remedies will or will not be available in the event of breach. Such contract provisions are not enforceable, however, if they are unreasonable or unconscionable. One important limitation is Section 2-719(2): "Where circumstances cause an exclusive or limited remedy to fail of its essential purpose, remedy may be had as provided in this Act." If, in other words, enforcement of the contract clause would mean that the injured party wound up with no real remedy at all, the Code's remedy sections apply. Further, subsection (3) of Section 2-719 provides that a limitation of consequential damages for personal injuries caused by defective consumer goods is prima facie unconscionable. The seller or manufacturer of the consumer goods would have a heavy presumption to overcome to make such a limitation enforceable. When a commercial loss

CASE 3

Mathias v. Accor Economy Lodging, Inc.

347 F.3d 672 (7 Cir. 2003)

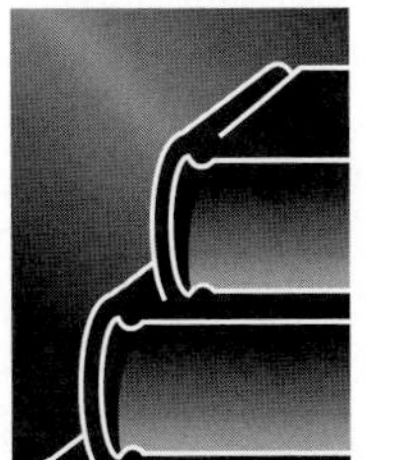

Facts: Burl and Desiree Mathias were severely bitten by bedbugs while they were guests in defendant's "Motel 6" in downtown Chicago. The motel had been aware of a serious bedbug infestation for several years, but had done nothing to deal with it. The manager's recommendation that the motel be closed and thoroughly sprayed was rejected. Complaining guests were moved to other rooms (on occasion, moved two or three times) or given refunds. Room clerks were instructed to call the bedbugs "ticks." Some rooms had been listed "Do not rent, bugs in room," or posted "DO NOT RENT UNTIL TREATED." On the evening in question, 190 of the 191 motel's rooms were rented, including those listed or posted as being infested. Plaintiffs were given one of these infested rooms. The jury awarded each Mathias $5,000 in actual damages, and $186,000 in punitive damages. The motel appealed the size of the punitive damages award.

Issue: Does the amount of this punitive damages award violate "due process of law"?

Decision: No. Judgment affirmed.

Opinion by Judge Posner: "[Motel 6's] failure either to warn guests or to take effective measures to eliminate the bedbugs amounted to fraud and probably to battery as well.... There was, in short, sufficient evidence of 'willful and wanton conduct' within the meaning that the Illinois courts assign to the term to permit an award of punitive damages in this case.

"But in what amount? In arguing that $20,000 was the maximum amount of punitive damages that a jury could constitutionally have awarded each plaintiff, the defendant points to the U.S. Supreme Court's recent statement that 'few awards [of punitive damages] exceeding a single-digit ratio between punitive and compensatory damages ... will satisfy due process.' ... The ratio of punitive to compensatory damages determined by [this] jury was, in contrast, 37.2 to 1.

"The Supreme Court did not, however, lay down a 4-to-1 or single-digit-ratio rule—it merely said that 'there is a presumption against an award that has a 145-to-1 ratio.' ... We must consider why punitive damages are awarded and why the Court has decided that due process requires that such awards be limited. The second question is easier to answer than the first. The term 'punitive damages' implies punishment, and a standard principle of penal theory is that 'the punishment should fit the crime' in the sense of being proportional to the wrongfulness of the defendant's action....

"Another penal precept is that a defendant should have reasonable notice of the sanction for unlawful acts....

"And a third precept ... is that sanctions should be based on the wrong done rather than the status of the defendant; a person is punished for what he does, not for who he is, even if the who is a huge corporation....

"[S]till today one function of punitive-damage awards is to relieve the pressures on an overloaded system of criminal justice by providing a civil alternative to criminal prosecution of minor crimes....

"The award of punitive damages in this case ... serves the additional purpose of limiting the defendant's ability to profit from its fraud by escaping detection and (private) prosecution....

"All things considered, we cannot say that the award of punitive damages was excessive, albeit the precise number chosen by the jury was arbitrary....

"[A] Chicago hotel that permits unsanitary conditions to exist is subject to revocation of its license, without which it cannot operate.... We are sure that the defendant would prefer to pay the punitive damages assessed in this case than to lose its license.

"AFFIRMED."

is caused by defective goods, there is no presumption that a contract clause limiting consequential damages is invalid. If an airline and a plane manufacturer included such a limitation in their contract, for example, the limitation would not be presumed unconscionable.

When the contract contains a liquidated damages provision, the amount specified must be "reasonable," under essentially the same test used prior to the Code. If the amount set is unreasonably large, it is void as a penalty.

Other Remedies

In addition to the damages remedy, several other remedies may be available to the injured plaintiff, depending on the facts of the case. Most of these alternative remedies were first developed by the courts of equity to deal with situations in which the "remedy at law," that is, damages, was felt to be inadequate to solve the plaintiff's problem. The main alternative remedies for breach of contract are discussed here; certain special remedies for breach of sale of goods contracts and secured financing contracts are discussed in later chapters.

Specific Performance

When the parties have contracted for the purchase and sale of a unique item, the buyer, particularly, may want the court to specifically enforce the contract, because it will usually be very hard to prove damages in the absence of an established market, and because even with damages, the buyer would still not be able to get the thing bargained for. In the eyes of the law, every piece of land is unique, so the **specific performance** remedy is available to either party to a real estate contract. Goods and securities are legally unique if no alternative source of supply is reasonably available. Fifty shares of stock in a small, closely held corporation might very well be unique; 50 shares of U.S. Steel would not be. A 2004 Ford is probably not unique; a 1904 Stanley Steamer almost certainly is.

As a general rule, specific performance is not available as a remedy for breach of personal services contracts, for two main reasons. First, courts traditionally have been reluctant to get involved in extensive supervision of contract performances on a day-to-day basis. And second, an order forcing one person to work for another smacks of "involuntary servitude," which is prohibited by the U.S. Constitution. Because performance under construction contracts can normally be judged against an agreed set of plans and specifications, specific performance is available in such cases.

Injunction

Injunction is another remedy that was developed by equity courts; a court orders someone to do something or to stop doing something. In breach of contract situations, a negative injunction may be granted to prevent a breaching party from performing for others while still under a contractual duty to perform for the plaintiff. For the reasons stated previously, the plaintiff does not get a positive decree ordering the defendant to perform; the plaintiff only gets a negative order directing the defendant not to perform for others.

CASE 4

Bander v. Grossman

611 N.Y.S.2d 985 (NY Sup. Ct. 1994)

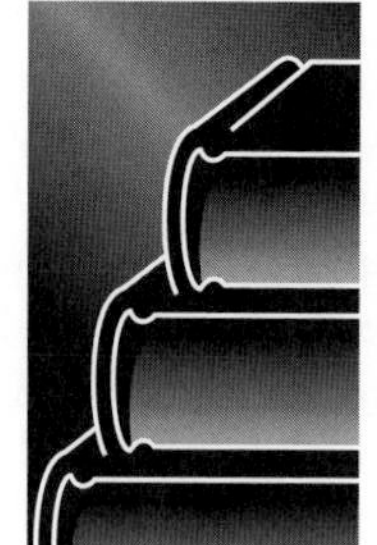

Facts: In the summer of 1987, plaintiff looked for a sports car to purchase for interim personal use and to resell when the price rose (a practice in which he had previously engaged). The defendant had in his inventory the subject 1965 DB5 Aston Martin convertible with left-hand drive. Plaintiff learned this particular model was 1 of only 20 in existence, with only 40 having been made, although those 20 cars seem to turn over with more frequency than their number might suggest. Plaintiff testified he thought the car was undervalued, based on his knowledge of sports car prices, and anticipated a price rise. A contract of sale was reached with a purchase price of $40,000, with plaintiff depositing $5,000.

The commercial agreement proceeded to unwind thereafter. The dealer could not obtain the title documents from the wholesaler from whom he had agreed to purchase the vehicle; the deposition testimony of the out-of-state wholesaler confirmed that the title had been misplaced. The defendant did not transmit this explanation to plaintiff, but instead told a story about problems of getting title from a different individual. In August of 1987, the defendant attempted to return the deposit, but advised that he would continue to try to resolve the title problems. Plaintiff pursued the purchase until, ultimately, in December of 1987, plaintiff's lawyer wrote defendant that the contract had been breached and plaintiff would commence litigation. However, no further action was taken by plaintiff until this case for specific performance was commenced in 1989, 4 months after defendant sold the car.

Issue: Can plaintiff receive "specific performance," in the form of the proceeds of the seller's resale of the unique car?

Decision: No. Judgment for defendant seller.

Opinion by Judge Lebedeff: "The request for specific performance raises a novel issue under the Uniform Commercial Code concerning entitlement to specific performance of a contract for the sale of unique goods with a fluctuating price. Section 2-716(1) of the Uniform Commercial Code, which is controlling, provides that '[s]pecific performance may be decreed where the goods are unique or in other proper circumstances.' The jury's advisory determined that the Aston Martin car at issue was unique.

"As noted above, the car was sold prior to the commencement of this litigation for a price of $185,000 more than the $40,000 contract price, and plaintiff requests that he be granted specific performance in the form of a constructive trust impressed upon the proceeds of sale, plus interest from the date of sale. As it developed, the defendant had not sold at the 'top of the market,' which peaked in July of 1989, approximately two years after the original contract, when the car had a value of $335,000, which was $295,000 over the contract price. Thereafter, collectible automobile values slumped and the sale price of a comparable Aston Martin vehicle by January of 1990 was $225,000 and, by the time of trial, was $80,000.

"Clearly, plaintiff's request for an award of specific performance monetary damages is legally cognizable, for every object has a price and even rare goods are subject to economic interchangeability.... Plaintiff urges that specific performance is particularly appropriate here for UCC 2-716 has been viewed as a statute enacted to liberalize the availability of specific performance of contracts of sale as a buyers' remedy.... Nonetheless, this change does not lessen the UCC's 'emphasis on the commercial feasibility of replacement' as the most desirable approach ... nor does it mean that typical equitable principles are inapplicable to consideration of the remedy....

"However, both on the facts and the law, the court determines that, if equitable monetary damages are to be awarded here, that award must be based upon value at the time of trial, rather than on an earlier valuation. Traditionally, equity 'give(s) relief adapted to the situation at the time of decree.' ... This position is consistent with the explicit goal of the Uniform Commercial Code that its remedies are to 'be liberally administered to the end that the aggrieved party may be put in as good a position as if the other party had fully performed' ... which, in the case of specific performance, has led to confining the remedy to restoration of the equivalent of the subject goods to a plaintiff's possession.... Here, if plaintiff were to be awarded enough to be able to acquire another Aston Martin at current prices, he would achieve the requisite equivalent.

"Plaintiff has fervently, but ultimately unconvincingly, argues that the larger amount is his due. While every litigant wishes to gain a maximum economic benefit, a court of equity should not grant an award which would be 'disproportionate in its harm to defendant and its assistance to plaintiff.' ...

"[S]pecfic performance rests upon the discretion of the trial court, reviewable under an abuse of discretion standard.... The use of a permissive 'may' in the text of UCC 2-716 does not modify that standard in any way or change the accepted concept ... that specific performance may be declined if it is concluded such relief 'would be a "drastic" or harsh remedy.' It should be noted in relation to price fluctuations that even an extreme rise in price is an insufficient reason, as a matter of law, to decline to consider this equitable remedy ... but, on the other hand, neither does a mere 'increase in the cost of a replacement ... merit the remedy.' ...

"With the passage of time, specific performance becomes disfavored. For example, because goods are subject to a rapid change in condition, or the cost of maintenance of the goods is important, time may be found to have been of the essence, and even a month's delay may defeat specific performance.... Even absent such special circumstances, with a greater delay, where a defendant has changed position or taken any economic risk, the court may conclude that 'the plaintiff will lose nothing but an uncontemplated opportunity to gather a windfall.' ... Particularly where some other transactions are available, it has been held that a 'customer [for resale] may not ... refuse to cover ... and thereby speculate on the market entirely at the risk of the [defendant]'....

"Turning to the facts in the instant case, the plaintiff did not sue in December of 1987, when it is likely a request for specific performance would have been granted. At that point, the defendant had disclaimed the contract and plaintiff was aware of his rights.... The court does not accept plaintiff's protest that he believed the commercial relationship was intact; the parties had already had a heated discussion and were communicating through attorneys. A more likely explanation of plaintiff's inaction is that he proceeded to complete the purchase in April of 1988 of a Ferrari Testarrosa for $128,000 and a Lamborghini for $40,000 in 1989.

"In short, the plaintiff abandoned any active claim of contract enforcement by late spring of 1988. Moreover, to the extent that his two sports cars constituted 'cover,' he did not present any evidence as to his treatment of those cars such that the court could evaluate damages or quantify what profits he expected to make on the Aston Martin which he regarded, in significant part, as a business transaction.... Finally, the court determines as a matter of credibility, that plaintiff would not have pursued this matter had the price fallen below the contract price.

"On this point, it is helpful to note that the initial burden of proving the proper remedy remains on the buyer.... In this instance, plaintiff's very attempt to prove qualifiable special performance damages has also proved: (a) the value of the disputed automobile was readily established by expert sources, (b) the adequacy of legal contract damages, and (c) the availability of 'a substitute transaction (which) is generally a more efficient way to prevent injury than is a suit for specific performance ... [and gives] a sound economic basis for limiting the injured party to damages.' ...

"In closing, the court does not fault plaintiff for his valiant attempt to reach for a higher level of damages. As two leading commentators have pointed out, in relation to the use of uniqueness as a basis for specific performance, the 'exact dimensions [of the concepts] are not fully known.' ... 'If only in the interest of commercial certainty, there is great wisdom in a rule of thumb that "uniqueness" continues to cover one-of-a-kind goods and items of special sentimental value, [and] goods that have particular market significance, such as goods covered by an output contract or which are being specially manufactured.' ...

"After full consideration of these factors, the court is satisfied that it would be inequitable and improper to grant specific performance in the form of a constructive trust upon the proceeds of sale."

Rescission and Restitution

Two remedies are really involved here, calling off the deal and returning any benefits already transferred. A court will not lightly undo the parties' whole agreement and order the restoration of benefits already given. The **rescission and restitution (R & R)** remedy is provided only if there has been fraud, material breach, or similar failure; only if the injured party asks for this remedy with reasonable promptness; and only if the rights of third parties or other equitable factors have not intervened. The objective of R & R is to terminate the contract *and* to put the parties back where they were before it was made. The more difficult and complex it is to achieve this objective, the less likely it is that R & R will be used as a remedy.

Quasi-Contract

Because the old common law courts heard only cases that fell into certain categories, lawyers became somewhat creative in constructing fact combinations to fit those categories. **Quasi-contract** means in essence "almost like a real contract, but not quite"; it describes a situation in which a party has received and retained benefits but has made no actual promise to pay for them. It is in fact a remedy that the courts developed to prevent such a party from being "unjustly enriched." The circumstances are such that it would not be fair for the person to keep the benefits without paying anything for them. The **unjust enrichment** principle is the justification for requiring a minor to pay the fair market value for necessaries received, even though the minor has exercised the option of disaffirming the contract made to pay for them. Quasi-contract also applies to all sorts of other situations, such as benefits conferred on the wrong person by mistake or partial performance given to one party prior to a breach of contract.

Contract Price for Goods

The seller of goods can sue and collect the full contract price from the buyer only in certain limited situations. The seller can, of course, sue for the full price on any goods that the buyer has accepted. The seller can also get the contract price for conforming goods that have been lost or damaged within a commercially reasonable time after the risk of loss passed to the buyer. Finally, the buyer owes the contract price for goods that have been identified to the contract and that cannot be resold at a reasonable price.

Possession of Goods

When the seller discovers that the buyer is insolvent, the seller may withhold delivery of the goods, unless the buyer is prepared to pay cash, including payment for all goods already delivered under the same contract. When the goods are already in transit, the seller can order the bailee to stop delivery if the bailee has not acknowledged the buyer's right to possession and if the buyer has not received a negotiable document of title covering the goods.

When the goods have already been delivered on credit to an insolvent buyer, the seller has a very limited right to reclaim them. The seller must demand their return within 10 days after the buyer received them, unless the buyer made a written statement of solvency within 3 months prior to the delivery; then the 10-day limitation does not apply. In any case, however, the seller's right of repossession is subject to the rights of buyers in the ordinary course of business or other good faith purchasers, and to the rights of lien creditors. When the seller decides on repossession, this remedy excludes all others.

If the buyer breaches before the seller has finished manufacturing the goods, the seller, if exercising "reasonable commercial judgment," has the options of completing the goods and identifying them to the contract, of selling the unfinished goods for scrap or salvage, or of pursuing any other reasonable alternative.

In the "extreme hardship" case, in which the seller has become insolvent within 10 days after receiving the first installment on the contract price, the buyer has the right to obtain possession of identified goods by tendering any unpaid part of the contract price. This is part of the buyer's special property in the goods once they have been identified to the contract. If the buyer has made the identification, this right to possession exists only if the goods conform to the contract.

A buyer in possession or control of goods that were rightfully rejected because of their nonconformity has a security interest in them for any payments already made on the price and for all reasonable expenses incurred in inspecting and handling them. The buyer can sell such goods and apply the proceeds to satisfy this claim.

Significance of This Chapter

As noted by the great Scots poet, Robert Burns, "the best laid plans of mice and men, gang aft a-glee." This chapter has indicated some of the reasons why the plans laid in a contract may "often go astray." Our discussion has covered at least the main bases for excuse or discharge of a party's contractual obligations. The parties themselves may provide for such excuses, either in the original contract, or in a subsequent modifying agreement, or through their subsequent conduct. Even without express contract excuse clauses, courts will sometimes grant relief from a contract duty in which the anticipated circumstances have changed very substantially. Because not every nonperformance is a breach of contract, the parties in many of these situations would be better served by a negotiated settlement than an extended litigation.

Because you are not reading this text to become lawyers, we have deemphasized most procedural aspects of the law and concentrated instead on the nature of your rights and liabilities. The purpose of our discussion of remedies is to acquaint you with the options you may have in the event the other party is guilty of a breach of contract. Because not every remedy is available for every situation, you need an appreciation of the limits of what the courts, and your lawyer, can do for you if you are successful in proving your case. You need to know what the possible outcomes might be to make a rational decision whether or not to bring the litigation or to continue it.

Because a court will not (and should not) give unrequested remedies, one of the lawyer's main jobs is to figure out the remedy or the combination of remedies that will best solve the client's problem. If you do go to litigation, make sure you fully understand what your options are and what your chances are of receiving each possible remedy.

IMPORTANT TERMS AND CONCEPTS

accord and satisfaction
account stated
adequate assurance
anticipatory repudiation
bankruptcy discharge
causation
certainty
compensatory damages
composition with creditors
concurrent conditions
condition
condition precedent
conditions subsequent
consequential damages
difference-money damages
novation
election of remedies
foreseeability
injunction
joint and several obligation
joint obligation
judgment
liquidated damages
merger
mitigation
mutual rescission
nominal damages
penalty
punitive damages
quasi-contract
release
res judicata
rescission and restitution (R & R)
special compensatory damages
specific performance
statute of limitations
substantial performance
unjust enrichment
waiver

QUESTIONS AND PROBLEMS FOR DISCUSSION

1. When will a liquidated damages clause be enforced?

2. When is specific performance available as a remedy for breach of contract?

3. What is the difference between a condition precedent and a condition subsequent?

4. What is the difference between a joint obligation and a joint and several obligation?

5. In 1992 the parties entered into a service station lease and retail gasoline dealer agreement. John Shaw agreed to buy not less than 200,000 gallons of gasoline per year, and

Mobil agreed to supply his requirements, up to a maximum of 500,000 gallons per year. Shaw agreed to pay rent on the station on the basis of 1.4 cents per gallon delivered, with a minimum of $470 per month. To meet the minimum rental, Mobil would have to deliver 33,572 gallons each month. In July 1993, Shaw ordered 34,000 gallons, but Mobil delivered 25,678 gallons, due to a gasoline shortage. The U.S. Energy office had required Mobil to allocate available supplies among its dealers, and Shaw's allocation was 25,678 gallons. Shaw sued for a declaratory judgment that he was not liable for the minimum rental for July. The trial court held for Mobil. Shaw appealed.

Does Mobil's failure to deliver the full order excuse Shaw's duty to pay the minimum rental for that month?

6. Ms. Stetzel sustained personal injuries as the result of an intersection collision in Iowa City on September 27. She was thrown sideways, and her head struck the window. She went to the University Student Health Center for treatment of her headache, was kept overnight, and was sent home the next day. Her headaches continued for several weeks, interfering with her studying; she was taking a prescribed medication for these headaches. After being pestered by an insurance adjuster, she finally signed a release on December 2, in return for $400. She admits she knew what the paper was when she signed it. Shortly thereafter, her symptoms became more serious; the headaches became more severe, she had difficulty picking things up; her eyes tired more easily; she seemed to be forgetful. Alleging that the release was invalid due to mutual mistake and/or undue influence, she sued for her injuries. The jury agreed and gave her $3,000. Defendant appealed.

   Was the release invalid due to mutual mistake? Was it invalid due to undue influence?

7. By written contract, Vidal agreed to buy four used airplanes from Transcontinental Airlines. Payment was to be made by certified check on delivery of the planes, which was to occur at the Kansas City Municipal Airport on June 1. Transcontinental was ready to deliver only one plane on June 1; the other three could have been delivered sometime before July 10. No offer of performance was ever made by either party. On October 8, Vidal sued for breach of contract.

   What is the result, and why?

8. For several years prior to April 30, 1992, the Storeys were partners in the petroleum products business at Cle Elum, doing business as Storey Distributing Company. On April 30, 1992, the defendants dissolved their partnership. At the time of dissolution of the partnership, defendants' account with plaintiff had a balance of $3,515.80.

   On December 27, 1993, plaintiff obtained a judgment against defendant Earl Storey for $3,735.47. Defendant William E. Storey was not a named defendant in that case. Having failed to collect that judgment, B-OK brought this suit on the same account. The trial court held for William Storey.

   Will this decision be sustained on appeal? Why or why not?

9. William E. Felch alleges, among other things, that he was employed by the defendant as a member of its faculty on a continuing basis and that contrary to and without compliance with the provisions for dismissal contained in administrative memoranda purporting to require certain hearings, the board of trustees of defendant on August 22, approved the action of its president on July 20, dismissing the plaintiff effective August 11. Plaintiff asks that "defendant be enjoined from carrying into effect the dismissal of this plaintiff as a member of the faculty . . . and that the defendant may be ordered to continue plaintiff as such member of the faculty of Findlay College, Findlay, Ohio, and that defendant be ordered to pay to this plaintiff the salary therefor agreed upon."

   Should the injunction be granted? Explain.

10. Ralph Nader was scheduled to make several appearances for the Connecticut Citizens Action Group (CCAG) on April 28, including a noon rally in Hartford and a speech on the Storrs campus of the University of Connecticut. On April 25, he bought a ticket for Allegheny's 10:15 am flight from Washington, D.C., to Hartford, which was scheduled to arrive at 11:15 am. His reservation was confirmed. When he arrived at the airport about 5 minutes before his flight, he was told there were no more seats. Only 100 seats were available for the 107 reservations that had been confirmed 1 hour before the flight. No one would give up a seat when Allegheny asked. Nader refused Allegheny's offer to fly him to Philadelphia, where he would have 10 minutes to catch a flight due to arrive in Hartford at 12:15. He flew to Boston, where a CCAG staff member picked him up and drove him to Storrs. Nader refused the $32.41 compensation offered to him under the Civil Aeronautics Board's rules and brought a common law suit for damages, alleging fraudulent misrepresentation. Nader was awarded $10 compensatory damages and $25,000 punitive damages; CCAG was awarded $51 compensatory damages and $25,000 punitive damages. The Court of Appeals reversed.

    On appeal, how should the U.S. Supreme Court decide this case? Discuss.

11. Riley purchased his new 1999 Lincoln from a Florida dealer at a cost of $38,476, and Ford Motor issued a self-styled "New Vehicle Warranty." Shortly thereafter he took the car to Robinson Brothers, an Alabama Ford dealer, for repair of a window and removal of a noise in the rear end. According to Riley, these defects were not corrected. At trial he testified that in the weeks following the requested repairs, and before the car was returned to Robinson Brothers for further repairs, these additional malfunctions developed: air conditioning did not work, speed control did not function, power seats became

inoperative, the radio aerial functioned spasmodically, the rear seat did not fit, headlight panels were not synchronized, the cigarette lighter was missing, windshield wipers were defective, engine knocked upon acceleration, the transmission did not function properly, gear shift lever would not function, and the left door would not close properly.

Riley wrote to Ford Motor setting forth in detail his complaints and requested Ford "to direct me to a dealer employing trained service personnel, or furnish me with someone capable of overseeing service personnel available in order to insure that the defects in my automobile are properly corrected in an expert and dependable manner." Ford dispatched a Technical Service Representative who road-tested the automobile, agreed that it was not functioning properly, and offered to take it to Robinson Brothers, where he would personally supervise its repair. Riley believed he had a better idea. He sued Ford and was awarded $130,000 by a U.S. District Court jury.

Was the jury's award of damages supported by the evidence?

PART 3

Law of Property

The law governing the acquisition, ownership, and disposition of property, both real and personal, is basic to the management of business and of nearly all our personal affairs. More than one person may have an ownership interest in real or personal property. Thus, ownership rights have to be defined, and different forms of ownership are needed to fit the various situations that may arise in co-ownership.

In our society, we often rent or borrow personal property and lease real property. We need to know the rights and duties each party has in those transactions. Also, because many areas where we live and work have become densely populated, we can no longer do with our property as we wish if it offends or injures our neighbors. We must, therefore, have land use and environmental regulations. For all these reasons, it is important to understand property rights.

In Part Three, we review the methods of acquisition and disposition of real and personal property and define the various forms of ownership. We examine the law regarding rental or use of personal property belonging to someone else (bailments), scrutinize the rights and duties of landlords and tenants, and discuss zoning laws and environmental regulations and how they affect the use of land.

A sale of goods is one particular type of contract, so the general rules of contract law apply, unless replaced by a specific rule from the Uniform Commercial Code (UCC). We have already seen many examples of such changes in the various chapters in Part Two. There were special goods rules for offer and acceptance, consideration, Statute of Frauds, assignment, and other topics. We will not repeat all those special rules in this part.

Our focus here is the other major areas of difference between general contract law and the UCC's rules for sales of goods. Chapter 17 discusses the rules for transferring the various ownership interests in the goods from the seller to the buyer. Chapter 17 also looks at two situations involving problems with the transfer of ownership—defects in the seller's title to the goods and claims of the bulk seller's unsecured creditors against the goods. Chapter 18 covers the very important area of products liability, one of the two or three most important legal developments in the past 50 years. Chapter 16 summarizes the special rules for ownership of intellectual property.

CHAPTER 15

Forms of Co-Ownership; Personal Property

Chapter Objectives

This Chapter will:

- **Define property.**
- **Describe the different classifications of property.**
- **Describe different types of ownership a person or people may have in property.**
- **Explain the process by which personal property can become real property, and real property can become personal property.**
- **Discuss the various ways title to personal property may be acquired.**

Human Rights, Property Rights, and Personal Rights

You will often hear people, particularly proponents of regulatory and wealth redistribution schemes, say that "human rights are more important than property rights." That statement is illogical and ridiculous. The *things* that are the subject matter of property rights—cars, books, TVs, parcels of real estate—have no "rights" at all, in and of themselves. Property rights belong to persons, including human beings, corporate persons, and various other kinds of legal entities. Among the most important rights of human beings are property rights—the right to acquire, possess, use, enjoy, and dispose of the things that are the subject of those rights. Your TV set has no rights; you do: the rights to acquire it, to watch it when you want to, to turn it off when you want to study, and to sell it or give it away (when it is paid for).

At least equally important is your property right in the results of your labor—the money and other rewards you earn through your physical and mental efforts. Those things are yours because you worked for them, and your "property rights" protect your freedom to save or spend, as you see fit, when you wish, where you wish. Property rights are very important to all of us. They enable us to enjoy music, art, poetry, literature, and all sorts of leisure and productive activity. In short, they are a large part of what separates us from the beasts of the jungle and makes life worth living.

Definition of Property

Property may be defined as the bundle of rights concerning a specific parcel of land or any other thing of value, tangible or intangible, visible or invisible. Some of the rights included in this bundle are the right to possess, to use, to sell, to lease, to dispose of, or to destroy the land or thing in a legal way, and the right to exclude others from trespassing or interfering with the land or thing.

Because property may be described as the bundle of rights concerning land or a thing, we often find that we do not have absolute or unconditional property because someone else may have certain rights in the land or thing. For example, the owner of a parcel of land may say, "That is my property," but the parcel of land may be leased to a tenant. Thus, the tenant has property rights in the land—the right to use it and the right to use the proceeds from it according to the terms of the lease contract. Also, a public utility company may have an easement across the parcel of land, allowing it to come in and repair or replace underground or overhead power lines. An easement is simply a right to enter someone else's land for a specific purpose. If there are mineral, oil, or gas deposits on the land, those deposits may be owned by a person or people other than the landowner. Moreover, if the purchaser of the land took out a purchase-money mortgage (i.e., a loan to buy the land), the mortgagee has certain rights in the land as security for payment of the mortgage. Thus, it is not uncommon for several persons to have property rights in the same land.

The *DePalma* case illustrates the rights of one co-owner where the other co-owner has destroyed their property. (This special form of co-ownership is discussed more fully later in the chapter.)

Classifications of Property

Real Property

When we speak of **real property**, we are referring to land, buildings, or permanent fixtures that have been erected on or affixed to the land. Crops, trees, or any other objects that are growing on land are generally considered real property until they are severed from the land or at least until they are sold separately.

Personal Property

This term designates anything of value that is subject to ownership and is not classified as real property. **Personal property** can be divided into two classifications, tangible and

CASE 1

DePalma v. Bates County Mutual Insurance
24 S.W.3d 766 (MO App. 2000)

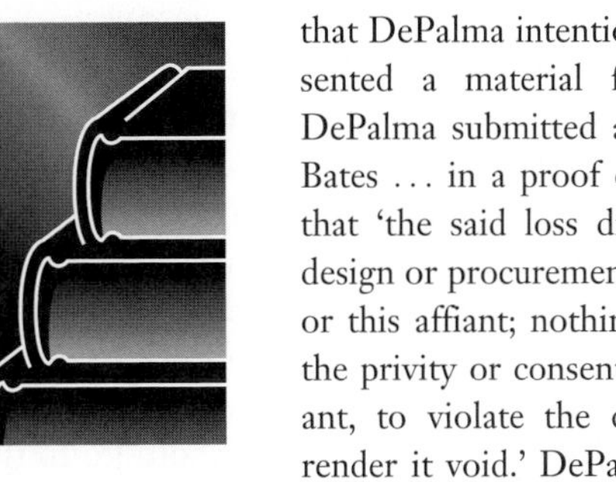

Facts: Bates Insurance appeals from a directed verdict in favor of Anthony DePalma, who sued Bates on a fire insurance claim for loss of his house and its contents. The house was owned by DePalma and his wife Janet, as tenants by the entirety. Janet intentionally started the fire, but Anthony filed a claim, as an innocent spouse, for compensation for loss of his interest in the property. Bates rejected several written "proof of loss" forms submitted by Anthony, and ultimately denied his claim.

The trial court initially granted summary judgment for Bates, but the appeals court reversed, holding that the right of an innocent spouse to recover must be determined by examining the insurance policy's language. After remand, and a trial, the trial court entered the directed verdict for Anthony because Bates had not proved that there had been any material misrepresentation in violation of the terms of the insurance policy.

Issue: Can an innocent spouse recover his interest in insured tenancy by the entirety property that was destroyed by the other spouse?

Decision: Yes. Judgment affirmed, as modified.

Opinion by Judge Howard: "The question of whether a spouse not participating [in] or ratifying an arson by the other spouse is barred as a matter of law from recovery was decided in [the first appeal]. That determination is, with limited exceptions, the law of the case as to issues that were raised or could have been raised in the first appeal.... Point I is denied.

"In its second point, Bates ... contends that the trial court erred in directing a verdict for DePalma ... because sufficient evidence existed from which a fact finder could have concluded that DePalma intentionally concealed or misrepresented a material fact. Bates ... asserts that DePalma submitted a signed, sworn statement to Bates ... in a proof of loss form and represented that 'the said loss did not originate by any act, design or procurement on the part of your insured, or this affiant; nothing has been done by or with the privity or consent of your insured or this affiant, to violate the conditions of the policy, or render it void.' DePalma also left blank the question which asked what was the cause and origin of the fire. Bates ... asserts that DePalma made these representations and concealments at a time when he knew that his wife, an insured, had intentionally set the house on fire....

"Because DePalma's proof of loss statements were rejected by Bates, ... they never became part of the claim. Therefore, we find that DePalma's assertions, or lack thereof, in his rejected proof of loss statements cannot be the basis for [Bates'] claim that DePalma concealed or misrepresented anything in violation of the insurance agreement....

"The amount of the dwelling coverage was $30,000. At the time of the trial, DePalma and his wife owned the dwelling as tenants by the entirety.... Because DePalma may only recover his interest in the property, we find that he is entitled to one-half of the amount of the dwelling coverage under the policy....

"The judgment of the trial court is affirmed as to the directed verdict in favor of DePalma, and reversed as to the award of damages and remanded to the trial court to enter a damages award in favor of DePalma for the dwelling coverage in the amount of $15,000, the personal property coverage in the amount of $6,788.95, prejudgment interest from January 8, 1994, and post-judgment interest as provided by law."

intangible. Tangible personal property includes such items as animals, furniture, books, clothes, jewelry, and business inventories. Intangible personal property includes a person's rights in patents, copyrights, shares of corporate stock, insurance policies, and many similar legal documents.

Public Property

Public property designates the land and things that are owned by the national government, a state government, a city, or some other political subdivision. Those things are, therefore, considered to be owned by the public. This classification includes parks, public buildings, and the national archives.

Private Property

In contrast to public property, **private property** belongs to an individual, a corporation, or other private legal entity. The property of Notre Dame University is private property, whereas the property of Iowa State University is public property.

Types of Ownership

Ownership in Severalty

Ownership in severalty is ownership in the name of one person. There is no co-owner of the property right.

Tenancy in Common

Here, there are two or more co-owners of real or personal property. Under this type of co-ownership, the co-owners or co-tenants have equal rights to possess and use the property. A co-owner's interest in a **tenancy in common** may be transferred by a last will and testament. It may be sold without the consent of the other co-owners, and is subject to judicial sale by a creditor who has secured a judgment against the owner.

Tenants in common need not be equal owners. For example, Grandfather had a will that said that all of his property would be divided equally among his children and that any deceased child's share should go to that child's children. When Grandfather died only one of his three children survived him. However, one of the deceased children had five children and the other had four. Thus, one third of Grandfather's real and personal property went to his surviving child, and the third, which was willed to each of his other children was co-owned by their children. All of the heirs are tenants in common, yet the tenants in common do not have equal shares.

In this example, the heirs could continue as tenants in common and any rents or profits from the property would have to be divided in proportion to the share of each person. Alternatively, the entire property or parts of the property could be sold and the money received from the sale would be divided according to each person's proportionate share. In some cases, the property itself must be divided among the tenants in common.

In addition to arising from inherited property, tenancy in common may arise when title to real or personal property is transferred to two or more persons and it is not declared to be joint tenancy or tenancy by the entirety.

Joint Tenancy

Joint tenancy is a second form of co-ownership in which land or personal property is owned by two or more persons. These persons enjoy equal rights to share in the use and profits of the property involved, but if any one of the joint tenants dies, the entire property passes to the surviving joint tenants. The interest of a joint tenant cannot be willed to the joint tenant's heirs because the deceased's interest terminates at death.

Joint tenants may sell and convey their separate shares in the joint tenancy. If this is done, the joint tenancy is severed, and the tenants or co-owners become tenants in common. Also, a joint tenant's interest is subject to the rights of creditors. The creditors of one joint tenant may secure judgment and have that co-owner's interest sold and the joint tenancy severed.

Historically, joint tenancy was only applicable to real estate. Today, however, one can have joint tenancy in almost any type of personal property—including bank accounts, stock shares, and automobiles.

Many states have passed specific joint tenancy statutes that modify the common law concept, and thus the applicable state law must be referred to in any case involving a joint tenancy relationship. The *Barboza* case discusses the California and Massachusetts rules on joint bank accounts.

Tenancy by the Entirety

Tenancy by the entirety is essentially a joint tenancy with the right of survivorship; however, the co-owners must be husband and wife to each other. The characteristic that distinguishes the two forms of property ownership is that tenancy by the entirety cannot be changed except by joint action of the husband and wife during their lifetimes, whereas a joint tenancy is terminated when any one of the tenants conveys his or her interest, or when a levy of execution is made by a creditor against a joint tenant's interest. If a husband and wife take title to a home as tenants by the entireties and the husband has a judgment rendered against him for damages that resulted from an automobile accident, the person

CASE 2

Barboza v. McLeod
853 N.E.2d 192 (MA 2006)

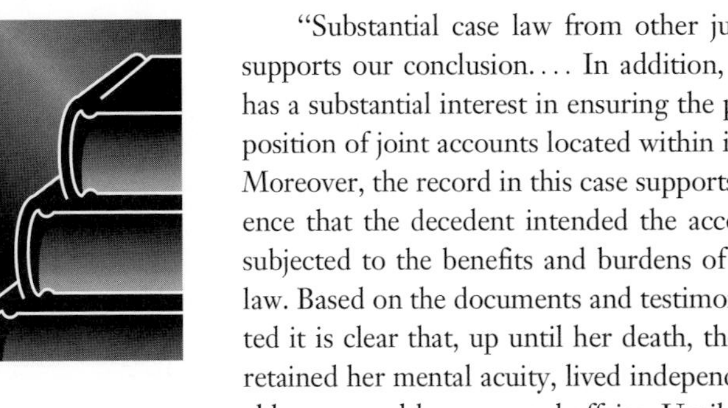

Facts: The decedent, Helen Zaborowski, had an account at a California credit union at the time of her death. She had been born and raised in Boston, but married Ralph Zaborowski in the 1940s and moved to the West Coast. The account was originally held in her name and her husband's name. When her husband died in 1994, Helen asked her nephew (the defendant, Andrew McLeod) to come to California to help her through the funeral arrangements. While he was there, Helen had him sign a signature card so that she could add his name to the account, which she did (after removing her deceased husband's name). Although the account was listed as "joint owner[s] with right of survivorship," McLeod had not had access to it and Helen had continued to manage the funds. Helen had moved back and forth between Massachusetts and California until her death in 2001. She left no valid will.

Shortly after Helen's death, McLeod withdrew the funds from the joint account. Helen's only brother, Stanley Barboza, and his son Robert were appointed as administrators of Helen's estate. Claiming that the California funds belonged to Helen's estate, they sued to force McLeod to turn over the money. The lower court agreed, and McLeod appealed.

Issue: Were the funds in the California bank part of the decedent's estate?

Decision: No. Judgment vacated and complaint dismissed.

Opinion by Judge Ireland: "The defendant, citing authority from several jurisdictions, argues that the question of ownership of the account should be governed by the law of the situs of the deposit and, therefore, California law should apply to determine whether the decedent intended to grant the defendant an interest in the joint account.... California law provides that funds in a joint account belong to the surviving party unless there is clear and convincing evidence of a different intent. There is no case law in Massachusetts that directly addresses this choice of law issue.... We conclude that the law of a joint account's situs at the time of decedent's death should apply to determine ownership of the account....

"Substantial case law from other jurisdictions supports our conclusion.... In addition, California has a substantial interest in ensuring the proper disposition of joint accounts located within its borders. Moreover, the record in this case supports the inference that the decedent intended the account to be subjected to the benefits and burdens of California law. Based on the documents and testimony submitted it is clear that, up until her death, the decedent retained her mental acuity, lived independently, and ably managed her personal affairs. Until her death, she continued diligently to maintain the account in California....

"The documents the plaintiffs produced do little to illuminate the issue. The putative draft will found in the decedent's home contains an itemized list of gifts to be given to her loved ones on her death. She lists the defendant, and none of her other nieces and nephews, as a beneficiary to receive $100,000. We think this fact militates against the plaintiffs and supports the defendant's argument that the decedent intended to give the defendant the proceeds of the account, approximately $142,000, on her death. The meaning of the putative draft will, of unknown origin and date, is unclear, and the fact of its existence does not advance the plaintiffs' position....

"[T]here are many ways the decedent could have rebutted the right of survivorship, but she did not. For example, she could have explicitly established the account as a joint account with 'no survivorship rights.' However, that account expressly granted to the defendant a joint interest in the account with a 'right of survivorship.' The decedent retained this designation long after her domicil had change to Massachusetts and when, presumably ... she was capable of changing the designation on the account and moving the entire proceeds of the account elsewhere. Given that plaintiffs have not illustrated by clear and convincing evidence the decedent's contrary intent, we must presume she intended her nephew to remain the joint owner of the account, with a right of survivorship. The proceeds of the account belong to the defendant, not to the estate....

"For the reasons set forth above, we vacate the judgment for the plaintiffs and dismiss the underlying complaint with prejudice."

who was awarded the damages cannot have the judgment executed against the home. If, however, both the husband and wife are jointly liable on a debt, then the creditor may secure a judgment and execute it against the home.

Like joint tenancy, tenancy by the entirety was historically confined to real estate ownership and did not extend to ownership of personal property. However, some states have extended the concept to personal property. About 20 states recognize tenancy by the entirety, but here again the state laws are not uniform and the individual state law must be referred to in each case.

CASE 3

United States v. Craft
535 U.S. 274 (2002)

Facts: Sandra Craft and her husband owned, as tenants by the entirety, a parcel of real estate located in Grand Rapids, Michigan. Claiming that Mr. Craft owed $482,446 in unpaid income taxes, the U.S. Internal Revenue Service (IRS) filed a tax lien against all his real and personal property. Under Michigan law, entireties property is owned by the "marital partnership;" neither spouse has individual rights to transfer it or to obligate it. Therefore, the creditors of an individual spouse have no claim against it.

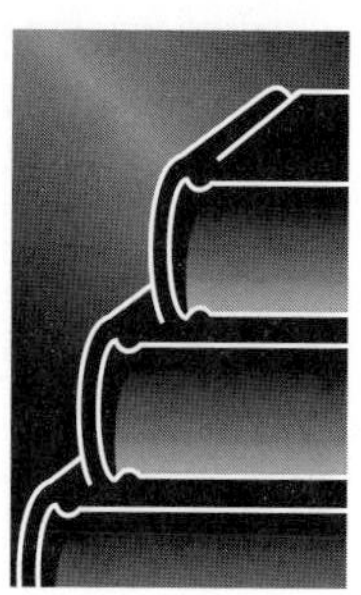

After notice of the tax lien had been filed, the Crafts signed a joint quitclaim deed that transferred the husband's interest in this land to Sandra, for $1.00. When Sandra tried to sell the land in 1992, the notice of the tax lien showed up as an unpaid claim against the land. The IRS agreed to release the lien so that the sale could go through, but required that half of the sale proceeds be placed in an escrow account, pending a court determination of the validity of the IRS lien. Sandra then filed this lawsuit to "quiet title," that is, to confirm her right to the land—free of the tax lien. The U.S. District Court granted the IRS's motion for summary judgment. The Sixth Circuit held that the tax lien could not attach to entireties property under Michigan law, but remanded to the District Court for a ruling on whether the transfer to Sandra was fraudulent. The District Court then decided that the transfer was not fraudulent, but that Mr. Craft's use of his separate funds to make mortgage payments on the property was fraudulent. The IRS was awarded a share of Sandra's sale proceeds equal to those mortgage payments. Both parties appealed; the Sixth Circuit affirmed the District Court's second decision. The IRS petitioned the U.S. Supreme Court for a further review.

Meanwhile, during the course of this litigation (in 1998), Mr. Craft died.

Issue: Can the ownership interest of one tenant by the entireties be subjected to a federal tax lien?

Decision: Yes. Judgment of the lower courts is reversed; case is remanded.

Opinion by Justice O'Connor: "Whether the interests of [Sandra's] husband in the property he held as a tenant by the entirety constitutes 'property and rights to property' for the purposes of the federal tax lien statute . . . is ultimately a question of federal law. The answer to this federal question, however, largely depends upon state law. The federal tax lien statute itself 'creates no property rights but merely attaches consequences, federally defined, to rights created under state law.' . . . Accordingly, 'we look initially to state law to determine what rights the taxpayer has in the property the Government seeks to reach, then to federal law to determine whether the taxpayer's state-delineated rights qualify as "property" or "rights to property" within the compass of the federal tax lien legislation.' . . .

"A common idiom describes property as a 'bundle of sticks'—a collection of individual rights which, in certain combinations, constitute property. . . . State law determines only which sticks are in a bundle. Whether those sticks qualify as 'property' for the purposes of the federal tax lien statute is a question of federal law.

"In looking to state law, we must be careful to consider the substance of the rights state law provides, not merely the labels the State gives these rights or the conclusions it draws from them. Such state law labels are irrelevant to the federal question of which bundles of rights constitute property that may be attached by a federal tax lien. . . .

"A tenancy by the entirety is a unique sort of concurrent ownership that can only exist between married persons. . . . Because of the common-law fiction that the husband and wife were one person at law (that person, practically speaking, was the husband . . .), Blackstone did not characterize the tenancy by the entirety as a form of concurrent ownership at all. Instead, he thought that entireties property was a form of single ownership by the marital unity. . . . Neither spouse was considered to own any individual interest in the estate; rather, it belonged to the couple. . . .

"With the passage of the Married Women's Property Acts in the late 19th century granting women distinct rights with respect to marital property, most States either abolished the tenancy by the entirety or altered it significantly. . . . Michigan's version of the estate is typical of the modern tenancy by the entirety. Following Blackstone, Michigan characterizes its tenancy by the entirety as creating no individual rights whatsoever. . . . And yet, in Michigan, each tenant by the entirety possesses the right of survivorship. . . . Each spouse—the wife as well as the husband—may also use the property, exclude third parties from it, and receive an equal share of the income produced by it. . . . Neither spouse may unilaterally alienate or encumber the property . . . although this may be accomplished with mutual consent. . . . Divorce ends the tenancy by the entirety, generally giving each spouse an equal interest in the property as a tenant in common, unless the divorce decree specifies otherwise. . . .

"In determining whether [Sandra's] husband possessed 'property' or 'rights to property' within the meaning of [the tax lien statute], we look to the individual rights created by these state law rules. According to Michigan law, [Sandra's] husband had, among other rights, the following rights with respect to the entireties property: the right to use the property, the right to exclude third parties from it, the right to a share of income produced from it, the right of survivorship, the right to become a tenant in common with equal shares upon divorce, the right to sell the property with [Sandra's] consent and to receive half the proceeds from such a sale, the right to place an encumbrance on the property with [Sandra's] consent, and the right to block [Sandra] from selling or encumbering the property unilaterally. . . .

"We turn now to the federal question of whether the rights Michigan law granted to [Sandra's] husband as a tenant by the entirety qualify as 'property' or 'rights to property' under S.6321 [the tax lien statute]. The statutory language authorizing the tax lien 'is broad and reveals on its face that Congress meant to reach every interest in property that a taxpayer might have.' . . . 'Stronger language could hardly have been selected to reveal a purpose to assure the collection of taxes.' . . . We conclude that the husband's rights in the entireties property fall within this broad statutory language. . . .

"This Court has already stated that federal tax liens may attach to property that cannot be unilaterally alienated. . . .

"That the rights of [Sandra's] husband in the entireties property constitute 'property' or 'rights to property' 'belonging to' him is further underscored by the fact that, if the conclusion were otherwise, the entireties property would belong to no one for the purposes of S.6321. [Sandra] had no more interest in the property than her husband; if neither of them had a property interest in the entireties property, who did? This result not only seems absurd, but would also allow spouses to shield their property from federal taxation by classifying it as entireties property, facilitating abuse of the federal tax system. . . .

"We therefore conclude that [the] husband's interest in the entireties property constituted 'property' or 'rights to property' for the purposes of the federal tax lien statute. We recognize that Michigan makes a different choice with respect to state law creditors. . . . But that by no means dictates our choice. The interpretation of 26 U.S.C. s.6321 is a federal question, and in answering that question we are in no way bound by state courts' answers to similar questions involving state law."

The *Craft* case discusses these rules, in the context of a lien for one spouse's unpaid income taxes.

Community Property

The main feature of the **community property** system is that most property acquired after marriage by either the husband or the wife automatically becomes the common property of the husband and wife. Under the common law, if a husband earned $50,000 per year, he was legally obligated to provide the necessities for his wife's support with that amount; however, his wife had no rights in any money over and above the amount required to provide these necessities. Also, under the common law, if a wife were employed outside the home, her income was also her husband's. Under the community property theory, most income and property acquired by either spouse is owned by both, share and share alike. Probable exceptions to the co-ownership rule would be property acquired by gift or inheritance or property received in exchange for property owned by one of the parties prior to the marriage. Income earned during the marriage by separately owned property may or may not be community property, depending on the state.

The community property system is a statutory type of ownership that, if adopted by a specific state, will cover all people in the relationship of husband and wife who are subject to the laws of that state. Unlike the previous types of ownership discussed in this chapter, it is not voluntary. Also, the states that have adopted this form of ownership have not followed any uniform pattern. Answers to such questions as whether a spouse's share in community property will descend to his or her heirs or will automatically go to the surviving spouse, or whether or not the spouse's share is subject to levy of execution by creditors, or how the property is to be divided in case of divorce, must be determined by looking at the specific statute of the state involved. The nine states that have community property laws are Arizona, California, Idaho, Louisiana, New Mexico, Nevada, Texas, Washington, and Wisconsin.

Condominium Ownership

Condominium ownership is a combination of ownership in severalty and tenancy in common. Condominiums are multiple-unit buildings or developments of several buildings in which an owner owns an individual unit, and all of these owners share the land and common areas used by all tenants as tenants in common. The owners of the various individual apartments or buildings pay a management fee to a condominium corporation to manage the complex and to keep the common areas repaired and cleaned.

Nearly all of the states have enacted some type of condominium law to regulate condominium ownership and construction. These laws vary from state to state, and a person should be familiar with the particular state condominium law before making any decisions regarding condominium ownership or construction.

Condominium owners are joint owners of the common areas, and as such are liable on a pro rata basis for costs, expenses, and even liability for claims for damages arising out of the use of the common areas.

Time-Sharing Ownership

This property concept has been developed particularly for resort properties. Time-sharing ownership is also called "interval ownership" in some areas.

The theory of **time-sharing ownership** is very simple. In the past, you purchased a condominium in Florida, hoping to rent it out for most of the year and to reserve it for yourself for 2 months in the winter. The problem was that the capital investment was quite sizable. Now, you can simply buy the right to use a condominium unit in a resort area for a specific period of time, perhaps 2 weeks a year; the other 50 weeks are sold to other individuals. You have purchased 2 weeks' use per year for your life or forever, as the case may be. You can trade your 2 weeks to one of the other time-share owners if you want to use the property at a different time, or you can sell or lease your right to use it. The obvious benefit of time-sharing ownership is that you have to pay only a fraction of the total price of the unit, yet you own an exclusive right to use it for a specific time every year.

As with condominium ownership, state laws regulating this type of ownership vary. Before any decision is made regarding such purchases, the laws of the state where the real estate is located should be reviewed.

Cooperative Ownership

The **cooperative** is a type of housing ownership in which the tenants must be owners of an interest in the cooperative, which is the landlord. However, they do not actually own the space in which they live, as does the person who owns a condominium or a time-share ownership. Typically the cooperative is a corporation and the tenants are the owners of shares of stock of the corporation. The stockholders as tenants then lease apartments from the corporation and the rent that each tenant pays is based on the tenant's share of the expenses of the corporation, such as mortgage payment, maintenance, real estate taxes, insurance, etc. The corporation is the owner of the real estate and the tenants are simply owners of personal property, namely the shares of stock of the corporation. Also most cooperatives require that if a tenant moves out, he or she must sell the shares of stock to a person who will then lease the apartment he or she is vacating, or some cooperatives might have a provision in their articles or bylaws requiring the tenant-stockholder to sell the shares back to the cooperative on moving out. Cooperatives are typically not-for-profit organizations and are created and regulated under specific statutes in most states.

Changes in Form

When purchasing a home the buyer may ask, "Do these drapes go with the house?" "Does this chandelier stay with the house?" "Does the carpet in the family room go with the house?" The crucial legal question here is whether or not these items, which were once personal property, now have become **fixtures** to the real property, and thus an inseparable part of the real property.

Personal Property to Real Property

Here again, the specific law of the state in which the property is located will determine whether a particular item is still movable personal property or whether it has become a fixture and part of the real property.

The best advice is: "put it in writing." Specify in your agreement to purchase what items go with the house.

Affixation

Has the item become permanently affixed to the land or the building? If an item has been attached to the land or the building in such a manner that it cannot be removed without damaging the building or the land or the item itself, then the item is usually considered part of the real property. If carpet is glued to the concrete slab in the family room of a house, it is typically considered part of the real estate because removing it would leave a bare, unusable floor and would no doubt destroy the carpet. Drapes or curtains can normally be removed from curtain rods or other types of hangers without damaging either the curtains or the fixtures on which they are hanging. However, the curtain rods themselves are considered permanent fixtures because they are permanently attached to the wall and cannot be removed without leaving holes in it.

Intent

What was the intent of the owner of the personal property when the personal property was affixed to the real property? Here, we may go beyond the actual physical method of affixing the property and look to the owner's intention when the property was affixed. Did the owner intend to add the fixture to the real property or to maintain it as personal property? If a person rents a store building and installs counters, showcases, and other equipment necessary to run the store, will these items be considered personal property, or will they be part of the real estate? Counters, showcases and similar equipment installed for business purposes are called "**trade fixtures**." The general rule is that, if a person affixes personal property to the land or building of another, the owner of the land or building becomes the owner of the affixed items. But in a situation such as the store, which involves installation of trade fixtures, most courts would probably say that the business tenant remains the owner of the items even though it becomes necessary to unbolt them from the floor or to disconnect electric wires or water pipes before the items can be removed from the building. It is normally not the intent of the business tenant to make a gift of such items to the landlord, and the landlord has either expressly or impliedly agreed to such removals.

Business Records

How is the property being carried on the books of a business? Is it still considered as personal property, or is it considered as an improvement of the real estate? Business records can be used as evidence of the parties' intent.

Courts are generally more liberal in permitting removal of items attached for the tenant's specific business or agricultural use or to add to the comfort and convenience of a residence. In all of these situations, however, it is advisable to have a clause in the lease specifying which items are removable by the tenant and are not to be considered part of the realty, even though permanently attached.

Real Property to Personal Property

When a fixture is severed from the real estate, it becomes personal property. A built-in stove in your kitchen is considered part of the real estate and goes with the house. However, if you decide to replace it with a new one, once the old stove has been physically severed from the real estate it returns to the status of personal property. Growing timber or crops are part of the real estate; however, once they are severed from the ground they become personal property. They can also be sold, as "goods" under the Uniform Commercial Code (UCC), without already having been physically detached from the land. Coal in the ground is part of the real estate; however, when it is mined and severed from the ground it becomes personal property.

Acquisition of Title to Personal Property

Title to personal property may be acquired in several different ways. Acquisition may be the result of voluntary action on the part of the former owner and the new owner, or it may occur simply by the operation of the law. Following are some of the common methods of acquiring title to personal property.

Purchase of Personal Property

When you go to the grocery store and buy groceries for the week, you have acquired personal property by purchase. No certificate of title is attached to each item in your grocery sack; mere possession is evidence of title to such items. If you purchase an automobile, a motorcycle, or a motor home, the seller will give you a bill of sale, which must be registered with the specific state authorities, so that title to the vehicle is registered in your name on state records. If you purchase the equipment and trade fixtures of a business, you will normally require that a bill of sale specifically describes each item or object that is part of the purchase. This bill of sale does not need to be recorded with the state or county; however, it will be your evidence of title.

Title to Personal Property by Gift

Title to personal property may be transferred from one person to other persons by gift. A gift is a voluntary action on the part of the giver, with no value in return from the person receiving the gift. The transfer of personal property by gift can be divided into three basic classifications. An *inter vivos* gift is a gift made by a living person to another living person. A gift *causa mortis* is a gift that is given in contemplation of the giver's death. A testamentary gift is a gift that is given in a person's will.

The three types of gifts differ mainly with regard to revocability. Once an inter vivos gift has been delivered, it is generally irrevocable. Because a gift causa mortis is made in contemplation of death, if the giver recovers, then the giver can have the property back. The causa mortis gift may be revoked by the giver during the giver's lifetime, and it may be revoked if the recipient dies before the giver dies. A testamentary gift may be revoked by revoking or amending the will.

The question often arises as to when an inter vivos gift becomes effective. Two tests must be met. First, it must be shown that the giver intended to divest certain rights in the property. It is not necessary that all rights be given for a gift to be valid. For example, an owner of corporate stock may give the dividends of the stock to another person, but retain ownership of the actual shares of stock. Intent may be evidenced by a written statement, by actions of the giver, or by other documents such as the signature card for a joint bank account.

The second test of a gift is delivery. Delivery is simply the transfer of possession or control from one person to another. Delivery does not have to be made to the recipient of the gift; it can be made to a third person as agent or trustee for the recipient. A bank will often be the trustee for the recipient if the recipient is a minor, or if the recipient is an elderly person who is incapable of handling the property. The key with regard to delivery is that the giver surrenders all rights to possession and control of the property that is the subject of the gift. In some instances, you cannot pick the gift up and hand it to the recipient. With an automobile, for example, delivery would consist of handing over the keys. This would be called symbolic delivery. If the gift involves intangible property, then delivery would consist of turning over some document that transfers title to the intangible property to the donee, such as an assignment of a patent or a copyright or a properly endorsed stock certificate.

The Uniform Gifts to Minors Act

In the past many parents who wanted to give money to their children would set up a savings account in a bank in the name of the minor child. The account would show one of the parents as parent and guardian, and normally the money could be taken out of the account only by the parent. The question arose as to whether or not there was an actual gift because the parent still retained control over the property. Was there really delivery? The **Uniform Gifts to Minors Act (UGMA)** was drafted to set up a procedure for making legal gifts to minors. This act has been adopted in nearly all of the states. It provides a method for making gifts of money and of registered and unregistered securities to minors.

If the gift is money, the money may simply be deposited in a bank in the name of the giver or some other adult, or of some corporate trustee, such as a bank, with the statement that the party in whose name the account is registered is a custodian for the minor under

CASE 4

KOHLER v. FLYNN
493 N.W.2d 647 (ND 1992)

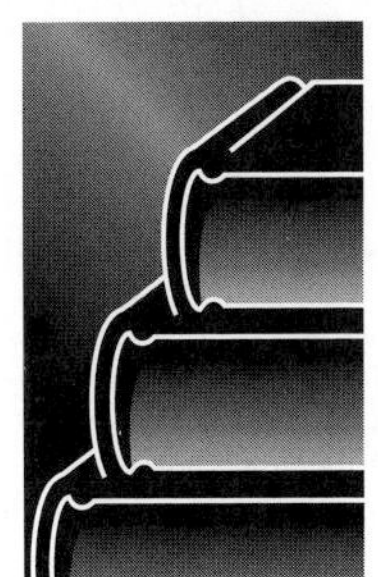

Facts: Don Kohler appeals a judgment dismissing his claim against Tangula Flynn for division of assets and debts after their cohabitation ended.

Don and Tangula began living together in May 1990. They kept separate checking accounts, although Don deposited a disputed amount of his sporadic earnings in Tangula's account, resulting in what the trial court termed a "common pot arrangement." The couple bought a mobile home in Tangula's name, with Don making the down payment and Tangula making subsequent payments. They occasionally paid one another's debts, including some incurred before they lived together. Intending to marry, Don and Tangula became engaged and bought an engagement ring for her.

In November 1990, the couple separated, not having married. Soon after, the mobile home and the engagement ring were destroyed by a fire. Tangula collected the fire insurance proceeds.

Don sued Tangula for an accounting of indebtedness and "an equitable share of their joint properties in the form of money," claiming that "the expenditures and pooling of monies and assets were done in anticipation of marriage which did not take place." Tangula counterclaimed, also seeking damages for her expenditures for Don's benefit, for some damage that Don did to the mobile home when he left and for personal property allegedly taken by Don.

After a trial without a jury, the trial court recognized that Don's claim was in the nature of "an audit or an accounting," but found the couple's funds to be "hopelessly intermingled."

The trial court concluded that Don and Tangula "parted with essentially the same assets, or their replacements, they had when they entered into the arrangement." The court dismissed both claims.

Issue: Should gifts, assets, and liabilities accumulated during an engagement be equitably divided when the marriage does not take place?

Decision: No. Judgment affirmed.

Opinion by Justice Meschke: "This is not a 'palimony' case like the notorious decision in *Marvin v. Marvin*.... The *Marvin* plaintiff gave up an entertainment career to live with a well-known actor for seven years, and she sought a share of the actor's property for her services as a 'companion, homemaker, housekeeper, and cook....' One scholar summarizes the *Marvin* holding: 'The meaning of the Marvin case thus seems to be that living together out of wedlock, *at least for a substantial period*, gives rise to claims on the part of both parties to share in each other's property on some unspecified equitable basis....' Here, Don and Tangula lived together for only six months, anything but 'a substantial period,' and neither gave up any personal or professional opportunity. Even if we were to consider the *Marvin* precedent, it has no bearing on this case.

"Our law on equitable distribution of martial property in a divorce does not fit the breakup of an engagement or living arrangement.... Rather, this case is controlled by the law on partition of property. ND 32-16-01 says:

> *When several cotenants hold and are in possession of real or personal property as partners, joint tenants, or tenants in common, in which one or more of them have an estate or inheritance, or for life or lives, or for years, an action may be brought by one or more of such persons for a partition thereof according to the respective rights of the persons interested therein....*

Thus, outside of marriage, judicial division of property ordinarily depends on common ownership. In this case, Don and Tangula did not hold any property 'as partners, joint tenants, or tenants in common.' Thus, Don and Tangula do not qualify for judicial division of their accumulated assets, debts, and mutual gifts.

"The general rule is that '[c]ohabitants may bring an action for partition of their property where the[ir] intention was clearly to own their property jointly. Conversely, mere cohabitation is not enough to support a right to partition in the absence of actual joint ownership....' If live-in companions intend to share property, they should express that intention in writing. In this case, there is neither evidence nor a finding that Don and Tangula intended to own any property together.

"The parties argue whether the engagement ring was an unconditional gift. Don cites the view, existing in many states, that an engagement ring is a conditional gift, returnable if the engagement is broken without justification by the donee or terminated by consent and sometimes irrespective of fault.... In some states, a specific statute governs the return of gifts made in contemplation of a marriage that does not take place.... Don alleges that 'the ring was thought of as Don's by Tangula,' despite the fact that 'she did not return it to him' when they separated. Don also claims that Tangula had the risk of the ring's loss by fire while it was in her possession, so that he is entitled to recover its value instead of its return. Tangula counters that Don deserves nothing more, because '[s]he paid on the ring while they were together, and ... would have returned it if she still had it, but the [trial] Court found it to be an unconditional gift.' Besides, she says, she lost much more in value than the insurance reimbursed her.

"Because the engagement ring was destroyed in the fire and is unavailable, we cannot consider its return. Furthermore, the trial court ruled that, factually neither party was indebted to the other. Since the court found that Don and Tangula each left 'with essentially the same assets' they had when they began living together, the possibility of fault by one of the parties in ending the engagement is not relevant to this case.

"North Dakota law defines a 'gift' as 'a transfer of personal property made voluntarily and without consideration. . . .' For a valid gift *inter vivos*, we have said:

> *There must be an intention on the part of the donor to relinquish the right of dominion on one hand and to create it on the other, and the delivery must be not only of possession but also of the dominion and control of the property. To have the effect of a valid gift, therefore, the transfer of possession and title must be absolute and go into immediate effect, so far as the donor can make it so by intent and delivery, and must be so complete that if he again resumes control over it without consent of the donee he becomes liable as a trespasser. . . .*

Here, both parties acknowledge that Don bought the ring for Tangula, despite her installment payments on it while they were together. Regardless of other arguments about the ring, the findings of the trial court control this case. Applying the law of gifts, the trial court found that 'whenever one party used identifiable funds belonging to that party for some purchase that was considered as belonging to the other party, that no loan was being made nor was there any expectation of receiving an ownership interest in the item purchased. If anything, they were unconditional mutual gifts.'"

the UGMA. If the gift is a registered security, then the giver registers the security as custodian for the minor under the UGMA. If the security is unregistered, it has to be delivered to another adult or to a bank or some other financial institution as trustee, together with a statement of the gift and an acknowledgment accepting the role of custodian of the security for and on behalf of the minor. The custodian has very broad powers as to the use and disposition of the property. The property can be exchanged or sold without the permission of the minor who is the beneficiary of the gift. Of course, the custodian is not permitted to use any of the property or any of the proceeds for personal benefit.

The Uniform Anatomical Gift Act

Traditionally, we do not think of the human body or parts of the human body as things of monetary value, so we were not concerned about property rights to our body or various parts of our body. Now that medical technology has developed processes for transplanting parts of one body to another body, the law must treat the human body and the parts thereof as property, and establish some procedure for making gifts of the human body or its parts. Under the **Uniform Anatomical Gift Act (UAGA)**, people 18 years of age or older may make a gift of their entire body or any specified part of their body. However, the gift does not take effect until the death of the giver. Such gifts are revocable at any time. They are usually included in the giver's last will and testament. Also, many states have included an anatomical gift statement on the back of the driver's license. People wishing to donate their bodies or specific organs can so specify and sign and date the statement in the presence of two witnesses, who must also sign.

People also may sell or donate blood, a kidney, an eye, or some other organ the loss of which does not automatically cause death. Such gifts are not covered by the UAGA because they are not given at death.

Title by Inheritance

As indicated previously, you may become the owner of personal property as a result of a specific bequest in a deceased person's will. You may also become the owner of personal property through the process of **intestate succession**. This means that you are an heir under state statute and that you will receive a designated share of the decedent's personal property if there is no valid will that disposes of it.

Title by Accession

Accession simply means an addition to what you already have. An example of accession would be a situation in which the lawn mower that your neighbor borrowed for the weekend broke down and he had to have it repaired. When your neighbor returned the lawn mower to you, you became the owner of the repairs by accession.

Problems of this type of acquisition of personal property arise when accession of considerable value is made without the property owner's consent and when the original item has been changed or altered so that identification is difficult. A trespasser cuts down small trees on my land, makes rustic lawn chairs from the trees, and sets up a stand along the highway to sell the lawn chairs. Who owns the lawn chairs that were previously my timber? There is no simple answer to this question because the courts have not agreed on one solution, especially if the original material was taken as the result of an innocent mistake.

Confusion

Title to personal property may be acquired when the property of different owners is so intermingled that the property of the individual owners cannot be identified or separated and returned to the specific owners. **Confusion** is most common when dealing with such fungible goods as corn, wheat, milk, and oil.

If three persons owning 1,000 bushels of wheat of the same grade and quality agree to intermingle their property for purposes of storage, there would be no problem because the intermingling was voluntary. Each party will simply have a one-third ownership in the total volume of wheat. The problem involving title to personal property arises when one owner intentionally and wrongfully intermingles goods with those of another person so that the goods of each owner can no longer be separated or distinguished. The majority of the courts, in a case where the commingling was deliberate and wrongful and without the permission of the other party, will simply grant the innocent party title to the entire volume of goods. The wrongdoer is punished by being deprived of any further right or title to the property. If the intermingling of the goods is not an intentional and wrongful act, and if the goods are of the same kind and quality, courts will usually hold that each owner now owns a proportionate share of the total mixed goods.

Title by Creation

Property is created when a new invention is made, when a new song or book is written, or when a new painting is created. These creations are the result of intellectual production. In **title by creation**, you are intellectually creating an expression of a new idea in which the law grants property rights. These complex issues are discussed in the next chapter.

Significance of This Chapter

Ownership of property is one of the most basic concepts of the law. At one time, it was said that "possession is nine-tenths of the law," but in a civilized society we must have rules regarding the ownership of property, how it can be transferred, and who inherits what rights. Possession in itself may not mean very much. Suppose, for example, that you found a wristwatch with a broken band. Obviously it accidentally fell off the person's arm when the band broke. Is the watch yours because you physically possess it? Clearly not. It is also important to understand the concept of the bundle of rights, because many things we say we own are not wholly owned by us; that is, we do not own all the rights in that thing. Another very important question concerns things that may be attached to, or detached from, real estate. Landlords and tenants, and buyers and sellers of land, need to know which things are part of the land. As a tenant, before you attach any item of personal property, get permission from the landlord to do so, reserve the right to remove the item, and "get it in writing."

IMPORTANT TERMS AND CONCEPTS

accession
community property
condominium ownership
confusion
cooperative
fixtures
intestate succession
joint tenancy
ownership in severalty
personal property
private property
public property
real property
tenancy by the entirety
tenancy in common
time-sharing ownership
title by creation
trade fixtures
Uniform Anatomical Gift Act (UAGA)
Uniform Gifts to Minors Act (UGMA)

QUESTIONS AND PROBLEMS FOR DISCUSSION

1. What are the different ways in which ownership of property can be acquired?

2. What are the two classifications of personal property, and what sort of things does each include?

3. What is the difference between joint tenancy and tenancy by the entirety?

4. How does the community property system work? How many states are now using this system?

5. Arthur Evans had rented a safe-deposit box in which he had stored valuables. His niece, Mrs. Kellows, had worked for the family since she was 16, and she continued to care for Evans until he died. Before Evans went into the hospital, just prior to his death, he gave the keys to the box to Kellows. Reverend Cummings visited Evans shortly before he died, and Evans told Cummings that he was giving $10,000 to the church and that he had given the rest of his possessions and the keys to the safe-deposit box to Kellows. The executor considered the contents of the safe-deposit box, valued at approximately $80,000, to be assets of the estate and not the specific property of Kellows. Kellows filed objections, stating that there had been a gift and that she owned the contents of the box. She had the keys; however, her name was not on the rental agreement and the bank had no notice that she had any interest in the box.

   Who owns the box contents, and why?

6. Plaintiff and defendant bought a house in 1982 and separated in 1991. The husband was seeking a divorce. The wife was seeking a separation and opposed a divorce on religious grounds. The husband had refused to share their marital home with the plaintiff, either by selling the house and dividing the proceeds, by paying the plaintiff her share of the equity of the house, or by renting the premises and dividing the proceeds. In support of his position, the husband pointed out that the property in question was held under a tenancy by the entirety that gave both him and his wife an indefeasible right of survivorship, but gave him the exclusive right to possession and control during his lifetime. He stated that he would grant the plaintiff one half of the equity in the house if she would grant him an uncontested divorce. She sued for her half.

   What result, and why?

7. Ralph Renter leased a commercial building from Owen Owner. Owen had been using the building for storage and so had never installed heating equipment. Ralph knew this when he leased the building. Ralph installed an oil burner and boiler in the basement so that he could heat the building because he intended to use it as his workshop. Owen sold the building to Betty Bucks. When Ralph's lease expired, Ralph and Betty were unable to agree on terms for a renewal, so Ralph planned to move out—with the heating equipment. On learning that Ralph planned to remove the oil burner and boiler, Betty sued for an injunction.

   Should the injunction be granted? Why or why not?

8. Annie and Dennie Cracker had been married for 6 years when they filed a joint petition for divorce. Annie had been employed full time throughout the marriage and had also done most of the couple's housework and cooking. Dennie had worked only part time and had gone to school full time for 4 of the 6 years. He had finished a BS in Engineering and had then received an MBA. The trial court found that the only marital "asset" of any value that the parties had accumulated during the marriage was Dennie's MBA degree. It placed a value of $82,000 on his future extra earnings due to the degree, and it awarded Annie $33,000 of this amount, which Dennie was to pay off at the rate of $100 per month. Dennie appealed from this award, saying his MBA is not really "property."

   How should the appeals court rule? Explain.

CHAPTER 16

Intellectual Property

Chapter Objectives

This chapter will:

- Explain the importance to business of "intellectual property."
- Define "trade secrets" and their significance.
- Summarize patent protection.
- Indicate how copyright applies in today's economy.
- Suggest the need to protect "trade dress."
- Discuss the international aspects of intellectual property.

It can be argued—with some justification—that **"intellectual property"** is the most important part of our modern internationalized economy. The term includes all those products of the human intellect that have potential commercial value. Many of our nation's major exports are based on intellectual property. Films, TV programs, music, and books are protected (usually) by copyright law. Franchisors of hamburgers and fried chicken rely on trademark protection to distinguish their heavily advertised products from domestic and foreign competitors, and the chicken colonel likewise uses trade secret law to protect his "11 secret herbs and spices." Certain formulas for cola drinks and drug products are also trade secrets. Alternatively, such formulas may be patented. Sellers of computers, jet planes, office furniture, automotive equipment, and similar goods have patents on various product designs and manufacturing processes. Intellectual property law thus provides protection for significant business assets that are the basis of many companies' competitive advantages. Understanding intellectual property law is therefore a key part of effective management in today's global business environment.

This chapter covers the four major subjects of intellectual property law—trade secrets, patents, copyrights, and trademarks. "Trade dress" law is included as a sub-part of trademark law. The chapter concludes with a brief overview of some of the international dimensions of intellectual property law.

Trade Secret Law

Unlike the other three major areas of intellectual property law, which are now governed primarily by national statutes and regulations, trade secret law is still basically state law. Originally part of the common law of "unfair competition" (which is discussed in Chapter 5), trade secret law is now subject to statutory definition in most states. About three-fourths of the states have adopted the **Uniform Trade Secrets Act (UTSA)**, a brief (but somewhat complex) statute defining the owner's rights and providing for monetary and injunctive relief.

Definition of Trade Secret

A **"trade secret"** is created when a business expends time or money to develop a concept or information that has commercial value, is kept confidential, and is not generally known in the trade. It is, in other words, a secret "competitive advantage." According to the UTSA, such information may include "a formula, pattern, compilation, program, device, method, technique, or process."

When deciding whether a particular set of data qualifies as a trade secret, courts usually consider several questions. To what extent are other businesses also aware of this information? Is this information widely shared within the company claiming the trade secret? What measures have been taken by the claimant company to preserve the secrecy of the information? How valuable is the information to the claimant company? How difficult would it be for competitors to (lawfully) acquire or duplicate the information? In light of these tests, one can understand the extreme security precautions taken by the cola drink company and the fried chicken franchisor to protect their product formulas. Each one of these examples is a mulitbillion-dollar global enterprise, with thousands of employees, but with only two or three people knowing the treasured product formula at one time.

Misappropriation

The UTSA says that a trade secret is misappropriated (and legal remedies can therefore be sought) in two circumstances. First, when it is acquired "by a person who knows or has reason to know that the trade secret was acquired by improper means." If the acquirer was buying the trade secret from a known industrial spy, there would be reason to know that it had been improperly acquired.

Second, misappropriation includes disclosure or use, without the owner's consent, by three groups of persons: (a) any person who used improper means to acquire knowledge of the secret; or (b) any person who knew or had reason to know that his or her knowledge of the secret was derived from a person who had learned it by improper means or who owed the secret's owner a duty to keep the secret, or was acquired "under circumstances giving rise to a duty to maintain its secrecy or limit its use;" or (c) any person who, before any material change in his or her position, knew or had reason to know that knowledge of the secret had been acquired by "accident or mistake."

With these comprehensive definitions, the UTSA is thus trying to cover all the possible circumstances in which wrongful use of the trade secret has occurred. The key to wrongful use is the unauthorized taking of someone else's trade secret. There is no violation if a second person independently develops a second version of the formula or process. Even if the second person discovers the trade secret by reverse engineering the first's product, there is no violation.

Trade secret law does not guarantee that no one else can manufacture and sell your product, only that they cannot use your secret process to do so. If you want exclusive rights to make and sell something, you need a patent or a copyright. This lack of protection against independent duplication is the major danger in relying on trade secret law.

Enforcement

When misappropriation has occurred, an injunction may be issued to prevent further wrongful use or disclosure. Money damages may be awarded to the secret owner for any

CASE 1

ConAgra Poultry Company v. Tyson Foods, Inc.

30 S.W.3d 725 (AK 2000)

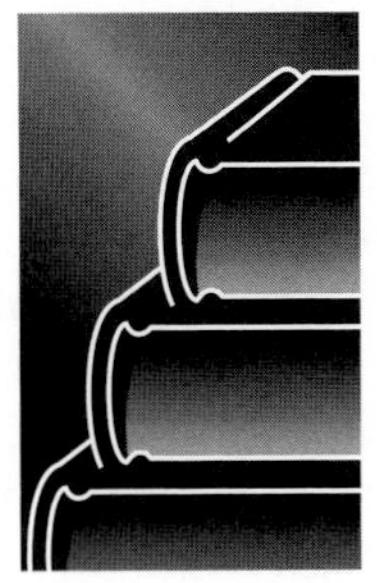

Facts: Both companies are major producers and marketers of poultry products—Tyson #1, ConAgra #5. Four senior executives of Tyson resigned and then were hired by ConAgra. Tyson claimed that they had access to trade secret information regarding pricing, cost of goods sold, profit margins, and marketing strategies. In this case, Tyson asked for and received an injunction against the continued employment of three of these executives in connection with sales of poultry products. ConAgra appealed on the basis that no trade secrets existed.

Issue: Did Tyson take reasonable steps to protect the secrecy of the relevant information, so as to qualify it as a trade secret?

Decision: No. Judgment reversed.

Opinion by Judge Brown: "Tyson neglected to include any restriction in its customer contracts which prevented disclosure to third parties. Regardless of whether proof was presented that such disclosure by Tyson customers had transpired, Tyson manifestly failed to take steps to guard the secrecy of this information. Moreover, without a curb or some restriction on its customers, the information was readily ascertainable by third parties from some, if not all, of Tyson's customers. This lapse is important to this court. If Tyson did not consider it necessary to preclude the dissemination of pricing information by its customers, why should this court ... enforce secrecy of that same information?

"But there is a second, more comprehensive aspect of the chancery court's decree which we believe is in error. In finding that Tyson met the criterion of guarding its secrets, the trial court relied solely on Tyson's Corporate Code of Conduct and Compliance Policy and 'verbal understandings' with its managers.... [W]e hold that the chancery court clearly erred in doing so.... The salient part of that Code ... relates only to Tyson employees and the requirement that they safeguard Tyson's confidential business and technical information. Tyson had not entered into a covenant not to compete with the three executives to be effective for a certain period of time after the three men left Tyson.... Nor did Tyson have a separate confidentiality agreement with these executives which extended the period of time for confidentiality of certain proprietary information for a period of one year after the three men left the company's employment.... In short, Tyson had in place no protection against postemployment revelation of confidential information by these executives....

"Though reasonable efforts to protect the secrecy of certain information is only one of the factors we look to in determining the status of a trade secret, it is a prominent one. To reiterate in part ... [the statute] requires that for information to qualify as a trade secret, it must be 'the subject of efforts that are reasonable under the circumstances to maintain its secrecy.'... As best we can tell, there were no efforts on Tyson's part to restrain disclosure of information post-employment.... Obviously, the failure of a business to protect against the disclosure of information it considers to be secret following employment is critical to our analysis and ultimate decision regarding whether the information is in fact a trade secret.

"Accordingly, we conclude that the trial court was clearly erroneous in finding that the information at issue qualified as a trade secret. We reverse the decree of the trial court ordering the one-year injunction and remand for an order to be entered forthwith voiding the injunction."

loss sustained as a result of the misappropriation. For intentional conduct, punitive damages may also be awarded. Criminal laws against theft and embezzlement may also be applicable to some wrongful takings.

Prevention

New employees ought to be required to sign confidentiality agreements as part of the hiring process. Clear disclosure policies, as to which people within the company have a need to know which trade secrets, need to be developed and monitored. Policies also need to be developed and enforced as to the presence of non-employees on the business premises. Company records that might contain trade secret information need to be carefully maintained. Exit interviews, reminding employees who are leaving of their post-employment obligations, are probably also a good idea.

The *ConAgra* case illustrates some of the difficulties in protecting trade secrets.

Patent Law

The Constitution (Article I, Section 8) gives Congress the power "To promote the progress of science and useful arts, by securing for limited times to authors and inventors the exclusive right to their respective writings and discoveries." Using this grant of authority, Congress has passed statutes providing for patents and copyrights, and establishing the process for awarding them. The first patent law was enacted in 1790, and has been subject to only three major revisions—1793, 1836, and 1952.

Definition of Patent

A **patent** gives the owner the exclusive right to make and sell the invention for the "limited times" specified by Congress. There are three basic categories of patents: **product or process patents**, **design patents**, and **plant patents**.

It is the product or process patent that most people are thinking of when they use the term *patent*. This first category applies to any "process, machine, manufacture, or composition of matter," and to improvements on any of these things. These are patents for the proverbial "better mousetrap." The inventor's rights extend for 20 years. Because of the extensive government testing requirements for new drugs and medical devices, before they can be sold, 1984 amendments to the patent law permit a 5-year extension of protection for these products, under certain conditions.

Design patents are granted to protect developers of original, ornamental product designs. The designer has exclusive rights of use for 14 years. Plant patents are granted to promote agricultural progress by protecting the rights of people who develop distinctive new plants by methods other than improved seeds. The Supreme Court decided in 1980 that developers of other new life forms (bacteria) could apply for product or process patents, even though they might not be eligible for a plant patent.

Patentability

What does the inventor have to show to qualify for a patent? No one can own an idea, so Einstein could not have patented $E = mc^2$. Likewise, patents cannot be granted for naturally occurring plants or animals, or for the "laws of nature." Printed matter and business methods are not patentable, although the former may be protectable by copyright. Ultimately, the Supreme Court will decide where to draw these lines.

For a product or process patent, the invention must be new, useful, and non-obvious. New in this context means, generally, that the invention was previously unknown and that no one has previously patented it or disclosed it through publication. Here again, there are some difficult, technical questions as to exactly what was known and when, where, and by whom it was known. Useful means that the inventor must show that the invention produces a specific, substantial beneficial result. Non-obvious means that the invention would not have been apparent to someone skilled in the particular field or industry. This third requirement causes particular difficulty when a patent claim is made for a new combination of elements that were already well known. On this point as well, the courts will have to make case-by-case decisions.

For a design patent, the claimant must show the design's ornamentality, rather than the utility required for a product or process patent. The novelty and non-obviousness requirements are the same. For a plant patent, the claimant must show the distinctiveness of the new plant, that is, that its characteristics are clearly different from those of existing types. Here again, the other two requirements are the same, but non-obvious in this context may mean little more than distinctive.

Application Process

A person claiming a patent files an application with the Patent and Trademark Office (PTO). The application must disclose, with words and diagrams, how to make and use the invention. Further, it must also explain how the invention differs from already known devices and processes (the "prior art" in the field). Finally, it must state precisely exactly what aspects of the invention are to be protected by the patent—the "claim."

Typically, there will be a considerable exchange of documents between the PTO and the inventor, as objections are raised and modifications to the application are made. There is an appeals process if the patent is denied.

Scope of Protection

Once granted, the patent gives the owner the right to prevent others from making or selling the invention within the United States. Because patents are still granted nation by nation, further applications will have to be filed in each country where protection is sought. Getting overseas protection may thus be a lengthy and expensive process, especially because procedures and protections may be quite different from nation to nation. These points will be discussed further in the last section of this chapter.

Because the patent process involves public disclosure of the invention, including how to make it and what it does, all the world now has access to this information. Anyone and everyone can now try to engineer their way around the patent, by trying to produce the same benefits with a different device or process.

Companies thus need to weigh very carefully the respective costs and benefits of patent protection versus trade secret protection.

Infringement

When a lawsuit claiming **infringement** is filed, the court will focus very closely on the claims made in the patent. Do they describe the allegedly offending device or product, as well as the patented one? As one court stated the test, the question is whether the defendant's product or process "performs substantially the same overall function or work, in substantially the same way, to obtain substantially the same overall result."

Infringement may occur by making, selling, or using a sufficiently similar product or process. Making, selling, or using a smaller, unpatented part of the patented product or process would not be a violation of the patent holder's rights. (Other persons are still free to use the Arrhenius equation in other contexts, despite the process patent held by Diehr and Lutton.) Good faith and ignorance are generally not excuses, although they may result in lower damages against the infringer.

Once a patented item has been sold to a buyer, that person may of course use it and re-sell it. It is likewise clear that the buyer may repair the purchased patented item, without violating the patent holder's rights. The difficulty is drawing the line between repairing an existing item and building a new one. Because only the patent holder has the right to "make" the patented item, making a new one would violate the holder's patent rights. Here too, some difficult legal and factual lines must be drawn by the courts.

Enforcement and Remedies

The Patent Act provides for a combination of remedies in which infringement has occurred. The patent owner may be entitled to an injunction against further wrongful manufacture, sale, or use. Damages are awarded to compensate the plaintiff's loss, in an amount at least equal to what would have been a reasonable royalty for use of the patent, plus interest. In an appropriate case (as for example, where the defendant has willfully infringed), damages may be trebled. Court costs will be awarded, but attorney fees are given only in "exceptional" cases. In design patent cases, the infringer's profits derived from the wrongful copying may be recovered by the patent owner.

The *eBay* case is the U.S. Supreme Court's most recent analysis of the use of injunctions in patent infringement cases.

CASE 2

EBAY INC. v. MERCEXCHANGE, L.L.C.

126 S.Ct. 1837 (2006)

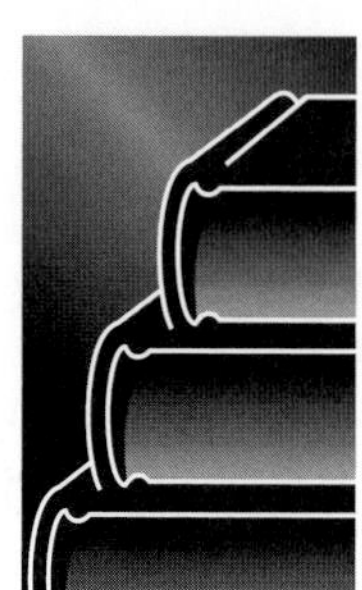

Facts: EBay and its subsidiary Half.com operate Web sites that allow private sellers to list goods they wish to sell, either at auction or for a fixed price. Mercexchange owns a number of patents, including a "business method" patent for an electronic marketplace. Mercexchange first sought to license that patent to defendants but was unable to reach an agreement with them. Mercexchange then filed a patent infringement suit against them, in U.S. District Court for the Eastern District of Virginia. A jury found that the patent was valid, that the defendants had infringed it, and that damages should be awarded. The District Court judge, however, denied Mercexchange's motion for a permanent injunction against the defendants' use of their infringing system. On appeal, the U.S. Circuit Court for the Federal Circuit reversed, saying that such injunctions should normally be granted.

Issue: Should injunctions normally be granted in patent infringement cases?

Decision: No. Judgment reversed, and case remanded.

Opinion by Justice Thomas: "According to well-established principles of equity, a plaintiff seeking a permanent injunction must satisfy a four-factor test before a court may grant such relief. A plaintiff must demonstrate: (1) that it has suffered an irreparable injury; (2) that remedies available at law, such as monetary damages, are inadequate to compensate for that injury; (3) that, considering the balance of hardships between the plaintiff and defendant, a remedy in equity is warranted; and (4) that the public interest would not be disserved by a permanent injunction.... The decision to grant or deny permanent injunctive relief is an act of equitable discretion by the district court, reviewable on appeal for abuse of discretion....

"These familiar principles apply with equal force to disputes arising under the Patent Act. As this Court has long recognized, 'a major departure from the long tradition of equity practice should not be lightly implied.'... Nothing in the Patent Act indicates that Congress intended such a departure. To the contrary, the Patent Act expressly provides that injunctions 'may' issue 'in accordance with the principles of equity.'...

"To be sure, the Patent Act also declares that 'patents shall have the attributes of personal property,'... including 'the right to exclude others from making, using, offering for sale, or selling the invention.'... According to the Court of Appeals, this statutory right to exclude alone justifies its general rule in favor of permanent injunctive relief.... But the creation of a right is distinct from the provision of remedies for violations of that right. Indeed, the Patent Act itself indicates that patents shall have the attributes of personal property '[s]ubject to the provisions of this title,'... including, presumably, the provision that injunctive relief 'may' issue only 'in accordance with the principles of equity.'

"This approach is consistent with our treatment of injunctions under the Copyright Act....

"Because we conclude that neither court below correctly applied the traditional four-factor framework that governs the award of injunctive relief, we vacate the judgment of the Court of Appeals, so that the District Court may apply that framework in the first instance.... We hold only that the decision to grant or deny injunctive relief rests within the equitable discretion of the district courts, and that such discretion must be exercised consistent with traditional principles of equity, in patent disputes no less than in other cases governed by such standards.

"Accordingly, we vacate the judgment of the Court of Appeals, and remand for further proceedings consistent with this opinion.

"It is so ordered."

Copyright Law

The first Congress also passed a Copyright Act in 1790. Major revisions occurred in 1831, 1870, 1909, and 1976. Important changes in the law were also made when the United States acceded to the international copyright treaty (the Berne Convention) in 1989.

Definition of Copyright

Copyright is exactly what the word says: the right to copy a tangible creative work, or "work of authorship." The underlying idea is not protected, only the specific manner or form in which it is expressed. No one can copyright the idea of having a chapter on "Intellectual Property" in a Business Law book, but we do have a copyright on the words you are reading at this very moment. Copyright gives the author the exclusive right to copy or reproduce the work for the statutory period, which is now generally the life of the author plus 70 years.

Copyrightability

Although the constitutional provision speaks of "writings," that word has been given a very broad interpretation. The Copyright Act of 1976 says that "works of authorship" include "literary works; musical works, including any accompanying words; dramatic works, including any accompanying music; pantomimes and choreographic works; pictorial, graphic, sculptural works; motion pictures and other audiovisual works; sound recordings; and architectural works." (Computer programs on microchips can also be protected, under the Semiconductor Chip Protection Act of 1984. The chip rules are quite different from normal copyright, although the same office administers both statutes.)

That is an impressive listing, but it is not intended to be exclusive. Protection is given to any original work of authorship that is expressed in tangible form and is capable of being communicated. The three requirements for copyright protection are that the work be original, that it be expressed in a tangible medium, and that it contain some element of creativity. It is the third requirement that distinguishes the copyrightability of the telephone book yellow pages from the non-copyrightability of the white pages. There is no "creativity" in an alphabetical listing of the names of people who have telephone numbers. There is at least some creativity in deciding how to categorize the multitude of businesses and services that are listed in the yellow pages.

What, then, is not copyrightable? The 1976 act says that protection cannot be given to "any idea, procedure, process, system, method of operation, concept, principle, or discovery." Such information will therefore have to be protected, if at all, as a trade secret or perhaps with a process patent.

Registration Process

Unlike patent rights, which require registration for protection, copyright protection exists from the moment when the author puts the "work" into a tangible form. These very lines are protected by copyright as they are being typed on the IBM laptop and are appearing on the computer screen. From that instant, only we—as the authors (and our publisher, to whom we have contractually transferred the right to publish)—have the right to reproduce these words, in this sequence.

Why then bother with registration at all? Registering the work with the U.S. Copyright Office is a necessary prerequisite to filing a lawsuit against an alleged infringer. In other words, although the author's exclusive right to copy the work is protected, he or she cannot sue to enforce that right without first having registered the copyright.

In addition, registration does give the author important advantages when it is necessary to sue an infringer. The copyright for a registered work is presumed valid. Registration prior to infringement permits the copyright owner to recover statutory damages (up to $100,000) without any proof of actual damages, and in appropriate cases, attorney fees.

On the cost side of the cost-benefit analysis, copyright registration (unlike patent registration) is simple, fast, and inexpensive. The author fills out the proper form and sends it, together with two copies of the work (or appropriate "identifying material" for non-printed works) and a $20 fee, to the Copyright Office. Because independent duplication does not violate copyright law, there is no need to search all the "prior art" (as is necessary for the issuance of a patent) to make sure there is no duplication. Consequently, registration is all but automatic. Unless there is an obvious omission or error on the form, it and the work will be filed, and a certificate of copyright will be issued to the author.

Scope of Protection

The author (or an assignee) is protected against unauthorized copying of the work. The author of a play has the exclusive right to have the play publicly performed. Authors of pictures and sculptures have exclusive rights to display their works to the public.

As previously noted, the normal protection period is the life of the author (or authors), plus 70 years. However, in the case of a work for hire, the employer of the author owns the copyright for 75 years after the first publication of the work, or 100 years after the creation of the work, whichever comes first. A person who fits the common law definition of employee (discussed in Chapter 29) is presumed to create any "works" that fall within the scope of employment for the benefit of the employer. Likewise, an independent contractor (also discussed in Chapter 29) specifically hired, by written contract, to create certain types of works also turns over copyright to the employer. Among the types of works specified in the 1976 act are textbooks, tests, and test answers. If we had specifically hired someone to prepare the test questions for this book, we would own the copyright on the tests.

Infringement

Because there is no protection against independent production of a very similar work, there would be no infringement in such a case. Conceivably, a person who had never read this chapter could develop an analysis of "intellectual property" very similar to ours, and write a very similar chapter. If that were the case, we would have no claim for copyright infringement. Nor would we have a case if someone did read this chapter, but then wrote a different analysis of intellectual property. The *Amistad* problem at the end of the chapter raises this "similarity" issue.

Fair Use. One of the most important concepts in copyright law is the doctrine of **fair use**. The basic idea here is that the copying is not done to exploit the work commercially and is incidental to some other legitimate purpose. According to the 1976 act, these purposes include "criticism, comment, news reporting, teaching (including multiple copies for classroom use), scholarship, or research." But—whether any particular use is fair ultimately depends on the court's analysis of the facts of the particular case.

The statute specifies that the factors to be considered will include (at least): "(1) the purpose and character of the use, including whether such use is of a commercial nature or is for nonprofit educational purposes; (2) the nature of the copyrighted work; (3) the amount and substantiality of the portion used in relation to the copyrighted work as a whole; and (4) the effect of the use upon the potential market for or value of the copyrighted work."

Using these tests, a U.S. Court of Appeals decided that a private, for-profit copy shop, which was preparing "course packs" based on professors' reading lists, was violating the copyright law. Presumably, the students could have each made personal photocopies without violating the law, or the professor could have made the copies and distributed them. But using the third party processor, who was making a profit on selling the course packs, pushed the case over the line.

Parodies. Another difficult copyright problem arises when a copyrighted work is parodied by someone else. By definition ("a song sung alongside another"—from the Greek), a **parody** involves the use of the parodied work. How much such "use" is fair use? Clearly, there must be enough use to identify the work being parodied. On the other hand, the claimed parody should not just use the copyrighted work "to get attention" or "to avoid the drudgery in working up something fresh." This difficult line-drawing is illustrated by the *Dr. Seuss* problem at the end of the chapter.

Enforcement and Remedies

Just as for patent infringement, injunctive relief is available to the copyright owner. In addition, the allegedly infringing copies and the equipment used to produce them may be seized under court order ("impounded") for the duration of the trial and then destroyed if the plaintiff wins the case. As a further special action, importation of infringing copies may be prohibited by the court or by the U.S. Customs Service.

The 1976 act provides for the recovery of both the plaintiff's actual damages and the defendant's illegally earned profits, to the extent these two do not overlap. (The plaintiff only has to prove defendant's gross profits; the defendant has the burden of proving any related expenses, to try to reduce the amount of the award.) If the copyright was registered prior to the infringement, the plaintiff may elect to receive statutory damages instead, without having to prove any actual loss at all. The court is empowered to award whatever amount is "just," with a minimum of $500 and a maximum of $20,000. For unknowing or mistaken infringement ("innocent" infringement), a defendant who acted in good faith can get the statutory damages reduced to $200. Contrariwise, if the defendant's infringement was willful, the court may award statutory damages up to $100,000.

Court costs will also be awarded. Reasonable attorneys' fees may be awarded to the winning party, at the court's discretion. Unlike the rules for patent and trademark cases, in which attorneys' fees are awarded only in "exceptional" cases, the court has the power to do so in any copyright case.

Criminal prosecution is also possible against willful infringers. Conviction may result in a fine up to $10,000, or imprisonment for up to 1 year. Conviction will also mean impoundment and destruction of the infringing copies. Because record and tape copying has become big business, 1982 amendments add harsher penalties for these "pirates"—fines up to $250,000, and up to 5 years in prison.

Modern technology for storage and retrieval of data has made application of copyright law much more complicated, as seen in the *MGM* case. Although all nine Justices agreed on the result, two different "concurring" opinions were filed, with three different Justices joining each concurrence. Each set of Justices had somewhat different views on the copyright implications of electronic "file sharing" via the Internet.

CASE 3

Metro-Goldwyn-Mayer Studios, Inc. v. Grokster, Ltd.

545 U.S. 913 (2005)

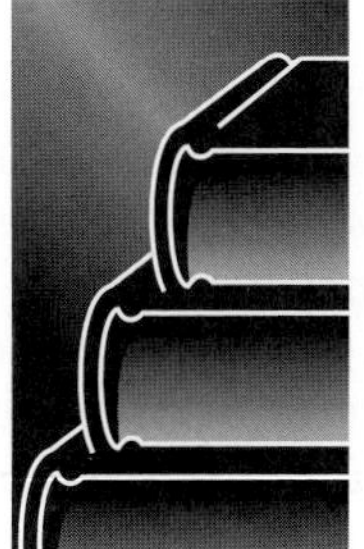

Facts: Owners of copyrights on movies and music sued Grokster and StreamCast Networks, distributors of file-sharing software, for copyright infringement by their software users. The software enables users to directly share movie and music files with each other. A statistical study showed that nearly 90 percent of the files available for download were copyrighted works. Defendants concede that most such downloads do violate copyright but argue that their software can also be used lawfully.

Relying on the Supreme Court's earlier decision that Sony was not guilty of similar charges simply because it manufactured video recorders, the U.S. District Court granted a summary judgment for the defendants. The Ninth Circuit Court of Appeals affirmed, and the plaintiffs asked for Supreme Court review.

Issue: Based on the stated facts, can the defendants be held liable for "contributory infringement"?

Decision: Yes. Summary judgment for defendants is vacated, and case is remanded.

Opinion by Justice Souter: "Grokster and StreamCast are not ... merely passive recipients of information about infringing use. The record is replete with evidence that from the moment Grokster and StreamCast began to distribute their free software, each one clearly voiced the objective that recipients use it to download copyrighted works, and each took active steps to encourage infringement....

"A kit developed by StreamCast to be delivered to advertisers, for example, contained press articles about StreamCast's potential to capture former Napster users ... and it introduced itself to some potential advertisers as a company 'which is similar to what Napster was.' ...

"Thus, StreamCast developed promotional materials to market its service as the best Napster alternative.... StreamCast even planned to flaunt the illegal uses of its software;

when it launched the OpenNap network, the chief technology officer of the company averred that '[t]he goal is to get in trouble with the law and get sued. It's the best way to get in the new[s].' . . .

"In addition to this evidence of express promotion, marketing, and intent to promote further, the business models employed by Grokster and StreamCast confirm that their principal object was use of their software to download copyrighted works. Grokster and StreamCast receive no revenue from users, who obtain the software itself for nothing. Instead, both companies generate income by selling advertising space, and they stream the advertising to . . . users while they are employing the programs. As the number of users of each program increases, advertising opportunities become worth more. . . .

"The argument for imposing indirect liability in this case is . . . a powerful one, given the number of infringing downloads that occur every day using Streamcast's and Grokster's software. When a widely shared device or product is used to commit infringement, it may be impossible to enforce rights in the protected work effectively against all direct infringers, the only practical alternative being to go against the distributor of the copying device for secondary liability on a theory of contributory or vicarious infringement. . . .

"One infringes contributorily by intentionally inducing or encouraging direct infringement . . . and infringes vicariously by profiting from direct infringement while declining to exercise a right to stop or limit it. . . . [T]hese doctrines of secondary liability emerged from common law principles and are well established in the law. . . .

"The rule on inducement of infringement as developed in the early cases is no different today. . . . Evidence of 'active steps . . . taken to encourage direct infringement' . . . such as advertising an infringing use or instructing how to engage in an infringing use, show an affirmative intent that the product be used to infringe, and a showing that infringement was encouraged overcomes the law's reluctance to find liability when a defendant merely sells a commercial product suitable for some lawful use. . . .

"There is substantial evidence in MGM's favor on all elements of inducement, and summary judgment in favor of Grokster and StreamCast was error. On remand, reconsideration of MGM's motion for summary judgment will be in order.

"The judgment of the Court of Appeals is vacated, and the case is remanded for further proceedings consistent with this opinion.

"It is so ordered."

Trademark Law

Artisans and craftsmen who take pride in their work have long used the practice of identifying their goods with some distinctive mark or symbol. One source indicates statutes regulating this trademark practice as early as the 13th century. The early common law rules were directed primarily against a second producer's copying the mark of the original producer to take advantage of the first's good reputation. Such "passing off" would be unfair both to the first producer and to the buyers.

Unlike patent and copyright, there is no express constitutional grant of trademark authority to Congress. The commerce clause is therefore the basis for national regulation in this area. The current statute is the Trademark Act of 1946, commonly known as the **Lanham Act**.

Definition

As was true historically, a **trademark** is a word, symbol, or other device used to identify the source of goods. Because the sale of services is such a large part of our modern economy, service marks have been developed to identify the source of services. They too are protected under the Lanham Act.

Trade dress refers to the total appearance of a product, including its size, shape, texture, color, and graphics. Such trade dress, when it is nonfunctional and distinctive (or has acquired a **secondary meaning**), is protected by law against copying. These rules were also noted in Chapter 5 as part of the law of **unfair competition**.

Registration

Unlike the rules for patents, the basis for trademark protection is actual use of the mark in connection with the sale of a product, rather than the registration of the mark. Common law rules protect the first user of a distinctive mark in connection with the sale of a product or service within a given geographic area.

Registration with the PTO does, however, provide important benefits. It gives "constructive" notice to all people marketing in the United States that the mark has been claimed. Thus, no later user of the registered mark can claim to be doing so in good faith.

Further, the validity of the registered mark becomes incontestable after 5 years. In addition, when it becomes necessary to enforce the registered mark, the national courts can be used, even without diversity of citizenship.

Even though a mark does not qualify for listing in the "primary register," because not distinctive, it may still be listed in the "supplemental register," if the mark is capable of becoming distinctive. Such supplementary registration may be advisable to protect use of the mark in other nations. Another nation might permit registration of the mark there, but require that it first be registered in its "home" country. U.S. "supplemental registration" meets this requirement.

For smaller companies operating within a single state, registration with the appropriate state official there may be sufficient.

Scope of Protection

What, then, can be registered as a trademark? As seen in the Supreme Court's 1995 ruling in the *Qualitex* case, the Lanham Act permits registration of any "word, name, symbol, or device, or any combination thereof." The mark must be inherently distinctive or have acquired a secondary meaning (i.e., buyers associate the non-distinctive mark with the product or service of a particular seller).

In the classic categorization of marks stated by one court, there are four types: arbitrary or fanciful marks, suggestive marks, descriptive marks, and generic marks. "Kodak" is the classic arbitrary mark—a word that has no meaning at all, apart from its use as a trademark. One source suggests that "Roach Motel" would be a suggestive mark for an insect trap. Both of these kinds of marks are distinctive, and thus registrable.

On the other hand, descriptive marks cannot be protected unless a secondary meaning is proved. A generic term cannot be protected, even if a secondary meaning has been developed. If a term within one of the other categories comes to be used generically, trademark protection may be lost. This has happened to aspirin and cellophane, for example. Xerox Corporation publishes advertisements every year to remind users that "Xerox" is a specific, copyrighted term, not a generic term for copier.

For several years, the U.S. Courts of Appeal had disagreed on whether a color could be trademarked. One circuit denied protection for a blue package for Nutrasweet's sugar substitute, finding that a secondary meaning had not been proved. But another circuit court held that Owens-Corning could trademark its pink fiberglass building insulation. The impasse was finally broken in 1995, when the U.S. Supreme Court decided (in *Qualitiex*) that a color could be trademarked, if it was in fact being used by buyers to identify the source of the goods, that is, if it had acquired a secondary meaning. There is nothing inherently distinctive about a gold letter M, but after "billions sold" and millions of dollars of advertising, nearly everyone in the world knows that the "golden arches" means McDonald's!

Infringement

Infringement occurs when a second seller uses a mark that is so similar to the first user's trademark that buyers are likely to be confused as to the source of the second product or service. The owner of the original trademark does not have to prove that any consumer has actually been confused, only that there is a reasonable likelihood of such confusion. Thus, all the facts need to be considered, such as the similarity of the marks, the similarity of the goods or services being sold, and the similarity of marketing channels used. If there *is* evidence of buyers' actually having been confused, that would normally be sufficient evidence of a "likelihood" of confusion.

The *Moseley* case illustrates the concept of "dilution" of a trademark, and interprets the 1995 Federal Trademark Dilution Act (FTDA)—an amendment to the Lanham Trademark Act of 1946.

Enforcement and Remedies

The remedy package for trademark violations is much the same as those for other intellectual property rights violations: injunction, destruction of violating materials, damages, and

CASE 4

Moseley d/b/a Victor's Little Secret v. Victoria's Secret Catalogue
537 U.S. 418 (2003)

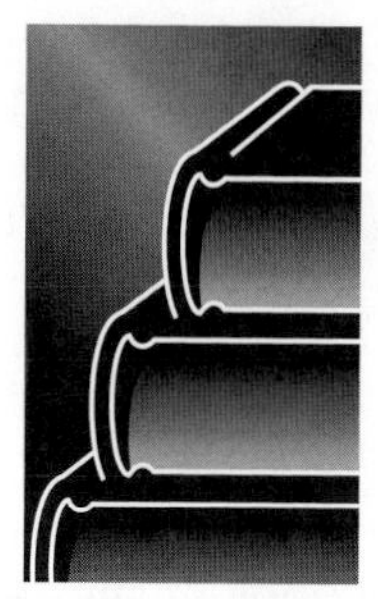

Facts: Victoria's Secret sells women's lingerie through its 750-plus retail stores and through some 400 million catalogs it distributes each year. It has two stores in Louisville, Kentucky. In 1998, it spent over $55 million on advertising. On February 12, 1998, an ad announcing the "GRAND OPENING" of "Victor's Secret," in nearby Elizabethtown, Kentucky, was distributed on the military base at Fort Knox, Kentucky. The ad said the new store featured lingerie, "Romantic Lighting," "Adult Novelties/Gifts," and other merchandise. An army colonel who found the ad objectionable sent a copy to Victoria's Secret, which in turn objected to "Victor's." The store's name was changed to "Victor's Little Secret," but that was not satisfactory to Victoria's Secret. This lawsuit resulted, alleging (1) trademark infringement; (2) unfair competition; (3) trademark dilution; and (4) state common law trademark infringement and unfair competition. Both parties moved for summary judgment. Finding no evidence of consumer confusion, the U.S. District Court dismissed the claims for infringement and unfair competition, but ruled for Victoria's on its dilution claim. The Sixth Circuit affirmed. Victor and Cathy Moseley petitioned for U.S. Supreme Court review.

Issue: Did Moseleys' business name unlawfully "dilute" Victoria's trademark?

Decision: No. Judgment reversed, and case remanded.

Opinion by Justice Stevens: "Unlike traditional infringement law, the prohibitions against trademark dilution are not the product of common-law development, and are not motivated by an interest in protecting consumers. The seminal discussion of dilution is found in Frank Schechter's 1927 law review article concluding 'that the preservation of the uniqueness of a trademark should constitute the only rational basis for its protection.'... Schechter supported his conclusion by referring to a German case protecting the owner of the well-known trademark 'Odol' for mouthwash from use on various noncompeting steel products. That case, and indeed the principal focus of the Schechter article, involved an established arbitrary mark that had been 'added to rather than withdrawn from the human vocabulary' and an infringement that made use of the identical mark. . . .

"The [House] committee's report stated that the 'purpose of H.R. 1295 [the 1995 FTDA] is to protect famous trademarks from subsequent uses that blur the distinctiveness of the mark or tarnish or disparage it, even in the absence of the likelihood of confusion.' . . . As examples of dilution, it stated that 'the use of DUPONT shoes, BUICK aspirin, and KODAK pianos would be actionable under this legislation.' . . .

"The contrast between the state statutes and the [FTDA]. . . sheds light on the precise question we must decide. For those state statutes, like several provisions in the federal Lanham Act, repeatedly refer to a 'likelihood' of harm, rather than to a completed harm. The relevant text of the FTDA . . . provides that 'the owner of a mark' is entitled to injunctive relief against another person's commercial use of a mark or trade name if that use 'causes dilution of the distinctive quality' of the famous mark. . . . This text unambiguously requires a showing of actual dilution, rather than a likelihood of dilution. . . .

"Of course, that does not mean that the consequences of dilution, such as an actual loss of sales or profits, must also be proved. . . . [A]t least where the marks at issue are not identical, the mere fact that consumers mentally associate the junior user's mark with a famous mark is not sufficient to establish actionable dilution. [S]uch mental association will not necessarily reduce the capacity of the famous mark to identify the goods of its owner, the statutory requirement for dilution under FTDA. For even though Utah drivers may be reminded of the circus when they see a license plate referring to the 'greatest snow on earth,' it by no means follows that they will associate 'the greatest show on earth' with skiing or snow sports, or associate it less strongly or exclusively with the circus. 'Blurring' is not a necessary consequence of mental association. (Nor, for that matter, is 'tarnishing.')

"The record in this case establishes that an army officer who saw the advertisement of the opening of a store named 'Victor's Secret' did make the mental association with 'Victoria's Secret,' but it also shows that he did not therefore form any different impression of the store that his wife and daughter patronized. There is a complete absence of evidence of any lessening of the capacity of the VICTORIA'S SECRET mark to identify and distinguish goods or services sold in Victoria's Secret stores or advertised in its catalogs. . . .

"Whatever difficulties of proof may be entailed, they are not an acceptable reason for dispensing with proof of an essential element of a statutory violation. The evidence in the present record is not sufficient to support the summary judgment on the dilution count. The judgment is therefore reversed, and the case is remanded for further proceedings consistent with this opinion."

attorneys' fees. Damages here include both the plaintiff's losses and the defendant's profits. The court has the discretion to adjust the award of (gross) profits up or down, to make sure that it is neither inadequate nor a "penalty." Likewise, the court may award up to three times the plaintiff's proved losses, if there is an indication that the actual losses were greater.

Here too, a trademark owner may be able to prevent the importation of infringing goods. However, if the goods have been lawfully manufactured and sold overseas, it may not be possible to do so. This problem is discussed more fully in the next section.

International Aspects

Two international problems with respect to the use of intellectual property arise with enough frequency to justify further discussion here. The first problem is the unauthorized importation into the United States of properly produced goods. The second is the unauthorized use of intellectual property to make and sell goods in other countries.

Gray Market Goods

The first problem is usually described as the sale of **gray market goods**. The goods themselves have been properly produced, either by the owner of the intellectual property, or by a licensee. The irregularity (the "grayness") arises from someone's violation of the original understanding on how the goods were to be distributed.

This situation arises because manufacturing costs, especially wages and environmental compliance, are substantially lower in many nations than they are here. A foreign licensee might be able to produce the same item for 60 percent of the U.S. cost, add on a 10 percent profit, and sell to a local distributor in that nation. The distributor adds on a 10 percent profit, and 10 percent for shipping costs to the U.S., and can still significantly undercut the U.S. producers. Alternatively, the United States producer sells goods to a foreign distributor, with a large discount because the buyer will assume all advertising and other distribution costs. Rather than reselling the product there, however, the foreign distributor brings it back to the United States for sale here at a discounted price. U.S. consumers (and large discount stores) are happy with these arrangements, but the U.S. producers are not.

Can the U.S. producer, as owner or licensee of the intellectual property connected to the product, prevent these "re-importations," these "Lassies" who always come home? The only answer to this complex question is "sometimes."

In 1988, in the *K-Mart* case, a five-Justice majority of the Supreme Court said that the U.S. owner of a trademark could prevent the unauthorized importation of goods that had been lawfully produced by an overseas licensee.

Pirated Intellectual Property

The second problem involves the out-and-out pirating of intellectual property by foreign producers. This is a huge problem; there are varying estimates of how many tens of billions or hundreds of billions of pirated products are sold each year. Governments of other nations vary in the vigor with which they enforce the intellectual property rights of foreign owners (or even those of their own citizens). In 1996, for example, the U.S. government threatened to impose trade sanctions against China for failing to protect intellectual property rights, especially rights on computer software.

Treaties/Conventions

To try to deal with the problem of international enforcement of intellectual property rights, several multination treaties (usually referred to as conventions) have been negotiated. Included here are the Berne Convention (for copyrights), the EC Patent Convention, the European Patent Convention, the Paris Convention (all intellectual property forms), the Patent Cooperation Treaty, the Universal Copyright Convention, the Vienna Trademark Registration Treaty, and others. Many nations have signed on to one or more of these agreements. Even within a nation that has agreed to the relevant treaty or convention, the intellectual property owner still needs to be aware of significant differences in local laws, and in the effectiveness of local enforcement.

Significance of This Chapter

It is difficult to imagine any single legal topic of more importance to today's global economy than intellectual property rights. Intellectual property is the source of significant competitive advantages for most companies. Protection of these major corporate assets has to be of primary concern to managers. This chapter provides an overview of the rules for doing so.

IMPORTANT TERMS AND CONCEPTS

copyright
design patents
fair use
gray market goods
infringement
intellectual property
Lanham Act
parody
patent
plant patents
product or process patents
secondary meaning
trade dress
trade secret
trademark
unfair competition
Uniform Trade Secrets Act (UTSA)

QUESTIONS AND PROBLEMS FOR DISCUSSION

1. What are the major advantages and disadvantages of patent protection as opposed to trade secret protection?

2. What is the difference between trade dress and trademark?

3. How much use of a copyrighted item is fair use?

4. Why is there protection against "dilution" of a trademark?

5. For over 30 years, Pepperidge Farm has sold its popular "Goldfish" snack crackers. They are fish-shaped, golden in color, and available in several flavors. They have a small, but distinct, share of the snack cracker market.

   Nabisco, a huge producer of crackers and other snack foods, plans to introduce a small cheese-flavored cracker shaped like various animals, including a golden-colored fish. Pepperidge Farm sued to enjoin the sale of the new Nabisco crackers.

   Should the injunction be granted? Why or why not?

6. Apple Computer manufactures and markets personal computers, related peripheral equipment, and computer programs. Franklin Computers makes and sells the ACE 100 personal computer, designed to be "Apple compatible," so that Apple software could be used on the ACE 100.

   Franklin admitted copying the Apple computer programs. Its vice president of engineering stated that it was not "feasible" for Franklin to create its own programs, and that there can be no infringement because Apple's programs are not copyrightable.

   If Apple sues, what result, and why?

7. Between 1931 and his death in 1991, Theodore Geisel wrote and published 47 children's books, with total worldwide sales of some 35 million copies. Geisel used "Dr. Seuss" as his pen name. One of his most popular characters was the "Cat in the Hat," who wore a large, floppy, red-and-white stovepipe hat.

   In 1995, Alan Katz and Chris Wrinn produced a satire on the O.J. Simpson murder trial, titled "The Cat NOT in the Hat." They used a rhyming style similar to Geisel's to tell the O.J. story, and O.J. is pictured 13 times wearing the Cat's distinctive stovepipe hat.

   Dr. Seuss Enterprises sued, to enjoin distribution of "The Cat NOT in the Hat." Should an injunction be issued by the court? Explain.

8. After 3 years of research, Chase Riboud wrote a historical novel (*Echo of Lions*) loosely based on the story of the revolt on the slave ship *Amistad.* Published in 1989, her book sold about 500,000 copies. She then tried to interest movie studios, including Steven Spielberg's company, in doing a film version. In 1993, Punch Productions took a 2-year option on the film rights, but then abandoned the project when no major studio showed any interest. In 1996, Spielberg announced that he would make the movie *Amistad.* His named screenplay-writer was David Franzoni, who had been involved in trying to sell the *Echo of Lions* project. In October 1997, shortly before the release of the Spielberg film, Riboud filed suit for an injunction.

   What sort of analysis should the court do in deciding whether or not to enjoin the showing of the film? Discuss.

9. Vicki Company, a Michigan corporation, owns the nationally registered trademark "LeGance" for its high-priced line of jewelry. Vicki has learned that a large shipment of jewelry bearing its trademark, produced by one of its European licensees who is authorized to make sales only within the European Community, is headed for the United States.

   What steps should Vicki take to protect its rights? Explain.

CHAPTER 17

Sales of Goods: Title and Risk of Loss

Chapter Objectives

This chapter will:

- Define "goods" as the subject of a sale contract.
- Identify and explain the six different ownership interests that can exist in goods.
- Explain the rules for transferring these ownership interests.
- Summarize the rules in four special sale arrangements.
- Indicate how documents of title are used in sale transactions.
- Discuss two special title problems.

Basic Concepts and Definitions

The sale of goods is certainly one of the most basic types of commercial transaction. Each of us probably enters into several such sales every day, buying school supplies, books, hamburgers, groceries, toothpaste, shoes, and similar items. Less frequently, we buy "big ticket" items such as TVs, furniture, cars, and boats. The transactions we are talking about in this chapter are familiar ones. But the problems we are discussing, and the technical language we are using, are probably less familiar. Most of us do not think about the problems discussed in this chapter as we do our daily business, and usually we don't have to do so. Most of the time, our sale transactions do go through as planned. Most of the time, the goods do not get lost or stolen between the time we buy them and the seller delivers them to us. Most of the time, no third parties try to assert rights against "our" new goods.

This chapter is concerned with the statistically unusual "what if" cases. What if something happens to the goods in transit, while they are on the way to the buyer? What if some third party has a claim against the goods? What if a third party alleges injury caused by someone with the goods? These problems do arise in the real world. Not every sale goes as planned, every time. Businesses and consumers need to know what the rules are for handling these problems when they arise. One "record-of-the-month" might not be worth a lawsuit, but a half-million-dollar shipment of computers might very well be worth arguing about. Businesses are also buyers and sellers, and some sales transactions involve millions of dollars of goods. Car manufacturers, for example, buy large amounts of steel, plastic, glass, machinery, and auto parts. They certainly need to know what is what in these dealings with their suppliers.

Uniform Commercial Code Coverage

Because a sale of goods is one specific type of contract, the general principles of contract law apply to such sales, but most of the rules relating specifically to sales of goods have been codified, supplemented, and sometimes changed by the Uniform Commercial Code (UCC). Article 2, the longest article in the UCC, specifically covers sales of goods, but other portions of the UCC may also apply. If the goods are to be stored or transported as part of the transaction, Article 7 may apply. The general principles and definitions stated in Article 1 apply to all Code transactions.

Many of the special sales rules have already been discussed in the contracts chapters covering offer and acceptance, consideration, the Statute of Frauds, and assignments. This chapter and the next chapter will focus on other major differences between the law of sales and general contract law.

Definitions

The basic purpose of a contract for the sale of goods is to pass the various ownership interests recognized by the Code from the seller to the buyer, for a consideration called the price. The transaction is not a gift of the goods because the seller is receiving a price for them; it is not a bailment of the goods because the buyer will become the owner of them. Whether a particular contract is a sale of goods or a services contract depends on which element—goods or services—predominates.

As defined in 2-105(1), **goods** means tangible, movable personal property. Investment securities, such as stocks and bonds, and other "things in action" personal property (intangibles) are excluded from the definition of goods; specifically included are such things as growing crops, the unborn young of animals, and specially manufactured goods. Goods that are not both existing and identified when the contract is made are called **future goods**, and a contract involving such goods is a **contract to sell**. **Fungible goods** are goods whose units are indistinguishable from one another, such as grain in a grain elevator, fuel oil in a tank car, or coal in a pile.

The **price** is whatever value is received by the seller for the goods; it may be money, other goods, services, or land—or a promise by the buyer to deliver any of these things.

A **merchant** (2-104[1]) is defined as a person who: (a) deals in goods of the kind being sold, or (b) by his or her occupation holds himself or herself out as having special knowledge about the goods or practices involved in the sale, or (c) is represented by someone

CASE 1

DAKOTA PORK INDUSTRIES V. CITY OF HURON
638 N.W.2D 884 (SD 2002)

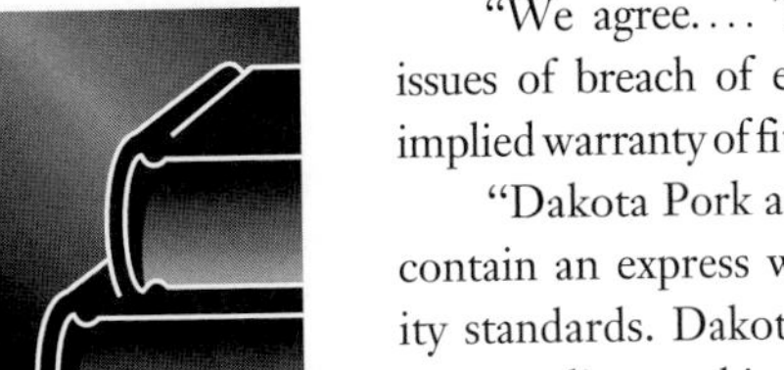

Facts: Dakota Pork operated a pork processing plant in Huron, South Dakota, from 1987 until it ceased operations in 1997. In 1991, Dakota Pork entered into an agreement with the city to provide Dakota Pork's water needs in exchange for Dakota Pork's water rights in the James River. Negotiations took place over the course of a year. No special conditions or uses for water were expressed in the written contract that resulted. Sometime prior to May 21, 1994, a foreign substance (later identified as calcium carbonate) appeared in Dakota Pork's meat products. Dakota Pork sued the city, claiming negligence, breach of express warranty, and breach of implied warranty of fitness for a particular purpose. City moved for summary judgment, which was granted by the trial court. Dakota Pork appealed the dismissal of its warranty claims.

Issues: Is a sale of water a sale of goods? Did Dakota Pork state a valid claim for breach of UCC warranties?

Decision: Yes. No. Judgment affirmed.

Opinion by Justice Gors: "The primary inquiry is whether City's furnishing of water to Dakota Pork constitutes a sale of goods under Article 2 of the [UCC]. Courts have adopted two conflicting viewpoints.

"One viewpoint is expressed in [a] pre-UCC case ... [in which] the New York Court of Appeals examined the sale of water under the Uniform Sales Act. Under that Act, goods were defined as 'all chattels personal other than things in action and money.' The court held that '[t]he furnishing of water, through a system of waterworks, by a water corporation, either private or municipal, to private customers, at a fixed compensation, is a sale of goods within the meaning of the statute.... It is a sale of goods as if the water were collected and delivered in bottles for a price.'...

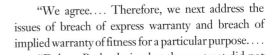

"We agree.... Therefore, we next address the issues of breach of express warranty and breach of implied warranty of fitness for a particular purpose....

"Dakota Pork admits that the contract did not contain an express warranty regarding water quality standards. Dakota Pork contends that, while it was not discussed in the contract, water quality was discussed in the negotiations and City was aware of the water needs and purposes....

"The CEO of Dakota Pork, Carl Kuehn, stated in his deposition that negotiations with City were extensive and addressed issues of quality, quantity, time and price. Kuehn testified that Dakota Pork's requirement for water was 'potable or drinkable water that fell within the guidelines [which] the Environmental Protection Agency had established for potable water.'...

"City denies making oral guarantees or express warranties regarding the water quality. City argues that because the contract is a complete and exclusive statement of the agreement between Dakota Pork and City, SDCL 57A-2-202(b) [the UCC's version of the parol evidence rule] precludes the supplementation of terms to the contract. We agree. Supplemental terms cannot be introduced through contemporaneous statements because, in this case, the written contract was a complete and exclusive statement of terms.... Dakota Pork's alleged oral understanding with City is not consistent with the written contract. The express terms of the contract control in the face of inconsistency....

"The next issue is whether an implied warranty of fitness for a particular purpose applies. In [the cited New York case] the court held that although the furnishing of water was a sale of goods, there are no implied warranties of merchantability and fitness for a particular purpose.... We agree....

"We therefore affirm the trial court's granting of summary judgment on both counts."

who is held out as having such special knowledge. The question of whether or not a farmer is a merchant for Code purposes has not been answered uniformly by the courts.

Another important difference between sales of goods, services, and land has to do with quality guarantees: What sort of performance standards does the law require of the seller? There are some very important distinctions between goods, on the one hand, and services or land, on the other. For land, although many states now follow a different rule (at least for the seller of a new home), the original rule is that the buyer takes the land as is; unless the buyer can prove that the seller committed fraud or made a specific guarantee as part of the contract, the buyer has no case for alleged defects in the real estate. For services, unless a specific guarantee of results has been made, the buyer-customer has to prove malpractice to recover; that is, the buyer-customer has to show that the seller's performance fell below the standard of a reasonably competent practitioner. For sales of goods, however, a merchant-seller is held to an automatic quality **warranty** that the goods are merchantable, even though the merchant-seller has said nothing specific about their quality and even though the merchant-seller is not guilty of any negligence in handling or delivering the goods. These warranty rules will be discussed more fully in the next chapter. The court in the *Dakota Pork* case is trying to decide whether they apply to a sale of water by a city. Their application depends on whether that sort of transaction is a sale of *goods*.

Passing of Ownership Interests in the Goods

One special (and somewhat complicated) problem in the law of sales is that of determining when the various ownership interests recognized by the Code pass from the seller to the buyer. The UCC recognizes six different ownership interests in the goods—**special property**, insurable interest, title, risk of loss, **right to possession**, and security interest. These six interests represent packages of rights and duties with respect to the goods. They can all exist at the same time, as to the same goods, and they may be parceled out among the seller, the buyer, and different third parties in any number of combinations. Part of the complexity in Article 2 is caused by the need to provide rules for all these situations.

The simplest case occurs when you buy a used book from a friend for cash, or items from a drugstore, or grocery store. If you pay by check, things get a bit more complicated because the check will only be paid by your bank if there is enough money in the account. If you use a credit card or some other credit arrangement, the seller is taking a still greater risk of nonpayment. When you order goods by mail, as many businesses do, all sorts of things can happen while the goods are in transit. When the goods are delivered to the buyer they may not conform to the contract, and either party may decide not to go through with the deal. The Code must provide appropriate rules to deal with all these "what if" situations.

Under the Code, most of the disputes between the buyer and the seller will be risk of loss cases, as shown by the examples in this chapter. When third parties are involved in the litigation, the solution will nearly always depend on the location of one of the other five interests. For example, title is frequently important in deciding liability claims by or against third parties.

Presumptions

Article 2 contains a rather extensive set of statutory presumptions as to when each of the various interests in the goods passes to the buyer; the most important sections are 2-401, 2-501, and 2-509. In general, these presumptions may be overcome by the parties' specific agreement. That is, the parties are free to make any specific agreement they wish as to when a particular ownership interest will pass to the buyer, but if they say nothing, the Code presumptions apply. In most cases the contract probably will not say anything specific about when these ownership interests pass.

One inflexible rule is stated in the Code (2-105[2]): "Goods must be both existing and identified before any interest in them can pass." In other words, even if they both agree to do so, the buyer and the seller cannot pass any interest to anyone unless the goods are both existing and identified. This is just common sense. Until we know whose goods are whose, no ownership in any goods can pass to anyone. Once the goods come into existence and are identified as the goods for the given contract, the buyer and the seller are free to parcel out the six ownership interests in any way they choose.

There is one other major exception to the parties' freedom of contract. As further discussed on page 308, the seller cannot retain *title* to goods once they have been shipped to or delivered to the buyer. Except for these two limitations, we are generally free to structure our contract as we see fit.

Identification

Identification is the act of specifying exactly which goods are to be delivered by the seller to the buyer to satisfy the terms of a particular contract. Identification may be made by either the seller or the buyer, in any manner they agree to have it made. As an important change from prior law, the goods do not necessarily have to be in "deliverable condition" per the terms of the contract, for identification to occur. If the parties so agree, individual shares of a mass of fungible goods can be "identified," and thus sold, even though these shares have not yet been parceled out. For example, the parties could agree to buy and sell half of the fuel oil in Penn-Central railroad car no. 35790; that would be a sufficient identification.

In the absence of any specific agreement, Section 2-501 says that identification is presumed to occur: (a) when the contract is made, if it is for goods already existing and identified in the parties' negotiations (a particular used car, for example); (b) for future goods generally, when the goods are "shipped, marked, or otherwise designated" by the seller (when the seller tags one new car in an inventory with the buyer's order number, for example); or (c) for agricultural products such as crops and the young of animals when the crops are planted and the as-yet-unborn young are conceived.

Once identification has occurred, ownership interests can then be passed to the buyer as the parties wish. Special property and insurable interest are presumed to pass to the buyer as soon as identification occurs.

Special Property

The special property interest, which the UCC gives to the buyer once particular goods have been identified to the contract, is a very different concept. Nothing like it existed under pre-Code law. The purpose of this new Code interest is to provide some protection for the buyer, both as to the seller and as to third parties, as soon as the buyer's goods have been identified, even though the buyer is not yet technically "the owner" of the goods, that is, legal title has not yet passed to the buyer.

In addition to an insurable interest, the buyer's special property interest gives the buyer a package of three rights against the goods:

1. The buyer has the right to inspect the goods at a reasonable time and place.
2. The buyer has the right to recover damages that the buyer sustains if a third party wrongfully interferes with the buyer's possession of the identified goods.
3. The buyer has a right to sue for possession of the identified goods when the seller refuses to deliver them and the buyer cannot get substitute goods or when the seller goes insolvent within 10 days after receiving the first installment on the contract price.

Insurable Interest

As soon as the goods are identified, the Code gives the buyer an **insurable interest**, meaning that the buyer can then get a valid insurance policy protecting the buyer against financial losses relating to these goods. The extent to which a preexisting "blanket" insurance policy on all property "owned" by the buyer would apply to such identified goods has not yet been determined in most states. Even so, this question can be resolved by a carefully drafted policy provision.

More than one person may have an insurable interest in the same goods at the same time. This does not mean that several persons will recover for the same damages, but that several persons may suffer different financial losses when the goods are lost or damaged. Each such person has an insurable interest to the extent of his or her potential loss. The seller, for example, retains an insurable interest so long as it holds title to the goods or a security interest against the goods. When the goods are shipped or stored, the **carrier** or the **warehouse** has an insurable interest in the goods while they are in its possession. Any party with an insurable interest in the goods can sue a third party who has caused a financial loss by injuring the goods.

Title

The concept of **title** generally refers to legal ownership, with all its attendant rights and liabilities. For the purpose of Article 2, however, title is given a much more restricted meaning because most of the litigations between the buyer and the seller, and even some litigations involving third parties, are solved by using other ownership interests and the location of the legal title is irrelevant. Title is still an important concept because even under the Code many cases involving third parties will depend on whether the buyer or the seller had title to the goods at some particular point in time. Such cases might involve

Exhibit 17.1: Passing of Title (presumptions)

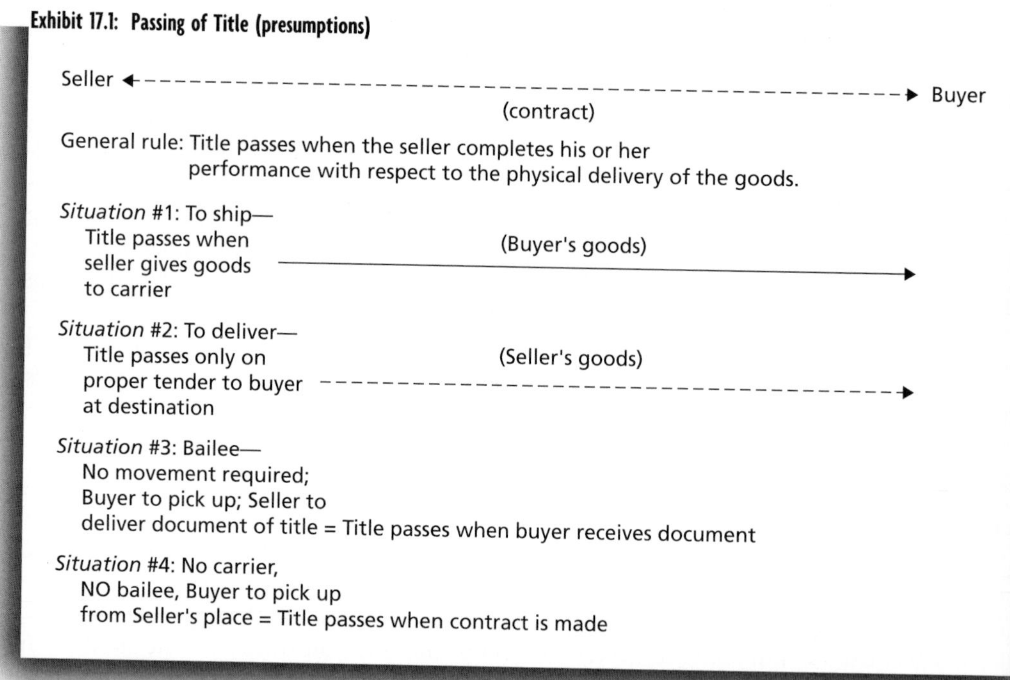

liability for required taxes, registration, or insurance on the goods, or liability resulting from use of the goods, or adverse claims against the goods by the creditors of the buyer or the seller.

Seller
Buyer
(contract)
General rule: Title passes when the seller completes his or her performance with respect to the physical delivery of the goods.
Situation #1: To ship—
Title passes when seller gives goods to carrier
(Buyer's goods)
Situation #2: To deliver—
Title passes only on proper tender to buyer at destination
(Seller's goods)
Situation #3: Bailee—
No movement required; Buyer to pick up; Seller to deliver document of title = Title passes when buyer receives document
Situation #4: No carrier, NO bailee, Buyer to pick up from Seller's place = Title passes when contract is made

The main presumptions as to when title passes are contained in Section 2-401; this section states a general rule and four specific applications. These presumptions are all based on common sense; if the parties want a special result, they will have to so expressly agree. On one point, however, the Code controls the parties' agreement: A seller cannot retain title to goods that have been shipped to, or delivered to, the buyer. The general rule is that title passes to the buyer "at the time and place at which the seller completes his [or her] performance with respect to the physical delivery of the goods." This rule applies even though, for financing reasons, using the goods as collateral for the unpaid balance of the purchase price, the seller has reserved a security interest in the goods, or even though a **document of title** (bill of lading or warehouse receipt) is to be delivered to the buyer at a different time or place. These documents are discussed more fully later in this chapter.

Four Specific Applications

The four specific rules cover the two common arrangements when the goods are to be moved as part of the contract for sale and the two common situations not involving any further movement of the goods by the seller. If the contract merely authorizes the seller to make the arrangement for shipping the goods to the buyer, but it does not require the seller to deliver the goods at their destination, title is presumed to pass at the time and place of shipment. In the other "movement" case, in which the seller is required to make delivery of the goods at their destination, a proper tender means that the seller must get the goods to the place where they are to be delivered to the buyer and give the buyer any notice reasonably necessary to enable the buyer to receive delivery.

In the two "nonmovement" cases, the goods are already at the location where the buyer is to take delivery. In one case, they are in the possession of a third party (usually a warehouse); in the other, they are in the seller's possession. If the seller is not required to move the goods but is required to deliver to the buyer a "document of title" (warehouse receipt or bill of lading) covering them, title is presumed to pass when the required document is delivered. (In this case the seller is only required to give the buyer the document. The buyer can then go over to the warehouse whenever he or she wants to and get the goods.)

When the seller is not required to move the goods or to deliver any documents, and the specific goods to which the contract applies have already been identified, title is presumed to pass "at the time and place of contracting;" that is, at the instant the contract is made. And the Code assumes that the place of delivery is the seller's place of business. In the typical used-car purchase, for example, title to the used car passes to the buyer at the instant he or she says, "I'll take it," because the seller has possession and is not required to move the car to any other location to make delivery. In most states this presumption would hold even though the state's motor vehicle registration requirements had not yet been complied with, as seen in the *Martin* case.

Return of Title to Seller

When title has already passed to the buyer under the aforementioned presumptions, it is passed back to the seller either by the buyer's rejection of the goods, whether the rejection is justified or not, or by the buyer's revocation of his or her previous acceptance, but only if such revocation is justified. In other words, if the buyer refuses delivery and sends the goods back, the goods again "belong to" the seller on the way back. But if the buyer has accepted the goods and *then* tries to revoke that acceptance by sending the goods back, title is not revested in the seller unless the buyer can show a justification for his or her action.

Risk of Loss

Article 2 treats risk of loss as a separate and distinct ownership interest. Stated most simply, **risk of loss** means responsibility for the goods. As between the buyer and the seller, who gets stuck for the value of the goods when they are destroyed or damaged by an "act of God" or by a third party? Who has to try to recover from the third party or from an insurance company?

Once the goods are identified, the parties can allocate the risk of loss on the goods in any way they wish. Merely giving the buyer a right to inspect the goods at a particular time and place does not postpone the passing of risk of loss, unless that result is also specified. If the parties have not made any specific agreement as to when risk of loss passes, Article 2 again provides a set of common sense presumptions in section 2-509.

In the two "movement" cases, the presumptions for risk of loss are basically the same as those for the passing of title. If the seller is authorized to ship but is not required to deliver, risk passes when the goods are delivered to the carrier, even though the seller has reserved the right to possession (collect on delivery [COD] shipment) or a security interest against the goods. A seller who is required to deliver keeps the risk of loss until the goods arrive at their destination and are duly tendered to the buyer.

When the goods are in the possession of a bailee, such as a warehouse or a carrier, and are to be delivered to the buyer without further movement to another place, risk of loss passes when any one of three things happens:

1. When the buyer receives a **negotiable document of title** on the goods.
2. When the buyer receives a non-negotiable document of title or other written delivery order on the goods *and* has had a reasonable amount of time to present the bailee with it and to pick up the goods.
3. When the bailee acknowledges the buyer's right to possession of the goods.

The reason for the difference between negotiable and non-negotiable documents is that the negotiable document requires the carrier or the warehouse to give the goods to the bearer of the document or to the order of someone named in the document. Whether issued to the bearer or to someone's order, the document itself thus indicates that someone other than the party who originally turned over the goods may present the document and demand redelivery. Because the carrier or warehouse is alerted to this possibility from the beginning of the transaction, no extra time is allowed for the buyer to present the document. Non-negotiable documents require that buyers be given a reasonable chance to identify themselves and explain why they, rather than the sellers, are picking up the goods.

CASE 2

Martin v. Nager

469 A.2d 519 (NJ Superior Ct. 1983)

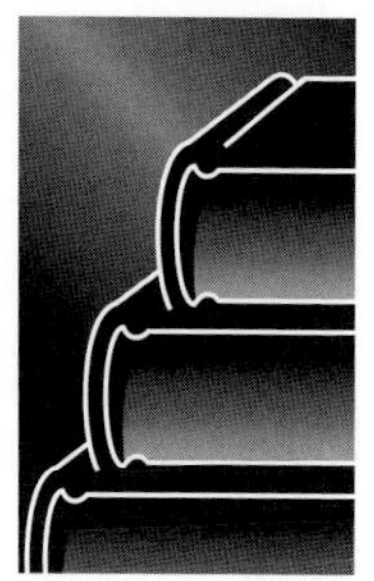

Facts: Plaintiffs Rose and Gary Martin bought an automobile owned by defendant George Norton Nager through a dealer, Bellbrook Volkswagen, Inc., who converted the purchase price and is now insolvent. Plaintiffs and defendant both are victims of Bellbrook's fraud. Plaintiffs have possession of the automobile; defendant has possession of the certificate of title, Bellbrook is in bankruptcy and its two principals are in jail. The court is aware of at least 21 more transactions with the same or similar scenario involving Bellbrook.

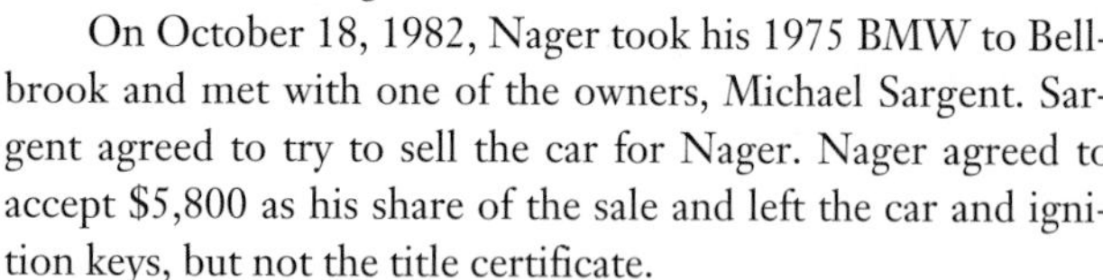

On October 18, 1982, Nager took his 1975 BMW to Bellbrook and met with one of the owners, Michael Sargent. Sargent agreed to try to sell the car for Nager. Nager agreed to accept $5,800 as his share of the sale and left the car and ignition keys, but not the title certificate.

On December 7, 1982, plaintiffs purchased defendant's vehicle from Bellbrook for $7,155. Bellbrook delivered the vehicle to the plaintiffs and assured them the certificate of title would be delivered promptly. After several unsuccessful attempts to get the certificate of title, on January 10, 1983, plaintiffs went to the Division of Motor Vehicles and, after presenting their proof of purchase, received a temporary registration that was effective only until January 31.

On January 25, 1983, defendant went to Bellbrook to retrieve his automobile because he had not been notified that it had been sold. He was shocked to learn that his automobile had been sold on December 7, 1982. He demanded his $5,800, but Sargent indicated that he was waiting for a check to clear the bank. Sargent gave defendant a check dated January 27, 1983. The check was deposited but returned with a notation that payment had been stopped. After several unsuccessful attempts to obtain payment from Bellbrook, defendant reported the matter to the Brooklawn chief of police.

On February 24, 1983, plaintiffs filed this action to restrain defendant from repossessing the automobile and to require transfer of the certificate of title to them. An order was entered restraining the defendant from repossessing the automobile. Subsequently, on defendant's application, an order was entered restraining plaintiffs from using the automobile and requiring them to provide for its storage and a certificate insuring defendant as a loss payee on their insurance policy.

Issue: Did title pass to plaintiff buyers?

Decision: Yes. Nager is ordered to sign and deliver the title certificate.

Opinion by Judge Deighan: "The arduousness of this decision is due to the fact that plaintiffs and defendant are both innocent victims of the fraud perpetrated by Bellbrook. The apparent conflict between the provisions of the UCC and the MVCOL arises because the transfer of a motor vehicle, unlike the transfer of other chattels, must be made in accordance with documentary evidence executed only in the method prescribed by the MVCOL.... But these statutes should be read and construed together and given fair effect to both if possible....

"The basic goals of the UCC and MVCOL are in perfect harmony; the UCC is to protect good faith purchasers and, as will be later discussed, the purpose of the MVCOL is to protect innocent purchasers of motor vehicles. Therefore, these statutes should complement and support each other rather than contradict or abrogate the other as suggested by defendant....

"The purpose of the Motor Vehicle Certificate of Ownership Law is to regulate and control titles and possession of motor vehicles and to prevent the sale and purchase of motor vehicles with fraudulent titles.... The MVCOL is largely designed to protect the ordinary automobile buyer.... The act seeks to accomplish this by requiring the vendor to transmit with the delivery of the car the original bill of sale as evidence of title....

"The UCC provisions substantially change pre-code law to enhance the protection given buyers in the ordinary course of business from dealers of such goods. Thus, under the code, delivery to a merchant for purposes of sale or resale expands the principle of prior law that delivery to a factor or dealer for such purposes confers on the latter power to make a valid sale even though made under circumstances violating the particular authority given.... Moreover, the UCC broadens pre-code law so that even a bailee, who has no authority whatever to make a sale, can confer good title to goods on a third party, if such bailee regularly sells the same kind of goods. In addition, a sale by a merchant-intermediary in violation of the terms under which the goods were entrusted to him will, nevertheless, confer good title on a buyer in the ordinary course of business....

"Under the UCC the retention of the certificate of title of the BMW by defendant and the reservation of the title as between defendant and Bellbrook is ineffective as against plaintiffs.... Defendant as an entruster gave Bellbrook, 'power to transfer all rights [of defendant] to a buyer in the ordinary course of business.'... The sale was valid but defendant failed to execute and deliver an assignment of the certificate of ownership as required by N.J.S.A. 39:10-9....

"In view of the foregoing, it is held that title to the BMW is vested in the plaintiffs. The purpose of the MVCOL is not circumvented by this holding but to the contrary is accomplished by requiring the defendant to fulfill an obligation to plaintiffs....

"An order may be presented by plaintiffs' attorney requiring defendant to execute and deliver the certificate of title to plaintiffs transferring title of the BMW to plaintiffs. Also, the prior order of the court requiring plaintiffs to store the motor vehicle and to carry insurance with the loss payee in favor of defendant will be vacated."

Exhibit 17.2: Passing of Risk of Loss (presumptions)

No general rule. As with title, a specific contract clause controls

Situation #1: To ship—
Risk passes when seller gives goods to carrier ——— (Goods at buyer's risk en route) ———→

Situation #2: To deliver—
Risk passes only on proper tender to buyer at destination - - - (Goods at seller's risk en route) - - -→

Situation #3: Bailee—
No movement required;
A. If negotiable document = When buyer gets document, buyer gets risk.
B. If non-negotiable document = Buyer gets risk when she/he gets document, and has had a reasonable time to present it to bailee.
C. If no document, when bailee acknowledges buyer's right to possession, buyer gets risk.

Situation #4: No carrier,
NO bailee, Buyer to pick up
A. Risk passes on tender of delivery by non-merchant seller
B. Risk passes on receipt of goods from merchant seller.

When the goods are in the seller's possession and the buyer is to come over and pick them up, there are two different rules as to when risk passes, depending on whether or not the seller is a merchant. Sellers who are not merchants pass risk when they tender delivery to the buyer; but sellers who are merchants do not pass risk to the buyer until actual receipt of goods by the buyer. This special "risk" rule where the seller is a merchant represents an important change from prior law.

When the seller's **tender of delivery** or the seller's delivery "fails to conform to the contract" so as to give the buyer the right to reject the goods, the risk of loss stays with the seller until the seller "cures" the problem or until the buyer agrees to accept the goods anyway. When the buyer rightfully revokes a prior acceptance, the seller must bear any loss not covered by the buyer's insurance. When the buyer breaches after conforming goods have been identified to the contract but before risk has passed to the buyer, the buyer must bear any loss not covered by the seller's insurance. In these breach cases, the basic risk of loss rule is: "The bad guy loses."

These risk of loss rules are at issue in the *Burnett* case.

Right to Possession of the Goods

The Code also recognized that a party may have title and risk of loss and yet not have an immediate right to the goods. One obvious case in which this result occurs is the COD contract: When the seller ships the goods as agreed, the buyer has title, risk of loss, and a special property interest and an insurable interest in the goods, but does not yet have the right to possession because the COD term requires payment to get delivery. Another common separation of the right to possession from title and risk occurs when goods are shipped or stored by a carrier or a warehouse. Article 7 of the Code gives such persons a possessory "lien" for their services, meaning that they can hold (and if necessary sell) the goods until their charges are paid. Either the buyer or the seller may have title and risk of loss, but neither of them has the right to possession of the goods until the carrier or warehouse gets paid.

Security Interest

Finally, where the goods are being used as collateral to secure payment of the balance due on the contract price, the financing agency, which could be the seller, a bank, or other lender, has a security interest in them. Stated most simply, this **security interest** means that if the debtor defaults, the creditor, the "secured party," has the right to get possession

CASE 3

Burnett v. Purtell
1992 OH App. LEXIS 3467

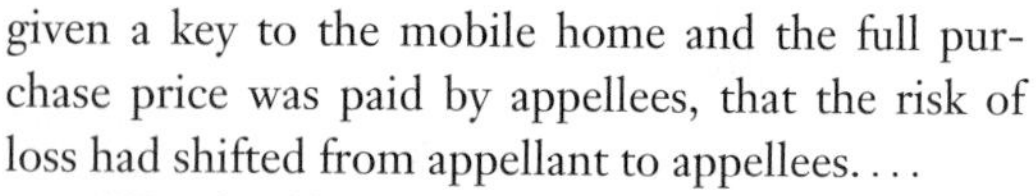

Facts: This appeal comes from the Painesville Municipal Court where appellant, Betty Jean Purtell, Executrix of the Estate of Lena M. Holland, was ordered to pay appellees, Richard Burnett, et al., $6,500 plus interest at 10 percent per annum from May 17, 1991.

Appellees agreed to purchase a mobile home with shed from appellant. On Saturday, March 3, 1990, appellees paid appellant $6,500 and in return were given the certificate of title to the mobile home and a key to the mobile home, but no keys to the shed.

At the time the certificate of title was transferred, the following items remained in the mobile home: the washer and dryer, mattress and box springs, two chairs, items in the refrigerator and the entire contents of the shed. These items were to be retained by appellant and removed by appellant. To facilitate removal, the estate retained one key to the mobile home and the only keys to the shed.

On Sunday, March 4, 1990, the mobile home was destroyed by fire through the fault of neither party. At the time of the fire, appellant still had a key to the mobile home and the keys to the shed, and she had not removed the contents of the mobile home nor the shed. The contents of the shed were not destroyed and have now been removed by appellant.

The referee determined that the risk of loss remained with appellant because there was no tender of delivery and entered judgment in favor of appellees.

Issue: Had the risk of loss passed to the buyer (appellee) at the time of the fire?

Decision: No. Judgment for buyer (for refund of the contract price) is affirmed.

Opinion by Judge Ford: "First, appellant argues that because the certificate of title was transferred, appellees were given a key to the mobile home and the full purchase price was paid by appellees, that the risk of loss had shifted from appellant to appellees. . . .

"[R]isk of loss is no longer determined by who holds title. . . .

"After reviewing [the UCC], it is clear that subsection (C) applies as appellant was neither to ship the mobile home by carrier nor was the mobile home to be held by a ballee. . . .

"It is clear that neither party meets the definition of merchant and therefore the second clause of (C) applies.

"The trial court found that there was no tender of delivery under the contract. If this determination is correct, then the risk of loss remained with appellant. . . . [T]ender of delivery requires that: (1) the goods be conforming, (2) the seller put and hold the goods at the buyer's disposition, and (3) the seller give the buyer any notification reasonably necessary to enable him to take delivery. . . .

"Analyzing the foregoing elements it is clear that . . . appellant did not tender delivery. The parties agreed that appellees would purchase the mobile home and shed from appellant. The contents of both the shed and the mobile home were to be retained by appellant and removed by appellant. At the time of the fire, appellant had not removed the items that she was required to remove from either the mobile home or the shed. Additionally, all keys to the mobile home were not surrendered and none of the keys to the shed were relinquished. Under this scenario, appellant did not tender conforming goods free of items belonging to her which remained in the trailer, nor did she put the mobile home at appellee's disposition without being fettered with the items previously enumerated. Accordingly, the trial court was correct in determining that appellant did not tender delivery within the meaning of the statute, and consequently the risk of loss remained with her."

of the goods, to resell them, and to apply the proceeds to pay off the balance due on the debt. Section 2-401(1) says that any attempt by the seller to withhold "title" on goods that are shipped or delivered to the buyer "is limited in effect to a reservation of a security interest." What the seller has to do is to make sure that there is a valid security interest. The legal requirements of such secured transactions are covered in Article 9 of the UCC; Chapters 23and 24 will discuss secured transactions at greater length.

Special Sale Arrangements

The Code also provides specific rules to cover several frequently used special sale arrangements: sale on approval, sale or return, consignment, and sale by auction. When the buyer has the option of returning goods even though they conform to the contract, the transaction is presumed to be a sale on approval if the buyer bought primarily for personal use, and a sale or return if the goods were purchased primarily for resale to others.

In a **sale on approval**, the buyer has possession of someone else's goods as a bailee, to use them according to the terms of the trial contract; the seller still "owns" the goods that is, the seller has both title and risk of loss. Title and risk do not pass to the buyer until the buyer accepts the goods, either expressly or by doing something that indicates an intent to exercise ownership, or until the agreed trial period expires with the buyer still in possession and not having notified the seller that they will be returned.

In a **sale or return**, title and risk pass to the buyer under the normal presumptions, but with the option of returning the goods in accordance with the terms of the contract. Any such return is at the buyer's risk and expense, unless otherwise agreed.

In a **consignment** arrangement, the "buyer" (a retail store, for example) is not really a buyer at all, but rather a bailee-agent who has possession of someone else's goods and the power to sell the goods to third parties. As between this **consignee**, the retail store, and the **consignor**, a manufacturer, for example, the consignor retains title and risk on the goods until they are sold to third parties. Out of fairness to the creditors of the consignee, however, the Code says that they can treat the transaction as if it were a sale or return, unless the consignee's creditors know generally that the consignee engages in such transactions or unless the consignor publicly files a financing statement under Article 9's provisions or posts a sign on the consignee's premises in accordance with an applicable state statute.

Section 2-328 contains some special "offer and acceptance" rules for sales by **auction**. When the auctioneer, Colonel Fasthammer, receives offers in the form of bids, his acceptance occurs when he raps his hammer (and hollers "Sold!") or in any other customary manner. Until the hammer falls, any bid can be withdrawn, but such a withdrawal does not revive any previous bid. Whether the goods have to be sold to the highest bidder depends on whether the sale is with reserve or **without reserve**. Unless specific notice is given otherwise, it is assumed that the auction is with reserve, meaning that the auctioneer "may withdraw the goods at any time until he announces completion of the sale." Because the goods are already identified and (usually) no further delivery by the seller is required, title and risk would be presumed to pass to the buyer when the auctioneer's acceptance occurs. In a sale without reserve, each bid is an acceptance of the auctioneer's offer to sell. Each such contract is conditional on there being no higher bid. The last, highest bid has thus formed a final contract, and title and risk would pass to that buyer when the auctioneer announces the end to bidding on that item.

U.N. Convention on Contracts for the International Sale of Goods (CISG) Risk of Loss Rules

For the international business-to-business goods contracts that it covers, the CISG provides a set or rules as to when risk of loss passes from the seller to the buyer. If the contract does not specify a particular place at which the seller is to turn over the goods, risk passes to the buyer when the seller gives the goods to the first carrier, for shipment to the buyer. If a particular place is specified, the seller bears the risk until the goods are turned over at that place. If the goods are already in transit when the sale is made, the buyer assumes the risk for the rest of the transportation period. If the goods are to be picked up by the buyer from a location other than the seller's place of business, the buyer has the risk when the goods are available for delivery and the buyer is notified of that fact. If the buyer is to pick up the goods at the seller's place of business, risk stays with the seller until the goods are physically turned over to the buyer. (See CISG Appendix D, Articles 66–69.)

The *St. Paul* case illustrates the CISG rules on risk of loss and the use of **"Incoterms"** (discussed on page 316).

Shipment and Storage of Goods

Bill of Lading—A Document of Title

Most goods shipped have no specific title registration certificates. The shipper simply delivers the goods to the common carrier with instructions to transport and deliver them, or the common carrier comes to the residence or business of the shipper and picks up the goods with instructions as to their transportation and delivery.

At the point when the shipper turns over possession to the common carrier, a document showing ownership of the particular goods is necessary. This document is called a

CASE 4

St. Paul Guardian Ins. Co. v. Neuromed Medical Systems GmbH

2002 U.S. Dist. LEXIS 5096 (S.D. NY 2002)

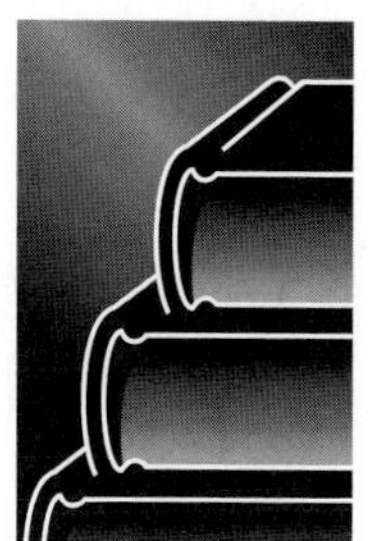

Facts: Shared Imaging (a U.S. corporation) bought a Siemens mobile magnetic resonance imaging (MRI) system from Neuromed, a German company. The contract specified that 10 percent of the $930,000 contract price would be paid immediately, with another 80 percent prior to shipment, and the final 10 percent after acceptance by the buyer—within 3 business days after the MRI arrived in Calumet City, Illinois. A handwritten note, allegedly initialed by Raymond Stachowiak of Shared Imaging, stated "Acceptance subject to Inspection." The contract also said that Neuromed retained title to the MRI until the price was paid in full. The shipment was to be made "CIF New York Seaport." The MRI was loaded onto the ship *Atlantic Carrier* undamaged and in good working order but was badly damaged when it arrived in Illinois. The two insurance companies that reimbursed Shared Imaging for $285,000 worth of repairs sued Neuromed. Neuromed has filed a motion to dismiss the complaint.

Issue: Which party had the risk of loss?

Decision: Shared Imaging—the buyer. Case dismissed.

Opinion by Judge Stein: "INCOTERMS define 'CIF' (named port of destination) to mean the seller delivers when the goods pass 'the ship's rail in the port of shipment.'... The seller is responsible for paying the cost, freight and insurance necessary to bring the goods to the named port of destination, but the risk of loss or damage to the goods passes from seller to buyer upon delivery to the port of shipment.... Further, 'CIF' requires the seller to obtain insurance only on minimum cover....

"Plaintiffs argue that Neuromed's explicit retention of title in the contract to the MRI machine modified the 'CIF' term, such that Neuromed retained title and assumed the risk of loss. INCOTERMS, however, only address passage of risk, not transfer of title.... Under the CISG, the passage of risk is likewise independent of the transfer of title....

"Moreover, according to Article 67(1), the passage of risk and the transfer of title need not occur at the same time, as the seller's retention of 'documents controlling the disposition of the goods does not affect the passage of risk.'...

"German law also recognizes passage of risk and transfer of title as two independent legal acts....

"Plaintiffs next contend that ... the other terms in the contract are that the parties' intention [was] to supercede and replace the 'CIF'" term such that Neuromed retained title and the risk of loss. That is incorrect....

"The 'CIF' term as defined by INCOTERMS only requires the seller to 'clear the goods for export' and is silent as to which party bears the obligation to arrange for customs clearance.... The parties are therefore left to negotiate these obligations. As such, a clause defining the terms of customs clearance neither alters nor affects the 'CIF' clause in the contract....

"INCOTERMS do not mandate a payment structure, but rather simply establish that the buyer bears an obligation to 'pay the price as provided in the contract of sale.'... Inclusion of the terms of payment in the contract does not modify the 'CIF' clause....

"Finally, plaintiffs emphasize the handwritten note, 'Acceptance upon inspection.'... [D]espite plaintiffs' arguments to the contrary, the handwritten note does not modify the 'CIF' clause; it instead serves to qualify the terms of the transfer of title....

"For the foregoing reasons, Neuromed's motion to dismiss for failure to state a cause of action is granted and the complaint is dismissed."

[In a very brief (2-paragraph) opinion, the U.S. Second Circuit affirmed "for substantially the reasons set forth in the district court's opinion."]

bill of lading if the transportation is by land or sea, and it is called an **air bill** if the transportation is by air. The bill of lading or air bill serves as both a receipt for the goods and as a contract that states the terms of the agreement to transport and deliver the goods. Title to the goods may be transferred from the shipper to another person or organization by transferring the bill of lading or air bill.

A bill of lading or an air bill can be negotiable or non-negotiable. If the bill is negotiable, it will state that the goods are to be delivered to the bearer of the bill or to the order of a specific person or organization. If the bill simply consigns the goods to a specific person or organization at the point of delivery, then it is non-negotiable and it is called a straight bill of lading or a straight air bill.

The bill of lading or air bill must describe the goods. Typically, it will state the weight of the goods and describe the number of items and the content of the shipment in such a manner that the person receiving the goods will be able to identify them as those that were entrusted to the carrier for shipment.

Article 7 of the UCC contains specific provisions governing the issuance and use of bills of lading. Normally, the bill of lading is issued to the shipper. The shipper can then mail the bill of lading to the person or organization that is to receive the goods at their final destination. However, UCC Section 7-305(1) allows the shipper to request that the common carrier issue the bill of lading directly to the person or organization receiving the goods at the final destination or at any other place that the shipper may request. Obviously, situations arise in which mailing the bill of lading to the receiver of the goods would be unwise. It would be better to have the bill of lading issued by the carrier directly to the person or organization receiving the goods prior to, or at the time of, delivery.

If the bill of lading is negotiable, then the carrier may not deliver the goods without getting the bill of lading properly endorsed by the person or organization receiving them. If the goods are shipped under a non-negotiable bill of lading, the carrier can simply deliver them to the person or organization named as consignee in the bill, and the bill of lading need not be endorsed by the receiving party. With a non-negotiable bill, the carrier must verify that the receiving party is in fact the party to whom the shipment was supposed to be delivered. If the carrier delivers the goods to the wrong person, the carrier will be responsible to the shipper.

Definition of a Warehouse

A public warehouse presents itself to the public as a business engaged in storing goods for members of the public for a fee. A private warehouse is a storage business that is not open to the public, but only leases storage space to one person or company or to a select number of persons or companies.

Warehouse Receipts—Another Document of Title

Every warehouse that stores goods for the public must issue a **warehouse receipt** to the bailor when the bailor leaves goods for storage. There is no specific statutory form that must be used. However, the receipt must contain certain essential terms, such as the location of the warehouse, the date the receipt was issued, and the consecutive number of the receipt. It also must contain a statement about delivery. Will the goods be delivered to the bearer of the receipt, or to the order of a specified person? If so, the receipt is negotiable. Or will the goods be delivered only to a specified person, thus making the receipt non-negotiable? The rates to be charged must also be stated and the goods described. The receipt must be signed by an agent of the warehouse, and if any advances have been made or any liabilities incurred, an explanation must be made on the receipt.

Common Shipping Terms

Because in the "movement" cases the location of title and risk will probably depend on whether the seller has met contractual duties, it is important to know what certain commonly used shipping terms require the seller to do. In addition to the **COD** term discussed earlier, the abbreviations **FOB** (free on board), **FAS** (free alongside), and **CIF** (cost, insurance, and freight) are commonly used.

The FOB term is used in combination with a named city, for example, FOB Chicago. The seller's obligation is to get the goods into the possession of a carrier and to get them to the specified place. Whether this is a **shipment contract** or a **delivery contract** depends on whether "Chicago" is the seller's city or the buyer's city. If the FOB contract also specifies a vessel, car, or other vehicle, the seller must also "at his own expense and risk load the goods on board"; in other words, the seller is responsible for getting the goods into the buyer's designated carrier.

The FAS term is used in connection with a particular vessel, for example, FAS *S.S. Mariner*. The seller must deliver the goods alongside that vessel in accordance with the port's custom or on a dock specified by the buyer. The seller must also get a receipt for the goods and tender it to the buyer so that the buyer can get a bill of lading from the vessel's operator.

The CIF contract provides the buyer with the convenience of making one lump sum payment to the seller, after the seller has made all the arrangements for shipping the goods. The seller is obligated to pay the carrier's freight charges (or to get credit from the carrier) and to obtain the customary insurance policy on the goods while they are in transit.

(A **C&F** contract omits the insurance requirement.) The seller then forwards to the buyer all the required paperwork: the freight receipt, the bill of lading, the insurance policy, the seller's own invoice for the package price, and a negotiable draft for the total invoice price. Normally these papers will be sent to a bank in the buyer's city where the buyer has made credit arrangements; the bank has instructions to give the buyer the negotiable bill of lading (without which the buyer cannot get the goods) only after the buyer signs the negotiable draft, thus indicating that the buyer will pay the draft when it becomes due. The bank then buys the draft from the seller and sends the seller the cash. Everyone's happy: The buyer has the goods and whatever credit period is specified in the draft in which to pay for them; the seller has the cash, with no risk of nonpayment; and the buyer's bank earns the interest rate provided for in the draft. This very common transaction shows how Articles 2, 3, 4, and 7 come together to cover the various aspects of a single commercial transaction.

Incoterms

For much of the international trade in goods, the delivery requirements are specified by the use of International Commercial Terms ("Incoterms") drafted by the International Chamber of Commerce (ICC). Of course, as a private party, the ICC cannot make "law." Widespread commercial use of Incoterms, however, does make them part of trade custom and usage, and many contracts do specify them as the controlling delivery term.

There are 13 Incoterms. For EXW, no carrier is required; seller makes the goods available at a designated factory or warehouse. There are seven "shipment" terms: FCA (seller obligated to deliver to the first carrier), FAS (seller obligated to deliver alongside a designated ship at a designated port), FOB (seller obligated to deliver on board a designated ship at a designated port), CIF (seller obligated to pay freight and insurance to destination port, but risk passes to buyer when goods are on board ship), CFR (same as CIF, expect that seller does not have to pay for insurance); CIP and CPT work the same as CIF/CFR, except they apply to other forms of transportation. There are five "delivery required" terms: DES—delivered ex ship (requires seller to make goods available to buyer at the destination port, but still on board ship); DEQ—delivered ex quay (requires seller to off-load the goods at destination port); DDU—delivered duty unpaid (means that buyer must pay any customs fees); DDP—delivered duty paid (means that seller must pay any customs fees); DAF—delivered at frontier, using ground transportation (means that buyer must pay any customs fees). The seller is generally required to notify the buyer that the goods are on the way.

The importance of the seller's complying exactly with the agreed shipping terms can be seen in the following case.

Two special situations involving claims by third parties against the goods have arisen frequently enough to require special legal rules. The "title" sections of Article 2 provide the rules for settling disputes that occur because of "defects" in the seller's title to the goods. "Bulk sales" problems are dealt with in Article 6.

Sale by Seller with Void or Voidable Title

Defects in Seller's Title

In any number of situations, a person might possess goods he or she does not own, or have a voidable title to such goods because someone else has the power to rescind a previous sale transaction. What happens when the person in possession of such goods sells them to a good faith purchaser? Which of the two innocent parties should the law protect—the original owner or the good faith purchaser? Because only one of these parties can win the litigation for ownership of the goods, the other party will sustain a loss unless he or she can find and collect against the "middleman." If you lend one of your books to a friend, and that person sells it along with some of his or her own books, either intentionally or by mistake, you can clearly sue your friend for the value of the book. The more basic question, however, is whether or not you can locate the buyer and get the book back.

The code's basic approach to this sort of problem is to distinguish between a seller who has a **void title**; that is, no title at all, and a seller whose title to the goods is **voidable**

CASE 5

Rheinberg Kellerei GmbH v. Brooksfield National Bank of Commerce Bank

901 F.2d 481 (5 Cir. 1990)

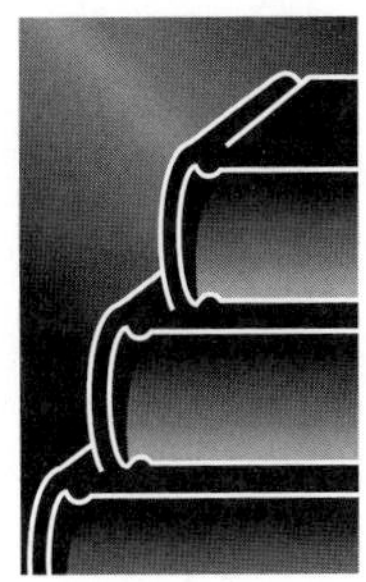

Facts: In January of 1986, J & J Wine, a U.S. company, ordered a shipment of wine from a German firm, Rheinberg Kellerei GmbH, through a U.S. importer, Frank Sutton & Co. Payment was to be made through an international letter of collection handled by Edekabank in Germany and Brooksfield National Bank of Commerce Bank in San Antonio ("NBC Bank"). On March 27, NBC Bank received the letter of collection, bill of lading, and invoices from Edeka. The letter of collection noted that payment was due "on arrival of goods in Houston harbor," and called for NBC Bank to notify Sutton "in case of any difficulty or lack of payment." The invoices noted an estimated time of arrival: April 2, 1986. NBC Bank then presented the documents to J & J Wine on March 27.

In a case like this one, international letters of collection are issued by the seller's bank (Edeka) and sent to the buyer's bank (NBC Bank), which in turn presents the letter and its documents to the buyer. To receive the documents and collect the goods, the buyer pays the amount due to its bank, which then forwards the funds to the seller's bank. Enforcement of these letters is governed by the International Chamber of Commerce's International Rules for Collection.

The bill of lading called for notification of Sutton and M.G. Maher & Co., the customs broker, on arrival of the goods in Houston. NBC Bank was not listed on the Bill of Lading or the invoices.

There is some dispute as to what, exactly, J & J Wine told NBC Bank about its financial situation at the time, but it is sure that J & J Wine did not pay the amount due, and instead asked NBC Bank to hold the letter for a time while J & J Wine worked to raise the money for payment. NBC Bank did not notify Edeka or Sutton of J & J Wine's failure to pay on presentment. In fact, NBC Bank did nothing further until early May, when Sutton informed them that the wine was still at the Houston port and NBC Bank cabled Edeka for further instructions.

The wine at arrived in Houston on March 31, but NBC Bank did not receive notice of that. Because J & J Wine had not taken delivery of it, the wine sat, exposed, at Houston harbor in metal containers until it had deteriorated completely. U.S. Customs agents eventually sold it at auction. J & J Wine subsequently went out of business, and Rheinberg Kellerei was never paid for the wine.

Rheinberg Kellerei then brought this suit. After a bench trial, the district court entered a judgment for NBC Bank.

Issue: Had risk of loss on the goods passed to the buyer? Did NBC Bank have a duty to notify Edeka Bank of the "difficulty"?

Decision: Yes. Yes. Judgment for Rheinberg Kellerei.

Opinion by Circuit Judge Garza: "NBC Bank presented the letter of collection and the other documents to J & J Wine for payment on March 27, 1986, before the wine had arrived and before the payment was due. Rheinberg Kellerei argues that, regardless of whether NBC Bank knew when the wine had arrived, once NBC Bank presented the documents, it had a duty to inform Edeka of any problem in collecting J & J Wine's payment. We agree. That duty arises both from the Rules and the collection letter itself. . . .

"The letter, which is the primary source of responsibility in this case, instructs NBC Bank to notify Sutton 'in case of any difficulty or lack of payment.' The district court found that section demanded notice only if there were a lack of payment or failure to pay. Likewise, NBC Bank emphasizes that the trigger for notice is a lack of payment.

"What the court below and NBC Bank ignore is the word 'difficulty.' The letter did not instruct NBC Bank to notify Sutton only if there were a default, or a failure to pay, or a lack of payment. Rather, NBC Bank was called on to act also if there were any difficulty in collecting payment. And the request that NBC Bank hold the letter while J & J Wine sought financing certainly posed a difficulty in collection. Once NBC Bank knew that J & J Wine had asked for time to come up with the money, it should have notified Sutton in accordance with the letter's instructions. . . .

"If [UCC] Section 4.502 were applied to our case, NBC Bank would have a duty to notify Edeka of J & J Wine's failure to pay the letter of collection when it was presented on March 27, even though the goods were not yet in Houston harbor and the payment was not yet due. This is not to say the J & J Wine was in default at that time or had dishonored the letter. Rather, the notice is an act of prudence, an exercise in due care. And, as the aims of the [international] Rules and the U.C.C. are more than consistent, and both demand the exercise of due care, we find that the Rules impose the same duty. NBC Bank should have notified Edeka of J & J Wine's failure to pay at presentment, as that failure constituted a 'non-payment.'. . .

"NBC Bank and the court below rely heavily on the fact that NBC Bank had no actual knowledge of the wine's arrival in Houston, and had no duty to inquire further. We agree with those premises, but do not feel they affect NBC Bank's duty to notify. That duty arose—under both the Rules and the letter itself—when J & J Wine failed to pay on presentment and asked for time. Arrival of the wine did not trigger it. And NBC Bank cannot avoid liability by hiding from knowledge of arrival and claiming that ignorance as a defense. . . .

"State law governs the measure of damages in a case such as this one. . . . [S]ec.2.709(a). . . gives the relevant standard: 'the seller may recover, together with any incidental damages under the next section, the price (1) of goods accepted or of conforming goods lost or damaged . . . after risk of their loss has passed to the buyer.' Risk of loss had passed to J & J Wine when the goods arrived at Houston harbor and were available for J & J Wine to take delivery. . . . The district court found that because the wine was exposed for such a long period in Houston harbor, it was '"over cooked" and had deteriorated, lost its original flavor, freshness, was flat and should not be sold into the market that it was intended.' Since the goods were so damaged, Rheinberg Kellerei is entitled to the contract price plus the unpaid freight costs, as provided in U.C.C. section 2.709(a)(1). . .

"The district court applied, and the parties refer to, U.C.C. sec. 2.708, which figures damages as the difference between market value at the time and place for tender and contract price, plus incidental damages. That section is inapposite here, as the wine's market value at the time of tender was destroyed by the long delay at Houston harbor. Section 2.708 is more properly used in cases where resale at a reasonable rate is possible. The wine's ultimate sale price here bears no resemblance to its market price at the time of tender. . . .

"NBC Bank is entitled to a credit for the net proceeds of any resale of the damaged wine. . . . Customs agents sold the wine at auction, but we have no evidence before us of the price paid or the net amount remaining after customs fees, wharfage, and the costs of the auction were paid. For that reason, we remand this case to the district court for the limited purpose of calculating that net amount. After finding that net amount, the district court should enter judgment for Rheinberg Kellerei for the contract price plus freight charges, less the net proceeds of the customs auction."

because of some irregularity in that person's acquisition of the goods. Except for the very special case you are about to read, the general rule is that a person with no title passes no title to his or her buyer. When your watch is lost, stolen, or lent and then sold by the finder, thief, or bailee, you get the watch back from the buyer if you can prove what happened, even if the buyer was acting in good faith. On the other hand, when there was in fact a sales transaction between the original owner and the reseller and the original owner intended at that time to make the reseller the owner of the goods, a **good faith purchaser (BFP or GFP)** from the reseller keeps the goods, even though the original sale is voidable because of minority, fraud, duress, nonpayment, or similar irregularity.

Appearance of Authority to Sell

However, when the original owner created a situation in which it appeared to reasonable third parties that a **bailee** was really the owner of the goods or that the bailee had the power to sell the goods for the owner, a good faith purchaser from the bailee would keep the goods. The main problem in such a case, both before and after the adoption of the Code, has been to determine what actions by the original owner are sufficient to create this **appearance of authority to sell**. Generally, the courts held that mere possession of goods by a bailee was not enough to create this appearance.

Entrusting to a Merchant

The Code creates a conclusive presumption of such an "appearance of authority" in only one situation—an "entrusting" of possession of goods to a merchant who deals in goods of that kind. **Entrusting** is defined in Section 2-403(3) as including any delivery of possession or any acquiescence in retention of possession. When such an entrusting occurs, the merchant has the power (not the right) to transfer all rights of the **entruster** to a **buyer in the ordinary course (BIOC)** of business. If you left your watch for repair at a jewelry store that sold watches, or if you bought a new watch at the store but left it there on a layaway plan until you could pay for it, you have given the watch merchant the power to transfer all your rights in the watch to a good faith purchaser (BIOC). The buyer keeps "your" watch; you have to sue the merchant for wrongfully selling your property. Notice, however, that if a thief stole your watch and left it for repair, you could still recover it from a BIOC because the merchant only had the power to pass whatever title the thief had (none). This section thus goes further than the law ever has in protecting good faith purchasers.

Bulk Sales

The Problem Defined

Bulk sales also involve third parties who may have claims against the seller's goods and who wish to assert those claims even though the goods are now in the hands of a good faith

Exhibit 17.3: Defects in Seller's Title

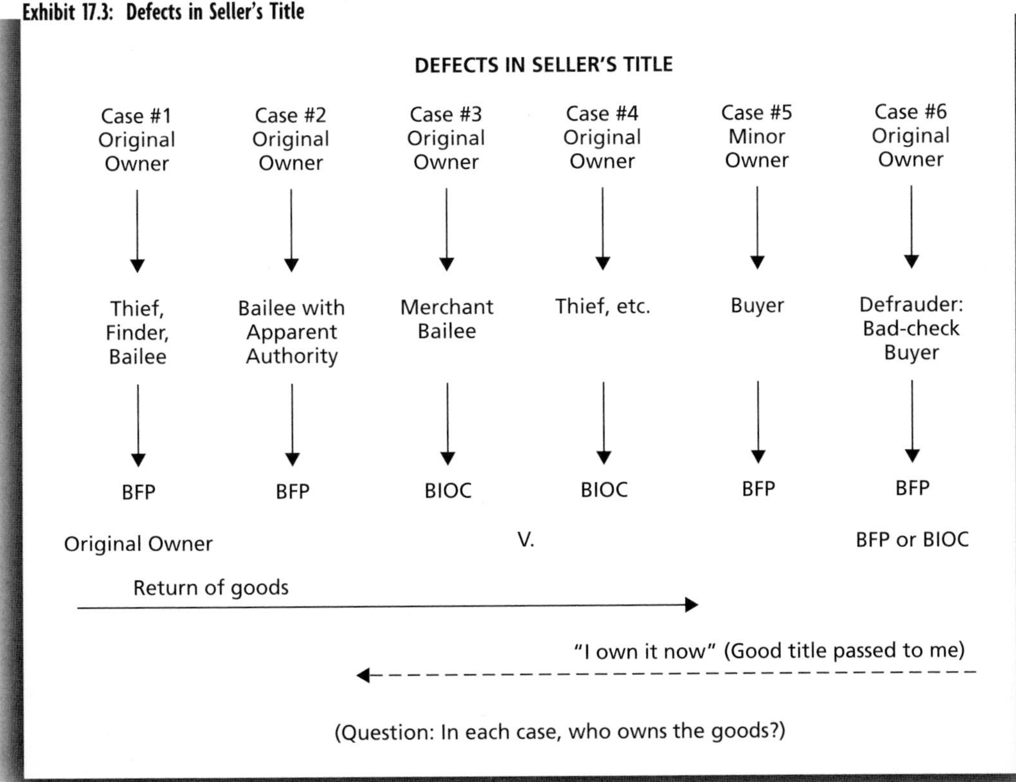

purchaser. This problem, however, arises in a different context. It occurs because some sellers want to play "take the money and run": They sell all their inventory to an innocent buyer, pocket the cash, and leave town without paying off their business creditors.

The seller here is a merchant "whose principal business is the sale of merchandise from stock, including those who manufacture what they sell." This definition excludes farmers, contractors, and service enterprises. The seller does own the goods involved—the inventory—but instead of selling it in the normal course of business, a bulk transfer is made; that is, a single transfer involving a "major part" of the inventory. The purpose of prior bulk sales laws and of Article 6 of the code is to try to protect both the seller's creditors and the buyer by specifying a required procedure for bulk transfers, with the main burden of compliance placed on the bulk seller.

Basic Requirements

In most cases the required procedure should be easy enough to follow. The buyer and seller prepare a schedule of the goods to be transferred. The seller furnishes the buyer with a list of the seller's creditors and their addresses; this list must be sworn to by the seller, and the buyer is not liable for any inaccuracies unless that person actually knows that a creditor's name has been omitted. The buyer is then responsible for notifying each listed creditor, either in person or by registered or certified mail, that the bulk transfer is to occur. This notice must be given at least 10 days before the buyer takes possession of the goods or makes a payment on the price. The notice must also contain the names and business addresses of the seller and the buyer and, if provision has been made for paying off the creditors, the address to which they should send their bills for payment. If no arrangement has been made for paying off the creditors, a "long form" notice must be used, which includes the estimated total of the seller's debts, the description and location of the goods to be transferred, the address where the creditor list and property schedule may be inspected, and the consideration received by the seller for the goods. The buyer must either preserve the schedule and list for 6 months, for inspection, or simply file this information with the specified public official.

Exhibit 17.4: Bulk Sales Rules

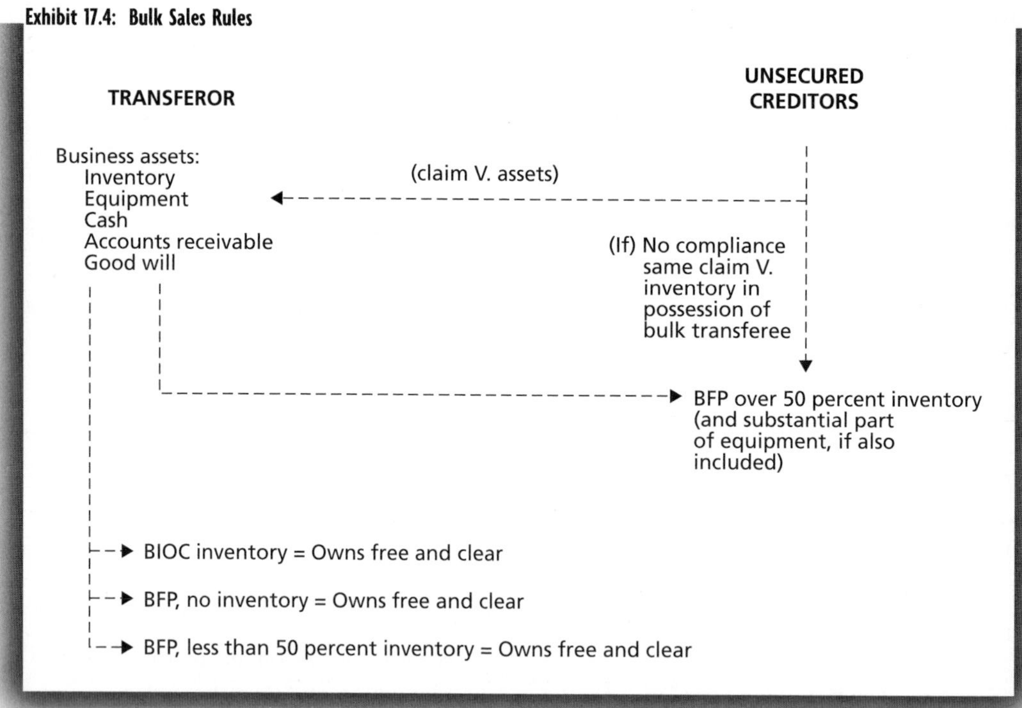

If these steps have been followed, the buyer owns the goods free and clear of any claims of the seller's unsecured creditors, except in those few states that have adopted optional Section 6-106. This part of the code makes the buyer personally responsible for seeing to it that the purchase price is applied to pay off the seller's creditors. If the required steps have not been followed, the seller's creditors can have the bulk goods seized and sold to satisfy their claims if they bring suit within 6 months after the transfer occurred or, if the transfer was concealed, within 6 months after they discover what happened. In any case, a good faith purchaser from the bulk transferee owns the goods free and clear of claims of the original seller's creditors.

In those states that have adopted optional Section 6-106, the bulk buyer needs to be much more careful because noncompliance can make the buyer personally liable to the unpaid creditors.

Exceptions

Certain extraordinary transfers are not subject to the requirements of Article 6. Transfers pursuant to judicial processes or to satisfy certain preexisting obligations and transfers of property that are exempt from creditors' claims can be made without complying with Article 6. Article 6 also contains two exemptions that were not found in most of the old bulk sales statutes.

These two new exemptions will permit the sale of a business, including its inventories, without the necessity of compliance, when the buyer has an established, solvent business and agrees to assume the seller's debts, or when the buyer is a new enterprise organized to take over and continue the seller's business and the seller receives nothing from the bulk transfer except an interest in the new enterprise that is subordinate to the claims of its creditors. In both cases an unspecified "public notice" must be given, but otherwise these exceptions should provide considerable flexibility in reorganizing an existing business.

Tax and Other Special Statutes

In addition to the bulk sale problems previously discussed, the buyer of a business will also need to be aware of possible claims against the business for unpaid taxes. Accrued social security and withholding taxes may be owed to the national government. Payments may be due to the state government for sales taxes, unemployment taxes, and workers' compensation coverage. Local real estate taxes and special assessments may not have been paid. In some cases, the tax statutes will provide that these accrued liabilities become liens against the business' assets. The buyer of the business may not be protected against such liens simply by complying with the Code's bulk sales requirements.

Also, if a transfer of real estate is involved in the sale of the business, the buyer needs to be aware of the possibility of adverse claims against the land. These matters are discussed more fully in Chapter 20. Article 6 has no application to transfers of land, only to bulk sales of inventory.

Repeal or Substantial Modification

Most recently, the National Conference of Commissioners on Uniform State Laws and the American Law Institute (ALI) have come to believe that Article 6 is no longer needed, and that it is imposing significant (and unnecessary) costs on businesses. Their current recommendation is for the complete repeal of Article 6.

As an alternative, for those states that want to continue some regulation in this area, the commissioners have recommended drastic changes to Article 6. Now renamed "Bulk Sales," Article 6 would apply only when the buyer has notice that the seller will not be continuing in the same or a similar business after the bulk sale. It would not apply where the sale involves property less than $10,000 or more than $25,000,000 in value. If the seller has 200 or more unsecured creditors, the buyer may simply file a disclosure with the secretary of state, rather than sending personal notice to each one. Notice must be given 45 days (rather than 10 days) before the sale. The seller's creditors have 1 year, rather than 6 months, within which to challenge the sale.

Businesses thus need to know which alternative is in force in their respective states: the old Article 6, the new Article 6, or no Article 6.

Significance of This Chapter

A modern economy cannot function effectively unless most buyers are assured that they will, in fact, own the goods they buy in good faith. The basic policy of the Code is to protect such good faith buyers against most adverse claims that might be made against the goods. When one buys goods from a merchant-dealer in an ordinary business transaction, the Code states a conclusive presumption that the merchant was authorized to sell them if the owner voluntarily left them in the merchant's possession. When one is buying a merchant's inventory "in bulk" and not in the ordinary course of business, Article 6 provides a relatively simple procedure to validate the transaction. In both cases, buyers are protected if they act in good faith and follow the law.

Although millions of sales contracts are made and performed each day without any problem arising, things go wrong in some cases. One of the parties fails to perform properly, or the goods are lost without the fault of either, or a third party asserts claims against the goods or otherwise tries to interfere with the transaction. The law needs to provide a set of rules to deal with these problem situations. The Code's approach is to provide a set of presumptions as to when the various ownership interests in the goods pass from the seller to the buyer or exist in favor of third parties.

As between the buyer and the seller, the most important presumptions are those dealing with risk of loss because most such cases will involve that issue. When one or more third parties are involved in the dispute, the case will usually require application of the presumptions for the other ownership interests: special property, insurable interest, title, right to possession, and security interest. A case pitting the seller or the buyer against a third party will usually have to be decided by applying the rules for one of these other five ownership interests. Both the parties to the sales transaction and third parties such as financing agencies thus need to know the rules governing the transfer of the various ownership interests from seller to buyer.

IMPORTANT TERMS AND CONCEPTS

air bill
appearance of authority to sell
auction
entrusting
entruster
bailee
bill of lading
bulk sales
buyer in the ordinary course (BIOC)
carrier
C&F
CIF
COD
consignee
consignment
consignor
contract to sell
delivery contract
document of title
FAS
FOB
fungible goods
future goods
good faith purchaser (BFP or GFP)
goods
identification
incoterms
insurable interest
merchant
price
right to possession
risk of loss
sale on approval
sale or return
security interest
shipment contract
special property
tender of delivery
title
void title
voidable
warehouse
warehouse receipt
warranty
without reserve

QUESTIONS AND PROBLEMS FOR DISCUSSION

1. What is identification in a sale of goods contract and when does it occur?

2. What is the buyer's special property in the goods, and when does it pass to the buyer?

3. When does the seller have an insurable interest in the goods that are the subject matter of a sale of goods contract?

4. When does a person in possession of goods, other than the owner, have an appearance of authority to sell them?

5. Couch, a dealer in new and used cars, sold a new Cadillac to Sartain, also a dealer. The registration papers on the car were to be sent to Sartain after Sartain's check cleared. After Couch had delivered the car, but before the check had cleared, Sartain sold the car to Cockroft, a bona fide purchaser (BFP). The check bounced. Couch filed for replevin, regained the Cadillac, and then resold it.

   The chancery court held that the seller had no right to replevy the car and that Cockroft was entitled to the value of the automobile from the seller for wrongful replevy. Couch appealed.

   Was Cockroft a BIOC even though he had not yet received a motor vehicle registration certificate?

6. Rheinberg-Kellerei, a German wine seller, sold a shipment to Vineyard Wines, a U.S. customer. The sale was made through Rheinberg's U.S. sales agent, Sutton, in North Carolina. The contract provided for shipment of the wine by sea, with notice to be given to Vineyard when the wine was turned over to a ship for transportation to the United States. Rheinberg sent the wine to Rotterdam, for shipment to the United States on board the *M.S. Munchen.* Rheinberg notified Sutton, but Sutton did not notify Vineyard. The *Munchen* went down with all hands and cargo in the North Sea. Vineyard refused to pay a draft for the contract price when it was presented for payment. Rheinberg sued for the contract price.

   Which party had the risk of loss when the ship sank? Discuss.

7. Ray Schock bought a used house trailer from Pablo and Collette Ronderos. Ray paid them the full contract price of $3,900 and received a signed bill of sale. Pablo said he would get the title registration certificate signed and notarized, and then mail it to Schock. Schock then removed the aluminum "skirting" around the bottom of the mobile home, and the cement blocks on which it had been resting, so that its wheels were back on the ground. He said he would be back to pick it up the following Monday, and that the sellers should remove their couch and piano before then and also get the gas and electricity and water lines disconnected. Pablo agreed to get these things done.

   Four days after the sale (Friday night of that same week), a tornado destroyed the mobile home. Schock did not come to pick up the remains on the following Monday, but did receive the certificate of title that Tuesday. Schock sued to get his money back.

   Who had risk of loss on the mobile home when it was destroyed? Explain.

8. Jane Zendman bought a diamond ring for $12,500 at an auction held at the gallery of Brand, Inc., on the boardwalk of Atlantic City, New Jersey.

   The ring had been entrusted to Brand by the defendant, Harry Winston, a diamond merchant located in New York City, under memorandums stating that the goods were for the jeweler's examination only and that title was not to pass until he had made his selection and had notified the defendant of his agreement to pay the stated price. Records disclosed that in the past other goods had been sent and later sold with payment accepted. A judgment in Zendman's favor in the trial court was reversed by the appellate division, and she appealed to the Court of Appeals.

What should the decision of the appeals court be, and why?

9. Lamborn as the buyer and the Seggermans as the sellers entered into a written contract for the sale of "1200/50 lb. boxes Calif. Evap. apples—Extra Choice Quality—1994 crop." (The Seggermans had, in turn, made arrangements to buy 1,200 boxes of dried apples from a supplier, Rosenberg Brothers.) Lamborn was to pay 22 1/2 cents per pound "FOB Pacific Coast Rail Shipping Point. . . . Payment to be made against draft with documents attached." The Rosenbergs loaded a Southern Pacific railroad car with 1,770 boxes of dried apples and received an "order" bill of lading that provided for shipment to New York. Once they knew the apples were on the way, the Seggermans billed Lamborn for 1,200 boxes and gave Lamborn an order addressed to their delivery clerk at their place of business. Seeing these documents, Lamborn paid the contract price as agreed—$13,377. The apples never arrived in New York; they were seized en route by agents of the U.S. government, for reasons not disclosed by the court. Lamborn sued for a refund but lost in the lower court.

If Lamborn appeals, how should the appeals court rule? Why?

10. Stanley Jakowski bought a new automobile from Carole Chevrolet. As part of the contract, Carole promised to undercoat the car and to apply a polymer sealant to the exterior finish. When Jakowski picked up the car on May 19, these two operations had not been done. Carole realized what had happened the next day, called Jakowski, and asked him to return the car for these treatments. Stanley brought the car back on May 22, and it was stolen from the lot that night, before the coatings had been applied.

Is Carole Chevrolet liable for the theft of the car? Why?

11. Three weeks before Christmas, Fink opened a family shoe store in Buffalo, New York. In May he still had $19,000 worth of winter-style shoes. He sold 1,300 pairs for $3,549 to Rubenstein to clear his shelves of off-season shoes and to obtain cash to pay his debts and thus obtain credit for the purchase of new summer stock. Fink continued in business for 6 months after the sale, until the filing of a petition in bankruptcy in November. The plaintiff, the trustee in bankruptcy acting on behalf of the creditors, sued to hold the defendant, Jack Rubenstein, accountable under the Bulk Sales Act. The trial court held for Rubenstein, but the appellate division reversed. Rubenstein appealed.

How should the final court of appeals decide?

12. Preparing to go on vacation, Ryta Kaher put her sterling silver dining ware, her jewelry, and several credit cards in bags in her attic. When she returned, she put the bags on the dining room table. Also on the table were several bags of clothes to be donated to Goodwill Industries. Her husband Tobey took all the bags to Goodwill; he did not ask for a receipt.

Julie Naylor, who had received the bags from Tobey, immediately started pricing the donated items and set them out for sale at the Goodwill "resale" store. Sorting through the clothing, she found a wallet, and called the Kahers to notify them of it. She recognized the silver set was "nice," but did not call the Kahers back about it because nice items were often donated.

Caren Carl had worked at Goodwill, and she often shopped there for bargains. She bought the silver set about 5 minutes after Julie Naylor put it on display. Caren refused to give the silver back to the Kahers, so they sued her.

Who owns the $4,000 silver set? Explain.

CHAPTER 18

Warranties and Products Liability

Chapter Objectives

This chapter will:

- Indicate the need for product liability rules.
- Summarize the traditional theories of product liability—fraud, innocent misrepresentation, mistake, and negligence.
- Explain the Uniform Commercial Code changes on express warranties.
- Define the implied warranty of merchantability and its application.
- Define the implied warranty of fitness.
- Explain the Uniform Commercial Code's limitations on disclaimers of warranties.
- Indicate how strict liability in tort applies to defective products.
- Discuss the defenses that may be available in a product liability case.
- Explain recent state and national changes in this area of the law.

Stop and think for a minute. How many times each day do you entrust your health and safety, and even your life, to a manufactured product? Your new electric blanket that you left on all night, the can of frozen orange juice that you opened for breakfast this morning (and the electric can opener that you used to open the orange juice), the car or bus that you used to get to school (and all the other motor vehicles that were on the highway at the same time)—a malfunction in any one of these or in thousands of other products that we encounter every day could produce sickness, injury, or even death. No product can be made absolutely safe, under any and all circumstances. Malfunctions do occur, with resulting personal injury, property damage, and financial loss. The law's function in this area is to provide the rules by which the burden of such losses will be allocated.

Earlier legal doctrine tended to "leave the loss where it was incurred"; that is, to force the injured parties to pay for their own injuries or to buy their own insurance to cover such losses. The modern legal trend, which has accelerated sharply during the past four decades, is to pass these losses back up the chain of distribution, to sellers and manufacturers, as one of the costs of doing business. The net result of the modern product liability rules is that all of us as consumers will pay higher prices for products and that some of the smaller manufacturers in high-risk industries, such as chemicals and machinery, may be forced out of business because they cannot absorb these additional overhead costs. The courts' willingness to apply these modern theories of liability and to disallow traditional defenses has produced a crisis of major proportions and worldwide impact.

Plaintiffs, Defendants, and Theories of Liability

In addition to the buyer of defective goods, other possible plaintiffs include members of the buyer's family and household, guests in the buyer's home, the buyer's employees and customers, and bystanders who have had no previous relationship with the buyer. In addition to the seller, possible defendants include the manufacturer or assembler of the product, the designer, the supplier of the defective component part, and any intermediate distributors. The availability of the manufacturer as a defendant becomes crucial in those cases in which the seller is unable to pay the judgment, or in which the injured buyer cannot remember where the brand name product that caused the injury was purchased, or when the injury resulted from long continued use of the brand name product, such as lung cancer from smoking.

Modern courts have a wide selection of theories of liability that can be used to impose damages back up the chain of distribution: fraud, innocent misrepresentation, negligence, breach of express or implied warranty, and strict liability. Although these different theories of liability require different forms of proof and are subject to different defenses and different statutes of limitations, the courts are not always careful to distinguish which theory is being applied to create liability in a particular case (see Exhibit 18-1).

Fraud and Innocent Misrepresentation

The most obvious case for **product liability** is against the seller (or manufacturer) who has fraudulently misrepresented the product. The defrauder should clearly be held liable for all the losses that are caused by the misrepresentation, and probably for punitive damages as well. However, as noted in Chapter 11, fraud is easy to allege, but difficult to prove, and it probably applies to only a tiny fraction of product liability cases.

As also noted in Chapter 11, most courts permit rescission (but not recovery of damages) when a buyer has been damaged because of reasonable reliance on the seller's honest, but mistaken, statement of fact, that is, an innocent misrepresentation. The most recent version of the **Restatement of the Law of Torts, Second**, includes a revised Section 402B, which would substantially modify this general rule for sales of goods. Under Section 402B, a seller of goods is liable for "physical harm to a consumer" that results from reliance on the seller's material misrepresentation, even though "not made fraudulently or negligently" and even though "the consumer has not bought the chattel from or entered into any contractual relation with the seller." Essentially, what this section does is to restate the law of express warranty, without the requirement of **privity** (relationship) of contract.

NEGLIGENCE

Like fraud, **negligence** is easy to allege but sometimes very difficult to prove. The fact that one part fails and causes injury is not much evidence of negligent manufacture, if tens of thousands of identical parts have been and are functioning properly. Indeed, in most cases such statistics would present a pretty convincing case that the manufacturer was doing an excellent job of product design, manufacture, and inspection. When negligence can be proved against either the manufacturer or the seller or both, the injured party should be able to collect all the damages that result. Courts today generally recognize that the manufacturer's liability for negligence extends not only to the buyer of the product but also to other people "whom he should expect to be endangered by its probable use" (if the product is not properly made). In a few situations, such as the case of the dead mouse in the bottle of cola, the courts may apply the doctrine of ***res ipsa loquitur*** ("the thing speaks for itself"), meaning that such things do not occur without negligent or purposeful conduct.

Exhibit 18.1: Theories of Liability and Defenses

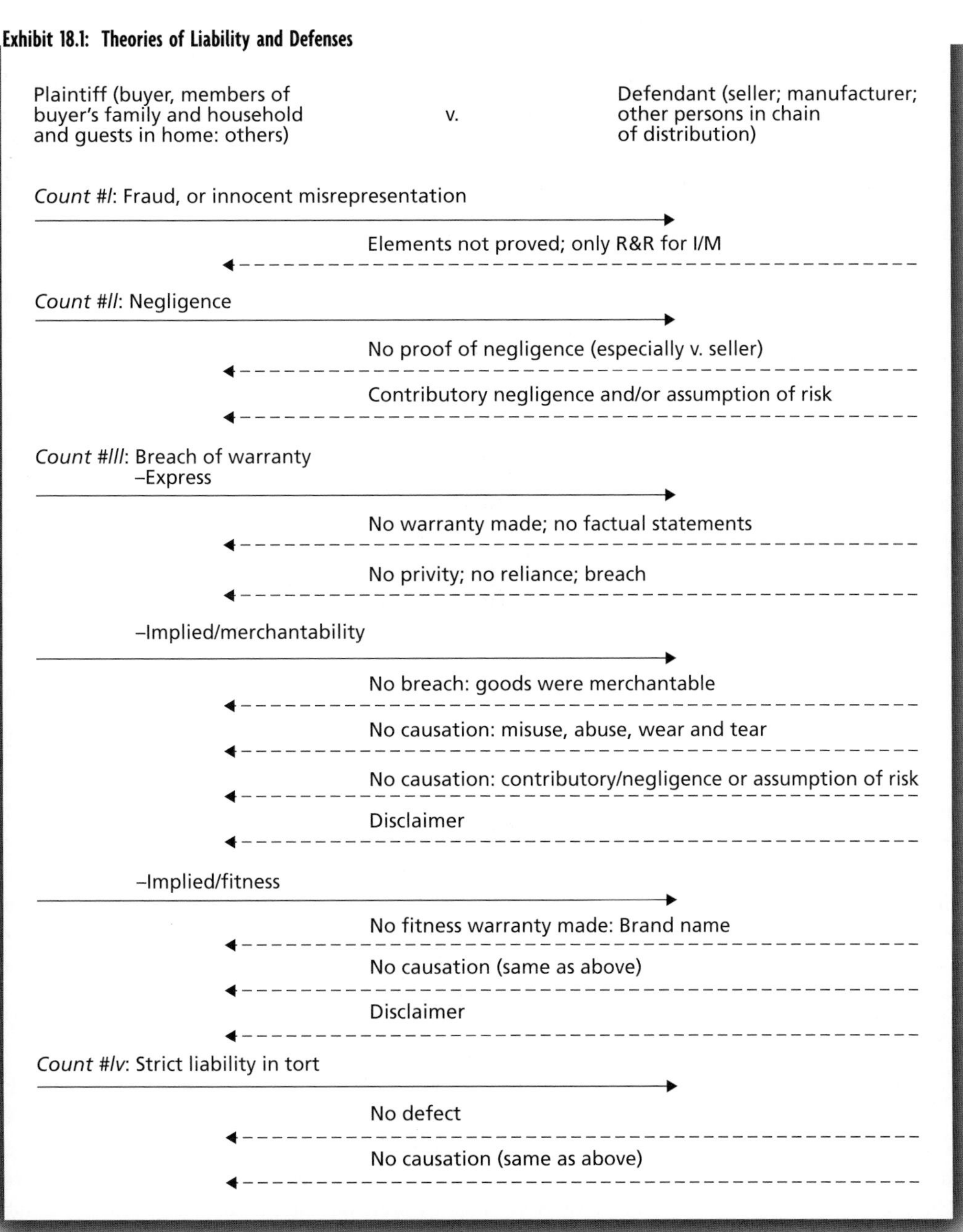

Manufacturers' liability began with cases in which careless production methods resulted in product defects that caused injuries. Courts then applied the negligence theory to improper labeling that resulted in injuries. The *Hamilton* case represents the next step in this progression—liability based negligent methods of product distribution that put potentially dangerous products in the wrong hands. Note that the *Hamilton* plaintiffs do not claim that the guns involved are in themselves "defective" in any way.

CASE 1

HAMILTON, *ET AL.* V. ACCU-TEK, *ET AL.*

62 F.Supp.2d 802 (E.D. NY 1999)

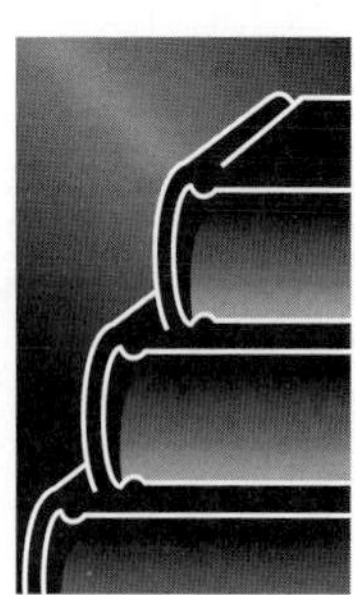

Facts: Relatives of six people killed by handguns, as well as one survivor and his mother, sued 25 handgun manufacturers for negligence. (Freddie Hamilton was the mother of one of the victims.) The plaintiffs claim that the manufacturers' indiscriminate marketing and distribution practices generated an underground market in handguns and provided youths and violent criminals like the shooters in these cases with easy access to guns. Defendants include foreign manufacturers, U.S. subsidiaries of foreign corporations, old-line U.S. manufacturers, and newer gun makers specializing in inexpensive small and medium caliber semiautomatic handguns. The trial court dismissed the claims based on product liability, but permitted the case for negligent marketing to proceed.

After a 4-week trial, the jury found 15 of the defendants to be negligent, and nine of these to have caused injury to one or more plaintiffs. Only plaintiff Steven Fox and his mother were awarded damages, against three defendants, based on their respective market shares. Defendants moved to have judgment entered in their favor, as a matter of law.

Issue: Have the plaintiffs stated a valid claim for recovery on the basis of negligence?

Decision: Yes. Judgment for plaintiff Fox.

Opinion by Judge Weinstein: "On state law issues of first impression, the district court must predict how the highest state court would rule were it presented with the same question. In making such a prediction, the precedents of intermediate state and federal courts are entitled to deference....

"Generally speaking, New York courts are reluctant to impose a duty to anticipate the criminal or tortious conduct of third parties.... This reluctance grows out of concerns of two types....

"The first is the specter of crushing liability on prospective defendants that may destroy their ability to deliver socially useful services....

"The second is the unfairness of imposing a duty on someone who, as a practical matter, could have done little to prevent the harm which occurred....

"New York courts have, however, recognized a duty predicated on the danger of a third person's tortious or criminal misconduct where a relationship between the defendant and either the plaintiff or the third party wrongdoer provides the defendant with the ability to minimize the risk....

"The law of New York imposes broad duties of care on manufacturers. Under parallel principles of strict products liability and negligence law, manufacturers owe a duty to design, produce and market non-defective products which are reasonably safe for their foreseeable use and are accompanied by warnings commensurate with the degree of reasonably foreseeable risk they present....

"While the New York Court of Appeals has not yet explicitly recognized a duty of care in connection with the marketing and distribution of a non-defective but highly dangerous product, imposition of such a duty is consistent with the expansive view of manufacturers' duties dating back to [the] MacPherson [case] and consistently reaffirmed since then....

"Where unavoidably hazardous products like handguns are distributed, it is not unfair for the law to minimize unreasonable risk of harm through the imposition of a duty on manufacturers to market and distribute responsibly....

"Decisions to impose collective liability have been grounded in both moral and pragmatic considerations. A primary motivating factor has been the injustice of barring innocent plaintiffs' recovery solely because of their inability to identify which of a number of wrongdoing defendants caused their injuries....

"Judgment is entered against American Arms, Inc. in favor of Steven Fox in the amount of $9,085 and for Gail Fox in the amount of $115; against Beretta U.S.A. Corp. in favor of Steven Fox in the amount of $238,185, and for Gail Fox in the amount of $3,015; and against Taurus International Manufacturing, Inc. in favor of Steven Fox in the amount of $268,600, and for Gail Fox in the amount of $3,400."

[On appeal, the U.S. Second Circuit asked the New York Court of Appeals two questions. Would state law impose a duty of care on the gun manufacturers, and would market share liability be appropriate? When New York's highest court answered "no" to both questions, the U.S. Second Circuit reversed the judgment, and remanded the case with instructions to dismiss the complaint.]

Permutations and offshoots of the basic negligence theory continue to develop. For several decades, smokers' suits against cigarette companies for tobacco-caused injuries were routinely dismissed on the basis of assumption of risk or contributory negligence. Because "everyone knew" of the dangers of smoking, people who voluntarily chose to smoke anyway had no one to blame but themselves when they contracted lung cancer or other smoking-related diseases. Then plaintiffs' lawyers began arguing that not everyone was aware that cigarettes were addictive and that cigarette companies may have been adjusting nicotine content to ensure addiction. Huge liability settlements resulted.

The McDonald's case is the first major attempt to extend some of the cigarette case arguments to "unhealthy" food. Although the plaintiffs lost the first round, we have surely not heard the last of this new group of product liability cases.

CASE 2

Pelman v. McDonald's Corporation

237 F.Supp.2d 512 (S.D. NY 2003)

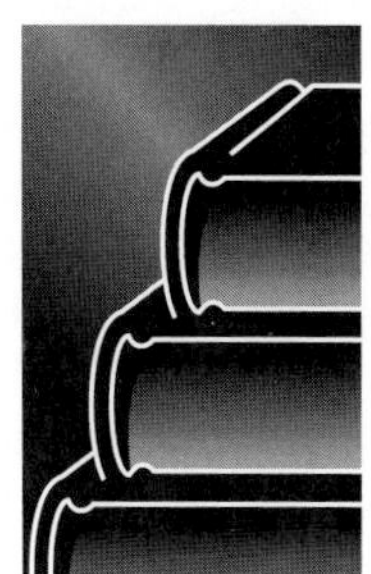

Facts: Two minor children—Ashley Pelman and Jazlen Bradley—sued McDonald's Corporation, McDonald's Restaurants of New York, and two local McDonald's restaurants. Plaintiffs filed the lawsuit in New York state supreme (trial) court; the McDonald's defendants had it removed to U.S. District Court. Plaintiffs alleged that McDonald's engaged in deceptive practices in making and selling its fast food products, and that this deception caused the plaintiffs to consume the products and thus injure their health by becoming obese. The defendants have moved to dismiss the complaint; the plaintiffs have moved to remand the case to state court because there is no diversity of citizenship.

Issue: Have the plaintiffs stated a case for recovery of damages?

Decision: No. Complaint is dismissed, but with leave to refile the case.

Opinion by Judge Sweet: "This action presents unique and challenging issues.... Questions of personal responsibility, common knowledge and public health are presented, and the role of society and the courts in addressing such issues.

"The issue of determining the breadth of personal responsibility underlies much of the law: where should the line be drawn between an individual's own responsibility to take care of herself, and society's responsibility to ensure that others shield her? Laws are created in those situations where individuals are somehow unable to protect themselves and where society needs to provide a buffer between the individual and some other entity—whether herself, another individual or a behemoth corporation that spans the globe. Thus Congress provided that essentially all packaged foods sold at retail shall be appropriately labeled and their contents described. [The Nutrition Labeling and Education Act.]...

"This opinion is guided by the principle that legal consequences should not attach to the consumption of hamburgers and other fast food fare unless consumers are unaware of the dangers of eating such food. As discussed,... this guiding principle comports with the law of products liability under New York law.... [O]ne important principle in assigning legal responsibility is the common knowledge of consumers. If consumers know (or reasonably should know) the potential ill health effects of eating at McDonald's, they cannot blame McDonald's if they, nonetheless, choose to satiate their appetite with a surfeit of supersized McDonald's products. On the other hand, consumers cannot be expected to protect against a danger that was solely within McDonalds' knowledge. Thus, one necessary element of any potentially viable claim must be that McDonalds' products involve a danger that is not within the common knowledge of consumers. As discussed later, plaintiffs have failed to allege with any specificity that such a danger exists....

"The interplay of these issues and forces has created public interest in this action, ranging from reports and letters to the Court to television satire. ["The reality is that anyone with an IQ higher than room temperature will understand that excessive consumption of food served in fast-food restaurants will lead to weight gain."] Obesity, personal liberty and public accountability affect virtually every American consumer....

"There is no dispute that all of the plaintiffs are New York residents and that three of the defendants ... are New York residents....

"In order to show that a non-diverse defendant was fraudulently joined to defeat diversity jurisdiction, the defendant must demonstrate, by clear and convincing evidence, either that there has been outright fraud committed in the plaintiffs' pleadings, or that there is no reasonable basis, based on the pleadings, for liability against the non-diverse defendants in light of the claims alleged....

"In order to state a claim against the outlets and McDonald's of New York, the plaintiffs must allege that they were in possession of information that the McDonald's Corp. products that they sold were more dangerous than a reasonable consumer would expect. Plaintiffs have failed to make such allegations. . . .

"Counts I and II allege that McDonald's violated the New York Consumer Protection Act, [sections] 349 and 350, by (1) deceptively advertising their food as not unhealthful and failing to provide consumers with nutritional information (Court I) and (2) inducing minors to eat at McDonald's through deceptive marketing ploys (Count II). . . .

"Because the Complaint does not identify a single instance of deceptive acts, Count I shall be dismissed to the extent it alleges deceptive practices of commission in violation of [sections] 349 and 350. . . .

"Count II, which focuses on representations targeting children, fails for the same reasons as discussed above. The Complaint does not identify a single specific advertisement, promotion or statement directed at infant consumers, and Count II must be dismissed in the absence of such specificity. . . .

"III. Counts III, IV and V: Negligence claims.

"The plaintiffs' common law claims against McDonald's sound in negligence, alleging that McDonald's was negligent in manufacturing and selling its products and negligent in failing to warn consumers of the potential hazards of eating its products. McDonald's argues that each of these claims fail as a matter of law because: (1) the attributes about which plaintiffs complain were so well-known that McDonald's had no duty either to eliminate such attributes or to warn plaintiffs about them, and (2) the plaintiffs cannot establish proximate cause. . . .

"Count III essentially alleges that McDonalds' products are inherently dangerous because of the inclusion of high levels of cholesterol, fat, salt and sugar. McDonald's argues that because the public is well aware that hamburgers, fries and other fast food fare have such attributes, McDonald's cannot be held liable. . . .

"[I]n order to state a claim, the Complaint must allege either that the attributes of McDonald's products are so extraordinarily unhealthy that they are outside the reasonable contemplation of the consuming public or that the products are so extraordinarily unhealthy as to be dangerous in their intended use. The Complaint—which merely alleges that the foods contain high levels of cholesterol, fat, salt and sugar, and that the foods are therefore unhealthy—fails to reach this bar. It is well-known that fast food in general, and McDonalds' products in particular, contain high levels of cholesterol, fat, salt and sugar, and that such attributes are bad for one. . . .

"As long as a consumer exercises free choice with appropriate knowledge, liability for negligence will not attach to a manufacturer. It is only when that free choice becomes but a chimera . . . that manufacturers should be held accountable. Plaintiffs have failed to allege in the Complaint that decisions to eat at McDonald's several times a week were anything but a choice freely made and which now may not be pinned on McDonald's. . . .

"[P]laintiffs argue that McDonalds' products have been so altered that their unhealthy attributes are now outside the ken of the average reasonable consumer. They point to McDonalds' ingredient lists to show that McDonalds' customers worldwide are getting much more than what is commonly considered to be a chicken finger, a hamburger, or a french fry. . . .

"For instance, Chicken McNuggets, rather than being merely chicken fried in a pan, are a McFrankenstein creation of various elements not utilized by the home cook. . . . In addition, Chicken McNuggets, while seemingly a healthier option than McDonald's hamburgers because they have 'chicken' in their names, actually contain twice the fat per ounce as a hamburger. . . . It is at least a question of fact as to whether a reasonable consumer would know—without recourse to the McDonalds' website—that a Chicken McNugget contained so many ingredients other than chicken and twice the fat of a hamburger. . . .

"This argument comes closest to overcoming the hurdle presented to plaintiffs. If plaintiffs were able to flesh out this argument in an amended complaint, it may establish that the dangers of McDonalds' products were not commonly well known and thus that McDonald's had a duty toward its customers. . . .

"Because the Complaint fails to allege that the danger of the McDonald's products were not well-known and fails to allege with sufficient specificity that the McDonald's products were a proximate cause of the plaintiffs' obesity and health problems, Count III shall be dismissed. . . .

"Count IV alleges a failure to warn of the unhealthy attributes of McDonalds' products. While the cause of action differs from Count III, McDonalds' arguments that the claim fails because the dangers of its fare were well-known and that plaintiffs have failed to show proximate cause are nonetheless applicable. . . .

"[T]heir theory is not supported in their Complaint, and thus cannot save Count IV from dismissal. . . .

"The exact basis of Count V is unclear. It appears to be a products liability claim, i.e., McDonalds' products are inherently dangerous in that they are addictive. The claim may also be read to allege that McDonald's failed to warn its customers that its products were addictive.

"This claim, unlike the one above based on unhealthy attributes, does not involve a danger so open and obvious, or so commonly well-known, that McDonalds' customers would be expected to know about it. In fact, such a hypothesis is even now the subject of current investigation. . . .

"In any case . . . the Complaint fails to allege sufficiently that the addictive nature of McDonalds' food and the plaintiffs' resulting ingestion thereof is a proximate cause of the plaintiffs' health problems. As a result, Count V is dismissed. . . .

"[Federal Rule] 15(a) requires that 'leave [to amend a complaint] shall be given freely when justice so requires.'. . . When a motion to dismiss is granted, 'the usual practice is to grant leave to amend the complaint.'. . . Although the decision whether to grant leave to amend is within the discretion of the district court, refusal to grant leave must be based on a valid ground. . . . As a result, the plaintiffs may amend their complaint to address the deficiencies listed above."

Breach of Warranty

Warranty is simply another word for guarantee. Depending on the facts and circumstances, the seller may make several different types of warranties on the goods being sold—warranties relating to the title to the goods or to the characteristics, qualities, or capabilities of the goods. In a simpler economy, in which most sellers produced what they sold, in which such manufactured goods as there were could be readily inspected and understood by the buyers, and in which there was a rough equality in the bargaining power of the parties, **caveat emptor** ("let the buyer beware") may have been a workable rule for the law of sales. As products became more intricate and the distribution system became more impersonal, courts and legislatures saw the necessity of changing this early rule to provide more protection to buyers and users. It is one thing to say that Walter Woodcutter ought to be able to tell a bad ax from a good one when he deals with the village blacksmith; it is quite another to apply the same standard to a weekend hobbyist who buys a gasoline-driven chainsaw from the local hardware store. The law of warranty has changed, and is still changing, to meet changes in the economy.

The Uniform Commercial Code (UCC) does not make any revolutionary changes in the law of warranties, but it does contain several provisions that extend warranty liability or that make such liability more difficult to disclaim. The code sections cover three types of warranties: **express warranty**, **implied warranty**, and **title warranty**.

Although the title warranties are not specifically labeled "implied," they are such, in the sense that they are automatically written into the transaction by the law unless the parties agree otherwise or the circumstances clearly indicate otherwise. The seller guarantees that he or she has a good title to the goods, that he or she has the right to sell them, and that there are no **liens** or **encumbrances** against them. In addition, when the seller is a merchant regularly dealing in such goods, there is also a warranty that the sale will not subject the buyer to suit by any third party claiming **infringement** on a patent, copyright, trademark, and the like.

Express Warranties

Under the Code, express warranties are created in one of three ways:

1. An **affirmation of fact** or a promise, which relates to the goods and becomes part of the basis of the bargain.
2. A **description of the goods**.
3. A **sample or model** of the goods.

In each of these three cases, the assumption is that the seller and the buyer have specifically included the guarantee as an integral part of their sales contract.

An express warranty is thus virtually impossible to disclaim by form language in a written sales contract. It is not necessary to prove that the seller used the word warranty or guarantee, or had the specific intent to make a warranty. If the statement is a factual one and it is made in the context of negotiations on the sales contract, it is assumed to be a warranty unless the facts clearly indicate otherwise. In the case of a description, sample, or model, there is an express warranty that the goods will conform to the description, sample, or model. Even statements made in advertisements, if factual, may be held to be express warranties.

Implied Warranty of Merchantability

When the seller is a merchant with respect to the type of goods involved in the contract, there is an implied warranty that the goods are "merchantable." This is a minimum quality guarantee, defined in UCC 2-314, which is imposed on the seller unless the buyer and the seller clearly agree otherwise. Among other requirements, to be merchantable goods must at least be "fit for the ordinary purposes for which goods are used;" be "adequately contained, packaged, and labeled as the agreement may require;" and "conform to the promises or affirmations of fact made on the container or label if any."

Merchantability of Food

Prior to the adoption of the Code, some courts drew a distinction between food purchased in carryout restaurants, to be consumed off the premises, and food purchased in service restaurants, where the diners ate on the premises. The latter case was held to be a services contract, not a sale of goods, and thus there was no implied warranty that food or drink purchased for consumption on the premises was merchantable. The Code specifically repudiates this distinction, so that your hamburger must be merchantable whether you eat it on or off the restaurant premises.

Whether a particular product is merchantable is a question of fact to be decided in each case. There is still a split of authority in which an injury is caused by the presence in a food product of something that is a natural part of the food at some stage of production. For example, is a chicken sandwich that contains a chicken bone unmerchantable? Some courts would say no because the chicken bone is a "natural" part of a chicken. The same reasoning would apply to a cherry pit in cherry pie or cherry ice cream. Other courts apply a different test: What should the consumer reasonably expect to find in the food product? Clearly, no one expects to find a piece of glass in a hot dog. But neither does one expect to find a sharp piece of bone there—even though bones are a natural part of the beef and pork from which the hot dog was made. The "naturalness" of the object is therefore merely one fact to be considered in determining whether the food product is merchantable. Under this second test, a chicken sandwich with a bone is not merchantable, but a serving of roast chicken containing a chicken bone would be.

CASE 3

Mexicali Rose v. Superior Court (Clark)

822 P.2d 1292 (CA 1992)

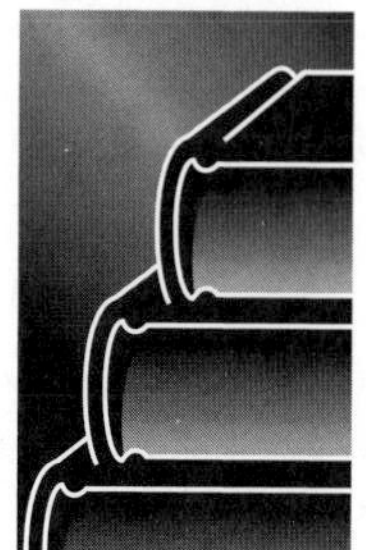

Facts: Real party in interest (plaintiff), Jack A. Clark, was a customer at petitioners' (defendants') restaurant. He ordered a chicken enchilada and sustained throat injuries when he swallowed a 1-inch chicken bone contained in the enchilada. He brought an action for damages based on theories of negligence, breach of implied warranty, and strict liability. He alleged defendant Mexicali Rose negligently left the bone in the enchilada and the food was unfit for human consumption. He also asserted he did not expect to find a bone, and it is not common knowledge there may be bones in chicken enchiladas. In addition, plaintiff sought punitive damages, alleging malice, fraud, and oppression based on the allegation defendants initially refused to obtain medical assistance for him.

The trial court overruled defendants' demurrer, but the Court of Appeal issued a writ of mandate, directing the trial court to sustain the demurrer on all causes of action. The Court of Appeal noted it was compelled, under principles of stare decisis, to follow the *Mix* rule precluding liability for injuries caused by naturally occurring substances in food.

Issue: Is a restaurant keeper liable for serving food containing substances natural to the product that when consumed by the patron cause injury?

Decision: Yes, but only if negligence is proved; not under the theories of implied warranty or strict liability. Court of Appeal is affirmed in part and reversed in part.

Opinion by Chief Justice Lucas: "An early rule of implied warranty in cases involving foreign or adulterated food substances was adopted, as of 1960, by seventeen jurisdictions, including California. . . . A review of the California cases reveals that the acceptance of an implied warranty rule against manufacturers in cases involving unfit foodstuffs was based on the rationale that a manufacturer that sold food items could no longer hide behind the shield of privity to absolve itself of liability. . . .

"This same implied warranty for foreign or adulterated substances in food was extended to independent restaurant owners who purchased the food from outside manufacturers. . . . We imposed on the restauranteur a burden to inspect the food, reasoning that: 'As between the patron, who has no means of determining whether the food served is safe for human consumption, and the seller, who has the opportunity of determining its fitness, the burden properly rests with the seller, who could have so cared for the food as to have made the injury to the customer impossible. . . . '

"A different rule developed when the injury was caused by an object deemed *natural* to the food being served. In *Mix*... the plaintiff swallowed a fragment of chicken bone contained in a chicken pot pie he consumed in the defendant's restaurant. *Mix* affirmed the trial court order dismissing the plaintiff's complaint for negligence and breach of implied warranty. We held there could be no liability under either an implied warranty or negligence theory, explaining that the statutory implied warranty of fitness of food does not make the purveyor an insurer, but merely requires that food be reasonably fit for human consumption. Although we conceded that it is frequently a question for the jury to determine whether an injury producing substance present in food makes the food unfit for consumption, we maintained that a court in appropriate cases may find *as a matter of law* that an alleged harmful substance in food does not make the food defective or unfit for consumption. We explained our holding as follows:

> *'Bones which are natural to the type of meat served cannot legitimately be called a foreign substance, and a consumer who eats meat dishes ought to anticipate and be on his guard against the presence of such bones. At least he cannot hold the restaurant keeper whose representation implied by law is that the meat dish is reasonably fit for human consumption, liable for any injury occurring as a result of the presence of a chicken bone in such chicken pie.... Certainly no liability would attach to a restaurant keeper for the serving of a T-bone steak, or a beef stew, which contained a bone natural to the type of meat served, or if a fish dish should contain a fish bone, or if a cherry pie should contain a cherry stone—although it be admitted that an ideal cherry pie would be stoneless....'*

"We concluded, as a matter of law, that a chicken pot pie containing chicken bones is reasonably fit for consumption and there could be no breach of the implied warranty ...

"As for the negligence claim, we concluded that because the restauranteur had no duty to offer a perfect chicken pie, he or she was not negligent in serving a pie with a bone in it.... *Mix* stated the negligence rule as follows: '[T]he restaurant keeper's obligation is limited to the exercise of the due care in the preparation and service of food furnished guests.... [A] duty of exercising due care in the furnishing and serving of food to guests exists on the part of a restaurant keeper, and ... he is liable in damages for any breach of such duty.'

"After recognizing the duty of care, however, the *Mix* court observed that injury due to a chicken bone in a chicken pie did not establish a lack of due care amounting to a breach of that duty. The court observed that the negligence issue involved 'a question of whether or not a restaurant keeper in the exercise of due care is required to serve in every instance a perfect chicken pie, in that all bones are entirely eliminated. If the customer has no right to expect such a perfect product, and we think he is not so entitled, then it cannot be said that it was negligence on the part of the restaurant keeper to fail to furnish an entirely boneless chicken pie.'

"If the injury-producing substance is natural to the preparation of the food served, it can be said that it was reasonably expected by its very nature and the food cannot be determined unfit or defective. A plaintiff in such a case has no cause of action in strict liability or implied warranty. If, however, the presence of the natural substance is due to a restaurateur's failure to exercise due care in food preparation, the injured patron may sue under a negligence theory.

"If the injury-causing substance is foreign to the food served, then the injured patron may also state a cause of action in implied warranty and strict liability, and the trier of fact will determine whether the substance: (i) would be reasonably expected by the average consumer, and (ii) rendered the food unfit or defective....

"Thus, we conclude that to the extent *Mix* precludes a cause of action in negligence when injuries are caused by substances natural to the preparation of the food served, it is overruled.

"Based on the foregoing, we affirm the Court of Appeal decision to the extent it directs the trial court to sustain defendants' demurrers to the implied warranty and strict liability causes of action, and we reverse the decision directing the demurrer to plaintiff's negligence cause of action be sustained. The cause is remanded to the Court of Appeal for further proceedings consistent with this holding."

Similar fact questions may arise when other products are alleged to be unmerchantable. The fact that someone was injured while a product was being used does not always mean that the product was not merchantable. The Code does not require that the goods must be perfect or that they will do anything and everything that the buyer wishes. They need only be fit for the ordinary purposes for which such goods are used. Experts in design and production may be called to testify on the safety and suitability of the goods. It may be appropriate to have the use of the goods demonstrated for the judge and jury. Even if the goods are found to be defective, it is also necessary to show that the injury complained of was caused by the defect, and not by the actions of the user or someone else.

Merchantability of Leased Goods and of Real Estate

As noted in the last chapter, courts have been extending the merchantability concept to cover other sorts of commercial transactions. Nearly all courts that have had to decide the question have imposed an implied warranty of merchantability on a business that rents goods to others. Many states now hold sellers of new houses to a similar standard. (See the discussion in Chapter 20.) Statutes in some states now require that real estate leased for residential purposes be reasonably "habitable." (See the discussion in Chapter 19.) In each of these situations, the courts and legislatures have determined that social policy requires that at least a minimum level of quality be guaranteed to the buyer or lessee. It now seems to be only a question of time until all states adopt similar rules.

Implied Warranty of Fitness

The Code has also made an important extension in the seller's liability under the **implied warranty of fitness**. When this warranty applies, the seller is not only guaranteeing that the goods are of fair, average quality and that they will do what most buyers expect them to do but also that they are suitable for the *particular* needs of the given buyer. The fitness warranty does not arise unless the buyer makes known to the seller some special needs and the fact that the buyer is relying on the seller to select or furnish suitable goods to meet those special needs. Prior to the Code, this fitness warranty could not apply where the goods were sold under a brand name or a trade name. Under UCC 2-315, a brand name on the goods is only one fact to be considered in determining whether the buyer relied on the seller to furnish suitable goods.

CASE 4

Morris v. Mack's Used Cars

824 S.W.2d 538 (TN 1992)

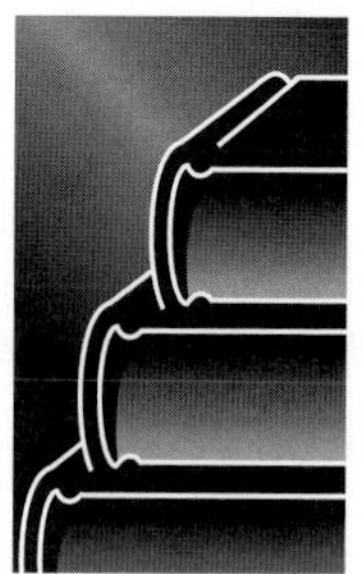

Facts: Darrell Morris sued the seller, Mack's Used Cars & Parts, Inc., for compensatory, treble, and punitive damages, alleging fraudulent concealment, breach of express warranty of title under T.C.A. § 47-2-312, breach of express warranty of description under T.C.A. § 47-2-313, breach of implied warranty of merchantability under T.C.A. § 47-2-314, and violation of the Tennessee Consumer Protection Act forbidding unfair or deceptive acts under T.C.A. § 47-18-104(b)(6),(7).

In September 1985, the defendant sold to Morris a vehicle described on the bill of sale as a 1979 Ford pickup truck. An older truck was traded in as a down payment, and the balance of the purchase price was financed over a term of 3 years with a retail installment contract and security agreement, pursuant to which the certificate of title was delivered by the defendant-seller directly to the lender. The bill of sale contained the following statement immediately above the purchaser's signature, "This unit sold as is. No warranties have been expressed or implied." At the time of sale, the truck had been wrecked or dismantled and was a "reconstructed" vehicle within the meaning of Title 55, Chapter 3, Part 2 of Tennessee Code Annotated. The seller knew but did not disclose to the purchaser that the pickup was a reconstructed vehicle. The purchaser obtained this information 3 years later when he received the certificate of title after paying the final installment on the sales contract. Being reconstructed reduced the vehicle's fair market value 30 to 50 percent.

The seller's defense was that the disclaimer contained in the bill of sale avoided any liability for its not disclosing to the purchaser the condition of the vehicle as revealed by the certificate of title.

The trial court agreed with the seller and dismissed the suit.

Issue: Does an "as is" disclaimer also avoid liability under a state's consumer protection statute?

Decision: No. Judgment reversed; case remanded.

Opinion by Chief Justice Reid: "The trial court and the Court of Appeals misconstrued these statutes as they relate to the Consumer Protection Act. Disclaimers permitted by § 47-2-316 of the Uniform Commercial Code (UCC) may limit or modify liability otherwise imposed by the code, but such disclaimers do not defeat separate causes of action for unfair or deceptive acts or practices under the Consumer Protection Act....

"The UCC contemplates the applicability of supplemental bodies of law to commercial transactions. Section 47-1-103, T.C.A. provides the following: 'Unless displaced by the particular provisions of Chapters 1 through 9 of this title, the principles of law and equity, including the law merchant and the law relative to capacity to contract, principal and agent, estoppel, fraud, misrepresentation, duress, coercion, mistake, bankruptcy, or other validating or invalidating cause shall supplement its provisions.'

"Also, the supplementary nature of the Consumer Protection Act is made clear by T.C.A. § 47-18-112, which states,

'The powers and remedies provided in this part shall be cumulative and supplementary to all other powers and remedies otherwise provided by law. The invocation of one power or remedy herein shall not be construed as excluding or prohibiting the use of any other available remedy.'

"A seller may disclaim all implied warranties pursuant to T.C.A. § 47-2-316. . . .

"The Consumer Protection Act recognizes this right of exclusion or modification of warranties under the UCC. Section 47-18-113, T.C.A., provides,

> ***Waiver of Rights.*** *(a) No provision of this part may be limited or waived by contract, agreement, or otherwise, notwithstanding any other provision of law to the contrary; provided, however, the provisions of this part shall not alter, amend, or repeal the provisions of the Uniform Commercial Code relative to express or implied warranties or the exclusion or modification of such warranties.*

"The above provision, however, also specifically precludes disclaimer of liability under the Consumer Protection Act. Furthermore, the UCC, pursuant to T.C.A. § 47-1-203, imposes an obligation of good faith in the performance or enforcement of every contract. Under T.C.A. § 47-1-102(3), this obligation may not be disclaimed.

"Claims under the UCC and the Consumer Protection Act are distinct causes of action, with different components and defenses. The Consumer Protection Act is applicable to commercial transactions, also regulated by the UCC. . . .

"The Tennessee Consumer Protection Act is to be liberally construed to protect consumers and others from those who engage in deceptive acts or practices. . . . In a case similar to the one before the Court, the seller's failure to disclose to the buyer that the vehicle had been in an accident and had been repaired constituted a violation of the Consumer Protection Act. To allow the seller here to avoid liability for unfair or deceptive acts or practices by disclaiming contractual warranties under the UCC would contravene the broad remedial intent of the Consumer Protection Act.

"In summary, disclaimers permitted by T.C.A. § 47-2-316 do not prevent application of the Consumer Protection Act. The Consumer Protection Act creates a separate and distinct cause of action for unfair or deceptive acts or practices."

United Nations Convention on Contracts for the International Sale of Goods (CISG) Quality Rules

CISG does not use the term *warranty*; rather, it refers to the "Obligations of the Seller." The seller's obligations with respect to the quality of the goods are spelled out primarily in CISG's Article 35, with some supplementation in Articles 36 and 37. (See Appendix D.) In general, the CISG quality rules parallel the UCC warranty rules very closely.

Article 35 first requires that the goods must conform to the terms of the contract as to quantity, quality, description, and packaging. It then goes on to say that, unless the parties have agreed otherwise, goods do not conform to the contract if they are not fit for the ordinary purposes for which such goods are used. (That requirement corresponds to the UCC's merchantability warranty.) Further, the goods must be fit for any particular purpose of the buyer made known to the seller, unless the buyer did not rely, or could not reasonably have relied, on the seller's skill and judgment. (That rule roughly corresponds to the UCC's fitness warranty.) The goods must also conform to any sample or model held out to the buyer, as is true under the UCC's express warranty to that effect. Finally, the goods must be contained or packaged in the usual manner, or if there is no such usual manner, "in a manner adequate to preserve and protect the goods." (A similar requirement is part of the UCC's merchantability warranty.) But, says Article 35, the seller is not liable under any of these specific rules if the buyer was aware of any nonconformity at the time the contract was made.

Article 36 says that the seller is liable for any nonconformity that exists when the risk of loss on the goods passes to the buyer, even though the nonconformity is not discovered until later. It also provides that the seller is liable for any agreed guarantee period.

Article 37 parallels the UCC's right to "cure" any defective delivery, although it is not quite as extensive as the UCC rule. If the CISG seller has delivered before the due date, it may deliver any missing portion or may replace or remedy any nonconforming goods up to the due date, provided that such "cure" does not cause any unreasonable inconvenience or expense. The buyer can still claim any damages that have been sustained due to the nonconformity.

The BP Oil case involves the application of the CISG quality rules and the risk of loss rules and the use of international "Incoterms."

European Union Product Liability Rules

While our state legislatures were passing statutory limitations on product liability, and our Congress was attempting to do so, the European Union (EU) was moving in the opposite

CASE 5

BP Oil Int'l., Ltd. v. Empresa Estatal Petroleos de Ecuador

332 F.3d 333 (5 Cir. 2003)

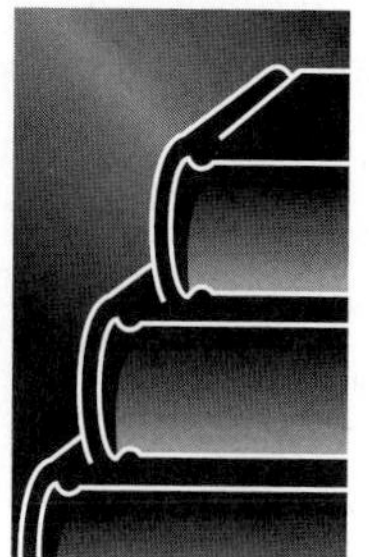

Facts: BP Oil contracted to sell 140,000 barrels of gasoline to Empresa Estatal Petroleos de Ecuador (PetroEcuador), "CFR La Libertad-Ecuador." The contract provided that the gasoline have a gum content of less than 3 milligrams per 100 milliliters, to be determined at the port of shipment, and that Ecuadorian law applied. BP bought the gasoline from Shell Oil and, after testing by Saybolt Inc., had it loaded on board the *M/T* TIBER at Shell's Deer Park, Texas refinery. Claiming that there was excessive gum content, PetroEcuador refused to accept delivery when the gasoline arrived. BP resold the gasoline at a loss, and then sued PetroEcuador and Saybolt for damages. The U.S. District Court, applying Ecuador's own civil code rather than the CISG, granted summary judgment for both defendants.

Issue: Did the gasoline meet the specifications in the contract? Which party had the risk of loss?

Decision: Yes. PetroEcuador, unless BP Oil *actually* knew of a "hidden defect." Judgment reversed, and case is remanded for fact-finding on what BP Oil actually knew at the time of shipment.

Opinion by Judge Smith: "A signatory's assent to the CISG necessarily incorporates the treaty as part of that nation's domestic law.... Given that the CISG is Ecuadorian law, a choice of law provision designating Ecuadorian law merely confirms that the treaty governs the transaction....

"PetroEcuador's invitation to bid for the procurement of 140,000 barrels of gasoline proposed 'CFR' delivery. The final agreement, drafted by PetroEcuador, again specified that the gasoline be sent 'CFR La Libertad-Ecuador' and that the cargo's gum content be tested pre-shipment. Shipments designated 'CFR' require the seller to pay costs and freight to transport the goods to the delivery port, but pass title and risk of loss to the buyer once the goods 'pass the ship's rail' at the port of shipment. The goods should be tested for conformity before the risk of loss passes to the buyer.... In the event of subsequent damage of loss, the buyer must generally seek a remedy against the carrier or insurer....

"In light of the parties' unambiguous use of the 'CFR,' BP fulfilled its contractual obligations if the gasoline met the contract's qualitative specifications when it passed the ship's rail and risk passed to PetroEcuador.... Indeed, Saybolt's testing confirmed that the gasoline's gum content was adequate before departure from Texas. Nevertheless, in its opposition to BP's motion for summary judgment, PetroEcuador contends that BP purchased the gasoline from Shell on an 'as is' basis and therefore failed to add sufficient gum inhibitor as a way to cut corners. In other words, the cargo contained a hidden defect.

"Having appointed Saybolt to test the gasoline, PetroEcuador 'ought to have discovered' the defect before the cargo left Texas.... Permitting PetroEcuador now to distance itself from Saybolt's test would negate the parties' selection of CFR delivery and would undermine the key role that reliance plays in international sales agreements. Nevertheless, BP could have breached the agreement if it provided goods that it 'knew or could not have been unaware' were defective when they 'passed over the ship's rail' and risk shifted to PetroEcuador.

"Therefore, there is a fact issue as to whether BP provided defective gasoline by failing to add sufficient gum inhibitor. The district court should permit the parties to conduct discovery as to this issue only....

"If PetroEcuador improperly refused CFR delivery, it is liable to BP for any consequential damages.... If Saybolt negligently misrepresented the gasoline's gum content, PetroEcuador (not BP) becomes the party with a potential claim [against Saybolt]....

"The judgment dismissing PetroEcuador is REVERSED and REMANDED for proceedings consistent with this opinion. The judgment dismissing Saybolt is AFFIRMED."

direction. An EU "directive" (regulation) required all member nations to provide legal recourse for consumers injured by defective products on the basis of strict liability in tort. As the European Commission (its regulatory body) defined the problem, trade within the "common market" was being distorted by the different product liability rules in the member nations. France and Germany, for instance, did have statutory rules that approximated strict liability in tort. Other nations, such as the United Kingdom, did not, but rather required proof of negligence, or privity of contract for warranty liability. All incoming member nations (Estonia, the Czech Republic, et al.) will likewise have to conform their product liability rules to this new requirement.

Separately, Japan has also adopted a version of strict liability for defective products, although the structure of the Japanese legal system still provides significant barriers to injured plaintiffs.

Exclusion or Modification of Warranties

The Code generally makes it more difficult for the seller to disclaim warranties once they are made. For all practical purposes, it is impossible for the seller to disclaim an express warranty unless the entire transaction is renegotiated or unless the parties agree on a final written contract that does not include the express warranty and that indicates that it is intended as a complete statement of all the terms of the contract. With such a clause in the final contract, any prior express warranty would be excluded by the operation of the parol evidence section of Article 2 (2-202). Otherwise, when an express warranty has been made it overrides any attempted disclaimer of warranty to the extent that the two provisions are inconsistent.

Theoretically, at least, a seller can disclaim the implied warranties of merchantability and fitness by complying with the appropriate Code sections. As a practical matter, however, courts have been reluctant to enforce such disclaimers unless there is evidence that the buyer understood and intended that result. An example would occur where a used item is bought **as is** or when the buyer is also a business, such as United buying jumbo jets from Boeing. To stand *any* chance of being enforceable, the disclaimer of warranties must comply with the Code's requirements. Merchantability may be disclaimed either orally or in writing, but the word merchantability must be used, unless the goods are being bought as is. Moreover, if the disclaimer is part of a written contract, it must be stated "conspicuously" in the writing. The fitness warranty cannot be excluded except by a writing, and the disclaimer must be a conspicuous part of the writing. UCC 1-201(10) defines **conspicuous** as being "so written that a reasonable person against whom it is to operate ought to have noticed it." A contrasting type style or color might be used to meet this requirement.

Even where all the Code's requirements for language and form of the disclaimer have been met, a court may still refuse to enforce the disclaimer, on the grounds that it is an attempt to avoid the seller's basic obligations of "good faith, diligence, reasonableness and care" (1-102[3]), or that it is **unconscionable** (2-302), or that it is against "public policy." The 1960 *Henningsen* case, from New Jersey, is perhaps the most significant single case on product liability. It started the modern trend by repudiating the "privity" requirement and by refusing to enforce the auto manufacturer's form disclaimer.

There are two other important limitations on warranty disclaimers. A seller who has made warranties to the buyer cannot "exclude or limit" the operation of Section 2-318, which extends the warranties automatically to "any natural person who is in the buyer's family or household or who is a guest in the buyer's home." Also, although Section 2-316 permits the parties to agree to limit the remedies for breach of warranty, Section 2-719 states that any limitation "of consequential damages for injury to the person in the case of consumer goods is prima facie unconscionable" (and therefore not enforceable).

The Code also provides that warranties, whether express or implied, are to be construed as consistent with each other and *cumulative*, (meaning that *all* the warranties that apply on the facts are made) unless such a construction is unreasonable.

Strict Liability in Tort

Historically, strict tort liability was imposed only on the keepers of dangerous wild animals and on persons who engaged in "extra-hazardous activities." What the courts have done, in effect, is to extend this theory of liability to manufacturers, sellers, and renters of products, so that the supplier of a defective product will be liable for the damage it causes, irrespective of any contract.

Of course, the plaintiff must still prove the case, but this is a much easier case to prove, and a much more difficult case to defend, than either negligence or breach of warranty. The fact that only this one product failed out of 5 million produced and used may prevent recovery for negligent manufacture, but it will not prevent recovery based on strict liability. The plaintiff need only prove that the product was made by the defendant, that it was "defective," that the defect caused the injury, and that damages have been sustained in a certain amount. The defendant can then try to show that the product was not defective, but instead failed as the result of normal wear and tear, or improper maintenance, or misuse by the plaintiff.

Although strict liability for defective products has been recognized for at least 40 years, the concept is not uniformly applied by all states. The types of transactions covered differ, as do the third parties protected, and ways possible defenses may apply. Results may vary because different triers of fact analyze similar situations in different ways. Opinions as to what constitutes a **defect**, legally and factually, may differ. Is a car "defective" if its gasoline tank explodes when the car is struck from behind by another vehicle? How about a car with an unpadded dashboard? Almost by definition, if the vehicle is not made in accordance with U.S. government safety standards, it would be defective in the legal sense. But is the reverse also true? Does compliance with these government standards mean that the product is *not* defective? The courts have generally said no; compliance with government or industry standards does not necessarily prevent liability.

The *Krutsch* case discusses alleged defects based on design and on lack of warnings.

CASE 6

KRUTSCH V. WALTER H. COLLIN GMBH

495 N.W.2d 208 (MN App. 1993)

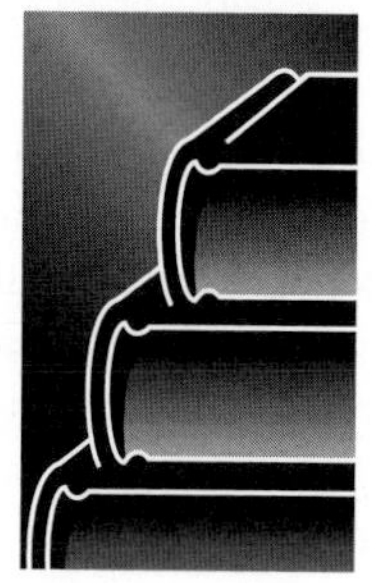

Facts: In 1982 Federal-Hoffman, Incorporated purchased a lead extruder machine from appellant Walter H. Collin GmbH Verfahrenstechnik Und Maschinenfabric ("Collin"), a German corporation. The machine is a large hydraulic press used to make lead bullets.

Respondent John H. Krutsch, an employee of Federal-Hoffman, was operating the machine when it broke down. Federal-Hoffman had trained Krutsch in the operation of the machine, but had not trained him to repair the machine. Krutsch discussed the machine's disrepair with fellow employees and opined that the machine was not functioning because there was air in its hydraulic cylinder and that he could fix the machine by "bleeding" the cylinder.

Krutsch consulted a partial copy of the machine's operation manual that Federal-Hoffman kept near the machine. Collin had provided Federal-Hoffman with a complete manual that included the procedure for "bleeding" the machine's hydraulic cylinder, but Federal-Hoffman kept the complete manual in its engineering office. The partial copy of the manual did not contain any information on "bleeding" the cylinder. Nevertheless, Krutsch attempted to repair the machine. He took a wrench and began to turn a pressure release bolt attached to the machine's hydraulic cylinder. The bolt contained a small hole through which fluid could flow from the cylinder. Krutsch turned the bolt too far and highly pressurized hydraulic fluid was injected into his thumb, causing severe injuries.

Krutsch sued Collin under negligence and strict liability theories. Collin asserted a contribution claim against Federal-Hoffman. Prior to the selection of a jury, Collin informed Krutsch and the trial court that it had settled its contribution claim with Federal-Hoffman, but did not provide Krutsch or the trial court with a signed copy of the settlement agreement until after the trial had begun. Federal-Hoffman did not participate in the trial.

The jury found that the machine was not defectively designed but was defective for failure to warn and that Krutsch, Collin, and Federal-Hoffman contributed to Krutsch's injuries. The jury awarded Krutsch damages for past pain, disability, disfigurement, and emotional distress; past medical expenses; past lost earnings; future pain, disfigurement, and emotional distress; future disability, future lost earnings; and future medical expenses. The jury also awarded Krutsch's wife damages for loss of consortium. Upon Collin's motion, the trial court reduced the jury's award for future medical expenses.

Issue: Did the trial court err in denying Collin's motion for judgment notwithstanding the verdict?

Decision: No. Judgment affirmed.

Opinion by Judge Huspeni: "The decision whether to grant JNOV is a pure question of law, and this court will review the trial court's decision de novo. . . .

> *[JNOV] may be granted only when the evidence is so overwhelmingly on one side that reasonable minds cannot differ as to the proper outcome. In applying this standard: (1) all the evidence, including that favoring the verdict, must be taken into account; (2) the evidence is to be viewed in the light most favorable to the verdict; and (3) the court may not weigh the evidence or judge the credibility of the witnesses. . . .*

"Collin claims that it is entitled to JNOV because it had no duty to warn of the dangers associated with 'bleeding' the cylinder. The question of whether a product manufacturer has a duty to warn of a particular danger is a question of law....

"[A] manufacturer's duty to warn in strict liability cases extends to all reasonably foreseeable users...." However, 'a manufacturer has no duty to warn when the dangers of a product are within the professional knowledge of the user....'

"Collin should have foreseen that the machine would be operated by individuals who were not fully trained in the machine's maintenance and repair procedures. The dangers associated with 'bleeding' the cylinder are not obvious to such a user. Thus, Collin had a duty to warn all foreseeable users of the machine of the dangers associated with 'bleeding' the machine's cylinder.

"Having concluded that Collin had a duty to warn, 'questions of a warning's adequacy, breach, and causation are usually jury questions....' Collin claims that even if it did have a duty to warn, it satisfied that duty by providing Federal-Hoffman with a manual which included the correct procedures for 'bleeding' the cylinder. Collin claims that Krutsch cannot challenge the adequacy of its warning because he never read the instructions contained in the complete manual. We disagree.

"Viewing the evidence in a light most favorable to the verdict, the evidence is not so overwhelmingly on one side that reasonable minds cannot differ as to the proper outcome.... Accordingly, the trial court did not err in denying Collin's motion for JNOV."

Defenses against Product Liability Claims

As indicated previously, it may be possible to avoid liability by disproving the main element of the plaintiff's case. For negligence, a defense would be proof that reasonable care was in fact exercised throughout the production and distribution process. For warranty, liability might be avoided by proving either that no warranty was made, that all warranties were disclaimed, or that all warranties were in fact met. For strict liability, the defense would be proving that the product was not in fact defective.

When evidence suggests that the product failed, and personal injuries were sustained, the courts have generally been reluctant to permit the seller and the manufacturer to escape liability on a "technicality." Even misuse of the product may not be a defense, if the misuse was foreseeable by the seller and the manufacturer. They may be held liable if they have not taken reasonable precautions to avoid foreseeable misuses, such as providing safety devices, warnings, and detailed instructions for use of the product.

Historically in a negligence case, **contributory negligence** on the part of the plaintiff was a complete defense. So was the plaintiff's voluntary **assumption of a known risk**. In product liability cases, these two defenses may not completely absolve the seller and the manufacturer. As noted in Chapter 7, many states have now adopted **comparative negligence** in place of contributory negligence. If the jury is permitted to offset the fault of the seller and the manufacturer of the defective car against the fault of the injured buyer, who happened to be speeding when the front tire fell off, clearly most of the buyer's damages will be awarded. When the product failure occurs due to abuse or misuse, however, the defendants may be able to convince the trier of the fact that there was really no defect, no breach of warranty, and no negligence in manufacture. The machine failed not because it was defective, but because it was used constantly without proper servicing. Likewise, even when a defect exists, if the buyer continues to use the product after discovering it, without service or repair, the defendants can argue that the defect did not really *cause* the buyer's injuries.

Magnuson-Moss Warranty Act

One might have imagined that if any field of law under the sun required additional "protective" legislation, it was not the law of product liability. Indeed, if a problem in this field required legislative attention, it was exactly the opposite problem: how to *limit* skyrocketing product liability costs before all but the very largest manufacturers were driven out of business. Congress, however, did not see it that way. Either unaware of or unimpressed by the product liability "revolution" that had occurred during the preceding 15 years, Congress in 1975 passed the **Magnuson-Moss Warranty Act**, thereby adding one more large straw to the already weakened camel's back.

The act does not provide that product warranties must be made; its basic purpose is to make warranties that are made more understandable. Warranty information must be made available prior to purchase of a product and must be displayed prominently with it. Moreover, the terms of the warranty must be stated in "plain English." The purpose of these requirements is to better enable buyers to shop for the best warranty, just as they shop for the best price and credit terms. Enforcement of the act is entrusted to the Federal Trade Commission (FTC), which has the power to adopt appropriate regulations to achieve the act's purposes.

For products over $15, any express warranty must be stated to be a full warranty or a limited warranty. The act provides standards for each type. A full warranty:

a. Must provide that the seller will remedy any defect, without charge, within a reasonable time.

b. Must provide that the buyer will have the choice of replacement or refund if the seller is unable to correct a defect after a reasonable number of attempts.

c. May not limit the duration of any implied warranty.

d. Must conspicuously state any clause that attempts to limit or exclude liability for consequential damages.

Such a full warranty, once made, extends for the entire time period specified, even if the product is resold. Injured third parties are protected by the warranty under its provisions and under applicable state law on warranties (UCC 2-318, for example).

Any other written warranty on a consumer product must be labeled as a limited warranty, no matter how broad its coverage or how liberal its remedies. Such a limited warranty must specify its coverage and duration, the procedures to be followed, and any mechanism provided for resolving disputes. These warranties cannot be made contingent on the consumer's return of a warranty card or on a requirement that the goods be serviced only by authorized dealers.

Like most "remedial" legislation, the act has high-minded objectives that are impossible to oppose: to provide consumers with clearer and truer warranties and to give dissatisfied consumers a remedy for defective products. The net result in the marketplace so far has been that very few manufacturers have tried to claim that they are giving full warranties on their products, and some have stopped giving written warranties altogether. Faced with the act's uncertainties, only the very hardiest (or foolhardiest) manufacturers will run the risk of extended jousting with the FTC staff. Whether this act represents a net gain for consumers remains to be seen.

New State Legislation

Confronted with manufacturers' and sellers' claims that they were being driven out of business by excessive judgments and by soaring premiums for liability insurance, state legislatures have been considering the need for statutory changes in product liability laws. Most of the product liability "crisis" is perceived to result from over-expansive judicial interpretations, and overgenerous jury verdicts. Several types of changes are being considered, and, in some states, have already been adopted.

One proposal is to create a strong statutory presumption that a product is not defective when a claim is made a certain number of years after the initial sale of the product—10 years, for example. Under existing law, an injured party could claim that a product that had been in use for 20 or 30 years was defective and thus have the benefit of the strict liability rules. Manufacturers and sellers would also like to see a specific statutory statement of contributory negligence and assumption of risk as defenses to product liability claims, even though most courts already do apply them in appropriate cases. Manufacturers would also like to be immune from liability in which they have complied with all applicable government regulations and industry standards, as of the date of manufacture. This is the **state-of-the-art defense**. They do not feel that they should be held liable if they fail to recall and modify a product that has already been sold. These and similar changes are being pushed hard by producer and seller organizations. Further legislative action seems likely.

A National Products Liability Statute?

In recent years, the Senate Commerce Committee has discussed proposals that would drastically change the products liability rules in the United States. They would require the injured party to prove that the manufacturer's negligence caused the injury. If adopted as reported, these proposals would thus preempt all state law on implied quality warranties and all state applications of strict liability to defective products. They would repeal nearly all of the judicial revolution that has taken place in this area over the last 40+ years. Obviously, this legislation is of vital concern to all U.S. manufacturers and sellers of products and to international firms interested in the U.S. market.

Significance of This Chapter

The product liability revolution is one of the two or three most important developments in commercial law in the last 50 years. A whole new range of potential liability exposure, of vast and unknown dimensions, has been created. Entire industries are threatened and have been forced to rethink completely their production and distribution processes. Some businesses have decided to terminate their operations. The consumer is king, with many new rights and protections. Some observers have suggested that the price (which we all are paying) may be too high. It is to deal with this question, and to strike a fair balance between rights and costs, that the state legislatures and Congress are now considering changes.

IMPORTANT TERMS AND CONCEPTS

affirmation of fact
as is
assumption of a known risk
caveat emptor
comparative negligence
conspicuous
contributory negligence
defect
description of the goods
encumbrances
express warranty
implied warranty
implied warranty of fitness
implied warranty of merchantability
infringement
liens
Magnuson-Moss Warranty Act
negligence
privity
product liability
res ipsa loquitur
Restatement of the Law of Torts, Second
sample or model
state-of-the-art defense
strict liability in tort
title warranty
unconscionable
warranty

QUESTIONS AND PROBLEMS FOR DISCUSSION

1. To what extent is contributory negligence or assumption of risk a defense against a product liability action based on strict liability in tort?

2. What is the difference between the implied warranty of merchantability and the implied warranty of fitness?

3. How can the implied warranties of merchantability and fitness be disclaimed?

4. What happens when an express warranty and an express disclaimer are both part of a sales contract, and they conflict with each other?

5. Millicent Innocent purchased a ski weekend vacation package at Nobby Nob Lodge. She was injured while using a rope-tow at the skiing facility operated by the lodge. She sued the lodge, on the theories of negligence, breach of warranty, and strict liability. The lodge moves to dismiss all three counts of the complaint. How should the trial judge rule, and why?

6. Clause bought his wife a new Plymouth as a Mother's Day present. Ten days later, while driving the car, she heard a loud noise from under the hood; she said it "felt as if something has cracked." The steering wheel spun in her hands, and the car veered sharply to the right and crashed into a brick wall. The plaintiffs sued Bloomfield (the dealer) and Chrysler (the manufacturer). The sales contract stated that the manufacturer's only warranty on the car was a promise to replace defective parts at the factory and that the warranty was given in lieu of all other warranties, express or implied. The trial court held for the plaintiffs, and the defendants appealed.

   How should the appeals court rule, and why?

7. On Saturday, April 25, about 1 pm, the plaintiff, accompanied by her sister and her aunt, entered the Blue

Ship Tea Room operated by the defendant. The group was seated at a table and supplied with menus.

This restaurant, which the plaintiff characterized as "quaint," was located in Boston "on the third floor of an old building on T Wharf, which overlooks the ocean."

The plaintiff, who had been born and brought up in New England, ordered clam chowder and crabmeat salad. Within a few minutes, she received tidings to the effect that "there was no more clam chowder." Presently, there was set before her "a small bowl of fish chowder." "The fish chowder contained haddock, potatoes, milk, water, and seasoning. The chowder was milky in color and not clear. The haddock and potatoes were in chunks." "She agitated it a little with a spoon and observed that it was a fairly full bowl.... After three or four spoonfuls, she was aware that something had lodged in her throat because she couldn't swallow and couldn't clear her throat by gulping and she could feel it." This misadventure led to two esophagoscopies.

Is Blue Ship liable for plaintiff's injury from the fish bone in her throat? Explain.

8. Baker bought a rifle from Rosemurgy. He paid for the gun even though he knew "there was something wrong with the safety" on it. He used the gun during the hunting seasons of 1989, 1990, and 1991. While he was deer hunting in 1991, he dropped the rifle, and it fired, even though the safety was in the "on" position. Baker sustained severe and permanent leg injuries. He sued Rosemurgy; Gamble-Skogmo, which had distributed the rifle to Rosemurgy; and Olin, the manufacturer. The trial court granted summary judgment for all three defendants.

   Will the trial court's ruling be upheld on appeal? Why or why not?

9. Gladys Flippo went into a ladies' clothing store in Batesville, Arkansas. The store, known as "Mode O'Day Frock Shops of Hollywood," was owned and operated by Rosie Goforth. Rosie showed Gladys two pairs of slacks. The first pair was too small. When Gladys tried on the second pair, she felt a sudden burning sensation in her thigh. She immediately took off the slacks and shook them. A spider fell out, which was later identified as a "brown recluse" spider—highly poisonous. Gladys was hospitalized for 30 days. She sued Rosie for negligence, breach of warranty, and strict liability in tort.

   How do these three theories of liability apply here? Explain.

CHAPTER 19

Bailments of Personalty and Leases of Realty

Chapter Objectives

This chapter will:

- Define "bailment."
- Discuss the four essential elements needed to create a bailment.
- Describe the three types of bailments.
- Discuss the duty of care required of a nonprofessional bailee.
- Define "lease."
- Describe the types of tenancies.
- Explain the landlord's rights and obligations.
- Explain the tenant's rights and obligations.
- Discuss termination of leases.
- Explain the purpose and use of security deposits.

Bailments of Personalty

In addition to professional bailees, such as the carriers and warehouses mentioned in Chapter 17, many other businesses and individuals are frequently involved in **bailments.** Have you ever loaned your car to a friend? Have you ever taken your stereo back to the dealer for repairs or checked your coat and hat at a restaurant? These are all bailments. A bailment exists when the possessor of personal property gives possession and control to another person with the agreement that there is no transfer of title to the object and that the transfer of possession is temporary. The person who is giving up possession is a **bailor,** and the person who is receiving the personal property is a **bailee.**

Essential Elements of Bailment

Four essential elements must be present to create a bailment: (1) an agreement between the parties, (2) possession of the object to be bailed by the bailor, (3) delivery of the object to be bailed, and (4) a duty on the part of the bailee to return the object to either the bailor or to someone else as instructed by the bailor.

Agreement

The first essential element of a bailment, an agreement between the parties, can be expressed either orally or in writing, or it may be implied from the facts and circumstances of the situation. An express agreement of bailment would normally cover the consideration, if any, to the bailor for the use of bailed property or to the bailee for caring for it, what the property is going to be used for or how it is going to be used; when, where, and how the bailed item is to be returned to the bailor, delivered to someone else, or disposed of in some other manner; and other rights and duties of the parties.

Many bailments involve contracts. Many do not. If you rent a car, a contract between you and the rental company covers the bailment of the car. If you borrow your friend's car, there is an agreement between you, but no contract.

Possession by the Bailor

To have a bailment, the bailor must have possession of the object to be bailed. The bailor need not be the owner of the property. In fact, the bailor may be a bailee. For example, as the bailee of the car you rented, you may entrust it to a parking attendant and thus become its bailor, as to the parking lot.

Delivery of the Object to be Bailed

There must be delivery of the object to be bailed from the bailor to the bailee, and the bailee must accept delivery of the object. As noted earlier, size, weight, and location prevent some items of personal property from being physically handed over to another person. Instead, we may have **constructive delivery,** such as handing a person the keys to a rental car in the parking lot and telling the person to go ahead and take the car. When the bailed property contains other items, there is no bailment as to those items unless the bailee knows, or has reason to know, of their existence.

Bailee's Duty to Return Object to Bailor

The bailee must have a duty to return the personal property to the bailor, to deliver the property to a third person, or to dispose the property in accordance with the bailor's wishes. Assume that you rent a truck to move your household goods from Los Angeles to New York. As the bailee, you will have a duty to return the specific property, the truck, to the bailor or to any person the bailor may designate. In this case, let us say that the bailor does not have an office in New York City, and therefore directs you to deliver the truck to a specific location in New York City where an employee of the bailor will pick it up and drive it back. The important factor here is that the object is still the bailor's property and that the bailee has the duty to give up possession of the object at the time and place that the bailor designates.

General Legal Rules

Types of Bailments

Basically, there are three types of bailment. First, there is a type in which both parties benefit from the bailment. Before leaving school, you rent a rug shampooer from a rental agency to clean your apartment. You are paying to use the rug shampooer so the bailor benefits and, in exchange for your payment, you receive the right to possess, use, and control the rug shampooer for a specified time.

In a second type of bailment the bailor is the only person who benefits from the arrangement. For example, your neighbor is going to the store where you bought your stereo and you ask that person to take your stereo back for adjustment. Your neighbor agrees, and you deliver the set to that person for the purpose of taking it to the store for repairs. Obviously, your neighbor is doing you a favor for no personal gain.

A third type of bailment is one in which only the bailee benefits. Your roommate borrows your car for the evening. No payment is to be made; the bailment is simply for the benefit of the bailee. In each of these last two situations, there is a bailment even though there is no contract.

Bailments also can be classified into two major categories: *gratuitous bailments*, in which no fee is charged for the use or care of the bailed object, and bailments in which a fee is charged. Bailments made in exchange for payment can be further broken down into two areas: **commercial bailors** such as automobile or equipment rental companies, and **professional bailees,** such as **common carriers,** innkeepers (hotels and motels), and warehouses.

Custody

Businesspeople need to understand the difference between bailments and custody situations in which a bailment will not exist. By knowing what creates a bailment, business owners can reduce liability for damage or theft of customers' property, by avoiding situations in which they would become bailees. For example, in the typical university parking lot you either pay by the month or get a claim check upon entering and pay when leaving. Because you park your own car and keep the keys, no bailment exists. You have not entrusted your car to the parking lot owner; you simply rent space. If, however, a parking lot attendant gives you a claim check, takes your car, parks it, and retains the keys, then there is a delivery to and acceptance by the bailee. In the case involving the university parking lot there was no delivery or acceptance by the university. You simply drove your car in and parked it.

The next case discusses the "bailment/no bailment" problem.

CASE 1

Sisters of Charity of the Incarnate Word v. Meaux

122 S.W.3d 428 (TX App. 2003)

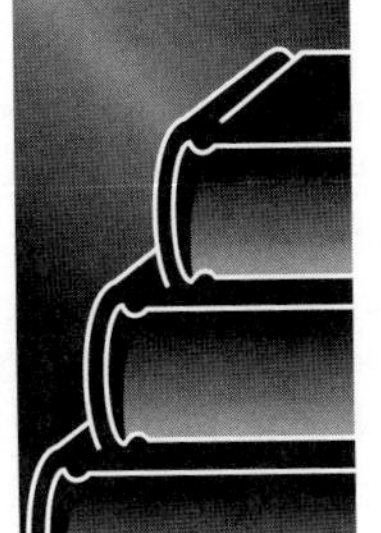

Facts: Sisters of Charity, d/b/a St. Elizabeth Hospital of Beaumont, operates a health and fitness center in connection with the Hospital. Phil Meaux was using the center's facilities when his locker was pried open and his Rolex watch, money clip, and $400 was stolen. He had been given a lock and key, but the center also had a master key for use if keys were lost or taken by mistake. The center's rules said that all personal property should be stored in a locker, but that the center "cannot assure the safety of your valuables and we suggest that you do not bring items of high personal or monetary value to the center." A sign to that effect was posted at the sign-in desk. Meaux admitted that he was aware of these rules but claimed that the center was liable as a bailee for the value of the stolen items. The jury found that the center was not guilty of any negligence, but was liable as a bailee—for $19,500. Sisters of Charity appealed.

Issue: Was a bailment created, as to the contents of the locker?

Decision: No. Judgment reversed.

Opinion by Judge Amidei: "A bailee has the duty to exercise ordinary care over the goods and is therefore 'responsible' for the bailor's goods.... In contrast, a lease is 'a transfer of an interest in and possession of property for a prescribed period of time in exchange for an agreed consideration called "rent".'... The lessor has the duty of ordinary care in maintaining the premises it controls, but does not have a duty to exercise care regarding the lessee's property stored on the premises.... The lessor is therefore not 'responsible' for the property of the lessee. As between the owner of premises and the owner of personal property left in a locker on the premises when exclusive possession thereof has not been delivered and control and dominion of the property is dependent in no degree upon the co-operation of the owner of the premises, a landlord and tenant relationship is created, not a bailment....

"[Meaux] claims the facts show an implied bailment agreement may be proved by direct or circumstantial evidence and it was not necessary that delivery and acceptance be formal. However, the cases cited by [Meaux] do not involve lockers used in situations as in this case where owner of the premises (locker) has no knowledge of the extent of the value of the property stored in the lockers, and suggests in its rules that items of high personal or monetary value not be brought to the premises. [Sisters] could reasonably expect that only ordinary personal belongings [would] be placed in the lockers, and would not have agreed to a violation of its rules by someone storing valuables of high personal or monetary value. The owners of the premises in the cases cited by [Meaux] had the opportunity to see the property they were to safe keep, and/or make an assessment of whether to accept the property and the responsibility in such connection....

"There was no evidence of delivery and acceptance of [Meaux's] property by [Sisters]. [Sisters] had no knowledge of what [Meaux] placed in the locker but had the right to expect no belongings of a high monetary value would be placed in the locker contrary to its rules, and that it would not be liable for the loss of [Meaux's] property by theft. We conclude there was no bailment agreement between [Sisters] and [Meaux], and the use of the locker by [him] created a landlord-tenant relationship between the parties. The parties' respective responsibilities and liability are governed by the rules of the ... Center and there is no presumption of negligence as ordinarily used in bailment cases.... There was no evidence from which an informal, constructive or implied bailment could have been established or inferred....

"[Sisters'] issue number two contends the trial court erred in rendering judgment for [Meaux] on his 'warranty' theory....

"The trial court erred.... There was no evidence of an express warranty, and there is no such implied warranty in Texas....

"We reverse and render judgment ... that [Meaux] take nothing against [Sisters]."

Rights of the Bailee

Because a bailment is based on an express or implied agreement between two parties, each party has rights and duties with regard to the use, care, and eventual return of the object of the bailment. The bailee has the right to possess, use, and control the object during the period of the bailment, subject to any legal restrictions and to the restrictions in any express or implied agreement. For example, a garage to which you had given your car for repairs would not have the right to make any other use of it.

Duty of Care for the Bailed Property

The general rule is that the bailee must take reasonable care of the bailed object while it is in the bailee's possession and control. If something happens to the bailed object, does the bailee have to reimburse the bailor for the cost of repairs if damaged, or the value of the object if it was lost or stolen? If, in fact, the bailee exercised reasonable care and still the damage or loss occurred, the bailee owes nothing to the bailor. If, however, the bailee failed to use reasonable care, then the bailee would be liable to the bailor for the damages or the value of the object if lost or stolen.

Now the question is: How much care is reasonable? The courts look at various factors when determining what level of care is reasonable. First, the court will look to see what type of bailment is involved. Is it a mutual benefit bailment, a bailment solely for the benefit of bailee, or a bailment solely for the benefit of the bailor? Next, courts take into consideration the type of object, and when appropriate, the skill level of the bailee.

Even in the case in which the bailment is for the sole benefit of the bailor, the bailee must still use reasonable care; however, some courts have required a lesser degree of care by a bailee when the sole benefit is for the bailor, than would be required in cases where there was a mutual benefit bailment or a bailment for the sole benefit of the bailee.

Contract Liability of the Bailee

In view of the uncertainty about what the common law liability of the bailee may be, in certain circumstances it is advisable to specify the bailee's liability in the bailment contract.

This is especially true for a commercial bailee, such as a garage or a repair shop. A parking garage will normally have a clause in the bailment contract stating that the garage will not be responsible for theft of, or damage to, the automobile while the automobile is in its custody. Typically, this clause is printed on a parking ticket that you receive as you enter the parking lot. Also, the terms are in very small print. This clause may be effective in relieving the bailee of liability for damage to your car if the clause is called to your attention when you leave the car, except in cases in which the bailee or its agents or employees negligently or willfully damage the bailed property. If the parking attendant backed your car into a post, for example, the bailee would be liable for the damages even though a clause in the bailment contract disclaimed all liability. If, on the other hand, the brakes of another parked car failed and that car ran into your parked car, no negligence would be attributed to the bailee or its employees or agents; the clause would relieve the bailee of liability.

Some courts have held such **disclaimers** to be against public policy, and thus not effective in limiting the professional bailee's liability.

The other extreme in contract clauses concerns the bailee's assumption of full liability for the bailed object. If you take your diamond ring to the jeweler for cleaning, the jeweler may issue a bailment contract which is, in effect, an insurance policy for the safety of your ring. If the jewelry store is broken into and your ring is stolen, the jeweler or its insurance company will reimburse you for the value of the ring. Rental contracts for cars, trailers, and equipment typically contain similar clauses, which purport to make the bailee liable for any loss to the property. They may or may not be fully effective.

Bailor's Liability for Defects

The traditional bailment litigation is that of a bailor suing a bailee for loss of, or damage to, the bailed property. Even though the amounts involved in many of these cases are relatively small, the results are important to the parties.

Increasingly people are renting all kinds of items from professional rental companies. Hundreds of thousands of cars are rented each year. Many businesses have discovered that it is more economical to rent trucks when they need them than to own and maintain their own fleets. College students rent furniture, TVs, and refrigerators. Do-it-yourselfers rent all types of tools and equipment. Businesses rent computers, software, and other office equipment. As a result, legal rules have been formulated to deal with cases in which the rented property is defective in some way and causes injury to the bailee or to third persons. Most recently, an entire Article (2A) has been added to the Uniform Commercial Code (UCC) to provide a more complete set of rules for such leases of personal property.

When the bailor simply loans an item to a friend, the bailor's only duty is to inform the friend-bailee of any known hazards or defects in the item. The bailor has no obligation to inspect the item or to discover existing defects. If the bailee has been informed of all known defects, the bailor has no further liability.

In the mutual benefit bailment, the bailor's obligation is much more extensive. Most courts that have looked at this problem in recent years have applied to the professional bailor the same three theories of product liability that are applied to the seller of goods. In such cases, a bailor may be held liable for negligence because of a failure to exercise reasonable care in maintaining, servicing, and inspecting equipment that is being rented for immediate use. The bailor may also be held liable for breach of warranty—either **express warranty** or the implied warranties of **merchantability** and **fitness**. The most recent development has been the extension to professional bailors of **strict liability in tort** for defects in their rented items.

Statutory Liability of the Bailee

In certain types of bailments, the bailee has a statutory duty rather than a common law duty of care. Common carriers and innkeepers are by law held to a higher degree of care with regard to bailed property. Some states also have special statutes for parking lots, repair shops, dry cleaners, and other specific categories of bailees. Such statutes typically give the bailee a lien for services performed and the power to sell the property, if necessary, to enforce the lien. The *Mulay* case discusses the liability of a carrier of goods.

CASE 2

Mulay Plastics, Inc. v. Grand Trunk Western Railroad Company

822 F.2d 676 (7 Cir. 1987)

Facts: Mulay's injection molding machine suffered damage from undetermined causes while being shipped. Mulay sued the seller, the rigger, and the carrier under the common law, the UCC, and the Carmack Amendment. The jury found for defendants. Mulay contended that the jury's verdict was not supported by the evidence and was inherently contradictory. The trial judge declined to grant a new trial or judgment notwithstanding the verdict, and Mulay appealed.

Mulay purchased a massive piece of machinery, a used injection-molding machine, from Prestolite in February of 1981. Prestolite had used the machine for 11 years and sold it to Mulay as is. The injection-molding machine consisted of an injection end, a clamp end, and a base. The clamp end and base were shipped as a single unit (the "machine") from Prestolite's plant in Bay City, Michigan, to Mulay's in Addison, Illinois. Together, the clamp end and base are 27 feet long and 15 feet high and weigh about 75 tons. The clamp end itself, which rests on the base, weighs 50 tons. Mulay hired Dobson to move the machine from the Prestolite plant to a Grand Trunk railway siding and to load it on a Grand Trunk flatcar.

Mulay took no part in transporting the machine, leaving the disassembly, loading, rigging, and carriage to the defendants. Dobson brought the machine by truck from Prestolite's plant to Grand Trunk's siding and loaded it by crane onto the flatcar. Dobson blocked and bolted the base of the machine to the flatcar but did not block the clamp end, leaving it simply in its position atop the base. Thus, the six 1-inch steel bolts and two 1 1/4-inch steel sleeve dowels that held the clamp end in place during operation were the only things holding the clamp end in place during shipment besides gravity and friction. The bolts guarded against vertical movement and the dowels against horizontal. The bolts and dowels can only be seen if a sheet metal cover is removed from the sides of the machine.

Grand Trunk's car man saw the machine four times. He took rough measurements of it in Prestolite's plant. He made a general inspection after it was loaded on the flatcar. Dobson's rigging foreman told him then how the machine would be secured and told him that there were parts above the base. He inspected it after rigging was finished and again before it left the siding. He approved the machine for transport as rigged.

Grand Trunk then transported it as far as Markham, Illinois. The machine was twice weighed underway at weigh stations of the Illinois Central Gulf Railroad Company. Illinois Central both times issued a weigh bill with instructions not to exceed 30 miles per hour, because the machine exceeded Illinois Central weight requirements for that type of load, flatcar, and track. Signs were put on the flatcar with the legend, "Do Not Hump." "Humping" means coupling railway cars at speeds greater than 4 miles per hour.

In Markham, the unit was found to be severely damaged. The clamp end had come loose and moved almost 6 feet, damaging the machine in various ways. No one ever determined when the clamp end had moved. The bolts had been cut in half by the clamp end's movement. One witness testified that the dowels were found intact at the bottom of the flatcar. Another testified that the dowels were sheared.

Issue: Is the railroad liable for the damage to the machine?

Decision: No. Judgment for defendants is affirmed.

Opinion by Circuit Judge Eschbach: "The jury found for Grand Trunk on the Carmack Amendment count and for Prestolite on the UCC count. Mulay argues as follows: The parties agree that the machine was delivered to Grand Trunk undamaged and became damaged en route. Therefore, the jury must have found that Grand Trunk proved its affirmative defense, which required finding that the damage was caused by a 'latent or hidden defect in the machine.' Thus, the machine was delivered to Grand Trunk with a latent defect. But on the UCC count, the jury must have found that Prestolite delivered the machine free from defects. The two findings are contradictory.

"Setting aside for a moment the wording of the instructions, we note first that a verdict for Grand Trunk on the Carmack Amendment count and a verdict for Prestolite on the UCC count are not inconsistent under the law. Grand Trunk establishes its defense if it proves that the damage was caused by an 'inherent vice' of the machine. Prestolite wins unless Mulay shows that Prestolite did not 'duly deliver' the machine. To say that verdicts for each defendant are inconsistent would be to say that the [seller's] duty to 'duly deliver' the goods includes the duty to ensure that the goods will not suffer damage as a result of an 'inherent vice.' Particularly here, where the machine was sold as-is, that would require more of the [seller] than the UCC intends....

"We turn to Grand Trunk. The Carmack Amendment absolves the carrier from liability when it can show both that it was not negligent and that the damage resulted from an inherent vice of the goods. The jury was entitled to find that Grand Trunk was not negligent....

"As to the second prong of Grand Trunk's defense, in some cases it is clear what damage from an inherent vice of goods means. Foods rot; iron rusts; some wines simply do not travel well. Where the carrier is not negligent in handling such goods, he is not held liable for the rot, rust or deterioration. An inherent vice, then, could be understood to mean a quality of the goods that causes damage to the goods during transport even in the absence of negligence. There was evidence that such a quality was present in this case.... Although the machine appeared solid and was normally securely held together by dowels, the dowels had a tendency to slip out during rail transport and permit the clamp end to shift on the base.

"[T]he instructions [to the jury] use the word 'defect' to refer both to an inherent vice of the goods for Carmack Amendment purposes and to a failure of the [seller] to duly deliver the goods for UCC purposes and thus hazard conflating two distinct concepts. Under the instructions, an inherent vice is a 'latent or hidden defect;' goods that are not duly delivered have a 'defect.' The jury found the machine to have the former but not the latter.

"We reconcile the two findings by holding that the jury was entitled to find that where the goods had a 'latent or hidden defect' for the purposes of the Carmack Amendment count, they did not necessarily have a 'defect' for the purposes of the UCC count. In other words, the jurors could have decided that the tendency of the dowels to slip loose and permit the clamp end to shift was a 'latent defect' for which the carrier was not responsible, but at the same time that condition was not a 'defect' the presence of which meant that the [seller] did not duly deliver the goods. The word defect would not be given the same meaning in the two instructions. That is not illogical; indeed, the word must be given different meanings in order to interpret the instructions accurately to reflect the law. This is a strained reading of the instructions, but a correct one. Such an understanding of the instructions is consistent with the law underlying the instructions and with the evidence in the case. As the trial judge put it, 'You cannot, in Gertrude Stein terms, say, "A defect is a defect is a defect".'"

Leases of Realty

The problems, rights, and duties involved in the landlord-tenant relationship are very relevant to the students reading this textbook because nearly all of you are involved in such a relationship. A student who lives in a dormitory is part of a landlord-tenant relationship in which the university is the **landlord** and the student is the **tenant.** For a student who lives in an apartment, the landlord is the owner of the apartment complex. In this section, we will try to answer some of the questions that are often asked about the landlord-tenant relationship. We will start by looking at tenancy—the right of the tenant, or lessee—to occupy the premises.

Types of Tenancies

Tenancies at Will

The simplest form of tenancy, **tenancy at will,** occurs when the landlord allows the tenant to occupy the premises and there is no agreement as to a specific time period. Either the landlord or the tenant may terminate the tenancy at any time. Also, a tenancy at will is automatically terminated by the death of either party.

Most states require that the terminating party give the other party advance notice. The length of this notice varies from state to state, but 30 days is typical. This, of course, assumes that the rent has been paid. If the tenant fails to pay the rent, then the landlord can simply give the tenant notice that the lease has been terminated for that reason. In this situation a different notice requirement would be imposed.

No reason need be given to terminate the tenancy at will. Landlords may terminate the tenancy at will simply because they do not want a tenant living there any longer. Tenants, on the other hand, may terminate it simply because they want to move out.

Tenancies for a Specified Period

The great majority of residential tenancies are for a period of 1 year. In a college community, however, the period of tenancy may be governed by the school year. For example, the landlord may lease an apartment from August to May to one student and then lease the apartment for 2 months during the summer to a student going to summer school. For expediency, a commercial lease usually will be for a period longer than 1 year. A tenancy for a specified time is automatically terminated by the expiration of its term, and there is no requirement that either party give any notice. Both parties are aware of the term, and when the term ends, the tenancy ends.

Normally, **tenancies for a specified period** will be in writing because it is in the best interest of both parties to have written evidence of their agreement and the term of the tenancy. In this type of tenancy, neither party may terminate the tenancy until the term expires, unless one of them breaches the agreement, in which case the other party may terminate the tenancy based on that breach. For example, if the landlord turns off the heat in subzero weather, the tenant certainly would have a right to terminate the lease and to move out of the premises because it would be unsafe to continue to live there.

Tenancies by Sufferance

This type of tenancy occurs after the tenancy for a specified period expires. For example, a student had a 10-month lease that expired on May 31. The student had a duty to move out on May 31, but for one reason or another needed to continue to occupy the premises. The student then became a **tenant by sufferance**. The landlord may treat the tenant by sufferance as a trespasser and have that person evicted, or the landlord may work out some type of rental agreement with such a tenant for the period of time that the tenant needs to stay. Until a landlord issues an eviction notice, or until the landlord and tenant agree to a new term of tenancy, the status of the tenant is that of a tenant by sufferance.

Nature of a Lease

The **lease** is a contract, and thus must comply with the requirements for the formation and enforcement of a contract. There must be an offer, acceptance, consideration, capacity to contract, and lawful purpose. The lease contract may be oral or written. If it is oral and for a term exceeding 1 year, it will not be legally enforceable in most states. A few states, however, allow the enforcement of oral lease contracts for a period of up to 3 years.

Many tenants have the misconception that an oral lease is better for them than a written one. Actually, a written lease provides better protection for both parties. A written lease states the rights and duties of both parties, and the landlord cannot raise the rent, evict the tenant, or impose any new rules during the term of the lease. In a college town where living space is limited, these protections can be very important. A written lease also prevents the tenant from moving out during the term of the lease except when the landlord has breached duties under terms of the lease. If the landlord fails to comply with the terms of the lease, then the tenant can move out legally, force the landlord to comply with the terms, or sue for damages.

The lease agreement must give the tenant-lessee the right to occupy, use, and enjoy the apartment or the parcel of land and the improvements thereon as defined in the agreement. Because the intent is not to permanently convey any rights to the lessee, the agreement must state when the landlord is allowed to retake possession. It must also state the rent the tenant is required to pay. The lease should specify what security deposit must be paid and when rental payments are due and to whom they are to be paid. There will also be lease terms that govern the tenant's use, enjoyment, and possession of the premises, and that preserve the landlord's right of inspection. Other terms may be inserted in a lease agreement. Many landlords do not want animals on the premises and, therefore, have a clause in the lease that prohibits the tenant from having a pet. Another common clause restricts the subletting of the premises. Normally, the tenant may sublet the premises to another person, provided the landlord agrees to the sublease. Landlords also frequently include clauses that purport to limit their liability for accidents on the premises.

Landlord's Rights and Obligations

Once a lease agreement has been made, the landlord has a duty to give the tenant possession of the premises specified in the lease agreement. The landlord also has the duty not to interfere with the right of the tenant to possess and enjoy the premises for the term of the agreement, provided that the tenant does not breach the lease. The landlord also has the right to inspect the premises at reasonable times, with the tenant's permission, to see that the premises are not being mistreated or damaged.

Condition of Premises

Under the common law, the landlord did not have to worry about the condition of the premises at the time they were rented to a tenant. The tenant was subject to the rule of caveat emptor and simply took the premises as they were or refused to rent them. If the premises were filthy or infested with rats and the tenant knowingly agreed to take them, then the tenant assumed the risk. The landlord would not be responsible for injuries and damages that the tenant might suffer as a result. The rule of caveat emptor has generally been replaced by the rule of caveat vendor—that is, "Let the seller (in this case, the landlord) beware." The landlord-tenant relationship has become the target of many consumer groups. As a result, many states, cities, and counties have enacted housing codes that set minimum standards with regard to the rental of premises for residential occupancy. Most cities and counties now have housing inspectors who will respond to the complaints of tenants. These inspectors check to see that rental units are in fact safe, habitable, and free from dangers such as bare electrical wires or other unhealthy and unsanitary conditions.

Injuries

In many recent cases, landlords have been found civilly liable for injury to tenants because the landlords failed to provide sufficient security or because the landlords' employees were responsible for theft from, or injury to, tenants. Whether or not the landlord is liable in such cases depends heavily on the circumstances. If the apartment complex advertises that it provides security for its tenants, then it has assumed that duty; if, however, no security has been promised or provided, then the tenant will be faced with caveat emptor. As to theft, the landlord will normally have a clause in the lease stating that the landlord is not responsible for theft. If an employee of the landlord commits a crime against a tenant, then the landlord will allege that the person who perpetrated the crime was not acting as an agent or employee, and that the employer is not responsible for criminal acts of employees. However, the pendulum of the law is swinging in favor of the consumer-tenant and against the seller-landlord. The wise landlord will insure adequately against such situations, because this is still a questionable area of landlord's rights and obligations. The Wright case illustrates a landlord's minimal responsibility to trespassers.

CASE 3

Wright v. Preston Resources, Inc.

639 N.W.2d 149 (NE App. 2002)

Facts: Patty Wright, personal representative of the estate of Raquel Woodruff, appeals from the trial court's granting summary judgment to Preston Resources. Wright had alleged that Raquel was "killed by a person or persons" while on the premises of an apartment building owned and operated by Preston Resources. Based on various exhibits presented at the motion hearing, the trial court found that Raquel was a trespasser, and that Preston Resources had not acted with "willful or wanton" disregard of her safety.

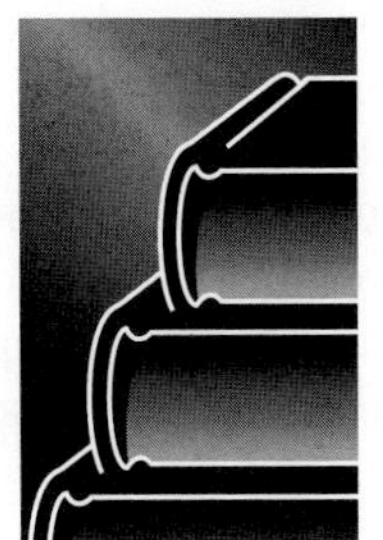

Issue: Did Preston Resources breach a duty of care owed to Woodruff?

Decision: No. Judgment affirmed.

Opinion by Chief Judge Erwin: "In premises liability actions, the duty owed by a landowner to another person depends on the person's status. To ascertain the duty owed by landowners to entrants upon their land, courts traditionally have classified entrants as either invitees, licensees, or trespassers. . . .

"A trespasser is legally defined as a person who enters or remains upon the premises of another without a privilege to do so as created by the possessor's consent, either express or implied. . . . An owner of premises owes only a very limited duty to refrain from willfully or wantonly injuring a trespasser. . . .

"In interrogatories, Preston requested that Wright disclose whom Woodruff might have visited on the premises, and Wright repeatedly answered that she '[did] not know.' The closest Wright was able to come in this regard was to indicate that Woodruff 'had a friend by the name of Carolyn Carson' who had resided on the premises. However, the tenant payment records established that Carson ceased being a tenant of Preston when she was evicted from the premises in April 1995, more than 1 month prior to the date of Woodruff's death. . . .

"Preston presented evidence . . . to establish that Woodruff was not a tenant, that she was not on the premises for any business purpose associated with Preston, and that she was not a guest of any tenant. The reasonable inferences deducible ... show no genuine issue of material fact concerning Woodruff's status.... Preston's evidence establishes that Woodruff was merely a trespasser on the property when she was killed....

"Wright asserts on appeal that testimony from the criminal trial of Woodruff's killer indicates that according to Woodruff's sister, Woodruff was visiting somebody named 'Jackie' or 'Nickie' '[o]n Howard Street' in the week preceding her death. However, Woodruff's sister testified that she was not sure of the name and did not have a specific address of where the person might have lived. As such, the evidence did not provide any reasonable inference that Woodruff was visiting or was a guest of anyone residing in the apartment building where she was killed, especially when it is noted that a review of the tenant listings ... does not indicate any tenant with a name comparable to Jackie or Nickie residing at the property between January and June 1995....

"Because Woodruff was a trespasser, Preston owed her a very limited duty with regard to her safety while on the property.... Preston was only obliged to refrain from willfully and wantonly injuring Woodruff.... A review of the record shows that no material issue of fact existed as to the willfulness and wantonness of Preston's conduct....

"For conduct to be willful and wanton, two criteria must be met.... First, the defendant must have actual knowledge of the danger.... Second, the defendant must have intentionally failed to act to prevent harm which was reasonably likely to result.... The record before us establishes that the second requirement is not met, and we will not further specifically address the first.

"Preston had security doors on the apartment building to keep trespassers out. These security doors required the entry of a numerical code to open the doors from the outside and automatically locked upon closing.... [W]hen trespassers were found on the premises by maintenance or other employees of Preston, they were instructed to leave the premises. On occasion, law enforcement was called to remove trespassers. The concern to be addressed is whether the evidence establishes that the premises owner took steps to prevent trespassers from entering the premises. Taking such measures precludes a finding that Preston acted with such reckless disregard of security and right as to imply bad faith....

"The evidence in the record before us and our review of applicable Nebraska law lead to only one conclusion: Preston refrained from willfully and wantonly injuring Woodruff. Reasonable minds cannot differ on this point. As such, the district court correctly granted Preston's motion for summary judgment."

Tenant's Rights and Obligations

The most important right that a tenant has is what the law terms **quiet enjoyment of the premises.** This means that, with a few exceptions, tenants have the right to use the house or apartment that they are renting in generally the same manner as if they owned the premises. To be more specific, if you are a tenant, you may invite anyone you wish to visit you, and you may carry on any activities they are not forbidden by the lease or by law. The key here is reasonable use of the premises.

For example, you rent a house with a large yard and the house is a considerable distance from other houses. In that case, you can play your stereo as loud as you want to and have loud parties, as long as you do not destroy or damage the rented property. On the other hand, if you live in an apartment building, your right to play the stereo loud and to have loud parties would be limited. As the tenant in an apartment, you not only have the right to quiet enjoyment of the premises, but you also have an obligation not to unreasonably disturb the other tenants, who also have the right to quiet enjoyment of the premises. The tenant should always read the fine print in the lease agreement because the agreement may prohibit many activities that are not expressly forbidden by law. Such provisions are contractual and will generally be enforced by courts.

Landlord Inspections

As stated earlier, the landlord has a right to inspect the rented premises. However, during the period of the lease the landlord does not have the right to enter the house or apartment at will and without the tenant's permission. The landlord who is going to inspect the premises must do so at reasonable times that will not interfere with the quiet enjoyment of the premises by the tenant. A landlord could be civilly liable in a trespass action for forcing entry into the rented premises or for entering the rented premises periodically when the tenant is not at home, simply to snoop.

Repairs

Another common problem experienced by tenants is that of liability for repairs. What repairs are the landlord's duty, and what repairs are the duty of the tenant? The landlord's obligation to make repairs inside the rented house or apartment will vary from state to state and from locality to locality and may also be dictated by the terms of the lease. As a general rule, however, the landlord is required to make major repairs except when the damage is caused by the tenant's negligence. If the tenant is having a wild party and something is thrown through the window, the tenant will be obligated to replace the window. If a windstorm blows off part of the roofing and water drips through the ceiling causing the plaster to fall, the landlord will be responsible for repairs.

A rule of thumb in these cases would be that the tenant has a duty to make minor repairs to keep the premises in as good a condition as when they were rented, excluding, of course, normal wear and tear. Most landlords require a security deposit for use in making such minor repairs when the tenant vacates the premises. If the tenant's furniture marked up the walls, then the tenant would be obligated to have the walls repainted to cover the damage. If the furnace broke down, that is a major repair that would be the landlord's obligation.

CASE 4

P.H. Investment v. Oliver
818 P.2d 1018 (UT 1994)

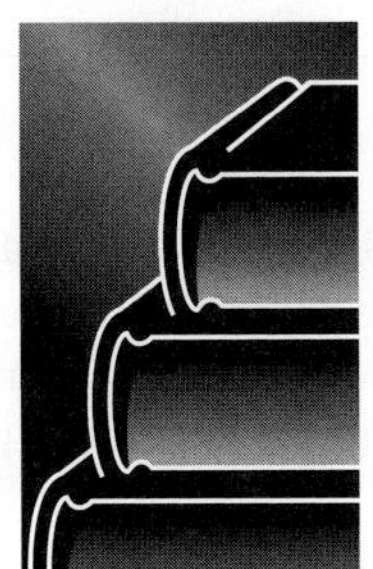

Facts: This is an unlawful detainer action by P.H. Investment (the landlord) against Cathy Oliver (the tenant) based on nonpayment of rent. Because of the deteriorated condition of the premises, the tenant argued that she owed no rent and counterclaimed for a rebate of rent paid. At trial, an officer with the Salt Lake City Building and Housing Services testified that there were 42 housing code violations on the rental premises. The violations included numerous electrical violations; a hazardous stairway without handrails; holes in the walls in every room; dilapidated and rotted floors and carpets; a collapsed bathroom ceiling; a collapsed bedroom ceiling; leaking faucets, shower, and toilets; broken and missing windows; no bathroom door; and inadequate protection from weather. The inspector declared the building a public nuisance and ordered it repaired or demolished.

The trial court granted judgment to the landlord against the tenant for rent, treble damages, and costs of court, together with an order of restitution of the premises. The tenant received an offset against the judgment for the value of her deposit, but her rent rebate counterclaim was dismissed. The court of appeals affirmed by a divided court.

Issue: Can a tenant who is sued for nonpayment of rent use the landlord's breach of the implied warranty of habitability as a defense?

Decision: Yes. Judgment reversed, and case remanded.

Opinion by Justice Durham: "Under contract principles, relief for a breach in the warranty of habitability is based on a failure of consideration rather than on some theory of eviction. As a result, the tenant should not have to vacate the premises to raise the claim. Especially where there is a shortage of rental housing, and given the cost and inconvenience of relocation, little would be accomplished if the tenant's only remedy for a breach of the warranty of habitability required vacation of the premises before taking action to recover for the breach. Thus, many courts allow the tenant to remain in possession, withhold rent installments accruing after the landlord's breach, and then raise the landlord's breach of the warranty of habitability as a counterclaim or defense when the landlord brings an eviction action for failure to pay rent.... We hold that no legal doctrine, substantive or procedural, bars a tenant from raising this critical issue in an unlawful detainer action in this jurisdiction.

"Utah's unlawful detainer statute ... takes away the landlord's common-law right to use self-help to remove a tenant. The statute grants the landlord a summary court proceeding to evict a tenant who has violated some express or implied provision of the lease. The statute provides five instances in which the tenant is in unlawful detainer, including the situation where the tenant defaults in the payment of rent and remains in possession.... The remedy for a successful landlord is restitution of the premises, treble damages, and recovery for waste or rent due.... If the unlawful detainer action is based on default in payment of rent, the judgment will also mandate forfeiture of the lease....

"[T]his court has recognized a defendant-tenant's right to raise proper counterclaims in unlawful detainer cases. The legislature, too, apparently has recognized this right.... Under the concept of dependence of covenants, a breach of the warranty of habitability is directly relevant to the issue of possession.... Having recognized a warranty of habitability, we conclude that a breach of that warranty must necessarily give rise to a counterclaim in an unlawful detainer action; otherwise, the tenant would be required to vacate before being able to raise the breach, a result entirely inconsistent with the policy behind our adoption of the implied warranty. While the state does have a significant interest in preserving a speedy repossession remedy, that interest is not strong enough to warrant a deprivation of a meaningful opportunity to raise a breach of the warranty of habitability. We reject, therefore, any limitation on the tenant's ability to raise a breach of the warranty of habitability as a defense or counterclaim to a landlord's unlawful detainer action for possession.

"The trial court held, as a matter of law, that the tenant had waived any defense or cause of action under a theory of warranty of habitability by agreeing to rent the premises in their deteriorated condition. Courts disagree on the propriety of waivers with regard to the warrant of habitability. A majority of courts prohibit them, reasoning that such a shift of responsibility is contrary to public policy....

"In the present case, the tenant is typical of the individuals we sought to protect by adopting the warranty of habitability. Ms. Oliver is a woman with little or no resources or income, with seven children, and pregnant with an eighth at the time of this action.... Because of a lack of bargaining power, low-income tenants often have no meaningful choice but to accept and continue to live in substandard housing. To protect persons similarly situated, our approach will invalidate boilerplate language, eliminate any duty of inspection, and protect against uninformed waivers of any latent defects. Moreover, because we will permit only express waivers of specifically listed defects, our approach should have the advantage of preventing much of the case-by-case litigation on the subject of implied waivers which may be generated by adherence to the Restatement approach. Our approach is, in this way, a workable compromise between those courts disallowing all waivers and those following the Restatement's broader language permitting implied waivers. Although we seek to protect parties' freedom to contract as they see fit, we must also recognize the undesirability of permitting landlords to lease uninhabitable dwellings.

"On remand, the trial court will need to determine if any specific defects were expressly waived by the tenant when she moved in. The burden of proving the waiver should be on the landlord. If such a waiver was made, the trial court will then need to determine if the waiver was contrary to public policy or unconscionable under comment e of the Restatement. The burden of proving this issue is on the tenant. We note that a finding upholding such a waiver must be supported by evidence that: (1) the waiver was express, and (2) the express waiver listed the specific defects waived."

A tenant's rights as to heat, water, and electricity will depend primarily on the lease. If a landlord who is to provide heat turns the thermostats down to an unsafe or intolerable temperature, then the tenant may terminate the lease and leave, pay to heat the premises and deduct the cost from the rent, or report the landlord to the local housing authority.

Tenant's Property

Another question that often arises is: Who bears the responsibility for the loss of the tenant's furniture, clothing, and personal effects if the rented apartment or house burns down? The lease will often expressly state that the tenants assume responsibility for carrying fire insurance on their personal belongings. If there is no such agreement in the lease, then the courts will usually hold the landlord responsible for damages to the tenants' contents if the fire or other damage was caused as a result of the landlord's negligence. The wise thing for the tenants to do is to carry renter's insurance on their contents because the law and the obligation of the landlord will vary. Also, it is often difficult to determine who, if anyone, was negligent in a major fire or catastrophe.

Ownership of Fixtures

Another common question concerns the extent to which tenants can make changes or additions, such as putting pictures on the walls, installing shelves, or changing curtain rods. Again, the lease often specifies that tenants may not paint the premises, hang pictures, or make any alterations to the premises without the landlord's permission. If there is no such provision in the lease, then a reasonableness rule applies. If tenants install such things as bookshelves or room dividers, the landlord automatically becomes the owner of those fixtures when the tenants leave, unless the fixtures can be removed without causing any damage to the rented property.

Termination of the Lease

If the lease is for a fixed period of time, it is rather difficult for the tenant to break it. However, a landlord and a tenant can always end the lease by mutual agreement, regardless of its terms. Thus, if the tenant and the landlord agree that the tenant may move out before the lease expires, then the lease may be terminated. It is a good idea to put this agreement in writing to prevent the landlord from coming back later and trying to enforce the original lease.

Breach of Lease

The tenant may also terminate the lease without the landlord's agreement if the landlord has interfered with the tenant's quiet enjoyment or if the landlord has in some way failed to meet obligations specified in the lease and such failure has caused the premises to be uninhabitable or below minimum health standards.

The landlord can evict a tenant for nonpayment of rent. The landlord can evict a tenant if the tenant stays in possession of the premises after the term of the lease has expired or if the tenant violates the rules and regulations of the lease. For example, if your lease states that no pets are allowed and you keep a cat, the landlord can evict you unless you get rid of it.

Security Deposits

Most leases provide that a lessee must pay a **security deposit,** also referred to as a damage deposit, when the lease is signed. This security deposit is to be held by the landlord and to be applied to any repairs required as a result of damage caused by the tenant, other than normal wear and tear. Two problems exist. First, the landlord takes two or three hundred dollars of each tenant's money and holds it for the lease period, which may be a year or longer. During that time the landlord can invest this money and secure interest on it. Some states require landlords to pay interest to tenants on the security deposit when it is returned. Most states, however, still do not have such a requirement. Thus, a landlord with 100 apartments has a large amount of cash to invest and the landlord can earn a good income from the tenants' money.

The second problem is what type of repairs and what type of cleanup should come out of the security deposit. Some landlords use the money for improvements such as repainting the entire apartment or purchasing new curtains on the contention that the walls were chipped or the drapes were stained. Obviously the walls could be patched and painted as necessary, but the landlord is not entitled to a complete paint job at the expense of the tenant. The same principle applies to the curtains and drapes. Cleaning may be allowable, but not the purchase of new drapes. The landlord is not supposed to gain by getting an improvement. The problem is that the landlord has the security deposit, and often refuses to return it, alleging it was used for repairs and cleanup. For years tenants simply grumbled but did not go to court because the cost of paying a lawyer, court costs and other expenses made collecting too expensive for the amount of money involved. Most jurisdictions now have small claims courts in which the tenant can, for a minimal filing fee, file a lawsuit and have the case heard promptly. Landlord-tenant cases comprise a major portion of the court docket in most small claims courts.

Landlord's Right to Damages

When a tenant simply defaults in the payment of rent, the landlord may file suit to evict and to collect the back rent. Depending on the particular state, the landlord may be entitled to hold the tenant's possessions under a "landlord lien statute."

What happens if the tenant moves out of the leased premises before the end of the lease? The landlord now sues the tenant for any unpaid rent due landlord at the time the tenant moved out, and for the balance of the rent due under the lease. What is the **landlord's duty to mitigate;** that is, to lessen, the amount due from the lessee by rerenting the premises to someone else? Traditionally, the landlord did not have a duty to rerent the premises and thus mitigate the loss. The trend in the recent landlord-tenant cases involving residential leases reflects a change in judicial thinking. Recent cases require the landlord in residential leases to make at least a reasonable effort to rerent the premises and thereby mitigate the damages.

With regard to commercial leases, the courts will not feel so sorry for the lessee. In a commercial lease situation the lease agreement is usually negotiated, with each party having legal counsel. Also in a commercial lease situation the parties will be on a more equal footing financially.

Significance of This Chapter

For professional bailees, such as warehouses and carriers, the UCC outlines the performance obligations of the parties and their available remedies in the event of breach in some detail. Generally, the parties are free to write the contract as they wish, but several Code sections try to ensure fair results in all cases. Parties who are aware of the Code's rules are in a better position to negotiate their own contract so that it recognizes their situations and provides for the variations they wish. If they are also aware of the outer limits set by the Code, they are in a better position to provide for a different, but still reasonable, package of remedies in the event of a breach. Parties to non-UCC bailments also need to consider many of these same points.

Most people will be involved in a lease at some time, either as a tenant, or as a landlord. This chapter reviews the contents of a lease and discusses the rights and duties of the tenant and the landlord. Here, too, the parties need a carefully drafted (and read) agreement.

Important Terms and Concepts

bailee
bailments
bailor
commercial bailors
common carriers
constructive delivery
disclaimers
express warranty
fitness
landlord
landlord's duty to mitigate
lease
merchantability
professional bailees
quiet enjoyment of the premises
security deposit
strict liability in tort
tenancies for a specified period
tenancy at will
tenant
tenant by sufferance

Questions and Problems for Discussion

1. Which is better, an oral lease or a written lease? Why?

2. What are the landlord's rights and duties?

3. Do tenants have any rights? What are they?

4. If a lease is for a fixed period of time, it will cease when that period has elapsed. However, in many cases either the landlord or the tenant may desire to terminate the lease before it expires. Can either of these parties terminate the lease before the term of the lease has expired? If so, how?

5. On September 12, Snyder bought a 27-foot sailboat from Four Winds. Under the contract he was given "free" storage for the winter. Four Winds' president refused to pay storage and said that the storage price was to be paid out of the salesman's commission on the sale. Snyder took delivery of his boat at the Four Winds marina in mid-October and took it out with the salesman on two or three short shake-down cruises, at the conclusion of which the salesman told Snyder where to tie up. After each cruise, Four Winds kept the keys to the four locks on the boat. Four Winds did not maintain dock guards, alarms, or other security devices. It did have three mercury vapor lights in the docking and office area. It also had a locked boat storage building with an alarm.

   On Sunday, November 4, Snyder told the salesman that he would not be using the boat any more and directed that it be put into the locked building. The salesman said the boat would be taken out of the water sometime that week.

   The last time the boat was seen was on Tuesday, November 6, by the president of Four Winds, who was checking the boats at his marina because someone had been reported as burglarizing another marina 100 feet away. He discovered the Snyder boat missing the following morning. Four Winds reported the theft to the police and the Coast Guard, but the boat was never seen again.

   Judge Mishler awarded Snyder the cost of the boat, \$32,261, plus interest. Four Winds appealed.

   Was there a bailment? If so, did the bailee exercise reasonable care for the safety of the bailed property?

6. In July 1993, Anthony and Grace Cucchi leased a burglar alarm system for their home. The Rollins salesman told Anthony that the system was "state of the art" and "almost unbeatable." The written contract signed by the Cucchis contained a clause that limited Rollins' liability to \$250 for any loss caused by the system's failure to operate. However, this contract also stated that it would not become effective until signed by Rollins' home office, and it was never so signed.

   The Cucchis' house was burglarized in 1998. The alarm system did not work, and some \$36,000 worth of property was taken. The Cucchis sued, alleging negligence, breach of warranty, and strict liability. The trial court held that strict liability did not apply to this case. After trial, the trial judge directed a verdict for Rollins on the negligence count, but permitted the jury to consider the Cucchis' claims for express and implied warranty. The jury awarded Grace Cucchi $20,000 and Anthony $10,000. On appeal, the Superior Court reversed on the basis that the UCC's 4-year statute of limitations applied and that the lawsuit had been filed more than 4 years after the lease commenced. The Cucchis appealed to the state Supreme Court.

Does a professional lessor of goods make implied warranties? Does the 4-year limitations period begin when the lease starts?

7. Rienecker leased a single-family house from Agnes Roseberry in 1990. Agnes had just had some remodeling done on the house, including the installation of a new roof. The roofers had removed the gutters from the front of the house but had not reinstalled them. Without gutters, water ran off the front side of the roof onto the front steps. On January 9, 1991, ice had accumulated on the steps and Rienecker worked that afternoon to clean them off. Gary Borders arrived at about 4 PM in response to a dinner invitation. When Gary left that evening, about 9 PM, he slipped and fell on the icy steps, and sustained personal injuries. Gary sued Agnes. He appealed from a trial court ruling that Agnes owed no duty to a social guest of the tenant in a single-family house where the injury was the result of a known hazard.

   What result, and why?

8. Gaspane Restaurant required its waitresses to wear uniforms while on the job. It provided a room, with a clothes rack and lockers, where the waitresses could change into their uniforms and leave their purses and other personal property. The room was unattended, although waitresses came in and out at various times, either on breaks or when their shift was over. The room was at the rear of the restaurant, which had a city alley running directly behind it. The rear window had been locked, but it had been jimmied open with a crowbar. Ms. Grana's new coat and purse were stolen. The coat was worth about $300 and the purse $45. Ms. Grana had just cashed her paycheck at the bank, and she had nearly $400 in the purse. Gaspane refused to reimburse her.

   Is Gaspane liable for the loss of any of this property? Discuss.

9. On December 24, Mae Theobald came to the beauty shop owned by Helen Swatterthwaite for a permanent wave. Mae hung her coat on a hook in the waiting room. On a prior visit, Mae had asked Helen whether it was safe to leave her coat there and Helen had told her that it was safe, that nothing had been stolen in 20 years. This time Mae's coat was stolen. The trial court gave Mae $300, the value of the coat, on the basis that there had been a bailment and that the waiting room was not a safe place because there was no bell or other warning device on the front door and because the waiting room was visible from the street. The Satterthwaites appealed.

   How should the appeals court rule, and why?

10. Kirsch and her son moved into a ground floor apartment in a building owned by Mendez. Mendez employed Middleton as caretaker for the building. Kirsch lived there for 1 month before she was required to sign a 1-year lease. The lease contained a clause disclaiming the landlord's liability for any damage done by plumbing, gas, steam, water, or other pipes. Kirsch did not read this clause at the time, nor was it explained to her. Her apartment had a "sleeve" for an air conditioning unit, but there was no air conditioning unit. Instead, a piece of cardboard covered the opening where the unit would have been. Hickman and Cramer moved into the apartment above Kirsch's in November. Their air conditioner was also missing, and during the winter they filed about 50 complaints with Middleton about the cardboard blowing off the hole and letting in cold air. Middleton did nothing about the problem. Kirsch received a call at work telling her to come back to her apartment. A copper tube in the baseboard radiation system had broken, and her apartment was flooded with water. The cold air coming in upstairs had apparently frozen the pipe, and it broke. Kirsch was paid by her insurance company, State Farm, and it sued Mendez's insurance company, Home. State Farm won a jury verdict, but the trial court entered a judgment N.O.V. for Home. State Farm appealed.

    Is the disclaimer in the lease effective here? Explain.

CHAPTER 20

Real Property—Acquisition of Ownership

Chapter Objectives

This chapter will:

- Define "real property."
- Explain the two basic methods of land description.
- Discuss the types of ownership in real property.
- Describe the ways in which ownership to real property may be acquired.
- Compare purchase of real property by land contract to purchase by deed and mortgage.
- Review the national laws that must be complied with when real property is purchased.

The law concerning the rights and duties of the owners of real property differs considerably from the law concerning the rights and duties of the owners of personal property. Some objects of personal property can be transported from state to state or even from country to country.

When dealing with real property, we are concerned with land and with the permanent fixtures and buildings attached to it. The land cannot be picked up and taken across state lines; it is part of the earth's surface. The fixtures and buildings on the land may depreciate, burn down, or otherwise be destroyed; however, the land itself remains basically the same, century after century. Also, the land cannot be possessed physically in the same way that an item of personal property is possessed.

Nature of Real Property

Real property is a term that describes the bundle of rights to a specific parcel of land. It includes not only buildings and other permanent fixtures attached to the surface of the land, but also rights to the ground below the surface of the land and rights to the air and sky above the land. Thus, the owner of a parcel of land has rights to the airspace above that parcel, to water on it, to things growing on or attached to its surface, and to the minerals, underground waters, and whatever else may be found below its surface.

Airspace

Technically, the owners of a tract of land, and therefore of the airspace above it, could prevent anyone from trespassing into their airspace. This presented a problem because landowners could have restricted interstate or even international air travel. The American Law Institute (ALI) formulated a rule to govern trespasses into the airspace above a landowner's parcel of land. Such an overflight is privileged if it is made at a reasonable height and if it is in accordance with all applicable government regulations. For example, the Federal Aviation Administration (FAA) regulations state that no aircraft may fly over a congested (populated) area at an altitude of less than 1,000 feet, and no aircraft may fly over a noncongested (farmland) area at an altitude of less than 500 feet. These rules do allow an exception for helicopters if they are operated without hazard and in accordance with specific regulations. An example would be the use of a helicopter for medical rescue operations in a congested populated area and the use of helicopters for crop spraying in a noncongested farm area.

The most obvious area of real property is the surface of the land. In Chapter 15, we discussed the question of when fixtures become real property and how certain things that are part of real property, such as growing crops, may be severed from the real property to become personal property. The rules are fairly clear concerning most of the land surface and the buildings, fixtures, trees, and other growing objects, which generally stay affixed until they are severed by people or by an act of God. The water that is present on the land surface is in constant motion, and it changes course and swells and shrinks in height and width with the seasons and the years.

Water

Water rights, called **riparian rights**, are a concern of those who own land that abuts a lake, river, or other body of water. Generally, the owner of the land next to a stream, river, or lake may take or use the water as needed for natural and domestic purposes on the land adjoining the water. For example, water could be taken for use in irrigation, for washing, or for drinking. A riparian owner would not, however, have the right to divert the entire stream and thus deprive landowners downstream of its use. Riparian rights also concern the property boundary lines of land next to a river, stream, or lake. Does your ownership extend to the edge of the river, 10 feet out into the river, or just where? The river or stream will run at different levels depending on the time of year. The general rule is that the property line will be at the point of normal flow of the river or stream.

The law concerning riparian rights varies from state to state because different areas of the country have different problems regarding water. In areas where water is scarce and irrigation is a necessity, rules governing the use of water from running streams will be strict. Also, different problems are involved if the property abuts a creek rather than a navigable river. In addition, many national and state statutes govern actions by a riparian landowner that might affect water quality.

Minerals

The law covering minerals, such as coal or metals, is quite clear. If you own the land, you own everything below the surface, unless the **mineral rights** were previously sold to someone else. Such sales of mineral rights are very common in Texas, Oklahoma, and other oil-producing states. If there is oil under your land and your neighbor's land, how much do you own? How much does your neighbor own? If you pump out the pool under your land, will you be taking your neighbor's oil? Because liquids seek their own level, you cannot just separate and take your part of the oil beneath your area of land if the pool extends beyond the boundaries of your property. Thus, the courts have often been called on to resolve disputes as to the ownership of oil and gas taken from below the surface of the ground. Now, an entire area of the law, known as "oil and gas law," specifically addresses the problems of oil and gas ownership. Although this is an area of interest, time and space do not permit a further discussion of this area of the law in this text.

Water rights are at issue in the next case.

CASE 1

In Re Big Horn River System

835 P.2d 273 (WY 1992)

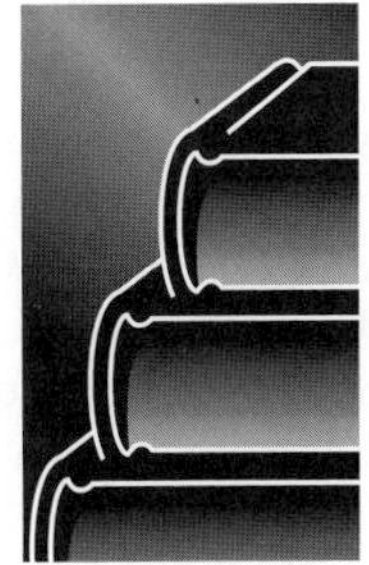

Facts: The state of Wyoming and non-Indian water users appeal from a judgment entered by the district court that: (1) decreed that the Shoshone and Northern Arapaho Tribes on the Wind River Indian Reservation may change the use of their reserved water right as they deem advisable without regard to Wyoming water law, and (2) substituted the tribal water agency for the state engineer as the administrator of both reserved and state-permitted water rights within the Wind River Indian Reservation.

This is another appeal of an ongoing general adjudication of all water rights in the Big Horn River System involving over 20,000 claimants. Because of its size and complexity, the adjudication is being conducted in phases. The dispute presently before this court relates to the interpretation of the amended judgment and decree entered on May 24, 1985, by Judge Alan B. Johnson (the 1985 decree) involving Phase 1, wherein the tribes were granted the right to divert water for agricultural purposes on reservation land historically irrigated and on reservation land included within certain future projects. In *Big Horn I*, this court affirmed the 1985 decree, granting the tribes the right to divert water from the Big Horn River System for agricultural purposes and subsuming livestock, municipal, domestic, and commercial uses within those purposes. This court also affirmed the district court's finding that an in-stream flow right for fisheries was not a subsuming use. The U.S. Supreme Court affirmed the *Big Horn I* decision in 1989. After the Supreme Court affirmed the Wyoming Supreme Court's decision, the tribes announced their intent to dedicate a portion of their reserved water right, which had been awarded for future projects, to instream flow for fisheries and other nonsubsumed uses in the Wind River. To that end, the tribes adopted a Wind River Interim Water Code, created the Wind River Water Resources Control Board, and on April 12, 1990, granted themselves Instream Flow Permit No. 90-001, which authorized the dedication for the 1990 irrigation season of up to 252 cubic feet per second of water in the Wind River for "fisheries restoration and enhancement, recreational uses, ground water recharge downstream benefits to irrigators and other water users."

Shortly after the issuance of Permit No. 90-001, the tribes complained to the state engineer that the diversion of water by holders of state-awarded water rights caused the Wind River flows to be less than that amount authorized by the permit. The state engineer informed the tribes that their permit was unenforceable because the tribes had been awarded only the right to divert water and that any change in the use of future project water covered by their reserved water right must be made following a diversion. The tribes nevertheless thereafter requested that the state-awarded water rights of Midvale Irrigation District be curtailed so that the in-stream flows could be maintained. The state engineer refused to honor this request, which he viewed as being an unlawful selective call.

On July 30, 1990, the tribes filed a motion in the district court for an order to show cause why the state engineer should not be held in contempt, why he should not be relieved of his duties, and why a special master should not be appointed to enforce the tribes' reserved water right. The state filed its own motion for a determination of certain administrative matters.

The district court referred the motions to a special master for a report. The special master agreed to hear all the issues raised except for the contempt issue involving the state engineer.

After hearing oral arguments on exceptions to the special master's report, the district court entered its judgment and decree on March 11, 1991, declaring that the tribes were entitled to use their reserved water right on the reservation as they deemed advisable, including in-stream flow use, without regard to Wyoming water law.

Issue:

1. May the tribes change their right to divert future project water for agricultural purposes to a right to maintain an instream flow for fishery purposes without regard to Wyoming water law?

2. Do the tribes have the right to administer all the water rights within the reservation to the exclusion of the Wyoming state engineer?

Decision: No. Judgment reversed.

Opinion by Justice Macy: "Our opinion clearly and unequivocally stated that the Tribes had the right to use a quantified amount of water on their reservation solely for agricultural and subsumed purposes and not for instream purposes. If we had intended to specify what the water could be used for merely as a methodology to determine the amount of water the Tribes could use for any purpose, we would have said so. The contrary is unmistakable.... *Big Horn I*, having been affirmed by the United States Supreme Court, is final and controlling. The Tribes do not have the unfettered right to use their quantified amount of future project water for any purpose they desire.

"We must now consider whether the district court erred when it decreed that the Tribes may change the use of their reserved future project water right from agriculture to any other purpose, including instream flows, without regard to Wyoming water law. The Tribes' first contention is that judgment and decree no. 8 in the 1983 decision gave them the right to change the 'use of the water covered by their reserved water rights' in any manner in which they deemed advisable. This position is simply not tenable. Our decision in *Big Horn I* is controlling. As we previously stated, the Tribes' reliance upon the 1983 decision for this proposition is not justified. It makes no sense whatsoever for this court to limit the use of the water for agricultural purposes and then to permit the Tribes to unilaterally change that use....

"The Wyoming legislature has for good reason precluded water right holders from unilaterally dedicating water to maintain instream flows. Water is the lifeblood of Wyoming. It is a scarce resource which must be effectively managed and efficiently used to meet the various demands of society. Wyoming's founding fathers also recognized the necessity of having state control over this vital resource.... Our decision today recognizes only that which has been the traditional wisdom relating to Wyoming water: Water is simply too precious to the well-being of society to permit water right holders unfettered control over its use....

"Article 1, § 31 of the Wyoming Constitution recognizes that state control of water is essential to the development and prosperity of Wyoming. To this end, the constitution declares that '[t]he water of all natural streams, springs, lakes, or other collections of still water' within the boundaries of Wyoming is the property of the state.... The constitution provides for the administration of state water....

"This court addressed the role of the state engineer as the administrator of the Tribes' reserved water right in *Big Horn I.* We limited the state engineer's authority as the administrator in two respects. We initially acknowledged that the Indian reserved water right existed independent of state law and procedure regarding the perfection of usufructuary rights to Wyoming water. We then determined that the state engineer, as the monitor of the Indian reserved water right, could not shut down tribal headgates once he believed that the Tribes had exceeded either the nature or the extent of their decreed right. We explained that, assuming cooperative efforts were of no avail, the state engineer would have to seek judicial enforcement of the decree against the United States and the Tribes....

"Our present decision is consistent with the duties and limitations imposed upon the state engineer in *Big Horn I.* The state engineer remains responsible to distribute the water within the Big Horn River System according to the nature, extent, and priority of right. When the nature, extent, and priority of the Indian reserved water right are clear and not respected by state appropriators, the state engineer must exercise his authority over the state appropriators to see that the tribal right is observed. When, on the other hand, it is impossible to determine if the tribal right is being violated because the right itself is in some respect ill-defined, the state engineer should promptly seek clarification from the district court so that appropriate remedial action, if needed, may be undertaken.... Should the state engineer determine that the Tribes violated the decree, he should execute an enforcement action as outlined in *Big Horn I* and summarized in the preceding paragraph."

Land Description and Title Registration

Personal property can be described fairly easily—for example, "a red 1990 Dodge Mirada two-door sedan." People can readily recognize the personal property in question by that description. On the other hand, if a man says that he owns 300 acres of land, we must have some method to designate the boundaries of the land. Moreover, the method of description must be similar to the method used to describe the adjoining parcels of land. For these reasons, some type of uniform system for describing and identifying land became necessary.

Basically there are two methods of land description—the metes and bounds description and the rectangular survey description. The metes and bounds description is the traditional method. It involves picking a starting point and marking it with a permanent stake or post so that it can always be referred to and then simply measuring distances and angles until you return to the starting point. This system was used for land description in the original 13 states of the United States.

In 1875, the U.S. government adopted a rectangular survey system that is now used in most of the states. This system divides the land into rectangular squares called sections. These sections are divided into quarter sections and can be further subdivided as needed. A section is a square mile. Where the rectangular survey system has been adopted, there will be maps or plats of the entire surface area of the land in a county, divided into 1-mile squares. Records of such plats are filed in the county courthouse. If the land involved lies within the limits of a city or town, it will be divided further into various subdivisions, which in turn are subdivided into lots.

Unlike personal property, for which physical possession is a strong indicator of ownership, ownership of land is proved by registration of title. If you purchase land, you will be given a deed transferring ownership from the previous owner to you. This deed has to be filed or registered with the proper authority in the county where the land is located. The title will then be public record, and anyone may check the county records to find out who owns that particular tract of land. Land registration is also needed for taxation purposes. Real estate is a prime source of tax revenue for municipal and county governments, and an ad valorem tax is imposed on the registered title holder of a tract of land.

Types of Ownership in Real Property

All of the rights of ownership to most objects of personal property are typically owned by one person. Seldom would a person have only a life interest in a book, a chair, or an automobile. This, of course, is because personal property typically does not have perpetual life; most items of personal property will be destroyed or deteriorate over time. Land, however, will always be there. This explains the need for a different set of ownership rights for real property than for personal property.

Fee Simple Estate

Fee simple title is the best title that an owner can have. This means that the owner has all of the rights associated with a parcel of real property and that the owner has these rights forever. The owner of the fee simple estate can sell all of these rights in the real property, or any part thereof. When the owner dies, the heirs will inherit the fee simple estate, and the title can be passed on through generations.

Life Estate

A **life estate** is an interest in real property that is limited to the life of a designated person or persons. The owner of the life estate may not cause permanent injury to the real property, but simply has the right to use it during the specified lifetime. An owner of a life estate may be viewed as a tenant who has free rent until he or she dies. When the life estate owner dies, ownership of the real property will revert to the owner who gave the life estate. If that owner is now dead, it will go to that owner's heirs or to whomever that owner has designated in his or her will.

Leasehold Estate

The owner of a **leasehold estate** has the right to occupy and use the described real property. A leasehold estate may be for a specified period, such as 1 year or 10 years, or it may be a tenancy at will, which means that either the tenant or the owner-landlord may terminate the leasehold at any time without reason, simply by giving a required notice. If you rent an apartment during the school year and you sign a lease, you will have acquired a leasehold interest in real property. Leasehold estates were discussed more fully in the previous chapter.

Easements

Easements may also be described as rights-of-way over real property. If you buy a lot in a subdivision on which you intend to build a home, no doubt there will be an easement across the back of the lot for the use of public utilities. The easement will allow the water company, the electric company, and the gas company to come on that specific area of land and erect poles, dig trenches for water lines, bury cable lines, and do other tasks associated with their business. You still own the land covered by an easement, but the easement allows another person or persons to come on that portion of the land for certain purposes. An easement is an interest in real property that is usually evidenced by a written document called a deed of easement, and this deed must be registered with the appropriate county official in the county where the real property is located. An exception to this general rule is called an **easement by prescription**. An easement by prescription is also known as an easement by adverse possession in many jurisdictions. Here there is no written easement and, in fact, there is no agreement that there should be an easement. This is simply a

CASE 2

Lowers v. United States of America

663 N.W.2d 408 (IA 2003)

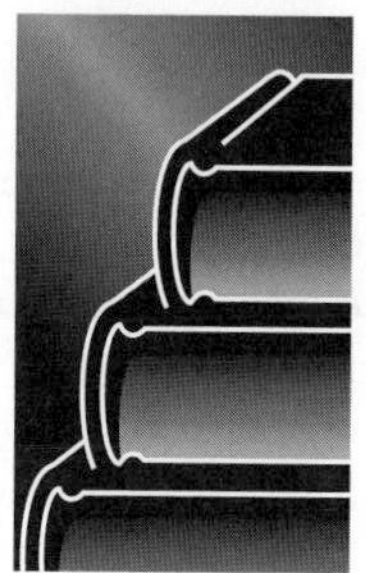

Facts: Lowers and others filed a class action in U.S. District Court, claiming that their property had been taken without just compensation. They claimed to be the successors in interest to the grantors of a 100-foot wide strip across certain farmland, which had been conveyed to a railroad company many years before. The deed provided that if the railroad company permanently abandoned the route, the strip of land "shall revert to, and become the property of the grantors, their heirs or assigns." In 1965, to try to clear up land title uncertainties, Iowa passed a statute that said that contingent claims based on deeds recorded more than 20 years previously would be invalid unless a verified claim was filed with the county recorder of deeds by July 4, 1966. No such verified claim had been filed as to the land involved here. However, the statute was amended in 1980 so as not to apply to railway abandonment claims if the abandonment occurs after July 1, 1980. The abandonment at issue here allegedly occurred in 1995. U.S. District Court asked the Iowa Supreme Court for an interpretation of Iowa law.

Issue: Were these land claims abandoned as per the 1965 Iowa statute?

Decision: Yes. Claimants have no interest in these lands.

Opinion by Justice Carter: "The federal class-action plaintiffs urge that the deed only granted an easement to the railroad company. They base that conclusion on [Iowa] cases ... in which this court concluded that a deed which specifies that the conveyance is for uses connected with construction and operation of a railroad conveys an easement rather than a fee. We are inclined to re-examine the logic underlying those conclusions. Determining the nature of the interest conveyed by reference to the intended use by the grantee seems frivolous in matters involving narrow tracts of land acquired by railroad companies. There is but one single reason for all such conveyances irrespective of whether the deed conveys a fee or an easement....

"We are satisfied that the reference in the deed to the use of the property for railroad purposes does not diminish the conveyance of all right, title, and interest of the grantor.... Nor does the fact that the deed bore a caption or title indicating 'Rt. of Way Deed' serve to limit the interest conveyed in the body of the deed....

"The federal class-action plaintiffs also rely on a line of cases that hold that a conveyance for right of way is presumed to grant only an easement.... To prevail under that line of cases, however, there must be some reference to right-of-way in the language defining the interest being conveyed....

"Our examination of the granting clause in the deed involved in the present case discloses that it grants a specified tract of land without limitation or qualification.... We are convinced that the deed conveyed a defeasible fee to the railroad company....

"We have previously considered the effect of this [Iowa] statute on reversionary interests contained in deeds conditioned on a continuing use for railway purposes. We have held in such cases that such reversionary interests created by deeds that were recorded more than twenty years prior to July 4, 1966, were extinguished if not asserted by verified claims filed with the county recorder on or before July 4, 1966.... Consequently, ... [the statute] operated to vest fee simple absolute ownership in the railroad company in 1966....

"We believe that [the 1980 amendment]... was not intended to revive property interests previously extinguished ... prior to the effective date of the amendment."

[The federal plaintiffs thus had no valid interest in the land.]

situation in which the owner of the land has allowed another person or persons to use a certain portion of the land continuously for a number of years, and the owner is now legally unable to deny the rights of that person or persons to continue to use the land. Most states have a specific statutory time before an easement by prescription will be effective.

The *Lowers* case interprets a deed, to see whether it created an easement or a fee simple (full ownership), and then interprets the state's forfeiture statute, to see how it effects the owner's rights.

Profits

In the law of real property, a **profit** is the right to remove part of someone else's land; for example, timber, crops, or minerals. Most modern cases treat profits under the same general rules as are applied to easements. Like easements, a profit may be appurtenant, attached to the ownership of other land, or in gross, owned by someone other than the adjoining landowner, regardless of whether or not that someone owns other real estate. An example of an appurtenant profit would be a neighbor who has the right to cut as much wood as he needs for his fireplace. A profit in gross would exist when the landowner has simply sold or given someone the right to remove firewood from the land.

Licenses

A **license** is permission to enter on the real property of another person. It is not an easement because it is not truly an interest in real property, but simply temporary permission to go on another person's real property for a specific purpose. A friend has an apple orchard, for example, and agrees to sell you all of the apples in the orchard for a specific price. Part of the agreement is that you will have to go into the orchard, pick the apples, and take them to market. You do not have a permanent easement to traverse that area at a later time or for any other reason.

Dower Rights

Under the common law, a widow had **dower rights** in her husband's real property. This meant that she had a life estate in one-third of all the real property that the husband had owned during his lifetime, provided she had not signed away her dower rights in a transfer of any of that real property to another person. The purpose of the dower interest was to ensure that the widow would have some means to support herself if her husband died. In those days, a woman typically was not a wage earner outside the home.

The widow's dower interest is still recognized in many states. However, some states have limited it to only that real property that the husband owned at the time of his death, thus preventing the widow from claiming an interest in real property that the husband had transferred to others during his lifetime.

Curtesy Rights

Under the common law, the husband, on the death of his wife, was entitled to a life estate in all of the real property his wife owned that was subject to inheritance. One requirement had to be met before the husband was granted **curtesy rights**: A child who could have inherited the real property had to have been born alive. Most states have replaced the common law right of curtesy with specific statutory provisions concerning a husband's right in his wife's estate.

Liens against Real Property

A lien is a claim that some person or persons may have against real property for the payment of some debt, obligation, or duty. A lien may be either voluntary or involuntary. An example of a **voluntary lien** would be the lien of a mortgage that is created when the owner of real estate borrows money and pledges the real estate as security for repayment of the loan. The lending institution, the mortgagee, then files the mortgage agreement with the county recorder in the county where the land is located, and thus has a lien against the property. The owner of the real property cannot sell the real property and give clear title until the mortgage lien is satisfied by full payment, or unless the mortgagee agrees to let the new buyer pay off the mortgage.

Examples of **involuntary liens** include a tax lien, a judgment lien, and a **mechanic's lien**. If the owner of real property fails to pay the property taxes, then the property taxes become a lien against the real property. As with a mortgage, the real property may not be sold with a clear title unless the lien is paid off. A **judgment lien** would involve a situation in which the owner of real property has been sued, the court has rendered a judgment against the owner, and the owner has not paid off the judgment. A mechanic's lien is a lien of a person or persons who furnish building materials or labor for the improvement of real property. Here again, the real property cannot be sold with a clear title unless the mechanic's lien is paid off. In some states, if a mechanic's lien is not satisfied within a specified period of time, the person holding the mechanic's lien may sue the owner, get a judgment, and have the real property sold at a sheriff's auction to satisfy the lien. Because mechanic's lien statutes differ from state to state, it is advisable to find out what the law is in your state. Otherwise, you might find your home sold for a very minor debt.

Acquisition of Ownership to Real Property

Real property may be acquired in various ways.

Legislative Grant

Real property may be acquired by legislative grant from the national government or by a patent. A patent is a document similar to a deed that the government issues to convey a portion of the public lands to one or more persons. In the early days of this nation, the national Homestead Act allowed settlers to establish their homestead on public land. After the passage of a specified period of time and compliance with the requirements of the act, the homesteader would be granted a patent to this land.

Purchase

Real property may be acquired by purchase. This, of course, is the most common method of acquisition.

Inheritance

Real property may be acquired by inheritance. You may inherit land from your parents, grandparents, or other persons who die and name you in their will, or if you are the legal heir, you would inherit by intestate succession.

Gift

Owners of land may decide to give a certain parcel of land to their children, to some other person or persons, or to some charity during their lifetime. A gift is not valid unless there is a proper deed that evidences a transfer of title from the donor, or giver, to the donee, that is, the person receiving the gift.

Accretion

Accretion simply means that the owner of land has acquired more land because of a change in the course of a river or stream that runs alongside the property. For example, over a period of years, sand and soil have been deposited on your side of a stream, thus increasing the actual land that you can use. A stream may also recede, giving more land between the previous bank and the present level of the stream.

Adverse Possession

After you use or occupy real property continuously for a statutory period of time, the original owner loses the right to object to your possession of the land. By your possession, which was adverse to the owner's interests, and the failure of the owner to enforce his or her rights to evict you, you have acquired ownership by **adverse possession**.

Eminent Domain

This method of acquiring land applies to governmental entities, such as school districts, cities, states, and the national government. This method of acquisition, **eminent domain**, also is often referred to as **condemnation**. It is the right of government to take private property for the use of the public. The owner of the private property must be paid a fair amount for the land taken.

Dedication

Acquisition through dedication is also a method of acquiring land that applies only to governmental entities. A real estate developer of a new subdivision dedicates the streets to the city. The streets then become public property. **Dedication** is a gift by the landowner to a governmental entity, and it is an effective acquisition only if the governmental entity accepts the gift. For example, a person may want to dedicate certain land to a city for use as a park that will be named after the donor. The city may or may not accept the gift with that condition. If the gift is accepted, then appropriate documents are executed and the land becomes public property that is owned and maintained by the city.

Process of Transfer of Ownership

The transfer of land from the present owner to the acquiring owner must be evidenced by a written document that can be recorded in the records of the county where the land is located.

Deeds

The transfer document used in an acquisition by purchase or by gift is a deed. This is a written document that is signed by the owner or owners of the real property and that conveys or transfers the owner's rights, title, and interest in specifically described real estate to the person or persons who are acquiring the ownership. The present owner or owners are called the grantors, and the person or persons acquiring ownership are called the grantees. The grantors must sign the deed in the presence of a notary public who will verify that they signed it. The deed may be in the form of a **warranty deed** or a **quitclaim deed**.

In a warranty deed, the grantor expressly guarantees that the ownership being transferred is free from the claims of others. That is, the grantor guarantees to the grantee that the grantor is transferring a clear and merchantable title. A quitclaim deed states that the grantor is transferring all of his or her rights, title, and interest in the real property to the grantee, but the grantor makes no guarantee that the grantee will have a clear title free from the claims of others.

The grantor or grantors in a warranty deed may reserve some rights or may make the warranty subject to certain rights of others. For example, the grantors in a warranty deed may reserve subsurface mineral rights. Then, if oil is ever found under the land, it belongs to the grantor. If there is a mortgage on the land, the grantor-seller may deed the title subject to the rights of the mortgagee, normally a bank or other lending institution. Thus, the new purchaser gets title subject to the lien of the mortgage. If there are private restrictions on the real estate, the deed will transfer title subject to those restrictions. Because taxes are a lien, the deed will also specify that the transfer of title is subject to unpaid taxes if any remain unpaid at the time of the transfer of title.

Warranties of Title in the Sale of Real Property

The person transferring title, the grantor, is presumed to have made certain warranties of title even though those warranties were not expressly stated in the deed. The grantor warrants that he or she owns the real property that is being conveyed, subject to restrictions, such as unpaid taxes, an unpaid mortgage, easements, or any other liens against the real property. The grantor also warrants that he or she has the right to convey the property. In the case of the transfer of title by a corporation, the officers signing the deed warrant that they have authority to act for the corporation. The grantor also guarantees that the land is not encumbered by any right or interest other than the liens or easements that are stated in the deed. Thus, the grantor is guaranteeing that the purchaser will have the right to enjoy the use of the property without interference by the grantor or others at a later date.

Even though the grantor guarantees that the buyer is being given a clear title, the buyer should request further assurances. After all, should there be problems later, the grantor who made those guarantees may have spent the money that the buyer paid for the real property, may have moved out of the area, may have died, may have filed bankruptcy, or may simply be judgment-proof. Before consummating the purchase of real property, the buyer should require from the seller either an **abstract of title** showing good and merchantable title certified to the date of the closing of the transaction or a policy of **title insurance** for the real estate.

An abstract of title is a history of the title to a piece of real estate. Usually beginning with the original transfer from the U.S. government to the homesteader, it then contains brief copies of every deed, mortgage, or other document that affects the title, from that date to the present. It also contains copies of any liens or encumbrances that have been filed against the real property. The abstract of title, however, covers only those documents that have been recorded in the county recorder's office in the county where the real property is situated. It does not cover any unrecorded documents that may have been agreed on by parties involved in the chain of title.

The abstractor, the person preparing the abstract, does not certify that the title is clear from liens and encumbrances and is merchantable. The abstract must be taken to an attorney who will examine it and then give an opinion stating whether or not the title is merchantable.

A policy of title insurance is an insurance policy that requires the insurance company to pay any judgment, legal fees, and court costs, in any action brought by someone claiming title against you. Before the title insurance company issues a policy, it first verifies that the title is clear and merchantable. Only then will it issue a policy of title insurance.

The warranties made by the seller-grantor, the issuance of a title insurance policy, and the preparation and examination of an abstract of title do not protect the buyer against any defects in the improvements on the real property, such as the house, the garage, or other buildings. The courts originally used the doctrine of caveat emptor, "Let the buyer beware," with regard to the condition of the improvements on the real property. Buyers have an opportunity to examine the real property, and if they do not request any express warranties or agreement as to the buildings, then they get what they see. Of course, an exception will be made when the seller is guilty of fraud or misrepresentation. If the seller lied to the buyer about some material fact and this concerned a condition that the buyer could not have checked with the use of ordinary inspection methods, then the courts will simply void the transaction. The buyer also may be able to secure additional monetary damages.

Another exception to the general rule of caveat emptor with regard to the buildings on the real property being transferred may occur when a new home has been constructed on the real property. Many states have specific laws that make the builder responsible for defects in the new home for a specific period of time, usually 1 year. Because this is a matter of state law, the buyer of real property should either secure an express warranty from the seller or check the statutory law in the given state.

National Regulation

The **U.S. Real Estate Settlement Procedures Act (RESPA)** requires the disclosure of the costs of a real estate transaction to the buyer prior to the consummation of such a transaction. The costs that must be disclosed are the loan origination fees, loan discount points, appraisal fees, attorney's fees, inspection fees, charges for title search or title insurance, and land survey fee. This law was passed in 1974 primarily to let buyers know just what they are paying for.

RESPA also prohibits certain practices that are not in the best interests of the buyer. The lending institution is not allowed to give a kickback to any person for referring the borrower to them, to charge or accept fees except for services actually performed, or to require that the borrower purchase title insurance from any specific title insurance company that the lender prefers. The parties also cannot be forced to use an attorney that the lending institution selects. They are free to hire one of their own choosing.

Financing of Real Estate Transactions

The great majority of real estate transactions involve some type of financing arrangement because few people have the cash required in exchange for the title to real property. Financing can be handled through either a land contract or a real estate mortgage.

Land Contracts

A **land contract** is an agreement between a buyer and a seller regarding the purchase of a parcel of land. The contract is a conditional sale of the land, subject to payment of the purchase price by the buyer. Typically, the buyer will make a down payment and will agree to make periodic payments of interest and principal for a specified period of time, either until the entire balance of the principal is paid or until the principal balance is paid down to a level that the buyer can secure a real estate mortgage from a lending institution. The down payment required for a land contract transaction is often less than that required in a transaction involving a real estate mortgage.

On execution of a land contract, the buyer is entitled to possession and control of the land and the improvements thereon. The buyer is the equitable owner of the rights to possess and control the land, subject to the legal rights of the fee simple titleholder who is selling the real property. In other words, the buyer may not use the real property in any way he or she wants to; however, the buyer does have the duty to keep the premises insured against fire and other risks of loss. The buyer may not add to or tear down the improvements without the specific permission of the seller. The buyer has the right to use, control, and enjoy the land and improvements, but may not materially change the land or improvements.

Mortgages

A real estate **mortgage** is a document wherein the owner of real property pledges that real property as security for the payment of a debt or some other obligation. The owner of the property, who is called the mortgagor, does not transfer title to the land in this document. The mortgagee, normally a bank or other lending institution, obtains a nonpossessory interest in the real estate. If the debt or obligation is not satisfied in accordance with the conditions for repayment set out in the mortgage document, the mortgagee may commence legal proceedings to foreclose on the mortgage and to have the real property sold. The proceeds will then be applied to the balance owed on the mortgage. The owner-mortgagor will receive any proceeds from the sale of the real property that are left after the payment of the mortgage balance, plus reasonable attorney's fees and court costs.

Filing and Recording Requirements

A mortgage need not be recorded in any public office to be valid between the mortgagor and the mortgagee. However, if a mortgage is not filed in the office of the recorder of the county where the real property is located, the mortgagee's lien will not be superior to any subsequent liens that may be placed against the real property. For example, an individual borrows money, executes a promissory note, and signs a mortgage on the real property, but the mortgagee does not record the mortgage. Later, a judgment is rendered against the owner as the result of an automobile accident. If the mortgage was not recorded properly, it would not have priority over the judgment. Thus, immediately after a mortgage is executed, it is very important to file and record the mortgage with the recorder of the county where the real property is located.

Defaults

The mortgagor may default on the mortgage by failing to pay the mortgage payments, the real property taxes, or the payments for insurance as they become due, or by doing an act that would endanger the security interest of the mortgagee.

CASE 3

Claflin v. Commercial State Bank
487 N.W.2d 242 (MN App. 1992)

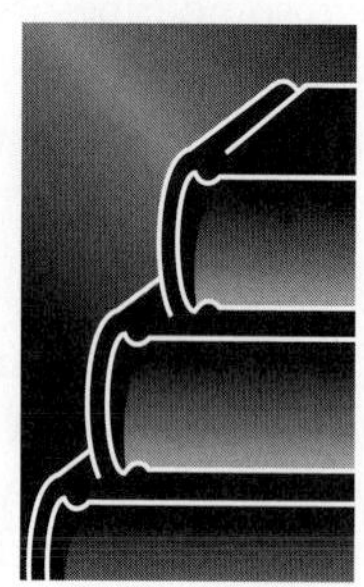

Facts: Appellant Margaret Claflin seeks review of a judgment dismissing her claims against respondent Commercial State Bank of Two Harbors. Margaret sought to have set aside two mortgages the bank had taken in exchange for loans granted to her son, Gregory, while he held record title to her home. Margaret also sought punitive damages. After presentation of Margaret's evidence in the jury trial, the bank's motion for a directed verdict was granted, dismissing all counts. The trial court held that the bank had no duty to investigate beyond the record title and that there was no evidence of any willful action by the bank against Margaret.

Greg's parents, Margaret and Amos Claflin, bought the real estate in question (the "Property") in 1973. The Property consists of a two-story home on about 40 acres in rural Two Harbors, Minnesota. In 1988, Amos died. Greg and his wife Mary returned to Two Harbors for Amos' funeral and decided to relocate there.

By January 1990, Greg convinced his mother to sign two documents. One was a note (the "Note") that Greg drafted by copying portions of the mortgage he and Mary gave her parents. Greg had his mother come to his office to sign the Note and have it notarized. Margaret's testimony indicates that she did not consider whether the Note should be recorded against the Property; she believed it was "official" because it was notarized.

Mother and son also went to the county recorder's office. There, Greg obtained a blank Minnesota Uniform Conveyancing Quit Claim Deed that he prepared, and had his mother execute before a notary. By this deed, which was duly recorded, Margaret quit-claimed the Property to Greg. Both documents were executed and notarized on January 25, 1990; only the deed was recorded.

On February 2, 1990, Greg applied to the bank for a loan to be secured by a mortgage on the Property (the "mortgage loan"). He told Bank Vice President Lance Schwanke that the purpose of the loan was to consolidate unsecured debt. Greg obtained a loan application and had his wife sign it before it was completed.

Schwanke went to Greg and Mary's home with the mortgage loan documents on the evening of February 9, 1990. The evidence demonstrates that portions of these documents were not completed when Mary signed them. Although it is not clear what information was contained at that time, none of the completed documents in evidence contain the street address of the Property; they contain a lengthy legal description. Mary testified that she did not read the documents, but simply executed them that evening. Mary and her infant son left Minnesota on February 13, 1990, to reside with Mary's parents in Philadelphia.

The mortgage loan documents were then dated March 21, 1990, and notarized by Schwanke, who had in fact witnessed the signatures on a much earlier date. The proceeds were disbursed to Greg, mainly through 14 cashier's checks issued to various unsecured creditors. Additional cashier's checks were disbursed for expenses related to the mortgage. After April 13, 1990, only $1,300 of the original $45,000 remained undisbursed.

One evening in June of 1990, Mary, still in Philadelphia, learned that Greg had acquired a new truck. Mary immediately called Schwanke at home regarding the source of these funds. Mary then learned for the first time that the documents she signed for Greg in February placed a mortgage on Margaret's home. Mary immediately insisted that all disbursements be stopped. Mary then arranged a trip to Minnesota.

When Mary arrived, the Claflin family held a meeting. Margaret learned for the first time that Greg had mortgaged the Property, contrary to their understanding. Mary learned that Margaret had conveyed the Property to Greg in a secret deal. Margaret retained an attorney who insisted that Greg and Mary immediately convey the Property back to Margaret. Greg and Mary gave Margaret a warranty deed, duly recorded on June 27, 1990.

Margaret then sought to assume the mortgage loan, submitting a financial statement to the Bank. The Bank instead elected to accelerate the mortgage loan, which contained a due-on-sale clause, because the property had been conveyed to Margaret. On September 10, 1990, Schwanke wrote to Greg and Mary indicating that the mortgage loan was more than 60 days past due. Seven days later, the bank's attorneys prepared a Notice of Mortgage Foreclosure Sale scheduled for November 14, 1990. On October 26, 1990, Margaret brought this suit against the bank.

Issue: Did the trial court err in granting a directed verdict in favor of the bank?

Decision: Yes. Judgment reversed.

Opinion by Judge Norton: "Minnesota law requires every conveyance of real estate to be recorded; unrecorded conveyances shall be void against any subsequent purchaser in good faith for valuable consideration.... Under the recording act, a purchaser in good faith is one who gives consideration without actual, implied or constructive notice of the inconsistent outstanding rights of others.... The purpose of the recording act is to protect those who purchase real estate in reliance upon the record.... Implied notice has been found where one has 'actual knowledge of facts which would put one on further inquiry....'

"If one is aware that someone other than the vendor is living on the land, one has a duty to inquire concerning the rights of the inhabitant of the property and is chargeable with notice of all facts which such inquiry would disclose.... One is not a bona fide purchaser if one had knowledge of facts which ought to have put one on an inquiry that would have led to knowledge of a conveyance....

"A purchaser who has actual, implied or constructive notice of the outstanding rights of another is not a bona fide purchaser entitled to the protection of the recording act.... Actual, open possession and use of property puts a subsequent purchaser on inquiry notice of the possessor's rights in the property.... Actual possession of real property is notice to all the world of the title and rights of the person so in possession and also of all facts connected therewith which reasonable inquiry would have developed.... Implied notice differs from constructive notice arising from the record of instruments because the record is notice only of what appears upon its face....

"In Minnesota, clear, actual, exclusive possession of the granted premises by the grantor, even after delivery and recording of the deed, is notice against purchasers and mortgagees of the grantor's possible interest in the property....

"In order to have status as a bona fide purchaser the mortgagee's inquiry must be directed to the person in possession; inquiry of the mortgagor, who may have reason to conceal the truth, is not sufficient. The supreme court has stated, 'Having made no inquiry, [the bank] is chargeable with notice of the actual condition of the title to the land.'

"Schwanke testified that he never contacted Margaret, although he knew she was living on the Property. Schwanke also acted to ensure that only Greg would be contacted by the others involved. Schwanke knew the title opinion contained an exception for the rights of occupants but he ignored it as 'boilerplate.' The Bank argues that it satisfied its duty of inquiry by asking Greg what interest his mother had in the Property. We disagree. Greg told the bank that his mother was simply living there with his permission. The Bank knowingly prevented and avoided inquiry directed to Margaret. The evidence demonstrates that, had the Bank inquired of Margaret, it could have learned that she asserted a superior interest. The Bank is therefore chargeable with notice of Margaret's unrecorded interests....

"In summary, most of the evidence presented clearly supports Margaret's claims; contrary evidence was generally impeached. Schwanke admitted that he had Mary pre-sign documents which were not complete, which were completed and notarized much later, and that he had previously made false statements about that. Schwanke admitted that he ignored the title opinion exception regarding the rights of occupants. He admitted that he inquired only of Greg regarding Margaret's possible rights in the Property. Greg admitted that he and his mother had intended to create a life estate. We must accept that evidence as true, including the reasonable inferences which may be drawn therefrom....

"In addition to her claim that the mortgage is invalid against her interests, Margaret sought punitive damages based on the Bank's conduct in taking the mortgage....

"The evidence establishes that the Bank was more than disinterested in Margaret's rights. The Bank, through Schwanke, not only avoided but actually prevented inquiry directed to Margaret. These acts effectively prevented her from learning that the Bank planned to grant Greg a mortgage loan against the Property. This cause of action arose when the mortgage became an encumbrance against the Property in March 1990. Therefore, while the Bank's conduct may demonstrate deliberate disregard for Margaret's rights, the standard applicable here is that of willful indifference. We hold that Margaret presented sufficient evidence to support a verdict that the Bank acted with willful indifference to her rights."

If the mortgagor defaults, then the mortgagee may file a suit of **foreclosure** against the mortgagor. At that time, the entire balance of the mortgage is due and payable, and if the court awards the mortgagee a judgment of foreclosure, the property will be sold at a sheriff's sale. The proceeds of the sale of the real estate will be applied first to the unpaid balance of the mortgage, interest, and the legal fees and court costs of the foreclosure suit. The balance will then be paid to the mortgagor. If the sale does not bring enough money to pay off the mortgage debt, the mortgagor will remain liable for the unpaid balance of the mortgage.

Many states have enacted statutes that allow the mortgagor to get a delay of foreclosure in certain hardship cases. Another statutory procedure that favors the mortgagor is called the right of **redemption**. This is the mortgagor's statutory right to repurchase the real estate within a specified time after the foreclosure. In other words, a mortgagor can have the property back by paying the amount for which it was sold plus the expenses incurred in the foreclosure and sale.

When the real property is sold by the sheriff, the sheriff is authorized by law to execute to the purchaser a sheriff's deed that is free and clear of the mortgage lien.

Trusts

Nature

A **trust** is any arrangement whereby the owner of property transfers its ownership to a natural or corporate person, called the **trustee**, who is instructed to hold the property for the benefit of a person or persons who are designated as **beneficiaries**. A trust can be created for any purpose that is legal and not against public policy. The owner of the property interest that is being transferred must instruct the trustee as to how that interest is to be administered for the beneficiaries. For example, an owner of an interest in property may transfer that interest to the trustee for a person's benefit and may instruct the trustee to distribute only the earnings on the property and not to distribute the principal, or **corpus**, of the trust until a later date. It is important that the trustee have specific instructions as to how the property is to be administered for the beneficiaries.

Types

Trusts are divided into two basic categories. A **living trust**, also called an inter vivos trust, is a trust that takes effect and is administered during the lifetime of the transferor of the property. A **testamentary trust** is created prior to the death of the person who sets it up but does not take effect until that person's death. These voluntary arrangements should be distinguished from a "constructive trust," which is a remedy for the fraudulent acquisition of property, imposed by a court of equity in favor of the real or intended owner. Equity says that the defrauder holds the property "in trust" for the rightful owner.

Creation

A trust is not necessarily a contract because no consideration is required from the beneficiaries. It is in effect a gift from the giver, also called the **settlor**, to the beneficiary through a middle person; namely, the trustee. To create an express trust, there must be a written document, which is normally called a **trust agreement** or a **deed of trust**. Although it is not necessary for any specific language to be used, certain requirements must be met. If the trust involves an interest in land, then the Statute of Frauds requires that the details of the transfer of that interest be set out in writing.

There is also a limit to how long a trust may exist before the interest vests in beneficiaries. The rule to be complied with here is called the **rule against perpetuities**. This rule prohibits a person from creating a trust that remains in existence forever. A general statement of the rule is that an interest in property, if conveyed for the benefit of a beneficiary, must be turned over or vested in the beneficiary no more than 21 years, plus the period of gestation of a new life, after the expiration of the life or lives of some person or people who were in being when the trust was created. There are exceptions to this rule if the purpose of the trust is charitable. Most states have a statutory maximum time during which a trust may remain operative. Here the specific state laws would govern.

Exhibit 20.1: Flowchart of a Trust

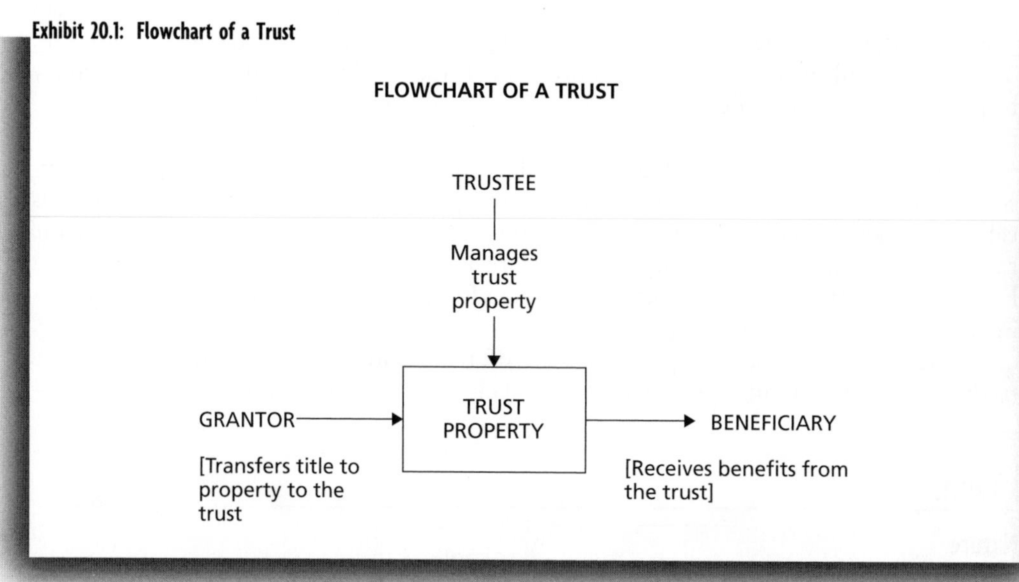

Revocability

An inter vivos trust may be declared either revocable or irrevocable. If a person sets up an **irrevocable trust** for the benefit of beneficiaries, then that person, the settlor, may not revoke or change the trust at a later date. Such a trust may be modified, with the consent of all the beneficiaries, provided such modification would not frustrate its original intent. However, this would only be possible in exceptional circumstances because the courts will not allow a change in a trust if this would change the trust's original intended purpose. If the settlor sets up a **revocable trust**, this means that this person transfers title to certain property to a trustee for the benefit of specific beneficiaries, but may at any time change his or her mind and take back the corpus of the trust from the trustee.

Many wealthy people deed property over to a trustee so that the trustee can manage it for them. Thus, these people are both settlor and beneficiary. Having a professional manage their property relieves them of the responsibilities of management and gives them the income, less a managerial service charge. If such a trust is revocable, the settlor can terminate the trust at any time.

Testamentary trusts do not become effective until the death of the settlor, and they are not revocable after the settlor's death. But anytime before the settlor's death, such a trust may be revoked simply by changing the last will and testament that contains or refers to it.

CASE 4

CHILDREN OF THE CHIPPEWA, OTTAWA, AND POTAWATOMY TRIBES v. THE UNIVERSITY OF MICHIGAN

305 N.W.2d 522 (MI 1981)

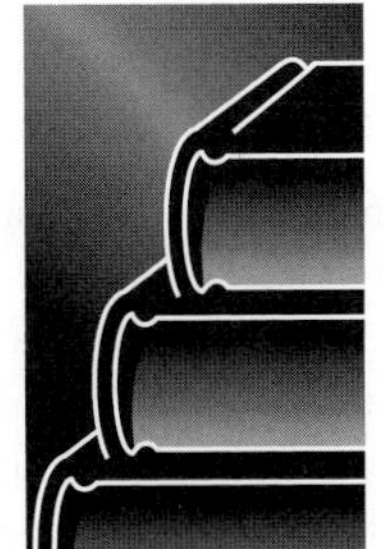

Facts: On September 29, 1817, the Treaty of Fort Meigs was executed. The Chippewa, Ottawa, and Potawatomy tribes were signatories of the first part, and the government of the United States of America was the signatory of the second part. The treaty was drafted entirely by the representative of the United States. The defendant, the University of Michigan, was not a party to the treaty.

Notwithstanding this latter fact, the plaintiffs, who are descendants of the members of the signatory tribes, brought an action in equity before the Circuit Court of Washtenaw County seeking to have a trust declared in their favor against defendant based on the provisions of this treaty. The trial court denied plaintiffs' request for a declaration of a trust in their favor. Plaintiffs appealed.

Issue: Did the evidence show an intent to create a trust?

Decision: No. Judgment affirmed.

Opinion Per Curiam: "The original complaint was filed August 5, 1971. It was claimed that Article 16 of the treaty created a trust whereby certain land, belonging to the Indians, was conveyed to defendant for purposes of ensuring that the Indians and their descendants would receive an education in the European fashion. In support of this contention, the complaint cited certain alleged historical events, including the vesting of title of the conveyed parcels of land in the defendant; the then-University president Lewis Cass's appointment of two trustees to locate and survey these lands; the patenting of these lands to defendant by the government of the United States in 1824; and the release by one Church of St. Anne of its interest of the lands in favor of defendant.

"The inclusion of St. Anne's Church in the complaint was occasioned by the plaintiffs' assertion that the treaty compelled the church to provide for the primary and secondary education of the Indians. The complaint then contends that the treaty imposed a concomitant duty upon defendant to ensure the Indians' college education. It is then claimed that the aforementioned conveyance by the church to the defendant merged the foregoing duties wholly into defendant's realm of responsibility. . . .

"The treaty provision that is the primary focus of the present dispute, Article 16, reads:

> *Some of the Ottawa, Chippewa, and Potawatomy Tribes, being attached to the Catholic religion, and believing they may wish some of their children hereafter educated, do grant to the rector of the Catholic church of St. Anne of Detroit, for the use of the said church, and to the corporation of the college at Detroit, for the use of the said college, to be retained or sold, as the said rector and corporation may judge expedient, each, one-half of three sections of land, to contain 640 acres, on the river Raisin, at a place called Macon; and three sections of land not yet located, which tracts were reserved, for the use of the said Indians, by the treaty of Detroit, in 1807; and the superintendent of Indian affairs, in the territory of Michigan, is authorized, on the part of the said Indians, to select the said tracts of land.*

"Trial commenced on August 21, 1978. During the trial, numerous exhibits were received along with much expert testimony from all sides. On February 28, 1979, the trial judge issued a meticulously researched and well drafted written opinion, thoroughly discussing the historical and procedural facets of this novel action and carefully setting forth the law which he believed controlling of this case. The opinion denied relief on all counts.

"We have painstakingly reviewed the findings of fact in that opinion and agree with the trial judge in respect to those findings. The task of leaping back over 160 years in time is most difficult, and the trial judge is to be commended for his efforts in that regard. . . .

"It is first asserted that the trial judge erred in finding that the Indians could not have owned fee simple title to any lands conveyed from the year 1790 forward. In so ruling, the trial court found *Oneida Indian Nation v. County of Oneida*, 414 U.S. 661... (1974), to be dispositive. We agree. The thrust of *Oneida* is that the 1790 Nonintercourse Act created a right of occupancy rather than a title in fee simple in the Indians as to lands held by them. The trial court held that the federal government possesses power to convey the fee as to lands occupied by Indian Tribes and all questions with respect to rights of occupancy and conditions of extinguishment of Indian title are solely for the federal government. The trial court went on to say:

> *This court will concede that in 1817 the Indians could have imposed an express trust on the lands possessed by them and granted to the Church and College by the 1817 Treaty, but this simply was not done at that time.*

"Given this recognition by the trial court, it is difficult to understand the plaintiffs' argument on the issue. The trial court's ultimate decision obviates further discussion in any event. . . .

"A third issue raised by plaintiffs is whether the trial court was justified in holding that Article 16 of the Treaty of Fort Meigs constituted a gift of lands to Father Richard and to defendant. We believe that it did. . . .

"The operative language in Article 16 provides that some of the plaintiffs' forefathers: 'do grant to the . . . church . . . for the use of the said church, and to the . . . college . . . for the use of the said college, *to be retained or sold, as the said rector and corporation may judge expedient. . . .* ' (Emphasis added.)

"Clearly, the grant itself is a completed one and not conditional in nature. Nor do its terms encompass more than one transaction. The land is donated jointly to the church, and to the corporation. The later division of the parcels was a consequence of Father Richard's discretion, a discretion Article 16 allowed him to exercise.

"The evidence points to an almost reverential attitude toward Father Richard on the Indians' part. This attitude was commingled with an attitude of filial affection. The evidence also points to a clear donative intent on the Indians' part as regards Father Richard and encompasses a similar attitude toward the educational institution which the Indians very properly regarded as an extension of Father Richard's personality and influence.

"We disagree with plaintiffs' continued assertions that the treaty, and particularly Article 16, were the sole product of Lewis Cass's efforts. The evidence does not support such a contention in any way. Rather, the treaty was the cumulative result of extended negotiations involving many leaders on both sides.

"Both the expert testimony and the language of the treaty itself reflect the likelihood of a present donative intent on the part of the Indians at the time of the treaty's execution. . . .

"The next claim of error challenges the trial court's decision that Article 16 created no express trust in the Indians' favor.

"It is a general principle of trust law that a trust is created only if the settlor manifests an intention to create a trust, and it is essential that there be an explicit declaration of trust accompanied by a transfer of property to one for the benefit of another. . . . Further, an express trust in real property must be in writing, under the hand of the party to be charged. . . .

"We find that the plaintiffs' substantive arguments in support of the theory of an express trust are based on speculation and irrelevancy. . . .

"The last claim on appeal concerns the issue of a constructive trust. The trial court rejected this theory for several reasons: (1) the university was not a party to the negotiations and committed no misconduct in the treaty negotiations; (2) the Indians were represented by competent interpreters and a trusted Indian agent; (3) the United States evidenced no unjust conduct at the negotiations, its main intent being to secure a cession of a significant area in Ohio; (4) the Article 16 land was of minimal value when conveyed and when the university tried to sell it; and (5) the two cases cited by plaintiffs are distinguishable. We agree.

"In a pristinely humane world, it might be honorable and fair to compel defendant to offer comprehensive scholarships in gratitude for the 1817 conveyance. Certainly, the cost of higher education is subject to the rigors of inflation as are all other things, and the plaintiffs, like everyone else, could benefit by the financial assistance they seek. However, constructive trusts are not used to requite obligations imposed by conscience alone. Rather, they are imposed solely where a balancing of equities discloses that it would be unfair to act otherwise. Where, as here, the language of the treaty and the historical evidence reflect a gift *inter vivos* and nothing more, the imposition of a constructive trust is neither equitably nor legally desirable.

"Based on the foregoing, it is readily apparent that the judgment of the trial court should be and the same is hereby affirmed. No costs, questions of novel impression, and public significance being involved."

Trustee

A trustee can be an individual or an institution, such as a bank, a trust company, or a similar financial institution. The trustee is governed by a given state's laws concerning the handling of trust funds. A trustee generally has the right to make decisions concerning the investment of the trust corpus in accordance with the settlor's directions, provided those directions are not contrary to the law of the particular jurisdiction. For example, a trustee must generally invest trust funds more conservatively than he or she would invest personal funds.

A trustee may not commingle the property of a trust with property that the trustee owns individually or with property that the trustee is administering as the trustee of another trust. Generally speaking, the trustee owes a duty of loyalty to the beneficiaries; that is, the trustee's job is to conserve the corpus for the beneficiaries' benefit and yet to secure the best income and growth possible. The trustee will be required to use the skill, judgment, and care reasonably expected of a person in that capacity. Banks, trust companies, and other corporate trustees will of course be required to use a high degree of skill, care, and judgment in the management of trusts because that is their profession. An individual who is acting as a trustee would not be required to use the same high degree of skill, care, and judgment but would be required to use reasonable care and judgment in the handling of the trust funds. Most trusts involving large sums of money or property will be administered by corporate trustees who have professional investment knowledge and expertise.

The last case involved an American Indian claim under a trust allegedly created by their ancestors.

Significance of This Chapter

Everyone needs to understand the various rights involved in ownership of real property because both individuals and businesses may become parties to many legal relationships involving land. This chapter answers many of the questions that relate to the ownership and transfer of real property.

IMPORTANT TERMS AND CONCEPTS

abstract of title
accretion
adverse possession
beneficiaries
condemnation
corpus
curtesy rights
dedication
deed of trust
dower rights
easement by prescription
easements
eminent domain
fee simple title
foreclosure
involuntary liens
irrevocable trust
judgment lien
land contract
leasehold estate
license
life estate
living trust
mechanic's lien
mineral rights
mortgage
profit
quitclaim deed
redemption
revocable trust
riparian rights
rule against perpetuities
settlor
testamentary trust
title insurance
trust
trust agreement
trustee
U.S. Real Estate Settlement Procedures Act (RESPA)
voluntary lien
warranty deed

QUESTIONS AND PROBLEMS FOR DISCUSSION

1. If you own an acre of land that fronts a lake, what are the boundaries of your real property ownership, above, below, and on the lakefront?

2. Under the rectangular survey method, land was divided into rectangular squares called sections. How large is a section?

3. What is eminent domain? Give an example when the legal process of condemnation would be used.

4. What is an abstract of title? Does the preparation of an abstract by an abstractor guarantee the title is merchantable? Discuss the use of an abstract of title in the purchase of real property.

5. J. P. Acker, Jr. brought this declaratory judgment action against M. M. Guinn to determine whether certain mineral rights passed under a deed executed in 1941. The deed conveyed "an undivided one-half interest in and to all of the oil, gas, and other minerals in and under, and that may be

produced from" a tract of 86 1/2 acres in Cherokee County. Acker, who held through the grantee, claimed that the deed included an interest in the iron ore on the land; Guinn, who held under the grantor, said that the deed did not include the iron ore. Over the years, the main use made of iron ore from Cherokee County had been as a foundation base for road construction; iron ore was also used in the manufacture of cement. Because of its high silica content, this iron ore had to be mixed with other ores to make pig iron. The ore deposits were solid beds, varying in thickness from a few inches to 3 or 4 feet. There were outcrops of the ore deposits at some places, and the deposits ranged in depth to as much as 50 feet below the surface. The ore had to be strip-mined, which would destroy or substantially impair the use of the surface for farming, ranching, or timber production. The trial court granted Acker's motion for summary judgment; the court of civil appeals reversed.

How should the Supreme Court rule, and why?

6. In 1957, James and Dolly Brown, husband and wife, purchased 80 acres of land from William and Faith Bost, joint tenants. The Bosts gave the Browns a statutory warranty deed. The deed was absolute on its face, and it purported to convey an estate in fee simple. In fact, a prior owner in the chain of title had conveyed a two-thirds interest in the mineral rights in 1947. This prior conveyance was not discovered in title searches that the Bosts had done in 1958 and 1968, when they used the land as collateral for loans. Faith Bost died in 1994; William had died before that. Naureen Lober was appointed as executor of Faith's estate. On May 8, 1994, the Browns granted a coal option to the Consolidated Coal Company for $6,000. On May 4, 1996, the Browns learned that they owned only one-third of the coal rights. They accepted $2,000 from the coal company and then sued Faith's estate for damages of $4,000. The trial court dismissed the lawsuit, holding that only the first two warranties in the Bosts' deed had been breached, that this had occurred in 1957, when the deed was delivered, and that the claim was thus barred by the 10-year statute of limitations. The Browns appealed.

Do the Browns still have a claim? Explain.

7. The city of Renton built a concrete reservoir. About once a year, from 1908 to 1929, the city had to drain and clean the reservoir to prevent the buildup of contamination. The wastewater pipe ran from the base of the reservoir and was discharged into a small gully. The wastewater then ran down into a small stream, which crossed Downie's land. Downie bought his two acres in 1981; it was then "unused, unimproved, unoccupied, unfenced, and covered with underbrush and second growth trees." In 1988, Downie dammed up the stream and created a one-third acre pond, which he stocked with 25,000 fish. The city's cleaning of the reservoir in September 1989 resulted in the discharge of wastewater, debris, and mud into Downie's pond. The trial court dismissed Downie's suit for an injunction, holding that the city had acquired an easement by prescription. Downie appealed.

What result, and why?

8. Medlin died in 1989, survived by his wife Minnie and nine children. Five of the children sued Minnie and the other four children for a declaratory judgment interpreting T. W.'s will. The will gave Minnie all of T. W.'s property "to have the use and benefit of the same during her natural life, and at her death, all of such property in her hands shall completely vest in my children, share and share alike." In another paragraph the will gave Minnie "the full and complete management, use and enjoyment of all of my property during her said lifetime, including all rents and revenues to be derived therefrom." The plaintiffs argued that Minnie received only a limited life estate, for her use and benefit, rather than a general life estate and that, similarly, the rents and revenues earned during her lifetime were not hers absolutely but were only to be used for her reasonable support. The trial court rejected both of these arguments. The plaintiffs appealed.

What was Minnie's ownership interest in the land? Explain.

CHAPTER 21

Real Property—Environmental Restrictions

Chapter Objectives

This chapter will:

- Discuss the need for environmental regulations for the use and occupancy of real property.
- Explain the purpose and effect of local zoning laws.
- Explain the use of private restrictive covenants that regulate the use of real property.
- Discuss national environmental policy and laws.

This chapter deals with the many problems involved in the use of real estate by its owner. The initial reaction from most people is: "It's my land, and I ought to be able to use it as I see fit." If we look back to the era of our grandfathers, or perhaps our great-grandfathers, we would find that owners of real estate could use their land in any way that they saw fit, provided their use did not cause a **nuisance** as defined by the law. Such a nuisance would do harm to the neighboring property owners or would interfere with their peaceable use and enjoyment of their real estate. There were no restrictions on house sizes, on the erection of fences or any outbuildings, on the number of families housed on a property, or on the use of a home to operate a beauty shop, a barbershop, a small appliance repair shop, or some similar type of business. In those days, we did not have the density problem or the traffic problem that we have today in most cities. Plenty of land was available, and far fewer people were making a demand for its use. Yet, cities grew and grew, in most cases without a master plan. Thus, we ended up with industrial plants, apartment complexes, and scattered commercial buildings in single-family residential areas.

Land Use Regulation

The increased population density in our cities has brought environmental problems: namely, contaminated air and water, solid waste pollution, traffic congestion, and noise pollution. To solve such problems, we have had to resort to governmental regulation of the use of various land areas. Today most cities develop industrial parks and encourage industry to build and operate within these areas. Most cities have developed zoning ordinances that restrict the use of the land in various areas. For example, single-family dwellings will be allowed in some areas; two-family dwellings will be allowed in other areas; multifamily dwellings, such as large apartment houses, will be allowed in still other areas; and commercial businesses will be excluded from certain areas.

At first glance, this may seem unfair to the owner of real estate because under these ordinances the owner is limited to the uses prescribed by the law. It is true that zoning ordinances do take away certain rights of the individual owner. However, when one looks at the overall picture, it is clear that some type of land use regulation is in the best interest of all the residents of the city. Such regulation guarantees a more peaceful enjoyment of the owners' premises for the purposes that are allowed in an area, and it also preserves the property values for the owners in that area. For example, if you live in an area of single-family dwellings, you certainly would object to having a developer put an apartment complex next to your home because this would increase the traffic in front of your residence, create a parking problem, and generally reduce the value of your real estate.

The first zoning law in the United States was an ordinance adopted in 1916 by New York City. It regulated both the location and the use of buildings in the city. The basic constitutionality of **zoning laws** was upheld as a valid exercise of the local government's police power in the landmark case of *Euclid v. Ambler Realty Co.*, which was decided by the U.S. Supreme Court in 1926. Zoning and land use restrictions of other kinds may still be held unconstitutional, if they unreasonably interfere with a property owner's rights or if they violate some other constitutional restriction.

Zoning Defined

Zoning can be defined as the division of a city, a township, or a county or other governmental unit into specific districts for the purpose of regulating the type of building structure that may be built in each district, the placement of the buildings on the land, and the permitted use or uses of the buildings and the land. For example, certain districts will be zoned R-l, which means that only single-family residential buildings would be allowed in them. Two-family buildings would be allowed in an R-2 district. Multifamily buildings, such as apartment houses, would be allowed in an R-3 district. A G-B district would allow general businesses, such as office buildings, stores, shopping centers, motels, and hotels. An L-I would allow light industry, such as assembly-type factories and warehouses. H-I zoning would allow heavy industry, such as manufacturing plants, with the potential for noise and air pollution. Typically, these industrial districts are located as far away from residential areas as possible. The use of the identifying terms R-l, R-2, R-3, G-B, L-I, and H-I is not universal. Some areas classify their zoning districts alphabetically, referring, for example, to A or B districts, or use other methods to identify their various zoning districts.

Within each zoning district there may be further regulations regarding the architecture, the location, and the occupancy of buildings. Examples of such regulations are restrictions on the height of buildings and regulations specifying a minimum distance from the front, side, and rear property lines within which no building may be constructed. This type of regulation helps control the density of buildings and protects property owners from encroachment on their airspace and access to sunlight. For example, a neighbor would not be allowed to construct a 16-foot fence that blocks your view or blocks sunlight from your windows, or to build an addition that brings the neighbor's house right up to your property line and thus reduces the space between the houses.

Most cities or counties now have specific building construction codes, primarily for safety and health purposes. These codes regulate construction methods and the use of construction materials, and typically set a minimum standard for the area. **Building codes** will differ throughout the country because different standards are dictated by regional characteristics, such as temperature, the density of buildings, the possibility of earthquakes, and freezing and thawing problems.

In addition to physical regulations regarding the structure and placement of buildings, many zoning districts may have regulations concerning businesses that may be undesirable to property owners. For example, certain districts may not allow bars or the selling of intoxicating beverages or may exclude funeral homes or cemeteries.

One of the problems that has plagued city planners is that zoning must be prospective rather than retroactive in effect. If a zoning ordinance zones a certain area exclusively for single-family residential dwellings, the little corner grocery store or the lady who has her beauty shop in her home cannot be forced to cease doing business. Thus, most zoning laws have a grandfather clause that allows a business that was in the area before the passage of the zoning ordinance to operate until it is sold or disposed of in some other manner.

Another exception to zoning regulations is the variance. Often there are situations in which the strict adherence to a zoning regulation would cause undue hardship to a property owner. In such situations the regulatory agency can grant a variance to allow the land to be used in a manner not in strict conformance with the zoning regulation. Variances are, however, not automatic but are granted only in exceptional situations.

Private Restrictive Covenants

Zoning laws are usually general in character and often do not cover certain specific areas of land use. For example, zoning laws do not forbid the parking of large boats or campers in a driveway, yet such action may be unsightly and disturbing to the adjoining residents. Thus, a land developer may place certain restrictions in the land deeds to protect the value of the real estate in a new residential subdivision. When the land is being developed and sold, the contract of sale and deed will contain certain restrictions, such as the requirement to submit house plans not only to the public agency for a building permit but also to a committee in the subdivision for its approval. Other restrictions might ban outside clotheslines, the construction of outbuildings, the construction of fences without prior approval, and the parking of boats and campers on driveways. Homeowners who violate these restrictions may be taken to court. The court may enjoin further violations and cause the party to tear down the building or fence, move the camper or trailer, or perhaps pay damages to neighbors if damages to them were incurred. Failure to comply with the court order could result in fines or imprisonment for civil contempt of court.

Thus, we have public zoning and private restrictive zoning. Before purchasing any parcel of real estate, purchasers should be aware not only of public zoning restrictions but of any private restrictions that may affect their future use of this land.

The *Nahrstadt* case concerns restrictions on ownership of pets.

CASE 1

NAHRSTEDT V. LAKESIDE VILLAGE CONDO

11 Cal. Rptr.2d 299 (CA App., 2 Dist. 1992)

Facts: This action concerns: (1) a plaintiff who wishes to continue living with her three pet cats in the condominium she owns; (2) a provision in the recorded covenants, conditions, and restrictions ("CC & R's") governing that condominium, which prohibits owners of the units in her condominium project from keeping most types of pets; and (3) the authority of the board of directors of her homeowners association to levy monetary fines on homeowners who violate that pet restriction. Natore Nahrstedt filed this action to obtain, among other things, a declaration that she: (1) is entitled to keep her pets in her condominium, notwithstanding the CC & R's and (2) has no legal obligation to pay the fines that have been assessed against her for her refusal to move her cats out of her condominium. Plaintiff appealed from a judgment of dismissal that was entered after the trial court sustained, without leave to amend, demurrers to all six causes of action in plaintiff's original complaint.

Issue: Has plaintiff stated a cause of action against the Homeowners Association?

Decision: Yes. Judgment reversed.

Opinion by Associate Justice Crosskey: "Plaintiff's first cause of action is for invasion of privacy. In it she alleges that Article VII, Section 11 of the CC & R's for the condominium project provides in part: 'No animals (which shall mean dogs and cats), livestock, reptiles, or poultry shall be kept in any unit except that usual and ordinary domestic fish and birds (and [sic] inside bird cages) may be kept as household pets within any unit; provided: (a) they are not kept, bred, or raised for commercial purposes or in unreasonable numbers; and (b) prior written approval of the Board [of Directors of the Condominium Association] is first obtained. As used herein, "unreasonable numbers" shall be determined by the Board, but in no event shall such term be construed so as to permit the maintenance by any owner of more than two (2) pets per unit. The Association shall have the right to prohibit maintenance of any pet which constitutes, in the opinion of the Board, a nuisance to any other owner.'

"Plaintiff alleges that her three cats at all times remain inside her unit and are noiseless and not a nuisance; that beginning in July 1988, defendants peered into and entered her condominium without a compelling reason to do so and in violation of the California Constitution's provision for privacy, found in Article 1, Section 1 thereof; that defendants have harassed plaintiff by assessing penalties against her in increasingly large amounts, (beginning with $25/month and increasing in steps to $500/month), to penalize her for keeping her pet cats; and that the assessments are in violation of the CC & R's and in violation of her right to privacy....

"The question of whether the pet restriction at issue in the case before us is an enforceable equitable servitude under Civil Code Section 1354 is a mixed issue of law and fact which can only be resolved in the context of the particular circumstances of this case....

"[T]he enforceability of the pet restriction will be decided in the trial court after the taking of evidence as to the relevant circumstances of this case. Restrictions in CC & R's regarding the ownership and possession of pets are reasonable and therefore are enforceable under Civil Code Section 1354 when they prohibit conduct which, while otherwise lawful, in fact interferes with, or has a reasonable likelihood of interfering with, the rights of other condominium owners to the peaceful and quiet enjoyment of their property.

"Defendants argue that the blanket pet restriction they seek to enforce against plaintiff is reasonable and enforceable because it avoids a situation where they must always take a 'wait and see' position on pets and then litigate over pets that are causing problems in the condominium project. We reject this contention.... Plaintiff's condominium home is her castle and her enjoyment of it should be by the least restrictive means possible, conducive with a harmonious communal living arrangement. Second, if carried to its logical conclusion, defendants' argument could be used to support all-inclusive bans on such diverse things as stereo equipment, social gatherings and visitors between the ages of two and eighteen. We cannot envision the courts finding that blanket restrictions against such things are reasonable; yet it is certainly conceivable that allowing Fluffin, Muffin, and Ruffin to live inside plaintiff's condominium will pose less of a threat to the peace and quiet of the parties' communal living arrangement than would stereo equipment, parties, or young visitors.

"As a final observation on the issue of Civil Code Section 1354, 'reasonableness,' we note its effect on defendants' contention that by purchasing a unit in the condominium project, plaintiff agreed to and became bound by the pet restriction and should not now be heard to complain of it. The contention is without merit because under Section 1354, defendants can only enforce restrictions in CC & R's that are reasonable. Thus, if the pet restriction at issue here is found to be unreasonable as applied to plaintiff because plaintiff's conduct in keeping her cats has not interfered with and does not have a reasonable likelihood of interfering with, the rights of other owners to the peaceful and quiet enjoyment of their property, then by the very terms of Section 1354, it is not enforceable against plaintiff, even though she bought her unit with at least constructive knowledge that keeping cats in the project was forbidden...

"Plaintiff should have been given an opportunity to revise the invasion of privacy cause of action by limiting it to the allegations regarding defendants' peering into and entering her home. She should also have been given the opportunity to advance these allegations as a basis for a cause of action for trespass. The other allegations pertaining to the pet restriction should be included in plaintiff's cause of action for declaratory relief, as a basis for her assertion that such a restriction is unreasonable and therefore unenforceable under Civil Code Section 1354. . . .

"[I]t appears to this court that the fines levied against plaintiff are not proper under the authority given to the Board in the portion of the CC & R's relied upon by defendants to support their demurrer to this fifth cause of action. We must therefore conclude that, absent such support in other positions of the CC & R's, not only did the trial court err in sustaining a demurrer to this cause of action (with or without leave to amend), but a request by plaintiff for a summary adjudication of issues on the question of the fines would, on the basis of the record before us, have to be resolved in her favor . . .

"The judgment of dismissal is reversed and, as to Homeowner's Association, a writ of mandate shall issue directing the trial court to vacate its order sustaining demurrers without leave to amend and to enter a new and different order. The cause is remanded to the trial court for further proceedings consistent with the views expressed herein. Costs on appeal to plaintiff."

Other Land Use Regulations

As we learned earlier in this chapter, each state has inherent rights to exercise police power to regulate private property for the public interest, convenience, and necessity. The states have delegated this regulatory power to the local governments: namely, counties and cities.

In addition to zoning regulations, housing codes, and building codes, most cities and counties now have subdivision controls and regulations because housing density is becoming increasingly a problem. When a group of new homes is to be built in an area, there must be a preliminary investigation to determine whether any health or other environmental hazard will be caused by this new group of dwellings. Today, many subdivisions are being created in areas where there are no public sewage systems or public water systems. In such areas it is important to make sure that the soil will allow proper drainage and filtering of wastes from the septic tanks of the new dwellings. It must also be determined that the water supply will not be contaminated by the septic systems. Another problem that must be considered is the drainage of storm water. For example, if a subdivision with 300 or 400 homes is built in a rural area that has had natural drainage across farmlands for years and no apparent drainage problems, each new home that is built changes the drainage situation by replacing land that ordinarily absorbs water with a concrete slab or basement and concrete or asphalt roadways. These changes reduce the absorptive capacity of the land. However, the storm water has to go somewhere, and because less of it is absorbed by the land, it will run across the land, where it may well cause damage to buildings, the erosion of topsoil, and other problems.

Environmental Concerns

The freedom of landowners to use their property as they wished was a cherished right in our country for many years. One day, only a few decades ago, people saw that our streams, rivers, and lakes had become polluted to such an extent that we could not enjoy the waters. The air had become hazy, smelly, and acrid, often burning our eyes. The landscape was cluttered with old car bodies, beer cans, and solid waste of every description. Citizen groups began calling for governmental regulation of the environment.

On the national level, Congress passed the **National Environmental Policy Act** and created the Environmental Protection Agency (EPA) to act as the watchdog against continued pollution of our air, water, and land. To control specific areas of pollution, Congress also passed the **Clean Air Act**, the **Water Pollution Control Act**, the **Noise Control Act**, and the **Solid Waste Disposal Act.**

Many states, counties, and cities have enacted environmental laws. In some instances these laws have set even more stringent pollution standards than the national pollution laws. Many states have also created their own environmental protection agencies to control and regulate pollution within their boundaries. A recent development in the control of solid waste pollution has been the passage of so-called bottle bills by several states. These laws require stores to take deposits from the customer on beverage containers and to return the deposit when the cans or bottles are returned empty. These same laws have also banned the use of pull-top cans for beverages.

Further environmental problems have been caused by the expansion of our cities into what was previously the domain of the farmer. No cattle or hog feedlot is pleasing to the nostrils, and we must accept the fact that such farming operations are not desirable next door to a residential area. What happens when the city expands to the point where the rights of the parties conflict?

Thus, we no longer have the cherished right to use our land, water, and airspace in any way we choose; there are too many of us, and we live too close together for that. You cannot burn trash in an outside incinerator anymore in most large cities. The burning of leaves may also be banned. You cannot install a septic system for your home unless it is approved by a local agency. You cannot use your backyard to store your collection of junk cars.

Regulation of Hazardous Waste Disposal

In one of the most important environmental cases ever, the U.S. Supreme Court majority recently ruled that the EPA did have the authority to issue mandatory regulations on the emission of "greenhouse gases," that it had not adequately explained its reasons for not doing so, and that it had a duty to provide an explanation for its refusal to adopt such regulations. The four dissenters filed two opinions. Chief Justice Roberts explained why the majority was wrong on the procedural issue of "standing to sue," and Justice Scalia indicated why the majority was wrong on the merits of the case.

CASE 2

Massachusetts v. Environmental Protection Agency

127 S.Ct. 1438 (2007)

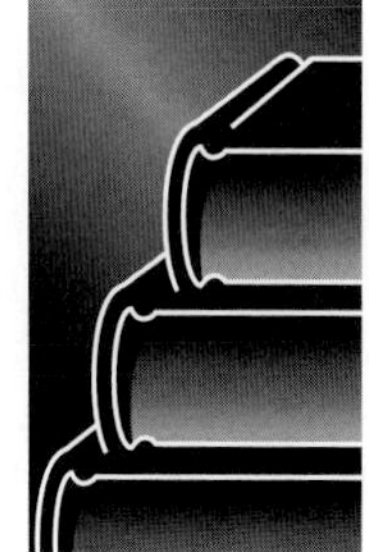

Facts: Section 202(a)(1) of the Clean Air Act ... provides: "The [EPA] Administrator shall by regulation prescribe (and from time to time revise) in accordance with the provisions of this section, standards applicable to the emission of any air pollutant from the class or classes of new motor vehicles or new motor vehicle engines, which in his judgment cause, or contribute to, air pollution which may reasonably be anticipated to endanger public health or welfare...." The Act defines "air pollutant" to include "any air pollution agent or combination of such agents, including any physical, chemical, biological, radioactive ... substance or matter which is emitted into or otherwise enters the ambient air." "Welfare" is also defined broadly: among other things, it includes "effects on ... weather ... and climate."

On October 20, 1999, a group of 19 private organizations filed a rulemaking petition asking EPA to regulate "greenhouse gas emissions from new motor vehicles under S. 202 of the Clean Air Act." Fifteen months later, EPA requested public comment on "all the issues raised in [the] petition," adding a "particular" request for comments on "any scientific, technical, legal, economic or other aspect of these issues that may be relevant to EPA's consideration of this petition." EPA received more than 50,000 comments over the next 5 months. On September 8, 2003, EPA entered an order denying the rule-making petition. The agency gave two reasons for its decision: (1) that the Clean Air Act does not authorize EPA to issue mandatory regulations to address global climate change, and (2) that even if the agency had such authority, it would be unwise to do so at this time. Petitioners, now joined by several states and local governments, sought review of the EPA's decision in the U.S. Court of Appeals for the District of Columbia Circuit. By a 2-1 vote, the D.C. Circuit said that "the EPA Administrator properly exercised his discretion under S. 202(a)(1) in denying the petition for rule making." Petitioners requested U.S. Supreme Court review.

Issue: Do the petitioners have "standing" to bring this lawsuit? Does the EPA have the authority to regulate "greenhouse gases"?

Decision: Yes. Judgment reversed, and case remanded.

Opinion by Justice Stevens: "The parties' dispute turns on the proper construction of a congressional statute, a question eminently suitable for resolution in federal court. Congress has moreover authorized this type of challenge to EPA action....

"EPA maintains that because greenhouse gas emissions inflict widespread harm, the doctrine of standing presents an insuperable jurisdictional obstacle. We do not agree. At bottom, 'the gist of the question of standing' is whether petitioners have 'such a personal stake in the outcome of the controversy as to assure that concrete adverseness which sharpens the presentation of issues upon which the court so largely depends for illumination.' ...

"To ensure the proper adversarial presentation ... a litigant must demonstrate that it has suffered a concrete and particularized injury that is either actual or imminent, that the injury is fairly traceable to the defendant, and that it is likely that a favorable decision will redress that injury.... However, a litigant to whom Congress has 'accorded a procedural right to protect his concrete interests ... can assert that right without meeting all the normal standards for redressability and immediacy.' ... When a litigant is vested with a procedural right, that litigant has standing if there is some possibility that the requested relief will prompt the injury-causing party to reconsider the decision that allegedly harmed the litigant....

"Only one of the petitioners needs to have standing to permit us to consider the petition for review.... We stress here ... the special position and interest of Massachusetts. It is of considerable relevance that the party seeking review here is a sovereign State and not ... a private individual.

"Well before the creation of the modern administrative state, we recognized that States are not normal litigants for the purposes for invoking federal jurisdiction [citing *Georgia v. Tennessee Copper Co.*, 206 U.S. 230 (1907)]....

"With that in mind, it is clear that petitioners' submissions as they pertain to Massachusetts have satisfied the most demanding standards of the adversarial process. EPA's steadfast refusal to regulate greenhouse gas emissions presents a risk of harm to Massachusetts that is both 'actual' and 'imminent.' ... There is, moreover, a 'substantial likelihood that the judicial relief requested' will prompt EPA to take steps to reduce that risk....

"That these climate-change risks are 'widely shared' does not minimize Massachusetts' interest in the outcome of this litigation.... [The] rising seas have already begun to swallow Massachusetts' coastal land.... Because the Commonwealth 'owns a substantial portion of the state's coastal property' ... it has alleged a particularized injury in its capacity as a landowner....

"The scope of our review of the merits of the statutory issues is narrow. As we have repeated time and again, an agency has broad discretion to choose how best to marshal its limited resources and personnel to carry out its delegated responsibilities.... That discretion is at its height when the agency decides not to bring an enforcement action.... Some debate remains, however, as to the rigor with which we review an agency's denial of a petition for rulemaking.

"There are key differences between a denial of a petition for rulemaking and an agency's decision not to initiate an enforcement action.... In contrast to nonenforcement decisions, agency refusals to initiate rulemaking 'are less frequent, more apt to involve legal as opposed to factual analysis, and subject to special formalities ... including a public explanation.' ... Refusals to promulgate rules are thus susceptible to judicial review, though such review is 'extremely limited' and 'highly deferential.' ...

"On the merits, the first question is whether S. 202 (a)(1) of the Clean Air Act authorizes EPA to regulate greenhouse gas emissions from new motor vehicles in the event that it forms a 'judgment' that such emissions contribute to climate change. We have little trouble concluding that it does....

"The broad language of S. 202(a)(1) reflects an intentional effort to confer the flexibility necessary to forestall [the Act's] obsolescence.... Because greenhouses gases fit well within the Clean Air Act's capacious definition of 'air pollutant,' we hold that EPA has the statutory authority to regulate the emission of such gases from new motor vehicles....

"The alternative basis for EPA's decision—that even if it does have statutory authority to regulate greenhouse gases, it would be unwise to do so at this time—rests on reasoning divorced from the statutory text. While the statute does condition the exercise of EPA's authority on its formation of a 'judgment,' ... the use of the word 'judgment' is not a roving license to ignore the statutory text. It is but a direction to exercise discretion within defined statutory limits.

"If EPA makes a finding of endangerment, the Clean Air Act requires the agency to regulate emission of the deleterious pollutant from new motor vehicles.... EPA no doubt has significant latitude as to the manner, timing, content, and coordination of its regulations with those of other agencies. But once EPA has responded to a petition for rulemaking, its reasons for action or inaction must conform to the authorizing statute....

"EPA has refused to comply with this clear statutory mandate. Instead, it has offered a laundry list of reasons not to regulate....

"Although we have neither the expertise nor the authority to evaluate these policy judgments, it is evident they have nothing to do with whether greenhouse gas emissions contribute to climate change. Still less do they amount to a reasoned justification for declining to form a scientific judgment....

"Nor can EPA avoid its statutory obligation by noting the uncertainty surrounding various features of climate change and concluding that it would therefore be better not to regulate at this time.... If the scientific uncertainty is so profound that it precludes EPA from making a reasoned judgment as to whether greenhouse gases contribute to global warming, EPA must say so....

"In short, EPA has offered no reasoned explanation for its refusal to decide whether greenhouse gases cause or contribute to climate change. Its action was therefore 'arbitrary, capricious ... or otherwise not in accordance with law.' ... We need not and do not reach the question whether on remand EPA must make an endangerment finding, or whether policy concerns can inform EPA's actions in the event it makes such a finding.... We hold only that EPA must ground its reasons for action or inaction in the statute....

"The judgment of the Court of Appeals is reversed, and the case is remanded for further proceedings consistent with this opinion."

Dissent by Chief Justice Roberts: "Global warming may be a 'crisis,' even 'the most pressing environmental problem of our time.' ... Indeed, it may ultimately affect nearly everyone on the planet in some potentially adverse way, and it may be that governments have done too little to address it. It is not a problem, however, that has escaped the attention of the policy-makers in the Executive and Legislative Branches of our Government, who continue to consider regulatory, legislative, and treaty-based means of addressing global climate change.

"Apparently dissatisfied with the pace of progress on the issue in the elected branches, petitioners have come to the courts claiming broad-ranging injury, and attempting to tie that injury to the Government's alleged failure to comply with a rather narrow statutory provision. I would reject these challenges as nonjusticiable. Such a conclusion involves no judgment on whether global warming exists, what causes it, or the extent of the problem. Nor does it render petitioners without recourse. This Court's standing jurisprudence simply recognizes that redress of grievances of the sort at issue here 'is the function of Congress and the Chief Executive,' not the federal courts.... I would vacate the judgment below and remand for dismissal of the petitions here for review....

"Our modern framework for addressing standing is familiar: 'A plaintiff must allege personal injury fairly traceable to the defendant's allegedly unlawful conduct and likely to be redressed by the requested relief.' ... Applying that standard here, petitioners bear the burden of alleging an injury that is fairly traceable to the [EPA's] failure to promulgate new motor vehicle greenhouse gas emission standards, and that is likely to be redressed by the prospective issuance of such standards.

"Before determining whether petitioners can meet this familiar test, however, the Court changes the rules. It asserts that 'States are not normal litigants for the purposes of invoking federal jurisdiction,' and that given 'Massachusetts' stake in protecting its quasi-sovereign interests, the Commonwealth is entitled to special solicitude in our standing analysis.' ...

"Relaxing Article III standing requirements because asserted injuries are pressed by a State, however, has no basis in our jurisprudence, and support for any such 'special solicitude' is conspicuously absent from the Court's opinion....

"Nor does the case law cited by the Court provide any support for the notion that Article III somehow implicitly treats public and private litigants differently. The Court has to go back a full century in an attempt to justify its novel standing rule, but even there it comes up short. The Court's analysis hinges on Georgia v. Tennessee Copper Co. ...—a case that did indeed draw a distinction between a State and private litigants, but solely with respect to available remedies. The case had nothing to do with Article III standing....

"It is not at all clear how the Court's 'special solicitude' for Massachusetts plays out in the standing analysis, except as an implicit concession that petitioners cannot establish standing on traditional terms. But the status of Massachusetts as a State cannot compensate for petitioners' failure to demonstrate injury in fact, causation, and redressability....

"Petitioners are never able to trace their alleged injuries back through this complex web to the fractional amount of global emissions that might have been limited with EPA standards. In light of the bit-part domestic new motor vehicle greenhouse gas emissions have played in what petitioners describe as a 150-year global phenomenon, and the myriad additional factors bearing on petitioners' alleged injury—the loss of Massachusetts coastal land—the connection is far too speculative to establish causation....

"No matter, the Court reasons, because any decrease in domestic emissions will 'slow the pace of global emissions increases, no matter what happens elsewhere.' ... Every little bit helps, so Massachusetts can sue over any little bit....

"The goods news is that the Court's 'special solicitude' for Massachusetts limits the future applicability of the diluted standing requirements applied in this case. The bad news is that the Court's self-professed relaxation of those Article III requirements has caused us to transgress 'the proper—and properly limited—role of the courts in a democratic society.' ...

"I respectfully dissent."

Dissent by Justice Scalia: "I join THE CHIEF JUSTICE's opinion in full, and would hold that this Court has no jurisdiction to decide this case because petitioners lack standing. The Court having decided otherwise, it is appropriate for me to note my dissent on the merits....

"As the Court recognizes, the statute 'conditions the exercise of EPA's authority on its formation of a "judgment".' ... There is no dispute that the Administrator has made no such judgment in this case....

"The question thus arises: Does anything require the Administrator to make a 'judgment' whenever a petition for rulemaking is filed? Without citation of the statute or any other authority, the Court says yes. Why is that so? When Congress wishes to make private action force an agency's hand, it knows how to do so....

"I am willing to assume, for the sake of argument, that the Administrator's discretion in this regard is not unbounded—that if he has no reasonable basis for deferring judgment he must grasp the nettle at once. The Court, however, with no basis in text or precedent, rejects all of EPA's stated 'policy judgments' as not 'amounting to a reasoned justification' ... effectively narrowing the universe of potentially reasonable bases to a single one: Judgment can be delayed only if the Administrator concludes that 'the scientific uncertainty is [too] profound.' ... The Administrator is precluded from concluding for other reasons 'that it would ... be better not to regulate at this time.' ... Such other reasons—perfectly valid reasons—were set forth in the agency's statement....

"EPA's interpretation of the discretion conferred by the statutory reference to 'its judgment' is not only reasonable, it is the most natural reading of the text. The Court nowhere explains why it is not entitled to deference.... As the Administrator acted within the law in declining to make a 'judgment' for the policy reasons [stated], I would uphold the decision to deny the rulemaking petition on that ground alone....

"I simply cannot conceive of what else the Court would like EPA to say....

"The Court's alarm over global warming may or may not be justified, but it ought not distort the outcome of this litigation. This is a straightforward administrative-law case, in which Congress has passed a malleable statute giving broad discretion, not to us but to an executive agency. No matter how important the underlying policy issues at stake, this Court has no business substituting its own desired outcome for the reasoned judgment of the responsible agency."

One of the strongest environmental statutes is the **Comprehensive Environmental Response, Compensation, and Liability Act (CERCLA).** Adopted in 1980, CERCLA is also known as the "Superfund" statute because it set up a fund, financed by taxes on hazardous products, to pay for cleaning up sites containing hazardous wastes. More importantly, CERCLA provides for recovery of cleanup costs from "responsible parties," including the person who generated the wastes, the person who transported the waste to the dump site, the owner of the site at the time of disposal, and the current owner and the current operator of the site.

Its liability rules are truly draconian. First, strict liability is imposed for the presence of hazardous wastes; fault or intentional wrong does not have to be shown. Second, the liability is retroactive; it can be imposed even though the disposal of hazardous waste was in full compliance with the law when it was done. And third, the liability is joint and several, meaning that a party responsible for only a small part of the waste at a particular site is fully liable for the entire cost of cleaning up the whole site.

With over 25,000 hazardous waste sites already identified by the EPA, the potential cleanup costs are enormous—tens of billions, even hundreds of billions of dollars. There is thus a strong financial motivation to litigate these cases. The first identified defendant wants to involve as many others as possible, to lower its proportionate share of the cleanup costs. All defendants want to avoid CERCLA liability in any way they can. Lawyers are certainly "cleaning up"; the real question is whether enough waste sites are being cleaned up, fast enough.

The *Bestfoods* case illustrates the application of CERCLA. The U.S. District Court is reanalyzing the extensive factual record developed in its initial trial of the case, after a remand of the case from the U.S. Supreme Court.

CASE 3

Bestfoods, f.k.a. CPC International v. Aerojet-General Corp.

173 F.Supp.2d 729 (W.D. MI 2001)

Facts: The site at issue in this case is 500 Agard Road, Dalton Township, near Muskegon, Michigan. From 1957 to 1965, Ott Chemical Company (Ott I) owned and operated a chemical plant there; from 1965 to 1972, Ott Chemical (Ott II) was a wholly-owned subsidiary of CPC International (formerly known as Corn Products, later known as Bestfoods). In 1972, Ott II sold the site to Story Chemical; Story went bankrupt in 1977. Story's bankruptcy trustee, with the support of the Michigan Department of Natural Resources, sold the site Cordova Chemical, a subsidiary of Aerojet-General. Cordova Chemical sold the site to its wholly-owned Michigan subsidiary in 1978. There have been no operations at the site since 1986.

The U.S. government and the MDNR (now the Michigan Department of Environmental Quality) filed CERCLA claims against the various corporations involved with the ownership and operation of the site. Settlements were reached with Arnold Ott, owner of the original Ott Chemical, and with Aerojet-General and its Cordova subsidiaries. After an extensive trial, with 29 live witnesses, dozens of depositions, and 2,300 trial exhibits, the U.S. District Court originally held that CPC, as the parent of Ott Chemical (Ott II), was an "operator," and thus liable for the cost of the cleanup. The U.S. Sixth Circuit reversed. The U.S. Supreme Court remanded for new findings as to operator liability. On remand, the District Court accepted 50 additional exhibits, heard oral arguments, and received extensive briefs.

Issue: Was CPC an "operator" of the facility?

Decision: No. Judgment for defendant CPC International.

Opinion by Judge Hillman: "In its 1991 opinion, this court held CPC directly liable as an operator of the facility, applying a modified standard of corporate parental liability that assessed the degree of parental involvement in the affairs of the subsidiary....

"With respect to direct operator liability, the Supreme Court rejected consideration of factors reflecting parental involvement in the affairs of the subsidiary. The Court held that the relevant question is '"not whether the parent operates the subsidiary, but rather whether it operates the facility, and that operation is evidenced by participation in the activities of the facility, not the subsidiary,"' ... (quoting Oswald, *Bifurcation of the Owner and Operator Analysis under CERCLA*, 72 WASH. U.L.Q. 223, 269 [1994]).... Direct operator liability does not depend on the ability to pierce the corporate veil and, therefore, does not depend on the facts relevant to derivative liability. Indeed, if a corporate parent actually acts to operate a facility, 'the existence of the parent-subsidiary relationship under state corporate law is simply irrelevant to the issue of direct liability.' . . .

"The Court thereafter defined the types of 'actions sufficient to constitute parental operation.' . . . The Court held that: 'under CERCLA, an operator is simply someone who directs the workings of, manages, or conducts the affairs of a facility. To sharpen the definition for purposes of CERCLA's concern with environmental contamination, an operator must manage, direct, or conduct operations specifically related to pollution, that is, operations having to do with the leakage or disposal of hazardous wastes, or decisions about compliance with environmental regulations.' . . .

"The Supreme Court held that upon remand, this court was to focus its analysis on the relationship between CPC and the Muskegon facility. . . . The Court rejected this court's reliance upon the interlocking directorships of CPC and Ott II, quoting with approval the 'well established principle [of corporate law] that directors and officers holding positions with a parent and its subsidiary can and do "change hats" to represent the two corporations separately, despite their common ownership.' . . . The Court held, therefore, that in order to establish liability based on the actions of directors and officers holding dual roles with both the parent and the subsidiary, the government must show that 'the officers and directors were acting in their capacities as CPC officers and directors, and not as Ott II officers and directors, when they committed these acts.' . . . The Court admonished that: '"Activities that involve the facility but which are consistent with the parent's investor status . . . should not give rise to direct liability." The critical question is whether, in degree and detail, actions directed to the facility by an agent of the parent alone are eccentric under accepted norms of parental oversight of a subsidiary's facility.' . . . (quoting Oswald, 72 WASH. U.L.Q., at 282). . . .

"Accordingly, applying the standards of *Bestfoods* on remand, the court must determine whether CPC may be held liable as an operator on the basis of its relationship with the Muskegon facility. . . . [T]o be relevant, any . . . dual officers or directors must have departed from the accepted norms of corporate behavior in discharging their duties. . . .

"In addition, the court must consider whether any agent of CPC actually 'directed the workings of, managed, or conducted the affairs of the facility.' . . . Further, the court must consider whether CPC actually operated the facility either alone or through some sort of joint venture with Ott II. Each of these questions turns on 'whether, in degree and detail, actions directed to the facility by an agent of the parent alone are eccentric under accepted norms of parental oversight of a subsidiary facility.' . . .

"Williams was a lawyer who coordinated air and water pollution programs for CPC. . . . Beginning in 1966, he was involved with the Muskegon facility of Ott II, upon the recommendation of dual-director Harold Hellman. . . .

"[T]he record reflects that while Williams may have advocated that Ott II delay implementation of waste treatment plans, his advice was rejected. Although delays in discharge compliance eventually occurred, and although the biological treatment facility was never built, those delays are not shown to have resulted from any influence Williams may have had on Ott II. . . . Instead, they reflect the Ott II decision to connect to the county waste water treatment system, and the record contains no evidence that Williams was involved in that decision.

"In sum, the record evidence is far too thin to conclude that Williams was responsible for any delays in compliance. . . .

"Similarly, the governments have failed to present sufficient evidence that any other CPC officer or dual office/director may have engaged in activities sufficiently 'eccentric' . . . as to impose operator liability. . . .

"Reviewing the asserted conduct both separately and together, I am satisfied that CPC's involvement with Ott II's product development does not demonstrate the requisite control over the facility to render CPC liable as an operator of the facility. . . .

"[W]hile the subsidiary (Ott II) may be considered a successor corporation to Ott I, the governments have failed to prove a basis under Michigan law for finding the parent corporation—CPC—a successor to Ott I. Accordingly, . . . the governments' theory of successor corporation fails for the reason that CPC's acquisition of Ott I did not constitute a de facto merger of the two corporations. . . .

"In sum, the governments have failed to prove that CPC is liable under CERCLA for environmental cleanup costs at the Muskegon site, either directly as an operator, or derivatively as a successor corporation to Ott I. . . . Accordingly, CPC is entitled to judgment in its favor as to all pending claims, cross-claims and counter-claims against it."

The next case involves a "takings" claim arising out of U.S. military responses to the terrorist bombings of two U.S. embassies.

Eminent Domain

The Fifth Amendment in the Bill of Rights of the U.S. Constitution provides that the national government shall not take private property without the payment of just compensation. The Fourteenth Amendment extended this provision to the various states. The states also have similar provisions in their constitutions, allowing them to exercise the power of eminent domain if just compensation is paid to the property owner.

Most simply stated, the power of **eminent domain** is the power of government to take real estate from a private owner for the use of the public. This very basic governmental

CASE 4

El-Shifa Pharm. Ind. Co. v. United States
378 F.3d 1346 (Fed.Cir. 2004)

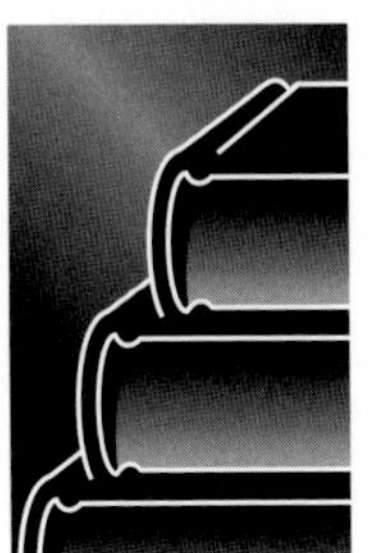

Facts: After the terrorist bombings of U.S. embassies in Kenya and Tanzania, President Clinton ordered the U.S. military to conduct attacks against designated terrorist locations. One location so destroyed was a manufacturing plant in Khartoum, Sudan. The plant was allegedly linked to Osama bin Ladin and al-Qaeda and to making a nerve gas ingredient. Claiming that the plant was merely making badly needed medicines and that the plant had been "taken" by the U.S. government, the plant owner (El-Shifa) and a major stockholder (Salah El Din Ahmed Mohammed Idris) sued for $50 million compensation as required by the Fifth Amendment to the U.S. Constitution. The Court of Federal Claims dismissed the case, and the plaintiffs appealed.

Issue: Does the president have the unreviewable power to make designations of "enemy property" as to things located outside the U.S.?

Decision: Yes. Dismissal of plaintiffs' complaint is affirmed.

Opinion by Judge Clevenger: "Without question, 'it is emphatically the province and duty of the judicial department to say what the law is.' Marbury v. Madison … (1803). 'Sometimes, however, the law is that the judicial department has no business entertaining [a] claim of unlawfulness—because the question is entrusted to one of the political branches or involves no judicially enforceable rights. Such questions are said to be "nonjusticiable" or "political questions".' …

"[W]hatever the Constitution says regarding the President's war powers, either explicitly in its text or by its structure, it need not say anything about the Takings Clause per se in order for us to conclude that it commits exclusively to the President the power to make extraterritorial enemy property designations. …

"We think consideration of the decisional law touching on the nature and scope of the President's war powers sheds important light on our present inquiry. … 'The Constitution … invests the President with the power to wage war' … .

"In exercising the power to wage war, the President finds authorization in the Constitution itself to 'direct the performance of those functions which may constitutionally be performed by the military arm of the nation in time of war.' … Within these functions are 'important incidents to the conduct of war' such as 'the adoption of measures by the military command … to repel and defeat the enemy.' … They also include 'the power to seize and subject to disciplinary measures those enemies who in their attempt to thwart or impede our military effort have violated the laws of war.' …

"In our view, the President's power to wage war must also necessarily include the power to make extraterritorial enemy property designations because such designations are also an important incident to the conduct of war. As much is borne out of the history of this nation's many declared and undeclared wars, part of which is documented in the cases where courts have applied the enemy property doctrine. The cases teach that the purpose of such designations is almost always to 'repel and defeat the enemy' by diminishing the sum of material resources it has at its disposal to prosecute hostilities against the United States and its citizens. … We cannot envision how a military commander, much less the Commander-in-Chief, could wage war successfully if he did not have the inherent power to decide what targets, i.e., property, belonged to the enemy and could therefore be destroyed free from takings liability. …

"The appellants' theory of takings liability centers on the alleged inaccuracy of the President's designation of the Plant as enemy property. This must be the case, because … if the Plant was in fact the property of al-Queda, the appellants would have no claim in takings against the United States for its destruction. … The appellants would have the [courts] … provide them with an opportunity to test [the President's] contention, and in the process, require this court to elucidate the constitutional standards that are to guide a President when he evaluates the veracity of military intelligence.

"We are of the opinion that the federal courts have no role in setting even minimal standards by which the President, or his commanders, are to measure the veracity of intelligence gathered with the aim of determining which assets, located beyond the borders of the United States, belong to the Nation's friends and which belong to its enemies. … Today, we need not decide whether and to what extent the Executive and Legislative branches share that responsibility. We conclude only that the Constitution does not contemplate or support the type of supervision over the President's extraterritorial enemy property designations the appellants request in this case. …

"For the foregoing reasons, the decision of the Court of Federal Claims to dismiss the complaint because it raises a nonjusticiable political question is affirmed."

power is necessary for the government to function properly and efficiently. For example, if the government is building a highway across the state, the highway must be laid out in as straight a line as possible, considering the topography of the land. It would not be in the best interest of the public if the highway had to jog around various pieces of property whose owners had decided not to sell to the government. The power of eminent domain is also used to acquire land for new school buildings, public parks, public housing projects, and other public buildings and projects.

The government simply must have the right to take over private property when doing so serves the best interest of the public. The owner of such property does, however, have a right to just compensation. The two key problems are: (1) that the land may be taken only for a public purpose, and (2) that the owner must receive just compensation. What constitutes a public purpose is often a question that must be resolved in the courts. What constitutes just compensation is also not an easy question to resolve in many cases, and thus a lawsuit may be filed and a jury called on to decide the issue.

Significance of This Chapter

In the early 1960s, we saw a movement in the United States to save the environment, to clean the air and water, to control solid waste dumping, and to stop other forms of pollution. We finally realized the results of uncontrolled and unregulated land use, which had occurred over a period of many years, and which left many cities with unnecessary traffic congestion problems, fire and safety hazards, and lowered property values. Most cities, both large and small, now have a system of land use regulation as well as local regulation of environmental problems.

This chapter gives an overview of the law concerning these areas. All citizens must realize the importance of this type of regulation and the continued need for regulation in the areas of land use and environment.

IMPORTANT TERMS AND CONCEPTS

building codes
Clean Air Act
Comprehensive Environmental Response, Compensation, and Liability Act (CERCLA)
eminent domain
National Environmental Policy Act
Noise Control Act
nuisance
Solid Waste Disposal Act
Water Pollution Control Act
zoning laws

QUESTIONS AND PROBLEMS FOR DISCUSSION

1. What happens if a zoning law is passed stating only single-family dwellings and no businesses are allowed in your area, and in fact a family grocery store operates in one of the houses in the neighborhood? Must the business immediately close up? If not, why not? Explain.

2. Describe a situation in which a zoning variance would be requested.

3. Who is affected by private restrictive covenants? Why are these restrictive covenants often used in real property transactions?

4. What are the so-called bottle bills? How does a typical bottle bill operate?

5. In 1991, the Oregon legislature passed a bottle bill. The bill prohibited the sale of pull-top beverage cans in the state and required deposits on all cans and bottles of beer and carbonated soft drinks. The plaintiffs in this suit included can and bottle manufacturers, bottlers of beer and soft drinks, and the Oregon Soft Drink Association. The plaintiffs alleged that the statute was invalid under the Due Process and Equal Protection clauses of the Fourteenth Amendment and under the Commerce Clause. They said that it also violated similar provisions in the state constitution. The trial court held that the statute was valid.

   Is the statute constitutional? Discuss.

6. The retirement community of Youngtown was founded in 1984, about 14 or 15 miles west of the urban area of Phoenix. Farming operations had been conducted in the area since 1911, and Spur's predecessors had started a feedlot about 2 1/2 miles south of Youngtown in 1986. By 1989, there were 25 cattle feeding or dairy operations in the area. In 1989, Del Webb began planning the development of a large retirement community, Sun City. One year later, 450 to 500 homes were completed or under construction. The units sold well, but sales resistance increased as the location of the homes got closer and closer to the feedlots. By 1992, Spur had expanded its operation from 35 to 114

acres. By 1993, Del Webb's housing manager said that it was impossible to sell any home in the southwestern portion of Del Webb's land. By 1996, the properties were within 500 feet of each other at one point, and Spur was feeding between 20,000 and 30,000 head of cattle on its lots, producing over a million pounds of wet manure per day. Del Webb sued to enjoin Spur as a public nuisance, due to the flies and odor. The trial court entered an injunction, and Spur appealed.

Should the injunction be upheld? Explain.

7. Residents of Hillcrest Heights sued to enjoin defendants from erecting two apartment buildings on a platted lot owned by defendants and located in Hillcrest Heights subdivision. Plaintiffs contended that defendants' proposed apartment buildings would violate the subdivision's protective covenants, based on the following clause of the covenants: "A. All lots in this subdivision shall be Residential One (R-1) only. . . ."

   Defendants admitted that this clause standing alone would prohibit them construction of the proposed apartment buildings. They contend, however, that because another clause in the restrictive covenants incorporates an existing zoning classification that allows apartment buildings, the apartment buildings would not violate the protective covenants. The clause relied on by defendants provides as follows: "L. None of the foregoing shall be construed as conflicting with any terms or regulations of the present or future Jefferson County zoning ordinance which shall form a part of this instrument and shall govern their use of all land herein described." The trial court entered judgment for plaintiffs.

   Does a zoning ordinance supersede any and all private restrictions on land use?

8. Mr. Reer requested a building permit to establish a "Good Times Pizza" parlor in the City of Midland. After the city's building inspector told Reer that a carryout restaurant was not a permissible use in the Business A zoning district where Reer proposed to build, Reer's request for an interpretation of the zoning ordinance was heard by the zoning board of appeals on March 29. By a 3 to 1 vote, the board determined that a carryout pizzeria was a permissible use. (The ordinance allowed restaurants, but not drive-ins.) On April 19, the city attorney requested the board to reconsider. The board took no action. On April 28, Reer obtained a building permit and began extensive renovation of the building he proposed to convert into a pizzeria. He also entered into a 10-year lease of the building.

   On May 17, the zoning board of appeals again took no action to reconsider. On June 6, a group of citizens filed suit against the city asking for a review of the zoning board's interpretation, contending that the notice requirement of the zoning ordinance had not been followed before the board's prior determination. After stipulation for another hearing following proper notice was entered into by the parties, the zoning board reconsidered its prior interpretation on June 28. By a 4 to 0 vote, the board found a carryout pizzeria was not a permissible use.

   Subsequently, the trial court affirmed the zoning board's interpretation. On grounds of estoppel, the trial judge enjoined the city from enforcing the ordinance. However, the trial court granted a group of private citizens, plaintiffs Talcott, Burks, and Boots, an injunction enjoining Reer from operating the pizzeria. Mr. Reer appealed.

   Does the zoning ordinance prevent Reer's pizzeria?

9. David Lucas bought two lots on an island off the coast of Georgia. He hired an architect to draw up plans for a single-family house on each lot. Two months later, before any building had occurred, the state legislature passed the Beachfront Management Act. The BMA prohibited owners from constructing any "occupiable improvements" within 20 feet of the coast at any point where erosion had occurred within the last 30 years. Thus, Lucas could not legally build any dwelling on either lot. He sued, claiming that his lots had been "taken" by the Georgia government and that he was owed compensation. The state trial court agreed, and awarded him $1.2 million. The state supreme court reversed. Lucas asked the U.S. Supreme Court for review.

   How should the Supreme Court rule, and why?

PART 4

Law of Finance

Because many sales of goods and real estate are made on credit, and because land, goods, and documents are frequently used as collateral in business financing arrangements, the material in Part Four logically follows Part Three. Here we review various aspects of commercial financing and risks of nonpayment.

The core of the legal rules for short-term commercial financing is found in Article 9 of the Uniform Commercial Code (UCC), "Secured Transactions." Article 9 covers all types of financing that use personal property or real estate fixtures as collateral. This very complex legal topic is covered in Chapters 23 and 24. Chapter 23 also covers the use of cosigners ("sureties") in credit transactions. To help you better appreciate the need for being a secured creditor rather than an unsecured one, the first chapter in this part summarizes the U.S. bankruptcy law. With hundreds of thousands of bankruptcies occurring each year, an unsecured creditor is taking a substantial risk of not receiving full payment. Bankruptcy is the problem; secured transactions are the solution.

In addition to establishing the legal rules in these two areas, both national and state governments have moved aggressively in the last two decades to protect consumers and debtors. Chapter 22 outlines the major consumer protection statutes now in force in the area of credit transactions.

This part also deals with the problems involved in using nonmoney pieces of paper as a method of payment. Article 3 of the UCC calls these pieces of paper commercial paper; the earlier term was negotiable esinstruments.

Nearly everyone is familiar with the use of personal checks as a payment instrument. The check is one form of commercial paper. This part covers the various types of liability on such instruments, the rules for enforcement of those liabilities, and the circumstances that will discharge such liabilities. Chapter 28 also covers the relationship between the customer and a bank when such instruments are deposited, or against which they have been issued.

Many students have signed promissory notes in loan transactions—for school expenses, car purchases, and the like. The promissory note is another form of commercial paper. Because it is a promise to pay, rather than an order to a bank to pay, some of the rules for a note are different than those for a check. These differences are also covered in this part.

The rules for dealing with these pieces of paper used as substitutes for money are complex, but very important to business operations. Millions of checks circulate through the banking system every day. Promissory notes are a key part of short-term financing arrangements, both for individuals and for businesses. A basic understanding of commercial paper rules is important to help you avoid or minimize liability and to protect your rights in transactions when these pieces of paper are used.

CHAPTER 22

Bankruptcy and Consumer Protection

Chapter Objectives

This chapter will:

- Explain the purpose and history of bankruptcy laws.
- Review the different types of proceedings in bankruptcy that are authorized by the law.
- Discuss the procedure for filing bankruptcy by a debtor or by a debtor's creditors.
- Explain the exemptions allowed to the debtor under national and state law.
- Review the rules of the bankruptcy law regarding discharge of debts.
- Explain the Consumer Credit Protection Act (the Truth in Lending Act).
- Indicate how the Equal Credit Opportunity Act protects credit applicants.
- Review the various prohibitions against misuse of credit information.
- Explain the new limitations on creditors' billing and collection practices.

Definition, Goals, Authority, and History

Bankruptcy is the process of settling the debts of persons or firms that are no longer able to meet their obligations. Under court supervision, the debtor's assets (or most of them) are collected and sold, and the proceeds are distributed to creditors. Creditors with equal **priority** status should receive the same proportion of their claims against the debtor. If the correct procedures have been followed, at the end of the process the debtor's obligations (or most of them) are discharged even though they have not been paid in full. The debtor gets a "fresh start."

Congress is empowered to establish uniform bankruptcy laws by the U.S. Constitution, Article I, Section 8. The first national bankruptcy law was passed in 1800. The Bankruptcy Act of 1898 was in force for 80 years, though it was substantially revised by the Chandler Act of 1938. To deal with the administrative problems that had arisen under the Bankruptcy Act and to better implement changes in consumer credit laws and in the UCC, Congress enacted the Bankruptcy Code of 1978, which became generally effective October 1, 1979. A new "Bankruptcy Reform Act" was passed by Congress in 2005. Its reforms include limits on the dollar amount of state homestead exemptions that debtors can claim, and the timing involved in changing one's "homestead" location, and requirements for some individuals to use Chapter 13 repayment plans rather than Chapter 7 liquidations. There are also many other detailed changes, including moving family support obligations to the number one priority for payment in personal bankruptcies.

Administration

The 1978 Code provided for a new system of bankruptcy courts as of April 1, 1984. The plan was that each U.S. judicial district would then have a bankruptcy court as an adjunct to the U.S. District Court, with one or more bankruptcy judges, each appointed for a 14-year term. These courts would have jurisdiction to decide all controversies affecting the debtor or the debtor's estate. In 1982, the Supreme Court in the *Northern Pipeline* case, found that the portion of the 1978 Bankruptcy Code, which created the new system of bankruptcy courts, violated Article III of the U.S. Constitution. The Supreme Court did state that its decision in this case would apply prospectively rather than retroactively, to avoid upsetting previously decided cases. In July 1984, the Bankruptcy Amendments and Federal Judgeship Act was adopted to replace those sections of the 1978 code that had been held unconstitutional. The 1984 amendments also made many other changes in the details of bankruptcy law.

Types of Proceedings

Chapter 7 of the 1978 code provides for **straight bankruptcy**, or **liquidation**. The trustee gathers and sells the debtor's property and pays the creditors; the debtor receives a discharge from all listed debts. Generally, straight bankruptcy proceedings may be voluntary or involuntary; that is, either the debtor or the creditors may institute such proceedings. Involuntary straight bankruptcy proceedings may not be commenced against a farmer or a nonprofit corporation.

Chapter 9 provides for adjustment of the debts of municipal corporations, where this is authorized by applicable state law.

Chapter 11 gives corporations in financial difficulty a chance to **reorganize** their financial affairs by staying in business and making periodic payments to their creditors. Chapter 11 proceedings may be voluntary or involuntary. Railroads are limited to Chapter 11 procedures.

Chapter 13 permits similar debt readjustments and payoffs for individuals with regular income. Chapter 13 proceedings can only be voluntary on the part of the debtor.

Insurance companies, banks, savings and loans, and similar financial institutions are governed by their own regulatory agencies and are not subject to the Bankruptcy Code.

In 1986, Congress added Chapter 12 to the Bankruptcy Code to provide for debt adjustment plans for "family farmers." As defined, a family farmer is an individual, or individual and spouse, engaged in a farming operation, whose total debts do not exceed $1,500,000 and at least 80 percent of which arise out of farming operations. In addition, such person(s) must have received more than 50 percent of the prior year's taxable income from farming operations. A corporation or partnership is included if more than 50 percent of the equity is owned by one family, or by one family and relatives, *and* the family or relatives conduct the farming operation. Additionally, more than 80 percent of the firm's business assets must be related to farming operations; its debts must not exceed $1,500,000 and must be 80 percent farming related; and if a corporation, its stock must not be publicly traded. *Farming operation* is defined as including ranching, raising of crops or livestock, and production of such unprocessed farm products as milk, eggs, and wool.

Chapter 12 provides for the filing and approval of a debt readjustment plan by the family farmer. The procedure is similar in most respects to the individual plans under Chapter 13, but it is specifically tailored to the needs of farmers. The family farmer is a business operation, and thus not quite the same as the typical consumer debtor who uses Chapter 13. Likewise, family farmers probably do need a slightly different procedure than the typical business reorganization under Chapter 11. In any event, Congress decided that a special procedure for **farm reorganizations** was justified.

Procedure

The debtor commences voluntary proceedings under Chapters 7, 9, 11, 12, or 13 by filing a petition, under the appropriate chapter, with the bankruptcy court. Spouses may file a joint petition to reduce administrative costs; the bankruptcy court has the power to allocate joint and separate property and debts.

When the debtor has 12 or more creditors, an involuntary petition under Chapters 7 or 11 must be joined in by 3 of them, who must have unsecured claims totaling at least $10,775. In determining this number, employees and insiders of the debtor are not counted. When there are fewer than 12 creditors, any one of them with an unsecured claim of $10,775 can file an involuntary petition. In addition, in an involuntary case the petitioning creditor or creditors must show either that the debtor is not paying his or her debts as they fall due or that the debtor has made a general assignment of assets for the benefit of creditors within 120 days before the filing of the petition.

In a voluntary case the court's "order for relief" is automatic; this operates to "stay" (prevent) collection proceedings against the debtor in state courts. In an involuntary petition the court must determine whether or not relief should be ordered. When the creditors' allegations are not proved, the debtor may be awarded court costs and damages for the lost use of property turned over to a trustee as well as actual and punitive damages if the filing was made in bad faith. Once an order for relief has been entered, the debtor is required to prepare schedules of creditors, assets, and liabilities. When the debtor is claiming personal exemptions, a schedule of those exemptions must also be filed with the court. Based on the list of creditors, the court sends out a notification of the first creditors' meeting.

The court may appoint an interim trustee to hold and manage the debtor's property until a trustee is elected by the creditors. If the creditors fail to elect a trustee, the interim trustee continues to administer the debtor's estate. The trustee's job is to collect all the debtor's property, to separate out **exempt property,** to determine whether creditors' claims are secured or unsecured, and finally to pay off claims according to their legal priority status.

The *Ellsworth* case discusses the possible consequences of omitting items of property from the Debtor's list of assets.

Debtor's Available Property

The 1898 act permitted each state to specify what items of property the debtor could exempt from the bankruptcy proceeding; these exemptions vary considerably from state to state. The Michigan exemptions, for example, include all family pictures, wearing apparel, "provisions and fuel" for comfortable subsistence for the family for 6 months, up to $1,000 of household goods and appliances, burial plots, up to $1,000 in the tools of the

CASE 1

Ellsworth v. Bauder

333 B.R. 828 (8 Cir. Bkrp. App. 2005)

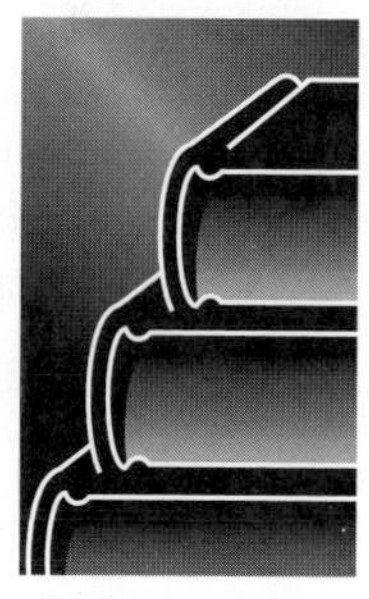

Facts: The debtor, Vicki Jo Bauder, is 52 years old. She did not complete high school and suffers from depression, anxiety, and adult attention deficit disorder. She filed for Chapter 7 bankruptcy on March 10, 2004. Her original list of personal property included household goods ($575), apparel ($300), pension ($15,595.78), tax refunds and accrued wages ($1,000), 1999 Grand Prix car ($3,700). She claimed exemptions for all these items except the car. She amended her property list 9 days after she had her first meeting with her creditors—this time including some additional personal items, plus several items in her possession that belonged to another person, and a diamond ring that was hers but was in her daughter's possession. (Bankruptcy Rule 1009 provides that property schedules "may be amended by the debtor as a matter of course at any time before the case is closed.")

The day after the amended filing, her former boyfriend (Michael Ellsworth) filed an objection to Bauder's being given a bankruptcy discharge from her debts because she had initially failed to disclose her ownership of the diamond ring. (Ellsworth had bought the ring for $1,000 and given it to Bauder while they were together.) Although she listed the ring's value as $300 on her amended schedule, Bauder said she had been told by a pawn shop that it was worth only $3 or $4 because a diamond was missing and several gem-holding prongs were bent. She said she had not listed it because an office employee of her lawyer had told her that she only had to list property in her possession. (She had apparently learned otherwise at the first creditors' meeting, and her daughter reminded her of the ring as they were filling out the amended schedule.)

The Bankruptcy Court denied Bauder a discharge of her debts, and she appealed.

Issue: Did the debtor "knowingly and fraudulently" make a false statement?

Decision: No. Judgment reversed, and case remanded for entry of a discharge.

Opinion by Bankruptcy Judge Venters: "Under 11 U.S.C. s.727(a)(4)(A), a debtor shall be granted a discharge unless 'the debtor knowingly and fraudulently, in ... the case—made a false oath.' To bar discharge, the false oath must be material. The subject matter is material if it concerns the discovery of assets or the existence and disposition of property. Intent under s.727 can be established by circumstantial evidence. Statements made with reckless indifference to the truth are regarded as intentionally false....

"The court based its denial of the Debtor's discharge solely on the Debtor's failure to list a diamond ring on her original schedules. 'Bauder's schedules were knowingly false because she failed to list her ownership of the diamond ring.' The court reached this conclusion after determining that her explanations for not listing the ring were not credible and were 'contradictory.'...

"First, the court found that 'the fact that her reasons for not listing the ring contradict each other, detract[s] from her credibility,' but the court's discussion of that contradiction indicates that the court's assessment of her credibility on that point was based on an erroneous review of the record. Specifically, it appears that the court confused the Debtor's explanations of why she did not list other 'valueless' property with the reasons given for why she failed to list the ring on her original schedules. The court found that the Debtor's testimony that the ring had only sentimental value was inconsistent with the decision to give it to her daughter to put into a safe-deposit box—an action which the court interpreted as suggesting that the Debtor believed that the ring had significant economic value. Rather, the Debtor offered only two explanations for why she failed to list the ring on her original schedules: (1) because she believed that she only had to list items in her possession, and (2) because she forgot about the ring at the time she filled out her schedules. And those explanations are complementary, not contradictory. If the Debtor believed (even if in error) that she only had to disclose items in her possession, it is logical, and likely, that she might not recall items that were in another's possession. These explanations are even more plausible given the Debtor's limited education and affliction with attention deficit disorder.

"Second, we find it problematic that the court did not give any weight to (or even mention) the fact that the Debtor disclosed the ring in her amended schedules shortly after the s.341 meeting of creditors and before this adversary proceeding was filed....

"The Plaintiff bears the burden of proof to establish fraudulent intent, so in the absence of any evidence indicating that the Debtor's disclosure was not self-motivated, we take the Debtor's prompt disclosure of the ring on her amended schedules—filed before this adversary proceeding and as authorized by Bankruptcy Rule 1009(a)—to be evidence of the Debtor's innocent intent which the court failed to consider....

"Third, we have reservations as to whether the omission, even if made knowingly, was material. The omission of property of trivial value is immaterial ... and the Debtor's testimony that the ring in its current condition is only worth a few dollars was uncontradicted....

"Finally, we are guided in our decision here by the Court of Appeals recent decision in In re Bren, where the Court granted a discharge to a significantly more sophisticated debtor who initially failed to list, but later disclosed prior to the filing of an objection to discharge, her interest in a 'modest' inheritance, and who claimed ignorance of other significant omissions related to property and business dealings allegedly managed entirely by her husband. Put simply, if Mrs. Bren qualifies for a discharge, then a person who has attention deficit disorder and other mental/emotional problems, and who omits but then timely discloses a worthless ring from her schedules certainly should. . . .

"For the reasons stated above, we reverse the bankruptcy court's denial of the Debtor's discharge . . . and remand for entry of an order of discharge."

debtor's trade, disability insurance benefits for sickness or injury, the cash surrender value of life insurance, benefits to be paid under workers' compensation, up to $3,500 for a "homestead" exemption (the debtor's equity in the family home), and to each householder "10 sheep, 2 cows, 5 swine, 100 hens, 5 roosters and sufficient hay and grain growing or otherwise to keep such animals and poultry for six months." The foregoing list seems fairly generous if one remembers that the debtor is getting a discharge from most debts and a fresh start.

The 1978 code gives the debtor the option of choosing the state exemptions or those provided in the 1978 code, unless the particular state specified its exemptions must be used. Some 30 states have done so. For most debtors with the option, the national exemptions will be a better choice.

Exempt Property

The exemptions of the 1978 code include a residence exemption of up to $7,500; up to $1,200 for one motor vehicle; and up to $200 per item, with a $4,000 limit on total value, for household goods, wearing apparel, appliances, animals, crops, or musical instruments. Additional exemptions include up to $500 in jewelry owned by the debtor or a dependent; up to $400 for any property plus up to $3,750 from any unused amount from the $7,500 residence exemption; up to $750 for the tools or books of the debtor's or a dependent's trade; any unmatured life insurance policy owned by the debtor other than a credit life policy; up to $4,000 in cash surrender or loan value for a life insurance policy owned by the debtor and on the debtor's life; professionally prescribed health aids for the debtor and dependents; alimony and child support payments; "future earnings" such as Social Security and veterans' benefits, unemployment compensation, disability payments, and pension plan payments; and up to $7,500 in payments from a personal injury lawsuit. The debtor is also given the power to avoid **judicial liens** and nonpossessory, **nonpurchase-money security interests** that impair his or her exemptions for most listed items of tangible personal property (but not liens against the motor vehicle).

The trustee may recover any items of property that the debtor **fraudulently transferred** to others within 1 year before the filing of the bankruptcy petition. A transfer is fraudulent if the debtor actually intended to hide the asset from his or her creditors' claims or if the debtor received less than fair consideration for the asset and was insolvent at the time (or became so as a result of the transfer). The trustee may also recover **preferential payments** made by the debtor 90 or fewer days prior to the petition. A payment is preferential if it is made for a prior unsecured debt, if it gives a creditor more than that creditor would have received in a bankruptcy proceeding, and if the debtor was insolvent at the time the payment was made. The debtor is presumed to have been insolvent during the 90-day period, and the creditor's good faith is irrelevant. A payment is not preferential if it was made in the ordinary course of business.

In the *Rousey* case, the U.S. Supreme Court interpreted the exemption provisions to include individual retirement accounts (IRAs), which are held by millions of people in this country.

Creditors' Claims and Priorities

A claim includes nearly any sort of right to payment, whether or not it is reduced to judgment, liquidated or unliquidated, fixed or contingent, matured or unmatured, disputed or undisputed, legal or equitable, secured or unsecured. It includes the right to equitable remedies when the breach also gives a right to payment. A creditor who has such a claim files a

CASE 2

Rousey v. Jacoway
544 U.S. 320 (2005)

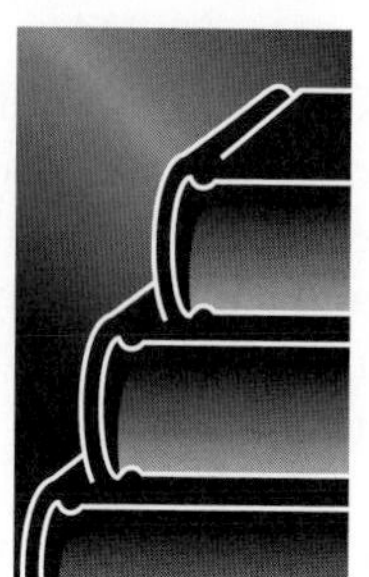

Facts: When Richard and Betty Jo Rousey ended their employment at Northrup Grumman Corp., they were required to take lump sum distributions from their employer-sponsored pension plans. They deposited these funds into two IRAs, one in each of their names. Several years later, they filed a joint Chapter 7 bankruptcy petition. They claimed their IRAs were exempt property, not part of the bankruptcy estate. Section 522(d)(10)(E) of the Bankruptcy Code provides an exemption for "(E) a payment under a stock bonus, pension, profitsharing, annuity, or similar plan or contract on account of illness, disability, death, age, or length of service, to the extent reasonably necessary for the support of the debtor and any dependent of the debtor. . . ." Jill Jacoway was appointed trustee; she objected to the exemption of the IRAs and moved for a court order turning those funds over to her as part of the bankruptcy estate. The Bankruptcy Court granted her motion, the bankruptcy appellate panel affirmed that ruling, and so did the Eighth Circuit Court of Appeals. The U.S. Supreme Court granted certiorari.

Issue: Can debtors exempt assets in their IRAs from their bankruptcy estates, pursuant to section 522(d)(10)(E)?

Decision: Yes. Judgment reversed, and case remanded.

Opinion by Justice Thomas: "Under the terms of the statute ... the Rouseys' right to receive payment under their IRAs must meet three requirements to be exempted ...: (1) the right to receive the payment must be from 'a stock bonus, pension, profitsharing, annuity, or similar plan or contract'; (2) the right to receive payment must be 'on account of illness, disability, death, age, or length of service'; and (3) even then, the right to receive payment may be exempted only 'to the extent' that it is 'reasonably necessary to support' the accountholder or his dependents. . . .

"The dispute in this case is whether the Rouseys' IRAs fulfill the first and second requirements. . . .

"We turn first to the requirement that the payment be 'on account of illness, disability, death, age, or length of service.' ... We have interpreted the phrase 'on account of' elsewhere within the Bankruptcy Code to mean 'because of,' thereby requiring a causal connection between the term that the phrase 'on account of' modifies and the factor specified in the statute at issue. . . . The context of this provision does not suggest that Congress deviated from the term's ordinary meaning. Thus, 'on account of' in s.522(d)(10)(E) requires that the right to receive payment be 'because of' illness, disability, death, age, or length of service. . . .

"The statutes governing IRAs persuade us that the Rouseys' right to payment from IRAs is causally connected to their age. Their right to receive payment of the entire balance is not in dispute. Because their accounts qualify as IRAs ... the Rouseys have a nonforfeitable right to the balance held in these accounts. . . . That right is restricted by a 10 percent tax penalty that applies to withdrawals from IRAs made before the accountholder turns 59 1/2. Contrary to Jacoway's contention, this tax penalty is substantial. . . . The low rates of early withdrawals are consistent with the notion that this penalty substantially deters early withdrawals from such accounts. . . . It therefore limits the Rouseys' right to 'payment' of the balance of their IRAs. And because this condition is removed when the accountholder turns age 59 1/2, the Rouseys' right to the balance of their IRAs is a right to payment 'on account of' age. . . .

"The [second] issue ... is whether the Rouseys' IRAs are 'similar plan[s] or contract[s]' within the meaning of s.522(d)(10(E). To be 'similar,' an IRA must be like, though not identical to, the specific plans or contracts listed ... and consequently share characteristics in common to the listed plans or contracts. . . .

"The Rouseys contend that IRAs are 'similar' to stock bonus, pension, profitsharing, or annuity plans or contracts, in that they have the same 'primary purpose,' namely, 'enabl[ing] Americans to save for their retirement.' ... We agree with the Rouseys that IRAs are similar to the plans specified in the statute. Those plans, like the Rouseys' IRAs, provide a substitute for wages ... and are not mere savings accounts. . . .

"The common feature of all of these plans is that they provide income that substitutes for wages earned as salary or hourly compensation. This understanding of the plans' similarities comports with the other types of payments that a debtor may exempt under s.522(d)(10)—all of which concern income that substitutes for wages. . . .

"We also reject Jacoway's argument that the availability of IRA withdrawals exempt from the 10 percent penalty renders the IRAs more like savings accounts. . . .

"These exceptions are limited in amount and scope. Even with these carveouts, an early withdrawal without penalty remains the exception, rather than the rule. . . .

"In sum, the Rouseys' IRAs fulfill both of S.522(d)(10(E)'s requirements at issue here. . . . The judgment of the Court of Appeals is therefore reversed, and the case is remanded for further proceedings consistent with this opinion.

"It is so ordered."

document called a **proof of claim.** A secured creditor need not do so unless the claim exceeds the value of the security and the creditor wishes to try to collect the balance in the bankruptcy proceeding. The creditor's "proof" is accepted as prima facie evidence of the existence and the amount of the debt, and such claims will be allowed and paid (to the extent that funds are available) unless objection is made to them by another creditor, the trustee, or the debtor. Under current practice, proofs of claim must be filed within 6 months after the first date set for the first meeting of creditors.

Not all claims are paid at the same time or to the same extent. **Secured creditors**, that is, creditors who have taken the proper steps to establish their rights against specific pieces of collateral, will be paid first from the proceeds of that collateral. If the value of their collateral is sufficient, secured creditors may be paid in full; if not, they are **unsecured creditors** for the remainder of their claims. In addition to the claims of secured creditors, there are other claims that are given priority under the Bankruptcy Code. One of the significant changes in the 2005 bankruptcy reform was to move **family support obligations** to priority number one—formerly it was sixth on the list. The feeling was that if there are any funds available from the debtor, they should go the family first, even before paying the processing costs of the bankruptcy. Expenses of administering the bankrupt's estate—accountants, attorneys, appraisers, trustees—are now second priority, along with creditors' expenses in discovering and recovering property that the debtor transferred or concealed.

Third priority now goes to unsecured claims for goods, services, or credit that arose in the normal course of the debtor's business between the filing of an involuntary petition and the court's order for relief or appointment of a trustee. Fourth priority goes to employees' claims (up to $10,000 per individual) for wages earned in the 180 days prior to filing of the petition or cessation of the debtor's business. Fifth in line are employees' claims for unpaid contributions to benefit plans, but each employee can claim no more than $10,000 total for unpaid wages and benefits.

The sixth priority group includes claims by grain sellers or bailees against a debtor owning or operating a grain elevator and claims by U.S. fishermen against a debtor operating a fish storage or processing facility for fish delivered to it. Seventh come consumer claims (up to $2,225 each) for deposits made in transactions to buy or rent property or to purchase consumer goods or services that have not been delivered by the debtor. Governments' claims for certain unpaid taxes have been lowered to eighth priority.

Only after all the aforementioned groups have been paid in full, in sequence, will the general unsecured creditors receive anything. In most bankruptcy cases this means that the general creditors will receive only a fraction of was what is due, if anything at all. And remember—the debtor has been allowed to keep all exempt property.

The 1978 Bankruptcy Code made one other significant priority change. The creditors of a **bankrupt partnership** are now entitled to share equally with the unsecured creditors of individual partners against the partners' personal assets. Under the old rule in the Uniform Partnership Act, the firm's unpaid creditors had no claim against personal assets until all the personal creditors had been paid in full. The Bankruptcy Code also contains special rules for community property, and it gives the court general power to change priorities on equitable grounds after a hearing.

Discharge, Objections, and Grounds for Refusal

Most of the individual debtors who file under Chapter 7 will receive a **discharge** from most of their previous debts at the conclusion of the bankruptcy proceedings. This is the whole idea of the fresh start. Generally, an individual can be so discharged only once within any 6-year period. However, when an individual has worked out a voluntary repayment plan under Chapter 13, has paid off at least 70 percent of the claims filed under it, and has made his or her best efforts in good faith, a discharge may be granted more frequently than once in 6 years.

Any single creditor or the trustee acting for all of them may file an **objection** to a discharge of the debtor. The court must then determine whether or not there is some reason for denying the discharge. The Bankruptcy Act lists several grounds for denial, including the debtor's destruction or concealment of property with the intent of delaying or

Exhibit 22.1: The Bankruptcy Process—Chapter 7 Liquidation

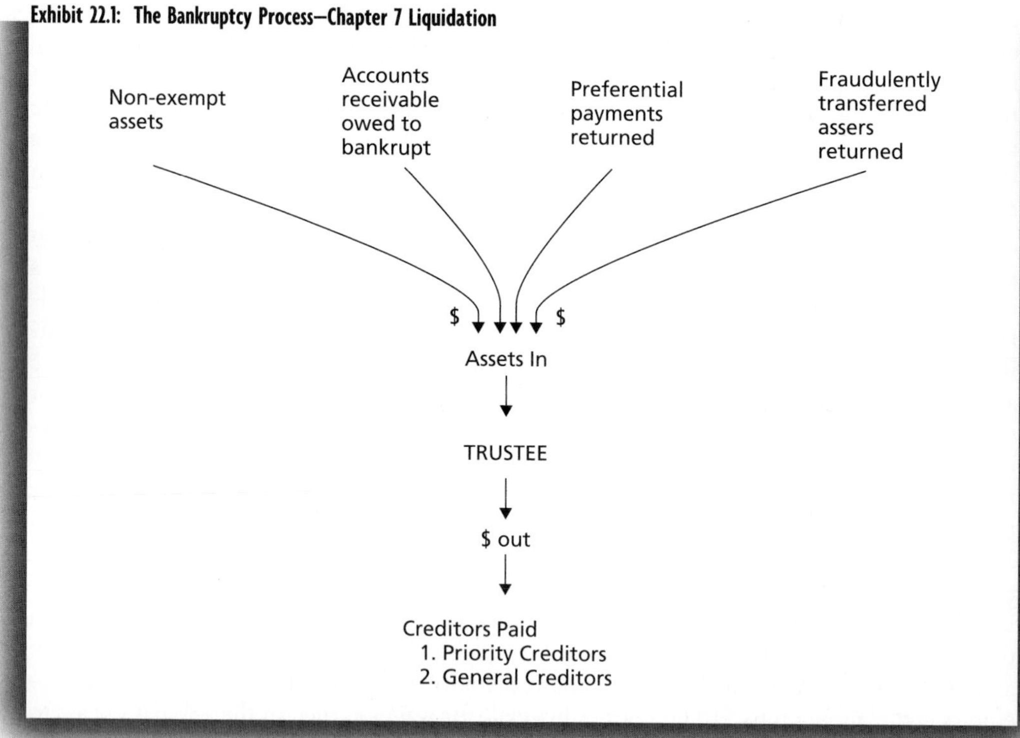

defrauding creditors; destroying, concealing, falsifying, or failing to keep books and records; committing a "bankruptcy crime," such as giving a false oath or participating in bribery to obtain some special advantage; failing to explain losses or deficiencies in existing assets; and failing to obey court orders or to answer questions (but *not* including refusals properly based on the constitutional privilege against self-incrimination). Also, even a debtor who is entitled to a discharge may in writing waive the right to one.

When a discharge has been properly granted, the 1978 code extends the protection given the debtor from the unpaid creditors' further collection efforts for discharged debts. The discharge, of course, voids all existing and future judgments based on such debts. The 1898 act also prohibited creditors from employing "any process" to collect discharged debts; the 1978 code forbids any *act* by creditors to recover such debts.

Debts Not Discharged

Some debts survive the bankruptcy discharge; that is, the debtor's liability still exists, and the creditor may use appropriate enforcement procedures. Such nondischargeable debts include taxes incurred for 3 years before the bankruptcy; **alimony and child support** payments; sums owed by a fiduciary because of fraud, misappropriation, or embezzlement; liability based on fraudulent representations or false pretenses; and liability for **intentional torts** ("willful and malicious injury"). As to debts in the last three groups, the creditor involved must specifically request a determination by the court that the debt is not dischargeable; if there is no such request, such debts would be discharged.

Because of the increasing frequency with which bankruptcies were being filed by recent college graduates, the 1978 code added another category of nondischargeable debts: **educational loans**, unless the first due date was more than 5 years before the filing of the bankruptcy petition or unless the continuing liability would impose an "undue hardship" on the debtor or the debtor's dependents. The 1984 amendments add liability for drunk driving to the list. Also, under the 1984 act, a debt of over $500 for **luxury items** bought within 40 days prior to the filing, and certain **cash advances** of over $1,000 made within 20 days prior to filing are presumed to be nondischargeable.

The *Karpinsky* case applies the phrase "willful and malicious injury."

CASE 3

DirecTV v. Karpinsky

328 B.R. 516 (Bkrp., E.D. MI 2005)

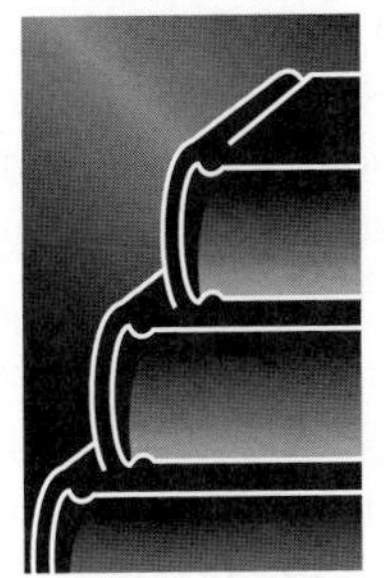

Facts: DirecTV is a direct broadcast satellite system, delivering 200+ channels of TV and other programming to more than 12 million homes and businesses in the United States. It encrypts (electronically scrambles) its satellite transmission to provide security and to prevent unauthorized viewing. It sells its services by subscription and pay-per-view. On October 1, 2002, DirecTV sued Eugene Karpinsky in U.S. District Court, alleging violations of several national statutes—unauthorized reception of satellite signals, unauthorized interception of electronic communications, and possession of pirate access devices—and (common law) conversion of property. On December 3, before the case went to trial, Karpinsky and his wife Ellen filed for bankruptcy. DirecTV filed their claim with the bankruptcy court and alleged that any debt arising from the alleged satellite piracy was nondischargeable. A trial was held on April 25, 2005. Defendant did not call any witnesses or present any evidence and acknowledged that DirecTV had proved its case. The court then had to decide on the amount of damages, and whether those damages were dischargeable in the bankruptcy proceeding.

Issue: Are these damages for satellite piracy nondischargeable?

Decision: Yes. Damages of $202,000 are awarded, Karpinsky is enjoined from committing further satellite piracy, and a hearing is scheduled to set attorney fees.

Opinion by Bankruptcy Judge McIvor: "Defendant argues that, to the extent courts have awarded statutory damages in similar DirecTV piracy cases, the courts have been lenient and, therefore, this Court should award only a small amount of damages, if any at all, to Plaintiff. Defendant cites three cases where damage awards have been relatively small....

"While the Court understands Defendant's desire to obtain a small damage award, this Court finds the above-listed cases distinguishable for two reasons. First all of the cited cases are default judgments where no evidence was presented. In contrast to those cases, this Court heard two days of trial testimony which demonstrated that Defendant's conduct was purposeful, planned, and willful. Second, there are factual differences between the instant case and these cases cited by Defendant. In Alvares and Andino, DirecTV alleged that the defendants possessed a single unlooper device.... In the instant cases, Defendant possessed at least seven devices used to intercept DirecTV satellite signals (three Unloopers, three Access Cards, and one Smart Card Programmer). In the Carpenter case, unlike the instant case, plaintiff DirecTV did not seek relief under s.605(a) [unauthorized reception of satellite signals].... Therefore, plaintiff was not entitled to seek relief under that statute. Because the cases cited by Defendant are distinguishable from the instant case, they are not particularly useful for helping this Court determine the appropriate amount of damages to be awarded....

"Defendant argues that any statutory damages awarded to Plaintiff, exceeding actual damages, are dischargeable in his bankruptcy because the statutory damage provisions that Plaintiff relies on ... are not set forth as enumerated exceptions to the general dischargeability provisions of s.523. In other words, even though the underlying activity (i.e., signal interception), and the actual damages flowing therefrom, may be non-dischargeable ... the damages resulting from the application of the statutory damage provision are dischargeable because s.523 contains no specific exception to discharge for statutory damages for signal theft. Defendant argues that, if Congress intended that statutory damages for signal theft be non-dischargeable, the Code would have specifically identified those damages as being non-dischargeable as Congress did in cases of criminal restitution ... and fines for drunken driving offenses....

"This Court finds that Defendant's intentional misappropriation of DirecTV's satellite signals constitutes larceny ... and a willful and malicious injury to Plaintiff ... and, therefore, Defendant's entire debt to Plaintiff—including the statutory damages awarded—is non-dischargeable.... The United States Supreme Court, in *Cohen v. De La Cruz* ... determined that the exception to discharge set forth in 11 U.S.C. s.523(a)(2)(A) applies to the underlying debt resulting from fraud along with any statutory damages and attorney's fees awarded on account of the debtor's fraud....

"Although ss.523(a)(4) & (a)(6) were not at issue in Cohen, the Supreme Court cited [them] as clear examples of instances in which statutory damages, including attorney's fess, that exceed actual damages would be non-dischargeable.... Based on the analysis set forth in *Cohen* ... this Court finds that all of the damages, including the attorney's fees authorized by statute, are non-dischargeable...."

Reaffirmation of Debts

The 1978 code changes the rules on debtor's new promises to pay scheduled bankruptcy debts by adding several extra requirements for such promises to be enforceable. First, the new promises must be enforceable under the applicable state (nonbankruptcy) law; you'll recall from Chapter 10 that many states require such new promises to be made in writing.

The 1978 code requires such new promises to have been made before the bankruptcy discharge becomes effective, and the code further states that such a promise may be rescinded by the debtor for 60 days after it becomes enforceable. In addition, when the debtor is an individual, the court must hold a hearing and advise the debtor of the legal effects of such a promise. The court also must tell the debtor that the promise is not required as a condition of the discharge. When the new promise relates to a consumer debt that is not secured by real property, the court in addition must approve the promise as being in the debtor's "best interest" and not imposing an "undue hardship" or as being part of a good faith agreement for the redemption of some of the debtor's property or for the settlement of a dispute as to whether the debt was or was not dischargeable.

Individual Repayment Plans

An individual in financial difficulty may file a voluntary petition for "adjustment" of debts under Chapter 13 of the 1978 code and thus prevent nearly all further actions by creditors to collect their claims. This Chapter 13 procedure is available to persons who have less than $269,250 in unsecured debts, less than $807,705 in secured debts, and a "regular income." Proprietors of businesses, Social Security recipients, and wage earners can file under Chapter 13. Within 10 days of filing the petition, the debtor must file with the court a plan that provides for payments of future income to a trustee, for full payment to creditors with priority, for equal treatment of all claims in the same class, and for retention of liens by secured creditors. Such plans usually ask for an extension of time within which to pay the debts; the plan maximum is 3 years unless the court grants an extension of up to 5 years for good cause. The debtor may also ask for a **composition** of debts in which the creditors may receive less than 100 percent of their claims.

A bankruptcy judge presides at the hearing for confirmation of the proposed plan. Unsecured creditors do not get to vote on confirming the plan, but the plan must give them at least what they would have received if the debtor had gone through a Chapter 7 bankruptcy/liquidation. Priority claimants must be paid in full, to the extent that money is available, unless these creditors agree to lesser payments. Secured creditors do get to vote on whether or not to accept the plan, but if a secured creditor disapproves, the court may confirm it anyway if the debtor gives the dissenting creditor the property that secures the claim or if the dissenting creditor retains a lien and the subject property is worth at least as much as the allowed amount of the secured claim. A secured claim against the debtor's principal residence cannot be modified by the plan; other secured claims may be. The payment arrangements of the plan itself may be modified after confirmation, subject to the aforementioned limitations, after proper notice and a hearing.

After completing the payments required by the plan, the debtor is discharged from all debts except long-term unsecured debts not covered by the plan and debts for child support, maintenance, and alimony. In cases of hardship, when modification of the plan is not practicable and when the amounts already paid are equal to Chapter 7 liquidation values, the debtor may receive a hardship discharge if the failure to complete the plan is not his or her fault. Such a hardship discharge does not affect any nondischargeable debts under Chapter 7 or long-term debts not dealt with by the plan, whether secured or unsecured; or debts incurred without the trustee's permission after confirmation of the plan. If the plan was a composition, the debtor cannot receive a second discharge for 6 years unless the amounts paid were his or her best effort, made in good faith, and at least 70 percent of the required payments were made.

Reorganization of Business Debtor

In many cases, businesses get into financial difficulty because of dislocations in the production/distribution/collection process over which they have little, if any, control. Embargoes, wars, strikes, materials shortages, defaults by major customers, and other economic occurrences may have serious impact on a business that does not have substantial financial reserves. If a basically sound firm has a temporary cash flow problem, it probably makes sense to try to save the firm rather than push it into a Chapter 7 liquidation. Most reorganizations under Chapter 11 are designed to salvage the debtor businesses, although the creditors sometimes require management changes and the business may be run temporarily by a trustee.

Chapter 11 cases, like Chapter 7 liquidations, may be voluntary or involuntary; most of the same rules apply to both types of proceedings. Under Chapter 11, however, the court must appoint a creditors' committee, usually composed of the seven largest unsecured creditors. This committee examines the affairs of the business to decide whether to continue the business, to ask the court for a liquidation, or to ask that a trustee be appointed to operate the business in place of the existing management. For the first 120 days after filing, only the debtor can propose a plan for reorganization, but the debtor would normally develop such a plan in consultation with the creditors. A debtor who files a plan within that time has a further 60 days to get the creditors to approve it. The court can reduce or extend these time periods for good cause. After the first 120 days, any party in interest (a creditor or the trustee) can propose a plan.

The proposed plan must classify claims and ownership interests and must spell out which will and which will not be impaired; it must provide equal treatment for all claims or interests in the same class unless the persons with that class of claims or interests agree otherwise; and it must provide adequate means for implementing the plan's payment arrangements. Further, when the debtor business is a corporation, the plan must require that stockholders' voting rights be protected, that no nonvoting stock be issued, and that directors and officers be selected so as to protect the interests of creditors and stockholders. Generally, the plan may modify the rights of creditors and owners, but these persons have the right to vote on whether or not to accept the plan. Normally the bankruptcy court will not confirm a reorganization plan unless it has received the required majority vote of each class of creditors or owners whose rights were modified ("impaired"). Two-thirds in dollar amount of each class of such owners must vote in favor of the plan. Each class of such creditors must approve by a majority in number and by two-thirds in the dollar amount of allowed claims. The plan may be confirmed without the consent of owners or creditors whose rights were not impaired.

It is possible for the court to confirm a plan that has not received the consent of an impaired class if the persons in that class are treated in a "fair and equitable" manner—for instance, if all members of the class will receive the full current value of their claims or if all members of the class will receive an equal proportion of their claims and classes whose claims and interests have lower priorities will receive nothing. This is a so-called "cram down" approval. In any case, dissenters are protected by the rule that they must receive from the plan at least what they would have received through a Chapter 7 liquidation. Moreover, to approve the plan, the court must find that it is "in the best interests of the creditors."

New Government Activism on Consumer Issues

Consumerism was surely one of the major social movements in the United States during the 1970s. The national government, and to a lesser extent the states, moved to correct what were seen as abuses by sellers and lenders. Inexperienced and unwary consumers were being pressured into paying for shoddy or undelivered merchandise, or misperformed or unperformed services. High-pressure sales tactics produced contracts with harsh and unfair provisions. Confronted with these marketplace manipulations, judges and legislators rebelled.

The ***Henningsen* case** (see Chapter 18) is probably the single most important piece of consumer law ever written. It was the opening salvo in the product liability revolution, which has continued from the 1960s and 1970s, into the new millennium. That part of consumer protection law is discussed throughout Chapter 18.

Other aspects of the consumer protection movement have also been discussed in previous chapters. The Federal Trade Commission's (FTC) authority over unfair trade practices and deceptive advertising is discussed in Chapter 5. The new legal rules on unordered goods and in-home sales are discussed in Chapter 8. Usury laws, limiting the rate of interest that can be charged, are covered in Chapter 12. Discussed in Chapter 9 is the concept of "unconscionability," which courts can use to invalidate contract provisions that are grossly unfair, although not specifically illegal.

Consumer Credit Protection Act (Truth in Lending Act)

Full Disclosure in Credit Transactions

As several philosophers have said, "knowledge is power." A consumer who was aware of the terms of a proposed credit transaction would be better able to compare them with those of other possible lenders and to object to those which were most unfair. Congress passed the Truth in Lending Act (TILA) in 1969, as the first major part of the **Consumer Credit Protection Act (CCPA)**, which now also includes sections on other topics, such as **consumer leasing** and **credit billing**. A required disclosure form must be given to the consumer at or before the signing of the credit contract. It must disclose the interest rate as an annual percentage and show the total dollar figure for the **finance charge,** which includes loan fees, credit report fees, and required insurance charges. TILA does not limit the amount of these charges; it only specifies that the amounts must be disclosed.

Similarly, ads for credit that mention a down payment, a monthly payment, or an interest rate must go on to specify the other terms as well.

When the purchaser's home is used as collateral, the purchaser is given 3 business days after the purchase, or after the creditor gives written notice of the right to cancel, within which to rescind the whole contract. This rescission rule does not apply to the first mortgage on the home, but only to later credit contracts, such as those for home improvements.

Under its rule-making authority, the Federal Reserve Board (FRB) has stated that TILA applies to any consumer transaction that calls for payment in more than four installments. This rule is found in **FRB Regulation Z**.

Because the original TILA covered only consumer purchases on credit, Congress added the consumer leasing sections to CCPA in 1976. Leasing of cars, computers, and other equipment has become increasingly common, even for people defined as consumers (personal users). Similar disclosures are required in these lease transactions.

When a creditor has violated TILA, the consumer may recover twice the finance charge, but not less than $100 nor more than $1,000, plus attorneys' fees. Criminal penalties for a willful and knowing failure to comply are a fine up to $1,000, or imprisonment up to 1 year, or both. Because of the detail and complexities involved in complying with TILA, amendments passed in 1980 exempt a creditor from liability if the error is corrected within 60 days after it is discovered.

Credit Card Liability

Other sections of the CCPA have drastically changed the law relating to the issuance and use of credit cards. Prior to the CCPA, gasoline companies and other issuers were free to send out cards by mass mailings, using computerized lists of potential customers. Under general contract law rules, retention and use of the credit card would constitute acceptance of the issuing company's offer. The issuer's terms could include a provision making the cardholder liable for its unauthorized use. These contract provisions were sometimes enforced by the courts, at least when the merchant taking the card as payment had made a reasonable effort to verify the identity of the person using the card.

It is now unlawful to issue cards that have not been requested by the customer. Further, the customer/cardholder's liability for unauthorized use is limited to $50. Even this $50 amount is conditioned on the card issuer's compliance with CCPA's requirements. The issuer must have notified the customer of this potential $50 liability, have provided a notification form to be sent to the issuer in the event of loss or theft of the card, and have provided either a signature or photo on the card so that the merchant can identify the user. If all these requirements have been met, the customer can be held liable for up to $50 of unauthorized charges that occur before the issuer is notified that the card has been lost or stolen.

Equal Credit Opportunity Act

Originally, the problems dealt with by the **Equal Credit Opportunity Act (ECOA)** were denials of credit on the basis of sex or marital status. Women who had been divorced or widowed were denied credit in many cases because they had had no separate credit history or because they had been codebtors with their husbands, who had defaulted on the debts.

Either way, they were unable to obtain credit in their own names. ECOA now prohibits such discrimination and also that based on race, color, religion, national origin, or age. These protections are similar to those given to employees under the national civil rights acts, as discussed in Chapter 30.

Creditors are prohibited from discouraging applications for credit, from refusing to grant a separate account to a married woman, and from asking the applicant's marital status when such a separate account is requested. Because marital property laws differ from state to state, however, a creditor may ask about marital status when collateral is required for the credit transaction. Similarly, minors cannot demand credit under ECOA because they lack full capacity to contract and can disaffirm contracts that they make while minors.

Use of Credit Information

It is true that businesses have always kept records about individuals, but recordkeeping was limited, due to the obvious problems of storage, access, and retrievability. The computer has minimized those problems, and consequently more and more information is kept about the individual. There is more possibility of error and less access by the individual to the records to determine just what they say. A major concern has been the gathering, storage, and retrieval of information about individuals by various credit bureaus and local merchants' associations, which have computerized their files and have dossiers on nearly every American adult.

Fair Credit Reporting Act

To curb the abuses of credit bureaus, Congress passed the **Fair Credit Reporting Act (FCRA)**, which became effective on April 25, 1971. The following is a summary of its major provisions.

1. Credit reporting agencies are authorized to furnish credit information only in connection with credit, insurance, and employment applications, a government license for which a consumer has applied, or any other business transaction in which a consumer is involved; or by written consent of the consumer concerned; or in compliance with a court order.
2. The reporting of adverse information more than 7 years old regarding suits, arrests, and other matters is generally prohibited. However, information on bankruptcies can be made available for 14 years, and if the inquiry concerns an application for a life insurance policy of $50,000 or more or an application for a job with an annual salary of $20,000 or more, then there is no age restriction on records and all information may be furnished. Thus the bureaus have an excuse not to clear out the computers periodically.
3. The reporting of adverse information from investigative reports more than 3 months old is generally prohibited unless the information is reverified.
4. All reporting agencies are required to "follow reasonable procedures to ensure maximum accuracy of the information" contained in reports.
5. The type of information that can be furnished to government agencies without a court order is limited.
6. Upon the request of a consumer, a reporting agency must disclose to the consumer all information about him or her in the agency's files, except for medical information or the sources of the information.
7. A person or business ordering an investigative report must notify the consumer that an investigation is being made.
8. An agency must disclose to a consumer on request the names of persons and businesses that have been furnished credit information about the consumer in the preceding 6 months (2 years for employment purposes).

9. An agency must reinvestigate information disputed by a consumer "within a reasonable period of time" unless "it has reasonable grounds to believe that the dispute by the consumer is frivolous or irrelevant." If the information is found to be inaccurate, then the agency must delete the information from the record. The consumer also has the right to have the agency put in the file a statement of not more than 100 words explaining that the information is disputed, and the agency, at the consumer's request, must send copies of the statement to the persons and businesses that had been sent the disputed information.
10. A person or business that "takes any adverse action" affecting a consumer with regard to credit, insurance, or employment on the basis of a credit report must advise the consumer of the reason for the rejection and identify the reporting agency.
11. A consumer is granted the right to file a civil action in U.S. District Court to recover damages resulting from willful and negligent noncompliance with the law.
12. Obtaining information under false pretenses for credit reporting and willfully giving out such information to unauthorized persons is punishable by a fine of up to $5,000 and imprisonment for up to 1 year.

As noted previously, this law gives the aggrieved individual the right to file an action charging that a credit bureau, its informant, or a user of its report violated the FCRA. The violation does not have to be intentional, but it must have caused demonstrable financial damage. In a successful action a consumer can collect actual damages, legal costs, and attorney's fees. For **willful violations**, a credit bureau may also have to pay punitive damages and may be subject to criminal penalties.

The *Safeco* case discusses the application of FCRA to insurance companies.

Privacy Act

In passing the **Privacy Act** of 1974, Congress recognized the problems of invasion of privacy caused by governmental computer recordkeeping. The act placed many restrictions on computerized recordkeeping and the handling of computerized records by the various governmental agencies. This act applies only to the records of national governmental agencies, not to those of state agencies or private businesses. In addition to placing restrictions on governmental recordkeeping and the handling of governmental records, the act gave individuals access to such records about themselves and the right to copy, correct, and challenge personal information held by the national government. The act also prohibited the nonroutine dissemination of records without notification to the individuals involved, and it placed restrictions on the expanded use of social security numbers.

Many states have passed privacy laws similar to the 1974 Privacy Act. These laws have placed restrictions on recordkeeping and the handling of computerized information by the various state agencies. The subject of computers and privacy is certainly a key issue in our society today. To date, the major thrust of the various privacy bills has been to regulate only national and state computerized recordkeeping, and there are still many unsolved legal problems concerning privacy and the recordkeeping practices of private business.

Electronic Funds Transfer Act

On November 10, 1978, Congress recognized the problems associated with electronic funds transfer (EFT) and passed the **Electronic Funds Transfer Act**. Congress stated that the purpose of this law was to provide a basic framework establishing the rights, liabilities, and responsibilities of participants in EFT systems. The primary objective of the law was to ensure a basic level of protection for the individual consumer's rights.

The Electronic Funds Transfer Act allows the various states to enact more comprehensive and more protective legislation if they desire to do so. A few states have enacted regulatory legislation in the EFT area, and many others are considering such legislation.

CASE 4

Safeco Insurance Co. of America v. Burr
127 S.Ct. 2201 (2007)

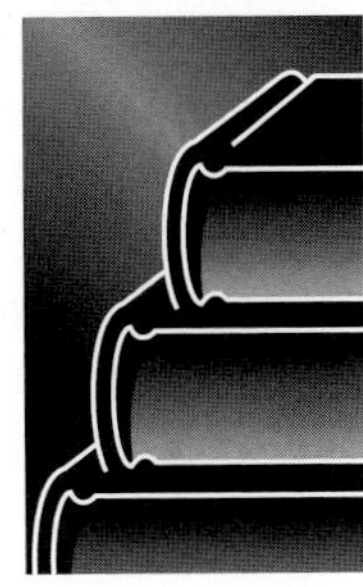

Facts: As it applies to insurance companies, an "adverse action" under FCRA is "a denial or cancellation of, an increase in any charge for, or a reduction or other adverse or unfavorable change in the terms of coverage or amount of, any insurance, existing or applied for." Safeco relies on credit reports to set initial insurance premiums, as it did for Charles Burr and Shannon Massey, who were offered higher rates than the best rates possible. Safeco sent them no adverse action notices, and they later joined a class action against Safeco, alleging willful violation of FCRA and seeking statutory and punitive damages.

Ajene Edo applied for auto insurance from GEICO. After seeing his credit score, GEICO offered him a policy at rates higher than the most favorable; he accepted. Due to other factors, GEICO would have given him the same rate if he had had a neutral credit score, so they did not send him an adverse action notice. Edo filed a similar class action against GEICO.

Both companies won summary judgments in U.S. District Court. The U.S. Ninth Circuit reversed both judgments. The Supreme Court agreed to review the cases together.

Issue: Was GEICO's decision based on Edo's credit report? Did Safeco act with reckless disregard of its duties under FCRA?

Decision: No. Judgments reversed, and cases remanded.

Opinion by Justice Souter: "GEICO and Safeco argue that liability under s.1681n(a) 'willfully fail[ing] to comply' with FCRA goes only to acts known to violate the Act, not to reckless disregard of statutory duty, but we think they are wrong.... [W]here willfulness is a statutory condition of civil liability, we have generally taken it to cover not only knowing violations of a standard, but reckless ones as well.... This construction reflects common law usage, which treated actions in 'reckless disregard' of the law as 'willful' violations....

"Before getting to the claims that the companies acted recklessly, we have the antecedent question whether either company violated the adverse action notice requirement at all. In both cases, respondent-plaintiffs' claims are premised on initial rates charged for new insurance policies, which are not 'adverse' actions unless quoting or charging a first-time premium is 'an increase in any charge for ... any insurance, existing or applied for.' ...

"[T]here is nothing about insurance contracts to suggest that Congress might have meant to differentiate applicants from existing customers when it set the notice requirement; the newly insured who gets charged more owing to an erroneous report is in the same boat with the renewal applicant.... We therefore hold that the 'increase' required for 'adverse action' ... speaks to a disadvantageous rate even with no prior dealing; the term reaches initial rates for new applicants....

"GEICO argues that in order to have adverse action 'based on' a credit report, consideration of the report must be a necessary condition for the increased rate....

"To the extent there is any disagreement on the issue, we accept GEICO's reading....

"The Government and respondent-plaintiffs argue that the baseline should be the rate that the applicant would have received with the best possible credit score, while GEICO contends it is what the applicant would have had if the company had not taken his credit score into account (the 'neutral score' GEICO used in Edo's case). We think GEICO has the better position....

"In GEICO's case, the initial rate offered to Edo was the one he would have received if his credit score had not been taken into account, and GEICO owed him no adverse action notice under s.1681n(a)....

"There being no indication that Congress had something different in mind, we have no reason to deviate from the common law understanding in applying the statute.... Thus, a company subject to FCRA does not act in reckless disregard of it unless the action is not only a violation under a reasonable reading of the statute's terms, but shows that the company ran a risk of violating the law substantially greater than the risk associated with a reading that was merely careless.

"Here, there is no need to pinpoint the negligence/recklessness line, for Safeco's reading of the statute, albeit erroneous, was not objectively unreasonable. As we said, s.1681a(k)(1)(B)(i) is silent on the point from which to measure 'increase.' On the rationale that 'increase' presupposes prior dealing, Safeco took the definition as excluding initial rate offers for new insurance, and so sent no adverse action notices to Burr and Massey. While we disagree with Safeco's analysis, we recognize that its reading has a foundation in the statutory text ... and a sufficiently convincing justification to have persuaded the District Court to adopt it and rule in Safeco's favor.

"The Court of Appeals correctly held that reckless disregard of a requirement of FCRA would qualify as a willful violation within the meaning of s.1681n(a). But there was no need for that court to remand the cases for factual development. GEICO's decision to issue no adverse action notice to Edo was not a violation ... and Safeco's misreading of the statute was not reckless. The judgments of the Court of Appeals are therefore reversed in both cases, which are remanded for further proceedings consistent with this opinion.

"It is so ordered."

Fair Credit Billing Act

Another area where abuses were thought to occur was disputes over charges to a credit account. Formerly, the creditor would bill charges it thought were valid, and then press the customer for payment. If the customer could not convince the creditor that disputed charges were incorrect, the creditor could report the delinquency to credit bureaus or take steps to collect the account through court process. Now, the **Fair Credit Billing Act (FCBA)** has set up certain procedures that must be followed if there is a dispute.

The consumer-debtor has 60 days after receiving a billing to notify the creditor of any claimed errors. The creditor then has 30 days to notify the debtor of receipt of the claim. The creditor must correct the account or investigate and explain its reasons for not correcting the account, within 90 days or two billing cycles. Claimed delinquencies cannot be reported to credit bureaus unless FCBA has been complied with. The debtor must be notified of the people to whom the delinquency has been reported. A creditor who fails to comply with FCBA forfeits its right to collect the first $50 of the disputed amount, including finance charges.

Federal Trade Commission Regulation 433

Another very important consumer protection law has already been noted in Chapter 13 and will be further discussed in Chapter 27. The FTC adopted a rule in 1976 that abolished the "**holder in due course**" concept for most consumer transactions. Basically, this is the concept that says that an assignee of an account receivable that is in negotiable form or that contains an express waiver of defenses clause, owns the account free and clear of most common defenses that the debtor might assert to try to avoid payment. The FTC has said, in effect, that a consumer-debtor can always assert any defense that can be proved.

Fair Debt Collection Practices Act

Finally, Congress took action in 1977 to curb some of the worst abuses in the credit field—collection agencies' scare tactics and harassment by passing the **Fair Debt Collection Practices Act (FDCPA)**. Most states had already acted to stop these abuses, and FDCPA allows these state regulations to continue if they contain adequate enforcement provisions. The national act covers only agencies that are collecting debts for others, not banks and businesses that are trying to collect their own accounts.

The FDCPA contains a number of restrictions on collection practices. The collector may not contact the consumer at work, if the employer objects, or at unusual or inconvenient times, or at all if the consumer has an attorney. The collector may not use harassing or intimidating tactics or abusive language against any person, or false or misleading tactics. Unless so authorized by a court, the collector may not contact third parties other than a spouse, parent, or financial adviser about the account. The collector may not contact the consumer-debtor about the account after receiving a written refusal to pay, except to notify the consumer of possible actions that may be taken. A debt collector may not deposit a postdated check before its effective date. These are significant limitations on previous practices.

Garnishment Limitations. **Garnishment** is a court process for seizing money or property belonging to the debtor but in the possession of third parties. Bank accounts and wages owed are typical subjects of garnishment.

Under its authority to interpret the constitutional phrase "due process of law," the U.S. Supreme Court has held that prejudgment garnishment of wages is unconstitutional (*Sniadach v. Family Finance Corp.*, 395 U.S. 337). It has also said, however, that some prejudgment remedies may be permissible (*Mitchell v. W.T. Grant*, 416 U.S. 600). Prejudgment garnishment of a bank account was specifically invalidated in *North Georgia Finishing, Inc. v. Di-Chem, Inc.*, (419 U.S. 601 [1975]).

The CCPA also limits garnishments of wages. No more than 25 percent of an individual's after-tax earnings, or the amount by which the wages exceed 30 times the minimum wage, whichever is less, can be garnished. These limits do not apply if the claim is for taxes, wife or child support, or subject to an order in a bankruptcy Chapter 13, adjustment of debts.

Significance of This Chapter

Even honest and hard-working people can suffer financial difficulties. Economic trends and technological changes can have adverse impacts on both businesses and individuals. When financial pressures become too severe, bankruptcy offers the debtor a fresh start.

All businesspersons must therefore be aware of the existence of the bankruptcy laws. They should know how the bankruptcy laws operate and who is covered by them. This chapter gives the reader a basic understanding of this area of the law.

Nearly everyone is a debtor, creditor, or both, at some time during their lives. Congress and the state legislatures have moved aggressively to regulate this aspect of commercial transactions. Important new protections have been developed for the consumer-debtor. This area of the law seems sure to expand further. Every businessperson needs to know the current debtor-creditor rules of the game.

IMPORTANT TERMS AND CONCEPTS

alimony and child support
bankruptcy
bankrupt partnership
cash advances
composition
Consumer Credit Protection Act (CCPA)
consumer leasing
consumerism
credit billing
discharge
educational loans
Electronic Funds Transfer Act
Equal Credit Opportunity Act (ECOA)
exempt property
Fair Credit Billing Act (FCBA)
Fair Credit Reporting Act (FCRA)
Fair Debt Collection Practices Act (FDCPA)
family support obligations
farm reorganizations
finance charge
fraudulently transferred
FRB Regulation Z
garnishment
Henningsen case
holder in due course
intentional torts
judicial liens
liquidation
luxury items
nonpurchase-money security interests
objection
preferential payments
priority
Privacy Act
proof of claim
reorganize
secured creditors
straight bankruptcy
unsecured creditors
willful violations

QUESTIONS AND PROBLEMS FOR DISCUSSION

1. When can credit reporting agencies legally furnish credit information about persons in their files?

2. What are the consumer's rights where he or she disagrees with information in a credit reporting agency's file?

3. How much of a debtor's property is exempt from a bankruptcy proceeding?

4. What debts are not discharged by bankruptcy?

5. Michael Hemmen has no accumulated wealth. He recently obtained a divorce, and his wife got everything. He has no savings account and only $40 in his checking account. He lives with his parents and pays them $60 per month room and board. He is unemployed and has made several unsuccessful attempts to obtain a job. He does not have a car. He only has 3 years of college with Business Administration as his major. He receives $90 per week unemployment. He owes $4,039 plus interest on several educational loans. The total unsecured debt less the educational loans is over $13,000.

   Is Michael entitled to a hardship discharge for educational loans? Discuss.

6. James Millstone applied to Firemen's Fund Insurance for insurance on his Volkswagen bus. Firemen's issued the policy but also ordered a credit report from O'Hanlon. About a month later, O'Hanlon furnished a report, based on information from Washington, D.C., where Millstone had previously lived. The report stated that he "was a hippie type person, with shoulder-length hair and with a beard on one occasion, who participated in many demonstrations in the Capitol, carried demonstrators back and forth to his home, where he housed them in his basement and wherever else there was room." It also said that "he was strongly suspected of being a drug user, that he was rumored by neighbors to have been evicted from three previous residences in Washington, D.C., and that he was very much disliked by his neighbors there." Based on this information, Firemen's ordered its agent to cancel the insurance policy on the VW. When the agent explained that Millstone was a highly respected assistant managing editor of the *St. Louis*

Post-Dispatch, and that he had been a White House reporter in Washington, Firemen's withdrew its cancellation order. When O'Hanlon refused to give satisfactory answers to him about the credit report, Millstone sued. The trial court awarded $2,500 actual damages and $25,000 punitive damages, plus $12,500 attorney's fees.

Did the trial court decide the case correctly? Explain.

7. Robert Isaac Lynn and Bonnie Marie Ryan had been married in 1981, while Robert was still in medical school. When they were divorced in 1989, the New Jersey court held that his medical degree and license to practice medicine were "property" and thus subject to "equitable distribution" between the spouses in the divorce proceeding. The New Jersey court then awarded Bonnie 20 percent of this "property," valued at $306,886. Robert was ordered to pay that amount ($61,377.20) in semiannual installments over the next 6 years. When Robert filed for bankruptcy, he indicated that he practiced medicine as a physician, but did not list his medical degree and license in his schedule of property owned. Bonnie and her attorney (Stephen Roth) objected to Robert's receiving a discharge in bankruptcy because he failed to schedule all his "property."

   Is Bonnie correct? Why or why not?

8. In November of 1999, Arland Boydston, a 40-year-old Army Lt. Colonel, married Carolyn Conner. Their financial downfall began in March 2000 when they borrowed $3,000 to start a wig business, the Chateau De Monique Wig Salon in Mineral Wells, Texas. By September, the shop's business had sharply deteriorated because of the projected closing of nearby Fort Wolters. At this time Boydston retired from the service, cutting his income by more than half, to $708 per month. Aside from his retirement income and the small amount of money the couple was taking in from the salon, the Boydstons had no other income. The bankrupt was also involved in a prospective low-income housing project from which he hoped to make a windfall by sharing in the net profits. In January 2001, the project fell through when Federal Housing Authority (FHA) approval was denied, again because of the closing of Fort Wolters.

   Despite their strained financial condition, however, the Boydstons went on a spending spree that lasted from the latter part of August 2000 until they filed their petition in bankruptcy on February 15, 2001. During this 6-month period they incurred almost $32,000 in new indebtedness, the overwhelming portion of which was for luxury items and nonessential personal expenses rather than for salvaging the wig business. Merchandise purchased included a new Cadillac, a mink coat, a very expensive shotgun, a houseful of new furniture, and $1,300 in personal travel expenses. A $6,000 bank loan ostensibly intended to acquire new inventory for the wig salon was diverted to the purchase of a new home in Dallas, and on several occasions personal financial statements submitted to creditors flagrantly failed to disclose a majority of their indebtedness. Most of the debt was incurred after the Boydstons were no longer able to meet existing obligations when due and had written at least two creditors requesting extension of payment deadlines.

   During this period, $2,923.73 worth of personal merchandise was charged at Sears and $2,540.03 at Neiman Marcus. No payments were ever made on either account. Appellants claim that the factors detailed previously clearly indicate a purpose to acquire merchandise on credit with no intention of paying for it. Sears also complains that, in completing a credit application with the store in November, Mrs. Boydston grossly overstated the wig salon's monthly earnings and omitted the family's major financial obligations to secure an extension of credit that otherwise would not have been granted. The application, however, contained only three blanks for listing present creditors.

   Neiman Marcus thwarted Mrs. Boydston's discharge from any of her debts under S. 14(c)(1) of the Bankruptcy Act by showing that she had altered documents pertaining to her bankruptcy for the purpose of deceiving the court and had given perjured testimony concerning the exhibits. The referee found that there was no evidence to show that Mr. Boydston participated in or knew of these changes, and granted him a discharge. The U.S. District Court affirmed.

   Is this result correct? Explain.

9. Thomas and Karen Norris lived on their 68-foot yacht as their only residence. The yacht was docked at a marina in Texas and received water, telephone service, and electricity through connections to the dock. They received mail through an address at a business postal center. Since they bought the boat in 1997, they had cruised to New Orleans, Florida, and Alabama. When they filed for bankruptcy in 2003, they listed the boat's value as $399,000. (It has four bedrooms, three bathrooms, a "galley" [kitchen], and an upper and lower salon.) Thomas and Karen claimed that the boat was their "homestead" and therefore not available to their creditors in the bankruptcy proceeding.

   How should the court decide this claim? Explain.

CHAPTER 23

Suretyship and Secured Transactions

Chapter Objectives

This chapter will:

- Explain the legal rights of cosigners.
- Define the term *secured transactions.*
- Review the Uniform Commercial Code provisions relating to secured transactions.
- Discuss the creation of security interests, their validity, and enforceability.
- Explain the use and contents of a financing statement.

Perhaps no single area is so crucial to the functioning of a modern economy, or so little understood by the "average" participant in the economic game, as secured financing. It is hard to imagine a modern business enterprise functioning effectively on a "cash on the barrelhead" basis; credit is the oil that keeps the economic wheels turning. Of course, some holdout consumers still insist that they always "pay cash for everything," but for most individuals this is just as much a credit economy as it is for business firms. The great majority of us will have an occasion, not just once but many times, to buy things on credit and to borrow money. Credit buying, borrowing, and financing is the name of the modern economic game, and that is what secured transactions are all about.

This chapter and the next are intended to convey to you the basic concepts and problems involved in secured financing and to give you some idea of what you need to do to protect your rights, either as an individual or as a businessperson. This chapter first explains the legal consequences of cosigning another person's obligations. It then focuses on the basic concepts involved in creating a **security interest** in personal property: What types of **collateral** may be involved? What has to be done to create a valid security interest in favor of the creditor in the debtor's property? Chapter 24 examines the requirements for "perfecting" a security interest against third-party claimants—usually the debtor's other creditors or a buyer of the collateral from the debtor. It also covers the rules for determining which creditor has the best claim to the collateral ("priority") when there is more than one claim and the rules for handling the collateral when the debtor defaults.

A significant revision of Article 9 was recommended to the states in 1999 and quickly adopted. All (or nearly all) have already adopted this "Revised Article 9" (R-9). R-9 has the effect of making a complicated area of the law even more complicated. Rather than attempting to explain all its intricacies, we will merely note several of its major changes at appropriate places in this chapter and the next.

Security and Pre-Code Law

Creditor's Need for Security

Creditors as a group are notoriously unwanted, unloved, misunderstood, and insecure. A **creditor** is someone who has permitted another party to receive his or her goods, services, or other value without their having been fully paid for by return value. This other party, the **debtor**, has been permitted to enjoy the benefits of the transaction but has not yet returned the full value that was promised to the creditor. The unsecured creditor thus has only the debtor's word that he or she will fulfill that promise, subject to all the human and economic infirmities that may come "twixt the cup and the lip."

In many personal business situations, the debtor's word may be good enough. The debtor's financial standing may be such that there is little risk of nonpayment. In many other situations the creditor has good reason to feel insecure, particularly because in the event of bankruptcy, general creditors are paid only after a long line of preferred claims.

Types of Security or Collateral

The creditor seeking the warm feeling of security may use any one of the three basic types of collateral to try to ensure the payment of the debt. A second person may be required to back up the debtor by also agreeing to pay the debt (a **surety**) or by agreeing to pay the debt if the debtor does not (a **guarantor**). The parties may agree that the creditor will have certain rights against some of the debtor's real estate if the debtor defaults. Finally, the parties may agree that the creditor will have certain rights against an item or items of personal property as collateral if the debtor defaults. It is this third situation that is defined by the Uniform Commercial Code (UCC) as a **secured transaction**.

Nature of Suretyship

When a lender or seller does not feel that the debtor's personal financial situation warrants the extension of credit, the lender or seller may require a **cosigner;** that is, another person who also agrees to become liable for payment of the debt. This sort of arrangement may be the only additional security the creditor requires, or it may be combined with personal property or real estate as specific collateral security for the debt. The person who actually receives the money or credit is spoken of as the **principal debtor;** the cosigner is the surety.

The other frequently occurring suretyship transaction involves bonding. Here a company issuing a surety bond promises to pay a certain sum of money if the debtor defaults on performance obligations. For example, with the performance bonds required of building contractors, the bonding company promises to pay the landowner/customer in the event of nonperformance or of improper performance by the builder. Because courts do not agree that such a bond also covers the claims of unpaid laborers or material suppliers, the builder may also be required to furnish a bond that specifically provides for the payment of these claims.

Many public officials, particularly those who have custody of public funds, must file bonds guaranteeing that the bonding company will replace any missing monies. Bonds are also required in many types of judicial proceedings to protect the other party and to guarantee performance of court-imposed obligations. An example is a bail bond to ensure a party's appearance for trial. Although perhaps not technically surety bonds, fidelity bonds are frequently required by employers for employees in "sensitive" jobs; specified defaults by such an employee give the employer the right to recover the amount of the bond from the bonding company.

Most courts continue to draw a distinction between suretyship, strictly defined, and guaranty. A surety makes the same promise to the creditor as does the principal debtor; the surety says, "I will pay." When the debt falls due, the creditor can sue the surety without first demanding payment from the principal debtor. A guarantor makes a different sort of promise; this person says, "If the principal debtor doesn't pay, then I'll pay." The creditor is required to demand the money from the principal debtor and to notify the guarantor of the principal debtor's default before the guarantor becomes liable to "pick up the check." The guarantor's promise is similar to the conditional contract liability of the endorser of a negotiable instrument. A **guarantor of collectibility** makes an even more limited promise; the creditor normally must get a judgment against the principal debtor and have the judgment returned unsatisfied before the guarantor of collectibility becomes liable. Many of the following legal rules, however, are applied by the courts to both suretyship and guaranty.

Contract Aspects of Suretyship

Because suretyship is a contract, an offer and acceptance, supported by consideration, must be present. Whether or not the creditor-offeree must give notice of acceptance to the surety-offeror depends on the facts and circumstances of the particular situation. In many cases, the creditor's acceptance of the surety's offer will be obvious. When a continuing guaranty of payment covers a number of possible transactions, many courts will require notice of a creditor's acceptance, so that the guarantor knows the extent of the obligations that the creditor has undertaken.

In the simplest transaction, both the principal debtor and the surety sign the loan agreement at the same time. The bank's payment of the loan funds to the principal debtor is consideration for both promises of payment. Because a contract of guaranty is typically a reassurance of payment sometime after the primary debt was made, new consideration is required to bind the guarantor to the promise. This new consideration may be an extension of the time for payment, smaller monthly installments, forbearance from suit, or any other agreed modification by the creditor, but some new consideration has to be present to hold the guarantor liable.

The precise form in which the "backstop" promise is made may also determine whether or not the Statute of Frauds applies. Clearly the guarantor's if-then promise is covered, and it must be evidenced by a signed writing. Courts may not always draw the technical distinction between suretyship and guaranty, however, and they may require a writing for suretyship contracts as well. Special state statutes may also produce the same result. As always, it is a good idea to get it in writing.

Special Rights of the Surety

The promise to pay someone else's debt places the surety in a rather special position. Therefore, the law gives the surety a set of special rights to produce fair ultimate results wherever possible.

Exoneration is the right of the surety to demand that the principal debtor pay the debt when it falls due and before the creditor collects it from the surety. The surety can also get a similar equity order against cosureties, forcing each to pay a proportionate share of the debt when the debtor is insolvent or otherwise in default.

The surety, after paying some or all of the debt, is entitled to **reimbursement** or **indemnification** from the debtor. This was really the debtor's obligation, and it is only fair that the debtor repay the surety. If there were two or more cosureties, any of them who paid more than a fair share is entitled to **contribution** from the cosureties, so that each surety bears the agreed proportionate part of the loss. To assist the surety in obtaining reimbursement from the principal debtor, the surety who has paid off the creditor acquires, through a process called **subrogation**, the same legal status that the creditor had. The surety automatically acquires whatever rights the creditor had in property, which served as collateral for the debt, and can take whatever enforcement steps the creditor could have taken against the collateral.

Defenses of the Surety

The law provides the surety with some special defenses because of the surety's unique situation. The surety can use some, but not all, of the defenses that can be used by the principal debtor as well as any defenses that may be personal to the surety.

Because of the surety's special legal situation, and to prevent unfair results, the courts generally hold that any of the following acts by the creditor will discharge the surety's liability.

Release of the Principal Debtor

A release of the principal debtor also releases the surety, *unless* the surety consents to such a release, or the creditor specifically reserves rights against the surety, or an arrangement is made to indemnify the surety, such as turning over to the surety sufficient collateral to cover the debt.

When the creditor releases the principal debtor but reserves the right to sue the surety, the surety's rights against the principal debtor must be preserved too, so that the principal debtor ultimately pays.

Release of Collateral

The courts have generally said that a release of rights against property held as collateral security for the debt also will release the surety *if* it can be shown that the surety's rights are prejudiced in some material way by such release. Some courts have reached similar results when the value of the items held as collateral has been substantially diminished by negligence of the creditor.

Material Alteration of Terms

The surety agrees to assume the debt of another person under certain terms and conditions. Therefore, any material change in those terms, if not agreed to by the surety, should discharge his or her liability. Materiality here is a fact question, but changes in the amount of the debt, the maturity date, or the place of payment would almost certainly be held to be material. Most modern cases require that a surety who has been paid for acting as such must show that the change in terms prejudices the surety's rights.

Rejection of Tender of Payment

When the creditor refuses a valid tender of payment by either the principal debtor or the surety, the surety is discharged. If the debtor is willing to pay the amount as agreed, and the tender is refused by the creditor, it certainly would not be fair for the creditor to then be able to sue the surety. If the surety's tender of payment is refused, it would not be fair to extend the liability any further because the surety could have sued the principal debtor immediately if the creditor had taken the money.

Like any other party liable on a contract, the surety has available any defense that applies to the individual situation. Some examples are lack of agreement, lack of consideration, lack of contractual capacity, and fraud. However, most courts will not allow a surety sued by a creditor to use fraud by the principal debtor against the surety as a defense unless the creditor is somehow responsible for the fraud.

The special suretyship arrangement entitles the surety to assert many of the defenses of the principal debtor, especially those relating to the formation or performance of the agreement. When a defense such as fraud or duress against the principal debtor makes the contract voidable, the surety can use the same defense if the principal debtor elects to avoid the contract. If the principal debtor elects to affirm the contract, the surety remains bound. When the whole contract is void because of illegality, that defense would, of course, be available to the surety. When the principal debtor's defense is a personal lack of capacity, the surety would still be bound. Such lack of capacity would in many cases be the very reason for having a cosigner. However, when a minor has disaffirmed the contract and returned the consideration received to the creditor, the surety is discharged, at least to the extent of the value of the consideration when returned. Bankruptcy of the principal debtor does not discharge the surety.

The *Beal Bank* case discusses the enforceability of a personal guaranty.

CASE 1

Beal Bank v. Siems, Fort, and Vokoun
670 N.W.2d 119 (IA 2003)

Facts: Edwin Siems, Wayne Catron, Timothy Titus, and Michael Fort organized Douglas Avenue Storage Limited (DASL) to build and operate a large storage facility in Urbandale. Fort's involvement was to be only construction and initial operation. The project was financed through Hartford Carlisle Savings Bank, collateralized by a mortgage on the facility, unlimited personal guaranties from Catron and Siems, and a $100,000 personal guaranty from Fort. These guaranties also covered future advances of funds to DASL and were effective until DASL's debts were paid or until the guarantor sent notice of revocation by certified mail. Siems' wife—Teresa Vokoun—also gave Hartford mortgages on two properties she owned. These mortgages were to be released when the building was completed, and that occurred in April 1998.

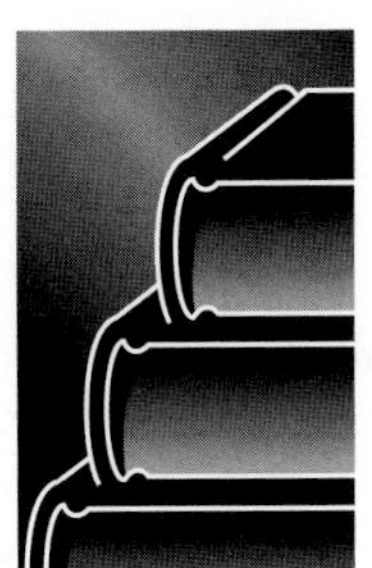

During the summer of 1998, Titus bought out Fort and Catron, with Hartford's approval. As part of the buyout, Fort was to be released from his guaranty. In September, a new loan was made to DASL by Hartford and the original loan was marked paid. The new loan was secured by a mortgage on the DASL property, new mortgages on Vokoun's properties, and personal guaranties from Siems, Vokoun, and Titus. Hartford became insolvent and was taken over by the Federal Deposit Insurance Corporation. The DASL notes, guaranties, and mortgages were bought from the FDIC by Beal Bank. When DASL defaulted on its loan, Beal Bank foreclosed on the DASL property but did not get enough from that sale to pay off the loan. Beal Bank then sued Siems, Vokoun, Titus, Catron, and Fort on their guaranties.

Issue: Does Beal Bank have a valid claim against Fort based on his guaranty?

Decision: No. Judgment for Fort is affirmed.

Opinion by Justice Ternes: "Beal Bank asserts that any discharge of Fort had to be in writing and signed by Hartford pursuant to the statute of frauds for credit agreements set forth in Iowa Code section 535.17(2). Even if that statute does not apply, contends the plaintiff, the evidence falls short of proving Hartford abandoned Fort's guaranty. In addition to this challenge to the sufficiency of the evidence, Beal Bank claims it is not bound by the allegedly undocumented release of Fort because it is a holder in due course. . . .

"Section 535.17(2) makes an oral modification of a credit agreement unenforceable only if 'the person asserting that modification [here Fort] has been notified in writing that oral or implied modifications to the credit agreement are unenforceable.' . . . Although 'this notification can be included among the terms of a credit agreement,' 'to be effective, the notification and its language must be conspicuous.' . . .

"Th[e] language [here] was not in boldface type, nor was the type larger than the type size of the surrounding paragraphs. There was nothing noticeable about this provision and it had no attributes that would have attracted the reader's attention to it. In short, the notification given to Fort was not conspicuous. . . . Under these circumstances, the restriction set forth in section 535.17(2) requiring that any modification to a credit agreement be in writing in order to be enforceable does not apply. . . .

"Having determined that any release of Fort from his guaranty need not be in a writing signed by Hartford, we now examine the record to decide whether there is substantial evidence to support the trial court's factual finding that Hartford abandoned Fort's agreement to guarantee future loans made to DASL. . . .

"Hartford's subsequent actions support the trial court's finding that Hartford . . . abandoned Fort's guaranty. When permanent financing was put into place, Fort's guaranty was not listed as collateral. Fort was not notified of the terms of this financing, as would be the normal banking practice if Fort had been considered a guarantor of the debt. . . . We think these . . . facts support the trial court's determination that Hartford abandoned Fort's guaranty when Fort sold his interest in DASL to Titus.

"Beal Bank argues that any abandonment of the Fort guaranty by Hartford is not binding on [it] because it is a holder in due course of the guaranty. In response, Fort contends Beal had notice of Hartford's abandonment of Fort's guaranty and therefore holds the guaranty subject to Fort's defense of discharge. . . .

"[W]e think the record provides substantial evidentiary support for the trial court's factual finding that Beal Bank had notice of Hartford's 1998 abandonment of the Fort guaranty. Fort's expert witness . . . testified that it was the custom and practice in [the banking] industry to list all guarantors in the promissory note. Yet, Beal Bank knew that the loan documents representing DASL's indebtedness to Hartford did not list Fort's guaranty as collateral. Beal Bank also knew that Fort had not been given a 'notice of final agreement,' as debtors and guarantors customarily are. Based on the information actually known by the plaintiff, it had 'reason to know' that Fort had been discharged from his obligation."

Secured Transactions, Article 9, Uniform Commercial Code

Purpose, Policy, and General Characteristics

The basic objectives of Article 9 in the field of personal property secured financing are uniformity, unity, and simplicity. Lawyers and nonlawyers struggling with the Code concepts and terminology may wonder whether the third objective has really been advanced very far, but it is clear that the first two have. The Code is now in force, with only relatively minor variations, in all U.S. jurisdictions, thus ending the pre-Code jungle of drastically conflicting state laws and the attendant conflict-of-laws problems. And even though it was necessary to make distinctions in Article 9 and to deal with different security situations and problems in different ways, such differences were placed within the context of an overall scheme of security law and their nature and effects were carefully calculated.

R-9 has recently been adopted by the states. It expands the coverage of Article 9 to include several newer forms of collateralized transactions, provides for electronic filing of financing statements, and makes many other changes in the rules for secured transactions. Our discussion in this chapter and the next will highlight some of the major changes.

The following hypothetical examples show the range of Article 9's coverage:

1. Carole Consumer wants to buy a new car on credit. Whether she arranges her own financing at her bank or credit union or signs a time payment contract that her car dealer sells to a bank or finance company, this is a secured transaction if the new car is used as collateral to secure payment of the balance of the purchase price.

2. Dan Debtor needs to borrow $1,500. His bank (or credit union, or finance company) will not make the loan on Dan's signature alone, but requires collateral. Dan owns an expensive stereo set and a refrigerator/freezer, which are both paid for, and which his bank accepts as sufficient collateral. This is a secured transaction.

3. Big Bennie's Appliance Store orders a shipment of new TVs on credit. This is a secured transaction if the credit seller (manufacturer or wholesaler) wants to use the TVs as collateral for the unpaid contract price. Alternatively, Bennie could borrow the contract price from a bank or finance company and use the TVs as collateral for the loan. Either way, because the creditor (the **"secured party"**) wants to use the TVs as collateral, this is a secured transaction.

4. Mr. Shatturglas (the home improvement king) needs to borrow $50,000 for added working capital. His bank (or finance company) will not lend him the money without collateral. His only available asset is his accounts receivable—the amounts due him for work performed. Whether Shatturglas merely pledges his accounts to the bank or sells the accounts outright for cash, this is a secured transaction.

5. Freddy Farmer leases a new tractor from an equipment rental company for 2 years for $300 per month. At the end of the 2-year lease term, Freddy has the option of buying the tractor for an additional $1. This is a secured transaction.

In sum, (nearly) all credit transactions in which **personal property** or a **fixture** is used as collateral are defined by the UCC as secured transactions.

Article 9, although comprehensive in intent and organization, does not embrace all the law dealing with interests in personal property. It is, after all, part of the Code; all the "General Provisions" of Article 1 apply to a particular transaction, and other parts of the Code may also be involved. For example, if the secured transaction involves a credit sale of goods, the warranty sections and other parts of Article 2 may be relevant.

In 9-109(a), the drafters reiterate their intent to cover all security interests created by contract: "[T]his article applies to: (1) a transaction, regardless of its form, that creates a security interest in personal property or fixtures by contract." Any contractual arrangement, new or old that is intended to create a security interest in personal property is included.

R-9 makes coverage even more comprehensive, by specifying several more types of personal property. "Software" is covered, as are "payment intangibles" (payment rights not represented by instruments), sales of promissory notes, "investment property" (securities, and commodity contracts or accounts), health-care insurance receivables, and commercial tort claims. R-9 also extends the definition of "accounts" to include payment obligations arising out of the sale or lease of all kinds of tangible or intangible property and to the use of credit card receivables as collateral.

Because in many cases Article 9's applicability is made dependent on the intent of the parties to the transaction, litigation frequently arises as to what the parties did intend. A third-party claimant will usually raise the question that the parties' arrangement is not effective as against third parties because it was really intended as a secured transaction, and it was not properly filed as such. The lease and consignment cases are particularly troublesome. The problem arose so often that a special new section on consignment was added by the 1972 amendments. In general, this section requires the consignor to give the same kind of notice to other inventory financiers as if it were selling on credit rather than consigning. R-9 includes consignors in its definition of secured party.

In 1-201(37), the Code also provides that leases are intended as security devices when the debtor can become the owner of the collateral by paying an additional nominal consideration.

The *Fleming* case involves this lease definition and the rules for obtaining a deficiency judgment against the debtor.

Exclusions

Having made such brave claims for the comprehensiveness of Article 9's coverage, we must now consider the lengthy list of specific exclusions that the Code enumerates. Generally, these exclusions refer to liens and transactions that are outside the scope of normal financing arrangements. For example, landlords' liens, wage assignments, and transfers of insurance claims, most tort claims, and payment intangibles being sold as part of a business are among the exclusions. Also excluded are security interests that are subject to a supervening national statute. The general theme underlying these exclusions is to omit Code coverage for transactions that are not normally used in commercial situations, particularly transactions that are already adequately covered under existing law.

Conflict-of-Law Rules

Part 3 of R-9 lays down a series of rules for dealing with complex multistate transactions. The validity and perfection of security interests against accounts, general intangibles, and mobile equipment is to be determined according to the law of the state where a multi-location business debtor has its chief executive office.

When personal property of other kinds already subject to a security interest is brought into a Code state, its validity is to be determined by the law of the state where the property was located when the security interest attached. If such an interest was already perfected when the property was brought into the state, it generally remains perfected in the new

CASE 2

Fleming v. Carroll Publishing Company
581 A.2d 1219 (D.C. App. 1990)

Facts: On December 29, 1980, Carroll Publishing Company entered into an "Equipment Lease Agreement" with three individual investors who had formed a partnership called Equity Leasing Joint Venture—80F. The lease covered certain computer hardware and software. These items were acquired through third-party vendors. Some of the software was "off-the-shelf" but at least two significant software packages were to be custom-written for Carroll by a third-party vendor. The lease term was for 5 years, with total payments of $87,328.25.

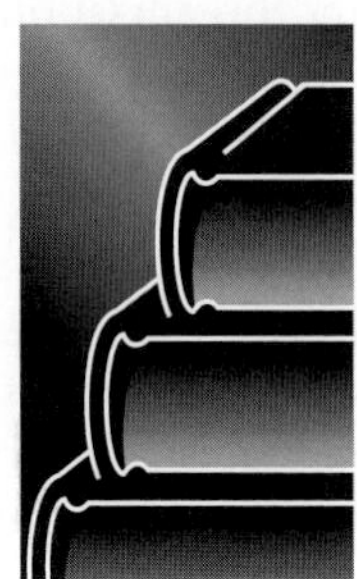

The lease did not provide for Carroll to purchase the equipment. In a subsequent purchase agreement of January 25, 1981, however, the parties agreed that "Buyer [Carroll] is hereby given the first right to purchase the Equipment at the estimated fair market value of 10 percent of the original value. Said purchase shall occur upon expiration of the lease." In addition, the purchase agreement provided that a "demand for purchase of the Equipment may be made by Equity or its successor or assigns at any time after the date hereof."

A series of difficulties of various kinds developed, and on August 25, 1982, Carroll wrote to Equity's agent terminating the agreement, on the ground of nondelivery of certain items called for by the lease. Up to that point, Carroll had made 16 regular lease payments totalling $26,198.46. On February 22, 1983, Equity filed the instant suit against Carroll, seeking recovery in the amount of $61,930.11 and attorney's fees. Carroll counterclaimed, alleging nondelivery of some of the leased items and seeking damages for fraud and for breach of contract.

While the case was pending, on September 29, 1983, Equity's agent went to Carroll's office armed with a court order and repossessed a number of pieces of hardware and one item of software, located in the drive of one of the repossessed machines. Subsequently, at least some of the repossessed hardware was sold at a private sale, of which Carroll was given no form of notice.

Following a bench trial, the trial court denied Equity any relief. The court concluded first that the agreement was not a "true lease" but a security agreement governed by Article 9. It concluded further that any claims for nondelivery were the sole responsibility of third-party vendors and not Equity; hence Equity was initially within its rights in proceeding under the agreement and under Article 9. However, it held, Equity's failure to give notice to Carroll of its proposed sale of repossessed collateral barred Equity from obtaining any deficiency judgment, and any rights in the software remaining in Carroll's possession had been lost because of the subsequent modification of the software. Hence, Equity took nothing by its complaint. Nonetheless, the court interpreted the agreement to permit Equity to recover reasonable attorney's fees and costs, which it awarded in the amount of $50,636.01.

Issue: Was this contract a security agreement?

Decision: Yes. Judgment affirmed (as to this Issue).

Opinion by Judge Steadman: "On appeal, Equity contends first that the trial court erred in concluding that the lease was not a 'true lease' but a security agreement governed by Article 9 of the District of Columbia Uniform Commercial Code....

"[I]n determining whether a lease is a 'true lease' or an Article 9 security agreement, the trial court must look to the intent of the parties, which depends on 'the facts of each case.' The trial court's determination as to the intent of the parties is essentially one of fact, ... and will not be upset unless it is 'plainly wrong or without evidence to support it.' ... Here, the trial court recognized that the intent of the parties is essential to a determination of whether a lease is a 'true lease' or security agreement and the court detailed its reasons for finding that the parties intended the lease as a security agreement. In particular, the court noted that the lease allocated to Carroll several burdens typically associated with ownership of property, such as the obligation to pay license fees and taxes on the equipment, the obligation to keep the equipment in good repair and the assumption of 'the entire risk of loss of and damage to Equipment from any and every cause whatsoever.' In addition, the court noted that Equity's status was as financier, rather than manufacturer or seller, and that Equity had no storage facilities for the equipment. These are among the 'factors' courts use in determining whether a lease is 'intended for security.' ... The court also noted that the total price Carroll was required to pay under the lease exceeded the purchase price of the equipment by $29,028 and that the customized system would be of little value to other potential lessees. 'Under the totality of the evidence presented,' the court found that the parties 'intended to create a security agreement.' We cannot say that this finding is 'plainly wrong or without evidence to support it.'

"Equity contends next that, even if the lease was a security agreement, the trial court erred in barring Equity from obtaining a deficiency judgment.... To the extent that paragraph 11 of the lease can be read to permit Equity to sell repossessed equipment without giving the statutory notice to Carroll, it is unenforceable under D.C. Code Section 28:9-501(3)(b)....

"It is true that the present case is somewhat unusual in that Equity did not repossess all the collateral in Carroll's possession, nor, apparently, did it sell all the collateral it did repossess. The trial court correctly held that these facts did not thereby entitle Equity to a deficiency judgement to which it was not otherwise entitled. While a secured creditor ordinarily has the right to sue on the debt as well as proceed against the collateral, ... if he proceeds against the collateral, he is obligated to follow the applicable rule for its disposition. At least under the circumstances here, a failure to do so acts as a bar to any deficiency judgment, whatever rights the creditor may retain in the collateral itself. Case law from other jurisdictions supports this conclusion. . . .

"Although Equity lost its rights to a deficiency judgment, it does not follow that it has lost rights in the remaining collateral, and especially to the collateral not repossessed (*viz.*, the bulk of the 'leased' software). . . .

"Accordingly, the case must be remanded for further consideration by the trial court of what rights, if any, Equity may still have with respect to the unrepossessed collateral, including replacements and modifications."

state for 4 months, within which time it may also be perfected in that state. When a certificate of title is issued on property under a state statute that requires notation on such a certificate to perfect a security interest, then perfection is governed by the law of the state that issued the certificate.

Although the adoption of the Code in all jurisdictions except Louisiana has had the effect of substantially minimizing the areas of interstate conflict, these conflict-of-laws rules retain considerable significance. One still needs to know where to file to perfect a security interest, whether or not to have a notation made on a vehicle's certificate of title, and what to do to protect the interest when the debtor will be using the collateral in more than one state.

The *Allete* case discusses the geographic scope of a security agreement.

CASE 3

Allete, Inc., d/b/a Minnesota Power v. GEC Engineering, Inc.

726 N.W.2d 520 (MN App. 2007)

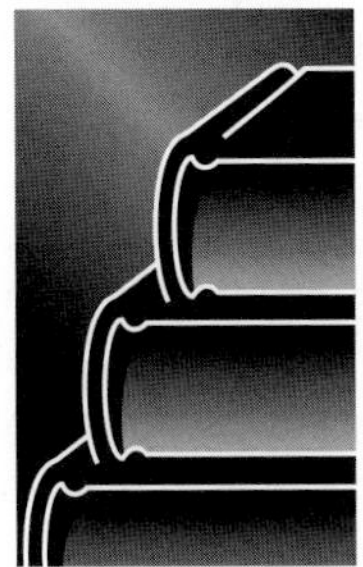

Facts: Allete/Minnesota Power loaned money to GEC Engineering, a start-up company that was attempting to develop technology to covert diesel engines to run on propane or natural gas. To secure the loan, on December 28, 2000, GEC executed a security agreement that gave Allete a security interest in "all equipment and inventory located at Borrower's facility at 510 W.3rd Avenue North, Aurora, Minnesota." A financing statement with a corresponding description of assets was filed in Minnesota. The loan agreement was based on the expectation that GEC would be moving to Aurora from its then location at Ballwin, Missouri. By the target moving date, April 15, 2001, GEC had not moved to Aurora and was experiencing financial difficulties. Allete then filed a financing statement in Missouri covering "All equipment and inventory located at 116 Holloway Road, Ballwin, MO." GEC is now insolvent. Allete got a default judgment against GEC and is trying to recover GEC's assets to pay the judgment.

The diesel engine at issue here was never located at Aurora but was purchased by GEC and shipped to the Ballwin location of CK Engineering (another company, which was working with GEC). GEC never paid CK for its services, but left the engine in CK's possession. To recover what it was owed, CK sold the engine to Danielle Dellhomme (an investor in and former director of GEC). Dellhomme has the engine in Texas. Allete asked a Minnesota court to order Dellhomme to turn the engine over to them. The trial court granted her a summary judgment.

Issue: Does Allete have a valid security interest in the diesel engine?

Decision: No. Summary judgment for Dellhomme is affirmed.

Opinion by Judge Minge: "[UCC 9-203] governs the attachment and enforceability of security interests. . . . Here, the parties do not dispute that value was given or that GEC had rights in the engine. The parties only dispute whether GEC 'authenticated' a security agreement that provides a description of the collateral, sufficient to create a security interest in the engine. . . .

"We do not understand [Allete] to claim that the parties' original security agreement created a security interest in the engine. Nor could it. The plain language of the security agreement only grants [Allete] a security interest in equipment 'located at Borrower's facility at 510 W. 3rd Avenue North, Aurora, Minnesota.' It is undisputed that the engine was never located in Aurora. We consistently give a contract its 'plain and ordinary meaning . . . even if the result is harsh.' . . .

"[Allete] seizes on the UCC's flexible definitions of 'security agreement' and 'agreement' to argue that the financing statement the parties filed in Missouri creates a material fact issue as to whether the parties amended the original security agreement to give [Allete] a security interest in the engine. Although the UCC does not explicitly address the question of whether a financing statement can boot strap a lender into a secured status, there are several provisions that are relevant to the answer.

"The language used in security agreements and financing statements reflects their functions. The security agreement must somehow state that a lien is created in identifiable collateral.... By contrast, the financing statement is a bare-bones document that simply gives names and addresses and a description of property. In fact, until recently, the Minnesota standard form financing statement had no language that mentioned the term 'security interest' or even referred to the described property as 'collateral.' ...

"[W]e are aware of no court that has held that a standard financing statement, standing alone or with only parol evidence, is sufficient as a matter of law to create a security interest in collateral, or to amend an unambiguous security agreement....

"Here, the security agreement contains an explicit description of property that is limited to equipment located at a specific address in Aurora, Minnesota, and other assets. There is nothing in the original security agreement that even implies that the security interest extends to equipment not located at that site.... [Allete's] argument has a certain appeal. But there is nothing from the debtor that grants [Allete] a security interest in the collateral located in Missouri. The financing statement used in this proceeding has no reference to the described property as collateral....

"Here, because there is no admissible evidence in the record that GEC actually granted a security interest in the equipment in Missouri to [Allete], we conclude that [Allete] has no security interest in the disputed engine as a matter of law and that the district court did not err in ordering summary judgment."

Classification of Collateral

Tangible

Collateral is classified generally into nine categories. The definitions used are essentially functional definitions, based on the nature of the item and/or the use to which it is being put by the debtor at the time the security interest attaches to it. The significance of these categories stems from the different treatment given the different types of collateral.

Such differences are observable: in the available methods of perfecting the security interest; in the place of filing and the necessity therefore; in the priority of claims against the collateral; in determining the rights of buyers from the debtor; and in the respective rights and remedies of the parties on default.

Section 9-109 recognizes four classes of "goods:"

1. **"Consumer goods"** if they are used or bought for use primarily for personal, family, or household purposes.
2. **"Equipment"** if they are used or bought for use primarily in business (including farming or a profession) or by a debtor who is a nonprofit organization or a governmental subdivision or agency or if the goods are not included in the definitions of inventory, farm products, or consumer goods.
3. **"Farm products"** if they are crops or livestock or supplies used or produced in farming operations or if they are products of crops or livestock in their unmanufactured states, and if they are in the possession of a debtor engaged in farming operations.
4. **"Inventory"** if they are held by a person who holds them for sale or lease or to be furnished under contracts of service or if he has so furnished them, or if they are raw materials, work in progress, or materials used or consumed in a business.

The comment to this section makes clear that these categories are mutually exclusive. Although the same goods can fall into different categories at different times, "the same property cannot at the same time and as to the same person be both equipment and inventory, for example." "Equipment" is the residuary category; if the goods do not fit one of the other definitions, they are equipment.

Intangible

Section 9-106 defines two kinds of intangible property that may serve as collateral: **account** and **general intangible**. The difference between an "account" and a **"contract right"** was eliminated by the 1972 amendments. As noted previously, R-9 now defines accounts as including payment obligations arising out of the sale or lease of all kinds of tangible or intangible property.

Account means any right to payment for goods sold or leased or for services rendered that is not evidenced by an instrument or chattel paper, whether or not it has been earned by performance. General intangibles means any personal property (including things in action) other than goods, accounts, chattel paper, documents, instruments, and money.

Documentary

The last three general types of collateral under Article 9 are also "intangible," but they relate to rights embodied in pieces of paper that are physically transferred from party to party as the rights they represent are sold, pledged, or mortgaged. In other words, these pieces of paper are used as a convenient way of handling any transfer of these intangible rights. These three categories are "documents," "instruments," and "chattel paper." **Document** means a document of title, defined as including bills of lading, warehouse receipts, and the like, covering goods in the possession of a bailee and giving the possessor of the document the right to dispose of it and of the goods it represents. **Instrument** means a negotiable instrument as defined (notes, drafts, checks, and certificates of deposit), or an investment security as defined (stocks and bonds), or any other similar writing. Under the UCC, "Chattel paper means a writing or writings which evidence both a monetary obligation and a security interest in or lease of specific goods." **Chattel paper** is thus the retail installment contract you sign when you buy your new car; you promise to pay the balance of the contract price in easy monthly installments, and the seller (or its financing agency) reserves a security interest in the goods in the event that you default. This piece of paper has value to the car dealer; it can be sold to a financing agency or used as collateral for the dealer's own loan.

Article 9 also singles out certain specific types of collateral for special treatment under some of the provisions to be discussed. Motor vehicles, fixtures, and the proceeds derived from the sale of collateral are examples of collateral to which such special treatment is applied.

Sufficiency of Description of Collateral

Both the immediate parties to the secured transaction and third parties need to know the identity of the collateral that it covers. Thus, both the security agreement itself and any financing statement that is to be publicly filed require a description of the collateral. Once again, the drafters of Article 9 clearly express their intent that this requirement should not become encumbered with extreme technicalities and legalisms. Section 9-108 (a) says:

> *Except as otherwise provided in subsections (c), (d), and (e), a description of personal or real property is sufficient, whether or not it is specific, if it reasonably identifies what is described.*

The *Waychus* end-of-chapter problem, involving "farm products," provides an illustration of the "reasonableness" approach of the courts to this Article 9 requirement.

Validity of Security Agreement and Rights of Parties Thereto

General Validity

As noted previously, both the Code generally and Article 9 specifically provide for a great deal of freedom of contract between the immediate parties to a transaction.

Section 9-201 says, in part:

> *(a) Except as otherwise provided in [this Act], a security agreement is effective according to its terms between the parties, against purchasers of the collateral, and against creditors.*

(As one authority put it, this may be "the biggest 'except' clause in the history of Western civilization.") The section then goes on to point out that Article 9 is not intended to modify in any way any existing *regulatory* legislation in the state pertaining to financial transactions.

Section 9-202 makes it clear that for the purposes of Article 9 distinctions based on whether the secured party has "title" to the collateral or "only" a lien on the collateral are no longer applicable. The parties are still free to structure their approach either way, but for the purposes of rights and remedies under Article 9 it makes no difference which form they choose to use. The location of "title" to the collateral may still be important for other reasons, however; tax, regulatory, and other non-Code liability problems may be solved by reference to the location of title.

Enforceability; Formal Requisites

Article 9 does include a "statute of frauds" requirement, in 9-203(b)(3), which states a general rule requiring a security interest to be in writing to be enforceable either against the debtor or against third parties. As an alternative to the writing (the "security agreement"), the secured party may keep possession/control of the collateral under an oral security agreement. There are also four other limited exceptions to this writing requirement: the security interest of a collecting bank in items it is handling for collection or of a securities intermediary, certain security interests against letters of credit, and security interests arising under Article 2 on Sales of Goods or Article 2A on leases of goods.

What is a sufficient writing to make the security interest enforceable under Article 9? On its face, Section 9-203 is deceptively simple. It provides that the security interest is not enforceable, generally, unless "the debtor has authenticated a security agreement which contains a description of the collateral and, if the security interest covers timber to be cut, a description of the land concerned." The deception arises because the term *security agreement* is itself defined in Section 9-102(73) as "an agreement that creates or provides for a security interest." In other words, to be effective as a security agreement, the writing signed by the debtor must not only describe the collateral, but it must also create or provide for a security interest in that collateral in favor of the creditor.

R-9 requires an "authenticated" "record," so as to recognize the validity of electronic transactions.

Financing Statements

The document that is publicly filed to give notice to all the world of the existence of the security interest is called a **financing statement**. This is not the lengthy and detailed financial statement often required from the debtor, showing all prior credit transactions, assets, and liabilities. The Code's financing statement is a simple, half-page form that merely announces the existence of a security interest in certain collateral.

Contents of Financing Statement

What must a financing statement contain to be effective? Because the only purpose of the financing statement is to serve as a "red flag" to third parties who may wish to deal with the collateral, the requirements are held to a minimum. A valid financing statement must contain the signature of the debtor, contains the names of both the debtor and the secured party, and "a statement indicating the types, or describing the items, of collateral." In addition, when timber or fixtures are involved, there must also be a description of the real estate involved. (Remember that any description is sufficient that "reasonably identifies" the collateral.) No legal mumbo-jumbo is required—no witnesses, no affidavits, no notarization. Moreover, substantial compliance is sufficient.

As previously noted, security agreement and financing statement are not used synonymously in Article 9; they are distinct terms, with distinct functions. It would be possible for a security agreement that contained the names and addresses of both parties to be filed as a valid financing statement. The disadvantage of this procedure is that it puts all the "gory details" of the transaction on the public record. But the greater potential danger to the secured party arises by attempting to have the financing statement do double duty as the security agreement. Because the typical financing statement form will not embody any agreement or provide for the creation of a security interest in the collateral, the secured party may very well wind up with an interest that is not even enforceable against the debtor. Courts are not willing to use the parties' "intent" to create a security interest, if they have not complied with Article 9.

The *Genoa* case discusses the effect of an incorrect listing of the debtor's name in the financing statement.

CASE 4

Genoa National Bank v. Southwest Implement, Inc.

353 B.R. 886 (NE Bkrp. 2006)

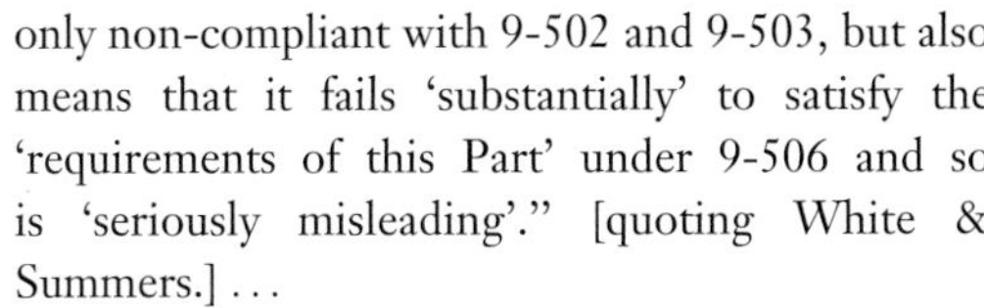

Facts: Genoa National Bank holds a perfected security interest on all of Michael Borden's personal property. Southwest Implements has security agreements on two pieces of Borden's farm equipment and filed financing statements identifying the debtor as "Mike Borden." He often signs his name that way, but his correct legal name is Michael Borden (or Michael R. Borden). A search of the publicly filed UCC documents under "Michael Borden" does not produce the Southwest Implements financing statements. Borden filed for bankruptcy, and Genoa asked the court for a determination of the validity of Southwest's filings. Genoa has moved for partial summary judgment on this point.

Issue: Were the financing statements naming "Mike Borden" as the debtor "seriously misleading"?

Decision: Yes. Partial summary judgment for Genoa National Bank.

Opinion by Bankruptcy Judge Mahoney: "The test of whether an error in a debtor's name on a financing statement is a fatal defect is whether a search of the filing office's records under the debtor's correct name, using the filing office's standard search logic, would disclose the financing statement. This differs from the earlier test of whether a reasonably diligent researcher would be able to locate the financing statement. 'Revised Article 9 requires more accuracy in filings, and places less burden on the searcher to seek out erroneous filings.... Revised Article 9 rejects the duty of a searcher to search using any names other than the name of the debtor indicated on the public record of the debtor's jurisdiction of organization [in the case of a corporate debtor].' ...

"[I]f the standard search logic (when instructed to use the correct name) fails to find a financing statement because the name is incorrect, that renders the financing statement not only non-compliant with 9-502 and 9-503, but also means that it fails 'substantially' to satisfy the 'requirements of this Part' under 9-506 and so is 'seriously misleading'." [quoting White & Summers.] ...

"A number of recent court decisions have addressed the scope of U.C.C. s.9-506(c) and whether the name used rendered the financing statement seriously misleading....

"[T]he Kinderknecht court enumerated four practical considerations for its conclusion: ... 'First, mandating the debtor's legal name sets a clear test so as [to] simplify the drafting of financial statements. Second, setting a clear test simplifies the parameters of U.C.C. searches.... Third, requiring the debtor's legal name will avoid litigation as to the commonality or appropriateness of a debtor's nickname, and as to whether a reasonable researcher would have or should have known to use the name. Finally, obtaining a debtor's legal name is not difficult or burdensome for the creditor taking a secured interest in a debtor's property. Indeed, knowing the individual's legal name will assure the accuracy of any search that creditor conducts prior to taking its secured interest in property.'

"As in Kinderknecht, the official Nebraska UCC1 form requires the 'debtor's exact full legal name.' The instructions further direct that the debtor's 'first given name' be entered in the form's 'First Name' box. An instruction to use the debtor's 'first given name' presumably serves to exclude the use of a nickname or short form of a given name....

"When the standard search logic of the filing office does not allow for expanded searches using wildcard functionality to cover all forms of a name, the searcher should not be required to separately search each possible name to ensure that all possibilities have been exhausted.... To adequately protect itself, the creditor should do its best to ensure that its Article 9 lien documents are filed under the debtor's legal name.

"A separate order will be entered granting Genoa National Bank's motion for partial summary judgment."

Continuation Statement; Termination Statement

When properly filed, the original financing statement is effective for the period it specifies, up to 5 years. It lapses at the end of the 5-year period or 60 days after the expiration date when a shorter period is specified. Upon such lapse, the security interest becomes unperfected.

If an extension of time is desired, a **continuation statement** may be filed by the secured party any time within the 6-month period prior to the specified expiration date or within the 60-day grace period referred to in the preceding paragraph. The requirements for this continuation statement are absolutely minimal: "Any such continuation statement must be signed by the secured party, identify the original statement by file number, and state that the original statement is still effective." As long as it complies with the provisions

Exhibit 23.1: Consumer Goods or Equipment–Motor Vehicle

Security Agreement for Consumer Goods or Equipment-Motor Vehicle

(Name) (Street Address) (City) (County) (State)

("Debtor"), hereby grants to ____________, ("Bank"), a security interest In the following described motor vehicle:

New ☐ Use ☐

Year________ Make ________ Mode ________ Serial No. ________

together with all parts, fitting, accessories, equipment, special tools, renewals and replacements of all or any part thereof, whether now owned or hereafter acquired by debtor (all hereinafter called "collateral"), to secure: (i) the payment of a note dated _______, executed and delivered by debtor to Bank, in the sum of $______, payable as to principal and interest as therein provided; (ii) further advances, to be evidenced by additional notes if such advances are made at Bank's option; (iii) all other liabilities (primary, secondary, direct, contingent, sole, joint, or general) due or to become due or which may be hereafter contracted or acquired, of debtor to Bank; and (iv) performance by debtor of the agreements hereinafter set forth.

Debtor warrants that:

1. He is or will be the owner of the collateral clear of all liens and security interests except the security interest granted herein.
2. He has the right to make this agreement.
3. He is using or will use the collateral primarily for the purpose checked below.
   ☐ Personal, family, or household purposes.
   ☐ Business purposes.
4. If checked here, ☐, the collateral is being acquired by debtor with the proceeds of the note and Bank is authorized to disburse said proceeds to the seller of the collateral.
5. The following statements, as checked, are true:
   a. ☐ Debtor's place of residence is at the address hereinabove stated.
   b. ☐ Debtor's chief place of business in Michigan is at the address hereinabove stated.
   c. ☐ If neither (a) nor (b) is checked, debtor has no residence or place of business in Michigan but the collateral will be kept in Michigan at:

   (Street Address) (City) (County)

Debtor agrees that he:

1. Will pay the Bank all amounts payable on the note mentioned above and all other notes held by Bank as and when the same shall be due and payable, whether at maturity, by acceleration, or otherwise, and will perform all terms of said notes and this or any other security or loan agreement between debtor and Bank, and will discharge all said liabilities.
2. Will defend the collateral against the claims and demands of all persons.
3. Will insure the collateral against all hazards requested by Bank in form and amount satisfactory to Bank. If debtor fails to obtain insurance. Bank shall have the right to obtain it at debtor's expense. Debtor assigns to Bank all right to receive proceeds of insurance not exceeding the unpaid balance under the note, directs any insurer to pay all proceeds directly to Bank, and authorizes Bank to endorse any draft for the proceeds.
4. Will keep the collateral in good condition and repair, reasonable wear and tear excepted, and will permit Bank and its agents to inspect the collateral at any time.
5. Will pay as part of the debt hereby secured all amounts, including attorneys' fees, with interest thereon, paid by Bank: (a) for taxes, levies, Insurance, repairs to, or maintenance of the collateral; and (b) in taking possession of, disposing of, or preserving the collateral after any default hereinafter described.
6. Will not permit the collateral to be removed from this state without the prior written consent of the Bank.
7. Will not: (a) permit any liens or security interest (other than Bank's security interest) to attach to the collateral, (b) permit the collateral to be levied upon under any legal process, (c) dispose of the collateral without the prior written consent of Bank, and (d) permit anything to be done that may impair the value of the collateral or the security intended to be afforded by this agreement.
8. Bank is hereby appointed debtor's attorney-in-fact to do all acts and things which Bank may deem necessary to perfect and continue perfected the security interest created by this security agreement and to protect the collateral.
9. Until default debtor may retain possession of the collateral and use it in any lawful manner not inconsistent with the agreements herein, or with the terms and conditions of any policy of insurance thereon.
10. Upon default by debtor in the performance of any covenant or agreement herein or in the discharge of any liability to Bank, or if any warranty should prove untrue, Bank shall have all of the rights and remedies of a secured party under the Uniform Commercial Code or other applicable law and all rights provided herein, in the notes mentioned above, or in any other applicable security or loan agreement, all of which rights and remedies shall, to the full extent permitted by law, be cumulative. Bank may require debtor to make the collateral available to Bank at a place to be designated by Bank which is reasonably convenient to Bank and debtor. Any notice of sale, disposition, or other intended action by Bank, sent to debtor at the address specified above, or such other address of debtor as may from time to time be shown on Bank's records, at least five days prior to such action, shall constitute reasonable notice to debtor. The waiver of any default hereunder shall not be a waiver of any subsequent default.

All rights of Bank hereunder shall inure to the benefit of its successors and assigns; and all obligations of debtor shall bind his heirs, executors, administrators, successors, and assigns. If there be more than one debtor their obligations hereunder shall be joint and several.

This agreement has been executed on ____________, 19 _____.

(Debtor)

each time, the secured party may renew the filing any number of times and thus preserve perfection against the collateral.

When the secured debt has been paid and the secured party has no obligation to make further advances of money or credit to the debtor, the secured party must on written

Exhibit 23.2: UCC Financing Statement

STATE OF INDIANA

FINANCING STATEMENT

UNIFORM COMMERCIAL CODE *FORM UCC-1*

Instructions:

1. This form may be used for filings with the Secretary of State and is also suitable for the following filings with the County Recorder: consumer goods, farm equipment, and farm products pursuant to IC26-1-9-401(1)(a) and (c).
2. Please type this form. Fold only along perforation for mailing.
3. Remove Secured Party and Debtor copies and send three copies with interleaved carbon paper to the filing officer. Enclose filing fee of ________ plus an additional fee of ________ for each of the following: (i) filing of an assignment of this form; and/or (ii) each additional debtor's name overone. Form UCC-3 should be used for any subsequent assignments.
4. If the space provided for any item is inadequate, the item may be continued on additional sheets, preferably 5"x 8". An additional fee of _____ is due for oversized sheets.
5. If the collateral is crops growing or to be grown, describe the collateral and also the real estate.
6. The filing officer will return the third page of this Form as an acknowledgment. Secured Party at a later time may use the third page as a Termination Statement by dating and signing the termination legend on that page.

This Financing Statement is presented to Filing Officer for filling pursuant to the Uniform Commercial Code.
Number of additional sheets provided

Debtor(s) (Last Name First) and Address(es)	Secured Part(ies) and Address(es)	For Filing Officer (Date, Time, Number, and Filing Office)
This Financing Statement covers the following types (or items) of property (include description of real estate when collateral is crops)	Name and Address of Assignee of Secured Party	
☐ Products of Collateral are also covered (see IC 26-1-9-315)		☐ Debtor is a transmitting utility as defined in IC 26-1-9-105.
Filed with: ☐ Secretary of State		☐ Recorder of County
____________________ By: ____________________ Signature of Debtor (or Secured Party in cases covered by IC 26-1-402[2]) **State Form 36751** **Form UCC-1—Indiana Uniform Commercial Code**		☐ Collateral was brought into this state subject to a security interest in another jurisdiction or the Debtor's location has been changed to this state. ☐ Filed in accordance with a security agreement signed by the Debtor authorizing the Secured Party to file this statement.
(1) FILING OFFICER COPY—ALPHABETICAL **JEBOP FINANCIAL SUPPLY. INC., EVANSVILLE, IN** Approved by: Secretary of State		

demand by the debtor send the debtor a **termination statement**, saying that "he no longer claims a security interest under the financing statement, which shall be identified by file number." A termination statement signed by someone other than the secured party of record must be accompanied by a statement of assignment from the secured party of record.

When the termination statement is presented to the filing officer, it must be noted in the index. The filing officer must then remove the financing statement, any continuation statement, and any statement of assignment or release. These are marked "terminated" and sent to the secured party.

Rights in the Collateral

Attachment of the Security Interest

The words ***attach*** and ***attachment*** as used in Article 9 merely refer to the coming into existence of the security interest with respect to the collateral involved. The point in time at which the security interest "attaches" to the collateral is significant for several reasons. It is at this point in time that the collateral is classified under the definitions discussed above. Some priority rules among conflicting claims to the collateral hinge on "attachment."

Section 9-203(a) and (b) also contain the rules determining when a security interest attaches. There must be an agreement, evidenced either by a writing authenticated by the debtor or by the creditor's possession or control of the collateral. Value must have been given by the secured creditor. And the debtor must have "rights" in the collateral. The security interest attaches to the collateral as soon as all three of these events have occurred unless the parties expressly agree to postpone the time of attaching. To rephrase the rules: the parties may provide that the security interest attaches to the collateral at any time *after* these three conditions exist. But even by agreement, they cannot provide for attachment *prior* to the occurrence of the three conditions.

The general rules of contract law and sales law would normally determine when the debtor had "rights" in the collateral. As pointed out in Chapter 17, for instance, UCC 2-105(2) provides: "Goods must be both existing and identified before any interest in them can pass." If you were borrowing money from your credit union to buy a new car, the credit union could not have an effective security against the new car until it had been "identified" (i.e., until you and the dealer had agreed on exactly which one you were buying). If the new car had to be ordered from the manufacturer, your credit union's security interest could not attach until your car was assembled and identified as yours—with your name or order number. In other words, even though a security agreement has been signed and cash or credit has been extended by the secured party, there can be no effective security interest until we know what things are being used as the collateral.

Subject to an exception for consumer goods, the Code expressly permits the parties to provide in their agreement "that collateral, whenever acquired, shall secure all obligations covered by the security agreement." For all subsequent creditors, the word is: "Look out for the person with this '**security blanket**.'"

This section also permits the secured agreement to cover "future advances" of value by the secured party, whether that party is obligated to make them or has the discretion to make them.

Use of Collateral by Debtor; Statement of Account

Article 9 expressly validates financing arrangements using a debtor's inventory or accounts, and it lets the parties determine to what extent the debtor should "police" the inventory or accounts. In general, third-party creditors in such situations should be adequately protected by the requirement that a financing statement on the shifting stock of collateral be publicly filed. When there has been no such filing and the validity of the security interest depends on possession of the collateral by the secured party, the common law rules on "pledge" still apply.

For the protection of both the debtor and any third parties involved, Section 9-208 provides that the debtor can require the secured party to verify periodic "progress reports" on the total amount the debtor believes to be due and on the collateral that is believed to be subject to the security agreement. The secured party must comply with such a request within 14 days after it is received by sending a written correction or approval and may become liable to the debtor and to third parties if it fails to comply without "reasonable excuse." The debtor can request one such statement without charge every 6 months; the secured party may charge a fee of up to $25 for each additional statement.

Collateral in Possession of Secured Party

In general, Section 9-207 continues the case law rules that had been developed under the common law of pledge. When the collateral is being held by the secured party, he or she has the obligation of using reasonable care in its custody and preservation—and of keeping collateral other than fungible goods identifiable. However, the risk of loss or damage to the collateral remains on the debtor to the extent of any deficiency in effective insurance coverage.

The secured party has the right to recover all reasonable expenses from the debtor, to hold any increase or profits (except money) received from the collateral as additional security for the debt, and to repledge the collateral so long as the debtor's right to redeem is not impaired. The secured party also has the right to use or operate the collateral to preserve it or its value, or pursuant to a court order, or in accordance with the provisions of the security agreement itself.

The secured party is liable for any loss caused by a failure to meet these obligations but does not thereby lose the security interest in the collateral.

Significance of This Chapter

Creditors require a second party's obligation on many personal and business loans or credit sales to ensure an additional source of payment if the principal debtor defaults. Any of us may be called on to cosign for another person or may be required to get a cosigner for our own obligation. Likewise, if we are representing the creditor company, we may want to require a cosigner. Whichever of the three parties we may be, it is nice to know the rules of the game.

Once again, the basis for suretyship law is general contract law, but some special rules apply. This chapter reviewed the special status of the surety/guarantor, the application of general contract rules, and the special rights and remedies of the surety/guarantor.

Because secured credit arrangements are so necessary and so frequently used in modern commercial society, it is important to know when and how they occur. All types of personal property may be used as collateral, and the debtor may be a single consumer or the very largest industrial corporation. The credit transaction may be structured as a sale, a loan, or a transfer of accounts receivable. For the purposes of Article 9, the form is generally irrelevant; what counts is the function: the extension of credit, with personal property used as collateral. This chapter discussed the rules for creating an effective security interest between the immediate parties. The next chapter will cover the secured party's rights against other persons who have claims against the same collateral, and the rights of both the secured party and the debtor when the debtor defaults on the credit contract.

IMPORTANT TERMS AND CONCEPTS

account
attach
attachment
chattel paper
collateral
consumer goods
continuation statement
contract right
contribution
cosigner
creditor
debtor
document
equipment
exoneration
farm products
financing statement
fixture
general intangible
guarantor
guarantor of collectibility
indemnification
instrument
inventory
personal property
principal debtor
reimbursement
secured party
secured transaction
security blanket
security interest
subrogation
surety
termination statement

QUESTIONS AND PROBLEMS FOR DISCUSSION

1. What is the difference between a secured transaction and a suretyship contract?

2. What types of property may be used as the collateral in a secured transaction?

3. What is the significance of defining certain collateral as being in one category of "goods" rather than another category?

4. What is the difference between a security agreement and a financing statement?

5. From time to time Waychus had borrowed money from the bank and had executed promissory notes and security agreements. A financing statement had been filed with the recorder of Cerro Gordo County. The financing statement identified the collateral as: "All Farm Machinery, All Brood Sows & the increase, All Crops, feed, and roughage." The financing statement also contained a real estate description of land located in Floyd County, whereas Waychus, in fact, resided in Cerro Gordo County.

   Johnson, who had no actual knowledge of the bank's interest, bought hogs from Waychus. The trial court held that Johnson was subject to the bank's perfected security interest. Johnson appealed.

   How should this appeal be decided? Explain.

6. Delilah filed for bankruptcy, listing among her secured creditors one Erlene Lertz. Erlene held a security agreement and had filed a financing statement, both of which described the collateral as "Lot 8, Lake Minotaur, & cabin at same location." Delilah leased Lot 8 and owned the cabin, so both were items of personal property rather than real estate. The trustee says that Erlene does not have a secured claim because the description of the collateral is insufficient.

   What is the result and why?

7. Dallas Entertainment operated a private club known as the Music Box. Dallas sold the entire club to Follies Buffet; included was a certain cash register. The parties prepared and filed a financing statement that described the collateral as including all equipment, but which did not specifically mention the cash register. Mosley bought the cash register from Follies, and then resold it. Dallas sued Mosley for conversion and received a judgment for $950.

   During the trial, Peggy Foley, the president of Dallas, testified that Dallas had received a promissory note and a security agreement from Follies at the time of the purchase. There was an objection to the introduction of the alleged security agreement because it had not been signed, and it does not appear in the trial court record. There was no other writing.

   Does Dallas have a valid security interest? Explain.

8. Floyd McLucas and his wife wanted to buy some furniture but were told by the store that the sale could not be made to them on credit. (Floyd was 22 years old; his wife 18.) Floyd was told he needed a cosigner. He brought his friend James McWilliams to the store, and McWilliams also signed the contract. The store was still not satisfied, so Floyd brought his mother, Catherine McLucas, and she cosigned too. At that point, the sale was made. The store assigned the contract to the plaintiff, Wexler, who sued Catherine when Floyd and his wife defaulted on their payments. The trial court held for Wexler, and Catherine McLucas appealed. After the complaint was served on Catherine, Floyd had gone to Wexler's office, and Wexler had agreed to let him pay off the account at $10 per week, thereby lengthening the term of the contract.

   How should this appeal be decided, and why?

9. Denver and Gary were both officers of Sunny Mobile Homes, Inc. Both of them had endorsed several of the company's notes for loans to it. They had also signed a guaranty agreement for the loans that stated: "Liability hereunder is not affected or impaired by any surrender, compromise, settlement, release, renewal, extension, authorization, substitution, exchange, modification, or other disposition of any said indebtedness and obligations." At one point, all of the company's outstanding loans were consolidated into one renewable note. Gary signed the renewal note, but Denver did not. Denver now claims that his liability as guarantor was discharged by a novation between the bank (lender), the company (Sunny), and Gary because the renewal note did not include his signature.

   What result, and why?

CHAPTER 24

Perfection, Priorities, and Remedies

Chapter Objectives

This chapter will:

- Explain the methods of making a security interest effective against third parties as well as the parties to the transaction.
- Review the Uniform Commercial Code rules that assign priorities with regard to creditors' claims against the secured collateral.
- Discuss the Uniform Commercial Code requirements for filing notice of a security interest in collateral.
- Explain the debtor's rights after default.
- Review the remedies available to the secured party after default.

Rights of Third Parties; Perfected and Unperfected Security Interests; Priorities

Reasons for Perfection

For the purpose of Article 9, the term **perfection** is used to describe a process—the steps that a secured party must take to make the security interest effective against third parties, particularly the debtor's general creditors or their representative in an insolvency proceeding. The very idea of security is to have an available source of funds from which the secured debt can be paid in the event of default by the debtor; that objective is defeated if the asset in question or its proceeds are distributed pro rata to all creditors.

To be more specific and more technically correct, perfection of the security interest in the collateral is necessary to beat a person who becomes a lien creditor before the security interest is perfected. **Lien creditor** is defined to include a creditor with a levy or attachment against the property involved, an assignee for the benefit of creditors, a receiver in equity, or a **trustee in bankruptcy**. Similar protection is given to certain unknowing transferees of goods, instruments, documents, chattel paper, accounts, and general intangibles; they too will beat the **unperfected security interest** of the would-be secured party to the extent that they give value without knowledge of the security interest.

Perfection will also assist the secured party in beating out some other kinds of third-party claimants, at least in some situations. But because it is possible to have more than one **perfected security interest** in the same collateral, and because even a perfected security interest is subordinate to certain types of third-party claims in certain situations, it must be remembered that a secured party with a perfected security interest is not always "the first to be paid." Priorities of payment under Article 9 will be discussed in this chapter.

The *Stanton* case illustrates the legal effect of an unperfected security interest.

CASE 1

Stanton v. 2001 Mazda V.I.N. 4F2YU08121KM57063

660 N.W.2d 137 (MN App. 2003)

Facts: On May 8, 2001, Anne Stanton co-signed an installment loan with her granddaughter, who was buying a 2001 Mazda automobile. The loan was guaranteed by Anne's savings account. That same day, her granddaughter wrote Anne a letter, pledging the car to Anne as collateral for Anne's potential liability on the loan. Anne's interest in the car was never registered with the state, as required to perfect a security interest against motor vehicles.

On September 9, 2001, her granddaughter was stopped by the police and arrested for driving under the influence of alcohol. This was granddaughter's third impaired driving offense within 10 years, for which the state law provides forfeiture of the vehicle involved. However, the statute also provided that the state's forfeiture interest was subject to "a bona fide security interest" in the vehicle.

Anne filed a petition with the court claiming an interest in the Mazda. The trial court agreed with her, and the state of Minnesota appealed.

Issue: Does Stanton's security interest have priority over the state's claim?

Decision: Yes. Judgment affirmed.

Opinion by Judge Schumacher: "This court has defined the plain meaning of the phrase 'bona fide' as 'made in good faith without fraud or deceit,' or 'in or with good faith; honest[l]y, openly, and sincerely; ... real, actual, genuine, and not feigned.' ... We conclude that Stanton had a bona fide security interest in the vehicle....

"The state claims that because Stanton's security interest was never perfected ... she does not have a bona fide security interest. That statute provides that a security interest in a vehicle of a type for which a certificate of title is required is not valid against creditors of the owner or subsequent transferees or secured parties of the vehicle unless perfected.... Failing to perfect the security interest may make the interest invalid against [the] granddaughter's creditors. However, the forfeiture statute provides for an interest in the vehicle even if the security interest is not perfected.... We conclude that by adding the phrase 'bona fide' the legislature intended that something less than a perfected security interest would suffice under the statute. The legislature intends to give effect to all words of a statute.... To have a 'bona fide security interest' ... does not require that the security interest be perfected....

"The district court did not err in ruling that Stanton had a bona fide security interest in the Mazda."

Methods of Perfection

There are three general methods of perfection—filing a financing statement, possession/control of the collateral, and automatic perfection—plus some variations (such as different places to file for different types of collateral). Filing is effective for every type of collateral except "instruments." Filing is the only method of perfecting against accounts and general intangibles because there is nothing in these situations that can really be effectively possessed. Possession of the item of collateral by the secured party is an effective method of perfection for all types of goods and for the "paper intangibles"—documents, instruments, and chattel paper. Because these pieces of paper are commonly dealt with in the commercial world as embodying the rights they represent, and because they are capable of being physically possessed, the drafters of Article 9 provided that a security interest in such pieces

CASE 2

In Re Baker

430 F.3d 858 (7 Cir. 2005)

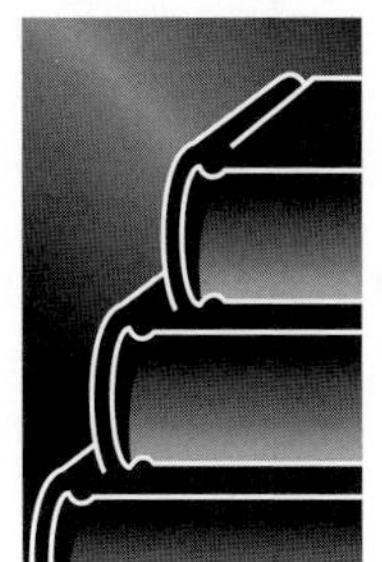

Facts: In 2001, Judith Baker bought a 2000 Oldsmobile Alero, financing it through Primus Financial Services. The New Mexico certificate of title listed Primus as secured party. Soon afterward, Baker moved to Wisconsin. She did register her car in Wisconsin but did not get a Wisconsin certificate of title.

In 2004, Baker filed for a Chapter 7 bankruptcy, and Claire Ann Resop was appointed trustee of Baker's bankruptcy estate. A trustee may seek to avoid unperfected liens against the debtor's property and distribute the value of such property to the debtor's general creditors. Resop's request to have the car turned over to her was rejected by the bankruptcy court, and on appeal, by the U.S. District Court. Resop appealed to the Seventh Circuit.

Issue: Is Primus Financial's security interest still perfected?

Decision: Yes. Judgment affirmed.

Opinion by Judge Evans: "Our starting point is the Wisconsin motor vehicle code. Wis. Stat. s.342.19(6) provides: 'If a vehicle is subject to a security interest when brought into this state, s. 409.316 states the rules which apply to determine the validity and perfection of the security interest in this state.'

"In turn, s.409.316 [UCC] tells us in relevant portion: 'A security interest perfected pursuant to the law of the jurisdiction designated in s.409.301(1) … remains perfected until the earliest of: … (b) The expiration of 4 months after a change of the debtor's location to another jurisdiction.' … Finally, we consult s.409.301(1), which instructs us that 'while a debtor is located in a jurisdiction, the local law of that jurisdiction governs perfection, the effect of perfection or nonperfection, and the priority of a security interest in collateral.' …

"S.409.301(1) cannot be read without reference to the limiting language in the introduction to s.409.301(1). That limiting language tells us that the subsections provide the rules governing perfection 'except as otherwise provided in ss.409.303 to 409.306.' …

"And so, turning to s.409.303 … we find the reason why the trustee's attempt to avoid the lien must fail. Section 409.303 provides the relevant law on the perfection and priority of security interest for 'goods covered by a certificate of title.' Specifically, s.409.303(3) states: 'The local law of the jurisdiction under whose certificate of title the goods are covered governs perfection, the effect of perfection or nonperfection, and the priority of a security interest in goods covered by a certificate of title from the time the goods become covered by the certificate of title until the goods cease to be covered by the certificate of title.' In nonlawyer speak, the 4-month period for reperfection provided by s.409.316(1)(b) does not apply to titled goods. Under Wisconsin law, as long as the New Mexico title continued in force, it was sufficient to protect Primus's interest. …

"We do not find any internal inconsistencies or absurdities in the operation of these statutes. …

"Indeed, it is the trustee's interpretation that would yield an absurd result. The rule that a security interest must be reperfected within 4 months after a debtor moves to a new jurisdiction makes sense in the context of untitled goods. But it is unreasonable to suggest that a lienholder's interest can become undone simply because an owner neglects her duty to apply for a new title when she changes states. Finance companies do not title vehicles, owners do. Had Baker retitled her vehicle in Wisconsin, Primus would have had to reperfect when its interest became unperfected under New Mexico law. … But we know of no authority for the notion, suggested by the trustee at oral argument, that a secured creditor is obligated to keep track of the domiciles of its debtors. An important function of a title is to record a secured creditor's interest, regardless of where the payments come from, or where the debtor and vehicle may roam. In this case, the New Mexico title is the only record available, and the Wisconsin statutes yield the sensible result that, under that valid title, the creditor's interest remains perfected. The judgment of the district court is AFFIRMED."

of paper could be perfected by the retention of them. Indeed, for instruments, except for a limited 21-day perfection against the debtor's other creditors, possession is the only acceptable method of perfection.

Revised Article 9 (R-9) uses a newer alternative method—"control"—for several newer types of collateral. R9-104 through R9-107 define control of bank deposit accounts, electronic chattel paper, investment property, and letter-of-credit payment rights.

Most states require the ownership of motor vehicles to be represented by a state-issued "certificate of title." For such vehicles, Article 9 requires that security interests be noted on the title certificate. The *Baker* case discusses the distinction between the title certificate and the (license plate) registration of the vehicle.

Place of Filing

The uniformity desired by the drafters of the Uniform Commercial Code (UCC) has broken down in the requirements for a valid filing to give notice to third parties of the existence of a security interest against the collateral. Solid policy arguments can be made both for central filing (there is only one place to check, particularly for a mobile debtor) and for local filing (it is much more convenient). The Code originally contained a simple filing scheme: for fixtures, file with the registrar of deeds in the county where the real estate is located; for motor vehicles required to be licensed, file by making a notation on the vehicle registration certificate; for all else, file with the secretary of state. Alternatives provided in the Code, combined with the effects of having each state legislature "do its own thing," produced some major variations in these filing requirements. Each state's filing requirements must be checked to ensure the validity of a filing there.

When the secured party makes a good faith attempt to file but files in an improper place or in only one of two required places, the filing is nonetheless effective as to anyone who has knowledge of the contents of the financing statement and also for any types of collateral as to which the filing is correct. An effective filing is not invalidated by a change in the debtor's residence or place of business or in the location of the collateral, but some states adopted alternative language that required a new filing in the new county, even within the same state. **Filing** is defined as meaning either communication of a record and tender of the filing fee or "acceptance of the statement by the filing officer." (The alternative language is included just in case the local filing officer gets funny and refuses to accept your financing statement for some reason, such as "it is not in proper form.") R-9 permits electronic filing, by changing the original word *presentation* to the word *communication.*

R-9 generally requires filing in only one place. It uses local filing only for timber and minerals and for fixtures. Filing is to be done in most cases in the state where the debtor is located.

Automatic Perfection

For **purchase-money security interests** in most **consumer goods**, Article 9 provides a third alternative. The "purchase-money person" (the seller or the financing agency that provided the cash or credit that the debtor used to buy the collateral) is given the benefit of an **automatic perfection** as soon as that person's security interest attaches to the collateral. (This automatic perfection alternative is *not* available when the consumer good is defined as a fixture or is a motor vehicle required to be licensed.) Even without filing and with the debtor in possession of the consumer good, the purchase-money person will still be protected against nearly all other possible claimants—lien creditors, other general creditors, the trustee in bankruptcy, another dealer to whom the collateral was given, or a buyer who had knowledge of the security interest.

Aside from the common priority problems, only one sort of claimant—a **bona fide purchaser (BFP)**—takes the collateral free and clear of the unfiled purchase-money security interest. The BFP must buy without knowledge of the unfiled security interest, for value, and for his or her own personal, family, or household purposes (consumer goods). Given this extensive protection of the unfiled security interest, the retailer or financier of these types of collateral can then decide whether or not protection against BFPs is worth the filing fee and the clerical expense involved in filing a financing statement. If the dealer does file, it will prevail even against a BFP, so buyers of consumer goods from other individuals do have to check these filing records to make sure that the item they are buying is indeed free and clear. Note again that this third perfection alternative applies only to the purchase-money person; all other secured parties must file or possess to perfect.

R-9 extends automatic perfection to several other types of secured transaction. It includes sales of "payment intangibles" and promissory notes, assignments of payment intangibles of security purposes, assignments of health-care-insurance receivables to health-care providers, and security interests of issuers of letters of credit in any documents presented to them to draw funds.

Perfection against Proceeds

Section 9-315 provides an extensive and careful coverage for security interests in **proceeds,** meaning "whatever is acquired upon the sale, lease, license, exchange, or other disposition of the collateral." Money, checks, and the like are "cash proceeds." All other proceeds are "noncash proceeds." The general intent of this section is to give the secured party with a security interest in collateral a similar security in anything that the debtor received from third parties in exchange for that collateral.

As a rule, unless the debtor was authorized to make the sale or exchange of the collateral, a secured party can elect to pursue the collateral in the hands of a third party as well as the proceeds in the hands of the debtor. A dealer who filed against a TV set that was bought on credit could, for example, repossess the TV from a third party to whom the set was sold if the debtor was in default under the original security agreement. The secured party will not get the debt paid twice but will have two sources to look to for payment. This general rule is subject to several exceptions, including the **buyer in the ordinary course (BIOC)** of business who buys goods (usually from a dealer's inventory). This BIOC takes the goods free and clear of a security interest created by the seller, even though that interest is perfected and even though the BIOC knows about it.

What does the secured party need to do to perfect a security interest against "proceeds"? If a financing statement that indicates the security interest applies to proceeds as well as the original collateral has been filed, nothing more need be done; there is a continuously perfected security interest against the proceeds. When the original financing statement does not so indicate, or when perfection against the original collateral occurred by another method, that perfection still applies to proceeds, continuously and automatically, for a 21-day grace period. Within that period, the secured party needs to file or to take possession of the proceeds to perfect.

Perfection against Fixtures

Many complex problems may arise when goods are attached to real estate and both the goods and the real estate are subject to the claims of financing agencies or good faith purchasers. The Code was not intended to regulate real property law, but in this area Article 9 does have an impact on real property doctrines. In general, fixtures are defined by the general law of the state where the realty is located. The Code does exclude ordinary building materials from the "fixtures" definition.

First, a construction mortgagee (who makes advances of funds to finance the building of structures on the land) is given a special priority over all fixture financiers even as to such items as dishwashers and refrigerators. As to other existing interests in the real estate (such as a land contract seller or the holder of the purchase mortgage), the fixture financier must make a **fixture filing** either before or within 20 days after the goods become attached to the real estate. This is a special rule for purchase-money security interests in the fixtures. Otherwise, there is a first-to-file rule for fixtures. For example, the seller of a new furnace on credit could obtain priority over the holder of an existing mortgage by making the proper fixture filing. But if the existing mortgage had already been properly recorded, a nonpurchase-money creditor who wished to use existing fixtures as collateral could not take priority over the mortgagee unless the latter agreed.

Financiers of "readily-removable factory or office machines" or readily-removable replacements of domestic appliances that are consumer goods are given priority over conflicting real estate interests if their security interest is perfected before the goods become fixtures. Most stoves, refrigerators, washers, and dryers would seem to be readily removable; most furnaces would not. A catchall provision indicates that a conflicting real estate interest takes priority against any security interest that is not properly perfected.

CASE 3

Rice v. Simmons First Bank of Searcy

308 B.R. 347 (8 Cir.Bkrp.App. 2004)

Facts: In 2001, Henry and Opal Renaud borrowed money from Simmons Bank to buy a Polaris ATV. Later that year, Opal signed a consolidation note at Simmons for the refinancing of the Polaris ATV and a 1994 Ford truck. Simmons had its lien noted on the truck title certificate and had Opal sign a security agreement covering the Polaris ATV. Simmons then filed a UCC-1 financing statement on the Polaris ATV with the Arkansas Secretary of State. Simmons did not note its lien on the ATV's title. Also in 2001, the debtors refinanced their Spirit mobile home and the real estate where it is located by borrowing $33,100.83 from Simmons Bank. The previous lienholder released its lien that had been noted on the Spirit's title certificate, but Simmons Bank did not note its new lien on the title certificate. Instead, Simmons recorded a mortgage against the real estate covering "all existing and future improvements, structures, fixtures, and replacements that may now, or at any time in the future, be part of the real estate." When Henry and Opal declared bankruptcy, trustee M. Randy Rice claimed both the Polaris ATV and the Spirit mobile home, alleging that Simmons Bank's security interests in both items were unperfected. The bankruptcy judge ruled in favor of Rice. Simmons Bank appealed.

Issues: Is notation on the vehicle title certificate the exclusive method of perfection for ATVs, which are not required to be registered for operation on the highway?

Can a security interest in a mobile home which is permanently attached to real estate be perfected by filing a mortgage against the real estate?

Decision: Yes. No. Judgments affirmed (in favor of trustee Rice).

Opinion by Bankruptcy Judge Venters: "The bankruptcy court held that an ATV is a motor vehicle subject to Arkansas' certificate of title laws. Simmons Bank argue that Arkansas law does not require ATVs to be registered as motor vehicles for operation on the public highways; thus, a notation on the ATV's certificate of title is not the exclusive method to perfect a lien....

"The Bank confuses the certificate of title and perfection laws with the statutes regulating the operation of ATVs on the public highways. In fact, under Arkansas law, not all ATVs are required to be registered as a motor vehicle for operation on the public highways, but 'all owners of [ATVs] that are not otherwise required to be registered by law shall register them with the Director of the Department of Finance and Administration within thirty (30) calendar days of acquiring them.' ... The Director of the Department of Finance then issues 'a certificate of title to the owner of [the ATV].' ... Accordingly, while an ATV does not have to be registered as a 'motor vehicle, motorcycle, or motor driven cycle for operation on the public streets and highways,' ... nothing in the statutes exempts ATVs from the certificate of title laws....

"Therefore, the bankruptcy court did not commit any error of law in concluding that Simmons Bank was an unperfected creditor in the Debtors' ATV and that the Chapter 7 Trustee was able to avoid Simmons Bank's lien....

"With respect to the mobile home, Simmons Bank ... contends that its mortgage on the real property encompassed the mobile home as soon as the mobile home became permanently affixed to the real property....

"There is no dispute that the Debtors' mobile home is subject to registration under Arkansas certificate of title laws.... The fact that a mobile home is without wheels and designed as permanent living quarters does not exempt owners of mobile homes from having to obtain a certificate of title.... In an apparent attempt to avoid the conundrum of when a mobile home is transmogrified into a fixture or structure affixed to the realty the Arkansas legislature has established a bright-line rule—the time of manufacture—to determine whether a mobile home is a mobile home or something else. Thus, it would appear that a house trailer or other vehicle designed for use as living quarters and capable of being towed or otherwise transported or drawn on a highway at the time of manufacture will always be a mobile home subject to the certificate of title laws.

"We can find no exception in Arkansas's certificate of title laws that exempt[s] mobile homes if they are affixed to realty, and counsel for Simmons Bank has pointed to no such exception.... We should not provide an extra-statutory exception to Arkansas law when the Arkansas legislature specifically made notation on the certificate of title on a mobile home the exclusive method of perfecting an interest therein.... If Simmons Bank is unhappy with the conclusion reached by the bankruptcy court, it should petition the Arkansas legislature to change the certificate of title laws pertaining to mobile homes affixed to realty.

"Accordingly, we affirm the rulings of the bankruptcy court."

A fixture filing must be made in the office designated for the filing of a mortgage on the related real estate. It must include a legal description of the real estate to which the fixture is being attached and also the name of the real estate owner if that person is not the debtor who is using the fixture as collateral. Thus, the fixture claim should appear in any title search of the real estate records.

The *Rice* case discusses the ambiguous status of a mobile home as a "fixture," and also another conflict between motor vehicle (all-terrain vehicle [ATV]) "registration" and "title certificate."

Priorities

For the creditor, priority of payment is what the security game is all about. Obviously, if the debtor had enough funds to go around, there would be no problem of who got paid first and no need for this sort of litigation. Litigation to establish priority occurs because someone who has extended credit to an insolvent debtor is going to get "stuck" for some or all of that claim against the debtor. Other types of claimants, such as good faith purchasers of collateral from the debtor, will also be interested in determining whether they hold the property in question free and clear, or subject to the claims of a creditor or creditors. Different potential claimants and different types of financing transactions combine to produce a great range of specific fact situations. Part of what appears to be a terrible complexity in Article 9's priority rules stems directly from the need to provide a number of different rules to deal with a number of quite different fact variations. We thus need to consider both the "general rules" and several special situations covered by special priority rules.

For the first general rule on priority, we return to 9-201(a):

> *Except as otherwise provided in [this Act], a security agreement is effective according to its terms between the parties, against purchasers of the collateral, and against creditors.*

In other words, the security agreement itself controls priority unless a Code provision covers the situation and provides otherwise. Nearly all typical priority situations are in fact covered by a Code rule, so that the security agreement itself operates only within a limited range with regard to priority rules.

Secured parties may agree among themselves as to their relative priority positions. Such an arrangement, of course, would be effective only as between the parties who agreed to it.

Even a secured party with an unfiled, unperfected security interest receives some protection in terms of priority. If the interest has attached to the collateral, the secured party does have rights in the collateral as against the debtor, and generally that interest will take priority as against buyers of the collateral or lien creditors who have knowledge of the security interest when they become such.

Section 9-322 is the basic priorities section. It provides the general rules for determining priorities between conflicting security interests in the same collateral, and it cross-references other sections containing special priority rules.

The general priority rules are simple and logical. As between competing perfected interests, priority is determined according to the time of filing or perfection. For example, Mabel is shopping for a new car. She agrees to buy a particular car from Big Bennie's dealership. Mabel goes to her credit union and borrows $8,000 to buy the car, giving her credit union a security interest against the car. The credit union files a financing statement that identifies the new car as collateral. Mabel then goes back to Bennie's and signs a purchase-money security agreement for the car—buying it on credit. Bennie's gives her the car, and then files a financing statement (without checking the records under Mabel's name). Mabel then drives back to her credit union and picks up her $8,000 check. Even though Bennie's security interest was perfected first, Mabel's credit union takes priority if she defaults on these two obligations. The credit union filed first, even though their interest was perfected after Bennie's. Bennie should have checked the records before giving Mabel the car.

So long as neither security interest has been perfected, priority is given in the order in which they attached to the collateral.

For the purposes of applying these priority rules, the date of filing or perfection as to the collateral is also the effective date as to any proceeds of that collateral.

Special purchase-money rules for inventory and noninventory collateral are set out in 9-324. A purchase-money security interest in **inventory collateral** has priority over a conflicting security interest in the same collateral if the purchase-money security interest is perfected when the debtor gets possession of the collateral; and written notification of the purchase-money security interest is received by any other "known" or "filed" secured party before the debtor gets possession of the collateral; and the notification states that the purchase-money person has or intends to acquire a purchase-money security interest in the debtor's inventory, "describing such inventory by item or type." Because there is much less of a commingling problem with **noninventory collateral**, the purchase-money person's requirements for priority in such collateral are much simpler. The interest just has to have been perfected when the debtor takes possession of the noninventory collateral, or within 20 days thereafter. Under this rule, Bennie could take priority over Mabel's credit union (in our last example) if he filed within the 10-day period.

Protection for Certain Good Faith Purchasers

Section 9-320 contains two special rules designed for the protection of good faith purchasers of goods. These rules were referred to in the preceding section of this chapter; and the *Nicolosi* problem at the end of this chapter illustrates their application in one fact situation.

Subsection (a) of 9-320 protects the "buyer in the ordinary course of business," who is defined by 1-201(9) as follows:

> *"Buyer in ordinary course of business" means a person who in good faith and without knowledge that the sale to him is in violation of the ownership rights or security interest of a third party in the goods buys in ordinary course from a person in the business of selling goods of that kind. . . .*

Stated more simply, the BIOC is a buyer from a dealer's inventory. The BIOC "takes free of a security interest created by the buyer's seller even if the security interest is perfected and the buyer knows of its existence."

The limitations inherent in this rule have been brought out by several car dealer cases. In one such case, the Supreme Court of New Hampshire held that BIOC Jones was not protected because a security interest had not been created by *his* seller and because the bank's security interest had been filed. Jones had bought the car in good faith from the dealer to whom it had been resold by the original buyer. When the original buyer went into default on his installment payments, the bank sued to foreclose on its security interest and won.

Moreover, where the BIOC not only knows of the existence of a security interest but also knows that the sale to him or her is in violation of it, he takes subject to the security interest.

Section 9-320(a) also specifically excludes from its protection "a person buying farm products from a person engaged in farming operations." Thus, buyer Johnson did not get BIOC protection in the *Waychus* problem in Chapter 23.

Equally significant is the limitation that 9-320(b) places on the operation of the automatic perfection alternative for consumer goods. When the secured party is relying on automatic perfection, a BFP takes free of the security interest if buying without knowledge and for personal, family, or household purposes.

Debtor's Defenses against Assignee

The great bulk of time-sale contracts are not held by the seller until maturity, but are transferred or "assigned" to a bank or other financing agency. The early common law absolutely prohibited such assignments because it was felt that they forced the debtor to do business with a stranger. Only within the last hundred years has their validity been accepted, and traces of the absolute common law prohibition have survived almost to our own day.

One of the most significant common law rules developed to protect account debtors in the assignment situation is the one that makes the assignee subject to all defenses the debtor has against the assignor (seller). The assignee steps into the assignor's shoes—they do not get any larger just because someone else is wearing them; if they pinch a little bit, too bad. For its own protection, the financial community has been able to get statutes passed in some states that modify this general rule. The seller could also insulate the financing agency from most of the debtor's usual defenses (nondelivery, defective merchandise, fraud in the inducement) by having the debtor sign a negotiable instrument and then negotiating it to the financing agency as a "holder in due course."

The drafters of Article 9 continued the general rule on debtors' defenses against the assignee in substantially unchanged form. As under the common law, therefore, the account debtor can assert any defense under the assigned contract against the assignee and can use any defense or claim against the assignor on totally unrelated matters, until receiving notice that the account has been assigned. For example, Biff Baker buys two cars, one new and one used, from Able's Auto Sales. Biff pays cash for the used car and finances the new car over 36 months. Able's Auto assigns the financing contract to the E-Z Money Company. If anything goes wrong with either car, Biff can use that defect (breach of warranty) as a defense when he is sued by E-Z Money, up to the point when Biff is notified of the assignment. After that, Biff can only assert claims he has under the new car contract against E-Z, and he has to go back to Able's Auto for any claims on the used car that arise after Biff gets notice.

However, Article 9 specifically validates a contractual agreement by the debtor-buyer not to assert against an assignee any claim or defense which may exist against the seller. For an assignee to claim the protection afforded by this section, it must take the assignment "for value, in good faith, and without notice of claim or defense." Moreover, this section does not prevent the debtor from asserting defenses that could be asserted against the holder in due course of a negotiable instrument, such as minority, illegality, and fraud in the execution. And finally, and perhaps most significantly, this rule is subject to "any statute or decision which establishes a different rule for buyers of consumer goods."

If a state wishes to modify the seeming harshness of this third section to protect consumers, this is easily done, either legislatively or judicially. Massachusetts took the lead by passing the bill that abolished the holder in due course concept for consumer sales; most states have now adopted such legislation. Under its rule-making powers, the Federal Trade Commission (FTC) held extensive hearings and then adopted an "unfair method of competition" rule at the national level. As a result, the **holder in due course doctrine** has been largely removed from the consumer-sales field. Such waiver clauses are valid for nonconsumer buyers (who, presumably, are better able to take care of themselves from a legal and contractual standpoint).

The UCC also makes it clear that any "disclaimer, limitation or modification of the seller's warranties" must be made in accordance with Article 2 and not under this section of Article 9.

The *Woffard* case in Chapter 13 was an illustration of these UCC rules on debtor's defenses.

Default and Remedies

Most of our discussion of secured transactions in this chapter has concerned the problems confronted by the secured party when third-party claimants contest the right to priority against the collateral. Most of Article 9 is directed toward those problems, but it does step into the transaction between the immediate parties, to regulate the rights and remedies as between them in the event that the debtor defaults.

Cumulative Remedies; Minimum Requirements after Default

The intent of the UCC drafters was that the secured party should be entitled to pursue all available remedies until the debt is satisfied. The secured party has the rights and remedies provided by Article 9, those provided in the security agreement itself (subject to certain limitations), and "any available judicial procedure" for debt enforcement under applicable state law.

Similarly, the debtor has the rights and remedies provided in Article 9 and in the security agreement. The policy of the Code and of Article 9 is to provide substantial freedom of contract between the immediate parties to the particular transaction. That policy is continued, to a degree, as regards default procedures, but Article 9 imposes a set of "minimum procedural requirements" on default, for the protection of the debtor. In addition to these prescribed minima, the parties' freedom to agree to "whatever they want" may also be limited by 1-102[3] and 2-302, as noted previously.

The objective in these default sections, then, is to balance the rights and remedies of both parties and to ensure that the debtor is protected by requiring that certain steps be taken when default occurs. Default, however, is not specifically defined; its definition is left to the agreement itself and to generally applicable legal principles.

Collection

On default, or whenever so agreed, the secured party has the right to notify an account debtor or the obligor on an instrument to start making payments directly and the right to take control of any proceeds. This rule applies even though the assignor, called the "debtor" in the security agreement, was previously making the collections and then remitting them to the secured party.

When the agreement provides that the secured party is entitled to charge back against the debtor any "uncollected" collateral and the secured party elects to collect personally, that must be done "in a commercially reasonable manner." The reasonable expenses incurred in the collection process can be recovered from the assignor-debtor. Provision is also made for both "deficiency" and "surplus" situations.

If the security agreement secures an indebtedness, the secured party must account to the debtor for any surplus, and the obligor is liable for any deficiency. But, if the underlying transaction was a sale of notes, accounts, payment intangibles, or chattel paper, the debtor is not entitled to any surplus and the obligor is not liable for any deficiency.

Repossession

The creditor's classic remedy on default has been to repossess the collateral. This remedy is continued for the secured party, pretty much as it existed under prior law, by Article 9. The secured party may use judicial process or use self-help—so long as there is no "breach of the peace."

Traditionally, the main question in these cases has been the definition of what constitutes a **breach of the peace** by the creditor repossessing without court order. Parked on the street or in a public parking lot, the debtor's car seems to be fair game for the repossession person. Even if it is in the debtor's driveway or parked on private property, the repossession person can probably still seize it and drive or tow it away. The line of demarcation seems to be the point at which the repossession person opens a door or gate, either by force or fraud, or threatens the debtor in any way. These lines of decision under prior law will presumably continue under Article 9.

Section 9-503 also provides two new repossession alternatives. The secured party may render the collateral inoperative, leave it on the debtor's premises, and sell it from there. Alternatively, the secured party can require the debtor to assemble the collateral at a mutually convenient location.

These two provisions give the secured party additional options under the general right to repossession.

Self-help repossession is at issue in the *Salisbury* case.

Disposition

After default by the debtor, the secured party has the right to dispose of the collateral and to apply the proceeds—first, to pay all reasonable selling expenses; second, to satisfy the security interest; and third, to pay any subordinate security interest as to which a written demand for payment is received prior to distribution of the proceeds.

As regards the disposition itself, Article 9 allows maximum flexibility as to details. The disposition may be made by public or private sale, in one or more contracts, as a unit or in parcels, at any time and place and on any terms. The secured party may buy the collateral at any public sale, or at a private sale if the collateral is of a type sold in a recognized market or subject to widely distributed standard price quotations. This considerable flexibility is, however, subject to a basic good faith limitation: "every aspect of the disposition including the method, manner, time, place and terms must be commercially reasonable." Except

CASE 4

Salisbury Livestock v. Colorado Central Credit Union
793 P.2d 470 (WY 1990)

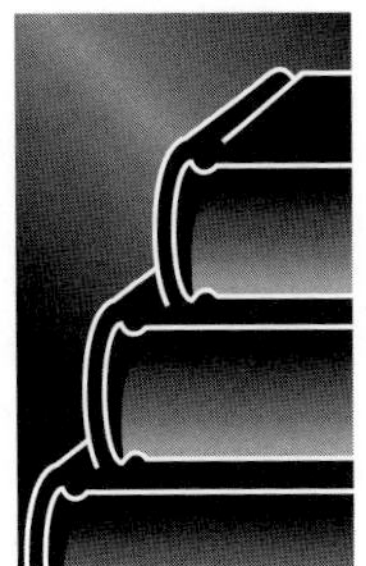

Facts: Salisbury Livestock Company (Salisbury Livestock) initiated a trespass action in response to Colorado Central's repossession of vehicles owned by George Salisbury, III (young Salisbury) from Wyoming property of Salisbury Livestock. Salisbury Livestock is a family corporation run by young Salisbury's father, George Salisbury, Jr.; it is registered in Wyoming and possesses land in Wyoming and Colorado. The disputed repossession of the vehicles took place on Salisbury Livestock's Ladder Ranch, which is on the Wyoming side of the Wyoming-Colorado state border.

Young Salisbury had pledged the repossessed vehicles, along with three others, as collateral for a $13,000 loan from Colorado Central in October 1984. This loan was made while he was living in the Denver area. He defaulted on the loan in March 1986. He had defaulted on the loan once before, in October 1985, and Colorado Central had repossessed one of his vehicles, which he subsequently redeemed. Colorado Central had then given young Salisbury an extension until February 15, 1986, meaning that he paid only interest from October 1985 until February 1986. He made the February 1986 payment, but did not make any further payments.

At some time in early 1986, young Salisbury left Denver and returned to Slater, Colorado, where he resided near the Salisbury Livestock Wyoming property on which his mother and father lived. Colorado Central sent notice of default to his Slater, Colorado mailing address in May 1986, but did not receive a response. In July 1986, Colorado Central decided to repossess the vehicles pledged as security on the loan. Welzheimer, Colorado Central's credit manager, hired C.A.R.S.-U.S.A., a car repossession company, to retrieve the vehicles.

On the evening of July 27, 1986, C.A.R.S.-U.S A. owner Clark and employees Srock and Boling (and one other C.A.R.S.-U.S.A. employee not made a party to the action) left Denver with two tow trucks to repossess young Salisbury's vehicles. Before leaving Denver, Clark had called young Salisbury's Slater, Colorado home and received directions for finding it from an unidentified woman. The repossession crew arrived at young Salisbury's home about 5:00 the next morning. They found one of the vehicles, a van, parked just off the highway in front of the house and with the key in the ignition. Clark looked inside a small shed or garage on the property and scouted the area around the house for the other vehicles, but did not find them.

Taking the van, they drove a short distance back up the road they had just traveled, Colorado Highway 129, to a large "Salisbury" sign that had been mentioned as a landmark by the unidentified woman Clark talked to on the telephone, and that they had noticed on their way to young Salisbury's home. The sign was adjacent to a private drive or roadway. Although they could not see any vehicles from the highway, the repossession crew turned down the drive. After traveling about 50 yards, they spotted several vehicles in the ranch yard. When they reached the vehicles, they identified two from their assignment form, a Corvette and a conversion van. They pushed the Corvette onto the drive so that they could reach it with one tow truck, backed up to the conversion van with the other tow truck, hooked both vehicles up, and towed them away.

At the time, it was light, and appellees reported that they heard people stirring in a nearby building. They did not attempt to obtain permission to enter the property or to take the vehicles. Clark testified that he did not plan on contacting anyone as it was his intention to avoid a confrontation. George Salisbury, Jr. testified that after the repossession, he discovered that the repossessors had apparently broken a 2-by-4 pole that was lying on the ground near the repossessed vehicles.

After the repossession, young Salisbury explained his financial problems to his father. The two agreed on a loan that permitted young Salisbury to redeem the vehicles on August 4, 1986, with a check drafted by his father. Salisbury Livestock, owner of the Wyoming property from which the Corvette and conversion van were towed, then initiated this trespass action. The trial court granted Colorado Central's motion for a directed verdict. Salisbury appealed.

Issue: Was this a proper self-help repossession?

Decision: Perhaps not. Judgment reversed. (A trial is necessary.)

Opinion by Justice Golden: "[W]e agree with the statement that 'courts disfavor self-help repossession because, if abused, it invades the legitimate conflict resolution function of the courts.' . . . While recognizing that W.S. 34-21-962 extends a conditional self-help privilege to secured parties, we will read the statute narrowly to reduce the risk to the public of extra judicial conflict resolution. Although it is apparent that the self-help remedy is efficient for creditors and results in reduced costs of credit for debtors, . . . we must seek a reasonable balancing of that interest against private property interests and society's interest in tranqui[lity].

"We then look to the language of W.S. 34-21-962 to establish the parameters of the protection it offers to secured parties who seek to repossess collateral without judicial process. The statute provides in pertinent part that '[i]n taking possession a secured party may proceed without judicial process if this can be done without breach of the peace. . . . ' Obviously, the key to whether a self-help repossession is privileged by the statute is whether the peace has been breached. Colorado Central agrees, but argues that the facts demonstrate that there was no breach of the peace. Salisbury Livestock would have us define breach of the peace as including simple trespass.

"W.S. 34-21-962 does not define breach of the peace, and there is no definition offered elsewhere in the Wyoming statutes that address rights of secured parties. In our review of decisions from other jurisdictions, we find no consistently applied definition but agree with the analysis of the Utah Supreme Court ... that, '[c]ourts have struggled in determining when a creditor's trespass onto a debtor's property rises to the level of a breach of the peace. The two primary factors considered in making this determination are the potential for immediate violence and the nature of the premises intruded upon.' These factors are interrelated in that the potential for violence increases as the creditor's trespass comes closer to a dwelling, and we will focus our analysis on them. It is necessary to evaluate the facts of each case to determine whether a breach of the peace has occurred....

"We agree with the trial court that the Restatement (Second) of Torts § 198 reasonableness requirement provides appropriate criteria for evaluating whether a creditor's entry has breached the peace. If, as here, there was no confrontation and the timing and manner, including notice or lack of notice, are found reasonable, the entry is privileged. If the jury should find that the manner or timing of this entry was unreasonable because it may have triggered a breach of the peace, it in effect finds the entry a breach of the peace and unprivileged. We foresee the possibility that a rational jury could reach the conclusion that this entry was unreasonable....

"[W]e cannot agree with Colorado Central's assertion that there can be no finding of a breach of the peace because there was no confrontation. Confrontation or violence is not necessary to finding a breach of the peace. The possibility of immediate violence is sufficient.... Two elements of this case create questions which we believe might lead reasonable jurors to a conclusion at odds with the trial court's directed verdict. First, this was an entry onto the premises of a third party not privy to the loan agreement. Particularly if there was no knowledge of young Salisbury's consent to repossession, this could trigger a breach of the peace. The few reported cases involving repossession from third party properties suggest that such entry is acceptable.... However, these cases do not address third party residential property. When entry onto third party property is coupled with the second unusual element, the location and the setting of this repossession, the possibility of a different verdict becomes more apparent.

"We have not located any cases addressing a creditor's entry into the secluded ranchyard of an isolated ranch where the vehicles sought are not even visible from a public place. The few cases involve urban or suburban driveways, urban parking lots, or business premises.... We believe that the location and setting of this entry to repossess is sufficiently distinct, and the privacy expectations of rural resident sufficiently different, that a jury should weigh the reasonableness of this entry, or whether the peace may have been breached by a real possibility of imminent violence, or even by mere entry into these premises: the area next to the residence in a secluded ranchyard.

"Because there are factual questions on which reasonable minds may differ, it was error to grant the motion for a directed verdict. The jury must determine whether the peace was breached by this creditor's entry because of the premises entered or the real possibility of immediate violence given the setting and location of the repossession. The reasonableness of the time and manner of the entry must be considered in the context of the third party property status and the rural setting. Whether notice is necessary is also an appropriate consideration when evaluating the manner of repossession. If either time or manner, or both, are found unreasonable then the entry is not privileged....

"We need not, and so do not, reach the question of exemplary damages. Any question of damages awaits a prerequisite finding that the repossessors committed an unprivileged trespass.

"Reversed and remanded for a new trial."

where the collateral is perishable, or threatens to decline speedily in value, or is customarily sold on a recognized market, the secured party must give the debtor reasonable notification of the intended sale. Except for consumer goods, notification must also be sent to any other secured party who had filed against the collateral or whose interest is known to the secured party. The debtor can thus challenge the legal effects of the sale either under the **commercially reasonable** requirement or on the basis that he or she did not get **reasonable notification**. The issue is most often raised when the debtor is sued for a **deficiency judgment**, in which the secured party says that the sale did not bring enough to pay off the debt.

Section 9-617 deals with the rights acquired by the purchaser of the collateral at the disposition sale. The disposition gives the purchaser all rights of the debtor, and it discharges the security interest under which the sale was made and any subordinate interest or lien. Even though the secured party does not follow proper sale procedures, the purchaser is protected at a public sale if there is no knowledge of the defects in the sale or collusion, and in any other case if acting in good faith.

Compulsory Disposition

A secured party who has repossessed the collateral must dispose of it in accordance with Section 9-620(e) when the consumer-debtor has paid 60 percent of the cash price or of the loan. If the secured party fails to comply with this section within 90 days after taking

CASE 5

Beardmore v. American Summit Financial Holdings, LLC

351 F.3d 352 (8 Cir. 2003)

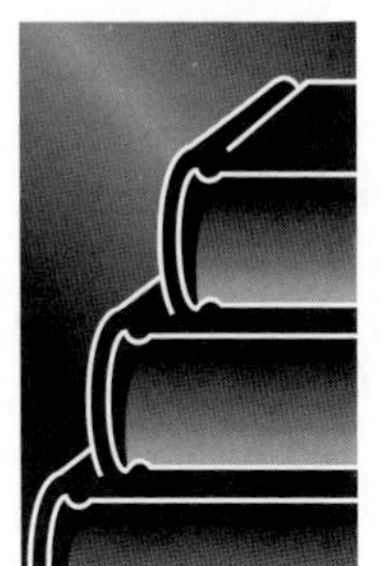

Facts: John and Kathrine Beardmore borrowed $2,500,000 from Founders Equity Group to buy 3.35 million shares of Superior Financial Holding Corporation. They signed a promissory note (Founders note) and a security agreement.... The security agreement granted Founders a security interest in 2.5 million Superior shares, the Innovative Financial Systems, Inc. (IFS) shares held by the Beardmores and at least one parcel of the Beardmores' real estate. Additionally, the Beardmores granted Founders an option to purchase 250,000 Superior shares for $250,000. All documents provided that Texas law governs. The Beardmores sold 1 million Superior shares and applied the proceeds to pay down the Founders note. Superior issued them a new stock certificate (#33) indicating ownership of 1.5 million shares, which they then delivered to Founders. After the Beardmores defaulted on their note, they agreed (the February 22, 2001 letter) with Founders on a public sale procedure for the collateral—Founders would first sell the Superior shares, and only sell the IFS shares if there was still a balance owing on the note. A week later, Founders assigned its rights to American Summit, who then sold the IFS shares on April 27, for $2,000. Seven days after the sale, the Beardmores tendered a $2,000,000 check to American Summit—as payment of the Founders Note. American Summit refused the check. The Beardmores filed a declaratory judgment action against American Summit, to determine their rights to the Superior shares at issue. The trial court ruled that American Summit had converted the shares when it refused the check offered as payment for the debt, and kept the Superior shares.

Issue: Did the secured party impliedly agree to take the collateral in satisfaction of the debt?

Decision: Yes. Judgment reversed, as to the Superior shares.

Opinion by Judge Riley: "Under Texas law, every aspect of a creditor's disposition of collateral must be commercially reasonable.... If the secured creditor disposes of the collateral in a commercially unreasonable manner, the secured creditor is deemed to have retained the collateral in complete satisfaction of the debt, prohibiting the secured creditor from pursuing a deficiency judgment....

"The Texas courts have not addressed the secured creditor's rights and the debtor's rights to repossessed, but not yet disposed of collateral, after the secured creditor has disposed of a portion of the collateral in a commercially unreasonable manner....

"The district court deemed American Summit's disposition of the collateral commercially unreasonable because American Summit breached the February 22 letter agreement.... American Summit agreed to first sell the Superior shares, apply the sale's proceeds to the Founders Note, and sell the IFS shares only if a deficiency remained. Despite [this] agreement, American Summit first sold the IFS shares, while retaining the Superior shares. Because American Summit's future disposition of the Superior shares will also be commercially unreasonable under the letter agreement, American Summit implicitly elected to retain both the IFS shares and the Superior shares in complete satisfaction of the Founders Note....

"The Beardmores' attempted tender did not divest American Summit of its rights to the Superior shares. After American Summit sold the IFS shares, the Beardmores tried to tender the amount outstanding on the Founders' Note. When a secured creditor ... elects to retain the collateral in full satisfaction of the debt, the debtor ... no longer has the right to redeem the collateral....

"Although we conclude American Summit retained the Superior shares in satisfaction of the debt, we note the Beardmores are not without recourse against American Summit if the fair market value of the Superior shares exceeds the amount outstanding. A debtor can recover any loss sustained due to the commercially unreasonable disposition of the debtor's collateral....

"American Summit seeks to foreclose its security interest in the Beardmores' realty. After disposing of personalty securing a debt, a secured creditor cannot foreclose a security interest in real estate to satisfy the same debt until the secured creditor demonstrates it can pursue a deficiency judgment.... Because American Summit is precluded from seeking a deficiency judgment, [it] cannot foreclose its security interest in the Beardmores' real estate."

possession, the debtor may either sue for conversion of the collateral or recover damages and a $500 penalty as specified.

Except for the previous consumer goods situation, a secured party who is in possession of the collateral may propose after default that he or she will retain it in satisfaction of the debt. The secured party must send written notice of this "proposal" to the debtor and, except for consumer goods, to any other secured party who has filed or who is known to the secured party with possession. The debtor or any secured party entitled to notification has 21 days from receipt of the notification to object in writing to the proposal; any other secured party claiming an interest in the collateral has 21 days from the time that secured party one obtained possession of the collateral. If anyone does object, secured party one cannot retain the collateral as proposed but must dispose of it; if there is no objection, the secured party can keep the collateral in satisfaction of the obligation.

Redemption by Debtor

At any time before the secured party has disposed or contracted to dispose of the collateral or has discharged the obligation by retention of the collateral, the debtor or any other secured party has the right to redeem the collateral. To redeem, there must be a tender to the secured party of: (a) all obligations secured by the collateral; (b) "the expenses reasonably incurred by the secured party in retaking, holding, and preparing the collateral for disposition, in arranging for the sale"; and (c) "to the extent provided in the agreement and not prohibited by law, his reasonable attorneys' fees and legal expenses." The debtor or any other secured party may agree in writing, after default, to waive this right to redeem.

The *Beardmore* case discusses the results when a secured party makes an unreasonable disposition of the collateral.

Secured Party Liability for Failure to Comply

Article 9 does two things. It defines more precisely the requirement that the secured party proceed after default in a "commercially reasonable" manner, and it provides remedies for the debtor where the secured party does not proceed in accordance with its default provisions.

Section 9-627 establishes several principles regarding "commercial reasonableness." When a violation of such standards has occurred the debtor is entitled to recover any financial damages caused by the violation. For some violations, the obligor or the consumer debtor is also entitled to an extra $500 as statutory damages. Also, depending on the nature of the violation, a court may order or prevent disposition of the collateral.

These Code sections thus provide significant protections for both consumer and nonconsumer debtors even after they have gone into default on their obligations under a security agreement.

Significance of This Chapter

Because debtors do default with some frequency, creditors need to be assured that they will have priority claims against "their" pieces of collateral. This priority is really the whole purpose of structuring the credit arrangement as a secured transaction. The entire motive for being a secured creditor is to have a specific source of funds in the event the debtor defaults, rather than having to rely on the debtor's general financial condition. Creditors thus need to know what to do to establish priority, and what payment sequences the Code provides.

Similarly, both debtors and creditors need to be aware of their rights when a default does occur. In general, a secured creditor who is proceeding in a reasonable manner is well protected by Article 9. On the other hand, the Code also tries to ensure that the debtor is treated fairly, even though guilty of a default. Because abuses occurred in the past, Article 9 gives consumer debtors the right to recover a penalty in the event their secured parties do not follow proper procedures. The Code has attempted to strike a fair balance between the parties in this very common and very important commercial transaction.

IMPORTANT TERMS AND CONCEPTS

automatic perfection
bona fide purchaser (BFP)
breach of the peace
buyer in the ordinary course (BIOC)
commercially reasonable
consumer goods
deficiency judgment
filing
fixture filing
holder in due course doctrine
inventory collateral
lien creditor
noninventory collateral
perfected security interest
perfection
proceeds
purchase-money security interests
reasonable notification
trustee in bankruptcy
unperfected security interest

QUESTIONS AND PROBLEMS FOR DISCUSSION

1. What is the difference between attachment and perfection?

2. What are the three different methods of perfecting a security interest?

3. What happens when a security interest is not perfected?

4. When does a buyer from a merchant take free and clear of a security interest that has been perfected against the goods being sold?

5. In 1998, Noyes Paving Company bought, on credit, two dump trucks and several other pieces of construction equipment from Northern Contractors, giving Northern a security interest in the two trucks and the equipment. Northern assigned its rights to James Talcott, Inc., a large finance company. Talcott filed a financing statement that named the collateral as "Construction Equipment, Motor Vehicles." Three months later, Noyes signed "equipment leases" for three more dump trucks and additional construction equipment at Franklin Bank. Franklin did not check the UCC filing records or file its own financing statement.

   In January 1999, having cash flow problems, Noyes asked Talcott for a modification of payment terms in their contract. Talcott agreed to accept lower monthly payments and a longer repayment schedule. In return, Noyes signed an amended security agreement, giving Talcott a security interest in "all goods whether now owned or hereafter acquired." Talcott did not file a new financing statement. When Noyes defaulted on all its obligations in May 2000, Franklin Bank filed a financing statement covering its collateral and repossessed its trucks and equipment. Talcott objected, claiming it had priority on all Noyes' goods.

   Who has payment priority, as to which goods? Explain.

6. Pedro Agricola, a farmer, bought a pickup for which he executed a promissory note to Flatland Bank. The note was secured by a properly executed and perfected security agreement. Pedro also had other loans outstanding with Flatland Bank that were secured by mortgages on other equipment and on his 16 pigs. Two years later, Pedro borrowed money from his neighbor Lilly White and gave her a promissory note but soon afterward he defaulted on both notes. Lilly took possession of the truck, claiming that the bank should satisfy its claim by taking possession of Pedro's other assets, namely the 10-year-old equipment and the sixteen 2-year-old pigs.

   Who has prior claim on the truck? Why?

7. On May 17, 1997, Esther Keidel borrowed $3,500 from the First National Bank of Wood River to finance the purchase of a mobile home. Keidel signed a security agreement with the bank and executed a promissory note. She received from the bank a check for $3,500 payable jointly to her, to Kenneth and Rose Mitchell (the sellers), and to Olin Employees' Credit Union (the prior lien holder). When the check was issued by the bank, it was taken to the business office of the credit union, where the money changed hands and various notations were made on the old certificate of title. Esther was advised immediately to apply for a new certificate of title. She attempted to apply for a new certificate of title but failed in (and finally desisted from) her efforts.

   Esther's petition in bankruptcy was filed on November 7, 1997. About 1 month later, the bank delivered an application for a new certificate of title to the secretary of state of Illinois. A new certificate was issued on December 15, 1997.

   The state's motor vehicle registration requires delivery of the old certificate of title and an application for a new one, with the claimed security interest noted thereon, to the secretary of state within 21 days of the sale to perfect the security interest.

   Who has the best claim to Esther's trailer? Explain.

8. Kelly Goodheart, registered owner of a highway tractor, leased his tractor to Morse Crash. However, the rental agreement was in actuality a conditional sales or title-retaining contract, under which Morse agreed to pay $300 for 15 weeks and then was to receive title. Morse also was to pay all repair bills and to provide insurance coverage. The vehicle was damaged in an accident and later repaired by Frank Hammer's Collision Service for $600. Morse decided to move for destinations unknown, leaving Kelly and Frank to fight over the tractor.

   How would you decide these conflicting claims? Why so?

9. Ned Ninepins, owner of Lucky Lane bowling alley, bought six automatic pinsetters from Leisure Equipment, Inc. He entered into a retail installment contract with the seller that specified that on default, the total contract price would become due. After several payments, Ned defaulted, and 6 months later Leisure Equipment, Inc. brought a foreclosure action against him. Under a warrant of seizure the local sheriff entered the building and rendered the pinsetters inoperative but left them in their place. Ned counterclaimed for damages, arguing that personal property had been converted and that the sheriff's failure to remove the seized equipment made it impossible for Ned to use the building in any other way.

   Was the seizure legal? Explain.

10. While Nancy Raffa and her husband were entertaining friends in their home at Lighthouse Point, her Cadillac Eldorado was taken by a "collection agent" (a repossession agent). She was over a month behind in making the 16th of

36 monthly payments on the car. The car was gone when Mrs. Raffa and her guests came out of the house, and she said she was embarrassed by the incident. She paid off the loan and retrieved the car, and is now suing for compensatory and punitive damages for wrongful repossession. She claims that the repossession agent committed an unlawful trespass, and that the Dania Bank failed to give her specific notice of their intent to repossess the car. The trial court granted summary judgment for the defendants. Nancy appealed.

How should the appeals court decide, and why?

11. James Brown sold his food store to Prang, Inc. As collateral to secure payment of the balance of the purchase price, Prang gave Brown a security agreement covering the store's fixtures and equipment, and its state-issued license to sell liquor that was being transferred from Brown to Prang as part of the sale. A proper financing statement was filed covering the fixtures and equipment, but it contained no mention of the liquor license. Two years later, a resale of the business was discussed with Fakhri Yousif. Yousif was made aware of Brown's security interest against the liquor license, and he asked Brown to consent to the retransfer of the liquor license. Brown refused to consent, but Yousif bought the business anyway and had the license transferred.

    Prang later defaulted on his payments to Brown, who then sued Prang and Yousif. Brown agreed to a partial settlement with Prang but maintained his claim against Yousif for the liquor license. Yousif moved for summary judgment because Brown's financing statement did not cover the liquor license.

    How should the court rule, and why?

12. Nicolosi bought his fiancée a diamond engagement ring for $1,237. He signed a security agreement in favor of the seller, Rike-Kumler Co., for the unpaid balance of the contract price. Rike-Kumler did not file a financing statement. After Nicolosi defaulted on his payments and filed for bankruptcy, his fiancée turned the ring over to the trustee in bankruptcy. Rike-Kumler says it did not have to file against "consumer goods" ("used or bought for use primarily for personal, family, or household use"). The trustee made two arguments: Nicolosi did not buy the ring to wear it himself, and even if the ring is consumer goods, the fiancée qualifies as another consumer who "bought" the ring for her own personal use and thus owned it free and clear—and she gave it to the trustee.

    How should the court decide these two issues, and why?

CHAPTER 25

Types of Instruments and Negotiability Requirements

Chapter Objectives

This chapter will:

- Indicate the need for negotiability in commercial credit transactions.
- Explain the concept of negotiability and the special results it produces.
- Outline the requirements an instrument must meet to be negotiable.
- Discuss each of these requirements.

Negotiable instruments were developed by Western European merchants several centuries ago to meet the needs of trade and commerce. Highwaymen and bandits made carrying large sums of money a risky operation. Goods and services conceivably could have been purchased on the buyer's credit, but that arrangement also entailed substantial risks of nonpayment in the days before Dun & Bradstreet and credit bureaus. What the merchant wanted was something as acceptable as money in most commercial transactions, which could be carried from place to place more safely than currency.

Through custom and usage, merchants and their special commercial courts came to agree that instruments written in the proper form would have the characteristics they desired. These traits were:

1. Such instruments would be freely transferable from person to person (under the old English common law, at least, a transferee of contract rights could not sue the debtor directly).
2. They would be presumed to have been issued for value, and the debtor would have the burden of proving otherwise.
3. The debtor would not be able to assert certain defenses (generally, "voidable" defenses) when a good faith purchaser ("holder in due course") sued to enforce an instrument and collect the money.

Negotiable instruments law, as part of the law merchant, was assimilated into English common law during the 17th and 18th centuries. An English statute codifying these practices was passed in 1882, and in 1896 the Uniform Negotiable Instruments Law (NIL) was proposed and later adopted by nearly all states in the United States. The Uniform Commercial Code's (UCC) Article 3, Commercial Paper, now supersedes the NIL. Article 4, Bank Deposits and Collections, brings together the rules regarding bank processing of such instruments. More recently, several states and the Federal Trade Commission have adopted new rules eliminating the "no defenses" result when the instrument was executed by a consumer-debtor. Article 3 and 4 were substantially amended in 1990. Article 4A on funds transfers was submitted to the states in 1989.

Major Legal Issues

Negotiable instruments law is technical and complex and tends to confuse many beginners. Because it is easy to get lost in the details of the cases and the UCC provisions, the student needs an overall picture of what is happening in these situations. One or more persons allegedly have signed a piece of paper that contains some sort of promise to pay money, and the plaintiff is trying to collect the money. The primary significance of that piece of paper's being negotiable is that a person to whom it was transferred as a good faith purchaser can force a party who is liable on it to pay the money even though that party has a defense against liability. If the instrument is negotiable, and it gets into the hands of the special sort of **bona fide purchaser (BFP)** called a **holder in due course (HDC)**, a business debtor who had signed it would have to pay it as promised. This is true even when the merchandise or services exchanged for the instrument were never delivered or were misrepresented. In other words, a negotiable instrument in the hands of an HDC can be enforced as written, despite the existence of certain defenses. The instrument's negotiability prevents the defendant from using some defenses, such as fraud or nonperformance, to avoid paying the HDC.

In analyzing a negotiable instruments problem, then, we need to determine whether or not this special "negotiability" result should occur. Should the person who signed the instrument have to pay it, even if the goods or services for which it was issued were not delivered or were misrepresented? First, to get these special negotiability results, the instrument must be in negotiable form. It must comply with the requirements for negotiability, as discussed later in this chapter. If the instrument is not negotiable, any defense against liability on it can be asserted as a reason for not paying it.

Second, to collect against a particular person, plaintiff must prove that that person is liable on the instrument in some way. In most cases, liability is based either on a defendant's having signed the instrument, thereby making a contractual promise to pay it, or having transferred it for value, thereby assuming certain implied warranties as to its validity. In some cases, a tort theory based on negligence or conversion may also be used to collect the amount of the instrument from a particular defendant. It is not enough, in other words, for plaintiff to prove that he or she is the proper party to be paid. To collect against a particular person, the plaintiff must prove that that person is liable, under some theory, for payment of the instrument. These theories of liability are discussed in Chapter 26.

Third, for the plaintiff to enforce the instrument and collect the money, the terms of the instrument must make the plaintiff the holder of the instrument. It must have been issued to the plaintiff or properly transferred ("negotiated") to the plaintiff. The requirements for becoming a holder of these instruments are discussed in Chapter 27. If the plaintiff is not a holder, the plaintiff should not collect on the instrument.

Fourth, if some of the persons who may be liable on the instrument have defenses against liability (reasons for not paying it), the plaintiff must also qualify as a HDC to overcome certain defenses and collect the money anyway. What it takes to become an HDC is also discussed in Chapter 27. If the plaintiff is not an HDC of the negotiable instrument, any defense that can be proved can be used to defeat or reduce the plaintiff's recovery on the instrument. If there are no reasons for not paying the instrument, plaintiff collects merely by being a holder. The significance of HDC status relates to cases where there are reasons for not paying the instrument or disputes over its ownership.

Finally, because some defenses against liability can be asserted against HDCs and some cannot, we need to know which are which. These two types of defenses are also discussed in Chapter 27, along with the events that discharge a party's liability on a negotiable instrument.

Text discussion in these chapters will follow the applicable sections of Article 3 of the UCC, which covers all these points in some detail. The cases in this area will focus on interpretation of the Code sections in particular fact situations.

Types of Commercial Paper

When someone issues a negotiable instrument in exchange for cash, goods, or services, the instrument is written in either of two basic ways. It may be a **promise** by the issuer to pay the indicated amount, or it may be an **order** to someone else (a bank, or some other party who owes the issuer money) to pay the stated amount. The UCC says that a promise is an "**undertaking to pay**." An "IOU" is therefore not a negotiable instrument, even though it is in writing and signed, because it is merely an acknowledgment of the debt. An order is defined as an instruction to pay. If you have a checking account, look at your checks—they do not say "Please pay," just "Pay." Some smart lawyer might otherwise try to argue that the use of courteous language made the order only a request, and that the check was thus not negotiable.

The Code identifies several specific types of commercial paper. A **note** is a promise by a **maker** to pay money to a payee. A **certificate of deposit** is "an acknowledgment by a bank" of receipt of money and a promise to repay it. A **draft** (or bill of exchange) is an order from a **drawer** directed to a **drawee** and ordering the drawee to pay the stated amount of money to a named payee. A **check** is an order directed to a bank as drawee and indicating that the money is to be paid "on demand," that is, any time the payee requests it.

In addition to these four basic types, several special kinds of negotiable instruments are widely used. Installment notes are frequently used for credit purchases of appliances, cars, and other large consumer items. Rather than being payable all at once, an installment note specifies monthly required payments. Mortgage notes are typically used in connection with the purchase of real estate. Again, monthly payments on the real estate mortgage are usually required. Businesses buying goods on credit also use the **trade acceptance**, which is a form of draft. Rather than ordering a bank to pay, the trade acceptance orders the buyer of the goods to pay the contract price of the goods, plus interest for the agreed credit period. The seller issues the trade acceptance as the drawer; the buyer is the drawee, who is ordered to pay the amount stated to the seller, as payee. When the buyer signs this order as well, meaning that the buyer promises to pay it according to its terms, the seller can then

Exhibit 25.1: Types of Commercial Paper

Note (Promissory note)

$__________ ____________________, ________
City State

On demand, for value received, I/We promise to pay to the order of____________________
the sum of____________________Dollars,
at____________________,
Address
together with interest at the rate of____________________ per year. If lawsuit be commenced to enforce payment of this note, I promise to pay such added sum as the court may determine as reasonable attorney's fees in connection with said lawsuit

Draft (Bill of exchange)

BIGGER BANK

TRADE ACCEPTANCE

NO. ________

__________ __________
City of Drawer Date

On ____________________, pay to the order of OURSELVES

____________________DOLLARS ($________________)

The transaction which gives rise to this instrument is the purchase of goods by the Acceptor from the Drawer

TO: ________________
Name of Drawee
____
Street Address
____
City of Drawee

sell the trade acceptance to a bank (usually a bank where the buyer of the goods has established credit). The buyer of the goods gets the time to pay for the goods, the seller of the goods gets cash, and the buyer of the trade acceptance gets the interest on it, plus any discount. Trade acceptances are very useful when the seller of the goods cannot afford to carry the buyer as an account receivable for the length of time the buyer requires. A **certified check** operates in much the same way as a trade acceptance. The order to pay the money is directed to the drawee bank. When the drawee bank agrees that it will pay the check, it "certifies" the check by writing its name on the face of the check. At that point, the bank has directly promised to pay the check. A **cashier's check** is a check written by a bank ordering itself to pay the stated amount. Again, the bank is directly liable for payment of the cashier's check.

Article 3 of the code specifically excludes "investment securities" (stocks and bonds) from its coverage, along with money and "documents of title." Article 8 covers investment securities, and documents of title are covered in Article 7. Both securities and documents may be issued in negotiable form, but they are not used as money substitutes in the same way as negotiable instruments.

The *State* case analyzes the negotiability of warrants for payment issued by a state to its creditors.

Requirements of Negotiability

Negotiability is strictly a matter of form. If an instrument is written to comply with the requirements of UCC 3-104(a), it is negotiable; if not, it is not negotiable, though it may

CASE 1

State v. Family Bank of Hallandale

623 So. 2d 474 (FL 1993)

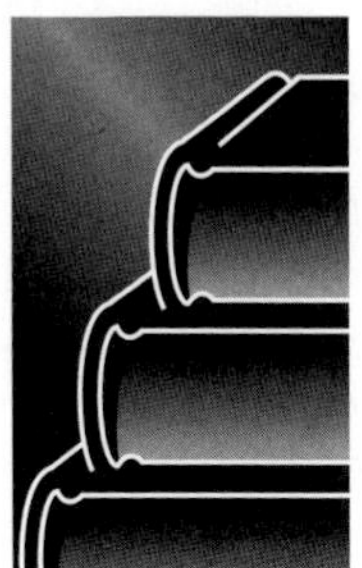

Facts: The Florida department of transportation awarded a contract to Ted's Sheds, Inc., for several metal buildings to be used at various service plazas on the Florida Turnpike. Ted's Sheds provided a Ft. Lauderdale address during the bidding process. When the buildings were delivered, the state received an invoice from Ted's Sheds, Inc., listing its address as Bonita Springs, Florida. The state approved the invoices for payment and, on February 5, 1987, the Comptroller issued a warrant, for $16,932 payable to the order of Ted's Sheds and sent it to the Ft. Lauderdale, Florida, address listed on the original bid.

On February 12, 1987, Ted's Sheds of Broward, Inc., presented the original warrant to Seminole National Bank. The warrant was endorsed "Ted's Sheds of Broward, Inc.," and was credited by the bank. Sometime thereafter, the agents of "Ted's Sheds Inc. in Bonita Springs stated that they had not received the warrant and requested a duplicate warrant. It was then discovered that there were two Ted's Sheds, one in Ft. Lauderdale known as Ted's Sheds of Broward, Inc." and one in Bonita Springs, known as "Ted's Sheds, Inc." These separate legal entitles shared common corporate officers. On February 19, 1987, the comptroller placed a stop payment on the original warrant, issued a duplicate warrant to Ted's Sheds and mailed it to Ted's Sheds Inc., in Bonita Springs. Subsequently, the Federal Reserve Bank of Miami returned the original warrant to the bank indicating that payment had been stopped by the state treasurer.

The bank initiated this action some 14 months after the original warrant was returned. In the intervening time, Ted's Sheds of Broward, Inc., was involuntarily dissolved. The bank argued that it had no knowledge of the stop payment order and asserted that it was an HDC entitled to reimbursement by the state of Florida on the theory that state warrants are negotiable instruments. The state maintained that state warrants are not negotiable instruments under the UCC and, thus, the bank was not entitled to repayment of these funds by the people of the state of Florida. The trial court entered summary judgment in favor of the bank as holder for value of a state warrant. On appeal, the district court affirmed.

Issue: Is a state warrant for payment a negotiable instrument?

Decision: No. Judgment reversed.

Opinion by Justice McDonald: "A brief examination of the meaning and use of warrants is desirable before addressing the issues in this case. In connection with state funds, the term 'warrant' has a well-defined meaning. Warrants are devices, prescribed by law, for drawing money from the state treasury. They are orders issued by the official whose duty it is to pass on claims to the treasurer to pay a specified sum from the treasury for the persons and purposes specified.... A warrant is not an order to pay absolutely, rather it is generally prime facie evidence of indebtedness payable out of a particular fund or appropriation.... Warrants have been regarded as negotiable in the restricted sense of the term in that they have the quality of easy or simple transferability.... But, in fact, there is much pre-code authority that a warrant possesses all of the qualities of negotiable paper but one (i.e., unlike negotiable paper, it is open to any defense which might have been made to the claim in the hands of the original holder).... Warrants drawn for ordinary governmental expenses are licenses authorizing payment and are not intended to have all the qualities of commercial paper. Warrants do not represent a pledge of the general credit of the issuing body, but are instruments authorized for convenience in conducting ordinary business and as a means of anticipating revenue.

"A warrant is best characterized as a chose in action, payable when funds are available for its purpose. This court has held that there is a 'vast distinction' between warrants and bonds.... A bond is basically an acknowledgement of indebtedness and a promise to pay, while a warrant is an order or direction to pay. The most noteworthy distinction between the two instruments is that a bond generally constitutes an absolute order to pay, while warrants generally are an order to pay out of a particular fund. Also, before the adoption of the Uniform Commercial Code, the point of distinction most often emphasized by the courts was the negotiability of bonds and the nonnegotiability of warrants.... 'A bond is a negotiable instrument, while a warrant is nonnegotiable. A warrant is subject at all times to the defenses it would be subject to were it in the hands of the original payee—not so with a negotiable bond.'

"Prior to the adoption of the Uniform Commercial Code in Florida, warrants issued by sovereign governmental entitles were expressly declared nonnegotiable for public policy reasons.... Under the pre-code law, the Uniform Negotiable Instruments Law (NIL) governed the negotiability of commercial paper.... During this stage, the law was clear, and there was no question as to the nonnegotiability of state treasury warrants.... The general rule regarding warrants under pre-code law expressly provided that a warrant drawn by a proper officer on the state treasury was not a negotiable instrument in the sense of the law merchant.... There are several reasons for this rule under the Uniform Negotiable Instruments Law; primarily, warrants are paid out of a particular fund and, therefore, are not unconditional. However, even though some warrants may have been in negotiable form under the NIL, Florida was among several jurisdictions that, because of public policy reasons, followed the rule that government warrants are not to be regarded as negotiable commercial paper so as to be free of all legal and equitable defenses of the particular governmental entity when in the hands of a holder in due course.... In its simplest terms, the public policy holding state warrants to be nonnegotiable instruments is the state's way of protecting the public treasury from crookedness and shady deals by dishonest officials. Warrants serve the dual purpose of safeguarding the public treasury and protecting the treasurer as to payments made in compliance therewith.... '[W]arrants, because of the nature of their creation, the purposes for which issued, the informal manner of their issue, the danger of mistakes, fraud, want of consideration, etc., are not given the protection of negotiable instruments.' [T]he policy of allowing the government to assert defenses against a holder of a warrant must outweigh any innocent purchaser notions; otherwise a few dishonest officials could bankrupt an entire town. 'It would overwhelm municipalities with ruin to hold that such warrants or orders have the qualities of negotiable paper, especially that quality which protects an innocent holder for value from defenses of which he has no notice, actual or constructive....'

"We hold that the district court erred in its finding that the Florida Legislature, in adopting the Uniform Commercial Code, intended to declare warrants to be commercial paper and abandon the public policy of nonnegotiability of governmental warrants....

"The Family Bank of Hallandale is not a holder in due course because the state treasury warrant involved is not a negotiable instrument to which the Uniform Commercial Code applies. As a result, the Family Bank took the warrant subject to the State's defense that it had issued a valid stop payment order."

be enforceable as an ordinary written contract. Negotiability, in other words, does not depend on the parties' intent, or their agreement, or their understanding, but on their compliance with the Code's requirements. The drafters of the Code have expressed this policy very clearly in several of their earlier official comments.

The courts were thus directed not to produce the very special negotiability results unless the debtor has signed a writing that clearly conforms to Article 3's requirements.

What are these requirements? As listed in Section 3-104(a), the writing must:

1. Be signed by the maker or drawer.
2. Contain an **unconditional promise or order** to pay a fixed amount of money, with or without interest or other charges.
3. Be **payable on demand** or **payable at a definite time**.
4. Be **payable to order** or **payable to bearer** at the time it is issued or first comes into possession of a holder.
5. Not state any other undertaking or instruction by the person promising or ordering payment to do any act in addition to the payment of money.

Each of these requirements is further defined and explained in other Code sections. Often, the defendant-debtor will argue against liability, claiming that the signed instrument is not negotiable. If true, the plaintiff-creditor would be subject to any provable defense.

Signed by Maker or Drawer

Signed, in the general definitions section of Article 1, includes "any symbol executed or adopted by a party with present intention to authenticate a writing." Thus, a signature need not be written out fully in script; it can be printed, typed, stamped, initialed, or reproduced mechanically by a check writer. Because of the special characteristics of negotiable instruments, Section 3-401(a) states a very important rule for them: "A person is not liable on an instrument unless (i) the person signed the instrument, or (ii) the person is represented by an agent ... who signed...." A person may be liable on some other basis to the plaintiff, but cannot be liable on an instrument unless that person's signature is on the instrument, though it does not necessarily have to appear at the bottom. It may be made by trade name, assumed name, mark (X), or even thumbprint. It may be made by a properly authorized agent, though the agent may be held personally liable to subsequent holders of the instrument if the agent does not clearly indicate that the signing is being done only on behalf of the principal. When someone who is not authorized to sign another's name does so, the signature operates as that of "the unauthorized signer in

CASE 2

Finnish Fur Sales v. Juliette Shulof Furs

770 F.Supp. 139 (S.D. NY 1991)

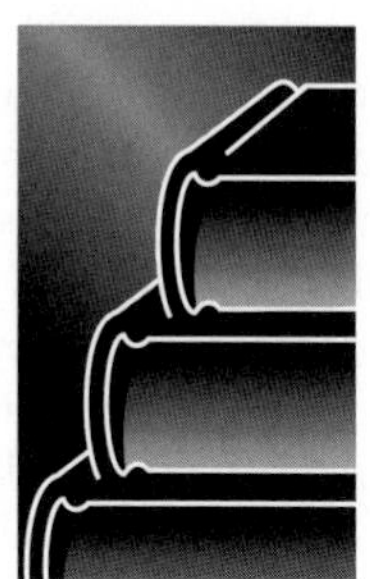

Facts: This is an action to collect sums allegedly owed in connection with furs purchased at two auctions in Vantaa, Finland. Plaintiff Finnish Fur Sales Co., Ltd. ("FFS"), asserts its claim of failure to pay for and clear 2,469 fox pelts against defendants Juliette Shulof Furs, Inc. ("JSF"), and George Shulof. Plaintiff Okobank Osuuspankkien Keskuspankki Oy ("Okobank") asserts its claim of failure to honor a bill of exchange against defendants JSF and Juliette Shulof.

Defendants George and Juliette Shulof asked the court for summary judgment dismissing the individual claims against each of them. Plaintiffs opposed defendants' motion and asked for summary judgment against all defendants.

FFS is a limited company organized under Finnish law, which sells fur pelts raised by Finnish breeders at public auctions held several times each year. The auctions are conducted under certain conditions of sale ("Conditions"), which are listed in the auction catalogue, a copy of which is given to each prospective bidder in advance of the auction. A one-page English translation of the Conditions appears on the inside front cover of the catalogue.

JSF is a New York corporation that has conducted a fur dealing business for approximately 15 years. George Shulof, an officer of JSF, has been in the fur business since 1935. Mr. Shulof attended the FFS auctions held in Vantaa, Finland, in January and May 1987. He purchased over $500,000 worth of skins at the January auction, and some $700,000 worth of skins at the May auction. It is undisputed that at each auction he was the actual bidder. JSF had not sent a bidder to the FFS auctions during the 25-year period from 1959 to 1984, but Mr. Shulof had personally attended the FFS auction in December 1986.

The parties apparently do not dispute the fact that JSF paid for and cleared the majority of the skins purchased at the two 1987 auctions, with the exception of 2,469 fox pelts worth $290,048.17. The parties also do not dispute that JSF made certain payments against the uncleared skins, leaving an unpaid balance of $202,416.85, plus interest.

Between December 1987 and December 1988, JSF gave FFS resale instructions regarding a number of the uncleared skins. FFS asserts that it was unable to sell the skins at the minimum resale prices set by JSF. Thereafter, FFS decided to liquidate JSF's account, to which JSF agreed in March 1989. FFS sold the remaining uncleared skins at its May and September 1989 auctions. FFS alleges damages of $153,502.39.

FFS claims that, in addition to the liability of JSF, Mr. Shulof is personally liable for this debt based on Finnish law, the custom and practice of the fur trade, and the provisions of Section 4 of the Conditions. Section 4 provides:

> *Any person bidding at the auction shall stand surety as for his own debt until full payment is made for purchased merchandise. If he has made the bid on behalf of another person, he is jointly and severally liable with the person for the purchase.*

George Shulof denies any personal liability on the grounds, inter alia, that the provision is unenforceable under both New York and Finnish law.

Okobank's claim arises from a line of credit arranged by FFS in November 1988 to allow JSF to clear some of the remaining skins. JSF made a cash down payment and accepted a bill of exchange (the "Bill of Exchange") for $30,328.39, due February 7, 1989.

According to plaintiffs, in January 1989, Okobank became HDC of the Bill of Exchange, which was presented for collection on or about February 7, 1989, at Bank Leumi in New York, but was dishonored. As of July 31, 1990, Okobank claimed principal and interest due amounting to $37,480.90.

The Bill of Exchange was signed "Juliette A. Shulof" above the printed name "Juliette Shulof Furs Inc." Okobank contends, and Mrs. Shulof denies, that this signature renders Mrs. Shulof liable in her individual capacity.

Issue: Is Juliette Shulof personally liable on the bill of exchange?

Decision: Yes.

Opinion by District Judge Leisure: "Section 15 of the Conditions provides that '[t]hese conditions are governed by Finnish law.' Choice of law clauses are routinely enforced by the courts of this Circuit, 'if there is a reasonable basis for the choice....'

"Finland's contacts with the transactions at issue are substantial, rendering the choice of law clause enforceable unless a strong public policy of New York is impaired by the application of Finnish law....

"FFS's expert, Vesa Majamaa ... a Doctor of Law and Professor of the Faculty of Law at the University of Helsinki, gives as his opinion that the provision of Section 4 of the Conditions imposing personal liability upon the bidder, regardless of whether he bids on behalf of another, is valid both as a term of the particular auctions at issue and as a general principle of Finnish and Scandinavian auction law....

"According to Majamaa, it is commonly accepted in Scandinavia that a bidder, by making a bid, accepts those conditions which have been announced at the auction....

"Majamaa also notes that under Danish law, which he maintains would be applied by a Finnish court in the absence of Finnish decisional or legislative law on point, 'it is taken for granted that someone who has bid on merchandise on someone else's account is responsible for the transaction, as he would be for his own obligation, together with his superior.... Hence the auction buyer's responsibility is not secondary, as is, for example, the responsibility of a guarantor....'

"[A] perusal of the Conditions reveals that their entire text is only a single page long, and that all of the Conditions, including Section 4, are printed in the same size print, which, although small, is legible. The catalogue was made available to Mr. Shulof at the beginning of the four-day period prior to the auction during which potential bidders were allowed to inspect the furs. Although Mr. Shulof contends that the urgent need to inspect large numbers of furs prevented him from reading the one-page list of Conditions, he admits that he knew where they were located in the catalogue and that he did read some of the Conditions before bidding. Further, Mr. Shulof does not dispute the fact that he was given a copy of the same Conditions at the time of the 1986 auction he attended.

"Under these circumstances, it seems unlikely that a New York court would refuse to enforce Section 4 in an arm's length commercial transaction involving a sophisticated defendant accustomed to bidding at fur auctions. Moreover, even if a New York court would not enforce such a provision in a transaction to which New York law clearly applied, this Court does not find New York's interest in protecting one of its residents against personal liability as a corporate officer to constitute so fundamental a policy that New York courts would refuse to enforce a contrary rule of foreign law....

"Thus, Mr. Shulof must be held jointly and severally liable with JSF for any damages owed to FFS for the furs purchased at its 1987 auctions, and his motion for summary judgment is denied....

"The parties agree that New York law governs the issue of the liability of Juliette Shulof on the Bill of Exchange, which was executed and payable in New York. The parties do not dispute that the Bill of Exchange is a negotiable instrument, and therefore subject to the provisions of Article 3 of the Uniform Commercial Code, as adopted by the state of New York.

"The relevant section of the Code is § 3-403, which governs signatures by authorized representatives....

"In the case at bar, Mrs. Shulof signed as 'Juliette A. Shulof' above a typed name of 'Juliette Shulof Furs Inc.,' which had been typed in by the preparer of the instrument, FFS. The cases interpreting signatures of this type demonstrate the special treatment of negotiable instruments under New York law. As reflected in the discussion in an earlier section of this opinion, New York has, as a general rule, a policy against imposing personal liability on corporate officers if the circumstances are ambiguous. However, this policy gives way before the policy considerations underlying N.Y.U.C.C. § 3-403, which 'aims to foster certainty and definiteness in the law of commercial paper, requirements deriving from the "necessity for takers of negotiable instruments to tell at a glance whose obligation they hold...."'

"Construing Section 3-403(2), the New York Court of Appeals held that 'the basic law is that resort to extrinsic proof is impermissible when the face of the instrument itself does not serve to put its holder on notice of the limited liability of a signer....'

"The Court finds the case at bar to be analogous to the holdings in *Javeri* and *Rotuba.* It is undisputed that Okobank never dealt with either of the Shulofs or JSF. Mrs. Shulof offers no evidence sufficient to raise a triable issue of fact as to either Okobank's status as a holder in due course or her allegations of fraud in the inducement on the part of FFS. Accordingly, the Court finds that Mrs. Shulof's signature on the Bill of Exchange did not give notice that she signed in a representative capacity only, and therefore she is personally liable for the amount of the bill. Her motion for summary judgment is denied, and the motion of Okobank for summary judgment against Juliette Shulof is granted."

favor of any person who in good faith pays the instrument or takes it for value" (3-403) (see Exhibit 25-2).

Unconditional Promise or Order to Pay

Section 3-106 lists a number of rules for determining when a promise or an order is or is not "unconditional"; most of these rules are designed to meet particular problems that have come up in prior cases. Instruments frequently refer to the transaction out of which they arose, or to the consideration received or to be received for them, or to the fact that payment is secured by mortgage or otherwise. Within limits, the code permits such references; the promise or order is still "unconditional," and the instrument is still negotiable. But when a promise or order states that it is "subject to or governed by" any other agreement, it is conditional and thus not negotiable. (The instrument may still be enforced like any ordinary written contract, however; not negotiable just means that the plaintiff's claim is subject to any defense that the defendant can prove.)

Similar rules are stated about the source of funds to pay the instrument. Under the latest version of Article 3, an instrument that is to be paid only out of a particular fund is still unconditional (and therefore negotiable). This is an important change from prior law, and it might very well change the results in cases such as *Family Bank of Hallandale*.

Exhibit 25.2: Requirements of Negotiability—Signatures by Agents

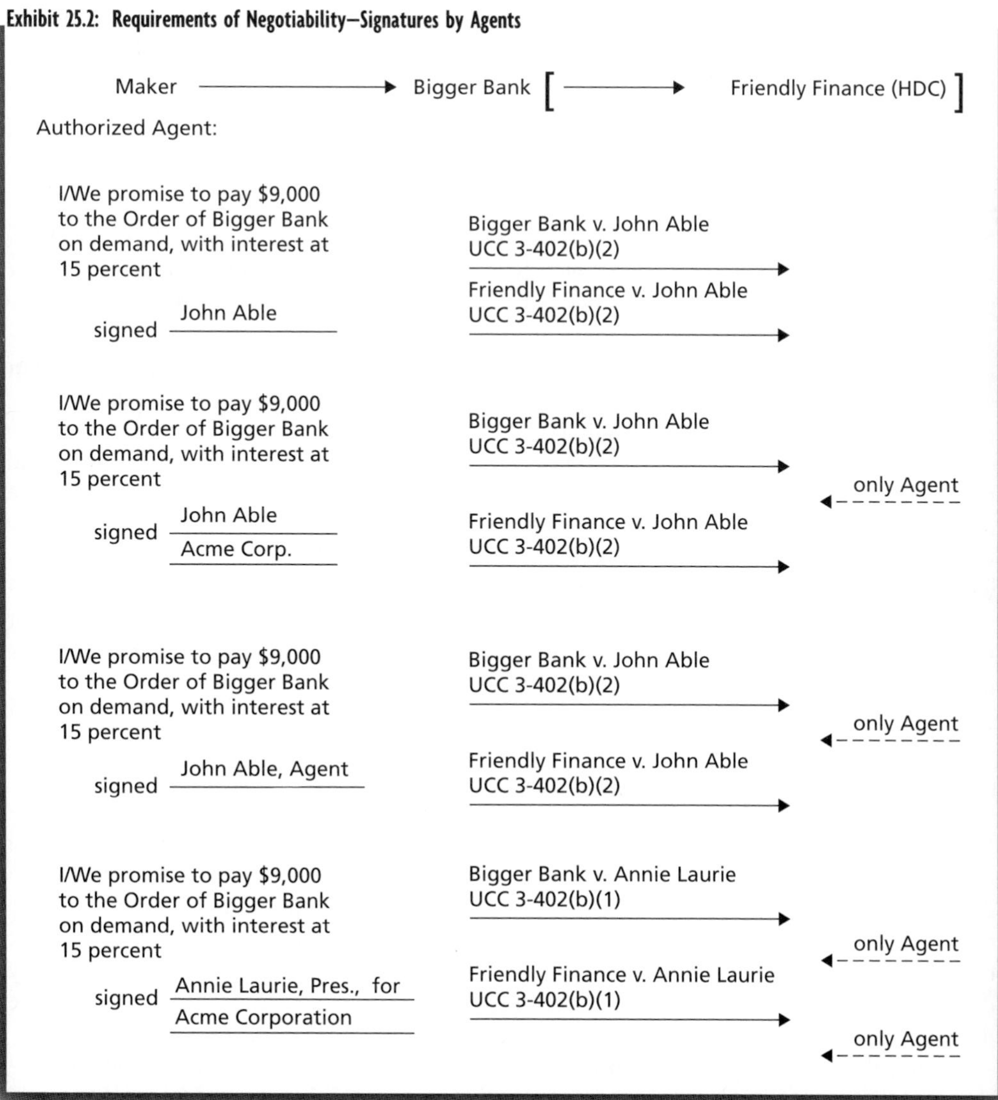

Fixed Amount

The Code also provides some detailed rules for determining when the amount to be paid is a fixed amount. Most typical provisions regarding interest, installment payments, and discounts or penalties for early payment require only a little mathematics to determine the "amount" due and are thus permissible. The interest rates and other percentages must be specified, however, so that the calculations can be made from the information appearing on the face of the instrument. Many instruments, particularly promissory notes, will include a provision requiring the payment of collection costs and attorney fees if the debtor defaults and litigation is necessary; the Code validates such provisions. Aside from the fact that attorneys drafted the Code, the rationale for this provision is that the basic sum due at maturity is "fixed" and that these additional costs arise only because of the debtor's default.

Of Money

Money is defined in the general definitions section of the Code as "a medium of exchange authorized or adopted by a domestic or foreign government as a part of its currency." The "official governmental currency" test is broader than just saying "legal tender"; thus an instrument is payable in "money" even though it is payable in the United States in foreign currency. Unless it specifies otherwise, such an instrument may be paid in dollars equivalent to the stated amount of foreign currency on the due date.

No Other Promise or Order except as Article 3 Authorizes

Negotiable instruments used to be described as "couriers without luggage." The obligations they imposed were to be stated clearly and simply; thus, any language providing for performances in addition to the payment of money was to be regarded with suspicion. The UCC continues that same basic policy, but it does state some rules more specifically. Section 3-106 lists provisions permitted to be included in (or omitted from) an instrument without destroying its negotiability. Provisions relating to collateral given to secure payment of the instrument may be included.

Section 3-104 permits the inclusion of terms that waive the benefit of any law intended to protect debtors and by which the debtor authorizes the creditor to go into court on the debtor's behalf and "confess judgment" (admit that the debtor owes the money). Many states would probably not permit their consumer protection laws to be overridden in this way, and only a few states recognize the confession of judgment procedure; Section 3-104 merely permits such provisions when they are otherwise lawful. An instrument need not state the consideration received for it, nor need it include any indication of where it was drawn or where it is to be paid.

Payable on Demand or at a Definite Time

For an instrument to be negotiable, its amount must be certain and the holder must be able to determine when the money may be demanded. When the instrument is payable "on demand," the money is due whenever the holder asks for it. **Demand instruments** include those payable "at sight" or "at the will of the holder" (essentially the same thing as saying on demand) and those in which no time for payment is stated. Checks, for example, usually do not include any statement as to when they are to be paid, so they are assumed to be demand instruments.

The rules for determining whether an instrument is payable at a definite time are a little more complicated. The clearest cases are those when the instrument is payable on or before a stated date or at a fixed period after a stated date. Also fairly easy to decide are those where the instruments are payable at a fixed period after sight. The **acceleration clause** and the **extension clause,** two provisions frequently inserted in instruments, may cause some difficulties with respect to the definite time requirement. An acceleration clause advances the due date; an extension clause delays it.

The UCC permits the use of acceleration clauses, within reason. If the acceleration of the date for payment can be made by the maker, a note is essentially payable "on or before" the due date, and thus still negotiable. Payment must be made at least by the due date but can be made earlier if the maker so wishes. If acceleration of the due date can be made by the holder of the instrument, such acceleration must be made in good faith. The holder must honestly believe that "the prospect of payment or performance is impaired." A default in paying several monthly installments, or perhaps only one installment, could produce such a good faith belief. The holder's good faith is presumed here; the party against whom the acceleration is occurring must prove that the holder acted in bad faith in advancing the due date. An instrument could also specify that acceleration would occur automatically when a specified event happens, such as filing of bankruptcy by the debtor, or sale of its business assets, or similar occurrences.

Because the holder of an instrument could always extend the time for payment anyway, giving the holder express permission to do so in the instrument does not affect its negotiability. If the maker is given an express option to extend the time for payment, it must be for a specified additional time. Similarly, if there is a provision for an automatic extension of the time for payment, it must be for a specified additional time. In these latter two cases, there is thus still a known date on which payment can definitely be demanded. If the holder

CASE 3

Waller v. Maryland Nat'l. Bank
620 A.2d 381 (MD App. 1993)

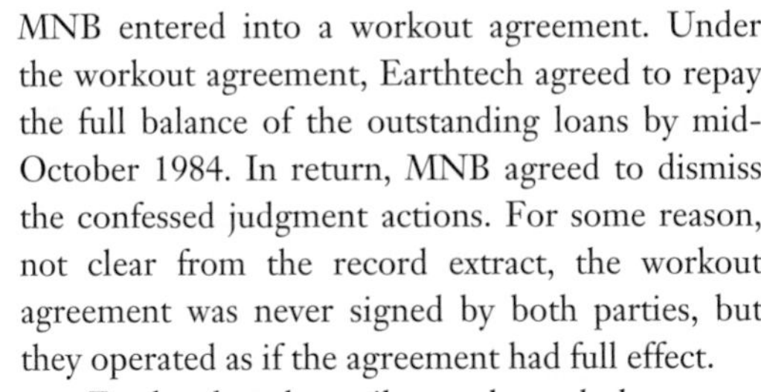

Facts: Earthtech is a Maryland corporation with technical expertise in earth measurement systems. In the early 1980s, Earthtech sought to develop two pieces of sophisticated equipment. To achieve this goal, Earthtech required additional working capital. On February 16, 1983, Earthtech obtained a loan from Maryland National Bank (MNB) for $50,000 evidenced by a revolving note that provided for a continuing line of credit. This revolving note also stated that it was payable "on demand." This note was executed by Earthtech's officers: Muriel Jennings Waller, President; John Millhiser, Vice President; and Jeffrey Bloom, Vice President. Each officer also personally and unconditionally guaranteed payment of Earthtech's obligations to MNB.

On May 20, 1983, Earthtech obtained a second loan for $5,000 from MNB. This loan was evidenced by an installment note and was payable in 35 equal monthly installments.

The parties' relationship appeared to run smoothly until late April 1984 when Earthtech requested an additional loan from MNB to cover its May payroll. MNB denied Earthtech's request. Subsequently, during the afternoon of April 30, 1984, Gary Tyrrell, an MNB officer, arrived at Earthtech's offices and requested that Earthtech's officers executed indemnity deeds of trust (IDOTs) on their residences in favor of MNB. Earthtech's officers were surprised and reminded Tyrrell that MNB already possessed adequate security for its loans. The officers refused to sign the IDOTS and, after much discussion, Tyrrell agreed to return the next morning to give the officers additional time to consider MNB's request.

The following day, May 1, 1984, Tyrrell arrived at Earthtech's offices by mid-morning and immediately presented Earthtech's officers with a letter demanding repayment of the outstanding balance on the revolving note. Earthtech was unable to meet this demand. As a consequence, on May 9, 1984, MNB advised Earthtech that it was also in default of the installment note because it included a cross default provision that provided that a default by Earthtech under any agreement with MNB could result in default under all agreements between Earthtech and MNB. MNB, therefore, was invoking its right under the agreement to accelerate and demand payment of the outstanding principal and accrued interest of the installment note.

In early May 1984, Waller learned that she required an emergency surgery. She entered the hospital on May 8 and underwent surgery the following day. Waller resumed active involvement in Earthtech, on a part-time basis, on June 5, 1984 and began working full-time on June 11, 1984. Appellants claim that MNB agreed to forbear from taking any action against Earthtech for the period of Waller's recovery. MNB, in contrast, claims that the forbearance agreement was contingent on Earthtech's officers executing IDOTs on their residences in favor of MNB.

On June 7, 1984, MNB filed confessed judgment actions against Earthtech and its officers. Subsequently, Earthtech and MNB entered into a workout agreement. Under the workout agreement, Earthtech agreed to repay the full balance of the outstanding loans by mid-October 1984. In return, MNB agreed to dismiss the confessed judgment actions. For some reason, not clear from the record extract, the workout agreement was never signed by both parties, but they operated as if the agreement had full effect.

Earthtech voluntarily accelerated the repayment period, and MNB was repaid in full by August 21, 1984. Approximately 3 weeks later, on September 13, 1984, MNB dismissed the confessed judgment actions.

On April 30, 1987, appellants, Earthtech, Inc. and its president and chief executive officer, Waller, filed a six count complaint against MNB, appellee, in the Circuit Court for Baltimore City.

Count I: Earthtech and Waller alleged breach of contract for violation by MNB of its duty of good faith and fair dealing;

Count II: Earthtech and Waller alleged "negligent breach of contract;"

Count III: Earthtech and Waller alleged conversion;

Count IV: Earthtech alleged breach of contract, claiming a breach of alleged forbearance and workout agreements;

Count V: Earthtech alleged intentional interference with contractual and business relations; and

Count VI: Waller alleged intentional infliction of emotional distress.

MNB filed a motion to dismiss for failure to state a claim on which relief can be granted and a motion for summary judgment. The circuit court granted MNB's motion to dismiss the claim for punitive damages under Count I and dismissed Count VI in its entirety. Later, the circuit court granted summary judgments on all the other claims.

Earthtech and Waller appealed.

Issue: Did the bank breach a duty of good faith?

Decision: No. Judgment for bank affirmed.

Opinion by Judge Harrell: "Appellants first argue that the circuit court erred because it failed to consider that MNB, as a party to a contract, was subject to a good faith duty not only in the *enforcement* of the Revolving Note, but also in its *performance*. Appellants claim that MNB breached its duty of good faith in the performance of the contract by engaging in 'collection activities' prior to MNB explicitly demanding payment of the Revolving Note....

"Maryland law implies a duty of good faith and fair dealing in certain contracts....

"This duty simply prohibits one party to a contract from acting in such a manner as to prevent the other party from performing his obligations under the contract.... Thus, the duty of good faith merely obligates a lender to exercise good faith in performing its contractual obligations; it does not obligate a lender to take affirmative actions that the lender is clearly not required to take under its loan documents....

"The implied duty of good faith does not change the terms of the contract. In addition, when the language of a contract is plain and unambiguous, there is no room for construction by the court. 'The clear and unambiguous language of an agreement will not give way to what the parties thought that the agreement meant or intended it to mean.' The actual contract, therefore, is the starting point for our analysis.

"Appellants and MNB entered into a loan agreement on 2 February 1983 that was evidenced by the Revolving Note. The clear and unambiguous language of the Revolving Note provides, in pertinent part:

> ON demand, *the Undersigned (whether one or more than one) promises—jointly and severally, if more than one—to pay to the order of MARYLAND NATIONAL BANK (the 'Bank') the principal sum of fifty thousand and 00/100 Dollars (the 'Principal Sum') or so much thereof as shall have been actually advanced by the Bank to the Undersigned....*

"As discussed [previously], the Revolving Note was clearly a demand note. As a demand note, it was payable immediately, without demand.... A demand loan may be called at any time by the lender because there is no fixed dated of maturity.... Although § 1-208 of the Commercial Law Article imposers a general requirement of good faith in an option to accelerate at will, the Official Comment states, 'Obviously this section has no application to demand instruments or obligations whose very nature permits call at any time with or without reason.'

"In addition, the weight of authority in other jurisdictions holds that the good faith requirement does not apply to a lender's decision to call a demand note....

"In summary, the Revolving Note was clearly a demand note, as evidenced by its clear and unambiguous language. A demand note by its very nature may be called at any time by the holder, with or without reason. Therefore, the circuit court did not err in holding that MNB was not required to act in good faith and thereby impose a reasonableness standard upon MNB's conduct. Instead, MNB could enforce the plain terms of the contract and call the demand note at anytime, with or without reason. The circuit court's grant of summary judgment as to Count I was proper."

is doing the extending, he or she can demand payment by simply refusing to give any further extensions. With both extensions and accelerations, the drafters of the Code wanted to give the parties some flexibility in making their payment arrangements, but subject always to reasonableness and good faith.

Payable to Order or to Bearer

These are "the magic words of negotiability;" they indicate clearly that an instrument is intended to pass freely from hand to hand, to circulate in commerce as a money substitute. Section 3-109 specifies the words and phrases used to achieve these results. Bearer instruments include those made payable to bearer, to the order of bearer, to a specified person or bearer, to cash, to the order or cash, or "otherwise indicates that it is not payable to an identified person." An instrument that indicates that the person in possession of it is entitled to payment is a bearer instrument. The revised Article 3 also says that an instrument that does not state a payee is bearer paper.

Order instruments are those payable to the order of an identified person or to an identified person or order.

Section 3-110 states that a person may be "identified" in any way on the instrument, including name, number, office, or account number.

The revised Article 3 does allow a check to be negotiable even if it is not payable to order or bearer, as long as it meets all the other requirements.

The *Schmitz* case illustrates one type of problem that may arise from an ambiguous payee designation.

Significance of This Chapter

The special negotiability results can occur only when the written promise to pay money is in negotiable form: a written, unconditional promise or order to pay a sum certain in

Exhibit 25.3: Requirements of Negotiability—Order or Bearer

ORDER INSTRUMENTS

Pay to the order of ___Maker___	
Pay to the order of ___Drawer___	Pay to the order of ___Drawee___
Pay to the order of ___John Smith___	Pay to the order of ___John and Jane Smith___
Pay to the order of bearer or ___John Smith___	Pay to the order of ___John and Jane Smith___
Pay to the order of ___Estate of John Smith___	Pay to the order of ___Ham Harbour City Treasurer___
Pay to the order of ___Redfront Grocery___	

BEARER INSTRUMENTS

Pay to the order of ___Bearer___	
Pay to the order of ___Bearer___	Pay to the order of ___John Smith or Bearer___
Pay to the order of ___Cash___	Pay to the order of ___Anybody___
Pay to the order of ___Cash___	Pay to the order of ___Superman___

CASE 4

Schmitz v. Firstar Bank Milwaukee

664 N.W.2d 594 (WI 2003)

Facts: The check in question was made payable to Eric Schmitz "in care of Georgetown Financial." Georgetown Financial deposited the unendorsed check in its account at Firstar Bank Milwaukee. Firstar accepted the deposit and credited Georgetown Financial's account. Schmitz claimed that the bank's actions were not in accordance with reasonable banking practice. Firstar Bank claimed that UCC 4-205 permits a bank to accept checks made out to customers for deposit to the customer's account, without the customer's endorsement. The court had stated that a bank could not legally take a check for deposit when the payee's signature was missing, but had then remanded the case to the lower court for determination of exactly who the payee of this check was. Firstar has asked the court to reconsider its prior opinion's statement of the law.

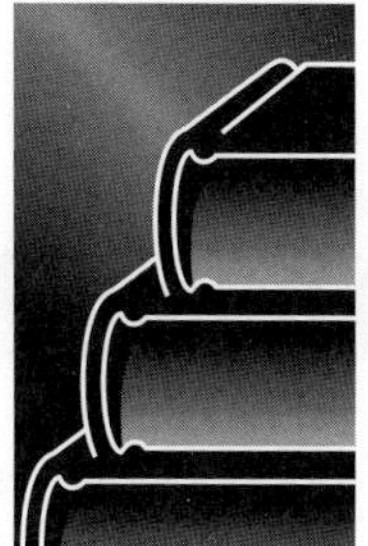

Issue: Did the prior opinion in this case correctly state the law?

Decision: Yes. Motion to reconsider the prior opinion is denied.

Opinion Per Curiam: "Firstar Bank [asks] the court to reconsider P35 of its opinion in Schmitz v. Firstar Bank Milwaukee . . . 658 N.W.2d 442. . . .

"Paragraph 35 of the Schmitz opinion reads as follows: 'While it appears that accepting a check when the payee's [i]ndorsement is missing is not in accordance with the reasonable commercial standards of banking and that the acceptance by a depositary bank of such a check for deposit is commercially unreasonable as a matter of law, n1 there is far less case law addressing who constitutes the payee when a check is made out to an individual in care of an investment company. n2 Accordingly, we remand the issue of liability on the . . . check to the circuit court for further proceedings.'

"Firstar Bank explains that [UCC 4-205] permits a depositary bank to accept a check for deposit with a missing

[i]ndorsement under 'lock-box' agreements with customers who receive a high volume of checks are irrelevant. . . .

"The plaintiff argues that under the prior statute, the payee was the plaintiff Schmitz, not Firstar Bank's customer Georgetown Financial, and that First Star Bank could supply only the [i]ndorsement of its customer. Under the newer version of [4.205], the plaintiff explains that a depositary bank may supply a missing [i]ndorsement only where the 'customer' is a 'holder' as defined in . . . [1.201] with respect to the negotiable instrument, and that in the present case, Georgetown Financial never became a holder because the check was payable to Schmitz, not Georgetown Financial and it was never [i]ndorsed over to Georgetown Financial.

"We conclude that the general rule is as stated in P35 of the Schmitz opinion. Accepting a check when the payee's [i]ndorsement is missing is not in accordance with the reasonable commercial standards of banking and the acceptance by a depositary bank of such a check for deposit is commercially unreasonable as a matter of law. Either version of . . . [4.205] excepts from the general rule depositary banks that receive un[i]ndorsed checks from customers when the missing [i]ndorsement is that of the customer. . . . Thus, the Schmitz opinion remanded to the circuit court the determination of who constitutes the payee when a check is made out to an individual in care of an investment company. . . .

"For the foregoing reasons, the motion for reconsideration is denied. . . ."

money, signed by the maker or drawer, payable on demand or at a definite time, payable to order or to bearer, and containing no other promise or order not authorized by the provisions of Article 3. The special HDC status, which is explained in Chapter 27, can only exist with respect to negotiable instruments. As a general rule, even an assignee who takes an account receivable in good faith and for value holds it subject to any defense that the debtor had against liability on the underlying contract. To prevent the debtor from asserting most voidable-type defenses, the instrument must be in negotiable form. Unless it is, the holder's good faith and lack of notice of the defenses is irrelevant.

On the other hand, just because an instrument is non-negotiable does not mean that it is totally invalid. If the debtor has no defenses to assert anyway or is estopped to assert them, the holder of the non-negotiable instrument will get the money represented by the instrument.

The requirements for negotiability are simply the first hurdle that the plaintiff must clear in establishing the special elimination-of-defenses result.

IMPORTANT TERMS AND CONCEPTS

acceleration clause
bona fide purchaser (BFP)
cashier's check
certificate of deposit
certified check
check
demand instruments
draft
drawee
drawer
extension clause
holder in due course (HDC)
maker
money
negotiable instruments
note
order
payable at a definite time
payable on demand
payable to bearer
payable to order
promise
signed
trade acceptance
unconditional promise or order
undertaking to pay

QUESTIONS AND PROBLEMS FOR DISCUSSION

1. From transferee's point of view, what are the advantages of an instrument's being negotiable, rather than nonnegotiable?

2. What is the difference between a note and a draft?

3. Why is a promise that is conditional not negotiable?

4. What is the difference between an instrument payable to order and one payable to bearer?

5. Charter sued to foreclose on a note and mortgage given by Holly Hill. The note contained the following provision: "The terms of said mortgage are by this reference made a part thereof." Rogers and Blythe had sold to Holly Hill, received the note and mortgage, and then assigned both to Charter. Holly Hill alleged that Rogers and Blythe had committed fraud in the sale. The trial court entered summary judgment against Holly Hill because it ruled that Charter was a HDC of a negotiable instrument.

   Was the note negotiable, so that Charter could be an HDC?

6. Albert and Dora Ingel had an aluminum siding job done on their home by Allied Aluminum Associates, Inc. In payment, they executed a promissory note for $1,890. The

note, together with a certificate indicating that the job had been completed, was transferred for value to the plaintiff. After making several monthly payments, the Ingels alleged that the job had not been done properly and that Allied was guilty of breach of warranties, breach of contract, and/or fraud. C.I.T. sued for the balance due, claiming that it was a HDC, and recovered $1,630.12 in the trial court. The Ingels appealed, alleging that the note was nonnegotiable and that the holder (C.I.T.) was subject to any defense that the Ingels could prove.

Are they correct? Why or not?

7. Barton signed a promissory note for $3,000 that would become due and payable "upon evidence of an acceptable permanent loan of $290,000 for Barton-Ludwig Cains Hill Place Office Building, Atlanta, Georgia, from one of SHRAM's investors and upon acceptance of the commitment by the undersigned." Barton admitted that SHRAM did get such a loan commitment and that Barton did execute the commitment. Barton claimed, however, that because the loan had not in fact been made, he did not owe the $3,000 loan fee. The trial court entered judgment for SHRAM on the pleadings. Barton appealed.

   Is the note negotiable? Can Barton avoid paying it? Explain.

8. Defendants entered into a franchise agreement with Great Land Nursery Corporation. Defendants, as the franchisees, were to grow and sell nursery stock and Christmas trees. The nursery was to provide and to deliver 65,000 trees as planting stock for the purchase price of $9,500. The franchisor, the nursery, under the agreement was to provide the number, size, and varieties therein specified, as well as to furnish replanting stock, chemicals, fertilizers, and other articles to be used in the production and sale of the trees; to root prune the trees; and to provide technical training and supervision necessary for the planting, shearing, pruning, marketing, and sale, and other technical information affecting the growth, production, harvest, and sale of the trees.

   Contemporaneously with the franchise agreement, the defendants, as makers, executed two promissory notes, each in the amount of $6,412. The notes were payable "to Great Lakes Nursery Corp." Nursery endorsed the notes to "First Investment Company or order."

   Defendants made no further payments on their notes for the reason that the nursery had failed to perform in accordance with the franchise agreement. In their answer, defendants pleaded a failure of consideration as an affirmative defense.

   Can First Investment collect from the makers? Discuss.

CHAPTER 26

Liabilities of Parties

Chapter Objectives

This chapter will:

- Explain the distinction between primary contract liability and secondary contract liability.
- Discuss the conditions—presentment, notice of dishonor, and protest—that are necessary to hold secondary parties liable for payment of the instrument.
- Define and explain warranty liability on commercial paper.
- Indicate how tort liability may arise from dealing with commercial paper.

Having determined that an instrument is negotiable, we next need to ascertain whether or not the defendant is liable on it and, if so, the nature of that liability. Negotiable instruments combine property and contract concepts, so liability may stem from the contract that a person has made concerning the instrument or from that person's transferal of a piece of property. In addition, persons who intentionally or negligently cause loss to others when dealing with such instruments may be held liable on a tort theory. We now proceed to examine each of these types of liability.

Distinctions between Primary and Secondary Liability

Primary Contract Liability

Someone who has made a direct, unqualified promise to pay an instrument when it is due has assumed **primary contract liability** on the instrument. Only two parties make such a primary promise—the **maker** of a promissory note and the **acceptor** of a draft or check. When the draft has not been presented to the **drawee** or **drawee bank** and **accepted** (**certified**) by the drawee, no one has primary contract liability on the draft or check. The draft or check is an order to the drawee to pay, and the drawer's normal assumption is that the order will be honored by the drawee.

If the payee or some later holder of the draft has some doubts about whether or not it will be honored, or if the payee refuses to send merchandise or to perform services without receiving a certified check, then the instrument can be presented to the drawee to find out whether or not the drawee will agree to pay it when it is presented for payment. A drawee who agrees to the order and directly promises to pay the money when due, writes "accepted" or "certified" on the instrument, signs his or her name, and gives the instrument back to the holder. By doing this, the drawee becomes an acceptor with primary contract liability; until the drawee does this, no one has primary contract liability on the draft or check, and the drawee or drawee bank is not liable on the instrument at all—to anyone.

How these rules apply to money orders is at issue in the *Trump Plaza* case.

CASE 1

Trump Plaza Associates v. Haas

692 A.2d 86 (NJ Superior Ct. 1997)

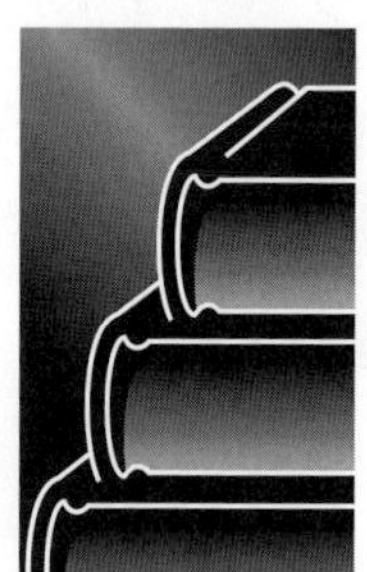

Facts: Trump Plaza appeals from a summary judgment dismissing its complaint against defendant Meridian Bank, New Jersey. In its complaint, Trump alleges that Meridian unlawfully stopped payment on a personal money order the bank had issued to a James Haas, Jr., in the amount of $35,000.

On December 13, 1994, Haas deposited two checks in the amount of $20,000 and $22,000, respectively, into the Meridian account of J. E. Haas–Mid-Way Equipment Co. The checks were drawn on a Mid-Way Equipment Co. account at Commerce Bank. Meridian credited the J. E. Haas-Mid-Way Equipment Co. account for the full amount of the two checks and forwarded them to Commerce Bank for payment.

On December 15, 1994, Haas purchased a $35,000 personal money order from Meridian. Meridian's name and logo are printed on the upper left-hand side of the money order. The money order is also stamped: "NOT VALID FOR MORE THAN $35,000." It is made payable to the order of "Jim Haas"; it is not clear from the record when the name of the payee "Jim Haas" was inserted. Haas signed the money order in the bottom right-hand comer of the document. On December 15, 1994, he presented the signed instrument to Trump and was given $35,000 in cash for use at Trump's gaming tables.

On December 16, 1994, the Mid-Way Equipment Co. checks drawn on the Commerce Bank account were returned to Meridian unpaid, with a notation that the Mid-Way Equipment Co. account had been closed. Meridian debited its J. E. Haas–Mid-Way Equipment Co. account for the amount of the returned checks, which resulted in a $38,584 overdraft. On December 20, 1994, Trump presented Haas' personal money order to Meridian for payment. Meridian dishonored the order, placing a "payment stopped" notation on it because the J. E. Haas–Mid-Way Equipment Co. account contained insufficient funds to cover the amount of the money order. It was thereupon returned to Trump.

The trial court dismissed Trump's complaint.

Issue: Is the drawee bank liable for payment of a money order it issued?

Decision: No, not unless it certifies it. Judgment of dismissal is affirmed.

Opinion by Judge Havey: "Th[e] statutory scheme makes clear that, despite a payee's expectation that the drawee bank will pay a check, the bank has no obligation to the check holder to pay it unless and until the bank has accepted it. . . . Even if the drawee 'arbitrarily dishonors a check, the payee or holder ordinarily has no cause of action against the drawee bank on the instrument.' . . .

"Although acceptance of an instrument is generally manifested by such words as 'accepted' in the case of a draft, or 'certified' in the case of a check, the Code expressly provides that an acceptance may consist of the drawee's signature alone. . . . However, it is essential that the instrument at least contain the signature of the drawee. . . . The money order purchased by [Haas] was not signed by any authorized representative of the bank, nor did it bear the signature of the bank. The mere fact that the printed name of the bank appeared on the face of the money order was not sufficient to constitute its signature and therefore was not an acceptance of the instrument for payment within the purview of [UCC] 3-401(l). . . .

"In our view, the name and logo were nothing more than a commercially acceptable means of identifying the institution issuing the instrument.

"Further, we reject plaintiff's argument that Meridian accepted the money order by stamping 'payment stopped' on its face. Meridian's action in stamping the money order 'payment stopped' is in fact a clear and obvious indication of an intent to dishonor the instrument, and nothing more. It logically cannot be deemed to constitute acceptance. Moreover, the fact the money order was stamped 'NOT VALID FOR MORE THAN $35,000' does not change the result. This notation can be fairly deemed merely as an expression of limitation on the authority of the party signing and delivering the money order. It certainly cannot be deemed 'a signed engagement to honor the draft as presented.' . . .

"[I]n purchasing a money order an individual deposits a sum with a bank and essentially receives one blank check. . . .

"The 1995 revisions to Articles 3 and 4, although not directly applicable here, lend support to our holding and the continued viability of Newman's analysis and result. Revised [UCC]3-104f defines a check to include a money order: 'An instrument may be a check even though it is described on its face by another term, such as "money order".' . . . The inclusion of personal money orders within the definition of an ordinary check (at Revised section 3-104f) rather than inclusion as a form of cashier's check (at section 3-411) means that such money orders are subject to customer stop payment orders and can be dishonored like an ordinary check. This applies only to money orders signed by the purchaser as drawer; of course a bank money order or similar bank draft (drawn by the issuing bank) would be treated as a cashier's or teller's check. . . .

"Trump next argues that, as a holder in due course of the money order 'it should not suffer due to Meridian's negligence in issuing the instrument as [Meridian] did not follow its own procedure nor use ordinary care.' This claim is predicated on the fact that Meridian purportedly failed to follow its own internal procedures requiring that, before a money order is sold, there are sufficient funds in the customer's account to cover it.

"Trump's status as a holder in due course meant that it took the instrument free from essentially all claims by others and all defenses of any party to the instrument with whom the holder has not dealt. . . . But these rights and protections do not come into play unless and until the drawee bank accepts the instrument. . . . Absent acceptance of the instrument by Meridian, Trump's sole remedy is against Haas, the drawer of the purchase money order.

"Moreover, we are satisfied that any claim of negligence based on Meridian's failure to adhere to its internal procedures was subsumed by former [UCC]4-402, which makes a payor bank liable to its 'customer' for damages proximately caused by the 'wrongful dishonor of an item.' Only the purchaser of a personal money order, the 'customer,' has a claim when the dishonor occurs through the 'mistake' of the payor bank. . . .

"It is true that [UCC] 1-103 provides that 'principles of law and equity' supplement the UCC, unless displaced by particular provisions. . . . This provision may be interpreted as permitting a claim of negligence under the UCC absent a specific provision preempting such a claim. But a party asserting that a bank has acted negligently must demonstrate that the bank owed a duty to that party which has been breached . . . and that there is a causal connection between the bank's action and the party's loss. . . .

"[H]ere, Meridian breached no statutory standard of care owed to its customer expressly established by the UCC."

Secondary Contract Liability

A party with **secondary contract liability** does not expect to pay the instrument; if everything goes right, someone else will pay. The drawer's signature on the instrument implies a kind of backstop promise: I will pay if necessary—*if* you make a proper, timely presentment of the instrument to the person who is supposed to pay, *and if* that person dishonors the instrument, *and if* you give me proper notice of the dishonor, *then* bring it to me and I will give you your money. This kind of if-then promise is quite different from that of the party who simply says, "I will pay." Drawers of drafts and checks and endorsers of all types of negotiable instruments make this secondary contract promise. (Even though the new Article 3 no longer calls the drawer a secondary party, the nature of the drawer's promise is the same.) Furthermore, the drawer of a noncheck draft and any endorser may disclaim even this secondary promise by drawing or endorsing "**without recourse**." If the instrument is an international draft governed by foreign law, there may be a further requirement:

The holder may also have to send the drawer and endorsers a **protest**, which is an official notarized statement of the fact of dishonor.

Failure to Meet Conditions

Implicit in the conditional promise of the drawer or endorser is the idea that if the aforementioned conditions are not met, the secondary liability is excused. For a drawer, this is true only to a limited extent. An unexcused failure to make a proper presentment or to send a notice of dishonor excuses the drawer only when the drawer "is deprived of funds maintained with the drawee or payor bank to cover the instrument" because the drawee or payor bank becomes insolvent during the delay. The drawer is now entitled to receive notice of dishonor only when a draft was accepted by a nonbank drawee and then dishonored.

When a bank insolvency occurs, the drawer can become free of any further liability for instruments by making a written assignment to the holder of any rights against the insolvent drawee bank. As a practical matter, this means that few drawers will be excused by a holder's failure to present or to give notice of dishonor. Any unexcused delay in complying with the requirements for presentment or notice, is a complete discharge of endorsers. Adhering to these requirements thus becomes very important to the holder. The holder must make sure that the secondary contract liability of drawers and endorsers is preserved to keep them available if the instrument is dishonored. (On many notes, there will be an express waiver of these requirements.) The details of these requirements are spelled out in other provisions of Article 3.

Presentment, Notice of Dishonor, and Protest

Presentment is the holder's demand for acceptance or payment of the instrument. It may be made by mail, through a clearinghouse, or in person at the place specified. The party to whom presentment is made may require the presenter to show the instrument, to provide personal identification, to note a receipt for partial or full payment on the instrument, and to surrender the instrument if it is paid in full.

When should presentment be made? If the instrument is payable on a specific date, presentment is also due then. If it is payable "after sight," it must "either be presented for acceptance or negotiated within a reasonable time after date or issue whichever is later." To enforce the instrument against a secondary party, presentment of any other instrument "is due within a reasonable time after such party becomes liable thereon." For an uncertified, domestic check, a "reasonable time" was presumed to be 30 days after date or issue, whichever is later, for the drawer to be held liable; for an endorser, 7 days after the endorsement. These presumptions do not appear in the revised Article 3. If presentment is due on a day that is not a full business day for either party, it is postponed to the next day that is a full business day for both. Presentment must be made at a reasonable hour; if it is made at a bank, during its banking day.

In some cases, the holder is required to present the instrument to hold secondary parties liable on it. In other situations, presentment is optional. Presentment for acceptance is necessary to charge the drawers and endorsers of a draft: (1) when it so provides, (2) when it is payable elsewhere than at the residence or place of business of the drawee, or (3) when its date of payment depends upon such presentment. Any other draft payable on a stated date may be presented for acceptance at the option of the holder.

Presentment for payment is necessary to charge any endorser, of any sort of instrument. To charge any drawer, or the acceptor of a draft payable at a bank, or the maker of a note payable at a bank, presentment for payment is required. As noted previously, however, such drawers, acceptors, and makers are discharged only to a limited extent if the required presentment for payment is not made or is delayed. Only in the situation in which they are deprived of funds due to the insolvency of the drawee or payor bank, during the delay period, will they be excused from further liability on the instrument.

Dishonor of the instrument occurs when it is properly presented and acceptance or payment is refused. The party to whom presentment is made has only a limited period to decide whether to pay or to accept. The time to decide whether or not to accept is limited to the close of the next business day, but the holder has the option of extending that deadline by 1 extra business day.

Payment, if requested, can be deferred "pending reasonable examination to determine whether it is properly payable," but only until the close of business on the day of presentment. There are only two exceptions to this "pay-same-day" rule: first, when the party to pay agrees to an earlier time for payment; second, when "documentary drafts" are being presented under a "letter of credit." In letter of credit cases, the bank to which such drafts are presented may defer honor until "the third banking day following receipt of the documents."

When an instrument has not been properly endorsed, returning it to the holder to obtain the required endorsement is not a dishonor, but a bank may or may not certify the instrument before returning it for the proper endorsement.

Because a check is a demand instrument that is normally intended to have only limited circulation and then to be paid, the drawee bank "has no obligation to certify a check." The bank's refusal to pay the check would, of course, be a dishonor. The holder is entitled to have the instrument accepted as presented and can treat any variation or qualification in the acceptance as a dishonor. If the holder does agree to take the acceptance with the changed terms, that act discharges the drawer and endorser. The holder then has only the obligation of the drawee/acceptor according to the changed terms. In this situation, the holder must decide which course is more likely to produce the money.

Notice Requirements

Something has obviously gone wrong when a proper presentment has been made and the instrument has been dishonored; the original expectations of the parties have somehow been frustrated. When such dishonor occurs, the drawer of a draft or check and endorsers of any sort of instrument are entitled to receive prompt notice, so that they can take steps to protect their rights. Notice is usually given by the holder, but 3-503(b) says that it may be given by "any other party who can be compelled to pay the instrument," such as a prior endorser.

"Any reasonable manner" of notification is sufficient; even oral notice is permitted, if it can be proved. The Uniform Commercial Code (UCC) also specifically recognizes the validity of the common banking procedure of simply returning the item with a stamp or attached ticket indicating the dishonor or just sending back a debit notice to the party who gave the instrument to the bank. Banks must give such required notice before their "midnight deadline," which means that a bank must send the word back up the line to others by midnight of the next banking day after the day of dishonor or the day of its own receipt from some other party of notice of dishonor. Nonbank parties are given until midnight of the third business day following dishonor or their receipt of notice.

Because a "written notice is given when sent although it is not received," it is important to be able to prove exactly when letters were posted or telegrams given to the telegraph company. Once properly given, "notice operates for the benefit of all parties who have rights on the instrument against the party notified." If a holder sent notice to prior endorsers Archie and Bernice, for example, Bernice's rights against Archie would be preserved even though she did not send Archie any notice.

Endorser rules also apply between banks, as seen in the *First Union* case.

Excuse for Failure to Meet Conditions

Parties with secondary contract liability may still be held on an instrument when there is an excuse for a delay in meeting these requirements or for a failure to meet them at all. If a holder does not know that an instrument has been accelerated by a prior holder, for example, a delay in making presentment would be excused. Similarly, when a delay is due to "circumstances beyond [his] control," a party has an excuse for late presentment, notice, or protest, so long as that person "exercised reasonable diligence after the cause of the delay ceased to operate."

Presentment is entirely excused when: (a) the party to be charged has waived it, or (b) there is no reason to expect the instrument to be paid or accepted, such as when the drawer of a check issues a stop pay order to his or her drawee bank, or (b) the requirement

CASE 2

First Union Nat. v. First Florida Bank
616 So.2d 1168 (FL App., 2 Dist. 1993)

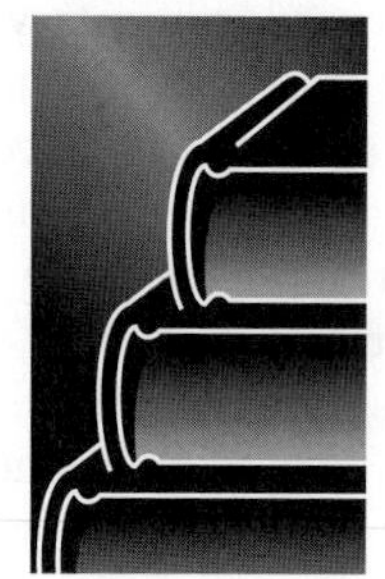

Facts: First Union National Bank appeals a monetary judgment in favor of First Florida Bank, N.A. The lawsuit was filed to determine whether the payor bank, First Florida, or the presenting bank, Union Bank, should be responsible for a dishonored check.

Victor Elias had a bank account with First Florida. On August 13, 1986, he wrote a $10,000 check payable to National Computer Consultants, Inc. National Computer endorsed the check and deposited the check in its account with Union Bank. Union Bank posted the check to National Computer's account on Thursday, August 14.

Union Bank presented this check to First Florida on the following day at the local clearinghouse. At the clearinghouse, Union Bank was credited $10,000 and First Florida was debited $10,000.The clearinghouse forwarded the check to First Florida.

On August 14, Mr. Elias gave a verbal stop-payment order to First Florida. Under statutory provisions discussed later in this opinion, First Florida had until midnight Monday, August 18, to notify Union Bank of its intention to dishonor this check. As a result, First Florida took steps on Monday, August 18, to return the check to Union Bank via the clearinghouse. The check was returned to the clearinghouse on either August 18 or August 19. Unfortunately, First Florida misrouted the check when it returned the item to the clearinghouse by addressing it to the wrong bank. That bank received the misrouted check and returned it to First Florida through the clearinghouse on August 20. First Florida did not return the check to the clearinghouse for Union Bank until August 21.

In addition to returning the check, First Florida attempted to give Union Bank notice of dishonor. In August 1986, First Florida was a member of a service offered by Security Pacific to give notice of dishonor on checks over $2,500. Security Pacific provided notice through a computer system to banks participating in its service. It telephonically informed nonmember banks of dishonored checks. Union Bank was not a member of the Security Pacific system. First Florida did not request Security Pacific to give notice of dishonor to Union Bank until 5:54 PM on August 18. Security Pacific gave that notice by telephone at 11:40 AM on August 19. The midnight deadline was midnight on August 18.

In the trial court, First Florida sued Union Bank for reimbursement of this check. Reimbursement was requested because the debits and credits at the clearinghouse had left responsibility for this check with First Florida. Union Bank argued that First Florida was responsible for this check because First Florida had not given timely notice of dishonor by telephone and the check was not timely returned by First Florida to Union Bank. The trial court determined that Sections 673.508 and 674.302, Florida Statutes (1985), should be controlled by a "rule of reasonableness." It decided that First Florida's efforts to provide telephonic notice had been reasonable and ordered Union Bank to reimburse First Florida $10,000, plus interest and costs.

Issue: Are reasonable efforts to comply with the midnight deadline sufficient to avoid liability on a dishonored check?

Decision: No. Judgment reversed.

Opinion by Judge Altenbernd: "By the midnight deadline, First Florida had delivered the check to the clearinghouse, but had routed this item to the wrong bank. It had notified Security Pacific of its intention to dishonor the check, but Security Pacific had not notified Union Bank. These efforts were insufficient to negate the payor bank's responsibility for the check.

"The payor bank must bear the responsibility of its error in misrouting this item. Section 674.301(4)(a) provides that an item received through a clearinghouse is returned 'when it is delivered to the presenting or last collecting bank or to the clearinghouse or is sent or delivered in accordance with its rules.' First Florida argues that it returned the check to the clearinghouse, and that its erroneous instructions to deliver the check to the wrong bank are irrelevant. The trial court rejected this argument and we agree with the trial court. The applicable rules and regulations of the Clearinghouse Association of Florida required a return item to be enclosed in an envelope indicating the identity of the 'first [i]ndorsing member.' Union Bank was the first [i]ndorsing member. By placing the check in an envelope to another bank, First Florida did not satisfy the rules of the local clearinghouse. The purposes of these statutes can be fulfilled only if they are interpreted to require delivery to the clearinghouse in a manner reasonably designed to result in an item's return to the presenting or last collecting bank.... In light of the substantial violation of the procedures established by the local clearinghouse, First Florida did not effectively return the item by the midnight deadline.

"First Florida's telephonic notification was also deficient because Union Bank did not receive it prior to the midnight deadline. First Florida argues that it provided notice of dishonor when it notified Security Pacific. We recognize that notice of dishonor may be given in any reasonable manner.... Nevertheless, Security Pacific was clearly the agent of First Florida, not Union Bank. Union Bank was not a member of the Security Pacific system of notification. Thus, Union Bank did not receive oral notice of dishonor until it received the telephone call on Tuesday, after the midnight deadline.

"The trial court acknowledged that First Florida had not fully satisfied these notice requirements prior to the midnight deadline, but was convinced that such noncompliance should not automatically place responsibility on First Florida. First Florida persuasively argued that the telephone call on Tuesday morning had a practical effect similar to an actual return of the check to the clearinghouse on the preceding day. Moreover, there was evidence that funds were disbursed from the National Computer account at Union Bank prior to the expiration of the normal hold period. First Florida maintains that the monetary problem for the two banks could have been avoided if Union Bank had utilized different procedures. The trial court concluded that the midnight deadline, under these circumstances, did not create a rule of strict liability but rather a rule requiring reasonable compliance. It concluded that First Florida had attempted reasonable compliance with the requirements for telephonic notification and that the loss should be borne by Union Bank.

"No Florida court has ever expressly held that the midnight deadline is a bright line rule that places responsibility for such a loss on the payor bank. In *First National Bank of Fla. v. Brandon State Bank*, 377 So.2d 990... this court held that the payor bank could revoke a provisional settlement of a check by either a timely notice of dishonor or a timely return of the item. In that case, the item was timely returned to the federal reserve but the notice of dishonor was not timely given. We held that the timely return of the check allowed the payor bank to avoid responsibility for the check. We at least implied that the payor bank would have had responsibility if neither option had been timely satisfied....

"In other states, it is well-established that Sections 4-301 and 4-302 of the Uniform Commercial Code create a statutory doctrine of strict accountability by the payor bank to the presenting bank if notice is not accomplished within the midnight deadline.... Under this doctrine, the payor bank is liable to the presenting bank for the full face amount of the check, absent a successful defense. This bright line test has been adopted under the rationale that the banking industry will better function with a rule establishing across-the-board certainty rather than case-by-case equity. We see no reason to depart from this application of the Uniform Commercial Code.

"Because First Florida presented no evidence in the trial court which might justify another basis for recovery from Union Bank, we reverse the judgment with instructions to enter judgment in favor of Union Bank."

cannot be met by "reasonable diligence." Presentment is also excused by the death or subsequent insolvency of the maker or acceptor, or when payment is refused but not for want of proper presentment.

In line with general commercial understanding, a waiver of presentment is also a waiver of notice. If the waiver language is part of the body of the instrument, it is binding on all secondary parties; if it is written above the signature of an endorser, it binds only that person. Notice may also be excused by a separate waiver. Either requirement may also be excused by the terms of the instrument itself.

Other Types of Liability

Liability of Accommodation Parties and Guarantors

In many cases the person desiring a loan or credit may not have sufficient income or assets to make the creditor feel reasonably secure about receiving repayment when it is due. One form of additional security that can be used is to have another person, someone who does have a good credit rating, also promise to pay the debt. These "backstop" promises on negotiable instruments can take several forms.

An **accommodation party** is someone who has signed an instrument in some capacity (maker, endorser, or acceptor) to lend his or her credit standing to another party to the instrument. Common sense and the Code dictate that the accommodation party be liable in whatever capacity he or she signs, to third parties who take the instrument for value. If Jones cannot get a bank loan in his own name and his friend Smith agrees to co-sign the note with him as a joint maker, Smith (the accommodation party) is liable to third parties as a maker. Had Smith endorsed the note after Jones signed as a sole maker, Smith would be liable to third parties as an endorser (and entitled to presentment and notice). Generally, these results occur even if the third party knows that Smith signed only to accommodate Jones. As between Smith and Jones, however, Smith has the right to demand reimbursement from Jones if Smith has to pay a third party, regardless of the order or the capacity in which they signed the instrument. The debt is really owed by Jones, and Jones should repay Smith.

Words of guarantee may also be added to a signature. Payment guaranteed means that the holder of the instrument can present it directly to the person so signing if it is not paid when due. In other words, the person making the guarantee is directly and immediately

Exhibit 26.1: Commercial Paper—Warranties

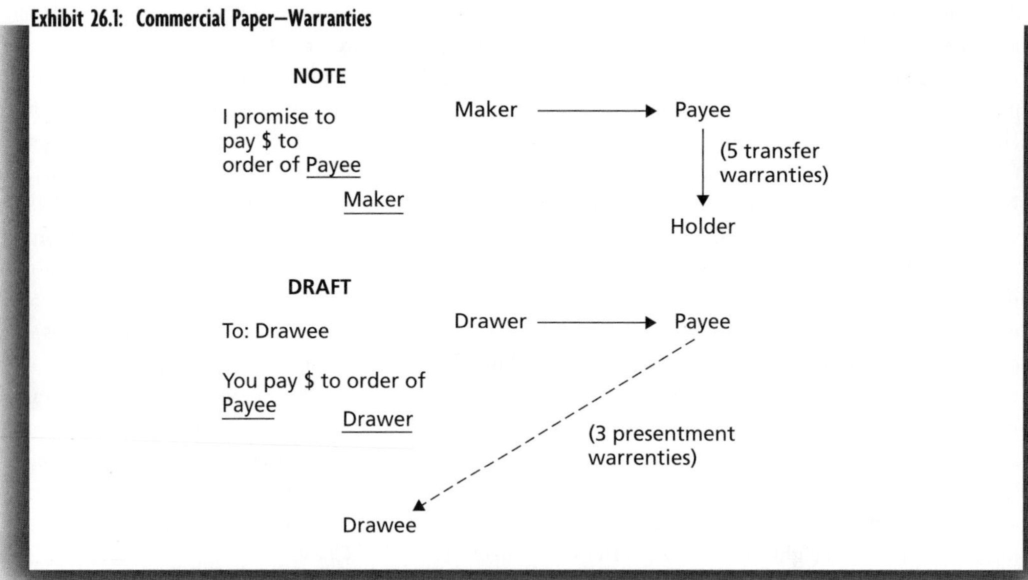

liable when the primary debtor defaults. Collection guaranteed means that before the signer-guarantor is obligated to pay, the holder must first get a judgment against the maker or acceptor and show that the judgment is uncollectible. When an endorser so guarantees payment or collection, presentment, notice, and protest are waived as to that endorser.

Warranty Liability

In addition to assuming contract liability by signing an instrument, a person may assume warranty liability by dealing with it as a piece of property. **Warranty liability** is imposed by the Code in two types of transactions—transfers of ownership of instruments and presentments of instruments for payment or acceptance. When a person transfers an instrument and receives consideration in return, that person makes five warranties about the instrument. This person is not collecting final payment but is simply transferring ownership of the instrument to someone else. If the transferee is a donee, receiving the instrument as a gift, the transferor makes no warranties. However, if the transferee is buying the instrument from the transferor, the five transfer warranties are made by the transferor. The details of these five transfer warranties are explained in the next section.

A person who presents the instrument for payment or acceptance (discussed previously in this chapter) also makes warranties to the party who in good faith pays or accepts. Someone who takes the instrument to the party who is supposed to pay it and gets the money from the party should at least make a guarantee that he or she is the proper party to be paid. The Code implies such a guarantee, as well as certain guarantees about the genuineness of the instrument. If the instrument is being presented for acceptance, the presenter is asking for a direct promise to pay it when it is finally presented for payment. In this case, too, the presenter should be required to guarantee ownership and validity, and the Code so requires. The details of the three **presentment warranties** are also spelled out here.

Transfer Warranties

Because the parties are dealing with the instrument as a piece of property, the Code provides that certain implied warranties are made when the instrument is transferred for value. Just as implied warranties are imposed against the seller of goods under Article 2, so, too, five implied warranties are imposed on the person who transfers an instrument and receives consideration. If the transfer is by endorsement, these five warranties run to all subsequent good faith holders of the instrument; if the transfer is by delivery alone, they run only to the immediate transferee. If the instrument is payable to someone's order, that person must endorse it to negotiate it to someone else. No endorsement is required to transfer a bearer instrument, but the transferor will often endorse anyway.

The transferor for value warrants:

1. That the warrantor is a person entitled to enforce the instrument.
2. That all signatures are authentic and authorized.
3. That the instrument has not been altered.
4. That no prior party who is liable on the instrument has a defense or claim that is good as against the warrantor.
5. That the warrantor has no knowledge of any insolvency proceeding instituted with respect to the maker, acceptor, or drawer of an unaccepted draft.

These warranties may be disclaimed by agreement between the immediate parties, but an endorser cannot escape such warranty liability to subsequent holders unless the disclaimer is part of the endorsement. Such a disclaimer might be stated as, "without warranty of any kind." These warranties may not be disclaimed by the transferor of a check.

CASE 3

Oak Park Currency Exchange, Inc. v. Maropoulos

363 N.E.2d 54 (IL 1977)

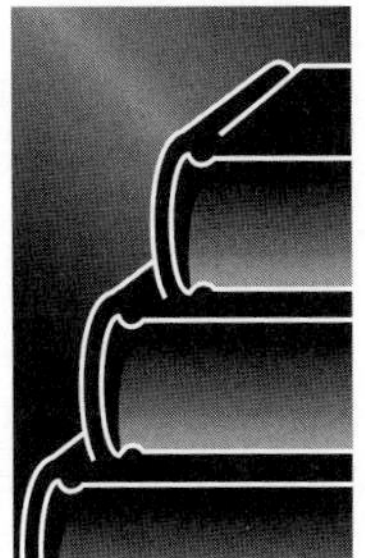

Facts: Oak Park Currency Exchange, Inc. (plaintiff) brought action against James Maropoulos (defendant). Plaintiff's theory was that a check for $3,564 had been endorsed by defendant and cashed by plaintiff and that the prior endorsement of the payee was a forgery. After all of the evidence was presented, the trial court directed a jury verdict for defendant. Plaintiff appealed.

Defendant testified that on several occasions, his friend, John Bugay, had asked for assistance in cashing checks. On these occasions, defendant had accompanied Bugay to a bank where defendant transacted his business and had endorsed the check as a favor. On July 24, 1971, Bugay again requested assistance in cashing a check. Defendant suggested that they go to plaintiff currency exchange where defendant often transacted business and was known to plaintiff's employees. The check in question was a certified check drawn on American National Bank payable to the order of "Henry Sherman, Inc." and endorsed "Henry Sherman" on the reverse side.

Defendant testified that at the currency exchange he identified himself and asked the clerk if she would cash his friend's check. Though she was not the woman with whom he usually dealt, she recognized him. She answered that she would cash the check if defendant would endorse it. He endorsed the check and handed it to the clerk. He observed that she examined both sides of the check. She then handed him the money. He did not count this but gave it immediately to Bugay. Defendant testified unequivocally that he received no money from Bugay in return for his help.

Some time later a claim was made against plaintiff by Belmont National Bank where plaintiff had deposited the check because the endorsement "Henry Sherman" had been forged. Plaintiff determined that it was liable to the bank and paid the claim. Subsequently plaintiff filed this action.

Issue: Is defendant liable for breach of warranty?

Decision: No. Judgment affirmed.

Opinion by Justice Goldberg: "In its judgment order directing the verdict, the trial court found that defendant was an accommodation endorser and as such made no warranty to plaintiff under the Uniform Commercial Code ... and that payment of the check discharged all endorsers so that defendant was not liable to plaintiff on his endorsement.

"In this court, plaintiff urges that defendant breached his warranty of good title when he obtained payment of a check on which the payee's endorsement was forged and that there was sufficient evidence to support a directed verdict in favor of plaintiff. Plaintiff's contentions are based exclusively on Section 3-417(1) [now 3-417(a)] of the Code. Defendant contends that an accommodation endorser does not make warranties under ... 3-417(1) and that the trial court properly directed a verdict for defendant.

"A party who signs an instrument 'for the purpose of lending his name to another party to'... that instrument is an accommodation party.... Such a party 'is liable in the capacity in which he has signed....' Therefore defendant is an accommodation endorser and would be liable to plaintiff under his endorser's contract, provided that he had received timely notice that the check had been presented to the drawee bank and dishonored.... Because these conditions precedent to the contractual liability of an endorser have not been met, defendant is not liable on his contract as an accommodation endorser.

"Furthermore, the drawee bank, American National, did not dishonor the check but paid it. This operated to discharge the liability of defendant as an accommodation endorser....

"The portion of the Code upon which plaintiff seeks to hold defendant liable is Section 3-417 entitled 'Warranties on

Presentment and Transfer. . . .' As shown above, the parties both confine their arguments to Subsection 3-417(1) of the Code and the judgment order refers specifically thereto. Section 3-417(1) sets out warranties which run only to a party who 'pays or accepts' an instrument upon presentment. . . . We note that presentment is defined as 'a demand for acceptance or payment made upon the maker, acceptor, drawee, or other payor. . . .' As applied to the instant case, the warranties contained in Section 3-417(1) are limited to run only to the payor bank and not to any other transferee who acquired the check. In the case before us, plaintiff is not a payor or acceptor of the draft. This interpretation is strongly supported by the official comment which details the reasons for distinguishing warranties made to a payor or acceptor of an instrument from those made to a transferee. . . . The case before us involves a transferee, not a party who paid or accepted the instrument. Thus it appears that reliance by plaintiff upon Subsection 3-417(1) was misplaced. The authorities cited by plaintiff do not support its contention as all of these cases were decided before the effective date of the Code.

"Defendant has cited no case bearing directly upon the situation before us. Our research has not disclosed any case construing this aspect of the pertinent subsection of the Code. Aside from the enactment itself and the comments above cited, we found only dicta to the effect that by this subsection the warranties pertaining to authenticity of endorsements run only 'to a person who in good faith pays or accepts'. . . the instrument. . . .

"An additional theory requires affirmance of the judgment appealed from. Subsection 3-417(2) [now 3-416(a)] of the Code provides that one 'who transfers an instrument and receives consideration warrants to his transferee . . .' that he has good title. . . . The Illinois comments to this portion of the Code confirm that this warranty is made only by any party who transfers an instrument for consideration. . . .

"The evidence presented in the case at bar establishes that defendant received no consideration for his endorsement. Though Mrs. Panveno testified that she saw Bugay hand defendant some money as the two left the currency exchange, she also testified that defendant stated that he was doing a favor for his friend; that she was not paying close attention to the two men and that she did not watch them as they walked away from her. Thus, her testimony was considerably weakened by her own qualifying statements and it was strongly and directly contradicted by the positive and unshaken testimony of defendant that he received nothing in return for his assistance. The simple fact standing alone that this witness saw Bugay hand some money to defendant, even if proved, would have no legal significance without additional proof of some type showing that the payment was consideration for defendant's endorsement. . . .

"In our opinion, the trial court correctly determined that no contrary verdict based on the testimony offered by plaintiff could ever stand and properly directed a verdict for defendant."

Presentment Warranties

Primarily to ensure that the proper party gets the money, Article 3 also imposes three warranties when the instrument is presented for payment or acceptance. These three warranties are imposed on both the person who obtains the payment or acceptance and on any prior transferor.

The warranties on presentment of an unaccepted draft to the drawee are:

1. That the warrantor is, or was at the time of transfer, a person entitled to enforce the draft or authorized to act for someone who is or was.
2. That the warrantor has no knowledge of any unauthorized signature of the drawer.
3. That the draft has not been altered.

The result under 2 is to ensure fairness and is based on the old English case of *Price v. Neal*, 3 Burr. 1354 (1762). The idea is that at some point payment should be final. The Code draws this line at the point when payment is made to a holder in due course (HDC), acting in good faith. If the drawee is not sharp enough to catch the fact that the drawer's signature has been forged, it is simply not fair to permit recovery of the money paid to an HDC who was acting in good faith. Probably the most typical situation in which the money has to be paid back and the instrument has to be kicked back up the chain of title is the case in which a required endorsement is missing, so that the person making the presentment did not really have a "good title."

Tort Liability

Article 3 also has special sections imposing liability for the torts of **negligence** and **conversion**. Section 3-406 says:

> *A person whose failure to exercise ordinary care substantially contributes to alteration of the instrument or to the making of a forged signature is precluded from asserting the alteration or the forgery against a person who pays the instrument or takes it for value or for collection.*

If you fill out a check with a blank space after "Six" and before "dollars," and you also leave a blank where you write "$6.00" and if someone alters that check to read "Six Hundred" and the check is paid by your bank, you could not claim the alteration as a basis for having the bank put $594 back in your account. However, if the words *six* and *hundred* were written in ink of a different color or if the handwritings were obviously dissimilar, your counterargument would be that the bank had not paid the check in good faith or had not exercised reasonable care in doing so.

Another fairly typical case of this sort would involve the negligence of a business that printed its checks on a checkwriter. If the business had not taken reasonable precautions to prevent unauthorized people from using the checkwriter, it could not assert their lack of authority when the drawee bank had paid the checks in good faith. The net result of this section is that the negligent party is stuck with the loss, unless that party can find and recover from the person who inserted the alteration or the unauthorized signature.

As with other types of personal property, a person who deals with an instrument in a manner inconsistent with the rights of the true owner commits the tort of conversion.

CASE 4

HSBC Bank USA v. F&M Bank—Northern Virginia

246 F.3d 335 (4 Cir. 2001)

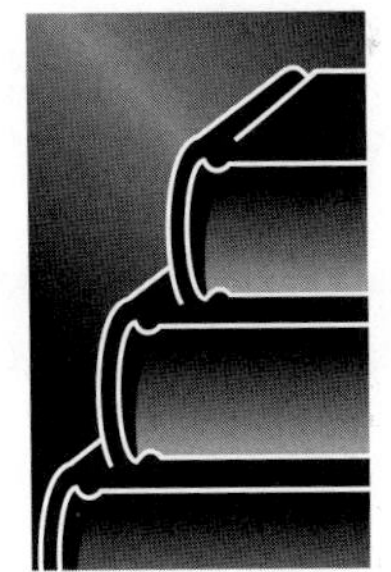

Facts: Donald Lynch bought a check from Allied Irish Bank (AIB) in Ireland. The check was payable to Advance Marketing and Investment Inc. (AMI). The amount of U.S. $250 was handwritten as "Two Hundred + Fifty" on the center line of the check with "US Dollars" handwritten on the line below, and "US $250.00" handwritten on the upper right-hand side of the check (the numerical portion of the check). As written, there was less than one-half inch of open space in the numerical portion and less than one inch of space in the written portion. The drawee bank was Marine Midland Bank, now known as HSBC Bank USA. Prior to being deposited into AMI's account at F&M Bank—Northern Virginia, the check was altered to $250,000, by adding three zeros and changing a period to a comma in the numerical part and adding the letters "Thoud" in the written portion. F&M presented the check to HSBC, who paid $250,000 and debited AIB's account. When told of the alteration, HSBC recredited AIB's account for $249,750, and sued F&M for that amount. F&M claimed it was not liable for breach of its presentment warranties because the drawer (AIB) had not used ordinary care in filling out the check. The U.S. District Court held F&M liable, and it appealed.

Issue: Was the trial court's decision on the facts "clearly erroneous"?

Decision: No. Judgment affirmed.

Opinion by Senior Circuit Judge Hamilton: "The district court ... found that AIB had exercised ordinary care in preparing the Check. In this ... regard, the district court stated:

'[T]he test has got to be is that line sufficiently filled in so that someone cannot come along and add into that writing in a way that just alters the check so that it will go through unnoticed.

'That certainly wasn't done on this check. This check was substantially written across the line. As a matter of fact, it was written far enough along the line that you could not write the word "thousand" in. It had to be scrawled up in the manner in which it was....

'There was sufficient writing there that any alteration that was made was obvious. And I can't find negligence in that regard.'

"The only evidence submitted by F&M in support of its burden of proving that AIB failed to exercise ordinary case in making out the Check was the Check itself. The district court physically examined the Check, including the just less than one-half inch of open space in the numerical portion of the check and the one inch of open space in the written portion of the Check. Based upon this physical examination, the district court found that AIB had filled in the open spaces in the numerical and written portions of the check sufficiently such that 'any alteration that was made was obvious.'...

"After reviewing a copy of the Check ... (the sole evidence on this issue presented below), we are not left with a definite and firm conviction that the district court's finding that AIB exercised ordinary care in making out the Check is wrong, mistaken, or implausible. Indeed, we see sound logic in the district court's rationale that if the written portion of the Check contained enough writing such that the Check's alteration could only be accomplished with the 'scrawled up,' abbreviated form of the word 'thousand,' i.e., 'Thoud,' ordinary care was used in making out the Check.... In short, we hold that the district court's factual finding that AIB exercised ordinary care in making out the check is not clearly erroneous....

"Because the district court's finding ... is not clearly erroneous, we affirm the judgment in favor of HSBC."

Section 3-420 says that an instrument is also converted if it is taken by transfer, other than a negotiation, from a person not entitled to enforce it, or if a bank makes or obtains payment of it for a person not entitled to payment. If any of these things occurs, the amount of tort damages that the owner can collect against the wrongdoer will usually be the face amount of the instrument.

The *HSBC Bank* case examines the question of whether the drawer was careless in making out the check, so that the presenting bank (F&M Bank) would not be liable for breaching its presentment warranties.

Significance of This Chapter

Both plaintiffs and defendants, creditors and debtors, need to know the circumstances under which they could become liable on a negotiable instrument. These rules are complicated because they encompass different types of liability. Perhaps no other single topic so clearly combines all the basic legal concepts: contract, property, tort, and crime.

Although negotiable instruments are involved in many fraudulent schemes in which criminal prosecution could occur, this chapter examined civil, rather than criminal, liability. We covered the contract liabilities of makers of notes, drawers and acceptors of drafts and checks, and endorsers of all types of instruments. Our discussion included warranties made by people who transfer instruments for value or who present them for payment or acceptance, and tort liability for negligence or conversion. Although these liabilities are primarily based on the provisions of Article 3 of the UCC, liabilities may also arise under general legal principles.

Because liability is easy to incur and hard to disclaim, extreme care should be exercised in signing, handling, transferring, and verifying all negotiable instruments.

IMPORTANT TERMS AND CONCEPTS

accepted
acceptor
accommodation party
certified
conversion
dishonor
drawee
drawee bank
maker
negligence
presentment
presentment warranties
primary contract liability
protest
secondary contract liability
warranty liability
without recourse

QUESTIONS AND PROBLEMS FOR DISCUSSION

1. What is the difference between primary and secondary contract liability?

2. What is the difference between warranty liability and contract liability?

3. What is tort liability as it relates to commercial paper?

4. What is the significance of endorsing an instrument with the words *without recourse*?

5. Sylvio, an independent insurance agent, received a check for $28,000, payable to one of his customers, Cobber Taxi Company. The check was issued by Rely Insurance Company to settle a claim filed by Cobber. Sylvio fraudulently endorsed the check with Cobber's name and then added his own endorsement. Sylvio then gave the check to his brother Lem and told Lem to use it as the initial deposit to the account of a car-rental business the brothers were starting up. Lem did so. Sylvio later withdrew these funds from the partnership account for his own use. Rely sued the bank where the check had been deposited. That bank sued Lem and the car-rental partnership.

   How should the court decide these lawsuits? Explain.

6. Billie Biggert had been buying sheep for her sheep ranch for several years from the Tremont Livestock Company, represented by Kevin Mummar. In 1999, Kevin told Billie that Tremont needed to buy back 100 sheep, so she sold them to him. Kevin gave her a check on Tremont's bank account for $42,000, which he had signed on behalf of Tremont. Billie thought Kevin was a partner, and therefore authorized to sign checks for Tremont, but in fact, he was only an employee in a sole proprietorship.

Billie deposited the check in her account, but when it was presented to Tremont's bank for payment, payment was refused because Kevin had no authority to sign checks on the account. When she got the check back, Billie immediately called up Tremont's bank to find out what the problem was. The bank's cashier told Billie to send the check through again and "we'll get the problem straightened out." Billie did so, but the bank bounced the check again. Tremont itself is now in bankruptcy, and Kevin is nowhere to be found.

Can Billie collect on this check against Tremont's bank? Discuss.

7. John B. Hane was the assignee-holder of a note issued by Theta Electronics Laboratories, Inc., in the amount of $15,377.07, plus 6 percent interest. The note, dated August 10, 1994, provided that the first monthly payment of $320.47 would be due on January 10, 1995. The note contained an acceleration clause. Gerald M. Exten, Emil L. O'Neil, James W. Hane, and their wives all endorsed the note. The original payees, George B. and Marguerite F. Thompson, assigned the note without recourse to Hane on November 26, 1995. Some $2,222.13 had been paid on the note up to that point. Exten had originally been the corporate president of Theta but had been removed in April or May 1995. Although no more than six payments were made (through June 1995), Hane took no action until June 7, 1997, when he filed a confession of judgment against all of the endorsers except the Thompsons. The Extens demanded and received a trial on the merits, after which the judge found them not liable. Hane appealed.

What result, and why?

8. Union Bank issued a personal money order to a customer who paid for it with an insufficient funds check. A personal money order is issued with blank spaces for the name of the payee, the date, and the signature of the purchaser; only the amount is filled in, usually, as in this case, with a checkwriting machine. When the check it had taken as payment was returned unpaid, Union issued a stop pay order on the personal money order. Meanwhile, Sequoyah Bank had taken the money order as an HDC. The trial court held that Union could issue a stop order itself, and that Sequoyah could not recover.

Can an issuing bank, on its own initiative, stop payment on a personal money order?

CHAPTER 27

Negotiation, Holders in Due Course, and Defenses

Chapter Objectives

This chapter will:

- Explain the difference between negotiation of commercial paper and assignment of an ordinary contract.
- Indicate why proper endorsement is needed to negotiate an instrument.
- Discuss the different types of endorsement.
- Define holder in due course.
- Discuss the requirements a transferee must meet to become a holder in due course.
- Explain the shelter rule for holders through a holder in due course.
- Define the major real and personal defenses to liability.
- Indicate how Federal Trade Commission Regulation 433 applies.
- Explain how liability may be discharged.

We now have an instrument that is negotiable and on which one or more parties are liable as signers. To get the special "negotiability" results, however, a plaintiff seeking to enforce the instrument must meet an additional set of requirements. Unless the plaintiff has taken the instrument through a special form of transfer called negotiation and under circumstances that qualify the plaintiff as a "holder in due course" (HDC), our plaintiff holds the instrument subject to all the defenses and claims that would be available against the assignee of a simple written contract. Only a person with the rights of an HDC holds the negotiable instrument free of adverse claims and defenses.

Negotiation

Today, as indicated in Chapter 13, most contracts can be assigned. Only a negotiable instrument, however, can be "negotiated." **Negotiation** is a transfer in such form that the transferee becomes a **holder**. There must be physical delivery of the instrument and, if the instrument is payable to order, it must be endorsed. A holder is a person who is in possession of an instrument "drawn, issued, or endorsed to him or to his order or to bearer or in blank." When you make your check payable to "cash," or when you endorse your paycheck on the back by simply signing your name, any person who subsequently gains possession of the instrument is a holder, even without any further endorsement. Not every holder is a **holder in due course (HDC)**, however. That status depends on the circumstances under which the holder acquired the instrument.

When an instrument is drawn to someone's order (e.g., your rent check to your landlord) or is endorsed to someone's order (you endorsed a dividend check to your bank as payment on a loan), negotiation cannot occur unless the person to whose order the instrument is now payable has properly endorsed the instrument. In other words, the finder of an unendorsed order instrument would not be a holder nor would any subsequent transferee from the finder. The missing required endorsement breaks the "chain of title" to the instrument, so that no later person, even though in possession of the instrument itself, is a holder.

To qualify as an HDC so as to own an instrument free of most claims and defenses, a person must first be a holder. The proper endorsement of an order instrument is therefore crucial to the HDC status of later possessors. If you simply sign your name on the back of your paycheck and then lose it on the way to the bank, the finder would not be an HDC (because that person gave no value for it), but the finder would be a holder and the store where he or she used it to buy merchandise could qualify as an HDC. The net result is that you lose the value represented by your paycheck just as if you had cashed it and then lost the cash.

To change this example: If you lost your paycheck before you endorsed it, the finder would not be a holder and neither would the store, even if the finder forged your endorsement on the back of the check. The net result is that you get your money back and the store gets stuck. For this reason, many stores and banks are reluctant to cash checks when the person asking for the money is not the original payee.

Endorsement

General Rules

An endorsement is made by signing your name on the instrument, normally on the back. An endorser could sign on the front of the instrument, but this would entail the risk of being held liable as a co-maker of the note or as a co-drawer of the draft if that is what the signature seemed to be. As a rule, unless the instrument clearly indicates that a signature is made in some other capacity it is an **endorsement**. It is usually assumed that endorsers are liable "in the order in which they endorse, which is presumed to be the order in which their signatures appear on the instrument." When an instrument has been transferred so many times that there is no room on it for further endorsement, these may be made on a "permanently" attached piece of paper called an allonge.

An endorsement is effective for negotiation only when it conveys the entire amount due on the instrument. Any attempt to endorse over only part of what's due is not a negotiation, rather a partial assignment. (Therefore, no transferee under such a partial endorsement could be an HDC.) When the name of the person to whose order the instrument is payable is misspelled or otherwise incorrect, he or she may endorse with the incorrect name or the correct name or both. Anyone giving value for the instrument can require the double endorsement of both the incorrect and the correct names. Unless the instrument is already payable to the bearer, any transferee **for value** can demand that the transferor endorse.

When an instrument is payable to two or more persons jointly ("pay to the order of Jones and Green"), all of them must endorse to be able to negotiate the instrument. When an instrument is payable to two or more persons in the alternative ("pay to the order of Jones or Green"), the single endorsement of either of them is sufficient to negotiate it.

Impostors and Defrauders

Article 3 contains some very special rules to cover situations when instruments are issued to impostors, crooked employees and agents, and other defrauders. In the impostor case, someone who is not Henry Forge comes into your office, says "I am Henry Forge," convinces you that he is, and persuades you to enter into a transaction that results in your making out a check payable to the order of "Henry Forge." He tricked you. The Uniform Commercial Code (UCC) says that *anyone* can effectively endorse this instrument by signing "Henry Forge." The fake Henry Forge can do so. If he loses it or it is stolen from him, the thief or finder can endorse "Henry Forge" and effectively negotiate the instrument. This does not mean that some or all of the persons cannot be prosecuted criminally; it just means that subsequent transferees can be holders and can therefore qualify as HDCs if they meet all of the other requirements.

The same rule applies when a corporation's bookkeeper or payroll clerk "pads the payroll" with extra fake names and then endorses and cashes these extra checks. The crook's endorsement in the names of the named payees are effective; the drawee bank honoring these checks when presented has paid the right party; and the corporation is stuck unless it can get the money back from the crook. Most simply, the Code's rule for these cases is: "The sucker always pays!"

These "fictitious payee" rules are applied by the court in the *Hinkle* case.

The Code also provides for similar results when the negotiation of an instrument is subject to rescission because of minority or other incapacity, illegality, breach of duty, or fraud, duress, or mistake. Such a negotiation is at least temporarily effective, and these "defects" in the transaction cannot be used to recover the instrument from a later HDC. A minor's negotiation of an instrument, for example, would make all later transferees holders, so that one of them could qualify as an HDC. If there were a subsequent HDC in the chain of title, the minor could not get the instrument back; if there were no subsequent HDC the minor could recover the instrument from the current holder. In either case, the minor could use minority as a defense against having to actually pay the instrument.

Types of Endorsement

Every endorsement has at least three features: the method it requires for making further negotiations, or at least the next one; the nature of the liability it imposes on the endorser; and the kind of restrictions, if any, that it attempts to place on further transfers. These three features may be combined in various ways.

Blank Endorsement and Special Endorsement

The last endorsement controls the status of the instrument as order paper or bearer paper, regardless of the form in which it was originally issued. A **blank endorsement** consists merely of the endorser's signature: "John Smith." If the last or the only endorsement is a blank endorsement, the instrument is now **bearer paper** and may be negotiated henceforth by delivery, without further endorsement. A **special endorsement** names the next transferee: "Pay to Judy Jones. John Smith." Regardless of how it was originally made payable, this instrument is now **order paper**, and Judy must now endorse to negotiate the

CASE 1

Hinkle v. Cornwell Quality Tool Co.

532 N.E.2d 772 (OH App. 1987)

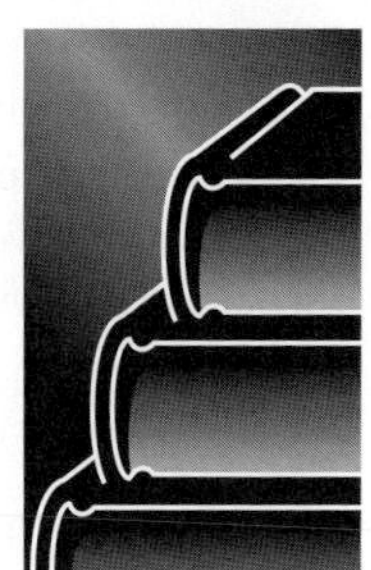

Facts: This case involves the appeal and cross-appeal of G. F. Hinkle, d/b/a Akron Novelty Co., and Cornwell Quality Tool Co., respectively. Cornwell's subrogee, Royal Insurance Company, intervened in the trial action and joins Cornwell in its appeal. Defendants-cross-appellees, Centran Bank and County of Summit, have filed cross-appellee briefs.

Linda Zelnar embezzled $57,000 from Akron Novelty while she was employed there as a bookkeeper. She was discovered and discharged.

Rather than prosecuting her for the crime of embezzlement, the Summit County Prosecutor's office referred Zelnar to its pretrial diversion program. After giving Zelnar a psychological examination, the director of the program, Mark Tully, enrolled her in the diversion program. One of the requirements of her participation in the program was her restitution of the stolen funds.

Zelnar told Tully she would be able to return Akron Novelty's funds by refinancing her home and borrowing from her parents. Zelnar presented Tully with two checks on two different occasions—one for $20,000 and a second for $37,000. The testimony contained in the trial transcript and depositions indicates that Hinkle had some concerns as to whether the first check was good. He had Tully and Zelnar get Centran to assure that there were sufficient funds in her account to cover the check. This Centran did. Zelnar got the second check for $37,000 certified. Hinkle deposited both checks in the accounts from which the funds had originally been taken.

Zelnar had been discharged from Akron Novelty on April 6, 1984. On April 30, 1984, she was employed, through Kelly Services, as an accounts payable clerk for Cornwell Quality Tools. She was eventually hired directly by Cornwell and filled out an application listing previous employment, including Akron Novelty. However, Cornwell never made its own inquiries into her previous employment, relying on the assumption that Kelly Services had already done so.

Zelnar's duties included the personal preparation of checks to Cornwell's creditors. While employed at Cornwell, Zelnar conceived a plan to embezzle money to pay back Hinkle, as well as for her own use. She established an account at Centran Bank in the name of "Linda R. Zelnar dba 'Model.'" She also purchased a kit and made a rubber stamp that read "For Deposit Only, Model."

Cornwell had regularly done business with Model Industries, Inc. of Chicago. When mailing more than one check, it was Cornwell's policy to make the first check in a group payable with the full name and address of the payee. The remaining checks were made payable only to "Model." Over a 3-month period, Zelnar prepared six checks payable to "Model," which were drawn on Cornwell's account at First National Bank. She presented the checks for the proper drawers' signatures and then took the checks, endorsed them with the stamp, and deposited them in the account at Centran. All six of the checks were accepted for payment by First National that charged them to Cornwell's account.

Zelnar drew two checks on the Centran account that were payable to Hinkle. When Centran notified Zelnar that one of the checks was going to be returned for uncollected funds, Zelnar obtained a letter from Centran explaining the delay and gave the letter to Mr. Tully of the diversion program. Zelnar was concerned because a check returned for insufficient funds would result in her ouster from the program. When the embezzlement scheme was discovered, the funds remaining in the Centran account were frozen and then returned to Cornwell.

Cornwell filed a complaint, seeking to enjoin the funds in the Centran account, and an amended complaint, alleging that Centran failed to exercise ordinary care in the establishment of the account and collection of the checks. Royal Insurance Company, which paid Cornwell $50,000, intervened in the suit as subrogee. Royal charged Centran and First National with conversion, pursuant to R.C. 1303.55 (UCC 3-419), and alleged that Centran failed to exercise ordinary care in the establishment of the account and collection of the checks. Centran filed motions for summary judgment against both plaintiffs. First National was voluntarily dismissed from the suit.

The trial court granted summary judgment to Centran.

Issue: Do the impostor rules apply here?

Decision: Yes. Judgment affirmed.

Opinion by Judge Cacioppo: "Application of the impostor rule . . . deems a forgery effective to pass good title to a negotiable instrument. The rule is an exception to the strict liability imposed on a bank that pays on a forged [i]ndorsement. The loss is shifted to the drawer because the responsibility for the payment can be attributed more to the drawer's actions than to the bank's failure to obtain a proper [i]ndorsement. . . .

"'The principle followed is that the loss should fall upon the employer as a risk of his business enterprise rather than upon the subsequent holder or drawee. The reasons are that the employer is normally in a better position to prevent such forgeries by reasonable care in the selection or supervision of his employees, or, if he is not, is at least in a better position to cover the loss by fidelity insurance; and that the cost of such insurance is properly an expense of his business rather than of the business of the holder or drawee.'

"To receive the protection of this rule, Centran has to meet both prongs of the statute, i.e.

1. That Linda Zelnar supplied the name of the payee, 'Model,' to her employer, Cornwell.

2. That Linda Zelnar intended the payee, 'Model,' to have no interest in the checks.

"In its attempt to meet the first prong, Centran uses a strained and contorted line of reasoning. Centran claims that the entity 'Model' was fictitious because Cornwell did not do business with any entity designated as such. For the purposes of the rule, a forger using the name of a fictitious payee obviously shows the name was 'supplied' to employer.

"Cornwell did, however, do business with 'Model Industries, Inc.' of Chicago. The record shows that 'Model' cannot be considered a fictitious entity, and even if it were, it would have been 'created' by Cornwell itself. Zelnar stated in her deposition that it was company policy to abbreviate the names of payees such as Model Industries, Inc.

"It was Cornwell's practice in a situation where several invoices were to be paid to one supplier on a single day—as was the case with Model Industries which was a constant supplier to Cornwell—that only the first check in the group would bear the full name and address of the payee. This check would be inserted in the window of the envelope, while the other checks would bear only the abbreviated name of the payee. There was nothing extraordinary about her use of the word 'Model' on the following checks, particularly since the invoices to which they applied were perfectly genuine. Thus, it is inaccurate to say that 'Cornwell never had done business with the fictitious entity called "Model"....' As used on these checks, 'Model' clearly pertained to Model Industries, Inc. of Chicago, from which the invoices attached to them had been received....

"To escape the application of the first prong of the rule, Cornwell uses a more plausible argument as to when an employee can be considered to have 'supplied' the name of the payee. Specifically, the issue is whether an employee can 'supply' a payee's name when the check is issued to a real person in payment of a genuine obligation of the employer. Several courts have held that where a check is issued to a bona fide creditor who had furnished legitimate invoices, the employee's action amounts to no more than theft of the check. An employee cannot be said to have 'supplied' the name of a payee in the course of a normal business transaction that would have occurred in any event....

"This theory has been criticized and the distinction between bona fide and fraudulent transactions has been considered inappropriate.... [T]he policy reasons for the rule apply to business atmospheres in general. An employer who delegates check processing duties must responsibly supervise employees. 'The business risk assumed by an employer who allows employees to process supporting documents or prepare checks is just as real whether the invoices presented are forged or authentic.'...

"The second prong of the rule requires that, in supplying the name, the employee must intend that the named payee have no interest in the check. Linda Zelnar freely admitted that, at the time she presented the checks to her superiors for their signatures, she never intended the true payee, Model Industries, Inc. of Chicago, to have any interest in the check.

"Having met the requirements of ... UCC 3-405[1][C], the forgery must be considered effective to pass good title on the instrument, and Cornwell must bear the loss. Therefore, summary judgment was appropriate in this case.

"Cornwell raises a second issue, asserting that the negligence of Centran precludes the benefits of R.C. 1303.41, making summary judgment improper. Cornwell claims that, in spite of Centran's relief from statutory liability by operation of R.C. 1303.41, a triable issue of fact remained as to Centran's actual negligence in failing to exercise ordinary care in the transaction.

"There are three Code provisions which allow a bank to escape strict liability for paying on a forged [i]ndorsement. R.C. 1303.42 (UCC 3-406) and R.C. 1304.29 (UCC 4-406) both specifically provide that where the drawer asserts and can prove that the bank failed to exercise reasonable commercial standards in handling the check, the bank loses its protection. R.C. 1303.41 (UCC 3-405) is silent on the issue of the bank's lack of care. We do not believe this silence to be inadvertent. The policy statements provided in the Official Comment denote an intent to place the loss on the party best able to prevent it.

"The interpretation of Section 3-405 as an *absolute* loss allocation device is also more consistent with the recognition that this section was conceived as a 'banker's provision *intended to narrow the liability of banks* and broaden the responsibility of their customers.'

"Such a 'banker's provision' was not likely to have been intended to leave the banks open to common-law liability. Therefore, since the Supreme Court has clearly expressed faith in and support of the policies advanced by the drafters, it can safely be said that R.C. 1303.41 (UCC 3-405) displaces any negligence claims against the depositary bank, common-law or otherwise.

"Since it was clear that Centran Bank met the requirements of R.C. 1303.41(A) (3), and that R.C. 1303.41(A)(3) is an absolute defense, regardless of negligence on the part of a bank, the trial court acted properly in granting Centran Bank's motion for summary judgment."

instrument further. (Note that the words of negotiability—*order* or *bearer*—do not have to be used in an endorsement. The preceding example is payable to the order of Judy Jones.)

Qualified and Unqualified Endorsement

An endorser may disclaim secondary contract liability by using the words *without recourse* or similar language. This is called a **qualified endorsement**. If such language is not used, the endorsement is unqualified, meaning that the endorser is assuming the normal

Exhibit 27.1: Types of Endorsement

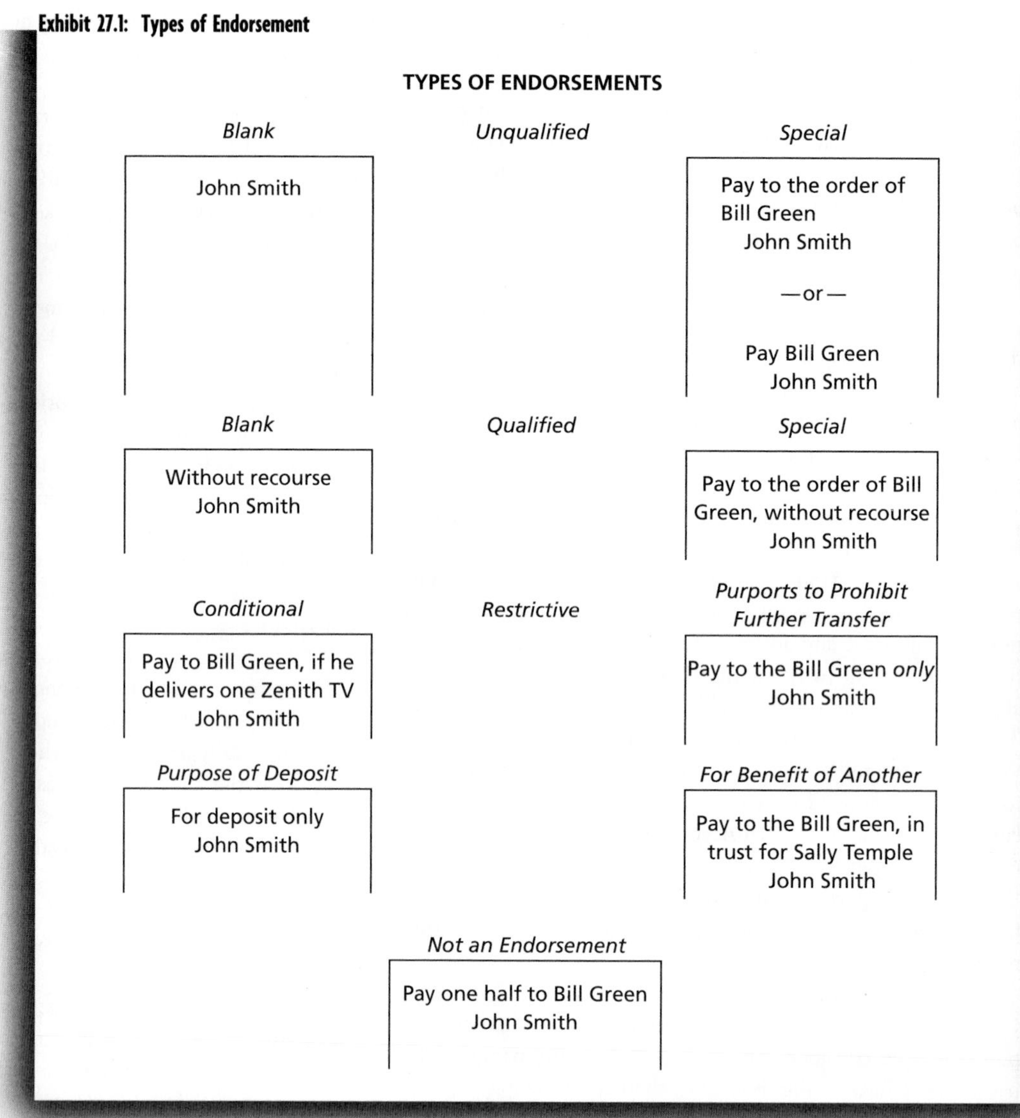

secondary contract liability—to pay the instrument on dishonor. These rules were discussed in detail in the last chapter.

Restrictive Endorsement

Endorsers sometimes attempt, in various ways, to restrict or limit the further negotiation of an instrument. Under the Code's rules, some such restrictions are fully effective, some are partially effective, and some are without legal effect. Section 3-206(a) states that no endorser can effectively prohibit the further negotiation of a negotiable instrument. If John Smith endorsed "Pay only Judy Jones" or "Pay Judy Jones and no one else," the "only" language is completely ineffective. Judy can endorse and renegotiate the instrument just as if John had endorsed "Pay to the order of Judy Jones."

The promise or order contained in the body of the instrument itself cannot be conditional without destroying its negotiability. This is not true, however, of endorsements. Conditions can be included in endorsements without affecting an instrument's negotiability. However, the Code makes such conditions effective only as between the immediate parties.

For example, Biff Bosox buys a new TV from Big Bennie's Appliance Store. As payment, Biff endorses his payroll check: "Pay to Big Bennie if he delivers one new Zenith TV to my home. Biff Bosox." Bennie is not supposed to get the money unless he delivers the TV as promised. The Code says that no later holder of the instrument is responsible for verifying that he or she has done so before taking the instrument. If Bennie has not delivered the TV but gets the money from someone anyway, that later holder of the instrument may still be an HDC. In contrast, all subsequent holders other than intermediary banks are fully bound by such language in the endorsement as "For deposit only" or "For collection." It is very hard to imagine a situation where a nonbank person taking an instrument after such an endorsement could ever qualify as an HDC. Such language clearly indicates that the instrument is intended to circulate only through the bank collection process.

When the **restrictive endorsement** indicates that the proceeds are to be paid to one person for the benefit of another ("Pay to Ollie Orkin for the benefit of Shirley Trample"), only the first taker after the endorsement is bound by it. To be the holder for value so as to (perhaps) qualify as an HDC, the immediate transferee must pay any value given "consistently with the endorsement." Unless later holders of the instrument actually know that the trustee or other fiduciary has misapplied these funds, they are not affected in any way by the "benefit" type of restrictive endorsement.

Holder in Due Course

Generally

The essence of the whole concept of negotiability is the elimination or nonassertability of most common defenses when the instrument gets into the hands of a good faith purchaser. The technical term for such a **bona fide purchasers (BFP)** in the negotiable instruments context is holder in due course. The requirements for becoming an HDC are set out in Section 3-302, and then they are more specifically defined in other sections. Whether or not a particular person has met this set of requirements presents a complex combination of legal and factual issues that have been subject to considerable litigation. Since, as previously noted, consumer debtors are now permitted to assert any defense they may have against anyone, HDC status has become virtually meaningless in consumer transactions. For businesses, however, these issues are still vital when merchandise has been fraudulently misrepresented or has not been delivered at all. Whether a business debtor will be able to assert such defenses or will be forced to pay for the proverbial "dead horse, will depend on a later holder's status as an HDC.

An HDC first has to be a holder (as previously discussed) and then must have taken the instrument for value, and in **good faith**, and without notice that it is overdue or has been dishonored or of any defense against or claim to it on the part of any person. Section 3-302 also contains several specific rules: A purchaser of a limited interest in an instrument can be an HDC only to that extent; and a person cannot become an HDC by buying an instrument at a judicial sale or as part of a bulk transaction not in the ordinary course of business or by acquiring it through legal process or in taking over an estate.

Value

As used here, value is a much more limited concept than consideration. A holder for value must have performed the agreed consideration for the note. If Axle Greez promises to buy a certain promissory note from Henna Rinz for $600, there is a contract, but Axle is not a holder for value until he actually pays Henna the $600. If he is notified of an existing defense before he pays, he cannot become an HDC. A person who acquires security interests or other liens against instruments, other than by judicial process, is a holder for value. So is a person who takes the instrument "as payment of, or as security for, an antecedent claim against any person whether or not the claim is due." Similarly, someone who makes an "irrevocable obligation to a third party" (e.g., a binding agreement for an extension of credit) is thereby a holder for value. Finally, value is given by giving another negotiable instrument. In the preceding example, if Axle had given Henna his check for $600 in payment for the promissory note he bought from her, Axle would be a holder "for value" of the note.

Good Faith

Article 3 contains no special definition of good faith other than that in the general definitions Section (1-201[19]). It is a subjective test, to be applied by the trier of fact: "honesty in fact in the conduct or transaction concerned." Such facts as the relationship between the parties, the size of any discount from the face amount of the instrument, the proximity of the transfer to the instrument's due date, the appearance of the instrument, and the time and place of the transfer would be relevant in deciding whether a particular holder had bought in good faith.

No Notice of Claim or Defense

Article 3 does contain several specific rules for determining when a purchaser has **notice** that an instrument is overdue, has been dishonored, or is subject to a claim or defense. The

CASE 2

United Catholic Parish Schools v. Card Services Center

636 N.W.2d 206 (WI App. 2001)

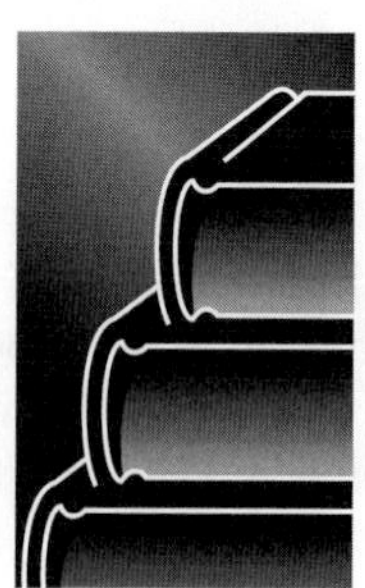

Facts: United Catholic Parish Schools of Beaver Dam Educational Association (UCPS) employed Janet Gittus as its bookkeeper. Over the course of 7 years Gittus wrote 37 checks, totaling $59,038.92, to Card Services Center (CSC)—a division of First Financial Bank. Gittus sent these checks to CSC in payment of her personal charge card account at CSC. These checks were "only a small part" of her total embezzlement of UCPS funds. UCPS sued CSC and First Financial based on a common law claim for conversion (wrongful use) of its property (the money represented by the 37 checks). First Financial says that it took the checks as an HDC, and thus is immune from such claims. The trial court ordered First Financial to repay the money, and First Financial appealed.

Issue: Is the defendant (CSC/First Financial) an HDC?

Decision: Yes. Judgment reversed, and case remanded with instructions to dismiss the complaint.

Opinion by Judge Roggensack: "On the record before us, whether First Financial is a holder in due course involves the application of [UCC 3-302] to undisputed facts and is therefore, a question of law that we review independently of the circuit court's decision. . . .

"In order to encourage the use of negotiable instruments in commercial transactions, a holder in due course is insulated from nearly all claims of any party. . . .

"Because the holder in due course defense is usually employed at the expense of an innocent party, [3-302] establishes strict requirements for determining holder in due course status. Those requirements attempt to identify holders that are worthy, in a commercial sense, of protection and to separate them from those who are not. . . .

"Here, the affidavit of Valentine Glytas establishes the uncontroverted fact that First Financial took the checks at issue in payment of Gittus's outstanding credit card balances. That satisfies the first part of the . . . test.

"Glytas avers that First Financial had no reason to suspect there was any problem with collecting payment on the checks when it accepted them, as they appeared to be authentic, did not have any facial irregularities and were accepted to pay Gittus's credit card debts. . . . We also note that the checks were drafted over a seven-year period, without any complaint from UCPS that Gittus had no authority to write them to pay her credit card debt. Therefore, we conclude that . . . First Financial took the checks in good faith. . . .

"Satisfying the statutory requirement of being 'without notice' requires First Financial to establish a negative, and therefore, the initial burden it must carry is slight. . . . Copies of the checks are attached to the complaint, and we note that all appear regular. Additionally, UCPS has submitted no affidavit to contradict Glytas's assertions. . . . Furthermore, the policy underlying Wisconsin's commercial code is to promote certainty in commercial transactions and to place the loss on the party in the best position to prevent it. . . . Therefore, . . . First Financial took the checks without notice, and accordingly, it has made a prima facie case for holder in due course status. . . .

"In contesting First Financial's status as a holder in due course, UCPS asserts that under [3-307] Gittus was a fiduciary and therefore, that First Financial cannot be a holder in due course. . . .

"UCPS submitted no proof that First Financial had actual knowledge that Gittus was a fiduciary of UCPS when these transactions occurred. . . . Accordingly, [3-307] provides no avenue for defeating First Financial's status as a holder in due course. . . .

"UCPS argues . . . that the law that has been applied to the conversion of personal property should be applied here rather than [the UCC]. . . . We are unpersuaded. . . . The policies of encouraging reliance on the face of negotiable instruments in order to facilitate commercial transactions in negotiable paper . . . are not parallel to those that drive a trover action for the possession of logs. Furthermore, while some claims for relief may exist side-by-side with claims under Wisconsin's commercial code, they cannot prevail if they conflict with code provisions. . . . Here, UCPS's claim for conversion would supplant the defenses available to a holder in due course, and this it cannot do. Accordingly, we reverse the judgment of the circuit court and remand with directions to dismiss UCPS's complaint."

basic rule is nothing more than common sense: A purchaser has notice of a claim or defense when the instrument bears "such apparent evidence of forgery or alteration," or is "otherwise so irregular or incomplete as to call into question its authenticity." A purchaser who is made aware "that the obligation of any party is voidable in whole or in part, or that all parties have been discharged" also has notice. When a fiduciary has negotiated an instrument for his or her own benefit, the purchaser must have had knowledge of that fact when taking the instrument. Remember the difference between knowledge and notice; knowledge means actual, "inside-the-head" information, whereas notice includes both acts from which a reasonable person should infer other information and the receipt of notices containing information, whether those notices are actually read or not. Knowledge is therefore only one form of notice. This section does say that the filing or recording of a document does not of itself constitute notice so as to prevent a person from being an HDC. It also says that for notice to be effective, it must be received "at a time and in a manner that gives a reasonable opportunity to act on it."

The application of these HDC rules can be seen in the *United Catholic* case.

No Notice That Instrument Is Overdue

Section 3-304 provides a few rules for determining when an instrument is "overdue." With a demand instrument, rather than one with a specific due date, it is overdue after a demand for payment has already been made by a prior holder or after more than a reasonable time from the date issued. The original section contains a presumption that 90 days is such a reasonable time for an uncertified check payable in the United States, but it does not contain similar guidelines for drafts or notes. (Presumably, the reasonable time for these other instruments would be longer than that for an uncertified check.)

The purchaser who is aware that a prior acceleration of the due date has been made also has such notice. Finally, there is notice that an instrument is overdue when the purchaser has reason to know that part of the principal is overdue (a missed installment payment, for example) or that "there is an uncured default in payment of another instrument of the same series." There is no stated rule for the most obvious case: The stated due date is July 1, and you buy the instrument on July 2. You can clearly see that the instrument is overdue when you buy it, and you are not an HDC.

Shelter Rule

Under the Code, a transferee of a negotiable instrument (including one who is not even a holder), in most instances, receives whatever rights its transferor had. A holder who is not an HDC (a donee, for example) would nevertheless have whatever enforcement rights the transferor had. Because of this general rule, any holder of an instrument after an HDC succeeds to all the rights of the HDC, even though the later holder or holders do not personally meet all the requirements for being an HDC. The donee of the instrument cannot personally qualify as an HDC because he or she gave no value for it. But if the donor or some prior party was an HDC, the donee would have all the rights to the instrument that the HDC did. In simplest terms, once there is an HDC in an instrument's chain of title, all later holders of the instrument receive the "shelter" of that person's HDC status even though they cannot meet the HDC tests personally.

There are two exceptions to this **shelter rule**. A person who is a party to some fraud or illegality affecting an instrument cannot improve his or her legal position by transferring the instrument to an HDC and then reacquiring it. Nor can a person who has notice of a claim or defense to an instrument, then transfers the instrument to an HDC, and then later reacquires the instrument.

The shelter rule is argued in the *Manufacturers* case.

Defenses and Discharge

The merchant community's main purpose in developing negotiable instruments and the main significance of negotiability today is the nonassertability of most common defenses

CASE 3

MANUFACTURERS HANOVER TRUST v. ROBINSON

597 N.Y.S.2d 986 (Sup. Ct. 1993)

Facts: Defendants are limited partners in 600 Grant Street Associates Limited Partnership that was organized to acquire, own, and operate a commercial office building in Pittsburgh, Pennsylvania. In connection with the purchase of their interests, defendants made cash down payments and executed promissory notes payable to the order of the partnership for the balance.

Defendants allege that they were induced to invest in the partnership as a result of certain misrepresentations made by the sponsor of the transaction, Integrated Resources, Inc., which allegedly failed to advise defendants of the presence of asbestos throughout the building and misrepresented that at the time of the sale there were 2.23 million square feet of vacant office space in downtown Pittsburgh, when in fact the vacant space was in excess of 12 million square feet.

In June and September 1986, plaintiff Manufacturers Hanover Trust Company acquired 39 of the promissory notes as collateral for an $80 million loan made to the partnership by it and five other banks for which it acted as agent.

Manufacturers alleges that in 1986 it accepted only the notes of limited partners who had met certain financial criteria, and then only if the notes were not in default. It also asserts that the partnership represented and warranted that none of the notes were overdue or had been dishonored and that no defense against or claim to the notes existed. Manufacturers also allegedly conducted a credit check of each limited partner who had executed a note.

Plaintiff asserts that at the time of the delivery of the notes to it in 1986, 37 were endorsed in blank by an officer of Marine Midland Bank, N.A. in the following form:

> *"PAY TO THE ORDER OF*
>
> *WITHOUT RECOURSE*
>
> *MARINE MIDLAND BANK, N.A.*
>
> *BY (signature of officer)*

Two of the notes were similarly endorsed in blank by an officer of Security Pacific National Bank. Previously the notes had been endorsed by the partnership to these two banks.

An exception to this scenario was the note made by defendant Russell D. Robinson, which was pledged in 1987 and endorsed by the partnership directly to Manufacturers.

Defendants were promised by the partnership and integrated in documents dated December 5, 1984, and March 15, 1985, that in the event of a reduction in the highest marginal federal income tax bracket, the purchase price of the property would be reduced, and the limited partners would be entitled to a reduction of their required capital contribution to the partnership. The October 1986 tax code amendments effected a reduction in such tax bracket, thereby triggering the capital reduction. The limited partners were notified that as a result they would receive a rebate of $21,552 per unit, which would be paid in annual installments in March 1988, 1989, 1990, and 1991. Integrated filed for bankruptcy thereafter in February 1990 and the promised capital reduction payments for the years 1990 and 1991 were never made.

In August 1990, Manufacturers removed the notes from its vault to inventory them, allegedly in anticipation of litigation. For reasons that are unclear, the removing bank officers then allegedly stamped on the 39 notes held in blank "600 GRANT STREET ASSOCIATES LIMITED PARTNERSHIP" in the blank space of each of the aforementioned endorsements, and then placed the following endorsement on these notes:

> *"600 Grant Street Associates Limited Partnership without recourse*
>
> *By: Manufacturers Hanover Trust Company as Agent, Attorney-in-fact for*
>
> *600 Grant Street Associates Limited Partnership*
>
> *By: (signature of officer) Vice President"*

Claiming that the notes were negotiated to it in 1986 and that it then took possession of them for value, in good faith and without knowledge of any claim or defense, Manufacturers moved for summary judgment asserting that it was an HDC thereof.

Issue: Does the shelter rule protect Manufacturers?

Decision: No. Motion for summary judgment denied, except as to the Robinson note.

Opinion by Justice Lehner: "Manufacturers contends that its 1986 holder in due course status was unaffected by the 1990 endorsements because there was no delivery of the instruments to the Partnership. However, Manufacturers functioned in a dual role, acting for itself and as the Partnership's agent. Once the notes were endorsed in favor of the Partnership, only the Partnership had the right to negotiate them. Manufacturers accomplished this by receiving the notes as the Partnership's agent and endorsing them in blank in that same capacity. The endorsement stamp used states that Manufacturers was signing as 'Agent, Attorney-in-fact for 600 Grant Street Associates Limited Partnership.' Therefore, albeit only for a brief period, the notes were upon such negotiation owned by the Partnership, although if the allegations against it are proven, not as a holder in due course.

"What then was Manufacturers' status when the notes were then renegotiated to it? It contends that even if it did not reacquire the notes as a holder in due course in 1990, summary judgment is still appropriate under the 'Shelter Rule' embodied in UCC § 3-201(1), which provides: 'Transfer of an instrument vests in the transferee such rights as the transferor has therein, except that a transferee who has himself been a party to any fraud or illegality affecting the instrument or who as a prior holder had notice of a defense or claim against it cannot improve his position by taking from a later holder in due course.'

"Under the Shelter Rule, a transferee obtains the rights, not the status, of the prior holder in due course.

"The Shelter Rule is designed to guarantee a holder in due course a ready market for its negotiable instrument....

"'Thus, when a transferee takes an instrument from a holder in due course the transferee takes free from all claims and defenses to the same extent as did the holder in due course even if the transferee is aware of those claims and defenses. If this was not the rule, a holder in due course could be deprived of a market for the instrument if the obligor widely disseminated notice of a claim or defense ... [which would] harm the holder in due course by destroying the market for the instrument....'

"The purpose behind this shelter principle is to protect the holder in due course so that he can sell what he has purchased. The statute therefore permits a holder with notice of defenses to acquire the rights of a holder in due course.

"The Shelter Rule, however, does not necessarily protect Manufacturers under the facts at bar. When the Partnership acquired title to the notes in 1990, it was allegedly a party to the asserted fraud and a prior holder who had notice of defenses against the notes. Therefore, if the allegations against it are proven, the Partnership is not eligible for the Shelter Rule protection or holder in due course status. Hence, the question arises whether Manufacturers can be sheltered under UCC § 3-201(1) if its transferor is specifically denied that protection.

"Since the same policy consideration in favor of a holder in due course does not apply to a party to a fraud or a prior holder who had knowledge of defenses, if the Partnership is found to have fallen within the exceptions of the Shelter Rule, it is consistent with the statutory policy to prohibit it from improving its position and the market for its instrument by also denying any transferee acquiring the notes from it (in this case Manufacturers) shelter under the statute. The fact that Manufacturers was a prior holder in due course does not aid it under the language of the section.

"Why Manufacturers endorsed the notes as it did in 1990 remains a mystery. Absent such endorsements, it could, based on the facts set forth in the submitted papers, enforce the notes as a holder in due course. But, as a consequence of its inexplicable unilateral actions it faces losing that substantive right, without having procured any seeming benefit from the endorsements, as the court finds no statutory provision governing commercial paper that entitles plaintiff, as a matter of law, to the rights of a holder in due course under the unusual circumstances presented herein.

"Accordingly, as there are numerous questions of fact concerning the Partnership's alleged fraudulent acts and Manufacturer's knowledge in 1990 of asserted defenses and claims, the motion for summary judgment, except as to the Robinson note, is denied.

"With respect to the Robinson note, which was endorsed directly to plaintiff in 1987, there is no evidence that plaintiff then had knowledge of any defense or infirmity with respect thereto, and thus it became a holder in due course upon acquiring the note. Consequently, plaintiff is entitled to summary judgment against Robinson for the outstanding principal on the note, plus interest, with the claim for attorneys' fees to be severed for an assessment of damages after the filing of a note of issue and statement of readiness."

against liability when an instrument gets into the hands of an HDC. HDC status does not, however, eliminate *all* defenses. Some defenses can still be asserted against an HDC and, if proved, will defeat or reduce recovery on an instrument. Those defenses that cannot be asserted against an HDC or a **holder through a holder in due course (HHDC)** are called **personal or limited defenses**. Personal defenses can still be asserted against anyone who is not an HDC or a holder through an HDC.

Those defenses that can be used against anyone, including an HDC or an HHDC, are called **real or universal defenses**. The most obvious example of these defenses is forgery; certainly a person whose name has been forged on an instrument should not be required to pay it, even to an HDC. The basic distinction is between **void-type** defenses (= real) and **voidable-type** defenses (= personal), except for minority, which is recognized as a real defense. If a defense is one that "makes the obligation a nullity," it is a real defense. If there is no contract, there is no contract, even if the instrument is in the hands of an HDC. On the other hand, if a defense merely relates to some problem between two of the parties on an instrument, it is a personal defense, and it cannot be asserted against an HDC.

Real Defenses

Article 3's main list of real defenses is found in Section 3-305. In addition, 3-403 (unauthorized signatures) and 3-407 (alteration) describe real defenses.

Unauthorized Signature or Forgery

When someone signs your name to an instrument without your permission, you are not liable, even to an HDC. The result is the same whether your name is simply forged or whether it is signed with an indication of agency authority that does not exist. The section says that this unauthorized signature is "wholly inoperative" against you unless you ratify it or are estopped by your conduct from denying its validity. It is, however, effective to impose full liability on the instrument against the forger, in favor of someone who pays or takes the instrument in good faith.

Material Alteration

When the contract of any party to an instrument has been changed "in any respect" by an alteration, Section 3-407 says that the alteration is material. If this material alteration is also fraudulent, the party whose contract is changed is discharged from further liability on the instrument unless that person assents to the change or is estopped from asserting it. As the one exception to this rule, an HDC can still enforce the instrument "according to its original tenor"; that is, the terms before the alteration. A nonmaterial or nonfraudulent alteration does not discharge any party.

As an example of these rules, if you signed a blank check and lost it, and the finder filled in $600 as the amount, an HDC could force you to pay the $600. If you signed a check and filled it in for $6.00 and someone found or stole the check and altered it to read $600, an HDC could force you to pay only the original $6.00. However, if you filled in the amount spaces with blanks after the number 6 and the word *Six*, so that the thief or finder could very easily add "00" and "Hundred," you would be estopped from asserting the alteration and would have to pay the full $600.

Minority

Although minority or infancy generally results in a voidable obligation rather than a void one, Section 3-305 makes it a real defense to liability on a negotiable instrument. Infancy is a defense to the same extent that it would be against liability on a simple contract. In other words, infancy can be asserted against an HDC. On the other hand, because this section distinguishes between "defenses" and "claims" and states that an HDC owns the instrument free of *all* adverse ownership claims, the minor cannot get back the instrument that he or she signed. Remember that the endorsement sections make the minor's endorsement fully effective to transfer ownership of the instrument, so that there can be later HDCs in the chain of title.

Other Incapacity

As to other types of contractual incapacity, Section 3-305 makes these a real defense only if they void the contract ("nullify the obligation of the obligor"). This rule thus refers us to the applicable state law on insanity, aliens, married women, and so on, as discussed in Chapter 11. Unauthorized acts by corporations or governmental agencies that resulted in the issuance of negotiable instruments would probably also fall into this category.

Void-Type Duress

Duress may be either a real or a personal defense, depending on whether it results in a void or a voidable obligation. "Gun-to-the-head" duress "renders the obligation of the party a nullity" and can thus be asserted against an HDC. The "threat-of-criminal-prosecution" type of duress would make a contract only voidable, not void, and thus it cannot be asserted against an HDC.

Void-Type Illegality

When some part of a transaction violates a criminal statute, the state's statutory and case law may make the contract involved either void or voidable. Section 3-305 again refers us to these state law distinctions to see whether the particular illegality is a real or only a personal defense.

Fraud in the Execution

The most obvious example of fraud in the execution occurs when the nature of the instrument itself is misrepresented. You are told you are merely signing a receipt for delivery of merchandise or an authorization form for repairs on your car, but the document is folded, or covered, or switched, so that you cannot see it is really a negotiable instrument. The section also extends this defense to the case when you do know you are signing a negotiable instrument but you do not have a reasonable opportunity to obtain knowledge of its "essential terms." In either of these cases, you must show that your ignorance of the character and terms of the instrument was "excusable ignorance"—in other words, that you acted reasonably under the circumstances. This is a fact question, depending on such things as the signer's age, education, business experience, and literacy; the nature of the representations made to the signer and the signer's reasons for relying on them; the availability of independent information; and the need to act quickly. If your ignorance was "excusable," you have a real defense, good even as against an HDC; otherwise, you do not.

Discharge in Bankruptcy

Section 3-305 also spells out a result that should be obvious anyway: The debtor's discharge in bankruptcy or other insolvency proceedings can be asserted against anyone, even the HDC of a negotiable instrument signed by the debtor.

Notice of Other Discharge

A holder cannot qualify as an HDC after taking the instrument with notice that all parties have been discharged. But it is possible to become an HDC with notice that one or more parties have been discharged, as long as there's no notice that all have been. The holder then qualifies as an HDC as to the remaining parties, but cannot collect against the ones known to have been discharged when the instrument was transferred. Discharge of an endorser by canceling his or her signature would be a typical example of this rule. The HDC could not collect against that endorser, but would still be an HDC as to all the remaining parties.

Personal Defenses

Because Section 3-305 says that an HDC can enforce an instrument free of "all defenses except" those listed, any other defense against liability on the instrument is only a personal defense. Some of these personal defenses are listed here.

Ordinary Contract Defenses

Any defense a party could assert in a simple contract suit can be asserted against anyone who does not have the rights of an HDC. This general rule would include such things as undue influence, breach of contract by the plaintiff (including any counterclaim by the defendant), and setoffs which the defendant might have from unrelated transactions.

Consideration Defenses

Section 3-303 mentions "issued without consideration" specifically because there is an initial presumption that the negotiable instrument was issued for legally sufficient consideration. If it was not or if the promised consideration was not properly delivered, the burden of proving the defense is on the defendant. These consideration defenses are only personal ones, and thus they cannot be used against an HDC.

Voidable Defenses

Tying back into Section 3-305, any defense based on lack of capacity, duress, or illegality that does not "render the obligation of the party a nullity" (void) is only a personal defense. Remember that minority is a real defense even though the minor's contracts are voidable rather than void.

Fraud in the Inducement

In contrast to fraud in the execution, fraud in the inducement, which is the typical fraud case, provides only a personal defense. Here the party does know that he or she is entering into a contract but is deceived as to the consideration to be received or the other terms and conditions of the contract. Fraud in the inducement also exists when a party could reasonably have discovered the nature of the contract that was signed, but simply did not bother to read it. The contract was misrepresented, but on the facts there is only a personal defense, and so the HDC collects.

Delivery Defenses

Numerous cases involve irregularities in the delivery or completion of an instrument. When an instrument has been signed or endorsed in bearer form, the fact that it has been negotiated by a thief or finder will not prevent a later party from being an HDC and collecting on the instrument. The fact that you just signed your check as drawer, intending to fill in the payee's name and the amount later, and that the check was completed by the thief or finder, will not change this result; the HDC still collects. An HDC would also collect when you signed a check and delivered it to your intended payee with instructions to fill in the amount you owed, but your payee filled it in for a larger, unauthorized amount. Finally, an HDC is also protected when a check has been properly filled in and delivered, but delivered subject to some oral condition that is not expressed in the instrument. If the condition is not fulfilled, a defense exists that could be asserted only against someone not having the rights of an HDC.

Agency Defenses

When someone signing on behalf of a corporation, a partnership, or an individual has general authority to sign negotiable instruments, the fact that a particular instrument was improperly signed is only a personal defense.

Federal Trade Commission Regulation

After the early 1970's, court decisions that the Federal Trade Commission (FTC) could issue rules with industrywide application, the FTC has been much more vigorous in the consumer protection field. One of the most important and widely discussed FTC rules relates to the HDC status of holders of consumer installment sales contracts. This rule, Regulation 433, was previously discussed in Chapters 13 and 24. It applies to a consumer's purchase or lease of goods with a price of $25,000 or less. Consumer purchases over that amount are subject to normal HDC rules. Regulation 433 does not apply to payments made by check or to purchases of land or securities.

Although the rule does not say so in so many words, the net effect is that in most cases all of a consumer's defenses are real defenses. Likewise, no waiver-of-defenses clause in an installment contract for the purchase of goods or services is effective against the consumer-buyer. Holders and assignees are thus remitted to their position under the old common law: The assignee "steps into the shoes of the assignor" and is subject to all available defenses that the debtor can prove. Although the exact dimensions of this FTC rule are still subject to litigation, revolving charge accounts (such as a Sears charge account) signed before August 1, 1977, and credit card accounts have been exempted from its operation.

Estoppel

It has been, and still is, true that a person with a claim or defense may be estopped by his or her conduct from asserting it. This is as true of real defenses as of personal defenses. If you typically signed your checks with a rubber stamp, and you lost the stamp and did not bother to alert your bank, you probably ought to get stuck when your bank continues to honor the checks that someone else has prepared in your name with your lost signature stamp. Estoppel clearly applies where you have made out your check or note in such a way

Exhibit 27.2: Defenses

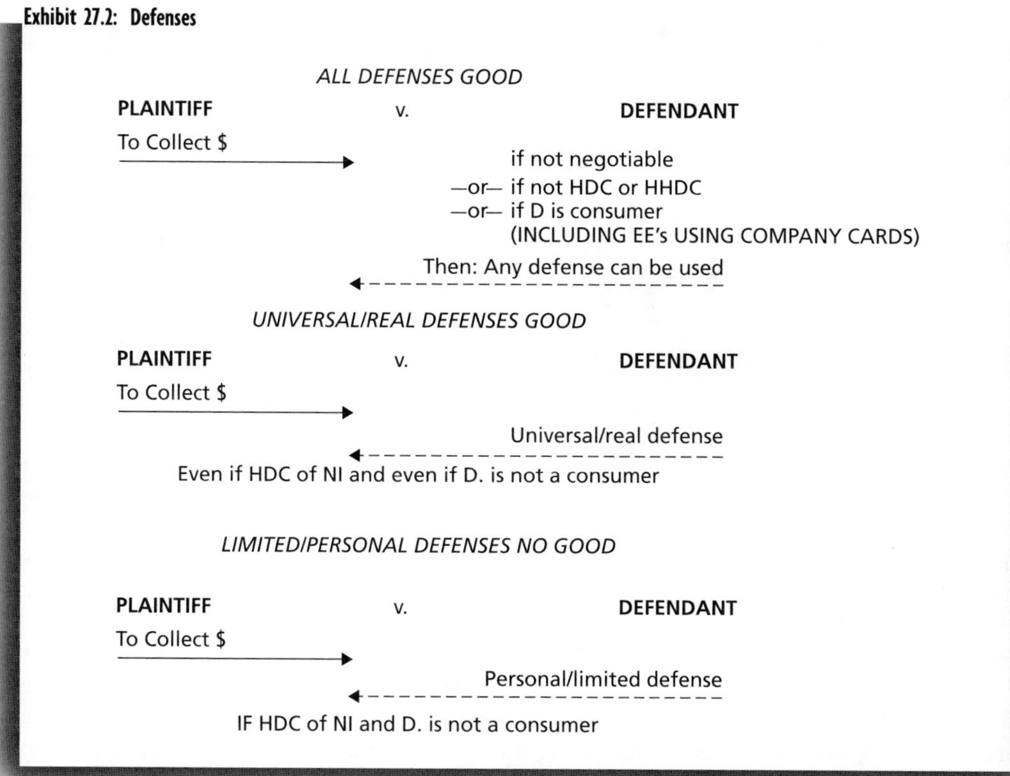

as to permit alteration very easily (e.g., large, inviting gaps after words and numbers). A more interesting question for litigation is whether gullible people ought to be permitted to assert the new FTC rule to avoid liability on the notes they signed, under circumstances in which the payee has obviously misrepresented the contents of the contract but the maker or drawer did not bother to read it.

Discharge

In addition to the defenses already discussed and the conditions precedent to endorsers' liability discussed previously, parties may be discharged from liability on an instrument in several other ways.

Payment

The most obvious and most frequent method of discharge is payment of the instrument to the holder. Perhaps the most important rule for most of us is found in Section 3-310(b)(1): "Payment . . . of the check results in discharge of the obligation to the extent of the amount of the check." In other words, when your check is paid by your bank, you are both discharged of liability on the check and liability on the underlying debt for which it was given as payment. The one danger point here is that this discharge is not effective against a later HDC of the instrument if the HDC does not have notice of it. If you pay your promissory note, but you do not get it back from the holder, and there is no indication on it that it has been paid or that it is overdue, a later HDC could make you pay it again.

The *Farmers National Bank* case illustrates the importance of maintaining clear records showing which business associate owes what and who has paid what.

Tender of Payment

When payment is offered to a holder on or after the due date of the instrument and the holder refuses payment for some reason, the party offering full payment is discharged only

CASE 4

Farmers National Bank v. Winfield Implement Co., Ltd. & Steele

702 N.W.2d 465 (IA 2005)

Facts: Jerry Dean Steele owned 49 percent of Winfield, and Jim Hassenfritz owned 51 percent. In 1997 Steele and Jeff Suter opened a corporate checking account for Winfield at Farmers National Bank. The account agreement stated: "Each of you also agrees to be jointly and severally (individually) liable for any account shortage resulting from charges or overdrafts, whether caused by you or another with access to this account." Steele and Suter signed the agreement. As of September 26, 2001, the account was overdrawn by $372,068.81. Hassenfritz owed Winfield some $290,000, so he and his wife signed a promissory note at Farmers for that amount and deposited the funds in the Winfield account. Steele and his wife signed a promissory note at Farmers for $83,000, and also deposited that money in the Winfield account. On April 18, 2002, Steele paid their note in full. After deducting payments and proceeds of sales of company assets, $217,934.08 remained unpaid on the Hassenfritz note. Farmers sued Winfield Implement and Steele for that amount, plus interest, costs, and attorney fees.

The trial court granted a summary judgment to defendants, but the court of appeals reversed and remanded. Defendants appealed.

Issue: Did the proceeds of the promissory notes constitute payment of the checking account overdrafts?

Decision: Yes. Court of Appeals reversed; trial court judgment affirmed.

Opinion by Chief Justice Lavorato: "It is undisputed that there were overdrafts in the Winfield Implement checking account that resulted in a negative account balance. However, when the cash proceeds from Steele's and Hassenfritz's promissory notes were applied to the account, the account balance was positive. As a result, the account overdrafts—the sole subject of the Bank's petition—no longer existed at the time the petition was filed. The defendants correctly argued in their motion for summary judgment that 'the overdrafts complained of in the petition have been fully satisfied and paid by virtue of the promissory notes executed by Jerry Steele and James Hassenfritz. Steele has fully paid his promissory note. Steele has no liability for the Hassenfritz note which remains in default. Plaintiff's only remedy should be against Hassenfirtz on the Hassenfritz note.'

"In their application for further review, the defendants also correctly argue that 'this is not just a replacement of one piece of paper for another representing a debt.' Rather, once the proceeds of the promissory notes were deposited into the Winfield Implement checking account, 'there was no longer a shortage upon which personal liability could occur under the language of the checking account agreement.'...

"Here, there was more than a 'mere promise in writing to pay.'... The proceeds of the promissory notes were applied to the checking account shortage in a manner described by the Bank as a 'customer deposit,' thereby completely eliminating the overdrafts and shortage.... 'If by agreement a note is taken in absolute payment of a debt, the debt is extinguished whether or [not] the note is paid, leaving the creditor's remedy on the note.'...

"The district court correctly concluded that the shortage resulting from the overdrafts was paid in full by the deposits of the proceeds of the two promissory notes.... We therefore vacate the court of appeals decision and affirm the district court judgment."

to the extent of any additional interest, court costs, or attorney fees later incurred. This rule also applies when the maker or acceptor of a nondemand instrument is ready and able to make payment on the due date at the place or places specified in the instrument, and payment is not demanded by the holder. The holder's refusal of tender discharges any party who has a right of recourse against the party making the tender.

Simple Contract Discharge

As between themselves, any two parties can agree that the liability of one to the other is discharged by any mechanism that is sufficient to discharge liability on a simple contract. All the forms of new agreements discussed in Chapter 14 also apply here: novation, rescission, release, waiver, and accord and satisfaction. Once again, no HDC unaware of these new arrangements is bound by them.

Cancellation or Renunciation

As a special negotiable instruments rule, Section 3-604 provides that any holder may discharge any party from further liability on an instrument by destruction or mutilation of the instrument, by cancelling the party's signature, by surrendering the instrument to the party, or by a separate writing signed and delivered to the party. All of these but the last would seem to be sufficient to put third parties on notice of the discharge.

Reacquisition Rules

Because of the very special nature of endorsers' liability, Section 3-207 provides some specific rules for the discharge of intermediate parties when someone reacquires an instrument. As against the reacquirer, such parties are discharged. If Arnie, Bernice, and Carole have signed an instrument as endorsers, and Arnie reacquires it, he cannot sue Bernice or Carole. Arnie could, however, renegotiate the instrument to Donald, who could sue Bernice or Carole if he qualified as an HDC. On the other hand, if Arnie crossed out the signatures of Bernice and Carole, Donald would be on notice that they had been discharged and so he could not sue them either.

Suretyship Rules

As is true under the law of suretyship generally (see Chapter 23), a holder of an obligation who impairs someone's rights of recourse or repayment from another person discharges the party whose rights are impaired. In the preceding example, if Donald had crossed out Bernice's signature, he would have discharged her from liability on the instrument, thus impairing Carole's rights against Bernice, and so Carole would have also been discharged. A holder can avoid such an "automatic discharge" by expressly reserving rights against the other party (Carole), but when he (Donald) does so, that has the effect of preserving the right of secondary recourse (by Carole against Bernice). Donald can say: "I won't sue Bernice, but I reserve my right to sue Carole." This also preserves Carole's right to sue Bernice if Carole has to pay Donald.

Likewise, when some piece of property is being used as collateral for an obligation, and through the negligence or intentional conduct of the holder its value is lessened or lost, secondary parties are discharged to that extent.

Significance of This Chapter

Because the major purpose of the merchant community in developing negotiable instruments was to protect HDCs to whom they had been transferred, and to permit HDCs to enforce them free of most common defenses, an understanding of how one becomes an HDC is crucial to understanding the uses and the significance of commercial paper.

The requirements for HDC status are relatively easy to list but sometimes more difficult in specific fact situations. Always, to be an HDC, one must first be a holder, which means that there can be no required endorsement missing. The holder's good faith is usually assumed, but circumstances may indicate otherwise. It is usually easy enough to determine whether the holder has given value for the instrument. Most litigation seems to center on whether or not the holder had notice of a claim or defense when the instrument was acquired. Generally, one who acquires an instrument from an HDC acquires all the HDC's rights to enforce it, even if the acquirer cannot personally qualify as an HDC. This shelter rule thus further protects the HDC, by providing greater marketability for the instrument. Although FTC Regulation 433 has made HDC status less significant in most consumer transactions, it is still very important in all other commercial transactions involving negotiable instruments.

Even HDCs will not necessarily collect every instrument from any party whose name appears on it. Some defenses, such as forgery and material alteration, involve such fundamental irregularities that they can be used against any plaintiff, including an HDC. Others, such as fraud in the inducement, are primarily just difficulties between two of the parties to the instrument and should not be available when an HDC sues to enforce the instrument. Under FTC Regulation 433, consumers are generally able to assert any defense that they can prove to defeat or reduce the claim of any plaintiff. For nonconsumers who have signed negotiable instruments, the distinction between real and personal defenses continues to be important.

In addition to defenses against liability that may be available, both claimants and obligors need to know the circumstances under which an existing liability may be discharged. Here, too, an HDC may be prevented from collecting the instrument from a particular party because that party's liability has been discharged.

IMPORTANT TERMS AND CONCEPTS

bearer paper
blank endorsement
bona fide purchasers (BFP)
endorsement
for value
good faith
holder
holder in due course (HDC)
holder through a holder in due course (HHDC)
negotiation
notice
order paper
personal or limited defense
qualified iendorsement
real or universal defense
restrictive endorsement
shelter rule
special endorsement
voidable-type
void-type

QUESTIONS AND PROBLEMS FOR DISCUSSION

1. Why can a person in possession of an unendorsed order instrument not be a holder of it?

2. What is the significance of the UCC's impostor rule?

3. Why must a person have given value to qualify as an HDC of commercial paper?

4. What is the meaning and significance of the shelter rule?

5. Emile, a state employee who had retired and was receiving monthly pension checks, died. The state, unaware of his death, continued to send checks to the same address. His daughter, Lillian, endorsed and cashed these checks each month. Her scheme was not discovered until she died some 8 years after her father. The state sues its drawee bank to recover the funds.

   How should the court decide this case? Explain. (Looking ahead, what other argument should the drawee bank make against being held liable?)

6. On October 31, Armand Korzenik's law firm had received $15,000 in trade acceptances from its client, Southern New England Distributing Corporation, "as a retainer for services to be performed." Korzenik had been retained by Southern on October 25 in connection with certain antitrust litigation. He did some work for Southern from October 25 to October 31, but there was no evidence as to its value. He also paid co-counsel in the antitrust case some money, but there was no indication of the specific amount. Korzenik sued to collect on two of the trade acceptances, due November 1 and December 1, in a total amount of $1,900. Southern had defrauded Supreme, although Korzenik did not know that when he took the trade acceptances. The lower courts found for Supreme Radio.

   What decision on appeal, and why?

7. Graff & Sons, a real estate brokerage partnership, represented Fred Klomann in his trading of certain real estate for the Countryside Shopping Plaza. The firm owed Klomann $13,000 as a result, and Robert Graff (a partner) gave him three notes, one for $5,000 and two for $4,000 each. Klomann hired Graff & Sons to manage the shopping center and orally promised that the commissions that the firm earned for that work could be offset against the amount that Graff owed him. Robert Graff estimated that his salary of $300 a month (total $14,700) more than offset the firm's debt to Klomann. Klomann specially endorsed the notes to his daughter, Candace Klomann. She examined them and then handed them back to her father so that he could collect them for her. Klomann later scratched out Candace's name, inserted his wife Georgia's name, and delivered the notes to Georgia. Georgia sued to collect. The trial court ruled that the money earned by Robert as manager of the shopping center could not be offset against the money that Graff & Sons owed Klomann, and it entered a summary judgment for Georgia.

   Is the trial court correct? Why or why not?

8. Money Mart cashes payroll and government checks for a fee. Epicycle Corporation is a Colorado employer that pays its employees by check. On February 16, Epicycle issued a payroll check payable to John Cronin in the amount of $278.59. During the term of his employment, Cronin had borrowed money from Epicycle to be offset by subsequent wages.

   The sequence of events is not clear, but Cronin's employment was terminated, and an Epicycle employee who was unaware of Cronin's indebtedness gave Cronin his final payroll check. Epicycle ordered payment on the check stopped. Cronin cashed the check at one of Money Mart's locations on February 22. Money Mart deposited the check, sending it through normal banking channels.

The check was returned to Money Mart marked "Payment Stopped."

Money Mart brought suit for the amount of the check, claiming that as an HDC of the dishonored check it was entitled to collect from Epicycle.

Is Money Mart correct? Explain.

9. Randum Bank did a large amount of business issuing certificates of deposit (CDs). When the CDs matured and were paid by the bank, they were stamped "PAID" and stored in file cabinets. The bank changed its storage procedures and sold the (supposedly) vacant file cabinets to Horace Zito, a used furniture dealer who regularly dealt with the bank. The cabinets were always sold "as is," including any that happened to be locked.

   Zito held a "parking lot sale" at his store, and sold the last four cabinets to Chuck Woode. (Woode had asked about buying one cabinet, and Zito said he could take it for nothing if he took all four.) Woode gave one (locked) cabinet to his friend Mickey Rich. When the cabinet later tipped over and popped open, Rich discovered about 1,500 CDs. Nearly all were stamped paid, but seven—with a total value of nearly $7 million—had not been cancelled.

   Randum Bank sues Rich for return of the seven CDs; Rich counterclaims for $7 million. Who wins, and why?

10. In 1991, Anthony Maggio invested in a limited partnership organized by a former astronaut to develop an optoelectronic scanner to provide perimeter security for sprawling properties such as airfields, oil fields, and pipelines. Maggio paid for his partnership interest with a promissory note for $75,000, to mature on October 1, 2000. The limited partnership negotiated the note to a venture capital company, who in turn negotiated it to Goldman Sachs. Goldman Sachs negotiated the note to Northwestern Insurance in 1998, along with a batch of other notes from the same limited partnership, at a 50 percent discount.

    At maturity, Maggio refused to pay the note, and Northwestern Insurance sued. Maggio claims that he was defrauded by the astronaut, and that Northwestern is not an HDC—for two reasons. Is he correct? Explain.

11. Fred Fentress contracted to install a flood control system for Eric and Beulah Hodge. Beulah wrote Fred a check for $500, as a down payment. When Fred and the system components did not show up at Hodges' home on the scheduled day, Eric called Fred and "cancelled" the contract. Eric also called the drawee, Citicorp Savings, and told them not to pay the check. Fred cashed the check at Kedzie & 103rd Currency Exchange, who presented it to Citicorp Savings, where it was dishonored. Claiming it was an HDC, Kedzie sued Beulah Hodge. Beulah claims that because Fred was not licensed as a plumber, as required by Illinois law, she has a real defense against her secondary contract liability as drawer of the check. Is she correct? Why or why not?

CHAPTER 28

Bank Deposits and Collections

Chapter Objectives

This chapter will:

- Explain the process of collecting checks through the banking system.
- Define the various types of banks involved in this process, as covered in Uniform Commercial Code, Article 4.
- Explain the relationship between the depositor and the depositary bank.
- Discuss the relationship between the depositor and the payor bank.
- Indicate when a drawee bank may charge its customer's account.
- Discuss a bank's liability to its customer for wrongful dishonor of an item properly payable.
- Alert the reader to the importance of electronic funds transfers.

Commercial banking in the United States is a huge industry. The nation's 10,000 plus commercial banks hold over $1 trillion in assets. Banks fund many business purchases of land, buildings, and equipment and provide many other services to business. The banking industry has been subjected to considerable governmental regulation, but the 1980s saw a movement toward deregulation of many banking operations. This chapter will not attempt to cover all of the various banking regulations but will focus instead on Article 4 of the Uniform Commercial Code (UCC), Bank Deposits and Collections. UCC Article 4 sets out the basic legal rules for the relationship between a bank and its customers and for the processing of negotiable (and non-negotiable) instruments.

Checks: The Collection Process

Clearinghouses and Federal Reserve Banks

The next time you get back a canceled check that you have sent to an out-of-state creditor (e.g., a book club or a record club), look at the back of it. All of those funny, multicolored stamps indicate that your humble little check has passed through several banks and been processed by goodness knows how many computers on its way back to you.

If both the payee and the drawer do business at the same bank, the collection process is quite simple: out of one account and into the other. If both are in the same city, but are customers of different banks, a local **clearinghouse** association of banks probably handles the collection of the check. At the end of each business day, if a bank has presented more (total dollar) items for payment than have been presented against it, it gets a check for the difference from the clearinghouse. If the reverse is true, it writes a check for the total dollar difference to the clearinghouse.

Many **correspondent bank** arrangements also exist for collecting checks and other items, particularly between large metropolitan banks and smaller banks in the same region. The small local bank receiving a check for collection would forward it to its large correspondent bank, which would in turn present it directly to the payor bank or would forward it through one of the 13 **Federal Reserve banks** if the payor bank were located in a different Federal Reserve district.

Your check to your out-of-state creditor might pass through a local bank, a large nearby metropolitan bank, a Federal Reserve bank in that district, a Federal Reserve bank in your district, a large metropolitan bank close to your bank, and finally get presented at your bank for payment (by which time you had better have the money in your account). Over $50 million worth of checks is probably "floating" through this national collection process on any given day. In 1990, when Article 4 was revised, the American Bankers Association estimated that 50 *billion* checks were being written each year. It is therefore obvious that banks (and their customers) need a set of legal rules to ensure that this process goes smoothly.

Dr. LaCombe's problem with his "business director" illustrates the kind of issues that can arise when the process does not go smoothly.

Banks under Article 4

To better spell out the rights and duties of banks in the collection process, Article 4 defines different categories of banks according to their function in the various stages of that process. A **depositary bank** is "the first bank to take an item even though it is also the payor bank," unless the item is presented for immediate payment over the counter. (The depositor, usually the payee/creditor of the drawer, or possibly a later holder of the instrument, takes the item to his or her bank and either cashes it or deposits it.)

The **payor bank** is the bank that is the drawee of a draft. (In the simplest case, when both the drawer and the "depositor" have accounts at the same bank, no other banks will be involved.) An **intermediary bank** is any bank "to which an item is transferred in course of collection except the depositary or payor bank." (In our earlier example, the correspondent banks and the Federal Reserve banks would be intermediary banks.)

When the depositary bank is not also the payor bank, it and all intermediary banks are also called **collecting banks.** (They are collecting, or trying to collect, your paycheck

CASE 1

LaCombe v. Bank One Corp.
953 So.2d 161 (LA App. 3 Cir. 2007)

Facts: Lana Slyfield was hired in 1998 as Dr. LaCombe's receptionist, eventually becoming the "business director," in charge of the front desk. Her duties did not include any accounting or bookkeeping because LaCombe Eye Center had both a bookkeeper and an office manager. Between 1999 and 2003, she stole 532 checks—totaling $69,767.41—from the Center's mail. She forged endorsements (or just wrote "For Deposit Only"), put her own personal account number underneath, and deposited them into her account at Bank One. LaCombe did not have any account at Bank One. Slyfield testified that no one at Bank One had ever questioned her about these deposits. Her scheme was discovered after she was fired for unrelated reasons, and Dr. LaCombe and his wife went over the books in preparation for hiring a replacement employee.

Dr. LaCombe sued Bank One and received a judgment for $63,855.79. Bank One appealed.

Issue: Did either party's negligence contribute to the success of the fraudulent scheme?

Decision: Yes, the bank's negligence did. Judgment affirmed, with damages amended to $68,747.37.

Opinion by Judge Pickett: "We first look at any possible fault on the part of Dr. LaCombe. Each side called an expert witness, a Certified Public Accountant/Certified Valuation Analyst—Robert C. Veasey testified for the plaintiff and Allen Hebert for the defense. Mr. Veasey has been Dr. LaCombe's accountant since the 1980's. He set up the accounting system used by Dr. LaCombe. The summary of his testimony is that there is no accounting system that would totally eliminate the possibility of theft, that one sets up an accounting system based upon a cost-benefit analysis, and that Dr. LaCombe's accounting system was reasonable under the circumstances.

"Mr. Hebert's testimony appeared to be based on hind-sight [sic]. He stated that Dr. LaCombe could have hired more employees and segregated their duties (i.e., instituted additional internal controls), thereby reducing the opportunity for any one employee to misdirect funds, or that Dr. LaCombe could have 'out-sourced' his billing and collection functions to an independent firm.

"Both of these 'solutions' would probably have kept Mrs. Slyfield from tapping the company coffer. However, considering the size of Dr. LaCombe's practice and applying a cost-benefit analysis, we find no error in the trial judge rejecting the Bank's expert opinion that the lack of internal controls in the accounting system in Dr. LaCombe's office contributed to the 'non-detection of the embezzlement scheme.' Accordingly, we find Dr. LaCombe exercised 'ordinary care' in the conduct of his practice and did not 'substantially contribute' to the making of his forged signature on the checks in question.

"In assessing the fault of the Bank, we take into account the Bank's failure to follow its own policies. Ms. Noy Kuy, an Assistant Banking Center Manager for the Bank, testified that the Bank recognized that a sole proprietorship was a form of business. She further testified that it was the Bank's policy that a check made out to a business, including a check made out to a sole proprietorship, had to be deposited into an account bearing the business's name. However, she stated that checks made out to Rick LaCombe, O.D., Dr. Rick LaCombe, or even Dr. Rick LaCombe d/b/a Lacombe Eye Center would be considered 'personal' rather than 'business' checks and would be handled accordingly. This appears to be in direct contravention of the Bank's own policies. Accordingly, we find the Bank failed to exercise ordinary care in taking the forged instruments and affirm the trial court's determination that the Bank was 100% at fault."

for you.) The last bank in the collection process, the one that actually presents the item to the payor/drawee for payment, is called the **presenting bank.** (A payor bank presenting the item to itself is excluded from this definition.)

Depositor and Depositary Bank

Agency Relationship

In the normal transaction, the depositor remains the owner of the check or other item that is being processed for collection by his or her bank. This rule protects the depositary and intermediary banks by leaving all the risks of ownership of the item with the depositor; all the banks in the collection process are protected so long as they exercise reasonable care in processing the item. This basic rule applies unless there is a clear agreement otherwise, regardless of the form of the endorsement or of the fact that the depositor is permitted to make withdrawals against these funds.

Withdrawals of Deposited Funds

A cash deposit can be withdrawn "as a matter of right" at the opening of the next banking day following its receipt by the bank unless the bank has the right to offset the deposited funds against amounts owed it by the depositor/customer. When the deposit is in the form of a check or other instrument, however, the credit to the customer's account is only **provisional;** that is, the credit is subject to revocation if the instrument is not honored when it is presented to the drawee bank. The depositor/customer thus does not have the right to withdraw these funds until the depositary bank has received a "final settlement" for the item. When the depositary bank is also the payor bank and the item is paid from the drawer's account, the depositor/customer has the right to withdraw the funds at the opening of the second banking day following receipt of the item.

Expedited Funds Availability Act

Congress passed the Expedited Funds Availability Act (EFAA) in 1987 to shorten the time period between the deposit of a check (or other item) and the availability of the dollars the check represents. The Federal Reserve Board has divided the country into check-processing regions. Any deposited check that is payable at another bank in the same region is a "local" check. As of September 1, 1990, the money from a local check must be available to the customer within 1 business day from the day of deposit. For checks drawn against banks outside the depositary bank's region, the funds must be available to the customer within 4 business days of the deposit.

There is also a 1 day rule for cash deposits, wire transfers of money, certified checks, cashier's checks, government checks, checks drawn on branches of the same bank, and the first $100 of a day's check deposits. (The balance of a nonlocal, ordinary check would have to be available within the 4 business days specified by the general rule.)

Longer delay periods are permitted for more unusual transactions or in special circumstances. Deposits made at automated teller machines that are not owned or operated by the depositary bank need not be made available for 6 days. Deposits in new accounts need not be available for 8 days. The bank has an extra 4 days to verify deposits to accounts with repeated **overdrafts** or when it suspects a check may not be collectible. It also has 4 extra days on deposits over $5,000, other than government or cashier's checks.

Customer/Depositor/Holder (and Collecting Banks as Agents) and Payor Banks

As between the holder of an instrument who is trying to collect on it and the payor/drawee bank that is supposedly going to pay it when it is presented, the most important rule is found in Article 3: "A check or other draft does not of itself operate as an assignment of any funds in the hands of the drawee available for its payment, and the drawee is not liable on the instrument until the drawee accepts it" [3-408]. Even if the money is in the drawer's checking account, in other words, the drawee bank owes no direct duty to the holder to pay the instrument. The drawee bank may be liable to its customer, the drawer, for a **wrongful dishonor** of the instrument, as discussed later in this chapter, but that does not mean that the holder/depositor has any direct claim against the payor bank.

Obviously, a drawee bank that has certified a check or accepted a draft is primarily liable on it to the holder thereof and can be sued if it does not pay the check or draft when it is properly presented.

Customer/Depositor/Holder and Drawer

If a deposited item is not paid, for whatever reason, the holder who deposited the item for collection may proceed against the drawer on the basis of secondary contract liability, subject to the rules discussed in Chapter 26. In addition, the depositor/holder may have a case against one or more of the collecting banks when their negligent mishandling of the instrument was the reason for its dishonor. However, a collecting bank is not liable solely on the basis of some prior bank's mishandling of the instrument; its own negligence must be established.

DRAWER/CUSTOMER AND DRAWEE/PAYOR BANK

Article 4 also provides some detailed rules for handling the problems that may occur between a drawer and the drawee bank.

Charging Items against Customer's Account

The drawee bank has a general contractual duty to its drawer/customer to pay items when presented, assuming that there are sufficient funds in the account. As a general rule, when the drawee bank does pay such items in good faith, it can charge the items against the customer's account. Even if an item causes an overdraft to a customer's account, the drawee/payor bank may honor the item anyway, and it has a claim against its customer for the amount of the overdraft.

The general rule for paying overdrafts is, however, subject to some important exceptions. The key phrase in Section 4-401 is "properly payable from that account." If the drawer's signature has been forged, the instrument is not "properly payable" from the drawer's account, and the bank will have to put the money back even if it paid in good faith. The same result occurs when the required signature of an endorser is forged; the money must be returned to the drawer's account because the bank has not paid the right party. If the instrument has been materially altered, the bank that has paid it can charge the drawer's account only "according to the original tenor of the altered item." The drawer's own negligence may prevent the assertion of any of these irregularities against the drawee bank unless the bank was also negligent in paying the item; that is, the bank did not pay in good faith and according to reasonable commercial standards.

Wrongful Dishonor

Whether mistakenly ("computer error") or intentionally, the drawee bank may dishonor an instrument that it should have paid. When this happens, the drawer is at least temporarily embarrassed because his or her good credit is impugned when the check bounces. If this happens by an honest mistake, Article 4 protects the drawee bank by providing that the drawer can recover only damages that were "proximately caused" and "actually proved;" there will be no punitive damages, in other words, for a simple mistake by the drawee bank. Further, the dishonor of a check is not per se defamation of a drawer's reputation, so that actual damages must be proved there, too. Finally, damages resulting from the arrest and prosecution of the drawer under an "insufficient funds" criminal statute may be recovered from the drawee bank *if* they are proved to have been proximately caused by the dishonor.

The issue in the *Grunwald* case is whether the bank had legal grounds for dishonoring the demand for payment against the letter of credit it had issued.

Stop Payment Orders

A check is an order by the customer/drawer to the drawee/payor bank to pay money to the order of the named payee. At least until the check is certified by the drawee bank, the drawer has the right to stop payment, in other words, to countermand the original order. An oral stop-pay order is valid for only 14 calendar days unless it is reconfirmed in writing within that period. A written stop-pay order is valid for 6 months unless it is similarly reconfirmed. In either case, the stop-pay order must be received by the drawee/payor bank "at a time and in a manner that affords the bank a reasonable opportunity to act on it before any action by the bank with respect to the item."

If the drawee/payor bank pays the item anyway, it can still charge its customer's account unless the customer can prove having suffered a loss as a result. (That would be the case, for example, when the customer had a defense that was valid against the holder,

CASE 2

Grunwald v. Wells Fargo Bank
725 N.W.2d 324 (IA 2005)

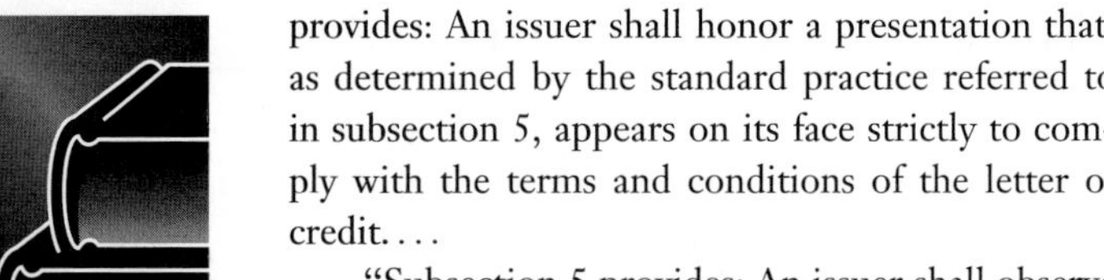

Facts: Dale Grunwald and his lawyer Robert Gallagher were beneficiaries under an irrevocable letter of credit issued by Wells Fargo Bank, at the request of Grunwald's ex-employer—Quad Cities Quality Service, Inc. The express terms of the letter of credit required: "The draft [demand for payment] must also be accompanied by the original of this Letter of Credit for our [i]ndorsement on this Letter of Credit of our payment of such draft." Plaintiffs' original payment demand was accompanied by a photocopy of the letter of credit and was refused. They then made a second demand, this time with their affidavits stating that the original letter of credit had never been delivered to them or that it had been lost. Refused payment again, they sued Wells Fargo for wrongful dishonor of the letter of credit. At the trial, plaintiffs' expert testified that standard banking practice in the area would be to accept a photocopy under these circumstances. Wells Fargo appealed from a summary judgment for plaintiffs.

Issue: Does application of the "strict compliance" rule in this case require an examination of local banking standards?

Decision: No. Judgment reversed, and case remanded for entry of summary judgment for Wells Fargo.

Opinion by Judge Mahan: "Our courts apply a rule of strict compliance to terms stipulated in letters of credit.. . .

"'If courts deviate from the rule of strict compliance and insist in certain undefined situations that banks make payments notwithstanding the fact that the beneficiary failed to comply with the terms stipulated in the letter of credit, the certainty that makes this device so attractive and useful may well be undermined, with the result that banks may become reluctant to assume the additional risks of litigation.'. . .

"The 1995 revisions to the [UCC], enacted in Iowa in 1996, codify the strict compliance standard.. . . [Section 5-108] provides: An issuer shall honor a presentation that, as determined by the standard practice referred to in subsection 5, appears on its face strictly to comply with the terms and conditions of the letter of credit. . . .

"Subsection 5 provides: An issuer shall observe the standard practice of financial institutions that regularly issue letters of credit. Determination of the issuer's observance of the standard of practice is a matter of interpretation for the court. The court shall offer the parties a reasonable opportunity to present evidence of the standard practice. . . .

"The parties differ as to whether a determination of 'standard practice' is necessary in this case. Wells Fargo argues section [5-108(5)] does not permit consideration of extrinsic evidence of standard practice in this case, where the unambiguous language in the letter of credit required presentment of the original letter of credit. . . .

"We think Wells Fargo has the better argument in this case. Central to the unique purpose of letters of credit is the 'independence principle,' which requires the issuer to pay a beneficiary on proper demand regardless of a breach or default on the underlying contract. . . . Thus, 'when a [letter of] credit's terms are clear, a court should not construe them at all.'. . .

"We recognize the revised UCC 'specifically adopts the strict compliance standard as determined by the "standard practice".'. . . However, 'by adopting standard practice as a way of measuring strict compliance,' the drafters endorsed only those cases in which minor typographical errors were overlooked by the court in applying the strict compliance rule. . . .

"Because we hold that application of the strict compliance rule does not require us to look beyond the express terms of the letter of credit in this case, we conclude the district court erred in granting summary judgment to Plaintiffs. We reverse the district court's decision and remand for entry of summary judgment in favor of Wells Fargo."

so that the holder really should not have gotten the money. The bank would have to put that money back in its customer's account.) Obviously, once a check has been certified, the customer loses the right to stop payment.

The *Mid Wisconsin Bank* case shows that a stop payment order does not necessarily relieve the drawer of liability for the check it issued.

Stale Checks

When an uncertified check has been circulating for more than 6 months, the drawee/payor bank is under no obligation to its checking account customer to pay the check. The bank may dishonor the check without any liability for damage even if there is enough money in the account to cover it. If the bank does pay the stale check, in good faith, it may charge the item against its customer's account. It is completely up to the bank, as long as the bank acts in good faith.

Exhibit 28.1: Bank Deposits and Collections

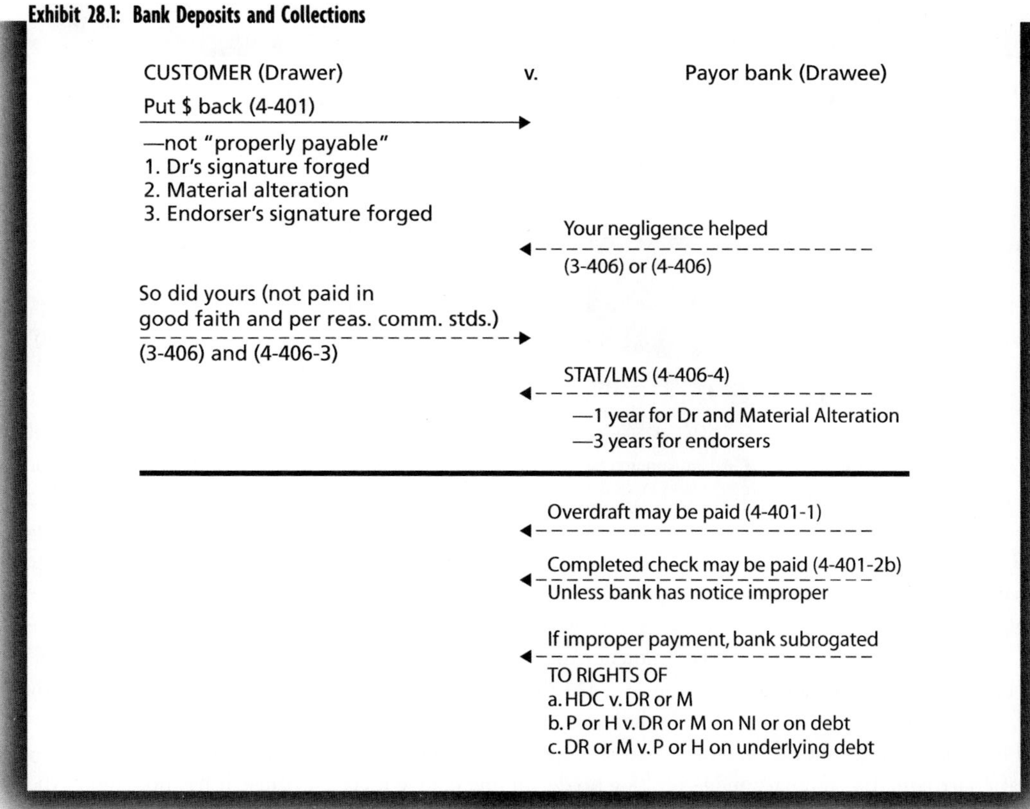

Customer's Death or Incompetence

The Code's rules generally protect a bank from liability in the case in which the customer dies or becomes legally incompetent. "Neither death nor incompetence of a customer revokes [a bank's] authority to accept, pay, collect or account until the bank knows of the fact of death or of an adjudication of incompetence and has reasonable opportunity to act on it" (4-405). Moreover, a bank, even after learning of its customer's death, may pay or certify previously issued checks for a period of 10 days, unless ordered not to by someone claiming an interest in the account. A customer's bankruptcy probably does not terminate the bank's authority to process items until the bank has knowledge or notice of it.

Customer's Duty to Inspect Statements

When a bank makes available an itemized statement and the cancelled items, its customer has a duty to exercise reasonable care and promptness in inspecting the charges and reporting any improper ones to the bank. Failure to do so may prevent a customer from forcing the bank to put money back in the account when an item has been altered or paid over a forged signature or endorsement. However, if the bank failed to exercise ordinary care in paying an item (e.g., if it paid an item that was obviously altered), the customer could still force the bank to put the money back into the account. Finally, whether the customer, the bank, or both were guilty of negligence, this section protects the bank by imposing a 1-year statute of limitations period for claims of alteration or forgery of the drawer's signature. In other words, if you do not notify the bank of the irregularities within that time period, you cannot make it put the money back in your account even if your signature on the check was forged. (A customer still has 3 years to demand recredit for an item paid over an unauthorized endorsement.) The lesson is clear: *Read your bank statement and verify your checks right away.*

The *Falk* case raises the question of how these time limits apply when the Bank has paid the check in "bad faith," and in effect has been a virtual participant in the scheme to defraud the customer.

CASE 3

Mid Wisconsin Bank v. Forsgard Trading, Inc., Forsgard, and Lakeshore Truck & Equipment, Inc.

668 N.W.2d 830 (WI App. 2003)

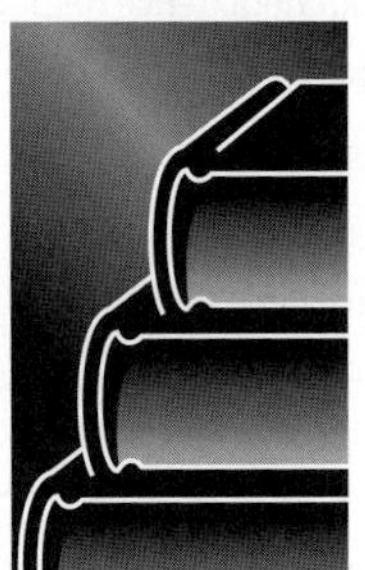

Facts: On May 7, 2001, Lakeshore wrote a check for $18,500 to Forsgard Trading; the drawee was a bank in Ironwood, Michigan. Forsgard Trading deposited the check in its account at Mid Wisconsin Bank. Mid Wisconsin gave Forsgard Trading immediate credit for the check, as they usually did—subject to their right to charge back if the check was dishonored. On May 8, Lakeshore issued a stop-pay order on the check to their Michigan bank; Mid Wisconsin was notified of the stop-pay on May 16. By that time, Forsgard Trading had made several draws against its account, so that when Mid Wisconsin deducted $18,500 for the dishonored Lakeshore check, there was an overdraft. The account had been overdrawn 24 times since it was opened in 1999, but Forsgard Trading had always made deposits to cover them when notified. This time, however, no added funds were deposited. Richard Forsgard (who is not a U.S. citizen) fled to Sweden. The trial court issued a summary judgment for Mid Wisconsin, and Lakeshore appealed.

Issue: Did Mid Wisconsin observe reasonable commercial standards in giving Forsgard Trading immediate credit for the deposited check?

Decision: Yes. Judgment affirmed.

Opinion by Judge Peterson: "Lakeshore maintains that under the circumstances, reasonable commercial standards of fair dealing should have led Mid Wisconsin to place a hold on the check instead of giving immediate credit. Lakeshore notes that Richard Forsgard was a foreign citizen, the check was drawn on an out-of-state account, the check was for greater than $5000, and Forsgard's account had been overdrawn many times in the past.

"To begin with, Wisconsin courts have approved the practice of extending immediate credit on deposited checks....

"Further, we are persuaded by the reasoning of the New Jersey Superior Court in a case with similar facts....

"'It would hinder commercial transactions if depositary banks refused to permit withdrawal prior to the clearance of checks. Apparently banking practice is to the contrary. It is clear that the Uniform Commercial Code was intended to permit the continuation of this practice and to protect banks who have given credit on deposited items prior to notice of a stop payment order....

'[A] depositary bank may properly charge an account by honoring a check drawn by a depositor even though it creates an overdraft. It would be anomalous for a bank to lose its status as a holder in due course merely because it has notice that the account of its depositor is overdrawn.'

"These cases teach that extending immediate credit is not contrary to reasonable commercial standards of fair dealing. Moreover, it does not matter whether, as here, the account had been overdrawn previously. Mid Wisconsin's policy is to place a hold on checks when it has reasonable doubt about the check based on the depositor's history. Here there was no reasonable doubt. Whenever Forsgard had been overdrawn previously, it always deposited funds to cover the overdraft when the bank alerted it to the problem. Mid Wisconsin had no reason to suspect there would be any problem if immediate credit was extended for this check. Consequently, we conclude that Mid Wisconsin observed reasonable commercial standards of fair dealing and therefore was a holder in due course. Under [UCC 3-305], Mid Wisconsin has the right to recover its losses from Lakeshore."

Bank's Right to Subrogation

The drawee/payor bank is further protected by being subrogated to the rights of other parties when it has made a payment despite a stop order or under other circumstances when the drawer or maker has "a basis for objection." When such an "improper" payment has occurred, the bank steps into the shoes of: (1) an holder in due course (HDC), as against the drawer or maker; (2) the payee or any other holder, as against the drawer or maker, either on the paid item itself or on the underlying transaction; and (3) the drawer or maker, as against the payee or any other holder on the underlying transaction. In other words, if the bank has paid someone when it should not have done so, it should not get stuck for the money but should have recourse against another party. The only problem may be finding that other party.

Electronic Funds Transfer

Just as the use of checks and credit cards has made us, to a very large extent, a "cashless" society, use of computer-controlled **electronic funds transfer (EFT)** systems could make

CASE 4

FALK v. THE NORTHERN TRUST COMPANY

763 N.E.2d 380 (IL App. 2001)

Facts: For over 13 years, Ralph Falk employed Patricia Podmokly as his personal assistant. She paid his personal bills, handled his bookkeeping, reported to his accountants, and communicated with his investment advisers. In 1984, she was made a signatory for his checking accounts at Northern Trust. In 1993, she began to take money from his accounts for her personal benefit. At Northern Trust, she drew checks in large amounts, payable to "Cash," and then used them to pay her personal debts, including her own loans and those of her business associates and friends. From 1993 to 1997, she embezzled over $2 million. Podmokly had her own accounts at Northern Trust, including a mortgage and a line of credit. The bank had reviewed her personal tax returns and other financial information in connection with her loans, so it knew that "her income was insufficient to support the account and loan activity she was generating."

Falk sued Northern Trust to recover the funds. The trial court dismissed the case on the basis that it was barred by the timely notice requirements of UCC 4-406(f). Falk appealed.

Issue: Do the 1-year notification requirements apply when the bank has been guilty of bad faith in paying the challenged items?

Decision: No. Judgment reversed, and case remanded for further proceedings.

Opinion by Justice Hall: "Prior to January 1, 1992, section 4-406 of the UCC provided that when a bank sent a statement to a customer accompanied by items paid in 'good faith,' the customer must exercise reasonable care and promptness to examine the statement and promptly notify the bank of an unauthorized signature or alteration. . . .

"In 1992, Section 4-406 was amended and renumbered. . . .

"Eliminated from Section 4-406(a) was the requirement contained in section 4-406(1) that the items be paid in 'good faith.' Section 4-406 goes on to provide that the customer is precluded from asserting the customer's unauthorized signature or any alteration of an item if the customer failed to examine the bank statement with reasonable promptness. . . . The 'preclusion' is treated differently depending on the bank's conduct. If the bank 'failed to exercise ordinary care' in paying the item, then the customer and the bank share the loss. However, if the customer proves that the bank did not pay the item in 'good faith,' the preclusion under subsection (d) does not apply. . . .

"Whether the time limitation set forth in Section 4-406(f) bars an action against a bank where the bank is alleged to have paid items in bad faith is a case of first impression in Illinois. . . .

"Our own examination of Section 4-406, as amended, in its entirety convinces us that Section 4-406(f) does not bar suits brought beyond the time limitation set forth in that section, where the customer alleges that the bank acted in 'bad faith' in paying the items that are the subject of the suit. . . .

"We believe that the legislature's use of the term 'care' in section 4-406(f) cannot be read to include 'good faith.' The fact that, in other parts of Section 4-406, the legislature drew a distinction between 'ordinary care' and 'good faith' in describing the consequences suffered, clearly indicates that the legislature did not intend to limit a bank's liability when it acted in 'bad faith' as opposed to acting with a lack of care when paying an item.

"In addition, we agree with the plaintiff that under the UCC every contract or duty contains an obligation of 'good faith' in its performance or enforcement, therefore, the Bank was required to pay the items in good faith. . . .

"In summary, we conclude that Section 4-406(f) requires that a bank act in 'good faith' when paying the items on the statement in order to claim the protection of the prerequisite of notice requirement contained in that section. As we stated earlier, the public policy behind placing the burden on the customer to determine unauthorized signatures or alterations is not served when the bank is a party, either actively or passively, to a scheme to defraud the customer. . . .

"[Plaintiff] alleged that the Bank had actual knowledge of the fiduciary relationship between Ms. Podmokly and the plaintiff. [He] further alleged that the Bank had accepted checks drawn by Ms. Podmokly on the plaintiff's account for payment of her loans at the Bank, for payment on her personal equity credit line at the Bank and for deposit into her own personal account at the Bank.

"Based upon the above allegations, the Bank was on notice that Ms. Podmokly was acting in breach of her fiduciary duties to the plaintiff. Given the number of years and the numerous transactions alleged by the plaintiff, the Bank's failure to investigate in light of its knowledge of the breach of fiduciary duty constitutes more than a lack of care for which it would be protected by Section 4-406(f). . . .

"We conclude that the plaintiff has set forth sufficient facts to establish that the Bank acted in bad faith rather than with a lack of care when it permitted Ms. Podmokly's check writing activities to continue without conducting an investigation in light of the fact that it was on notice that she was in breach of her fiduciary duties to the plaintiff."

us a "checkless" society. With billions of checks being processed each year, the practical need for such a system is very clear. Properly implemented, it could speed payments, reduce errors, and lower costs. However, EFT presents its own set of problems, which the law is just beginning to confront.

Some phases of EFT are already in widespread use; probably the most common is the "24-hour money machine," located at bank branches and even many supermarkets. The machine enables a customer to use a magnetic card to receive cash, make deposits, pay bills, and transfer funds between accounts. Another frequently used EFT system makes direct deposits of paychecks to employees' bank accounts. More recently, banks have begun to offer their customers the option of paying bills with a telephone call to the bank's computer system; this method saves the customer's time and money. Not yet widely adopted is the most revolutionary EFT system: immediate payment from the customer's checking account through point-of-sale computer terminals located in stores.

It is not hard to imagine some of the problems involved in implementing each of these EFT systems. Inevitably, some customers who fear that they will lose control of their money will resist the change. Some workers like to see their actual paycheck, if only for a few minutes on the way to the bank. (Anyone who has ever been paid by an employer in cash can probably appreciate the different feeling you get from being able to actually see what you have earned in your own hands.)

The money machines are a great convenience, but they also involve security risks late at night and the possibility of lost cards and unauthorized withdrawals. The major difficulty involved with the point-of-sale payment, aside from the loss of the float period that would exist if the bills were totaled once a month and mailed out, is preserving consumer defenses when defective merchandise or services are delivered.

New legal rules to deal with these and other problems have been proposed, both as amendments to the UCC and as separate legislation. New laws have such provisions as: (1) the bank must send each customer a written agreement that includes rights of EFT card users, (2) the bank must provide a monthly statement of all EFT transactions to the customer, (3) the customer must be given a receipt for each EFT transaction, (4) the bank is liable for unauthorized use of the EFT card in the machine unless the customer has been negligent, (5) the bank may not send out unsolicited EFT cards unless the recipients are already its customers, and (6) the bank may not release a customer's financial records without the customer's permission or a court order. These statutes may provide civil and criminal penalties for violation by the bank.

Electronic Fund Transfer Act

Congress passed the Electronic Funds Transfer Act (EFTA) in 1978 to protect consumers who were using these electronic banking services. Commercial accounts are not covered by the EFTA, only those used for personal, family, or household purposes. Nearly all types of consumer cash accounts, at nearly all kinds of financial institutions, are covered by EFTA. The major purpose of the EFTA is to provide information to the consumers who are using such services. Financial institutions must disclose the nature of the systems available; any limits on amounts or frequency of use; the charges for use; the right to see written receipts; how to correct errors; how to report a loss or theft; how to stop payment; the customer's liability for unauthorized use; the bank's liability to the customer; and the rules on disclosure of account information to third parties. The bank must provide monthly statements in any month in which transactions have occurred; otherwise, quarterly statements for the account must be provided.

EFTA limits the customer's liability for any unauthorized use to $50—*if* the customer notifies the institution within 2 business days after learning of the loss or theft of the access card. If the customer does not notify within that 2-day limit, the liability goes up to $500. When the customer receives a statement showing an unauthorized transfer of funds and does not notify the institution of the problem within 60 days, the customer may be held liable for the full amount of the loss. Of course, the bank must prove that the loss would not have occurred if the customer had notified it.

For commercial accounts, a Uniform New Payments Code (UNPC) is being developed by the American Law Institute (ALI) and the Permanent Editorial Board for the UCC.

The entire area of EFT will continue to challenge the ingenuity of judges, lawyers, and legislators.

Significance of This Chapter

Because most individuals and nearly all businesses issue and receive checks in significant numbers, we must have a clear set of rules for processing these instruments. Article 4 of the UCC supplements the general rules for commercial paper found in Article 3 by outlining the relationships between check issuers, check depositors, and the banks involved in the check collection process. Article 4 spells out the rules for charging a customer's checking account, and the circumstances under which the drawee bank has to put the money back in the account. In general, in dealing with their customers, banks will not incur liability if they act in good faith and with reasonable care. Even if they do, however, they may still be liable in cases involving forgery or alteration of instruments. For customer-depositors, it is important to have adequate internal financial controls and to verify bank statements and canceled items promptly.

IMPORTANT TERMS AND CONCEPTS

clearinghouse
collecting banks
correspondent bank
depositary bank
electronic funds transfer (EFT)
Federal Reserve banks
intermediary bank
overdrafts
payor bank
presenting bank
provisional
wrongful dishonor

QUESTIONS AND PROBLEMS FOR DISCUSSION

1. What is the difference between a payor bank and a depositary bank?

2. What is the difference between a collecting bank and a presenting bank?

3. What happens when an item payable from a customer's account is presented to the payor bank and paying it would create an overdraft?

4. What happens when a payor bank wrongfully dishonors an item?

5. John Mahoney had prepared Antone Silvia's tax returns for over 25 years. Mahoney would make out the return and a check for any tax due to the IRS and would then take the documents to Silvia for his signature. In 1987, "apparently in need of some extra cash," Mahoney added $7,000 of nonexistent business profits to Silvia's return, thereby increasing Silvia's tax liability from about $2,000 to $4,625. Mahoney made out one of Silvia's checks to "Internal Revenue Services" and had Silvia sign the check and the return. Mahoney then added "by John J. Mahoney" in the space for the payee's name, endorsed the check "Internal Revenue Services by John J. Mahoney," and exchanged Silvia's check for several cashier's checks at Industrial National Bank. Mahoney used these cashier's checks to pay his personal creditors. Silvia did not notice the alterations made by his accountant when he received the canceled check with his bank statement in February 1988. Silvia first became aware of the problem in April 1989, when the IRS notified him that he had not paid his taxes for 1987. By that time, Mahoney had died. Silvia sued Industrial to force it to recredit his account. The trial court held for the bank; Silvia appealed.

   How should the Appeals Court rule? Explain.

6. Edward and Christine McSweeney, husband and wife, opened a joint checking account with the plaintiff bank in September 1996. Overdrafts commenced almost immediately, but the plaintiff regularly honored the checks. Edward gave the plaintiff two notes, totaling $181,000, to cover the overdrafts and some loans that the bank had made to him. The notes were given in April 1998. Between then and July 1998, when the account was closed, 195 checks were written, totalling $99,063.74. Christine wrote 95, totaling $16,811.43; Edward wrote 100, totaling $82,252.31. After deducting deposits to the account, the cumulative overdraft for this period was $75,983.06. The bank sued Edward on the two notes and sued both McSweeneys for the later overdrafts. The trial court gave summary judgment against Edward on both theories but refused to enter summary judgment against Christine. Plaintiff bank appeals from this refusal.

   Is Christine liable? Why or why not?

7. On October 10, Granite drew a check against its account at Hempstead, made payable to Overseas Equipment Company. Five days later, when Overseas notified Granite that it had not received the check, Granite issued a written stop-pay order on the check and directed Hempstead to simply wire the funds directly to Overseas. Hempstead did so. Granite never renewed its stop-pay order. On November 10, the original check was presented for payment. Without any notice or inquiry to Granite, Hempstead simply paid the stale check and charged Granite's account.

   Was Hempstead correct in doing so? Explain.

8. Zepka drew a check for $4,800 on his account at Socie Bank, payable to SAB Company, and gave the check to Mishmash, one of SAB's sales agents. Mishmash forged SAB's endorsement, signed his own name, and exchanged the check for a cashier's check for the same amount at Socie Bank. The cashier's check was also made out to SAB, so Mishmash again forged SAB's signature and then deposited the check in an account titled "Doors, Inc.," which he had at Capie Bank. Capie Bank sent the check to Commie Bank for collection. Commie Bank collected on the check from Socie Bank. More than a year later, Zepka told Socie Bank that the endorsement on his original check had been forged and Socie put the money back in his account. Socie now sues Capie and Commie.

   What is the result, and why?

PART 5

Law of Organizations

Persons who intend to start a business may choose which form of business organizations to use in conducting their business. These choices range from the sole proprietorship, which is the least expensive to create, is not subject to extensive regulation, but it has the disadvantage of unlimited liability against the owner; to the corporation, which is more expensive to create, may be subject to more extensive regulation, but it offers limited liability. Part Five reviews the various types of business organizations and discusses the pros and cons of each. In Part Five, we also discuss the law of agency that allows us to have others, our agents, conduct business on our behalf. In this part we also review the law governing the issuance and sale of securities, in connection with the legal liabilities of officers and directors.

CHAPTER 29

Agency Law

Chapter Objectives

This chapter will:

- Define "agency."
- Distinguish independent contractors from agents and employees.
- Explain the methods of creating an agency relationship.
- Review the principal's liability for the agent's torts.
- Explain the methods of termination of an agency relationship.
- Discuss the mutual duties between a principal and an agent.
- Outline the potential liabilities between agents and third parties.

Agency is an ancient and very important legal concept. Agency law and contract law describe the two most basic legal relationships. On this foundation many of the other, more specialized legal relationships are erected. The modern law of agency can be traced to the Roman law concerning the owner and slave; the law merchant, a private system of rules and courts that traders and merchants established to govern themselves during the Middle Ages; and the English common law. Because individuals and businesses everywhere must on many occasions conduct their affairs through others, every legal system must somehow deal with the concept of agency. Every contract entered into by corporations and partnerships and many of the contracts made by individuals and unincorporated associations involve the principles of agency law.

Although the law of agency obviously has great "commercial" significance, it is not covered in the Uniform Commercial Code (UCC). One reason for this omission may be that when the UCC was formulated, the basic rules of agency law were already pretty well agreed on by the states and were already summarized in the Restatement of the Law of Agency, Second. The Restatement does not have the force of law, but it is considered to be an authoritative source and it is followed most of the time by most courts.

Basic Definitions

An **agent** is one who has been authorized to act for another person, to conduct that other person's business dealings with one or more third parties. The person who authorizes another as agent is called the **principal.** The "third party" is the other person with whom the negotiations are to be conducted. The third party may also be represented in the transaction by an agent. All corporations must rely on human beings to conduct their actual business affairs, so any contract between two corporations will be negotiated and finalized (and performed) by their agents.

An **employee** is a person who has been hired by someone to do a particular job for that person. Employees, as such, do not have the power to act as agents and make contracts with third persons on behalf of their employer. The same person, however, may be both an agent and an employee. The sales clerk in a retail store is clearly an employee of the store, but is also an agent, with the authority to make sales to customers and to receive payment for the goods sold. A friend taking your coat to the dry cleaners for you would be your agent, but not your employee. A factory worker with no authority to deal with third parties is an employee, but not also an agent.

Before we look at the various ways in which the agency relationship can be created (and terminated), it is necessary to distinguish another arrangement that involves the use of others to conduct one's affairs—the independent contractor.

Independent Contractors

Independent Contractors Distinguished from Agents/Employees

As a rule, a person who employs an **independent contractor** to perform services is liable neither for torts committed by the independent contractor in performing the job nor for subcontracts made by the independent contractor to get the job done. Independent contractors are, of course, liable for their own torts (and for the torts of their agents and employees) and for their own contracts. Litigation frequently arises, however, when the independent contractor has gone out of business, lacks the financial resources to cover a substantial claim, or is simply out of the jurisdiction and not available, or at least not conveniently available, for suit. The key issue in these cases is whether the relationship in question was really an independent contractor-employer relationship, which results in nonliability, or was a principal-agent, which results in the principal/employer's being held liable in tort and/or contract.

The primary test used by the courts to distinguish these legal relationships is the degree of control the employer/principal exercises over the person in the middle; that is, the independent contractor or the agent/employee. The general idea is that with independent contractors the employer contracts only for results and leaves the details of the job to the independent contractors, although given the right set of facts, these too could be agents/employees.

Put in the simplest terms, a person using an independent contractor controls *what* gets done, but the independent contractor decides *how* it gets done. With an agent/employee, the principal/employer not only determines *what* gets done but also has the power to determine *how* it gets done. If you hire an employee to help you put aluminum siding on your house, you can tell that person what size hammer to use, what size nails to use, where to place the nails, and so on. If you hire Mr. Shatturglas, "the aluminum siding king," to do the job for you, you contract only for a good, skillful job, and Shatturglas determines the nail placement and all the other details of how the job gets done.

The nature of the relationship the parties have created is essentially a fact question, for determination by the court. The label that the parties have attached to that relationship is not conclusive, nor is the "intent" of the parties, nor is what the parties "thought" they were creating. The facts speak for themselves in each case because the parties may easily be mistaken as to what the law is or they may be attempting to avoid legal responsibilities by using the independent contractor label as a smoke screen. Among the factors that a court may consider significant are "whether the one employed is engaged in a distinct business, whether in the locality the work is usually done under supervision or by a specialist without supervision, skill required, furnishing of tools and equipment, time limit of employment, method of payment, whether [the] work is a part of [the] regular business of [the] employer, whether [the] parties believe they are creating one or the other relationship, and whether the principal is or is not in business."

CASE 1

Zimmerman v. Elm Hill Marina
839 S.W.2d 760 (TN App. 1992)

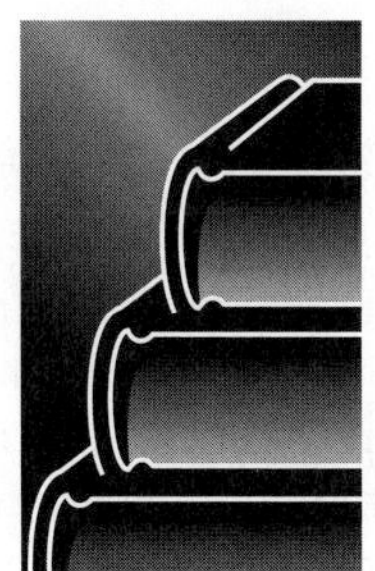

Facts: Plaintiff, Emily Zimmerman, appeals from the trial court's order granting the defendant Elm Hill Marina's motion for summary judgment. Also named as defendants are Ed Rafalowski, individually and d/b/a Elm Hill Marina, L & R Incorporated d/b/a Elm Hill Marina, Brentwood Bodyguard and Security, Inc., and Roy Tanner.

Elm Hill Marina entered into a lease agreement with the Secretary of the Army for the marina to operate a business within the J. Percy Priest Dam and Reservoir Project Area. The lease, which authorized the marina to furnish docking facilities for privately owned boats, prohibited the marina from using the premises or permitting them to be used for "any illegal or immoral business or purpose" and from permitting "any activity which would constitute a nuisance" on the premises.

Under a separate agreement, the defendant, Brentwood Bodyguard and Security, Inc. provided security services for the Marina. The defendant, Roy Tanner, was employed by the security company as a guard.

At about 10:30 AM on Sunday, March 26, 1989, Tanner, while on duty at the marina, observed Plaintiff's decedent, Dr. Daniel P. McCoy, go from the parking lot to his boat. According to Mr. Tanner, Dr. McCoy was staggering and did not have good control of his faculties. Dr. McCoy fell while getting out of his car, while crossing the parking lot, and again while approaching the marina ramp. Dr. McCoy then crawled out on the pier to his boat and passed out on its bow. Mr. Tanner followed Dr. McCoy to make sure he did not fall in the water and drown. Mr. Tanner then returned to his normal duties.

Another witness observed Dr. McCoy lying on the deck of his boat at about 11:30 AM the same day. The witness stated that Dr. McCoy appeared to be intoxicated in that when he tried to sit up, he would fall over and hit his head on the deck. The witness also reported that at about 3:45 PM he saw Dr. McCoy's keys, t-shirt, and newspaper, but he did not see Dr. McCoy.

On Monday, March 27, 1989, Dr. McCoy's body was found in Percy Priest Lake. An autopsy revealed that his death was caused by drowning and that his blood alcohol level was 0.26 percent.

Plaintiff, the personal representative of Dr. McCoy's estate and the guardian of his sole surviving heir at law, filed this lawsuit against the defendants for Dr. McCoy's death. Plaintiff's theory of liability as to the marina was predicated on the argument that the lease agreement between the marina and the Secretary of the Army created a duty to Dr. McCoy in tort. Specifically, plaintiff argued that the duty was not to permit the premises to be used for any illegal purpose and not to permit on the premises any nuisance. Because Dr. McCoy's level of intoxication was illegal and constituted a nuisance, plaintiff reasoned, the marina breached its duty to Dr. McCoy by failing to deny him access to the marina and, thus, proximately caused his death. Further, plaintiff argued that the marina was liable under the theory of respondeat superior in that the marina's agents, the security company and Roy Tanner, breached the aforementioned duty.

Issue: Was the security company an independent contractor?

Decision: Yes. Judgment affirmed.

Opinion by Judge Farmer: "In determining liability under the theory of respondeat superior, the courts have recognized the decisive question to be whether the defendant had the power or right to control the wrongdoer's specific conduct or manner of doing work.... The question of control is one of fact, and each case must depend on its own facts.... Factors considered by this Court have included, but are not limited to, whether the defendant paid the worker's salary and Social Security taxes; whether the defendant provided the worker with employee benefits, such as an optional retirement fund; and whether the defendant had the power to terminate the worker's employment at that time....

"In support of its motion for summary judgment, the Marina submitted the affidavit of its president, Edward C. Rafalowski. In his affidavit, Mr. Rafalowski stated that the Marina entered into a contract with the security company to provide security services for the Marina on an independent contractor basis. Additionally, he stated that the Marina did not control the manner in which the security guard performed his duties nor did it pay the security guard. Instead, pursuant to the contract, the Marina paid the security company, which in turn paid the security guard.

"Plaintiff filed a memorandum in opposition to the Marina's motion for summary judgment. In her memorandum, Plaintiff neither contradicted the affidavit of Mr. Rafalowski nor filed opposing affidavits or depositions thereto. On appeal, Plaintiff chooses to rely on her pleadings and on the written contract between the Marina and the security company. Although this contract clearly specifies that the security company is an independent contractor, Plaintiff points to provisions which state that the Marina will set the schedule of the hours and numbers of guards needed, that the Marina will make payments to the security company, and that the security guards will perform their services pursuant to guidelines furnished by the Marina. We note, however, that this last provision reiterates that the security company and its guards are independent contractors....

"Plaintiff has failed to respond by affidavit or otherwise setting forth facts which would show that either the security company or security guard was an employee of the Marina. Once the Marina filed its affidavit demonstrating an independent contractor relationship, Plaintiff's reliance on her pleadings and the security agreement was insufficient to create a genuine issue of fact regarding an essential element of her claim, the theory of respondeat superior. Further, in her amended complaint Plaintiff alleged that Roy Tanner was an employee of the security company, and the Marina admitted this fact in its answer. Since this fact was admitted, Plaintiff cannot now take a position to the contrary. Under these circumstances, we hold that the trial court did not err in granting the Marina's motion for summary judgment."

Independent Contractors under Statutes Regulating Employer-Employee Relationships

The nonliability aspects of the independent contractor relationship as compared to the agent/employee relationship tend to make businesses and individuals prefer to conduct their affairs through independent contractors whenever possible. However, the tort and contract areas are not the only places in which the law deals differently with independent contractors and their employers. In general, employers of independent contractors escape regulation under statutes designed to "protect" employees. Employers of independent contractors do not have to withhold state or national income tax, do not have to withhold or pay social security taxes, do not have to pay unemployment compensation taxes, do not have to provide workers' compensation coverage for the independent contractors, and are not subject to minimum wage or employment discrimination statutes. Moreover, independent contractors have no rights to organization and collective bargaining under the National Labor Relations Act (NLRA).

Statutes often contain their own definition, for their purposes, of who is an employee and who is an independent contractor. Typically the board or agency charged with the enforcement of such a statute may make its own administrative determination as to who is subject to the statute's provisions, and often employers have to challenge the board or agency in court if they wish to claim an exemption for independent contractors employed by them.

Franchisees as Independent Contractors

A business that sells a widely advertised product or service through local franchised "dealers" (e.g., McDonald's, Kentucky Fried Chicken, and General Motors) must avoid overstepping the boundaries that separate the independent contractor relationship from the principal-agent relationship. The business wants to minimize its legal liability and regulatory exposures by using independent contractors to sell its products or services. At the same time, however, it wants to ensure that certain quality standards are met by each franchisee-dealer. The dilemma is that the greater the degree of quality control it exercises, the more likely it is that the franchisee will be held to be an agent-employee rather than an independent contractor for both liability and regulatory purposes. Ultimately, each case presents a fact question for the court.

Exceptions to the Nonliability Rule for Contracts and Torts of Independent Contractors

There are at least three well-recognized exceptions to the nonliability aspects of employing independent contractors.

Contracts by the Independent Contractor

Nearly all states have mechanic's lien statutes, which provide that persons who supply labor or materials for improvements on real estate can file claims against the real estate if they are not paid. These laws generally do not make the owners of the real estate personally liable for the debts their independent contractors owe to laborers or material suppliers, but the results have almost the same effect: Owners must pay off the claims to clear the title to the real estate. Of course, the landowner who is forced to pay off such third-party claims can recover from the independent contractor, if the contractor is still solvent and available for suit.

Extra-Hazardous Activities

When the work for which the contractor is hired involves a clear risk of injury to others, the employer will be liable when such injuries occur. Examples of such activities include construction of dams and reservoirs, blasting, excavations near a highway, spraying of poisons, clearing land by fire, and razing buildings. These kinds of operations call for special precautions, and the employer should remain liable for any contractor negligence when such jobs are being done.

Nondelegable Duties

Nondelegable duties may be created by statute, by contract, or by case law. In Chapter 13, we discussed contractual duties that could not be delegated due to their personal nature. Statutory and case law rules create nondelegable duties on the part of a railroad to keep its crossings in good repair, a city to keep its streets in good repair, a business to provide a safe place for employees and customers, and others. In each of these cases, the employer can be held liable for the negligence of a contractor hired to perform the duty, at least when the negligence relates directly to the job itself. Of course, the employer could also be held liable for any personal negligence, such as providing the contractor with improper plans for the job or hiring a contractor who was not qualified to do the job. Most courts would also disallow the exemption when the employer reserved the right to supervise, or did in fact supervise, the performance of the job.

Personal Negligence by Employer of Independent Contractor

Quite apart from the issue of employer's liability for torts by the independent contractor, the employer can clearly be held liable for his or her own torts. The employer is liable for any personal negligence in connection with the work being done. The employer can be held liable for negligence in failing to select a qualified contractor, for failing to require the contractor to take needed safety precautions, or for inadequate instructions or equipment furnished to the contractor. If the employer directs or controls part of the job, negligence in doing so would also make the employer liable. The employer would also be held negligent for failing to make a proper inspection after the job was done to make sure it had been done properly. In any of these cases, the negligence is the employer's own, not that of the independent contractor.

Creation of the Agency Relationship

In General

The agency relationship is created by the mutual consent of the parties thereto, the principal and the agent, but whether it exists or not depends on the legal significance of what the parties actually said and did rather than what they "really intended." In other words, a court may find that agency exists even though the parties did not really intend that result. As a general rule, agency may be created by oral or written words or by conduct. There is no generally applicable Statute of Frauds section for agency agreements, although many states require written authority when an agent is to execute real estate documents for the principal. Depending on the state, other particular types of agency agreements may also have to be in writing. A signed, written statement of agency authority is usually called a **power of attorney,** making the agent an "attorney in fact" for his or her principal as to the matters contained in the document.

Although agency is usually based on a contract, with the agent being compensated for his or her services, the relationship can also exist without any contract at all. For example, your roommate is going to the cleaner and agrees to take your coat there for you as well. Your roommate is acting as your agent when making the contract with the cleaner to have the coat cleaned, even though he or she is just doing it as a favor, with no compensation. If the cleaner ruins your coat, you could sue it for breach of contract. An agency was created. Your agent made an offer on your behalf, and the cleaner accepted the coat for cleaning. You would not, however, be able to sue your roommate for breach of contract if he or she decided not to take your coat to the cleaner after all, because there was no agency contract.

Because the agent is to contract on behalf of the principal, the principal is the party who must have contractual capacity. Principals who are minors have the same rights of disaffirmance as they would have if they had made a contract in person, including the right to disaffirm whatever contract they may have made with their agents. The fact that agents are minors, or lack capacity for some other reason, would not generally have any impact on the contracts that they made on behalf of their principals. However, agents who are minors can disaffirm any employment contract that they made with their principals.

The burden of proving that an agency relationship exists is on the person alleging it, typically the third party who dealt with the alleged agent. The third party has no case against the alleged principal unless it can be shown that the principal gave the agent the authority to do the acts in question. To hold the principal liable for the agent's actions, the third party must show that the agent had express authority, implied authority, apparent authority, or authority by ratification.

Express Authority

Express authority is authority that has been given specifically. Orally or in writing, the principal has told the agent to perform some specific act: "Sell my GM stock"; or "Go over to the lumberyard, and buy us ten more two-by-fours." In these simple examples it is pretty clear what is intended, but there are many situations in which the principal's meaning is not so easy to determine. When the words used are more general, when the agent is to conduct a series of complicated transactions, or when the agent is left "in charge" for a period of time, a court may be called on to see whether the principal's instructions did or did not include the acts in question.

The Restatement of Agency, Second, is of some help here, at least as to what is involved in "managing" a business. Section 73 lists these things: buying supplies and equipment, making repairs, hiring and firing employees, selling goods held for sale, paying and receiving payment of debts, and doing those things that are incidental, usual, necessary, or ordinary in such a business.

Courts are usually reluctant to imply the power to issue negotiable instruments because such a power, quite literally, gives the agent a blank check with the principal's name on it. As a general rule, third parties should not take such instruments signed by an alleged agent unless these parties have so dealt with the agent in the past or unless they have a clear, express statement of authority from the principal.

Implied Authority

Not every detail needs to be stated expressly for actual authority to exist. Once an agent has been given the express authority to do a particular job, the implication is that the principal also intended the agent to have the authority to do whatever was necessary and appropriate to get the main job done. This **implied authority** gives the agent the authority to take care of all incidental details. Also, when an emergency threatens the success of the enterprise, the agent on the spot, in charge of the principal's affairs, is assumed to have the authority to meet and deal with the emergency. And finally, implied authority may exist on the basis of a course of prior transactions between the principal and the agent or on the basis of custom in their trade or business.

Any implied authority that might otherwise exist would be negated by express instructions to the contrary, but third parties might still be able to rely on the "appearance" of authority unless they were aware of the specific instructions.

In addition to these fundamental ideas on implied authority, many rules as to whether particular powers have been given to the agent are generally agreed on, through long-established usage and custom and by expression in the Restatement of Agency. For instance, once an agency relationship has been established, notice to the agent is effectively notice to the principal, as to those facts related to the conduct of the agency. Likewise, admission by the agent, as to matters within the scope of that person's authority, bind the principal. And, although there are some earlier cases to the contrary, most courts today would probably hold the principal liable for representations made by the agent about the subject matter of the agency.

Third parties dealing with agents should be particularly careful about making payments to them because the courts are reluctant to imply the power to receive payment unless there is a clear industry custom or a history of prior dealing between the parties. Store clerks who sell merchandise usually have the power to receive payments; traveling salespeople who merely solicit orders for goods or services usually do not. An agent who does have authority to receive payments can accept only money, checks (usually), or credit cards (in accordance with the principal's policies). The agent cannot take other forms of property or services in payment unless expressly authorized to do so.

Apparent Authority

Even though the principal did not actually give the alleged agent the express or implied authority to do the acts in question, the principal may be held liable nonetheless if he or she has created the "appearance" of authority. That is, if the principal has created a situation in which it appears to a reasonable third party that the agent was authorized to do what he or she did, the principal is estopped to deny that an agency relationship existed once the third party has changed legal position in reliance on the appearances. This may also be called agency by **estoppel.**

Apparent authority may arise when secret instructions or limitations of authority are communicated to the agent but not to third parties. Or it may arise when actual authority was terminated (as when the agent was fired) but third parties were not notified of the termination. Apparent authority may also arise from some other business relationship between the principal and the agent and even in a situation in which there is no business relationship between them at all.

Notice in the following case that there is no "appearance" of agency authority simply because of the existence of a marital relationship.

Ratification

Finally, the principal may be held liable for an agent's actions on the basis of **ratification.** When the agent acted without authority but the principal wishes to accept the results of the agent's action anyway, the principal has the power to do so. In most states the principal must act to ratify before the third party discovers the agent's lack of authority and decides to repudiate the contract. If the principal does so, the third party ends up with exactly the contract he thought he was making and should have no basis for complaint.

Ratification may be express ("I agree to be bound on this contract"), or it may be implied from the principal's retention of the benefits of the unauthorized transaction or

CASE 2

Citibank (S.D.), N.A. v. Hauff
668 N.W.2d 528 (SD 2003)

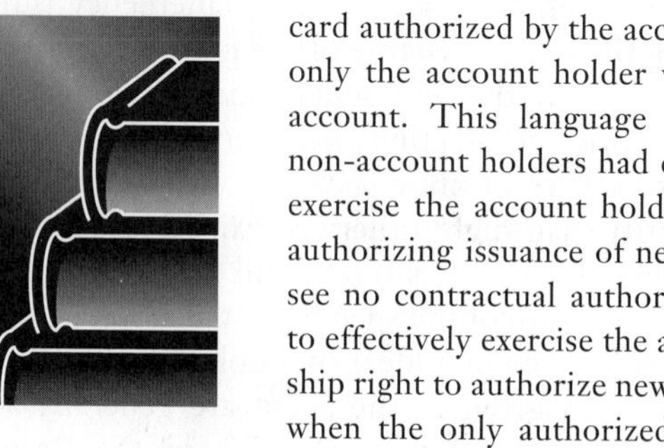

Facts: While she was married to David Hauff, Tonette Hauff opened a Citibank credit card account. She authorized David to use the account and got him a card. Pending their divorce, they paid off their credit card accounts, including Citibank. Their other accounts were closed, but Citibank was not, although Tonette says she requested that it be closed. After the divorce, the Citibank cards expired. Citibank sent renewal cards to their original address, but Tonette was no longer living there. David activated the new cards with a telephone call, without telling Tonette, and proceeded to use them. After making aggressive collection efforts, Citibank sued Tonette for the account balance. She denied liability and counterclaimed for barratry and intentional infliction of emotional distress. Both parties moved for summary judgment. The trial court granted Tonette's motion for summary judgment on the account balance and denied Citibank's motion for summary judgment on the counterclaim. Citibank appealed.

Issue: Does one spouse, as a spouse, have implied or apparent authority to act as agent for the other?

Decision: No. Summary judgment for Tonette is affirmed.

Opinion by Justice Zinter: "[T]he terms of the Citibank agreement control the disposition of this dispute. In that agreement, Citibank created two separate and distinct classifications of users. That distinction is seen in the burdens and privileges given the 'account holder,' but denied to a mere 'authorized user' in the 'Additional Cards'" provision of the agreement. That provision allowed an account holder like Tonette to name another person as an authorized user of the card. However, the authorized user's privileges were specifically limited to the right of access and use of 'the card' and account. The agreement did not also make an authorized user an 'account holder,' nor did it grant the authorized user any of the other rights that the owner of the account possessed. . . .

"Thus, under the agreement, an 'authorized user' was only given the privilege of access and use of the account and card authorized by the account holder. Moreover, only the account holder was responsible for the account. This language does not suggest that non-account holders had contractual authority to exercise the account holder's ownership right of authorizing issuance of new cards. Therefore, we see no contractual authorization for a mere user to effectively exercise the account holder's ownership right to authorize new renewal cards at a time when the only authorized cards had expired on their face.

"This conclusion is supported by Citibank's own testimony. . . .

"Citibank was entitled to summary judgment on Tonette's counterclaim for intentional infliction of emotional distress and barratry. . . .

"For conduct to be 'outrageous,' it must be so extreme in degree as to go beyond all possible bounds of decency, and to be regarded as atrocious, and utterly intolerable in a civilized community. . . .

"The conduct that Tonette relies upon . . . does not rise to this level: it only involves collection contacts reasonably made by collecting creditors. . . .

"Tonette . . . asserts that Citibank collection representatives yelled, made her feel like a criminal, and threatened garnishment. Although Tonette and her friends testified that Tonette was very upset by these collection calls, a reasonable person is expected to be able to withstand some extent of collection activity . . .

"Civil barratry exists when a party brings a frivolous or malicious claim. . . .

"Although we hold today that Citibank did not have a legal claim against Tonette, Citibank's action was not frivolous or malicious. Citibank raised rational arguments based on the evidence and law in support of its claim. . . .

"Consequently, we reverse the denial of Citibank's motion for summary judgment on the intentional infliction of emotional distress and barratry claims. We affirm the summary judgment in favor of Tonette on the collection claim."

from other conduct of the principal that indicates an intent to be bound to the contract. Obviously, the principal must have knowledge of the transaction when it speaks or acts to ratify; the principal generally will not be held to have ratified something it did not know about. Equally obviously, the principal has to ratify the entire transaction; the principal cannot just accept the benefits and refuse to assume the reciprocal obligations. Generally, when the principal does ratify an unauthorized contract, the courts say that the principal has also agreed to accept responsibility for whatever conduct of the agent produced the contract, including false warranties and fraud.

Ratification, like any of the other cases against the alleged principal, must be proved by evidence; agency is not necessarily assumed just because some other relationship exists.

Generally, to be ratifiable, the act must be one which the principal could have authorized when it was done and when it is ratified.

Undisclosed Principal

A principal is "undisclosed" when the third party is unaware of the principal's existence or identity; that is, the third party either does not know that an agent is being dealt with or knows that an agent is being dealt with but does not know whom the agent represents. In most cases it probably makes no difference to the third party who is being dealt with, as long as the third party gets the contracted return performance. An **undisclosed principal** is given substantially the same rights to enforce the contract as is a disclosed principal.

Because in certain circumstances it would be unfair to force the third party to do business with an undisclosed principal, the courts have worked out some limitations. These limitations are much the same as the limitations covering the assignment of contract rights. For instance, a third party cannot be forced to perform personal services for an undisclosed principal, to loan an undisclosed principal money, or to sell to an undisclosed principal on credit. In such cases the third party's rights might be prejudiced by being forced to do business with someone other than the party believed to have been contracted with—the agent. A court may also refuse to force the third party to perform for an undisclosed principal when both the principal and the agent were aware that the third party would have refused to make the contract if the principal's identity had been disclosed.

To make sure that the third party's rights are fully protected, the third party is given the choice of holding either the agent or the undisclosed principal liable for the promised return performance, once the third party discovers the principal's identity. This election may be made either expressly or impliedly after the principal becomes known. The undisclosed principal is not liable to the third party under such an election when the third party has already received full performance under the contract, when the principal has already settled accounts with the agent on the basis of conduct by the third party, or when the principal's name does not appear on a negotiable instrument (because of the special liability rules for negotiable instruments).

Principal's Liability for Agent's Torts

When a person conducts affairs through agents or employees, the doctrine of respondeat superior holds the person liable for any wrongs they commit in trying to accomplish that person's business. Agents or employees are, of course, always liable for their own torts. The only question is whether the torts were committed within the "scope of employment" or the "scope of authority," so that the principal/employer is also liable. This is a form of vicarious liability—that is, liability for the wrongful acts of another, not for one's own conduct.

The main question to be decided in such cases is one of fact: Was the tort committed by the agent or employee within the scope of employment? If the answer is yes, both the principal/employer and the agent/employee are liable for the tort; if the answer is no, the agent/employee is liable but the principal/employer is not. An agent/employee may have been within the "scope of employment" even when that person violated direct instructions, so long as the trier of fact feels that the agent or employee was attempting to accomplish the assigned job. On the other hand, if agents are "off on a frolic of their own," or "doing their own thing," the principal is not liable for their actions. The "frolic" rule, however, may be subject to special motor vehicle statutory liabilities.

Two other important variables in deciding the scope-of-authority question are the character and the location of the tort. If the tort was intentionally committed, rather than just negligence, the agent/employee may have been motivated by personal reasons rather than the employer's needs; if the intentional tort was so motivated, the employer ought not be held liable. The place where the tort occurred may be important in proving its connection with the principal/employer's business. However, acts on the "premises" may not be within the scope of employment.

Sexual harassment cases present especially difficult issues, as seen in the *Burlington* case.

CASE 3

Burlington Industries v. Ellerth
524 U.S. 742 (1998)

Facts: From March 1993 until May 1994, Kimberly Ellerth worked in a two-person office in Chicago as a salesperson in one of Burlington's five divisions. She alleges constant sexual harassment by Ted Slowik, her second-level supervisor. Slowik was a unit vice-president within the division; he had authority to hire and promote, subject to his supervisor's approval.

Ellerth emphasized three specific instances: an invitation to a hotel lounge while they were both on a business trip, at which time Slowik told her to "loosen up" and warned her, "you know, Kim, I could make your life very hard or very easy at Burlington"; a promotion interview during which Slowik told her she was not "loose enough," and then rubbed her knee—and told her after she got the promotion "you're gonna be out there with men who work in factories, and they certainly like women with pretty legs"; and two business telephone calls, during which he said, "I don't have time for you right now, Kim—unless you want to tell me what you're wearing" and "are you wearing shorter skirts yet, Kim, because it would make your job a whole heck of a lot easier." Even though she knew that Burlington had an anti-harassment policy, she told no one in authority about these incidents.

Ellerth sued Burlington Industries. Burlington denied it was legally responsible for Slowik's actions. The U.S. District Court for the Northern District of Illinois granted summary judgment for Burlington. The Seventh Circuit, sitting en banc, reversed.

Issue: Is an employer vicariously liable for a supervisor's sexual harassment if the employee suffers no tangible adverse job action?

Decision: Yes, *if* the supervisor is "aided by the agency position." Summary judgment for employer is reversed, and case is remanded for trial.

Opinion by Justice Kennedy: "[A] supervisor acting out of gender-based animus or a desire to fulfill sexual urges may not be actuated by a purpose to serve the employer.... The harassing supervisor often acts for personal motives, motives unrelated and even antithetical to the objectives of the employer.... There are instances, of course, where a supervisor engages in unlawful discrimination with the purpose, mistaken or otherwise, to serve the employer....

"The general rule is that sexual harassment by a supervisor is not conduct within the scope of employment.

"Scope of employment does not define the only basis for employer liability under agency principles. In limited circumstances, agency principles impose liability on employers even where employees commit torts outside the scope of employment. The principles are set forth in the much-cited S.219(2) of the Restatement: '(2) A master is not subject to liability for the torts of his servants acting outside the scope of their employment unless ... (d) the servant ... was aided in accomplishing the tort by the existence of the agency relation.'...

"In a sense, most workplace tortfeasors are aided in accomplishing their tortious objective by the existence of the agency relation: Proximity and regular contact may afford a captive pool of potential victims.... Were this to satisfy the aided in the agency relation standard, an employer would be subject to vicarious liability not only for all supervisor harassment, but also for all co-worker harassment, a result enforced by neither the EEOC nor any court of appeals to have considered the issue.... The aided in the agency relation standard, therefore, requires the existence of something more than the employment relation itself....

"Whether the agency relation aids in commission of supervisor harassment which does not culminate in a tangible employment action is less obvious. Application of the standard is made difficult by its malleable terminology, which can be read to either expand or limit liability in the context of supervisor harassment. On the one hand, a supervisor's power and authority invests his or her harassing conduct with a particular threatening character, and in this sense, a supervisor is always aided by the agency relation.... On the other hand, there are acts of harassment a supervisor might commit which might be the same acts a co-employee would commit, and there may be some circumstances where the supervisor's status makes little difference....

"In order to accommodate the agency principles of vicarious liability for harm caused by misuse of supervisory authority, as well as Title VII's equally basic policies of encouraging forethought by employers and saving action by objecting employees, we adopt the following holding.... An employer is subject to vicarious liability to a victimized employee for an actionable hostile environment created by a supervisor with immediate (or successively higher) authority over the employee. When no tangible employment action is taken, a defending employer may raise an affirmative defense to liability or damages, subject to proof by a preponderance of the evidence.... The defense comprises two necessary elements: (a) that the employer exercised reasonable care to prevent and correct promptly any sexually harassing behavior, and (b) that the plaintiff employee unreasonably failed to take advantage of any preventative or corrective opportunities provided by the employer or to avoid harm otherwise. While proof that an employer had promulgated an anti-harassment policy with complaint procedure is not necessary in every instance as a matter of law, the need for a stated policy suitable to the employment circumstances may appropriately be addressed in any case when litigating the first element of the defense. And while proof that an employee failed to fulfill the corresponding obligation of reasonable care to avoid harm is not limited to showing any unreasonable failure to use any complaint procedure provided by the employer, a demonstration of such failure will normally suffice to satisfy the employer's burden under the second element of the defense. No affirmative defense is available, however, when the supervisor's harassment culminates in a tangible employment action, such as discharge, demotion, or undesirable reassignment."

Termination of the Agency Relationship

In discussing the termination of the agency relationship, we must first distinguish between the principal's power to terminate and the principal's right to do so. As a rule, the principal has the power to terminate the agency at any time by revocation, provided the principal gives proper notice of termination to the agent and to third parties. Whether the principal also has the right to do so depends on the principal's arrangement with the agent. If there is a contract between them, the principal's wrongful termination may make the principal liable to the agent for breach, even though the agent's power to make contracts with third parties has been effectively terminated. The same distinction applies to the agent; the agent can effectively terminate the relationship at any time by simply refusing to continue as agent but may be liable to the principal for breach of contract.

The agency relationship may also be terminated, without liability for breach, by mutual agreement between the principal and the agent, by fulfillment of the purpose of the agency, or by expiration of an agreed duration. An agency may also be terminated without liability by the same sort of "impossibility" excuses as apply to contracts generally: the death, insanity, or bankruptcy of either party; the subsequent illegality of the agency's purpose; the destruction of the subject matter of the agency; a substantial change in business conditions; or war.

The *Capuzzi* case involves a slightly more complicated question regarding the death of a principal.

Notice of Termination

Generally, when termination has occurred by the act of either the principal or the agent, or by their mutual agreement, notice of the termination must be given to third parties. Otherwise, the agent may still have apparent authority to continue business as usual. Any third party who has actually dealt with the agent as an agent in the past must be given actual notice, either orally or in writing. A newspaper ad or similar "constructive notice" is sufficient for all other third parties, whether or not they ever read the ad or have it called to their attention. When the termination of an agency occurs by "operation of law," no notice at all need be given to third parties, except that an insane principal is bound on contracts made by third parties in good faith before that person is judicially declared incompetent or before the third parties receive other notice of the principal's incapacity.

Agency Coupled with an Interest

As an exception to the general rule that gives the principal the power to revoke an agency at any time, the principal cannot revoke an agency in which the agent has a personal interest in the subject matter—an **agency coupled with an interest.** This phrase describes the cases where the agent is more than just a hired hand, where there is some other underlying relationship between the parties—most typically, a debtor-creditor relationship. The agency power has been given to the agent as the creditor of the principal to try to make sure that the agent gets paid. In such cases, the principal cannot revoke the agent's power and the agent's power is not terminated by the subsequent incapacity of either party.

Most courts have held that the agent's power is terminated by the principal's death unless the principal has also transferred some sort of ownership interest in the subject

CASE 4

Capuzzi and Capuzzi v. Fisher

684 N.W.2d 677 (MI 2004)

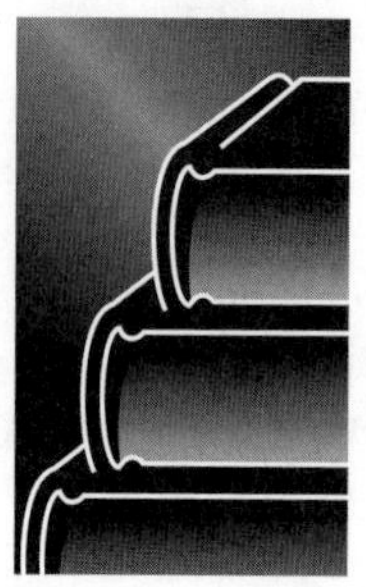

Facts: Dr. Eugene Capuzzi died, leaving a will which directed that his shares in a limited partnership go to his three children, equally. Before he died, he had given his son Michael a durable power of attorney authorizing Michael to have ownership of the shares transferred to himself and the other son Eugene Jr., thereby excluding daughter Christina Fisher. Michael contacted the limited partnership on August 10 and 11, 1998, and instructed them to make the transfer. They had not yet done so when Dr. Capuzzi died on August 14. On August 19, they wrote Michael a letter, refusing to transfer the shares to him and Eugene Jr. The probate court granted a summary judgment to the sons, but the Court of Appeals reversed. The sons appealed.

Issue: Can the third party refuse to complete performance when the principal dies after the agent has completed all the principal's performance requirements?

Decision: No. Judgment of the Court of Appeals is reversed.

Opinion by Justice Cavanaugh: "It is a longstanding legal principle that a duly authorized agent has the power to act and bind the principal to the same extent as if the principal acted.... A power of attorney provides the agent with all the rights and responsibilities of the principal as outlined in the agreement.... In effect, the agent stands in the shoes of the principal....

"It is also well-settled that the death of the principal revokes the authority of the agent, unless the agency is coupled with an interest.... Any act done by the agent after the principal dies cannot affect the estate.... This is true even if an agent has performed some of the acts necessary in a single transaction but not all of them.... If an agent is in the midst of a transaction when the principal dies, the transaction cannot continue, regardless of the principal's previously stated wishes....

"However, when an agent has completed all necessary actions and all that is left is for a third party to act to complete the transaction, we hold that the principal's death has no effect on the validity of the transaction and does not relieve the requirement on the third party to act. This is because the agent's actions were complete at the time of the principal's death....

"When all necessary actions have been completed, just as the third party would be required to follow the directive of the principal, the third party is also required to follow the directive of the agent.... Although the agent's authority to act terminates when the principal dies, actions completed before the termination no longer require the agent to exercise authority. Therefore, the principal's death does not revoke already completed actions by the agent.... ('A revocation of the agent's authority cannot retroactively affect the completed acts of the agent.')

"In this case, in accord with Dr. Capuzzi's wishes and acting as Dr. Capuzzi's agent pursuant to a durable power of attorney, Michael contacted the third party and directed that the shares be transferred. Just as Dr. Capuzzi had the authority to compel the third party to transfer the shares, Michael, as Dr. Capuzzi's agent, possessed the same authority. Once he ordered the third party to transfer the shares, this concluded the agent's actions that were necessary to complete the transaction. All that remained was for the third party to act. Again, in this case, the agent did all that was required to transfer the shares. The failure to transfer the shares was solely the result of the third party's delay and had nothing to do with the third party's internal procedures or concerns that the agent did not have the proper authority....

"We hold that an agent's completed actions are not revoked by the death of the principal when all necessary actions have been taken by the principal before the agent's death. Accordingly, we reverse the decision of the Court of Appeals and affirm the decision of the trial court."

matter to the agent. In other words, if the principal had merely authorized the agent to sell a specific piece of property to pay the principal's debt to the agent, the principal's death would terminate the power to sell; if the principal had given the agent a mortgage on the property (an "interest") plus the power to sell, the principal's death would not terminate that power.

Because the intent of the parties is basically the same in both cases, some modern decisions do not follow this distinction and hold that either a power given as security or a power "coupled with an interest" would survive the principal's death.

Such powers to sell collateral in the event of default would be terminated by the principal's bankruptcy, unless a proper filing of the security agreement or a financing statement has been made or other steps have been taken in accordance with bankruptcy law to establish priority over other creditors.

Duties and Liabilities of Principal to Agent

Principal's Duty to Compensate Agent

Many of the cases in which an agent is suing a principal involve the principal's duty to compensate the agent. Based on their contract, the principal owes the agent whatever salary or commission was agreed on for doing the acts required. It is assumed that the principal should reimburse the agent for any expenses that the agent reasonably and necessarily incurred in carrying out the principal's instructions. If the agent is to pay expenses, this should be stated in the contract. In the absence of any specific agreement, it is also assumed that the agent should be reimbursed for any personal loss or damage sustained as a result of following the principal's instructions.

Special compensation rules apply to real estate brokers. Usually the broker does not actually have the power to sell the listed property but only to conduct negotiations with prospective buyers. The broker, therefore, has normally earned the commission by "bringing in a deal," that is, when the broker produces a buyer who is ready, willing, and able to meet the purchase terms specified by the seller in the listing agreement.

Principal's Liability for Breach of Agency Contract

If the principal wrongfully prevents the agent from carrying out their contract and thus earning the agreed compensation, the principal, like any other employer, is liable to the agent for breach. Some of these cases involve an unjustified discharge of the agent; others result from the principal's improper interference with the agent's conduct of the agency, such as failing to provide the agent with new price and product information or attempting to impose arbitrary and discriminatory paperwork requirements.

If the agent fails to meet duties under the contract, the principal may be justified in firing the agent. Generally, if the agency has not been set up for a specific period of time, and therefore is "at will," the agent may be fired at any time, with or without reason, and the agent will have no case for breach of contract. Recent cases have held that there are some "outer limits" on the right to discharge an employee even when the term of employment is "at will." The courts in many states have recognized similar limitations on the **at-will employment** doctrine. Some of the state legislatures are considering legislation to prohibit arbitrary dismissals of "at-will" employees. The law on this point is changing very rapidly. Lawsuits may be filed claiming breach of express or implied contract or under various tort theories. The *Wholey* case illustrates some of these arguments.

Principal's Liability for Defamation

One way to avoid liability for wrongful or discriminatory discharge of an agent or employee is to show that there was cause for the discharge. To prove that the discharged person's job performance had been unsatisfactory, the principal/employer usually has to produce a written record of warnings and reprimands. Employers are thus motivated to document all wrongful or improper employee actions in each individual's personnel file, just in case. In doing so, however, the employer faces something of a dilemma because liability can also arise when defamatory statements about the employee are communicated to a third person.

The problem arises in many cases when a former employer is asked for a reference on one of its former employees. In answering such requests, the former employer must make sure that any statements made are absolutely true and can be verified if necessary.

Employer's Liability under Workers' Compensation

As noted in Chapter 7, an employer may also be held liable for an employee's on-the-job injuries. The employer owes a duty to provide a reasonably safe workplace. This duty is now expressed in state workers' compensation statutes, under which the employer is presumed to be liable for any job-related injuries. These statutes, and the state courts' decisions interpreting them, are not completely uniform. Chronic, long-term conditions, such as black lung disease and asbestosis, and mental illness resulting from job pressures may or may not be covered. In general, state courts have been quite liberal in applying statutory coverage.

CASE 5

Wholey v. Sears Roebuck & Co.
803 A.2d 482 (MD 2002)

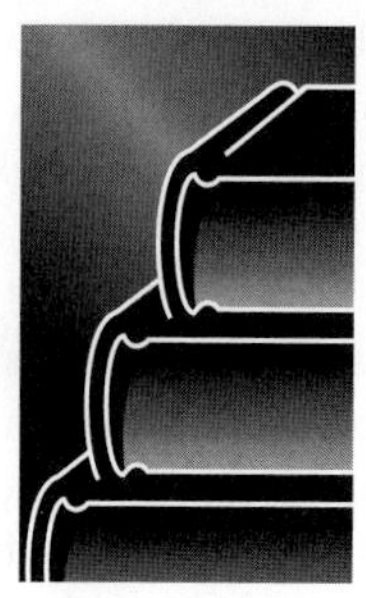

Facts: Edward Wholey had been a security officer at the Sears store in Glen Burnie, Maryland, for 24 years (the last 16 as the store's security manager), when he was discharged in 1996. Wholey had observed the store manager take merchandise into his office, which was in violation of company policy. The items would then "disappear" from the manager's office. This happened several times during 1995. Wholey reported these actions to the District Manager for Security, John Eiseman. Eiseman told him to continue observing. The manager's conduct continued, and Wholey alleges that Eiseman agreed to the installation of a surveillance camera. A short time later, Eiseman told Wholey to remove the camera. Wholey was fired less than 2 months later.

The trial court refused Sears' motion to dismiss the case, and the jury returned a verdict for Wholey. The Court of Special Appeals reversed, and Wholey petitioned for further review.

Issue: Does Maryland recognize a "public policy" exception that covers this situation?

Decision: No. Judgment of the Court of Special Appeals is affirmed.

Opinion by Judge Battaglia: "An at-will employee … has an employment contract of infinite duration which is terminable for any reason by either party.… The tort of wrongful discharge is one exception to the well-established principle that an at-will employee may be discharged for any reason, or no reason at all.… When this Court recognized the wrongful discharge tort …, we joined the growing number of states which have adopted a 'public policy exception' to the common notion of at-will employment by holding, specifically, that an employee who has been 'discharged in a manner that contravenes public policy' may 'maintain a cause of action for abusive or wrongful discharge against his former employer.'…

"Our task is to consider whether a clear mandate of public policy exists in Maryland which would prohibit the discharge of an at-will employee for his investigation of suspected criminal activity of a co-worker and reporting to his supervisors thereof.…

"The first limiting factor with respect to adopting a 'new' public policy mandate for a wrongful discharge claim is derived from the generally accepted purpose behind recognizing the tort in the first place: to provide a remedy for an otherwise unremedied violation of public policy.… For example, we [have] held that the tort of wrongful discharge is inapplicable where the public policy sought to be vindicated—in that case, sex discrimination in the workplace—is expressed in a statute which carries its own remedy for violation of that public policy.…

"A second limiting factor in defining a public policy mandate as a cause of action in tort is the notion that the policies should be reasonably discernible from prescribed constitutional or statutory mandates.… [W]e have … recognized that the establishment of 'an otherwise undeclared public policy as a basis for a judicial decision involves the application of a very nebulous concept to the facts of a given case,' and that declaration of public policy is normally the function of the legislative branch.…

"Constitutional provisions and principles also provide clear public policy mandates, under which a termination may be grounds for a wrongful discharge claim.…

"First, no statutory impediment to the tort cause of action sought by the petitioner exists because the Legislature, quite simply, has declined to provide a statutory remedy for private whistleblowers.…

"Second, and most significantly, an express statutory mandate provides a discernible foundation for the public policy exception sought by petitioner; namely, the Legislature has created a misdemeanor offense for a person who harms or injures another's person or property in retaliation for reporting a crime.…

"From this clearly definable public policy, we are able to adopt a civil cause of action in wrongful discharge for employees who are discharged for reporting suspected criminal activity to the appropriate authorities.…

"That we so hold, however, does not mean that the petitioner has a successful claim for wrongful discharge. To qualify for the public policy exception to at-will employment, the employee must report the suspected criminal activity to the appropriate law enforcement or judicial official, not merely investigate suspected wrong-doing and discuss that investigation with co-employees or supervisors.…

"We believe that the proper balance is achieved by proceeding cautiously when called upon to declare public policy absent some legislative or judicial expression on the subject and in so doing, we limit the adoption of a tort cause of action for wrongful discharge to circumstances where an employee reports criminal activity to the proper authorities and is discharged as a result of this reporting."

Duties and Liabilities of Agent to Principal

In General

The agency relationship is based on the trust and confidence that the principal has placed in the agent by giving the agent the power to manage the principal's affairs. The agent is thus a fiduciary, owing to the principal a duty of honesty and fair dealing in their relationship. The following specific aspects of this fiduciary duty may be easier to remember if you recall the boy scout's pledge: "Trustworthy, Loyal, Helpful, Friendly, Courteous, Kind, Obedient, Cheerful, Thrifty, Brave, Clean, and Reverent." Nearly all of these desirable characteristics of a successful scout also apply to the agent.

Loyalty and Good Faith

Loyalty to the principal's interests and good faith in dealing with that person are the most basic parts of the agent's fiduciary duty. Under the rule that a person "cannot faithfully serve two masters," an agent is prohibited from representing two persons with opposing interests, such as the two parties of a business transaction, unless both of them know of the dual agency and agree to it. A principal who does not know of the dual agency can rescind the resulting transaction on learning the truth. Likewise, the agent can neither buy from, or sell to, himself or herself nor derive any other secret benefit from conducting the principal's affairs. The receipt of secret bribes, payoffs, or presents by the agent from third parties will justify dismissal of the agent and may also involve civil or criminal penalties against the agent.

A related problem, and one which arises with some frequency in a technological society, is the conflict between employer and employee over who owns patents developed by the employee and other "secret" information used by the employee on the job (e.g., customer lists). Courts generally hold that the fiduciary duty does not end simply because employment is terminated, and thus the employee (or agent) does not have the right to use formulas, processes, customer lists, or other trade secrets in competition with a former employer. As to patented devices and processes that the employee developed on the job, the employee may become the owner by having them patented in his or her own name, but the employer has a "shop right" to make use of them in the employer's business without paying royalties. Specific language in the employment contract will probably head off most of these problems.

Employment contracts may also contain an agreement by the agent/employee not to compete with the principal/employer after the relationship is terminated. As noted in Chapter 12, such agreements are lawful and enforceable so long as the area and the duration of the restraint are both reasonable. If an unreasonable restraint is included, courts are split as to what should happen. Some courts refuse to enforce the unreasonable restraint at all; others are willing to rewrite it so as to make it reasonable. If the employer materially breaches the employment contract, as by wrongfully discharging the employee, a court could decide that such a restraint clause in the contract was no longer enforceable by the employer. In the absence of such an agreement, an employee (after termination) could go to work for a competitor but would still not be able to use the former employer's trade secrets.

Care and Skill in a Calling

A person, after accepting appointment as an agent, has the duty to use that degree of care and skill possessed by a reasonably competent practitioner in that line of business. A salesperson, for example, would be required to have and to exercise the knowledge, training, and diligence of "average" salespeople in the field involved. The existence of this duty means that an agent can be held liable for **misfeasance** (not doing lawful acts in a proper manner), **malfeasance** (doing a wrongful act), or **nonfeasance** (not being diligent in performing the job).

Personal Performance

A person is chosen as an agent of a principal, and placed in a position of trust and confidence, on the basis of his or her unique personal characteristics. It therefore follows logically that the agent owes a duty to the principal to use those personal qualities in performing the assigned job and that the agent should not be able to delegate to others the exercise of his or her discretionary powers as an agent. Absent any specific agreement, delegation by the agent is permitted only when the nature of the business requires it, when a known and established custom permits it, or when the delegation involves purely ministerial or mechanical acts (e.g., answering the telephone or typing correspondence). Except in these situations, the principal will not be liable to third parties for the acts of such "subagents," and their appointment by the original agent would be a breach of his or her duty to the principal.

Obedience to Instructions and Good Conduct

Like the boy scout, a good agent is obedient. The agent must obey the principal's instructions, even if they seem stupid or unreasonable; this control over methods, remember, is the main distinction between the agent/employee and the independent contractor. In general, the agent's only excuses for not obeying instructions are that they require doing something illegal or that it has become impossible to comply with them. The law is not too clear on the degree to which agents must subject themselves to personal danger to comply with the principal's instructions, although the Restatement of Agency does indicate that agents can disregard such instructions to "protect the agent's own superior interests." It is clear that the agent will have to follow instructions that are merely "unreasonable," unless the relationship involves an agency coupled with an interest and the unreasonable instructions would interfere with the agent's rights in the subject matter of the agency.

As far as third parties are concerned, the agent is the principal. This holds true particularly for agents who represent business concerns. The image and reputation of a business are in large part determined by the way its agents and employees conduct themselves toward third parties. The agent, and to some extent even the employee, therefore owes a duty of "good conduct." This requirement clearly covers on-the-job conduct, so things like dress codes can be enforced if they are reasonably and uniformly applied. The Restatement of Agency also indicates that this duty extends to off-the-job conduct that might affect the principal's business, such as the conduct of the bank teller who becomes known in the community as the "patron of the races." The exact degree to which agents can be legally required to surrender their personality to keep their jobs remains an open question.

Use of Principal's Property

The agent is liable for any misuse of property that the principal has entrusted to the agent or that comes into the agent's possession in the course of acting as agent. As part of this duty, the agent is not to commingle money or other property of the principal with personal money or other property, and the agent is required to provide the principal with correct and reasonably detailed statements of account.

The agent also has a duty to communicate to the principal any information that the agent possesses that might materially affect the agency.

Principal's Ratification of Agent's Unauthorized Act

Typically when the principal has a clear choice and ratifies with full knowledge that the agent's actions were unauthorized, the agent is excused of any further liability to the principal. The Restatement says that the agent will remain liable for breach of duty either when the principal "is obliged to affirm the act in order to protect his own interest" or when the principal is induced to ratify by the agent's fraud or duress.

Liability of Agent to Third Party

Agent Acts beyond Authority

In most states, when the agent in a disclosed agency transaction acts beyond the scope of his or her authority, so that the third party has no contract with the principal, the third party has no contract with the agent either. In these states the third party's remedy against the agent is a tort claim for fraud, provided the agent knowingly misrepresented his or her authority, or a case for breach by the agent of an "implied warranty of authority." As a rule, it is assumed that the agent makes such a warranty to the third party. There is no such warranty, however, if the third party knew that the agent was unauthorized, if the agent in good faith disclosed to the third party all the facts regarding the extent of the authority, or if the contract contains a disclaimer of the agent's liability. In a minority of states, the agent could also be sued directly on the contract that the agent was not authorized to make for the principal.

Principal Nonexistent or Incompetent

The two most common examples of the "nonexistent" principal are the corporation that has not yet been formed, and the unincorporated association, which is usually not recognized as a separate legal person. In these cases, the agent is personally liable on the contracts made with the third party, even if the third party knows of the "nonexistence," unless the contracts specifically exempt the agent from personal liability.

When the principal totally lacks contractual capacity at the time the contract is made (for instance, a person who has been judicially declared insane), most courts will probably arrive at the same result as would be reached if the principal were "nonexistent." Also, the agent would clearly be liable if the agent fraudulently misrepresented or concealed the principal's lack of capacity. When the principal has merely exercised an option to disaffirm the contract, however, the results are not so clear cut, but even in such cases many courts would hold the agent liable.

Agent Pledges Personal Credit

An agent who has pledged his or her personal credit on the contract, as surety for the principal, is also clearly liable to the third party. This occurs frequently when the agent is acting on behalf of a small, brand-new corporation that has not yet established its own credit standing; in such cases the third party will often demand that the agent-promoter-shareholder cosign the contract. If the agent does so, the agent is liable according to the terms of the contract.

Because this situation is so common, the agent may also be held personally liable when the contract language or the signatures on the contract indicate such liability. If it appears that the agent was a party (or the other party) to the contract, the agent may be prevented by the parol evidence rule from proving otherwise. If the principal's name does not appear on a negotiable instrument, and the agent's does, the agent is liable on it and the principal is not. To avoid these unintended results, the agent should always sign "Peter Principal, by John Able, agent"—thus clearly indicating that he or she is signing in a representative capacity.

Agent Commits Tort against Third Party

As stated earlier in the chapter, an agent is personally liable for torts committed against third parties. When the agent's tort is within the scope of authority, the third party can sue both the agent and the principal and they are both liable, although the third party cannot collect damages twice.

As a rule, the agent is not liable to third parties for breach of a duty that is owed only to the principal, at least if the breach involves only nonfeasance or misfeasance.

Undisclosed Principal

As also indicated earlier in the chapter, when the existence or identity of the principal is not disclosed at the time the contract is made, the third party has the option of holding the agent personally liable on the contract. The courts do not agree on when the third party must make an election to hold one to the exclusion of the other, although of course all do agree that no double recovery is permitted. The only way for an agent to avoid being held liable on this basis is to disclose the principal when the contract is made.

Liability of Third Party to Agent

Agent Suing on Own Behalf

There are only a few situations in which the agent will sue the third party on his or her own behalf. If the agent was also made a party to the original contract or if the agent owns the contract rights by assignment from the principal, the agent can sue the third party. The agent can also sue a third party for wrongful interference in the contract relationship between the agent and the principal or for any other tort that the third party commits against the agent. Finally, when the agent has delivered money or goods to the third party under circumstances when the third party would be unjustly enriched at the agent's expense (e.g., the agent by mistake pays the third party more than the principal owes the third party), the agent can sue in his or her own name to prevent such unjust enrichment.

Agent Suing for the Principal

Generally, an agent cannot sue in his or her own name to enforce a contract that the agent made on behalf of the principal; the principal has to sue the third party. If specifically authorized to do so, an agent may be able to bring suit as an agent for collection, and an assignment may be made to such an agent for the purpose of collection only. An agent can also sue on the principal's behalf to recover goods the agent delivered to the third party by mistake or for interference by the third party with the agent's possession of the principal's goods.

Thus, although the main agency is the third party's suit against the principal, based on an alleged contract or on the agent's tort, any of the three parties to this relationship may have a case against either of the other two.

Significance of This Chapter

Many business activities are carried on through other persons. Each of us, living in a complex society, needs to be aware of the basic rules for determining when one person is responsible for the actions of another. An important distinction exists between principals who employ agents and persons who employ independent contractors. Likewise, there are different rules for determining contract and tort liability for the actions of agents. Because we will all be dealing with and through agents on many occasions, we need to know how these basic rules work.

Because many of us will be employed as agents and will also be employing agents of our own, we also need to know the rights and duties that exist between principal and agent. Whether we are acting as agents or are the third parties with whom the agents are dealing, we should be aware of the rights and duties involved in that relationship as well. Although the major litigation pattern is a suit by the third party against the principal, based on actions of the agent, any of the three parties involved may have grounds for a suit against either of the others.

IMPORTANT TERMS AND CONCEPTS

agency
agency coupled with an interest.
agent
apparent authority
at-will employment
employee
estoppel
express authority
implied authority
independent contractor
malfeasance
misfeasance
nondelegable duties
nonfeasance
power of attorney
principal
ratification
undisclosed principal

QUESTIONS AND PROBLEMS FOR DISCUSSION

1. How is an agency relationship created? How can an agency relationship be terminated?

2. What duties does an agent owe to the principal? List each and discuss.

3. When the existence of the principal is not revealed in negotiations between the agent and the third party and later after a breach of the contract, the third party learns of the existence of the principal, whom can the third party sue? Why?

4. If an employee invents a new process or a new device while working for the employer, who has the right to patent this process or device? Who gets the royalties? Discuss.

5. Defendant JC Penney hired plaintiff David Patton in 1979. Plaintiff worked in Eugene until 1990 when he was transferred to Portland where he worked as a merchandising manager. In 1991 the store manager, defendant McKay, told plaintiff to break off a social relationship with a female coemployee. Plaintiff responded by telling McKay that he did not socialize with the coemployee at work and that he intended to continue seeing her on his own time. Apparently, the social relationship did not interfere with the plaintiff's performance at work, for during this time he earned several awards for "Merchant of the Month" and one for "Merchant of the Year."

   McKay later, while interrogating other employees about whether plaintiff had broken off the relationship, made statements to the effect that if plaintiff wanted to keep working he had to discontinue the relationship. Although no written or unwritten policy, rule, or regulation proscribed socializing between employees, other employees told plaintiff that McKay disfavored plaintiff's fraternization with the female coemployee. Nevertheless, plaintiff continued seeing the coemployee. When McKay warned plaintiff in late 1991 that his job performance was unsatisfactory and that he would be fired if there was no improvement, plaintiff asked for a transfer to another department. McKay denied the request. In February, McKay terminated plaintiff's employment for unsatisfactory job performance. The district manager, defendant Chapin, approved the termination.

   Does Patton have a case for wrongful discharge? Explain.

6. Cloris James opened a Servu Revolving Charge Account at the local Servu Store. She signed the application "Mrs. Ralph James." Cloris made over $600 worth of credit purchases on the account before Servu terminated her charging privileges because of nonpayment. Cloris had no separate job and no available personal assets. Servu sued her husband, Ralph, for the balance due on the account. There is no indication that Ralph ever used the charge account or that he ever made any of the payments credited on it.

   What is the result, and why?

7. K-Mart hired Cadillac Window Cleaning Company to wash the windows at K-Mart's world headquarters building. John Szymanski and two other Cadillac employees were on a 40-foot high scaffold doing the job, when Szymanski fell off and was seriously injured. None of the men was wearing a safety belt—standard industry practice—at the time. Szymanski sued K-Mart for his injuries, claiming it was liable under the "inherently dangerous activity" exception, even though Cadillac was an independent contractor.

   Does Szymanski have a valid claim? Discuss.

8. Plaintiffs Wagner Brothers operate four retail clothing stores in the greater New York City area. Defendant Appendagez, Inc. is a Massachusetts corporation that manufactured and sold wholesale a line of jeans, tops, and sweaters under the brand name "Faded Glory."

   The Wagners wished to feature the "Faded Glory" line at their new Cedarhurst location, which was in a high-income, sophisticated area. Aaron Wagner telephoned the corporate offices of Appendagez and asked to be placed in communication with the Appendagez salesman covering that area. This inquiry produced a visit, at the Cedarhurst location, from one Alan Friedman, who identified himself to Aaron Wagner as the Long Island salesman for Appendagez. On hearing of the other three stores, Friedman advised that he would write orders for all four stores, billing them through the Wagner Bros. Haberdashery account in Cedarhurst, so that the Wagners could examine the entire line at one time and there would be only one billing address. The Wagners agreed to this procedure. A number of orders were placed with Appendagez, through Friedman, for the four stores. To the extent that those orders were unfilled, they form the subject matter of this action.

   Orders were written up by Friedman on a printed order form prepared by Appendagez. There is no statement to the effect that orders are subject to acceptance by Appendagez at Norwood before they become binding on the seller. Some sellers in the industry had such a statement on their order forms; others did not. The Wagners sued for breach of contract.

   How should this case be analyzed? Explain.

9. Parke Davis, a pharmaceutical manufacturer, employed Neil Stuempges as one of its Minneapolis sales representatives from 1978 until February 25, 1994, when it asked him to resign or be fired. During the first 15 years of his employment, Stuempges had never been disparaged for his lack of ability as a salesperson and had even received commendations over the years for his outstanding sales record.

   In July 1993, Robert Jones became the new district manager of the Minneapolis area in which Stuempges' sales territory was located. From the beginning, they clashed in their approaches to a number of issues.

On February 25, 1994, at Jones's request, Stuempges met with him and Donald Burgett, Jones's immediate supervisor. At this meeting Stuempges was asked to resign and was promised a good recommendation if he did so. If he refused to resign, however, Jones told him that he would be "blackballed" in the industry. Shortly thereafter, Stuempges submitted his resignation.

On March 5, 1994, Stuempges sought assistance in finding another job through Sales Consultants, Inc., an employment agency specializing in sales personnel. He was interviewed by Robert Hammer, at which time he listed Parke Davis as his most recent employer and Jones as his most recent supervisor and gave him permission for Sales Consultants to check his references at Parke Davis. Hammer called Jones for a reference. Jones told Hammer that Stuempges was a poor salesman, not industrious, hard to motivate, could not sell, and that he had been fired and had not just resigned. Hammer refused to try to place Stuempges in a job as a result of this poor recommendation. Stuempges sued Parke Davis & Company alleging he had been defamed by Parke Davis employees.

Has Parke Davis defamed Stuempges? Discuss.

CHAPTER 30

Employment Law

Chapter Objectives

This chapter will:

- Introduce the sources of law regulating employment relationships.
- Discuss major problem areas of labor relations law.
- Review labor standards legislation.
- Discuss the laws governing occupational safety.
- Discuss antidiscrimination legislation.

We have already discussed many of the basic legal rules involved in the employer-employee relationship in Chapter 29. We assumed in that discussion that the employer was negotiating with each employee or prospective employee on an individual basis. Many employees, of course, are union members and rely on their unions to negotiate on their behalf for improved wages, hours, and conditions of employment. To promote peaceful collective bargaining, the national government regulates this process in some detail. Although the states may not enact regulations that conflict with the national labor law system, they are free to regulate collective bargaining by state and local government employees and by any other whose activities do not affect interstate commerce.

National and state governments have also enacted a variety of laws that provide benefits and safety standards for employees. Minimum wage laws, the Social Security system, the Employee Retirement Income Security Act (ERISA), the Occupational Safety and Health Act (OSHA), and similar laws provide required standards for the employee-employer relationship. National and state governments have also enacted employment discrimination laws with which employers must comply.

Labor Laws

Originally, the employment contract was treated by the common law in much the same way as other types of contracts; it required offer and acceptance, consideration, and the other elements of a valid contract. It was a two-party contract, with each party having the freedom to accept or reject the bargain offered by the other and with the parties being pretty much free to agree on any terms they chose. Specific legal rules also developed to cover this "master-servant" relationship, such as the employer's liability for torts committed by his or her servant within the scope of the employment and the employer's responsibility for furnishing a reasonably safe place in which to work. Much of the common law has now been displaced in this area because both national and state governments have moved in aggressively to redefine this relationship.

Several broad, comprehensive national statutes exist in each of the two major divisions of labor law—labor relations and labor standards. There is also considerable state regulation of both areas, and the Fourteenth Amendment to the U.S. Constitution may be invoked if the state itself, or one of its agencies or instrumentalities, is directly involved in the relationship as the employer.

Labor Relations Laws

Wagner Act. In the area of labor relations, the basic piece of national legislation is the National Labor Relations Act of 1935 (NLRA) as amended. The NLRA (also known as the **Wagner Act**) laid the cornerstone of national labor policy: belief in the process of collective bargaining between the employer and a representative freely chosen by his or her employees. The original act set out a series of forbidden employer **"unfair labor practices,"** so that employers would not interfere with the selection of the **bargaining representative** and would be required to bargain. The governmental interference here was limited to providing the employees with a freely chosen bargaining representative; it was then up to the union to work out the terms and conditions of employment by bargaining with the employer.

Taft-Hartley Act. Concern over excessive union power and abuses, coupled with a wave of strikes after World War II, led to the adoption of a series of comprehensive amendments in 1947—the **Taft-Hartley Act** (or Labor-Management Relations Act). Taft-Hartley set out a series of forbidden union unfair labor practices and attempted to ensure certain basic employer and employee rights—such as the employer's right to tell his or her side of the story to the employees and the employee's right to refrain from participating in union activity if he or she so chose. These amendments also permitted the several states to prohibit agreements between employer and union that required union membership as a condition of employment **(state right-to-work laws)**.

Landrum-Griffin Act. Further disenchantment with union operations and evidence of widespread corruption in the internal management of unions, provided by nationally televised hearings of the McClellan subcommittee, resulted in 1959 in a second substantial revision of the

NLRA. The Labor-Management Reporting and Disclosure Act (LMRDA), or **Landrum-Griffin Act,** again attempted to protect employers, individual employees, and the public from certain union abuses, particularly the abuse of exerting indirect pressure on a recalcitrant employer by involving third parties in the bargaining dispute. The LMRDA also placed certain requirements on the internal management of unions and union funds and provided machinery for dealing with so-called national emergency strikes.

As a result of these two sets of amendments, a good deal of the spirit of the original Wagner Act ("Let the union do it") has been dissipated. The rather considerable limitations contained in Taft-Hartley and Landrum-Griffin are not fully consistent with the free collective bargaining envisaged by the Wagner Act, and the law of labor relations thus becomes susceptible to radically different interpretations at several important points.

Railway Labor Act. The NLRA does not cover railroad employees or airline employees, they are covered by the **Railway Labor Act,** passed by Congress in 1926. Also the National Labor Relations Law does not cover public employees on the national, state, or local level. Employees of our national government are covered by the Federal Service Labor-Management and Employee Relations Act of 1978, which gives them the right to organize and be represented by a union for collective bargaining, but denies them the right to strike. Many states have enacted statutes authorizing and regulating collective bargaining by public employees. These laws usually deny such employees the right to strike. Since a strike is not allowed, many of these statutes provide for compulsory arbitration of the dispute if the parties cannot resolve the dispute between themselves.

Labor Standards Laws

Labor standards legislation provides direct regulation of the terms and conditions of employment; in that sense, it limits the freedom of the employer and the union, as well as the individual employee, to set their own terms of association with each other. The Wagner Act represented a basic commitment of national labor policy to the collective bargaining process, but the commitment has never been complete or without qualification. The mandatory "social security" system is itself an important piece of labor standards legislation because it provides a required arrangement for retirement, disability, and dependent benefits. Social security can be supplemented, but not displaced, through collective bargaining.

Fair Labor Standards Act. The main piece of national wages and hours legislation is the **Fair Labor Standards Act (FLSA)** of 1938, as amended. Once again, it sets boundaries to the parties' freedom of contract by specifying certain minimum wages and required overtime that must be paid (even if there are people ready and willing to work for less). Also included in this general category are several national statutes requiring the payment of "prevailing minimum wages" in a particular industry, as determined by the Secretary of Labor. The two such acts with broadest scope are the Walsh-Healy Act, for manufacturers and dealers supplying the national government with supplies valued at $10,000 or more, and the Davis-Bacon Act, covering building contracts with the national government for more than $2,000. Similar provisions have been inserted in national grant-in-aid legislation for the construction of airports, highways, housing for defense personnel, and urban renewal projects.

Occupational Safety and Health Act. One of the most far-reaching (and therefore the most costly) piece of "labor standards" legislation ever enacted became law in 1970: the **Occupational Safety and Health Act (OSHA).** This act is designed to "assure as far as possible every working man and woman in the nation safe and healthful working conditions," by giving the Secretary of Labor very broad powers to adopt "standards" that will in effect be mandatory health and safety practices. To ensure compliance, the employer's premises are subject to unannounced inspection by "the man from OSHA," either on employee complaint or by random selection. Injunctive relief and criminal penalties are provided for violations.

Employment Retirement Income Security Act. In 1974 Congress passed another important piece of labor legislation—the **Employment Retirement Income Security Act (ERISA).** ERISA establishes a new government agency, financed by contributions from employers with pension plans, to guarantee payment of earned pension benefits. It does not require any employer to establish a pension plan, but when he or she does, the plan must meet certain standards for the funding and management of assets and for the vesting of benefits. ERISA is thus a significant new protection for the more than 30 million workers who are covered by its provisions.

State Laws. Labor legislation in a particular state may include all of the aforementioned types plus some additions. Many states now have statutes regulating collective bargaining by public employees, some of which provide for compulsory arbitration of bargaining disputes that the parties are unable to resolve themselves. The states have also enacted workers' compensation laws that provide a statutory scheme for compensating employees for virtually all job-related injuries. (A similar national statute, the Federal Employees' Compensation Act, covers U.S. government employees.) Finally, workers who have lost their jobs are provided with at least some temporary help though state systems of unemployment compensation.

The *GARD* case illustrates some of ERISA's complexities.

Labor Relations: Major Problem Areas

Selection of Bargaining Agent. Assuming that a group of employees have indicated a desire for union representation and that they are subject to NLRA jurisdiction, the first step in the procedure for selecting a bargaining agent is to define the extent of the bargaining unit. In some cases, when there is only one business location and when there is a substantial identity of interests among all concerned employees, this is an easy job.

Multiple job sites create some definitional problems. What if one plant votes "no union" but a majority for all plants operated by the company votes in favor of a union? Do we decide plant by plant or companywide? The National Labor Relations Board (NLRB) has generally favored the companywide approach.

How about employees with substantially different skills, interests, and professional identification? Are they all to be lumped together as an amorphous mass ("one big union"), or are they somehow to be split up (so that some smaller craft unions or even "no union" might have a better chance of winning the separate elections)? Conflicting equities can make it difficult to arrive at a "fair" resolution of these questions. The NLRB's general approach has been "one big union," meaning that a group of employees wishing to be excluded from the employerwide unit must have some strong evidence of their "uniqueness."

In addition to determining the appropriate bargaining unit, the NLRB's preelection hearing also decides which employees are entitled to vote and which unions will appear on the ballot. The original union petitioning for the election is required to present evidence of 30 percent support, typically by means of signature cards from the requisite number of employees. Any other union wishing to appear on the ballot need only show substantial interest, and the "no union" choice will appear automatically. The election is by secret ballot. The winner need only receive a majority of the votes actually cast. If there is no majority, a runoff election is held between the two choices receiving the highest vote totals. Although a secret ballot election is clearly the preferred method and the one normally used, the board does have the power to grant bargaining rights to a union presenting signature cards from a majority, when the cards clearly indicate such an intent, when there has been no union misrepresentation of the purpose of the cards to the individual employees, and when the possibility of holding a fair election is lessened by the employer's serious unfair labor practices.

Section 7 of the NLRA gives employees "the right to self-organization, to form, join, or assist labor organizations." Section 8(a)(1) then makes it an unfair labor practice for an employer to "interfere with, restrain, or coerce employees in the exercises of the rights guaranteed in Section 7." Labor history contains many cases where unscrupulous employers used puppet unions to forestall genuine representation and to exploit their workers still further. The NLRB is vigorous and vigilant, therefore, in protecting these important organizing rights, so that the employer's conduct during an organizing campaign must now be circumspect to avoid an unfair labor practice charge. Taft-Hartley

CASE 1

Gard v. Blankenberg

2002 U.S.App. LEXIS 2963 (6 Cir. 2002)

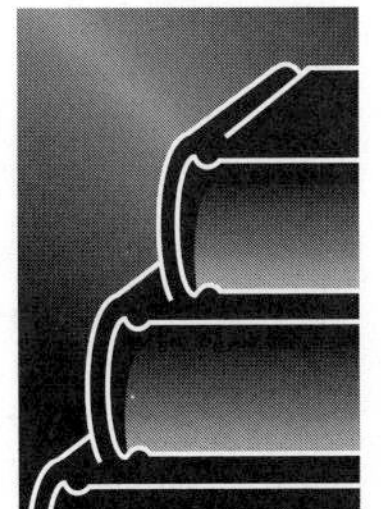

Facts: Paul Gard, a trustee of a multiemployer defined benefit (DB) pension plan, sued the plan's former trustees, alleging violations of ERISA. Specifically, he alleged that they had violated their fiduciary duty under ERISA by adopting modifications to the plan that provided for a 100 percent joint and survivor benefit option and for a 90-hour break-in-service "cure" for inactive participants. The changes were made pursuant to an agreement between the employers and the union to "freeze" the defined benefit plan and to begin a defined contribution (DC) plan and a 401k plan. As a result of these changes, the DB plan became seriously underfunded, even though the plan's actuary had said it would be fully funded in perpetuity on the basis of several actuarial assumptions. The trustees either did not understand or disregarded these stated assumptions when they adopted the changes. Gard also claimed that the trustees violated their ERISA duties by permitting the DB plan to pay certain fees incurred by the DC plan and the 401k plan.

The U.S. District Court for the Northern District of Ohio initially found in favor of Gard on both claims. On reconsideration in light of the U.S. Supreme Court's decision in the *Lockheed* case, however, District Judge Nugent held that the former trustees were not acting as ERISA fiduciaries when they amended the plan. Gard appealed.

Issue: Were the former trustees acting as ERISA fiduciaries?

Decision: No. Judgment affirmed.

Opinion by Judge Guy: "Plaintiff's first claim is that the District Court erred in finding that it had incorrectly applied the fiduciary standard of care to the trustees' conduct in amending the DB Plan to include the 100 percent joint survivor benefit and the 90-hour cure. After reviewing this question of law de novo, we find that the trustees did not act as fiduciaries in adopting these provisions and, therefore, were not subject to ERISA's fiduciary duties in this regard....

"[O]ur starting point must be ERISA's definition of a fiduciary. ERISA provides ... that 'a person is a fiduciary with respect to a plan' to the extent that he 'exercises any discretionary authority or discretionary control respecting management,' or 'has any discretionary authority or discretionary responsibility in the administration' of the plan.... Under this functional approach, the act of the employer or other plan sponsor in amending, modifying, or terminating a plan does not constitute an act of plan management or administration.... Consequently, employers or other plan sponsors 'who alter the terms of a plan do not fall into the category of fiduciaries.'...

"We ... reject the ... argument that *Lockheed* applies only when the employer, acting as a settlor of the plan, takes the action of amending or modifying the plan.... As the Court explained in *Hughes:* 'Although trust law may offer a "starting point" for analysis in some situations, it must give way if it is inconsistent with "the language of the statute, its structure, or its purposes".'...

"Given the functional nature of the definition of fiduciary, we believe that it is the nature of these actions—not the status of the actor as employer or settlor—that takes the conduct outside the defined functions of an ERISA fiduciary. Moreover, the Court's holding in *Lockheed* encompassed not only employers, but also 'other plan sponsors' who alter the terms of a pension benefit plan.... ERISA, in turn, specifically defines the term 'plan sponsor' to include the trustees of a multi-employer plan.... [W]e hold ... that trustees of a multi-employer pension benefit plan do not act as fiduciaries under ERISA when they amend, modify, or terminate the plan....

"Taking a different tack, plaintiff argues that the trustees were acting as fiduciaries because 'plan design' had been dictated by agreement between the union and the [employers]. As a result, plaintiff contends, the trustees' actions in amending the DB plan were functionally no more than an exercise of discretionary authority in the management or administration of the plan.... When the nature of the authority exercised by the trustees in this case is considered, it is clear that their decisions ... were acts of plan design and, therefore, not actions giving rise to fiduciary obligations under ERISA....

"Alternatively, the plaintiff argues ... that even if the trustees were not acting as fiduciaries in amending the plan, they acted as fiduciaries when they implemented or carried out the challenged amendments. In support of this fiduciary claim, plaintiff relies on the decision in *Varity*..., and an academic discussion suggesting that standards need to be developed to distinguish between actions taken to amend plans and actions taken to implement those amendments, see Dana M. Muir, *The Plan Amendment Trilogy: Settling the Scope of the Settlor Doctrine*, 15 LAB. LAW. 205 (Fall 1999). We are satisfied that the facts of this case do not present a distinct challenge to the actions taken to implement the amended DB plan....

"AFFIRMED."

guarantees the employer's (and others') right of "free speech," so long as the employer does not make any threat of reprisal or promise any benefit, but the board has ruled that such conduct may be a basis for invalidating a no-union vote, thus requiring a new election.

CASE 2

Hoffman Plastic Compounds, Inc. v. National Labor Relations Board
535 U.S. 137 (2002)

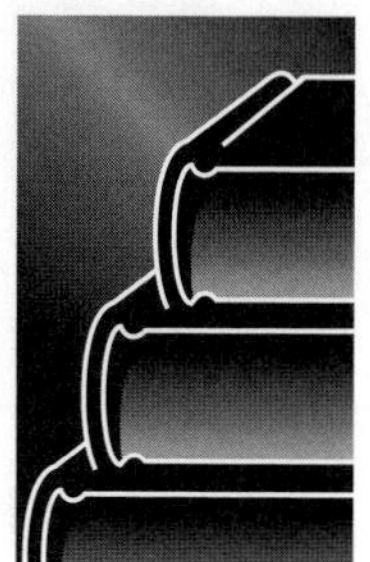

Facts: In 1992, the NLRB ruled that Jose Castro and three other employees had been laid off by Hoffman Plastic in retaliation for union organizing activities. The board issued a cease-and-desist order, required posting of appropriate notices at the plant, and ordered back pay for Castro and the others. At a compliance hearing before an administrative law judge (ALJ) in June 1993, Castro admitted that he had never been legally admitted to the United States or authorized to work here. The ALJ then decided that Castro could not be awarded back pay. The board reversed. A three-judge panel of the Court of Appeals denied Hoffman's petition for review, and the Court en banc affirmed that denial. Hoffman petitioned the Supreme Court.

Issue: Does IRCA prevent the NLRB from issuing a back pay award to a wrongfully discharged employee who is in the country illegally?

Decision: Yes. Judgment of the Court of Appeals (and the NLRB) is reversed.

Opinion by Chief Justice Rehnquist: "[W]here the Board's chosen remedy trenches upon a federal statute or policy outside the Board's competence to administer, the Board's remedy may be required to yield. Whether or not this was the situation at the time of [the] *Sure-Tan* [case], it is precisely the situation today. In 1986, two years after *Sure-Tan*, Congress enacted IRCA, a comprehensive scheme prohibiting the employment of illegal aliens.... IRCA 'forcefully' made combating the employment of illegal aliens central to 'the policy of immigration law.'... It did so by establishing an extensive 'employment verification system,'... designed to deny employment to aliens who (a) are not lawfully present in the United States, or (b) are not lawfully authorized to work in the United States.... This verification system is critical to the IRCA regime. To enforce it, IRCA mandates that employers verify the identity and eligibility of all new hires by examining specified documents before they begin work.... If an alien applicant is unable to present the required documents, the unauthorized alien cannot be hired....

"Similarly, if an employer unknowingly hires an unauthorized alien, or if the alien becomes unauthorized while employed, the employer is compelled to discharge the worker upon discovery of the worker's undocumented status.... Employers who violate IRCA are punished by civil fines ... and may be subject to criminal prosecution.... IRCA also makes it a crime for an unauthorized alien to subvert the employer verification system by tendering fraudulent documents.... It thus prohibits aliens from using or attempting to use 'any forged, counterfeit, altered, or falsely made document' or 'any document lawfully issued to or with respect to a person other than the possessor' for purposes of obtaining employment in the United States.... Aliens who use or attempt to use such documents are subject to fines and criminal prosecution.... There is no dispute that Castro's use of false documents to obtain employment with Hoffman violated these provisions....

"The Board asks that we overlook this fact and allow it to award backpay to an illegal alien for years of work not performed, for wages that could not lawfully have been earned, and for a job obtained in the first instance by a criminal fraud. We find, however, that awarding backpay to illegal aliens runs counter to policies underlying IRCA, policies the Board has no authority to enforce or administer. Therefore, as we have consistently held in these circumstances, the award lies beyond the bounds of the Board's remedial discretion.

"Indeed, awarding backpay in a case like this not only trivializes the immigration laws, it also condones and encourages future violations. The Board admits that had the INS detained Castro, or had Castro obeyed the law and departed to Mexico, Castro would have lost his right to backpay.... Similarly, Castro cannot mitigate damages, a duty our cases require ... without triggering new IRCA violations.... The Board here has failed to even consider this tension....

"However broad the Board's discretion to fashion remedies when dealing only with the NLRA, it is not so unbounded as to authorize this sort of an award....

"The judgment of the Court of Appeals is reversed."

The *Hoffman* case involves the availability of back pay as a sanction against an employer who fired employees for engaging in union organizing activities. The complication here is that one of the employees was in the United States illegally and had presented false documents to the company—a violation of the Immigration Reform and Control Act of 1986 (IRCA).

Union Security and Membership. Once selected as the official bargaining agent, the union is then legally required to bargain for all employees in the unit, union and nonunion alike, as well as to process the grievances of all employees on an equal basis. Violation of this duty of equal and fair representation could lead to decertification of the union by the NLRB or to charges before the **Equal Employment Opportunity Commission (EEOC).**

Because it is legally required to represent all, the union makes the superficially logical argument that all employees in the unit should be required to become union members to keep their jobs. This is the so-called **free rider argument:** No nonunion employee should get a free ride on union-won benefits at the expense of dues-paying fellow employees. The first answer to this argument is that the union not only agreed to accept this status; it aggressively sought it. And second, it should be possible to work up some fair compensation to the union for benefits actually conferred by it on nonunion employees, without forcing them to join and financially support an organization with which they may disagree violently—philosophically, politically, and economically.

From a union's standpoint, the best union-security arrangement is the **closed shop,** where only union members are hired and where employees must remain union members to keep their jobs. The closed shop has been outlawed for nearly all industries, but the legally permitted union shop is almost as good. Under a **union shop,** the employee has an initial period of time after hiring, typically 30 days, to decide whether or not to join the union to keep the job. An employee who decides not to join is fired at the end of the trial period. In addition to the union shop, the union will probably also negotiate a contract provision for automatic payroll deduction of union dues.

Section 14(b) of Taft-Hartley gave the states the authority to ban compulsory unionism if they wished to do so; slightly more than one-third of the states have such right-to-work laws. Because Section 14(b) speaks of required "membership" in a union, some of these states permit the **agency shop** under which an employee is not required to join the union but instead pays it a fee that supposedly represents the value of the union's services to him or her as a member of the bargaining unit. Other states in this group hold that the agency shop is illegal, too, and in those states the original open shop prevails. With an **open shop** each individual employee is legally free to decide whether or not to become, or remain, a union member, and the union leaders are thus responsible to the membership on a continuing basis. Labor's annual drive in Congress to repeal 14(b) has thus far been unsuccessful.

Scope of Duty to Bargain. Section 8(a)(5) of the NLRA makes it an unfair labor practice for the employer to refuse to bargain collectively with the representative of his or her employees; Section 8(b)(3) contains a similar requirement for the chosen union representative. But the parties are required to bargain only as to items that are classified as **mandatory subjects** of collective bargaining. As to those items, not only is it a violation of the NLRA to refuse to bargain, but it is also legally permissible to insist on one's bargaining position as the price of an agreement. That is, when a mandatory subject is involved, either party can use all of the weapons at its command—strike, lockout, picketing, and so on—to enforce the bargaining demand.

What are these mandatory subjects? Generally, they comprise items designated as "wages, hours, and other terms and conditions of employment." Very few bargaining demands would not fall into this category. Pension, profit-sharing, and stock-purchase plans; bonuses and merit raises; seniority and retirement rules; prices for meals and housing furnished by the company; and union security arrangements—all have been ruled mandatory subjects.

Permissive subjects of collective bargaining are those that the parties are free to discuss if they both wish to, but which neither can insist on as the price of an agreement. Such insistence or the use of bargaining weapons would be a violation of the Section 8 duty to bargain and would subject the wrongdoer to unfair labor practice charges. Nearly all demands held to be merely permissive have related to the mechanics of the bargaining process itself, such as the size of the bargaining teams, the requirement of a secret employee vote on ratification of the employer's last offer before a strike, or a secret ballot vote on ratification of the new contract. Product selection, distribution, and pricing have likewise thus far been held to be **management prerogatives** and thus not mandatory subjects for collective bargaining. But the contracting out of work that was formerly performed by members of the bargaining unit is a mandatory subject, and the NLRB has ordered the resumption of maintenance operations that were so terminated by the company without prior bargaining.

There are a few provisions, such as closed shop and "hot cargo" agreements, that may not be lawfully included in the collective bargaining contract even if both parties so desire.

The duty imposed by the NLRA means that the parties must bargain in "good faith." This at least includes meeting with each other, listening to the other side's proposals, and discussing them. In the case of the employer, the duty to bargain also means providing the union with such relevant information as is within its possession and reasonably available. The NLRA does not require any party to agree to a proposal from the other side or even to make any concession. Despite these clearly stated rules, however, both the NLRB and the U.S. Second Circuit Court of Appeals held that General Electric committed the unfair labor practice of refusing to bargain by making its "last, best offer" at the start of negotiations and indicating to the employees that that was the best it could do.

Union Tactics and Unfair Labor Practices. The union's main weapons in support of its bargaining demands are the strike, picketing, and the boycott. There are some significant legal limitations (and economic ones) on the use of each. In general, both the objectives sought and the tactics used must be lawful.

Both Taft-Hartley and Landrum-Griffin tried to restrict union conduct that had the effect of dragging neutral employers, and their employees, into the primary dispute. The main relevant section of the amended NLRA is Section 8(b)(4). Strikes, refusals to handle or work on certain ("hot") goods, or any other union conduct that threatens, coerces, or restrains any person is illegal if its objective is:

(a) To force any employer or self-employed person to enter a labor organization or to enter into a "hot cargo" agreement, illegal under 8(e).

(b) To force any person to cease doing business with any other person.

(c) To force any employer to bargain with one union where another union has already been certified.

(d) To force an employer to assign particular work to one group of employees rather than another.

Section 8(b)(7) further limits the permissible objectives of picketing. Picketing is unlawful when it is done to force an employer to recognize a union or to force his or her employees to accept it as their agent if:

(a) Another union has already been recognized and there is no legal question as to its status.

(b) A valid election has been held within the past twelve months.

(c) Such picketing has been conducted for a reasonable time (not to exceed 30 days) and the union has not filed a petition for an election.

In addition to the above legal restrictions on the purposes for which union collective-action weapons may be used, any such concerted activities must themselves be conducted in a lawful manner. In general, this means that the union's tactics must be "peaceful." Violence or threats of violence directed against the employer, his or her premises, employees who choose to go to work, or customers or others who wish to continue to do business with the "target" employer would clearly be illegal. Access to and egress from the target premises must not be impeded. The laws of libel and slander presumably still apply to picket signs and other information media. And so on.

Illegality of the union's objectives or tactics not only subjects it to unfair labor practice charges; there may also be other consequences. The union itself may be liable for the damages caused and/or subject to an injunction to prohibit the unlawful conduct. Civil rights violations could conceivably be involved in the union's conduct. Employees engaging in an "unprotected" strike are subject to lawful dismissal by the employer, with no right to reinstatement when the strike ends. The 1947 and 1959 amendments, coupled with a more critical public attitude toward unions, now make it reasonably clear that union hooliganism will be punished. However, the public still shows a high tolerance level for illegal, but peaceful, union conduct, such as illegal boycotts and illegal public employee strikes. These issues remain unresolved.

Employer Tactics and Unfair Labor Practices. The employer's arsenal of weapons includes some that are roughly comparable to those used by the union, as well as some for which the union has no real equivalent. The counterpart of the union's denial of services through a strike is the employer's denial of access to the workplace (and therefore wages) by means of a **lock-out.** In lieu of picketing, the employer advises employees, customers, and other members of the public of his or her side of the dispute by advertising, typically in a local newspaper. There is no real employer counterpart to the boycott. In addition to the aforementioned "corresponding" weapons, the employer also possesses the ultimate sanctions of **plant relocation** and termination of the business, though the use of either is severely limited by the board and the courts. Management may also do some forward planning to cushion the effects of a strike, by stockpiling inventories, readjusting contract schedules, or transferring work from one plant to another. The employer may also attempt to restrict the scope of the union's collective action by means of a court injunction.

A lockout designed to prevent unionization or to discourage union membership would be an unfair labor practice, but an employer may use the lockout to protect his or her own legitimate economic interests. When there is a bargaining impasse, the employer may lock out in support of his or her bargaining position. Or, if the union calls or threatens to call a strike, the employer can lock out in retaliation and also lock out to prevent "economic hardship" to the business.

An employer has an absolute right to go out of business at any time, for any reason, even if the employer's sole reason for doing so is his or her antiunion bias. When an employer closes only part of an operation, however, the employer's motives must be economic ones and not a desire to "chill unionism" at his or her other locations. In general, the legality of a plant relocation **(runaway shop)** would be tested in the same manner as that of a partial closing.

Throughout most of the early history of unionism, the courts were on the employer's side. The standard operating procedure when confronted with union collective action was to ask for a court injunction to restrict or terminate the union activities. Employers got an unexpected bonanza when the courts applied the **Sherman Antitrust Act** to union activities, thus further restricting employee collective action.

Congress attempted to limit the use of the courts in labor disputes by including Sections 6 and 20 in the **Clayton Act** of 1914. Unfortunately, from the union viewpoint, Section 20 said that an injunction could be issued if "necessary to prevent irreparable injury to property, or to a property right," and the courts were very liberal in construing this qualifying phrase. It took the **Norris-LaGuardia Act** of 1932 to substantially eliminate the labor injunction from the U.S. District Courts. (Many states copied this act.) It is still theoretically possible for an employer to get an injunction in a labor dispute, but the strict jurisdictional requirements make this very unlikely. The one exceptional case in which the employer will be granted an injunction is when there is a strike in violation of a no-strike clause in an existing collective agreement. (An employer can also get a specific performance order to enforce an arbitration clause in an existing contract.) In addition, the NLRB and the Attorney General are not bound by Norris-LaGuardia and can get injunctions issued.

Conflict Resolution. As indicated previously, the government's basic approach to management-union disputes is merely to see to it that the parties meet their obligation to bargain with each other in good faith and then to let the economic chips fall where they may. In 1947, however, Congress opted for additional governmental participation in the bargaining process, with the creation of the Federal Mediation and Conciliation Service (FMCS), an independent administrative agency.

The primary responsibility of bargaining out and living with their agreement is still left up to the parties. But the services of the FMCS are available at the request of either party or on its own initiative when the labor dispute involves the public safety and interest or when it threatens to have a substantial adverse impact on interstate commerce. If the parties want to submit their dispute to binding arbitration, the FMCS will also make available to them a list of qualified labor arbitrators from which to select.

Arbitration provides a more civilized method of settling disputes than strikes, lockouts, and the like. It is usually less formal, less complicated, and therefore less time-consuming and less expensive than a court trial. Nearly all arbitration is voluntarily agreed to by the parties, but some states have compulsory arbitration laws for public employees, particularly firefighters and police officers, and the Taft-Hartley Act contains special procedures for compulsory government action in "national emergency strikes." Today the courts recognize and enforce awards made by third-party arbitrators on matters submitted to them by the parties, and as indicated previously, arbitration clauses in existing contracts are specifically enforceable, despite the Norris-LaGuardia Act.

Internal Union Management; Reporting and Disclosure Requirements. The Landrum-Griffin amendments to the NLRA ushered in a new era in union organization and administration. The Landrum-Griffin Act was passed following the sensational disclosures of the McClellan subcommittee on the extent of corruption and gangster control in the labor movement. The findings received widespread publicity because many of the hearings were televised and because of the popularity of *The Enemy Within*, a book written by subcommittee counsel Robert Kennedy. The result was the passage of the Landrum-Griffin Act, which set out a "bill of rights" for labor union members and imposed substantial reporting and disclosure requirements on unions.

The bill of rights is an attempt to provide guarantees of minimum participatory access to the union's decision-making process and to protect the individual member's status within the union. Subject to the union's "reasonable rules," all members are to have equal rights to attend and vote at meetings, to nominate candidates, to vote in elections, and to exercise their freedoms of speech and assembly. Dues increases must be voted by secret ballot at a special membership meeting or by referendum. Except for failure to pay dues, an individual union member cannot be disciplined by his or her union unless served with written, specific charges and given a reasonable time to prepare a defense and a full and fair hearing. If a grievance against the union or its officers or agents is not resolved by internal procedures within 4 months, the member can bring a civil suit in a U.S. District Court to enforce any rights under the act. The member can demand a copy of any collective contract that affects him or her, and the Secretary of Labor is directed to bring suit on the member's behalf if a copy is not provided.

The union itself is required to file two major types of reports with the Secretary of Labor—procedural and financial. Each union must adopt a constitution and bylaws, and both must be filed. Existing provisions covering such things as membership qualifications, initiation fees, selection and removal of officers, contract ratification, and strike authorization must also be filed if such matters are not covered in the constitution and bylaws. Yearly financial reports must be filed, covering such matters as assets and liabilities; receipts and their sources; salaries, loans, and other payments to officers and employees; and loans to any business. Full, periodic reports must also be filed when the national union places a local under "trusteeship." To try to prevent conflicts of interest, union officers and employees must file personal financial reports covering transactions with companies that the union has organized or is trying to organize.

The Landrum-Griffin Act thus contains important new legal protections for the individual union member and for the public.

Employment Discrimination Laws

Beginning in the early 1960s, Congress recognized the need to eliminate discrimination in employment. Several anti-discrimination laws have now been passed by Congress. The first of these laws, the **Equal Pay Act of 1963,** which was an amendment to the FLSA, required employers to pay equal pay to men and women for doing equal work. The next law was the **Civil Rights Act of 1964,** which was amended in 1972 and 1991. Title VII of that act forbids discrimination by either an employer or a union against an applicant for employment, an employee, or an applicant for membership or benefits in a union if such discrimination is based on race, color, religion, sex, or national origin. Discrimination by an employment agency in the referral of applications is also prohibited. Congress, under the 1991 amendments, added that victims of intentional discrimination may be eligible for both compensatory damages and punitive damages under certain circumstances. Also, in cases in which the employer alleges that the discrimination was unintentional, the burden of proof will be on the employer to prove that the discrimination was unintentional. In these cases, the plaintiff may be awarded attorney fees if he or she prevails in the lawsuit. In 1967, the Congress added a prohibition of discrimination based on age when they passed the **Age Discrimination in Employment Act (ADEA),** which was also an amendment to the FLSA. The ADEA has been amended several times. In 1973, Congress enacted the **Vocational Rehabilitation Act,** which extends protection to handicapped workers but only applies to employees and prospective employees of employers who have federal contracts of $2,500 or more. In 1990, Congress passed the **Americans with Disabilities Act (ADA),** which generally protects people with disabilities from discrimination. In 1974, Congress passed the **Vietnam Veterans Readjustment Act.** This law requires certain federal contractors to develop an **affirmative action** plan to hire Vietnam veterans. In 1978 Congress passed the **Pregnancy Disability Act,** which amended Title VII of the Civil Rights Act of 1964. This law prohibits discrimination in employment based on pregnancy or pregnancy-related conditions.

In addition to these laws, Presidential Executive Order 11246 directs the Secretary of Labor to supervise the various federal contracting agencies to see that there is equal opportunity afforded to employees of certain federal contractors. The Secretary of Labor created the **Office of Federal Contract Compliance Programs (OFCCP)** to supervise both the awards of federal contracts and the required affirmative action.

Equal Pay Act

The Equal Pay Act of 1963 prohibits pay differentials based solely on sex. As indicated previously, it was an amendment to the FLSA and applies only to those employees who are covered by the provisions of the FLSA. Union conduct that causes or attempts to cause such employer discrimination is likewise prohibited.

To show a violation, the government must prove that the jobs in question require equal skill, equal effort, and equal responsibility and are performed under similar working conditions, and that males and females are paid different wages for performing them. If the employer wishes to raise one of the exceptions permitted by the Equal Pay Act as a defense, namely seniority, merit, quality of production, and any other factor other than sex, the employer then has the burden of proving that the differential is based on the alleged exception. Equal does not mean identical, but minor; insignificant job differences will not justify wage discrimination.

When a violation is shown to exist, the employer is prohibited from reducing anyone's wages to eliminate the differential; someone's wages must be raised. Aside from this provision, all the standard FLSA enforcement procedures apply to the equal pay provisions, including criminal penalties. Originally enforcement of this law was the responsibility of the Secretary of Labor; however, in 1978, as a result of a presidential order, the enforcement of this law was transferred to the EEOC.

Civil Rights Act

Title VII of the Civil Rights Act of 1964 as amended by the Equal Employment Opportunity Act of 1972 forbids discrimination by employers in hiring, promotion, discharge, and with regard to compensation, terms, conditions, and privileges of employment. This law also forbids discrimination by unions with regard to union membership and representation. In addition to the prohibitions against employers and unions, the law also extends its prohibition to discrimination by employment agencies. They must not discriminate in the referral of applicants for employment. Unlawful discrimination under Title VII is discrimination based on a person's race, color, religion, sex, or national origin.

There are, however, several statutory exceptions. Discriminatory hiring on the basis of religion, sex, or national origin is permitted when such limitations can be justified as a

bona fide occupational qualification (BFOQ) that is reasonably necessary to the normal operation of that particular business or enterprise.

An example of a religious BFOQ would be the requirement that the person hired as a minister for a specific church be a person who has the necessary religious training in the specific faith of that church. Also certain jobs may have a valid BFOQ that would require the employee to be of a specific sex.

Other jobs may have a BFOQ requiring a specific national origin. It must be noted however that an employer may not legally use a BFOQ to discriminate against an applicant or employee because of the applicant's race or color.

In addition to the BFOQ exception, there is a specific exemption for businesses located on or near an American Indian reservation; such businesses are permitted to have employment practices that give "preferential treatment" to American Indians. Similarly, the U.S. Bureau of Indian Affairs can conduct preferential hiring for American Indians.

Not all employers are covered by Title VII provisions. Private sector employers who employ fewer than 15 employees are exempt from Title VII provisions; however, many states have enacted their own civil rights laws that cover employers with fewer than 15 employees. Also, not all unions are covered by this law. Unions with fewer than 15 members are not subject to the provisions of Title VII unless they operate a hiring hall. Unions that operate hiring halls and employment agencies are subject to the provisions of Title VII regardless of the number of members in the union or the number of employees employed by the employment agency or the volume of their referrals. The Civil Rights Act of 1964 also exempted state and local employees; however, the amendments passed by Congress in 1972 extended the coverage of Title VII to most state and local employees.

The Civil Rights Act of 1964 set up the EEOC. The EEOC was granted authority by the 1964 act to investigate and conciliate grievances by individuals that allege discrimination based on race, color, religion, sex, or national origin. The amendments to the Civil Rights Act passed in 1972 gave the EEOC the added authority to not only investigate and conciliate but to file litigation on behalf of the complaining party or parties if they deemed it necessary and proper. If the EEOC investigation reveals that there is reasonable evidence to support the complainant's charge that unlawful discrimination has occurred and that the party charged is not willing to negotiate and conciliate, then the EEOC attorneys may commence litigation in the U.S. District Court on behalf of the complainant, at the expense of the EEOC. If the EEOC attorneys decide not to litigate the case, the EEOC will issue a "right-to-sue letter," which authorizes the complainant to file suit, but the suit must be filed at the complainant's expense.

There is a statutory time limit for filing of a complaint by a person who feels he or she has been discriminated against. The complaint (referred to as a charge) must be filed with the EEOC within 180 days after the discriminatory act occurred. If there is a state or local civil rights agency and the local or state law requires that the complaining party file with the state or local agency first before filing with the EEOC, then the time period is extended to 300 days. There is also a time limit for the filing of a lawsuit in U.S. District Court by a complainant in the case where the EEOC decides not to pursue litigation but issues the right-to-sue letter. The complaining party only has 90 days to file his or her lawsuit after receiving a right-to-sue letter.

The district courts that hear these Title VII actions are empowered to issue an injunction to stop an unlawful discriminatory practice if it is a continuing practice, and in certain cases they may also order affirmative action by the guilty party. Also the court may order the hiring or reinstatement of the people who were discriminated against with or without back pay. The law does, however, limit back pay awards to a period of 2 years prior to the date the charge was filed.

The 1972 amendments to the Civil Rights Act of 1964 not only gave the EEOC the right to commence litigation on behalf of complainants at the government's expense, the amendments also gave the EEOC a new and very important power to combat discrimination. Before the 1972 amendments, the EEOC was primarily concerned with individual grievances concerning alleged discrimination. With the passage of the 1972 amendments, the EEOC was given the power to bring class actions to litigate allegations of "pattern or practice" of discrimination.

The **Civil Rights Act of 1991** did not change the people and entities covered by the act. The primary thrust of this act was to expand the scope of damages that can be awarded to a victim of intentional discrimination and to reverse a trend set by several recent U.S. Supreme Court cases that were viewed as being very pro-employer and thus watering down the effect and purpose of the 1964 Act. This new law made many changes and additions to the civil rights laws of which employers must be aware.

The *Ledbetter* case interprets the 180-day filing limitation. The strict interpretation of the statutory language is a significant legal victory for employers. The decision was 5-4, with a strongly worded dissent.

Age Discrimination in Employment Act

In 1967, Congress enacted the ADEA. This act was passed as an amendment to the FLSA. An amendment to the law enacted in 1974 extended the act's protection to state and local governmental employees. An amendment enacted in 1978 extended the coverage to workers between the ages 40 and 70. An amendment enacted in 1980 prohibited mandatory retirement before 70 years of age. In 1986, as previously noted in this chapter, Congress again amended the ADEA making it unlawful for an employer to require an individual to retire at any age. Congress did make an exception regarding the mandatory retirement age for airline pilots, college professors, firefighters, and law enforcement officers stating that these types of employees could be required to retire at age 70 until December 31, 1993. Congress amended the ADEA again in 1990 with the passage of the **Older Workers Benefit Protection Act (OWBPA)**, which forbids age discrimination with regard to employee benefits. The OWBPA also established minimum standards for determining the validity of a waiver, which an employee may be requested to sign to waive his or her rights under the ADEA. It is legal for an employer to make an agreement with an employee to retire early. However, because this agreement is a waiver of the employee's rights it must meet the minimum standards of the OWBPA. The ADEA was originally enforced through FLSA procedures. However, in 1978 under a presidential reorganization plan, the enforcement of this law was transferred from the labor department to the EEOC.

As with religion, sex, and national origin under Title VII, there is a BFOQ exception to the ADEA. In addition, the employer may differentiate on the basis of **reasonable factors other than age (RFOTA).** For example, a 40-year-old professional football player who was no longer able to run, block, and tackle with the necessary vigor could presumably be fired on the basis of RFOTA, even though age as such was not a BFOQ for a position on the team. The employer may also observe the terms of any bona fide seniority system or employee benefit plan, but an employer cannot use the benefit plan as an excuse for refusing to hire an older employee. Of course, an employer can still discharge or discipline an employee for good cause.

Vocational Rehabilitation Act

With the passage of the Vocational Rehabilitation Act of 1973 Congress provided protection from private sector discrimination against the handicapped; however, such protection is limited only to the private sector employers making a contract with the U.S. government for $2,500 or more. Even so, coverage extends to most major companies and perhaps half of all the businesses in the country. All such companies must have an affirmative action plan for hiring and promoting qualified handicapped people at all levels, so in that sense the 1973 act requires more than Title VII of the 1964 act. All departments and agencies of the executive branch of the national government are likewise covered by the 1973 act.

Americans with Disabilities Act

This law is perhaps the most important and comprehensive legislation in the area of employment discrimination since the passage of the original civil rights act in 1964. The Vocational Rehabilitation Act of 1973 only applies to a relatively small group of employers, namely only those employers with contracts of at least $2,500 with the U.S. government. The ADA of 1990, effective July 1, 1992, covers all employers with 25 or more

CASE 3

Ledbetter v. Goodyear Tire & Rubber Co., Inc.

127 S.Ct. 2162 (2007)

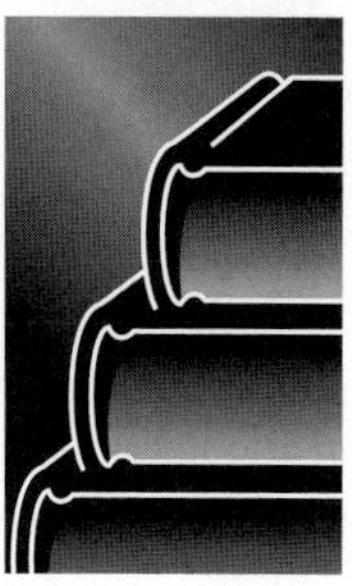

Facts: Shortly after her retirement from Goodyear in 1998, Lilly Ledbetter brought a pay discrimination lawsuit under Title VII of the 1964 Civil Rights Act. She had filed her charge with the EEOC in July 1998, alleging that discriminatory performance evaluations by her supervisors, years before, had resulted in her lower pay level throughout the rest of her career at Goodyear. Although there was no discriminatory intent against her in these later years, she claimed that the effects of the earlier gender-based discrimination continued to impact each subsequent salary decision. The U.S. District Court allowed the pay claim to proceed to trial, with a jury award in her favor. The 11th Circuit Court reversed, finding that her claims were time-barred by the 180-day limitation because she had never filed an EEOC charge when the original discrimination occurred. She was granted review by the Supreme Court.

Issue: Can an employee recover for discriminatory pay received within the 180-period, which is the result of intentionally discriminatory pay decisions made more than 180 days before the filing of an EEOC charge?

Decision: No. Judgment of the 11th Circuit Court is affirmed.

Opinion by Justice Alito: "In addressing the issue whether an EEOC charge was filed on time, we have stressed the need to identify with care the specific employment practice that is at issue.... Ledbetter points to two different employment practices as possible candidates. Primarily, she urges us to focus on the paychecks that were issued to her during the EEOC charging period (the 180-day period preceding the filing of her EEOC questionnaire), each of which, she contends, was a separate act of discrimination. Alternatively, Ledbetter directs us to the 1998 decision denying her a raise, and she argues that this decision was 'unlawful because it carried forward intentionally discriminatory disparities from prior years.... Both these arguments fail because they would require us in effect to jettison the defining element of the legal claim on which her Title VII recovery was based.

"Ledbetter asserted disparate treatment, the central element of which is discriminatory intent.... However, Ledbetter does not assert that the relevant Goodyear decision-makers acted with actual discriminatory intent either when they issued her checks during the EEOC charging period or when they denied her a raise in 1998. Rather, she argues that the paychecks were unlawful because they would have been larger if she had been evaluated in a nondiscriminatory manner prior to the EEOC charging period.... Similarly, she maintains that the 1998 decision was unlawful because it 'carried forward' the effects of prior, uncharged discriminatory decisions.... In essence, she suggests that it is sufficient that discriminatory acts that occurred prior to the charging period had continuing effects during that period.... This argument is squarely foreclosed by our precedents....

"The instruction provided by [the precedents] is clear. The EEOC charging period is triggered when a discrete unlawful practice takes place. A new violation does not occur, and a new charging period does not commence, upon occurrence of subsequent nondiscriminatory acts that entail adverse effects resulting from the past discrimination. But of course, if an employer engages in a series of acts each of which is intentionally discriminatory, then a fresh violation takes place when each act is committed....

"Ledbetter's arguments here ... cannot be reconciled with [the precedents]. Ledbetter ... makes no claim that intentionally discriminatory conduct occurred during the charging period or that discriminatory decisions that occurred prior to that were not communicated to her.... [C]urrent effects alone cannot breathe life into prior, unchanged discrimination; as we held in Evans, such effects themselves have 'no present legal consequences.'...

"Ledbetter's attempt to take the intent associated with the prior pay decisions and shift it to the 1998 pay decision is unsound.... The effect of this shift would be to impose liability in the absence of the requisite intent....

"We therefore reject the suggestion that an employment practice committed with no improper purpose and no discriminatory intent is rendered unlawful nonetheless because it gives some effect to an intentional discriminatory act that occurred outside the charging period. Ledbetter's claim is, for this reason, untimely....

"We are not in a position to evaluate Ledbetter's policy arguments, and it is not our prerogative to change the way in which Title VII balances the interests of aggrieved employees and the interest in encouraging the 'prompt processing of all charges of employment discrimination.'...

"Ledbetter's policy arguments for giving special treatment to pay claims find no support in the statute and are inconsistent with our precedents.... We apply the statute as written, and this means that any unlawful employment practice, including those involving compensation, must be presented to the EEOC within the period prescribed by statute....

"For these reasons, the judgment of the Court of Appeals for the Eleventh Circuit is affirmed.

"It is so ordered."

employees, and as of July 1, 1994, this law covers all employers with 15 or more employees. The title that primarily concerns employment discrimination is Title I. Title I of the Act states that: "No covered entities shall discriminate against a qualified individual with a disability because of the disability of such individual in regard to job application procedures, the hiring, advancement or discharge of employees, employee compensations, job training, and other terms, conditions, and privileges of employment." The EEOC is responsible for the enforcement of this law. Disability under the act includes both "physical and mental impairment that substantially limits one or more of the major life activities of such individuals: or being regarded as having such an impairment." This definition is more encompassing than the handicapped definition under the Vocational Rehabilitation Act of 1973. Under this new law the employer must be concerned not only about the person with the obvious disability, such as the blind or hearing impaired or the person with a loss of use of a limb, and so forth, but also the employer must be concerned with mental disabilities. For example, drug addiction, alcoholism, AIDS, and various psychological disorders are often not identifiable during the interview of a person for employment. The law bans preemployment medical examinations and prohibits inquiries of job applicants regarding whether or not a disability exists. The employer can require a medical examination but only after an offer of employment has been made and then subject to several conditions and requirements. If an employee is known to have a disability then the employer has an obligation to make reasonable accommodations to enable the person to perform the tasks required of the person. Reasonable accommodations will no doubt also require physical changes to the employer's buildings, such as wheelchair ramps, restroom availability to handicapped, and so on.

As these various new employment statutes have been adopted, the courts have been confronted with an increasingly complex problem of interpretation: How do they relate to each other? The *Hoffman* case earlier in this chapter provided one example—the interface between the NLRA and the IRCA—and resulted in a 5-to-4 split on the Supreme Court. Difficult cases have also arisen from employers' attempts to reconcile the duty to provide a safe workplace (OSHA) with the nondiscrimination requirements of Title VII and ADA. In 1991, the Supreme Court ruled that Johnson Controls had violated Title VII when it prohibited women who were or could become pregnant from taking certain jobs where they could be exposed to lead (which may cause serious birth defects). The company claimed it was simply trying to avoid workplace injuries, but the Court held that there was illegal gender discrimination.

There is a similar tension between the ADA and OSHA. The EEOC has adopted regulations interpreting the ADA and attempting to minimize the seeming conflict. The validity of one of those regulations is at issue in the *Chevron* case.

Vietnam Veterans Readjustment Act

Congress passed the Vietnam Veterans Readjustment Act to give Vietnam veterans a special priority with regard to employment; however, only employers with government contracts of $10,000 or more are required to take affirmative action to employ and advance disabled and qualified veterans of the Vietnam era. No other employers are required by law to give such preference or priority to the veterans of the Vietnam era. All covered employers have an obligation to list all suitable job openings with the appropriate local employment service. Referral priority will then be given to Vietnam era veterans.

Pregnancy Discrimination Act

A recent major addition to the antidiscrimination laws is the Pregnancy Discrimination Act. This act prohibits discrimination in any aspect of the employment relationship because of a female employee's pregnancy. Health and disability plans for employees, in particular, must provide coverage of pregnancy and childbirth on the same basis as other medical conditions.

State Antidiscrimination Laws

Many states have passed civil rights laws that extend coverage to more employers than the national law. For example, the national Civil Rights Act only covers employers with

CASE 4

Chevron U.S.A., Inc. v. Echazabal
536 U.S. 73 (2002)

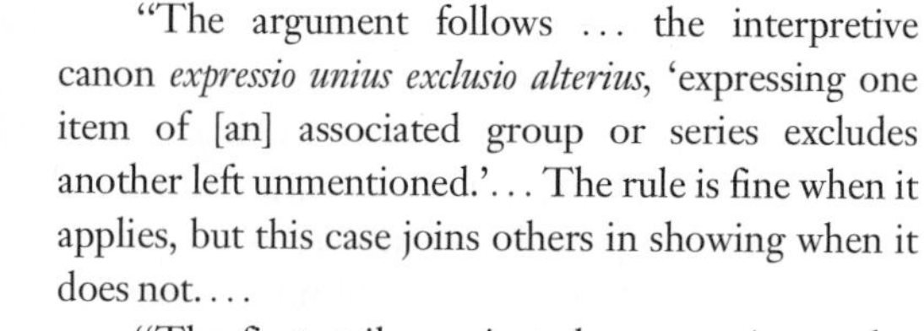

Facts: Mario Echazabal worked for an independent contractor at one of Chevron's oil refineries. When he applied for a job with Chevron, his physical examination revealed a liver disease, which the doctors said could be aggravated by exposure to the toxins at the refinery. Chevron refused to hire him and told the contractor that Mario had to be reassigned to a job where he would not be exposed or else be completely removed from the refinery. Mario was laid off and filed a lawsuit under the ADA. The U.S. District Court granted Chevron's motion for summary judgment, but the Ninth Circuit reversed. Chevron asked for U.S. Supreme Court review.

Issue: Does the ADA justify an employer's refusal to permit an employee to work on a job that poses a direct threat to his health?

Decision: Yes. Judgment of the Ninth Circuit reversed, and case remanded.

Opinion by Justice Souter: "[T]he [ADA] creates an affirmative defense for action under a qualification standard 'shown to be job-related for the position in question and consistent with business necessity.' Such a standard may include 'a requirement that an individual shall not pose a direct threat to the health or safety of other individuals in the workplace,'. . . if the individual cannot perform the job safely with reasonable accommodation. . . . By regulation, the EEOC carries the defense one step further, in allowing an employer to screen out a potential worker with a disability not only for risks he would pose to others in the workplace but for risks on the job to his own health or safety as well. . . .

"Chevron relies on the regulation here, since it says a job in the refinery would pose a 'direct threat' to Echazabal's health. . . . Echazabal, on the contrary, argues that as a matter of law the statute precludes the regulation. . . .

"The argument follows . . . the interpretive canon *expressio unius exclusio alterius*, 'expressing one item of [an] associated group or series excludes another left unmentioned.'. . . The rule is fine when it applies, but this case joins others in showing when it does not. . . .

"The first strike against the expression-exclusion rule is right in the text that Echazabal quotes. Congress included the harm-to-others provision as an example of legitimate qualifications that are 'job-related and consistent with business necessity.' These are spacious defensive categories, which seem to give an agency . . . a good deal of discretion in setting the limits of permissible qualification standards. . . . Far from supporting Echazabal's position, the expansive phrasing of 'may include' points directly away from the sort of exclusive specification he claims. . . .

"Strike two in this case is the failure to identify any such established series, including both threats to others and threats to self, from which Congress appears to have made a deliberate choice to omit the latter item as a signal of the affirmative defense's scope. . . .

"It would be a stretch . . . to say that there was a standard usage, with its source in agency practice or elsewhere, that connected threats to others so closely to threats to self that leaving out one was like ignoring a twin. . . .

"Nor can the EEOC's resolution be fairly called unreasonable as allowing the kind of workplace paternalism the ADA was meant to outlaw. . . . Its regulation disallows just this sort of sham protection, through demands for a particularized inquiry into the harms the employee would probably face. . . . The EEOC was certainly acting within the reasonable zone when it saw a difference between rejecting workplace paternalism and ignoring specific and documented risks to the employee himself, even if the employee would take his chances for the sake of getting a job. . . .

"Accordingly, we reverse the judgment of the Court of Appeals and remand the case for proceedings consistent with this opinion."

15 or more employees. Some states' civil rights laws cover those employers with 6 or more employees. Many states also have their own civil rights commissions to enforce these laws.

Civil Rights Laws: Major Problem Areas

Job Testing and Educational Requirements

Title VII of the Civil Rights Act of 1964, as amended in 1972, does not prohibit employers from testing applicants or current employees. Tests may be used to measure the applicant's or employee's ability to do the job, provided the test does not discriminate against minorities or women. For example, an employer wants to hire a typist. A typing test would be a legal test if it simply tested the accuracy and speed of typing that could be performed by the applicant. With regard to requiring a certain level of education before a person will be considered for employment, any such requirement must be shown to be job related.

In 1971, the U.S. Supreme Court decided the now famous *Griggs v. Duke Power* case. In that case, the employer used preemployment tests and had a job requirement stating that all applicants had to have a high school diploma to be hired. Neither the tests nor the requirement of a high school diploma were found to be job related. In that case, both the tests and the educational requirements had the effect of disqualifying a disproportionate number of African Americans.

Generally speaking, employers may use tests and may have educational requirements for certain jobs, but the burden is on the employer to prove that the tests and educational requirements are job related.

Sexual Harassment

Section 703 of Title VII of the Civil Rights Act of 1964 as amended prohibits sexual harassment. **Sexual harassment** has been defined as conduct involving unwelcome sexual advances, requests for sexual favors, and other verbal or physical conduct of a sexual nature. Typically, a supervisor makes such advances, in return for a promotion, raise, or other job-related benefit.

There is no question that the person guilty of the sexual harassment, such as a supervisor who requests sexual favors as a condition for hiring an applicant, continued employment, a salary increase, or a promotion, is guilty of violating the law. Recently the courts have also held the employer liable for civil damages if it can be shown that the employer knew or should have known of the illegal conduct.

Employer Benefit Plans

Most employers provide some type of medical payment plan for employees and their families and some type of retirement plan. These plans can be financed entirely by contributions by the employer, or their cost may be shared between employer and employee. The discrimination problems with regard to these plans have been primarily in the area of sex discrimination. One question that arose was: Does a medical plan have to provide coverage for pregnancy? The Supreme Court of the United States answered that question in the negative in 1976. Then the U.S. Congress stepped in and in 1978 enacted the Pregnancy Discrimination Act, which now makes it unlawful for an employer to exclude pregnancy-related disabilities from any medical, hospital, or disability benefits plan or any company plan or program that allows sick leaves.

In 1983, the U.S. Supreme Court further defined the required "neutrality" in its decision in *Newport News Shipbuilding and Dry Dock Co. v. EEOC.* In that case, the employer gave women employees paid leave time to give birth to a child, and the question was raised as to whether the granting of such benefits to females was discriminatory against males. The Supreme Court held that the employer must also give paid leave time to any male employee whose wife gives birth to a child.

Statistically, women have had a longer life expectancy than men. Pension plans, insurance annuity plans, and other forms of retirement plans have traditionally based contribution rates on life expectancy. That is, because women statistically have a longer life expectancy after retirement than men, it can be expected that they will have to be paid more benefits than would be paid to men, who have a shorter life expectancy. Insurance companies, to have adequate funding, either increased the contribution to be made by women to offset the fact that they may receive benefits for a longer time, or the companies charged the same contribution rate but then paid the retired women a lower monthly retirement benefit than retired men who had made similar contributions. These practices were based on the contention that the woman would live longer and thus there would be more monthly payments to be made in the case of a retired woman than to a retired man. The Supreme Court has declared both of these practices discriminatory under Title VII.

Thus, after these decisions any contributions by employees to a retirement plan must be sex-neutral, and any distribution to retired employees from such plans must also be calculated without regard to the sex of the party receiving the distribution benefits.

Comparable Worth Doctrine

We have previously discussed the Equal Pay Act of 1963. As previously stated, that law requires an employer to pay equal pay for equal work. For a claimant to collect back pay under that law it must be shown that one sex (usually the males) is being paid more than members of the opposite sex who are doing the same job. If the job performed by one sex is not substantially equal to the job performed by the opposite sex, then there is no violation.

Recently the proponents of equal pay for the sexes came up with the concept of "comparable worth." This concept would make the employer not only pay equal pay to both sexes for doing substantially equal work but also for doing jobs which are of comparable worth or value to the company. In 1981 the U.S. Supreme Court, in *County of Washington v. Gunther*, found that women who were not doing substantially the same job as their male counterparts could bring a lawsuit under Title VII for back wages based on alleged intentional sexual discrimination in payment of wages to women.

That case involved complaints by four female prison guards who were being paid less than male prison guards. However, the evidence showed the jobs of the female prison guards and the male prison guards were not substantially the same because the male guards supervised 10 times as many prisoners per guard as did the female guards and also a substantial part of the female guards' job was spent doing clerical work. Thus, the jobs were not substantially equal. The Supreme Court found that there was sexual discrimination with regard to the wages paid to the women and remanded the case to provide for payment of back wages, but without basing their decision on the **comparable worth doctrine.** The advocates of comparable worth felt that the case was a first step in the acceptance of the comparable worth doctrine even though the court did not specifically address the comparable worth issue.

The state legislature of the state of Washington was favorably impressed with the fairness of the comparable worth concept and passed a law in applying the doctrine of comparable worth to the state employees' jobs, effective in June 1983.

Although this doctrine on its face seems to be a fair doctrine and certainly a doctrine that would promote the cause of reducing discrimination against women in the workplace, it has not been widely accepted. The primary reason, of course, is not only the difficulty of deciding comparable worth of the various jobs, but also the bottom line of the dollars and cents cost of making such adjustments. Obviously you could not reduce the pay of one job to the level of the comparative job so it would mean increasing the pay for the lower paying job. Thus, the future of comparative worth is still uncertain at this time.

Affirmative Action Required by Government Contractors

We have previously referred to the Rehabilitation Act of 1973 and the Vietnam Veterans Readjustment Act of 1974. Both of these acts are legislative enactments that specify that government contractors with contracts exceeding a specific amount must take affirmative action with regard to hiring the people protected by those laws, namely, the handicapped and Vietnam veterans.

In 1965, President Johnson issued Executive Order No. 11246; and in 1967, he issued Executive Order 11375. These executive orders set up the OFCCP. They also require a contractor who accepts a U.S. government contract of $50,000 or more with 50 employees to file a written affirmative action plan with the OFCCP. This plan involves a complete review of the contractor's workforce and a breakdown of the workforce into categories of race, color, sex, and national origin. The surrounding area from which employees are recruited is then reviewed with regard to the same categories. The contractor is then reviewed with regard to the same categories. The contractor is then required to prepare a plan to take affirmative action to increase the numbers of employees in these various categories, so that the percentage of people in the various categories in the workforce of the employer is comparable to the percentage of the available workers in such categories in the recruiting area. Contractors are not required to fire nonminorities or males or to hire more people than necessary, nor are they required to hire people who are not qualified for the job.

In addition to the contractors who accept U.S. contracts of $50,000 or more and who have 50 or more employees, several other groups are affected by Executive Orders 11246 and 11375. Those groups are: (1) contractors or subcontractors that provide the government with more than $10,000 worth of supplies, services, or work, (2) contractors or

CASE 5

Morrison v. Circuit City Stores, Inc.

317 F.3d 646 (6 Cir. 2003)

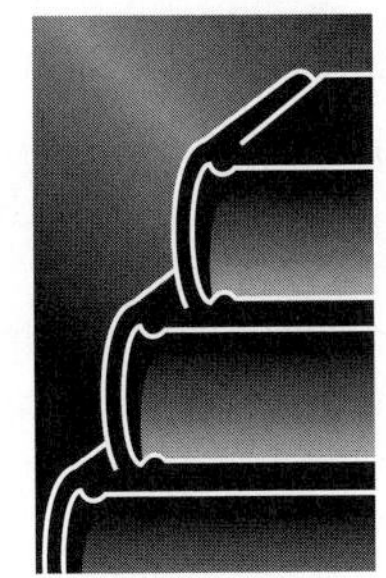

Facts: Lillian Morrison was fired after she had worked at Circuit City for 2 years. Claiming race and sex discrimination, she filed a lawsuit in Ohio state courts. The company had the case removed to a U.S. District Court and then asked for enforcement of the arbitration agreement that Lillian had signed when she was hired. The court ordered arbitration, and Lillian appealed.

Mark Shankle quit his job at Pep Boys and asked for arbitration of his claim for severance pay. Shankle changed lawyers, tried to withdraw his arbitration request, and filed suit in Tennessee state court for additional wrongs—including Title VII violations. Pep Boys removed the case to a U.S. District Court and asked for enforcement of the arbitration agreement Shankle had signed. The court refused to enforce the arbitration agreement, and Pep Boys appealed.

The Sixth Circuit judges decide to hear the appeals together, en banc (all judges participating).

Issue: Are cost-splitting provisions in arbitration agreements on employment discrimination claims enforceable?

Decision: No. Morrison judgment affirmed (on other grounds); Shankle case remanded for arbitration, without the cost-splitting provision.

Opinion by Judge Moore: "The proper resolution of these [two] appeals requires that we carefully reconcile the 'liberal federal policy favoring arbitration agreements,'... with the important rights created and protected by federal civil rights legislation. In the past, many have viewed mandatory arbitration in the employment context and the goals of civil rights legislation as irreconcilable, with the former understood as a means for employers to evade the purpose of the latter. The Supreme Court, however, has repeatedly rejected generalized attacks on arbitration that rest on suspicion of arbitration as a method of weakening the protections afforded in the substantive law....

"[U]nder the correct reconciliation of the sometimes-perceived conflict between arbitration agreements in the employment contract and federal anti-discrimination laws, the choice to arbitrate statutory claims will change only the forum of decision and not the substantive protections afforded by the statutes in question....

"Both Morrison and Shankle argue on appeal that the cost-splitting provisions in the arbitration agreements at issue in their respective cases have the effect of denying them effective fora for the vindication of their statutory rights. The Supreme Court has made clear that statutory rights, such as those created by Title VII, may be subject to mandatory arbitration only if the arbitral forum permits effective vindication of those rights.... If, then, the splitting or sharing of the costs of the arbitral forum under a particular arbitration effectively prevents the vindication of a plaintiff's statutory rights, those rights cannot be subject to mandatory arbitration under that agreement....

"The arbitration of statutory claims must be accessible to potential litigants as well as adequate to protect the rights in question so that arbitration, like the judicial resolution of disputes, will 'further broader social purposes.'... To put the matter in a slightly different way, employers should not be permitted to draft arbitration agreements that deter a substantial number of potential litigants from seeking any forum for the vindication of their rights....

"[T]he Supreme Court [has] adopted a case-by-case approach to determining whether a cost-splitting provision in an arbitration agreement denies potential litigants the opportunity to vindicate their statutory rights.... 'Where ... a party seeks to invalidate an arbitration agreement on the ground that arbitration would be prohibitively expensive, that party bears the burden of showing the likelihood of incurring such costs.'...

"The issue is whether the terms of the arbitration agreement itself would deter a substantial number of similarly situated employees from bringing their claims to the arbitral forum, and thus the court must consider the decision-making process of these potential litigants. In many cases, if not most, employees considering the consequences of bringing their claims in the arbitral forum will be inclined to err on the side of caution, especially when the worst-case scenario would mean not only losing on their substantive claims but also the imposition of the costs of the arbitration....

"[W]e conclude that the cost-splitting provision in the Circuit City arbitration agreement was unenforceable....

"We also conclude that the limitations that the Circuit City arbitration agreement places on the damages a claimant may recover are unenforceable....

"[H]owever, the [Morrison] arbitration has already taken place, and we have been informed by the parties that Morrison was not required to pay any share of the costs of the arbitration and that the arbitrator did not apply the limitation on remedies. Given these facts, remand is not necessary, and thus we will affirm the district court's order compelling arbitration, on these different grounds."

[Shankle's case was remanded for a District Court order requiring arbitration in conformity with the agreement, but without the cost-splitting provision.]

subcontractors that have had more than $10,000 worth of government business in any 12-month period, (3) anyone who has government bills of lading in any amount, (4) any firm that serves as an issuing or paying agent of U.S. savings bonds and notes, (5) any firm that serves as a depository of U.S. funds in any amount, (6) all contractors and subcontractors that hold U.S. assisted contracts in excess of $10,000, and (7) any construction contractor's or subcontractor's construction employees who are engaged in on-site construction including those construction employees who work on a nonfederal or nonfederally assisted construction site.

The theory of affirmative action is to seek out women and people from the minority categories to fill new and vacant positions to thus increase the percentage of women and minority people in the employment of the contractor. OFCCP will periodically review the plan and the progress made. Failure to comply with the plan may cause cancellation of the government contract and disbarment from future government contracts for a period of time. One of the problems of most concern with regard to affirmative action plans is the problem of "reverse discrimination," primarily against white males.

Arbitration Clauses

Confronted with this vast array of liability-producing statutes and regulations, many employers are requiring employees to sign arbitration agreements as a condition of employment. The Federal Arbitration Act of 1925 was adopted to validate arbitration as a method of settling legal disputes. Over the last several decades, the U.S. Supreme Court has enforced arbitration clauses in a number of different contexts, including claims arising under national regulatory statutes (antitrust, securities, ocean transportation). In 1991, the Court ordered arbitration of a broker-employee's claim under the ADEA, and in 2001 the Court ruled that the Federal Aviation Administration's (FAA) exemption for "seamen, railroad employees, or any other class of workers engaged in foreign or interstate commerce" only exempted the employment contracts of other transportation workers. All other employees are thus subject to the FAA if they sign arbitration agreements. The *Morrison* case examines some of the outer limits as to just what can be included in an arbitration agreement.

Significance of This Chapter

The relationship between employer and employee is a significant area of government regulation. Prior to such regulation, we saw blatant discrimination with regard to employees' rights concerning unionism and considerable discrimination as to employees' civil rights. Every manager needs to have knowledge of at least the major laws that regulate the employer-employee relationship. This chapter gives the manager a basic knowledge of those laws.

IMPORTANT TERMS AND CONCEPTS

affirmative action
Age Discrimination in Employment Act (ADEA)
agency shop
Americans with Disabilities Act (ADA)
arbitration
bargaining representative
bona fide occupational qualification (BFOQ)
Civil Rights Act of 1964
Civil Rights Act of 1991
Clayton Act
closed shop
comparable worth doctrine
Employment Retirement Income Security Act (ERISA)
Equal Employment Opportunity Commission (EEOC)
Equal Pay Act of 1963
Fair Labor Standards Act (FLSA)
free rider argument
Landrum-Griffin Act
lockout
management prerogatives
mandatory subjects
Norris-LaGuardia Act
Occupational Safety and Health Act (OSHA)
Office of Federal Contract Compliance Programs (OFCCP)
Older Workers Benefit Protection Act (OWBPA)
open shop
permissive subjects
plant relocation
Pregnancy Disability Act
Railway Labor Act
reasonable factors other than age (RFOTA)
runaway shop
Section 14(b) of Taft-Hartley
sexual harassment
Sherman Antitrust Act
state right-to-work laws
Taft-Hartley Act
unfair labor practices
union shop
Vietnam Veterans Readjustment Act
Vocational Rehabilitation Act
Wagner Act

QUESTIONS AND PROBLEMS FOR DISCUSSION

1. How does the NLRB determine the scope of the appropriate bargaining unit?

2. What topics are mandatory subjects to collective bargaining?

3. What is the difference between a BFOQ and an RFOTA?

4. What is the OFCCP? What is its role?

5. Johnson Controls manufactures batteries; lead is a primary ingredient in the process. Lead is a toxic element, especially harmful to the unborn. When eight of its female employees with blood lead levels exceeding the OSHA standard became pregnant, Johnson adopted a policy that prevented fertile women from working on jobs where they would be exposed to lead. The International Union, United Automobile, Aerospace and Agricultural Implement Workers of America (UAW) filed a class action in U.S. District Court alleging sex discrimination. The District Court granted summary judgment for Johnson, based on "business necessity," and the Court of Appeals affirmed.

   Can an employer exclude fertile females from certain jobs because of its concern for the fetuses that the women employees might conceive?

6. Illinois Coil Spring Company decided to move its assembly operations formerly conducted at its Milwaukee Division to its McHenry Division. The labor costs at Milwaukee were $8 an hour in wages and $2 an hour in fringe benefits; at McHenry, $4.50 in wages and $1.35 in fringes. A labor contract was in force at Milwaukee but not at McHenry. Illinois did bargain with its Milwaukee union about the change by asking for wage concessions to keep the Milwaukee location viable. After the union rejected any concessions Illinois did begin to relocate its assembly operations to McHenry. The union filed unfair labor practice charges alleging a violation of Section 8(d), 8(a)(1), 8(a)(3), and 8(a)(5).

   Is the union correct? Explain.

7. Captain Carl Stotts, an African American employed by the Memphis Tennessee Fire Department, filed a class action in U.S. District Court in Tennessee alleging that the fire department, the local union, and certain city officials of Memphis, Tennessee, were engaged in a pattern or practice of discrimination on the basis of race and color. This case was settled by consent of the parties, and a consent decree was entered by the court ordering the fire department to remedy the department's hiring and promotion practice with regard to African Americans. The consent decree required the city to promote 13 individuals and to provide back pay to 81 employees of the fire department. It also required the city to adopt a long-term goal to increase the amount of minority representation in each job classification. The next year, the city announced a budget cut that would require layoffs throughout city government. Layoffs were to be on the "last hired first fired" basis. The plaintiff Stotts went back to court and requested an injunction forbidding the layoffs of any African American employees.

   Should the injunction be granted? Why or why not?

8. The University of Nebraska at Omaha appealed an order of the state's Court of Industrial Relations (CIR) that established a collective bargaining unit at the University of Nebraska at Omaha. The university contended that: (1) the CIR had no jurisdiction over it; (2) the bargaining unit was inappropriate because it included only employees of University of Nebraska at Omaha; and (3) the bargaining unit was inappropriate because it should not have included department chairs, librarians, counselors, assistant instructors, or academic personnel holding special appointments. The University of Nebraska at Omaha College of Business Administration Faculty Association also appealed from the dismissal of its petition for intervention that had asked for the establishment of a separate bargaining unit. Intercollegiate athletic coaches and trainers were excluded from the bargaining unit.

   Will the CIR's decision be upheld? Explain.

9. Celio Diaz applied for the job of flight cabin attendant (also known as the job of stewardess). Pan Am refused to hire him. Pan Am contended that a BFOQ applied. Diaz filed suit on behalf of himself and all other males as a class being denied access to these jobs, alleging Pan Am had violated the Civil Rights Act of 1964 by refusing to hire him. Pan Am's primary contention was that it was the passengers' preference to be served by females rather than males. The trial court found that being a female was a proper BFOQ for the job. Diaz appealed.

   Is there a BFOQ here? Discuss.

CHAPTER 31

Partnership Law

Chapter Objectives

This chapter will:

- Define a partnership.
- Describe the creation of a partnership.
- Discuss the classifications of partnerships.
- Review the process of dissolution, winding up, and termination of a partnership.
- Describe a partner's rights and duties to the other partners.
- Explain the relationship of partners to third process.
- Review the liability of a partner for torts.
- Discuss possible criminal liability of partners.

Nature of Partnership

Origins

The partnership is perhaps the oldest and most common form of business organization involving more than one person. The partnership form of organization dates as far back as the Middle Ages and perhaps even before that. Traditionally the partnership was a nonstatutory form of business organization, whose creation was comparatively simple, inexpensive, and informal.

The body of law governing the partnership business organization was developed on a case-by-case basis throughout the court system over the years. Whenever law is developed by the case method, there are bound to be variations in decisions by judges, a lack of uniformity from state to state, and a lack of real clarity as to what the law is on a particular point. Thus, the National Conference of Commissioners on Uniform State Laws, which was referred to in an earlier chapter, drafted the **Uniform Partnership Act (UPA)** in 1914. The purpose of this act was to clarify and codify the maze of court decisions on partnership law into a workable statutory form. The great majority of the states have adopted the UPA. Thus, references will be made to the UPA throughout the chapters on partnership law.

Legal Entity

Under the common law, a partnership was not considered a separate **legal entity**, or person, but merely a collection of persons who were doing business together. There was no separate "it," but merely "them." In contrast, a corporation is clearly a separate legal person, even though it has no actual physical existence. All of a corporation's business affairs are conducted in its name, even though it must use agents.

Failure to recognize a partnership as a separate entity makes the conduct of its business unnecessarily cumbersome. Under common law, for example, a partnership could not hold title to real estate in its firm name; it had to be held in the name of one or more partners. Suits by or against large partnerships can be terribly complex if the rules require each partner to be specifically named, and so on.

Recognizing these problems, the UPA's drafters reached a compromise. For certain purposes, but not completely, the partnership is now recognized as a separate entity. Its property is treated as separate from that of the individual partners (as discussed later in the chapter), and it can own real estate in the firm name if it wishes. It keeps separate books and records and prepares separate (informational) tax returns. It does not, however, pay a separate tax, as it would if it were a separate entity. Many states, with newer civil procedure rules, now also permit suits by or against a partnership in the firm name. Separate bankruptcy proceedings can also be instituted by or against a partnership.

Definition

Section 6 of the UPA defines a partnership as follows: "a partnership is an association of two or more persons to carry on as co-owners, a business for profit." This definition contains several requirements that must be met before there can be a partnership. First, the partnership must be an association of two or more persons. The word *association* implies that an agreement has been made. Thus, we are talking about contract law with regard to whether or not a legal agreement exists. Second, the association must consist of two or more persons. A person can be a natural person or a legal entity such as a corporation. Third, persons must carry on a business as co-owners. A partnership is not simply two or more people working together; it must be two or more people, each of whom has some rights of ownership in the business. It is not required that all of these people have equal rights of ownership; however, each must be a co-owner. Finally, the business must be for profit. This rules out the many organizations that have been established for religious, charitable, educational, and other not-for-profit purposes.

It is interesting to note that for tax purposes the Internal Revenue Code, Section 761(a), defines a partnership as a "syndicate, group, pool, joint venture, or other unincorporated organization through . . . which any business . . . is carried on, and which is not . . . a corporation or a trust or estate." The Internal Revenue Service (IRS) is not concerned about the rights and duties between partners or between partners and third persons; it is only trying to classify business organizations for taxing purposes.

Joint Ventures

A **joint venture** is similar to a partnership in that it also involves two or more persona who are engaged in some business activity. Joint ventures differ from partnerships mainly in purpose and duration. A partnership is created to carry on a business for profit for an indefinite period of time and is dissolved by the death or resignation of one of the partners. A joint venture, on the other hand, is created to conduct a specific business activity over a specific period of time. An example of a joint venture would be a situation in which two persons purchased an apartment house as an investment for resale and hired a manager to run it until it was sold. The purpose of this venture is specific, and the duration is limited. No general agency is created between the parties; they are simply joint investors.

A **syndicate**, like a partnership, involves two or more persons who are involved in some business activity. However, a syndicate differs from a partnership in that, like a joint venture, it is formed for a specific business activity and a specific duration. The parties involved in a syndicate can be classified as investors rather than as persons carrying on a business as co-owners. A syndicate was defined in the case of *Hambleton v. Rhind*, 84 Md. 456, as "[A]n association of individuals, formed for the purpose of conducting and carrying out some particular business transaction, ordinarily of a financial character, in which the members are mutually interested."

The terms *group* and *pool* as used in Section 761(a) are really just Internal Revenue Code language used to describe a group of persons who are participating in a business activity or a situation in which persons pool their money to conduct a business for profit.

Qualifications of Partners

Part I, Section 2 of the UPA states that the word *persons* includes individuals, partners, corporations, and other associations. This means that not only individuals but also corporations, partnerships, and other associations may be partners in a partnership. Because individual states may have specific rules and regulations regarding participation in partnerships by corporations, other partnerships, and other associations, whether these can be partners depends on state law.

Any natural person having the capacity to contract can become a partner. In Part Two, we dealt with the question of what persons are competent to contract. Insane people may not become partners. Minors do not have full contractual capacity; however, they may become partners in a partnership. But, as with simple contracts, minors have the right to disaffirm their partnership contracts at any time before they reach majority and for a reasonable time thereafter. By such disaffirmance, a minor may avoid certain liability to partnership creditors. Also, a minor who disaffirms the partnership agreement is generally entitled to get back his or her capital investment and share of the profits up to that time, provided that such a distribution will not adversely affect the interest of existing partnership creditors. In some states, the disaffirming minor may be able to withdraw capital before creditors are paid.

Because a partnership is a voluntary association, the general rule is that no one can be forced to become a partner with another; there must be an agreement to be partners. This rule is summed up in the Latin phrase *delectus personae* (choice of persons). Each of us has the right to choose the persons with whom we will be partners, and we are not partners unless we agree to be partners. In contrast, the shares of stock in a corporation are presumed to be fully and freely transferable, so that a person could become involved in a corporate business with someone who was a total stranger of unknown abilities and personality.

In cases involving alleged discrimination by large law firms or accounting firms the courts have tried to balance the partners' freedom to choose new associates with the individual's right to be free from discriminatory evaluations.

Classification

Partnerships may be classified as **general partnerships** or **limited partnerships**. The general partnership is the more familiar form. It is a partnership in which all of the partners have unlimited liability for partnership debts. A limited partnership is a partnership in which one or more of the partners are general partners with unlimited liability. However, one or more of the other partners are limited partners, and their liabilities for partnership debts are limited to the extent of their investment in the partnership. Like persons who buy stock in a corporation, they cannot be liable for more than their investment in the business.

Partnerships may be further classified as **trading partnerships** or **nontrading partnerships**. A trading partnership is engaged in the business of buying or selling goods or real estate for a profit. A nontrading partnership is a business that provides services, such as a law partnership or an accounting partnership.

The law of limited partnerships will be dealt with in detail in Chapter 32.

Creating a General Partnership

The association requirement in Section 6 of the UPA means that for a partnership to exist there must be some sort of agreement among the persons involved in it. As is true under general contract law, however, this agreement may be express—either oral or written—or implied. Most courts would refuse to enforce, at least as between the partners themselves, an oral partnership agreement that was to last longer than 1 year. The Statute of Frauds might also be applicable when the partnership agreement called for the transfer of land, goods over $500, or miscellaneous intangibles over $5,000.

Intent

Although the parties' intent is certainly important in creating a partnership, it is not conclusive. If the parties wanted to create a partnership but left out one of the required elements, they did not form a partnership. Likewise, if the parties did not intend to create a partnership but in fact voluntarily entered into a relationship that contained all of the elements of a partnership, they become partners. No state action is required to form a partnership, though most states do require some sort of registration of the firm, at least when it is using a fictitious name. Failure to register under such a statute does not preclude a firm's existence, though it may prevent the firm from suing.

Estoppel

Section 16 of the UPA provides that persons who are not actual partners as to each other may be held liable to third parties as if they were partners when they have held themselves out as partners or when they have consented to having another hold them out as partners and when the third party has relied on such representations in making a decision to extend credit to the firm. When the representation of partnership has been made publicly, no specific proof of reliance is required; reliance is assumed. Section 16 calls this sort of situation a **partnership by estoppel**.

Contents of Partnership Agreement

A **partnership agreement**, also called articles of partnership or articles of copartnership, should contain the basic provisions required to form a contract, as a partnership agreement is in fact a contract. In addition to these basic provisions, there will usually be certain provisions that relate to the type of business and to special problems connected with the management of that particular business. For example, a considerable number of the provisions in the articles of partnership of a large law firm would not be found in the articles of partnership of a family manufacturing firm.

Partners' Mutual Rights and Duties

Right to Participate in Management Decisions

In a general partnership unless there is a specific agreement to the contrary, each partner has the right to participate in the partnership's management activities and management decisions. Each partner also has an equal vote with the other partners in the management

CASE 1

TRALMER SALES AND SERVICE, INC. v. ERICKSON
521 N.W.2d 182 (WI App. 1994)

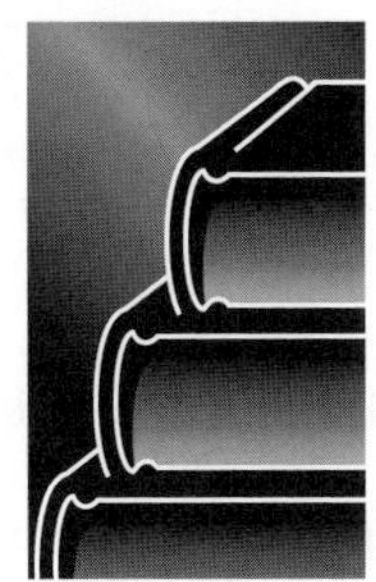

Facts: Section 815.18 of the Wisconsin statutes allows debtors to claim certain property as exempt from execution. This case involves a judgment creditor's challenge to the debtors' claim that property comes within the business property exemption.

The Ericksons own their home in Tomah, Wisconsin. In 1990, Sandra obtained a state permit to operate a bed and breakfast, the "Victoriana," in their home. Tralmer, a building contractor, provided home improvement labor and materials to the Ericksons in 1990 and 1991. The Ericksons failed to pay the balance due Tralmer. In December 1991, Tralmer took judgment against them for $11,637.23. On March 1992, the county sheriff levied execution on goods in the Ericksons' home.

In April 1992, the Ericksons affirmatively claimed that all the items seized were exempt from execution, some as business property under § 815.18(3)(b), STATS., and the rest as consumer goods under § 815.18 (3)(d). They requested an appraisal of the property under § 815.19(1), STATS., and received it in June. In early July, they moved for an order, determining their right to the claimed exemptions.

While the judgment was still unsatisfied, Sandra sold and gave away some unseized property still in their possession. In late July, Tralmer moved the court to appoint a supplementary receiver to exercise control over the goods still in the Ericksons' possession and to prohibit them from amending the claim they had filed in April. In August, the Ericksons amended their claim of exemptions, asserting that some items they originally claimed as exempt consumer goods were actually exempt business property and some items they originally claimed as exempt business property were actually exempt consumer goods. The sheriff did not sell or dispose of the seized property.

Following hearings in September, the trial court: (1) concluded that the Ericksons were entitled to claim business property exemptions because the Victoriana was a business, (2) determined that some seized items were business property and the rest were consumer goods, (3) denied Tralmer's motion to prohibit the Ericksons from amending their claimed exemptions, (4) denied Tralmer's motion to appoint a receiver, and (5) required the Ericksons to designate and select their claimed exemptions within 10 days of the last hearing. They did so, claiming as exempt $9,862.50 worth of consumer goods and $14,707.50 worth of business property. Tralmer appealed.

Issue: Was the business a "sole proprietorship" under the statute?

Decision: Yes. Judgment affirmed.

Opinion by Justice Gartzke: "We begin our discussion by acknowledging the legislature's charge to the courts in § 815.18(1), STATS.: 'This section shall be construed to secure its full benefit to debtors and to advance the humane purpose of preserving to debtors and their dependents the means of obtaining a livelihood, the enjoyment of property necessary to sustain life and the opportunity to avoid becoming public charges.'

"The direction in § 815.18(1), STATS., is consistent with judicial decisions over the years requiring a liberal construction of the exemption laws in favor of the debtor....

"Tralmer argues that if the Victoriana was a business, it was a partnership consisting of Sandra and Daniel, and therefore the Ericksons cannot claim business exemptions under § 815.18(3)(b).... Section 815.18(3)(b) allows a debtor to exempt up to $7,500 worth of business property used in the business of the 'debtor.' Section 815.18(2)(c) defines a debtor as 'an individual;' the definition excludes a 'partnership.'

"Because the exemption statute does not define a partnership, we look to ch. 178, STATS., the Uniform Partnership Act, for guidance. That act defines a partnership as 'an association of two or more persons to carry on as co-owners a business for profit....' Case law establishes the elements the contracting parties must satisfy to create a partnership. The parties must: (1) intend to form a bona fide partnership and accept the accompanying legal requirements and duties, (2) have a community of interest in the capital employed, (3) have an equal voice in the partnership's management, and (4) share and distribute profits and losses.... If any of the four elements is not satisfied, the parties have not created a partnership.

"Because it claims that a partnership exists, Tralmer bears the burden of proof.... Tralmer fails to meet its burden. It has not established the existence of the first element, that the Ericksons intended to create a partnership.

"To establish the first element, Tralmer relies on Daniel's testimony that '[t]his is a partnership as it relates to a marriage; she and I lived in that house and we operated it on that basis.' Tralmer also relies on Sandra's testimony:

Q. *[You] ran this business as a partnership with your husband, did you not?*
A. *[We] were into it together just as we are in marri[age] that-in the partnership in that sense.*
Q. *All right. So it was a partnership between you and your husband, something the two of you engaged in together.*
A. *Yes, we did it together.*

"The trial court made no explicit finding that Daniel and Sandra used 'partnership' simply to mean their marriage rather than a business organization. However, we may assume that the trial court decided the missing finding consistently with its order.... The court concluded that the Ericksons are entitled to claim property under the business exemption. Only a debtor can claim exemptions under § 815.18, STATS., and, under § 815.18(2)(c), a partnership is not a debtor. We infer that the trial court concluded that Daniel and Sandra used 'partnership' to mean their marriage.

"Other evidence supports the trial court's implied finding that the Ericksons used 'partnership' in its marriage sense. Their 1990 and 1991 tax returns describe the bed and breakfast as a sole proprietorship and name Sandra the sole proprietor. . . .

"Tralmer argues that even if the Ericksons did not create a partnership, they publicly held themselves out as a partnership and are therefore estopped under 178.13(1), STATS., from claiming otherwise. Tralmer claims that the Ericksons represented the Victoriana as a partnership by naming Sandra and Daniel as its hosts in advertising brochures. . . .

"Tralmer's estoppel claim fails. A party claiming partnership by statutory estoppel must prove the elements of estoppel. . . . Reliance is an element of estoppel under § 178.13(1), STATS. Tralmer did not establish that it relied on the Ericksons' advertising brochures when it extended credit to them."

and decision making of the partnership. Here a partnership differs from a corporation because in a corporation a stockholder will have votes for directors in proportion to ownership of stock, whereas in a partnership every partner has an equal voice and vote regardless of the amount of money or services the partner has contributed to the business.

With regard to day-to-day business decisions, it is not uncommon for partners to delegate certain decision-making authority to a **managing partner**. This partner will act as a general manager of the business. In a large law or accounting firm, for example, it is not possible for the partners to get together daily to make decisions on business matters. Typically the partners will meet on a regular basis to make policy and general management decisions other than the day-to-day decisions that are delegated to the managing partner. Usually a simple majority vote is needed on such matters. Certain types of decisions, however, require **unanimous action** of the partners. These include decisions involving an amendment of the original articles of partnership, the addition of a new partner, major changes in the business activities of the partnership, and any changes in the division of profits. Again, we must emphasize that a partnership is a contractual arrangement and that the partners may, if they so desire, provide in the partnership agreement that certain changes shall require only a majority vote, a two-thirds vote, a unanimous vote, and so on. Again, we emphasize the desirability of having specific provisions in the partnership agreement to cover these kinds of matters. Especially when there are only two partners, provisions should be included for deciding issues on which the partners are evenly divided.

Right to Share Profits and Duty to Share Losses

Generally speaking, each partner has a right to share in the profits of the partnership and is liable for its losses. The problem to be resolved is how much each partner's share is. If there is no agreement with regard to the sharing of profits, then the partners would share equally. However, it is best to have an agreement specifying a formula for sharing profits. This formula can be based on the various partners' contributions of capital or services.

If there is no specific agreement on the sharing of losses, then the partners will share losses in the same ratio as they share profits. However, if there is a formula for sharing losses, then that formula will be followed as between the partners. A partner with a large income from other sources might be willing to accept a larger allocation of losses because such losses would be set off against the other income for tax purposes.

Once determined, the profit-sharing ratio must be applied to all aspects of the firm's business.

The next case emphasizes the importance of the profit-sharing arrangement in determining potential application of employment discrimination laws to at least some "partners."

Rights to Salary or Other Compensation

A partner is not, as a matter of right, entitled to a salary or to other compensation for services rendered to the partnership. Absent an agreement, which provides for salaries to the various partners, it is assumed that the partners have agreed to share the profits. Obviously, salaries would reduce the total profits. Thus, if salaries or other forms of compensation are contemplated, then a special agreement should be made with regard to these items. It is not uncommon for partners to be paid regular salaries, with profits then being distributed at the end of the calendar or fiscal year.

CASE 2

Equal Employment Opportunity Commission v. Sidley Austin Brown & Wood
315 F.3d 696 (7 Cir. 2002)

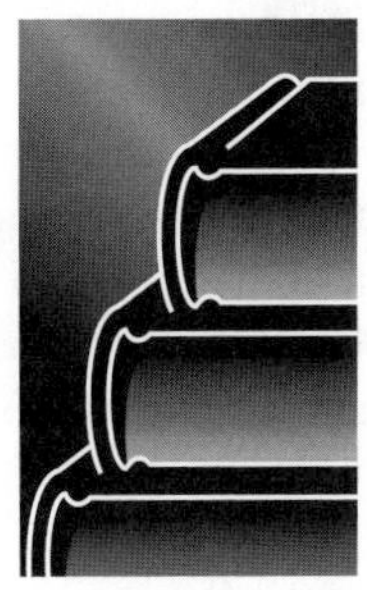

Facts: Sidley Austin, with over 500 lawyer-partners, is controlled by a 36-member self-perpetuating (unelected) executive committee. Some other partners do have authority, delegated to them by the executive committee, to make personnel decisions as to their subordinates. Each of the demoted partners had a capital account, averaging about $400,000. Their income was determined by the executive committee as a percentage share in the firm's profits. Each served on one or more of the firm's other committees, but all of these were controlled by the executive committee.

In 1999, Sidley Austin demoted 32 of its equity partners to "counsel" or "senior counsel." There is no dispute that these terms signify a demotion and are therefore adverse personnel action within the meaning of the Age Discrimination in Employment Act (ADEA). The Equal Employment Opportunity Commission (EEOC) began an investigation and issued a subpoena against the law firm, seeking documentation relevant to whether the 32 partners were covered by the ADEA and whether there had been a violation. The law firm provided most, but not all of the requested information, so the EEOC sought a court order enforcing the subpoena. The court ordered full compliance, and the law firm appealed.

Issue: Should full compliance with the EEOC subpoena be ordered?

Decision: Only as to the "coverage" documentation/information as of this point in time. Judgment affirmed in part; deferred in part.

Opinion by Judge Posner: "Employers are not protected by discrimination laws such as Title VII and the ADEA, but are partners employers? Always? Always for purposes of Title VII and ADEA, or the other federal laws that prohibit employment discrimination? Statutory purpose is relevant ...

"An individual who was classified as a partner-employer under state partnership law might be classified as an employee for other purposes, including the purpose for which federal antidiscrimination law extends protection to employees but not employers.... This is not the occasion on which to come down on one side or the other of the issue....

"Perhaps the most partneresque feature of the 32 partners' relation to the firm is their personal liability for the firm's debts.... Is this enough to pin the partner tail on the donkey? Wheeler ... comes close to saying it is.... Yet it does not quite deny the necessity of other factors. And tugging the other way are Strother ... and Simpson.... Simpson classified partners as employers in circumstances broadly similar to, though distinguishable from, those of the present case....

"The matter of liability for partnership debts illustrates the importance of referring the question whether a partner in a particular firm is an employer or an employee to statutory purpose. If implicit in the ADEA's exemption for employers is recognition that partners ordinarily have adequate remedies under partnership law to protect themselves against oppression (including age and other forms of discrimination) by the partnership, then exposure to liability can hardly be decisive. These 32 partners were not empowered by virtue of bearing large potential liabilities! The 32 were virtually defenseless; they had no power over their fate. If other partners shirked and as a result imposed liability on the 32, the 32 could not, as partners in a conventional partnership could do, vote to expel them. They had no voting power.... To repeat, the issue is not whether the 32 before their demotion were partners, an issue to which their liability for firm debts is germane; the issue is whether they were employers. The two classes, partners under state law and employers under federal discrimination law, may not coincide.

"Of course firms have broad freedom of election among the different forms of doing business, such as the corporate, partnership, LLC, and so forth.... But the question ... is not whether Sidley is a partnership; it is. The question is whether, when a firm employs the latitude allowed to it by state law to reconfigure a partnership in the direction of making it a de facto corporation, a federal agency enforcing federal antidiscrimination law is compelled to treat all the 'partners' as employers....

"All that is clear amidst this welter of cases is that the coverage issue in the present case remains murky despite Sidley's partial compliance with the subpoena. The Commission is therefore entitled to full compliance, at least with regard to coverage, unless the additional documents the Commission is seeking are obviously irrelevant. What the Commission particularly wants to know is how unevenly the profits are spread across the entire firm. Are profits so concentrated in members of the executive committee, or in some smaller or larger set of partners, in relation to the profits that the executive committee allocated to the 32, that the latter occupied the same position they would have if they had been working at a comparable rank for one of the investment banks that once were partnerships but now are corporations? This might not be decisive but it would bear on the unavoidably multi-factored determination of whether this large law firm—which in recognition that conventional partnership is designed for much smaller and simpler firms has contractually altered the structure of the firm in the direction of the corporate form—should for purposes of antidiscrimination law be deemed the employer of some at least of the individuals whom it designates as partners....

"We are not ruling that the 32 demoted partners were in fact employees within the meaning of the age discrimination law. Such a ruling would be premature.... We hold only that there is enough doubt about [this question] to entitle the EEOC to full compliance with that part, at least, of its subpoena.

"VACATED AND REMANDED WITH DIRECTIONS."

Right to Inspect Partnership Books of Account

Each partner has the right to inspect the partnership books and to make copies of those books for his or her own records. The partnership books must be kept at the principal office of the partnership unless the partnership agreement specifies otherwise.

Rights in Partnership Property

Section 8 of the UPA indicates that all property that is contributed when the partnership is formed and all property that the partnership later acquires by purchase or otherwise is considered **partnership property** and not the property of any individual partner. Whether a particular asset has been contributed to the firm is a question of fact. Partners may permit the firm to use their personal assets, as for example, space in a building or a vehicle or other piece of equipment. The name listed on the deed or other registration document is some evidence on this question, but certainly not conclusive, because firm assets are sometimes held in the name of one or more individual partners. The fact that the firm is paying taxes, insurance, and license fees on the asset is likewise not conclusive because these are sometimes paid by the firm in place of a monthly rental to the partner-owner. If there is a specific agreement, either in the articles of partnership or elsewhere, that should nearly always control. In the absence of a specific agreement, the way the asset is treated in the firm's books is probably the best indicator of ownership.

Section 24 of the UPA says that a partner has three property rights in the firm: (1) rights as to specific pieces of the firm's property; (2) an "interest" in the firm; and (3) the right to participate in management. We have already discussed a partner's management rights. What about the other two of these "property rights?"

As to specific pieces of property owned by the firm, the partners are co-owners in a special form of joint ownership known as "tenancy in partnership." As defined in Section 25, this co-ownership gives each partner an equal right to possess and use the firm's assets for the firm's business. A partner has no right to make any personal use of the firm's assets for personal purposes. A partner would have to get the other partners' permission to take the firm's delivery truck on a camping trip, for instance. Further, this right to make business use of the firm's property is personal in each partner and cannot be transferred to anyone else by an individual partner. Of course, the firm's rights of ownership of its assets can be sold to someone else by the firm. It is just that a single partner cannot separately transfer that person's individual right to use the asset as a partner. As a corollary to that rule, the personal creditor of an individual partner has no claim against any specific firm asset. Partnership assets, in other words, cannot be seized and sold to satisfy personal claims against individual partners. Partnership creditors can seize the firm's assets; creditors of the partners as individuals cannot do so.

When a partner dies, that partner's right in specific firm assets passes to the surviving partner or partners, for partnership purposes. As indicated later in the chapter, when such a dissolution occurs, the firm will either be terminated or continued. In either case, the firm's assets will stay in the firm. There may be a payout to the estate of the deceased partner by the firm, as part of the process of settling up accounts, but the firm's assets as such do not pass directly into the deceased partner's estate.

What is being paid over to the deceased partner's estate is actually the third thing mentioned in UPA Section 24: the partner's "**interest in the partnership**." This phrase has a very precise, technical meaning in the UPA. It means a partner's "share of the profits and surplus." This right to receive money from the firm (profits and surplus) is an item of property owned by each partner as an individual. This claim against the firm for money can thus be voluntarily transferred or assigned by each partner without the consent of the other partners. Likewise, this claim for money can be garnisheed by the creditor of an individual partner. Neither a voluntary assignment nor a garnishment order ("**charging order**") automatically dissolves the firm. In either case, the firm is free to continue its business; one partner's share of the profits is simply being paid to someone else. That other person is not a partner, has no liability as a partner, and has no right to participate in management. An assignee is not even entitled to receive periodic information on the firm's business or to inspect the books. Further, the assignee can ask for an accounting, if the firm is dissolved, only back to the time of the assignment. When a court has entered a charging order against a partner's

Exhibit 31.1: Partnership Property

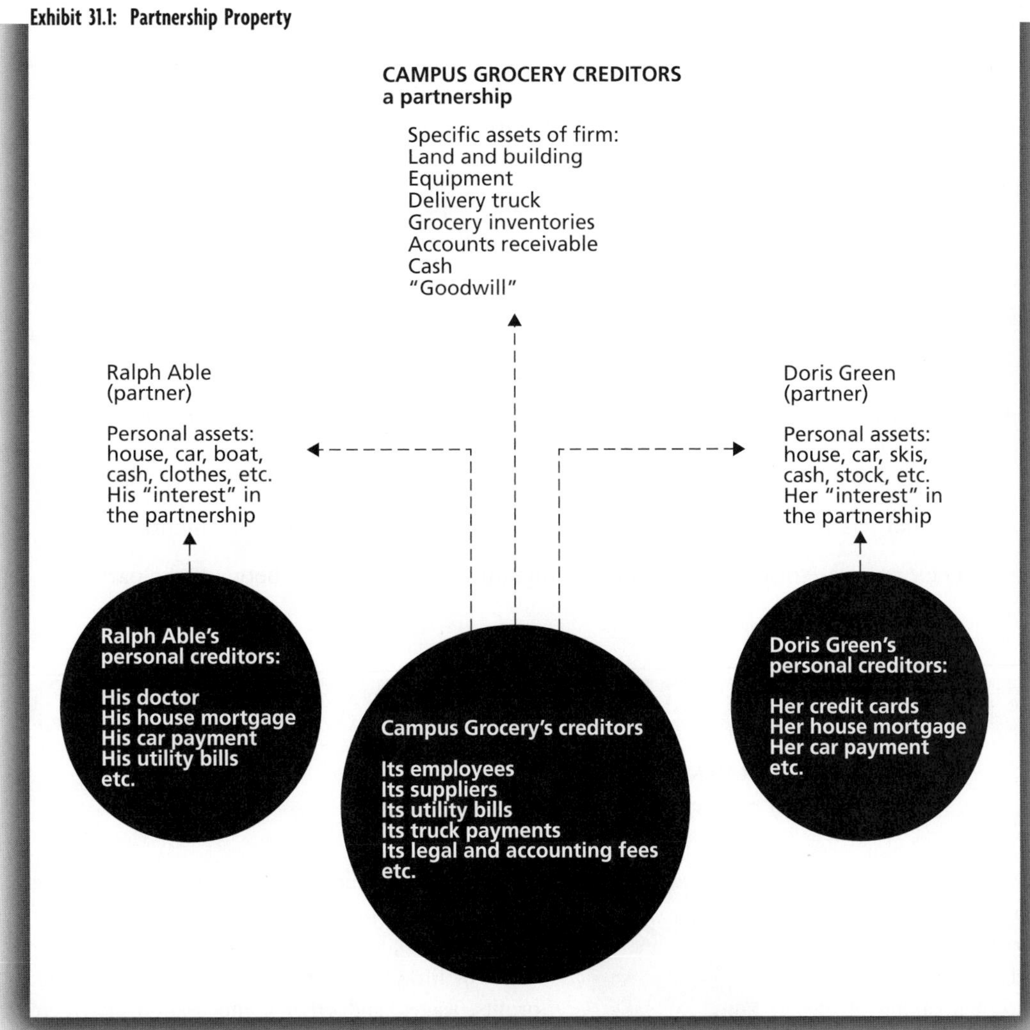

interest, the court can require any information from the firm that is necessary to make sure its order is being obeyed. When the partner's interest is transferred either voluntarily or involuntarily, the transferee may petition a court for a dissolution. Such a petition could be filed at any time if the partnership is one at will. If the partnership agreement specified a duration, the transferee could petition for dissolution at the end of that period.

Right to Return of Capital Contributions

Section 18 of the UPA provides that absent any agreement to the contrary among the partners, each partner shall be legally entitled to repayment of any capital contribution to the partnership. The repayment of capital contributions is considered a liability of the partnership. Unless otherwise agreed, a partner is not entitled to interest on a capital contribution. If, however, a partner contributes more than the required share, then the amount in excess of the required contribution will be treated as a loan, and interest will be paid on it.

Right to Repayment of Expenses

Each partner has a right to be indemnified for payments that he or she makes and personal liabilities that he or she reasonably incurs in the ordinary and proper conduct of the partnership business or to preserve the partnership business or its property.

Right to Decide Who Will Be a Partner

No new partners may be admitted to a partnership without the consent of all present partners unless there is an agreed procedure to the contrary in the partnership agreement.

Duties of One Partner to the Other Partner

Each partner is an agent of the partnership and thus, in effect, an agent of every other partner in the partnership. As an agent, the partner has a **fiduciary** relationship with the partnership and with the other partners. This relationship carries with it a number of duties. Among these duties are the following:

1. A partner must be loyal to the partnership and to his or her partners. A partner may not conduct business that will conflict with the partnership unless he or she has the other partners' permission to do so.
2. A partner has a duty to account to the other partners.
3. A partner must use reasonable care in conducting partnership business.
4. If the activities in which a partner engages or the information that a partner has acquired may affect the partnership, the partner has a duty to keep the other partners advised of them.
5. A partner has a legal duty to abide by the terms of the partnership agreement.

The *Frank* case discusses the rules for dividing the firm's assets between the partners.

CASE 3

FRANK V. BIRKY
817 P.2d 696 (MT 1991)

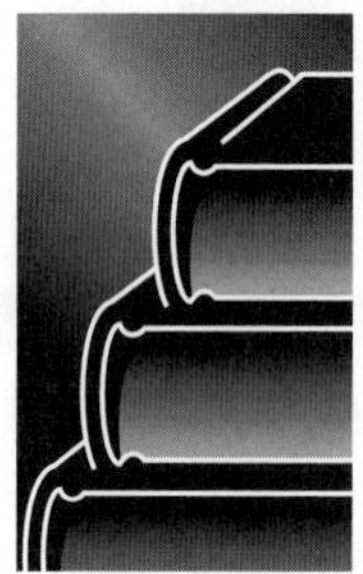

Facts: On July 1, 1978, Lawrence Birky (appellant/defendant) and Alan Frank (respondent/plaintiff) entered into a written partnership agreement to engage in logging and related industries. The agreement provided that the initial capital of the partnership would be contributed equally, that individual capital accounts would be kept for each partner, and that in the event of termination, the assets would be divided equally. In October 1983, Frank filed a lawsuit alleging that Birky had breached the partnership agreement and requested that the court dissolve the partnership and award Frank his partnership share plus damages.

The trial court determined that the partnership was composed of the following assets: 1976 Barko Loader mounted on a Kenworth truck complete with winch; 1978 Kenworth Truck and Trailer; 1978 450 Timberjack rubber-tire Skidder with chains, air compressor, and fuel tank. The court also found that the partnership was dissolved by mutual agreement in May 1983 and ordered that the aforementioned property be divided equally between the parties. A Special Master was appointed by the court to provide an accounting of the partnership property. Birky was unable to provide books containing a record of individual capital accounts and admitted that such a record did not exist.

The court adopted the findings of the Special Master, which included the following distribution of the partnership property. The Barko loader (sold by Birky for $42,000)—$9,000 allowed to Birky for repairs necessary to make the sale, $15,500 to Frank, $15,500 to Birky; the Kenworth truck and trailer (sold for $42,000)—$21,000 to Frank, $21,000 retained by Birky (including responsibility for collecting $6,000 owed by purchaser); the Timberjack skidder (value of $40,000 at dissolution)—$20,000 owed Frank by Birky, who retained control and later sold; profits, wages, and other compensation generated during the partnership—$22,325 owed Frank by Birky.

Birky believes the equal distribution of the assets as delineated is inequitable in light of the evidence presented.

Issue: Was equal distribution of the assets proper in the absence of written proof to the contrary?

Decision: Yes. Judgment affirmed.

Opinion by Justice McDonough: "First, appellant Birky contends that the court committed prejudicial error by ordering (in the absence of individual capital accounts on the partnership books) the capital contributions of the partners to be deemed equal.... Birky argues that by failing to remunerate him for his alleged capital contributions the District Court has circumvented the mandate of [the UPA] Birky further argues that to ignore [his alleged] capital contributions creates an inequitable distribution of the property which results in the unjust enrichment of Frank. A substantial portion of his alleged capital contributions would have to be proved by parol or extrinsic evidence....

"Birky contends that the court abused its discretion by not allowing him to present evidence pertaining to his capital contributions other than the business records.

"In the dissolution of a partnership and the sale and distribution of the partnership's assets, a partner against whom an action was brought and who failed to keep records [is] estopped from objecting to the court's finding of value of each party's contribution to the venture.... Here Birky kept the records of the partnership. We conclude that the court did not abuse its discretion in refusing to allow parol or extrinsic evidence to be presented by Birky in determining capital contributions....

"There are ample facts in the record to support the District Court's finding that the capital contributions should be deemed equal. First, the partnership agreement itself clearly indicates that the contributions would be equal. Second, in the event that contributions were made they were to be documented in the capital accounts as part of the partnership records. As previously indicated, there were no such records. Third, the record of the proceeding before the District Court reflects evidence to support such a finding. The findings as supported above are not clearly erroneous and therefore cannot be set aside.

"The appellant raises the additional claim that the manner in which the court provided the accounting and distribution of the partnership was inconsistent with the evidence on record. We disagree. Specifically, the appellant finds error with the District Court's reliance on expert testimony, the court's lack of consideration of draws taken by Frank, the court's lack of consideration of partnership obligations, and the court's valuation of the skidder. Each of these four related issues is a question of fact to be determined by the trial court....

"Both parties had opportunity to present expert testimony and thereby opportunity to provide a manner for the court to calculate the value of wages and profits generated by the partnership. The appellant takes exception with the court's acceptance of Frank's expert's method. Both experts testified that it was difficult to impossible to accurately verify the partnership's expenses. The finder of fact weighs the evidence and we conclude the findings are not clearly erroneous and are therefore affirmed.

"Lastly, appellant asks for review of the determination of the value of the skidder because he believes it was valued at an improper date. It is uncontested that the net value of assets is generally made at or near the time of dissolution.... Once again, decisions regarding valuation of partnership property will be overturned only if they are clearly erroneous. The decision of the court to adhere to the general rule is not clearly erroneous."

Partnership Liabilities

Contracts

Unless there is a contrary agreement, every partner in a general partnership is an agent of the partnership for the purpose of conducting the partnership's business. It is not uncommon for articles of partnership to limit or to restrict the agency power of the various partners. This is an agreement between the partners, and such internal limitations or restrictions among the partners themselves would not relieve the partnership of liability to a third person who dealt with a partner who exceeded them unless that third person knew that the partner was limited in his or her authority. Because, generally speaking, each partner is an agent of the partnership, the basic law of agency is applicable to the relationship between partners and third persons.

It is a general rule of agency that third persons who deal with an agent have the duty to ascertain the nature and the extent of the alleged agent's authority. Third persons cannot simply rely on a person's statement that he or she is an agent and has certain authority. In the case of a partnership, if a third person verifies that a person is a partner, then the third person has a right to believe that the partner-agent has the normal authority of a partner unless he or she is told otherwise. In other words, if a partnership is going to restrict or limit a partner's authority, then the partnership is responsible for notifying all persons who might be dealing with the partner-agent that the partner-agent does not have the full authority that would ordinarily be expected of a person in that capacity.

The partnership is also a principal and the individual partner an agent with regard to any information that the individual partnership may secure that relates to the partnership's business affairs. If a partner acquires certain information, then the partnership as the principal is automatically charged with the same information. It is also a general rule of agency that statements and representations made by an agent will bind the principal even though the statements may be untrue, provided the statements were made in the course of the agent's business for the principal and provided the statements were within the normally expected authority of such an agent.

Limitations on Partner's Authority by Law

Because each partner is an agent of the partnership, it would seem that as long as a partner's acts or transactions are within the scope of the partnership business, then the partnership would be liable for the contracts made by a partner on behalf of the partnership. However, there are a number of legal limitations on the authority of individual partners to act for the partnership.

The first such limitation concerns a partner's right to act as an agent with regard to the purchase and conveyance of real estate. Section 10 of the UPA deals with the right to convey real property owned by the partnership. When the partnership holds title to real property in the partnership name, any partner may convey the title to that property by a deed executed in the partnership name by that partner as agent. However, if the other partners have not authorized the partner to make such a conveyance, then the partnership can recover the property from the person to whom it was conveyed. An exception would be made to this right of the partnership to recover the property when the person to whom the conveyance was made transferred the title to an innocent third person who had no knowledge of the situation. Then the innocent third person would prevail over the partnership, provided there was not fraud in the transaction. Another exception would be made when certain acts or past practices of the partnership had created the apparent authority of the particular agent to convey the real estate.

The only safe way to purchase real estate from a partnership is to secure both a deed signed by one of the partners and a resolution signed by all of the partners that authorizes the sale of the real estate and also authorizes a specific partner to sign on behalf of the partnership.

Section 9(3) of the UPA sets out these further restrictions:

> *Unless authorized by the other partners or unless they have abandoned the business, one or more but less than all the partners have no authority to: (a) assign the partnership property in trust for creditors or on the assignee's promise to pay the debts of the partnership, (b) dispose of the good-will of the business, (c) do any other act which would make it impossible to carry on the ordinary business of a partnership, (d) confess a judgment, (e) submit a partnership claim or liability to arbitration or reference.*

Section 9(4) of the UPA further confirms that no act of a partner in contravention of a restriction on the partner's authority shall bind the partnership to persons having knowledge of the restriction. Thus, as indicated previously, if there are so-called internal restrictions on the power and authority of a partnership's various agents and if those restrictions have been revealed to third persons, such third persons have no recourse against the partnership for the partner's unauthorized acts.

Authority to Hire and Fire Employees

Going back to the basic authority of the partner, as set out in Section 9 of the UPA, every partner is an agent of the partnership for the purpose of its business. Every act of a partner, including the execution in the partnership name of any instrument apparently necessary for carrying on the business of the partnership in the usual way, binds the partnership unless the partner has no authority to act for the partnership in that particular matter and the person with whom he or she is dealing knows the lack of authority.

The articles of partnership could very well state that certain partners are charged with the duty of hiring and firing personnel and that the other partners have no direct authority to do so but have the right to be consulted on matters concerning the employment and tenure of personnel. For example, in a 50-partner law or accounting firm, you could not have each and every partner hiring and firing as he or she saw fit. In a two- or three-member partnership, on the other hand, each of the partners may be involved in the hiring and firing of personnel.

Absent an agreement to the contrary between partners, each partner would have the authority to hire persons whose services were reasonably necessary to carry on the partnership business and the further authority to bind the partnership for a reasonable salary for such persons. Each partner would also have the right to dismiss any employee whose services he or she felt were not reasonably necessary to carry on the partnership business. One can immediately see the problems that could arise if such authority were exercised in a firm with a large number of partners. This is why some internal agreement between the partners should specify which partner or partners have the authority to hire and fire personnel and should restrict the other partners accordingly.

Borrowing Money and Mortgaging the Partnership Property

Going back to the general authority clause to which we referred briefly, any partner has the authority to borrow money and execute a mortgage on behalf of the partnership, provided this is done for the purpose of carrying on the partnership business in the usual way. The UPA does not differentiate between the authority of an agent in a trading partnership and that of an agent in a nontrading partnership. However, in interpreting a partner's authority, courts in many jurisdictions have generally found that partners in a trading partnership that is engaged in buying and selling goods and property have greater implied and apparent authority to buy and sell property, to borrow in the partnership name, and to indorse or execute negotiable instruments in the partnership name if this is reasonably necessary to carry on the partnership business.

In partnerships that are considered to be engaged in a nontrading business, such as law firms or accounting firms, courts generally do not feel that individual partners should have the implied and apparent authority to borrow money or to execute or indorse negotiable instruments in the partnership name. Generally speaking, courts have held that the partners in nontrading partnerships do not have the authority to bind the partnership in such situations unless it was customary to do so in a given partnership or unless there was an actual necessity to do so. Thus, trading partnerships are governed by standards different from the standards that govern partners in nontrading partnerships, insofar as their authority with relation to third parties is concerned.

Lawsuits Involving Partnerships

Under the common law, a partnership was not a legal entity, and therefore a partnership could not sue or be sued in the partnership name. If a third person wanted to sue a partnership, the complaint had to name all of the partners as individual defendants, and each partner had to be individually served with a summons. This could be accomplished without too much effort when dealing with simple father-son partnerships or three- or four-member partnerships. However, if it had to be done with a modern accounting firm having more than a hundred partners, not all of whom lived in the same jurisdiction, the chore could prove very frustrating. Many states have enacted statutes that allow a partnership to be sued as an entity by simply naming the partnership by its firm name. These statutes also allow a partnership to bring action as a legal entity against third persons. Most statutes, however, require that the partners be named as defendants and be served personally with process if this is at all possible. Most statutes also permit the petitioner to secure a judgment against the partnership if the petitioner served at least one of the partners even though several other partners were not served. In a case in which the partnership entity was sued and at least one of the partners was named and served process, the judgment can be collected from the partnership assets. However, any judgment amount not collectible from the partnership assets cannot be collected from the individual partners unless the individual partners were sued, made a party to the lawsuit, and properly served with a summons.

Getting a judgment against a partnership is the first step. The next step is to collect it. Section 40(h) of the UPA states: "When partnership property and the individual properties of the partners are in possession of a court for distribution, partnership creditors shall have priority on partnership property and separate creditors on individual property, saving the rights of lien or secured creditors as heretofore." In other words, lienholders and secured creditors come first; the partner's individual creditors for his or her individual bills come next; and then the balance can be taken for partnership debts. The new bankruptcy code, which became law in October 1979, changes the law of distribution with regard to the assets of partners. It provides that in a case concerning the partnership, if the assets of the partnership are insufficient to satisfy the claims allowed, then each general partner in the partnership will be liable to the trustee in bankruptcy for the full amount of the deficiency. Thus, in the case of a bankrupt partnership the trustee in bankruptcy may now seek to recover the entire deficiency from any one of the general partners on a pro rata basis with the partner's personal creditors.

Liability for Torts

Section 13 of the UPA provides that when a partner is acting in the ordinary course of the business of the partnership or is acting with the authority of the co-partners of the partnership, then if that partner commits a tort, the partnership will be liable for damages to the same extent that the partner committing the tort was liable. If, however, the injured person was another partner in the partnership, then the partnership would not be liable for the claims of the injured partner.

What if the person who committed the tort was not a partner, but was an employee of the partnership? The UPA does not specifically state that the partnership is liable for the torts of its employees. However, Section 4(3) of the UPA states that the law of agency shall apply under this act. Thus, the partnership is the employer and is liable for the tortious acts of its employees, provided the employee was acting within the scope of employment.

Section 15 of the UPA provides that all partners are liable not only jointly but severally for any liability chargeable to the partnership under Section 13 of the UPA. Thus, if there are insufficient funds in the partnership to pay the damages resulting from the tort, then the partners may jointly pay for the loss. Or, if the partnership has assets and one partner has personal assets and the others do not, that partner may be held severally liable for the entire loss. This should be a serious concern whenever you enter into a general partnership because you could end up losing your personal assets, such as your home and your life savings, simply because of the negligence of some other person. This is one of the primary reasons that persons with individual assets over and above their investment in the business should consider being a limited partner in a limited partnership or forming a corporation. If there are unexpected tort losses, the most you as an investor will lose is your original investment, not your home and your life savings. It is, of course, recommended that the partnership carry liability insurance to cover tort losses. However, people sometimes forget to pay insurance policy premiums when due, and often the loss exceeds the policy limits.

Liability for Crimes

As previously stated, under the common law a partnership was not viewed as a legal entity, and it could not sue or be sued. Any legal action had to be taken by or against the individual partners. Thus, if the partnership was not a legal entity, it could neither commit nor be charged with a crime. Again, most states have now enacted statutes that allow a partnership to be sued as a legal entity by simply naming the partnership by its firm name. Many states have gone further and found that a partnership can be a legal entity for criminal purposes and can be guilty of a crime. The criminal penalty is simply a fine to be paid by the partnership from partnership funds. The nonacting partners normally could not be jailed for a crime committed by the partnership, particularly if the crime requires proof of a specific wrongful intent. If the partners are to be punished, they must be separately charged and have separate trials.

An individual partner who commits a crime while in the course of activities on behalf of and in the scope of the partnership will be criminally liable. But neither the partnership as an entity nor any other partner will be criminally liable unless the other partner or partners and/or the partnership participated in the criminal actions. For example, Jerry Jones is a partner in Jones and Son Construction Co. Jerry is discussing a construction bid with a client, and they get into a heated argument. Jerry, an ex-professional boxer now weighing 275 pounds, strikes the client in the face, breaking his glasses, and injuring him. Jerry is arrested for criminal assault and battery. Neither the two other partners nor the partnership is guilty of any crime, although they could very likely be held liable in tort.

Let us change the facts. Say Jerry was hired as an "enforcer" to "convince" clients to accept the bids from Jones and Son Construction Co., and it was understood by the partners that Jerry would use force to get a desired result: a signed contract. In that case, the other partners would be found to be accessories to the criminal act and would be criminally liable.

Some of these issues are raised in the *Kansallis* case.

The widely respected Arthur Andersen accounting firm was essentially destroyed when it was indicted for and convicted of "obstruction of justice." The firm and several of its members were accused of improperly destroying (shredding) a large number of documents relevant to the collapse of energy giant Enron. Even though the U.S. Supreme Court ultimately reversed the conviction, by that time the firm had melted away. The following case is reported in Chapter 6.

CASE 4

KANSALLIS FINANCE LTD. v. FERN
659 N.E.2d 731 (MA 1996)

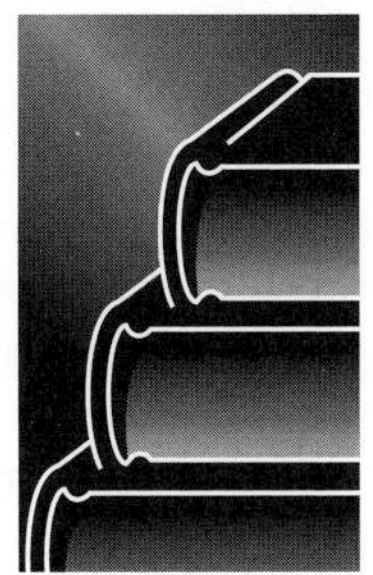

Facts: Stephen Jones and the four defendants were law partners in Massachusetts when, in connection with a loan and lease financing transaction, the plaintiff sought and obtained an opinion letter from Jones. In the order of certification, the U.S. Court of Appeals states that the letter, executed in Massachusetts and issued on "Fern, Anderson, Donahue, Jones & Sabatt, P.A." letterhead, "contained several intentional misrepresentations concerning the transaction and was part of a conspiracy by Jones and others (though not any of the defendants here) to defraud Kansallis." Although Jones did not personally sign the letter, he arranged for a third party to do so, and both the U.S. District Court judge and the jury found that Jones adopted or ratified the issuance of the letter. Jones was later convicted on criminal charges for his part in the fraud, but the plaintiff was unable to collect its $880,000 loss from Jones or his co-conspirators.

In an effort to recover its loss, the plaintiff brought suit in the U.S. District Court against Jones's law partners on the theory that the partners were liable for the damage caused by the fraudulent letter. Advancing the claim on essentially three grounds, the plaintiff asserted that defendants are liable for the letter because: (1) the defendants gave Jones apparent authority to issue the letter, (2) Jones acted within the scope of the partnership in issuing the letter, and (3) the issuance of the letter violated G.L.c. 93A, under which the partners are vicariously liable. The District Court submitted the first two common law claims to the jury and reserved the c. 93A count to itself. Both the judge and jury, for different reasons, decided that defendants were not liable for Jones's conduct. The Court of Appeals affirmed both the judge's and the jury's factual findings and certified two questions to this Massachusetts Supreme Court to resolve the legal issues.

Issue: To impose vicarious liability, must the acting partner intend to benefit the firm? Can partners be held vicariously liable for criminal actions of their partner?

Decision: No. Yes. (These answers are sent to the U.S. Court of Appeals.)

Opinion by Judge Fried: "[I]f we take the first certified question to ask whether a partner must necessarily at least in part act for the benefit of the partnership if the partnership is to be liable for his actions, the answer is 'no'. But the answer is 'no' only because under our law—and the law of partnership and agency generally—there are two routes by which vicarious liability may be found. If the partner has apparent authority to do the act, that will be sufficient to ground vicarious liability, whether or not he acted to benefit the partnership. It is only where there is no apparent authority, which is what the jury found on the common law counts here, that there may yet be vicarious liability on the alternative ground requiring such an intent to benefit the partnership. Since there is no evidence that Jones was acting to benefit the partnership, the District Court's judgment for the defendants on the common law counts accords with our statutes and precedents. The jury instructions on the common law claims were correct.

"The second question asks whether there must be a finding that the partners were at all aware of or involved in Jones's misconduct before they may be held liable to Jones's victim under G.L.c. 93A. This question raises a difficulty of a different order, because it arises under a statute ... which was designed to offer broader and more comprehensive relief to victims of dishonesty than may be available at common law.... Accordingly, it is not surprising that neither the statutory language nor our cases suggest that vicarious liability under the statute is measured by any less comprehensive standards than those we have set out above in considering the common law cause of action. Plaintiffs point out for example that c. 93A recoveries are routinely had against corporate defendants, all of whom, of course, have been landed in liability by the acts—often not actually authorized—of their agents....

"As G.L.c. 93A, S.1, defines 'persons' subject to liability under S.11 to include both partnerships and corporations, the standard for determining liability under c. 93A is the same for both. Vicarious liability may be imposed by either of the two routes that we have set out above with respect to the common law cause of action. Neither route contains a requirement of awareness or personal involvement by the person held vicariously liable beyond that implicit in the two sets of rules themselves: (a) did the actor have apparent or actual authority for the acts on which liability is predicated, or (b) did the actor act within the scope of the partnership business with some intent to benefit the partnership. To the extent that either of these tests is met, there is liability under the statute....

"The statute does, however, by its terms make a distinction between cases where simple compensatory damages are paid to the plaintiff and where there are double or treble—that is, punitive—damages. In those latter cases, the statute requires that the court find that 'the act or practice was a willful or knowing violation.' Thus the Legislature envisaged multiple damage awards against those defendants with a higher degree of culpability than that sufficient to ground simple liability....

"We must, however, approach this question with some caution, lest we unsettle a large body of accepted practice under c. 93A. As we have noted, the definition section of c. 93A equates partnerships to corporations and natural persons; and S.13 of the Uniform Partnership Act makes partnerships liable for penalties incurred by an errant partner. Moreover, our cases have routinely held corporations liable for multiple damages because of the knowing and wilful acts of their agents. Nevertheless, we are not persuaded that partners should automatically be equated to corporations for the purpose of assessing multiple damages for the knowing and wilful act of their agents. A corporation is an impersonal entity that can act only through agents, and so requiring some measure of personal culpability would exempt businesses operating in corporate form from multiple damages. Partnerships differ from corporations in that those held vicariously liable for multiple damages are often themselves natural persons, capable of personal culpability. It makes sense then to consider the partners' knowledge or wilfulness. Moreover, corporations exist in part just to insulate from and limit the liability of natural persons associated with them as investors, while partners are generally subject to unlimited personal liability. . . .

"Of the six States that have addressed this issue, Texas, Maryland, and Missouri hold innocent partners liable for punitive damages, and New Mexico, Indiana and Hawaii do not.

"We acknowledge that to make such a distinction between corporations on the one hand and partnerships and perhaps other natural persons in the position of master or principal on the other engrafts on the statute a middle degree of responsibility, and we shall not lay out here a comprehensive set of rules to govern this heretofore unexplored territory. It is only in the course of further adjudication that the courts can develop a sensible approach to this freshly raised problem. Suffice it to say that the jury's finding that there was no apparent authority in this case . . . might have some bearing on whether double or triple damages are appropriate. . . .

"To summarize, . . . a partnership may be liable by one of two routes for the unauthorized acts of a partner: if there is apparent authority, or if the partner acts within the scope of the partnership at least in part to benefit the partnership. Where there is neither apparent authority nor action intended at least in part to benefit the partnership, there cannot be vicarious liability. Accordingly, we answer the first question 'no', but only because even if a partner acts with no purpose to benefit the partnership, vicarious liability may yet be appropriate, if he is clothed with apparent authority. . . . We answer the second question 'yes', but add that, while c. 93A permits a finding that an innocent and uninvolved partner may be vicariously liable for the acts of his partner, some further showing of culpability or involvement must be made to justify multiple damages."

Liability for Partner's Breach of Trust

As previously stated, each partner is an agent of the other partners. As such, each is responsible for the acts or omissions of the other partners, provided such acts or omissions are in the ordinary course of business of the partnership. If any partner acting in the course of the partnership business, or acting within the scope of apparent authority, receives money or property in its custody and such money or property is misapplied by one of the partners, then in both situations the partnership is liable and must make good the loss.

Dissolution, Winding Up, and Termination

A partnership is based on a contract, which may be superseded by the parties' later actions. The firm may be dissolved by agreement of the partners, by acts of the partners, by a decree of court, or by operation of law. In the case of a partnership with a specific time span, it is dissolved at the end of the stipulated period of time. The partnership contract does, however, differ from many other contracts in that it concerns not only the contractual relationship between the parties to the contract but also the contractual relationship between the partnership and its various creditors. Thus, even though the partners may decide to dissolve their contractual relationship between themselves, the partnership is not really terminated until all of its debts are paid and all of its assets are distributed. This procedure is commonly called "winding up." Once the winding-up process has been completed, the partnership is considered terminated. Thus, we have a three-step process: dissolution, winding up, and **termination**.

Dissolution is defined by Section 29 of the UPA as "the change in the relation of the partners caused by any partner ceasing to be associated in the carrying on as distinguished from the winding up of the business." This change in relation can be voluntary or involuntary. An example of voluntary dissolution would be one in which the partners simply decide to end their relationship and go their separate ways. An example of involuntary dissolution would be one that occurred because a partner died or became mentally or physically incapacitated.

The key legal point to remember is that dissolution in itself does not terminate the partnership entity. Dissolution may trigger the next step; namely, the winding-up process. During the winding-up process, the partnership agreement is still legally in force.

However, the authority of each partner to act as an agent of the partnership has been legally terminated except as necessary to wind up partnership affairs.

Agreement

The partners may decide to dissolve their partnership for various reasons. This decision must be unanimous unless the partnership agreement specifies otherwise. For example, the agreement could specify that only a majority vote of the partners is needed to dissolve the partnership. Remember, a partnership is a voluntary agreement.

Acts of the Partners

Various actions by one or more partners may also cause dissolution.

1. Withdrawal by a Partner. If a partner withdraws from the business, that action causes a dissolution of the partnership. This does not necessarily mean that the business will have to be terminated. If the partnership agreement has been drawn with this problem in mind, it will contain provisions that give the remaining partners the right to buy the withdrawing partner's interest so that they can continue the business.

   Although a partner has the power to withdraw from the partnership for any reason that he or she may choose, the withdrawing partner may still be liable to the remaining partners for breach of contract. After all, the partnership agreement is a contract, and if its breach causes damage to the other contracting parties, then the violating party should be liable for such damages. Here again, a well-drawn partnership agreement should anticipate and provide a solution for such problems.

2. Expulsion of a Partner. Section 31(1)(d) of the UPA states that a partnership is dissolved "by the expulsion of any partner from the business bona fide in accordance with such a power conferred by the agreement between the partners." Thus, if the agreement provides for the expulsion of a member under certain circumstances and the remaining partners exercise that power for good and valid cause, then the partnership is dissolved.

3. Death of a Partner. The UPA, Section 31(4), states that the death of any partner will cause dissolution.

4. Bankruptcy of a Partner. The UPA, Section 31(5), states that the bankruptcy of any partner will cause dissolution.

5. Addition of a Partner. The addition of a partner dissolves the partnership, technically, but in few situations would there be a winding up and termination.

6. Assignment of a Partner's Interest for the Benefit of Creditors. Under the old common law rule, the voluntary or involuntary sale or assignment of a partner's interest would have dissolved the partnership. Section 27 of the UPA specifically provides that neither a voluntary nor an involuntary sale for the benefit of creditors automatically dissolves the partnership. The creditors will simply receive the profits that the partner would have received. If, however, a dissolution did occur, then the assignees could get the capital interest of the partner. A few states still follow the old common law rule of automatic dissolution.

As a general rule of law, a partnership is dissolved whenever its membership changes. When informed of this rule of law, the layperson asks, "If this is true, then how do large law firm and accounting firm partnerships handle the problem, as they are constantly bringing in partners, retiring partners, and so forth?" The answer is that the partnership agreement of such firms specifies the procedure to be followed in case of expulsion, voluntary withdrawal, the addition, death, or retirement of a partner, or any other change in membership. In effect, the old partnership is technically dissolved and reorganized in accordance with the provisions of the agreement each time such a situation occurs.

Operation of Law

The UPA, Section 31(3) states, "Dissolution is caused: By any event which makes it unlawful for the business of the partnership to be carried on or for the members to carry it on in the partnership." This simply means that if by either legislative enactment or a court decision the business that the partnership was carrying on is no longer legal, then the partnership is dissolved by operation of the law. The partnership agreement has become an illegal bargain and therefore void. As an illustration, let's say that a partnership is operating a casino in Atlantic City and the gaming commission takes away its license or the gambling law is repealed, making gambling illegal. The partnership will then be dissolved by operation of law.

Court Decree

Often circumstances arise that require a court to determine whether or not a partnership should be dissolved. For example, if an affliction has caused a partner to be of unsound mind and incapable of handling the partnership's affairs, then a remaining partner may petition the court to order the dissolution of the partnership. A court determination might also be desirable if one of the partners has become a drunkard or a drug addict and no longer assumes his or her share of the work and responsibility but refuses to dissolve the partnership voluntarily. Or, if fewer than the number of partners required for voluntary dissolution under the agreement will agree to dissolution, then the partners requesting dissolution may request that the court review the situation.

Expiration

A partnership may be created for a specified period of time, such as 1, 5, or 10 years. When that period expires, the partnership is dissolved.

After Dissolution

Dissolution does not change either the existing liability of the partnership or the existing liabilities of the individual partners. Dissolution may be likened to the death of an individual. The person dies, and then an administrator is appointed to settle the affairs of the deceased's estate. The administration of the deceased's estate is a process similar to the winding-up process previously referred to.

The rights of the partners may be likened to the rights of the heirs of a deceased person's estate. The partners have a right to an accounting to see that their interests are being handled properly, and after all the debts have been paid, whatever is left is distributed to them.

All partnership creditors and all other persons who have any current relationship with the partnership should be notified of the dissolution immediately. If these persons are not notified and if they continue to deal with the business after dissolution, the partnership and the individual partners may be liable as if the transaction had occurred prior to dissolution. Thus, once the decision has been made to dissolve the partnership, once an act of dissolution has occurred, or once a court decree of dissolution has been entered, the first step is to notify in writing everyone who could possibly be concerned with the dissolution and termination of the business.

There are different liability rules for withdrawing and incoming partners. The withdrawing partner remains fully personally liable for all debts of the firm that were incurred prior to withdrawal. Even if there is an agreement that the continuing partners will pay off all existing liabilities without any further contribution from the withdrawing partner, the third-party creditors are not bound by such agreement. Third-party creditors of the firm can, if necessary, impose full personal liability on any person who was a member of the firm when the debt was incurred. To avoid such continuing liability, the withdrawing partner would have to get the agreement of the third-party creditors of the firm. Notice of dissolution, in other words, does not terminate existing liabilities, it merely avoids additional future liabilities.

The incoming partner will, of course, assume full personal liability for all debts of the firm incurred after becoming a member. As to preexisting debts of the firm, the incoming partner is liable only to the extent of any capital contribution. Here again, if the firm's creditors wanted to have the new partner assume full liability for preexisting debts, a specific agreement to that effect would be necessary.

Winding Up

Winding up, the second step in ending a partnership, is the process of liquidating the partnership assets, that is, selling the real and personal property the partnership owned, collecting any outstanding accounts, paying any outstanding debts, and closing out any loose ends of the business—canceling orders not yet delivered, canceling any lease or rental agreements, terminating any relationships that the partnership may have had with persons who were not partners, and so on.

After all the outstanding accounts have been collected, all the assets have been turned into cash, and all the outstanding bills and claims against the partnership have been paid and settled, then any cash remaining has to be divided among the partners. First, if any of the partners have loaned money to the partnership, those loans are repaid with whatever interest was agreed on. Next, the partners will be given back their initial investment. Finally, if there is still some cash left, it will be divided among the partners as profits, and the distribution will be in the same proportions as the distribution of profits in the past and in accordance with the proportions set out in the partnership agreement.

The preceding discussion of the dissolution assumes that the assets of the partnership exceed its outstanding debts. This, of course, is not always the situation of a dissolved partnership that is in the process of winding up. If the assets are insufficient to pay its debts, then the personal assets of the various partners may be called on to pay them. It must be noted, however, that the personal creditors of an individual partner with personal debts may have priority over creditors who are attempting to collect partnership debts from that partner. If a bankruptcy proceeding is instituted, both groups of creditors will have equal priority against a partner's personal assets.

The *Gull* case involves the winding up of a law firm.

CASE 5

Gull v. Van Epps
517 N.W.2d 531 (WI App. 1994)

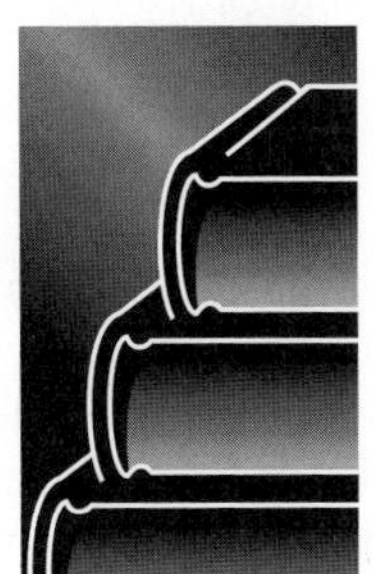

Facts: Jerome E. Gull, Ruth E. Van Epps, and David L. Berth practiced law in an at-will partnership from January 1, 1984, until Gull withdrew effective December 31, 1987. Gull continued to serve his clients in the partnership offices until February 19, 1988, when he opened his own office in the same city. He took with him his clients and his files.

Despite serious attempts, the parties were unable to wind up the affairs of the partnership. Gull began this action for an accounting December 11, 1990. On December 10, 1991, during trial, the parties stipulated to Gull's share of the accounts receivable and the furniture, furnishings, and library. However, the parties were unable to settle Gull's claim that he is entitled to his customary percentage of the "profits" of the partnership earned during the wind-up period, January 1, 1988 to December 10, 1991.

On December 23, 1992, the trial court entered judgment in favor of Gull according to the stipulation. However, the court denied Gull's claim for any share of the fees earned by Van Epps and Werth during the wind-up period. The court concluded that it would be unethical fee-splitting for Van Epps and Werth to share such fees with Gull.

Issue: Is a withdrawing partner entitled to a share of profits earned during the winding-up period?

Decision: Yes, but only as to ongoing business.

Opinion by Judge Sundby: "We first address the fee-splitting issue. Van Epps and Berth cite Wisconsin Supreme Court Rule 20:1.5(e) (Callaghan 1994) which provides in part: 'A division of fees between lawyers *who are not in the same firm* may be made only if:... ' (Emphasis added.) None of the enumerated exceptions apply here.

"Section 178.25(2), STATS., of the Uniform Partnership Act, provides: 'On dissolution the partnership is not terminated, but continues until the winding up of partnership affairs is completed.' After Gull's withdrawal, the partnership was dissolved, but until its affairs were wound up, the partnership remained intact for that purpose. Supreme Court Rule 20:1.5(e) does not apply to the division of fees concluding the affairs of the partnership because, until that process is completed, the lawyers are in the same firm. We recognize that winding up the affairs of a law partnership involves non-economic responsibilities which the partners have to their clients. The discharge of those responsibilities does not present issues in this appeal.

"We next consider Gull's claim that he consented to the continuation of the partnership and therefore ... he may elect to share in the 'profits' of the partnership earned after dissolution. We construe his claim to extend to fees earned by Van Epps and Werth on new work contracted for and performed during wind-up....

"While fees from new work normally do not belong to a dissolved partnership, . . . all partners of the dissolved firm are generally entitled to share in fees for predissolution work in progress earned after dissolution, even if the client has exercised a right to discharge the attorney or attorneys who are sharing in the fees. . . . The dissolution of a partnership operates only with respect to future transactions; the partnership continues as to all existing matters until they are terminated. . . . On dissolution, the partnership remains in existence for the purpose of performing existing executory contracts. . . . The partnership entity continues in existence after dissolution until termination. . . . Until termination of the partnership, the interests of the partners in partnership assets, profits, liabilities and losses do not change. . . .

"Perhaps the most difficult problem with regard to completion of work in progress concerns compensation for the partner who must complete the work. . . . Section 178.15(6), STATS., and U.P.A. § 18(F) (1914) provide: 'No partner is entitled to remuneration for acting in the partnership business, except that a surviving partner is entitled to reasonable compensation for his services in winding up the partnership affairs.' Section 178.15(6) allows extra compensation only when the partnership is dissolved due to the death of a partner and there is a surviving partner. It appears to be the rule in inter vivos cases—those in which a partner retires or withdraws—that the partner who completes work in progress is not entitled to any compensation beyond the fee he or she would have received for that work had the partnership not dissolved. . . . However, the former partners of a dissolved law firm are entitled to reasonable overhead expenses, excluding partners' salaries, attributable to the production of postdissolution partnership income. . . .

"We therefore conclude that during wind-up, net fees from work in progress by Van Epps, Werth and Gull constitute an asset of the partnership and shall be allocated to each partner according to the partnership formula without any additional compensation to any partner.

"When law partners cannot agree as to how the affairs of the law partnership are to be wound up, judicial resources in accomplishing wind-up may be considerably strained, depending on the size of the partnership and the nature of the partnership's practice. Fortunately, the trial court has broad discretion to accomplish a fair accounting between the parties because an action for the dissolution of a partnership and the liquidation of its affairs is a proceeding in equity. . . . We affirm the portion of the judgment based upon the parties' stipulation and reverse the judgment as to Gull's claim to fees earned during the wind-up, and remand for the trial court to apply ch. 178, STATS, and its equitable powers to complete the wind-up of the affairs of this law partnership."

The UPA, Section 35(1)(a), allows a partner to do "any act appropriate for winding up partnership affairs or completing transactions unfinished at dissolution." Thus, the winding up can be done by any of the partners, or by a partner whom the other partners designate as the winding-up partner, or by an outsider who is appointed as a receiver for the purpose of winding up the partnership and making the final distribution of its assets. When one partner has wrongfully caused the dissolution, the other partners have the right to do the winding up.

Continuing the Business

As indicated previously, the dissolution of a partnership does not automatically mean the termination of its business. Among the common situations that cause dissolution are the death or withdrawal of a partner. In such cases the remaining partners do not necessarily want to terminate the business. Winding up in such situations will simply be an internal process of buying out the interest of the deceased or withdrawing partner and of making appropriate bookkeeping changes for the reorganization and continued operation of the business. Creditors and persons dealing with the firm may not even know that any changes were made when a partnership has been legally dissolved by death of one of the partners. However, if a partner withdraws from the firm, it is wise to so notify all creditors and all persons and firms that deal with the partnership.

Remember, in a general partnership each partner is an agent of the partnership. Although dissolution terminates that relationship as between the partners, people who have been doing business with the partnership will not know that the person who has withdrawn is no longer a partner. Until such third parties are notified otherwise, the partnership may be liable for certain acts and dealings of the former partner. Thus, even though the business is to continue after dissolution, it is still necessary to give proper notification of the dissolution to all creditors and all persons who might be dealing with the continuing business.

Significance of This Chapter

The partnership is still the most simple and most commonly used form of business organization for small businesses. It is, therefore, important for the future business person to know what a partnership is, how a partnership is created, and how it can be terminated, either by some intentional act of the partners or some unexpected event such as death of a partner.

Once a partnership is created and begins transacting business, many problems regarding day-to-day operation will arise. It becomes important to know what each partner's rights and duties are regarding the day-to-day business operation. This chapter sets out the partners' rights and duties to each other and also discusses the relationship of the partner to third persons.

IMPORTANT TERMS AND CONCEPTS

charging order
dissolution
fiduciary
general partnerships
interest in the partnership
joint venture
legal entity
limited partnerships
managing partner
nontrading partnerships
partnership agreement
partnership by estoppel
partnership property
syndicate
termination
trading partnerships
unanimous action
Uniform Partnership Act (UPA)
winding up

QUESTIONS AND PROBLEMS FOR DISCUSSION

1. What types of decisions require unanimous consent of all the partners?

2. What are the presumptions as to the sharing of profits and losses among partners?

3. What is the difference between a partner's rights in specific firm assets and his or her interest in the partnership?

4. What authority does one partner have to make contracts for the firm?

5. Ellingson was the receiver of the landlord; the suit was to enforce a lease executed by a partnership. Barneson, one of the partners, disputed his personal liability on the lease because it was executed by the firm before he became a member. After Barneson became a general partner in the firm, it subleased the premises in question for a time and collected rent from the sublessee and paid its own rent to the landlord. The firm owed $2,374.13 for the period from March 1, 1992, to January 25, 1993. The trial court judgment imposed full liability on Barneson along with the other general partners.

   Will the trial court decision be upheld when Barneson appeals? Why or why not?

6. Daniel Phillips and Isadore Harris were equal partners in a business known as Dan's Used Cars. Neither of them owned a personal car. They had agreed that Harris would use the firm's cars for transportation to and from home. He could demonstrate and sell such cars, and they had "for sale" signs placed in them at various times. He could also use such cars to visit other dealerships and buy cars for the firm's inventory and to stop at the Department of Motor Vehicles so that necessary paperwork could be done for the firm's business. On January 7, while driving one of the firm's cars, Harris hit a car driven by Smith, which in turn hit a car driven by Dolores Cook. Harris was on his way home at the time. About a week later, the partnership was terminated. Dolores and her husband, Marshall, sued the partnership and received a judgment. Phillips appealed.

   Is Phillips liable? Explain.

7. Amerco got a judgment against Jerry Bohonus, who was acting as his own attorney. The trial court ruled that his attempt to appeal from the summary judgment was not timely and granted Amerco's request for a charging order against Bohonus's interest in a partnership. As part of that process, the trial court ordered a sale of Bohonus's interest in the assets of the partnership, which included a liquor license. The sheriff proceeded with the sale. Bohonus appealed.

   What is the result, and why?

8. C. N. Stroud and Earl Freeman were equal partners in a grocery store business known as Stroud's Food Center. During 1992, 1993, and 1994, the plaintiff regularly sold bread to the store. Several months prior to February 1994 Stroud told one of the plaintiff's agents that he did not want any more of its bread in the store and that he would not be personally responsible for any more bread purchases from it. From February 6 through February 25, 1994, the plaintiff sold $171.04 worth of bread to the store through this agent. The partnership was dissolved, and Stroud took over the business and paid off all of its existing debts ($12,014.45) except for "his" half of the bread bill, $85.52. The plaintiff recovered a judgment for $171.04, and Stroud appealed.

   How should the appeals court rule? Discuss.

CHAPTER 32

Limited Partnership Law

Chapter Objectives

This chapter will:

- Explain the differences between a limited partnership and a general partnership.
- Review the process of formation of a limited partnership.
- Discuss the changes under the Revised Uniform Limited Partnership Act.
- Discuss other forms of business organizations.

Limited Partnerships

A limited partnership differs from a general partnership in two major respects. First, a limited partnership allows certain partners to have limited liability for the debts and other liabilities of the partnership. Second, a general partnership may be formed by an express oral or written agreement or by an implied agreement, whereas a limited partnership agreement must be in writing and must conform to the statutory requirements for the formation of such a partnership.

The National Conference of Commissioners on Uniform State Laws, after finding that limited partnership laws varied from state to state, recognized the need for uniformity. In 1916 the commissioners drafted the **Uniform Limited Partnership Act (ULPA)**. This act was adopted by every state except Louisiana, which has its own limited partnership law.

In 1976, the commissioners revised the ULPA. Nearly all states have adopted the revised act, but it is still important to note what state is involved and whether the new act or the old act is the effective statutory law in that state. Our primary focus in this chapter will be the **Revised Uniform Limited Partnership Act (RULPA)**.

Limited partnerships have become a very popular form of business organization for people who wish to invest but want limited liability and who also wish to have their profits treated as partnership profits and not as corporate profits subject to the corporate income tax. There is no income tax on the profits of a limited partnership. The partners divide the profits in accordance with the partnership agreement. The partnership files with the Internal Revenue Service (IRS) a partnership return that is merely an informational return. The individual partner's profit is then shown on his or her income tax return, and the individual pays tax on that profit along with the tax on his or her other income. The limited partnership form of business organization is found mostly in so-called tax shelter ventures, such as land development organizations, oil exploration ventures, and cattle feeding ventures.

Definition

Section 101(7) of RULPA defines a limited partnership as a "partnership formed by two or more persons . . . having as members one or more general partners and one or more limited partners." Thus, each limited partnership must have at least one general partner with unlimited liability for the business of the partnership and at least one partner with limited liability. The limited partner, like a stockholder in a corporation, cannot be liable for more than his or her investment. However, unlike the corporation stockholder, who has a voice in the control of the business through votes for directors based on the number of shares owned, the limited partner has no voice in the control of the business. In fact, a limited partner who does take a part in the management or control of the business may be held personally liable for the firm's debts. Thus, if a limited partner wants to retain complete limited liability, he or she should not become involved in any way in the operation of the business.

Under RULPA, a limited partner who acts substantially like a general partner is liable as a general partner to all the firm's creditors. But if the limited partner merely participates in control, he or she has full liability only to those third parties with actual knowledge of that participation.

Creation

A **limited partnership certificate** must be prepared. This certificate must state the name of the limited partnership—for example, Wildcat Oil Exploration Associates, Ltd. If RULPA has been adopted by the state where the limited partnership is being formed, then the name of the limited partnership would have to be Wildcat Oil Exploration Associates, Limited Partnership. In other words the letters Ltd. are no longer allowed because many consumers do not know what Ltd. means. If the words *Limited Partnership* are written out in full, the public should be aware of the limited liability of some partners.

Next, the certificate must state the purpose of the limited partnership. In this case the purpose would be to conduct oil explorations in the state of Texas. The principal place of business of the limited partnership, the names and addresses of each general and limited partner, the duration of the partnership, and the amount of the contribution that is to be received from each partner must also be stated. Other requirements include a statement as to whether other limited partners can be admitted to the partnership and whether the limited partners may sell and assign their interests to other people. The limited partnership certificate must be filed and recorded in a designated office such as the office of the county recorder or the county clerk in the county where the principal office is located. The filing gives people who deal with the limited partnership public notice as to the items of information that are provided on the certificate of limited partnership. In most states it is also necessary to file the limited partnership certificate with a state authority, such as the secretary of state's office.

Once the limited partnership certificate has been filed and recorded, the limited partnership may proceed to do business. If the statutory requirements were properly adhered to, the limited partners should be free from liability beyond their investment. However, the partners may desire to draft more detailed articles of partnership to provide for matters not considered in the limited partnership certificate.

Defective Formation

What happens if the business associates fail to comply with the required procedures for becoming a limited partnership? Of course, any of them who are doing anything knowingly, with fraudulent intent, would be fully liable personally for all claims against the firm. But suppose one or more of the associates is acting in good faith, assuming that he or she is a limited partner, when in fact the statutory requirements have not been met. What happens to those good faith investors?

Potentially, each investor in the business would have full, unlimited personal liability for all the debts of the business. If they have failed to achieve the status of a limited partnership, they must then be general partners in a general partnership. They meet all the definitional elements as a partnership, so they will be held liable as general partners. Recognizing that this result is potentially unfair to an investor who acts in good faith, ULPA included an "escape hatch" in Section 11. Such an investor is not held personally liable if he or she promptly renounces any interest in the profits of the business as soon as the mistake is discovered.

RULPA gives an investor a choice. When he or she discovers the mistake, he or she can either withdraw from future equity participation in the firm or file a proper limited partnership certificate or an amendment to correct the error. This rule is probably fairer to the investor because it would permit the firm to proceed as planned once the correction was made. RULPA does provide, however, that such an investor continues to be fully personally liable to persons who thought the investor was a general partner before the correction was made.

General Partners

The general partner or partners have essentially the same rights and duties as any partner in a general partnership insofar as the partnership's day-to-day business operations are concerned. There is, however, one difference. Such partners cannot, on their own, take in other general partners or other limited partners unless this right has been granted to them in the limited partnership certificate.

The *Bennett* case examines the nature of a managing partner's fiduciary duties.

Limited Partners

Basically the limited partner has no specific duties. He or she is simply an investor. However, Section 305 of RULPA gives the limited partner the right to inspect and copy the partnership certificate, list of partners, tax returns, and partnership agreement. The limited partner also has the right to demand full information on all matters affecting the partnership. Thus, the limited partner may not have a voice as such in the management of the limited partnership, but he or she need not stand by and watch as fraudulent or wasteful acts are being committed by the general partner. In addition, a limited partner may petition a court of proper jurisdiction to have a dissolution and **winding up** of the limited partnership. If that occurs, the limited partner is entitled to receive a share of the profits as income

CASE 1

Matter of Bennett

989 F.2d 779 (5 Cir. 1993)

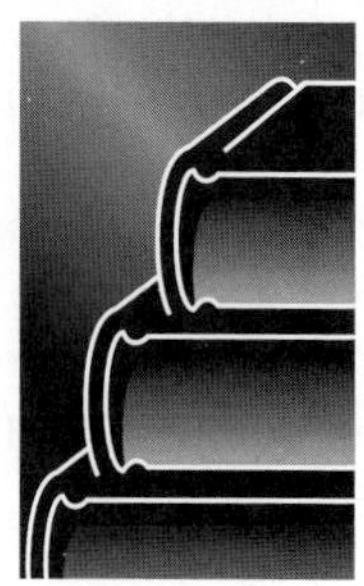

Facts: This appeal arises out of an adversary proceeding in a bankruptcy case, in which the bankruptcy court entered an order granting a discharge to the appellee, Archie Bennett, Jr., over the objection of the appellants that certain of Mr. Bennett's debts were not dischargeable. In support of their argument, the appellants rely solely on 11 U.S.C. § 523(a)(4), which provides that debts resulting from a defalcation by the debtor while acting in a fiduciary capacity are not dischargeable in bankruptcy.

In approximately March of 1980, Bennett and the appellants formed a Texas limited partnership known as Mariner/Greenspoint, Ltd. ("MG"). The appellants in this case are, and were at all relevant times, limited partners of MG. The sole general partner of MG was another limited partnership, known as Mariner Interest No. 20, Ltd. ("No. 20"). The sole general partner of No. 20 was the appellee, Archie Bennett, Jr.

The purpose of the MG partnership was to construct and operate a Marriott hotel near the Greenspoint Mall in Houston, Texas. The hotel was completed on time and opened in January of 1981. At that time Bennett made a $1 million distribution to himself for completing the project for less than the budgeted $22 million.

Subsequently, several problems with the hotel came to light. First, in approximately April of 1981, mildew began to occur in the guest rooms of the hotel. This mildew was evidently caused by a "negative pressure" problem, which in turn was caused by the design of the heating, ventilation, and air conditioning (HVAC) system in the hotel. As a result of the mildew problem, virtually all of the guest rooms in the hotel had to be revinyled and resheetrocked twice, during 1981 and 1982. The bankruptcy court also reviewed numerous equipment leases that were entered into by the general partner for the purpose of providing various types of equipment to the hotel. The bankruptcy court concluded that the misapplication of partnership funds to pay for the mildew repairs and the equipment leases described were the result of defalcations by the general partner of MG in the total amount of $904,204.40. The bankruptcy court also found, however, that Bennett, as the general partner of the general partner, did not owe a fiduciary duty to the limited partners of MG. The district court, in a brief opinion, affirmed the order of the bankruptcy court granting a discharge to Bennett.

Issue: Did Bennett owe a fiduciary duty to the limited partners?

Decision: Yes. Judgment reversed.

Opinion by Judge Prado: "The first issue that we address is whether the scope of the fiduciary duty owed by the managing general partner of a limited partnership to the limited partners is sufficient to meet the narrow requirements of Section 523(a)(4). Next, we must decide if such a duty also applies to the managing partner of the managing partner....

"We find ... that these obligations are more than a fiduciary relationship created in response to some wrongdoing. Texas law clearly and expressly imposes trust obligations on managing partners of limited partnerships and these obligations are sufficient to meet the narrow requirements of Section 523(a)(4).

"However, this is only the first step in the analysis, because it is undisputed that Bennett was not the managing partner of MG. He was instead, the managing partner *of the managing partner* of MG. Therefore, this Court must now address the more difficult question of whether Texas law imposes these same trust-type obligations on the managing partner in a two-tiered partnership arrangement (i.e., the managing partner of the managing partner)....

"In reviewing the line of cases that gave rise to the rule in Texas that the managing partner of a partnership owes to his copartners the highest fiduciary obligations known at law, it is clear that the issue of control has always been the critical fact looked to by the courts in imposing this high level of responsibility....

"[I]n *Meinhard v. Salmon*, a case cited extensively in Texas and elsewhere for establishing the fundamental fiduciary duty rules governing managing partners, Justice Cardozo focused on the control that one 'coadventurer' exercised over the business enterprise at issue:

> *The very fact that Salmon was in control with exclusive powers of direction charged him the more obviously with the duty of disclosure....*
>
> "The court observed:
>
> *[T]here may be no abuse of special opportunities growing out of a special trust as manager or agent.... Salmon had put himself in a position in which thought of self was to be renounced, however hard the abnegation. He was much more than a coadventurer. He was a managing coadventurer. For him and for those like him the rule of undivided loyalty is relentless and supreme....*

"Therefore, again in the *Meinhard* case the fact of control or management is vital to the court's analysis....

"The *Crenshaw* court, analyzing the issue in a manner consistent with the way in which Texas jurisprudence has developed in this area, concluded that ... the managing partner of the managing partner of the limited partnership, owed to the limited partners the highest fiduciary duty known at law, a duty analogous to that owed by a trustee to the beneficiaries of the trust.... Therefore, based on the holding in

Crenshaw and the cases cited therein, we find that Bennett, as the managing partner of the managing partner, owed to the MG limited partners 'the highest fiduciary duty recognized in the law.' We find further that this fiduciary obligation is sufficient to meet the requirement of Section 523(a)(4). . . .

"In conclusion, we find that the question of the nondischargeability of Bennett's debts to the limited partners under 11 U.S.C. § 523(a)(4) was wrongly decided. We therefore reverse the decisions of the bankruptcy and district courts on that issue and render judgment in favor of the limited partners in the amount of $1,904,204.40."

and may also be entitled to have his or her contribution returned in accordance with the limited partnership certificate, subject of course to any exceptions under local law. As an alternative to a lawsuit for dissolution, RULPA permits a limited partner to bring a derivative suit for damages on behalf of the firm. Such a suit might be brought against a general partner for injuries caused to the firm by a breach of fiduciary duty.

Dissolution, Winding Up, and Termination

In Chapter 31, it was noted that the death, bankruptcy, or withdrawal of a partner were causes for dissolution of the partnership. These rules do not apply to a limited partnership. Because limited partners are simply limited liability investors, they have no voice in management and are not liable for more than their investment. Thus, there is no specific loss to the limited partnership if a limited partner dies or becomes bankrupt. For these reasons, the substitution of a new limited partner for an old limited partner or the addition of a limited partner will not cause dissolution of a limited partnership. Only if all the limited partners have either died or withdrawn and no substitutions have been made would the death or withdrawal of limited partners necessitate the dissolution of a limited partnership. A limited partnership must have a minimum of one limited partner. Without the limited partner there is no limited partnership.

The death or withdrawal of a general partner from a limited partnership will cause the limited partnership to be dissolved unless there is a provision in the certificate to substitute another person for the deceased or withdrawing general partner.

Thus, a limited partnership will normally not be dissolved until the general partners or their replacements decide to dissolve the partnership or until a specific term expires, if the limited partnership was created for a specified term.

Although the limited partnership need not be dissolved on the death or withdrawal of a general partner if provisions were made for that partner's replacement, the limited partnership still has to file and record an amended limited partnership certificate to inform the public of the change. If a limited partner dies or withdraws and is not replaced, no amendments need be filed and recorded. However, if another person is substituted or added as a limited partner, then the certificate must be amended. Also, if a limited partnership decides to go into a different business or to make any other major changes in the business that concern matters covered in its certificate, it must file and record an amended certificate that gives the public full notice of these changes. Section 24 of RULPA specifies the various changes in the business that requires an amended certificate be filed.

Under RULPA, amendments to the certificate must be filed within 30 days after: (1) the admission of a new partner, (2) the withdrawal of a partner, (3) the continuation of the firm's operations after a judicial dissolution due to withdrawal of the last general partner, or (4) any change in a partner's contribution to the firm. Changes in the addresses of limited partners need only be filed once a year.

Changes under the Revised Uniform Limited Partnership Act

RULPA has now been adopted by nearly all states. A major reason for the revision of ULPA was to clarify the question of control. ULPA states that a limited partner may not participate in the control of the limited partnership. A limited partner who does participate in the control of the business will be treated in the same way as a general partner and thus will lose limited liability. The problem is simply: What is control? Can a limited partner make suggestions to the general partner? Can a limited partner have a vote? Conflicting court decisions have been reached in the various states as to what a limited partner may or may not do insofar as participation in the control of the business is concerned. Some states even amended their limited partnership statute to grant limited partners a right to vote on certain types of major business decisions.

Because of the concern over the growing nonuniformity of ULPA laws, RULPA was drafted. This act specifically allows the limited partner to do certain acts with the understanding that these acts do not constitute participation in the control of the business. The following acts are permitted by RULPA:

1. Being a contractor for, or an agent of, the partnership.
2. Consulting with and advising a partner with respect to the business.
3. Acting as a surety for the partnership.
4. Approving or disapproving of an amendment to the partnership agreement.
5. Voting on such matters as dissolution, winding up, the transfer of all or substantially all of the assets, the incurrence of debt other than in the ordinary course of business, a change in the nature of the business, and the removal of a general partner.

In addition to allowing the limited partner to do the aforementioned acts, RULPA also provides that if a limited partner does actively participate in the control of the partnership by doing acts other than those mentioned, the limited partner will only be liable to those people who did business with the partnership and who had knowledge of the limited partner's participation in its control. RULPA also makes some general changes in the filing requirements for limited partnerships. It requires that the certificate of limited partnership be filed in the office of the secretary of state in the state where the limited partnership is doing business, and it also requires that the limited partnership designate a resident in the state where it is doing business as the registered agent for the service of process for lawsuits that may be filed against it.These requirements are similar to the filing requirements for corporations.

ULPA restricted the limited partner's capital contribution to cash or other property. Under RULPA the limited partner may contribute services as a capital contribution or in place of cash or other property. This is a very important change because it means that the consulting expertise or other specialized talents of limited partners can now be contributed as a capital contribution to a limited partnership.

Another change in RULPA was previously referred to. That change requires that the full words *limited partnership* be used in the firm name rather than the abbreviation "Ltd.," which is allowed under ULPA.

Other Organizational Forms

Joint Stock Company

The **joint stock company** is a form of business organization in which the management of the business is placed in the hands of trustees or directors. Shares represented by certificates are then issued to the members of the company, who are in effect joint owners of the enterprise. These certificate holders then elect the board of directors or the board of trustees. Like the shares of a corporation, the shares or certificates are transferable, and their transfer does not cause dissolution, as it would in a partnership. Also the death of a shareholder does not dissolve the organization, as would be the case for a partnership. The joint stock company exists for the period of time stated in its bylaws. In reality, the joint stock company is a partnership; however, it has many of the advantages of the corporation. Its principle disadvantage is that there is still unlimited personal liability, as in a partnership. Depending on the state statute, the joint stock company may or may not be considered a legal entity for purposes of litigation.

One may wonder why the law recognizes a business organization such as the joint stock company. The joint stock company is a compromise between the partnership and the corporation. It has the partnership's tax advantages because it pays no separate corporation tax, and it has the corporation's advantages of transferability and duration, but it also has the partnership's disadvantage of unlimited liability. At one time, the joint stock company was a popular form of business. However, with the advent of the subchapter S corporation, it no longer has great appeal.

CASE 2

Pavlov v. Bank of New York Co., Inc.

135 F.Supp.2d 426 (S.D. NY 2001)

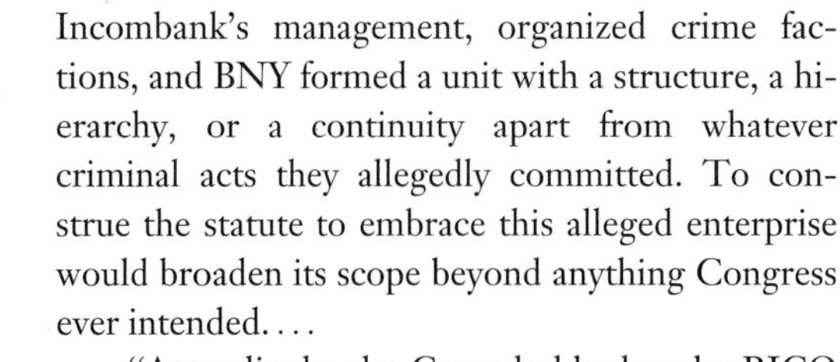

Facts: Plaintiffs brought a class action on behalf of the depositors in the now insolvent Joint Stock Bank Incombank, which did business in Russia. Plaintiffs allege that Bank of New York (BNY), several of its senior managers, Incombank's senior managers, and Russian organized crime factions joined together to take money from Incombank and send it to overseas accounts. Plaintiffs claimed damages for violations of the RICO Act and conversion of property and aiding and abetting conversion. Defendants moved to dismiss on the grounds that there was no RICO "enterprise," that there was no diversity of citizenship jurisdiction, and that Russia was a more convenient forum for the lawsuit.

Issue: Did this conspiracy constitute an "enterprise" under the RICO Act?

Decision: No. Complaint dismissed (for all the defendants' reasons).

Opinion by Judge Kaplan: "Plaintiffs allege that defendants violated [RICO], which ... makes it unlawful 'for any person employed by or associated with any enterprise ... to conduct or participate ... in the conduct of such enterprise's affairs through a pattern of racketeering activity....' 'Enterprise' is defined ... to include 'any individual, partnership, corporation, association, or other legal entity, and any union or group of individuals associated in fact although not a legal entity.'...

"While RICO applies equally to legitimate and illegitimate groups, it is well in construing the term 'enterprise' to remember the statute's overriding purpose—to create a weapon useful in combating organized crime.... [T]he Supreme Court long ago held that a RICO enterprise is a 'group of persons associated together for a common purpose of engaging in a course of conduct' that 'is proved by evidence of an ongoing organization, formal or informal, and by evidence that the various associates function as a continuing unit.' In other words, it has a 'hierarchy, organization and activities' and it 'must exhibit structural continuity' which 'exists where there is an organizational pattern or system of authority that provides a mechanism for directing the group's affairs on a continuing, rather than an ad hoc, basis.'...

"It 'cannot simply be the undertaking of the acts of racketeering, neither can it be the minimal association which surrounds these acts.'

"These requirements are not satisfied here.... [T]here is nothing in the complaint to suggest that the members of Incombank's management, organized crime factions, and BNY formed a unit with a structure, a hierarchy, or a continuity apart from whatever criminal acts they allegedly committed. To construe the statute to embrace this alleged enterprise would broaden its scope beyond anything Congress ever intended....

"Accordingly, the Court holds that the RICO count fails to state a claim upon which relief may be granted....

"In order to exercise jurisdiction based on diversity of citizenship, the matter in controversy ... must exceed $75,000...

"[T]he claim of each individual plaintiff and class member must meet the jurisdictional amount requirement.... Accordingly, plaintiffs may not maintain a class action, and the conversion and aiding and abetting claims must be dismissed as to all plaintiffs other than Onara Partners and S&K Trust, the two plaintiffs who allege claims in excess of $75,000....

"The ... complaint alleges that Onara Partners and S&K Trust are both business trusts organized and existing under the laws of Bulgaria and that the current trustee of each is a Greek citizen domiciled in Bulgaria. These allegations, however, are insufficient to establish diversity of citizenship.

"As the Supreme Court made clear in Carden ... business entities other than corporations are not treated as citizens. Rather, such an entity is regarded as a citizen of every state of which 'the several persons composing such association' is a citizen. No exception has been made for business trusts. In consequence, the allegation of Bulgarian citizenship, to the extent it rests on the alleged existence of these trusts as business entities under Bulgarian law, is insufficient....

"Accordingly, the Court lacks subject matter jurisdiction over the conversion and aiding and abetting claims....

"This at root is predominantly a Russian affair. A few depositors of a Russian bank, most of them located in Russia, claim that the Russian principals of the bank, joined by a handful of BNY employees, engaged in activity in Russia to convert the plaintiffs' deposits and then to ship the money out of the country. They claim that a key part of this activity was the infiltration of the bank by Russian organized crime.... This is a private dispute about monetary loss allegedly suffered by depositors in a Russian bank. There is little justification for imposing it on U.S. courts and jurors....

"In sum, this Court concludes that Russia is an adequate alternative forum for this dispute....

"For the foregoing reasons, defendants' motion to dismiss the complaint is granted."

Business Trust

The **business trust**, or the Massachusetts trust,as it is often called, is a business organization in which title to certain property is deeded over to a trustee or a board of trustees who manage and operate the business for the benefit of those parties who contributed property in the form of money or other assets to the trust. The people who contributed money or other assets to the trust are called **beneficiaries**. They no longer have any legal title to the trust corpus; however, they do have an equitable or beneficial interest in the trust. They are given trust certificates as evidence of their interest in it. As beneficiaries of the trust, the certificate holders will receive the profits from the operations and investments of the trust properties. However, the key factor is that the certificate holders do not have any right to control the enterprise. If, in fact, they do have a right to control the actions of the trustees, the courts will normally hold that the business is a partnership and not a trust.

The main purpose of the business trust is to ensure limited liability to the beneficiaries and yet avoid some of the statutory regulations and reporting procedures of a corporation.

This form of business organization, like the joint stock company, is not used extensively today, at least not in this country. Both forms may be used more widely in other nations. The looted bank in the prior case was some sort of joint stock company doing business in Russia, and some of the plaintiffs were Bulgarian business trusts. The court also had to consider the meaning of the word "enterprise" in the U.S. Racketeer Influenced and Corrupt Organizations (RICO) Act.

Cooperative Association

One often hears of farm co-ops or student co-ops. A **cooperative association** is a union of individuals formed for the purpose of operating an enterprise to make profits or to provide benefits for its members. If it is a profit-making business, the legal rules governing it will be very similar to those that govern a partnership or a joint venture.

If a cooperative is nonprofit and unincorporated, the legal rules governing it are quite different, particularly those relating to the personal liability of the associates. Personal liability for the contract and tort debts of the organization is not automatically assumed on the basis of membership in a nonprofit cooperative. The liability of individual members must be based on proof of an agency relationship; that is, the members whom it is sought to hold personally liable must be shown to have authorized the liability producing act. Such personal authorization may be proved by showing that the act in question is part of the organization's purposes or that the act was specifically authorized by the persons sought to be held liable or that those persons were active participants in the act.

The status of an individual member is at issue in the *Cox* case.

Limited Liability Companies

History and mythology abound with stories of searches for the ultimate prize. Jason and the Argonauts searched for the Golden Fleece. King Arthur's Knights of the Round Table searched for the Holy Grail. Columbus searched for the Indies. Henry Cabot searched for the Northwest Passage.

Like these historical and mythical searchers, investors seek the ultimate organizational form for their business ventures. Generally, they want single taxation of profits, limited liability, transferability of ownership interests, perpetual existence, and professional management. Finding an organizational form that embodies all of these desired features has been difficult, to say the least.

The corporation provides four of the five characteristics but is subject to potentially devastating double taxation. It pays its own income taxes on its profits, and its stockholders are then taxed again when those profits are distributed as dividends. Subchapter S offers relief from this double tax, as noted previously, but is subject to many limitations. Limited partnership offers single taxation, but the investors cannot actively participate in management, dissolution may occur, and someone has to assume unlimited personal liability. The joint stock company and the business trust have limited utility, as noted previously. So what is the answer?

CASE 3

Cox v. Thee Evergreen Church
836 S.W.2d 167 (TX 1992)

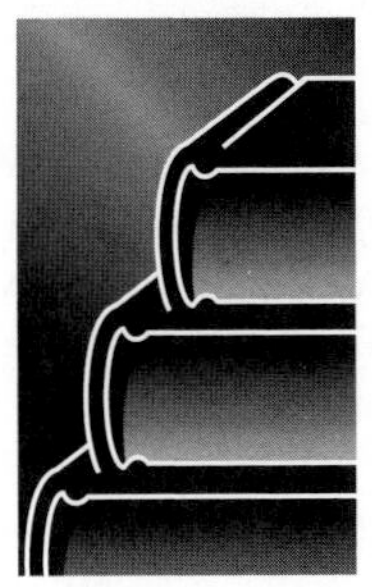

Facts: Karen Cox was a member of Thee Evergreen Church, an unincorporated charitable association. Cox had been a member for 4 years and held a position on Evergreen's administrative board. On November 4, 1986, Cox dropped her son off at a "mother's day out" program, for which she paid a nominal fee, operated on Evergreen premises by volunteer members of the church. On entering the church, Cox slipped and fell, injuring her back and head. Cox brought an action against Evergreen alleging negligence and gross negligence. The trial court granted a motion for summary judgment filed on behalf of Evergreen on the ground that a member of an unincorporated charitable association lacks standing to maintain an action against the association. The Court of Appeals affirmed.

Issue: Can a member sue his or her unincorporated association?

Decision: Yes. Judgment reversed.

Opinion by Justice Hightower: "An unincorporated association is a voluntary group of persons, without a charter, formed by mutual consent for the purpose of promoting a common enterprise or prosecuting a common objective.... Historically, unincorporated associations were not considered separate legal entities and had no existence apart from their individual members.... Because of the lack of a separate legal status, it was generally considered that unincorporated associations could only hold property through the intervention of trustees.... For the same reason, a judgment could not be rendered against such an association....

"Consequent to the lack of legal identity, special rules arose concerning liability in actions involving unincorporated associations. In regard to contracts, members incurring the debt on behalf of the association or assenting to its creation were personally liable.... In regard to tort actions, member liability depended upon such factors as the nature of the association and the individual member's involvement in the conduct giving rise to the cause of action....

"The rule of law also developed that an unincorporated association was not liable to one of its members for damages occasioned by the wrongful act of another member or agent of the association.... Such immunity was grounded on the concept that the injured member and the association were regarded as coprincipals, with the tort feasor as their common agent. The wrongful conduct was thus 'imputed' to the plaintiff for purposes of his action against the association.... In effect, it was considered that the plaintiff was suing himself.... It is this rule of law that Evergreen contends precludes Cox's claim.

"Cox advances three arguments for allowing her to maintain a cause of action. First, Cox argues that the common-law principles have been modified by a series of statutes concerning suits by and against unincorporated joint stock companies and associations....

"Cox next looks to Rule 28 of the Texas Rules of Civil Procedure. Rule 28 has been interpreted as treating unincorporated associations as legal entities, at least to the extent of obtaining and enforcing judgments against them....

"Lastly, Cox argues that the common-law principle precluding her from bringing a negligence action solely because of her membership in the association should be abolished. We agree.

"As discussed above, an unincorporated association was historically not liable to one of its members for damages occasioned by the wrongful act of another member or agent of the association.... This court, however, has recognized various situations in which membership alone is an insufficient reason to preclude a member of an unincorporated association from asserting a cause of action against the association....

"So what remains of the early common-law rules regarding unincorporated associations and the imputed negligence doctrine? Apparently, very little. We allow suits by and against unincorporated associations in their own name.... We allow nonmembers to bring suits, including those for negligence, against unincorporated associations.... We allow members to sue unincorporated associations for acts committed that are strictly adverse to the member's interests.... We allow members to sue unincorporated associations when the association conspires to bring about or ratifies the wrongful conduct....We refuse to apply the imputed negligence doctrine in the analogous joint enterprise context when there is no business or pecuniary purpose.... And lastly, a number of states allow suits against unincorporated associations by their members for injuries resulting from the association's negligence.... Nevertheless, one vestige of the common law survives—our obedience to an ancient precept automatically imputing the negligence of an unincorporated association to an injured member. Considering the development of the law in regard to our treatment of unincorporated associations, ... combined with our refusal to apply the imputed negligence doctrine in other contexts, ... we perceive no compelling reason for retaining this remnant of the original common-law rules.... Consequently, we hold that a member of an unincorporated charitable association is not precluded from bringing a negligence action against the association solely because of the individual's membership in the association. Any assets of the unincorporated charitable association, held either by the association or in trust by a member of the association, may be reached in satisfaction of a judgment against the association."

Under German law, the answer is the *Geschellschaft mit beschrenkter Haftung* (GmbH)—an enterprise with limited liability. By analogy, the GmbH is an "incorporated partnership." Members can exercise full management authority and still enjoy limited liability. Similar business organizations exist in other countries, the *Limitada* in most Latin American countries, for example. No comparable organizational form was available in this country until 1977, when Wyoming passed an act authorizing the formation of **limited liability companies (LLCs)**. The act was apparently passed in response to the request of an oil company.

Although adopted by one state (with a very small population), LLCs remained virtually unknown until 1988. In that year, the IRS issued Revenue Ruling 88-76, which said that LLCs would be treated as partnerships for IRS purposes. A Wyoming LLC, in other words, would not be subjected to double taxation on profits. With that ruling, the floodgates opened, and 40 plus states passed statutes authorizing the formation of LLCs. Many states also authorized a variation called "**limited liability partnerships (LLPs)**."

Just what is an LLC? It is a business organization in which the members have limited liability, but are not subject to double taxation on profits. To gain this favorable tax treatment, the IRS originally ruled that an organization may not possess more than two of the following four characteristics: limited liability, continuity of life, free transferability of interest, and central management. Because limited liability is the much-sought-after "Holy Grail," along with single taxation, an LLC can posses only one of the other three characteristics. In practice, that means that limitations must be placed on two of the three remaining features. If the organization has unlimited life, then there must be restrictions on the transfer of ownership interests and on centralized management. If there is to be centralized management (as in a corporation), then there must be restrictions on free transferability of ownership interests and unlimited life. Just how restrictive these various "restrictions" had to be for tax purposes was an open question. Faced with the prospect of extended litigation on these points and the possible disabling of the LLC as a viable organizational alternative, the IRS has adopted regulations that generally permit noncorporate entities to choose their tax status.

Partnerships, limited partnerships, LLCs, and LLPs are taxed as partnerships (flow through to owners; no separate entity tax), unless they file Form 8832, indicating an intent to be taxed as a corporation. Sole proprietorships are taxed as part of the proprietor's personal income, unless the owner elects to have the business income taxed as if it were earned by a corporation. Corporations are taxed as such, unless a qualifying corporation elects subchapter S status, as discussed previously.

The next case shows the kind of technical questions that are likely to arise.

Limited Liability Partnerships

Many licensed professionals, especially accountants and attorneys, traditionally practiced together as partners. Some states even prohibited such professionals from incorporating. With the widespread adoption of the LLC as a possible organization form, the professionals asked: "Why shouldn't we have that sort of choice, too?" Depending on the specific state's legislation, the LLC form may be available to certified public accountants (CPAs) and lawyers, but many of them would still prefer the "partnership" label. (It just sounds more "professional.")

Thus was born another hybrid organizational form—the LLP. Unlike the traditional limited partnership, *all* members have limited personal liability, even though they are taking an active part in the business of the firm. Most of the these LLPs are virtually identical in organization and operation to LLCs—only the name has been changed ("to protect the innocent"?)

LLPs have become very popular with the accounting and legal professions, but one or two reminders are in order, in light of the Enron affair. Arthur Andersen, the "Big Five" accounting firm, was organized as an LLP. *But*—every individual at Arthur Andersen (and at the Enron *corporation*) who committed negligent or intentional wrongful acts is personally liable to the injured parties. Moreover, even the totally innocent partners, associates, and employees at Arthur Andersen and Enron suffered significant personal financial losses.

CASE 4

McConnell v. HuntSports Enterprise

725 N.E.2d 1193 (OH 1999)

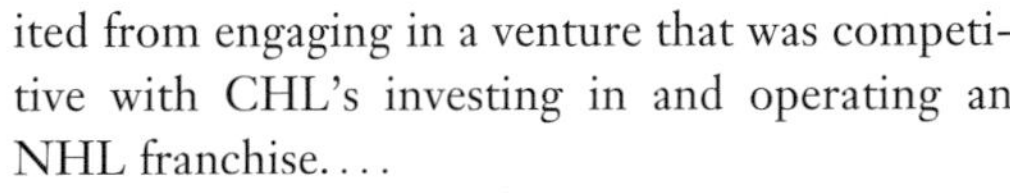

Facts: Having decided to expand to several new cities, the National Hockey League (NHL) telephoned Gregory Lashutka, the mayor of Columbus, Ohio, to see if the city was interested in obtaining a hockey franchise. The mayor called several civic leaders, including John McConnell and Ronald Pizzuti. Pizzuti in turn contacted Lamar Hunt, his co-investor (along with McConnell and Wolfe Enterprises) in the city's professional soccer team. As a result, Hunt, Pizzuti, McConnell, Wolfe, and Buckeye Sports organized a new LLC, Columbus Hockey Limited (CHL). (Ameritech also invested the required $25,000, although it was not listed as a member.)

To qualify for an NHL franchise, CHL needed a suitable arena. The city's attempt to fund one with a bond issue was voted down, so Nationwide Insurance agreed to build an arena for the team. Nationwide's proposed lease terms were rejected several times by Hunt, Buckeye Hockey, and Ameritech. After removing CHL's name from the lease, McConnell signed it personally as the proposed NHL franchise owner. He then organized COLHOC, a limited partnership, with his family corporation as the majority owner and Pizzuti and Wolfe participating. COLHOC now owns the Columbus NHL franchise.

McConnell and Wolfe asked the Ohio court for a declaratory judgment interpreting the CHL operating agreement and defining their right to compete with CHL. The trial court found in their favor on all issues, including those raised by HuntSports' counterclaims. HuntSports appealed.

Issue: Did McConnell breach a fiduciary duty to the LLC in which he was a member?

Decision: No. Judgment affirmed.

Opinion by Judge Tyack: "Section 3.3 of the [CHL] operating agreement states: 'Members May Compete. Members shall not in any way be prohibited from or restricted in engaging or owning an interest in any other business venture of any nature, including any venture which might be competitive with the business of the Company....' [HuntSports] contends that members may only engage in or own an interest in a venture that is not in the business of investing in and operating a franchise within the NHL.

"Appellant's interpretation of Section 3.3 goes beyond the plain language of the agreement and adds words or meanings not stated in the provision.... The words 'any nature' could not be broader, and the inclusion of the words '... any venture which might be competitive with the business of the Company ...' makes it clear that members were not prohibited from engaging in a venture that was competitive with CHL's investing in and operating an NHL franchise....

"Accordingly, summary judgment in favor of appellees [McConnell] was appropriate, and appellees were entitled to a declaration that Section 3.3 of the operating agreement permitted appellees to request and obtain an NHL hockey franchise to the exclusion of CHL....

"In forming COLHOC and in obtaining the NHL franchise, Mr. McConnell was obviously not taking action on behalf of CHL. Therefore, [he] did not breach [CHL's operating agreement] in failing to obtain the vote of all CHL members prior to taking such action....

"Mr. McConnell was not obligated to call for or provide additional capital to fund CHL....

"The term 'fiduciary relationship' has been defined as a relationship in which special confidence and trust is reposed in the integrity and fidelity of another, and there is a resulting position of superiority or influence acquired by virtue of this special trust.... In the case at bar, a limited liability company is involved which, like a partnership, involves a fiduciary relationship. Normally, the presence of such a relationship would preclude direct competition between members of the company. However, here we have an operating agreement which by its very terms allows members to compete with the business of the company. Hence, the question we are presented with is whether an operating agreement of a limited liability company may, in essence, limit or define the scope of the fiduciary duties imposed upon its members. We answer this question in the affirmative....

"[T]he evidence does not show that appellees tortiously interfered with appellant's prospective business relationships with Nationwide and the NHL. The evidence does not show that appellees induced or otherwise purposely caused Nationwide and the NHL to not enter into or continue a business relationship with appellant. Indeed, ... the evidence shows Mr. McConnell stated he would lease the arena and obtain the franchise only if appellant did not. It was only after appellant rejected the lease proposal on several occasions that Mr. McConnell stepped in. Appellant had yet another opportunity on June 9, 1997 to participate in the Nationwide arena lease and the NHL franchise. Appellant again found the lease proposed unacceptable, and without a signed lease sheet, there would have been no franchise from the NHL....

"In conclusion, there was not sufficient material evidence presented at trial so as to create a factual question for the jury on the issues of breach of fiduciary duty and tortious interference with business relationships. Therefore, a directed verdict in favor of appellees on count three of the second amended complaint was appropriate."

Thousands of jobs were lost. Enron's pension plan was apparently funded primarily with Enron's own stock. When the stock's price dropped from $90 to pennies a share, Enron employees saw the value of their retirement portfolios disappear almost overnight. (There has as yet been little publicity on how Arthur Andersen's pension plan is funded, or if the situation there is as serious as that at Enron.). The point is that "no personal liability" may be cold comfort to an innocent employee who has just lost both job and pension. (The U.S. Supreme Court decision in this case is presented in chapter 6.)

Significance of This Chapter

In the last few decades, limited partnerships have become a very important form of business organization, particularly for use in tax shelter business operations. It is therefore important for the businessperson to know what a limited partnership is, how it is formed, what the limited partners can and cannot do and still retain limited liability status, and also how a limited partnership can be terminated. Although the limited partnership has been the most significant of these alternative forms of organization, there are several other possibilities. Because the rights and liabilities of the associates vary from one form to another, this chapter has also included a summary of the differences between the joint stock company, the business trust, the for-profit unincorporated association, and the nonprofit unincorporated association. Newer forms, the LLC and the LLP, are now in widespread use. Not only the associates, but also the third parties dealing with various organizations, need to know the basic rules for who can do what and who's liable for what.

IMPORTANT TERMS AND CONCEPTS

beneficiaries
business trust
cooperative association
joint stock company
limited liability companies (LLCs)
limited liability partnerships (LLPs)
limited partnership certificate
Revised Uniform Limited Partnership Act (RULPA)
Uniform Limited Partnership Act (ULPA)
winding up

QUESTIONS AND PROBLEMS FOR DISCUSSION

1. How does a limited partnership differ from a general partnership?

2. Why are limited partnerships a popular form of organization?

3. What are the disadvantages of the limited partnership?

4. Why have so many states moved so quickly to permit LLCs?

5. Plaintiff was injured by carbon monoxide fumes while attending a fish fry at Post 650. The petition alleges that the defendants, American Legion Post No. 650 Realty Co., Inc., and the individual members of the American Legion Post No. 650 "jointly and severally, conducted or caused to be conducted within said building a social affair known as a fish fry for which they charged each person attending the sum of one dollar ($1)," and that "defendants, each of them, were negligent in failing to provide a safe heating system in the building; in equipping and maintaining the building with a defective heating system; in failing to adequately inspect said heating system; in failing to provide proper ventilation in the building; and in failing to warn invitees in the building, including decedent, of the presence of carbon monoxide fumes therein."

   Are the individual members of Post 650 personally liable, as well as the organization? Explain.

6. Ricardo de Escamilla was raising beans on a farm near Escondido when he organized Hacienda Farms, a limited partnership, with James Russell and H. W. Andrews. Russell and Andrews were the limited partners; Ricardo was the general partner. Hacienda Farms operated only from February to December 1993, when it went bankrupt. Holzman, Hacienda's trustee in bankruptcy, sought to hold Russell and Andrews personally liable for its debts. Russell and Andrews had participated substantially in the operation of Hacienda Farms. When asked whether he had had conversations with them prior to deciding to plant tomatoes, Ricardo said: "We also conferred and agreed as

to what crops we would put in." He also said: "There . . . was never any crop that was planted or contemplated in planting that wasn't thoroughly discussed and agreed upon by the three of us; particularly Andrews and myself." In fact, Andrews and Russell overruled de Escamilla on the planting of peppers, watermelons, and eggplant. They also asked him to resign as manager of Hacienda and replaced him with Harry Miller. Russell and Andrews also seemed to have control of Hacienda's finances.

The two men had absolute power to withdraw all the partnership funds in the banks without the knowledge or consent of the general partner. Either Russell or Andrews could take control of the business from de Escamilla by refusing to sign checks for bills contracted by him and thus limit his activities in the management of the business. They were active in dictating the crops to be planted, some of them against the wish of de Escamilla.

Are Russell and Andrews personally liable for the debts of the business? Why or why not?

7. Dr. Vidricksen intended, when he turned over $25,000 to Thom in July 1998, to become a limited partner with Thom, the general manager, in a Chevrolet car agency business at Dunsmuir, California. Articles of partnership were drawn up, but no effort was made to comply with the California statutory requirement of recording a certificate of limited partnership. Bankruptcy overtook Thom in September 1999. Apparently the agency developed financial difficulties in March 1999, and the doctor consulted successively two different lawyers. From them, although they could not represent him because of conflict of interest, he did learn he had a problem; to wit, whether in his venture he had attained a real limited partnership and therefore limited liability under California law.

   On September 19, 1999 (8 days after the bankruptcy proceedings started), Dr. Vidricksen filed in the bankruptcy proceedings a renunciation under Section 15511 of the Corporations Code of California, that state's version of the ULPA.

   Is the doctor now free of liability? Explain.

8. Steinberg and his two general partners owned 84 acres of land in Baltimore County, which land they had encumbered with $365,000 worth of mortgages. To get operating capital, they solicited investments from persons who would become limited partners.

   Allen, the plaintiff's husband, was one of those solicited. He said that he and his wife would not be interested in any construction project but that they would be interested in a land deal. Mrs. Allen sent a check for $10,000, after being assured that they were investing in land and that the building operation on the land would be separate. The partnership agreement that Mrs. Allen signed had been redrafted by her husband so that the definition of the firm's business was "the ownership and promotion for development of a tract of land" rather than "the ownership and development of a tract of land." Through various manipulations, the general partners had the firm assume $275,000 worth of utility installation costs and also mortgaged part of the tract for $140,000, all without the knowledge or consent of the limited partners. The firm's assets were lost, and Mrs. Allen sued the general partners for an accounting and for damages resulting from their mismanagement. She appealed from the trial court's dismissal of her suit.

   How should the appeals court rule? Discuss.

CHAPTER 33

Corporation Law—Nature and Formation

Chapter Objectives

This chapter will:

- Describe the various classifications of corporations.
- Outline the procedure for formation of a corporation and discuss the problems that result from defective formation.
- Discuss "piercing the corporate veil" to hold corporate officers, directors, and stockholders liable for corporate actions.
- Review the requirements for adopting promoters' contracts.
- Explain the states' jurisdiction to tax and regulate foreign corporations.
- Discuss procedures for filing as a foreign corporation and penalties for failure to file.

A **corporation** is called a legal person or a **legal entity.** It may also be called a "child of the state," because its birth, existence, and termination are regulated by statutory law. On the completion of certain requirements a state will grant a charter of incorporation, which is in effect a "birth certificate" for the corporation. The corporation must abide by the specific statutory law during its existence. If the corporation is to be terminated, then the termination must also comply with the statutory law. Each state has specific statutes governing the creation, regulation, and termination of corporations and also regulating corporations created in other states but doing local business in that state.

The **Model Business Corporation Act (MBCA)** was drafted by the Committee of Corporation Laws of the Section of Corporation Banking and Business Law of the American Bar Association in 1950 with the hope that the various states would pattern their state corporate statutes after it. The MBCA is similar to the Uniform Acts we have discussed earlier in the text in that they are not law until adopted by a specific state legislature. The MBCA has been reviewed and revised periodically, and in 1984 the committee completed a comprehensive revision of it.

Classifications of Corporations

Private Corporation for Profit

This is the most common type of corporation. Such a corporation is created for the purpose of conducting private, nongovernmental business.

Private corporations for profit may be further classified as **close corporations** or **publicly held corporations.** A close corporation is a corporation in which the stock is owned by a small number of shareholders, and the stock is not offered for sale to the general public. It is called a close corporation because it is closed to the general public. Its shares are not for sale on any stock exchange. A publicly held corporation is a corporation whose shares are offered for sale to the general public. These shares of stock are traded regularly on the various stock exchanges.

Publicly held corporations must comply with very strict rules and regulations as to their procedure in offering their shares of stock for sale to the public. These rules and regulations are made and enforced by the various state securities commissions and the Securities Exchange Commission (SEC). These procedures and requirements will be discussed further in Chapter 35.

A subclassification of the close corporation is the (subchapter) S corporation.

Subchapter S is simply a subdivision of the Internal Revenue Code that permits small close corporations to be exempt from payment of corporate income tax. The shareholders are allocated shares of the profits and then declare those profits as income. Also, if the corporation has losses, the shareholder can deduct his or her share of those losses from other personal income. The corporation files a corporate tax return, but it is simply an informational return similar to the return required to be filed by a general partnership. Thus, the shareholders gain the benefits of incorporation, such as limited liability, ease of transferability of their interest, and perpetual duration, but are not subjected to double taxation. There is no separate taxation of corporate income or a second tax when dividends are distributed as individual income.

Subchapter S status is a tax status granted by the Internal Revenue Service (IRS) on application and IRS approval. There are several requirements that a corporation must meet before it will be granted subchapter S status by the IRS. The first requirement refers to the number of shareholders. Second, the S corporation can have only one class of stock. (But stockholders need not have equal voting rights because they may own different numbers of shares.) Third, the corporation must be a U.S. corporation. And fourth, shareholders may not be nonresident aliens or (generally) nonhuman entities. However, there are exceptions for estates, some trusts, and **subchapter S corporations;** these entities can own stock in a subchapter S corporation.

There are also limitations as to the percentage of non-U.S. income and investment income the corporation may receive and still retain S status. Another requirement is that all shareholders must join in the application for S status. However, if the shareholders decide to terminate the S status, they may do so. Only the consent of a majority of the stockholders is needed for revocation of subchapter S status.

Subchapter S status is advantageous only as long as it is in the best interests of the shareholders from a tax standpoint. For example, if the shareholders in a small corporation were three shareholders who all had other incomes that put them in the top tax bracket for their individual income taxes, then they would not want S status. Their preference would be to have the corporation profits taxed at corporation tax levels and then have the after-tax profits reinvested, rather than distributed as dividends. Then later, when they wanted to take their money out of the corporation, they could sell their stock and only have to pay capital gains taxes. However, if the corporation was sustaining losses, the three shareholders might want to use S status, so that they could offset the losses against their other income.

Public Corporation

This is a corporation created for governmental purposes. An example of a **public corporation** would be a municipal corporation, a school corporation, and other corporations created by the state government or the national government for governmental purposes.

Not-for-Profit Corporation

This is a corporation for a civic, charitable, or educational purpose. For example, a fraternity or sorority, if incorporated, would be incorporated as a **not-for-profit corporation** because its purposes would be social and civic rather than the conduct of a profit-making business. Special tax considerations are given to not-for-profit corporations.

Domestic Corporation

In the state where it was originally incorporated, a corporation is a domestic corporation. Acting in any other state, it is doing so as a "foreign" corporation.

Foreign Corporation

This is a corporation that is incorporated in one state and is doing business in another state. Foreign corporations must file certain documents and pay certain fees before doing local business in states other than the state in which they are incorporated. This topic is discussed in more detail later in the chapter.

Professional Corporation

Many states now have specific incorporation laws that allow the incorporation of certain professionals, for example, a medical corporation. Such a corporation can be one doctor or many doctors. Dentists, veterinarians, architects, accountants, and lawyers may also incorporate their businesses under **professional corporation** statutes. Typically there are different requirements for incorporation and different provisions for regulation under the professional corporation statutes.

The *Clackamas* case illustrates a continuing problem: What is the status of the "professional" owners/operators of a professional corporation?

Relationship with State of Incorporation

Formation

Incorporators. **Incorporators** are the people who actually apply to the state for the incorporation of a business. The incorporators sign a document, usually called **articles of incorporation,** and file it with the secretary of state of the state where they are requesting incorporation. Some states require the incorporators to be citizens of the incorporation state; others do not. The MBCA, which has been followed by many states, now allows a single incorporator to apply. Thus an individual may incorporate a business and may be the sole shareholder.

Procedure for Incorporation. Although each state has its own individual incorporation statute, the requirements for incorporation are similar in all states. Generally speaking, the incorporator or incorporators execute and sign articles of incorporation and file this document with

CASE 1

Clackamas Gastro Assoc. v. Wells
538 U.S. 440 (2003)

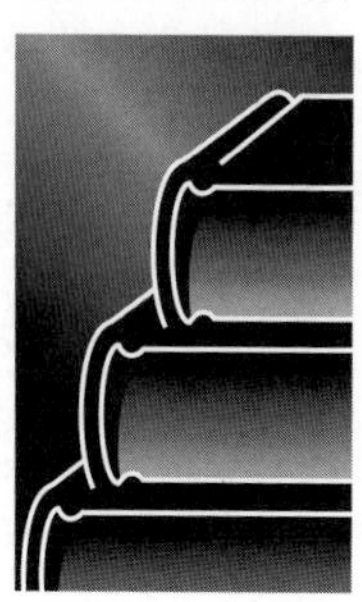

Facts: Clackamas is a medical clinic, organized as an Oregon professional corporation, with four doctor-shareholder/directors and 14 employees. Deborah Wells filed a lawsuit, claiming that the termination of her employment at the clinic violated the Americans with Disabilities Act (ADA) of 1990. The ADA does not apply to organizations with fewer than 15 employees, so Wells claimed that the four doctor-shareholder directors were also "employees." ADA defines "employee" as "an individual employed by an employer."

The U.S. District Court granted Clackamas' motion for summary judgment, but the U.S. Ninth Circuit Court of Appeals reversed, holding that the four doctors were "employees" of their corporation. Clackamas petitioned for U.S. Supreme Court review.

Issue: Are the four doctor/shareholders employees for ADA purposes?

Decision: No. Judgment of the Ninth Circuit is reversed, and case is remanded.

Opinion by Justice Stevens: "'[W]hen Congress has used the term 'employee' without defining it, we have concluded that Congress intended to describe the conventional master-servant relationship as understood by common-law agency doctrine'.…

"[O]ur inquiry is whether a shareholder-director is an employee or, alternatively, the kind of person that the common law would consider an employee.…

"Perhaps the Courts of Appeals' and the parties' failure to look to the common law for guidance in this case stems from the fact that we are dealing with a new type of business entity that has no exact precedent in the common law. State statutes now permit incorporation for the purpose of practicing a profession, but in the past 'the so-called learned professions were not permitted to organize as corporate entities.' … Thus, professional corporations are relatively young participants in the market, and their features vary from State to State.…

"Nonetheless, the common law's definition of the master-servant relationship does provide helpful guidance. At common law the relevant factors defining the master-servant relationship focus on the master's control over the servant.…

"This is the position that is advocated by the Equal Employment Opportunity Commission (EEOC), the agency that has special enforcement responsibilities under the ADA and other federal statutes containing similar threshold issues for determining coverage.…

"Specific EEOC guidelines discuss both the broad question of who is an 'employee' and the narrower question of when partners, officers, members of boards of directors, and major shareholders qualify as employees.… The guidelines list six factors to be considered in answering the narrower question, which they frame as 'whether the individual acts independently and participates in managing the organization, or whether the individual is subject to the organization's control.' … We are persuaded by the EEOC's focus on the common-law touchstone of control … and specifically by its submission that each of the following six factors is relevant to the inquiry whether a shareholder-director is an employee:

'Whether the organization can hire or fire the individual or set the rules and regulations of the individual's work

'Whether and, if so, to what extent the organization supervises the individual's work

'Whether the individual reports to someone higher in the organization

'Whether and, if so, to what extent the individual is able to influence the organization

'Whether the parties intended that the individual be an employee, as expressed in written agreements or contracts

'Whether the individual shares in the profits, losses, and liabilities of the organization.' EEOC Compliance Manual s. 605.0009.

"As the EEOC's standard reflects, an employer is the person, or group of persons, who owns and manages the enterprise. The employer can hire and fire employees, can assign tasks to employees and supervise their performance, and can decide how the profits and losses of the business are to be distributed. The mere fact that a person has a particular title—such as partner, director, or vice president—should not necessarily be used to determine whether he or she is an employee or a proprietor.… Nor should the mere existence of a document styled 'employment agreement' lead inexorably to the conclusion that either party is an employee.… Rather … the answer to whether a shareholder-director is an employee depends on 'all of the incidents of the relationship … with no one factor being decisive.' …

"Some of the District Court's findings—when considered in light of the EEOC's standard—appear to weigh in favor of a conclusion that the four director-shareholder physicians in this case are not employees of the clinic.… There may, however, be evidence in the record that would contradict those findings or support a contrary conclusion under the EEOC's standard that we endorse today. Accordingly … we reverse the judgment of the Court of Appeals and remand the case to that court for further proceedings consistent with this opinion."

the appropriate state official, usually the secretary of state. A filing fee is required, which, of course, varies from state to state. The corporation division of the secretary of state's office will review the articles, and if they comply with the applicable statute, the secretary of state's office will issue a certificate of incorporation that officially gives birth to the corporation. Many states require that a minimum amount of capital be paid into the corporation before it can legally commence business. Some states require that the articles of incorporation be filed in the recorder's office of any county where the corporation holds real estate, or where it has its home office.

1. *Name.* The corporation, like a new baby, must be given a legal name. The incorporators are free to choose nearly any name, so long as it is not the same as or similar to the name of another corporation doing business in the state. Thus, before approving a name for the corporation, the state must run a check of all the corporations on file to find out whether this name is the same as or similar to the names of other corporations. Also, the name of the corporation must include the word *Incorporated* or the abbreviation *Inc.*, so that people will know that when they deal with this organization they are dealing with a limited liability organization.
2. *The purpose for which the corporation is formed.* The purpose for which the corporation is formed can be stated in general terms. In most states it is not necessary to state the specific business the corporation intends to participate in. For example, the purpose may be stated as follows: "to transact any and all lawful business for which a corporation may be incorporated" (under the specific state corporation act).
3. *The address of the corporation's principal office and the name of its registered agent.* The principal office, of course, will be the mailing address for all corporate correspondence, and the resident agent is the person who can officially accept service of process for lawsuits against the corporation.
4. *The duration of the corporation.* A corporation has perpetual existence unless its articles of incorporation provide otherwise.
5. *Issuance of shares of stock.* The incorporator or incorporators must here state the total number of shares of stock the corporation requests authority to issue, the number of shares of stock that are to have a par value, and the number of shares that are to have no par value. If there are to be different classes of stock, different series of stock, and different rights and preferences with regard to different classes of stock, then this information must also be provided. Some states require the names and addresses of the original subscribers to the capital stock and the amount of their subscriptions.
6. *Directors and officers and qualifications of directors.* Many states require the articles of incorporation to include the names of the members of the first board of directors, and often the names of the officers of the corporation are also required. Most states do not require their corporations' directors to be residents of that state.
7. *Provisions for regulation of business and conduct of affairs of the corporation.* Many states require specific statements as to the conduct and scheduling of annual and special meetings of shareholders and directors and as to other provisions concerning the conduct of the business.
8. *Requirements prior to doing business.* Many states have specific requirements that must be complied with prior to the commencement of business by the corporation. The most common requirement is the payment of a minimum amount of money, typically $1,000, by subscribers to the corporation before the corporation commences doing business.

Charter as a Contract

When the articles are approved or the **corporate charter** is issued by the state of incorporation, a "contract" is formed between the state and the corporation. As a contract, the corporate charter is protected by Article I, Section 10 of the U.S. Constitution, which prohibits a state from passing any law "impairing the obligation of contracts." In the days when each corporate charter was the result of a special statute, this decision barred much state regulation of corporations. Today, however, general corporation laws contain provisions that reserve to the state the power to amend or repeal the statute. The state's power to change the corporate rules thus becomes part of every contract formed with every corporation pursuant to the statute.

The corporate charter also acts as a contract between the corporation and its stockholders, in the sense that it states the nature of the corporation's business. The bylaws adopted by the corporation also become part of this contract. To avoid unnecessary litigation, clear procedures for amending the corporate charter/articles and the corporate bylaws should be spelled out, and the power to amend should be specifically stated.

Other Obligations

The obligations of the corporation to its home state do not end with the issuance of the charter. Typically, annual reports to the state are required, and the corporation must pay an annual fee for the privilege of exercising its corporate powers. Corporation statutes usually provide for suspension or termination of the corporation's privileges for noncompliance with these annual requirements, at least when the default continues for an extended period of time. The *Williams* case shows the kind of complications that may arise when this happens.

Corporation as Person and Citizen

The corporation is, by definition, a legal person. As such, it enjoys the same constitutional protections as humans. Under the Fifth Amendment, its life, liberty, and property cannot

CASE 2

Williams v. Martin Lakes Condominiums Assoc., Inc.

644 S.E.2d 424 (GA App. 2007)

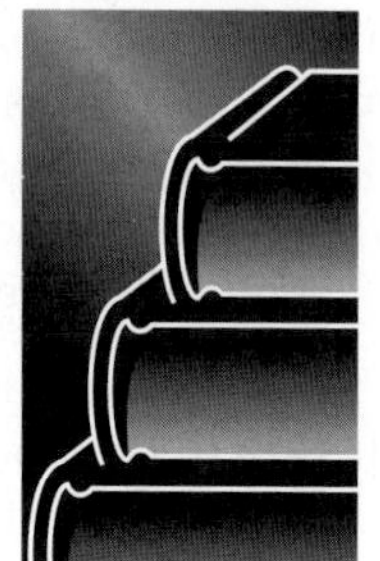

Facts: On November 8, 1999, the Association sued Mary Ann Williams to collect $1,220 in past due fees and assessments on her condominium unit. A nonprofit corporation, the Association had been administratively dissolved on July 1, 1993. Its charter was reinstated on June 1, 2000. When Williams filed her motion for summary judgment, the Association was in legal compliance, so the trial court denied the motion. Williams appealed.

Issue: Did the Association lack legal capacity to maintain its lawsuit?

Decision: No. Judgment affirmed.

Opinion by Judge Ellington: "Under Georgia law, when a nonprofit corporation is administratively dissolved, it 'continues its corporate existence but may not carry on any business except that necessary to wind up and liquidate its business affairs.... A corporation that has been administratively dissolved may apply for reinstatement, and this may be done at any time.... At present, Georgia law does not limit the period during which a corporation may apply for reinstatement.... When an administratively dissolved corporation has been reinstated, the reinstatement 'relates back to and takes effect as of the effective date of the administrative dissolution and the corporation resumes carrying on its business as if the administrative dissolution had never occurred....

"Although the appellate courts of this State have not addressed whether reinstatement ... revives the corporation such that it has the capacity to sue in that period between dissolution and reinstatement, we find case law from other jurisdictions persuasive. The Court of Appeals of Tennessee, considering a statute identical to ours, concluded that a reinstated homeowners association that had filed suit during its dissolution 'possessed the legal capacity to pursue its appeal.' ...

"When considering whether a reinstated corporation had the capacity to contract during its dissolution, the Court of Appeals of Kentucky also found that reinstatement validates a dissolved corporation's interim acts.... The court reasoned that ...

> *'In good conscience the defendants, who are strangers to the dealings between plaintiff and the State, should not be allowed to take advantage of the plaintiff's default in paying its taxes to escape their own obligation to the plaintiff, when its default has been cured by its subsequent compliance with the statutory requirements.'* ...

"We find this reasoning persuasive and hold that because the Association in the instant case was effectively reinstated, it possessed the legal capacity to sue at the time the complaint was filed."

be taken, without due process of law, by the national government or any of its agencies. Under the Fourteenth Amendment, the same due process protection exists against the state governments. Likewise, states cannot deny corporate people the equal protection of the law. (*Equal* here does not mean identical. It only means that distinctions must have a rational basis; arbitrary, invidious discrimination against corporations is prohibited.)

Corporations are not considered citizens for the purpose of Fourteenth Amendment "privileges and immunities of citizenship." Most obviously, this means that corporations cannot vote in political elections, hold political office, or serve on juries. More important, corporations do not have a citizen's right to conduct business in states other than the domicile state. Corporations wishing to do local business in a second state must secure that state's permission to do so; human persons, as citizens, are exempt from this requirement.

To determine whether or not diversity of citizenship exists (so that an ordinary civil case may be brought into U.S. District Court), a corporation *is* considered to be a "citizen" of its state of incorporation. Courts have also recognized that a corporation may acquire a kind of "double citizenship" in the state where it has its principal place of business. If any of the opposing parties in a litigation were a citizen of either of those two states, there would not be complete diversity of citizenship, and the case could not be brought into the U.S. courts on that basis, no matter how large an amount was involved.

Defective Formation

Mistakes are sometimes made during the incorporation process. Forms are filled out incorrectly, or some procedural step is omitted. The effect of such errors on the corporation's existence varies, depending on the seriousness of the mistake and on the intent of the human beings who were representing the corporation.

De Jure Corporation

Perfection is not required to attain full de jure corporate status. As long as any errors are minor, immaterial ones, the corporation's existence cannot be challenged by anyone, including the state of incorporation. Substantial compliance with all mandatory state requirements, in good faith, is all that is required. A mistake as to the last digit in the zip code on the corporation's mailing address would almost certainly be of this nature. If the corporation's name, street number, city, county, and state were correct, its mail would be delivered despite the (slightly) incorrect zip code.

De Facto Corporation

Even though the mandatory requirements of the corporation law have not been substantially complied with, so that the corporation has not attained de jure status, the corporation's de facto ("in fact") existence may nevertheless be recognized. Only very limited challenges against a **de facto corporation** are permitted. Subscribers cannot be forced to take and pay for stock in a de facto corporation; they are entitled to full de jure status. The state of incorporation, in a direct proceeding (usually called a *quo warranto*, "by whose authority") can force the suspension of a de facto corporation's business until the error is corrected. To attain de facto status, the promoters/incorporators must have made a good faith attempt to comply with a statute under which the corporation could be organized; they must be in at least "colorable" compliance with the statutory requirements (no mandatory step has been omitted); and the corporation must actually have used its powers. The stockholders of a de facto corporation have limited liability, and the de facto corporation can conduct its business free of third-party challenges.

Corporation by Estoppel

Courts sometimes apply the principle of estoppel against persons who have received benefits from a purported, but really nonexistent, corporation. The recipient of goods and services should have to pay for them, whether or not the provider was validly organized as a corporation. Similarly, insiders who were responsible for the defective organization but then dealt with it to their advantage should be prevented from asserting its defects.

The principle of estoppel can also be used to prevent persons who have held themselves out as a corporation from later trying to deny they were in fact a corporation.

No Corporation: Partnership Liability

When the promoters acted in bad faith, omitted a mandatory procedural step, or for any other reason failed to achieve at least de facto status for the corporation, the result is partnership liability for all the business associates. In such situations stockholders could be held fully liable personally for all the debts of the business. Persons trying to assert claims against the corporation would normally not be estopped from proving that it was not really a corporation and that all associates in the enterprise were personally liable for its torts and contracts.

Separate Corporate Entity/Piercing the Corporate Veil

Once a corporation has been successfully organized, it is recognized as a separate and distinct legal person or entity. It owns its own property, makes its own contracts, and pays its own taxes. So long as a corporation's separate identity is preserved by the persons who operate the corporation, that identity should be respected and upheld by the courts and other agencies of government. The fact that all of a corporation's stock is held by only a few persons is not, in itself, a basis for disregarding the separate corporate entity. A court should take this drastic step only when the corporation is being used to produce illegal or fraudulent results or when its human operators are themselves disregarding its existence. Severe under-capitalization of the new corporation may lead a court to infer fraud on the part of its organizers. Some regulatory and taxation statutes permit enforcement agencies to impose liability on other persons for acts by a corporation. Although this is not quite the same as piercing the corporate veil, in effect, the separate corporate entity is disregarded.

The next case shows how these rules may affect the parent/subsidiary relationship, at least when third parties are involved.

CASE 3

United States Leather, Inc. v. Mitchell Mfg. Group, Inc.

276 F.3d 782 (6 Cir. 2002)

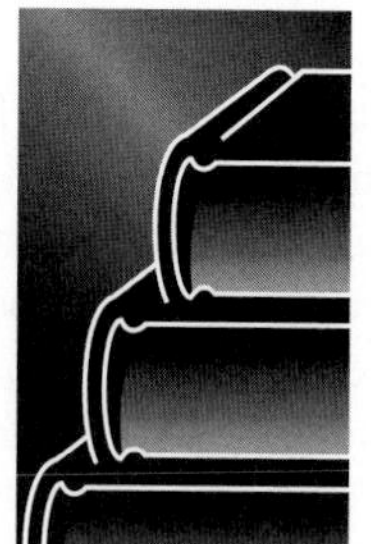

Facts: Mitchell Manufacturing Group, Inc. (now known as Mitchell Automotive) is a subsidiary of Mitchell Corporation of Owosso (MCO). The subsidiary manufactured leather products for use in automobile interiors and had purchased a large amount of leather from U.S. Leather (USL). By early 1998, the subsidiary owed USL over $1.5 million on account and also owed its parent (MCO) over $4.5 million. In an attempt to solve its financial problems, the subsidiary sold its assets (including its plant in Clare, Michigan) to Lamont Group, Inc., for $27.5 million. Lamont paid $6.5 million in cash and signed two promissory notes for the balance. As security for the notes, Lamont gave Mitchell Automotive a security interest in the purchased assets and a mortgage on the Clare plant. Mitchell Automotive in turn gave MCO a security interest in all its personal property, including the promissory notes from Lamont. When Lamont defaulted on its payments, it transferred all assets back to Mitchell Automotive. Lamont's deed to the Clare facility said that the deed was not intended to merge with the original mortgage and that the mortgage was intended to remain in full force and effect. USL sued to collect its account, received a judgment, and demanded that the current tenant of the Clare facility pay the rent to USL.

USL filed this lawsuit to determine who had first priority to the assets of Mitchell Automotive. The district court ruled in its favor, and MCO appealed.

Issue: Should the parent corporation's security interest be recognized as a first priority claim against its subsidiary's assets?

Decision: No. Judgment for USL is affirmed.

Opinion by Judge Guy: "The general rule ... is that when a holder of a mortgage becomes the owner ..., the mortgage and the [title] are merged and the mortgage is extinguished.... 'This rule is, however, subject to the exception that when it is to the interest of the mortgagee and [it] is his intention to keep the mortgage alive, there is no merger, unless the rights of the mortgagor or third persons are affected thereby.' ...

"As the district court explained, however, the exception is in turn subject to equitable consideration of its effect on the rights of the mortgagor or a third party[:]

> *For example, there will be no merger 'where to decree a merger would cause injustice or violate equitable principles, as is generally the case where the conflicting rights of a third person have intervened.' ... Likewise, the exception to the merger doctrine will not be applied when doing so violates equitable principles. Thus, even where the parties express an interest in keeping the mortgage alive, courts will decline to apply the exception where the rights of third persons would otherwise be lost....*
>
> *Applying these principles to the case at bar, the Court agrees with the Magistrate that the parties' expressed intent cannot be enforced in light of equitable considerations. Allowing an exception to [the] merger rule in this instance would do grave injustice. Such a finding would permit Defendant [Mitchell Automotive] to avoid paying an uncontested $1.5 million dollar debt to [USL] in favor of its parent corporation, Defendant [Mitchell Corp.]. The fact that these two corporations are run by the same President who originally incurred to debt to [USL] only highlights the inequity of applying the exception.*
>
> *Further, the Court finds its conclusion to be most consistent with the purpose of the exception to the merger rules.... In the present case, [Mitchell Automotive] is not in the position of a mortgagee trying to protect itself from junior lienholders of the Lamont Defendants, it is attempting to protect itself from having to pay a debt it acknowledges owing to Plaintiff....*

"Mitchell Corp. claims its rights should be protected as a 'third party' because it is the entity 'most affected by merger or non-merger.' In fact, USL is equally affected by the outcome of the merger issue. Mitchell Corp. also argues that the district court erred in its balancing of the equities by 'lumping' Mitchell Corp. and Mitchell Automotive together without determining whether the corporate veil could be pierced. While the Mitchell defendants maintain that they observed their separate corporate formalities, it is also undisputed that the companies had their offices in the same building, used the same computers, shared or leased the same employees, and had the same officers. Significantly, William Mitchell, President, Chairman of the board, and principal shareholder in both companies, incurred the debt to USL on behalf of Mitchell Automotive and was on both sides of the debt that arose between Mitchell Corp. and Mitchell Automotive.

"Since USL had abandoned its effort to attempt to collect the debts of Mitchell Automotive from the assets of its parent, it was not necessary to decide whether the facts would justify piercing the corporate veil. Instead, the district court was called upon to weigh the equities between USL and Mitchell Corp. as secured creditors competing for the sole asset of the debtor. In weighing those equities, it was proper to consider the relationship between Mitchell Automotive and its respective creditors. We find no error in the district court's determination that the equities weighed against allowing Mitchell Automotive to rely on the exception to the merger rule to favor the debt owed to its parent company over USL's judgment lien."

Corporate Powers

Because a corporation is a creature of the law, it possesses only those powers given to it by the law. It can only do those things it has been authorized to do. Authorization for particular acts of a corporation must be found either in its state's corporation statute or in its own charter. Powers that result from the corporation's existence as a legal person, such as the power to sue and be sued in its corporate name and the power to hold and convey property, are called **inherent powers.** These powers and others specifically stated in the corporation statute are also referred to as **statutory powers.** All corporations formed in the state have them.

Express powers are the powers specifically granted to a particular corporation by its charter. Many states permit such powers to be stated very broadly—for example, "to conduct any lawful business which may be conducted by corporations in this state." Corporations also have **implied powers;** that is, the powers that are necessary and appropriate to help carry out their express powers. When a corporation has not used a very broad statement of its express powers, litigation may occur over whether a particular corporate activity is or is not within its implied powers.

Problems have arisen, for example, over whether a corporation has the inherent or implied power to reacquire its own shares of stock, to be a partner in a partnership, to acquire shares of stock in other corporations not in the same line of business, and to make charitable contributions. Some state corporation statutes contain a long list of things that corporations formed thereunder are permitted to do. Section 302 of the MBCA contains such a list. If the corporation's powers/purpose clause has been stated as "any lawful business," there should be little chance of a successful court challenge to any of the aforementioned activities. Although some state statutes are still rather restrictive, the modern tendency seems to be to take a liberal view of the corporation's powers. If specific investors/promoters wish to limit *their* corporation's operations, they would be free to do so by adopting a restrictive purpose clause and statement of powers.

Acts that do not fall within one of the aforementioned categories are said to be **ultra vires,** "outside" the corporation's powers. Courts have not agreed as to what should happen when a corporation engages in such unauthorized activity. The modern tendency is to severely limit such challenges to corporate acts. If a contract has been fully performed by both parties, neither party can raise the ultra vires claim so as to force rescission. If a contract is completely executory, neither party can sue for enforcement. When only one party has performed, the courts disagree on what should happen; most courts permit the party that has performed to enforce the contract. In any case, the state should be able to enjoin the performance of unauthorized acts; a shareholder should be able to sue for an injunction and damages, and the corporation itself should be able to collect damages against the directors and officers who were responsible for the violation of the charter. Both the MCBA and the Revised MCBA follow this modern approach.

Promoters

Definition

The classic definition of a **promoter** is found in the *Old Dominion* case: "those who undertake to form a corporation and to procure for it the rights, instrumentalities, and capital by which it is to carry out the purposes set forth in its charter and to establish it as fully able to do business." The promoters are the "idea people"; they conceive the idea of incorporation, and then they attempt to implement it. The incorporators, the persons who sign the documents specifically requesting the state of incorporation to recognize the corporation's existence, may or may not be promoters. Persons whose only function in the incorporation process is a professional one, such as lawyers, accountants, or engineers, are not necessarily promoters. The promoters are the driving force behind the corporation.

Liability Inter Se

As between themselves, promoters are in a sense partners or at least joint venturers. Once agreement has been reached as to what will be done and how it will be done, they owe each other a fiduciary duty. This fiduciary duty does not arise, however, unless and until some agreement has been reached. A person who discloses a "good idea" to another person before any agreement has been reached therefore runs the risk that the other person will appropriate the idea without compensation.

Liability to the Corporation and/or Shareholders

Promoters also occupy a fiduciary relationship to their corporation and its subscribers/shareholders. Promoters should, of course, recover all reasonable expenses they have incurred during the incorporation process. They are not, however, entitled to retain secret profits that they have made during the incorporation process, for example, by reselling assets to the corporation for more than they paid for them. Full disclosure of such proposed profits must be made. The question is: To whom? By the majority rule, disclosure to only the original promoters/subscribers is not sufficient, at least when there is a plan to sell more shares to the public. Full disclosure must be made to an independent (nonpromoters) board of directors, to all subscribers, or to all shareholders, unless the promoters making the profits have themselves subscribed to all the shares to be issued.

Corporation's Liability on Promoter's Contracts

Because the corporation does not yet legally exist, the promoters cannot be its agents when they make preincorporation contracts. The promoters are thus personally liable on all preincorporation contracts (with suppliers, landlords, employees, and so on), unless and until the new corporation comes into existence and "adopts" these contracts as its own. If and when that happens, the states disagree on whether the promoter's liability on the contract is impliedly discharged. If the third party knew that the corporation had not yet been formed and did intend to deal with it through the promoter and the corporation then comes into existence and adopts the contract, there would seem to be no reason to hold the promoter liable any further. Both parties got exactly the contract they intended and wanted. Some states so hold, but others do not. In this other group of states, the promoter is not discharged unless the third party agrees to a novation, either expressly or impliedly agreeing to accept the corporation in place of the promoter and to discharge the promoter. This second rule seems to give the third party more than he or she bargained for and more than the promoter originally agreed to. Because of these uncertainties, the preincorporation contract should be very carefully drafted, with a specific statement on when the promoter's liability ends.

Foreign Corporations

Definition

When we see the term ***foreign corporation*** we normally think of a corporation from some country other than the United States. Actually any corporation for profit, organized and created in one state and doing business in another state, is a foreign corporation. For example, a corporation organized and created in Illinois is a foreign corporation when it is transacting intrastate business in Wisconsin or Iowa. Corporations organized in foreign countries and doing business in a state of the United States would technically be classified as **alien corporations** but are also usually regulated as foreign corporations. Simply stated, any corporation not organized in the specific state in which it is doing local business or requesting to do local business is a foreign corporation insofar as that state's law is concerned. A corporation organized and doing business in the state in which it is organized is termed a **domestic corporation.** Thus, a corporation can be both a domestic corporation and a foreign corporation, depending on where it is doing business.

Exhibit 33.1: Promoters Preincorporation Contracts

Promoters ←-- (contracts) --→ Subscribers

Promoters ←-- (contracts) --→ Landowners, Lenders, Builders, Suppliers, Employees, Franchisors, Franchisees

↓

Proposed new corporation

(incorporation process)

New corporation

↕

Stockholders

↕

Directors ←----→ Directors vote to have corporation "adopt" promoters' contracts

↕

Officers ←-- (new contracts) --→ Third parties

↕

Agents ←-- (new contracts) --→ Third parties

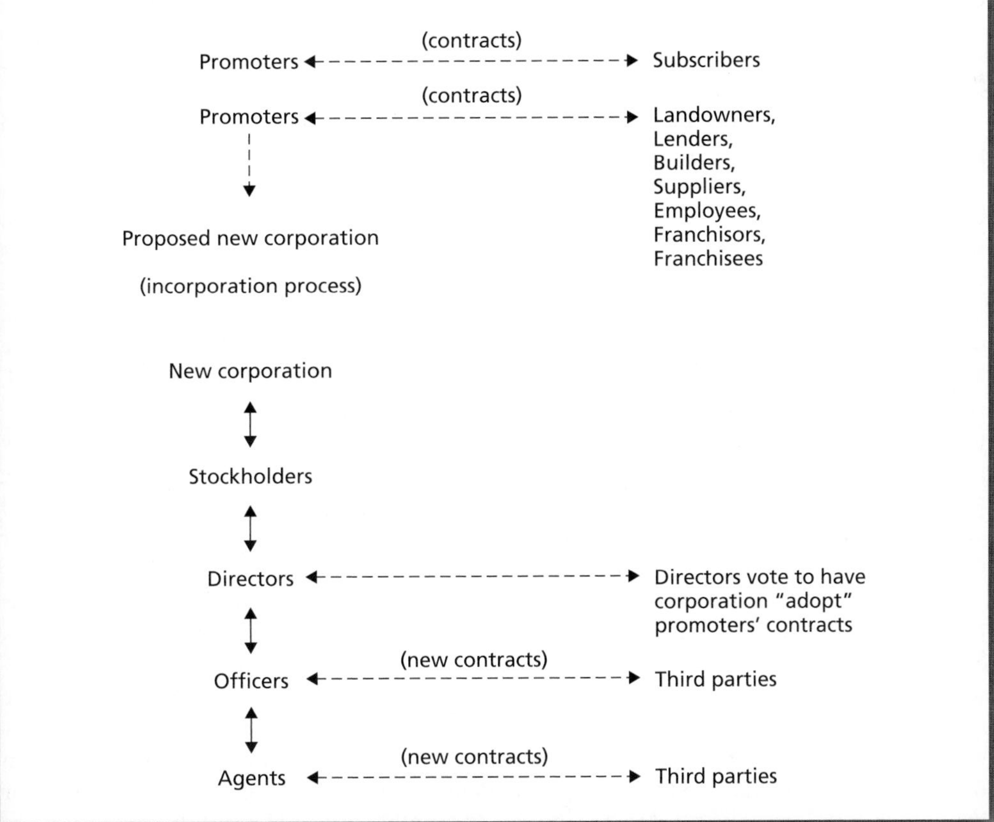

Degrees of "Doing Business"

A foreign corporation may be subject to the jurisdiction of a state other than its state of incorporation for litigation, for taxation, or for regulation on the basis of having done business in the second state. The **degree of "doing business"** necessary to sustain jurisdiction is not the same, however, in the three cases. One transaction may be sufficient to provide jurisdiction for litigation relating to that transaction. For taxation, the event or relationship being taxed must have occurred within the taxing state. For a corporation to be subject to a second state's regulatory system for foreign corporations, it must conduct some more substantial amount of local business in that state.

Jurisdiction for Litigation

If a foreign corporation has been granted a certificate of authority and it does business within a state, then the foreign corporation must designate a person or another corporation as a resident agent for service of process. Thus, there is no problem in securing service of process against a foreign corporation that is admitted and qualified to do business in the state.

A problem arises when a foreign corporation is doing business within a state but has not secured a certificate of authority and does not have an office nor any employees or agents within the state boundaries. In Chapter 4, we indicated that most states now have long-arm civil procedure statutes. These statutes allow service of process on foreign corporations even though they have not registered and have not appointed an agent to receive service of process within the state. Some statutes provide for service of process to the litigation state's secretary of state (who will then forward the notice to the defendant foreign corporation). Other statutes require the plaintiff to send copies of the summons and complaint directly to the out-of-state corporate defendant by registered or certified mail. In any event, for the long-arm process to be constitutionally valid, the defendant foreign corporation must have had some **minimum contact** with people or property in the plaintiff's state. Exactly how minimal these contacts can be is still not completely clear, as we saw in Chapter 4.

Jurisdiction for Taxation

To tax a foreign corporation, the taxing state must show that the corporation has entered into the relationship, within the state, which the tax is designed to reach. Further, if challenged on constitutional grounds, the taxing state must show that the tax does not unfairly discriminate against interstate commerce. When multistate relationships are involved, some rational apportionment formula must be used to allocate appropriate taxable shares to each state.

With real estate that a foreign corporation owns in the taxing state, the relationship, or **nexus,** is clear. The foreign corporation, like any other landowner, will have to pay the assessed real estate taxes. When personal property of a foreign corporation is being taxed, conflicts may arise if the property is being used in more than one state. For example, trucking companies, airlines, and railroads all have equipment that simply cannot stay in one place all year long. How much of their equipment can be taxed by each of the states where the equipment lands or travels? No uniform or standardized formula for taxing personal property is used in all states. The threat of multiple taxation continues to be a problem for corporations using property in more than one state.

Many difficulties also exist in the area of income taxation. Each state of course wants to tax as much of the foreign corporation's income as possible. In a landmark case the U.S. Supreme Court upheld the state of Minnesota in its taxation of income that the Northwestern States Portland Cement Company derived from sales in interstate commerce rather than intrastate business. After the decision in that case Congress enacted the interstate income law, which provides that a tax cannot be imposed on net income of a person or a corporation engaged in interstate business in which the only activity of the person or the corporation is to solicit orders for the sale of tangible personal property, the orders are sent outside the state for approval or rejection, and approved orders are shipped or delivered from a point outside the state. The law also exempts income that a foreign corporation derives from selling or soliciting sales through independent contractors, even though the independent contractor may have an office within the state. There will continue to be many litigations in this area because the revenue needs of the taxing state must be balanced against the discriminatory effect of the tax on interstate commerce and because the tax statute must provide a rational apportionment formula for multistate income.

The *Barclay's Bank* case is one of the key precedents on state taxation of a corporation's worldwide income.

CASE 4

Barclay's Bank, PLC. v. Franchise Tax Board of California
512 U.S. 298 (1994)

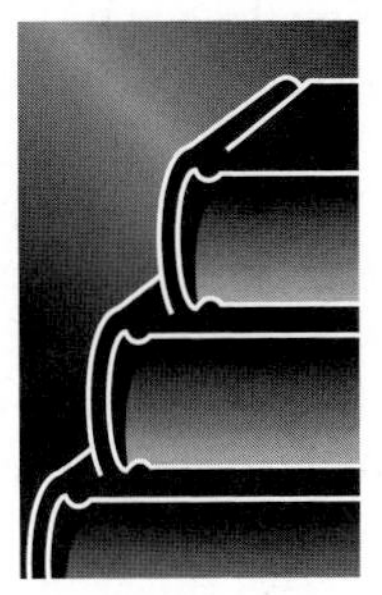

Facts: Barclays Bank, PLC. is a United Kingdom corporation that is part of Barclays Group, a multinational banking enterprise of over 220 companies doing business in some 60 nations. It conducts local business in California, which imposes a franchise tax on privilege of doing so. The state first determines the worldwide income of the unitary business and then allocates a portion of that income to California operations as a basis for taxation. The taxable income is equal to the average of the proportions of worldwide payroll, property, and sales located in California. Barclays paid the tax under protest and then sued for a refund. They won in the lower courts, but the California Supreme Court held the tax was valid and remanded the case. After further consideration, the California Court of Appeals denied the refund claim. Barclays petitioned for U.S. Supreme Court review.

Issue: Does this tax violate the Commerce Clause?

Decision: No. Judgment affirmed.

Opinion by Justice Ginsburg: "The [Commerce] Clause does not shield interstate (or foreign) commerce from 'its fair share of the state tax burden.' ... Absent congressional approval, however, a state tax on such commerce will not survive Commerce Clause scrutiny if the taxpayer demonstrates that the tax (1) applies to an activity lacking a substantial nexus to the taxing State; (2) is not fairly apportioned; (3) discriminates against interstate commerce; or (4) is not fairly related to services provided by the State....

"A tax affecting foreign commerce ... raises two concerns in addition to the four delineated [above]. The first is prompted by 'the enhanced risk of multiple taxation.' ... The second relates to the Federal Government's capacity to 'speak with one voice when regulating commercial relations with foreign governments.' ...

"Barclays ... vigorously contends ... that California's worldwide combined reporting scheme violates the antidiscrimination component of the ... test. Barclays maintains that a foreign owner of a taxpayer filing a California tax return 'is forced to convert its diverse financial and accounting records from around the world into the language, currency, and accounting principles of the United States' at 'prohibitive' expense.... Domestic-owned taxpayers, by contrast, need not incur such expense because they 'already keep most of their records in English, in United States currency, and in accord with United States accounting principles.' ...

"Compliance burdens, if disproportionately imposed on out-of-jurisdiction enterprises, may indeed be inconsistent with the Commerce Clause....

"California's regulations, however, also provide that the Tax Board 'shall consider the effort and expense required to obtain the necessary information,' and, in 'appropriate cases, such as when the necessary data cannot be developed from financial records maintained in the regular course of business,' may accept 'reasonable approximations.' ...

"We do not question Barclays' assertion that multinational enterprises with a high proportion of income taxed by jurisdictions with wage rates, property values, and sales prices lower than California's face a correspondingly high risk of multiple international taxation....

"[M]ultiple taxation is not the 'inevitable result' of the California tax; and ... the 'alternative reasonably available to the taxing State' ... 'could not eliminate the risk of double taxation' and might in some cases enhance that risk....

"We turn, finally, to the question ultimately and most energetically presented: Did California's worldwide combined reporting requirement ... 'impair federal uniformity in an area where federal uniformity is essential' ...; in particular, did the State's taxing scheme 'prevent the Federal Government from "speaking with one voice" in international trade'? ...

"[W]e discern no 'specific indication of congressional intent' to bar the state action here challenged. Our decision in *Container Corp.* left the ball in Congress' court; had Congress ... considered nationally uniform use of separate accounting 'essential,' ... it could have enacted legislation prohibiting the States from taxing corporate income based on the worldwide combined reporting method. In the 11 years that have elapsed since our decision in *Container Corp.*, Congress has failed to enact such legislation....

"Accordingly, the judgment of the California Court of Appeals is affirmed."

Jurisdiction for Regulation

Because a foreign corporation is not a "citizen" under the Fourteenth Amendment, it has no right to transact intrastate business in states other than the state of its creation. However, all of the states have provisions in their corporation laws that allow foreign corporations to do intrastate business on compliance with certain filing and licensing requirements. Moreover, a foreign corporation may transact interstate business across a state's borders without being required to file and comply with the state's requirements for foreign corporations.

Interstate commerce, that is, commerce among the states, is regulated by the national government under the authority of the Interstate Commerce Clause of the U.S. Constitution (Article I, Section 8). The individual states may not interfere with, burden, or discriminate against interstate commerce by their laws or regulations. The question which then arises is: What is interstate commerce, and what is intrastate commerce? The MBCA set out some general guidelines as to the activities of foreign corporations that will not be regarded as doing business in a state and will not require filing as a foreign corporation. These activities include selling goods through an independent contractor in another state; soliciting or procuring by mail orders, which will be accepted in a home state rather than in the state where they are solicited; conducting isolated transactions; maintaining a bank account; maintaining an office or agency for the transfer, exchange, and registration of the corporation's securities; holding meetings of directors or shareholders; maintaining or defending a lawsuit; or taking out loans or mortgages.

The common element in all of these examples is that the foreign corporation is not intending to conduct a long-term business in the state; does not have employees, agents, or property within the state; and thus is dealing in interstate commerce only. Section 15.01 of the Revised MCBA specifically states that the list it sets out is not exclusive. There is no clear rule of thumb as to what is and what is not interstate commerce. Thus, each case is going to have to review separately the amount of business conducted, the type of business conducted, the time span, and so on.

Procedure for Admission

Chapter 15 of the Revised MBCA sets out procedures for the admission of foreign corporations and regulations concerning the doing of local business in a particular state. Similar provisions have been adopted by most of the states. However, it must be remembered that this was a "model" act and that not all states adopted it verbatim. Many states have made specific changes to take care of specific problems.

Generally speaking, a foreign corporation doing local business within a state must apply for a **certificate of authority.** Such an application will normally require the name of the corporation, when and where it was incorporated, the names and addresses of the directors and corporate officers, a breakdown of the number and types of shares issued, and authorization the corporation has regarding the further issuance of stock. The corporation will also be required to estimate the value of the property, both real and personal, that it intends to own within the state and the gross amount of the business that it will transact within the state in the coming year. In addition, it will have to designate some person within the state to be the **registered agent** on whom service of process for lawsuits can be made, and it will have to maintain a registered office within the state. A license fee must accompany the application. This license fee will differ from state to state. A **franchise tax** may be assessed annually based on the corporation's property within the state and the business it conducts there. The foreign corporation must file an annual report similar to the annual reports filed by domestic corporations.

Penalties

The MBCA states that a foreign corporation that transacts business within a state without first obtaining a certificate of authority will not be permitted to bring any lawsuit in a court of that state until it has obtained a certificate of authority. The compliance with the requirements for the certificate of authority can be retroactive, thus allowing the corporation to sue on transactions that were consummated prior to the granting of the certificate of authority.

The MBCA goes on to state that the failure of a foreign corporation to obtain a certificate of authority to transact business in a state will not impair the validity of any contracts or acts of the corporation and will not prevent the corporation from defending any action brought against it in a court in the state. Thus, a corporation does not have the right to bring action as a plaintiff in the courts in a state where it is not authorized to do business; however, it does have the right to defend itself.

The foreign corporation will, of course, be liable for all fees and franchise taxes, which it would have paid had it duly applied for a certificate of authority and received it. Also, many states have statutory penalties for doing business without first obtaining permission. These penalties may be fines imposed on the corporation or its individual officers, directors, or resident agents. Another penalty imposed by some states is to make the officers, the directors, and any agents involved in contracts personally liable on the contracts, in effect taking away the corporate shield against liability. Again, it must be noted that not all states adopted the MBCA in its entirety, and thus there are still differences in the treatment of foreign corporations which fail to comply with the requirements of a particular state. Before doing business in a state, a foreign corporation should check out the state's law carefully.

Significance of This Chapter

The corporation is not only for big business. It is an organizational form that can be used by small family businesses, farmers, and professionals, such as doctors, accountants, lawyers, and architects. Nonprofit organizations also may have corporate status.

This chapter first discusses classifications of corporations and then goes through a typical procedure to be followed in establishing a corporation. The chapter discusses what happens when a mistake is made and who may be liable. Corporate powers also are discussed.

Nearly all large corporations do business in more than one state and thus are foreign corporations when they do business in states other than the state that granted their charter. This chapter defines what a foreign corporation is, reviews the filing procedures for registration as a foreign corporation, discusses the rights and duties a foreign corporation has, and reviews the penalty for failure of a foreign corporation to comply with the registration and filing procedures.

Any corporation operating across state lines needs to be aware of these rules because the consequences of noncompliance can be very serious. Not being licensed as required can result in the invalidation of contracts made in the other state. Failure to pay properly assessed taxes can result in large fines. Failure to defend a properly filed lawsuit can result in a default judgment, which can then be brought to the corporation's home state and enforced. For some of these violations, the human beings representing the foreign corporation may be subject to fines or imprisonment. Foreign corporation rules should definitely be factored into the decision to do business in another state.

IMPORTANT TERMS AND CONCEPTS

alien corporations
articles of incorporation
certificate of authority
close corporations
corporate charter
corporation
de facto corporation
degree of "doing business"
domestic corporation
express powers
foreign corporation
franchise tax
implied powers
Incorporators
inherent powers
legal entity
minimum contact
Model Business Corporation Act (MBCA)
nexus
not-for-profit corporations
professional corporation
promoter
public corporation
publicly help corporations
registered agent
statutory powers
subchapter S corporations
ultra vires

QUESTIONS AND PROBLEMS FOR DISCUSSION

1. What is a subchapter S corporation?

2. What is the difference between the incorporators and the promoters?

3. How can a corporation be a "citizen" for some purposes but not for others?

4. What is the difference between a de jure corporation and a de facto corporation?

5. Rochester Leasing, a New York corporation with its principal place of business in Rochester, New York, was in the business of leasing machines and equipment. Schilling, located in Tennessee, had leased 25 postage stamp vending machines at $55.35 a month for 5 years. The machines were delivered, but Schilling claimed that he had been defrauded by the salesman of a Florida company that had initially arranged the lease contract. Schilling refused to pay, and Rochester sued. Rochester was not registered to do business as a foreign corporation in Tennessee. It had no agents or employees there, and all dealings with it in this case had been by mail. The lease contract had been approved by Rochester at its New York office and had provided that all payments should be made there. The trial court dismissed the suit because Rochester was not registered to do business; the Court of Appeals affirmed; and Rochester then appealed to the Supreme Court.

   How should the Tennessee Supreme Court rule, and why?

6. Plaintiff-appellant, John Hyland, M.D., claiming a violation of the Age Discrimination in Employment Act (ADEA) alleges that he was forced to resign as an employee, officer, and director of defendant-appellee, New Haven Radiology Associates, P.C. ("NHRA") because he was 51 years of age. Following extensive discovery, NHRA, a professional corporation, moved for summary judgment, asserting that Hyland lacked the necessary standing to invoke the protections afforded by the ADEA. Applying an "economic realities" test, the District Court granted the motion, finding that NHRA "amounts to a partnership in all but name," and that Hyland was, in effect, a partner in the enterprise. According to the District Court, Hyland therefore was not an employee entitled to claim the benefits provided by the ADEA.

   Appellant and four other radiologists organized NHRA in 1992 as a professional services corporation under the laws of the state of Connecticut to conduct the practice of radiology. Pursuant to the terms of a stockholder's agreement, each of the five founding members contributed the same amount of capital for equal shares in the corporation and an equal voice in management. Profits and losses were divided evenly among the members, all of whom served as corporate officers and directors. The stockholders agreed that stock could be held only by shareholder-members, who were required to be licensed physicians. On the death, withdrawal or termination of any member, the member or his estate was required to sell, and NHRA to purchase, that shareholder's stock at a price fixed in accordance with the valuation provisions of the agreement. No stock could be held in the corporation by a nonmember or nonemployee. The stockholders' agreement provided for the admission to membership of additional "Stockholder-Employees," who would enjoy the benefits of the corporation and participate in the management of its affairs equally with the other shareholders.

   Is Hyland "really" still a "partner," so that he has no claim as an employee under ADEA? Explain.

7. Prior to March 17, Dr. Valencia and eight other medical doctors agreed to staff the emergency room at St. Mary's. On that date, the doctors executed articles of incorporation for Mercy Medical Associates, Inc. On April 6, the articles were approved by the secretary of state. Eugene Birt was treated by Dr. Valencia on May 13, at which time Birt claims malpractice occurred. On May 13, Associates had not received the required certificate of registration from the Board of Medical Registration and Examination because they had not sent the board a copy of their corporate bylaws. When Birt sued for malpractice, he named the eight nontreating doctors along with Dr. Valencia, St. Mary's, and Associates. Birt appeals from a summary judgment for the eight doctors.

   Are other eight doctors personally liable for Dr. Valencia's negligence? Why or why not?

8. Ill health forced James Bukacek to sell his dairy business. His personal problems resulted in a divorce from his wife, Virginia. His financial affairs were also in bad shape. The sheriff was advertising his 300-acre farm for sale, to pay three judgments; he owed the state $15,000 for back taxes; and his mortgage payment was overdue. Bukacek was also unable to exercise the option that Virginia had given him on the 180 acres she owned. At this point, Bukacek went to see Burttram "about saving 'my farm.'" Together with Kelly and Wyatt, they agreed to organize Pell City Farms, Inc. Bukacek conveyed his 300 acres to Pell City, which also exercised the option on Virginia's 180 acres. Pell City (or its promoters) paid off all the back claims and personally assumed the old mortgage and executed a new one. When the deeds from James and Virginia were executed, Pell City's articles had not been filed with the local judge of probate as required by Alabama law. James filed an action to quiet title to the land in himself because Pell City was not incorporated and therefore could not take title. The trial court held for Pell City, and James appealed.

   How should his appeal be decided? Explain.

CHAPTER 34

Corporation Law—Shareholders

Chapter Objectives

This chapter will:

- Describe the classes of capital stock a corporation may be authorized to issue.
- Discuss the legal rules concerning subscriptions for shares of stock and the issuance of shares of corporate stock.
- Review the process of registration and transfer of shares.
- Discuss shareholders' rights.
- Discuss management rights of shareholders.
- Describe the legal procedure that must be followed to expand or terminate a corporation.

The legal structure of a corporation differs substantially from that of a partnership. As discussed in Chapter 31, each partner is assumed to have an equal voice in managing the business, the right to an equal share of the profits, and the liability for an equal share of the losses. If necessary, any partner can be forced to pay the firm's debts in full. Each partner is assumed to be a general agent of the firm, with full authority to conduct all of its normal business operations. The partners' investments in the firm are governed by their own partnership agreement. These management and ownership rights and liabilities inhere in each partner individually as the result of their partnership agreement. Partnership status cannot be transferred to someone else by the act of a single partner.

Nearly all these ownership and management rules are different for a corporation. The primary mechanism for corporation investment and control purposes is the share of stock. A corporation, as a separate legal person, can of course borrow money in much the same way as an individual or a partnership can. The equity investment in the corporation, however, is done by buying shares of stock. The investor agrees to buy a certain number of shares and receives a certificate indicating how many shares have been purchased. The investor, now a stockholder or shareholder, has the right to vote the number of shares owned at stockholders' meetings. The investor also has the right to receive dividends, as earned and declared, based on the number of shares owned. Although the stockholder is not considered an agent of the corporation, and generally has no authority to conduct its business operations, the shares of stock are assumed to be freely transferable. The shares can be sold to someone else without the consent of the other shareholders or of the corporation, and the transferee becomes a shareholder with the same rights as all other shareholders.

As a separate legal person, the corporation owns its own assets. Individual stockholders have no right to possess or use these assets just because they are stockholders. Their shares of stock simply make them the "owners" of proportionate parts of the corporation's net worth.

Although a corporation's stockholders normally do not have any rights against third parties who have had dealings with the corporation, there are some exceptions, as seen in the *Sabey* case.

Classes of Stock

In some corporations there is normally only one type of stock. Typically all of the shares in a small corporation have the same value, and all of the shareholders have the same rights. This is not true in large corporations where it is not uncommon to have several classes and series of stock. Some stock may have a par value, and other stock may have no-par value. Some stock may have voting rights, and other stock may not have voting rights. Some stock may be preferred, and other stock may be common.

Common Stock

Common stock is the basic class of stock issued by corporations. Typically a shareholder has one vote for each share of stock, and the shareholder is entitled to receive a pro rata share of the corporation's profits in the form of dividends. The common stockholder is given no guarantees, no special preference. If the business succeeds, the common stockholders receive dividends and their share value will increase. If the business fails, the common stockholders get no return on their investment, and they may lose the investment itself because they share in the balance of the assets after creditors and preferred stockholders have been paid off.

Preferred Stock

As the term **preferred stock** indicates, this class of stockholders gets special preference. Typically the preferred stockholder receives a specific, guaranteed dividend before any dividends are paid to the persons owning the corporation's common stock. In case of **dissolution** of the corporation the preferred stockholders get their money back before any money is returned to the common stockholders. Usually, preferred stock is nonvoting.

The preferred stockholder is not a creditor of the corporation, and normally the dividend on preferred stock does not have to be paid if the board of directors decides not to declare a dividend.

CASE 1

Sabey v. Howard Johnson & Company
5 P.3D 730 (WA App. 2000)

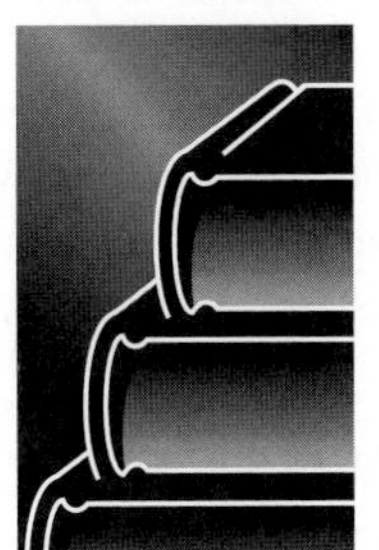

Facts: In 1986, Frederick and Nelson Acquisition Corp. (FNAC) hired Howard Johnson & Co. (HoJoCo), an actuarial firm, to assist in the termination of FNAC's pension plan. In 1988, FNAC began the formal termination process required by the Employment Retirement Income Security Act (ERISA), the national statute regulating pension plans. HoJoCo certified to the national regulatory agency—the Pension Benefit Guaranty Corporation (PBGC)—that the FNAC pension plan was fully funded. In its annual report, filed later that year, FNAC listed a $150,000 shortage in the plan.

David Sabey, president and sole shareholder of Sabey Corporation, was interested in buying FNAC. His personal lawyer did a due diligence investigation of FNAC's financial condition, and was assured—in writing—by HoJoCo that FNAC's pension plan would be terminated with no significant shortage of funds. Based on this assurance, Sabey had his new company, F & N Holding, Inc., buy FNAC in July 1989. When the bids from annuity companies for taking over the pension obligations were received, however, all the bids were $1,400,000 or more higher than HoJoCo had estimated. On September 7, 1989, HoJoCo notified the PBGC that the FNAC pension fund was insolvent, and FNAC filed for bankruptcy in 1991. The PBGC informed Sabey that he and Sabey Corporation might be held liable for any deficiency. Sabey Corporation, FNAC, and its pension fund sued HoJoCo. That lawsuit was dismissed when the plaintiffs failed to proceed with it, but Sabey Corporation was given permission to refile at a later date. When the PGBC claimed that Sabey and Sabey Corporation were liable for $3.75 million, Sabey settled the claim for $1.95 million. Sabey then sued HoJoCo. Because he was a stockholder in F & N Holding, the trial court dismissed all his claims. Sabey appealed.

Issue: Does Sabey have a sufficient personal interest, apart from his status as a stockholder, to bring his individual lawsuit?

Decision: Yes. Judgment reversed, and case remanded.

Opinion by Judge Ellington: "ERISA provides that 'all ... trades and business ... under common control shall be treated as a single employer.'... 'Common control' is 'one or more chains of organizations conducting trades or businesses connected through ownership of a controlling interest.'...

"[T]he PBGC apparently pursued Sabey and Sabey Corporation because ... Sabey had ownership interests in F&N Holding and in Sabey Corporation such that both he and Sabey Corporation fell within the 'controlled group' definition....[1]

"The 'standing' doctrine requires that a plaintiff have a personal stake in the outcome of the case in order to bring suit. Ordinarily, a shareholder cannot sue for wrongs done to a corporation, because the corporation is a separate entity: the shareholder's interest is viewed as too removed to meet the standing requirements. Even a shareholder who owns all or most of the stock, but suffers damages only indirectly as a shareholder, cannot sue as an individual. Howard Johnson argues that Sabey was merely a shareholder in F&N Holding and therefore lacks standing.

"There are two often overlapping exceptions to the general rule: (1) where there is a special duty, such as a contractual duty, between the wrongdoer and the shareholder; and (2) where the shareholder suffered an injury separate and distinct from that suffered by other shareholders. Sabey asserts both exceptions here....

"The purpose of the letter [relating to the solvency of the pension plan] was to confirm previous discussions between Howard Johnson and Sabey's personal counsel. Under the RESTATEMENT, this representation, and those that preceded it, could be found to create (and breach) a duty to Sabey personally.

"As to the second exception to the shareholder standing rule, Sabey alleges individual injury. When Sabey was identified as a member of the controlled group and paid $1.95 million to the PBGC in exchange for release of his and Sabey Corporation's liability, he suffered an injury separate and distinct from that of other shareholders. Thus, both exceptions to the shareholder standing rule are applicable, and the rule does not preclude Sabey's standing....

"Summary judgment is reversed. We remand for further proceedings consistent with this opinion."

1. Personal liability under ERISA is a complex subject. See, e.g., D[ana] M. Muir & Cindy A. Schipani, *The Intersection of State Corporation Law and Employee Compensation Programs: Is It Curtains for Veil Piercing?*, 1996 U. ILL. L. REV. 1059, 1101 ("To an even greater degree than other federal statutes such as CERCLA, ERISA's myriad regulatory requirements provide a number of potential settings where a variety of parties may attempt to reach through the curtain of protection typically accorded to corporations."...)

Cumulative Preferred Stock

In some lean years the corporation may not have enough profits to declare a dividend for either the preferred stockholders or the common stockholder. This question then arises: Does the preferred stockholder lose out on the unpaid dividend for such years? Unless the articles of incorporation state otherwise, the unpaid dividends on preferred stock would accumulate, creating **cumulative preferred stock.** Thus, it is important that preferred stock be declared either noncumulative or cumulative. If the preferred stock is noncumulative, then, of course, if no dividends are declared by the board of directors during a given year, the preferred stockholders simply lose out for that year. If the stock is cumulative, then the next year they will get the past year's dividends plus the new year's dividends before any money is distributed to the common stockholders.

Participating Preferred Stock

The preferred stockholder has the advantage of receiving dividends prior to the distribution of dividends to the common stockholder. Typically, however, the preferred stockholder is entitled to receive only a specific, guaranteed dividend, for example, 6 percent. If the corporation had a good year, the amount left to divide among the common stockholders might well exceed the percentage awarded to the preferred stockholders. However, if the preferred stockholder has **participating preferred stock,** then the preferred stockholder would share in the amount divided after the common stockholders received a dividend equal to the dividend paid to the preferred stockholders. Thus, if the preferred stockholders get 6 percent on their stock, then the common stockholders would get 6 percent on their stock and if there was extra money left over, it would be shared equally on a pro rata basis between the two classes of shared stock. This special feature, however, would have to be expressly stated.

In addition to the cumulative or noncumulative and participating or nonparticipating provisions of preferred stock, it is not uncommon to find **redeemable** or **convertible** provisions. Such provisions say, in effect, that at the election of the corporation or of the stockholder, preferred shares may be converted into another class of shares or may be redeemable by the corporation.

Par Value and No-Par-Value Stock

A corporation may issue stock with or without a par value. The certificates for **par value stock** state an amount that must be paid per share for the stock by the subscriber. The amount paid per share of no-par-value stock is simply determined by the board of directors.

The issuance of par value stock often creates misunderstanding. For example, if a new corporation issues 1,000 shares at a par value of $100 each, and you buy 10 shares at $100 each, you will be given stock certificates that show a face value of $1,000. The corporation, however, proceeds to buy equipment and inventory and to pay the expenses of incorporation and other expenses of doing business, and thus the corporation no longer has a net worth of $100,000 or 1,000 times $100 per share of par value stock. As a result, even though your certificate of stock shows a par value of $100 per share, you could not necessarily sell the stock for $100 per share as the stock is now only worth 1/1,000 of the net worth or book value of the corporation. The Revised Model Business Corporation Act (MBCA) eliminates the concept of par value.

Issuance of Shares

Authorized Stock

Authorized stock is the number of shares and the kind of stock that the corporation is authorized to issue. The original charter issued to the corporation by the state of its creation states the number of shares authorized and also the kind of shares authorized. If the corporation desires to increase its authority to issue more shares or different kinds of stock, it must apply to the state of its creation. Such approval will be granted if the request complies with the requirements of the state's corporation laws. A minimal filing fee will be charged.

Unissued Stock

This term refers to the authorized stock that is not yet issued.

Issued Stock

Issued stock refers to the shares of stock that have been sold and delivered to shareholders. It includes shares that have been reacquired by the corporation as treasury shares.

Outstanding Stock

Outstanding stock describes that stock that has been issued and is currently owned by stockholders.

Treasury Stock

This term refers to stock that was issued to shareholders and was later repurchased by the corporation. **Treasury stock** must be paid for with the corporation's surplus funds; the corporation cannot use original capital funds to repurchase stock. Also, the shares of treasury stock, although they are held in the corporation's name, are not votable, and such shares cannot earn dividends. Treasury stock may be resold, held, or canceled. Cancelling these shares reduces the number of shares issued, and the corporation can then issue new stock as long as it does not exceed the total number of shares authorized. The Revised MBCA provides that such shares become authorized, unissued stock, unless their reissue is prohibited by the articles of incorporation.

Subscriptions for Shares

One of the promoters' most important preincorporation functions is to make arrangements for acquiring the capital necessary to commence the firm's business. Persons making preincorporation offers to buy shares of the firm's stock are called subscribers. Because these offers are made to the corporation, they cannot be accepted until after incorporation. Unfortunately, in many cases proposed corporations fail before they ever commence business or after a very short period of operation. If there are unpaid creditors of the now insolvent corporation, it thus becomes very important to know exactly when subscribers become liable for their shares and the extent of that liability.

Revocable Offer

The general rule is that a stock **subscription,** like any offer, is revocable prior to acceptance. This rule creates problems for the promoters because they cannot count on having any set amount of capital until the corporation is formed and accepts the subscription offers. Some courts have found particular subscriptions to be irrevocable because the promoters' efforts provided consideration for an implied promise by the subscriber not to revoke. Some cases find mutual promise between the several subscribers not to revoke. Section 17 of the MBCA, which has been adopted in many states, makes the subscription offer irrevocable for 6 months without consideration. Of course, when fraud was committed against the subscriber, the offer can be revoked despite Section 17 or the presence of consideration. The Revised MBCA contains a similar provision.

Implied Conditions Precedent

For a subscriber to be held liable on a subscription contract, the courts have generally agreed that three conditions must be met. First, the corporation must be fully organized de jure. Second, it must be substantially like the one proposed to the subscriber. And finally, the shares subscribed for must be legally issuable by the corporation (in other words, must not be shares representing an oversubscription).

Express Conditions Precedent/Subscriptions on Special Terms

Some potential subscribers may not be interested in investing in the proposed corporation unless certain return promises are made. These special promises could relate to the corporation's method of operation, the location of its place of business, or other matters. What happens when the corporation is organized, accepts the subscriptions, but goes into bankruptcy before it builds its main plant in Keokuk, as it promised one subscriber? Is that subscriber liable anyway, or was the "plant in Keokuk" an express condition precedent that has not been fulfilled? As between risk-taking investors and unpaid corporate creditors, the equities are all with the creditors. Courts will try as hard as possible to label these special deals as subscriptions on special terms, so as to hold the subscriber liable for the full price of the contracted shares. After paying in full, the subscriber then has a claim for damages, if any can be proved, for the corporation's breach of its promise to build the plant. If the parties' intent and the "no contract if no plant" results are spelled out clearly enough in the subscription, the subscriber may avoid liability.

Subscription versus Contract to Purchase Shares

Particularly in cases in which the stock is being paid for in installments, it may also be important to distinguish between a subscription and a contract to purchase shares. A subscriber becomes liable for the full price of the shares when the subscription offer is effectively accepted by the corporation. A purchaser does not become a shareholder (and thus become liable for the price of the shares) until a certificate is delivered or tendered. When corporations have gone into bankruptcy before issuance of the certificates, many courts have held that the purchasers were excused from further liability because they would never receive their certificates. Subscribers in such a case would be bound to pay any balance due on their shares.

Once again, in figuring out which is which, it is a question of the parties' intent and of some legal presumptions and rules. Prior to incorporation, the transaction can only be a subscription, not a purchase. After incorporation, the agreement to buy original, unissued shares may be either. Generally, a purchase is an individual agreement, whereas a subscription may involve several purchasers. If there is any ambiguity at all, most courts will try to impose full liability by classifying the transaction as a subscription. The Revised MBCA makes all postincorporation agreements "contracts to purchase."

Minimum Liability Equals Full Par Value

In some instances subscribers may not be willing to pay the full par value per share, and the promoters may agree to sell shares at a discount. This is a dangerous practice at best because all states agree, on one theory or another, that every subscriber must pay at least the full par value for each share taken. One early case held that the corporation's capital was sort of a "trust fund" for the benefit of its creditors. A few states analyze the discount to subscribers as a fraud on the firm's creditors. The most sensible analysis simply says that payment of at least full par is the price the state demands for the privilege of doing business in the corporate form with limited personal liability.

Under any of these theories, creditors can force payment of the difference between the discounted contract price and the full par value. Creditors who knew about the discount when they extended credit, however, might have some difficulty in recovering in a fraud theory state. Stockholders who have paid full par for their shares might also sue to force the discounter to pay up. In some cases the corporation itself or the state of incorporation may bring the suit.

In addition to the original subscriber who bought at a discount (whether or not still a stockholder), possible defendants include knowing transferees of the discounted shares, the directors who approved the sale, and the promoters. As states adopt the Revised MBCA, these lawsuits will be almost completely eliminated because there will be no par value for shares.

Payment in Property or Services

Another potential area of liability arises when shares are paid for with noncash items. Property or services, to be valid payment for shares, must be usable by the corporation in operating its business. Generally, promises to perform services or to deliver property in the future do not constitute proper payment for shares, and subscribers who receive shares in exchange for such promises could be sued for the full par value of the shares they receive. The Revised MBCA permits payment with promissory notes and with promises to perform services.

Complications arise not only from questions as to whether or not the corporation was authorized to receive the noncash items but also as to the valuation of those items. States use two very different rules in determining whether at least full par has been paid. The MBCA and most of the newer corporation statutes have adopted the **good faith rule:** The valuation of the board of directors is conclusive. Whatever the board says the property or services were worth binds the corporation and all its creditors, unless the board was acting fraudulently or was grossly negligent. Some of the states still follow the older **true value rule,** which holds that any such noncash item had a true market value when it was transferred to the firm in payment for shares, that such value presents a question of fact, and that a jury can thus determine the true value of the noncash item. The result of this rule is that jurors are second-guessing the parties, sometimes after a lapse of several years, on the basis of less than perfect information.

No-Par Shares

As noted previously, **no-par stock** does not have any specific dollar figure indicated on the share certificate. Thus, most "valuation" problems are avoided when no-par stock is exchanged for a noncash item. Most statutes permit no-par shares to be issued for such consideration as is agreed to by the directors (or the existing stockholders). The no-par's price is thus permitted to fluctuate with market conditions, and the no-par stockholders would not be held liable for any "discount." No-par shares cannot, however, be issued as a gift. Moreover, there is case law that indicates that after the initial issue, if the price paid for no-par is not "fair" to the existing stockholders, they can bring suit to enjoin the dilution of their interest in the firm's net assets. Again, this difference in treatment will be eliminated under the Revised MBCA, which eliminates the idea of par value.

Treasury Shares

Treasury shares (which were issued but then reacquired by the corporation) generally may be resold for any consideration fixed by the board of directors. Once again, there should be no "valuation" problem or "discount" liability as long as the directors were acting in good faith. The Revised MBCA simply makes such stock additional authorized but unissued shares.

Shares Issued by Going Concern

What if the corporation needs additional capital after it has been in operation for some period of time? If it still has original, unissued par stock, can it sell that stock to investors at the market price, or is it still bound to receive at least par value per share? Only in a few states do the corporation statutes recognize this problem and specifically permit the directors, in this case, to sell par stock at the going market price. This problem, too, should be solved by the adoption of the Revised MBCA.

Repurchase of Shares

Having required the payment of at least par value per share by subscribers/investors, courts do not want these risk takers to be able to escape easily if the firm gets into financial difficulties. Creditors should be paid in full before stockholders recover any part of their investment. Thus, a contract for the repurchase of shares is valid only if the corporation has earned surplus when the contract is made, and for such a contract to be enforceable in court by the shareholder, the corporation must also have earned surplus when payment is to be made to the shareholder. At both points in time, the earned surplus shown on the books must be sufficient to cover the repurchase.

Registration and Transfer of Shares

Registration

Many securities issues must be registered with either the Securities and Exchange Commission (SEC), a similar state agency, or both. This is a very complex area of the law. Chapter 35 discusses the nature of these registration requirements and the potential liabilities involved.

Mechanics of Transfer

Article 8 of the Uniform Commercial Code (UCC) contains many of the rules covering the transfer of corporate securities (both stocks and bonds). Many customary practices are also involved—stockbrokers' rules for dealing with each other and their customers, regulations adopted by the stock exchanges, and administrative rulings from the SEC. Large corporations usually appoint a bank or trust company to act as their transfer agent; that is, to record transfer of their securities and to issue new certificates in the new owner's names. Securities, particularly bonds, may also be issued in bearer form, in which case ownership transfers are not registered with the corporation. Bearer bonds are often called coupon bonds because interest coupons attached to such bonds must be clipped and sent in by the bondholder to receive the interest due on the bonds.

The Revised MBCA does not require that a corporation issue paper certificates as evidence of ownership of its shares. Most corporations have done so, and continue to do so, but computerized share transfers may become more popular in the near future. If used, share certificates provide proof of ownership of the shares they represent and furnish a handy means of dealing with the shares. When shares are sold, the certificate is endorsed over to the buyer or simply endorsed in blank. When shares are used as collateral in a credit transaction, the certificate is usually left with the creditor.

Someone who transfers a certificate for value warrants to the purchaser that: (1) the transfer is effective and rightful, (2) the certificate is genuine and has not been materially altered, and (3) the transferor knows of no fact that would impair the validity of the certificate. However, if the transfer is made by an intermediary, that person warrants only that the transfer is authorized and is made in good faith.

Registration of Transfer

When securities have been issued in registered form, the corporation may continue to treat as owner the person whom they have registered as owner. That registered owner would, for instance, continue to receive dividends on the shares. A buyer of registered shares, therefore, may wish to have the transfer of ownership registered on the corporation's books. The corporation has a duty to do so if: (1) the certificate has been properly endorsed, (2) reasonable assurance is given that the endorsement is valid, (3) no adverse ownership claims to the shares have been presented to the corporation and are still pending, (4) all applicable tax laws have been satisfied, and (5) the transfer was in fact rightful or was made to a bona fide purchaser (BFP) who received the certificate free of adverse claims. A BFP of the certificate is a person who took it for value, in good faith, and without notice of any adverse claims. For the transferee to receive this BFP protection, the certificate must have been issued in bearer form or have been properly endorsed.

Lost or Stolen Securities

When the missing securities were in bearer form or had been properly endorsed by the former registered owner, a good faith purchaser from the thief or finder owns the securities. If registered securities are involved, the BFP is entitled to be registered on the corporation's books as the new owner.

When the securities were in registered form but the thief or finder forged the endorsement/assignment of the owner, the BFP does not own the certificates and must return them. If the BFP sends in an old certificate to the transfer agent, however, and the old certificate is canceled and a new one issued to the BFP, the BFP does own the new certificate. In this last situation the former owner has a claim against the corporation and its transfer agent for not catching the forgery. Because of the potential liabilities resulting from such a "double issuance" of a new certificate, corporations will uniformly require that persons who claim that their certificates have been lost or stolen post bonds protecting the corporation against the "reappearance" of the missing securities.

Restrictions

Corporate securities are generally freely transferable by the owner. In special situations, however, the persons, operating the firm may wish to place limitations on the retransfer of its stock. In a small closely held corporation, for example, the stockholders might want to give the corporation itself or the other stockholders a right of first refusal before any stock is resold to outsiders. Similarly, there might be a requirement that shares issued to key employees be resold to the firm rather than to outsiders when the employment ends. For such restrictions to be effective against buyers who do not know about them, they must be noted conspicuously on the certificate.

Shareholder Rights

Vested Rights

As noted in Chapter 33, the charter of the corporation is a contract. This means that the shareholders' rights the charter establishes cannot be changed without their consent. When the power to amend the articles and the bylaws has been reserved, however, and the amendment procedure is followed, changes can be made in the respective rights and liabilities of the stockholders.

Preemptive Rights

One right recognized in many older cases is the right to maintain one's proportionate investment in the corporation. The original stock issue gave each stockholder a certain percentage of the votes and of any dividends declared. To protect this relationship among the stockholders, courts required that existing stockholders be given a right of first refusal for a proportionate part of any new issue. That is, the new stock had to be offered to existing stockholders first, before it could be sold to others. Courts did not agree as to whether this preemptive right also applied to originally authorized but unissued stock.

Insistence on such **preemptive rights** makes it very difficult for a firm to authorize a new stock issue for executive bonuses, acquisition of assets, mergers with other firms, or other possible business needs. The modern tendency is to limit or eliminate such preemptive rights unless they are specifically provided for in the articles or by agreement among the stockholders.

Voting Rights

Except perhaps in Illinois, corporations are permitted to issue both voting and nonvoting stock. As previously noted, typically common stock has the right to vote, whereas preferred stock does not. Unlike partnerships, where each partner is presumed to have one vote regardless of the amount invested, in corporations each share is entitled to one vote.

To facilitate minority representation on the board of directors, some corporations provide for **cumulative voting.** (In some states, in fact, cumulative voting for directors is required by law.) Under this voting system, all directors' vacancies that are to be filled in a given year are voted for at the same time, with each share having as many votes as there are directors to be elected. The idea is that by massing their votes for only one (or a few) candidates, minority stockholders may be able to get at least some representation on the board. A seat on the board enables the minority to obtain information and to present alternative proposals and views. To find out how many shares they need to assemble to be assured of electing their candidates, minority stockholders can use the following formula:

$$X = \frac{a \times c + 1}{b + 1}$$

where *X* equals the number of shares needed, *a* equals the number of shares voting in the election, *b* equals the number of directors to be elected, and *c* equals the number of directors the minority want to elect.

To assemble the number of shares needed to obtain board representation or to gain or maintain control, shareholder groups can use one of three devices: the proxy, the voting control agreement, or the voting trust. A **proxy** is merely a revocable agency authority to vote shares. Changing conditions or new information could lead stockholders to withdraw their proxies or to give later proxies to the opposing side. Proxies thus do not provide a very stable coalition.

Some or all of the stockholders, particularly in closely held corporations, may enter into **voting control agreements.** Such agreements usually provide for reciprocal voting for the board of directors; A, B, and C agree to vote for each other, so that each retains a seat on the board. Such agreements are permitted in most states, at least for a limited period of time. They are not, however, binding on the corporation or on unknowing transferees of stock. A stockholder wishing to break up such an agreement could simply transfer shares to a BFP, who would then be free to vote them as he or she pleased.

The **voting trust** is the most durable arrangement for accumulating the votes necessary to maintain control of a corporation. Stockholders, the corporation itself, and transferees are all bound by the voting trust because shares of stock are actually turned over to the voting trustees, who are registered as the owners of the shares on the corporation's books. In return for their shares, the (former) stockholders receive voting trust certificates, which give them all the rights of stockholders except the right to vote. Many voting trusts are set up by demand of the firm's creditors as a condition to the extension of further credit. The creditors want to ensure continuity of management, and a voting trust is a good way to do so.

Dividend Rights

Many persons who invest in corporate stock are mainly motivated by the expectation of dividends The firm's directors generally determine the timing and amount of dividends, subject to the requirements of the particular state. Most states require that there be earned surplus before dividends may be lawfully declared and paid, but a few states permit the payment of dividends from current earnings even though prior years' losses have not been made up. Once declared, cash dividends become debts of the corporation. If a dividend has been illegally declared, the directors who voted in favor are jointly and severally liable for the entire amount of the dividend. All of the states agree that shareholders who know that a dividend was illegal can be forced to return it, but there is disagreement as to whether innocent stockholders can also be forced to return an illegal dividend.

Stock dividends are not debts of the corporation, and they may be rescinded by the board before the new shares are issued.

Right of Access to Information

Stockholders have the right to receive information regarding the operation of "their" corporation. This right, however, is not unlimited. All of the states agree that financial information, such as the firm's annual balance sheet and its profit and loss statement, should be available to the stockholders. There is some disagreement as to when an individual stockholder should have access to other information, particularly the firm's general books and business records. With unlimited rights of access, minority stockholders might be able to disrupt normal business operations. Competitors could simply buy one share of a firm's stock and then demand access to all of its trade secrets, formulas, and customer lists. "Junk mailers" of various sorts could buy one share and ask for lists of stockholders. For these reasons, courts have generally required that a stockholder must have a "proper purpose" in asking for access to corporate books and records. Some states require ownership of a certain percentage of a class of stock, and some also require that the stock have been owned for some minimum period of time (such as 6 months) prior to the demand for information. When the demand is proper and the officers refuse to provide the information, some statutes make them liable for 10 percent of the value of the stock owned, in addition to any other appropriate remedy to which the stockholder may be entitled. The Revised MBCA

CASE 2

SANDERS V. MCMULLEN
868 F.2d 1465 (5 Cir. 1989)

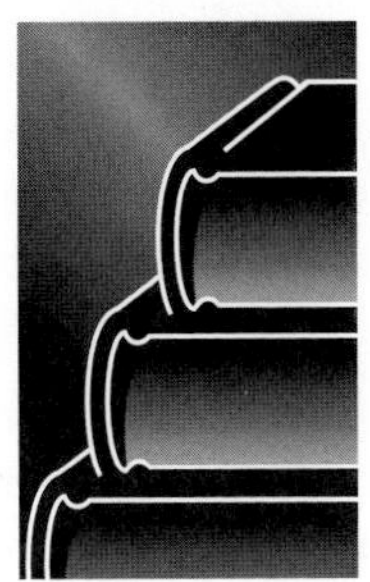

Facts: The Houston Sports Association (HSA) is a Texas corporation that owns and operates the Astrodome and the Houston Astros Baseball Club. In 1979, the defendant-appellee, John J. McMullen, formed the Houston Astros Limited Partnership (HALP) to purchase the capital stock of HSA from its creditors. McMullen was a general partner of HALP and personally owned 25 percent of the partnership. His family owned an additional 8 percent. The plaintiff, Don A. Sanders, as one of 25 other investors, owned a 2 percent interest in HALP.

After the 1980 baseball season, investors sought to oust McMullen as a general partner of HALP, and the organization was dissolved. HSA, however, was recapitalized and the partners of HALP received HSA stock. The result was that McMullen controlled 34 percent of the stock and became chairman of the board. Sanders still owned 2 percent.

In 1984, minority shareholders tried to enter a voting agreement with 51 percent of the stockholders to remove McMullen from management of HSA. Sanders' 2 percent interest was included in the 51 percent, but he decided to withdraw from the agreement, leaving the shareholders with only 49 percent. Sanders claims he agreed to withdraw because of promises made by McMullen. McMullen was able to retain control of HSA and even purchased more shares when the organization was restructured. McMullen then controlled 63 percent of the shares and Sanders increased his share to 13 percent with a $4 million stock purchase.

Sanders contends that McMullen promised him the following items in exchange for withdrawing from the voting trust:

(1) Participation in all management decisions involving the baseball team.

(2) Access to all operational information.

(3) The baseball manager and staff would be advised of Sanders' status.

(4) Participation in league meetings, World Series, and All Star Game activities.

(5) Access to all baseball facilities.

(6) Inclusion of his shares in the control block for any sale.

(7) McMullen would vote his shares to keep Sanders on the board of directors.

Sanders contends that he purchased the additional stock and withdrew from the voting trust that would have ousted McMullen in reliance on these promises. A continuing shareholder's agreement and a collateral agreement were both signed by the parties. The agreements represented Sanders' additional investment of $4 million. The promises are not contained in the documents or mentioned on the stock certificates.

In November 1986, Sanders was not reelected to the board of directors of HSA, and McMullen sent him a letter stating that he was not entitled to any special privileges as a shareholder. Sanders sued McMullen for breaching the agreement and for fraudulent misrepresentation. He sought specific performance or an injunction requiring McMullen to honor his agreement. The trial court granted McMullen's motion for summary judgment, finding that there was no genuine issue of material fact.

Issue: Was this agreement required to be in writing?

Decision: Only as to point 7. Judgment reversed as to all other points.

Opinion by Circuit Judge Gee: "The trial court determined that the oral agreement between McMullen and Sanders was a 'voting agreement' subject to the requirements of Article 2.30(13). Since the promises were not in writing, the court granted summary judgment on the issue. The trial court treated all of the issues as constituting a voting agreement, although not all of them related to voting. In fact, of the seven alleged promises, only the one that required McMullen to vote his shares so as to keep Sanders on the Board is without question controlled by Article 2.30(B). The trial court's summary judgment on alleged promises not relating to the voting of shares is therefore reversed and remanded.

"With regard to the alleged agreement that McMullen vote so as to keep Sanders on the Board, the appellant argues that the doctrine of part performance removes it from the statute of frauds. The part performance by Sanders would be his purchase of the shares. The appellant contends McMullen's alleged agreement would then be enforceable without meeting the writing requirement of Article 2.30(B).

"The appellant's argument is not persuasive. Part performance must be specifically referable to an agreement. As Cardozo wrote, 'There must be performance "unequivocally referable" to the agreement, performance which alone and without the aid of words of promise is unintelligible or at least extraordinary unless as an incident of ownership, assured, if not existing.'...

"The other cause of action, fraudulent misrepresentation, sounds in tort. The order of the trial court fails completely to address the fraud complaint....

"Perhaps the trial court considered the tort claim moot since the contract claim failed. This, however, would not eliminate the tort claim....

"Alternatively, both in its original complaint and on appeal, the appellant sought specific enforcement of the agreement or an injunction. The trial court will be able to consider these remedies on remand. The plaintiff has stated a cause of action on the tort claim, and granting the motion for summary judgment was error. . . .

"Summary judgment for the appellee on the alleged promise of McMullen to vote so as to keep Sanders on the Board is AFFIRMED. The agreement was properly characterized as a voting agreement subject to the strictures of the Texas Business Corporation Act, Article 2.30(B). The appellee, however, has presented a prima facie case for fraudulent misrepresentation. All alleged promises not relating to the voting of shares must therefore be heard at trial."

makes the corporation liable for the stockholder's legal fees in getting a court order for inspection, unless the corporation had a good faith doubt about the stockholder's right to inspect.

Shareholder Lawsuits

Individual shareholders can of course bring lawsuits, as individuals, to enforce their rights as shareholders. They may sue to enforce their right to dividends, to vote, to subscribe to additional shares, to receive corporate information, and other similar stockholder rights. A group of shareholders together may file a class action lawsuit if they meet the test outlined in Chapter 4. Such lawsuits by one or more shareholders are directed against the corporation, and any remedies given are directed against the corporation and for the benefit of the stockholders as individuals.

Derivative Suits

In certain extraordinary situations, individual stockholders may be able to bring lawsuits on behalf of their corporation. In these cases, they are suing for their own benefit only

Exhibit 34.1: Shareholders: Voting Control Mechanisms

1. Voting by proxy

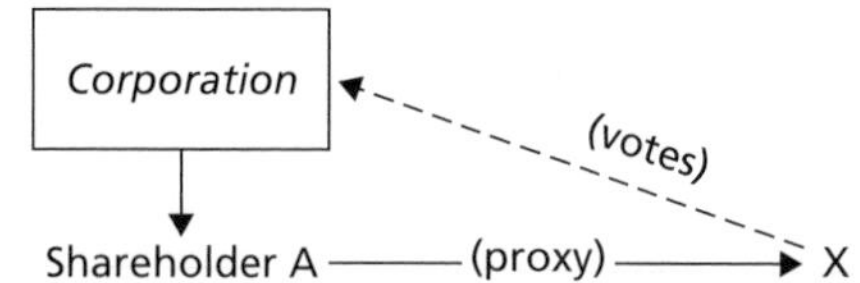

2. Voting control agreement

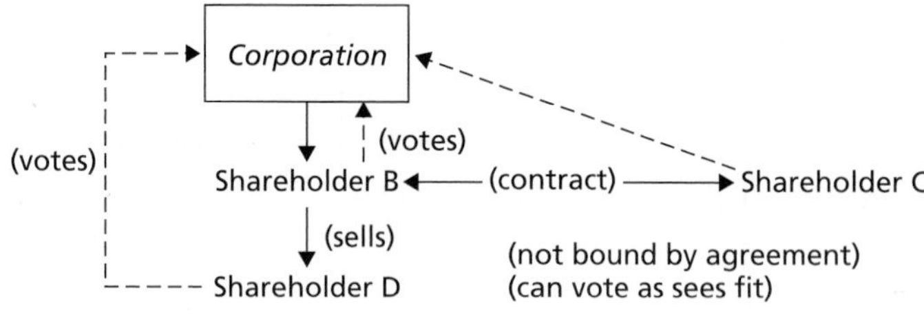

3. Voting trust

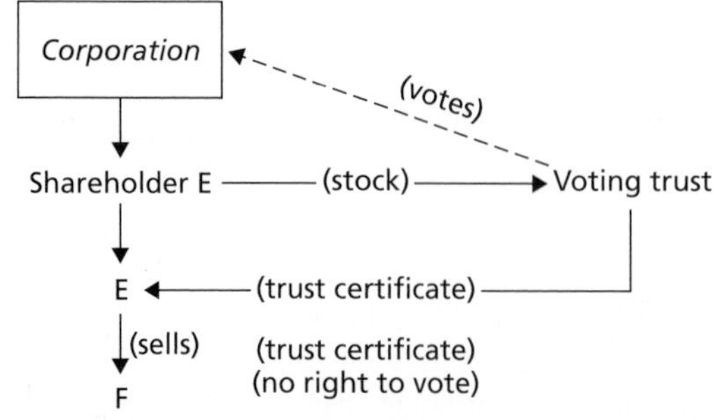

Exhibit 34.2: Proxy Statement

FOLD * * *FOLD*

PROXY • • *SOLICITED BY THE COMMITTEE OF SEPARATE ACCOUNT II*

SEPARATE ACCOUNT II OF EQUITABLE VARIABLE LIFE INSURANCE COMPANY

Annual Meeting of Policyholders—April 25, 1984

The undersigned Owner of a Policy supported by assets of Separate Account II of Equitable Life Insurance Company ("Separate Account II") hereby appoints Donald J. Mooney, James W. Mason, and Kevin Keefe, and each of them to act with full power without the other and with power of substitution, the attorneys and proxies of the undersigned, for and in the name of the undersigned, to exercise all the voting rights which the undersigned would be entitled to exercise if personally present at the Annual Meeting of Policy owners of Separate Account II to be held at 1285 Avenue of the Americas, New York, New York, on April 25, 1984 at 11 :15 A.M., and any adjournments thereof, hereby ratifying and confirming all that each of said attorneys and proxies, or any substitute, shall lawfully do or cause to be done by virtue hereof, with respect to the following matters:

1. ELECTION OF MEMBERS OF THE COMMITTEE OF SEPARATE ACCOUNT II:

   FOR all nominees listed below (except as marked to the contrary below) ☐ WITHHOLD AUTHORITY To vote for all nominees listed below ☐

   (*INSTRUCTION*: To withhold authority to vote for any individual nominee strike a line through the nominee's name in the list below.)

   Howard E. Hassler, Walter C. Kronke, Donald R. Kurtz, Gordon W. McKinley, and Donald J. Mooney

2. PROPOSAL TO RATIFY THE SELECTION OF DELOITTE HASKINS & SELLS as the independent auditors of Separate Account II for the year 1984:

   ☐ *FOR* ☐ *AGAINST* ☐ *ABSTAIN*

3. PROPOSAL TO APPROVE THE INVESTMENT ADVISORY AGREEMENT of Separate Account II as described in the accompanying Proxy Statement.

   ☐ *FOR* ☐ *AGAINST* ☐ *ABSTAIN*

4. In their discretion, the Proxies are authorized to vote upon such other matters as may properly come before the meeting or any adjournments thereof.

This proxy when properly executed will be voted in the manner directed herein by the undersigned. If no direction is made, this Proxy will be voted for Proposals 1, 2, and 3.

Receipt to the Notice of Meeting and Proxy Statement accompanying this Proxy is acknowledged by the undersigned.

Dated: ____________________, 1984

____

Signature

The Policyholder should enter date, sign his/her name and return the signed Proxy in the enclosed envelope.

indirectly; the real plaintiff is the corporation. Any remedies given are for the corporation and against the third parties who are defendants—directors, officers, majority shareholders, or outsiders. Any benefits received by the corporation as plaintiff will indirectly benefit the shareholders who brought the case, but the primary purpose of the lawsuit is to protect the corporation. Normally, of course, the shareholders have no right as such to manage the corporation directly. That rule would include the lack of stockholder authority to decide to bring a lawsuit on behalf of the corporation. What then are the "extraordinary circumstances" that justify a derivative suit? Typically, the wrongdoers are officers, directors, or majority stockholders. Because they control the corporation's decision-making process, the corporation is unlikely to sue. If there is an independent board of directors, which could take action to correct the problem (as by firing the officer), the stockholder must make a demand to the board that it act. If such a demand would be "futile," because the wrongdoers also control the board, the stockholder can proceed to file the **derivative lawsuit** without making any demand. If a demand is made and the board decides that the corporation should sue, the complaining stockholders could not bring a second lawsuit in the name of the corporation. If a demand is made and the board decides that the corporation should not sue, that decision would also prevent the complaining stockholders from bringing a derivative suit. If the board is acting in good faith, its business judgment in deciding that the corporation should not sue would be upheld by the courts. Of course, if the board is the alleged wrongdoer, its decision that the corporation should not sue would not prevent the complaining shareholders from bringing the derivative suit against the board itself.

Some corporations have attempted to use a special board committee—the "stockholder litigation committee"—to convince the courts that it acted in good faith. Use of such a separate committee will not necessarily prevent a court from second-guessing the board's decision not to sue. When a derivative lawsuit is successful, the corporation will probably be ordered to reimburse the complaining stockholders for any reasonable litigation expenses, including attorneys' fees. On the other hand, when the lawsuit is unsuccessful and has been brought without "reasonable cause," many corporation statutes require the complaining stockholders to pay the defendants' litigation expenses, including attorneys' fees.

Management Rights

In small, closely held corporations, in which the stockholders are also the directors, officers, and managers, the stockholders may participate in the daily operations of the business. With large corporations like IBM or GM, however, stockholders will usually have only one annual meeting to attend. Special meetings other than the regular annual meeting may be called, but only after proper notice has been sent to all of the stockholders so that they all have a chance to attend. The MBCA specifies that a quorum at a stockholders' meeting is a majority of the voting shares (represented in person or by proxy), unless the articles of the particular firm specify a lower percentage. Some of the newer statutes permit the stockholders to transact business if any shares are represented, as long as proper notice has been sent. Once a quorum has been established, stockholders cannot prevent the transaction of business by leaving the meeting and then having someone make another quorum call.

The main item of business to be transacted at the stockholders' meeting is the election of directors. As noted previously, the cumulative voting system may be used. In most cases the slate of candidates proposed by management is elected without much, if any, opposition. When a firm has had bad financial results, dissident stockholders may propose their own slate of directors and try to take control of the firm. Each side will solicit support from the rest of the stockholders through personal letters, ads in *The Wall Street Journal*, and other methods. The SEC has extensive regulations on the solicitation and use of proxies in such control battles.

The stockholders generally have no say in making ordinary business decisions for "their" company. By custom and statute, the responsibility for day-to-day management is vested in the board of directors, which in turn delegates much of this authority to the officers. The directors and officers are usually called on to report to the stockholders at the annual meeting, and the stockholders can question them at that time about the decisions made during the year. The stockholders will also usually vote on the selection of the corporation's outside auditors. The independent certified public accountant (CPA) firm auditing the corporation's books provides another source of information to the stockholders and another method of checking on the directors' and officers' conduct of the firm's business. If changes in a corporation's bylaws are proposed, those will also have to be voted on by the stockholders. Extraordinary business decisions, such as amending the articles to change the nature of the firm's business or voluntary dissolution of the corporation, or merger or consolidation with another company, must also be presented for stockholder vote. Although the MBCA now requires only a majority vote on such extraordinary decisions, many states still require a two-thirds or even a three-fourths favorable vote.

Generally, the majority stockholders have the right to determine corporate policy as they see fit, through the directors they elect and through the officers those directors appoint. The majority control group, however, must act within the limits set by the charter and must act in good faith as far as the rights of the minority stockholders are concerned. Several cases have held that the majority control group occupies a fiduciary position with respect to the minority and that its acts can be challenged when it is abusing its control powers.

The *Chambers* case applies some of the SEC's proxy regulations to a directors' election.

CASE 3

CHAMBERS v. BRIGGS & STRATTON CORP.

863 F.Supp. 900 (E.D. WI 1994)

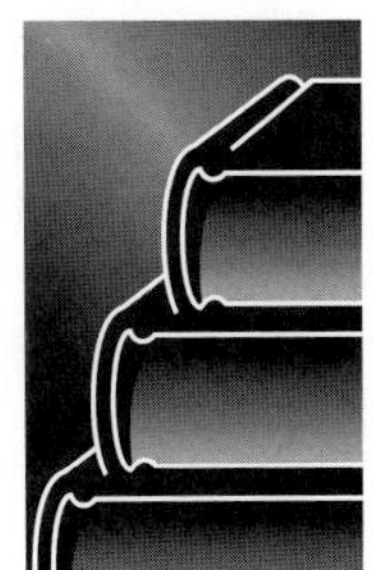

Facts: The plaintiff, Joseph G. Chambers, a shareholder of 17 shares of stock in the defendant corporation, Briggs & Stratton Corporation, commenced this action for declaratory and injunctive relief on September 14, 1994. Along with his complaint, Mr. Chambers filed a "Motion for Temporary Restraining Order/Preliminary Injunction."

The defendant's annual meeting was scheduled to be held on October 19, 1994. On September 8, 1994, the defendant sent to shareholders a "Notice of Annual Meeting of Shareholders," a "Proxy Statement," and a form of proxy. One of the items of business identified in the notice and proxy statement is the election of directors. Three of the nine seats on the defendant's board of directors are now up for election.

The proxy statement identifies the three candidates put forth as nominees by the current directors, but it omits the name of William P. Dixon, who the plaintiff claims he nominated pursuant to Article II, Section 2.01 of the defendant's bylaws. Mr. Dixon is described by the plaintiff as a lawyer who has formerly served as commissioner of banking of Wisconsin, chief of staff to United States Senator Gary Hart, and the United States alternative executive director to the World Bank.

Notwithstanding the fact that Mr. Dixon had been properly nominated in accordance with Article II, Section 2.01, his name was not included in the proxy statement or the form of proxy that was mailed to the shareholders by the defendant on September 8, 1994. Mr. Chambers alleges that this omission renders the proxy materials materially false and misleading under the regulations of the SEC. As a result of such material omission, the plaintiff contends that the defendant may acquire a sufficient number of proxies such that Mr. Dixon will not gain election to the board of directors.

Issue: Does the omission of the name of a candidate for director make the proxy statement materially false?

Decision: Yes. Injunctive order to require correction.

Opinion by District Judge Gordon: "Contrary to the defendant's reading, I believe that these [SEC] regulations place upon the defendant the obligation of disclosing in its proxy statement the existence of candidates who are not nominated by management. In instances involving the election of directors, persons other than management are obligated to disclose information only concerning their own nominees.... However, this same limitation does not apply to solicitations by management. Rather, the express language of Instruction 5 to §229.401(a) and Item 7 of §240.14a-101 requires management to provide information as to: (1) directors, (2) persons nominated for election, and (3) persons chosen by management. Had the SEC intended the same limitation to apply to solicitations by both management and persons other than management, it would not have distinguished between the two types of solicitations as it did in these regulations....

"Since the defendant's proxy statement contained a material omission, the shareholder vote will go forward on the basis of potentially misleading information unless the court grants the plaintiff's request for injunctive relief. The Supreme Court has recognized the 'use of solicitation which is materially misleading poses the kind of irreparable injury to stockholders which can justify injunctive relief prior to a shareholder's meeting....'

"Given the overriding public interest in the full and accurate disclosure of information to shareholders of public corporations to ensure that a shareholder's vote is based upon accurate and complete information, I believe that this factor weighs in favor of granting a preliminary injunction. Allowing a shareholder vote based on incomplete and inaccurate information undermines the purpose underlying SEC Rule 14a-9.

"I have considered the several forms of relief sought by the plaintiff in this action and have determined that the equitable course is to require the defendant to cure the material omission in its proxy statement. In addition, the defendant will be directed not to vote any proxy it solicited prior to October 1, 1994, at the annual meeting of its shareholders.

"Consistent with the identification of its own nominees in the initial proxy statement, Briggs & Stratton Corporation's revised proxy statement should name Mr. Dixon and include the following information: (1) Mr. Dixon's age (50); (2) that he is presently a partner in the law firm of Davis, Miner, Barnhill & Galland, P.D. in Madison, Wisconsin; (3) that he served as the commissioner of banking of Wisconsin from 1983 to 1985; (4) that he served as chief of staff to United States Senator Gary Hart in 1987; and (5) that he served as the alternative executive director to the World Bank from 1977 to 1979.

"I decline Mr. Chambers' invitation to require Briggs & Stratton Corporation to disseminate a new proxy form that identifies Mr. Dixon as a candidate. Mr. Chambers is entitled to have Briggs & Stratton Corporation correct its proxy statement, but the corporation does not have to provide its shareholders with the form which solicits an actual proxy for Mr. Chambers' nominee. In other words, after (or simultaneously with) the transmission of a corrected proxy statement, the defendant is free to submit to its shareholders a proxy form which invites shareholders to select the nominees favored by Briggs & Stratton Corporation. If Mr. Chambers chooses to seek proxies from shareholders, he has to do so at his own expense."

Extraordinary Business Decisions

Substantial changes in economic circumstances or regulatory policies may indicate the need for a firm to expand or to terminate its business. The MBCA and most state statutes contain fairly detailed procedures to cover each of these special situations and the stockholders' role in deciding how to deal with them.

Methods of Expansion

In addition to growing gradually by selling more of its product or service year by year, a corporation may wish to expand rapidly by entering into various sorts of combinations with other firms. It may wish to buy or lease all the assets of a second firm. It may wish to merge or consolidate with one or more other firms. Or it may wish to simply buy a controlling stock interest in other firms.

In general, the legality of any of the aforementioned sorts of combinations would be tested under the national antitrust laws if the firm is engaged in interstate commerce or if its activities have a substantial impact on interstate commerce. Even if a combination met all of the state procedural requirements, the Federal Trade Commission (FTC) or the U.S. attorney general could still prevent the combination if it would have substantial anticompetitive effects. Antitrust law is discussed more thoroughly in Chapter 5.

Purchase or Lease of Assets

When one corporation buys or leases all the existing assets of another, there is no change in the corporate identity of either; they both continue to exist as before. The seller or lessor firm has simply decided to liquidate its operations in one line of business and to reinvest in its funds and efforts elsewhere. A TV manufacturer, for example, feels that the present and future competition is too tough, so it sells its TV manufacturing assets and starts making business machines. The stockholders of the seller or lessor firm must approve this extraordinary transaction by majority vote, after recommendation and proper notice of the special meeting from the board of directors. Once shareholder authorization has been given, however, the board may cancel the sale or lease, if conditions change, without further shareholder action. Assuming that all actions have been taken in good faith, the creditors of the seller or lessor firm would have no basis for objecting to the transaction. Because the buyer or lessee is paying fair value for the assets, it should own them free and clear of the seller/lessor's creditors.

Merger and Consolidation

Two or more firms may decide to combine by means of a **merger** or a **consolidation.** In a merger, one of the original firms survives and the others end. In a consolidation, all of the original firms end; a new corporation is formed, and the original ones all become parts of it. In either case, all assets and all liabilities are turned over to the surviving firm. In each case, the MBCA requires approval by the board and by a majority of each class of stock entitled to vote as a class. Because all liabilities are being assumed by the survivor firm, consent of the creditors of the original firms would generally not be required.

Purchase of Controlling Stock Interest

When the directors of X Corporation decide to have X buy a controlling stock interest in Y Corporation, both firms continue to exist as before. X Corporation offers to buy shares from Y's stockholders. This is a tender offer and is subject to extensive regulation by the SEC and the states. See Chapter 35 for further discussion of this concept.

Rights of Dissenting Shareholders

The MBCA requires approval by majority stockholder vote in the case of sale or lease of all the firm's assets, merger, or consolidation. In the tender offer, each stockholder makes an individual decision as to whether to sell at the price offered. Generally, consent of the firm's creditors is not required. But what about the minority shareholders who object to this drastic change in their firm's operations? The Revised MBCA tries to protect the

CASE 4

First American Bank v. Shivers
629 A.2d 1334 (MD App. 1993)

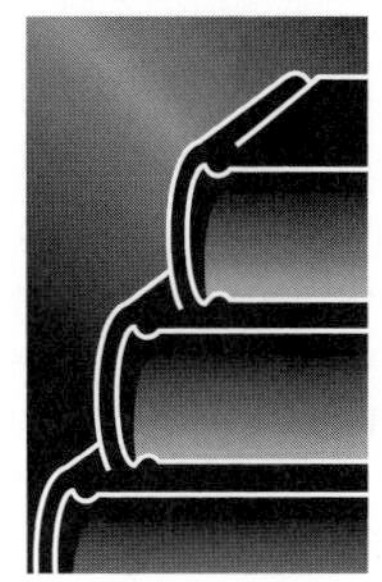

Facts: On or about March 29, 1988, First American Bank of Maryland (First American), appellant, entered into a merger agreement with First American Bank of Maryland (FABM) Acquisition Bank. The proposal was constructed with First American as the surviving, or successor, bank. On May 25, 1988, Rufus W. Shivers (the Shareholder), appellee, voted by proxy his 1,178 shares of First American common stock against the proposed merger. His objection was to no avail, however, because he and his fellow dissentients comprised less than the number of First American's shareholders needed to defeat the proposal. The merger was approved on June 14, 1988.

Some time in August 1988 First American sent, by regular mail, a "Notice of Effective Date of Merger" to its shareholders. The notice was dated August 8, 1988 but there is no evidence as to when the notice was actually mailed. The notice informed the shareholders that the merger was approved on June 14 and became effective on August 8. The notice also stated that objecting shareholders who did not perfect their "dissenter's rights" would be entitled to receive only the amount offered by First American for each share of First American stock.

Finally, the notice directed shareholders who had voted against the merger and desired to perfect their dissenter's rights to follow the procedures set forth in FI §3-719. By perfecting dissenter's rights within the 30-day time frame indicated in that section, an objecting shareholder can elect to receive the appraised fair value of the shares rather than accept the dollar amount per share offered by the successor bank. The offered price per share was $42.00. The fair market value of First American's shares was eventually determined to be $55.00 per share.

The 30-day period in the instant case began on August 8, 1988 and ended on September 7, 1988. The Shareholder, however, was away from his Alexandria, Virginia home on out-of-town trips for over half of those 30 days. On August 11, he embarked on a 13-day business trip to several locations around the country; he returned home on August 23. He left again on September 2 to oversee rental property that he owned in Delaware. He returned home from that trip on September 6. He opened and read the August 8, 1988 Notice of Effective Date of Merger on the evening of September 8, one day after the statutory time period ended. The next morning, he called the office of the First American's corporate secretary, Nancy R. Lewis, whose name and number appeared on the notice. Because Ms. Lewis was not in her office, the Shareholder spoke to an unidentified woman. He explained to this person the circumstances surrounding his discovery of the merger notice, his status as a dissenting shareholder, and his desire to inform Ms. Lewis of these facts. Later that day, the Shareholder sent a letter addressed to Ms. Lewis, explaining the events leading to his discovery of the notice and expressing his desire to maintain his dissenter's rights. He added that his stock certificates were then being used as security for a loan, but that he would immediately take action to obtain them.

One week later, the Shareholder spoke to Ms. Lewis by telephone to restate his position as a dissenting shareholder and explain again the reason for his delay in perfecting his dissenter's rights. On September 21 and 26, 1988, however, the Shareholder received letters from First American's president, Paul G. Adams, III, denying his requests for fair value for his shares.

The Shareholder filed a complaint against First American in the Circuit Court for Montgomery County on August 8, 1991. He sought to be included among First American's list of objecting stockholders who had perfected their dissenter's rights and to receive the fair value for his shares. The Shareholder based his claim on First American's failure to send the merger notice via certified mail pursuant to CA §3-207(b), which, he asserted, applied to bank mergers by way of FI §1-201.

First American argued that the Financial Institutions Article contained specific provisions that prevailed over the Corporations and Associations Article, rendering CA §3-207 inapplicable.

The trial court granted the Shareholder's motion for summary judgment, denied First American's motion for summary judgment, and awarded the Shareholder $64,790.00 plus interest. First American appealed.

Issue: Was the bank's notice of the merger sufficient?

Decision: No. Judgment affirmed.

Opinion by Judge Harrell: "The Financial Institutions Article of the Annotated Code of Maryland contains specific provisions governing mergers of banks. Section 3-719 of the article sets forth the procedures that a stockholder who objects to an approved merger must follow to perfect his right to fair value of his shares. . . .

"The Financial Institutions Article is silent on the questions of who is to give bank shareholders notice of a merger's effective date and in what manner such notice is to be given.

"The Maryland General Corporation Law, on the other hand, not only imposes specific duties on objecting stockholders with regard to exercising their statutory rights generally, but also provides clear directions to a successor corporation with regard to providing notice of the event that triggers the time period within which the stockholders may exercise those rights.

"The Bank's first argument is simple: There is no certified mail requirement in the merger provisions of the Financial

Institutions Article, §§3-701 to 3-721. In the Bank's view, these provisions set forth a statutory scheme that is self-contained and completely separate from that found in the Corporations and Associations Article....

"Although we agree with the Bank's assertion that the bank merger provisions of the Financial Institutions Article represent the General Assembly's separate treatment of this particular class of corporations, we disagree that these provisions are self-contained and not governed in any respect by the general corporation law. We believe, as did the circuit court, that the plain language of FI §1-201 compels the conclusion that CA §3-207(b) requires a bank to use personal delivery or certified mail as the manner of sending notice of the effective date of a merger to the bank's shareholders....

"In sum, we hold that, pursuant to FI §1-201 and CA §3-207(b), a bank must notify its objecting shareholders of the effective date of an approved merger by delivering the notice personally or mailing it by certified mail, return receipt requested. This conclusion follows seamlessly and naturally from the plain and unambiguous language of FI §1-201. It also affords the same protection to dissenting shareholders of a bank that is given to dissenting shareholders of an ordinary corporation. Absent an express directive to the contrary from the legislature, we see no basis for differentiating between such similar classes of dissenting stockholders with regard to the protection of their dissenter's rights. Objecting shareholders of a merging corporation clearly are entitled to be notified, in a specified manner, of the date of the event—the acceptance by the State Department of Assessments and Taxation of the articles of merger—that triggers the running of the period within which such shareholders must perfect their statutory rights. We believe that, in the absence of any statute or other law providing otherwise, dissenting shareholders of a merging bank are entitled to the same notice, in the same specified manner, of the analogous triggering event—the date the merger becomes effective....

"Technical or not, the requirement of certified mail is mandated by CA §3-207(b). The breach of this requirement renders the given notice ineffective....

"For that reason, the Shareholder's alleged lack of diligence is of no moment. He did not receive notice consistent with the requirements of the Maryland Code. Accordingly, we affirm the circuit court's grant of summary judgment in the Shareholder's favor."

minority by providing a mandatory buyout procedure. Prior to attendance at the special stockholders' meeting, the dissenter must file written notice of objection to the proposed action. At the meeting, of course, the dissenter must not vote for the proposal. If the proposal is passed by the necessary majority vote, the dissenter may then file a written demand with the firm for payment of the fair value of his or her shares as of the day prior to the vote, "excluding any appreciation or depreciation in anticipation of such corporate action." This demand for payment must be made within the time period specified in the notice sent by the corporation to the dissenters. The theory of this procedure is that the individual should not be forced to maintain an investment in a substantially different firm.

This procedure is discussed in the *First American* case.

Dissolution

Assuming that it retained the power to amend, the legislature of the state of incorporation would presumably have the power to terminate the existence of that state's corporations. The state's attorney general or corporation commissioner could ask a court to decree dissolution when a corporation was in continuing default on its duties to file reports and to pay taxes and fees. In those rare cases in which the articles did not provide for perpetual existence, the end of the specified time period or the occurrence of the specified event would cause a dissolution of the firm. The shareholders may act voluntarily to terminate their corporation, either by unanimous action or by majority vote, after a recommendation from the board of directors. Normally courts will not interfere with the shareholders' decision.

Modern corporation law treats a dissolved corporation in much the same way as a dissolved partnership. That is, the corporation continues to operate for the limited purpose of winding up its affairs—collecting money owed to it, selling off its assets, and paying off its creditors. After the creditors have been paid in full, the preferred stockholders have the first claim on any assets remaining and then, finally, the common stockholders are paid.

Reorganization

Financial reorganizations under the Bankruptcy Act are covered in Chapter 22. An attempt may be made to save the firm by adjusting its debts, or the firm may be dissolved and its assets sold to pay off as many of its creditors as possible.

Significance of This Chapter

This chapter defines and discusses the various kinds of stock that corporations may issue, the process of subscribing to purchase shares, the issuance and transfer of such shares, and shareholders' rights. Thus, this chapter provides an overview of the methods by which stockholders own and control a corporation.

Corporations also have financial difficulties and often must be dissolved or perhaps reorganized under bankruptcy law, and procedures are needed for these changes. Also, corporations often desire to expand by purchasing other corporations and merging them within the parent corporation. This chapter also reviews these procedures and the rights of the stockholders in these matters.

IMPORTANT TERMS AND CONCEPTS

authorized stock
common stock
consolidation
convertible
cumulative preferred stock
cumulative voting
derivative lawsuit
dissolution
good faith rule
merger
no-par stock
par value stock
participating preferred stock
preemptive rights
preferred stock
proxy
redeemable
subscription
treasury stock
true value rule
voting control agreements
voting trust

QUESTIONS AND PROBLEMS FOR DISCUSSION

1. What is the difference between common stock and preferred stock?

2. What is the difference between cumulative preferred stock and participating preferred stock?

3. What is the difference between par and no-par stock?

4. What is treasury stock?

5. Wallazz Eaton owned and operated a frozen foods business. He organized a corporation and transferred the business to it in return for 4,500 shares of $10 par stock. The corporations commissioner required that 1,022 shares of the stock be placed in escrow and not transferred without his written consent; 1,022 shares were put in escrow in Eaton's name, and the other 3,478 shares were issued directly to him. The plaintiff had a judgment against the corporation for $21,246.42, of which some $15,000 was still unpaid. The corporation was insolvent. The trial court found that the value of the transferred business was $34,780.83 and gave the plaintiff a judgment against Eaton for $10,219.17. Because it had failed to make a finding that the plaintiff relied on some misrepresentation in connection with the watered stock, the trial court granted Eaton a new trial. The plaintiff appealed the order granting a new trial.

   How should the appeals court decide? Explain.

6. On August 5, 1991, the plaintiff (Wilkes) filed a bill in equity for declaratory judgment in the Probate Court for Berkshire County, naming as defendants T. Edward Quinn (Quinn), Leon L. Riche (Riche), the First Agricultural Bank of Berkshire County, and Frank Sutherland MacShane as executors under the will of Lawrence R. Connor (Connor), and the Springside Nursing Home, Inc. (Springside or the corporation). Wilkes alleged that he, Quinn, Riche, and Dr. Hubert A. Pipkin (Pipkin) entered into a partnership agreement in 1981, prior to the incorporation of Springside, which agreement was breached in 1987 when Wilkes's salary was terminated and he was voted out as an officer and director of the corporation. Wilkes sought, among other forms of relief, damages in the amount of the salary he would have received had he continued as a director and officer of Springside subsequent to March 1987. A judge of the probate court referred the suit to a master, who, after a lengthy hearing, issued his final report in late 1993. Wilkes's objections to the master's report were overruled after a hearing, and the master's report was confirmed in late 1994. A judgment was entered dismissing Wilkes's action on the merits. The state supreme court granted direct appellate review.

   How should Wilkes' appeal be decided? Discuss.

7. Minority stockholders sued to force the directors to declare an additional special dividend. Horace and John Dodge, the plaintiffs, were two of the original stockholders in Ford Motor Company, along with Horace Rackham, James Couzens, and Henry Ford himself. On the capitalization of $2 million, Ford Motor had been paying a quarterly

dividend equal to 60 percent per year; it had also paid out a total of $41 million in special dividends. Ford Motor still had a capital surplus of nearly $112 million, however, and sales and profits were up. Henry proposed a massive capital expansion to produce iron and steel (the Rouge plant) and a lowering of the price of the Model T from $440 to $360. At one point, Henry was quoted as saying: "My ambition is to employ still more men, to spread the benefits of this industrial system to the greatest possible number, to help them build up their lives and their homes. To do this, we are putting the greatest share of our profits back in the business." Ford Motor appealed from the trial court's decision ordering payment of a special dividend and enjoining the building of the Rouge plant.

Will the trial court decision be upheld on appeal? Why or why not?

8. On July 3, Pillsbury attended a meeting of a group involved in a so-called Honeywell Project. He had long opposed the Vietnam War, but it was at this meeting that he first learned of Honeywell's involvement as a manufacturer of antipersonnel fragmentation bombs. "Upset" and "shocked" by this information, he determined to stop Honeywell's munitions production. On July 14, he told his fiscal agent to buy 100 shares of Honeywell. The agent, not knowing that Pillsbury wanted the shares in his own name, put them in the name of Quad & Co., a family holding company, as he always did. On learning that the 100 shares had not been registered in his name, Pillsbury bought one share in his own name. Meanwhile, he learned that his grandmother's trust, of which he was a beneficiary, owned 242 Honeywell shares. He then made a written demand that Honeywell give him its original shareholder ledger, its current shareholder ledger, and "all corporate records dealing with weapons and munitions manufacture." Honeywell refused, and Pillsbury filed a petition to order disclosure. He appealed from the trial court's denial of his petition.

   Should the court order disclosure of this information? Why or why not?

CHAPTER 35

Corporation Law—Securities Regulation and Management Duties

Chapter Objectives

This chapter will:

- Explain the duties and responsibilities of corporate directors.
- Explain the duties and responsibilities of corporate officers.
- Discuss the liabilities of directors and officers.
- Review the Foreign Corrupt Practices Act.
- Discuss the regulation of securities by the states.
- Explain the national securities acts.

Directors

Authority and Qualifications

The **directors** are given management control of the normal business operations of the corporation. They are more than just agents for the shareholders because a large part of their authority and duties flows from the state's corporation statute. Shareholders may try to influence or replace the directors, but shareholders as such have no right to participate in corporate management. So long as the directors are acting in good faith and within the statute, articles, and bylaws, they have exclusive control of the corporation's ordinary business decisions.

Older statutes required three or more directors. Recognizing the reality of the "one-person" corporation, modern corporation codes require only one director. Some states still require directors to be shareholders and/or residents of the state of incorporation. Again, the modern tendency, as seen in Section 8.02 of the Revised **Model Business Corporation Act (MBCA)**, is to require neither unless the articles or bylaws of the particular corporation so specify. In other words, let each corporation decide for itself what qualifications its directors must have.

Selection and Removal

As noted in the last chapter, selection of the board of directors is the shareholders' most important management function. Although some states require cumulative voting, most statutes permit it but do not require it. Most states also permit corporations to provide for staggered terms for directors, similar to those of U.S. senators. Electing only part of the board each year provides continuity of management and also prevents an outside group from taking over the board all at once, in one election.

The rule in most states is that directors may be removed by the shareholders at any time, with or without cause. Directors, in other words, serve at the pleasure of the shareholders. In this sense, they are like agents. In a few states, such as New York, directors can be removed only if good cause is shown. In any corporation in which cumulative voting is in force, a director could not be removed unless he or she failed to get enough votes to win a seat under the cumulative voting system.

Nearly all statutes provide for the replacement of directors by the remaining board members, where vacancies occur, at least until the next shareholders' meeting at which directors are elected. These procedural steps must be followed exactly.

Meetings of the Board

The general rule is that the directors must meet as a board to take official action for the corporation. Proxy voting is not permitted. Most states today permit the directors to meet outside the state of incorporation; this allows the board to select the most convenient location. Some modern statutes are even more flexible; they permit the directors to have a "meeting" by means of a conference telephone call. Some statutes also permit the directors to take official action by means of a signed document: If they all read and sign the same document, why require them to waste transportation facilities to come together in a meeting room?

Section 8.25 of the Revised MBCA and the laws in some states permit the directors to designate some board members as an executive committee and to delegate some decision-making authority to the smaller committee. Other similar committees may also be created. The modern tendency is toward flexible management.

If a director wishes to dissent from a decision of the board, the normal rule is that the dissent must be officially entered in the minutes of the board. Otherwise, concurrence with the majority decision is presumed. This rule is significant when a later lawsuit challenges board actions.

Management Authority

As noted previously, some extraordinary business decisions are left to the shareholders, but the directors have exclusive control of the ordinary business of the firm. In making these ordinary business decisions, the directors are given the widest possible discretion as long as they are acting in good faith. The individual directors are selected for their business skill and judgment, and courts do not feel that they should second-guess the directors when the directors exercise that judgment. There is, therefore, a very strong presumption in favor of the directors' decisions unless some abuse is shown.

This principle of nonintervention in corporate affairs is summarized as the **business judgment rule.** The business decisions of the directors cannot be challenged in court so long as the directors are acting in good faith and with reasonable care. They cannot guarantee satisfactory results for the corporation in every case; there are too many uncertainties and factors beyond their control. All that can be required of directors is that they are honest and diligent. If they are, but nevertheless make a bad decision, they should not be held liable for the unfavorable results.

On the other hand, when there is evidence that the directors are acting in a totally arbitrary and capricious way, to the corporation's detriment, their actions may be overturned. Henry Ford's arbitrary policy on dividends was successfully challenged by the stockholders in the classic *Dodge* case in 1919.

The following case looks at the business judgment rule in the context of a **hostile takeover** attempt. The directors' defensive tactics are being questioned.

Fiduciary Duties

The directors are fiduciaries, and as such, they owe their corporation and its stockholders responsibility and loyalty. Responsibility means that the directors must be more than just personally honest; they must "direct." They must be diligent and careful in managing the firm's business. They are responsible for knowing what's going on, and they may be held personally liable if they do not know but should.

A fiduciary must also be loyal. This means at least that the director cannot use his or her position for personal gain at the expense of the corporation. Most states today permit the directors to set their own compensation, but courts would be willing to review such arrangements to make sure there was no abuse of discretion. In any case in which the director is dealing with the corporation and receiving a personal benefit, the transaction would be subject to very close judicial review.

One specific aspect of the duty of loyalty owed by directors and officers is described as the **corporate opportunity rule.** A director or officer may not take, for personal benefit, a business opportunity that should rightfully belong to the corporation. If the director or officer does so, a court will order any profits from the "opportunity" turned over to the corporation. In deciding whether the opportunity rightfully belongs to the corporation, the courts will examine whether: (1) it is within the scope of the corporation's business; (2) the director or officer learned of the opportunity while acting as such; or (3) corporate funds, equipment, or personnel were used to develop the opportunity. Under the strictest application of the rule, if any of these three conditions exist, the opportunity belongs to the corporation.

Corporate "Constituency" Statutes

Perhaps in the belief that corporate directors needed assurance that they could legally take a broader view of their responsibilities, most states enacted corporate "constituency" statutes in the 1980s. Nearly all of these laws permit, but do not require, the directors to consider the effects of their official decisions on groups other than the corporation's stockholders—the "owners" of the company. In deciding whether to relocate a plant from Michigan to South Carolina, or to Mexico or China, the directors could take into account the effects of the relocation on employees, suppliers, creditors, customers, and the local community. It's hard to believe that the directors would not have the power to do so anyway because the company's long-term viability is certainly connected to its relations with each of these groups. In any event, these statutes at least reinforce the directors' authority to weigh long-term factors as well as the next quarter's earnings in making corporate decisions. The extent to which such weighing has actually occurred is not clear. Despite the statutes, business relocations and plant closures continue to occur because firms struggle to survive in an increasingly competitive global economy.

CASE 1

Paramount Communications v. QVC Network
637 A.2d 34 (DE 1993)

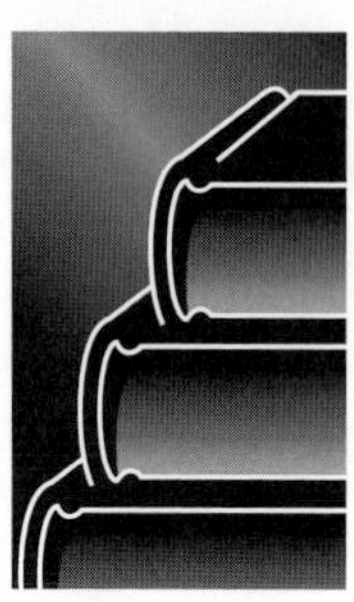

Facts: Paramount is a Delaware corporation with its principal offices in New York City. Approximately 118 million shares of Paramount's common stock are outstanding and traded on the New York Stock Exchange. The majority of Paramount's stock is publicly held by numerous unaffiliated investors. Paramount owns and operates a diverse group of entertainment businesses, including motion picture and television studios, book publishers, professional sports teams, and amusement parks.

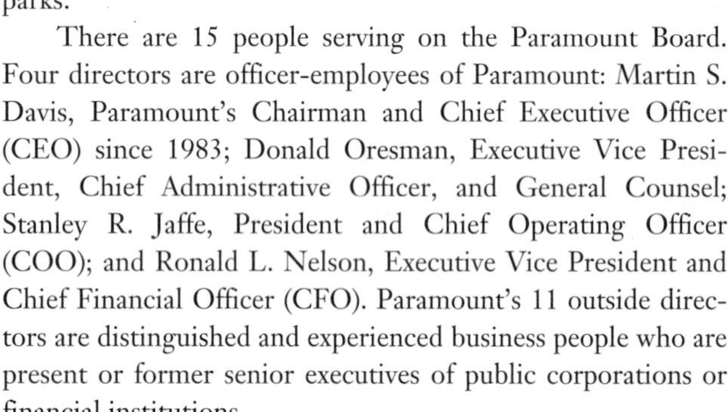

There are 15 people serving on the Paramount Board. Four directors are officer-employees of Paramount: Martin S. Davis, Paramount's Chairman and Chief Executive Officer (CEO) since 1983; Donald Oresman, Executive Vice President, Chief Administrative Officer, and General Counsel; Stanley R. Jaffe, President and Chief Operating Officer (COO); and Ronald L. Nelson, Executive Vice President and Chief Financial Officer (CFO). Paramount's 11 outside directors are distinguished and experienced business people who are present or former senior executives of public corporations or financial institutions.

Viacom is a Delaware corporation with its headquarters in Massachusetts. Viacom is controlled by Sumner M. Redstone, its Chairman and CEO, who owns indirectly approximately 85.2 percent of Viacom's voting Class A stock and approximately 69.2 percent of Viacom's nonvoting Class B stock through National Amusements, Inc. ("NAI"), an entity 91.7 percent owned by Redstone. Viacom has a wide range of entertainment operations, including a number of well-known cable television channels such as MTV, Nickelodeon, Showtime, and The Movie Channel. Viacom's equity co-investors in the ParamountViacom transaction include NYNEX Corporation and Blockbuster Entertainment Corporation.

QVC is a Delaware corporation with its headquarters in West Chester, PA. QVC has several large stockholders, including Liberty Media Corporation, Comcast Corporation, Advance Publications, Inc., and Cox Enterprises Inc. Barry Diller ("Diller"), the Chairman and CEO of QVC, is also a substantial stockholder. QVC sells a variety of merchandise through a televised shopping channel. QVC has several equity co-investors in its proposed combination with Paramount including BellSouth Corporation and Comcast Corporation.

QVC and certain stockholders of Paramount commenced separate actions (later consolidated) in the Court of Chancery seeking preliminary and permanent injunctive relief against Paramount, certain members of the Paramount Board, and Viacom. This action arises out of a proposed acquisition of Paramount by Viacom through a tender offer followed by a second-step merger (the "Paramount-Viacom transaction"), and a competing unsolicited tender offer by QVC. The Court of Chancery granted a preliminary injunction.

The Court of Chancery found that the Paramount directors violated their fiduciary duties by favoring the Paramount-Viacom transaction over the more valuable unsolicited offer of QVC. The Court of Chancery preliminarily enjoined Paramount and the individual defendants from amending or modifying Paramount's stockholder rights agreement, including the redemption of the rights, or taking other action to facilitate the consummation of the pending tender offer by Viacom or any proposed second-step merger.

Issue: Does the business judgment rule protect the directors here?

Decision: No. Judgment affirmed.

Opinion by Chief Justice Veasey: "The General Corporation Law of the State of Delaware and the decisions of this Court have repeatedly recognized the fundamental principle that the management of the business and affairs of a Delaware corporation is entrusted to its directors, who are the duly elected and authorized representatives of the stockholders.... Under normal circumstances, neither the courts nor the stockholders should interfere with the managerial decisions of the directors. The business judgment rule embodies the deference to which such decisions are entitled....

"Nevertheless, there are rare situations which mandate that a court take a more direct and active role in overseeing the decisions made and actions taken by directors. In these situations, a court subjects the directors' conduct to enhanced scrutiny to ensure that it is reasonable. The decisions of this Court have clearly established the circumstances where such enhanced scrutiny will be applied.... The case at bar implicates two such circumstances: (1) the approval of a transaction resulting in a sale of control, and (2) the adoption of defensive measures in response to a threat to corporate control....

"In the case before us, the public stockholders (in the aggregate) currently own a majority of Paramount's voting stock. Control of the corporation is not vested in a single person, entity, or group, but vested in the fluid aggregation of unaffiliated stockholders. In the event the Paramount-Viacom transaction is consummated, the public stockholders will receive cash and a minority equity voting position in the surviving corporation. Following such consummation, there will be a controlling stockholder who will have the voting power to: (a) elect directors, (b) cause a break-up of the corporation, (c) merge it with another company, (d) cash-out the public stockholders, (e) amend the certificate of incorporation, (f) sell all or substantially all of the corporate assets, or (g) otherwise alter materially the nature of the corporation and the public stockholders' interests. Irrespective of the present Paramount Board's vision of a long-term strategic alliance with Viacom, the proposed sale of control would provide the new controlling stockholder with the power to alter that vision.

"Because of the intended sale of control, the Paramount-Viacom transaction has economic consequences of considerable significance to the Paramount stockholders. Once control has shifted, the current Paramount stockholders will have no leverage in the future to demand another control premium. As a result, the Paramount stockholders are entitled to receive, and should receive, a control premium and/or protective devices of significant value. There being no such protective provisions in the Viacom-Paramount transaction, the Paramount directors had an obligation to take the maximum advantage of the current opportunity to realize for the stockholders the best value reasonably available.

"The consequences of a sale of control impose special obligations on the directors of a corporation. In particular, they have the obligation of acting reasonably to seek the transaction offering the best value reasonably available to the stockholders. The courts will apply enhanced scrutiny to ensure that the directors have acted reasonably. The obligations of the directors and the enhanced scrutiny of the courts are well-established by the decisions of this Court. The directors' fiduciary duties in a sale of control context are those which generally attach. In short, 'the directors must act in accordance with their fundamental duties of care and loyalty. . . .'

"The key features of an enhanced scrutiny test are: (a) a judicial determination regarding the adequacy of the decision-making process employed by the directors, including the information on which the directors based their decision; and (b) a judicial examination of the reasonableness of the directors' action in light of the circumstances then existing. The directors have the burden of proving that they were adequately informed and acted reasonably.

"Although an enhanced scrutiny test involves a review of the reasonableness of the substantive merits of a board's actions, a court should not ignore the complexity of the directors' task in a sale of control. There are many business and financial considerations implicated in investigating and selecting the best value reasonably available. The board of directors is the corporate decision making body best equipped to make these judgments. Accordingly, a court applying enhanced judicial scrutiny should be deciding whether the directors made a **reasonable** decision, not a **perfect** decision. If a board selected one of several reasonable alternatives, a court should not second-guess that choice even though it might have decided otherwise or subsequent events may have cast doubt on the board's determination. Thus, courts will not substitute their business judgment for that of the directors, but will determine if the directors' decision was, on balance, within a range of reasonableness. . . .

"Under the facts of this case, the Paramount directors had the obligation: (a) to be diligent and vigilant in examining critically the Paramount-Viacom transaction and the QVC tender offers; (b) to act in good faith; (c) to obtain, and act with due care on, all material information reasonably available, including information necessary to compare the two offers to determine which of these transactions, or an alternative course of action, would provide the best value reasonable available to the stockholders; and (d) to negotiate actively and in good faith with both Viacom and QVC to that end. . . .

"By November 12, 1993, the value of the revised QVC offer on its face exceeded that of the Viacom offer by over $1 billion at then current values. This significant disparity of value cannot be justified on the basis of the directors' vision of future strategy, primarily because the change of control would supplant the authority of the current Paramount Board to continue to hold and implement their strategic vision in any meaningful way. Moreover, their uninformed process had deprived their strategic vision of much of its credibility. . . .

"The realization of the best value reasonably available to the stockholders became the Paramount directors' primary obligation under these facts in light of the change of control. That obligation was not satisfied, and the Paramount Board's process was deficient. The directors' initial hope and expectation for a strategic alliance with Viacom was allowed to dominate their decision making process to the point where the arsenal of defensive measures established at the outset was perpetuated (not modified or eliminated) when the situation was dramatically altered. QVC's unsolicited bid presented the opportunity for significantly greater value for the stockholders and enhanced negotiating leverage for the directors. Rather than seizing those opportunities, the Paramount directors chose to wall themselves off from material information which was reasonably available and to hide behind the defensive measures as a rationalization for refusing to negotiate with QVC or seeking other alternatives. Their view of the strategic alliance likewise became an empty rationalization as the opportunities for higher value for the stockholders continued to develop. For the reasons set forth herein, the November 24, 1993, Order of the Court of Chancery has been AFFIRMED, and this matter has been REMANDED for proceedings consistent herewith, as set forth in the December 9, 1993, Order of this Court."

Officers

Authority

To a more limited extent, the firm's **officers** may also get some of their authority from the state's corporation statute. For the most part, the officers derive their authority from the corporation's articles and bylaws and from specific board resolutions. The states do not agree on the amount of power that is given to the corporation's president merely by appointment as such. In some states, the president is presumed to be a kind of "general

CASE 2

Wetzel v. Schlenvogt
705 N.W.2d 836 (ND 2005)

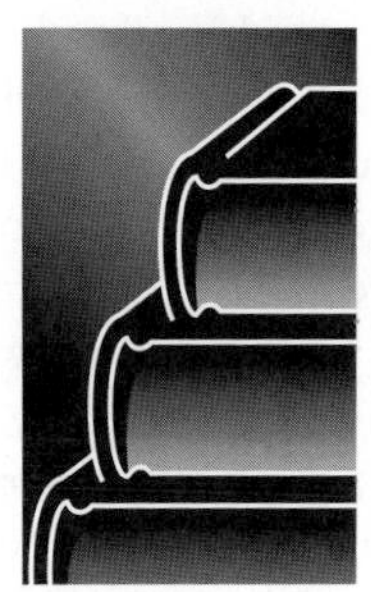

Facts: On December 29, 2004, Orville Schlenvogt telephoned Cenex Oil of Glen Ullin to complain about their servicing of a pickup truck tire. He said they had tightened the lug nuts too much. A Cenex Oil employee told him that could not have happened. The conversation became heated, and Schlenvogt hung up. Later that day, he came in with the tire and continued arguing with three Cenex employees about what had happened to his tire. At one point, he hit Curt Wetzel. One of the other employees tended to Wetzel, and the third one pushed Schlenvogt away and out of the building. On January 3, 2005, Wetzel and Cenex Oil filed petitions for restraining orders against Schlenvogt (requiring him to stay away from the Cenex property). Wetzel represented himself; Cenex Oil was represented by Brian Schneider, a nonlawyer Cenex manager. State law prohibits nonlawyers from practicing law—including legal representation of other persons, but the trial court granted restraining orders to both Wetzel and Cenex Oil. Schlenvogt appealed.

Issue: Is the restraining order in favor of Cenex Oil valid?

Decision: No. Judgment for Cenex Oil is reversed.

Opinion by Justice Sandstrom: "A corporation is an artificial person that must act through its agents. . . . This Court has firmly adhered to the common law rule that a corporation my not be represented by a non-attorney agent in a legal proceeding. . . . This rule is born out of the necessity to have a court system that functions effectively. Attorneys are knowledgeable of the law, the court system, and its rules of procedure, which keep legal matters moving smoothly through the courts. . . . Just as one unlicensed natural person may not act as attorney for another natural person in his or her cause, an unlicensed natural person cannot attorn for an artificial person, such as a corporation. . . .

"This Court, however, has not decided what must happen to an underlying case or documents when a corporation in represented by a non-attorney agent. . . .

"We are persuaded by [the] body of case law. We hold that when a case is commenced on behalf of a corporation by a non-attorney agent, the case and all documents signed by the non-attorney agent are void from the beginning. Cenex is a corporation. It is undisputed that Schneider is not an attorney. He signed and filed the restraining order petition on behalf of Cenex as its manager. Filing the petition began the action for a restraining order. Cenex also never appeared at the hearing because it was not represented by a lawyer. The district court found that Schneider's appearance was as a witness. Because Cenex was never represented by an attorney, its petition was void from the beginning. Since the district court allowed Cenex to proceed with its petition, its decision was not in accordance with the law. . . . Cenex's restraining order against Schlenvogt is vacated."

manager," with automatic authority to make all contracts that are within the scope of the firm's normal business. In other states, the corporation president is only a "figurehead," unless specific powers have been given to the officeholder by articles, bylaws, or resolution. Third parties need to check carefully on whether the individual with whom they are negotiating has authority to bind the corporation. In no state would the president have the authority to execute unusual or extraordinary contracts without specific resolutions.

As the above case shows, the powers of corporate officers may also be subject to limitations in other state regulations.

Selection, Compensation, and Removal

Corporate officers are selected by the board of directors unless the articles provide otherwise. Officers are usually appointed for 1-year, renewable terms, but they continue to serve at the will of the board. In other words, the general rule is that the board can remove an officer at any time, with or without cause. If an officer is removed without good cause, any employment contract with the firm would probably require compensation for the remainder of the appointment period, but that person would no longer be permitted to function as a corporate officer. Most modern corporation statutes do not require more than one officer, though there may be requirements that more than one person sign certain documents for the corporation (e.g., deeds to land).

Officers' compensation is determined by the board of directors, and their decision will generally not be second-guessed by a court. A director who is also an officer should not be present when the directors set the salary for that office. As with any other decision in which the board's business judgment is involved, there are limits to the discretion that is given to the board with regard to officers' compensation.

Liabilities of Directors and Officers

Most of the specific sources of directors' and officers' liability have already been discussed, in this and previous chapters. Directors are liable for the issuance of watered stock and for the declaration of illegal dividends. They may be held liable for refusing a stockholder's justified demand for corporate information or for breaching their fiduciary duty by self-dealing or by stealing a corporate opportunity. Directors and officers may also incur liability under state regulatory statutes for failure to file required reports and income statements. Under the national securities laws, such corporate **insiders** as directors and officers may be held liable for making personal profits at the expense of the corporation or its shareholders. And directors and officers may be held liable to their firm and its shareholders for failing to take reasonable care in the operation of its business.

In recent years, directors and officers have also been subjected to an increasing criminal liability exposure. Criminal prosecutions against the directors and officers responsible for antitrust and other regulatory violations have been becoming more common, as have prison terms for people convicted of willful violations.

Foreign Corrupt Practices Act

After Securities and Exchange Commission (SEC) investigations disclosed that over 300 U.S. firms had made various kinds of payments and gifts to foreign officials to get contracts or favorable regulations, Congress passed the **Foreign Corrupt Practices Act (FCPA)** in 1977. The FCPA amends the 1934 Securities Exchange Act in three main areas: a U.S. firm, whether or not subject to the 1934 act's registration and disclosure requirements, is prohibited from bribing foreign officials to misuse their official position to benefit the firm; a firm subject to the 1934 act must maintain books and records that, in reasonable detail, accurately and fairly reflect the firm's transactions, and must also maintain a system of internal accounting controls that reasonably ensures that transactions are properly executed and recorded and that corporate assets are protected; new criminal penalties of up to \$1 million for the firm and of up to \$10,000 and 5 years' imprisonment for the individuals involved may be imposed for willful violations.

Sarbanes-Oxley Act

Congress responded to the demands for action following the Enron, Worldcom, and other corporate scandals by passing the Corporate Responsibility Act of 2002—frequently referred to as the Sarbanes-Oxley Act, after its Senate and House sponsors. The act's basic purpose is "to protect investors by improving the accuracy and reliability of corporate disclosures made pursuant to the securities laws." Its focus is the publicly traded companies who file financial reports with the SEC.

Like the FCPA, the emphasis in the 2002 act is on corporate financial information and corporate financial controls. Requirements include (1) creation of an audit committee of the board, with committee members who satisfy certain criteria, such as being independent directors; (2) certification of the accuracy of SEC filings by the CEO and the CFO; (3) SEC penalties against any person attempting to improperly influence a corporate audit; (4) repayment of bonuses paid to the CEO and the CFO for any period represented by misleading financial reports due to misconduct, even if the CEO or CFO did not participate in the misconduct; (5) "fitness" standards for directors and officers, with equitable relief available to protect investors; (6) prohibition of insider trading during periods when the company's pension funds cannot trade; (7) SEC standards for corporate attorney reporting of security law violations by their corporate clients; and (8) creation of an SEC special fund into which bonus repayments and civil penalties will be paid, for the benefit of the company's stockholders.

This is a seemingly impressive list, but not all commentators are convinced it will solve the problem. It's worth noting that Enron did have both an internal financial control system and an audit committee composed of outside directors—as required by the new act. Despite the existence of these structures, the Enron board apparently ignored the warning signs, failed to ask questions, and plowed blindly on with its approval of "creative" accounting and questionable practices. As one critic put it: "[N]ot only does the new legislation do little to change existing law, it imposes high costs on corporate shareholders without any corresponding gain." At the very least, it seems that shareholders still need to be wary investors and diligent monitors.

The *Sussberg* case discusses liabilities under Sarbanes-Oxley.

CASE 3

SUSSBERG V. K-MART HOLDING CORP.

463 F.Supp.2d 704 (ED MI 2006)

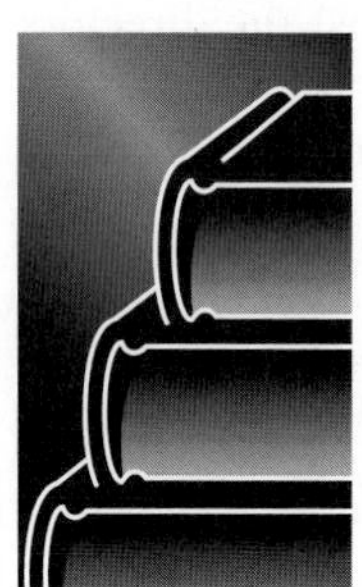

Facts: Sussberg began working as an apparel buyer for K-Mart in 1996. His performance reviews were generally satisfactory, but his supervisors noted that he had strained working relationships with co-buyers and assistants. In September 2002, he told the Human Relations Director (Rachel Bradford) that his new supervisor (Michael Lewis) had a reputation for accepting kickbacks and pushing buyers to deal with Lewis's friends. When she asked for details, Sussberg provided only third-hand stories. In June 2003, Sussberg sent a letter with the same allegations to K-Mart president Julian Day. Day told the Director of Investigations (Joseph Sinischo) to investigate. Lewis testified that he had no knowledge of the investigation until December 2004.

Meanwhile, in June/July 2003, Lewis prepared his review of Sussberg's 2002 performance, rating him "unsatisfactory" in five of eight categories and "unsatisfactory" overall, and sent the review to Bradford. Bradford told Lewis to revise the review and to reduce the "unsatisfactories" to three. Lewis did so, with an overall "effective" rating. Bradford asked him to make further revisions. He did so, but included co-workers' complaints about Sussberg's poor relationships with them and others. That September, K-Mart decided to emphasize fashion-oriented apparel and to concentrate on internally produced merchandise. Lewis adamantly disagreed with this approach and refused to participate in a meeting on the new strategy. Lewis was terminated in October 2003 and replaced by Kathy Douglas. She also received complaints from Sussberg's co-workers about his relationships with them. About the same time, she was told by Senior Vice President and Chief Apparel Officer John Goodman that he was not impressed with Sussberg's basic knowledge of the clothing business and implementation of the new strategy. In March 2004, Sussberg was sent to Florida to do some comparison shopping and prepare a report. He came back with only two pieces of swimwear and prepared a "woefully inadequate" report. Douglas and Goodman decided to fire Sussberg, Bradford approved the decision, and Sussberg was fired on April 12, 2004. He filed a complaint under the Sarbanes-Oxley Act in June 2004, and this case on October 4, 2004.

Issue: Was Sussberg fired because he engaged in a "protected activity" under Sarbanes-Oxley?

Decision: No. Summary judgment for K-Mart.

Opinion by Judge Cohn: "The Court recognizes that there is substantial debate but relatively little guidance in the case law (in the way of set principles) regarding the scope of protected activity. The Court, however, finds it unnecessary to determine whether Sussberg's activities were in fact protected because even assuming ... that Sussberg has engaged in protected activity, he has still failed to establish a causal connection between these activities and his termination....

"It is undisputed that Bradford, Douglas, and Goodman were involved in the decision to terminate Sussberg. Sussberg says that only Bradford and Douglas actively participated in the decision to terminate him and that both had a motive to retaliate against him for his involvement in the investigation of Lewis. Sussberg says the Bradford was angry at him for sending the anonymous letter to Day after she dismissed his allegations ... and also because he complained to Sinischo that she had failed to respond to the allegations. Sussberg says that Bradford retaliated against him by telling Lewis to change the Sussberg's 2002 ... performance review from 'effective' to 'unsatisfactory.' ... Moreover, Sussberg says that it was Bradford's complaints that prompted Goodman and Douglas to hold the March 9, 2004, meeting. Finally, Bradford approved the request from Goodman and Douglas to terminate Sussberg....

"K-Mart says that there is no connection between Sussberg's protected activity and his termination.... K-Mart says that all of Sussberg's allegedly protected activities occurred approximately five months or more prior to his termination. In fact, he had reported the allegations to Bradford some 20 months before his termination.

"Next, K-Mart refutes that Bradford or Douglas had a retaliatory motive and argue[s] that intervening events sever the causal connection between Sussberg's allegedly protected activities and his termination.... K-Mart says Sussberg's difficulty dealing with co-workers in early 2004, Goodman's observations that Sussberg lacked requisite business knowledge,

Sussberg's deficient trip to Florida, and his argumentative and disrespectful treatment of Douglas and Rothstein at the subsequent meeting all legitimately contributed to the decision to terminate him. . . .

"Sussberg has failed to show by a preponderance of the evidence that there is a causal connection between his allegedly protected activities and his termination. First, while passage of time is not a conclusive factor, at some point Sussberg's involvement in the Lewis investigation can no longer shield him from being discharged. . . .

"Second, Sussberg has failed to establish that there exists a genuine issue of fact as to whether he was subjected to a pattern of retaliation for his part in Lewis' investigation. . . . While Sussberg asserts that Bradford encouraged Lewis to give Sussberg a more negative review for the fiscal year 2002, it appears that Bradford in fact encouraged Lewis to give Sussberg a more positive review. . . .

"Next, Sussberg's contention that Douglas was motivated to complain about Sussberg because she and Lewis were close friends is far too attenuated to create a genuine issue of fact. . . . Sussberg has grossly exaggerated Douglas' testimony in his briefs and has failed to create a genuine issue of fact about the relationship between Lewis and Douglas. . . .

"Moreover, Douglas explained that shortly after she began to supervise Sussberg she witnessed him being rude to co-workers, received complaints about Sussberg from Sussberg's assistant and a co-buyer, and had discussions with Goodman about Sussberg's poor performance. All of these events occurred before Douglas knew about Sussberg's role in Lewis' investigation and refute Sussberg's conclusion that Douglas had retaliatory motive.

"Third, it is apparent from Goodman's deposition testimony that he was intricately involved with the decision to terminate Sussberg, and that the decision was based on far more than just Douglas' assessment of Sussberg's performance. In particular, Goodman pointed out two occasions where he felt that Sussberg lacked basic knowledge of the clothing buying business and depended far too much on his assistant for information Goodman believed Sussberg should have known. . . .

"K-Mart's motion for summary judgment is GRANTED. . . ."

Securities Law

The securities industry is one of the most heavily regulated areas of business. With certain exemptions, both the original issue of securities and subsequent trading are subject to detailed and complicated regulations at both the national and state levels. These regulations impose duties and liabilities not only on buyers and sellers of securities but also on the corporate issuer, its officers and directors, and its attorneys, accountants, and other experts. Noncompliance may result in serious civil and criminal penalties and the loss of millions of dollars of value.

State Regulation

The great surge of economic development during the late 1800s and early 1900s and the greatly increased use of the corporate form of business organization brought with them many abuses. Promoters of dubious background and resources sold investments to a gullible public in all sorts of "speculative schemes which have no more basis than as many feet of blue sky," as one judge put it. To deal with these abuses, the states passed **blue-sky laws,** regulating transactions in securities. Standing alone, the state laws were not very effective. Some states had no such law; others did not enforce their statute very effectively. The simplest method for the fraudulent promoter was to operate across state lines from a "friendly" state, beyond the reach of state officials who were trying to enforce their statute. Moreover, the early state laws had many exemptions and were thus relatively easy to evade. Finally, because enforcement depended primarily on the victims' willingness to pursue a lawsuit, the promoters who did get "caught" could escape simply by reaching a financial settlement with the plaintiffs in the lawsuit.

Because the national securities laws specifically permit concurrent regulation by the several states, blue-sky statutes are on the books in nearly all states. The effectiveness with which these statutes are enforced still varies. About half the states have adopted the **Uniform Securities Act.** The Uniform Securities Act attempts to combine three types of state regulation:

1. *Antifraud provisions,* which prohibit fraud in the sale of securities and provide for injunctions and criminal penalties.
2. *Full-disclosure provisions,* similar to those in the national act, which require the disclosure of all material information to prospective purchasers of the security.
3. *Broker-licensing provisions,* which require registration and licensing for people marketing securities.

Most of the states that have not adopted the Uniform Securities Act have at least adopted a full-disclosure statute. Even with the Uniform Securities Act in force, an individual state would have difficulty in preventing securities frauds without the cooperation of other states. As business merged, reorganized, and relocated, many states became concerned with the possibility of the loss of jobs. The older industrial states of the Northeast and Midwest were particularly unhappy about the movement of factories to the South and Southwest. Several states tried to protect their businesses from being taken over by outside companies by passing **state tender offer statutes** that imposed certain requirements that the offeror company had to meet before the buyout could occur.

Liability for Brokers' Wrongful Actions

As several large trading scandals have shown, one of the recurring problems in regulation of the securities industry is determining the extent to which the brokerage firm is liable for the wrongful acts of its individual brokers. An overeager or greedy broker may disregard specific instructions, violate industry standards, or—in extreme cases—even commit torts and crimes. The wrongdoer is of course personally liable for his or her conduct. At the point of discovery, however, the wrongdoer may not have sufficient personal assets to reimburse all the injured parties or may not be available for lawsuits in the places where the injured parties want to sue. And so the brokerage firm becomes the main target of the injured customer-clients.

In general, vicarious liability in these cases follows the rules discussed earlier in the tort and agency chapters. The firm is liable for the acts of its agents committed within the scope of their agency authority, that is, while they are acting *as agents*. The *Millan* case illustrates the potential difficulty in deciding just where to draw that line.

National Regulation

The fantastic boom times of the 1920s turned into the depression of the 1930s. Many an investment bubble was punctured by the great stock market crash of 1929. The 1929 crash exposed to the public for the first time the widespread price manipulations and credit abuses that had characterized the stock market of the 1920s. The first New Deal Congress passed the two main pieces of national securities legislation—the **Securities Act of 1933** and the **Securities Exchange Act of 1934.** Other legislation followed, such as the Public Utility Holding Company Act of 1935, the Trust Indenture Act of 1939, the Investment Company Act of 1940, and the Investment Advisors Act of 1940. More recently, Congress passed the Securities Investor Protection Act of 1970 (designed to protect investors against the insolvency of their stockbroker) and the 1975 amendments to the 1933 act, which extend the antifraud provisions of the act to dealers in municipal securities.

The Securities and Exchange Commission

The Securities Act of 1933 entrusted enforcement of securities regulation to the Federal Trade Commission (FTC), but Congress decided by the next year that this specialized area needed its own specialized regulatory body. The Securities Exchange Act of 1934 thus created the SEC and gave it the responsibility for enforcing both acts. Over the years the SEC has accumulated jurisdiction under the various other new securities laws, and it also exercises important functions in corporate reorganizations in bankruptcy proceedings.

The SEC is headed by five commissioners, appointed for staggered 5-year terms by the President with the advice and consent of the Senate. No more than three commissioners may be members of the same political party, but the President does have the power to name the commission's chairperson. The SEC's headquarters is in Washington, but it has regional offices throughout the country, particularly in the large cities where corporate financing operations are concentrated. The commissioners are assisted by a large organizational staff of lawyers, accountants, economists, securities analysts, and other experts.

CASE 4

Millan v. Dean Witter Reynolds, Inc.

90 S.W.3d 760 (TX App. 2002)

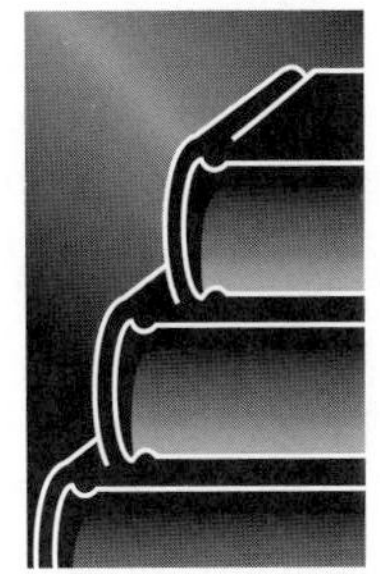

Facts: On July 7, 1993, Maria Millan opened two brokerage accounts at Dean Witter—one for herself and one as trustee for her son James. She used her other son Miguel as her Dean Witter broker, even though she knew that Miguel was in debt and had difficulty managing his own finances. Maria's sister had also opened an account, and Maria had her account statements mailed to her sister's home. Over the next 3 years, Miguel looted Maria's account of over $287,000. (Miguel opened a new account with check-writing privileges and a credit card—in his mother's name, forging her signature on the application. He used the card "liberally" and forged his mother's name on checks that he stole from her. He also diverted her deposits into the fake account. He forged her signature on a change of address to a post office box and sent her fake account statements from Dean Witter.) Maria's sister noticed irregularities in the statements and told Maria about them, but Maria did nothing.

Maria sued Miguel and Dean Witter for conversion, fraud, breach of fiduciary duty, unauthorized transactions, negligence, and gross negligence. The trial court ultimately ruled in favor of Dean Witter on all counts. Maria filed an appeal, naming 12 "issues."

Issue: Was Miguel acting a Dean Witter's agent in defrauding his mother?

Decision: No. Judgment affirmed.

Opinion by Justice Angelini: "The discovery rule doctrine provides that an action does not accrue until a plaintiff knew or in the exercise of reasonable diligence should have known of a wrongful act and resulting injury.... In response to jury question three, the jury found Millan should have discovered the irregularities in her Dean Witter accounts in July 1994. Millan filed suit June 3, 1998. Assuming the evidence was sufficient to support the jury's answer to question three, limitations bars recovery for Millian's claims of negligence, gross negligence, conversion, and breach of fiduciary duty. It does not, however, bar recovery for fraud, because Millan filed suit before limitations had run on this cause of action....

"There is more than a scintilla of evidence, reviewed in the light most favorable to the jury's findings, to support the jury's findings that Millan should have known by July 1994 that something was amiss with her accounts and that she bore 85% of the responsibility. Moreover, these findings are not so against the great weight and preponderance of the evidence as to shock the conscience or render the findings manifestly unjust.

"We overrule [Millan's appeal] issues five and seven....

"At trial, Millan alleged that Dean Witter is vicariously liable for Miguel's fraudulent acts under the doctrine of respondeat superior because he was acting in the course and scope of his employment.... Dean Witter moved for directed verdict on [this] issue.... The trial court ... [found] that Dean Witter was not vicariously liable for Miguel's actions. In her sixth [appeal] issue, Millan maintains the trial court erred in granting Dean Witter's motion and should have, instead, submitted the issue of Dean Witter's vicarious liability for fraud to the jury....

"'Under the doctrine of respondeat superior, an employer is vicariously liable for the negligence of an agent or employee acting within the scope of his or her agency or employment.' ... To determine whether an employee's acts are within the scope of his or her employment, we ask whether the employee's actions fall within the scope of the employee's general authority, are in furtherance of the employer's business, and are for the accomplishment of the object for which the employee was hired.... In cases involving serious criminal activity, an employer is not liable for intentional and malicious acts that are unforeseeable considering the employee's duties.... Our inquiry, therefore, must first focus on the scope of Miguel's general authority.

"Miguel ... opened a brokerage account for his mother. It was within Miguel's general authority to open such accounts for clients, receive deposits to these accounts, and purchase and sell securities as directed by clients. Miguel's activities, however, went far beyond these general brokerage duties. Miguel greatly exceeded the scope of his authority when, through a litany of deceitful acts, he stole money from his mother. These acts include stealing checks from his mother's bathroom drawer, writing checks on his mother's account, depositing his mother's checks into his own account, forging his mother's signature on numerous occasions, stealing statements from his mother's mailbox, and opening a post office box so he could receive his mother's actual statements. These acts were not related to Miguel's duties and were not within his general scope of authority as a broker for Dean Witter.

"We hold there was no evidence that Miguel acted within the scope of his authority as a broker for Dean Witter. Accordingly, there is no evidence to support the submission of the issue of Dean Witter's vicarious liability for fraud to the jury. Issue six [of Millan's appeal] is overruled....

"Having overruled issues one, two, three, four, five, seven, eight, [ten,] eleven and twelve, we affirm the jury's findings and those portions of the directed verdict dealing with apparent authority, unauthorized trading, NASD violations, breach of fiduciary duty, conversion, negligence, and gross negligence. We also overrule that part of issue nine addressing breach of fiduciary duty, because we have held that this claim has a two year statute of limitations. Even though Millan's fraud claim against Dean Witter is not limitations barred, there was no evidence to support submission of the issue to the jury. Accordingly, the trial court's judgment is affirmed."

[In 2003, the Texas Supreme Court refused to review this decision.]

Going Public: The 1933 Securities Act

Basic Purposes

The 1933 act was aimed solely at the first offering of a securities issue, not at later trading on the stock exchanges or over the counter. Its primary objective was truth in securities: to provide the potential investor with all the information needed to make a rational decision when purchasing a security. The 1933 act did not provide for governmental "approval" of securities, in the sense of deciding whether they were good or bad investments. Its main objective was to require full disclosure by the offering company, so that the potential investor could make an informed decision. Only secondarily did the 1933 act prohibit fraud and deceit in securities transactions generally.

Even this somewhat limited approach was a big change from the common law rules. You will recall from Chapter 11 that mere nondisclosure was not usually regarded as a fraudulent misrepresentation unless some special facts were present in the case. The 1933 act imposed on the offering corporation a positive legal duty to speak out and tell the truth, and the whole truth, about the offered security.

Definition of "Security"

The costs of complying with the full-disclosure requirement can be very high. When paying lawyers, accountants, experts, printers, and others, a quarter of a million dollars does not go very far. Because these costs have to be deducted from profits, promoters are always looking for "moneymaking" schemes that do not have to comply with the requirements of the 1933 act.

Only **securities** are covered by the 1933 act, but the courts have given that term a very broad definition. So does the act:

> *The term "security" means any note, stock, treasury stock, bond, debenture, evidence of indebtedness, certificate of interest or participation in any profit-sharing agreement, collateral-trust certificate, preorganization certificate or subscription, transferable share, investment contract, voting-trust certificate, certificate of deposit for a security, fractional undivided interest in oil, gas, or other mineral rights, or, in general, any interest or instrument commonly known as a "security," or any certificate of interest or participation in, temporary or interim certificate for, receipt for, guarantee of, or warrant or right to subscribe to or purchase, any of the foregoing. . . .*

With that definition, it is hard to imagine any investment that is not a security, but promoters keep trying.

Many states now have statutes regulating franchise investments that prohibit or strictly limit the use of multilevel plans. Given the ingenuity of promoters, the definition of a security has to be flexible.

Exemptions

Not every offering of securities is subject to the 1933 act. Some types of securities and some transactions in securities are exempted. These exemptions eliminate only the need to register the security through SEC procedures; the antifraud (and other) provisions still apply.

Short-term commercial paper, ordinarily bought by banks rather than being issued to the general public, is exempt from SEC registration. Securities issued by governmental agencies and nonprofit organizations, such as churches and schools, are exempt. Transactions that involve only a private offering or that are exclusively intrastate in nature are exempt; in both of these cases the process of qualifying the securities for the exemption requires expert advice. Most individual sales of securities are exempt; the 1933 act is aimed at the issuer, underwriter, and broker making the initial offering. The SEC is authorized by statute to provide a simplified registration procedure for issues that do not involve more than a minimal amount, currently set at $5 million.

Registration Statement and Prospectus

The corporation issuing nonexempt securities must file multiple copies of a registration statement with the SEC before offering the securities for sale to investors. The

registration statement is the basic document for making full disclosure. It must include such information as the company's business, organizational structure, and financial structure and condition; how the proceeds of the new issue are to be used; agreements for the distribution of the new issue; and extraordinary business contracts. The registration statement must be signed by the issuing company, its principal officers, at least a majority of the board of directors, and any expert named as having prepared or certified part of the statement. Certified financial statements for the current year and the last 2 years must also be filed.

The registration statement becomes effective 20 days after filing unless the SEC advances the effective date or requires further data, in which case the 20 days starts again when the supplement is filed. Technically, the SEC does not have the power to "disapprove" a security because it is a bad investment, but by delaying and by requiring many negative disclosure statements, the SEC can certainly try to discourage the issuer. When there are any delays in the final effective date, all materials in the registration statement must be reviewed to make sure they are still completely accurate.

The **prospectus** contains most of the information noted previously, but not necessarily all of the exhibits or all of the details on how the securities are to be distributed. The prospectus is the document given directly to offeree-buyers. Like the registration statement, it must be accurate and complete; literally true information, which is misleading in the context in which it is stated, is a violation.

Rescission by Investors

Section 12(2) of the 1933 act permits investors to rescind their transactions if they can prove that false statements or significant omissions were made "by means of a prospectus or oral communication." This section is especially favorable to investors because they do not have to prove fraud; mere negligence, if proved, permits rescission. Likewise, the investor-plaintiff need not prove personal reliance on the false statement.

Section 12(2) became very popular with plaintiffs after the 1976 ruling by the U.S. Supreme Court in the *Hochfelder* case. Investors, alleging a negligent audit, sued Ernst & Ernst. The claim was based on Section 10(b) of the 1934 act and **SEC Rule 10(b)5.** The Supreme Court decided that 10(b) required proof of fraud, not just professional negligence.

Because Section 12(2) of the 1933 act only requires proof of negligence, dissatisfied investors began to allege that it had been violated, in their claims, rather than Section 10(b) of the 1934 act. Courts disagreed as to whether Section 12(2) applied to *all* securities transactions or only to initial public offerings (IPOs). The disagreement was resolved in a 5-to-4 Supreme Court decisions—*Alloyd*—in 1995.

Antifraud Provisions

In addition to its disclosure requirements, the 1933 act also contains a very broad prohibition in Section 17 against securities fraud. This section covers "any device, scheme, or artifice to defraud" and "any transaction, practice, or course of business which operates or would operate as a fraud or deceit upon the purchaser." It includes both false statements and material omissions that make otherwise true statements misleading. Securities that are exempt from registration are not exempt from these **antifraud provisions.**

Being Public: The 1934 Securities Exchange Act

Basic Purposes. Whereas the 1933 act dealt primarily with the initial offering of a securities issue, the 1934 act attempted to deal with the abuses and manipulations that occurred once the stock got into the market. The original basis for regulation was that the security was traded on one of the national stock exchanges and was clearly "interstate commerce." More recent amendments require registration when the corporation has total assets of $1 million or more and a class of equity securities held by 500 or more peersons. (Bonds are not equity securities; bondholders are creditors, so a company could have a class of bonds held by more than 500 persons and not have to register under the 1934 act.) Once these minimum standards apply, the corporation and its stockholders become subject to all sorts

CASE 5

Gustafson et al. v. Alloyd Co., Inc.
513 U.S. 561 (1995)

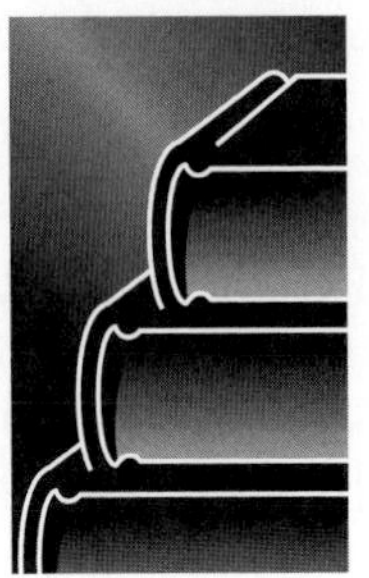

Facts: Petitioners (collectively Gustafson), the sole shareholders of Alloyd, Inc., sold substantially all of its stock to respondents and other buyers in a private sale agreement. The purchase price included a payment reflecting an estimated increase in the company's net worth from the end of the previous year through the closing because hard financial data was unavailable. The contract provided that if a year-end audit and financial statements revealed variances between estimated and actual increased value, the disappointed party would receive an adjustment. As a result of the audit, respondents were entitled to recover an adjustment, but instead sought relief under §12(2) of the Securities Act of 1933, which gives buyers an express right of rescission against sellers who make material misstatements or omissions "by means of a prospectus." In granting Gustafson's motion for summary judgment, the District Court held that §12(2) claims can only arise out of initial stock offerings and not a private sale agreement. The Court of Appeals vacated the judgment and remanded the case. The sellers petitioned for Supreme Court review.

Issue: Is this sale transaction covered by Section 12(2)?

Decision: No. Court of Appeals judgment reversed; and case remanded.

Opinion by Justice Kennedy: "Under §12(2) of the Securities Act of 1933 buyers have an express cause of action for rescission against sellers who make material misstatements or omissions 'by means of a prospectus.' The question presented is whether this right of rescission extends to a private, secondary transaction, on the theory that recitations in the purchase agreement are part of a 'prospectus....'

"Three sections of the 1933 Act are critical in resolving the definitional question on which the case turns: §2(10), which defines a prospectus; §10, which sets forth the information that must be contained in a prospectus; and §12, which imposes liability based on misstatements in a prospectus. In seeking to interpret the term 'prospectus,' we adopt the premise that the term should be construed, if possible, to give it a consistent meaning throughout the Act. That principle follows from our duty to construe statutes, not isolated provisions....

"Although §10 does not define what a prospectus is, it does instruct us what a prospectus cannot be if the Act is to be interpreted as a symmetrical and coherent regulatory scheme, one in which the operative words have a consistent meaning throughout. There is no dispute that the contract in this case was not required to contain the information contained in a registration statement and that no statutory exemption was required to take the document out of §10's coverage.... It follows that the contract is not a prospectus under §10. That does not mean that a document ceases to be a prospectus whenever it omits a required piece of information. It does mean that a document is not a prospectus within the meaning of that section if, absent an exemption, it need not comply with §10's requirements in the first place.

"An examination of §10 reveals that, whatever else 'prospectus' may mean, the term is confined to a document that, absent an overriding exemption, must include the 'information contained in the registration statement.' By and large, only public offerings by an issuer of a security, or by controlling shareholders of an issuer, require the preparation and filing of registration statements.... It follows, we conclude, that a prospectus under §10 is confined to documents related to public offerings by an issuer or its controlling shareholders.

"This much (the meaning of prospectus in §10) seems not to be in dispute. Where the courts are in disagreement is with the implications of this proposition for the entirety of the Act, and for §12 in particular.... We conclude that the term 'prospectus' must have the same meaning under §§10 and 12. In so holding, we do not, as the dissent by JUSTICE GINSBURG suggests, make the mistake of treating §10 as a definitional section.... Instead, we find in §10 guidance and instruction for giving the term a consistent meaning throughout the Act.

"The Securities Act of 1933, like every Act of Congress, should not be read as a series of unrelated and isolated provisions. Only last term we adhered to the 'normal rule of statutory construction' that 'identical words used in different parts of the same act are intended to have the same meaning....' That principle applies here. If the contract before us is not a prospectus for purposes of §10—as all must and do concede—it is not a prospectus for purposes of §12 either.

"The primary innovation of the 1933 Act was the creation of federal duties—for the most part, registration and disclosure obligations—in connection with public offerings.... We are reluctant to conclude that §12(2) creates vast additional liabilities that are quite independent of the new substantive obligations the Act imposes. It is more reasonable to interpret the liability provisions of the 1933 Act as designed for the primary purpose of providing remedies for violations of the obligations it had created. Indeed, §§11 and 12(1)—the statutory neighbors of §12(2)—afford remedies for violations of those obligations.... Under our interpretation of 'prospectus,' §12(2) in similar manner is linked to the new duties created by the Act....

"It is understandable that Congress would provide buyers with a right to rescind, without proof of fraud or reliance, as to misstatements contained in a document prepared with care, following well established procedures relating to investigations with due diligence and in the context of a public offering by an issuer or its controlling shareholders. It is not plausible to infer that Congress created this extensive liability for every casual communication between buyer and seller in the secondary market. It is often difficult, if not altogether impractical, for those engaged in casual communications not to omit some fact that would, if included, qualify the accuracy of a statement. Under Alloyd's view, any casual communication between buyer and seller in the aftermarket could give rise to an action for rescission, with no evidence of fraud on the part of the seller or reliance on the part of the buyer. In many instances, buyers in practical effect would have an option to rescind, impairing the stability of past transactions where neither fraud nor detrimental reliance on misstatements or omissions occurred. We find no basis for interpreting the statute to reach so far....

"In light of the care that Congress took to justify the imposition of liability without proof of either fraud or reliance on 'those whose moral responsibility to the public is particularly heavy'—the 'originators of securities'—we cannot conclude that Congress would have extended that liability to every private or secondary sale without a whisper of explanation....

"In sum, the word 'prospectus' is a term of art referring to a document that describes a public offering of securities by an issuer or controlling shareholder. The contract of sale, and its recitations, were not held out to the public and were not a prospectus as the term is used in the 1933 Act."

of burdensome and costly regulations. For this reason, there has been a considerable movement in recent years to "go private;" that is, to buy back enough shares to reduce the number of stockholders below 500 and "deregister" the stock.

If the 1934 act applies, the stock must be registered with the SEC, and if the stock is traded on an exchange, it must be registered with the exchange as well. These registration requirements are similar to those under the 1933 act. In addition, certified annual reports must be filed each year, disclosing such matters as management changes, important legal proceedings, significant asset changes, and other material business events.

Ownership and Proxy Regulations. The SEC has adopted extensive regulations to prevent injury to the corporation or its shareholders by a few dominant insiders or by an outside group trying to take control. Within 10 days after becoming the **beneficial owner** of more than 5 percent of a registered equity security, the owner must file a disclosure statement with the SEC and send copies to the issuing corporation and to any stock exchange on which the shares are traded. The owner must disclose who he or she is, why he or she bought the shares, how many shares are owned, and where the funds came from to buy them. Updated reports must be filed 10 days after the end of any month in which the owner has changed the amount of holdings.

Such beneficial owners must turn over to the corporation any **short-swing profits** if the owner holds more than 10 percent of the stock. Short-swing profits result from the purchase and sale of their company's shares within a 6-month period. A stockholder with only 9 percent ownership could keep the profits. The corporation's directors and officers are also covered by this rule (Section 16 of the 1934 act). If the buying and selling transactions extend beyond 6 months, all of these people (directors, officers, 10 percent owners) could keep their profits. The reason for this short-swing rule is that insiders should not be allowed to take financial advantage of inside corporate information until there is a fair chance for it to be circulated to all investors.

In recent years there have been many criminal prosecutions of people who used insider information to make a profit in the stock market. The question arises as to just who is an insider. The Supreme Court has generally said that, to be an insider, the person must owe a duty to shareholders.

Whether they are the existing management insiders or a group of outsiders seeking to gain control, people soliciting proxies from stockholders must file an extensive disclosure statement with the SEC. This information must also be available to the stockholders being solicited. Since the 1968 amendments to the 1934 act, similar disclosures must be made in connection with a cash offer to the stockholders to buy all or part of a class of shares. The SEC's proxy rules also attempt to promote "shareholder democracy" by requiring management to include most shareholder proposals in the company's proxy statement and to provide shareholder lists or send out supporting material for the sponsors of such proposals. The *Chambers* case in Chapter 34 illustrated a stockholder's use of these rules.

Antifraud Provisions. Although all of the foregoing rules are important and have probably contributed to better corporate management, the most sweeping and revolutionary section of the 1934 act is 10(b), the antifraud section. Together with the SEC's rule 10(b)5, as interpreted by the courts, this section potentially covers nearly any aspect of the securities markets one can imagine. It applies not only to the actual buyers and sellers of securities but to all other involved parties as well. It applies not only to the actual purchase and sale of securities but to any transaction in connection with their purchase and sale. It includes transactions in any securities, whether or not they are required to be listed and whether or not they are traded on an exchange. It covers much more than just common law fraud, including such things as failure to comply with other securities law requirements, arbitrary withholding of dividends, breaches of fiduciary duty, and disclosure of too much or too little information.

Rule 10b(5) reads as follows:

> It shall be unlawful for any person, directly or indirectly, by the use of any means or instrumentality of interstate commerce, or of the mails, or of any facility of any national securities exchange,
>
> (a) to employ any device, scheme, or artifice to defraud.
>
> (b) to make any untrue statement of a material fact or to omit to state a material fact necessary in order to make the statements made, in the light of the circumstances under which they were made, not misleading.
>
> (c) to engage in any act, practice, or course of business which operates or would operate as a fraud or deceit upon any person, in connection with the purchase or sale of any security.

As noted earlier, this rule's application was narrowed considerably in 1976, when the Supreme Court held that it applied only to cases of fraud.

Remedies, Liabilities, and Penalties.

The SEC uses a variety of court and administrative remedies to enforce the securities laws. It may seek an injunction to halt the sale of unregistered securities. It may ask a court to order the return of illegally received profits. Administratively, it may try to prevent employment of known violators by securities firms. The SEC enters into many voluntary settlements ("consent decrees") with firms and individuals accused of violations. The accused does not admit guilt but agrees to refrain from certain specified practices, or to do certain things, in the future. Sometimes a penalty is accepted as part of the consent decree; sometimes not. Because the courts are usually quite lenient with securities law violators, the SEC feels these consent decrees are justified in many cases.

Under Rule 2(e) of its rules of practice, the SEC may also bring disciplinary proceedings against professionals, such as accountants and attorneys, who are involved in securities transactions under the commission's jurisdiction. The SEC, after giving the accused offender the opportunity for a hearing on the charges, may revoke the privilege of practicing before the commission. Persons who lack the qualifications to represent others, who have engaged in unethical professional conduct or otherwise lack character or integrity, or who have willfully violated or aided and abetted violations of the securities laws, may be prohibited from appearing before the commission. Rule 2(e) also provides for automatic suspension of any attorney who has been suspended or disbarred, and any person whose state license has been suspended or revoked, and any person who has been convicted of a felony or of a misdemeanor involving moral turpitude. Temporary suspension may also occur when a professional has been subjected to an injunction against further violations of the securities laws. Commencing in 1975, the SEC has used this rule against corporate officers who also happened to be accountants or attorneys. In such a case, the corporate officer who could not practice before the SEC would be unable to sign the required filing documents for his company, and would thus be prevented from continuing to serve as the officer required to sign those documents. Because the rule states that it applies to "any person," the SEC could conceivably try to apply it to officers who were neither accountants nor attorneys. Further litigation on the validity and scope of this rule seems inevitable.

Individual investors who have been damaged financially as a result of violations of the securities laws may bring their own lawsuits against those responsible. The problem of suing for individual relief is the same here as in any other case—legal fees. It will undoubtedly cost several thousand dollars to get a securities case instituted, and perhaps as much as $50,000 to see it through all the possible appeals and rehearings. Class action lawsuits are still possible, although the U.S. Supreme Court ruled in 1974 that each member of a "class" of potential plaintiffs has to be notified personally of the lawsuit, so that he or she can decide whether to join in as a plaintiff. When such a class action is brought, with thousands of plaintiffs, including large institutional investors, damages can add up to millions of dollars very quickly.

Both the 1933 act and the 1934 act provide for criminal penalties—up to 5 years in prison and fines of up to $10,000 for most violations. Failure to file any report under the 1984 act makes the issuing corporation liable for a fine of $100 per day until the required filing occurs. (A corporation cannot be imprisoned, of course, but it can certainly be fined and enjoined.) Criminal cases are brought for the SEC by the U.S. Justice Department, so these two agencies must work together to prepare and present an effective criminal case. The *United States v. Natelli* case is one of the rare criminal cases that have been brought against accountants for securities law violations.

Defenses to Civil Liability

There are several possible defenses that may be used to avoid liability under the securities laws. First, the 1933 act has a relatively short statute of limitations: Suit must be brought within 1 year from the discovery of the violation or from the date when it would have been discovered using reasonable diligence; in no case, however, can suit be brought more than 3 years after the sale. With many analysts constantly studying the markets, most large frauds would probably be discovered within that time, but in the famous *Hochfelder* case, Nay defrauded people for some 25 years and was "discovered" only when he committed suicide.

It is at least theoretically possible for the courts to hold that a particular misstatement or omission was not material, but that is unlikely if investors have in fact sustained damage. The definition of **materiality** used in the cases is quite liberal: "any fact which might reasonably affect the value of the security."

Although plaintiffs in securities cases do not have to prove that they specifically relied on a misstatement (as they would in a common law fraud case), they cannot recover if the defendant can prove that they knew when they entered into the securities transaction that the statement was false.

Probably the most important defense, and the one most open to interpretation, is the **due diligence defense.** This defense may be proved by any person other than the issuing corporation. As to parts of a registration statement not based on an expert's authority, the defendant is not liable if he or she can show that he or she "had, after reasonable investigation, reasonable ground to believe and did believe, at the time such part of the registration statement became effective, that the statements therein were true" (and not misleading). The standard of reasonableness specified is "that required of a prudent person in the management of his or her own property." As to the "expertised" sections of the registration statement (e.g., those certified by certified public accountants [CPAs], engineers, or appraisers), the defendant is not liable if he or she "had no reasonable ground to believe, and did not believe," that the statements were untrue or misleading. In other words, the statements made by experts can be relied on unless the defendant knew or reasonably should have known that the statements were false or misleading. However, lawyers are not necessarily "experts" on everything, under this definition. The court in the landmark *Escott* case rejected the defendants' claim that they could rely on everything in the registration statement because it had been prepared by lawyers. Under this definition, lawyers would only be experts as to specifically legal questions; for example, the nature of the company's contingent liabilities.

Significance of This Chapter

Regulation of the issuance and sale of securities is a very important phase of government regulation on both the state and national level. It is not only the very rich, who obviously have access to excellent legal advice and valuable market information, who invest in securities. Investors include people from all walks of life and from all income levels. They must be protected from persons who would defraud them or take their money by deceptive practices. Also, the public buyer should be protected against the insider who because of special knowledge would get an unfair advantage as to new stock issues, stock splits, and similar material developments.

From the issuing company's standpoint, compliance with the securities law is burdensome in time, effort, and money. There are no easy shortcuts. But full and accurate compliance is clearly in the company's best interests. For all responsible individuals, the company's compliance should be checked and rechecked to avoid the possibility of ruinous damage suits by angry investors.

The corporation is simply a legal entity, a piece of paper, a charter from the state. Thus, it must be managed by people. This chapter identifies those people as directors and officers, and reviews the process of their selection and removal, and their powers, duties, authority, compensation, and possible personal liability.

IMPORTANT TERMS AND CONCEPTS

antifraud provisions
beneficial owner
blue-sky laws
business judgment rule
corporate opportunity rule
directors
due diligence defense
Foreign Corrupt Practices Act (FCPA)
hostile takeover
insiders
materiality
Model Business Corporation Act (MBCA)
officers
prospectus
registration statement
SEC Rule 10(b)5
securities
Securities Act of 1933
Securities Exchange Act of 1934
short-swing profits
state tender offer statutes
Uniform Securities Act

QUESTIONS AND PROBLEMS FOR DISCUSSION

1. Why can't directors vote by proxy, the way stockholders do?

2. What is the business judgment rule?

3. What is a tender offer? Why do states want to regulate it?

4. What is the difference between the 1933 act and the 1934 act?

5. Chiarella was a printer by trade. He worked as a "markup man" in the New York composing room of Pandick Press, a financial printer. Among documents that Chiarella handled were five announcements of corporate takeover bids. When these documents were delivered to the printer, the identities of the acquiring and target corporations were concealed by blank spaces or false names. The true names were sent to the printer on the night of the final printing.

   Chiarella, however, was able to deduce the names of the target companies before the final printing from other information contained in the documents. Without disclosing his knowledge, he purchased stock in the target companies and sold shares immediately after the takeover attempts were made public. By this method, he realized a gain of slightly more than $30,000 in the course of 14 months.

   Has Chiarella violated the Securities Acts? Discuss.

6. Liberty was a Delaware corporation, with its main operations in Chicago. The plaintiffs and their families owned about 20 percent of Liberty's stock. Grossman was president and treasurer; Gross, executive vice president and secretary. They were directors, along with Sachnoff and Myers. Liberty's bylaws called for five directors and permitted the directors to amend the bylaws and fill vacancies on the board. The four were unable to agree on a candidate for the single vacancy, but they agreed to amend the bylaws to increase the number of directors to seven and to elect Malkin, Haas, and Roland to fill the three vacancies. The next day Grossman and Gross said that they wanted to rescind the board actions, but Sachnoff (an attorney) told them that this could not be done. At a later board meeting, Grossman and Gross were dismissed as officers and Malkin, Roland, and Haas were elected to the main offices. Grossman and Gross brought suit to declare that both the election of the three new directors and all subsequent board actions were invalid.

   Are these board actions valid? Why or why not?

7. The SEC asked for an injunction to stop the sale of unregistered securities and to prohibit fraudulent practices in connection with their sale. The U.S. District Court denied the injunction, and the SEC appealed.

Koscot was one of the subsidiaries of Glen W. Turner Enterprises; it was organized as a multilevel network of distributors for a line of cosmetics. Distributors received cash bonuses ranging up to $3,000 for each new person who was brought into the plan and advanced up the distribution chain. Prospective distributors were introduced to the plan at "Opportunity Meetings," which were to be run exactly according to a company-prepared script. Distributors were told to dress and live as if they had a very large income, so as to impress the prospects. At the Opportunity Meetings, films were shown, speeches were made, and high-pressure sales tactics were used to try to get the prospects to "make a decision."

How should the SEC's appeal be decided, and why?

8. Audit Services, a collection agency, sued on behalf of three union trust funds for monies owing pursuant to certain collective bargaining agreements and declarations of trust. Roy Winslow, Elmo Road's general manager, signed the collective agreements for the corporation, which was then obligated to make certain payments to the pension and welfare trusts for its employees' benefit. Elmo Road made these payments from April to October 1992, and then stopped. When further payments were refused, the trust funds assigned their claims to the plaintiff, which sued for $31,842.53 due, plus $1,802.02 attorney fees. The trial court gave judgment for Elmo Road, holding that Winslow had no express, implied, or apparent authority to sign for the corporation. Plaintiff appealed.

   How should the appeals court decide? Explain.

The Declaration of Independence

Thomas Jefferson

A Declaration by the Representatives of the United States of America in Congress Assembled, July 4, 1776

When in the course of human events, it becomes necessary for one people to dissolve the political bands which have connected them with another, and to assume, among the powers of the earth, the separate and equal station to which the laws of nature and of nature's God entitle them, a decent respect to the opinions of mankind requires that they should declare the causes which impel them to the separation.

We hold these truths to be self-evident, that all men are created equal; that they are endowed by their Creator with certain unalienable rights; that among these are life, liberty, and the pursuit of happiness. That, to secure these rights, governments are instituted among men, deriving their just powers from the consent of the governed; that, whenever any form of government becomes destructive of these ends, it is the right of the people to alter or to abolish it, and to institute a new government, laying its foundation on such principles, and organizing its powers in such form, as to them shall seem most likely to effect their safety and happiness. Prudence, indeed, will dictate that governments long established should not be changed for light and transient causes; and, accordingly, all experience hath shown, that mankind are more disposed to suffer, while evils are sufferable, than to right themselves by abolishing the forms to which they are accustomed. But, when a long train of abuses and usurpations, pursuing invariably the same object, evinces a design to reduce them under absolute despotism, it is their right, it is their duty, to throw off such government, and to provide new guards for their future security. Such has been the patient sufferance of these colonies, and such is now the necessity which constrains them to alter their former systems of government. The history of the present King of Great Britain is a history of repeated injuries and usurpations, all having, in direct object, the establishment of an absolute tyranny over these States. To prove this, let facts be submitted to a candid world:

He has refused his assent to laws the most wholesome and necessary for the public good.

He has forbidden his governors to pass laws of immediate and pressing importance, unless suspended in their operation till his assent should be obtained; and, when so suspended, he has utterly neglected to attend them.

He has refused to pass other laws for the accommodation of large districts of people, unless those people would relinquish the right of representation in the legislature; a right inestimable to them, and formidable to tyrants only.

He has called together legislative bodies at places unusual, uncomfortable, and distant from the depository of their public records, for the sole purpose of fatiguing them into compliance with his measures.

He has dissolved representative houses repeatedly, for opposing, with manly firmness, his invasions on the rights of the people.

He has refused, for a long time after such dissolutions, to cause others to be elected; whereby the legislative powers, incapable of annihilation, have returned to the people at large for their exercise; the state remaining, in the meantime, exposed to all the danger of invasion from without, and convulsions within.

He has endeavored to prevent the population of these States; for that purpose, obstructing the laws for naturalization of foreigners, refusing to pass others to encourage their migration hither, and raising the conditions of new appropriations of lands.

He has obstructed the administration of justice, by refusing his assent to laws for establishing judiciary powers.

He has made judges dependent on his will alone, for the tenure of their offices, and the amount and payment of their salaries.

He has erected a multitude of new offices, and sent hither swarms of officers to harass our people, and eat out their substance.

He has kept among us, in time of peace, standing armies, without the consent of our legislatures.

He has affected to render the military independent of, and superior to, the civil power.

He has combined, with others, to subject us to a jurisdiction foreign to our Constitution, and unacknowledged by our laws; giving his assent to their acts of pretended legislation:

For quartering large bodies of armed troops among us:

For protecting them by a mock trial, from punishment, for any murders which they should commit on the inhabitants of these States:

For cutting off our trade with all parts of the world:

For imposing taxes on us without our consent:

For depriving us, in many cases, of the benefit of trial by jury:

For transporting us beyond seas to be tried for pretended offenses:

For abolishing the free system of English laws in a neighboring province, establishing therein an arbitrary government, and enlarging its boundaries, so as to render it at once an example and fit instrument for introducing the same absolute rule into these colonies:

For taking away our charters, abolishing our most valuable laws, and altering, fundamentally, the forms of our governments:

For suspending our own legislatures, and declaring themselves invested with power to legislate for us in all cases whatsoever.

He has abdicated government here, by declaring us out of his protection, and waging war against us.

He has plundered our seas, ravaged our coasts, burnt our towns, and destroyed the lives of our people.

He is, at this time, transporting large armies of foreign mercenaries to complete the works of death, desolation, and tyranny, already begun, with circumstances of cruelty and perfidy scarcely paralleled in the most barbarous ages, and totally unworthy the head of a civilized nation.

He has constrained our fellow-citizens, taken captive on the high seas, to bear arms against their country, to become the executioners of their friends and brethren, or to fall themselves by their hands.

He has excited domestic insurrections amongst us, and has endeavored to bring on the inhabitants of our frontiers, the merciless Indian savages, whose known rule of warfare is an undistinguished destruction of all ages, sexes, and conditions.

In every stage of these oppressions, we have petitioned for redress, in the most humble terms; our repeated petitions have been answered only by repeated injury. A prince, whose character is thus marked by every act which may define a tyrant, is unfit to be the ruler of a free people.

Nor have we been wanting in attention to our British brethren. We have warned them, from time to time, of attempts by their legislature to extend an unwarrantable jurisdiction over us. We have reminded them of the circumstances of our emigration and settlement here. We have appealed to their native justice and magnanimity, and we have conjured them, by the ties of our common kindred, to disavow these usurpations, which would inevitably interrupt our connections and correspondence. They, too, have been deaf to the voice of justice and consanguinity. We must, therefore, acquiesce in the necessity which denounces our separation, and hold them, as we hold the rest of mankind, enemies in war, in peace, friends.

We, therefore, the representatives of the United States of America, in general Congress assembled, appealing to the Supreme Judge of the world for the rectitude of our intentions, do, in the name, and by the authority of the good people of these colonies, solemnly publish and declare, that these united colonies are, and of right ought to be, free and independent states; that they are absolved from all allegiance to the British Crown, and that all political connection between them and the state of Great Britain is, and ought to be, totally dissolved; and that, as free and independent states, they have full power to levy war, conclude peace, contract alliances, establish commerce, and to do all other acts and things which independent states may of right do. And, for the support of this declaration, with a firm reliance on the protection of Divine Providence, we mutually pledge to each other our lives, our fortunes, and our sacred honour.

The Constitution of the United States

Preamble

We the People of the United States, in Order to form a more perfect Union, establish Justice, insure domestic Tranquility, provide for the common Defence, promote the general Welfare, and secure the Blessings of Liberty to ourselves and our Posterity, do ordain and establish this Constitution for the United States of America.

ARTICLE 1

Section 1. All legislative Powers herein granted shall be vested in a Congress of the United States, which shall consist of a Senate and House of Representatives.

Section 2. [1] The House of Representatives shall be composed of Members chosen every second Year by the People of the several States, and the Electors in each State shall have the Qualifications requisite for Electors of the most numerous Branch of the State Legislature.

[2] No Person shall be a Representative who shall not have attained to the Age of twenty five Years, and been seven Years a Citizen of the United States, and who shall not, when elected, be an Inhabitant of that State in which he shall be chosen.

[3] Representatives and direct Taxes shall be apportioned among the several States which may be included within this Union, according to their respective Numbers, which shall be determined by adding to the whole Number of free Persons, including those bound to Service for a Term of Years, and excluding Indians not taxed, three fifths of all other Persons The actual Enumeration shall be made within three Years after the first Meeting of the Congress of the United States, and within every subsequent Term of ten Years, in such Manner as they shall by Law direct. The Number of Representatives shall not exceed one for every thirty Thousand, but each State shall have at Least one Representative; and until such enumeration shall be made, the State of New Hampshire shall be entitled to chose three, Massachusetts eight, Rhode Island and Providence Plantations one, Connecticut five, New York six, New Jersey four, Pennsylvania eight, Delaware one, Maryland six, Virginia ten, North Carolina five, South Carolina five, and Georgia three.

[4] When vacancies happen in the Representation from any State, the Executive Authority thereof shall issue Writs of Election to fill such Vacancies.

[5] The House of Representatives shall chose their Speaker and other Officers; and shall have the sole Power of Impeachment.

Section 3. [1] The Senate of the United States shall be composed of two Senators from each State, chosen by the Legislature thereof, for six Years; and each Senator shall have one Vote.

[2] Immediately after they shall be assembled in Consequence of the first Election, they shall be divided as equally as may be into three Classes. The Seats of the Senators of the first Class shall be vacated at the Expiration of the Second Year, of the second Class at the Expiration of the fourth Year, and of the third Class at the Expiration of the sixth Year, so that one third may be chosen every second Year; and if Vacancies happen by

Resignation, or otherwise, during the Recess of the Legislature of any State, the Executive thereof may make temporary Appointments until the next Meeting of the Legislature, which shall then fill such Vacancies.

[3] No Person shall be a Senator who shall not have attained to the Age of thirty Years, and been nine Years a Citizen of the United States, and who shall not, when elected, be an Inhabitant of that State for which he shall be chosen.

[4] The Vice President of the United States shall be President of the Senate, but shall have no Vote, unless they be equally divided.

[5] The Senate shall chose their other Officers, and also a President pro tempore, in the Absence of the Vice President, or when he shall exercise the Office of President of the United States.

[6] The Senate shall have the sole Power to try all Impeachments. When sitting for that Purpose, they shall be on Oath or Affirmation. When the President of the United States is tried, the Chief Justice shall preside: And no Person shall be convicted without the Concurrence of two thirds of the Members present.

[7] Judgment in Cases of Impeachment shall not extend further than to removal from Office, and disqualification to hold and enjoy any Office of Honor, Trust, or Profit under the United States: but the Party convicted shall nevertheless be liable and subject to Indictment, Trial, Judgment, and Punishment, according to Law.

Section 4. **[1]** The Times, Places and Manner of holding elections for Senators and Representatives, shall be prescribed in each State by the Legislature thereof; but the Congress may at any time by Law make or alter such Regulations, except as to the Places of choosing Senators.

[2] The Congress shall assemble at least once in every Year, and such Meeting shall be on the first Monday in December, unless they shall by Law appoint a different Day.

Section 5. **[1]** Each House shall be the Judge of the Elections, Returns, and Qualifications of its own Members, and a Majority of each shall constitute a Quorum to do Business; but a smaller Number may adjourn from day to day, and may be authorized to compel the Attendance of absent Members, in such Manner, and under such Penalties as each House may provide.

[2] Each House may determine the Rules of its Proceedings, punish its Members for disorderly Behavior, and, with the Concurrence of two thirds, expel a Member.

[3] Each House shall keep a Journal of its Proceedings, and from time to time publish the same, excepting such Parts as may in their Judgment require Secrecy; and the Yeas and Nays of the Members of either House on any question shall, at the Desire of one fifth of those Present, be entered on the Journal.

[4] Neither House, during the Session of Congress, shall, without the Consent of the other, adjourn for more than three days, nor to any other Place than that in which the two Houses shall be sitting.

Section 6. **[1]** The Senators and Representatives shall receive a Compensation for their Services, to be ascertained by Law, and paid out of the Treasury of the United States. They shall in all Cases, except Treason, Felony and Breach of the Peace, be privileged from Arrest during their Attendance at the Session of their respective Houses, and in going to and returning from the same; and for any Speech or Debate in either House, they shall not be questioned in any other Place.

[2] No Senator or Representative shall, during the Time for which he was elected, be appointed to any civil Office under the Authority of the United States, which shall have been created, or the Emoluments whereof shall have been increased during such time; and no Person holding any Office under the United States, shall be a Member of either House during his Continuance in Office.

Section 7. **[1]** All Bills for raising Revenue shall originate in the House of Representatives; but the Senate may propose or concur with Amendments as on other Bills.

[2] Every Bill which shall have passed the House of Representatives and the Senate, shall, before it becomes a Law, be presented to the President of the United States; If he approve he shall sign it, but if not he shall return it, with his Objections to the House in which it shall have originated, who shall enter the Objections at large on their Journal, and proceed to reconsider it. If after such Reconsideration two thirds of that House shall agree to pass the Bill, it shall be sent together with the Objections, to the other House, by which it shall likewise be reconsidered, and if approved by two thirds of that House, it shall become a Law. But in all such Cases the Votes of both Houses shall be determined by Yeas and Nays, and the Names of the Persons voting for and against the Bill shall be entered on the Journal of each House respectively. If any Bill shall not be returned by the President within ten Days (Sundays excepted) after it shall have been presented to him, the Same shall be a Law, in like Manner as if he had signed it unless the Congress by their Adjournment prevent its Return in which Case it shall not be a Law.

[3] Every Order, Resolution, or Vote, to Which the Concurrence of the Senate and House of Representatives may be necessary (except on a question of Adjournment) shall be presented to the President of the United States; and before the Same shall take Effect, shall be approved by him, or being disapproved by him, shall be repassed by two thirds of the Senate and House of Representatives, according to the Rules and Limitations prescribed in the Case of a Bill.

Section 8. **[1]** The Congress shall have Power To lay and collect Taxes, Duties, Imposts and Excises, to pay the Debts and provide for the common Defence and general Welfare of the United States; but all Duties, Imposts and Excises shall be uniform throughout the United States;

[2] To borrow money on the credit of the United States;

[3] To regulate Commerce with foreign Nations, and among the several States, and with the Indian Tribes;

[4] To establish an uniform Rule of Naturalization, and uniform Laws on the subject of Bankruptcies throughout the United States;

[5] To coin Money, regulate the Value thereof, and of foreign Coin, and fix the Standard of Weights and Measures;

[6] To provide for the Punishment of counterfeiting the Securities and current Coin of the United States;

[7] To Establish Post Offices and Post Roads;

[8] To promote the Progress of Science and useful Arts, by securing for limited Times to Authors and Inventors the exclusive Right to their respective Writings and Discoveries;

[9] To constitute Tribunals inferior to the supreme Court;

[10] To define and punish Piracies and Felonies committed on the high Seas, and Offenses against the Law of Nations;

[11] To declare War, grant Letters of Marque and Reprisal, and make Rules concerning Captures on Land and Water;

[12] To raise and support Armies, but no Appropriation of Money to that Use shall be for a longer Term than two Years;

[13] To provide and maintain a Navy;

[14] To make Rules for the Government and Regulation of the land and naval Forces;

[15] To provide for calling forth the Militia to execute the Laws of the Union, suppress Insurrections and repel Invasions;

[16] To provide for organizing, arming, and disciplining, the Militia, and for governing such Part of them as may be employed in the Service of the United States, reserving to the States respectively, the Appointment of the Officers, and the Authority of training the Militia according to the discipline prescribed by Congress;

[17] To exercise exclusive Legislation in all Cases whatsoever, over such District (not exceeding ten Miles square) as may, by Cession of particular States, and the Acceptance of Congress, become the Seat of the Government of the United States, and to exercise like Authority over all Places purchased by the Consent of the Legislature of the State in which the Same shall be, for the Erection of Forts, Magazines, Arsenals, dock Yards and other needful Buildings;—And

[18] To make all Laws which shall be necessary and proper for carrying into Execution the foregoing Powers, and all other Powers vested by this Constitution in the Government of the United States, or in any Department or Officer thereof.

Section 9. **[1]** The Migration or Importation of Such Persons as any of the States now existing shall think proper to admit, shall not be prohibited by the Congress prior to the Year one thousand eight hundred and eight, but a Tax or duty may be imposed on such Importation, not exceeding ten dollars for each Person.

[2] The privilege of the Writ of Habeas Corpus shall not be suspended, unless when in Cases of Rebellion or Invasion the public Safety may require it.

[3] No Bill of Attainder or ex post facto Law shall be passed.

[4] No Capitation, or other direct, Tax shall be laid, unless in Proportion to the Census or Enumeration herein before directed to be taken.

[5] No Tax or Duty shall be laid on Articles exported from any State.

[6] No Preference shall be given by any Regulation of Commerce or Revenue to the Ports of one State over those of another: nor shall Vessels bound to, or from, one State be obliged to enter, clear, or pay Duties in another.

[7] No money shall be drawn from the Treasury, but in Consequence of Appropriations made by Law; and a regular Statement and Account of the Receipts and Expenditures of all public Money shall be published from time to time.

[8] No Title of Nobility shall be granted by the United States: And no Person holding any Office of Profit or Trust under them. shall, without the Consent of the Congress, accept of any present, Emolument, Office, or Title, of any kind whatever, from any King, Prince, or foreign State.

Section 10. **[1]** No State shall enter into any Treaty, Alliance, or Confederation; grant Letters of Marque and Reprisal; coin Money; emit Bills of Credit; make any Thing but gold and silver Coin a Tender in Payment of Debts; pass any Bill of Attainder, ex post facto Law, or Law impairing the Obligation of Contracts, or grant any Title of Nobility.

[2] No State shall, without the Consent of the Congress, lay any Imposts or Duties on Imports or Exports, except what may be absolutely necessary for executing its inspection Laws: and the net Produce of all Duties and Imposts, laid by any State on Imports or Exports, shall be for the Use of the Treasury of the United States; and all such Laws shall be subject to the Revision and Control of the Congress.

[3] No State shall, without the Consent of Congress, lay any Duty of Tonnage, keep Troops, or Ships of War in time of Peace, enter into any Agreement or Compact with another State, or with a foreign Power, or engage in War, unless actually invaded, or in such imminent Danger as will not admit of delay.

Article II

Section 1. **[1]** The executive Power shall be vested in a President of the United States of America. He shall hold his Office during the Term of four Years, and, together with the Vice President, chosen for the same Term, be elected, as follows:

[2] Each State shall appoint, in such Manner as the Legislature thereof may direct, a Number of Electors, equal to the whole Number of Senators and Representatives to which the State may be entitled in the Congress; but no Senator or Representative, or Person holding an Office of Trust or Profit under the United States, shall be appointed an Elector.

[3] The Electors shall meet in their respective States, and vote by Ballot for two Persons, of whom one at least shall not be an Inhabitant of the same State with themselves. And they shall make a List of all the Persons voted for, and of the Number of Votes for each; which List they shall sign and certify, and transmit sealed to the Seat of the Government of the United States, directed to the President of the Senate. The President of the Senate shall, in the Presence of the Senate and House of Representatives, open all the Certificates, and the Votes shall then be counted. The Person having the greatest Number of Votes shall be the President, if such Number be a Majority of the whole Number of Electors appointed; and if there be more than one who have such Majority, and have an equal Number of Votes, then the House of Representatives shall immediately chose by Ballot one of them for President; and if no Person have a Majority, then from the five highest on the List the said House shall in like Manner chose the President. But in choosing the President, the Votes shall be taken by States the Representation from each State having one

Vote; A quorum for this Purpose shall consist of a Member or Members from two thirds of the States, and a Majority of all the States shall be necessary to a Choice. In every Case, after the Choice of the President, the Person having the greater Number of Votes of the Electors shall be the Vice President. But if there shall remain two or more who have equal Votes, the Senate shall chose from them by Ballot the Vice President.

[4] The Congress may determine the Time of chosing the Electors, and the Day on which they shall give their Votes; which Day shall be the same throughout the United States.

[5] No person except a natural born Citizen, or a Citizen of the United States, at the time of the Adoption of this Constitution, shall be eligible to the Office of President; neither shall any Person be eligible to that Office who shall not have attained to the Age of thirty five Years, and been fourteen Years a Resident within the United States.

[6] In case of the removal of the President from Office, or of his Death, Resignation or Inability to discharge the Powers and Duties of the said Office, the Same shall devolve on the Vice President, and the Congress may by Law provide for the Case of Removal, Death, Resignation or Inability, both of the President and Vice President, declaring what Officer shall then act as President, and such Officer shall act accordingly, until the Disability be removed, or a President shall be elected.

[7] The President shall, at stated Times, receive for his Services, a Compensation, which shall neither be increased nor diminished during the Period for which he shall have been elected, and he shall not receive within that Period any other Emolument from the United States, or any of them.

[8] Before he enter on the Execution of his Office, he shall take the following Oath or Affirmation: "I do solemnly swear (or affirm) that I will faithfully execute the Office of President of the United States, and will to the best of my Ability, preserve, protect and defend the Constitution of the United States."

Section 2. **[1]** The President shall be Commander in Chief of the Army and Navy of the United States, and of the militia of the several States, when called into the actual Service of the United States; he may require the Opinion, in writing, of the principal Officer in each of the Executive Departments, upon any Subject relating to the Duties of their respective Offices, and he shall have Power to grant Reprieves and Pardons for Offenses against the United States, except in Cases of Impeachment.

[2] He shall have Power, by and with the Advice and Consent of the Senate to make Treaties, provided two thirds of the Senators present concur; and he shall nominate, and by and with the Advice and Consent of the Senate, shall appoint Ambassadors, other public Ministers and Consuls, Judges of the supreme Court, and all other Officers of the United States, whose Appointments are not herein otherwise provided for, and which shall be established by Law; but the Congress may by Law vest the Appointment of such inferior Officers, as they think proper, in the President alone, in the Courts of Law, or in the Heads of Departments.

[3] The President shall have Power to fill up all Vacancies that may happen during the Recess of the Senate, by granting Commissions which shall expire at the End of their next Session.

Section 3. He shall from time to time give to the Congress Information of the State of the Union, and recommend to their Consideration such Measures as he shall judge necessary and expendient; he may, on extraordinary Occasions, convene both Houses, or either of them, and in Case of Disagreement between them, with Respect to the Time of Adjournment, he may adjourn them to such Time as he shall think proper; he shall receive Ambassadors and other public Ministers; he shall take Care that the Laws be faithfully executed, and shall Commission all the Officers of the United States.

Section 4. The President, Vice President and all civil Officers of the United States, shall be removed from Office on Impeachment for, and Conviction of, Treason, Bribery, or other high Crimes and Misdemeanors.

Article III

Section 1. The judicial Power of the United States, shall be vested in one supreme Court, and in such inferior Courts as the Congress may from time to time ordain and establish. The

Judges, both of the supreme and inferior Courts, shall hold their Offices during good Behaviour, and shall, at stated Times, receive for their Services a Compensation, which shall not be diminished during their Continuance in Office.

Section 2. [1] The judicial Power shall extend to all Cases, in Law and Equity, arising under this Constitution, the Laws of the United States, and Treaties made, or which shall be made, under their Authority; to all Cases affecting Ambassadors, other public Ministers and Consuls; to all Cases of admiralty and maritime Jurisdiction; to Controversies to which the United States shall be a Party; to Controversies between two or more States; between a State and Citizens of another State; between Citizens of different States; between Citizens of the same State claiming Lands under the Grants of different States, and between a State, or the Citizens thereof, and foreign States, Citizens or Subjects.

[2] In all Cases affecting Ambassadors, other public Ministers and Consuls, and those in which a State shall be a Party, the supreme Court shall have original Jurisdiction. In all the other Cases before mentioned, the supreme Court shall have appellate Jurisdiction, both as to Law and Fact, with such Exceptions, and under such Regulations as the Congress shall make.

[3] The trial of all Crimes, except in Cases of Impeachment, shall be by Jury; and such Trial shall be held in the State where the said Crimes shall have been committed; but when not committed within any State, the Trial shall be at such Place or Places as the Congress may by Law have directed.

Section 3. [1] Treason against the United States, shall consist only in levying War against them, or, in adhering to their Enemies, giving them Aid and Comfort. No Person shall be convicted of Treason unless on the Testimony of two Witnesses to the same overt Act, or on Confession in open Court.

[2] The Congress shall have Power to declare the Punishment of Treason, but no Attainder of Treason shall work Corruption of Blood, or Forfeiture except during the Life of the Person attainted.

Article IV

Section 1. Full Faith and Credit shall be given in each State to the public Acts, Records, and judicial Proceedings of every other State. And the Congress may by general Laws prescribe the Manner in which such Acts, Records and Proceedings shall be proved, and the Effect thereof.

Section 2. [1] The Citizens of each State shall be entitled to all Privileges and Immunities of Citizens in the several States.

[2] A Person charged in any State with Treason, Felony, or other Crime, who shall flee from Justice, and be found in another State, shall on demand of the executive Authority of the State from which he fled, be delivered up, to be removed to the State having Jurisdiction of the Crime.

[3] No Person held to Service or Labour in one State, under the Laws thereof, escaping into another, shall, in Consequence of any Law or Regulation therein, be discharged from such Service or Labour, but shall be delivered up on Claim of the Party to whom such Service or Labour may be due.

Section 3. [1] New States may be admitted by the Congress into this Union; but no new State shall be formed or erected within the Jurisdiction of any other State; nor any State be formed by the Junction of two or more States, or Parts of States, without the Consent of the Legislatures of the States concerned as well as of the Congress.

[2] The Congress shall have Power to dispose of and make all needful Rules and Regulations respecting the Territory or other Property belonging to the United States; and nothing in this Constitution shall be so construed as to Prejudice any Claims of the United States, or of any particular State.

Section 4. The United States shall guarantee to every State in this Union a Republican Form of Government, and shall protect each of them against Invasion; and on Application of the

Legislature, or of the Executive (when the Legislature cannot be convened) against domestic Violence.

Article V

The Congress, whenever two thirds of both Houses shall deem it necessary, shall propose Amendments to this Constitution, or, on the Application of the Legislatures of two thirds of the several States, shall call a Convention for proposing Amendments, which, in either case, shall be valid to all Intents and Purposes, as part of this Constitution, when ratified by the Legislatures of three fourths of the several States, or by Conventions in three fourths thereof, as the one or the other Mode of Ratification may be proposed by the Congress; Provided that no Amendment which may be made prior to the Year One thousand eight hundred and eight shall in any Manner affect the first and fourth Clauses in the Ninth Section of the first Article; and that no State, without its Consent, shall be deprived of its equal Suffrage in the Senate.

Article VI

[1] All Debts contracted and Engagements entered into, before the Adoption of this Constitution shall be as valid against the United States under this Constitution, as under the Confederation.

[2] This Constitution, and the Laws of the United States which shall be made in Pursuance thereof; and all Treaties made, or which shall be made, under the Authority of the United States, shall be the supreme Law of the Land; and the Judges in every State shall be bound thereby, any Thing in the Constitution or Laws of any State to the Contrary notwithstanding.

[3] The Senators and Representatives before mentioned, and the Members of the several State Legislatures, and all executive and judicial Officers, both of the United States and of the several States, shall be bound by Oath or Affirmation, to support this Constitution; but no religious Test shall ever be required as a Qualification to any Office or public Trust under the United States.

Article VII

The Ratification of the Conventions of nine States shall be sufficient for the Establishment of this Constitution between the States so ratifying the Same.

ARTICLES IN ADDITION TO, AND AMENDMENT OF, THE CONSTITUTION OF THE UNITED STATES OF AMERICA, PROPOSED BY CONGRESS, AND RATIFIED BY THE LEGISLATURES OF THE SEVERAL STATES PURSUANT TO THE FIFTH ARTICLE OF THE ORIGINAL CONSTITUTION.

Amendment I [1791]

Congress shall make no law respecting an establishment of religion, or prohibiting the free exercise thereof; or abridging the freedom of speech, or of the press; or the right of the people peaceably to assemble, and to petition the Government for a redress of grievances.

Amendment II [1791]

A well regulated Militia, being necessary to the security of a free State, the right of the people to keep and bear Arms, shall not be infringed.

Amendment III [1791]

No Soldier shall, in time of peace be quartered in any house, without the consent of the Owner, nor in time of war, but in a manner to be prescribed by law.

Amendment IV [1791]

The right of the people to be secure in their persons, houses, papers, and effects, against unreasonable searches and seizures, shall not be violated, and no Warrants shall issue, but upon probable cause, supported by Oath or affirmation, and particularly describing the place to be searched, and the persons or things to be seized.

Amendment V [1791]

No person shall be held to answer for a capital, or otherwise infamous crime, unless on a presentment or indictment of a Grand Jury, except in cases arising in the land or naval forces, or in the Militia, when in actual service in time of War or public danger; nor shall any person be subject for the same offence to be twice put in jeopardy of life or limb; nor shall be compelled in any criminal case to be a witness against himself, nor be deprived of life, liberty, or property, without due process of law; nor shall private property be taken for public use, without just compensation.

Amendment VI [1791]

In all criminal prosecutions, the accused shall enjoy the right to a speedy and public trial, by an impartial jury of the State and district wherein the crime shall have been committed, which district shall have been previously ascertained by law, and to be informed of the nature and cause of the accusation; to be confronted with the witnesses against him; to have compulsory process for obtaining witnesses in his favor, and to have the Assistance of Counsel for his defence.

Amendment VII [1791]

In Suits at common law, where the value in controversy shall exceed twenty dollars, the right of trial by jury shall be preserved, and no fact tried by jury, shall be otherwise reexamined in any Court of the United States, than according to the rules of common law.

Amendment VIII [1791]

Excessive bail shall not be required, nor excessive fines imposed, nor cruel and unusual punishments inflicted.

Amendment IX [1791]

The enumeration in the Constitution, of certain rights, shall not be construed to deny or disparage others retained by the people.

Amendment X [1791]

The powers not delegated to the United States by the Constitution, nor prohibited by it to the States, are reserved to the States respectively, or to the people.

Amendment XI [1798]

The Judicial power of the United States shall not be construed to extend to any suit in law or equity, commenced or prosecuted against one of the United States by Citizens of another State, or by Citizens or Subjects of any Foreign State.

Amendment XII [1804]

The Electors shall meet in their respective states and vote by ballot for President and Vice President, one of whom, at least, shall not be an inhabitant of the same state with themselves; they shall name in their ballots the person voted for as President, and in distinct ballots the person voted for as Vice President, and they shall make distinct lists of all persons voted for as President, and of all persons voted for as Vice President, and of the number of votes for each, which lists they shall sign and certify, and transmit sealed to the seat of the government of the United States, directed to the President of the Senate; The President of the Senate shall, in the presence of the Senate and House of Representatives, open all the certificates and the votes shall then be counted; The person having the greatest number of votes for President, shall be the President, if such number be a majority of the whole number of Electors appointed; and if no person have such majority, then from the persons having the highest numbers not exceeding three on the list of those voted for as President, the House of Representatives shall choose immediately, by ballot, the President. But in choosing the President, the votes shall be taken by states, the representation from each state having one vote; a quorum for this purpose shall consist of a member or members from two thirds of the states, and a majority of all states shall be necessary to a choice. And if the House of Representatives shall not choose a President whenever the right of choice shall devolve upon them before the fourth day of March next following, then the Vice President shall act as President, as in the case of the death or other constitutional disability of the President. The person having the greatest number of votes as Vice President, shall be the Vice President, if such number be a majority of the whole number of Electors appointed, and if no person have a majority, then from the two highest numbers on the list, the Senate shall choose the Vice President; a quorum for the purpose shall consist of two thirds of the whole number of Senators, and a majority of the whole number shall be necessary to a choice. But no person constitutionally ineligible to the office of President shall be eligible to that of Vice President of the United States.

Amendment XIII [1865]

Section 1. Neither slavery nor involuntary servitude, except as a punishment for crime whereof the party shall have been duly convicted, shall exist within the United States, or any place subject to their jurisdiction.

Section 2. Congress shall have power to enforce this article by appropriate legislation.

Amendment XIV [1868]

Section 1. All persons born or naturalized in the United States, and subject to the jurisdiction thereof, are citizens of the United States and of the State wherein they reside. No State shall make or enforce any law which shall abridge the privileges or immunities of citizens of the United States; nor shall any State deprive any person of life, liberty, or property, without due process of law; nor deny to any person within its jurisdiction the equal protection of the laws.

Section 2. Representatives shall be apportioned among the several States according to their respective numbers, counting the whole number of persons in each State, excluding Indians not taxed. But when the right to vote at any election for the choice of electors for President and Vice President of the United States, Representatives in Congress, the Executive and Judicial officers of a State, or the members of the Legislature thereof, is denied to any of the male inhabitants of such State, being twenty one years of age, and citizens of the United States, or in any way abridged, except for participation in rebellion, or other crime, the basis of representation therein shall be reduced in the proportion which the number of such male citizens shall bear to the whole number of male citizens twenty one years of age in such State.

Section 3. No person shall be a Senator or Representative in Congress, or elector of President and Vice President, or hold any office, civil or military, under the United States, or under any State, who having previously taken an oath, as a member of Congress, or as an officer of the United States, or as a member of any State legislature, or as an executive or judicial officer of any State, to support the Constitution of the United States, shall have engaged in insurrection or rebellion against the same, or given aid or comfort to the enemies thereof. But Congress may by a vote of two thirds of each House, remove such disability.

Section 4. The validity of the public debt of the United States, authorized by law, including debts incurred for payment of pensions and bounties for services in suppressing insurrection or rebellion, shall not be questioned. But neither the United States nor any State shall assume or pay any debt or obligation incurred in aid of insurrection or rebellion against the United States, or any claim for the loss or emancipation of any slave; but all such debts, obligations and claims shall be held illegal and void.

Section 5. The Congress shall have power to enforce, by appropriate legislation, the provisions of this article.

Amendment XV [1870]

Section 1. The right of citizens of the United States to vote shall not be denied or abridged by the United States or by any State on account of race, color, or previous condition of servitude.

Section 2. The Congress shall have power to enforce this article by appropriate legislation.

Amendment XVI [1913]

The Congress shall have power to lay and collect taxes on incomes, from whatever source derived, without apportionment among the several States, and without regard to any census or enumeration.

Amendment XVII [1913]

[1] The Senate of the United States shall be composed of two Senators from each State elected by the people thereof, for six years; and each Senator shall have one vote. The electors in each State shall have the qualifications requisite for electors of the most numerous branch of the State legislatures.

[2] When vacancies happen in the representation of any State in the Senate, the executive authority of such State shall issue writs of election to fill such vacancies: Provided, That the legislature of any State may empower the executive thereof to make temporary appointments until the people fill the vacancies by election as the legislature may direct.

[3] This amendment shall not be so construed as to affect the election or term of any Senator chosen before it becomes valid as part of the Constitution.

Amendment XVIII [1919]

Section 1. After one year from the ratification of this article the manufacture, sale, or transportation of intoxicating liquors within, the importation thereof into, or the exportation thereof from the United States and all territory subject to the jurisdiction thereof for beverage purposes is hereby prohibited.

Section 2. The Congress and the several States shall have concurrent power to enforce this article by appropriate legislation.

Section 3. This article shall be inoperative unless it shall have been ratified as an amendment to the Constitution by the legislatures of the several States, as provided in the Constitution, within seven years from the date of the submission hereof to the States by the Congress.

AMENDMENT XIX [1920]

[1] The right of citizens of the United States to vote shall not be denied or abridged by the United States or by any State on account of sex.

[2] Congress shall have power to enforce this article by appropriate legislation.

AMENDMENT XX [1933]

Section 1. the terms of the President and Vice President shall end at noon on the 20th day of January, and the terms of Senators and Representatives at noon on the 3d day of January, of the years in which such terms would have ended if this article had not been ratified; and the terms of their successors shall then begin.

Section 2. The Congress shall assemble at least once in every year, and such meeting shall begin at noon on the 3d day of January, unless they shall by law appoint a different day.

Section 3. If, at the time fixed for the beginning of the term of the President, the President elect shall have died, the Vice President elect shall become President. If the President shall not have been chosen before the time fixed for the beginning of his term, or if the President elect shall have failed to qualify, then the Vice President elect shall act as President until a President shall have qualified; and the Congress may by law provide for the case wherein neither a President elect nor a Vice President elect shall have qualified, declaring who shall then act as President, or the manner in which one who is to act shall be selected, and such person shall act accordingly until a President or Vice President shall have qualified.

Section 4. The Congress may by law provide for the case of the death of any of the persons from whom the House of Representatives may choose a President whenever the right of choice shall have devolved upon them, and for the case of the death of any of the persons from whom the Senate may choose a Vice President whenever the right of choice shall have developed upon them.

Section 5. Sections 1 and 2 shall take effect on the 15th day of October following the ratification of this article.

Section 6. This article shall be inoperative unless it shall have been ratified as an amendment to the Constitution by the legislatures of three fourths of the several States within seven years from the date of its submission.

AMENDMENT XXI [1933]

Section 1. The eighteenth article of amendment to the Constitution of the United States is hereby repealed.

Section 2. The transportation or importation into any State, Territory, or possession of the United States for delivery or use therein of intoxicating liquors, in violation of the laws thereof, is hereby prohibited.

Section 3. This article shall be inoperative unless it shall have been ratified as an amendment to the Constitution by conventions in the several States, as provided in the Constitution, within seven years from the date of the submission hereof to the States by the Congress.

AMENDMENT XXII [1951]

Section 1. No person shall be elected to the office of the President more than twice, and no person who has held the office of President, or acted as President, for more than two years of a term to which some other person was elected President shall be elected to the office of President more than once. But this Article shall not apply to any person holding the office of President when this Article was proposed by the Congress, and shall not prevent any person who may be holding the office of President, or acting as President, during the term within which this Article becomes operative from holding the office of President or acting as President during the remainder of such term.

Section 2. This article shall be inoperative unless it shall have been ratified as an amendment to the Constitution by the legislatures of three fourths of the several States within seven years from the date of its submission to the States by the Congress.

Amendment XXIII [1961]

Section 1. The District constituting the seat of Government of the United States shall appoint in such manner as the Congress may direct:

A number of electors of President and Vice President equal to the whole number of Senators and Representatives in Congress to which the District would be entitled if it were a State, but in no event more than the least populous state; they shall be in addition to those appointed by the states, but they shall be considered, for the purposes of the election of President and Vice President, to be electors appointed by a state; and they shall meet in the District and perform such duties as provided by the twelfth article of amendment.

Section 2. The Congress shall have power to enforce this article by appropriate legislation.

Amendment XXIV [1964]

Section 1. The right of citizens of the United States to vote in any primary or other election for President or Vice President, for electors for President or Vice President or for Senator or Representative in Congress, shall not be denied or abridged by the United States, or any State by reason of failure to pay any poll tax or other tax.

Section 2. The Congress shall have power to enforce this article by appropriate legislation.

Amendment XXV [1967]

Section 1. In case of the removal of the President from office or of his death or resignation, the Vice President shall become President.

Section 2. Whenever there is a vacancy in the office of the Vice President, the President shall nominate a Vice President who shall take office upon confirmation by a majority vote of both Houses of Congress.

Section 3. Whenever the President transmits to the President pro tempore of the Senate and the Speaker of the House of Representatives his written declaration that he is unable to discharge the powers and duties of his office, and until he transmits to them a written declaration to the contrary, such powers and duties shall be discharged by the Vice President as Acting President.

Section 4. Whenever the Vice President and a majority of either the principal officers of the executive departments or of such other body as Congress may by law provide, transmit to the President pro tempore of the Senate and the Speaker of the House of Representatives their written declaration that the President is unable to discharge the powers and duties of his office, the Vice President shall immediately assume the powers and duties of the office as Acting President.

Thereafter, when the President transmits to the President pro tempore of the Senate and the Speaker of the House of Representatives his written declaration that no inability exists, he shall resume the powers and duties of his office unless the Vice President and a majority of either the principal officers of the executive department or of such other body as Congress may by law provide, transmit within four days to the President pro tempore of the Senate and the Speaker of the House of Representatives their written declaration and the President is unable to discharge the powers and duties of his office. Thereupon Congress shall decide the issue, assembling within forty eight hours for that purpose if not in session. If the Congress, within twenty one days after receipt of the latter written declaration, or, if Congress is not in session, within twenty one days after Congress is required to assemble, determines by two thirds vote of both Houses that the President is unable to discharge the powers and duties ties of his office, the Vice President shall continue to discharge the same as Acting President; otherwise, the President shall resume the powers and duties of his office.

Amendment XXVI [1971]

Section 1. The right of citizens of the United States, who are eighteen years of age or older, to vote shall not be denied or abridged by the United States or by any State on account of age.

Section 2. The Congress shall have power to enforce this article by appropriate legislation.

Amendment XXVII [1992]

No law, varying the compensation for the services of the Senators and Representatives, shall take effect, until an election of Representatives shall have intervened.

Uniform Commercial Code (selected sections)*

Title.

An Act.

To be known as the Uniform Commercial Code, Relating to Certain Commercial Transactions in or regarding Personal Property and Contracts and other Documents concerning them, including Sales, Commercial Paper, Bank Deposits and Collections, Letters of Credit, Bulk Transfers, Warehouse Receipts, Bills of Lading, other Documents of Title, Investment Securities, and Secured Transactions, including certain Sales of Accounts, Chattel Paper, and Contract Rights; Providing for Public Notice to Third Parties in Certain Circumstances; Regulating Procedure, Evidence, and Damages in Certain Court Actions Involving such Transactions, Contracts or Documents; to Make Uniform the Law with Respect Thereto; and Repealing Inconsistent Legislation.

Article 1. General Provisions.

Part 1. Short Title, Construction, Application, and Subject Matter of the Act.

Section 1-101. Short Title.

This Act shall be known and may be cited as Uniform Commercial Code.

Section 1-102. Purposes; Rules of Construction; Variation by Agreement.

(1) This Act shall be liberally construed and applied to promote its underlying purposes and policies.

(2) Underlying purposes and policies of this Act are:

(a) to simplify, clarify, and modernize the law governing commercial transactions;

(b) to permit the continued expansion of commercial practices through custom, usage and agreement of the parties;

(c) to make uniform the law among the various jurisdictions.

(3) The effect of provisions of this Act may be varied by agreement, except as otherwise provided in this Act and except that the obligations of good faith, diligence, reasonableness and care prescribed by this Act may not be disclaimed by agreement but the parties may by agreement determine the standards by which the performance of such obligations is to be measured if such standards are not manifestly unreasonable.

Authors' note: The texts of some sections have been omitted.

(4) The presence in certain provisions of this Act of the word "unless otherwise agreed" or words of similar import does not imply that the effect of other provisions may not be varied by agreement under subsection (3).

(5) In this Act unless the context otherwise requires

(a) words in the singular number include the plural, and in the plural include the singular;

(b) indicates words of the masculine gender incude the feminine and the neuter, and when the sense so indicates of the neuter gender may refer to any gender.

Section 1-103. Supplementary General Principles of Law Applicable.

Unless displaced by the particular provisions of this Act, the principles of law and equity, including the law merchant and the law relative to capacity to contract, principal and agent, estoppel, fraud, misrepresentation, duress, coercion, mistake, bankruptcy, or other validating or invalidating cause shall supplement its provision.

Section 1-104. Construction Against Implicit Repeal.

[Text omitted]

Section 1-105. Territorial Application of the Act; Parties' Power to Choose Applicable Law.

[Text omitted]

Section 1-106. Remedies to Be Liberally Administered.

[Text omitted]

Section 1-107. Waiver or Renunciation of Claim or Right After Breach.

Any claim or right arising out of an alleged breach can be discharged in whole or in part without consideration by a written waiver or renunciation signed and delivered by the aggrieved party.

Section 1-108. Severability.

[Text omitted]

Section 1-109. Section Captions.

[Text omitted]

Part 2. General Definitions and Principles of Interpretation.

Section 1-201. General Definitions.

Subject to additional definitions contained in the subsequent Articles of this Act which are applicable to specific Articles or Parts thereof, and unless the context otherwise requires, in this Act:

(1) "Action" in the sense of a judicial proceeding includes recoupment, counterclaim, set off, suit in equity and any other proceedings in which rights are determined.

(2) "Aggrieved party" means a party entitled to resort to a remedy.

(3) "Agreement" means the bargain of the parties in fact as found in their language or by implication from other circumstances including course of dealing or usage of trade or course of performance as provided in this Act (Sections 1-205 and 2-208). Whether an agreement has legal consequences is determined by the provisions of this Act, if applicable; otherwise by the law of contracts (Section 1-103). (Compare "Contract.")

(4) "Bank" means any person engaged in the business of banking.

(5) "Bearer" means the person in possession of an instrument, document of title, or certificated security payable to bearer or indorsed in blank.

(6) "Bill of lading" means a document evidencing the receipt of goods for shipment issued by a person engaged in the business of transporting or forwarding goods, and includes an airbill. "Airbill" means a document serving for air transportation as a bill of lading does for marine or rail transportation, and includes an air consignment note or air waybill.

(7) "Branch" includes a separately incorporated foreign branch of a bank.

(8) "Burden of establishing" a fact means the burden of persuading the triers of fact that the existence of the fact is more probable than its non existence.

(9) "Buyer in ordinary course of business" means a person who in good faith and without knowledge that the sale to him is in violation of the ownership rights or security interest of a third party in the goods buys in ordinary course from a person in the business of selling goods of that kind but does not include a pawnbroker. All persons who sell minerals or the like (including oil and gas) at wellhead or minehead shall be deemed to be persons in the business of selling goods of that kind. "Buying" may be for cash or by exchange of other property or on secured or unsecured credit and includes receiving goods or documents of title under a pre-existing contract for sale but does not include a transfer in bulk or as security for or in total or partial satisfaction of a money debt.

(10) "Conspicuous": A term or clause is conspicuous when it is so written that a reasonable person against whom it is to operate ought to have noticed it. A printed heading in capitals (as: NON-NEGOTIABLE BILL OF LADING) is conspicuous. Language in the body of a form is "conspicuous" if it is in larger or other contrasting type or color. But in a telegram any stated term is "conspicuous." Whether a term or clause is "conspicuous" or not is for decision by the court.

(11) "Contract" means the total legal obligation which results from the parties' agreement as affected by this Act and any other applicable rules of law. (Compare "Agreement.")

(12) "Creditor" includes a general creditor, a secured creditor, a lien creditor and any representative of creditors, including an assignee for the benefit of creditors, a trustee in bankruptcy, a receiver in equity and an executor or administrator of an insolvent debtor's or assignor's estate.

(13) "Defendant" includes a person in the position of defendant in a cross-action or counterclaim.

(14) "Delivery" with respect to instruments, documents of title, chattel paper, or certificated securities means voluntary transfer of possession.

(15) "Document of title" includes bill of lading, dock warrant, dock receipt, warehouse receipt or order for the delivery of goods, and also any other document which in the regular course of business or financing is treated as adequately evidencing that the person in possession of it is entitled to receive, hold and dispose of the document and the goods it covers. To be a document of title a document must purport to be issued by or addressed to a bailee and purport to cover goods in the bailee's possession which are either identified or are fungible portions of an identified mass.

(16) "Fault" means wrongful act, omission or breach.

(17) "Fungible" with respect to goods or securities means goods or securities of which any unit is, by nature or usage of trade, the equivalent of any other like unit. Goods which are not fungible shall be deemed fungible for the purposes of this Act to the extent that under a particular agreement or document unlike units are treated as equivalents.

(18) "Genuine" means free of forgery or counterfeiting.

(19) "Good faith" means honesty in fact in the conduct or transaction concerned.

(20) "Holder," with respect to a negotiable instrument, means the person in possession if the instrument is payable to bearer or, in the case of an instrument payable to an identified person, if the identified person is in possession. "Holder" with respect to a document of title means the person in possession if the goods are deliverable to bearer or to the order of the person in possession.

(21) To "honor" is to pay or to accept and pay, or where a credit so engages to purchase or discount a draft complying with the terms of the credit.

(22) "Insolvency proceedings" includes any assignment for the benefit of creditors or other proceedings intended to liquidate or rehabilitate the estate of the person involved.

(23) A person is "insolvent" who either has ceased to pay his debts in the ordinary course of business or cannot pay his debts as they become due or is insolvent within the meaning of the federal bankruptcy law.

(24) "Money" means a medium of exchange authorized or adopted by a domestic or foreign government and includes a monetary unit of account established by an intergovernmental organization or by agreement between two or more nations.

(25) A person has "notice" of a fact when

(a) he has actual knowledge of it; or

(b) he has received a notice or notification of it; or

(c) from all the facts and circumstances known to him at the time in question he has reason to know that it exists.
A person "knows" or has "knowledge" of a fact when he has actual knowledge of it. "Discover" or "learn" or a word or phrase of similar import refers to knowledge rather than to reason to know. The time and circumstances under which a notice or notification may cease to be effective are not determined by this Act.

(26) A person "notifies" or "gives" a notice or notification to another by taking such steps as may be reasonably required to inform the other in ordinary course whether or not such other actually comes to know of it. A person "receives" a notice or notification when

(a) it comes to his attention; or

(b) it is duly delivered at the place of business through which the contract was made or at any other place held out by him as the place for receipt of such communications.

(27) Notice, knowledge or a notice or notification received by an organization is effective for a particular transaction from the time when it is brought to the attention of the individual conducting that transaction, and in any event from the time when it would have been brought to his attention if the organization had exercised due diligence. An organization exercises due diligence if it maintains reasonable routines for communicating significant information to the person conducting the transaction and there is reasonable compliance with the routines. Due diligence does not require an individual acting for the organization to communicate information unless such communication is part of his regular duties or unless he has reason to know of the transaction and that the transaction would be materially affected by the information.

(28) "Organization" includes a corporation, government or governmental subdivision or agency, business trust, estate, trust, partnership or association, two or more persons having a joint or common interest, or any other legal or commercial entity.

(29) "Party," as distinct from "third party," means a person who has engaged in a transaction or made an agreement within this Act.

(30) "Person" includes an individual or an organization (See Section 1-102).

(31) "Presumption" or "presumed" means that the trier of fact must find the existence of the fact presumed unless and until evidence is introduced which would support a finding of its nonexistence.

(32) "Purchase" includes taking by sale, discount, negotiation, mortgage, pledge, lien, issue or re issue, gift or any other voluntary transaction creating an interest in property.

(33) "Purchaser" means a person who takes by purchase.

(34) "Remedy" means any remedial right to which an aggrieved party is entitled with or without resort to a tribunal.

(35) "Representative" includes an agent, an officer of a corporation or association, and a trustee, executor or administrator of an estate, or any other person empowered to act for another.

(36) "Rights" includes remedies.

(37) "Security interest" means an interest in personal property or fixtures which secures payment or performance of an obligation. The retention or reservation of title by a seller of goods notwithstanding shipment or delivery to the buyer (Section 2-401) is limited in effect to a reservation of a "security interest." The term also includes any interest of a buyer of accounts or chattel paper which is subject to Article 9. The special property interest of a buyer of goods on identification of those goods to a contract for sale under Section 2-401 is not a "security interest" but a buyer may also acquire a "security interest" by complying with Article 9. Unless a lease or consignment is intended as security, reservation of title thereunder is not a "security interest" but a consignment in any event is subject to the provisions on consignment sales (Section 2-326).

Whether a transaction creates a lease or security interest is determined by the facts of each case; however, a transaction creates a security interest if the consideration the lessee is to pay the lessor for the right to possession and use of the goods is an obligation for the term of the lease not subject to termination by the lessee, and

(a) the original term of the lease is equal to or greater than the remaining economic life of the goods,

(b) the lessee is bound to renew the lease for the remaining economic life of the goods or is bound to become the owner of the goods,

(c) the lessee has an option to renew the lease for the remaining economic life of the goods for no additional consideration or nominal additional consideration upon compliance with the lease agreement, or

(d) the lessee has an option to become the owner of the goods for no additional consideration or nominal additional consideration upon compliance with the lease agreement.

A transaction does not create a security interest merely because it provides that

(a) the present value of the consideration the lessee is obligated to pay the lessor for the right to possession and use of the goods is substantially equal to or is greater than the fair market value of the goods at the time the lease is entered into,

(b) the lessee assumes risk of loss of the goods, or agrees to pay taxes, insurance, filing, recording, or registration fees, or service or maintenance costs with respect to the goods,

(c) the lessee has an option to renew the lease or to become the owner of the goods,

(d) the lessee has an option to renew the lease for a fixed rent that is equal to or greater than the reasonably predictable fair market rent for the use of the goods for the term of the renewal at the time the option is to be performed, or

(e) the lessee has an option to become the owner of the goods for a fixed price that is equal to or greater than the reasonably predictable fair market value of the goods at the time the option is to be performed.

For purposes of this subsection (37):

(x) Additional consideration is not nominal if (i) when the option to renew the lease is granted to the lessee the rent is stated to be the fair market rent for the use of the goods for the term of the renewal determined at the time the option is to be performed, or (ii) when the option to become the owner of the goods is granted to the lessee the price is stated to be the fair market value of the goods determined at the time the option is to be performed. Additional consideration is nominal if it is less than the lessee's reasonably predictable cost of performing under the lease agreement if the option is not exercised;

(y) "Reasonably predictable" and "remaining economic life of the goods" are to be determined with reference to the facts and circumstances at the time the transaction is entered into; and

(z) "Present value" means the amount as of a date certain of one or more sums payable in the future, discounted to the date certain. The discount is determined by the interest rate specified by the parties if the rate is not manifestly unreasonable at the time the transaction is entered into; otherwise, the discount is determined by a commercially reasonable rate that takes into account the facts and circumstances of each case at the time the transaction was entered into.

(38) "Send" in connection with any writing or notice means to deposit in the mail or deliver for transmission by any other usual means of communication with postage or cost of transmission provided for and properly addressed and in the case of an instrument to an address specified thereon or otherwise agreed, or if there be none to any address reasonable under the circumstances. The receipt of any writing or notice within the time at which it would have arrived if properly sent has the effect of a proper sending.

(39) "Signed" includes any symbol executed or adopted by a party with present intention to authenticate a writing.

(40) "Surety" includes guarantor.

(41) "Telegram" includes a message transmitted by radio, teletype, cable, any mechanical method of transmission, or the like.

(42) "Term" means that portion of an agreement which relates to a particular matter.

(43) "Unauthorized" signature or indorsement means one made without actual, implied or apparent authority and includes a forgery.

(44) "Value." Except as otherwise provided with respect to negotiable instruments and bank collections (Sections 3-303, 4-208 and 4-209) a person gives "value" for rights if he acquires them

(a) in return for a binding commitment to extend credit or for the extension of immediately available credit whether or not drawn upon and whether or not a chargeback is provided for in the event of difficulties in collection; or

(b) as security for or in total or partial satisfaction of a pre-existing claim; or

(c) by accepting delivery pursuant to a pre-existing contract purchase; or

(d) generally, in return for any consideration sufficient to support a simple contract.

(45) "Warehouse receipt" means a receipt issued by a person engaged in the business of storing goods for hire.

(46) "Written" or "writing" includes printing, typewriting or any other intentional reduction to tangible form.

Section 1-202. Prima Facie Evidence by Third Party Documents.

[Text omitted]

Section 1-203. Obligation of Good Faith.

Every contract or duty within this Act imposes an obligation of good faith in its performance or enforcement.

Section 1-204. Time; Reasonable Time; "Seasonably."

(1) Whenever this Act requires any action to be taken within a reasonable time, any time which is not manifestly unreasonable may be fixed by agreement.

(2) What is a reasonable time for taking any action depends on the nature, purpose and circumstance of such action.

(3) An action is taken "seasonably" when it is taken at or within the time agreed or if no time is agreed at or within a reasonable time.

Section 1-205. Course of Dealing and Usage of Trade.

(1) A course of dealing is a sequence of previous conduct between the parties to a particular transaction which is fairly to be regarded as establishing a common basis of understanding for interpreting their expressions and other conduct.

(2) A usage of trade is any practice or method of dealing having such regularity of observance in a place, vocation or trade as to justify an expectation that it will be observed with respect to the transaction in question. The existence and scope of such a usage are to be proved as facts. If it is established that such a usage is embodied in a written trade code or similar writing the interpretation of the writing is for the court.

(3) A course of dealing between parties and any usage of trade in the vocation or trade in which they are engaged or of which they are or should be aware give particular meaning to and supplement or qualify terms of an agreement.

(4) The express terms of an agreement and an applicable course of dealing or usage of trade shall be construed wherever reasonable as consistent with each other; but when such construction is unreasonable express terms control both course of dealing and usage of trade and course of dealing controls usage of trade.

(5) An applicable usage of trade in the place where any part of performance is to occur shall be used in interpreting the agreement as to that part of the performance.

(6) Evidence of a relevant usage of trade offered by one party is not admissible unless and until he has given the other party such notice as the court finds sufficient to prevent unfair surprise to the latter.

Section 1-206. Statute of Frauds for Kinds of Personal Property Not Otherwise Covered.

Except in the cases described in subsection

(1) Subsection (2) of this section a contract for the sale of personal property is not enforceable by way of action or defense beyond five thousand dollars in amount or value of remedy unless there is some writing which indicates that a contract for sale has been made between the parties at a defined or stated price, reasonably identifies the subject matter, and is signed by the party against whom enforcement is sought or by his authorized agent.

(2) Subsection (1) of this section does not apply to contracts for the sale of goods (Section 2-201) nor of securities (Section 8-319) nor to security agreements (Section 9-203).

Section 1-207. Performance or Acceptance Under Reservation of Rights.

A party who with explicit reservation of rights performs or promises performance or assents to performance in a manner demanded or offered by the other party does not thereby prejudice the rights reserved. Such words as "without prejudice," "under protest" or the like are sufficient.

Section 1-208. Option to Accelerate at Will.

A term providing that one party or his successor in interest may accelerate payment or performance or require collateral or additional collaterral "at will" or "when he deems himself insecure" or in words of similar import shall be construed to mean that he shall have power to do so only if he is good faith believes that the prospect of payment or performance is impaired. The burden of establishing lack of good faith is on the party against whom the power had been exercised.

Section 1-209. Subordinated Obligations.

[Text omitted]

Article 2. Sales.

Part 1. Short Title, General Construction and Subject Matter.

Section 2-101. Short Title.

This Article shall be known and may be cited as Uniform Commercial Code—Sales.

Section 2-102. Scope; Certain Security and Other Transactions Excluded From This Article.

Unless the context otherwise requires, this Article applies to transactions in goods; it does not apply to any transaction which although in the form of an unconditional contract to sell or present sale is intended to operate only as a security transaction nor does this Article impair or repeal any statute regulating sales to consumers, farmers or other specified classes of buyers.

Section 2-103. Definitions and Index of Definitions.

(1) In this Article unless the context otherwise requires

(a) "Buyer" means a person who buys or contracts to buy goods.

(b) "Good faith" in the case of a merchant means honesty in fact and the observance of reasonable commercial standards of fair dealing in the trade.

(c) "Receipt" of goods means taking physical possession of them.

(d) "Seller" means a person who sells or contracts to sell goods.

(2) Other definitions applying to this Article or to specific Parts thereof, and the sections in which they appear are:

"Acceptance," Section 2-606.

"Banker's credit," Section 2-325.

"Between merchants," Section 2-104.

"Cancellation," Section 2-106(4).

"Commercial unit," Section 2-105.

"Confirmed credit," Section 2-325.

"Conforming to contract," Section 2-106.

"Contract for sale," Section 2-106.

"Cover," Section 2-712.

"Entrusting," Section 2-403.

"Financing agency," Section 2-104.

"Future goods," Section 2-105.

"Goods," Section 2-105.

"Identification," Section 2-501.
"Installment contract," Section 2-612.
"Letter of Credit," Section 2-325.
"Lot," Section 2-105.
"Merchant," Section 2-104.
"Overseas," Section 2-323.
"Person in position of seller," Section 2-707.
"Present sale," Section 2-106.
"Sale," Section 2-106.
"Sale on approval," Section 2-326.
"Sale or return," Section 2-326.
"Termination," Section 2-106.

(3) The following definitions in other Articles apply to this Article:

"Check," Section 3-104.
"Consignee," Section 7-102.
"Consignor," Section 7-102.
"Consumer goods," Section 9-109.
"Dishonor," Section 3-507.
"Draft," Section 3-104.

(4) In addition Article I contains general definitions and principles of construction and interpretation applicable throughout this Article.

Section 2-104. Definitions: "Merchant;" "Between Merchants;" "Financing Agency."

(1) "Merchant" means a person who deals in goods of the kind or otherwise by his occupation holds himself out as having knowledge or skill peculiar to the practices or goods involved in the transaction or to whom such knowledge or skill may be attributed by his employment of an agent or broker or other intermediary who by his occupation holds himself out as having such knowledge or skill.

(2) "Financing agency" means a bank, finance company or other person who in the ordinary course of business makes advances against goods or documents of title or who by arrangement with either the seller or the buyer intervenes in ordinary course to make or collect payment due or claimed under the contract for sale, as by purchasing or paying the seller's draft or making advances against it or by merely taking it for collection whether or not documents of title accompany the draft. "Financing agency" includes also a bank or other person who similarly intervenes between persons who are in the position of seller and buyer in respect to the goods (Section 2-707).

(3) "Between merchants" means in any transaction with respect to which both parties are chargeable with the knowledge or skill of merchants.

Section 2-105. Definitions: Transferability; "Goods;" "Future" Goods; "Lot;" "Commercial Unit."

(1) "Goods" means all things (including specially manufactured goods) which are movable at the time of identification to the contract for sale other than the money in which the price is to be paid, investment securities (Article 8) and things in action. "Goods" also includes the unborn young of animals and growing crops and other identified things attached to realty as described in the section on goods to be severed from realty (Section 2-107).

(2) Goods must be both existing and identified before any interest in them can pass. Goods which are not both existing and identified are "future" goods. A purported present sale of future goods or of any interest therein operates as a contract to sell.

(3) There may be a sale of a part interest in existing identified goods.

(4) An undivided share in an identified bulk of fungible goods is sufficiently identified to be sold although the quantity of the bulk is not determined. Any agreed proportion of such a bulk or any quantity thereof agreed upon by number, weight or other measure may to the extent of the seller's interest in the bulk be sold to the buyer who then becomes an owner in common.

(5) "Lot" means a parcel or a single article which is the subject matter of a separate sale or delivery, whether or not it is sufficient to perform the contract.

(6) "Commercial unit" means such a unit of goods as by commercial usage is a single whole for purposes of sale and division of which materially impairs its character or value on the market or in use. A commercial unit may be a single article (as a machine) or a set of articles (as a suite of furniture or an assortment of sizes) or a quantity (as a bale, gross, or carload) or any other unit treated in use or in the relevant market as a single whole.

Section 2-106. Definitions: "Contract;" "Agreement;" "Contract for Sale;" "Sale;" "Present Sale;" "Conforming to Contract;" "Termination;" "Cancellation."

(1) In this Article unless the context otherwise requires "contract" and "agreement" are limited to those relating to the present or future sale of goods. "Contract for sale" includes both a present sale of goods and a contract to sell goods at a future time. A "sale" consists in the passing of title from the seller to the buyer for a price (Section 2-401). A "present sale" means a sale which is accomplished by the making of the contract.

(2) Goods or conduct including any part of a performance are "conforming" or conform to the contract when they are in accordance with the obligations under the contract.

(3) "Termination" occurs when either party pursuant to a power created by agreement or law puts an end to the contract otherwise than for its breach. On "termination" all obligations which are still executory on both sides are discharged but any right based on prior breach or performance survives.

(4) "Cancellation" occurs when either party puts an end to the contract for breach by the other and its effect is the same as that of "termination" except that the cancelling party also retains any remedy for breach of the whole contract or any unperformed balance.

Section 2-107. Goods to Be Severed From Realty: Recording.

(1) A contract for the sale of minerals or the like (including oil and gas) or a structure or its materials to be removed from realty is a contract for the sale of goods within this Article if they are to be severed by the seller but until severance a purported present sale thereof which is not effective as a transfer of an interest in land is effective only as a contract to sell.

(2) A contract for the sale apart from the land of growing crops or other things attached to realty and capable of severance without material harm thereto but not described in subsection (1) or of timber to be cut is a contract for the sale of goods within this Article whether the subject matter is to be severed by the buyer or by the seller even though it forms part of the realty at the time of contracting, and the parties can by identification effect a present sale before severance.

(3) The provisions of this section are subject to any third party rights provided by the law relating to realty records, and the contract for sale may be executed and recorded as a document transferring an interest in land and shall then constitute notice to third parties of the buyer's rights under the contract for sale.

Part 2. Form, Formation and Readjustment of Contract.

Section 2-201. Formal Requirements; Statute of Frauds.

(1) Except as otherwise provided in this section a contract for the sale of goods for the price of $500 or more is not enforceable by way of action or defense unless

there is some writing sufficient to indicate that a contract for sale has been made between the parties and signed by the party against whom enforcement is sought or by his authorized agent or broker. A writing is not insufficient because it omits or incorrectly states a term agreed upon but the contract is not enforceable under this paragraph beyond the quantity of goods shown in such writing.

(2) Between merchants if within a reasonable time a writing in confirmation of the contract and sufficient against the sender is received and the party receiving it has reason to know its contents, it satisfies the requirements of subsection (1) against such party unless written notice of objection to its contents is given within 10 days after it is received.

(3) A contract which does not satisfy the requirements of subsection (1) but which is valid in other respects is enforceable

(a) if the goods are to be specially manufactured for the buyer and are not suitable for sale to others in the ordinary course of the seller's business and the seller, before notice of repudiation is received and under circumstances which reasonably indicate that the goods are for the buyer, has made either a substantial beginning of their manufacture or commitments for their procurement; or

(b) if the party against whom enforcement is sought admits in his pleading, testimony or otherwise in court that a contract for sale was made, but the contract is not enforceable under this provision beyond the quantity of goods admitted; or

(c) with respect to goods for which payment has been made and accepted or which have been received and accepted (Section 2-606).

Section 2-202. Final Written Expression: Parol or Extrinsic Evidence

Terms with respect to which the confirmatory memoranda of the parties agree or which are otherwise set forth in a writing intended by the parties as a final expression of their agreement with respect to such terms as are included therein may not be contradicted by evidence of any prior agreement or of a contemporaneous oral agreement but may be explained or supplemented

(a) by course of dealing or usage of trade (Section 1-205) or by course of performance (Section 2-208); and

(b) by evidence of consistent additional terms unless the court finds the writing to have been intended also as a complete and exclusive statement of the terms of the agreement.

Section 2-203. Seals Inoperative.

The affixing of a seal to a writing evidencing a contract for sale or an offer to buy or sell goods does not constitute the writing a sealed instrument and the law with respect to sealed instruments does not apply to such a contract or offer.

Section 2-204. Formation in General.

(1) A contract for sale of goods may be made in any manner sufficient to show agreement, including conduct by both parties which recognizes the existence of such a contract.

(2) An agreement sufficient to constitute a contract for sale may be found even though the moment of its making is undetermined.

(3) Even though one or more terms are left open a contract for sale does not fail for indefiniteness if the parties have intended to make a contract and there is a reasonably certain basis for giving an appropriate remedy.

Section 2-205. Firm Offers.

An offer by a merchant to buy or sell goods in a signed writing which by its terms give assurance that it will be held open is not revocable, for lack of consideration, during the time stated or if no time is stated for a reasonable time, but in no event may such period of irrevocability exceed three months; but any such term of assurance on a form supplied by the offeree must be separately signed by the offeror.

Section 2-206. Offer and Acceptance in Formation of Contract.

(1) Unless otherwise unambiguously indicated by the language or circumstances

(a) an offer to make a contract shall be construed as inviting acceptance in any manner and by any medium reasonable in the circumstances;

(b) an order or other offer to buy goods for prompt or current shipment shall be construed as inviting acceptance either by a prompt promise to ship or by the prompt or current shipment of conforming or nonconforming goods, but such a shipment of nonconforming goods does not constitute an acceptance if the seller seasonably notifies the buyer that the shipment is offered only as an accommodation to the buyer.

(2) Where the beginning of a requested performance is a reasonable mode of acceptance an offeror who is not notified of acceptance within a reasonable time may treat the offer as having lapsed before acceptance.

Section 2-207. Additional Terms in Acceptance or Confirmation.

(1) A definite and seasonable expression of acceptance or a written confirmation which is sent within a reasonable time operates as an acceptance even though it states terms additional to or different from those offered or agreed upon, unless acceptance is expressly made conditional on assent to the additional or different terms.

(2) The additional terms are to be construed as proposals for addition to the contract. Between merchants such terms become part of the contract unless:

(a) the offer expressly limits acceptance to the terms of the offer;

(b) they materially alter it; or

(c) notification of objection to them has already been given or is given within a reasonable time after notice of them is received.

(3) Conduct by both parties which recognizes the existence of a contract is sufficient to establish a contract for sale although the writings of the parties do not otherwise establish a contract. In such case the terms of the particular contract consist of those terms on which the writings of the parties agree, together with any supplementary terms incorporated under any other provisions of this Act.

Section 2-208. Course of Performance or Practical Construction.

(1) Where the contract for sale involves repeated occasions for performance by either party with knowledge of the nature of the performance and opportunity for objection to it by the other, any course of performance accepted or acquiesced in without objection shall be relevant to determine the meaning of the agreement.

(2) The express terms of the agreement and any such course of performance, as well as any course of dealing and usage of trade, shall be construed whenever reasonable as consistent with each other, but when such construction is unreasonable, express terms shall control course of performance and course of performance shall control both course of dealing and usage of trade (Section 1-205).

(3) Subject to the provisions of the next section on modification and waiver, such course of performance shall be relevant to show a waiver or modification of any term inconsistent with such course of performance.

Section 2-209. Modification, Rescission and Waiver.

(1) An agreement modifying a contract within this Article needs no consideration to be binding.

(2) A signed agreement which excludes modification or rescission except by a signed writing cannot be otherwise modified or rescinded, but except as between merchants such a requirement on a form supplied by the merchant must be separately signed by the other party.

(3) The requirements of the statute of frauds section of this Article (Section 2-201) must be satisfied if the contract as modified is within its provisions.

(4) Although an attempt at modification or rescission does not satisfy the requirements of subsection (2) or (3) it can operate as a waiver.

(5) A party who has made a waiver affecting an executory portion of the contract may retract the waiver by reasonable notification received by the other party that strict performance will be required of any term waived, unless the retraction would be unjust in view of a material change of position in reliance on the waiver.

Section 2-210. Delegation of Performance; Assignment of Rights.

(1) A party may perform his duty through a delegate unless otherwise agreed or unless the other party has a substantial interest in having his original promisor perform or control the acts required by the contract. No delegation of performance relieves the party delegating of any duty to perform or any liability for breach.

(2) Unless otherwise agreed all rights of either seller or buyer can be assigned except where the assignment would materially change the duty of the other party, or increase materially the burden or risk imposed on him by his contract, or impair materially his chance of obtaining return performance. A right to damages for breach of the whole contract or a right arising out of the assignor's due performance of his entire obligation can be assigned despite agreement otherwise.

(3) Unless the circumstances indicate the contrary a prohibition of assignment of "the contract" is to be construed as barring only the delegation to the assignee of the assignor's performance.

(4) An assignment of "the contract" or of "all my rights under the contract" or an assignment in similar general terms is an assignment of rights and unless the language or the circumstances (as in an assignment for security) indicate the contrary, it is a delegation of performance of the duties of the assignor and its acceptance by the assignee constitutes a promise by him to perform those duties. This promise is enforceable by either the assignor or the other party to the original contract.

(5) The other party may treat any assignment which delegates performance as creating reasonable grounds for insecurity and may without prejudice to his rights against the assignor demand assurances from the assignee (Section 2-609).

Part 3. General Obligations and Construction of Contract.

Section 2-301. General Obligations of Parties.

The obligation of the seller is to transfer and deliver and that of the buyer is to accept and pay in accordance with the contract.

Section 2-302. Unconscionable Contract or Clause.

(1) If the court as a matter of law finds the contract or any clause of the contract to have been unconscionable at the time it was made the court may refuse to enforce the contract, or it may enforce the remainder of the contract without the unconscionable clause, or it may so limit the application of any unconscionable clause as to avoid any unconscionable result.

(2) When it is claimed or appears to the court that the contract or any clause thereof may be unconscionable the parties shall be afforded a reasonable opportunity to present evidence as to its commercial setting, purpose and effect to aid the court in making the determination.

Section 2-303. Allocation or Division of Risks.

Where this Article allocates a risk or a burden as between the parties "unless otherwise agreed," the agreement may not only shift the allocation but may also divide the risk or burden.

Section 2-304. Price Payable in Money, Goods, Realty, or Otherwise.

(1) The price can be made payable in money or otherwise. If it is payable in whole or in part in goods each party is a seller of the goods which he is to transfer.

(2) Even though all or part of the price is payable in an interest in realty the transfer of the goods and the seller's obligations with reference to them are subject to this Article, but not the transfer of the interest in realty or the transferor's obligations in connection therewith.

Section 2-305. Open Price Term.

(1) The parties if they so intend can conclude a contract for sale even though the price is not settled. In such a case the price is a reasonable price at the time for delivery if

(a) nothing is said as to price; or

(b) the price is left to be agreed by the parties and they fail to agree; or

(c) the price is to be fixed in terms of some agreed market or other standard as set or recorded by a third person or agency and it is not so set or recorded.

(2) A price to be fixed by the seller or by the buyer means a price for him to fix in good faith.

(3) When a price left to be fixed otherwise than by agreement of the parties fails to be fixed through fault of one party the other may at his option treat the contract as cancelled or himself fix a reasonable price.

(4) Where, however, the parties intend not to be bound unless the price be fixed or agreed and it is not fixed or agreed there is no contract. In such a case the buyer must return any goods already received or if unable so to do must pay their reasonable value at the time of delivery and the seller must return any portion of the price paid on account.

Section 2-306. Output, Requirements and Exclusive Dealings.

(1) A term which measures the quantity by the output of the seller or the requirements of the buyer means such actual output or requirements as may occur in good faith, except that no quantity unreasonably disproportionate to any stated estimate or in the absence of a stated estimate to any normal or otherwise comparable prior output or requirements may be tendered or demanded.

(2) A lawful agreement by either the seller or the buyer for exclusive dealing in the kind of goods concerned imposes unless otherwise agreed an obligation by the seller to use best efforts to supply the goods and by the buyer to use best efforts to promote their sale.

Section 2-307. Delivery in Single Lot or Several Lots.

Unless otherwise agreed all goods called for by a contract for sale must be tendered in a single delivery and payment is due only on such tender but where the circumstances give either party the right to make or demand delivery in lots the price if it can be apportioned may be demanded for each lot.

Section 2-308. Absence of Specified Place for Delivery.

Unless otherwise agreed

(a) the place for delivery of goods is the seller's place of business or if he has none his residence; but

(b) in a contract for sale of identified goods which to the knowledge of the parties at the time of contracting are in some other place, that place is the place for their delivery; and

(c) documents of title may be delivered through customary banking channels.

Section 2-309. Absence of Specific Time Provisions; Notice of Termination.

(1) The time for shipment or delivery or any other action under a contract if not provided in this Article or agreed upon shall be a reasonable time.

(2) Where the contract provides for successive performances but is indefinite in duration it is valid for a reasonable time but unless otherwise agreed may be terminated at any time by either Party.

(3) Termination of a contract by one party except on the happening of an agreed event requires that reasonable notification be received by the other party and an agreement dispensing with notification is invalid if its operation would be unconscionable.

Section 2-310. Open Time for Payment or Running of Credit: Authority to Ship Under Reservation.

Unless otherwise agreed

(a) payment is due at the time and place at which the buyer is to receive the goods even though the place of shipment is the place of delivery; and

(b) if the seller is authorized to send the goods he may ship them under reservation, and may tender the documents of title, but the buyer may inspect the goods after their arrival before payment is due unless such inspection is inconsistent with the terms of the contract (Section 2-513); and

(c) if delivery is authorized and made by way of documents of title otherwise than by subsection (b) then payment is due at the time and place at which the buyer is to receive the documents regardless of where the goods are to be received; and

(d) where the seller is required or authorized to ship the goods on credit the credit period runs from the time of shipment but postdating the invoice or delaying its dispatch will correspondingly delay the starting of the credit period.

Section 2-311. Options and Cooperation Respecting Performance.

(1) An agreement for sale which is otherwise sufficiently definite (subsection (3) of Section 2-204) to be a contract is not made invalid by the fact that it leaves particulars of performance to be specified by one of the parties. Any such specification must be made in good faith and within limits set by commercial reasonableness.

(2) Unless otherwise agreed specifications relating to assortment of the goods are at the buyer's option and except as otherwise provided in subsections (1) (c) and (3) of Section 2-319 specifications or arrangements relating to shipment are at the seller's option.

(3) Where such specification would materially affect the other party's performance but is not seasonably made or where one party's cooperation is necessary to the agreed performance of the other but is not seasonably forthcoming, the other party in addition to all other remedies

  (a) is excused for any resulting delay in his own performance; and

  (b) may also either proceed to perform in any reasonable manner or after the time for a material part of his own performance treat the failure to specify or to cooperate as a breach by failure to deliver or accept the goods.

Section 2-312. Warranty of Title and Against Infringement; Buyer's Obligation Against Infringement.

(1) Subject to subsection (2) there is in a contract for sale a warranty by the seller that

(a) the title conveyed shall be good, and its transfer rightful; and

(b) the goods shall be delivered free from any security interest or other lien or encumbrance of which the buyer at the time of contracting has no knowledge.

(2) A warranty under subsection (1) will be excluded or modified only by specific language or by circumstances which give the buyer reason to know that the person selling does not claim title in himself or that he is purporting to sell only such right or title as he or a third person may have.

(3) Unless otherwise agreed a seller who is a merchant regularly dealing in goods of the kind warrants that the goods shall be delivered free of the rightful claim of any third person by way of infringement or the like but a buyer who furnishes specifications to the seller must hold the seller harmless against any such claim which arises out of compliance with the specifications.

Section 2-313. Express Warranties by Affirmation, Promise, Description, Sample.

(1) Express warranties by the seller are created as follows:

(a) Any affirmation of fact or promise made by the seller to the buyer which relates to the goods and becomes part of the basis of the bargain creates an express warranty that the goods shall conform to the affirmation or promise.

(b) Any description of the goods which is made part of the basis of the bargain creates an express warranty that the goods shall conform to the description.

(c) Any sample or model which is made part of the basis of the bargain creates an express warranty that the whole of the goods shall conform to the sample or model.

(2) It is not necessary to the creation of an express warranty that the seller use formal words such as "warrant" or "guarantee" or that he have a specific intention to make a warranty, but an affirmation merely of the value of the goods or a statement purporting to be merely the seller's opinion or commendation of the goods does not create a warranty.

Section 2-314. Implied Warranty: Merchantability; Usage of Trade.

(1) Unless excluded or modified (Section 2-316), a warranty that the goods shall be merchantable is implied in a contract for their sale if the seller is a merchant with respect to goods of that kind. Under this section the serving for value of food or drink to be consumed either on the premises or elsewhere is a sale.

(2) Goods to be merchantable must be at least such as

(a) pass without objection in the trade under the contract description; and

(b) in the case of fungible goods, are of fair, average quality within the description; and

(c) are fit for the ordinary purposes for which such goods are used; and

(d) run, within the variations permitted by the agreement, of even kind, quality and quantity within each unit and among all units involved; and

(e) are adequately contained, packaged, and labeled as the agreement may require; and

(f) conform to the promises or affirmations of fact made on the container or label if any.

(3) Unless excluded or modified (Section 2-316) other implied warranties may arise from course of dealing or usage of trade.

Section 2-315. Implied Warranty: Fitness for Particular Purpose.

Where the seller at the time of contracting has reason to know any particular purpose for which the goods are required and that the buyer is relying on the seller's skill or judgment to select or furnish suitable goods, there is unless excluded or modified under the next section an implied warranty that the goods shall be fit for such purpose.

Section 2-316. Exclusion or Modification of Warranties.

(1) Words or conduct relevant to the creation of an express warranty and words or conduct tending to negate or limit warranty shall be construed wherever reasonable as consistent with each other; but subject to the provisions of this Article on parol or extrinsic evidence (Section 2-202) negation or limitation is inoperative to the extent that such construction is unreasonable.

(2) Subject to subsection (3), to exclude or modify the implied warranty or merchantability or any part of it the language must mention merchantability and in case of a writing must be conspicuous, and to exclude or modify any implied warranty of fitness the exclusion must be by a writing and conspicuous. Language to exclude all implied warranties of fitness is sufficient if it states, for example, that "There are no warranties which extend beyond the description on the face hereof."

(3) Notwithstanding subsection (2)

  (a) unless the circumstances indicate otherwise, all implied warranties are excluded by expressions like "as is," "with all faults" or other language which in common understanding calls the buyer's attention to the exclusion of warranties and makes plain that there is no implied warranty; and

  (b) when the buyer before entering into the contract has examined the goods or the sample or model as fully as he desired or has refused to examine the goods there is no implied warranty with regard to defects which an examination ought in the circumstances to have revealed to him; and

  (c) implied warranty can also be excluded or modified by course of dealing or course of performance or usage of trade.

(4) Remedies for breach of warranty can be limited in accordance with the provisions of this Article on liquidation or limitation of damages and on contractual modification of remedy (Sections 2-718 and 2-719).

Section 2-317. Cumulation and Conflict of Warranties Express or Implied.

Warranties whether express or implied shall be construed as consistent with each other and as cumulative, but if such construction is unreasonable the intention of the parties shall determine which warranty is dominant. In ascertaining that intention the following rules apply:

(a) Exact or technical specifications displace an inconsistent sample or model or general language of description.

(b) A sample from an existing bulk displaces inconsistent general language of description.

(c) Express warranties displace inconsistent implied warranties other than an implied warranty of fitness for a particular purpose.

Section 2-318. Third Party Beneficiaries of Warranties Express or Implied.

Note: *If this Act is introduced in the Congress of the United States this section should be omitted. (States to select one alternative.)*

Alternative A A seller's warranty whether express or implied extends to any natural person who is in the family or household of his buyer or who is a guest in his home if it is reasonable to expect that such person may use, consume or be affected by the goods and who is injured in person by breach of the warranty. A seller may not exclude or limit the operation of this section.

Alternative B A seller's warranty whether express or implied extends to any natural person who may reasonably be expected to use, consume or be affected by the goods and who is injured in person by breach of the warranty. A seller may not exclude or limit the operation of this section.

Alternative C A seller's warranty whether express or implied extends to any person who may reasonably be expected to use, consume or be affected by the goods and who is injured by breach of the warranty. A seller may not exclude or limit the operation of this section with respect to injury to the person of an individual to whom the warranty extends.

Section 2-319. F.O.B. AND F.A.S. Terms.

(1) Unless otherwise agreed the term F.O.B. (which means "free on board") at a named place, even though used only in connection with the stated price, is a delivery term under which

(a) when the term is F.O.B. the place of shipment, the seller must at that place ship the goods in the manner provided in this Article (Section 2-504) and bear the expense and risk of putting them into the possession of the carrier; or

(b) when the term is F.O.B. the place of destination, the seller must at his own expense and risk transport the goods to that place and there tender delivery of them in the manner provided in this Article (Section 2-503);

(c) when under either (a) or (b) the term is also F.O.B. vessel, car or other vehicle, the seller must in addition at his own expense and risk load the goods on board. If the term is F.O.B. vessel the buyer must name the vessel and in an appropriate case the seller must comply with the provisions of this Article on the form of bill of lading (Section 2-323).

(2) Unless otherwise agreed the term F.A.S. vessel (which means "free alongside") at a named port, even though used only in connection with the stated price, is a delivery term under which the seller must

(a) at his own expense and risk deliver the goods alongside the vessel in the manner usual in that port or on a dock designated and provided by the buyer; and

(b) obtain and tender a receipt for the goods in exchange for which the carrier is under a duty to issue a bill of lading.

(3) Unless otherwise agreed in any case falling within subsection (1) (a) or (c) or subsection (2) the buyer must seasonably give any needed instructions for making delivery, including when the term is F.A.S. or F.O.B. the loading berth of the vessel and in an appropriate case its name and sailing date. The seller may treat the failure of needed instructions as a failure of cooperation under this Article (Section 2-311). He may also at his option move the goods in any reasonable manner preparatory to delivery or shipment.

(4) Under the term F.O.B. vessel or F.A.S. unless otherwise agreed the buyer must make payment against tender of the required documents and the seller may not tender nor the buyer demand delivery of the goods in substitution for the documents.

Section 2-320. C.I.F. AND C. & F. Terms.

(1) The term C.I.F. means that the price includes in a lump sum the cost of the goods and the insurance and freight to the named destination. The term C. & F. or C.F. means that the price so includes cost and freight to the named destination.

(2) Unless otherwise agreed and even though used only in connection with the stated price and destination, the term C.I.F. destination or its equivalent requires the seller at his own expense and risk to

(a) put the goods into the possession of a carrier at the port for shipment and obtain a negotiable bill or bills of lading covering the entire transportation to the named destination; and

(b) load the goods and obtain a receipt from the carrier (which may be contained in the bill of lading) showing that the freight has been paid or provided for; and

(c) obtain a policy or certificate of insurance, including any war risk insurance, of a kind and on terms then current at the port of shipment in the usual amount, in the currency of the contract, shown to cover the same goods covered by the bill of lading and providing for payment of loss to the order of the buyer or for the account of whom it may concern; but the seller may add to the price the amount of the premium for any such war risk insurance; and

(d) prepare an invoice of the goods and procure any other documents required to effect shipment or to comply with the contract; and

(e) forward and tender with commercial promptness all the documents in due form and with any indorsement necessary to perfect the buyer's rights.

(3) Unless otherwise agreed the term C. & F. or its equivalent has the same effect and imposes upon the seller the same obligations and risks as a C.I.F. term except the obligation as to insurance.

(4) Under the term C.I.F. or C. & F. unless otherwise agreed the buyer must make payment against tender of the required documents and the seller may not tender nor the buyer demand delivery of the goods in substitution for the documents.

Section 2-321. C.I.F. or C. & F.: "Net Landed Weights;" "Payment on Arrival;" Warranty of Condition on Arrival.

Under a contract containing a term C.I.F. or C. & F.

(1) Where the price is based on or is to be adjusted according to "net landed weights," "delivered weights," "out turn" quantity or quality or the like, unless otherwise agreed the seller must reasonably estimate the price. The payment due on tender of the documents called for by the contract is the amount so estimated, but after final adjustment of the price a settlement must be made with commercial promptness.

(2) An agreement described in subsection (1) or any warranty of quality or condition of the goods on arrival places upon the seller the risk of ordinary deterioration, shrinkage and the like in transportation but has no effect on the place or time of identification to the contract for sale or delivery or on the passing of the risk of loss.

(3) Unless otherwise agreed where the contract provides for payment on or after arrival of the goods the seller must before payment allow such preliminary inspection as is feasible; but if the goods are lost delivery of the documents and payment are due when the goods should have arrived.

Section 2-322. Delivery "Ex Ship."

(1) Unless otherwise agreed a term for delivery of goods "ex ship" (which means from the carrying vessel) or in equivalent language is not restricted to a particular ship and requires delivery from a ship which has reached a place at the named port of destination where goods of the kind are usually discharged.

(2) Under such a term unless otherwise agreed

(a) the seller must discharge all liens arising out of the carriage and furnish the buyer with a direction which puts the carrier under a duty to deliver the goods; and

(b) the risk of loss does not pass to the buyer until the goods leave the ship's tackle or are otherwise properly unloaded.

Section 2-323. Form of Bill of Lading Required in Overseas Shipment; "Overseas."

(1) Where the contract contemplates overseas shipment and contains a term C.I.F. or C. & F. or F.O.B. vessel, the seller unless otherwise agreed must obtain a negotiable bill of lading stating that the goods have been loaded on board or, in the case of a term C.I.F. or C. & F., received for shipment.

(2) Where in a case within subsection (1) a bill of lading has been issued in a set of parts, unless otherwise agreed if the documents are not to be sent from aboard the buyer may demand tender of the full set; otherwise only one part of the bill of lading need be tendered. Even if the agreement expressly requires a full set

(a) due tender of a single part is acceptable within the provisions of this Article on cure of improper delivery (subsection (1) of Section 2-508); and

(b) even though the full set is demanded, if the documents are sent from abroad the person tendering an incomplete set may nevertheless require payment upon furnishing an indemnity which the buyer in good faith deems adequate.

(3) A shipment by water or by air or a contract contemplating such shipment "overseas" insofar as by usage of trade or agreement it is subject to the commercial, financing or shipping practices characteristic of international deep water commerce.

Section 2-324. "No Arrival, No Sale" Term.

Under a term "no arrival, no sale" or terms of like meaning, unless otherwise agreed,

(a) the seller must properly ship conforming goods and if they arrive by any means he must tender them on arrival but he assumes no obligation that the goods will arrive unless he has caused the nonarrival; and

(b) where without fault of the seller the goods are in part lost or have so deteriorated as no longer to conform to the contract or arrive after the contract time, the buyer may proceed as if there had been casualty to identified goods (Section 2-613).

Section 2-325. "Letter of Credit" Term; "Confirmed Credit."

(1) Failure of the buyer seasonably to furnish an agreed letter of credit is a breach of the contract for sale.

(2) The delivery to seller of a proper letter of credit suspends the buyer's obligation to pay. If the letter of credit is dishonored, the seller may on seasonable notification to the buyer require payment directly from him.

(3) Unless otherwise agreed the term "letter of credit" or "banker's credit" in a contract for sale means an irrevocable credit issued by a financing agency of good repute and, where the shipment is overseas, of good international repute. The term "confirmed credit" means that the credit must also carry the direct obligation of such an agency which does business in the seller's financial market.

Section 2-326. Sale on Approval and Sale or Return; Consignment Sales and Rights of Creditors.

(1) Unless otherwise agreed, if delivered goods may be returned by the buyer even though they conform to the contract, the transaction is

(a) a "sale on approval" if the goods are delivered primarily for use, and

(b) a "sale or return" if the goods are delivered primarily for resale.

(2) Except as provided in subsection (3), goods held on approval are not subject to the claims of the buyer's creditors until acceptance; goods held on sale or return are subject to such claims while in the buyer's possession.

(3) Where goods are delivered to a person for sale and such person maintains a place of business at which he deals in goods of the kind involved, under a name other than the name of the person making delivery, then with respect to claims of creditors of the person conducting the business the goods are deemed to be on sale or return. The provisions of this subsection are applicable even though an agreement purports to reserve title to the person making delivery until payment or resale or uses such words as "on consignment" or "on memorandum." However, this subsection is not applicable if the person making delivery

(a) complies with an applicable law providing for a consignor's interest or the like to be evidenced by a sign, or

(b) establishes that the person conducting the business is generally known by his creditors to be substantially engaged in selling the goods of others, or

(c) complies with the filing provisions of the Article on Secured Transactions (Article 9).

(4) Any "or return" term of a contract for sale is to be treated as a separate contract for sale within the statute of frauds section of this Article (Section 2-201) and as contradicting the sale aspect of the contract within the provisions of this Article on parol or extrinsic evidence (Section 2-202).

Section 2-327. Special Incidents of Sale on Approval and Sale or Return.

(1) Under a sale on approval unless otherwise agreed

(a) although the goods are identified to the contract the risk of loss and the title do not pass to the buyer until acceptance; and

(b) use of the goods consistent with the purpose of trial is not acceptance but failure seasonably to notify the seller of election to return the goods is acceptance, and if the goods conform to the contract acceptance of any part is acceptance of the whole; and

(c) after due notification of election to return, the return is at the seller's risk and expense but a merchant buyer must follow any reasonable instructions.

(2) Under a sale or return unless otherwise agreed

(a) the option to return extends to the whole or any commercial unit of the goods while in substantially their original condition, but must be exercised seasonably; and

(b) the return is at the buyer's risk and expense.

Section 2-328. Sale by Auction.

(1) In a sale by auction if goods are put up in lots each lot is the subject of a separate sale.

(2) A sale by auction is complete when the auctioneer so announces by the fall of the hammer or in other customary manner. Where a bid is made while the hammer is falling in acceptance of a prior bid the auctioneer may in his discretion reopen the bidding or declare the goods sold under the bid on which the hammer was falling.

(3) Such a sale is with reserve unless the goods are in explicit terms put up without reserve. In an auction with reserve the auctioneer may withdraw the goods at any time until he announces completion of the sale. In an auction without reserve, after the auctioneer calls for bids on an article or lot, that article or lot cannot be withdrawn unless no bid is made within a reasonable time. In either case a bidder may retract his bid until the auctioneer's announcement of completion of sale, but a bidder's retraction does not revive any previous bid.

(4) If the auctioneer knowingly receives a bid on the seller's behalf or the seller makes or procures such a bid, and notice has not been given that liberty for such bidding is reserved, the buyer may at his option avoid the sale or take the goods at the price of the last good faith bid prior to the completion of the sale. This subsection shall not apply to any bid at a forced sale.

Part 4. Title, Creditors and Good Faith Purchasers.

Section 2-401. Passing of Title; Reservation for Security; Limited Application of This Section.

Each provision of this Article with regard to the rights, obligations and remedies of the seller, the buyer, purchasers or other third parties applies irrespective of title to the goods except where the provision refers to such title. Insofar as situations are not covered by the other provisions of this Article and matters concerning title become material the following rules apply:

(1) Title to goods cannot pass under a contract for sale prior to their identification to the contract (Section 2-501), and unless otherwise explicitly agreed the buyer acquires by their identification a special property as limited by this Act. Any retention or reservation by the seller of the title (property) in goods shipped or delivered to the buyer is limited in effect to a reservation of a security interest. Subject to these provisions and to the provisions of the Article on Secured Transactions (Article 9), title to goods passes from the seller to the buyer in any manner and on any conditions explicitly agreed on by the parties.

(2) Unless otherwise explicitly agreed title passes to the buyer at the time and place at which the seller completes his performance with reference to the physical delivery of the goods, despite any reservation of a security interest and even though a document of title is to be delivered at a different time or place; and in particular and despite any reservation of a security interest by the bill of lading

(a) if the contract requires or authorizes the seller to send the goods to the buyer but does not require him to deliver them at destination, title passes to the buyer at the time and place of shipment; but

(b) if the contract requires delivery at destination, title passes on tender there.

(3) Unless otherwise explicitly agreed where delivery is to be made without moving the goods.

(a) if the seller is to deliver a document of title, title passes at the time when and the place where he delivers such documents; or

(b) if the goods are at the time of contracting already identified and no documents are to be delivered, title passes at the time and place of contracting.

(4) A rejection or other refusal by the buyer to receive or retain the goods, whether or not justified, or a justified revocation of acceptance revests title to the goods in the seller. Such revesting occurs by operation of law and is not a "sale."

Section 2-402. Rights of Seller's Creditors Against Sold Goods.

(1) Except as provided in subsections (2) and (3), rights of unsecured creditors of the seller with respect to goods which have been identified to a contract for sale are subject to the buyer's rights to recover the goods under this Article (Sections 2-502 and 2-716).

(2) A creditor of the seller may treat a sale or an identification of goods to a contract for sale as void if as against him a retention of possession by the seller is fraudulent under any rule of law of the state where the goods are situated, except that retention of possession in good faith and current course of trade by a merchant seller for a commercially reasonable time after a sale or identification is not fraudulent.

(3) Nothing in this Article shall be deemed to impair the rights of creditors of the seller

(a) under the provision of the Article on Secured Transactions (Article 9); or

(b) where identification to the contract or delivery is made not in current course of trade but in satisfaction of or as security for a pre-existing claim for money, security or the like and is made under circumstances which under any rule of law of the state where the goods are situated would apart from this Article constitute the transaction a fraudulent transfer or voidable preference.

Section 2-403. Power to Transfer; Good Faith Purchase of Goods: "Entrusting."

(1) A purchaser of goods acquires all title which his transferor had or had power to transfer except that a purchaser of a limited interest acquires rights only to the extent of the interest purchased. A person with voidable title has power to transfer a good

title to a good faith purchaser for value. When goods have been delivered under a transaction of purchase the purchaser has such power even though

(a) the transferor was deceived as to the identity of the purchaser, or

(b) the delivery was in exchange for a check which is later dishonored, or

(c) it was agreed that the transaction was to be a "cash sale," or

(d) the delivery was procured through fraud punishable as larcenous under the criminal law.

(2) Any entrusting of possession of goods to a merchant who deals in goods of that kind gives him power to transfer all rights of the entruster to a buyer in ordinary course of business.

(3) "Entrusting" includes any delivery and any acquiescence in retention of possession regardless of any condition expressed between the parties to the delivery or acquiescence and regardless of whether the procurement of the entrusting or the possessor's disposition of the goods have been such as to be larcenous under the criminal law.

(4) The rights of other purchasers of goods and of lien creditors are governed by the Articles on Secured Transactions (Article 9), Bulk Transfers (Article 6) and Documents of Title (Article 7).

Part 5. Performance.

Section 2-501. Insurable Interest in Goods; Manner of Identification of Goods.

(1) The buyer obtains a special property and an insurable interest in goods by identification of existing goods as goods to which the contract refers even though the goods so identified are nonconforming and he has an option to return or reject them. Such identification can be made at any time and in any manner explicitly agreed to by the parties. In the absence of explicit agreement identification occurs

(a) when the contract is made if it is for the sale of goods already existing and identified;

(b) if the contract is for the sale of future goods other than those described in paragraph (c), when goods are shipped, marked or otherwise designated by the seller as goods to which the contract refers;

(c) when the crops are planted or otherwise become growing crops or the young are conceived if the contract is for the sale of unborn young to be born within twelve months after contracting or for the sale of crops to be harvested within twelve months or the next normal harvest season after contracting whichever is longer.

(2) The seller retains an insurable interest in goods so long as title to or any security interest in the goods remains in him and where the identification is by the seller alone he may until default or insolvency or notification to the buyer that the identification is final substitute other goods for those identified.

(3) Nothing in this section impairs any insurable interest recognized under any other statute or rule of law.

Section 2-502. Buyer's Right to Goods on Seller's Insolvency.

(1) Subject to subsection (2) and even though the goods have not been shipped a buyer who has paid a part or all of the price of goods in which he has a special property under the provisions of the immediately preceding section may on making and keeping good a tender of any unpaid portion of their price recover them from the seller if the seller becomes insolvent within ten days after receipt of the first installment on their price.

(2) If the identification creating his special property has been made by the buyer he acquires the right to recover the goods only if they conform to the contract for sale.

Section 2-503. Manner of Seller's Tender of Delivery.

(1) Tender of delivery requires that the seller put and hold conforming goods at the buyer's disposition and give the buyer any notification reasonably necessary to enable him to take delivery. The manner, time and place for tender are determined by the agreement and this Article, and in particular

(a) tender must be at a reasonable hour, and if it is of goods they must be kept available for the period reasonably necessary to enable the buyer to take possession; but

(b) unless otherwise agreed the buyer must furnish facilities reasonably suited to the receipt of the goods.

(2) Where the case is within the next section respecting shipment tender requires that the seller comply with its provisions.

(3) Where the seller is required to deliver at a particular destination tender requires that he comply with subsection (1) and also in any appropriate case tender documents as described in subsections (4) and (5) of this section.

(4) Where goods are in the possession of a bailee and are to be delivered without being moved

(a) tender requires that the seller either tender a negotiable document of title covering such goods or procure acknowledgement by the bailee of the buyer's right to possession of the goods; but

(b) tender to the buyer of a non-negotiable document of title or of a written direction to the bailee to deliver is sufficient tender unless the buyer seasonably objects, and receipt by the bailee of notification of the buyer's rights fixes those rights as against the bailee and all third persons; but risk of loss of the goods and of any failure by the bailee to honor the non-negotiable document of title or to obey the direction remains on the seller until the buyer has had a reasonable time to present the document or direction, and a refusal by the bailee to honor the document or to obey the direction defeats the tender.

(5) Where the contract requires the seller to deliver documents

(a) he must tender all such documents in correct form, except as provided in this Article with respect to bills of lading in a set (subsection (2) of Section 2-323); and

(b) tender through customary banking channels is sufficient and dishonor of a draft accompanying the documents constitutes nonacceptance or rejection.

Section 2-504. Shipment by Seller.

Where the seller is required or authorized to send the goods to the buyer and the contract does not require him to deliver them at a particular destination, then unless otherwise agreed he must

(a) put the goods in the possession of such a carrier and make such a contract for their transportation as may be reasonable having regard to the nature of the goods and other circumstances of the case; and

(b) obtain and promptly deliver or tender in due form any document necessary to enable the buyer to obtain possession of the goods or otherwise required by the agreement or by usage of trade; and

(c) promptly notify the buyer of the shipment.

Failure to notify the buyer under paragraph (c) or to make a proper contract under paragraph (a) is a ground for rejection only if material delay or loss ensues.

Section 2-505. Seller's Shipment Under Reservation.

(1) Where the seller has identified goods to the contract by or before shipment:

(a) his procurement of a negotiable bill of lading to his own order or otherwise reserves in him a security interest in the goods. His procurement of the bill to the order of a financing agency or of the buyer indicates in addition only the seller's expectation of transferring that interest to the person named.

(b) a non-negotiable bill of lading to himself or his nominee reserves possession of the goods as security but except in a case of conditional delivery (subsection (2) of Section 2-507) a non-negotiable bill of lading naming the buyer as consignee reserves no security interest even though the seller retains possession of the bill of lading.

(2) When shipment by the seller with reservation of a security interest is in violation of the contract for sale it constitutes an improper contract for transportation within the preceding section but impairs neither the rights given to the buyer by shipment and identification of the goods to the contract nor the seller's powers as a holder of a negotiable document.

Section 2-506. Rights of Financing Agency.

(1) A financing agency by paying or purchasing for value a draft which relates to a shipment of goods acquires to the extent of the payment or purchase and in addition to its own rights under the draft and any document of title securing it any rights of the shipper in the goods including the right to stop delivery and the shipper's right to have the draft honored by the buyer.

(2) The right to reimbursement of a financing agency which has in good faith honored or purchased the draft under commitment to or authority from the buyer is not impaired by subsequent discovery of defects with reference to any relevant document which was apparently regular on its face.

Section 2-507. Effect of Seller's Tender; Delivery on Condition.

(1) Tender of delivery is a condition to the buyer's duty to accept the goods and, unless otherwise agreed, to his duty to pay for them. Tender entitles the seller to acceptance of the goods and to payment according to the contract.

(2) Where payment is due and demanded on the delivery to the buyer of goods or documents of title, his right as against the seller to retain or dispose of them is conditional upon his making the payment due.

Section 2-508. Cure by Seller of Improper Tender or Delivery; Replacement.

(1) Where any tender or delivery by the seller is rejected because nonconforming and the time for performance has not yet expired, the seller may seasonably notify the buyer of his intention to cure and may then within the contract time make a conforming delivery.

(2) Where the buyer rejects a non-conforming tender which the seller had reasonable grounds to believe would be acceptable with or without money allowance the seller may if he seasonably notifies the buyer have a further reasonable time to substitute a conforming tender.

Section 2-509. Risk of Loss in the Absence of Breach.

(1) Where the contract requires or authorizes the seller to ship the goods by carrier

(a) if it does not require him to deliver them at a particular destination, the risk of loss passes to the buyer when the goods are duly delivered to the carrier even though the shipment is under reservation (Section 2-505); but

(b) if it does require him to deliver them at a particular destination and the goods are there duly tendered while in the possession of the carrier, the risk of loss passes to the buyer when the goods are there duly so tendered as to enable the buyer to take delivery.

(2) Where the goods are held by a bailee to be delivered without being moved, the risk of loss passes to the buyer

(a) on his receipt of a negotiable document of title covering the goods; or

(b) on acknowledgment by the bailee of the buyer's right to possession of the goods; or

(c) after his receipt of a non-negotiable document of title or other written direction to deliver, as provided in subsection (4) (b) of Section 2-503.

(3) In any case not within subsection (1) or (2), the risk of loss passes to the buyer on his receipt of the goods if the seller is a merchant; otherwise the risk passes to the buyer on tender of delivery.

(4) The provisions of this section are subject to contrary agreement of the parties and to the provisions of this Article on sale on approval (Section 2-327) and on effect of breach on risk of loss (Section 2-510).

Section 2-510. Effect of Breach on Risk of Loss.

(1) Where a tender or delivery of goods so fails to conform to the contract as to give a right of rejection the risk of their loss remains on the seller until cure or acceptance.

(2) Where the buyer rightfully revokes acceptance he may to the extent of any deficiency in his effective insurance coverage treat the risk of loss as having rested on the seller from the beginning.

(3) Where the buyer as to conforming goods already identified to the contract for sale repudiates or is otherwise in breach before risk of their loss has passed to him, the seller may to the extent of any deficiency in his effective insurance coverage treat the risk of loss as resting on the buyer for a commercially reasonable time.

Section 2-511. Tender of Payment by Buyer; Payment of Check.

(1) Unless otherwise agreed tender of payment is a condition to the seller's duty to tender and complete any delivery.

(2) Tender of payment is sufficient when made by any means or in any manner current in the ordinary course of business unless the seller demands payment in legal tender and gives any extension of time reasonably necessary to procure it.

(3) Subject to the provisions of this Act on the effect of an instrument on an obligation (Section 3-802), payment by check is conditional and is defeated as between the parties by dishonor of the check on due presentment.

Section 2-512. Payment by Buyer Before Inspection.

(1) Where the contract requires payment before inspection nonconformity of the goods does not excuse the buyer from so making payment unless

(a) the non-conformity appears without inspection; or

(b) despite tender of the required documents the circumstances would justify injunction against honor under the provisions of this Act (Section 5-114).

(2) Payment pursuant to subsection (1) does not constitute an acceptance of goods or impair the buyer's right to inspect or any of his remedies.

Section 2-513. Buyer's Right to Inspection of Goods.

(1) Unless otherwise agreed and subject to subsection (3), where goods are tendered or delivered or identified to the contract for sale, the buyer has a right before payment or acceptance to inspect them at any reasonable place and time and in any reasonable manner. When the seller is required or authorized to send the goods to the buyer, the inspection may be after their arrival.

(2) Expenses of inspection must be borne by the buyer but may be recovered from the seller if the goods do not conform and are rejected.

(3) Unless otherwise agreed and subject to the provisions of this Article on C.I.F. contracts (subsection (3) of Section 2-321), the buyer is not entitled to inspect the goods before payment of the price when the contract provides

(a) for delivery "C.O.D." or on other like terms; or

(b) for payment against documents of title, except where such payment is due only after the goods are to become available for inspection.

(4) A place or method of inspection fixed by the parties is presumed to be exclusive but unless otherwise expressly agreed it does not postpone identification or shift the place for delivery or for passing the risk of loss. If compliance becomes impossible, inspection shall be as provided in this section unless the place or method fixed was clearly intended as an indispensable condition failure of which avoids the contract.

Section 2-514. When Documents Deliverable on Acceptance; When on Payment.

Unless otherwise agreed documents against which a draft is drawn are to be delivered to the drawee on acceptance of the draft if it is payable more than three days after presentment; otherwise, only on payment.

Section 2-515. Preserving Evidence of Goods in Dispute.

In furtherance of the adjustment of any claim or dispute

(a) either party on reasonable notification to the other and for the purpose of ascertaining the facts and preserving evidence has the right to inspect, test and sample the goods including such of them as may be in the possession or control of the other; and

(b) the parties may agree to a third party inspection or survey to determine the conformity or condition of the goods and may agree that the findings shall be binding upon them in any subsequent litigation or adjustment.

Part 6. Breach, Repudiation, and Excuse.

Section 2-601. Buyer's Rights on Improper Delivery.

Subject to the provisions of this Article on breach in installment contracts (Section 2-612) and unless otherwise agreed under the sections on contractual limitations of remedy (Sections 2-718 and 2-719), if the goods or the tender of delivery fail in any respect to conform to the contract, the buyer may

(a) reject the whole; or

(b) accept the whole; or

(c) accept any commercial unit or units and reject the rest.

Section 2-602. Manner and Effect of Rightful Rejection.

(1) Rejection of goods must be within a reasonable time after their delivery or tender. It is ineffective unless the buyer seasonably notifies the seller.

(2) Subject to the provisions of the two following sections on rejected goods (Sections 2-603 and 2-604).

(a) after rejection any exercise of ownership by the buyer with respect to any commercial unit is wrongful as against the seller; and

(b) if the buyer has before rejection taken physical possession of goods in which he does not have a security interest under the provisions of this Article (subsection (3) of Section 2-711), he is under a duty after rejection to hold them with reasonable care at the seller's disposition for a time sufficient to permit the seller to remove them; but

(c) the buyer has no further obligations with regard to goods rightfully rejected.

(3) The seller's rights with respect to goods wrongfully rejected are governed by the provisions of this Article on Seller's remedies in general (Section 2-703).

Section 2-603. Merchant Buyer's Duties as to Rightfully Rejected Goods.

(1) Subject to any security interest in the buyer (subsection (3) of Section 2-711), when the seller has no agent or place of business at the market of rejection a merchant buyer is under a duty after rejection of goods in his possession or control to follow any reasonable instructions received from the seller with respect to the goods and in the absence of such instructions to make reasonable efforts to sell them for the seller's account if they are perishable or threaten to decline in value speedily. Instructions are not reasonable if on demand indemnity for expenses is not forthcoming.

(2) When the buyer sells goods under subsection (1), he is entitled to reimbursement from the seller or out of the proceeds for reasonable expenses of caring for and selling them, and if the expenses include no selling commission then to such commission as is usual in the trade or if there is none to a reasonable sum not exceeding ten per cent on the gross proceeds.

(3) In complying with this section the buyer is held only to good faith and good faith conduct hereunder is neither acceptance nor conversion nor the basis of an action for damages.

Section 2-604. Buyer's Options as to Salvage of Rightfully Rejected Goods.

Subject to the provisions of the immediately preceding section on perishables if the seller gives no instructions within a reasonable time after notification of rejection the buyer may store the rejected goods for the seller's account or reship them to him or resell them for the seller's account with reimbursement as provided in the preceding section. Such action is not acceptance or conversion.

Section 2-605. Waiver of Buyer's Objections by Failure to Particularize.

(1) The buyer's failure to state in connection with rejection a particular defect which is ascertainable by reasonable inspection precludes him from relying on the unstated defect to justify rejection or to establish breach

(a) where the seller could have cured it if stated seasonably; or

(b) between merchants when the seller has after rejection made a request in writing for a full and final written statement of all defects on which the buyer proposes to rely.

(2) Payment against documents made without reservation of rights precludes recovery of the payment for defects apparent on the face of the documents.

Section 2-606. What Constitutes Acceptance of Goods.

(1) Acceptance of goods occurs when the buyer

(a) after a reasonable opportunity to inspect the goods signifies to the seller that the goods are conforming or that he will take or retain them in spite of their nonconformity; or

(b) fails to make an effective rejection (subsection (1) of Section 2-602), but such acceptance does not occur until the buyer has had a reasonable opportunity to inspect them; or

(c) does any act inconsistent with the seller's ownership; but if such act is wrongful as against the seller it is an acceptance only if ratified by him.

(2) Acceptance of a part of any commercial unit is acceptance of that entire unit.

Section 2-607. Effect of Acceptance; Notice of Breach; Burden of Establishing Breach After Acceptance; Notice of Claim or Litigation to Person Answerable Over.

(1) The buyer must pay at the contract rate for any goods accepted.

(2) Acceptance of goods by the buyer precludes rejection of the goods accepted and if made with knowledge of a nonconformity cannot be revoked because of it unless the acceptance was on the reasonable assumption that the nonconformity would be seasonably cured but acceptance does not of itself impair any other remedy provided by this Article for nonconformity.

(3) Where a tender has been accepted

(a) the buyer must within a reasonable time after he discovers or should have discovered any breach notify the seller of breach or be barred from any remedy; and

(b) if the claim is one for infringement or the like (subsection (3) of Section 2-312) and the buyer is sued as a result of such a breach he must so notify the seller within a reasonable time after he receives notice of the litigation or be barred from any remedy over for liability established by the litigation.

(4) The burden is on the buyer to establish any breach with respect to the goods accepted.

(5) Where the buyer is sued for breach of a warranty or other obligation for which his seller is answerable over

(a) he may give his seller written notice of the litigation. If the notice states that the seller may come in and defend and that if the seller does not do so he will be bound in any action against him by his buyer by any determination of fact common to the two litigations, then unless the seller after seasonable receipt of the notice does come in and defend he is so bound.

(b) if the claim is one for infringement or the like (subsection (3) of Section 2-312) the original seller may demand in writing that his buyer turn over to him control of the litigation including settlement or else be barred from any remedy over and if he also agrees to bear all expense and to satisfy any adverse judgment, then unless the buyer after seasonable receipt of the demand does turn over control the buyer is so barred.

(6) The provisions of subsections (3), (4) and (5) apply to any obligation of a buyer to hold the seller harmless against infringement or the like (subsection (3) of Section 2-312).

Section 2-608. Revocation of Acceptance in Whole or in Part.

(1) The buyer may revoke his acceptance of a lot or commercial unit whose nonconformity substantially impairs its value to him if he has accepted it

(a) on the reasonable assumption that its nonconformity would be cured and it has not been seasonably cured; or

(b) without discovery of such nonconformity if his acceptance was reasonably induced either by the difficulty of discovery before acceptance or by the seller's assurances.

(2) Revocation of acceptance must occur within a reasonable time after the buyer discovers or should have discovered the ground for it and before any substantial change in conditions of the goods which is not caused by their own defects. It is not effective until the buyer notifies the seller of it.

(3) A buyer who so revokes has the same rights and duties with regard to the goods involved as if he had rejected them.

Section 2-609. Right to Adequate Assurance of Performance.

(1) A contract for sale imposes an obligation on each party that the other's expectation of receiving due performance will not be impaired. When reasonable grounds for

insecurity arise with respect to the performance of either party the other may in writing demand adequate assurance of due performance and until he receives such assurance may if commercially reasonable suspend any performance for which he has not already received the agreed return.

(2) Between merchants the reasonableness of grounds for insecurity and the adequacy of any assurance offered shall be determined according to commercial standards.

(3) Acceptance of any improper delivery or payment does not prejudice the aggrieved party's right to demand adequate assurance of future performance.

(4) After receipt of a justified demand failure to provide within a reasonable time not exceeding thirty days such assurance of due performance as is adequate under the circumstances of the particular case is a repudiation of the contract.

Section 2-610. Anticipatory Repudiation.

When either party repudiates the contract with respect to a performance not yet due the loss of which will substantially impair the value of the contract to the other, the aggrieved party may

(a) for a commercially reasonable time await performance by the repudiating party; or

(b) resort to any remedy for breach (Section 2-703 or Section 2-711), even though he has notified the repudiating party that he would await the latter's performance and has urged retraction; and

(c) in either case suspend his own performance or proceed in accordance with the provisions of this Article on the seller's right to identify goods to the contract notwithstanding breach or to salvage unfinished goods (Section 2-704).

Section 2-611. Retraction of Anticipatory Repudiation.

(1) Until the repudiating party's next performance is due he can retract his repudiation unless the aggrieved party has since the repudiation cancelled or materially changed his position or otherwise indicated that he considers the repudiation final.

(2) Retraction may be by any method which clearly indicates to the aggrieved party that the repudiating party intends to perform, but must include any assurance justifiably demanded under the provisions of this Article (Section 2-609).

(3) Retraction reinstates the repudiating party's rights under the contract with due excuse and allowance to the aggrieved party for any delay occasioned by the repudiation.

Section 2-612. "Installment Contract;" Breach.

(1) An "installment contract" is one which requires or authorizes the delivery of goods in separate lots to be separately accepted, even though the contract contains a clause "each delivery is a separate contract" or its equivalent.

(2) The buyer may reject any installment which is nonconforming if the non-conformity substantially impairs the value of that installment and cannot be cured or if the nonconformity is a defect in the required documents; but if the non-conformity does not fall within subsection (3) and the seller gives adequate assurance of its cure the buyer must accept that installment.

(3) Whenever nonconformity or default with respect to one or more installments substantially impairs the value of the whole contract there is a breach of the whole. But the aggrieved party reinstates the contract if he accepts a nonconforming installment without seasonably notifying of cancellation or if he brings an action with respect only to past installments or demands performance as to future installments.

Section 2-613. Casualty to Identified Goods.

Where the contract requires for its performance goods identified when the contract is made, and the goods suffer casualty without fault of either party before the risk of loss passes to the buyer, or in a proper case under a "no arrival, no sale" term (Section 2-324) then

(a) if the loss is total the contract is avoided; and

(b) if the loss is partial or the goods have so deteriorated as no longer to conform to the contract the buyer may nevertheless demand inspection and at his option either treat the contract as avoided or accept the goods with due allowance from the contract price for the deterioration or the deficiency in quantity but without further right against the seller.

Section 2-614. Substituted Performance.

(1) Where without fault of either party the agreed berthing, loading, or unloading facilities fail or an agreed type of carrier becomes unavailable or the agreed manner of delivery otherwise becomes commercially impracticable but a commercially reasonable substitute is available, such substitute performance must be tendered and accepted.

(2) If the agreed means or manner of payment fails because of domestic or foreign governmental regulation, the seller may withhold or stop delivery unless the buyer provides a means or manner of payment which is commercially a substantial equivalent. If delivery has already been taken, payment by the means or in the manner provided by the regulation discharges the buyer's obligation unless the regulation is discriminatory, oppressive or predatory.

Section 2-615. Excuse by Failure of Presupposed Conditions.

Except so far as a seller may have assumed a greater obligation and subject to the preceding section on substitute performance:

(a) Delay in delivery or nondelivery in whole or in part by a seller who complies with paragraphs (b) and (c) is not a breach of his duty under a contract for sale if performance as agreed has been made impracticable by the occurrence of a contingency the nonoccurrence of which was a basic assumption on which the contract was made or by compliance in good faith with any applicable foreign or domestic governmental regulation or order whether or not it later proves to be invalid.

(b) Where the causes mentioned in paragraph (a) affect only a part of the seller's capacity to perform, he must allocate production and deliveries among his customers but may at his option include regular customers not then under contract as well as his own requirements for further manufacture. He may so allocate in any manner which is fair and reasonable.

(c) The seller must notify the buyer seasonably that there will be delay or nondelivery and, when allocation is required under paragraph (b), of the estimated quota thus made available for the buyer.

Section 2-616. Procedure on Notice Claiming Excuse.

(1) Where the buyer receives notification of a material or indefinite delay or an allocation justified under the preceding section he may by written notification to the seller as to any delivery concerned, and where the prospective deficiency substantially impairs the value of the whole contract under the provisions of this Article relating to breach of installment contracts (Section 2-612), then also as to the whole,

   (a) terminate and thereby discharge any unexecuted portion of the contract; or

   (b) modify the contract by agreeing to take his available quota in substitution.

(2) If after receipt of such notification from the seller the buyer fails so to modify the contract within a reasonable time not exceeding thirty days the contract lapses with respect to any deliveries affected.

(3) The provisions of this section may not be negated by agreement except in so far as the seller has assumed a greater obligation under the preceding section.

Part 7. Remedies.

Section 2-701. Remedies for Breach of Collateral Contracts Not Impaired.

Remedies for breach of any obligation or promise collateral or ancillary to a contract for sale are not impaired by the provisions of this Article.

Section 2-702. Seller's Remedies on Discovery of Buyer's Insolvency.

(1) Where the seller discovers the buyer to be insolvent he may refuse delivery except for cash including payment for all goods theretofore delivered under the contract, and stop delivery under this Article (Section 2-705).

(2) Where the seller discovers that the buyer has received goods on credit while insolvent he may reclaim the goods upon demand made within ten days after the receipt, but if misrepresentation of solvency has been made to the particular seller in writing within three months before delivery the ten day limitation does not apply. Except as provided in this subsection the seller may not base a right to reclaim goods on the buyer's fraudulent or innocent misrepresentation of solvency or of intent to pay.

(3) The seller's right to reclaim under subsection (2) is subject to the rights of a buyer in ordinary course or other good faith purchaser under this Article (Section 2-403). Successful reclamation of goods excludes all other remedies with respect to them.

Section 2-703. Seller's Remedies in General.

Where the buyer wrongfully rejects or revokes acceptance of goods or fails to make a payment due on or before delivery or repudiates with respect to a part or the whole, then with respect to any goods directly affected and, if the breach is of the whole contract (Section 2-612), then also with respect to the whole undelivered balance, the aggrieved seller may

(a) withhold delivery of such goods;

(b) stop delivery by any bailee as hereafter provided (Section 2-705);

(c) proceed under the next section respecting goods still unidentified to the contract;

(d) resell and recover damages as hereafter provided (Section 2-706);

(e) recover damages for nonacceptance (Section 2-708) or in a proper case the price (Section 2-709);

(f) cancel.

Section 2-704. Seller's Right to Identify Goods to the Contract Notwithstanding Breach or to Salvage Unfinished Goods.

(1) An aggrieved seller under the preceding section may

(a) identify to the contract conforming goods not already identified if at the time he learned of the breach they are in his possession or control;

(b) treat as the subject of resale goods which have demonstrably been intended for the particular contract even though those goods are unfinished.

(2) Where the goods are unfinished an aggrieved seller may in the exercise of reasonable commercial judgment for the purposes of avoiding loss and of effective realization either complete the manufacture and wholly identify the goods to the contract or cease manufacture and resell for scrap or salvage value or proceed in any other reasonable manner.

Section 2-705. Seller's Stoppage of Delivery in Transit or Otherwise.

(1) The seller may stop delivery of goods in the possession of a carrier or other bailee when he discovers the buyer to be insolvent (Section 2-702) and may stop delivery of

carload, truckload, planeload or larger shipments of express or freight when the buyer repudiates or fails to make a payment due before delivery or if for any other reason the seller has a right to withhold or reclaim the goods.

(2) As against such buyer the seller may stop delivery until

(a) receipt of the goods by the buyer; or

(b) acknowledgment to the buyer by any bailee of the goods except a carrier that the bailee holds the goods for the buyer; or

(c) such acknowledgment to the buyer by a carrier by reshipment or as warehouseman; or

(d) negotiation to the buyer of any negotiable document of title covering the goods.

(3) (a) To stop delivery the seller must so notify as to enable the bailee by reasonable diligence to prevent delivery of the goods.

(b) After such notification the bailee must hold and deliver the goods according to the directions of the seller but the seller is liable to the bailee for any ensuing charges or damages.

(c) If a negotiable document of title has been issued for goods the bailee is not obliged to obey a notification to stop until surrender of the document.

(d) A carrier who has issued a non-negotiable bill of lading is not obliged to obey a notification to stop received from a person other than the consignor.

Section 2-706. Seller's Resale Including Contract for Resale.

(1) Under the conditions stated in Section 2-703 on seller's remedies, the seller may resell the goods concerned or the undelivered balance thereof. Where the resale is made in good faith and in a commercially reasonable manner the seller may recover the difference between the resale price and the contract price together with any incidental damages allowed under the provisions of this Article (Section 2-710), but less expenses saved in consequence of the buyer's breach.

(2) Except as otherwise provided in subsection (3) or unless otherwise agreed resale may be at public or private sale including sale by way of one or more contracts to sell or of identification to an existing contract of the seller. Sale may be as a unit or in parcels and at any time and place and on any terms but every aspect of the sale including the method, manner, time, place and terms must be commercially reasonable. The resale must be reasonably identified as referring to the broken contract, but it is not necessary that the goods be in existence or that any or all of them have been identified to the contract before the breach.

(3) Where the resale is at private sale the seller must give the buyer reasonable notification of his intention to resell.

(4) Where the resale is at public sale

(a) only identified goods can be sold except where there is a recognized market for a public sale of futures in goods of the kind; and

(b) it must be made at a usual place or market for public sale if one is reasonably available and except in the case of goods which are perishable or threaten to decline in value speedily the seller must give the buyer reasonable notice of the time and place of the resale; and

(c) if the goods are not to be within the view of those attending the sale the notification of sale must state the place where the goods are located and provide for their reasonable inspection by prospective bidders; and

(d) the seller may buy.

(5) A purchaser who buys in good faith at a resale take the goods free of any rights of the original buyer even though the seller fails to comply with one or more of the requirements of this section.

(6) The seller is not accountable to the buyer for any profit made on any resale. A person in the position of a seller (Section 2-707) or a buyer who has rightfully rejected or justifiably revoked acceptance must account for any excess over the amount of his security interest, as hereinafter defined (subsection (3) of Section 2-711).

Section 2-707. "Person in the Position of a Seller."

(1) A "person in the position of a seller" includes as against a principal an agent who has paid or become responsible for the price of goods on behalf of his principal or anyone who otherwise holds a security interest or other right in goods similar to that of a seller.

(2) A person in the position of a seller may as provided in this Article withhold or stop delivery (Section 2-705) and resell (Section 2-706) and recover incidental damages (Section 2-710).

Section 2-708. Seller's Damages for Nonacceptance or Repudiation.

(1) Subject to subsection (2) and to the provisions of this Article with respect to proof of market price (Section 2-723), the measure of damages for nonacceptance or repudiation by the buyer is the difference between the market price at the time and place for tender and the unpaid contract price together with any incidental damages provided in this Article (Section 2-710), but less expenses saved in consequence of the buyer's breach.

(2) If the measure of damages provided in subsection (1) is inadequate to put the seller in as good a position as performance would have done then the measure of damages is the profit (including reasonable overhead) which the seller would have made from full performance by the buyer, together with any incidental damages provided in this Article (Section 2-710), due allowance for costs reasonably incurred and due credit for payments or proceeds of resale.

Section 2-709. Action for the Price.

(1) When the buyer fails to pay the price as it becomes due the seller may recover, together with any incidental damages under the next section, the price

  (a) of goods accepted or of conforming goods lost or damaged within a commercially reasonable time after risk of their loss has passed to the buyer; and

  (b) of goods identified to the contract if the seller is unable after reasonable effort to resell them at a reasonable price or the circumstances reasonably indicate that such effort will be unavailing.

(2) Where the seller sues for the price he must hold for the buyer any goods which have been identified to the contract and are still in his control except that if resale becomes possible he may resell them at any time prior to the collection of the judgment. The net proceeds of any such resale must be credited to the buyer and payment of the judgment entitles him to any goods not resold.

(3) After the buyer has wrongfully rejected or revoked acceptance of the goods or has failed to make a payment due or has repudiated (Section 2-610), a seller who is held not entitled to the price under this section shall nevertheless be awarded damages for nonacceptance under the preceding section.

Section 2-710. Seller's Incidental Damages.

Incidental damages to an aggrieved seller include any commercially reasonable charges, expenses or commissions incurred in stopping delivery, in the transportation, care and custody of goods after the buyer's breach, in connection with return or resale of the goods or otherwise resulting from the breach.

Section 2-711. Buyer's Remedies in General; Buyer's Security Interest in Rejected Goods.

(1) Where the seller fails to make delivery or repudiates or the buyer rightfully rejects or justifiably revokes acceptance then with respect to any goods involved, and with respect to the whole if the breach goes to the whole contract (Section 2-612), the buyer may cancel and whether or not he has done so may in addition to recovering so much of the price as has been paid

(a) "cover" and have damages under the next section as to all the goods affected whether or not they have been identified to the contract; or

(b) recover damages for nondelivery as provided in this Article (Section 2-713).

(2) Where the seller fails to deliver or repudiates the buyer may also

(a) if the goods have been identified recover them as provided in this Article (Section 2-502); or

(b) in a proper case obtain specific performance or replevy the goods as provided in this Article (Section 2-716).

(3) On rightful rejection or justifiable revocation of acceptance a buyer has a security interest in goods in his possession or control for any payments made on their price and any expenses reasonably incurred in their inspection, receipt, transportation, care and custody and may hold such goods and resell them in like manner as an aggrieved seller (Section 2-706).

Section 2-712. "Cover;" Buyer's Procurement of Substitute Goods.

(1) After a breach within the preceding section the buyer may "cover" by making in good faith and without unreasonable delay any reasonable purchase of or contract to purchase goods in substitution for those due from the seller.

(2) The buyer may recover from the seller as damages the difference between the cost of cover and the contract price together with any incidental or consequential damages as hereinafter defined (Section 2-715), but less expenses saved in consequence of the seller's breach.

(3) Failure of the buyer to effect cover within this section does not bar him from any other remedy.

Section 2-713. Buyer's Damages for Nondelivery or Repudiation.

(1) Subject to the provisions of this Article with respect to proof of market price (Section 2-723), the measure of damages for nondelivery or repudiation by the seller is the difference between the market price at the time when the buyer learned of the breach and the contract price together with any incidental and consequential damages provided in this Article (Section 2-715), but less expenses saved in consequence of the seller's breach.

(2) Market price is to be determined as of the place for tender or, in cases of rejection after arrival or revocation of acceptance, as of the place of arrival.

Section 2-714. Buyer's Damages for Breach in Regard to Accepted Goods.

(1) Where the buyer has accepted goods and given notification (subsection (3) of Section 2-607) he may recover as damages for any nonconformity of tender the loss resulting in the ordinary course of events from the seller's breach as determined in any manner which is reasonable.

(2) The measure of damages for breach of warranty is the difference at the time and place of acceptance between the value of the goods accepted and the value they

would have had if they had been as warranted, unless special circumstances show proximate damages of a different amount

(3) In a proper case any incidental and consequential damages under the next section may also be recovered.

Section 2-715. Buyer's Incidental and Consequential Damages.

(1) Incidental damages resulting from the seller's breach include expenses reasonably incurred in inspection, receipt, transportation and care and custody of goods rightfully rejected, any commercially reasonable charges, expenses or commissions in connection with effecting cover and any other reasonable expense incident to the delay or other breach.

(2) Consequential damages resulting from the seller's breach include

(a) any loss resulting from general or particular requirements and needs of which the seller at the time of contracting had reason to know and which could not reasonably be prevented by cover or otherwise; and

(b) injury to person or property proximately resulting from any breach of warranty.

Section 2-716. Buyer's Right to Specific Performance or Replevin.

(1) Specific performance may be decreed where the goods are unique or in other proper circumstances.

(2) The decree for specific performance may include such terms and conditions as to payment of the price, damages, or other relief as the court may deem just.

(3) The buyer has a right of replevin for goods identified to the contract if after reasonable effort he is unable to effect cover for such goods or the circumstances reasonably indicate that such effort will be unavailing or if the goods have been shipped under reservation and satisfaction of the security interest in them has been made or tendered.

Section 2-717. Deduction of Damages From the Price.

The buyer on notifying the seller of his intention to do so may deduct all or any part of the damages resulting from any breach of the contract from any part of the price still due under the same contract.

Section 2-718. Liquidation or Limitation of Damages; Deposits.

(1) Damages for breach by either party may be liquidated in the agreement but only at an amount which is reasonable in the light of the anticipated or actual harm caused by the breach, the difficulties of proof of loss, and the inconvenience or nonfeasibility of otherwise obtaining an adequate remedy. A term fixing unreasonably large liquidated damages is void as a penalty.

(2) Where the seller justifiably withholds delivery of goods because of the buyer's breach, the buyer is entitled to restitution of any amount by which the sum of his payments exceeds

(a) the amount to which the seller is entitled by virtue of terms liquidating the seller's damages in accordance with subsection (1), or

(b) in the absence of such terms, twenty percent of the value of the total performance for which the buyer is obligated under the contract or $500, whichever is smaller.

(3) The buyer's right to restitution under subsection (2) is subject to offset to the extent that the seller establishes

(a) a right to recover damages under the provisions of this Article other than subsection (1), and

(b) the amount or value of any benefits received by the buyer directly or indirectly by reason of the contract.

(4) Where a seller has received payment in goods their reasonable value or the proceeds of their resale shall be treated as payments for the purposes of subsection (2); but if the seller has notice of the buyer's breach before reselling goods received in part performance, his resale is subject to the conditions laid down in this Article on resale by an aggrieved seller (Section 2-706).

Section 2-719. Contractual Modification or Limitation of Remedy.

(1) Subject to the provisions of subsections (2) and (3) of this section and of the preceding section on liquidation and limitation of damages,

(a) the agreement may provide for remedies in addition to or in substitution for those provided in this Article and may limit or alter the measure of damages recoverable under this Article, as by limiting the buyer's remedies to return of the goods and repayment of the price or to repair and replacement of nonconforming goods or parts; and

(b) resort to a remedy as provided is optional unless the remedy is expressly agreed to be exclusive, in which case it is the sole remedy.

(2) Where circumstances cause an exclusive or limited remedy to fail of its essential purpose, remedy may be had as provided in this Act.

(3) Consequential damages may be limited or excluded unless the limitation or exclusion is unconscionable. Limitation of consequential damages for injury to the person in the case of consumer goods is prima facie unconscionable but limitation of damages where the loss is commercial is not.

Section 2-720. Effect of "Cancellation" or "Rescission" on Claims for Antecedent Breach.

Unless the contrary intention clearly appears, expressions of "cancellation" or "rescission" of the contract or the like shall not be construed as a renunciation or discharge or any claim in damages for an antecedent breach.

Section 2-721. Remedies for Fraud.

Remedies for material misrepresentation or fraud include all remedies available under this Article for nonfraudulent breach. Neither rescission or a claim for rescission of the contract for sale nor rejection or return of the goods shall bar or be deemed inconsistent with a claim for damages or other remedy.

Section 2-722. Who Can Sue Third Parties for Injury to Goods.

Where a third party so deals with goods which have been identified to a contract for sale as to cause actionable injury to a party to that contract

(a) a right of action against the third party is in either party to the contract for sale who has title to or a security interest or a special property or an insurable interest in the goods; and if the goods have been destroyed or converted a right of action is also in the party who either bore the risk of loss under the contract for sale or has since the injury assumed that risk as against the other;

(b) if at the time of the injury the party plaintiff did not bear the risk of loss as against the other party to the contract for sale and there is no arrangement between them for disposition of the recovery, his suit or settlement is, subject to his own interest, as a fiduciary for the other party to the contract;

(c) either party may with the consent of the other sue for the benefit of whom it may concern.

Section 2-723. Proof of Market Price: Time and Place.

(1) If an action based on anticipatory repudiation comes to trial before the time for performance with respect to some or all of the goods, any damages based on market

price (Section 2-708 or Section 2-713) shall be determined according to the price of such goods prevailing at the time when the aggrieved party learned of the repudiation.

(2) If evidence of a price prevailing at the times or places described in this Article is not readily available the price prevailing within any reasonable time before or after the time described or at any other place which in commercial judgment or under usage of trade would serve as a reasonable substitute for the one described may be used, making any proper allowance for the cost of transporting the goods to or from such other place.

(3) Evidence of a relevant price prevailing at a time or place other than the one described in this Article offered by one party is not admissible unless and until he has given the other party such notice as the court finds sufficient to prevent unfair surprise.

Section 2-724. Admissibility of Market Quotations.

Whenever the prevailing price or value of any goods regularly bought and sold in any established commodity market is in issue, reports in official publications or trade journals or in newspapers or periodicals of general circulation published as the reports of such market shall be admissible in evidence. The circumstances of the preparation of such a report maybe shown to affect its weight but not its admissibility.

Section 2-725. Statute of Limitations in Contracts for Sale.

(1) An action for breach of any contract for sale must be commenced within four years after the cause of action has accrued. By the original agreement the parties may reduce the period of limitation to not less than one year but may not extend it.

(2) A cause of action accrues when the breach occurs, regardless of the aggrieved party's lack of knowledge of the breach. A breach of warranty occurs when tender of delivery is made, except that where a warranty explicitly extends to future performance of the goods and discovery of the breach must await the time of such performance the cause of action accrues when the breach is or should have been discovered.

(3) Where an action commenced within the time limited by subsection (1) is so terminated as to leave available a remedy by another action for the same breach such other action may be commenced after the expiration of the time limited and within six months after the termination of the first action unless the termination resulted from voluntary discontinuance or from dismissal for failure or neglect to prosecute.

(4) This section does not alter the law on tolling of the statute of limitations nor does it apply to causes of action which have accrued before this Act becomes effective.

Article 2A. Leases.

Authors' note: *Article 2A has been omitted as unnecessary for the purposes of this text.*

Article 3. Negotiable Instruments. [Revised]

Part 1. General Provisions and Definitions.

Section 3-101. Short Title.

This Article may be cited as Uniform Commercial Code—Negotiable Instruments.

Section 3-102. Subject Matter.

(a) This Article applies to negotiable instruments. It does not apply to money, to payment orders governed by Article 4A, or to securities governed by Article 8.

(b) If there is conflict between this Article and Article 4 or 9, Articles 4 and 9 govern.

(c) Regulations of the Board of Governors of the Federal Reserve System and operating circulars of the Federal Reserve Banks supersede any inconsistent provision of this Article to the extent of the inconsistency.

Section 3-103. Definitions.

(a) In this Article:

(1) "Acceptor" means a drawee who has accepted a draft.

(2) "Drawee" means a person ordered in a draft to make payment.

(3) "Drawer" means a person who signs or is identified in a draft as a person ordering payment.

(4) "Good faith" means honesty in fact and the observance of reasonable commercial standards of fair dealing.

(5) "Maker" means a person who signs or is identified in a note as a person undertaking to pay.

(6) "Order" means a written instruction to pay money signed by the person giving the instruction. The instruction may be addressed to any person, including the person giving the instruction, or to one or more persons jointly or in the alternative but not in succession. An authorization to pay is not an order unless the person authorized to pay is also instructed to pay.

(7) "Ordinary care" in the case of a person engaged in business means observance of reasonable commercial standards, prevailing in the area in which the person is located, with respect to the business in which the person is engaged. In the case of a bank that takes an instrument for processing for collection or payment by automated means, reasonable commercial standards do not require the bank to examine the instrument if the failure to examine does not violate the bank's prescribed procedures and the bank's procedures do not vary unreasonably from general banking usage not disapproved by this Article or Article 4.

(8) "Party" means a party to an instrument.

(9) "Promise" means a written undertaking to pay money signed by the person undertaking to pay. An acknowledgment of an obligation by the obligor is not a promise unless the obligor also undertakes to pay the obligation.

(10) "Prove" with respect to a fact means to meet the burden of establishing the fact (Section 1-201(8)).

(11) "Remitter" means a person who purchases an instrument from its issuer if the instrument is payable to an identified person other than the purchaser.

(b) Other definitions applying to this Article and the sections which they appear are:

"Acceptance," Section 3-409.

"Accommodated party," Section 3-419.

"Accommodation party," Section 3-419.

"Alteration," Section 3-407.

"Anomalous indorsement," Section 3-205.

"Blank indorsement," Section 3-205.

"Cashier's check," Section 3-104.

"Certificate of deposit," Section 3-104.

"Certified check," Section 3-409.

"Check," Section 3-104.

"Consideration," Section 3-303.

"Draft," Section 3-104.

"Holder in due course," Section 3-302.
"Incomplete instrument," Section 3-115.
"Indorsement," Section 3-204.
"Indorser," Section 3-204.
"Instrument," Section 3-104.
"Issue," Section 3-105.
"Issuer," Section 3-105.
"Negotiable instrument," Section 3-104.
"Negotiation," Section 3-201.
"Note," Section 3-104.
"Payable at a definite time," Section 3-108.
"Payable on demand," Section 3-108.
"Payable to bearer," Section 3-109.
"Payable to order," Section 3-109.
"Payment," Section 3-602.
"Person entitled to enforce," Section 3-301.
"Presentment," Section 3-501.
"Reacquisition," Section 3-207.
"Special indorsement," Section 3-205.
"Teller's check," Section 3-104.
"Transfer of instrument," Section 3-203.
"Traveler's check," Section 3-104.
"Value," Section 3-303.

(c) The following definitions in other Articles apply to this Article:

"Bank," Section 4-105.
"Banking day," Section 4-104.
"Clearing house," Section 4-104.
"Collecting bank," Section 4-105.
"Depositary bank," Section 4-105.
"Documentary draft," Section 4-104.
"Intermediary bank," Section 4-105.
"Item," Section 4-104.
"Payor bank," Section 4-105.
"Suspends payments," Section 4-104.

(d) In addition, Article 1 contains general definitions and principles of construction and interpretation applicable throughout this Article.

Section 3-104. Negotiable Instrument.

(a) Except as provided in subsections (c) and (d), "negotiable instrument" means an unconditional promise or order to pay a fixed amount of money, with or without interest or other charges described In the promise or order, if it:

(1) is payable to bearer or to order at the time it is issued or first comes into possession of a holder;

(2) is payable on demand or at a definite time; and

(3) does not state any other undertaking or instruction by the person promising or ordering payment to do any act in addition to the payment of money, but the

promise or order may contain (i) an undertaking or power to give, maintain, or protect collateral to secure payment, (ii) an authorization or power to the holder to confess judgment or realize on or dispose of collateral, or (iii) a waiver of the benefit of any law intended for the advantage or protection of an obligor.

(b) "Instrument" means a negotiable instrument.

(c) An order that meets all of the requirements of subsection (a), except paragraph (1), and otherwise falls within the definition of "check" in subsection (f) is a negotiable instrument and a check.

(d) A promise or order other than a check is not an instrument if, at the time it is issued or first comes into possession of a holder, it contains a conspicuous statement, however expressed, to the effect that the promise or order is not negotiable or is not an instrument governed by this Article.

(e) An instrument is a "note" if it is a promise and is a "draft" if it is an order. If an instrument falls within the definition of both "note" and "draft," a person entitled to enforce the instrument may treat it as either.

(f) "Check" means (i) a draft, other than a documentary draft, payable on demand and drawn on a bank or (ii) a cashier's check or teller's check. An instrument may be a check even though it is described on its face by another term, such as "money order."

(g) "Cashier's check" means a draft with respect to which the drawer and drawee are the same bank or branches of the same bank.

(h) "Teller's check" means a draft drawn by a bank (i) on another bank, or (ii) payable at or through a bank.

(i) "Traveler's check" means an instrument that (i) is payable on demand, (ii) is drawn on or payable at or through a bank, (iii) is designated by the term "traveler's check" or by a substantially similar term, and (iv) requires, as a condition to payment, a countersignature by a person whose specimen signature appears on the instrument.

(j) "Certificate of deposit" means an instrument containing an acknowledgment by a bank that a sum of money has been received by the bank and a promise by the bank to repay the sum of money. A certificate of deposit is a note of the bank.

Section 3-105. Issue of Instrument.

(a) "Issue" means the first delivery of an instrument by the maker or drawer, whether to a holder or nonholder, for the purpose of giving rights on the instrument to any person.

(b) An unissued instrument, or an unissued incomplete instrument that is completed, is binding on the maker or drawer, but nonissuance is a defense. An instrument that is conditionally issued or is issued for a special purpose is binding on the maker or drawer, but failure of the condition or special purpose to be fulfilled is a defense.

(c) "Issuer" applies to issued and unissued instruments and means a maker or drawer of an instrument.

Section 3-106. Unconditional Promise or Order.

(a) Except as provided in this section, for the purposes of Section 3-104(a), a promise or order is unconditional unless it states (i) an express condition to payment, (ii) that the promise or order is subject to or governed by another writing, or (iii) that rights or obligations with respect to the promise or order are stated in another writing. A reference to another writing does not of itself make the promise or order conditional.

(b) A promise or order is not made conditional (i) by a reference to another writing for a statement of rights with respect to collateral, or acceleration, or (ii) because payment is limited to resort to a particular fund or source.

(c) If a promise or order requires, as a condition to payment, a countersignature by a person whose specimen signature appears on the promise or order, the condition does not make the promise or order conditional for the purposes of Section 3-104(a). If the person whose specimen signature appears on an instrument fails to countersign the instrument, the failure to countersign is a defense to the obligation of the issuer, but the failure does not prevent a transferee of the instrument from becoming a holder of the instrument.

(d) If a promise or order at the time it is issued or first comes into possession of a holder contains a statement, required by applicable statutory or administrative law, to the effect that the rights of a holder or transferee are subject to claims or defenses that the issuer could assert against the original payee, the promise or order is not thereby made conditional for the purposes of Section 3-104(a); but if the promise or order is an instrument, there cannot be a holder in due course of the instrument.

Section 3-107. Instrument Payable in Foreign Money.

Unless the instrument otherwise provides, an instrument that states the amount payable in foreign money may be paid in the foreign money or in an equivalent amount in dollars calculated by using the current bank offered spot rate at the place of payment for the purchase of dollars on the day on which the instrument is paid.

Section 3-108. Payable on Demand or at Definite Time.

(a) A promise or order is "payable on demand" if it (i) states that it is payable on demand or at sight, or otherwise indicates that it is payable at the will of the holder, or (ii) does not state any time of payment.

(b) A promise or order is "payable at a definite time" if it is payable on elapse of a definite period of time after sight or acceptance or at a fixed date or dates or at a time or times readily ascertainable at the time the promise or order is issued, subject to rights of (i) prepayment, (ii) acceleration, (iii) extension at the option of the holder or (iv) extension to a further definite time at the option of the maker or acceptor or automatically upon or after a specified act or event.

(c) If an instrument, payable at a fixed date, is also payable upon demand made before the fixed date, the instrument is payable on demand until the fixed date and, if demand for payment is not made before that date, becomes payable at a definite time on the fixed date.

Section 3-109. Payable to Bearer or to Order.

(a) A promise or order is payable to bearer if it:

(1) states that it is payable to bearer or to the order of bearer or otherwise indicates that the person in possession of the promise or order is entitled to payment;

(2) does not state a payee; or

(3) states that it is payable to or to the order of cash or otherwise indicates that it is not payable to an identified person.

(b) A promise or order that is not payable to bearer is payable to order if it is payable (i) to the order of an identified person or (ii) to an identified person or order. A promise or order that is payable to order is payable to the identified person.

(c) An instrument payable to bearer may become payable to an identified person if it is specially indorsed pursuant to Section 3-205(a). An instrument payable to an identified person may become payable to bearer if it is indorsed in blank pursuant to Section 3-205(b).

Section 3-110. Identification of Person to Whom Instrument Is Payable.

(a) The person to whom an instrument is initially payable is determined by the intent of the person, whether or not authorized, signing as, or in the name or behalf of, the issuer of the instrument. The instrument is payable to the person intended by the signer even if that person is identified in the instrument by a name or other identification that is not that of the intended person. If more than one person signs in the name or behalf of the issuer of an instrument and all the signers do not intend the same person as payee, the instrument is payable to any person intended by one or more of the signers.

(b) If the signature of the issuer of an instrument is made by automated means, such as a check writing machine, the payee of the instrument is determined by the intent of the person who supplied the name or identification of the payee, whether or not authorized to do so.

(c) A person to whom an instrument is payable may be identified in any way, including by name, identifying number, office, or account number. For the purpose of determining the holder of an instrument, the following rules apply:

(1) If an instrument is payable to an account and the account is identified only by number, the instrument is payable to the person to whom the account is payable. If an instrument is payable to an account identified by number and by the name of a person, the instrument is payable to the named person, whether or not that person is the owner of the account identified by number.

(2) If an instrument is payable to:

(i) a trust, an estate, or a person described as trustee or representative of a trust or estate, the instrument is payable to the trustee, the representative, or a successor of either, whether or not the beneficiary or estate is also named;

(ii) a person described as agent or similar representative of a named or identified person, the instrument is payable to the represented person, the representative, or a successor of the representative;

(iii) a fund or organization that is not a legal entity, the instrument is payable to a representative of the members of the fund or organization: or

(iv) an office or to a person described as holding an office the instrument is payable to the named person, the incumbent of the office, or a successor to the incumbent.

(d) If an instrument is payable to two or more persons alternatively, it is payable to any of them and may be negotiated, discharged, or enforced by any or all of them in possession of the instrument If an instrument is payable to two or more persons not alternatively, it is payable to all of them and may be negotiated, discharged, or enforced only by all of them. If an instrument payable to two or more persons is ambiguous as to whether it is payable to the persons alternatively, the instrument is payable to the persons alternatively.

Section 3-111. Place of Payment.

Except as otherwise provided for items in Article 4, an instrument is payable at the place of payment stated in the instrument. If no place of payment is stated, an instrument is payable at the address of the drawee or maker stated in the instrument. If no address is stated, the place of payment is the place of business of the drawee or maker. If a drawee or maker has more than one place of business, the place of payment is any place of business of the drawee or maker chosen by the person entitled to enforce the instrument. If the drawee or maker has no place of business, the place of payment is the residence of the drawee or maker.

Section 3-112. Interest.

(a) Unless otherwise provided in the instrument, (i) an instrument is not payable with interest, and (ii) interest on an interest bearing instrument is payable from the date of the instrument.

(b) Interest may be stated in an instrument as a fixed or variable amount of money or it may be expressed as a fixed or variable rate or rates. The amount or rate of interest may be stated or described in the instrument in any manner and may require reference to information not contained in the instrument. If an instrument provides for interest, but the amount of interest payable cannot be ascertained from the description, interest is payable at the judgment rate in effect at the place of payment of the instrument and at the time interest first accrues.

Section 3-113. Date of Instrument.

(a) An instrument may be antedated or postdated. The date stated determines the time of payment if the instrument is payable at a fixed period after date. Except as provided in Section 4-401(c), an instrument payable on demand is not payable before the date of the instrument.

(b) If an instrument is undated, its date is the date of its issue or, in the case of an unissued instrument, the date it first comes into possession of a holder.

Section 3-114. Contradictory Terms of Instrument.

If an instrument contains contradictory terms, typewritten terms prevail over printed terms, handwritten terms prevail over both, and words prevail over numbers.

Section 3-115. Incomplete Instrument.

(a) "Incomplete instrument" means a signed writing, whether or not issued by the signer, the contents of which show at the time of signing that it is incomplete but that the signer intended it to be completed by the addition of words or numbers.

(b) Subject to subsection (c), if an incomplete instrument is an instrument under Section 3-104, it may be enforced according to its terms if it is not completed, or according to its terms as augmented by completion. If an incomplete instrument is not an instrument under Section 3-104, but, after completion, the requirements of Section 3-104 are met, the instrument may be enforced according to its terms as augmented by completion.

(c) If words or numbers are added to an incomplete instrument without authority of the signer, there is an alteration of the incomplete instrument under Section 3-407.

(d) The burden of establishing that words or numbers were added to an incomplete instrument without authority of the signer is on the person asserting the lack of authority.

Section 3-116. Joint and Several Liability; Contribution.

(a) Except as otherwise provided in the instrument, two or more persons who have the same liability on an instrument as makers, drawers, acceptors, indorsers who indorse as joint payees, or anomalous indorsers are jointly and severally liable in the capacity in which they [sign].

(b) Except as provided in Section 3-419(e) or by agreement of the affected parties, a party having joint and several liability who pays the instrument is entitled to receive from any party having the same joint and several liability contribution in accordance with applicable law.

(c) Discharge of one party having joint and several liability by a person entitled to enforce the instrument does not affect the right under subsection (b) of a party having the same joint and several liability to receive contribution from the party discharged.

Section 3-117. Other Agreements Affecting Instrument.

Subject to applicable law regarding exclusion of proof of contemporaneous or previous agreements, the obligation of a party to an instrument to pay the instrument may be modified, supplemented, or nullified by a separate agreement of the obligor and a person entitled to enforce the instrument, if the instrument is issued or the obligation is incurred in reliance on the agreement or as part of the same transaction giving rise to the agreement. To the extent an obligation is modified, supplemented, or nullified by an agreement under this section, the agreement is a defense to the obligation.

Section 3-118. Statute of Limitations.

(a) Except as provided in subsection (e), an action to enforce the obligation of a party to pay a note payable at a definite time must be commenced within six years after the due date or dates stated in the note or, if a due date is accelerated, within six years after the accelerated due date.

(b) Except as provided in subsection (d) or (e), if demand for payment is made to the maker of a note payable on demand, an action to enforce the obligation of a party to pay the note must be commenced within six years after the demand. If no demand for payment is made to the maker, an action to enforce the note is barred if neither principal nor interest on the note has been paid for a continuous period of 10 years.

(c) Except as provided in subsection (d), an action to enforce the obligation of a party to an unaccepted draft to pay the draft must be commenced within three years after dishonor of the draft or 10 years after the date of the draft, whichever period expires first.

(d) An action to enforce the obligation of the acceptor of a certified check or the issuer of a teller's check, cashier's check, or traveler's check must be commenced within three years after demand for payment is made to the acceptor or issuer, as the case may be.

(e) An action to enforce the obligation of a party to a certificate of deposit to pay the instrument must be commenced within six years after demand for payment is made to the maker, but if the instrument states a due date and the maker is not required to pay before that date, the six year period begins when a demand for payment is in effect and the due date has passed.

(f) An action to enforce the obligation of a party to pay an accepted draft, other than a certified check, must be commenced (i) within six years after the due date or dates stated in the draft or acceptance if the obligation of the acceptor is payable at a definite time, or (ii) within six years after the date of the acceptance if the obligation of the acceptor is payable on demand.

(g) Unless governed by other law regarding claims for indemnity or contribution, an action (i) for conversion of an instrument, for money had and received, or like action based on conversion, (ii) for breach of warranty, or (iii) to enforce an obligation, duty, or right arising under this Article and not governed by this section must be commenced within three years after the [cause of action] accrues.

Section 3-119. Notice of Right to Defend Action.

In an action for breach of an obligation for which a third person is answerable over pursuant to this Article or Article 4, the defendant may give the third person written notice of the litigation, and the person notified may then give similar notice to any other person who is answerable over. If the notice states (i) that the person notified may come in and defend and (ii) that failure to do so will bind the person notified in an action later brought by the person giving the notice as to any determination of fact common to the two litigations, the person notified is so bound unless after seasonable receipt of the notice the person notified does come in and defend.

Part 2. Negotiation, Transfer, and Indorsement.

Section 3-201. Negotiation.

(a) "Negotiation" means a transfer of possession, whether voluntary or involuntary, of an instrument by a person other than the issuer to a person who thereby becomes its holder.

(b) Except for negotiation by a remitter, if an instrument is payable to an identified person, negotiation requires transfer of possession of the instrument and its indorsement by the holder. If an instrument is payable to bearer, it may be negotiated by transfer of possession alone.

Section 3-202. Negotiation Subject to Rescission.

(a) Negotiation is effective even if obtained (i) from an infant, a corporation exceeding its powers, or a person without capacity, (ii) by fraud, duress, or mistake, or (iii) in breach of duty or as part of an illegal transaction.

(b) To the extent permitted by other law, negotiation may be rescinded or may be subject to other remedies, but those remedies may not be asserted against a subsequent holder in due course or a person paying the instrument in good faith and without knowledge of facts that are a basis for rescission or other remedy.

Section 3-203. Transfer of Instrument; Rights Acquired by Transfer.

(a) An instrument is transferred when it is delivered by a person other than its issuer for the purpose of giving to the person receiving delivery the right to enforce the instrument.

(b) Transfer of an instrument, whether or not the transfer is a negotiation, vests in the transferee any right of the transferor to enforce the instrument, including any right as a holder in due course, but the transferee cannot acquire rights of a holder in due course by a transfer, directly or indirectly, from a holder in due course if the transferee engaged in fraud or illegality affecting the instrument.

(c) Unless otherwise agreed, if an instrument is transferred for value and the transferee does not become a holder because of lack of indorsement by the transferor, the transferee has a specifically enforceable right to the unqualified indorsement of the transferor, but negotiation of the instrument does not occur until the indorsement is made.

(d) If a transferor purports to transfer less than the entire instrument, negotiation of the instrument does not occur. The transferee obtains no rights under this Article and has only the rights of a partial assignee.

Section 3-204. Indorsement.

(a) "Indorsement" means a signature, other than that of a signer as maker, drawer, or acceptor, that alone or accompanied by other words is made on an instrument for the purpose of (i) negotiating the instrument, (ii) restricting payment of the instrument, or (iii) incurring indorser's liability on the instrument, but regardless of the intent of the signer, a signature and its accompanying words is an indorsement unless the accompanying words, terms of the instrument, place of the signature, or other circumstances unambiguously indicate that the signature was made for a purpose other than indorsement. For the purpose of determining whether a signature is made on an instrument, a paper affixed to the instrument is a part of the instrument.

(b) "Indorser" means a person who makes an indorsement.

(c) For the purpose of determining whether the transferee of an instrument is a holder, an indorsement that transfers a security interest in the instrument is effective as an unqualified indorsement of the instrument.

(d) If an instrument is payable to a holder under a name that is not the name of the holder, indorsement may be made by the holder in the name stated in the instrument or in the holder's name or both, but signature in both names may be required by a person paying or taking the instrument for value or collection.

Section 3-205. Special Indorsement; Blank Indorsement; Anomalous Indorsement.

(a) If an indorsement is made by the holder of an instrument, whether payable to an identified person or payable to bearer, and the indorsement identifies a person to whom it makes the instrument payable, it is a "special indorsement." When specially indorsed, an instrument becomes payable to the identified person and may be negotiated only by the indorsement of that person. The principles stated in Section 3-110 apply to special indorsements.

(b) If an indorsement is made by the holder of an instrument and it is not a special indorsement, it is a "blank indorsement." When indorsed in blank, an instrument becomes payable to bearer and may be negotiated by transfer of possession alone until specially indorsed.

(c) The holder may convert a blank indorsement that consists only of a signature into a special indorsement by writing, above the signature of the indorser, words identifying the person to whom the instrument is made payable.

(d) "Anomalous indorsement" means an indorsement made by a person who is not the holder of the instrument. An anomalous indorsement does not affect the manner in which the instrument may be negotiated.

Section 3-206. Restrictive Indorsement.

(a) An indorsement limiting payment to a particular person or otherwise prohibiting further transfer or negotiation of the instrument is not effective to prevent further transfer or negotiation of the instrument.

(b) An indorsement stating a condition to the right of the indorsee to receive payment does not affect the right of the indorsee to enforce the instrument. A person paying the instrument or taking it for value or collection may disregard the condition, and the rights and liabilities of that person are not affected by whether the condition has been fulfilled.

(c) If an instrument bears an indorsement (i) described in Section 4-201(b), or (ii) in blank or to a particular bank using the words "for deposit," "for collection," or other words indicating a purpose of having the instrument collected by a bank for the indorser or for a particular account, the following rules apply:

(1) A person, other than a bank, who purchases the instrument when so indorsed converts the instrument unless the amount paid for the instrument is received by the indorser or applied consistently with the indorsement.

(2) A depositary bank that purchases the instrument or takes it for collection when so indorsed converts the instrument unless the amount paid by the bank with respect to the instrument Is received by the indorser or applied consistently with the indorsement.

(3) A payor bank that is also the depositary bank or that takes the instrument for immediate payment over the counter from a person other than a collecting bank converts the instrument unless the proceeds of the instrument are received by the indorser or applied consistently with the indorsement.

(4) Except as otherwise provided in paragraph (3), a payor bank or intermediary bank may disregard the indorsement and is not liable if the proceeds of the instrument are not received by the indorser or applied consistently with the indorsement.

(d) Except for an indorsement covered by subsection (c), if an instrument bears an indorsement using words to the effect that payment is to be made to the indorsee as agent, trustee, or other fiduciary for the benefit of the indorser or another person, the following rules apply:

(1) Unless there is notice of breach of fiduciary duty as provided in Section 3-307, a person who purchases the instrument from the indorsee or takes the instrument from the indorsee for collection or payment may pay the proceeds of payment or the value given for the instrument to the indorsee without regard to whether the indorsee violates a fiduciary duty to the indorser.

(2) A subsequent transferee of the instrument or person who pays the instrument is neither given notice nor otherwise affected by the restriction in the indorsement unless the transferee or payor knows that the fiduciary dealt with the instrument or its proceeds in breach of fiduciary duty.

(e) The presence on an instrument of an indorsement to which this section applies does not prevent a purchaser of the instrument from becoming a holder in due course of the instrument unless the purchaser is a converter under subsection (c) or has notice or knowledge of breach of fiduciary duty as stated in subsection (d).

(f) In an action to enforce the obligation of a party to pay the instrument, the obligor has a defense if payment would violate an indorsement to which this section applies and the payment is not permitted by this section.

Section 3-207. Reacquisition.

Reacquisition of an instrument occurs if it is transferred to a former holder, by negotiation or otherwise. A former holder who reacquires the instrument may cancel indorsements made after the reacquirer first became a holder of the instrument. If the cancellation causes the instrument to be payable to the reacquirer or to bearer, the reacquirer may negotiate the instrument. An indorser whose indorsement is cancelled is discharged, and the discharge is effective against any subsequent holder.

Part 3. Enforcement of Instruments.

Section 3-301. Person Entitled to Enforce Instrument.

"Person entitled to enforce" an instrument means (i) the holder of the instrument, (ii) a nonholder in possession of the instrument who has the rights of a holder, or (iii) a person not in possession of the instrument who is entitled to enforce the instrument pursuant to Section 3-309 or 3-418(d). A person may be a person entitled to enforce the instrument even though the person is not the owner of the instrument or is in wrongful possession of the instrument.

Section 3-302. Holder in Due Course.

(a) Subject to subsection (c) and Section 3-106
(d), "holder in due course" means the holder of an instrument if:

(1) the instrument when issued or negotiated to the holder does not bear such apparent evidence of forgery or alteration or is not otherwise so irregular or incomplete as to call into question its authenticity; and

(2) the holder took the instrument (i) for value, (ii) in good faith, (iii) without notice that the instrument is overdue or has been dishonored or that there is an uncured default with respect to payment of another instrument issued as part of the same series, (iv) without notice that the instrument contains an unauthorized signature or has been altered, (v) without notice of any claim to the instrument described in Section 3-306, and (vi) without notice that any party has a defense or claim in recoupment described in Section 3-305(a).

(b) Notice of discharge of a party, other than discharge in an insolvency proceeding, is not notice of a defense under subsection (a), but discharge is effective against a person who became a holder in due course with notice of the discharge. Public filing or recording of a document does not of itself constitute notice of a defense, claim in recoupment, or claim to the instrument.

(c) Except to the extent a transferor or predecessor in interest has rights as a holder in due course, a person does not acquire rights of a holder in due course of an instrument taken (i) by legal process or by purchase in an execution, bankruptcy, or creditor's sale or similar proceeding, (ii) by purchase as part of a bulk transaction not in ordinary course of business of the transferor, or (iii) as the successor in interest to an estate or other organization.

(d) If, under Section 3-303(a) (1), the promise of performance that is the consideration for an instrument has been partially performed, the holder may assert rights as a holder in due course of the instrument only to the fraction of the amount payable under the instrument equal to the value of the partial performance divided by the value of the promised performance.

(e) If (i) the person entitled to enforce an instrument has only a security interest in the instrument and (ii) the person obliged to pay the instrument has a defense, claim in recoupment, or claim to the instrument that may be asserted against the person who granted the security interest, the person entitled to enforce the instrument may assert rights as a holder in due course only to an amount payable under the instrument which, at the time of enforcement of the instrument, does not exceed the amount of the unpaid obligation secured.

(f) To be effective, notice must be received at a time and in a manner that gives a reasonable opportunity to act on it.

(g) This section is subject to any law limiting status as a holder in due course in particular classes of transactions.

Section 3-303. Value and Consideration.

(a) An instrument is issued or transferred for value if:

(1) the instrument is issued or transferred for a promise of performance, to the extent the promise has been performed;

(2) the transferee acquires a security interest or other lien in the instrument other than a lien obtained by judicial proceeding;

(3) the instrument is issued or transferred as payment of, or as security for, an antecedent claim against any person, whether or not the claim is due;

(4) the instrument is issued or transferred in exchange for a negotiable instrument; or

(5) the instrument is issued or transferred in exchange for the incurring of an irrevocable obligation to a third party by the person taking the instrument.

(b) "Consideration" means any consideration sufficient to support a simple contract. The drawer or maker of an instrument has a defense if the instrument is issued without consideration. If an instrument is issued for a promise of performance, the issuer has a defense to the extent performance of the promise is due and the promise has not been performed. If an instrument is issued for value as stated in subsection (a). the instrument is also issued for consideration.

Section 3-304. Overdue Instrument.

(a) An instrument payable on demand becomes overdue at the earliest of the following times:

(1) on the day after the day demand for payment is duly made;

(2) if the instrument is a check, 90 days after its date; or

(3) if the instrument is not a check, when the instrument has been outstanding for a period of time after its date which is unreasonably long under the circumstances of the particular case in light of the nature of the instrument and usage of the trade.

(b) With respect to an instrument payable at a definite time the following rules apply:

(1) If the principal is payable in installments and a due date has not been accelerated, the instrument becomes overdue upon default under the instrument for nonpayment of an installment, and the instrument remains overdue until the default is cured.

(2) If the principal is not payable in installments and the due date has not been accelerated, the instrument becomes overdue on the day after the due date.

(3) If a due date with respect to principal has been accelerated, the instrument becomes overdue on the day after the accelerated due date.

(c) Unless the due date of principal has been accelerated, an instrument does not become overdue if there is default in payment of interest but no default in payment of principal.

Section 3-305. Defenses and Claims in Recoupment.

(a) Except as stated in subsection (b), the right to enforce the obligation of a party to pay an instrument is subject to the following:

(1) a defense of the obligor based on (i) infancy of the obligor to the extent it is a defense to a simple contract. (ii) duress, lack of legal capacity, or illegality of the transaction which, under other law, nullifies the obligation of the obligor, (iii) fraud that induced the obligor to sign the instrument with neither knowledge nor reasonable opportunity to learn of its character or its essential terms, or (iv) discharge of the obligor in insolvency proceedings;

(2) a defense of the obligor stated in another section of this Article or a defense of the obligor that would be available if the person entitled to enforce the instrument were enforcing a right to payment under a simple contract; and

(3) a claim in recoupment of the obligor against the original payee of the instrument if the claim arose from the transaction that gave rise to the instrument; but the claim of the obligor may be asserted against a transferee of the instrument only to reduce the amount owing on the instrument at the time the action is brought.

(b) The right of a holder in due course to enforce the obligation of a party to pay the instrument is subject to defenses of the obligor stated in subsection (a) (1), but is not subject to defenses of the obligor stated in subsection (a) (2) or claims in recoupment stated in subsection (a) (3) against a person other than the holder.

(c) Except as stated in subsection (d), in an action to enforce the obligation of a party to pay the instrument, the obligor may not assert against the person entitled to enforce the instrument a defense, claim in recoupment, or claim to the instrument (Section 3-306) of another person, but the other person's claim to the instrument may be asserted by the obligor if the other person is joined in the action and personally asserts the claim against the person entitled to enforce the instrument. An obligor is not obliged to pay the instrument if the person seeking enforcement of the instrument does not have rights of a holder in due course and the obligor proves that the instrument is a lost or stolen instrument.

(d) In an action to enforce the obligation of an accommodation party to pay an instrument, the accommodation party may assert against the person entitled to enforce the instrument any defense or claim in recoupment under subsection (a) that the accommodated party could assert against the person entitled to enforce the instrument, except the defenses of discharge in insolvency proceedings, infancy, and of legal capacity.

Section 3-306. Claims to an Instrument.

A person taking an instrument, other than a person having rights of a holder in due course, is subject to a claim of a property or possessory right in the instrument or its proceeds, including a claim to rescind a negotiation and to recover the instrument or its proceeds. A person having rights of a holder in due course takes free of the claim to the instrument.

Section 3-307. Notice of Breach of Fiduciary Duty.

(a) In this section:

(1) "Fiduciary" means an agent, trustee, partner, corporate officer or director, or other representative owing a fiduciary duty with respect to an instrument.

(2) "Represented person" means the principal, beneficiary, partnership, corporation, or other person to whom the duty stated in paragraph (1) is owed.

(b) If (i) an instrument is taken from a fiduciary for payment or collection or for value, (ii) the taker has knowledge of the fiduciary status of the fiduciary, and (iii) the represented person makes a claim to the instrument or its proceeds on the basis that the transaction of the fiduciary is a breach of fiduciary duty, the following rules apply:

(1) Notice of breach of fiduciary duty by the fiduciary is notice of the claim of the represented person.

(2) In the case of an instrument payable to the represented person or the fiduciary as such, the taker has notice of the breach of fiduciary duty if the instrument is (i) taken in payment of or as security for a debt known by the taker to be the personal debt of the fiduciary, (ii) taken in a transaction known by the taker to be for the personal benefit of the fiduciary, or (iii) deposited to an account other than an account of the fiduciary, as such, or an account of the represented person.

(3) If an instrument is issued by the represented person or the fiduciary as such, and made payable to the fiduciary personally, the taker does not have notice of the breach of fiduciary duty unless the taker knows of the breach of fiduciary duty.

(4) If an instrument is issued by the represented person or the fiduciary as such, to the taker as payee, the taker has notice of the breach of fiduciary duty if the instrument is (i) taken in payment of or as security for a debt known by the taker to be the personal debt of the fiduciary, (ii) taken in a transaction known by the taker to be for the personal benefit of the fiduciary, or (iii) deposited to an account of the represented person.

Section 3-308. Proof of Signatures and Status as Holder in Due Course.

(a) In an action with respect to an instrument, the authenticity of, and authority to make, each signature on the instrument is admitted unless specifically denied in the pleadings. If the validity of a signature is denied in the pleadings, the burden of establishing validity is on the person claiming validity, but the signature is presumed to be authentic and authorized unless the action is to enforce the liability of the purported signer and the signer is dead or incompetent at the time of trial of the issue of validity of the signature. If an action to enforce the instrument is brought against a person as the undisclosed principal of a person who signed the instrument as a party to the instrument, the plaintiff has the burden of establishing that the defendant is liable on the instrument as a represented person under Section 3-402(a)

(b) If the validity of signatures is admitted or proved and there is compliance with subsection (a), a plaintiff producing the instrument is entitled to payment if the plaintiff proves entitlement to enforce the instrument under Section 3-301, unless the defendant proves a defense or claim in recoupment. If a defense or claim in recoupment is proved, the right to payment of the plaintiff is subject to the defense or claim, except to the extent the plaintiff proves that the plaintiff has rights of a holder in due course which are not subject to the defense or claim.

Section 3-309. Enforcement of Lost, Destroyed, or Stolen Instrument.

(a) A person not in possession of an instrument is entitled to enforce the instrument if (i) the person was in possession of the instrument and entitled to enforce it when loss of possession occurred, (ii) the loss of possession was not the result of a transfer by the person or a lawful seizure, and (iii) the person cannot reasonably obtain possession of the instrument because the instrument was destroyed, its whereabouts cannot be determined, or it is in the wrongful possession of an unknown person or a person that cannot be found or is not amenable to service of process.

(b) A person seeking enforcement of an instrument under subsection (a) must prove the terms of the instrument and the person's right to enforce the instrument. If that proof is made, Section 3-308 applies to the case as if the person seeking enforcement had produced the instrument. The court may not enter judgment in favor of the person seeking enforcement unless it finds that the person required to pay the instrument is adequately protected against loss that might occur by reason of a claim by another person to enforce the instrument. Adequate protection may be provided by any reasonable means.

Section 3-310. Effect of Instrument on Obligation for Which Taken.

(a) Unless otherwise agreed, if a certified check, cashier's check, or teller's check is taken for an obligation, the obligation is discharged to the same extent discharge would result if an amount of money equal to the amount of the instrument were taken in payment of the obligation. Discharge of the obligation does not affect any liability that the obligor may have as an indorser of the instrument.

(b) Unless otherwise agreed and except as provided in subsection (a) if a note or an uncertified check is taken for an obligation, the obligation is suspended to the same extent the obligation would be discharged if an amount of money equal to the amount of the instrument were taken, and the following rules apply:

(1) In the case of an uncertified check, suspension of the obligation continues until dishonor of the check or until it is paid or certified. Payment or certification of the check results in discharge of the obligation to the extent of the amount of the check.

(2) In the case of a note, suspension of the obligation continues until dishonor of the note or until it is paid. Payment of the note results in discharge of the obligation to the extent of the payment.

(3) Except as provided in paragraph (4), if the check or note is dishonored and the obligee of the obligation for which the instrument was taken is the person entitled to enforce the instrument, the obligee may enforce either the instrument or the obligation. In the case of an instrument of a third person which is negotiated to the obligee by the obligor, discharge of the obligor on the instrument also discharges the obligation.

(4) If the person entitled to enforce the instrument taken for an obligation is a person other than the obligee, the obligee may not enforce the obligation to the extent the obligation is suspended. If the obligee is the person entitled to enforce the instrument but no longer has possession of it because it was lost, stolen, or destroyed, the obligation may not be enforced to the extent of the amount payable on the instrument, and to that extent the obligee's rights against the obligor are limited to enforcement of the instrument.

(c) If an instrument other than one described in subsection (a) or (b) is taken for an obligation, the effect is (i) that stated in subsection (a) if the instrument is one on which a bank is liable as maker or acceptor, or (ii) that stated in subsection (b) in any other case.

Section 3-311. Accord and Satisfaction by Use of Instrument.

(a) If a person against whom a claim is asserted proves that (i) that person in good faith tendered an instrument to the claimant as full satisfaction of the claim, (ii) the amount of the claim was unliquidated or subject to a bona fide dispute, and (iii) the claimant obtained payment of the instrument, the following subsections apply.

(b) Unless subsection (c) applies, the claim is discharged if the person against whom the claim is asserted proves that the instrument or an accompanying written communication contained a conspicuous statement to the effect that the instrument was tendered as full satisfaction of the claim.

(c) Subject to subsection (d), a claim is not discharged under subsection (b) if either of the following applies:

(1) The claimant, if an organization, proves that (i) within a reasonable time before the tender, the claimant sent a conspicuous statement to the person against whom

the claim is asserted that communications concerning disputed debts, including an instrument tendered as full satisfaction of a debt, are to be sent to a designated person, office, or place, and (ii) the instrument or accompanying communication was not received by that designated person, office, or place.

(2) The claimant, whether or not an organization, proves that within 90 days after payment of the instrument, the claimant tendered repayment of the amount of the instrument to the person against whom the claim is asserted. This paragraph does not apply if the claimant is an organization that sent a statement complying with paragraph (1) (i).

(d) A claim is discharged if the person against whom the claim is asserted proves that within a reasonable time before collection of the instrument was initiated, the claimant, or an agent of the claimant having direct responsibility with respect to the disputed obligation, knew that the instrument was tendered in full satisfaction of the claim.

Part 4. Liability of Parties.

Section 3-401. Signature.

(a) A person is not liable on an instrument unless (i) the person signed the instrument, or (ii) the person is represented by an agent or representative who signed the instrument and the signature is binding on the represented person under Section 3-402.

(b) A signature may be made (i) manually or by means of a device or machine, and (ii) by the use of any name, including a trade or assumed name, or by a word, mark, or symbol executed or adopted by a person with present intention to authenticate a writing.

Section 3-402. Signature by Representative.

(a) If a person acting, or purporting to act, as a representative signs an instrument by signing either the name of the represented person or the name of the signer, the represented person is bound by the signature to the same extent the represented person would be bound if the signature were on a simple contract. If the represented person is bound, the signature of the representative is the "authorized signature of the represented person" and the represented person is liable on the instrument, whether or not identified in the instrument.

(b) If a representative signs the name of the representative to an instrument and the signature is an authorized signature of the represented person, the following rules apply:

(1) If the form of the signature shows unambiguously that the signature is made on behalf of the represented person who is identified in the instrument, the representative is not liable on the instrument.

(2) Subject to subsection (c), if (i) the form of the signature does not show unambiguously that the signature is made in a representative capacity or (ii) the represented person is not identified in the instrument, the representative is liable on the instrument to a holder in due course that took the instrument without notice that the representative was not intended to be liable on the instrument. With respect to any other person, the representative is liable on the instrument unless the representative proves that the original parties did not intend the representative to be liable on the instrument.

(c) If a representative signs the name of the representative as drawer of a check without indication of the representative status and the check is payable from an account of the represented person who is on the check, the signer is not liable on the check if the signature is an authorized signature of the represented person.

Section 3-403. Unauthorized Signature.

(a) Unless otherwise provided in this Article or Article 4, an unauthorized signature is ineffective except as the signature of the unauthorized signer in favor of a person who in good faith pays the or takes it for value. An unauthorized signature may be ratified for all purposes of this Article.

(b) If the signature of more than one person is required to constitute the authorized signature of an organization, the signature of the organization is unauthorized if one of the required signatures is lacking.

(c) The civil or criminal liability of a person who makes an unauthorized signature is not affected by any provision of this Article which makes the unauthorized signature effective for the purposes of this Article.

Section 3-404 Impostors; Fictitious Payees.

(a) If an impostor, by use of the mails or otherwise, induces the issuer of an instrument to issue the instrument to the impostor, or to a person acting in concert with the impostor, by impersonating the payee of the instrument or a person authorized to act for the payee, an indorsement of the instrument by any person in the name of the payee is effective as the indorsement of the payee in favor of a person who, in good faith, pays the instrument or takes it for value or for collection.

(b) If (i) a person whose intent determines to whom an instrument is payable (Section 3-110(a) or (b)) does not intend the person identified as payee to have any interest in the instrument, or (ii) the person identified as payee of an instrument is a fictitious person, the following rules apply until the instrument is negotiated by special indorsement:

(1) Any person in possession of the instrument is its holder.

(2) An indorsement by any person in the name of the payee stated in the instrument is effective as the indorsement of the payee in favor of a person who, in good faith, pays the instrument or takes it for value or for collection.

(c) Under subsection (a) or (b), an indorsement is made in the name of a payee if (i) it is made in a name substantially similar to that of the payee or (ii) the instrument, whether or not indorsed, is deposited in a depositary bank to an account in a name substantially similar to that of the payee.

(d) With respect to an instrument to which subsection (a) or (b) applies, if a person paying the instrument or taking it for value or for collection fails to exercise ordinary care in paying or taking the instrument and that failure substantially contributes to loss resulting from payment of the instrument, the person bearing the loss may recover from the person failing to exercise ordinary care to the extent the failure to exercise ordinary care contributed to the loss.

Section 3-405. Employer's Responsibility for Fraudulent Indorsement by Employee.

(a) In this section:

(1) "Employee" includes an independent contractor and employee of an independent contractor retained by the employer.

(2) "Fraudulent indorsement" means (i) in the case of an instrument payable to the employer, a forged indorsement purporting to be that of the employer, or (ii) in the case of an instrument with respect to which the employer is the issuer, a forged indorsement purporting to be that of the person identified as payee.

(3) "Responsibility" with respect to instruments means authority (i) to sign or indorse instruments on behalf of the employer, (ii) to process instruments received by the employer for bookkeeping purposes, for deposit to an account, or for other disposition, (iii) to prepare or process instruments for issue in the name of the employer, (iv) to supply information determining the names or addresses of payees of instruments to be issued in the name of the employer, (v) to control the disposition of instruments to be issued in the name of the employer, or (vi) to act otherwise with respect to instruments in a responsible capacity. "Responsibility" does not include authority that merely allows an employee to have access to

instruments or blank or incomplete instrument forms that are being stored or transported or are part of incoming or outgoing mail, or similar access.

(b) For the purpose of determining the rights and liabilities of a person who, in good faith, pays an instrument or takes it for value or for collection, if an employer entrusted an employee with responsibility with respect to the instrument and the employee or a person acting in concert with the employee makes a fraudulent indorsement of the instrument, the indorsement is effective as the indorsement of the person to whom the instrument is payable if it is made in the name of that person. If the person paying the instrument or taking it for value or for collection fails to exercise ordinary care in paying or taking the instrument and that failure substantially contributes to loss resulting from the fraud, the person bearing the loss may recover from the person failing to exercise ordinary care to the extent the failure to exercise ordinary care contributed to the loss.

(c) Under subsection (b), an indorsement is made in the name of the person to whom an instrument is payable if (i) it is made in a name substantially similar to the name of that person or (ii) the instrument, whether or not indorsed, is deposited in a depositary bank to an account in a name substantially similar to the name of that person.

Section 3-406. Negligence Contributing to Forged Signature or Alteration of Instrument.

(a) A person whose failure to exercise ordinary care substantially contributes to an alteration of an instrument or to the making of a forged signature on an instrument is precluded from asserting the alteration or the forgery against a person who, in good faith, pays the instrument or takes it for value or for collection.

(b) Under subsection (a), if the person asserting the preclusion fails to exercise ordinary care in paying or taking the instrument and that failure substantially contributes to loss, the loss is allocated between the person precluded and the person asserting the preclusion according to the extent to which the failure of each to exercise ordinary care contributed to the loss.

(c) Under subsection (a), the burden of proving failure to exercise ordinary care is on the person asserting the preclusion. Under subsection (b), the burden of proving failure to exercise ordinary care is on the person precluded.

Section 3-407. Alteration.

(a) "Alteration" means (i) an unauthorized change in an instrument that purports to modify in any respect the obligation of a party, or (ii) an unauthorized addition of words or numbers or other change to an incomplete instrument relating to the obligation of a party.

(b) Except as provided in subsection (c), an alteration fraudulently made discharges a party whose obligation is affected by the alteration unless that party assents or is precluded from asserting the alteration. No other alteration discharges a party, and the instrument may be enforced according to its original terms.

(c) A payor bank or drawee paying a fraudulently altered instrument or a person taking it for value, in good faith and without notice of the alteration, may enforce rights with respect to the instrument (i) according to its original terms, or (ii) in the case of an incomplete instrument altered by unauthorized completion, according to its terms as completed.

Section 3-408. Drawee Not Liable on Unaccepted Draft.

A check or other draft does not of itself operate as an assignment of funds in the hands of the drawee available for its payment, and the drawee is not liable on the instrument until the drawee accepts it.

Section 3-409. Acceptance of Draft; Certified Check.

(a) "Acceptance" means the drawee's signed agreement to pay a draft as presented. It must be written on the Draft; Certified Check and may consist of the drawee's signature alone. Acceptance may be made at any time and becomes effective when notification pursuant to instructions is given or the accepted draft is delivered for the purpose of giving rights on the acceptance to any person.

(b) A draft may be accepted although it has not been signed by the drawer, is otherwise incomplete, is overdue, or has been dishonored.

(c) If a draft is payable at a fixed period after sight and the acceptor fails to date the acceptance, the holder may complete the acceptance by supplying a date in good faith.

(d) "Certified check" means a check accepted by the bank on which it is drawn. Acceptance may be made as stated in subsection (a) or by a writing on the check which indicates that the check is certified. The drawee of a check has no obligation to certify the check, and refusal to certify is not dishonor of the check.

Section 3-410. Acceptance Varying Draft.

(a) If the terms of a drawee's acceptance vary from the terms of the draft as presented, the holder may refuse the acceptance and treat the draft as dishonored. In that case, the drawee may cancel the acceptance.

(b) The terms of a draft are not varied by an acceptance to pay at a particular bank or place in the United States, unless the acceptance states that the draft is to be paid only at that bank or place.

(c) If the holder assents to an acceptance varying the terms of a draft, the obligation of each drawer and indorser that does not expressly assent to the acceptance is discharged.

Section 3-411. Refusal to Pay Cashier's Checks, Teller's Checks, and Certified Checks.

(a) In this section, "obligated bank" means the acceptor of a certified check or the issuer of a cashier's check or teller's check bought from the issuer.

(b) If the obligated bank wrongfully (i) refuses to pay a cashier's check or certified check, (ii) stops payment of a teller's check, or (iii) refuses to pay a dishonored teller's check, the person asserting the right to enforce the check is entitled to compensation for expenses and loss of interest resulting from the nonpayment and may recover consequential damages if the obligated bank refuses to pay after receiving notice of particular circumstances giving rise to the damages.

(c) Expenses or consequential damages under subsection (b) are not recoverable if the refusal of the obligated bank to pay occurs because (i) the bank suspends payments, (ii) the obligated bank asserts a claim or defense of the bank that it has reasonable grounds to believe is available against the person entitled to enforce the instrument, (iii) the obligated bank has a reasonable doubt whether the person demanding payment is the person entitled to enforce the instrument, or (iv) payment is prohibited by law.

Section 3-412. Obligation of Issuer of Note or Cashiers Check.

The issuer of a note or Cashier's Check or other draft drawn on the drawer is obliged to pay the instrument (i) according to its terms at the time it was issued or, if not issued, at the time it first came into possession of a holder, or (ii) if the issuer signed an incomplete instrument, according to its terms when completed, to the extent stated in Sections 3-115 and 3-407. The obligation is owed to a person entitled to enforce the instrument or to an indorser who paid the instrument under Section 3-415.

Section 3-413. Obligation of Acceptor.

(a) The acceptor of a draft is obliged to pay the draft (i) according to its terms at the time it was accepted, even though the acceptance states that the draft is payable "as originally drawn" or equivalent terms, (ii) if the acceptance varies the terms of the draft, according to the terms of the draft as varied, or (iii) if the acceptance is of a draft that is an incomplete instrument, according to its terms when completed, to the extent stated in Sections 3-115 and 3-407. The obligation is owed to a person entitled to enforce the draft or to the drawer or an indorser who paid the draft under Section 3-414 or 3-415.

(b) If the certification of a check or other acceptance of a draft states the amount certified or accepted, the obligation of the acceptor is that amount. If (i) the certification or acceptance does not state an amount, (ii) the amount of the instrument is subsequently raised, and (iii) the instrument is then negotiated to a holder in due course, the obligation of the acceptor is the amount of the instrument at the time it was taken by the holder in due course.

Section 3-414. Obligation of Drawer.

(a) This section does not apply to cashier's checks or other drafts drawn on the drawer.

(b) If an unaccepted draft is dishonored, the drawer is obliged to pay the draft (i) according to its terms at the time it was issued or, if not issued, at the time it first came into possession of a holder, or (ii) if the drawer signed an incomplete instrument, according to its terms when completed, to the extent stated in Sections 3-115 and 3-407. The obligation is owed to a person entitled to enforce the draft or to an indorser who paid the draft under Section 3-415.

(c) If a draft is accepted by a bank, the drawer is discharged, regardless of when or by whom acceptance was obtained.

(d) If a draft is accepted and the acceptor is not a bank, the obligation of the drawer to pay the draft if the draft is dishonored by the acceptor is the same as the obligation of an indorser under Section 3-415(a) and (c).

(e) If a draft states that it is drawn "without recourse" or otherwise disclaims liability of the drawer to pay the draft, the drawer is not liable under subsection (b) to pay the draft if the draft is not a check. A disclaimer of the liability stated in subsection (b) is not effective if the draft is a check.

(f) If (i) a check is not presented for payment or given to a depositary bank for collection within 30 days after its date, (ii) the drawee suspends payments after expiration of the 30 day period without paying the check, and (iii) because of the suspension of payments, the drawer is deprived of funds maintained with the drawee to cover payment of the check, the drawer to the extent deprived of funds may discharge its obligation to pay the check by assigning to the person entitled to enforce the check the rights of the drawer against the drawee with respect to the funds.

Section 3-415. Obligation of Indorser.

(a) Subject to subsections (b), (c), and (d) and to Section 3-419(d), if an instrument is dishonored, an indorser is obliged to pay the amount due on the instrument (i) according to the terms of the instrument at the time it was indorsed, or (ii) if the indorser indorsed an incomplete instrument, according to its terms when completed, to the extent stated in Sections 3-115 and 3-407. The obligation of the indorser is owed to a person entitled to enforce the instrument or to a subsequent indorser who paid the instrument under this section.

(b) If an indorsement states that it is made "without recourse" or otherwise disclaims liability of the indorser, the indorser is not liable under subsection (a) to pay the instrument.

(c) If notice of dishonor of an instrument is required by Section 3-503 and notice of dishonor complying with that section is not given to an indorser, the liability of the indorser under subsection (a) is discharged.

(d) If a draft is accepted by a bank after an indorsement is made, the liability of the indorser under subsection (a) is discharged.

(e) If an indorser of a check is liable under subsection (a) and the check is not presented for payment, or given to a depositary bank for collection, within 30 days after the day the indorsement was made, the liability of the indorser under subsection (a) is discharged.

Section 3-416. Transfer Warranties.

(a) A person who transfers an instrument for consideration warrants to the transferee and, if the transfer is by indorsement, to any subsequent transferee that:

(1) the warrantor is a person entitled to enforce the instrument;

(2) all signatures on the instrument are authentic and authorized;

(3) the instrument has not been altered;

(4) the instrument is not subject to a defense or claim in recoupment of any party which can be asserted against the warrantor; and

(5) the warrantor has no knowledge of any insolvency proceeding commenced with respect to the maker or acceptor or, in the case of an unaccepted draft, the drawer.

(b) A person to whom the warranties under subsection (a) are made and who took the instrument in good faith may recover from the warrantor as damages for breach of warranty an amount equal to the loss suffered as a result of the breach, but not more than the amount of the instrument plus expenses and loss of interest incurred as a result of the breach.

(c) The warranties stated in subsection (a) cannot be disclaimed with respect to checks. Unless notice of a claim for breach of warranty is given to the warrantor within 30 days after the claimant has reason to know of the breach and the identity of the warrantor, the liability of the warrantor under subsection (b) is discharged to the extent of any loss caused by the delay in giving notice of the claim.

(d) A [cause of action] for breach of warranty under this section accrues when the claimant has reason to know of the breach.

Section 3-417. Presentment Warranties.

(a) If an unaccepted draft is presented to the drawee for payment or acceptance and the drawee pays or accepts the draft, (i) the person obtaining payment or acceptance, at the time of presentment, and (ii) a previous transferor of the draft, at the time of transfer, warrant to the drawee making payment or accepting the draft in good faith that:

(1) the warrantor is, or was, at the time the warrantor transferred the draft, a person entitled to enforce the draft or authorized to obtain payment or acceptance of the draft on behalf of a person entitled to enforce the draft;

(2) the draft has not been altered; and

(3) the warrantor has no knowledge that the signature of the drawer of the draft is unauthorized.

(b) A drawee making payment may recover from any warrantor damages for breach of warranty equal to the amount paid by the drawee less the amount the drawee received or is entitled to receive from the drawer because of the payment. In addition, the drawee is entitled to compensation for expenses and loss of interest resulting from the breach. The right of the drawee to recover damages under this subsection is not affected by any failure of the drawee to exercise ordinary care in making payment. If the drawee accepts the draft, breach of warranty is a defense to the obligation of the acceptor. If the acceptor makes payment with respect to the draft, the acceptor is entitled to recover from any warrantor for breach of warranty the amounts stated in this subsection

(c) If a drawee asserts a claim for breach of warranty under subsection (a) based on an unauthorized indorsement of the draft or an alteration of the draft, the warrantor may defend by proving that the indorsement is effective under Section 3-404 or 3-405 or the drawer is precluded under Section 3-406 or 4-406 from asserting against the drawee the unauthorized indorsement or alteration.

(d) If (i) a dishonored draft is presented for payment to the drawer or an indorser or (ii) any other instrument is presented for payment to a party obliged to pay the instrument, and (iii) payment is received, the following rules apply:

(1) The person obtaining payment and a prior transferor of the instrument warrant to the person making payment in good faith that the warrantor is, or was, at the time the warrantor transferred the instrument, a person entitled to enforce the instrument or authorized to obtain payment on behalf of a person entitled to enforce the instrument.

(2) The person making payment may recover from any warrantor for breach of warranty an amount equal to the amount paid plus expenses and loss of interest resulting from the breach.

(e) The warranties stated in subsections (a) and (d) cannot be disclaimed with respect to checks. Unless notice of a claim for breach of warranty is given to the warrantor within 30 days after the claimant has reason to know of the breach and the identity of the warrantor, the liability of the warrantor under subsection (b) or (d) is discharged to the extent of any loss caused by the delay in giving notice of the claim.

(f) A [cause of action] for breach of warranty under this section accrues when the claimant has reason to know of the breach.

Section 3-418. Payment or Acceptance by Mistake.

(a) Except as provided in subsection (c), if the drawee of a draft pays or accepts the draft and the drawee acted on the mistaken belief that (i) payment of the draft had not been stopped pursuant to Section 4-403 or (ii) the signature of the drawer of the draft was authorized, the drawee may recover the amount of the draft from the person to whom or for whose benefit payment was made or, in the case of acceptance, may revoke the acceptance. Rights of the drawee under this subsection are not affected by failure of the drawee to exercise ordinary care in paying or accepting the draft.

(b) Except as provided in subsection (c), if an instrument has been paid or accepted by mistake and the case is not covered by subsection (a), the person paying or accepting may, to the extent permitted by the law governing mistake and restitution, (i) recover the payment from the person to whom or for whose benefit payment was made or (ii) in the case of acceptance, may revoke the acceptance.

(c) The remedies provided by subsection (a) or (b) may not be asserted against a person who took the instrument in good faith and for value or who in good faith changed position in reliance on the payment or acceptance. This subsection does not limit remedies provided by Section 3-417 or 4-407.

(d) Notwithstanding Section 4-215, if an instrument is paid or accepted by mistake and the payor or acceptor recovers payment or revokes acceptance under subsection (a) or (b), the instrument is deemed not to have been paid or accepted and is treated as dishonored, and the person from whom payment is recovered has rights as a person entitled to enforce the dishonored instrument

Section 3-419. Instruments Signed for Accommodation.

(a) If an instrument is issued for value given for the benefit of a party to the instrument ("accommodated party") and another party to the instrument ("accommodation party") signs the instrument for the purpose of incurring liability on the instrument without being a direct beneficiary of the value given for the instrument, the instrument is signed by the accommodation party "for accommodation."

(b) An accommodation party may sign the instrument as maker, drawer, acceptor, or indorser and, subject to subsection (d), is obliged to the instrument in the capacity in which the accommodation party signs. The obligation of an accommodation party may be enforced notwithstanding any statute of frauds and whether or not the accommodation party receives consideration for the accommodation.

(c) A person signing an instrument is presumed to be an accommodation party and there is notice that the instrument is signed for accommodation if the signature is an anomalous indorsement or is accompanied by words indicating that the signer is acting as surety or guarantor with respect to the obligation of another party to the instrument. Except as provided in Section 3-605, the obligation of an accommodation party to pay the instrument is not affected by the fact that the person enforcing the obligation had notice when the instrument was taken by that person that the accommodation party signed the instrument for accommodation.

(d) If the signature of a party to an instrument is accompanied by words indicating unambiguously that the party is guaranteeing collection rather than payment of the obligation of another party to the instrument, the signer is obliged to pay the amount due on the instrument to a person entitled to enforce the instrument only if (i) execution of judgment against the other party has been returned unsatisfied, (ii) the other party is insolvent or in an insolvency proceeding, (iii) the other party cannot be served with process, or (iv) it is otherwise apparent that payment cannot be obtained from the other party.

(e) An accommodation party who pays the instrument is entitled to reimbursement from the accommodated party and is entitled to enforce the instrument against the accommodated party. An accommodated party who pays the instrument has no right of recourse against, and is not entitled to contribution from, an accommodation party.

Section 3-420. Conversion of Instrument.

(a) The law applicable to conversion of personal property applies to instruments. An instrument is also converted if it is taken by transfer, other than a negotiation, from a person not entitled to enforce the instrument or a bank makes or obtains payment with respect to the instrument for a person not entitled to enforce the instrument or receive payment. An action for conversion of an instrument may not be brought by (i) the issuer or acceptor of the instrument or (ii) a payee or indorsee who did not receive delivery of the instrument either directly or through delivery to an agent or a copayee.

(b) In an action under subsection (a), the measure of liability is presumed to be the amount payable on the instrument, but recovery may not exceed the amount of the plaintiff's interest in the instrument.

(c) A representative, other than a depositary bank, who has in good faith dealt with an instrument or its proceeds on behalf of one who was not the person entitled to enforce the instrument is not liable in conversion to that person beyond the amount of any proceeds that it has not paid out.

Part 5. Dishonor.

3-501. Presentment.

(a) "Presentment" means a demand made by or on behalf of a person entitled to enforce an instrument (i) to pay the instrument made to the drawee or a party obliged to pay the instrument or, in the case of a note or accepted draft payable at a bank, to the bank, or (ii) to accept a draft made to the drawee.

(b) The following rules are subject to Article 4, agreement of the parties, and clearinghouse rules and the like:

  (1) Presentment may be made at the place of payment of the instrument and must be made at the place of payment if the instrument is payable at a bank in the United States; may be made by any commercially reasonable means, including an oral, written, or electronic communication; is effective when the demand for payment or acceptance is received by the person to whom presentment is made; and is effective if made to any one of two or more makers, acceptors, drawees, or other payors.

(2) Upon demand of the person to whom presentment is made, the person making presentment must (i) exhibit the instrument, (ii) give reasonable identification and, if presentment is made on behalf of another person, reasonable evidence of authority to do so, and (iii) sign a receipt on the instrument for any payment made or surrender the instrument if full payment is made.

(3) Without dishonoring the instrument, the party to whom presentment is made may (i) return the instrument for lack of a necessary indorsement, or (ii) refuse payment or for failure of the presentment to comply with the terms of the instrument, an agreement of the parties, or other applicable law or rule.

(4) The party to whom presentment is made may treat presentment as occurring on the next business day after the day of presentment if the party to whom presentment is made has established a cut off hour not earlier than 2 p.m. for the receipt and processing of instruments presented for payment or acceptance and presentment is made after the cutoff hour.

Section 3-502. Dishonor.

(a) Dishonor of a note is governed by the following rules:

(1) If the note is payable on demand, the note is dishonored if presentment is duly made to the maker and the note is not paid on the day of presentment.

(2) If the note is not payable on demand and is payable at or through a bank or the terms of the note require presentment, the note is dishonored if presentment is duly made and the note is not paid on the day it becomes payable or the day of presentment, whichever is later.

(3) If the note is not payable on demand and paragraph (2) does not apply, the note is dishonored if it is not paid on the day it becomes payable.

(b) Dishonor of an unaccepted draft other than a documentary draft is governed by the following rules:

(1) If a check is duly presented for payment to the payor bank otherwise than for immediate payment over the counter, the check is dishonored if the payor bank makes timely return of the check or sends timely notice of dishonor or nonpayment under Section 4-301 or 4-302, or becomes accountable for the amount of the check under Section 4-302.

(2) If a draft is payable on demand and paragraph (1) does not apply, the draft is dishonored if presentment for payment is duly made to the drawee and the draft is not paid on the day of presentment.

(3) If a draft is payable on a date stated in the draft, the draft is dishonored if (i) presentment for payment is duly made to the drawee and payment is not made on the day the draft becomes payable or the day of presentment, whichever is later, or (ii) presentment for acceptance is duly made before the day the draft becomes payable and the draft is not accepted on the day of presentment.

(4) If a draft is payable on elapse of a period of time after sight or acceptance, the draft is dishonored if presentment for acceptance is duly made and the draft is not accepted on the day of presentment.

(c) Dishonor of an unaccepted documentary draft occurs according to the rules stated in subsection (b) (2), (3), and (4), except that payment or acceptance may be delayed without dishonor until no later than the close of the third business day of the drawee following the day on which payment or acceptance is required by those paragraphs.

(d) Dishonor of an accepted draft is governed by the following rules:

(1) If the draft is payable on demand, the draft is dishonored if presentment for payment is duly made to the acceptor and the draft is not paid on the day of presentment.

(2) If the draft is not payable on demand, the draft is dishonored if presentment for payment is duly made to the acceptor and payment is not made on the day it becomes payable or the day of presentment, whichever is later.

(e) In any case in which presentment is otherwise required for dishonor under this section and presentment is excused under Section 3-504, dishonor occurs without presentment if the instrument is not duly accepted or paid.

(f) If a draft is dishonored because timely acceptance of the draft was not made and the person entitled to demand acceptance consents to a late acceptance, from the time of acceptance the draft is treated as never having been dishonored.

Section 3-503 Notice of Dishonor.

(a) The obligation of an indorser stated in Section 3-415(a) and the obligation of a drawer stated in Section 3-414(d) may not be enforced unless (i) the indorser or drawer is given notice of dishonor of the instrument complying with this section or (ii) notice of dishonor is excused under Section 3-504(b).

(b) Notice of dishonor may be given by any person; may be given by any commercially reasonable means, including an oral, written, or electronic communication; and is sufficient if it reasonably identifies the instrument and indicates that the instrument has been dishonored or has not been paid or accepted. Return of an instrument given to a bank for collection is sufficient notice of dishonor.

(c) Subject to Section 3-504(c), with respect to an instrument taken for collection by a collecting bank, notice of dishonor must be given (i) by the bank before midnight of the next banking day following the banking day on which the bank receives notice of dishonor of the instrument, or (ii) by any other person within 30 days following the day on which the person receives notice of dishonor. With respect to any other instrument, notice of dishonor must be given within 30 days following the day on which dishonor occurs.

Section 3-504. Excused Presentment and Notice of Dishonor.

(a) Presentment for payment or acceptance of an instrument is excused if (i) the person entitled to present the instrument cannot with reasonable diligence make presentment, (ii) the maker or acceptor has repudiated an obligation to pay the instrument or is dead or in insolvency proceedings, (iii) by the terms of the instrument presentment is not necessary to enforce the obligation of indorsers or the drawer, (iv) the drawer or indorser whose obligation is being enforced has waived presentment or otherwise has no reason to expect or right to require that the instrument be paid or accepted, or (v) the drawer instructed the drawee not to pay or accept the draft or the drawee was not obligated to the drawer to pay the draft.

(b) Notice of dishonor is excused if (i) by the term of the instrument notice of dishonor is not necessary to enforce the obligation of a party to pay the instrument, or (ii) the party whose obligation is being enforced waived notice of dishonor. A waiver of presentment is also a waiver of notice of dishonor.

(c) Delay in giving notice of dishonor is excused if the delay was caused by circumstances beyond the control of the person giving the notice and the person giving the notice exercised reasonable diligence after the cause of the delay ceased to operate.

Section 3-505. Evidence of Dishonor.

(a) The following are admissible as evidence and create a presumption of dishonor and of any notice of dishonor stated:

(1) a document regular in form as provided in subsection (b) which purports to be a protest;

(2) a purported stamp or writing of the drawee, payor bank, or presenting bank on or accompanying the instrument stating that acceptance or payment has been refused

unless reasons for the refusal are stated and the reasons are not consistent with dishonor;

(3) a book or record of the drawee, payor bank, or collecting bank, kept in the usual course of business which shows dishonor, even if there is no evidence of who made the entry.

(b) A protest is a certificate of dishonor made by a United States consul or vice consul, or a notary public or other person authorized to administer oaths by the law of the place where dishonor occurs. It may be made upon information satisfactory to that person. The protest must identify the instrument and certify either that presentment has been made or, if not made, the reason why it was not made, and that the instrument has been dishonored by nonacceptance or nonpayment. The protest may also certify that notice of dishonor has been given to some or all parties.

Part 6. Discharge and Payment.

Section 3-601. Discharge and Effect of Discharge.

(a) The obligation of a party to pay the instrument is discharged as stated in this Article or by an act or agreement with the party which would discharge an obligation to pay money under a simple contract.

(b) Discharge of the obligation of a party is not effective against a person acquiring rights of a holder in due course of the instrument without notice of the discharge.

Section 3-602. Payment.

(a) Subject to subsection (b), an instrument is paid to the extent payment is made (i) by or on behalf of a party obliged to pay the instrument, and (ii) to a person entitled to enforce the instrument. To the extent of the payment, the obligation of the party obliged to pay the instrument is discharged even though payment is made with knowledge of a claim to the instrument under Section 3-306 by another person.

(b) The obligation of a party to pay the instrument is not discharged under subsection (a) if:

(1) a claim to the instrument under Section 3-306 is enforceable against the party receiving payment and (i) payment is made with knowledge by the payor that payment is prohibited by injunction or similar process of a court of competent jurisdiction, or (ii) in the case of an instrument other than a cashier's check, teller's check, or certified check, the party making payment accepted, from the person having a claim to the instrument, indemnity against loss resulting from refusal to pay the person entitled to enforce the instrument; or

(2) the person making payment knows that the instrument is a stolen instrument and pays a person it knows is in wrongful possession of the instrument.

Section 3-603. Tender of Payment.

(a) If tender of payment of an obligation to pay an instrument is made to a person entitled to enforce the instrument, the effect of tender is governed by principles of law applicable to tender of payment under a simple contract.

(b) If tender of payment of an obligation to pay an instrument is made to a person entitled to enforce the instrument and the tender is refused, there is discharge, to the extent of the amount of the tender, of the obligation of an indorser or accommodation party having a right of recourse with respect to the obligation to which the tender relates.

(c) If tender of payment of an amount due on an instrument is made to a person entitled to enforce the instrument, the obligation of the obligor to pay interest after the due date on the amount tendered is discharged. If presentment is required with respect to an instrument and the obligor is able and ready to pay on the due date at every place of payment stated in the instrument, the obligor is deemed to have made tender of payment on the due date to the person entitled to enforce the instrument.

Section 3-604. Discharge by Cancellation or Renunciation.

(a) A person entitled to enforce an instrument, with or without consideration, may discharge the obligation of a party to pay the instrument (i) by an intentional voluntary act, such as surrender of the instrument to the party, destruction, mutilation, or cancellation of the instrument, cancellation or striking out of the party's signature, or the addition of words to the instrument indicating discharge, or (ii) by agreeing not to sue or otherwise renouncing rights against the party by a signed writing.

(b) Cancellation or striking out of an indorsement pursuant to subsection (a) does not affect the status and rights of a party derived from the indorsement.

Section 3-605. Discharge of Indorsers and Accommodation Parties.

(a) In this section, the term "indorser" includes a drawer having the obligation described in Section 3-414(d).

(b) Discharge, under Section 3-604, of the obligation of a party to pay an instrument does not discharge the obligation of an indorser or accommodation party having a right of recourse against the discharged party.

(c) If a person entitled to enforce an instrument agrees, with or without consideration, to an extension of the due date of the obligation of a party to pay the instrument, the extension discharges an indorser or accommodation party having a right of recourse against the party whose obligation is extended to the extent the indorser or accommodation party proves that the extension caused loss to the indorser or accommodation party with respect to the right of recourse.

(d) If a person entitled to enforce an instrument agrees, with or without consideration, to a material modification of the obligation of a party other than an extension of the due date, the modification discharges the obligation of an indorser or accommodation party having a right of recourse against the person whose obligation is modified to the extent the modification causes loss to the indorser or accommodation party with respect to the right of recourse. The loss suffered by the indorser or accommodation party as a result of the modification is equal to the amount of the right of recourse unless the person enforcing the instrument proves that no loss was caused by the modification or that the loss caused by the modification was an amount less than the amount of the right of recourse.

(e) If the obligation of a party to pay an instrument is secured by an interest in collateral and a person entitled to enforce the instrument impairs the value of the interest in collateral, the obligation of an indorser or accommodation party having a right of recourse against the obligor is discharged to the extent of the impairment. The value of an interest in collateral is impaired to the extent (i) the value of the interest is reduced to an amount less than the amount of the right of recourse of the party asserting discharge, or (ii) the reduction in value of the interest causes an increase in the amount by which the amount of the right of recourse exceeds the value of the interest. The burden of proving impairment is on the party asserting discharge.

(f) If the obligation of a party is secured by an interest in collateral not provided by an accommodation party and a person entitled to enforce the instrument impairs the value of the interest in collateral, the obligation of any party who is jointly and severally liable with respect to the secured obligation is discharged to the extent the impairment causes the party asserting discharge to pay more than that party would have been obliged to pay, taking into account rights of contribution, if impairment had not occurred. If the party asserting discharge is an accommodation party not entitled to discharge under subsection (e), the party is deemed to have a right to contribution based on joint and several liability rather than a right to reimbursement. The burden of proving impairment is on the party asserting discharge.

(g) Under subsection (e) or (f), impairing value of an interest in collateral includes (i) failure to obtain or maintain perfection or recordation of the interest in collateral,

(ii) release of collateral without substitution of collateral of equal value, (iii) failure to perform a duty to preserve the value of collateral owed, under Article 9 or other law, to a debtor or surety or other person secondarily liable, or (iv) failure to comply with applicable law in disposing of collateral.

(h) An accommodation party is not discharged under subsection (c), (d), or (e) unless the person entitled to enforce the instrument knows of the accommodation or has notice under Section 3-419(c) that the instrument was signed for accommodation.

(i) A party is not discharged under this section if (i) the party asserting discharge consents to the event or conduct that is the basis of the discharge, or (ii) the instrument or a separate agreement of the party provides for waiver of discharge under this section either specifically or by general language indicating that parties waive defenses based on suretyship or impairment of collateral.

Article 4. Bank Deposits and Collections.

Part I. General Provisions and Definitions.

Section 4-101. Short Title.

This Article shall be known and may be cited as Uniform Commercial Code—Bank Deposits and Collections.

Section 4-102. Applicability.

(a) To the extent that items within this Article are also within Articles 3 and 8, they are subject to those Articles. If there is conflict, this Article governs Article 3, but Article 8 governs this Article.

(b) The liability of a bank for action or nonaction with respect to an item handled by it for purposes of presentment, payment, or collection is governed by the law of the place where the bank is located. In the case of action or nonaction by or at a branch or separate office of a bank, its liability is governed by the law of the place where the branch or separate office is located.

Section 4-103. Variation by Agreement; Measure of Damages; Action Constituting Ordinary Care.

(a) The effect of the provisions of this Article may be varied by agreement, but the parties to the agreement cannot disclaim a bank's responsibility for its lack of good faith or failure to exercise ordinary care or limit the measure of damages for the lack or failure. However, the parties may determine by agreement the standards by which the bank's responsibility is to be measured if those standards are not manifestly unreasonable.

(b) Federal Reserve regulations and operating circulars, clearinghouse rules, and the like have the effect of agreements under subsection (a), whether or not specifically assented to by all parties interested in items handled.

(c) Action or nonaction approved by this Article or pursuant to Federal Reserve regulations or operating circulars is the exercise of ordinary care and, in the absence of special instructions, action or nonaction consistent with clearinghouse rules and the like or with a general banking usage not disapproved by this Article, is prima facie the exercise of ordinary care.

(d) The specification or approval of certain procedures by this Article is not disapproval of other procedures that may be reasonable under the circumstances.

(e) The measure of damages for failure to exercise ordinary care in handling an item is the amount of the item reduced by an amount that could not have been realized by the exercise of ordinary care. If there is also bad faith it includes any other damages the party suffered as a proximate consequence.

Section 4-104. Definitions and Index of Definitions.

(a) In this Article, unless the context otherwise requires

(1) "Account" means any deposit or credit account with a bank, including a demand, time, savings, passbook, share draft, or like account, other than an account evidenced by a certificate of deposit;

(2) "Afternoon" means the period of a day between noon and midnight;

(3) "Banking day" means the part of a day on which a bank is open to the public for carrying on substantially all of its banking functions;

(4) "Clearing house" means an association of banks or other payors regularly clearing items;

(5) "Customer" means a person having an account with a bank or for whom a bank has agreed to collect items, including a bank that maintains an account at another bank:

(6) "Documentary draft" means a draft to be presented for acceptance or payment if specified documents, certificated securities (Section 8-102) or instructions for uncertificated securities (Section 8-308), or other certificates, statements, or the like are to be received by the drawee or other payor before acceptance or payment of the draft;

(7) "Draft" means a draft as defined in Section 3-l04 or an item, other than an instrument, that is an order.

(8) "Drawee" means a person ordered in a draft to make payment.

(9) "Item" means an instrument or a promise or order to pay money handled by a bank for collection or payment. The term does not include a payment order governed by Article 4A or a credit or debit card slip;

(10) "Midnight deadline" with respect to a bank is midnight on its next banking day following the banking day on which it receives the relevant item or notice or from which the time for taking action commences to run, whichever is later;

(11) "Settle" means to pay in cash, by clearinghouse settlement, in a charge or credit or by remittance, or otherwise as agreed. A settlement may be either provisional or final.

(12) "Suspends payments" with respect to a bank means that it has been closed by order of the supervisory authorities, that a public officer has been appointed to take it over, or that it ceases or refuses to make payments in the ordinary course of business.

(b) Other definitions applying to this Article and the sections in which they appear are:

"Agreement for electronic presentment,"
Section 4-110.
"Bank," Section 4-105.
"Collecting bank," Section 4-105.
"Depositary bank," Section 4-105.
"Intermediary bank," Section 4-105.
"Payor bank," Section 4-105.
"Presenting bank," Section 4-105.
"Presentment notice," Section 4-110.

(c) The following definitions in other Articles apply to this Article:

"Acceptance," Section 3-409.
"Alteration," Section 3-407.

"Cashier's check," Section 3-104.
"Certificate of deposit," Section 3-104.
"Certified check," Section 3-409.
"Check," Section 3-104.
"Good faith," Section 3-103.
"Holder in due course," Section 3-302.
"Instrument," Section 3-104.
"Notice of dishonor," Section 3-503.
"Order," Section 3-103.
"Ordinary care," Section 3-103.
"Person entitled to enforce," Section 3-301.
"Presentment," Section 3-501.
"Promise," Section 3-103.
"Prove," Section 3-103.
"Teller's check," Section 3-104.
"Unauthorized signature," Section 3-403.

(d) In addition, Article 1 contains general definitions and principles of construction and interpretation applicable throughout this Article.

Section 4-105. "Bank"; "Depositary Bank"; "Payor Bank;" "Intermediary Bank;" "Collecting Bank;" "Presenting Bank."

In this Article:

(1) "Bank" means a person engaged in the business of banking, including a savings bank, savings and loan association, credit union, or trust company.

(2) "Depositary bank" means the first bank to take an item even though it is also the payor bank, unless the item is presented for immediate payment over the counter;

(3) "Payor bank" means a bank that is the drawee of a draft;

(4) "Intermediary bank" means a bank to which an item is transferred in course of collection except the depositary or payor bank;

(5) "Collecting bank" means a bank handling an item for collection except the payor bank;

(6) "Presenting bank" means a bank presenting an item except a payor bank.

Section 4-106. Payable Through or Payable at Bank Collecting.

(a) If an item states that it is "payable through" a bank identified in the item, (i) the item designates the bank as a collecting bank and does not by itself authorize the bank to pay the item, and (ii) the item may be presented for payment only by or through the bank.

Alternative A

(b) If an item states that it is "payable at" a bank identified in the item. the item is equivalent to a draft drawn on the bank.

Alternative B

(b) If an item states that it is "payable at" a bank identified in the item, (i) the item designates the bank as a collecting bank and does not by itself authorize the bank to pay the item, and (ii) the item may be presented for payment only by or through the bank.

(c) If a draft names a nonbank drawee and it is unclear whether a bank named in the draft is a codrawee or a collecting bank, the bank is a collecting bank.

Section 4-107. Separate Office of Bank.

A branch or separate office of a bank is a separate bank for the purpose of computing the time within which and determining the place at or to which action may be taken or notices or orders shall be given under this Article and under Article 3.

Section 4-108. Time of Receipt of Items.

(a) For the purpose of allowing time to process items, prove balances, and make the necessary entries on its books to determine its position for the day, a bank may fix an afternoon hour of 2 p.m. or later as a cutoff hour for the handling of money and items and the making of entries on its books.

(b) An item or deposit of money received on any day after a cutoff hour so fixed or after the close of the banking day may be treated as being received at the opening of the next banking day.

Section 4-109. Delays.

(a) Unless otherwise instructed, a collecting bank in a good faith effort to secure payment of a specific item drawn on a payor other than a bank, and with or without the approval of any person involved, may waive, modify, or extend time limits imposed or permitted by this [Act] for a period not exceeding two additional banking days without discharge of drawers or indorsers or liability to its transferor or a prior party.

(b) Delay by a collecting bank or payor bank beyond time limits prescribed or permitted by this [Act] or by instructions is excused if (i) the delay is caused by interruption of communication or computer facilities, suspension of payments by another bank, war, emergency conditions, failure of equipment, or other circumstances beyond the control of the bank, and (ii) the bank exercises such diligence as the circumstances require.

Section 4-110. Electronic Presentment.

(a) "Agreement for electronic presentment" means an agreement, clearing house rule, or Federal Reserve regulation or operating circular, providing that presentment of an item may be made by transmission of an image of an item or information describing the item ("presentment notice") rather than delivery of the item it self. The agreement may provide for procedures governing retention, presentment, payment, dishonor, and other matters concerning items subject to the agreement.

(b) Presentment of an item pursuant to an agreement for presentment is made when the presentment notice is received.

(c) If presentment is made by presentment notice, a reference to "item" or "check" in this Article means the presentment notice unless the context otherwise indicates.

Section 4-111. Statute of Limitations.

An action to enforce an obligation, duty, or right arising under this Article must be commenced within three years after the [cause of action] accrues.

Part 2. Collection of Items: Depository and Collecting Banks.

Section 4-201. Status of Collecting Bank as Agent and Provisional Status of Credits; Applicability of Article; Item Indorsed "Pay Any Bank."

(a) Unless a contrary intent clearly appears and before the time that a settlement given by a collecting bank for an item is or becomes final, the bank, with respect to an item, is an agent or sub agent of the owner of the item and any settlement given for the item is provisional. This provision applies regardless of the form of indorsement or lack of indorsement and even though credit given for the item is subject to immediate withdrawal as of right or is in fact withdrawn; but the continuance of ownership of an item by its owner and any rights of the owner to proceeds of the item are subject to rights of a collecting bank, such as those resulting from outstanding advances on the item and rights of recoupment or setoff. If an item is handled by banks for purposes of presentment, payment, collection, or return, the relevant provisions of this Article apply even though action of the parties clearly establishes that a particular bank has purchased the item and is the owner of it.

(b) After an item has been indorsed with the words "pay any bank" or the like, only a bank may acquire the rights of a holder until the item has been:

  (1) returned to the customer initiating collection; or

  (2) specially indorsed by a bank to a person who is not a bank.

Section 4-202. Responsibility for Collection or Return; When Action Timely.

(a) A collecting bank must exercise ordinary care in:

  (1) presenting an item or sending it for presentment;

  (2) sending notice of dishonor or nonpayment or returning an item other than a documentary draft to the bank's transferor after learning that the item has not been paid or accepted, as the case may be;

  (3) settling for an item when the bank receives final settlement; and

  (4) notifying its transferor of any loss or delay in transit within a reasonable time after discovery thereof.

(b) A collecting bank exercises ordinary care under subsection (a) by taking proper action before its midnight deadline following receipt of an item, notice, or settlement. Taking proper action within a reasonably longer time may constitute the exercise of ordinary care, but the bank has the burden of establishing timeliness.

(c) Subject to subsection (a) (1), a bank is not liable for the insolvency, neglect, misconduct, mistake, or default of another bank or person or for loss or destruction of an item in the possession of others or in transit.

Section 4-203. Effect of Instructions.

Subject to Article 3 concerning conversion of instruments (Section 3-420) and restrictive indorsements (Section 3-206), only a collecting bank's transferor can give instructions that affect the bank or constitute notice to it, and a collecting bank is not liable to prior parties for any action taken pursuant to the instructions or in accordance with any agreement with its transferor.

Section 4-204. Methods of Sending and Presenting; Sending Directly to Payor Bank.

(a) A collecting bank shall send items by a reasonably prompt method, taking into consideration relevant instructions, the nature of the item, the number of those items on hand, the cost of collection involved, and the method generally used by it or others to present those items.

(b) A collecting bank may send:

  (1) an item directly to the payor bank;

  (2) an item to a nonbank payor if authorized by its transferor; and

  (3) an item other than documentary drafts to a nonbank payor, if authorized by Federal Reserve regulation or operating circular, clearinghouse rule, or the like.

(c) Presentment may be made by a presenting bank at a place where the payor bank or other payor has requested that presentment be made.

Section 4-205. Depositary Bank Holder of Unindorsed Item.

If a customer delivers an item to a depositary bank for collection:

(1) the depositary bank becomes a holder of the item at the time it receives the item for collection if the customer at the time of delivery was a holder of the item, whether or not the customer indorses the item, and, if the bank satisfies the other requirements of Section 3-302, it is a holder in due course; and

(2) the depositary bank warrants to collecting banks, the payor bank or other payor, and the drawer that the amount of the item was paid to the customer or deposited to the customer's account.

Section 4-206. Transfer Between Banks.

Any agreed method that identifies the transferor bank is sufficient for the item's further transfer to another bank

Section 4-207. Transfer Warranties.

(a) A customer or collecting bank that transfers an item and receives a settlement or other consideration warrants to the transferee and to any subsequent collecting bank that:

(1) the warrantor is a person entitled to enforce the item;

(2) all signatures on the item are authentic and authorized;

(3) the item has not been altered;

(4) the item is not subject to a defense or claim in recoupment (Section 3-305(a)) of any party that can be asserted against the warrantor; and

(5) the warrantor has no knowledge of any insolvency proceeding commenced with respect to the maker or acceptor or, in the case of an unaccepted draft, the drawer.

(b) If an item is dishonored, a customer or collecting bank transferring the item and receiving settlement or other consideration is obliged to pay the amount due on the item (i) according to the terms of the item at the time it was transferred, or (ii) if the transfer was of an incomplete item, according to its terms when completed as stated in Sections 3-115 and 3-407. The obligation of a transferor is owed to the transferee and to any subsequent collecting bank that takes the item in good faith. A transferor cannot disclaim its obligation under this subsection by an indorsement stating that it is made "without recourse" or otherwise disclaiming liability.

(c) A person to whom the warranties under subsection (a) are made and who took the item in good faith may recover from the warrantor as damages for breach of warranty an amount equal to the loss suffered as a result of the breach, but not more than the amount of the item plus expenses and loss of interest incurred as a result of the breach.

(d) The warranties stated in subsection (a) cannot be disclaimed with respect to checks. Unless notice of a claim for breach of warranty is given to the warrantor within 30 days after the claimant has reason to know of the breach and the identity of the warrantor, the warrantor is discharged to the extent of any loss caused by the delay in giving notice of the claim.

(e) A cause of action for breach of warranty under this section accrues when the claimant has reason to know of the breach.

Section 4-208. Presentment Warranties.

(a) If an unaccepted draft is presented to the drawee for payment or acceptance and the drawee pays or accepts the draft, (i) the person obtaining payment or acceptance, at the time of presentment, and (ii) a previous transferor of the draft, at the time of transfer, warrant to the drawee that pays or accepts the draft in good faith that:

(1) the warrantor is, or was, at the time the warrantor transferred the draft, a person entitled to enforce the draft or authorized to obtain payment or acceptance of the draft on behalf of a person entitled to enforce the draft;

(2) the draft has not been altered; and

(3) the warrantor has no knowledge that the signature of the purported drawer of the draft is unauthorized.

(b) A drawee making payment may recover from a warrantor damages for breach of warranty equal to the amount paid by the drawee less the amount the drawee received or is entitled to receive from the drawer because of the payment. In addition, the drawee is entitled to compensation for expenses and loss of interest resulting from the breach. The right of the drawee to recover damages under this subsection is not affected by any failure of the drawee to exercise ordinary care in making payment. If the drawee accepts the draft (i) breach of warranty is a defense to the obligation of the acceptor, and (ii) if the acceptor makes payment with respect to the draft, the acceptor is entitled to recover from a warrantor for breach of warranty the amounts stated in this subsection.

(c) If a drawee asserts a claim for breach of warranty under subsection (a) based on an unauthorized indorsement of the draft or an alteration of the draft, the warrantor may defend by proving that the indorsement is effective under Section 3-404 or 3-405 or the drawer is precluded under Section 3-406 or 4-406 from asserting against the drawee the unauthorized indorsement or alteration.

(d) If (i) a dishonored draft is presented for payment to the drawer or an indorser or (ii) any other item is presented for payment to a party obliged to pay the item, and the item is paid, the person obtaining payment and a prior transferor of the item warrant to the person making payment in good faith that the warrantor is, or was, at the time the warrantor transferred the item, a person entitled to enforce the item or authorized to obtain payment on behalf of a person entitled to enforce the item. The person making payment may recover from any warrantor for breach of warranty an amount equal to the amount paid plus expenses and loss of interest resulting from the breach.

(e) The warranties stated in subsections (a) and (d) cannot be disclaimed with respect to checks. Unless notice of a claim for breach of warranty is given to the warrantor within 30 days after the claimant has reason to know of the breach and the identity of the warrantor, the warrantor is discharged to the extent of any loss caused by the delay in giving notice of the claim.

(f) A cause of action for breach of warranty under this section accrues when the claimant has reason to know of the breach.

Section 4-209. Encoding and Retention Warranties.

(a) A person who encodes information on or with respect to an item after issue warrants to any subsequent collecting bank and to the payor bank or other payor that the information is correctly encoded. If the customer of a depositary bank encodes, that bank also makes the warranty.

(b) A person who undertakes to retain an item pursuant to an agreement for electronic presentment warrants to any subsequent collecting bank and to the payor bank or other payor that retention and presentment of the item comply with the agreement. If a customer of a depositary bank undertakes to retain an item, that bank also makes this warranty.

(c) A person to whom warranties are made under this section and who took the item in good faith may recover from the warrantor as damages for breach of warranty an amount equal to the loss suffered as a result of the breach, plus expenses and loss of interest incurred as a result of the breach.

Section 4-210. Security Interest of Collecting Bank in Items, Accompanying Documents, and Proceeds.

(a) A collecting bank has a security interest in an item and any accompanying documents or the proceeds of either:

(1) in case of an item deposited in an account, to the extent to which credit given for the item has been withdrawn or applied;

(2) in case of an item for which it has given credit available for withdrawal as of right, to the extent of the credit given, whether or not the credit is drawn upon or there is a right of chargeback; or

(3) if it makes an advance on or against the item.

(b) If credit given for several items received at one time or pursuant to a single agreement is withdrawn or applied in part, the security interest remains upon all the items, any accompanying documents or the proceeds of either. For the purpose of this section, credits first given are first withdrawn.

(c) Receipt by a collecting bank of a final settlement for an item is a realization on its security interest in the item, accompanying documents, and proceeds. So long as the bank does not receive final settlement for the item or give up possession of the item or accompanying documents for purposes other than collection, the security interest continues to that extent and is subject to Article 9, but.

(1) no security agreement is necessary to make the security interest enforceable (Section 9-203(1) (a));

(2) no filing is required to perfect the security interest; and

(3) the security interest has priority over conflicting perfected security interests in the item, accompanying documents or proceeds.

Section 4-211. When Bank Gives Value for Purposes of Holder in Due Course.

For purposes of determining its status as a holder in due course, a bank has given value to the extent it has a security interest in an item if the bank otherwise complies with the requirements of Section 3-302 on what constitutes a holder in due course.

Section 4-212. Presentment by Notice of Item Not Payable by, Through, or at Bank; Liability of Drawer or Indorser.

(a) Unless otherwise instructed, a collecting bank may present an item not payable by, through, or at a bank by sending to the party to accept or pay a written notice that the bank holds the item for acceptance or payment. The notice must be sent in time to be received on or before the day when presentment is due and the bank must meet any requirement of the party to accept or pay under Section 3-501 by the close of the bank's next banking day after it knows of the requirement (b) If presentment is made by notice and payment, acceptance, or request for compliance with a requirement under Section 3-501 is not received by the close of business on the day after maturity or, in the case of demand items, by the close of business on the third banking day after notice was sent, the presenting bank may treat the item as dishonored and charge any drawer or indorser by sending it notice of the facts.

Section 4-213. Medium and Time of Settlement by Bank.

(a) With respect to settlement by a bank, the medium and time of settlement may be prescribed by Federal Reserve regulations or circulars, clearing house rules, and the like, or agreement. In the absence of such prescription:

(1) the medium of settlement is cash or credit to an account in a Federal Reserve bank of or specified by the person to receive settlement; and

(2) the time of settlement, is:

(i) with respect to tender of settlement by cash, a cashier's check, or teller's check, when the cash or check is sent or delivered;

(ii) with respect to tender of settlement by credit in an account in a Federal Reserve Bank, when the credit is made;

(iii) with respect to tender of settlement by a credit or debit to an account in a bank, when the credit or debit is made or, in the case of tender of settlement by authority to charge an account, when the authority is sent or delivered; or

(iv) with respect to tender of settlement by a funds transfer, when payment is made pursuant to Section 4A-406(a) to the person receiving settlement.

(b) If the tender of settlement is not by a medium authorized by subsection (a) or the time of settlement is not fixed by subsection (a), no settlement occurs until the tender of settlement is accepted by the person receiving settlement.

(c) If settlement for an item is made by cashier's check or teller's check and the person receiving settlement, before its midnight deadline:

(1) presents or forwards the check for collection, settlement is when the check is finally paid; or

(2) fails to present or forward the check for collection, settlement is final at the midnight deadline of the person receiving settlement.

(d) If settlement for an item is made by giving authority to charge the account of the bank giving settlement in the bank receiving settlement, settlement is final when the charge is made by the bank receiving settlement if there are funds available in the account for the amount of the item.

Section 4-214. Right of Charge Back or Refund; Liability of Collecting Bank: Return of Item.

(a) If a collecting bank has made provisional settlement with its customer for an item and fails by reason of dishonor, suspension of payments by a bank, or otherwise to receive settlement for the item which is or becomes final, the bank may revoke the settlement given by it, charge back the amount of any credit given for the item to its customer's account, or obtain refund from its customer, whether or not it is able to return the item, if by its midnight deadline or within a longer reasonable time after it learns the facts it returns the item or sends notification of the facts. If the return or notice is delayed beyond the bank's midnight deadline or a longer reasonable time after it learns the facts, the bank may revoke the settlement, charge back the credit, or obtain refund from its customer, but it is liable for any loss resulting from the delay. These rights to revoke, charge back, and obtain refund terminate if and when a settlement for the item received by the bank is or becomes final.

(b) A collecting bank returns an item when it is sent or delivered to the bank's customer or transferor or pursuant to its instructions.

(c) A depositary bank that is also the payor may charge back the amount of an item to its customer's account or obtain refund in accordance with the section governing return of an item received by a payor bank for credit on its books (Section 4-301).

(d) The right to charge back is not affected by

(1) previous use of a credit given for the item; or

(2) failure by any bank to exercise ordinary care with respect to the item, but a bank so failing remains liable.

(e) A failure to charge back or claim refund does not affect other rights of the bank against the customer or any other party.

(f) If credit is given in dollars as the equivalent of the value of an item payable in foreign money, the dollar amount of any charge back or refund must be calculated on the basis of the bank offered spot rate for the foreign money prevailing on the day when the person entitled to the charge back or refund learns that it will not receive payment in ordinary course.

Section 4-215. Final Payment of Item by Payor Bank; When Professional Debits and Credits Become Final; When Certain Credits Become Available for Withdrawal.

(a) An item is finally paid by a payor bank when the bank has first done any of the following:

(1) paid the item in cash;

(2) settled for the item without having a right to revoke the settlement under statute, clearinghouse rule, or agreement; or

(3) made a provisional settlement for the item and failed to revoke the settlement in the time and manner permitted by statute, clearinghouse rule, or agreement.

(b) If provisional settlement for an item does not become final, the item is not finally paid.

(c) If provisional settlement for an item between the presenting and payor banks is made through a clearing house or by debits or credits in an account between them, then to the extent that provisional debits or credits for the item are entered in accounts between the presenting and payor banks or between the presenting and successive prior collecting banks seriatim, they become final upon final payment of the item by the payor bank.

(d) If a collecting bank receives a settlement for an item which is or becomes final, the bank is accountable to its customer for the amount of the item and any provisional credit given for the item in an account with its customer becomes final.

(e) Subject to (i) applicable law stating a time for availability of funds and (ii) any right of the bank to apply the credit to an obligation of the customer, credit given by a bank for an item in a customer's account becomes available for withdrawal as of right:

(1) if the bank has received a provisional settlement for the item, when the settlement becomes final and the bank has had a reasonable time to receive return of the item and the item has not been received within that time;

(2) if the bank is both the depositary bank and the payor bank, and the item is finally paid, at the opening of the bank's second banking day following receipt of the item.

(f) Subject to applicable law stating a time for availability of funds and any right of a bank to apply a deposit to an obligation of the depositor, a deposit of money becomes available for withdrawal as of right at the opening of the bank's next banking day after receipt of the deposit.

Section 4-216. Insolvency and Preference.

(a) If an item is in or comes into the possession of a payor or collecting bank that suspends payment and the item has not been finally paid, the item must be returned by the receiver, trustee, or agent in charge of the closed bank to the presenting bank or the closed bank's customer.

(b) If a payor bank finally pays an item and suspends payments without making a settlement for the item with its customer or the presenting bank which settlement is or becomes final, the owner of the item has a preferred claim against the payor bank.

(c) If a payor bank gives or a collecting bank gives or receives a provisional settlement for an item and thereafter suspends payments, the suspension does not prevent or interfere with the settlement's becoming final if the finality occurs automatically upon the lapse of certain time or the happening of certain events.

(d) If a collecting bank receives from subsequent parties settlement for an item, which settlement is or becomes final and the bank suspends payments without making a settlement for the item with its customer which settlement is or becomes final, the owner of the item has a preferred claim against the collecting bank.

Part 3. Collection of Items: Payor Banks.

Section 4-301. Deferred Posting; Recovery of Payment by Return of Items; Time of Dishonor, Return of Items by Payor Bank.

(a) If a payor bank settles for a demand item other than a documentary draft presented otherwise than for immediate payment over the counter before midnight of the banking day of receipt, the payor bank may revoke the settlement and recover the settlement if, before it has made final payment and before its midnight deadline, it

(1) returns the item; or

(2) sends written notice of dishonor or nonpayment if the item is unavailable for return.

(b) If a demand item is received by a payor bank for credit on its books, it may return the item or send notice of dishonor and may revoke any credit given or recover the amount thereof withdrawn by its customer, if it acts within the time limit and in the manner specified in subsection (a).

(c) Unless previous notice of dishonor has been sent, an item is dishonored at the time when for purposes of dishonor it is returned or notice sent in accordance with this section.

(d) An item is returned:

(1) as to an item presented through a clearing house, when it is delivered to the presenting or last collecting bank or to the clearing house or is sent or delivered in accordance with clearinghouse rules; or

(2) in all other cases, when it is sent or delivered to the bank's customer or transferor or pursuant to instructions.

Section 4-302. Payor Bank's Responsibility for Late Return of Item.

(a) If an item is presented to and received by a payor bank, the bank is accountable for the amount of:

(1) a demand item, other than a documentary draft, whether properly payable or not, if the bank, in any case in which it is not also the depositary bank, retains the item beyond midnight of the banking day of receipt without settling for it or, whether or not it is also the depositary bank, does not pay or return the item or send notice of dishonor until after its midnight deadline; or

(2) any other properly payable item unless, within the time allowed for acceptance or payment of that item, the bank either accepts or pays the item or returns it and accompanying documents.

(b) The liability of a payor bank to pay an item pursuant to subsection (a) is subject to defenses based on breach of a presentment warranty (Section 4-208) or proof that the person seeking enforcement of the liability presented or transferred the item for the purpose of defrauding the payor bank.

Section 4-303. When Items Subject to Notice, Stop Payment Order, Legal Process, or Setoff; Order in Which Items May Be Charged or Certified.

(a) Any knowledge, notice, or stop payment order received by, legal process served upon, or setoff exercised by a payor bank comes too late to terminate, suspend, or modify the bank's right or duty to pay an item or to charge its customer's account for the item if the knowledge, notice, stop payment order, or legal process is received or served and a reasonable time for the bank to act thereon expires or the setoff is exercised after the earliest of the following:

(1) the bank accepts or certifies the item;

(2) the bank pays the item in cash;

(3) the bank settles for the item without having a right to revoke the settlement under statute, clearing house rule, or agreement;

(4) the bank becomes accountable for the amount of the item under Section 4-302 dealing with the payor bank's responsibility for late return of items; or

(5) with respect to checks, a cutoff hour no earlier than one hour after the opening of the next banking day after the banking day on which the bank received the check

and no later than the close of that next banking day or, if no cutoff hour is fixed, the close of the next banking day after the banking day on which the bank received the check.

(b) Subject to subsection (a), items may be accepted, paid, certified, or charged to the indicated account of its customer in any order.

Part 4. Relationship Between Payor Bank and Its Customer.

Section 4-401. When Bank May Charge Customer's Account.

(a) A bank may charge against the account of a customer an item that is properly payable from the account even though the charge creates an overdraft. An item is properly payable if it is authorized by the customer and is in accordance with any agreement between the customer and bank.

(b) A customer is not liable for the amount of an overdraft if the customer neither signed the item nor benefitted from the proceeds of the item.

(c) A bank may charge against the account of a customer a check that is otherwise properly payable from the account, even though payment was made before the date of the check, unless the customer has given notice to the bank of the postdating describing the check with reasonable certainty. The notice is effective for the period stated in Section 4-403(b) for stop payment orders, and must be received at such time and in such manner as to afford the bank a reasonable opportunity to act on it before the bank takes any action with respect to the check described in Section 4-303. If a bank charges against the account of a customer a check before the date stated in the notice of postdating, the bank is liable for damages for the loss resulting from its act. The loss may include damages for dishonor of subsequent items under Section 4-402.

(d) A bank that in good faith makes payment to a holder may charge the indicated account of its customer according to:

(1) the original terms of the altered item; or

(2) the terms of the completed item, even though the bank knows the item has been completed unless the bank has notice that the completion was improper.

Section 4-402. Bank's Liability to Customer for Wrongful Dishonor; Time of Determining Insufficiency of Account.

(a) Except as otherwise provided in this Article, a payor bank wrongfully dishonors an item if it dishonors an item that is properly payable, but a bank may dishonor an item that would create an overdraft unless it has agreed to pay the overdraft.

(b) A payor bank is liable to its customer for damages proximately caused by the wrongful dishonor of an item. Liability is limited to actual damages proved and may include damages for an arrest or prosecution of the customer or other consequential damages. Whether any consequential damages are proximately caused by the wrongful dishonor is a question of fact to be determined in each case.

(c) A payor bank's determination of the customer's account balance on which a decision to dishonor for insufficiency of available funds is based may be made at any time between the time the item is received by the payor bank and the time that the payor bank returns the item or gives notice in lieu of return, and no more than one determination need be made. If, at the election of the payor bank, a subsequent balance determination is made for the purpose of reevaluating the bank's decision to dishonor the item, the account balance at that time is determinative of whether a dishonor for insufficiency of available funds is wrongful.

Section 4-403. Customer's Right to Stop Payment; Burden of Proof.

(a) A customer or any person authorized to draw on the account if there is more than one person may stop payment of any item drawn on the customer's account or close the account by an order to the bank describing the item or account with reasonable certainty received at a time and in a manner that affords the bank a reasonable opportunity to act on it before any action by the bank with respect to the item described in Section 4-303. If the signature of more than one person is required to draw on an account, any of these persons may stop payment or close the account.

(b) A stop payment order is effective for six months, but it lapses after 14 calendar days if the original order was oral and was not in writing within that period. A stop payment order may be renewed for additional six month periods by a writing given to the bank within a period during which the stop payment order is effective.

(c) The burden of establishing the fact and amount of loss resulting from the payment of an item contrary to a stop payment order or order to close an account is on the customer. The loss from payment of an item contrary to a stop payment order may include damages for dishonor of subsequent items under Section 4-402.

Section 4-404. Bank Not Obliged to Pay Check More Than Six Months Old.

A bank is under no obligation to a customer having a checking account to pay a check, other than a certified check, which is presented more than six months after its date, but it may charge its customer's account for a payment made thereafter in good faith.

Section 4-405. Death or Incompetence of Customer.

(a) A payor or collecting bank's authority to accept, pay, or collect an item or to account for proceeds of its collection, if otherwise effective, is not rendered ineffective by incompetence of a customer of either bank existing at the time the item is issued or its collection is undertaken if the bank does not know of an adjudication of incompetence. Neither death nor incompetence of a customer revokes the authority to accept, pay, collect, or account until the bank knows of the fact of death or of an adjudication of incompetence and has reasonable opportunity to act on it.

(b) Even with knowledge, a bank may for 10 days after the date of death pay or certify checks drawn on or before that date unless ordered to stop payment by a person claiming an interest in the account.

Section 4-406. Customer's Duty to Discover and Report Unauthorized Signature or Alteration.

(a) A bank that sends or makes available to a customer a statement of account showing payment of items for the account shall either return or make available to the customer the items paid or provide information in the statement of account sufficient to allow the customer reasonably to identify the items paid. The statement of account provides sufficient information if the item is described by item number, amount, and date of payment.

(b) If the items are not returned to the customer, the person retaining the items shall either retain the items or, if the items are destroyed, maintain the capacity to furnish legible copies of the items until the expiration of seven years after receipt of the items. A customer may request an item from the bank that paid the item, and that bank must provide in a reasonable time either the item or, if the item has been destroyed or is not otherwise obtainable, a legible copy of the item.

(c) If a bank sends or makes available a statement of account or items pursuant to subsection (a), the customer must exercise reasonable promptness in examining the statement or the items to determine whether any payment was not authorized because of an alteration of an item or because a purported signature by or on behalf of the customer was not authorized. If, based on the statement or items provided, the customer should reasonably have discovered the unauthorized payment, the customer must promptly notify the bank of the relevant facts.

(d) If the bank proves that the customer failed, with respect to an item, to comply with the duties imposed on the customer by subsection (c), the customer is precluded from asserting against the bank:

(1) the customer's unauthorized signature or any alteration on the item, if the bank also proves that it suffered a loss by reason of the failure; and

(2) the customer's unauthorized signature or alteration by the same wrongdoer on any other item paid in good faith by the bank if the payment was made before the bank received notice from the customer of the unauthorized signature or alteration and after the customer had been afforded a reasonable period of time, not exceeding 30 days, in which to examine the item or statement of account and notify the bank.

(e) If subsection (d) applies and the customer proves that the bank failed to exercise ordinary care in paying the item and that the failure substantially contributed to loss, the loss is allocated between the customer precluded and the bank asserting the preclusion according to the extent to which the failure of the customer to comply with subsection (c) and the failure of the bank to exercise ordinary care contributed to the loss. If the customer proves that the bank did not pay the item in good faith, the preclusion under subsection (d) does not apply.

(f) Without regard to care or lack of care of either the customer or the bank, a customer who does not within one year after the statement or items are made available to the customer (subsection (a)) discover and report the customer's unauthorized signature on or any alteration on the item is precluded from asserting against the bank the unauthorized signature or alteration. If there is a preclusion under this subsection, the payor bank may not recover for breach or warranty under Section 4-208 with respect to the unauthorized signature or alteration to which the preclusion applies.

Section 4-407. Payor Bank's Right to Subrogation on Improper.

If a payor bank has paid an item over the order of the drawer or maker to stop payment, or after an account has been closed, or otherwise under circumstances giving a basis for objection by the drawer or maker, to prevent unjust enrichment and only to the extent necessary to prevent loss to the bank by reason of its payment of the item, the payor bank is subrogated to the rights

(1) of any holder in due course on the item against the drawer or maker;

(2) of the payee or any other holder of the item against the drawer or maker either on the item or under the transaction out of which the item arose; and

(3) of the drawer or maker against the payee or any other holder of the item with respect to the transaction out of which the item arose.

Part 5. Collection of Documentary Drafts.

Section 4-501. Handling of Documentary Drafts; Duty to Send for Presentment and to Notify Customer of Dishonor.

A bank that takes. a documentary draft for collection shall present or send the draft and accompanying documents for presentment and, upon learning that the draft has not been paid or accepted in due course, shall seasonably notify its customer of the fact even though it may have discounted or bought the draft or extended credit available for withdrawal as of right.

Section 4-502. Presentment of "On Arrival" Drafts.

If a draft or the relevant instructions require presentment "on arrival", "when goods arrive" or the like, the collecting bank need not present until in its judgment a reasonable time for arrival of the goods has expired. Refusal to pay or accept because the goods have not arrived is not dishonor; the bank must notify its transferor of the refusal but need not present the draft again until it is instructed to do so or learns of the arrival of the goods.

Section 4-503. Responsibility of Presenting Bank for Documents and Goods; Report of Reasons for Dishonor; Referee in Case of Need.

Unless otherwise instructed and except as provided in Article 5, a bank presenting a documentary draft:

(1) must deliver the documents to the drawee on acceptance of the draft if it is payable more than three days after presentment; otherwise, only on payment; and

(2) upon dishonor, either in the case of presentment for acceptance or presentment for payment, may seek and follow instructions from any referee in case of need designated in the draft or, if the presenting bank does not choose to utilize the referee's services, it must use diligence and good faith to ascertain the reason for dishonor, must notify its transferor of the dishonor and of the results of its effort to ascertain the reasons therefore, and must request instructions. However, the presenting bank is under no obligation with respect to goods represented by the documents except to follow any reasonable instructions seasonably received; it has a right to reimbursement for any expense incurred in following instructions and to prepayment of or indemnity for those expenses.

Section 4-504. Privilege of Presenting Bank to Deal with Goods; Security Interest for Expenses.

(a) A presenting bank that, following the dishonor of a documentary draft has seasonably requested instructions but does not receive them within a reasonable time may store, sell or otherwise deal with the goods in any reasonable manner.

(b) For its reasonable expenses incurred by action under subsection (a) the presenting bank has a lien upon the goods or their proceeds, which may be foreclosed in the same manner as an unpaid seller's lien.

Authors' note: *Articles 4A, 5, 6, 7, and 8 have been omitted as unnecessary for the purposes of this text.*

Article 9. Secured Transactions. [Revised]

Part 1. General Provisions

[Subpart 1. Short Title, Definitions, and General Concepts]

Section 9-101. Short Title.

This article may be cited as Uniform Commercial Code—Secured Transactions.

Section 9-102. Definitions and Index of Definitions.

(a) In this article:

(1) "Accession" means goods that are physically united with other goods in such a manner that the identity of the original goods is not lost.

(2) "Account", except as used in "account for", means a right to payment of a monetary obligation, whether or not earned by performance, (i) for property that has been or is to be sold, leased, licensed, assigned, or otherwise disposed of, (ii) for services rendered or to be rendered, (iii) for a policy of insurance issued or to be issued, (iv) for a secondary obligation incurred or to be incurred, (v) for energy provided or to be provided, (vi) for the use or hire of a vessel under a charter or other contract, (vii) arising out of the use of a credit or charge card or information contained on or for use with the card, or (viii) as winnings in a lottery or other game of chance operated or sponsored by a State, governmental unit of a State, or person licensed or authorized to operate the game by a State or governmental unit of a State. The term includes health-care insurance receivables. The term does not include (i) rights to payment evidenced by chattel paper or an instrument, (ii) commercial tort claims, (iii) deposit accounts, (iv) investment property, (v) letter-of-credit rights or letters of credit, or (vi) rights to payment for money or funds advanced or sold, other than rights arising out of the use of a credit or charge card or information contained on or for use with the card.

(3) "Account debtor" means a person obligated on an account, chattel paper, or general intangible. The term does not include persons obligated to pay a negotiable instrument, even if the instrument constitutes part of chattel paper.

(4) "Accounting," except as used in "accounting for", means a record:

(A) authenticated by a secured party;

(B) indicating the aggregate unpaid secured obligations as of a date not more than 35 days earlier or 35 days later than the date of the record; and

(C) identifying the components of the obligations in reasonable detail.

(5) "Agricultural lien" means an interest, other than a security interest, in farm products:

(A) which secures payment or performance of an obligation for:

(i) goods or services furnished in connection with a debtor's farming operation; or

(ii) rent on real property leased by a debtor in connection with its farming operation;

(B) which is created by statute in favor of a person that:

(i) in the ordinary course of its business furnished goods or services to a debtor in connection with a debtor's farming operation; or

(ii) leased real property to a debtor in connection with the debtor's farming operation; and

(C) whose effectiveness does not depend on the person's possession of the personal property.

(6) "As-extracted collateral" means:

(A) oil, gas, or other minerals that are subject to a security interest that:

(i) is created by a debtor having an interest in the minerals before extraction; and

(ii) attaches to the minerals as extracted; or

(B) accounts arising out of the sale at the wellhead or minehead of oil, gas, or other minerals in which the debtor had an interest before extraction.

(7) "Authenticate" means:

(A) to sign; or

(B) to execute or otherwise adopt a symbol, or encrypt or similarly process a record in whole or in part, with the present intent of the authenticating person to identify the person and adopt or accept a record.

(8) "Bank" means an organization that is engaged in the business of banking. The term includes savings banks, savings and loan associations, credit unions, and trust companies.

(9) "Cash proceeds" means proceeds that are money, checks, deposit accounts, or the like.

(10) "Certificate of title" means a certificate of title with respect to which a statute provides for the security interest in question to be indicated on the certificate as a condition or result of the security interest's obtaining priority over the rights of a lien creditor with respect to the collateral.

(11) "Chattel paper" means a record or records that evidence both a monetary obligation and a security interest in specific goods, a security interest in specific goods and software used in the goods, a security interest in specific goods and license of software used in the goods, a lease of specific goods, or a lease of specific goods and license of software used in the goods. In this paragraph, "monetary

obligation" means a monetary obligation secured by the goods or owed under a lease of the goods and includes a monetary obligation with respect to software used in the goods. The term does not include (i) charters or other contracts involving the use or hire of a vessel or (ii) records that evidence a right to payment arising out of the use of a credit or charge card or information contained on or for use with the card. If a transaction is evidenced by records that include an instrument or series of instruments, the group of records taken together constitutes chattel paper.

(12) "Collateral" means the property subject to a security interest or agricultural lien. The term includes:

(A) proceeds to which a security interest attaches;

(B) accounts, chattel paper, payment intangibles, and promissory notes that have been sold; and

(C) goods that are the subject of a consignment.

(13) "Commercial tort claim" means a claim arising in tort with respect to which:

(A) the claimant is an organization; or

(B) the claimant is an individual and the claim:

(i) arose in the course of the claimant's business or profession; and

(ii) does not include damages arising out of personal injury to or the death of an individual.

(14) "Commodity account" means an account maintained by a commodity intermediary in which a commodity contract is carried for a commodity customer.

(15) "Commodity contract" means a commodity futures contract, an option on a commodity futures contract, a commodity option, or another contract if the contract or option is:

(A) traded on or subject to the rules of a board of trade that has been designated as a contract market for such a contract pursuant to federal commodities laws; or

(B) traded on a foreign commodity board of trade, exchange, or market, and is carried on the books of a commodity intermediary for a commodity customer.

(16) "Commodity customer" means a person for which a commodity intermediary carries a commodity contract on its books.

(17) "Commodity intermediary" means a person that:

(A) is registered as a futures commission merchant under federal commodities law; or

(B) in the ordinary course of its business provides clearance or settlement services for a board of trade that has been designated as a contract market pursuant to federal commodities law.

(18) "Communicate" means:

(A) to send a written or other tangible record;

(B) to transmit a record by any means agreed upon by the persons sending and receiving the record; or

(C) in the case of transmission of a record to or by a filing office, to transmit a record by any means prescribed by filing-office rule.

(19) "Consignee" means a merchant to which goods are delivered in a consignment.

(20) "Consignment" means a transaction, regardless of its form, in which a person delivers goods to a merchant for the purpose of sale and:

(A) the merchant:

(i) deals in goods of that kind under a name other than the name of the person making delivery;

(ii) is not an auctioneer; and

(iii) is not generally known by its creditors to be substantially engaged in selling the goods of others;

(B) with respect to each delivery, the aggregate value of the goods is $1,000 or more at the time of delivery;

(C) the goods are not consumer goods immediately before delivery; and

(D) the transaction does not create a security interest that secures an obligation.

(21) "Consignor" means a person that delivers goods to a consignee in a consignment.

(22) "Consumer debtor" means a debtor in a consumer transaction.

(23) "Consumer goods" means goods that are used or bought for use primarily for personal, family, or household purposes.

(24) "Consumer-goods transaction" means a consumer transaction in which:

(A) an individual incurs an obligation primarily for personal, family, or household purposes; and

(B) a security interest in consumer goods secures the obligation.

(25) "Consumer obligor" means an obligor who is an individual and who incurred the obligation as part of a transaction entered into primarily for personal, family, or household purposes.

(26) "Consumer transaction" means a transaction in which (i) an individual incurs an obligation primarily for personal, family, or household purposes, (ii) a security interest secures the obligation, and (iii) the collateral is held or acquired primarily for personal, family, or household purposes. The term includes consumer-goods transactions.

(27) "Continuation statement" means an amendment of a financing statement which:

(A) identifies, by its file number, the initial financing statement to which it relates; and

(B) indicates that it is a continuation statement for, or that it is filed to continue the effectiveness of, the identified financing statement.

(28) "Debtor" means:

(A) a person having an interest, other than a security interest or other lien, in the collateral, whether or not the person is an obligor;

(B) a seller of accounts, chattel paper, payment intangibles, or promissory notes; or

(C) a consignee.

(29) "Deposit account" means a demand, time, savings, passbook, or similar account maintained with a bank. The term does not include investment property or accounts evidenced by an instrument.

(30) "Document" means a document of title or a receipt of the type described in Section 7-201(2).

(31) "Electronic chattel paper" means chattel paper evidenced by a record or records consisting of information stored in an electronic medium.

(32) "Encumbrance" means a right, other than an ownership interest, in real property. The term includes mortgages and other liens on real property.

(33) "Equipment" means goods other than inventory, farm products, or consumer goods.

(34) "Farm products" means goods, other than standing timber, with respect to which the debtor is engaged in a farming operation and which are:

(A) crops grown, growing, or to be grown, including:

(i) crops produced on trees, vines, and bushes; and

(ii) aquatic goods produced in aquacultural operations;

(B) livestock, born or unborn, including aquatic goods produced in aquacultural operations;

(C) supplies used or produced in a farming operation; or

(D) products of crops or livestock in their unmanufactured states.

(35) "Farming operation" means raising, cultivating, propagating, fattening, grazing, or any other farming, livestock, or aquacultural operation.

(36) "File number" means the number assigned to an initial financing statement pursuant to Section 9-519(a).

(37) "Filing office" means an office designated in Section 9-501 as the place to file a financing statement.

(38) "Filing-office rule" means a rule adopted pursuant to Section 9-526.

(39) "Financing statement" means a record or records composed of an initial financing statement and any filed record relating to the initial financing statement.

(40) "Fixture filing" means the filing of a financing statement covering goods that are or are to become fixtures and satisfying Section 9-502(a) and (b). The term includes the filing of a financing statement covering goods of a transmitting utility which are or are to become fixtures.

(41) "Fixtures" means goods that have become so related to particular real property that an interest in them arises under real property law.

(42) "General intangible" means any personal property, including things in action, other than accounts, chattel paper, commercial tort claims, deposit accounts, documents, goods, instruments, investment property, letter-of-credit rights, letters of credit, money, and oil, gas, or other minerals before extraction. The term includes payment intangibles and software.

(43) "Good faith" means honesty in fact and the observance of reasonable commercial standards of fair dealing.

(44) "Goods" means all things that are movable when a security interest attaches. The term includes (i) fixtures, (ii) standing timber that is to be cut and removed under a conveyance or contract for sale, (iii) the unborn young of animals, (iv) crops grown, growing, or to be grown, even if the crops are produced on trees, vines, or bushes, and (v) manufactured homes. The term also includes a computer program embedded in goods and any supporting information provided in connection with a transaction relating to the program if (i) the program is associated with the goods in such a manner that it customarily is considered part of the goods, or (ii) by becoming the owner of the goods, a person acquires a right to use the program in connection with the goods. The term does not include a computer program embedded in goods that consist solely of the medium in which the program is embedded. The term also does not include accounts, chattel paper, commercial tort claims, deposit accounts, documents, general intangibles, instruments,

investment property, letter-of-credit rights, letters of credit, money, or oil, gas, or other minerals before extraction.

(45) "Governmental unit" means a subdivision, agency, department, county, parish, municipality, or other unit of the government of the United States, a State, or a foreign country. The term includes an organization having a separate corporate existence if the organization is eligible to issue debt on which interest is exempt from income taxation under the laws of the United States.

(46) "Health-care-insurance receivable" means an interest in or claim under a policy of insurance which is a right to payment of a monetary obligation for health-care goods or services provided.

(47) "Instrument" means a negotiable instrument or any other writing that evidences a right to the payment of a monetary obligation, is not itself a security agreement or lease, and is of a type that in ordinary course of business is transferred by delivery with any necessary indorsement or assignment. The term does not include (i) investment property, (ii) letters of credit, or (iii) writings that evidence a right to payment arising out of the use of a credit or charge card or information contained on or for use with the card.

(48) "Inventory" means goods, other than farm products, which:

(A) are leased by a person as lessor;

(B) are held by a person for sale or lease or to be furnished under a contract of service;

(C) are furnished by a person under a contract of service; or

(D) consist of raw materials, work in process, or materials used or consumed in a business.

(49) "Investment property" means a security, whether certificated or uncertificated, security entitlement, securities account, commodity contract, or commodity account.

(50) "Jurisdiction of organization", with respect to a registered organization, means the jurisdiction under whose law the organization is organized.

(51) "Letter-of-credit right" means a right to payment or performance under a letter of credit, whether or not the beneficiary has demanded or is at the time entitled to demand payment or performance. The term does not include the right of a beneficiary to demand payment or performance under a letter of credit.

(52) "Lien creditor" means:

(A) a creditor that has acquired a lien on the property involved by attachment, levy, or the like;

(B) an assignee for benefit of creditors from the time of assignment;

(C) a trustee in bankruptcy from the date of the filing of the petition; or

(D) a receiver in equity from the time of appointment.

(53) "Manufactured home" means a structure, transportable in one or more sections, which, in the traveling mode, is eight body feet or more in width or 40 body feet or more in length, or, when erected on site, is 320 or more square feet, and which is built on a permanent chassis and designed to be used as a dwelling with or without a permanent foundation when connected to the required utilities, and includes the plumb ing, heating, air-conditioning, and electrical systems contained therein. The term includes any structure that meets all of the requirements of this paragraph except the size requirements and with respect to which the manufacturer voluntarily files a certification required by the United States Secretary of Housing and Urban Development and complies with the standards established under Title 42 of the United States Code.

(54) "Manufactured-home transaction" means a secured transaction:

(A) that creates a purchase-money security interest in a manufactured home, other than a manufactured home held as inventory; or

(B) in which a manufactured home, other than a manufactured home held as inventory, is the primary collateral.

(55) "Mortgage" means a consensual interest in real property, including fixtures, which secures payment or performance of an obligation.

(56) "New debtor" means a person that becomes bound as debtor under Section 9-203(d) by a security agreement previously entered into by another person.

(57) "New value" means (i) money, (ii) money's worth in property, services, or new credit, or (iii) release by a transferee of an interest in property previously transferred to the transferee. The term does not include an obligation substituted for another obligation.

(58) "Noncash proceeds" means proceeds other than cash proceeds.

(59) "Obligor" means a person that, with respect to an obligation secured by a security interest in or an agricultural lien on the collateral, (i) owes payment or other performance of the obligation, (ii) has provided property other than the collateral to secure payment or other performance of the obligation, or (iii) is otherwise accountable in whole or in part for payment or other performance of the obligation. The term does not include issuers or nominated persons under a letter of credit.

(60) "Original debtor", except as used in Section 9-310(c), means a person that, as debtor, entered into a security agreement to which a new debtor has become bound under Section 9-203(d).

(61) "Payment intangible" means a general intangible under which the account debtor's principal obligation is a monetary obligation.

(62) "Person related to", with respect to an individual, means:

(A) the spouse of the individual;

(B) a brother, brother-in-law, sister, or sister-in-law of the individual;

(C) an ancestor or lineal descendant of the individual or the individual's spouse; or

(D) any other relative, by blood or marriage, of the individual or the individual's spouse who shares the same home with the individual.

(63) "Person related to", with respect to an organization, means:

(A) a person directly or indirectly controlling, controlled by, or under common control with the organization;

(B) an officer or director of, or a person performing similar functions with respect to, the organization;

(C) an officer or director of, or a person performing similar functions with respect to, a person described in subparagraph (A);

(D) the spouse of an individual described in subparagraph (A), (B), or (C); or

(E) an individual who is related by blood or marriage to an individual described in subparagraph (A), (B), (C), or (D) and shares the same home with the individual.

(64) "Proceeds", except as used in Section 9-609(b), means the following property:

(A) whatever is acquired upon the sale, lease, license, exchange, or other disposition of collateral;

(B) whatever is collected on, or distributed on account of, collateral;

(C) rights arising out of collateral;

(D) to the extent of the value of collateral, claims arising out of the loss, nonconformity, or interference with the use of, defects or infringement of rights in, or damage to, the collateral; or

(E) to the extent of the value of collateral and to the extent payable to the debtor or the secured party, insurance payable by reason of the loss or nonconformity of, defects or infringement of rights in, or damage to, the collateral.

(65) "Promissory note" means an instrument that evidences a promise to pay a monetary obligation, does not evi dence an order to pay, and does not contain an acknowledgment by a bank that the bank has received for deposit a sum of money or funds.

(66) "Proposal" means a record authenticated by a secured party which in cludes the terms on which the secured party is willing to accept collateral in full or partial satisfaction of the obligation it secures pursuant to Sections 9-620, 9-621, and 9-622.

(67) "Public-finance transaction" means a secured transaction in connection with which:

(A) debt securities are issued;

(B) all or a portion of the securities issued have an initial stated maturity of at least 20 years; and

(C) the debtor, obligor, secured party, account debtor or other person obligated on collateral, assignor or assignee of a secured obligation, or assignor or assignee of a security interest is a State or a governmental unit of a State.

(68) "Pursuant to commitment", with respect to an advance made or other value given by a secured party, means pursuant to the secured party's obligation, whether or not a subsequent event of default or other event not within the secured party's control has relieved or may relieve the secured party from its obligation.

(69) "Record", except as used in "for record", "of record", "record or legal title", and "record owner", means information that is inscribed on a tangible medium or which is stored in an electronic or other medium and is retrievable in perceivable form.

(70) "Registered organization" means an organization organized solely under the law of a single State or the United States and as to which the State or the United States must maintain a public record showing the organization to have been organized.

(71) "Secondary obligor" means an obligor to the extent that:

(A) the obligor's obligation is secondary; or

(B) the obligor has a right of recourse with respect to an obligation secured by collateral against the debtor, another obligor, or property of either.

(72) "Secured party" means:

(A) a person in whose favor a security interest is created or provided for under a security agreement, whether or not any obligation to be secured is outstanding;

(B) a person that holds an agricultural lien;

(C) a consignor;

(D) a person to which accounts, chattel paper, payment intangibles, or promissory notes have been sold;

(E) a trustee, indenture trustee, agent, collateral agent, or other representative in whose favor a security interest or agricultural lien is created or provided for; or

(F) a person that holds a security interest arising under Section 2-401, 2-505, 2-711(3), 2A-508(5), 4-210, or 5-118.

(73) "Security agreement" means an agreement that creates or provides for a security interest.

(74) "Send", in connection with a record or notification, means:

(A) to deposit in the mail, deliver for transmission, or transmit by any other usual means of communication, with postage or cost of transmission provided for, addressed to any address reasonable under the circumstances; or

(B) to cause the record or notification to be received within the time that it would have been received if properly sent under subparagraph (A).

(75) "Software" means a computer program and any supporting information provided in connection with a transaction relating to the program. The term does not include a computer program that is included in the definition of goods.

(76) "State" means a State of the United States, the District of Columbia, Puerto Rico, the United States Virgin Islands, or any territory or insular possession subject to the jurisdiction of the United States.

(77) "Supporting obligation" means a letter-of-credit right or secondary obligation that supports the payment or performance of an account, chattel paper, a document, a general intangible, an instrument, or investment property.

(78) "Tangible chattel paper" means chattel paper evidenced by a record or records consisting of information that is inscribed on a tangible medium.

(79) "Termination statement" means an amendment of a financing statement which:

(A) identifies, by its file number, the initial financing statement to which it relates; and

(B) indicates either that it is a termination statement or that the identified financing statement is no longer effective.

(80) "Transmitting utility" means a person primarily engaged in the business of:

(A) operating a railroad, subway, stre et railway, or trolley bus;

(B) transmitting communications electrically, electromagnetically, or by light;

(C) transmitting goods by pipeline or sewer; or

(D) transmitting or producing and transmitting electricity, steam, gas, or water.

(b) The following definitions in other articles apply to this article:

"Applicant." Section 5-102
"Beneficiary." Section 5-102
"Broker." Section 8-102
"Certificated security." Section 8-102
"Check." Section 3-104
"Clearing corporation." Section 8-102
"Contract for sale." Section 2-106
"Customer." Section 4-104
"Entitlement holder." Section 8-102
"Financial asset." Section 8-102
"Holder in due course." Section 3-302

"Issuer" (with respect to a letter of credit or letter-of-credit right). Section 5-102
"Issuer" (with respect to a security). Section 8-201
"Lease." Section 2A-103
"Lease agreement." Section 2A-103
"Lease contract." Section 2A-103
"Leasehold interest." Section 2A-103
"Lessee." Section 2A-103
"Lessee in ordinary course of business." Section 2A-103
"Lessor." Section 2A-103
"Lessor's residual interest." Section 2A-103
"Letter of credit." Section 5-102
"Merchant." Section 2-104
"Negotiable instrument." Section 3-104
"Nominated person." Section 5-102
"Note." Section 3-104
"Proceeds of a letter of credit." Section 5-114
"Prove." Section 3-103
"Sale." Section 2-106
"Securities account." Section 8-501
"Securities intermediary." Section 8-102
"Security." Section 8-102
"Security certificate." Section 8-102
"Security entitlement." Section 8-102
"Uncertificated security."Section 8-102

(c) Article 1 contains general definitions and principles of construction and interpretation applicable throughout this article.

Amended in 1999 and 2000.

Section 9-103. Purchase-Money Security Interest; Application of Payments; Burden of Establishing.

(a) In this section:

(1) "purchase-money collateral" means goods or software that secures a purchase-money obligation incurred with respect to that collateral; and

(2) "purchase-money obligation" means an obligation of an obligor incurred as all or part of the price of the collateral or for value given to enable the debtor to acquire rights in or the use of the collateral if the value is in fact so used.

(b) A security interest in goods is a purchase-money security interest:

(1) to the extent that the goods are purchase-money collateral with respect to that security interest;

(2) if the security interest is in inventory that is or was purchase-money collateral, also to the extent that the security interest secures a purchase-money obligation incurred with respect to other inventory in which the secured party holds or held a purchase-money security interest; and

(3) also to the extent that the security interest secures a purchase-money obligation incurred with respect to software in which the secured party holds or held a purchase-money security interest.

(c) A security interest in software is a purchase-money security interest to the extent that the security interest also secures a purchase-money obligation incurred with respect to goods in which the secured party holds or held a purchase-money security interest if:

(1) the debtor acquired its interest in the software in an integrated transaction in which it acquired an interest in the goods; and

(2) the debtor acquired its interest in the software for the principal purpose of using the software in the goods.

(d) The security interest of a consignor in goods that are the subject of a consignment is a purchase-money security interest in inventory.

(e) In a transaction other than a consumer-goods transaction, if the extent to which a security interest is a purchase-money security interest depends on the application of a payment to a particular obligation, the payment must be applied:

(1) in accordance with any reasonable method of application to which the parties agree;

(2) in the absence of the parties' agreement to a reasonable method, in accordance with any intention of the obligor manifested at or before the time of payment; or

(3) in the absence of an agreement to a reasonable method and a timely manifestation of the obligor's intention, in the following order:

(A) to obligations that are not se cured; and

(B) if more than one obligation is secured, to obligations secured by purchase-money security interests in the order in which those obligations were incurred.

(f) In a transaction other than a consumer-goods transaction, a purchase-money security interest does not lose its status as such, even if:

(1) the purchase-money collateral also secures an obligation that is not a purchase-money obligation;

(2) collateral that is not purchase-money collateral also secures the purchase-money obligation; or

(3) the purchase-money obligation has been renewed, refinanced, consolidated, or restructured.

(g) In a transaction other than a consumer-goods transaction, a secured party claiming a purchase-money security interest has the burden of establishing the extent to which the security interest is a purchase-money security interest.

(h) The limitation of the rules in subsections (e), (f), and (g) to transactions other than consumer-goods transactions is intended to leave to the court the determination of the proper rules in consumer-goods transactions. The court may not infer from that limitation the nature of the proper rule in consumer-goods transactions and may continue to apply established approaches.

Section 9-104. Control of Deposit Account.

(a) A secured party has control of a deposit account if:

(1) the secured party is the bank with which the deposit account is maintained;

(2) the debtor, secured party, and bank have agreed in an authenticated record that the bank will comply with instructions originated by the secured party directing disposition of the funds in the deposit account without further consent by the debtor; or

(3) the secured party becomes the bank's customer with respect to the deposit account.

(b) A secured party that has satisfied subsection (a) has control, even if the debtor retains the right to direct the disposition of funds from the deposit account.

Section 9-105. Control of Electronic Chattel Paper.

A secured party has control of electronic chattel paper if the record or records comprising the chattel paper are created, stored, and assigned in such a manner that:

(1) a single authoritative copy of the record or records exists which is unique, identifiable and, except as otherwise provided in paragraphs (4), (5), and (6), unalterable;

(2) the authoritative copy identifies the secured party as the assignee of the record or records;

(3) the authoritative copy is communicated to and maintained by the secured party or its designated custodian;

(4) copies or revisions that add or change an identified assignee of the authoritative copy can be made only with the participation of the secured party;

(5) each copy of the authoritative copy and any copy of a copy is readily identifiable as a copy that is not the authoritative copy; and

(6) any revision of the authoritative copy is readily identifiable as an authorized or unauthorized revision.

Section 9-106. Control of Investment Property.

(a) A person has control of a certificated security, uncertificated security, or security entitlement as provided in Section 8-106.

(b) A secured party has control of a commodity contract if:

(1) the secured party is the commodity intermediary with which the commodity contract is carried; or

(2) the commodity customer, secured party, and commodity intermediary have agreed that the commodity intermediary will apply any value distributed on account of the commodity contract as directed by the secured party without further consent by the commodity customer.

(3) A secured party having control of all security entitlements or commodity contracts carried in a securities account or commodity account has control over the securities account or commodity account.

Section 9-107. Control of Letter-of-Credit Right.

A secured party has control of a letter-of-credit right to the extent of any right to payment or performance by the issuer or any nominated person if the issuer or nominated person has consented to an assignment of proceeds of the letter of credit under Section 5-114(c) or otherwise applicable law or practice.

Section 9-108. Sufficiency of Description.

(a) Except as otherwise provided in subsections (c), (d), and (e), a description of personal or real property is sufficient, whether or not it is specific, if it reasonably identifies what is described.

(b) Except as otherwise provided in subsection (d), a description of collateral reasonably identifies the collateral if it identifies the collateral by:

(1) specific listing;

(2) category;

(3) except as otherwise provided in subsection (e), a type of collateral defined in [the Uniform Commercial Code];

(4) quantity;

(5) computational or allocational formula or procedure; or

(6) except as otherwise provided in subsection (c), any other method, if the identity of the collateral is objectively determinable.

(c) A description of collateral as "all the debtor's assets" or "all the debtor's personal property" or using words of similar import does not reasonably identify the collateral.

(d) Except as otherwise provided in subsection

(e) a description of a security entitlement, securities account, or commodity account is sufficient if it describes:

(1) the collateral by those terms or as investment property; or

(2) the underlying financial asset or commodity contract.

(f) A description only by type of collateral defined in [the Uniform Commercial Code] is an insufficient description of:

(1) a commercial tort claim; or

(2) in a consumer transaction, consumer goods, a security entitlement, a securities account, or a commodity account.

[Subpart 2. Applicability of Article]

Section 9-109. Scope.

(a) Except as otherwise provided in subsections (c) and (d), this article applies to:

(1) a transaction, regardless of its form, that creates a security interest in personal property or fixtures by contract;

(2) an agricultural lien;

(3) a sale of accounts, chattel paper, payment intangibles, or promissory notes;

(4) a consignment;

(5) a security interest arising under Section 2-401, 2-505, 2-711(3), or 2A-508(5), as provided in Section 9-110; and

(6) a security interest arising under Section 4-210 or 5-118.

(b) The application of this article to a security interest in a secured obligation is not affected by the fact that the obligation is itself secured by a transaction or interest to which this article does not apply.

(c) This article does not apply to the extent that:

(1) a statute, regulation, or treaty of the United States preempts this article;

(2) another statute of this State expressly governs the creation, perfection, priority, or enforcement of a security interest created by this State or a governmental unit of this State;

(3) a statute of another State, a foreign country, or a governmental unit of another State or a foreign country, other than a statute generally applicable to security interests, expressly governs creation, perfection, priority, or enforcement of a security interest created by the State, country, or governmental unit; or

(4) the rights of a transferee beneficiary or nominated person under a letter of credit are independent and superior under Section 5-114.

(d) This article does not apply to:

(1) a landlord's lien, other than an agricultural lien;

(2) a lien, other than an agricultural lien, given by statute or other rule of law for services or materials, but Section 9-333 applies with respect to priority of the lien;

(3) an assignment of a claim for wages, salary, or other compensation of an employee;

(4) a sale of accounts, chattel paper, payment intangibles, or promissory notes as part of a sale of the business out of which they arose;

(5) an assignment of accounts, chattel paper, payment intangibles, or promissory notes which is for the purpose of collection only;

(6) an assignment of a right to payment under a contract to an assignee that is also obligated to perform under the contract;

(7) an assignment of a single account, payment intangible, or promissory note to an assignee in full or partial satisfaction of a preexisting indebtedness;

(8) a transfer of an interest in or an assignment of a claim under a policy of insurance, other than an assignment by or to a health-care provider of a health-care-insurance receivable and any subsequent assignment of the right to payment, but Sections 9-315 and 9-322 apply with respect to proceeds and priorities in proceeds;

(9) an assignment of a right represented by a judgment, other than a judgment taken on a right to payment that was collateral;

(10) a right of recoupment or set-off, but:

(A) Section 9-340 applies with respect to the effectiveness of rights of recoupment or set-off against deposit accounts; and

(B) Section 9-404 applies with respect to defenses or claims of an ac count debtor;

(11) the creation or transfer of an interest in or lien on real property, including a lease or rents thereunder, except to the extent that provision is made for:

(A) liens on real property in Sections 9-203 and 9-308;

(B) fixtures in Section 9-334;

(C) fixture filings in Sections 9-501, 9-502, 9-512, 9-516, and 9-519; and

(D) security agreements covering personal and real property in Section 9-604;

(12) an assignment of a claim arising in tort, other than a commercial tort claim, but Sections 9-315 and 9-322 apply with respect to proceeds and priorities in proceeds; or

(13) an assignment of a deposit account in a consumer transaction, but Sections 9-315 and 9-322 apply with respect to proceeds and priorities in proceeds.

Section 9-110. Security Interests Arising under Article 2 or 2A.

A security interest arising under Section 2-401, 2-505, 2-711(3), or 2A-508(5) is subject to this article. However, until the debtor obtains possession of the goods:

(1) the security interest is enforceable, even if Section 9-203(b)(3) has not been satisfied;

(2) filing is not required to perfect the security interest;

(3) the rights of the secured party after default by the debtor are governed by Article 2 or 2A; and

(4) the security interest has priority over a conflicting security interest created by the debtor.

Part 2. Effectiveness of Security Agreement; Attachment of Security Interest; Rights of Parties to Security Agreement

[Subpart 1. Effectiveness and Attachment]

Section 9-201. General Effectiveness of Security Agreement.

(a) Except as otherwise provided in [the Uniform Commercial Code], a security agreement is effective according to its terms between the parties, against purchasers of the collateral, and against creditors.

(b) A transaction subject to this article is subject to any applicable rule of law which establishes a different rule for consumers and [insert reference to (i) any other statute or regulation that regulates the rates, charges, agreements, and practices for loans, credit sales, or other extensions of credit and (ii) any consumer-protection statute or regulation].

(c) In case of conflict between this article and a rule of law, statute, or regulation described in subsection (b), the rule of law, statute, or regulation controls. Failure to comply with a statute or regulation described in subsection (b) has only the effect the statute or regulation specifies.

(d) This article does not:

  (1) validate any rate, charge, agreement, or practice that violates a rule of law, statute, or regulation described in subsection (b); or

  (2) extend the application of the rule of law, statute, or regulation to a transaction not otherwise subject to it.

Section 9-202. Title to Collateral Immaterial.

Except as otherwise provided with respect to consignments or sales of accounts, chattel paper, payment intangibles, or promissory notes, the provisions of this article with regard to rights and obligations apply whether title to collateral is in the secured party or the debtor.

Section 9-203. Attachment and Enforceability of Security Interest; Proceeds; Supporting Obligations; Formal Requisites.

(a) A security interest attaches to collateral when it becomes enforceable against the debtor with respect to the collateral, unless an agreement expressly postpones the time of attachment.

(b) Except as otherwise provided in subsections (c) through (i), a security interest is enforceable against the debtor and third parties with respect to the collateral only if:

  (1) value has been given;

  (2) the debtor has rights in the collateral or the power to transfer rights in the collateral to a secured party; and

  (3) one of the following conditions is met:

    (A) the debtor has authenticated a security agreement that provides a description of the collateral and, if the security interest covers timber to be cut, a description of the land concerned;

    (B) the collateral is not a certificated security and is in the possession of the secured party under Section 9-313 pursuant to the debtor's security agreement;

    (C) the collateral is a certificated security in registered form and the security certificate has been delivered to the secured party under Section 8-301 pursuant to the debtor's security agreement; or

    (D) the collateral is deposit accounts, electronic chattel paper, investment property, or letter-of-credit rights, and the secured party has control under Section 9-104, 9-105, 9-106, or 9-107 pursuant to the debtor's security agreement.

(c) Subsection (b) is subject to Section 4-210 on the security interest of a collecting bank, Section 5-118 on the security interest of a letter-of-credit issuer or nominated person,

Section 9-110 on a security interest arising under Article 2 or 2A, and Section 9-206 on security interests in investment property.

(d) A person becomes bound as debtor by a security agreement entered into by another person if, by operation of law other than this article or by contract:

(1) the security agreement becomes effective to create a security interest in the person's property; or

(2) the person becomes generally obligated for the obligations of the other person, including the obligation secured under the security agreement, and acquires or succeeds to all or substantially all of the assets of the other person.

(e) If a new debtor becomes bound as debtor by a security agreement entered into by another person:

(1) the agreement satisfies subsection (b)(3) with respect to existing or after-acquired property of the new debtor to the extent the property is described in the agreement; and

(2) another agreement is not necessary to make a security interest in the property enforceable.

(f) The attachment of a security interest in collateral gives the secured party the rights to proceeds provided by Section 9-315 and is also attachment of a security interest in a supporting obligation for the collateral.

(g) The attachment of a security interest in a right to payment or performance secured by a security interest or other lien on personal or real property is also attachment of a security interest in the security interest, mortgage, or other lien.

(h) The attachment of a security interest in a securities account is also attachment of a security interest in the security entitlements carried in the securities account.

(i) The attachment of a security interest in a commodity account is also attachment of a security interest in the commodity contracts carried in the commodity account.

Section 9-204. After-Acquired Property; Future Advances.

(a) Except as otherwise provided in subsection (b), a security agreement may create or provide for a security interest in after-acquired collateral.

(b) A security interest does not attach under a term constituting an after-acquired property clause to:

(1) consumer goods, other than an accession when given as additional security, unless the debtor acquires rights in them within 10 days after the secured party gives value; or

(2) a commercial tort claim.

(c) A security agreement may provide that collateral secures, or that accounts, chattel paper, payment intangibles, or promissory notes are sold in connection with, future advances or other value, whether or not the advances or value are given pursuant to commitment.

Section 9-205. Use or Disposition of Collateral Permissible.

(a) A security interest is not invalid or fraudulent against creditors solely because:

(1) the debtor has the right or ability to:

(A) use, commingle, or dispose of all or part of the collateral, including returned or repossessed goods;

(B) collect, compromise, enforce, or otherwise deal with collateral;

(C) accept the return of collateral or make repossessions; or

(D) use, commingle, or dispose of proceeds; or

(2) the secured party fails to require the debtor to account for proceeds or replace collateral.

(b) This section does not relax the requirements of possession if attachment, perfection, or enforcement of a security interest depends upon possession of the collateral by the secured party.

Section 9-206. Security Interest Arising in Purchase or Delivery of Financial Asset.

(a) A security interest in favor of a securities intermediary attaches to a person's security entitlement if:

(1) the person buys a financial asset through the securities intermediary in a transaction in which the person is obligated to pay the purchase price to the securities intermediary at the time of the purchase; and

(2) the securities intermediary credits the financial asset to the buyer's securities account before the buyer pays the securities intermediary.

(b) The security interest described in subsection (a) secures the person's obligation to pay for the financial asset.

(c) A security interest in favor of a person that delivers a certificated security or other financial asset represented by a writing attaches to the security or other financial asset if:

(1) the security or other financial asset:

(A) in the ordinary course of business is transferred by delivery with any necessary indorsement or assignment; and

(B) is delivered under an agreement between persons in the business of dealing with such securities or financial assets; and

(2) the agreement calls for delivery against payment.

(d) The security interest described in subsection (c) secures the obligation to make payment for the delivery.

[Subpart 2. Rights and Duties]

Section 9-207. Rights and Duties of Secured Party Having Possession or Control of Collateral.

(a) Except as otherwise provided in subsection (d), a secured party shall use reasonable care in the custody and preservation of collateral in the secured party's possession. In the case of chattel paper or an instrument, reasonable care includes taking necessary steps to preserve rights against prior parties unless otherwise agreed.

(b) Except as otherwise provided in subsection (d), if a secured party has possession of collateral:

(1) reasonable expenses, including the cost of insurance and payment of taxes or other charges, incurred in the custody, preservation, use, or operation of the collateral are chargeable to the debtor and are secured by the collateral;

(2) the risk of accidental loss or damage is on the debtor to the extent of a deficiency in any effective insurance coverage;

(3) the secured party shall keep the collateral identifiable, but fungible collateral may be commingled; and

(4) the secured party may use or operate the collateral:

(A) for the purpose of preserving the collateral or its value;

(B) as permitted by an order of a court having competent jurisdiction; or

(C) except in the case of consumer goods, in the manner and to the extent agreed by the debtor.

(c) Except as otherwise provided in subsection (d), a secured party having possession of collateral or control of collateral under Section 9-104, 9-105, 9-106, or 9-107:

(1) may hold as additional security any proceeds, except money or funds, received from the collateral;

(2) shall apply money or funds received from the collateral to reduce the secured obligation, unless remitted to the debtor; and

(3) may create a security interest in the collateral.

(d) If the secured party is a buyer of accounts, chattel paper, payment intangibles, or promissory notes or a consignor:

(1) subsection (a) does not apply unless the secured party is entitled under an agreement:

(A) to charge back uncollected collateral; or

(B) otherwise to full or limited recourse against the debtor or a secondary obligor based on the nonpayment or other default of an account debtor or other obligor on the collateral; and

(2) subsections (b) and (c) do not apply.

Section 9-208. Additional Duties of Secured Party Having Control of Collateral.

(a) This section applies to cases in which there is no outstanding secured obligation and the secured party is not committed to make advances, incur obligations, or otherwise give value.

(b) Within 10 days after receiving an authenticated demand by the debtor:

(1) a secured party having control of a deposit account under Section 9-104(a)(2) shall send to the bank with which the deposit account is maintained an authenticated statement that releases the bank from any further obligation to comply with instructions originated by the secured party;

(2) a secured party having control of a deposit account under Section 9-104(a)(3) shall:

(A) pay the debtor the balance on deposit in the deposit account; or

(B) transfer the balance on deposit into a deposit account in the debtor's name;

(3) a secured party, other than a buyer, having control of electronic chattel paper under Section 9-105 shall:

(A) communicate the authoritative copy of the electronic chattel paper to the debtor or its designated custodian;

(B) if the debtor designates a custodian that is the designated custodian with which the authoritative copy of the electronic chattel paper is maintained for the secured party, communicate to the custodian an authenticated record releasing the designated custodian from any further obligation to comply with instructions originated by the secured party and instructing the custodian to comply with instructions originated by the debto r; and

(C) take appropriate action to enable the debtor or its designated custodian to make copies of or revisions to the authoritative copy which add or change an identified assignee of the authoritative copy without the consent of the secured party;

(4) a secured party having control of investment property under Section 8-106(d)(2) or 9-106(b) shall send to the securities intermediary or commodity intermediary with which the security entitlement or commodity contract is maintained an authenticated record that releases the securities intermediary or commodity

intermediary from any further obligation to comply with entitlement orders or directions originated by the secured party; and

(5) a secured party having control of a letter-of-credit right under Section 9-107 shall send to each person having an unfulfilled obligation to pay or deliver proceeds of the letter of credit to the secured party an authenticated release from any further obligation to pay or deliver proceeds of the letter of credit to the secured party.

Section 9-209. Duties of Secured Party If Account Debtor Has Been Notified of Assignment.

(a) Except as otherwise provided in subsection (c), this section applies if:

(1) there is no outstanding secured obligation; and

(2) the secured party is not committed to make advances, incur obligations, or otherwise give value.

(b) Within 10 days after receiving an authenticated demand by the debtor, a secured party shall send to an account debtor that has received notification of an assignment to the secured party as assignee under Section 9-406(a) an authenticated record that releases the account debtor from any further obligation to the secured party.

(c) This section does not apply to an assignment constituting the sale of an account, chattel paper, or payment intangible.

Section 9-210. Request for Accounting; Request Regarding List of Collateral or Statement of Account.

(a) In this section:

(1) "Request" means a record of a type described in paragraph (2), (3), or (4).

(2) "Request for an accounting" means a record authenticated by a debtor requesting that the recipient provide an accounting of the unpaid obligations secured by collateral and reasonably identifying the transaction or relationship that is the subject of the request.

(3) "Request regarding a list of collateral" means a record authenticated by a debtor requesting that the recipient approve or correct a list of what the debtor believes to be the collateral securing an obligation and reasonably identifying the transaction or relationship that is the subject of the request.

(4) "Request regarding a statement of account" means a record authenticated by a debtor requesting that the recipient approve or correct a statement indicating what the debtor believes to be the aggregate amount of unpaid obligations secured by collateral as of a specified date and reasonably identifying the transaction or relationship that is the subject of the request.

(b) Subject to subsections (c), (d), (e), and (f), a secured party, other than a buyer of ac counts, chattel paper, payment intangibles, or promissory notes or a consignor, shall comply with a request within 14 days after receipt:

(1) in the case of a request for an accounting, by authenticating and sending to the debtor an accounting; and

(2) in the case of a request regarding a list of collateral or a request regarding a statement of account, by authenticating and sending to the debtor an approval or correction.

(c) A secured party that claims a security interest in all of a particular type of collateral owned by the debtor may comply with a request regarding a list of collateral by sending to the debtor an authenticated record including a statement to that effect within 14 days after receipt.

(d) A person that receives a request regarding a list of collateral, claims no interest in the collateral when it receives the request, and claimed an interest in the collateral at an earlier time shall comply with the request within 14 days after receipt by sending to the debtor an authenticated record:

(1) disclaiming any interest in the collateral; and

(2) if known to the recipient, providing the name and mailing address of any assignee of or successor to the recipient's interest in the collateral.

(e) A person that receives a request for an accounting or a request regarding a statement of account, claims no interest in the obligations when it receives the request, and claimed an interest in the obligations at an earlier time shall comply with the request within 14 days after receipt by sending to the debtor an authenticated record:

(1) disclaiming any interest in the obligations; and

(2) if known to the recipient, providing the name and mailing address of any assignee of or successor to the recipient's interest in the obligations.

(f) A debtor is entitled without charge to one response to a request under this section during any six-month period. The secured party may require payment of a charge not exceeding $25 for each additional response.

As amended in 1999.

Part 3. Perfection and Priority.

[Subpart 1. Law Governing Perfection and Priority].

Section 9-301. Law Governing Perfection and Priority of Security Interests.

Except as otherwise provided in Sections 9-303 through 9-306, the following rules determine the law governing perfection, the effect of perfection or nonperfection, and the priority of a security interest in collateral:

(1) Except as otherwise provided in this section, while a debtor is located in a jurisdiction, the local law of that jurisdiction governs perfection, the effect of perfection or nonperfection, and the priority of a security interest in collateral.

(2) While collateral is located in a jurisdiction, the local law of that jurisdiction governs perfection, the effect of perfection or nonperfection, and the priority of a possessory security interest in that collateral.

(3) Except as otherwise provided in paragraph (4), while negotiable documents, goods, instruments, money, or tangible chattel paper is located in a jurisdiction, the local law of that jurisdiction governs:

(A) perfection of a security interest in the goods by filing a fixture filing;

(B) perfection of a security interest in timber to be cut; and

(C) the effect of perfection or nonperfection and the priority of a nonpossessory security interest in the collateral.

(4) The local law of the jurisdiction in which the wellhead or minehead is located governs perfection, the effect of perfection or nonperfection, and the priority of a security interest in as-extracted collateral.

Section 9-302. Law Governing Perfection and Priority of Agricultural Liens.

While farm products are located in a jurisdiction, the local law of that jurisdiction governs perfection, the effect of perfection or nonperfection, and the priority of an agricultural lien on the farm products.

Section 9-303. Law Governing Perfection and Priority of Security Interests in Goods Covered by a Certificate of Title.

(a) This section applies to goods covered by a certificate of title, even if there is no other relationship between the jurisdiction under whose certificate of title the goods are covered and the goods or the debtor.

(b) Goods become covered by a certificate of title when a valid application for the certificate of title and the applicable fee are delivered to the appropriate authority. Goods cease to be covered by a certificate of title at the earlier of the time the certificate of title ceases to be effective under the law of the issuing jurisdiction or the time the goods become covered subsequently by a certificate of title issued by another jurisdiction.

(c) The local law of the jurisdiction under whose certificate of title the goods are covered governs perfection, the effect of perfection or nonperfection, and the priority of a security interest in goods covered by a certificate of title from the time the goods become covered by the certificate of title until the goods cease to be covered by the certificate of title.

Section 9-304. Law Governing Perfection and Priority of Security Interests in Deposit Accounts.

(a) The local law of a bank's jurisdiction governs perfection, the effect of perfection or nonperfection, and the priority of a security interest in a deposit account maintained with that bank.

(b) The following rules determine a bank's jurisdiction for purposes of this part:

(1) If an agreement between the bank and the debtor governing the deposit account expressly provides that a particular jurisdiction is the bank's jurisdiction for purposes of this part, this article, or [the Uniform Commercial Code], that jurisdiction is the bank's jurisdiction.

(2) If paragraph (1) does not apply and an agreement between the bank and its customer governing the deposit account expressly provides that the agree ment is governed by the law of a particular jurisdiction, that jurisdiction is the bank's jurisdiction.

(3) If neither paragraph (1) nor paragraph (2) applies and an agreement between the bank and its customer governing the deposit account expressly provides that the deposit account is maintained at an office in a particular jurisdiction, that jurisdiction is the bank's jurisdiction.

(4) If none of the preceding paragraphs applies, the bank's jurisdiction is the jurisdiction in which the office identified in an account statement as the office serving the customer's account is located.

(5) If none of the preceding paragraphs applies, the bank's jurisdiction is the jurisdiction in which the chief executive office of the bank is located.

Section 9-305. Law Governing Perfection and Priority of Security Interests in Investment Property.

(a) Except as otherwise provided in subsection (c), the following rules apply:

(1) While a security certificate is located in a jurisdiction, the local law of that jurisdiction governs perfection, the effect of perfection or nonperfection, and the priority of a security interest in the certificated security represented thereby.

(2) The local law of the issuer's jurisdiction as specified in Section 8-110(d) governs perfection, the effect of perfection or nonperfection, and the priority of a security interest in an uncertificated security.

(3) The local law of the securities intermediary's jurisdiction as specified in Section 8-110(e) governs perfection, the effect of perfection or nonperfection, and the priority of a security interest in a security entitlement or securities account.

(4) The local law of the commodity intermediary's jurisdiction governs perfection, the effect of perfection or nonperfection, and the priority of a security interest in a commodity contract or commodity account.

(b) The following rules determine a commodity intermediary's jurisdiction for purposes of this part:

(1) If an agreement between the commodity intermediary and commodity customer governing the commodity account expressly provides that a particular jurisdiction is the commodity intermediary's jurisdiction for purposes of this part, this article, or [the Uniform Commercial Code], that jurisdiction is the commodity intermediary's jurisdiction.

(2) If paragraph (1) does not apply and an agreement between the commodity intermediary and commodity customer governing the commodity account expressly provides that the agreement is governed by the law of a particular jurisdiction, that jurisdiction is the commodity intermediary's jurisdiction.

(3) If neither paragraph (1) nor paragraph (2) applies and an agreement between the commodity intermediary and commodity customer governing the commodity account expressly provides that the commodity account is maintained at an office in a particular jurisdiction, that jurisdiction is the commodity intermediary's jurisdiction.

(4) If none of the preceding paragraphs applies, the commodity intermediary's jurisdiction is the jurisdiction in which the office identified in an account statement as the office serving the commodity customer's account is located.

(5) If none of the preceding paragraphs applies, the commodity intermediary's jurisdiction is the jurisdiction in which the chief executive office of the commodity intermediary is located.

(c) The local law of the jurisdiction in which the debtor is located governs:

(1) perfection of a security interest in investment property by filing;

(2) automatic perfection of a security interest in investment property created by a broker or securities intermediary; and

(3) automatic perfection of a security interest in a commodity contract or commodity account created by a commodity intermediary.

Section 9-306. Law Governing Perfection and Priority of Security Interests in Letter-of-Credit Rights.

(a) Subject to subsection (c), the local law of the issuer's jurisdiction or a nominated person's jurisdiction governs perfection, the effect of perfection or nonperfection, and the priority of a security interest in a letter-of-credit right if the issuer's jurisdiction or nominated person's jurisdiction is a State.

(b) For purposes of this part, an issuer's jurisdiction or nominated person's jurisdiction is the jurisdiction whose law governs the liability of the issuer or nominated person with respect to the letter-of-credit right as provided in Section 5-116.

(c) This section does not apply to a security interest that is perfected only under Section 9-308(d).

Section 9-307. Location of Debtor.

(a) In this section, "place of business" means a place where a debtor conducts its affairs.

(b) Except as otherwise provided in this section, the following rules determine a debtor's location:

(1) A debtor who is an individual is located at the individual's principal residence.

(2) A debtor that is an organization and has only one place of business is located at its place of business.

(3) A debtor that is an organization and has more than one place of business is located at its chief executive office.

(c) Subsection (b) applies only if a debtor's residence, place of business, or chief executive office, as applicable, is located in a jurisdiction whose law generally requires information concerning the existence of a nonpossessory security interest to be made generally available in a filing, recording, or registration system as a condition or result of the security interest's obtaining priority over the rights of a lien creditor with respect to the collateral. If subsection (b) does not apply, the debtor is located in the District of Columbia.

(d) A person that ceases to exist, have a residence, or have a place of business continues to be located in the jurisdiction specified by subsections (b) and (c).

(e) A registered organization that is organized under the law of a State is located in that State.

(f) Except as otherwise provided in subsection (i), a registered organization that is organized under the law of the United States and a branch or agency of a bank that is not organized under the law of the United States or a State are located:

(1) in the State that the law of the United States designates, if the law designates a State of location;

(2) in the State that the registered organization, branch, or agency designates, if the law of the United States authorizes the registered organization, branch, or agency to designate its State of location; or

(3) in the District of Columbia, if neither paragraph (1) nor paragraph (2) applies.

(g) A registered organization continues to be located in the jurisdiction specified by subsection (e) or (f) notwithstanding:

(1) the suspension, revocation, forfeiture, or lapse of the registered organization's status as such in its jurisdiction of organization; or

(2) the dissolution, winding up, or cancellation of the existence of the registered organization.

(h) The United States is located in the District of Columbia.

(i) A branch or agency of a bank that is not organized under the law of the United States or a State is located in the State in which the branch or agency is licensed, if all branches and agencies of the bank are licensed in only one State.

(j) A foreign air carrier under the Federal Aviation Act of 1958, as amended, is located at the designated office of the agent upon which service of process may be made on behalf of the carrier.

(k) This section applies only for purposes of this part.

[Subpart 2. Perfection].

Section 9-308. When Security Interest or Agricultural Lien Is Perfected; Continuity of Perfection.

(a) Except as otherwise provided in this section and Section 9-309, a security interest is perfected if it has attached and all of the applicable requirements for perfection in Sections 9-310 through 9-316 have been satisfied. A security interest is perfected when it attaches if the applicable requirements are satisfied before the security interest attaches.

(b) An agricultural lien is perfected if it has become effective and all of the applicable requirements for perfection in Section 9-310 have been satisfied. An agricultural lien is perfected when it becomes effective if the applicable requirements are satisfied before the agricultural lien becomes effective.

(c) A security interest or agricultural lien is perfected continuously if it is originally perfected by one method under this article and is later perfected by another method under this article, without an intermediate period when it was unperfected.

(d) Perfection of a security interest in collateral also perfects a security interest in a supporting obligation for the collateral.

(e) Perfection of a security interest in a right to payment or performance also perfects a security interest in a security interest, mortgage, or other lien on personal or real property securing the right.

(f) Perfection of a security interest in a securities account also perfects a security interest in the security entitlements carried in the securities account.

(g) Perfection of a security interest in a commodity account also perfects a security interest in the commodity contracts carried in the commodity account.

Legislative Note: Any statute conflicting with subsection (e) must be made expressly subject to that subsection.

Section 9-309. Security Interest Perfected upon Attachment.

The following security interests are perfected when they attach:

(1) a purchase-money security interest in consumer goods, except as otherwise provided in Section 9-311(b) with respect to consumer goods that are subject to a statute or treaty described in Section 9-311(a);

(2) an assignment of accounts or payment intangibles which does not by itself or in conjunction with other assignments to the same assignee transfer a significant part of the assignor's outstanding accounts or payment intangibles;

(3) a sale of a payment intangible;

(4) a sale of a promissory note;

(5) a security interest created by the assignment of a health-care-insurance receivable to the provider of the health-care goods or services;

(6) a security interest arising under Section 2-401, 2-505, 2-711(3), or 2A-508(5), until the debtor obtains possession of the collateral;

(7) a security interest of a collecting bank arising under Section 4-210;

(8) a security interest of an issuer or nominated person arising under Section 5-118;

(9) a security interest arising in the delivery of a financial asset under Section 9-206(c);

(10) a security interest in investment property created by a broker or securities intermediary;

(11) a security interest in a commodity contract or a commodity account created by a commodity intermediary;

(12) an assignment for the benefit of all creditors of the transferor and subsequent transfers by the assignee thereunder; and

(13) a security interest created by an assignment of a beneficial interest in a decedent's estate; and

(14) a sale by an individual of an account that is a right to payment of winnings in a lottery or other game of chance.

Section 9-310. When Filing Required to Perfect Security Interest or Agricultural Lien; Security Interests and Agricultural Liens to Which Filing Provisions Do Not Apply.

(a) Except as otherwise provided in subsection (b) and Section 9-312(b), a financing statement must be filed to perfect all security interests and agricultural liens.

(b) The filing of a financing statement is not necessary to perfect a security interest:

(1) that is perfected under Section 9-308(d), (e), (f), or (g);

(2) that is perfected under Section 9-309 when it attaches;

(3) in property subject to a statute, regulation, or treaty described in Section 9-311(a);

(4) in goods in possession of a bailee which is perfected under Section 9-312(d)(1) or (2);

(5) in certificated securities, documents, goods, or instruments which is perfected without filing or possession under Section 9-312(e), (f), or (g);

(6) in collateral in the secured party's possession under Section 9-313;

(7) in a certificated security which is perfected by delivery of the security certificate to the secured party under Section 9-313;

(8) in deposit accounts, electronic chattel paper, investment property, or letter-of-credit rights which is perfected by control under Section 9-314;

(9) in proceeds which is perfected under Section 9-315; or

(10) that is perfected under Section 9-316.

(c) If a secured party assigns a perfected security interest or agricultural lien, a filing under this article is not required to continue the perfected status of the security interest against creditors of and transferees from the original debtor.

Section 9-311. Perfection of Security Interests in Property Subject to Certain Statutes, Regulations, and Treaties.

(a) Except as otherwise provided in subsection (d), the filing of a financing statement is not necessary or effective to perfect a security interest in property subject to:

(1) a statute, regulation, or treaty of the United States whose requirements for a security interest's obtaining priority over the rights of a lien creditor with respect to the property preempt Section 9-310(a);

(2) [list any certificate-of-title statute covering automobiles, trailers, mobile home s, boats, farm tractors, or the like, which provides for a security interest to be indicated on the certificate as a condition or result of perfection, and any non-Uniform Commercial Code central filing statute]; or

(3) a certificate-of-title statute of another jurisdiction which provides for a security interest to be indicated on the certificate as a condition or result of the security interest's obtaining priority over the rights of a lien creditor with respect to the property.

(b) Compliance with the requirements of a statute, regulation, or treaty described in subsection (a) for obtaining priority over the rights of a lien creditor is equivalent to the filing of a financing statement under this article. Except as otherwise provided in subsection (d) and Sections 9-313 and 9-316(d) and (e) for goods covered by a certificate of title, a security interest in property subject to a statute, regulation, or treaty described in subsection (a) may be perfected only by compliance with those requirements, and a security interest so perfected remains perfected notwithstanding a change in the use or transfer of possession of the collateral.

(c) Except as otherwise provided in subsection (d) and Section 9-316(d) and (e), duration and renewal of perfection of a security interest perfected by compliance with the requirements prescribed by a statute, regulation, or treaty described in subsection (a) are governed by the statute, regulation, or treaty. In other respects, the security interest is subject to this article.

(d) During any period in which collateral subject to a statute specified in subsection (a)(2) is inventory held for sale or lease by a person or leased by that person as lessor and that person is in the business of selling goods of that kind, this section does not apply to a security interest in that collateral created by that person.

Legislative Note: This Article contemplates that perfection of a security interest in goods covered by a certificate of title occurs upon receipt by appropriate State officials of a properly tendered application for a certificate of title on which the security interest is to be indicated, without a relation back to an earlier time. States whose certificate-of-title statutes provide for perfection at a different time or contain a relation-back provision should amend the statutes accordingly.

Section 9-312. Perfection of Security Interests in Chattel Paper, Deposit Accounts, Documents, Goods Covered by Documents, Instruments, Investment Property, Letter-of-Credit Rights, and Money; Perfection by Permissive Filing; Temporary Perfection without Filing or Transfer of Possession.

(a) A security interest in chattel paper, negotiable documents, instruments, or investment property may be perfected by filing.

(b) Except as otherwise provided in Section 9-315(c) and (d) for proceeds:

(1) a security interest in a deposit account may be perfected only by control under Section 9-314;

(2) and except as otherwise provided in Section 9-308(d), a security interest in a letter-of-credit right may be perfected only by control under Section 9-314; and

(3) a security interest in money may be perfected only by the secured party's taking possession under Section 9-313.

(c) While goods are in the possession of a bailee that has issued a negotiable document covering the goods:

(1) a security interest in the goods may be perfected by perfecting a security interest in the document; and

(2) a security interest perfected in the document has priority over any security interest that becomes perfected in the goods by another method during that time.

(d) While goods are in the possession of a bailee that has issued a nonnegotiable document covering the goods, a security interest in the goods may be perfected by:

(1) issuance of a document in the name of the secured party;

(2) the bailee's receipt of notification of the secured party's interest; or

(3) filing as to the goods.

(e) A security interest in certificated securities, negotiable documents, or instruments is perfected without filing or the taking of possession for a period of 20 days from the time it attaches to the extent that it arises for new value given under an authenticated security agreement.

(f) A perfected security interest in a negotiable document or goods in possession of a bailee, other than one that has issued a negotiable document for the goods, remains perfected for 20 days without filing if the secured party makes available to the debtor the goods or documents representing the goods for the purpose of:

(1) ultimate sale or exchange; or

(2) loading, unloading, storing, shipping, transshipping, manufacturing, processing, or otherwise dealing with them in a manner preliminary to their sale or exchange.

(g) A perfected security interest in a certificated security or instrument remains perfected for 20 days without filing if the secured party delivers the security certificate or instrument to the debtor for the purpose of:

(1) ultimate sale or exchange; or

(2) presentation, collection, enforcement, renewal, or registration of transfer.

(h) After the 20-day period specified in subsection (e), (f), or (g) expires, perfection depends upon compliance with this article.

Section 9-313. When Possession by or Delivery to Secured Party Perfects Security Interest without Filing.

(a) Except as otherwise provided in subsection (b), a secured party may perfect a security interest in negotiable documents, goods, instruments, money, or tangible chattel paper by taking possession of the collateral. A secured party may perfect a security interest in certificated securities by taking delivery of the certificated securities under Section 8-301.

(b) With respect to goods covered by a certificate of title issued by this State, a secured party may perfect a security interest in the goods by taking possession of the goods only in the circumstances described in Section 9-316(d).

(c) With respect to collateral other than certificated securities and goods covered by a document, a secured party takes possession of collateral in the possession of a person other than the debtor, the secured party, or a lessee of the collateral from the debtor in the ordinary course of the debtor's business, when:

(1) the person in possession authenticates a record acknowledging that it holds possession of the collateral for the secured party's benefit; or

(2) the person takes possession of the collateral after having authenticated a record acknowledging that it will hold possession of collateral for the secured party's benefit.

(d) If perfection of a security interest depends upon possession of the collateral by a secured party, perfection occurs no earlier than the time the secured party takes possession and continues only while the secured party retains possession.

(e) A security interest in a certificated security in registered form is perfected by delivery when delivery of the certificated security occurs under Section 8-301 and remains perfected by delivery until the debtor obtains possession of the security certificate.

(f) A person in possession of collateral is not required to acknowledge that it holds possession for a secured party's benefit.

(g) If a person acknowledges that it holds possession for the secured party's benefit:

(1) the acknowledgment is effective under subsection (c) or Section 8-301(a), even if the acknowledgment violates the rights of a debtor; and

(2) unless the person otherwise agrees or law other than this article otherwise provides, the person does not owe any duty to the secured party and is not required to confirm the acknowledgment to another person.

(h) A secured party having possession of collateral does not relinquish possession by delivering the collateral to a person other than the debtor or a lessee of the collateral from the debtor in the ordinary course of the debtor's business if the person was instructed before the delivery or is instructed contemporaneously with the delivery:

(1) to hold possession of the collateral for the secured party's benefit; or

(2) to redeliver the collateral to the secured party.

(i) A secured party does not relinquish possession, even if a delivery under subsection (h) violates the rights of a debtor. A person to which collateral is delivered under subsection (h) does not owe any duty to the secured party and is not required to confirm the delivery to another person unless the person otherwise agrees or law other than this article otherwise provides.

Section 9-314. Perfection by Control.

(a) A security interest in investment property, deposit accounts, letter-of-credit rights, or electronic chattel paper may be perfected by control of the collateral under Section 9-104, 9-105, 9-106, or 9-107.

(b) A security interest in deposit accounts, electronic chattel paper, or letter-of-credit rights is perfected by control under Section 9-104, 9-105, or 9-107 when the secured party obtains control and remains perfected by control only while the secured party retains control.

(c) A security interest in investment property is perfected by control under Section 9-106 from the time the secured party obtains control and remains perfected by control until:

(1) the secured party does not have control; and

(2) one of the following occurs:

(A) if the collateral is a certificated security, the debtor has or acquires possession of the security certificate;

(B) if the collateral is an uncertificated security, the issuer has registered or registers the debtor as the registered owner; or

(C) if the collateral is a security entitlement, the debtor is or becomes the entitlement holder.

Section 9-315. Secured Party's Rights on Disposition of Collateral and in Proceeds.

(a) Except as otherwise provided in this article and in Section 2-403(2):

(1) a security interest or agricultural lien continues in collateral notwithstanding sale, lease, license, exchange, or other disposition thereof unless the secured party authorized the disposition free of the security interest or agricultural lien; and

(2) a security interest attaches to any identifiable proceeds of collateral.

(b) Proceeds that are commingled with other property are identifiable proceeds:

(1) if the proceeds are goods, to the extent provided by Section 9-336; and

(2) if the proceeds are not goods, to the extent that the secured party identifies the proceeds by a method of tracing, including application of equitable principles, that is permitted under law other than this article with respect to commingled property of the type involved.

(c) A security interest in proceeds is a perfected security interest if the security interest in the original collateral was perfected.

(d) A perfected security interest in proceeds becomes unperfected on the 21st day after the security interest attaches to the proceeds unless:

(1) the following conditions are satisfied:

(A) a filed financing statement covers the original collateral;

(B) the proceeds are collateral in which a security interest may be perfected by filing in the office in which the financing statement has been filed; and

(C) the proceeds are not acquired with cash proceeds;

(2) the proceeds are identifiable cash proceeds; or

(3) the security interest in the proceeds is perfected other than under subsection (c) when the security interest attaches to the proceeds or within 20 days thereafter.

(e) If a filed financing statement covers the original collateral, a security interest in proceeds which remains perfected under subsection (d)(1) becomes unperfected at the later of:

(1) when the effectiveness of the filed financing statement lapses under Section 9-515 or is terminated under Section 9-513; or

(2) the 21st day after the security interest attaches to the proceeds.

Section 9-316. Continued Perfection of Security Interest Following Change in Governing Law.

(a) A security interest perfected pursuant to the law of the jurisdiction designated in Section 9-301(1) or 9-305(c) remains perfected until the earliest of:

(1) the time perfection would have ceased under the law of that jurisdiction;

(2) the expiration of four months after a change of the debtor's location to another jurisdiction; or

(3) the expiration of one year after a transfer of collateral to a person that thereby becomes a debtor and is located in another jurisdiction.

(b) If a security interest described in subsection (a) becomes perfected under the law of the other jurisdiction before the earliest time or event described in that subsection, it remains perfected thereafter. If the security interest does not become perfected under the law of the other jurisdiction before the earliest time or event, it becomes unperfected and is deemed never to have been perfected as against a purchaser of the collateral for value.

(c) A possessory security interest in collateral, other than goods covered by a certificate of title and as-extracted collateral consisting of goods, remains continuously perfected if:

(1) the collateral is located in one jurisdiction and subject to a security interest perfected under the law of that jurisdiction;

(2) thereafter the collateral is brought into another jurisdiction; and

(3) upon entry into the other jurisdiction, the security interest is perfected under the law of the other jurisdiction.

(d) Except as otherwise provided in subsection (e), a security interest in goods covered by a certificate of title which is perfected by any method under the law of another jurisdiction when the goods become covered by a certificate of title from this State remains perfected until the security interest would have become unperfected under the law of the other jurisdiction had the goods not become so covered.

(e) A security interest described in subsection (d) becomes unperfected as against a purchaser of the goods for value and is deemed never to have been perfected as against a purchaser of the goods for value if the applicable requirements for perfection under Section 9-311(b) or 9-313 are not satisfied before the earlier of:

(1) the time the security interest would have become unperfected under the law of the other jurisdiction had the goods not become covered by a certificate of title from this State; or

(2) the expiration of four months after the goods had become so covered.

(f) A security interest in deposit accounts, letter-of-credit rights, or investment property which is perfected under the law of the bank's jurisdiction, the issuer's jurisdiction, a nominated person's jurisdiction, the securities intermediary's jurisdiction, or the commodity intermediary's jurisdiction, as applicable, remains perfected until the earlier of:

(1) the time the security interest would have become unperfected under the law of that jurisdiction; or

(2) the expiration of four months after a change of the applicable jurisdiction to another jurisdiction.

(g) If a security interest described in subsection (f) becomes perfected under the law of the other jurisdiction before the earlier of the time or the end of the period described in that subsection, it remains perfected thereafter. If the security interest does not become perfected under the law of the other jurisdiction before the earlier of that time or the end of that period, it becomes unperfected and is deemed never to have been perfected as against a purchaser of the collateral for value.

[Subpart 3. Priority].

Section 9-317. Interests That Take Priority over or Take Free of Security Interest or Agricultural Lien.

(a) A security interest or agricultural lien is subordinate to the rights of:

(1) a person entitled to priority under Section 9-322; and

(2) except as otherwise provided in subsection (e), a person that becomes a lien creditor before the earlier of the time:

(A) the security interest or agricultural lien is perfected; or

(B) one of the conditions specified in Section 9-203(b)(3) is met and a financing statement covering the collateral is filed.

(b) Except as otherwise provided in subsection (e), a buyer, other than a secured party, of tangible chattel paper, documents, goods, instruments, or a security certificate takes free of a security interest or agricultural lien if the buyer gives value and receives delivery of the collateral without knowledge of the security interest or agricultural lien and before it is perfected.

(c) Except as otherwise provided in subsection (e), a lessee of goods takes free of a security interest or agricultural lien if the lessee gives value and receives delivery of the collateral without knowledge of the security interest or agricultural lien and before it is perfected.

(d) A licensee of a general intangible or a buyer, other than a secured party, of accounts, electronic chattel paper, general intangibles, or investment property other than a certificated security takes free of a security interest if the licensee or buyer gives value without knowledge of the security interest and before it is perfected.

(e) Except as otherwise provided in Sections 9-320 and 9-321, if a person files a financing statement with respect to a purchase-money security interest before or within 20 days after the debtor receives delivery of the collateral, the security interest takes priority over the rights of a buyer, lessee, or lien creditor which arise between the time the security interest attaches and the time of filing.

As amended in 2000.

Section 9-318. No Interest Retained in Right to Payment That Is Sold; Rights and Title of Seller of Account or Chattel Paper with Respect to Creditors and Purchasers.

(a) A debtor that has sold an account, chattel paper, payment intangible, or promissory note does not retain a legal or equitable interest in the collateral sold.

(b) For purposes of determining the rights of creditors of, and purchasers for value of an account or chattel paper from, a debtor that has sold an account or chattel paper, while the buyer's security interest is unperfected, the debtor is deemed to have rights and title to the account or chattel paper identical to those the debtor sold.

Section 9-319. Rights and Title of Consignee with Respect to Creditors and Purchasers.

(a) Except as otherwise provided in subsection (b), for purposes of determining the rights of creditors of, and purchasers for value of goods from, a consignee, while the goods are in the possession of the consignee, the consignee is deemed to have rights and title to the goods identical to those the consignor had or had power to transfer.

(b) For purposes of determining the rights of a creditor of a consignee, law other than this article determines the rights and title of a consignee while goods are in the con signee's possession if, under this part, a perfected security interest held by the consignor would have priority over the rights of the creditor.

Section 9-320. Buyer of Goods.

(a) Except as otherwise provided in subsection (e), a buyer in ordinary course of business, other than a person buying farm products from a person engaged in farming operations, takes free of a security interest created by the buyer's seller, even if the security interest is perfected and the buyer knows of its existence.

(b) Except as otherwise provided in subsection (e), a buyer of goods from a person who used or bought the goods for use primarily for personal, family, or household purposes takes free of a security interest, even if perfected, if the buyer buys:

(1) without knowledge of the security interest;

(2) for value;

(3) primarily for the buyer's personal, family, or household purposes; and

(4) before the filing of a financing statement covering the goods.

(c) To the extent that it affects the priority of a security interest over a buyer of goods under subsection (b), the period of effectiveness of a filing made in the jurisdiction in which the seller is located is governed by Section 9-316(a) and (b).

(d) A buyer in ordinary course of business buying oil, gas, or other minerals at the wellhead or minehead or after extraction takes free of an interest arising out of an encumbrance.

(e) Subsections (a) and (b) do not affect a security interest in goods in the possession of the secured party under Section 9-313.

Section 9-321. Licensee of General Intangible and Lessee of Goods in Ordinary Course of Business.

(a) In this section, "licensee in ordinary course of business" means a person that becomes a licensee of a general intangible in good faith, without knowledge that the license violates the rights of another person in the general intangible, and in the ordinary course from a person in the business of licensing general intangibles of that kind. A person becomes a licensee in the ordinary course if the license to the person comports with the usual or customary practices in the kind of business in which the licensor is engaged or with the licensor's own usual or customary practices.

(b) A licensee in ordinary course of business takes its rights under a nonexclusive license free of a security interest in the general intangible created by the licensor, even if the security interest is perfected and the licensee knows of its existence.

(c) A lessee in ordinary course of business takes its leasehold interest free of a security interest in the goods created by the lessor, even if the security interest is perfected and the lessee knows of its existence.

Section 9-322. Priorities among Conflicting Security Interests in and Agricultural Liens on Same Collateral.

(a) Except as otherwise provided in this section, priority among conflicting security interests and agricultural liens in the same collateral is determined according to the following rules:

  (1) Conflicting perfected security interests and agricultural liens rank according to priority in time of filing or perfection. Priority dates from the earlier of the time a filing covering the collateral is first made or the security interest or agricultural lien is first perfected, if there is no period thereafter when there is neither filing nor perfection.

  (2) A perfected security interest or agricultural lien has priority over a conflicting unperfected security interest or agricultural lien.

  (3) The first security interest or agricultural lien to attach or become effective has priority if conflicting security interests and agricultural liens are unperfected.

(b) For the purposes of subsection (a)(1):

  (1) the time of filing or perfection as to a security interest in collateral is also the time of filing or perfection as to a security interest in proceeds; and

  (2) the time of filing or perfection as to a security interest in collateral supported by a supporting obligation is also the time of filing or perfection as to a security interest in the supporting obligation.

(c) Except as otherwise provided in subsection (f), a security interest in collateral which qualifies for priority over a conflicting security interest under Section 9-327, 9-328, 9-329, 9-330, or 9-331 also has priority over a conflicting security interest in:

  (1) any supporting obligation for the collateral; and

  (2) proceeds of the collateral if:

    (A) the security interest in proceeds is perfected;

    (B) the proceeds are cash proceeds or of the same type as the collateral; and

(C) in the case of proceeds that are proceeds of proceeds, all intervening proceeds are cash proceeds, proceeds of the same type as the collateral, or an account relating to the collateral.

(d) Subject to subsection (e) and except as otherwise provided in subsection (f), if a security interest in chattel paper, deposit accounts, negotiable documents, instruments, investment property, or letter-of-credit rights is perfected by a method other than filing, conflicting perfected security interests in proceeds of the collateral rank according to priority in time of filing.

(e) Subsection (d) applies only if the proceeds of the collateral are not cash proceeds, chattel paper, negotiable documents, instruments, investment property, or letter-of-credit rights.

(f) Subsections (a) through (e) are subject to:

(1) subsection (g) and the other provisions of this part;

(2) Section 4-210 with respect to a security interest of a collecting bank;

(3) Section 5-118 with respect to a security interest of an issuer or nominated person; and

(4) Section 9-110 with respect to a security interest arising under Article 2 or 2A.

(g) A perfected agricultural lien on collateral has priority over a conflicting security interest in or agricultural lien on the same collateral if the statute creating the agricultural lien so provides.

Section 9-323. Future Advances.

(a) Except as otherwise provided in subsection (c), for purposes of determining the priority of a perfected security interest under Section 9-322(a)(1), perfection of the security interest dates from the time an advance is made to the extent that the security interest secures an advance that:

(1) is made while the security interest is perfected only:

(A) under Section 9-309 when it attaches; or

(B) temporarily under Section 9-312(e), (f), or (g); and

(2) is not made pursuant to a commitment entered into before or while the security interest is perfected by a method other than under Section 9-309 or 9-312(e), (f), or (g).

(b) Except as otherwise provided in subsection (c), a security interest is subordinate to the rights of a person that becomes a lien creditor to the extent that the security interest secures an advance made more than 45 days after the person becomes a lien creditor unless the advance is made:

(1) without knowledge of the lien; or

(2) pursuant to a commitment entered into without knowledge of the lien.

(c) Subsections (a) and (b) do not apply to a security interest held by a secured party that is a buyer of accounts, chattel paper, payment intangibles, or promissory notes or a consignor.

(d) Except as otherwise provided in subsection (e), a buyer of goods other than a buyer in ordinary course of business takes free of a security interest to the extent that it secures advances made after the earlier of:

(1) the time the secured party acquires knowledge of the buyer's purchase; or

(2) 45 days after the purchase.

(e) Subsection (d) does not apply if the advance is made pursuant to a commitment entered into without knowledge of the buyer's purchase and before the expiration of the 45-day period.

(f) Except as otherwise provided in subsection (g), a lessee of goods, other than a lessee in ordinary course of business, takes the leasehold interest free of a security interest to the extent that it secures advances made after the earlier of:

(1) the time the secured party acquires knowledge of the lease; or

(2) 45 days after the lease contract becomes enforceable.

(g) Subsection (f) does not apply if the advance is made pursuant to a commitment entered into without knowledge of the lease and before the expiration of the 45-day period.

As amended in 1999.

Section 9-324. Priority of Purchase-Money Security Interests.

(a) Except as otherwise provided in subsection (g), a perfected purchase-money security interest in goods other than inventory or livestock has priority over a conflicting security interest in the same goods, and, except as otherwise provided in Section 9-327, a perfected security interest in its identifiable proceeds also has priority, if the purchase-money security interest is perfected when the debtor receives possession of the collateral or within 20 days thereafter.

(b) Subject to subsection (c) and except as otherwise provided in subsection (g), a perfected purchase-money security interest in inventory has priority over a conflicting security interest in the same inventory, has priority over a conflicting security interest in chattel paper or an instrument constituting proceeds of the inventory and in proceeds of the chattel paper, if so provided in Section 9-330, and, except as otherwise provided in Section 9-327, also has priority in identifiable cash proceeds of the inventory to the extent the identifiable cash proceeds are received on or before the delivery of the inventory to a buyer, if:

(1) the purchase-money security interest is perfected when the debtor receives possession of the inventory;

(2) the purchase-money secured party sends an authenticated notification to the holder of the conflicting security interest;

(3) the holder of the conflicting security interest receives the notification within five years before the debtor receives possession of the inventory; and

(4) the notification states that the person sending the notification has or expects to acquire a purchase-money security interest in inventory of the debtor and describes the inventory.

(c) Subsections (b)(2) through (4) apply only if the holder of the conflicting security interest had filed a financing statement covering the same types of inventory:

(1) if the purchase-money security interest is perfected by filing, before the date of the filing; or

(2) if the purchase-money security interest is temporarily perfected without filing or possession under Section 9-312(f), before the beginning of the 20-day period thereunder.

(d) Subject to subsection (e) and except as otherwise provided in subsection (g), a perfected purchase-money security interest in livestock that are farm products has priority over a conflicting security interest in the same livestock, and, except as otherwise provided in Section 9-327, a perfected security interest in their identifiable proceeds and identifiable products in their unmanufactured states also has priority, if:

(1) the purchase-money security interest is perfected when the debtor receives possession of the livestock;

(2) the purchase-money secured party sends an authenticated notification to the holder of the conflicting security interest;

(3) the holder of the conflicting security interest receives the notification within six months before the debtor receives possession of the livestock; and

(4) the notification states that the person sending the notification has or expects to acquire a purchase-money security interest in livestock of the debtor and describes the livestock.

(e) Subsections (d)(2) through (4) apply only if the holder of the conflicting security interest had filed a financing statement covering the same types of livestock:

(1) if the purchase-money security interest is perfected by filing, before the date of the filing; or

(2) if the purchase-money security interest is temporarily perfected without filing or possession under Section 9-312(f), before the beginning of the 20-day period thereunder.

(f) Except as otherwise provided in subsection (g), a perfected purchase-money security interest in software has priority over a conflicting security interest in the same collateral, and, except as otherwise provided in Section 9-327, a perfected security interest in its identifiable proceeds also has priority, to the extent that the purchase-money security interest in the goods in which the software was acquired for use has priority in the goods and proceeds of the goods under this section.

(g) If more than one security interest qualifies for priority in the same collateral under subsection (a), (b), (d), or (f):

(1) a security interest securing an obligation incurred as all or part of the price of the collateral has priority over a security interest securing an obligation incurred for value given to enable the debtor to acquire rights in or the use of collateral; and

(2) in all other cases, Section 9-322(a) applies to the qualifying security interests.

Section 9-325. Priority of Security Interests in Transferred Collateral.

(a) Except as otherwise provided in subsection (b), a security interest created by a debtor is subordinate to a security interest in the same collateral created by another person if:

(1) the debtor acquired the collateral subject to the security interest created by the other person;

(2) the security interest created by the other person was perfected when the debtor acquired the collateral; and

(3) there is no period thereafter when the security interest is unperfected.

(b) Subsection (a) subordinates a security interest only if the security interest:

(1) otherwise would have priority solely under Section 9-322(a) or 9-324; or

(2) arose solely under Section 2-711(3) or 2A-508(5).

Section 9-326. Priority of Security Interests Created by New Debtor.

(a) Subject to subsection (b), a security interest created by a new debtor which is perfected by a filed financing statement that is effective solely under Section 9-508 in collateral in which a new debtor has or acquires rights is subordinate to a security interest in the same collateral which is perfected other than by a filed financing statement that is effective solely under Section 9-508.

(b) The other provisions of this part determine the priority among conflicting security interests in the same collateral perfected by filed financing statements that are effective solely under Section 9-508. However, if the security agreements to which a new debtor became bound as debtor were not entered into by the same original debtor, the conflicting security interests rank according to priority in time of the new debtor's having become bound.

Section 9-327. Priority of Security Interests in Deposit Account.

The following rules govern priority among conflicting security interests in the same deposit account:

(1) A security interest held by a secured party having control of the deposit account under Section 9-104 has priority over a conflicting security interest held by a secured party that does not have control.

(2) Except as otherwise provided in paragraphs (3) and (4), security interests perfected by control under Section 9-314 rank according to priority in time of obtaining control.

(3) Except as otherwise provided in paragraph (4), a security interest held by the bank with which the deposit account is maintained has priority over a conflicting security interest held by another secured party.

(4) A security interest perfected by control under Section 9-104(a)(3) has priority over a security interest held by the bank with which the deposit account is maintained.

Section 9-328. Priority of Security Interests in Investment Property.

The following rules govern priority among conflicting security interests in the same investment property:

(1) A security interest held by a secured party having control of investment property under Section 9-106 has priority over a security interest held by a secured party that does not have control of the investment property.

(2) Except as otherwise provided in paragraphs (3) and (4), conflicting security interests held by secured parties each of which has control under Section 9-106 rank according to priority in time of:

 (A) if the collateral is a security, obtaining control;

 (B) if the collateral is a security entitlement carried in a securities ac count and:

  (i) if the secured party obtained control under Section 8-106(d)(1), the secured party's becoming the person for which the securities account is maintained;

  (ii) if the secured party obtained control under Section 8-106(d)(2), the securities intermediary's agreement to comply with the secured party's entitlement orders with respect to security entitlements carried or to be carried in the securities account; or

  (iii) if the secured party obtained control through another person under Section 8-106(d)(3), the time on which priority would be based under this paragraph if the other person were the secured party; or

 (C) if the collateral is a commodity contract carried with a commodity intermediary, the satisfaction of the requirement for control specified in Section 9-106(b)(2) with respect to commodity contracts carried or to be carried with the commodity intermediary.

(3) A security interest held by a securities intermediary in a security entitlement or a securities account maintained with the securities intermediary has priority over a conflicting security interest held by another secured party.

(4) A security interest held by a commodity intermediary in a commodity contract or a commodity account maintained with the commodity intermediary has priority over a conflicting security interest held by another secured party.

(5) A security interest in a certificated security in registered form which is perfected by taking delivery under Section 9-313(a) and not by control under Section 9-314 has priority over a conflicting security interest perfected by a method other than control.

(6) Conflicting security interests created by a broker, securities intermediary, or commodity intermediary which are perfected without control under Section 9-106 rank equally.

(7) In all other cases, priority among conflicting security interests in investment property is governed by Sections 9-322 and 9-323.

Section 9-329. Priority of Security Interests in Letter-of-Credit Right.

The following rules govern priority among conflicting security interests in the same letter-of-credit right:

(1) A security interest held by a secured party having control of the letter-of-credit right under Section 9-107 has priority to the extent of its control over a conflicting security interest held by a secured party that does not have control.

(2) Security interests perfected by control under Section 9-314 rank according to priority in time of obtaining control.

Section 9-330. Priority of Purchaser of Chattel Paper or Instrument.

(a) A purchaser of chattel paper has priority over a security interest in the chattel paper which is claimed merely as proceeds of inventory subject to a security interest if:

(1) in good faith and in the ordinary course of the purchaser's business, the purchaser gives new value and takes possession of the chattel paper or obtains control of the chattel paper under Section 9-105; and

(2) the chattel paper does not indicate that it has been assigned to an identified assignee other than the purchaser.

(b) A purchaser of chattel paper has priority over a security interest in the chattel paper which is claimed other than merely as proceeds of inventory subject to a security interest if the purchaser gives new value and takes possession of the chattel paper or obtains control of the chattel paper under Section 9-105 in good faith, in the ordinary course of the purchaser's business, and without knowledge that the purchase violates the rights of the secured party.

(c) Except as otherwise provided in Section 9-327, a purchaser having priority in chattel paper under subsection (a) or (b) also has priority in proceeds of the chattel paper to the extent that:

(1) Section 9-322 provides for priority in the proceeds; or

(2) the proceeds consist of the specific goods covered by the chattel paper or cash proceeds of the specific goods, even if the purchaser's security interest in the proceeds is unperfected.

(d) Except as otherwise provided in Section 9-331(a), a purchaser of an instrument has priority over a security interest in the instrument perfected by a method other than possession if the purchaser gives value and takes possession of the instrument in good faith and without knowledge that the purchase violates the rights of the secured party.

(e) For purposes of subsections (a) and (b), the holder of a purchase-money security interest in inventory gives new value for chattel paper constituting proceeds of the inventory.

(f) For purposes of subsections (b) and (d), if chattel paper or an instrument indicates that it has been assigned to an identified secured party other than the purchaser, a purchaser of the chattel paper or instrument has knowledge that the purchase violates the rights of the secured party.

Section 9-331. Priority of Rights of Purchasers of Instruments, Documents, and Securities under Other Articles; Priority of Interests in Financial Assets and Security Entitlements under Article 8.

(a) This article does not limit the rights of a holder in due course of a negotiable instrument, a holder to which a negotiable document of title has been duly negotiated, or a protected purchaser of a security. These holders or purchasers take priority over an earlier security interest, even if perfected, to the extent provided in Articles 3, 7, and 8.

(b) This article does not limit the rights of or impose liability on a person to the extent that the person is protected against the assertion of a claim under Article 8.

(c) Filing under this article does not constitute notice of a claim or defense to the holders, or purchasers, or persons described in subsections (a) and (b).

Section 9-332. Transfer of Money; Transfer of Funds from Deposit Account.

(a) A transferee of money takes the money free of a security interest unless the transferee acts in collusion with the debtor in violating the rights of the secured party.

(b) A transferee of funds from a deposit account takes the funds free of a security interest in the deposit account unless the transferee acts in collusion with the debtor in violating the rights of the secured party.

Section 9-333. Priority of Certain Liens Arising by Operation of Law.

(a) In this section, "possessory lien" means an interest, other than a security interest or an agricultural lien:

(1) which secures payment or performance of an obligation for services or materials furnished with respect to goods by a person in the ordinary course of the person's business;

(2) which is created by statute or rule of law in favor of the person; and

(3) whose effectiveness depends on the person's possession of the goods.

(b) A possessory lien on goods has priority over a security interest in the goods unless the lien is created by a statute that expressly provides otherwise.

Section 9-334. Priority of Security Interests in Fixtures and Crops.

(a) A security interest under this article may be created in goods that are fixtures or may continue in goods that become fixtures. A security interest does not exist under this article in ordinary building materials incorporated into an improvement on land.

(b) This article does not prevent creation of an encumbrance upon fixtures under real property law.

(c) In cases not governed by subsections (d) through (h), a security interest in fixtures is subordinate to a conflicting interest of an encumbrancer or owner of the related real property other than the debtor.

(d) Except as otherwise provided in subsection (h), a perfected security interest in fixtures has priority over a conflicting interest of an encumbrancer or owner of the real property if the debtor has an interest of record in or is in possession of the real property and:

(1) the security interest is a purchase-money security interest;

(2) the interest of the encumbrancer or owner arises before the goods become fixtures; and

(3) the security interest is perfected by a fixture filing before the goods become fixtures or within 20 days thereafter.

(e) A perfected security interest in fixtures has priority over a conflicting interest of an encumbrancer or owner of the real property if:

(1) the debtor has an interest of record in the real property or is in possession of the real property and the security interest:

(A) is perfected by a fixture filing before the interest of the encumbrancer or owner is of record; and

(B) has priority over any conflicting interest of a predecessor in title of the encumbrancer or owner;

(2) before the goods become fixtures, the security interest is perfected by any method permitted by this article and the fixtures are readily removable:

(A) factory or office machines;

(B) equipment that is not primarily used or leased for use in the operation of the real property; or

(C) replacements of domestic appliances that are consumer goods;

(3) the conflicting interest is a lien on the real property obtained by legal or equitable proceedings after the security interest was perfected by any method permitted by this article; or

(4) the security interest is:

(A) created in a manufactured home in a manufactured-home transaction; and

(B) perfected pursuant to a statute described in Section 9-311(a)(2).

(f) A security interest in fixtures, whether or not perfected, has priority over a conflicting interest of an encumbrancer or owner of the real property if:

(1) the encumbrancer or owner has, in an authenticated record, consented to the security interest or disclaimed an interest in the goods as fixtures; or

(2) the debtor has a right to remove the goods as against the encumbrancer or owner.

(g) The priority of the security interest under paragraph (f)(2) continues for a reasonable time if the debtor's right to remove the goods as against the encumbrancer or owner terminates.

(h) A mortgage is a construction mortgage to the extent that it secures an obligation incurred for the construction of an improvement on land, including the acquisition cost of the land, if a recorded record of the mortgage so indicates. Except as otherwise provided in subsections (e) and (f), a security interest in fixtures is subordinate to a construction mortgage if a record of the mortgage is recorded before the goods become fixtures and the goods become fixtures before the completion of the construction. A mortgage has this priority to the same extent as a construction mortgage to the extent that it is given to refinance a construction mortgage.

(i) A perfected security interest in crops growing on real property has priority over a conflicting interest of an encumbrancer or owner of the real property if the debtor has an interest of record in or is in possession of the real property.

(j) Subsection (i) prevails over any inconsistent provisions of the following statutes:

[List here any statutes containing provisions inconsistent with subsection (i).]

Legislative Note: States that amend statutes to remove provisions inconsistent with subsection (i) need not enact subsection (j).

Section 9-335. Accessions.

(a) A security interest may be created in an accession and continues in collateral that becomes an accession.

(b) If a security interest is perfected when the collateral becomes an accession, the security interest remains perfected in the collateral.

(c) Except as otherwise provided in subsection (d), the other provisions of this part determine the priority of a security interest in an accession.

(d) A security interest in an accession is subordinate to a security interest in the whole which is perfected by compliance with the requirements of a certificate-of-title statute under Section 9-311(b).

(e) After default, subject to Part 6, a secured party may remove an accession from other goods if the security interest in the accession has priority over the claims of every person having an interest in the whole.

(f) A secured party that removes an accession from other goods under subsection (e) shall promptly reimburse any holder of a security interest or other lien on, or owner of, the whole or of the other goods, other than the debtor, for the cost of repair of any physical injury to the whole or the other goods. The secured party need not reimburse the holder or owner for any diminution in value of the whole or the other goods caused by the absence of the accession removed or by any necessity for replacing it. A person entitled to reimbursement may refuse permission to remove until the secured party gives adequate assurance for the performance of the obligation to reimburse.

Section 9-336. Commingled Goods.

(a) In this section, "commingled goods" means goods that are physically united with other goods in such a manner that their identity is lost in a product or mass.

(b) A security interest does not exist in commingled goods as such. However, a security interest may attach to a product or mass that results when goods become commingled goods.

(c) If collateral becomes commingled goods, a security interest attaches to the product or mass.

(d) If a security interest in collateral is perfected before the collateral becomes commingled goods, the security interest that attaches to the product or mass under subsection (c) is perfected.

(e) Except as otherwise provided in subsection (f), the other provisions of this part determine the priority of a security interest that attaches to the product or mass under subsection (c).

(f) If more than one security interest attaches to the product or mass under subsection (c), the following rules determine priority:

(1) A security interest that is perfected under subsection (d) has priority over a security interest that is unperfected at the time the collateral becomes commingled goods.

(2) If more than one security interest is perfected under subsection (d), the security interests rank equally in proportion to the value of the collateral at the time it became commingled goods.

Section 9-337. Priority of Security Interests in Goods Covered by Certificate of Title.

If, while a security interest in goods is perfected by any method under the law of another jurisdiction, this State issues a certificate of title that does not show that the goods are subject to the security interest or contain a statement that they may be subject to security interests not shown on the certificate:

(1) a buyer of the goods, other than a person in the business of selling goods of that kind, takes free of the security interest if the buyer gives value and receives delivery of the goods after issuance of the certificate and without knowledge of the security interest; and

(2) the security interest is subordinate to a conflicting security interest in the goods that attaches, and is perfected under Section 9-311(b), after issuance of the certificate and without the conflicting secured party's knowledge of the security interest.

Section 9-338. Priority of Security Interest or Agricultural Lien Perfected by Filed Financing Statement Providing Certain Incorrect Information.

If a security interest or agricultural lien is perfected by a filed financing statement providing information described in Section 9-516(b)(5) which is incorrect at the time the financing statement is filed:

(1) the security interest or agricultural lien is subordinate to a conflicting per fected security interest in the collateral to the extent that the holder of the conflicting security interest gives value in reasonable reliance upon the incorrect information; and

(2) a purchaser, other than a secured party, of the collateral takes free of the security interest or agricultural lien to the extent that, in reasonable reliance upon the incorrect information, the purchaser gives value and, in the case of chattel paper, documents, goods, instruments, or a security certificate, receives delivery of the collateral.

Section 9-339. Priority Subject to Subordination.

This article does not preclude subordination by agreement by a person entitled to priority. [Subpart 4. Rights of Bank].

Section 9-340. Effectiveness of Right of Recoupment or Set-Off against Deposit Account.

(a) Except as otherwise provided in subsection (c), a bank with which a deposit account is maintained may exercise any right of recoupment or set-off against a secured party that holds a security interest in the deposit account.

(b) Except as otherwise provided in subsection (c), the application of this article to a security interest in a deposit account does not affect a right of recoupment or set-off of the secured party as to a deposit account maintained with the secured party.

(c) The exercise by a bank of a set-off against a deposit account is ineffective against a secured party that holds a security interest in the deposit account which is perfected by control under Section 9-104(a)(3), if the set-off is based on a claim against the debtor.

Section 9-341. Bank's Rights and Duties with Respect to Deposit Account.

Except as otherwise provided in Section 9-340(c), and unless the bank otherwise agrees in an authenticated record, a bank's rights and duties with respect to a deposit account maintained with the bank are not terminated, suspended, or modified by:

(1) the creation, attachment, or perfection of a security interest in the deposit account;

(2) the bank's knowledge of the security interest; or

(3) the bank's receipt of instructions from the secured party.

Section 9-342. Bank's Right to Refuse to Enter into or Disclose Existence of Control Agreement.

This article does not require a bank to enter into an agreement of the kind described in Section 9-104(a)(2), even if its customer so requests or directs. A bank that has entered into such an agreement is not required to confirm the existence of the agreement to another person unless requested to do so by its customer.

Part 4. Rights of Third Parties.

Section 9-401. Alienability of Debtor's Rights.

(a) Except as otherwise provided in subsection (b) and Sections 9-406, 9-407, 9-408, and 9-409, whether a debtor's rights in collateral may be voluntarily or involuntarily transferred is governed by law other than this article.

(b) An agreement between the debtor and secured party which prohibits a transfer of the debtor's rights in collateral or makes the transfer a default does not prevent the transfer from taking effect.

Section 9-402. Secured Party Not Obligated on Contract of Debtor or in Tort.

The existence of a security interest, agricultural lien, or authority given to a debtor to dispose of or use collateral, without more, does not subject a secured party to liability in contract or tort for the debtor's acts or omissions.

Section 9-403. Agreement Not to Assert Defenses against Assignee.

(a) In this section, "value" has the meaning provided in Section 3-303(a).

(b) Except as otherwise provided in this section, an agreement between an account debtor and an assignor not to assert against an assignee any claim or defense that the account debtor may have against the assignor is enforceable by an assignee that takes an assignment:

(1) for value;

(2) in good faith;

(3) without notice of a claim of a property or possessory right to the property assigned; and

(4) without notice of a defense or claim in recoupment of the type that may be asserted against a person entitled to enforce a negotiable instrument under Section 3-305(a).

(c) Subsection (b) does not apply to defenses of a type that may be asserted against a holder in due course of a negotiable instrument under Section 3-305(b).

(d) In a consumer transaction, if a record evidences the account debtor's obligation, law other than this article requires that the record include a statement to the effect that the rights of an assignee are subject to claims or defenses that the account debtor could assert against the original obligee, and the record does not include such a statement:

(1) the record has the same effect as if the record included such a statement; and

(2) the account debtor may assert against an assignee those claims and defenses that would have been available if the record included such a statement.

(e) This section is subject to law other than this article which establishes a different rule for an account debtor who is an individual and who incurred the obligation primarily for personal, family, or household purposes.

(f) Except as otherwise provided in subsection (d), this section does not displace law other than this article which gives effect to an agreement by an account debtor not to assert a claim or defense against an assignee.

Section 9-404. Rights Acquired by Assignee; Claims and Defenses against Assignee.

(a) Unless an account debtor has made an enforceable agreement not to assert defenses or claims, and subject to subsections (b) through (e), the rights of an assignee are subject to:

(1) all terms of the agreement between the account debtor and assignor and any defense or claim in recoupment arising from the transaction that gave rise to the contract; and

(2) any other defense or claim of the account debtor against the assignor which accrues before the account debt or receives a notification of the assignment authenticated by the assignor or the assignee.

(b) Subject to subsection (c) and except as otherwise provided in subsection (d), the claim of an account debtor against an assignor may be asserted against an assignee under subsection (a) only to reduce the amount the account debtor owes.

(c) This section is subject to law other than this article which establishes a different rule for an account debtor who is an individual and who incurred the obligation primarily for personal, family, or household purposes.

(d) In a consumer transaction, if a record evidences the account debtor's obligation, law other than this article requires that the record include a statement to the effect that the account debtor's recovery against an assignee with respect to claims and defenses against the assignor may not exceed amounts paid by the account debtor under the record, and the record does not include such a statement, the extent to which a claim of an account debtor against the assignor may be asserted against an assignee is determined as if the record included such a statement.

(e) This section does not apply to an assignment of a health-care-insurance receivable.

Section 9-405. Modification of Assigned Contract.

(a) A modification of or substitution for an assigned contract is effective against an assignee if made in good faith. The assignee acquires corresponding rights under the modified or substituted contract. The assignment may provide that the modification or substitution is a breach of contract by the assignor. This subsection is subject to subsections (b) through (d).

(b) Subsection (a) applies to the extent that:

(1) the right to payment or a part thereof under an assigned contract has not been fully earned by performance; or

(2) the right to payment or a part thereof has been fully earned by performance and the account debtor has not received notification of the assignment under Section 9-406(a).

(c) This section is subject to law other than this article which establishes a different rule for an account debtor who is an individual and who incurred the obligation primarily for personal, family, or household purposes.

(d) This section does not apply to an assignment of a health-care-insurance receivable.

Section 9-406. Discharge of Account Debtor; Notification of Assignment; Identification and Proof of Assignment; Restrictions on Assignment of Accounts, Chattel Paper, Payment Intangibles, and Promissory Notes Ineffective.

(a) Subject to subsections (b) through (i), an account debtor on an account, chattel paper, or a payment intangible may discharge its obligation by paying the assignor until, but not after, the account debtor receives a notification, authenticated by the assignor or the assignee, that the amount due or to become due has been assigned and that payment is to be made to the assignee. After receipt of the notification, the account debtor may discharge its obligation by paying the assignee and may not discharge the obligation by paying the assignor.

(b) Subject to subsection (h), notification is ineffective under subsection (a):

(1) if it does not reasonably identify the rights assigned;

(2) to the extent that an agreement between an account debtor and a seller of a payment intangible limits the account debtor's duty to pay a person other than the seller and the limitation is effective under law other than this article; or

(3) at the option of an account debtor, if the notification notifies the account debtor to make less than the full amount of any installment or other periodic payment to the assignee, even if:

(A) only a portion of the account, chat tel paper, or payment intangible has been assigned to that as signee;

(B) a portion has been assigned to another assignee; or

(C) the account debtor knows that the assignment to that assignee is limited.

(c) Subject to subsection (h), if requested by the account debtor, an assignee shall seasonably furnish reasonable proof that the assignment has been made. Unless the assignee complies, the account debtor may discharge its obligation by paying the assignor, even if the account debtor has received a notification under subsection (a).

(d) Except as otherwise provided in subsection (e) and Sections 2A-303 and 9-407, and subject to subsection (h), a term in an agreement between an account debtor and an assignor or in a promissory note is ineffective to the extent that it:

(1) prohibits, restricts, or requires the consent of the account debtor or person obligated on the promissory note to the assignment or transfer of, or the creation, attachment, perfection, or enforcement of a security interest in, the account, chattel paper, payment intangible, or promissory note; or

(2) provides that the assignment or transfer or the creation, attachment, perfection, or enforcement of the security interest may give rise to a default, breach, right of recoupment, claim, defense, termination, right of termination, or remedy under the account, chattel paper, payment intangible, or promissory note.

(e) Subsection (d) does not apply to the sale of a payment intangible or promissory note.

(f) Except as otherwise provided in Sections 2A-303 and 9-407 and subject to subsections (h) and (i), a rule of law, statute, or regulation that prohibits, restricts, or requires the consent of a government, governmental body or official, or account debtor to the assignment or transfer of, or creation of a security interest in, an account or chattel paper is ineffective to the extent that the rule of law, statute, or regulation:

(1) prohibits, restricts, or requires the consent of the government, governmental body or official, or account debtor to the assignment or transfer of, or the creation, attachment, perfection, or enforcement of a security interest in the account or chattel paper; or

(2) provides that the assignment or transfer or the creation, attachment, perfection, or enforcement of the security interest may give rise to a default, breach, right of recoupment, claim, defense, termination, right of termination, or remedy under the account or chattel paper.

(g) Subject to subsection (h), an account debtor may not waive or vary its option under subsection (b)(3).

(h) This section is subject to law other than this article which establishes a different rule for an account debtor who is an individual and who incurred the obligation primarily for personal, family, or household purposes.

(i) This section does not apply to an assignment of a health-care-insurance receivable.

(j) This section prevails over any inconsistent provisions of the following statutes, rules, and regulations:

[List here any statutes, rules, and regulations containing provisions inconsistent with this section.]

Legislative Note: States that amend statutes, rules, and regulations to remove provisions inconsistent with this section need not enact subsection (j).

As amended in 1999 and 2000.

Section 9-407. Restrictions on Creation or Enforcement of Security Interest in Leasehold Interest or in Lessor's Residual Interest.

(a) Except as otherwise provided in subsection (b), a term in a lease agreement is ineffective to the extent that it:

(1) prohibits, restricts, or requires the consent of a party to the lease to the assignment or transfer of, or the creation, attachment, perfection, or enforcement of a security interest in an interest of a party under the lease contract or in the lessor's residual interest in the goods; or

(2) provides that the assignment or transfer or the creation, attachment, perfection, or enforcement of the security interest may give rise to a default, breach, right of recoupment, claim, defense, termination, right of termination, or remedy under the lease.

(b) Except as otherwise provided in Section 2A-303(7), a term described in subsection (a)(2) is effective to the extent that there is:

(1) a transfer by the lessee of the lessee's right of possession or use of the goods in violation of the term; or

(2) a delegation of a material performance of either party to the lease contract in violation of the term.

(c) The creation, attachment, perfection, or enforcement of a security interest in the lessor's interest under the lease contract or the lessor's residual interest in the goods is not a transfer that materially impairs the lessee's prospect of obtaining return performance or materially changes the duty of or materially increases the burden or risk imposed on the lessee within the purview of Section 2A-303(4) unless, and then only to the extent that, enforcement actually results in a delegation of material performance of the lessor.

As amended in 1999.

Section 9-408. Restrictions on Assignment of Promissory Notes, Health-Care-Insurance Receivables, and Certain General Intangibles Ineffective.

(a) Except as otherwise provided in subsection (b), a term in a promissory note or in an agreement between an account debtor and a debtor which relates to a health-care-insurance receivable or a general intangible, including a contract, permit, license, or franchise, and which term prohibits, restricts, or requires the consent of the person obligated on the promissory note or the account debtor to, the assignment or transfer of, or creation, attachment, or perfection of a security interest in, the promissory note, health-care-insurance receivable, or general intangible, is ineffective to the extent that the term:

(1) would impair the creation, attachment, or perfection of a security interest; or

(2) provides that the assignment or transfer or the creation, attachment, or perfection of the security interest may give rise to a default, breach, right of recoupment, claim, defense, termination, right of termination, or remedy under the promissory note, health-care-insurance receivable, or general intangible.

(b) Subsection (a) applies to a security interest in a payment intangible or promissory note only if the security interest arises out of a sale of the payment intangible or promissory note.

(c) A rule of law, statute, or regulation that prohibits, restricts, or requires the consent of a government, governmental body or official, person obligated on a promissory note, or account debtor to the assignment or transfer of, or creation of a security interest in, a promissory note, health-care-insurance receivable, or general intangible, including a contract, permit, license, or franchise between an account debtor and a debtor, is ineffective to the extent that the rule of law, statute, or regulation:

(1) would impair the creation, attachment, or perfection of a security interest; or

(2) provides that the assignment or transfer or the creation, attachment, or perfection of the security interest may give rise to a default, breach, right of recoupment, claim, defense, termination, right of termination, or remedy under the promissory note, health-care-insurance receivable, or general intangible.

(d) To the extent that a term in a promissory note or in an agreement between an account debtor and a debtor which relates to a health-care-insurance receivable or general intangible or a rule of law, statute, or regulation described in subsection (c) would be effective under law other than this article but is ineffective under subsection (a) or (c), the creation, attachment, or perfection of a security interest in the promissory note, health-care-insurance receivable, or general intangible:

(1) is not enforceable against the person obligated on the promissory note or the account debtor;

(2) does not impose a duty or obligation on the person obligated on the promissory note or the account debtor;

(3) does not require the person obligated on the promissory note or the account debtor to recognize the security interest, pay or render performance to the secured party, or accept payment or performance from the secured party;

(4) does not entitle the secured party to use or assign the debtor's rights under the promissory note, health-care-insurance receivable, or general intangible, including any related information or materials furnished to the debtor in the transaction giving rise to the promissory note, health-care-insurance receivable, or general intangible;

(5) does not entitle the secured party to use, assign, possess, or have access to any trade secrets or confidential information of the person obligated on the promissory note or the account debtor; and

(6) does not entitle the secured party to enforce the security interest in the promissory note, health-care-insurance receivable, or general intangible.

(e) This section prevails over any inconsistent provisions of the following statutes, rules, and regulations:

[List here any statutes, rules, and regulations containing provisions inconsistent with this section.]

Legislative Note: States that amend statutes, rules, and regulations to remove provisions inconsistent with this section need not enact subsection (e).

As amended in 1999.

Section 9-409. Restrictions on Assignment of Letter-of-Credit Rights Ineffective.

(a) A term in a letter of credit or a rule of law, statute, regulation, custom, or practice applicable to the letter of credit which prohibits, restricts, or requires the consent of an applicant, issuer, or nominated person to a beneficiary's assignment of or creation of a security interest in a letter-of-credit right is ineffective to the extent that the term or rule of law, statute, regulation, custom, or practice:

(1) would impair the creation, attachment, or perfection of a security interest in the letter-of-credit right; or

(2) provides that the assignment or the creation, attachment, or perfection of the security interest may give rise to a default, breach, right of recoupment, claim, defense, termination, right of termination, or remedy under the letter-of-credit right.

(b) To the extent that a term in a letter of credit is ineffective under subsection (a) but would be effective under law other than this article or a custom or practice applicable to the letter-of-credit, to the transfer of a right to draw or otherwise demand performance under the letter of credit, or to the assignment of a right to proceeds of the letter of credit, the creation, attachment, or perfection of a security interest in the letter-of-credit right:

(1) is not enforceable against the applicant, issuer, nominated person, or transferee beneficiary;

(2) imposes no duties or obligations on the applicant, issuer, nominated person, or transferee beneficiary; and

(3) does not require the applicant, issuer, nominated person, or transferee beneficiary to recognize the security interest, pay or render performance to the secured party, or accept payment or other performance from the secured party.

As amended in 1999.

Part 5. Filing.

[Subpart 1. Filing Office; Contents and Effectiveness of Financing Statement].

Section 9-501. Filing Office.

(a) Except as otherwise provided in subsection (b), if the local law of this State governs perfection of a security interest or agricultural lien, the office in which to file a financing statement to perfect the security interest or agricultural lien is:

(1) the office designated for the filing or recording of a record of a mortgage on the related real property, if:

(A) the collateral is as-extracted collateral or timber to be cut; or

(B) the financing statement is filed as a fixture filing and the collateral is goods that are or are to become fixtures; or

(2) the office of [ ] [or any office duly authorized by [ ]], in all other cases, including a case in which the collateral is goods that are or are to become fixtures and the financing statement is not filed as a fixture filing.

(b) The office in which to file a financing statement to perfect a security interest in collateral, including fixtures, of a transmitting utility is the office of [ ]. The financing statement also constitutes a fixture filing as to the collateral indicated in the financing statement which is or is to become fixtures.

Legislative Note: The State should designate the filing office where the brackets appear. The filing office may be that of a governmental official (e.g., the Secretary of State) or a private party that maintains the State's filing system.

Section 9-502. Contents of Financing Statement; Record of Mortgage as Financing Statement; Time of Filing Financing Statement.

(a) Subject to subsection (b), a financing statement is sufficient only if it:

(1) provides the name of the debtor;

(2) provides the name of the secured party or a representative of the secured part y; and

(3) indicates the collateral covered by the financing statement.

(b) Except as otherwise provided in Section 9-501(b), to be sufficient, a financing statement that covers as-extracted collateral or timber to be cut, or which is filed as a fixture filing and covers goods that are or are to become fixtures, must satisfy subsection (a) and also:

(1) indicate that it covers this type of collateral;

(2) indicate that it is to be filed [for record] in the real property records;

(3) provide a description of the real property to which the collateral is related [sufficient to give constructive notice of a mortgage under the law of this State if the description were contained in a record of the mortgage of the real property]; and

(4) if the debtor does not have an interest of record in the real property, provide the name of a record owner.

(c) A record of a mortgage is effective, from the date of recording, as a financing statement filed as a fixture filing or as a financing statement covering as-extracted collateral or timber to be cut only if:

(1) the record indicates the goods or accounts that it covers;

(2) the goods are or are to become fixtures related to the real property described in the record or the collateral is related to the real property described in the record and is as-extracted collateral or timber to be cut;

(3) the record satisfies the requirements for a financing statement in this section other than an indication that it is to be filed in the real property records; and

(4) the record is [duly] recorded.

(d) A financing statement may be filed before a security agreement is made or a security interest otherwise attaches.

Legislative Note: Language in brackets is optional. Where the State has any special recording system for real property other than the usual grantor-grantee index (as, for instance, a tract system or a title registration or Torrens system) local adaptations of subsection (b) and Section 9-519(d) and (e) may be necessary. See, e.g., Mass. Gen. Laws Chapter 106, Section 9-410.

Section 9-503. Name of Debtor and Secured Party.

(a) A financing statement sufficiently provides the name of the debtor:

(1) if the debtor is a registered organization, only if the financing statement provides the name of the debtor indicated on the public record of the debtor's jurisdiction of organization which shows the debtor to have been organized;

(2) if the debtor is a decedent's estate, only if the financing statement provides the name of the decedent and indicates that the debtor is an estate;

(3) if the debtor is a trust or a trustee acting with respect to property held in trust, only if the financing statement:

(A) provides the name specified for the trust in its organic documents or, if no name is specified, provides the name of the settlor and additional information sufficient to distinguish the debtor from other trusts having one or more of the same settlers; and

(B) indicates, in the debtor's name or otherwise, that the debtor is a trust or is a trustee acting with respect to property held in trust; and

(4) in other cases:

(A) if the debtor has a name, only if it provides the individual or organizational name of the debtor; and

(B) if the debtor does not have a name, only if it provides the names of the partners, members, associates, or other persons comprising the debtor.

(b) A financing statement that provides the name of the debtor in accordance with subsection (a) is not rendered ineffective by the absence of:

(1) a trade name or other name of the debtor; or

(2) unless required under subsection (a)(4)(B), names of partners, members, associates, or other persons comprising the debtor.

(c) A financing statement that provides only the debtor's trade name does not sufficiently provide the name of the debtor.

(d) Failure to indicate the representative capacity of a secured party or representative of a secured party does not affect the sufficiency of a financing statement.

(e) A financing statement may provide the name of more than one debtor and the name of more than one secured party.

Section 9-504. Indication of Collateral.

A financing statement sufficiently indicates the collateral that it covers if the financing statement provides:

(1) a description of the collateral pursuant to Section 9-108; or

(2) an indication that the financing statement covers all assets or all personal property.

As amended in 1999.

Section 9-505. Filing and Compliance with Other Statutes and Treaties for Consignments, Leases, Other Bailments, and Other Transactions.

(a) A consignor, lessor, or other bailor of goods, a licensor, or a buyer of a payment intangible or promissory note may file a financing statement, or may comply with a statute or treaty described in Section 9-311(a), using the terms "consignor", "consignee", "lessor", "lessee", "bailor", "bailee", "licensor", "licensee", "owner", "registered owner", "buyer", "seller", or words of similar import, instead of the terms "secured party" and "debtor".

(b) This part applies to the filing of a financing statement under subsection (a) and, as appropriate, to compliance that is equivalent to filing a financing statement under Section 9-311(b), but the filing or compliance is not of itself a factor in determining whether the collateral secures an obligation. If it is determined for another reason that the collateral secures an obligation, a security interest held by the consignor, lessor, bailor, licensor, owner, or buyer which attaches to the collateral is perfected by the filing or compliance.

Section 9-506. Effect of Errors or Omissions.

(a) A financing statement substantially satisfying the requirements of this part is effective, even if it has minor errors or omissions, unless the errors or omissions make the financing statement seriously misleading.

(b) Except as otherwise provided in subsection (c), a financing statement that fails sufficiently to provide the name of the debtor in accordance with Section 9-503(a) is seriously misleading.

(c) If a search of the records of the filing office under the debtor's correct name, using the filing office's standard search logic, if any, would disclose a financing statement that fails sufficiently to provide the name of the debtor in accordance with Section 9-503(a), the name provided does not make the financing statement seriously misleading.

(d) For purposes of Section 9-508(b), the "debtor's correct name" in subsection (c) means the correct name of the new debtor.

Section 9-507. Effect of Certain Events on Effectiveness of Financing Statement.

(a) A filed financing statement remains effective with respect to collateral that is sold, exchanged, leased, licensed, or otherwise disposed of and in which a security interest or agricultural lien continues, even if the secured party knows of or consents to the disposition.

(b) Except as otherwise provided in subsection (c) and Section 9-508, a financing statement is not rendered ineffective if, after the financing statement is filed, the information provided in the financing statement becomes seriously misleading under Section 9-506.

(c) If a debtor so changes its name that a filed financing statement becomes seriously misleading under Section 9-506:

   (1) the financing statement is effective to perfect a security interest in collateral acquired by the debtor before, or with in four months after, the change; and

   (2) the financing statement is not effective to perfect a security interest in collateral acquired by the debtor more than four months after the change, unless an amendment to the financing statement which renders the financing statement not seriously misleading is filed within four months after the change.

Section 9-508. Effectiveness of Financing Statement If New Debtor Becomes Bound by Security Agreement.

(a) Except as otherwise provided in this section, a filed financing statement naming an original debtor is effective to perfect a security interest in collateral in which a new debtor has or acquires rights to the extent that the financing statement would have been effective had the original debtor acquired rights in the collateral.

(b) If the difference between the name of the original debtor and that of the new debtor causes a filed financing statement that is effective under subsection (a) to be seriously misleading under Section 9-506:

(1) the financing statement is effective to perfect a security interest in collateral acquired by the new debtor before, and within four months after, the new debtor becomes bound under Section 9B-203(d); and

(2) the financing statement is not effective to perfect a security interest in collateral acquired by the new debtor more than four months after the new debtor becomes bound under Section 9-203(d) unless an initial financing statement providing the name of the new debtor is filed before the expiration of that time.

(c) This section does not apply to collateral as to which a filed financing statement remains effective against the new debtor under Section 9-507(a).

Section 9-509. Persons Entitled to File a Record.

(a) A person may file an initial financing statement, amendment that adds collateral covered by a financing statement, or amendment that adds a debtor to a financing statement only if:

(1) the debtor authorizes the filing in an authenticated record or pursuant to subsection (b) or (c); or

(2) the person holds an agricultural lien that has become effective at the time of filing and the financing statement covers only collateral in which the person holds an agricultural lien.

(b) By authenticating or becoming bound as debtor by a security agreement, a debtor or new debtor authorizes the filing of an initial financing statement, and an amendment, covering:

(1) the collateral described in the security agreement; and

(2) property that becomes collateral under Section 9-315(a)(2), whether or not the security agreement expressly covers proceeds.

(c) By acquiring collateral in which a security interest or agricultural lien continues under Section 9-315(a)(1), a debtor authorizes the filing of an initial financing statement, and an amendment, covering the collateral and property that becomes collateral under Section 9-315(a)(2).

(d) A person may file an amendment other than an amendment that adds collateral covered by a financing statement or an amendment that adds a debtor to a financing statement only if:

(1) the secured party of record authorizes the filing; or

(2) the amendment is a termination statement for a financing statement as to which the secured party of record has failed to file or send a termination statement as required by Section 9-513(a) or (c), the debtor authorizes the filing, and the termination statement indicates that the debtor authorized it to be filed.

(e) If there is more than one secured party of record for a financing statement, each secured party of record may authorize the filing of an amendment under subsection (d).

As amended in 2000.

Section 9-510. Effectiveness of Filed Record.

(a) A filed record is effective only to the extent that it was filed by a person that may file it under Section 9-509.

(b) A record authorized by one secured party of record does not affect the financing statement with respect to another secured party of record.

(c) A continuation statement that is not filed within the six-month period prescribed by Section 9-515(d) is ineffective.

Section 9-511. Secured Party of Record.

(a) A secured party of record with respect to a financing statement is a person whose name is provided as the name of the secured party or a representative of the secured party in an initial financing statement that has been filed. If an initial financing statement is filed under Section 9-514(a), the assignee named in the initial financing statement is the secured party of record with respect to the financing statement.

(b) If an amendment of a financing statement which provides the name of a person as a secured party or a representative of a secured party is filed, the person named in the amendment is a secured party of record. If an amend ment is filed under Section 9-514(b), the assignee named in the amendment is a secured party of record.

(c) A person remains a secured party of record until the filing of an amendment of the financing statement which deletes the person.

Section 9-512. Amendment of Financing Statement.

[Alternative A]

(a) Subject to Section 9-509, a person may add or delete collateral covered by, continue or terminate the effectiveness of, or, subject to subsection (e), otherwise amend the information provided in, a financing statement by filing an amendment that:

(1) identifies, by its file number, the initial financing statement to which the amendment relates; and

(2) if the amendment relates to an initial financing statement filed [or recorded] in a filing office described in Section 9-501(a)(1), provides the information specified in Section 9-502(b).

[Alternative B]

(a) Subject to Section 9-509, a person may add or delete collateral covered by, continue or terminate the effectiveness of, or, subject to subsection (e), otherwise amend the information provided in, a financing statement by filing an amendment that:

(1) identifies, by its file number, the initial financing statement to which the amendment relates; and

(2) if the amendment relates to an initial financing statement filed [or recorded] in a filing office described in Section 9-501(a)(1), provides the date [and time] that the initial financing statement was filed [or recorded] and the information specified in Section 9-502(b).

[End of Alternatives]

(b) Except as otherwise provided in Section 9-515, the filing of an amendment does not extend the period of effectiveness of the financing statement.

(c) A financing statement that is amended by an amendment that adds collateral is effective as to the added collateral only from the date of the filing of the amendment.

(d) A financing statement that is amended by an amendment that adds a debtor is effective as to the added debtor only from the date of the filing of the amendment.

(e) An amendment is ineffective to the extent it:

(1) purports to delete all debtors and fails to provide the name of a debtor to be covered by the financing statement; or

(2) purports to delete all secured parties of record and fails to provide the name of a new secured party of record.

Legislative Note: States whose real-estate filing offices require additional information in amendments and cannot search their records by both the name of the debtor and the file number should enact Alternative B to Sections 9-512(a), 9-518(b), 9-519(f), and 9-522(a).

Section 9-513. Termination Statement.

(a) A secured party shall cause the secured party of record for a financing statement to file a termination statement for the financing statement if the financing statement covers consumer goods and:

(1) there is no obligation secured by the collateral covered by the financing statement and no commitment to make an advance, incur an obligation, or otherwise give value; or

(2) the debtor did not authorize the filing of the initial financing statement.

(b) To comply with subsection (a), a secured party shall cause the secured party of record to file the termination statement:

(1) within one month after there is no obligation secured by the collateral covered by the financing statement and no commitment to make an advance, incur an obligation, or otherwise give value; or

(2) if earlier, within 20 days after the secured party receives an authenticated demand from a debtor.

(c) In cases not governed by subsection (a), within 20 days after a secured party receives an authenticated demand from a debtor, the secured party shall cause the secured party of record for a financing statement to send to the debtor a termination statement for the financing statement or file the termination statement in the filing office if:

(1) except in the case of a financing statement covering accounts or chattel paper that has been sold or goods that are the subject of a consignment, there is no obligation secured by the collateral covered by the financing statement and no commitment to make an advance, incur an obligation, or otherwise give value;

(2) the financing statement covers ac counts or chattel paper that has been sold but as to which the account debt or or other person obligated has discharged its obligation;

(3) the financing statement covers goods that were the subject of a consignment to the debtor but are not in the debtor's possession; or

(4) the debtor did not authorize the filing of the initial financing statement.

(d) Except as otherwise provided in Section 9-510, upon the filing of a termination statement with the filing office, the financing statement to which the termination statement relates ceases to be effective. Except as otherwise provided in Section 9-510, for purposes of Sections 9-519(g), 9-522(a), and 9-523(c), the filing with the filing office of a termination statement relating to a financing statement that indicates that the debtor is a transmitting utility also causes the effectiveness of the financing statement to lapse.

As amended in 2000.

Section 9-514. Assignment of Powers of Secured Party of Record.

(a) Except as otherwise provided in subsection (c), an initial financing statement may reflect an assignment of all of the secured party's power to authorize an amendment to the financing statement by providing the name and mailing address of the assignee as the name and address of the secured party.

(b) Except as otherwise provided in subsection (c), a secured party of record may assign of record all or part of its power to authorize an amendment to a financing statement by filing in the filing office an amendment of the financing statement which:

(1) identifies, by its file number, the initial financing statement to which it relates;

(2) provides the name of the assignor; and

(3) provides the name and mailing address of the assignee.

(c) An assignment of record of a security interest in a fixture covered by a record of a mortgage which is effective as a financing statement filed as a fixture filing under Section 9-502(c) may be made only by an assignment of record of the mortgage in the manner provided by law of this State other than [the Uniform Commercial Code].

Section 9-515. Duration and Effectiveness of Financing Statement; Effect of Lapsed Financing Statement.

(a) Except as otherwise provided in subsections (b), (e), (f), and (g), a filed financing statement is effective for a period of five years after the date of filing.

(b) Except as otherwise provided in subsections (e), (f), and (g), an initial financing statement filed in connection with a public-finance transaction or manufactured-home transaction is effective for a period of 30 years after the date of filing if it indicates that it is filed in connection with a public-finance transaction or manufactured-home transaction.

(c) The effectiveness of a filed financing statement lapses on the expiration of the period of its effectiveness unless before the lapse a continuation statement is filed pursuant to subsection (d). Upon lapse, a financing statement ceases to be effective and any security interest or agricultural lien that was perfected by the financing statement becomes unperfected, unless the security interest is perfected otherwise. If the security interest or agricultural lien becomes unperfected upon lapse, it is deemed never to have been perfected as against a purchaser of the collateral for value.

(d) A continuation statement may be filed only within six months before the expiration of the five-year period specified in subsection (a) or the 30-year period specified in subsection (b), whichever is applicable.

(e) Except as otherwise provided in Section 9-510, upon timely filing of a continuation statement, the effectiveness of the initial financing statement continues for a period of five years commencing on the day on which the financing statement would have become ineffective in the absence of the filing. Upon the expiration of the five-year period, the financing statement lapses in the same manner as provided in subsection (c), unless, before the lapse, another continuation statement is filed pursuant to subsection (d). Succeeding continuation statements may be filed in the same manner to continue the effectiveness of the initial financing statement.

(f) If a debtor is a transmitting utility and a filed financing statement so indicates, the financing statement is effective until a termination statement is filed.

(g) A record of a mortgage that is effective as a financing statement filed as a fixture filing under Section 9-502(c) remains effective as a financing statement filed as a fixture filing until the mortgage is released or satisfied of record or its effectiveness otherwise terminates as to the real property.

Section 9-516. What Constitutes Filing; Effectiveness of Filing.

(a) Except as otherwise provided in subsection (b), communication of a record to a filing office and tender of the filing fee or acceptance of the record by the filing office constitutes filing.

(b) Filing does not occur with respect to a record that a filing office refuses to accept because:

(1) the record is not communicated by a method or medium of communication authorized by the filing office;

(2) an amount equal to or greater than the applicable filing fee is not tendered;

(3) the filing office is unable to index the record because:

(A) in the case of an initial financing statement, the record does not provide a name for the debtor;

(B) in the case of an amendment or correction statement, the record:

(i) does not identify the initial financing statement as required by Section 9-512 or 9-518, as applicable; or

(ii) identifies an initial financing statement whose effectiveness has lapsed under Section 9-515;

(C) in the case of an initial financing statement that provides the name of a debtor identified as an individual or an amendment that provides a name of a debtor identified as an individual which was not previously provided in the financing statement to which the record relates, the record does not identify the debtor's last name; or

(D) in the case of a record filed [or recorded] in the filing office described in Section 9-501(a)(1), the record does not provide a sufficient description of the real property to which it relates;

(4) in the case of an initial financing statement or an amendment that adds a secured party of record, the record does not provide a name and mailing address for the secured party of record;

(5) in the case of an initial financing statement or an amendment that provides a name of a debtor which was not previously provided in the financing statement to which the amendment relates, the record does not:

(A) provide a mailing address for the debtor;

(B) indicate whether the debtor is an individual or an organization; or

(C) if the financing statement indicates that the debtor is an organization, provide:

(i) a type of organization for the debtor;

(ii) a jurisdiction of organization for the debtor; or

(iii) an organizational identification number for the debtor or indicate that the debtor has none;

(6) in the case of an assignment reflected in an initial financing statement under Section 9-514(a) or an amendment filed under Section 9-514(b), the record does not provide a name and mailing address for the assignee; or

(7) in the case of a continuation statement, the record is not filed within the six-month period prescribed by Section 9-515(d).

(c) For purposes of subsection (b):

(1) a record does not provide information if the filing office is unable to read or decipher the information; and

(2) a record that does not indicate that it is an amendment or identify an initial financing statement to which it relates, as required by Section 9-512, 9-514, or 9-518, is an initial financing statement.

(d) A record that is communicated to the filing office with tender of the filing fee, but which the filing office refuses to accept for a reason other than one set forth in subsection (b), is effective as a filed record except as against a purchaser of the collateral which gives value in reasonable reliance upon the absence of the record from the files.

Section 9-517. Effect of Indexing Errors.

The failure of the filing office to index a record correctly does not affect the effectiveness of the filed record.

Section 9-518. Claim Concerning Inaccurate or Wrongfully Filed Record.

(a) A person may file in the filing office a correction statement with respect to a record indexed there under the person's name if the person believes that the record is inaccurate or was wrongfully filed.

[Alternative A]

(b) A correction statement must:

(1) identify the record to which it relates by the file number assigned to the initial financing statement to which the record relates;

(2) indicate that it is a correction statement; and

(3) provide the basis for the person's belief that the record is inaccurate and indicate the manner in which the person believes the record should be amend ed to cure any inaccuracy or provide the basis for the person's belief that the record was wrongfully filed.

[Alternative B]

(b) A correction statement must:

(1) identify the record to which it relates by:

(A) the file number assigned to the initial financing statement to which the record relates; and

(B) if the correction statement relates to a record filed [or recorded] in a filing office described in Section 9-501(a)(1), the date [and time] that the initial financing statement was filed [or recorded] and the information specified in Section 9-502(b);

(2) indicate that it is a correction statement; and

(3) provide the basis for the person's belief that the record is inaccurate and indicate the manner in which the person believes the record should be amend ed to cure any inaccuracy or provide the basis for the person's belief that the record was wrongfully filed.

[End of Alternatives]

(c) The filing of a correction statement does not affect the effectiveness of an initial financing statement or other filed record.

Legislative Note: States whose real-estate filing offices require additional information in amendments and cannot search their records by both the name of the debtor and the file number should enact Alternative B to Sections 9-512(a), 9-518(b), 9-519(f), and 9-522(a).

[Subpart 2. Duties and Operation of Filing Office].

Section 9-519. Numbering, Maintaining, and Indexing Records; Communicating Information Provided in Records.

(a) For each record filed in a filing office, the filing office shall:

(1) assign a unique number to the filed record;

(2) create a record that bears the number assigned to the filed record and the date and time of filing;

(3) maintain the filed record for public inspection; and

(4) index the filed record in accordance with subsections (c), (d), and (e).

(b) A file number [assigned after January 1, 2002,] must include a digit that:

(1) is mathematically derived from or related to the other digits of the file number; and

(2) aids the filing office in determining whether a number communicated as the file number includes a single-digit or transpositional error.

(c) Except as otherwise provided in subsections (d) and (e), the filing office shall:

(1) index an initial financing statement according to the name of the debtor and index all filed records relating to the initial financing statement in a manner that associates with one another an initial financing statement and all filed records relating to the initial financing statement; and

(2) index a record that provides a name of a debtor which was not previously provided in the financing statement to which the record relates also according to the name that was not previously provided.

(d) If a financing statement is filed as a fixture filing or covers as-extracted collateral or timber to be cut, [it must be filed for record and] the filing office shall index it:

(1) under the names of the debtor and of each owner of record shown on the financing statement as if they were the mortgagors under a mortgage of the real property described; and

(2) to the extent that the law of this State provides for indexing of records of mortgages under the name of the mortgagee, under the name of the secured party as if the secured party were the mortgagee thereunder, or, if indexing is by description, as if the financing statement were a record of a mortgage of the real property described.

(e) If a financing statement is filed as a fixture filing or covers as-extracted collateral or timber to be cut, the filing office shall index an assignment filed under Section 9-514(a) or an amendment filed under Section 9-514(b):

(1) under the name of the assignor as grantor; and

(2) to the extent that the law of this State provides for indexing a record of the assignment of a mortgage under the name of the assignee, under the name of the assignee.

[Alternative A]

(f) The filing office shall maintain a capability:

(1) to retrieve a record by the name of the debtor and by the file number assigned to the initial financing statement to which the record relates; and

(2) to associate and retrieve with one another an initial financing statement and each filed record relating to the initial financing statement.

[Alternative B]

(f) The filing office shall maintain a capability:

(1) to retrieve a record by the name of the debtor and:

(A) if the filing office is described in Section 9-501(a)(1), by the file number assigned to the initial financing statement to which the record relates and the date [and time] that the record was filed [or recorded]; or

(B) if the filing office is described in Section 9-501(a)(2), by the file number assigned to the initial financing statement to which the record relates; and

(2) to associate and retrieve with one another an initial financing statement and each filed record relating to the initial financing statement.

[End of Alternatives]

(g) The filing office may not remove a debtor's name from the index until one year after the effectiveness of a financing statement naming the debtor lapses under Section 9-515 with respect to all secured parties of record.

(h) The filing office shall perform the acts required by subsections (a) through (e) at the time and in the manner prescribed by filing-office rule, but not later than two business days after the filing office receives the record in question.

(i) Subsection[s] [(b)] [and] [(h)] do[es] not apply to a filing office described in Section 9-501(a)(1).]

Legislative Notes:

1. *States whose filing offices currently assign file numbers that include a verification number, commonly known as a "check digit," or can implement this requirement before the effective date of this Article should omit the bracketed language in subsection (b).*
2. *In States in which writings will not appear in the real property records and indices unless actually recorded the bracketed language in subsection (d) should be used.*
3. *States whose real-estate filing offices require additional information in amendments and cannot search their records by both the name of the debtor and the file number should en act Alternative B to Sections 9-512(a), 9-518(b), 9-519(f), and 9-522(a).*
4. *A State that elects not to require real-estate filing offices to comply with either or both of subsections (b) and (h) may adopt an applicable variation of subsection (i) and add "Except as otherwise provided in subsection (i)," to the appropriate subsection or subsections.*

Section 9-520. Acceptance and Refusal to Accept Record.

(a) A filing office shall refuse to accept a record for filing for a reason set forth in Section 9-516(b) and may refuse to accept a record for filing only for a reason set forth in Section 9-516(b).

(b) If a filing office refuses to accept a record for filing, it shall communicate to the person that presented the record the fact of and reason for the refusal and the date and time the record would have been filed had the filing office accepted it. The communication must be made at the time and in the manner prescribed by filing-office rule but [, in the case of a filing office described in Section 9-501(a)(2),] in no event more than two business days after the filing office receives the record.

(c) A filed financing statement satisfying Section 9-502(a) and (b) is effective, even if the filing office is required to refuse to accept it for filing under subsection (a). However, Section 9-338 applies to a filed financing statement providing information described in Section 9-516(b)(5) which is incorrect at the time the financing statement is filed.

(d) If a record communicated to a filing office provides information that relates to more than one debtor, this part applies as to each debtor separately.

Legislative Note: A State that elects not to require real-property filing offices to comply with subsection (b) should include the bracketed language.

Section 9-521. Uniform Form of Written Financing Statement and Amendment.

(a) A filing office that accepts written records may not refuse to accept a written initial financing statement in the following form and format except for a reason set forth in Section 9-516(b):

[NATIONAL UCC FINANCING STATEMENT (FORM UCC1)(REV. 7/29/98)]

[NATIONAL UCC FINANCING STATEMENT ADDENDUM (FORM UCC1Ad) (REV. 07/29/98)]

(b) A filing office that accepts written records may not refuse to accept a written record in the following form and format except for a reason set forth in Section 9-516(b):

[NATIONAL UCC FINANCING STATEMENT AMENDMENT (FORM UCC3) REV. 07/29/98)]

[NATIONAL UCC FINANCING STATEMENT AMENDMENT ADDENDUM (FORM UCC3Ad) (REV. 07/29/98)]

Section 9-522. Maintenance and Destruction of Records.

[Alternative A]

(a) The filing office shall maintain a record of the information provided in a filed financing statement for at least one year after the effectiveness of the financing statement has lapsed under Section 9-515 with respect to all secured parties of record. The record must be retrievable by using the name of the debt or and by using the file number assigned to the initial financing statement to which the record relates.

[Alternative B]

(a) The filing office shall maintain a record of the information provided in a filed financing statement for at least one year after the effectiveness of the financing statement has lapsed under Section 9-515 with respect to all secured parties of record. The record must be retrievable by using the name of the debt or and:

(1) if the record was filed [or recorded] in the filing office described in Section 9-501(a)(1), by using the file number assigned to the initial financing statement to which the record relates and the date [and time] that the record was filed [or recorded]; or

(2) if the record was filed in the filing office described in Section 9-501(a)(2), by using the file number assigned to the initial financing statement to which the record relates.

[End of Alternatives]

(b) Except to the extent that a statute governing disposition of public records provides otherwise, the filing office immediately may destroy any written record evidencing a financing statement. However, if the filing office destroys a written record, it shall maintain another record of the financing statement which complies with subsection (a).

Legislative Note: States whose real-estate filing offices require additional information in amendments and cannot search their records by both the name of the debtor and the file number should enact Alternative B to Sections 9-512(a), 9-518(b), 9-519(f), and 9-522(a).

Section 9-523. Information from Filing Office; Sale or License of Records.

(a) If a person that files a written record requests an acknowledgment of the filing, the filing office shall send to the person an image of the record showing the number assigned to the record pursuant to Section 9-519(a)(1) and the date and time of the filing of the record. However, if the person furnishes a copy of the record to the filing office, the filing office may instead:

(1) note upon the copy the number assigned to the record pursuant to Section 9-519(a)(1) and the date and time of the filing of the record; and

(2) send the copy to the person.

(b) If a person files a record other than a written record, the filing office shall communicate to the person an acknowledgment that provides:

(1) the information in the record;

(2) the number assigned to the record pursuant to Section 9-519(a)(1); and

(3) the date and time of the filing of the record.

(c) The filing office shall communicate or otherwise make available in a record the following information to any person that requests it:

(1) whether there is on file on a date and time specified by the filing office, but not a date earlier than three business days before the filing office receives the request, any financing statement that:

(A) designates a particular debtor [or, if the request so states, designates a particular debtor at the address specified in the request];

(B) has not lapsed under Section 9-515 with respect to all secured parties of record; and

(C) if the request so states, has lapsed under Section 9-515 and a record of which is maintained by the filing office under Section 9-522(a);

(2) the date and time of filing of each financing statement; and

(3) the information provided in each financing statement.

(d) In complying with its duty under subsection (c), the filing office may communicate information in any medium. However, if requested, the filing office shall communicate information by issuing [its written certificate] [a record that can be admitted into evidence in the courts of this State without extrinsic evidence of its authenticity].

(e) The filing office shall perform the acts required by subsections (a) through (d) at the time and in the manner prescribed by filing-office rule, but not later than two business days after the filing office receives the request.

(f) At least weekly, the [insert appropriate official or governmental agency] [filing office] shall offer to sell or license to the public on a nonexclusive basis, in bulk, copies of all records filed in it under this part, in every medium from time to time available to the filing office.

Legislative Notes:

1. *States whose filing office does not offer the additional service of responding to search requests limited to a particular address should omit the bracketed language in subsection (c)(1)(A).*

2. *A State that elects not to require real-estate filing offices to comply with either or both of subsections (e) and (f) should specify in the appropriate subsection(s) only the filing office described in Section 9-501(a)(2).*

Section 9-524. Delay by Filing Office.

Delay by the filing office beyond a time limit prescribed by this part is excused if:

(1) the delay is caused by interruption of communication or computer facilities, war, emergency conditions, failure of equipment, or other circumstances beyond control of the filing office; and

(2) the filing office exercises reasonable diligence under the circumstances.

Section 9-525. Fees.

(a) Except as otherwise provided in subsection (e), the fee for filing and indexing a record under this part, other than an initial financing statement of the kind described in subsection (b), is [the amount specified in subsection (c), if applicable, plus]:

(1) $[X] if the record is communicated in writing and consists of one or two pages;

(2) $[2X] if the record is communicated in writing and consists of more than two pages; and

(3) $[1/2X] if the record is communicated by another medium authorized by filing-office rule.

(b) Except as otherwise provided in subsection (e), the fee for filing and indexing an initial financing statement of the following kind is [the amount specified in subsection (c), if applicable, plus]:

(1) $______ if the financing statement indicates that it is filed in connection with a public-finance transaction;

(2) $______ if the financing statement indicates that it is filed in connection with a manufactured-home transaction.

[Alternative A]

(c) The number of names required to be indexed does not affect the amount of the fee in subsections (a) and (b).

[Alternative B]

(c) Except as otherwise provided in subsection (e), if a record is communicated in writing, the fee for each name more than two required to be indexed is $_______.

[End of Alternatives]

(d) The fee for responding to a request for information from the filing office, including for [issuing a certificate showing] [communicating] whether there is on file any financing statement naming a particular debtor, is:

(1) $_______ if the request is communicated in writing; and

(2) $_______ if the request is communicated by another medium authorized by filing-office rule.

(e) This section does not require a fee with respect to a record of a mortgage which is effective as a financing statement filed as a fixture filing or as a financing statement covering as-extracted collateral or timber to be cut under Section 9-502(c). However, the recording and satisfaction fees that otherwise would be applicable to the record of the mortgage apply.

Legislative Notes:

1. *To preserve uniformity, a State that places the provisions of this section together with statutes setting fees for other services should do so without modification.*

2. *A State should enact subsection (c), Alternative A, and omit the bracketed language in subsections (a) and (b) unless its indexing system entails a substantial additional cost when indexing additional names.*

As amended in 2000.

Section 9-526. Filing-Office Rules.

(a) The [insert appropriate governmental official or agency] shall adopt and publish rules to implement this article. The filing-office rules must be]:

(1) consistent with this article[; and

(2) adopted and published in accordance with the [insert any applicable state administrative procedure act]].

(b) To keep the filing-office rules and practices of the filing office in harmony with the rules and practices of filing offices in other jurisdictions that enact substantially this part, and to keep the technology used by the filing office compatible with the technology used by filing offices in other jurisdictions that enact substantially this part, the [insert appropriate governmental official or agency], so far as is consistent with the purposes, policies, and provisions of this article, in adopting, amending, and repealing filing-office rules, shall:

(1) consult with filing offices in other jurisdictions that enact substantially this part; and

(2) consult the most recent version of the Model Rules promulgated by the International Association of Corporate Administrators or any successor organization; and

(3) take into consideration the rules and practices of, and the technology used by, filing offices in other jurisdictions that enact substantially this part.

Section 9-527. Duty to Report.

The [insert appropriate governmental official or agency] shall report [annually on or before _______] to the [Governor and Legislature] on the operation of the filing office. The report must contain a statement of the extent to which:

(1) the filing-office rules are not in harmony with the rules of filing offices in other jurisdictions that enact substantially this part and the reasons for these variations; and

(2) the filing-office rules are not in harmony with the most recent version of the Model Rules promulgated by the International Association of Corporate Administrators, or any successor organization, and the reasons for these variations.

Part 6. Default

[Subpart 1. Default and Enforcement of Security Interest].

Section 9-601. Rights after Default; Judicial Enforcement; Consignor or Buyer of Accounts, Chattel Paper, Payment Intangibles, or Promissory Notes.

(a) After default, a secured party has the rights provided in this part and, except as otherwise provided in Section 9-602, those provided by agreement of the parties. A secured party:

(1) may reduce a claim to judgment, foreclose, or otherwise enforce the claim, security interest, or agricultural lien by any available judicial procedure; and

(2) if the collateral is documents, may proceed either as to the documents or as to the goods they cover.

(b) A secured party in possession of collateral or control of collateral under Section 9-104, 9-105, 9-106, or 9-107 has the rights and duties provided in Section 9-207.

(c) The rights under subsections (a) and (b) are cumulative and may be exercised simultaneously.

(d) Except as otherwise provided in subsection (g) and Section 9-605, after default, a debtor and an obligor have the rights provided in this part and by agreement of the parties.

(e) If a secured party has reduced its claim to judgment, the lien of any levy that may be made upon the collateral by virtue of an execution based upon the judgment relates back to the earliest of:

(1) the date of perfection of the security interest or agricultural lien in the collateral;

(2) the date of filing a financing statement covering the collateral; or

(3) any date specified in a statute under which the agricultural lien was created.

(f) A sale pursuant to an execution is a foreclosure of the security interest or agricultural lien by judicial procedure within the meaning of this section. A secured party may purchase at the sale and thereafter hold the collateral free of any other requirements of this article.

(g) Except as otherwise provided in Section 9-607(c), this part imposes no duties upon a secured party that is a consignor or is a buyer of accounts, chattel paper, payment intangibles, or promissory notes.

Section 9-602. Waiver and Variance of Rights and Duties.

Except as otherwise provided in Section 9-624, to the extent that they give rights to a debtor or obligor and impose duties on a secured party, the debtor or obligor may not waive or vary the rules stated in the following listed sections:

(1) Section 9-207(b)(4)(C), which deals with use and operation of the collateral by the secured party;

(2) Section 9-210, which deals with requests for an accounting and requests concerning a list of collateral and statement of account;

(3) Section 9-607(c), which deals with collection and enforcement of collateral;

(4) Sections 9-608(a) and 9-615(c) to the extent that they deal with application or payment of noncash proceeds of collection, enforcement, or disposition;

(5) Sections 9-608(a) and 9-615(d) to the extent that they require accounting for or payment of surplus proceeds of collateral;

(6) Section 9-609 to the extent that it imposes upon a secured party that takes possession of collateral without judicial process the duty to do so without breach of the peace;

(7) Sections 9-610(b), 9-611, 9-613, and 9-614, which deal with disposition of collateral;

(8) Section 9-615(f), which deals with calculation of a deficiency or surplus when a disposition is made to the secured party, a person related to the secured party, or a secondary obligor;

(9) Section 9-616, which deals with explanation of the calculation of a surplus or deficiency;

(10) Sections 9-620, 9-621, and 9-622, which deal with acceptance of collateral in satisfaction of obligation;

(11) Section 9-623, which deals with redemption of collateral;

(12) Section 9-624, which deals with permissible waivers; and

(13) Sections 9-625 and 9-626, which deal with the secured party's liability for failure to comply with this article.

Section 9-603. Agreement on Standards Concerning Rights and Duties.

(a) The parties may determine by agreement the standards measuring the fulfillment of the rights of a debtor or obligor and the duties of a secured party under a rule stated in Section 9-602 if the standards are not manifestly unreasonable.

(b) Subsection (a) does not apply to the duty under Section 9-609 to refrain from breaching the peace.

Section 9-604. Procedure If Security Agreement Covers Real Property or Fixtures.

(a) If a security agreement covers both personal and real property, a secured party may proceed:

  (1) under this part as to the personal property without prejudicing any rights with respect to the real property; or

  (2) as to both the personal property and the real property in accordance with the rights with respect to the real property, in which case the other provisions of this part do not apply.

(b) Subject to subsection (c), if a security agreement covers goods that are or become fixtures, a secured party may proceed:

  (1) under this part; or

  (2) in accordance with the rights with respect to real property, in which case the other provisions of this part do not apply.

(c) Subject to the other provisions of this part, if a secured party holding a security interest in fixtures has priority over all owners and encumbrancers of the real property, the secured party, after default, may remove the collateral from the real property.

(d) A secured party that removes collateral shall promptly reimburse any encumbrancer or owner of the real property, other than the debtor, for the cost of repair of any physical injury caused by the removal. The secured party need not reimburse the encumbrancer or owner for any diminution in value of the real property caused by the absence of the goods removed or by any necessity of replacing them. A person entitled to reimbursement may refuse permission to remove until the secured party gives adequate assurance for the performance of the obligation to reimburse.

Section 9-605. Unknown Debtor or Secondary Obligor.

A secured party does not owe a duty based on its status as secured party:

(1) to a person that is a debtor or obligor, unless the secured party knows:

(A) that the person is a debtor or obligor;

(B) the identity of the person; and

(C) how to communicate with the person; or

(2) to a secured party or lienholder that has filed a financing statement against a person, unless the secured party knows:

(A) that the person is a debtor; and

(B) the identity of the person.

Section 9-606. Time of Default for Agricultural Lien.

For purposes of this part, a default occurs in connection with an agricultural lien at the time the secured party becomes entitled to enforce the lien in accordance with the statute under which it was created.

Section 9-607. Collection and Enforcement by Secured Party.

(a) If so agreed, and in any event after default, a secured party:

(1) may notify an account debtor or other person obligated on collateral to make payment or otherwise render performance to or for the benefit of the secured party;

(2) may take any proceeds to which the secured party is entitled under Section 9-315;

(3) may enforce the obligations of an account debtor or other person obligated on collateral and exercise the rights of the debtor with respect to the obligation of the account debtor or other person obligated on collateral to make payment or otherwise render performance to the debtor, and with respect to any property that secures the obligations of the account debtor or other person obligated on the collateral;

(4) if it holds a security interest in a deposit account perfected by control under Section 9-104(a)(1), may apply the balance of the deposit account to the obligation secured by the deposit account; and

(5) if it holds a security interest in a deposit account perfected by control under Section 9-104(a)(2) or (3), may instruct the bank to pay the balance of the deposit account to or for the benefit of the secured party.

(b) If necessary to enable a secured party to exercise under subsection (a)(3) the right of a debtor to enforce a mortgage nonjudicially, the secured party may record in the office in which a record of the mortgage is recorded:

(1) a copy of the security agreement that creates or provides for a security interest in the obligation secured by the mortgage; and

(2) the secured party's sworn affidavit in recordable form stating that:

(A) a default has occurred; and

(B) the secured party is entitled to enforce the mortgage nonjudicially.

(c) A secured party shall proceed in a commercially reasonable manner if the secured party:

(1) undertakes to collect from or enforce an obligation of an account debtor or other person obligated on collateral; and

(2) is entitled to charge back uncollected collateral or otherwise to full or limited recourse against the debtor or a secondary obligor.

(d) A secured party may deduct from the collections made pursuant to subsection (c) reasonable expenses of collection and enforcement, including reasonable attorney's fees and legal expenses incurred by the secured party.

(e) This section does not determine whether an account debtor, bank, or other person obligated on collateral owes a duty to a secured party.

As amended in 2000.

Section 9-608. Application of Proceeds of Collection or Enforcement; Liability for Deficiency and Right to Surplus.

(a) If a security interest or agricultural lien secures payment or performance of an obligation, the following rules apply:

(1) A secured party shall apply or pay over for application the cash proceeds of collection or enforcement under Section 9-607 in the following order to:

(A) the reasonable expenses of collection and enforcement and, to the extent provided for by agreement and not prohibited by law, reasonable attorney's fees and legal expenses incurred by the secured party;

(B) the satisfaction of obligations secured by the security interest or agricultural lien under which the collection or enforcement is made; and

(C) the satisfaction of obligations secured by any subordinate security interest in or other lien on the collateral subject to the security interest or agricultural lien under which the collection or enforcement is made if the secured party receives an authenticated demand for proceeds before distribution of the proceeds is completed.

(2) If requested by a secured party, a holder of a subordinate security interest or other lien shall furnish reasonable proof of the interest or lien within a reasonable time. Unless the holder complies, the secured party need not comply with the holder's demand under paragraph (1)(C).

(3) A secured party need not apply or pay over for application noncash proceeds of collection and enforcement under Section 9-607 unless the failure to do so would be commercially unreasonable. A secured party that applies or pays over for application noncash proceeds shall do so in a commercially reasonable manner.

(4) A secured party shall account to and pay a debtor for any surplus, and the obligor is liable for any deficiency.

(b) If the underlying transaction is a sale of accounts, chattel paper, payment intangibles, or promissory notes, the debtor is not entitled to any surplus, and the obligor is not liable for any deficiency.

As amended in 2000.

Section 9-609. Secured Party's Right to Take Possession after Default.

(a) After default, a secured party:

(1) may take possession of the collateral; and

(2) without removal, may render equipment unusable and dispose of collateral on a debtor's premises under Section 9-610.

(b) A secured party may proceed under subsection (a):

(1) pursuant to judicial process; or

(2) without judicial process, if it proceeds without breach of the peace.

(c) If so agreed, and in any event after default, a secured party may require the debtor to assemble the collateral and make it available to the secured party at a place to be designated by the secured party which is reasonably convenient to both parties.

Section 9-610. Disposition of Collateral after Default.

(a) After default, a secured party may sell, lease, license, or otherwise dispose of any or all of the collateral in its present condition or following any commercially reasonable preparation or processing.

(b) Every aspect of a disposition of collateral, including the method, manner, time, place, and other terms, must be commercially reasonable. If commercially reasonable, a secured party may dispose of collateral by public or private proceedings, by one or more contracts, as a unit or in parcels, and at any time and place and on any terms.

(c) A secured party may purchase collateral:

(1) at a public disposition; or

(2) at a private disposition only if the collateral is of a kind that is customarily sold on a recognized market or the subject of widely distributed standard price quotations.

(d) A contract for sale, lease, license, or other disposition includes the warranties relating to title, possession, quiet enjoyment, and the like which by operation of law accompany a voluntary disposition of property of the kind subject to the contract.

(e) A secured party may disclaim or modify warranties under subsection (d):

(1) in a manner that would be effective to disclaim or modify the warranties in a voluntary disposition of property of the kind subject to the contract of disposition; or

(2) by communicating to the purchaser a record evidencing the contract for disposition and including an express disclaimer or modification of the warranties.

(f) A record is sufficient to disclaim warranties under subsection (e) if it indicates "There is no warranty relating to title, possession, quiet enjoyment, or the like in this disposition" or uses words of similar import.

Section 9-611. Notification before Disposition of Collateral.

(a) In this section, "notification date" means the earlier of the date on which:

(1) a secured party sends to the debtor and any secondary obligor an authenticated notification of disposition; or

(2) the debtor and any secondary obligor waive the right to notification.

(b) Except as otherwise provided in subsection (d), a secured party that disposes of collateral under Section 9-610 shall send to the persons specified in subsection (c) a reasonable authenticated notification of disposition.

(c) To comply with subsection (b), the secured party shall send an authenticated notification of disposition to:

(1) the debtor;

(2) any secondary obligor; and

(3) if the collateral is other than consumer goods:

(A) any other person from which the secured party has received, before the notification date, an authenticated notification of a claim of an interest in the collateral;

(B) any other secured party or lienholder that, 10 days before the notification date, held a security interest in or other lien on the collateral perfected by the filing of a financing statement that:

(i) identified the collateral;

(ii) was indexed under the debtor's name as of that date; and

(iii) was filed in the office in which to file a financing statement against the debtor covering the collateral as of that date; and

(C) any other secured party that, 10 days before the notification date, held a security interest in the collateral perfected by compliance with a statute, regulation, or treaty described in Section 9-311(a).

(d) Subsection (b) does not apply if the collateral is perishable or threatens to decline speedily in value or is of a type customarily sold on a recognized market.

(e) A secured party complies with the requirement for notification prescribed by subsection (c)(3)(B) if:

(1) not later than 20 days or earlier than 30 days before the notification date, the secured party requests, in a commercially reasonable manner, information concerning financing statements indexed under the debtor's name in the office indicated in subsection (c)(3)(B); and

(2) before the notification date, the secured party:

(A) did not receive a response to the request for information; or

(B) received a response to the request for information and sent an authenticated notification of disposition to each secured party or other lienholder named in that response whose financing statement covered the collateral.

Section 9-612. Timeliness of Notification before Disposition of Collateral.

(a) Except as otherwise provided in subsection (b), whether a notification is sent within a reasonable time is a question of fact.

(b) In a transaction other than a consumer transaction, a notification of disposition sent after default and 10 days or more before the earliest time of disposition set forth in the notification is sent within a reasonable time before the disposition.

Section 9-613. Contents and Form of Notification before Disposition of Collateral: General. Except in a consumer-goods transaction.

The following rules apply:

(1) The contents of a notification of disposition are sufficient if the notification:

(A) describes the debtor and the secured party;

(B) describes the collateral that is the subject of the intended disposition;

(C) states the method of intended disposition;

(D) states that the debtor is entitled to an accounting of the unpaid indebtedness and states the charge, if any, for an accounting; and

(E) states the time and place of a public disposition or the time after which any other disposition is to be made.

(2) Whether the contents of a notification that lacks any of the information specified in paragraph (1) are nevertheless sufficient is a question of fact.

(3) The contents of a notification providing substantially the information specified in paragraph (1) are sufficient, even if the notification includes:

(A) information not specified by that paragraph; or

(B) minor errors that are not seriously misleading.

(4) A particular phrasing of the notification is not required.

(5) The following form of notification and the form appearing in Section 9-614(3), when completed, each provides sufficient information:

NOTIFICATION OF DISPOSITION OF COLLATERAL

To: [*Name of debtor, obligor, or other person to which the notification is sent*]

From: [*Name, address, and telephone number of secured party*]

Name of Debtor(s): [*Include only if debtor(s) are not an addressee*]

[*For a public disposition:*]

We will sell [or lease or license, *as applicable*] the [*describe collateral*] [to the highest qualified bidder] in public as follows:

Day and Date: __________
Time: __________
Place: __________

[*For a private disposition:*]

We will sell [or lease or license, *as applicable*] the [*describe collateral*] privately sometime after [*day and date*].

You are entitled to an accounting of the unpaid indebtedness secured by the property that we intend to sell [or lease or license, *as applicable*] [for a charge of $_______]. You may request an accounting by calling us at [*telephone number*].

[End of Form]
As amended in 2000.

Section 9-614. Contents and Form of Notification before Disposition of Collateral: Consumer-Goods Transaction.

In a consumer-goods transaction, the following rules apply:

(1) A notification of disposition must provide the following information:

  (A) the information specified in Section 9-613(1);

  (B) a description of any liability for a deficiency of the person to which the notification is sent;

  (C) a telephone number from which the amount that must be paid to the secured party to redeem the collateral under Section 9-623 is available; and

  (D) a telephone number or mailing address from which additional information concerning the disposition and the obligation secured is available.

(2) A particular phrasing of the notification is not required.

(3) The following form of notification, when completed, provides sufficient information:

[*Name and address of secured party*]
[*Date*]

NOTICE OF OUR PLAN TO SELL PROPERTY

[*Name and address of any obligor who is also a debtor*]
Subject: [*Identification of Transaction*]

We have your [*describe collateral*], because you broke promises in our agreement.

[*For a public disposition:*]

We will sell [*describe collateral*] at public sale. A sale could include a lease or license. The sale will be held as follows:

Date: __________
Time: __________
Place: __________

You may attend the sale and bring bidders if you want.

[*For a private disposition:*]

We will sell [*describe collateral*] at private sale sometime after [*date*]. A sale could include a lease or license.

The money that we get from the sale (after paying our costs) will reduce the amount you owe. If we get less money than you owe, you [*will or will not, as applicable*] still owe us the difference. If we get more money than you owe, you will get the extra money, unless we must pay it to someone else.

You can get the property back at any time before we sell it by paying us the full amount you owe (not just the past due payments), including our expenses. To learn the exact amount you must pay, call us at [*telephone number*].

If you want us to explain to you in writing how we have figured the amount that you owe us, you may call us at [*telephone number*] [or write us at [*secured party's address*]] and request a written explanation. [We will charge you $_______ for the explanation if we sent you another written explanation of the amount you owe us within the last six months.]

If you need more information about the sale call us at [*telephone number*] [or write us at [*secured party's address*]].

We are sending this notice to the following other people who have an interest in [*describe collateral*] or who owe money under your agreement:

[*Names of all other debtors and obligors, if any*]

[End of Form]

(4) A notification in the form of paragraph (3) is sufficient, even if additional information appears at the end of the form.

(5) A notification in the form of paragraph (3) is sufficient, even if it includes errors in information not required by paragraph (1), unless the error is misleading with respect to rights arising under this article.

(6) If a notification under this section is not in the form of paragraph (3), law other than this article determines the effect of including information not required by paragraph (1).

Section 9-615. Application of Proceeds of Disposition; Liability for Deficiency and Right to Surplus.

(a) A secured party shall apply or pay over for application the cash proceeds of disposition under Section 9-610 in the following order to:

(1) the reasonable expenses of retaking, holding, preparing for disposition, processing, and disposing, and, to the extent provided for by agreement and not prohibited by law, reasonable attorney's fees and legal expenses incurred by the secured party;

(2) the satisfaction of obligations secured by the security interest or agricultural lien under which the disposition is made;

(3) the satisfaction of obligations secured by any subordinate security interest in or other subordinate lien on the collateral if:

(A) the secured party receives from the holder of the subordinate security interest or other lien an authenticated demand for proceeds before distribution of the proceeds is completed; and

(B) in a case in which a consignor has an interest in the collateral, the subordinate security interest or other lien is senior to the interest of the consignor; and

(4) a secured party that is a consignor of the collateral if the secured party receives from the consignor an authenticated demand for proceeds before distribution of the proceeds is completed.

(b) If requested by a secured party, a holder of a subordinate security interest or other lien shall furnish reasonable proof of the interest or lien within a reasonable time. Unless the holder does so, the secured party need not comply with the holder's demand under subsection (a)(3).

(c) A secured party need not apply or pay over for application noncash proceeds of disposition under Section 9-610 unless the failure to do so would be commercially unreasonable. A secured party that applies or pays over for application noncash proceeds shall do so in a commercially reasonable manner.

(d) If the security interest under which a disposition is made secures payment or performance of an obligation, after making the payments and applications required by subsection (a) and permitted by subsection (c):

(1) unless subsection (a)(4) requires the secured party to apply or pay over cash proceeds to a consignor, the secured party shall account to and pay a debtor for any surplus; and

(2) the obligor is liable for any deficiency.

(e) If the underlying transaction is a sale of accounts, chattel paper, payment intangibles, or promissory notes:

(1) the debtor is not entitled to any surplus; and

(2) the obligor is not liable for any deficiency.

(f) The surplus or deficiency following a disposition is calculated based on the amount of proceeds that would have been realized in a disposition complying with this part to a transferee other than the secured party, a person related to the secured party, or a secondary obligor if:

(1) the transferee in the disposition is the secured party, a person related to the secured party, or a secondary obligor; and

(2) the amount of proceeds of the disposition is significantly below the range of proceeds that a complying disposition to a person other than the secured party, a person related to the secured party, or a secondary obligor would have brought.

(g) A secured party that receives cash proceeds of a disposition in good faith and without knowledge that the receipt violates the rights of the holder of a security interest or other lien that is not subordinate to the security interest or agricultural lien under which the disposition is made:

(1) takes the cash proceeds free of the security interest or other lien;

(2) is not obligated to apply the proceeds of the disposition to the satisfaction of obligations secured by the security interest or other lien; and

(3) is not obligated to account to or pay the holder of the security interest or other lien for any surplus.

As amended in 2000.

Section 9-616. Explanation of Calculation of Surplus or Deficiency.

(a) In this section:

(1) "Explanation" means a writing that:

(A) states the amount of the surplus or deficiency;

(B) provides an explanation in accordance with subsection (c) of how the secured party calculated the surplus or deficiency;

(C) states, if applicable, that future debits, credits, charges, including additional credit service charges or interest, rebates, and expenses may affect the amount of the surplus or deficiency; and

(D) provides a telephone number or mailing address from which additional information concerning the transaction is available.

(2) "Request" means a record:

(A) authenticated by a debtor or consumer obligor;

(B) requesting that the recipient provide an explanation; and

(C) sent after disposition of the collateral under Section 9-610.

(b) In a consumer-goods transaction in which the debtor is entitled to a surplus or a consumer obligor is liable for a deficiency under Section 9-615, the secured party shall:

(1) send an explanation to the debtor or consumer obligor, as applicable, after the disposition and:

(A) before or when the secured party accounts to the debtor and pays any surplus or first makes written demand on the consumer obligor after the disposition for payment of the deficiency; and

(B) within 14 days after receipt of a request; or

(2) in the case of a consumer obligor who is liable for a deficiency, within 14 days after receipt of a request, send to the consumer obligor a record waiving the secured party's right to a deficiency.

(c) To comply with subsection (a)(1)(B), a writing must provide the following information in the following order:

(1) the aggregate amount of obligations secured by the security interest under which the disposition was made, and, if the amount reflects a rebate of unearned interest or credit service charge, an indication of that fact, calculated as of a specified date:

(A) if the secured party takes or receives possession of the collateral after default, not more than 35 days before the secured party takes or receives possession; or

(B) if the secured party takes or receives possession of the collateral before default or does not take possession of the collateral, not more than 35 days before the disposition;

(2) the amount of proceeds of the disposition;

(3) the aggregate amount of the obligations after deducting the amount of proceeds;

(4) the amount, in the aggregate or by type, and types of expenses, including expenses of retaking, holding, preparing for disposition, processing, and disposing of the collateral, and attorney's fees secured by the collateral which are known to the secured party and relate to the current disposition;

(5) the amount, in the aggregate or by type, and types of credits, including rebates of interest or credit service charges, to which the obligor is known to be entitled and which are not reflected in the amount in paragraph (1); and

(6) the amount of the surplus or defi ciency.

(d) A particular phrasing of the explanation is not required. An explanation complying substantially with the requirements of subsection (a) is sufficient, even if it includes minor errors that are not seriously misleading.

(e) A debtor or consumer obligor is entitled without charge to one response to a request under this section during any six-month period in which the secured party did not send to the debtor or consumer obligor an explanation pursuant to subsection (b)(1). The secured party may require payment of a charge not exceeding $25 for each additional response.

Section 9-617. Rights of Transferee of Collateral.

(a) A secured party's disposition of collateral after default:

(1) transfers to a transferee for value all of the debtor's rights in the collateral;

(2) discharges the security interest under which the disposition is made; and

(3) discharges any subordinate security interest or other subordinate lien [other than liens created under [cite acts or statutes providing for liens, if any, that are not to be discharged]].

(b) A transferee that acts in good faith takes free of the rights and interests described in subsection (a), even if the secured party fails to comply with this article or the requirements of any judicial proceeding.

(c) If a transferee does not take free of the rights and interests described in subsection (a), the transferee takes the collateral subject to:

(1) the debtor's rights in the collateral;

(2) the security interest or agricultural lien under which the disposition is made; and

(3) any other security interest or other lien.

Section 9-618. Rights and Duties of Certain Secondary Obligors.

(a) A secondary obligor acquires the rights and becomes obligated to perform the duties of the secured party after the secondary obligo r:

(1) receives an assignment of a secured obligation from the secured party;

(2) receives a transfer of collateral from the secured party and agrees to accept the rights and assume the duties of the secured party; or

(3) is subrogated to the rights of a secured party with respect to collateral.

(b) An assignment, transfer, or subrogation described in subsection (a):

(1) is not a disposition of collateral under Section 9-610; and

(2) relieves the secured party of further duties under this article.

Section 9-619. Transfer of Record or Legal Title.

(a) In this section, "transfer statement" means a record authenticated by a secured party stating:

(1) that the debtor has defaulted in connection with an obligation secured by specified collateral;

(2) that the secured party has exercised its post-default remedies with respect to the collateral;

(3) that, by reason of the exercise, a transferee has acquired the rights of the debtor in the collateral; and

(4) the name and mailing address of the secured party, debtor, and transferee.

(b) A transfer statement entitles the transferee to the transfer of record of all rights of the debtor in the collateral specified in the statement in any official filing, recording, registration, or certificate-of-title system covering the collateral. If a transfer statement is presented with the applicable fee and request form to the official or office responsible for maintaining the system, the official or office shall:

(1) accept the transfer statement;

(2) promptly amend its records to reflect the transfer; and

(3) if applicable, issue a new appropriate certificate of title in the name of the transferee.

(c) A transfer of the record or legal title to collateral to a secured party under subsection (b) or otherwise is not of itself a disposition of collateral under this article and does not of itself relieve the secured party of its duties under this article.

Section 9-620. Acceptance of Collateral in Full or Partial Satisfaction of Obligation; Compulsory Disposition of Collateral.

(a) Except as otherwise provided in subsection (g), a secured party may accept collateral in full or partial satisfaction of the obligation it secures only if:

(1) the debtor consents to the acceptance under subsection (c);

(2) the secured party does not receive, within the time set forth in subsection (d), a notification of objection to the proposal authenticated by:

(A) a person to which the secured party was required to send a proposal under Section 9-621; or

(B) any other person, other than the debtor, holding an interest in the collateral subordinate to the security interest that is the subject of the proposal;

(3) if the collateral is consumer goods, the collateral is not in the possession of the debtor when the debtor consents to the acceptance; and

(4) subsection (e) does not require the secured party to dispose of the collateral or the debtor waives the requirement pursuant to Section 9-624.

(b) A purported or apparent acceptance of collateral under this section is ineffective unless:

(1) the secured party consents to the acceptance in an authenticated record or sends a proposal to the debtor; and

(2) the conditions of subsection (a) are met.

(c) For purposes of this section:

(1) a debtor consents to an acceptance of collateral in partial satisfaction of the obligation it secures only if the debtor agrees to the terms of the acceptance in a record authenticated after default; and

(2) a debtor consents to an acceptance of collateral in full satisfaction of the obligation it secures only if the debtor agrees to the terms of the acceptance in a record authenticated after default or the secured party:

(A) sends to the debtor after default a proposal that is unconditional or subject only to a condition that collateral not in the possession of the secured party be preserved or maintained;

(B) in the proposal, proposes to accept collateral in full satisfaction of the obligation it secures; and

(C) does not receive a notification of objection authenticated by the debtor within 20 days after the proposal is sent.

(d) To be effective under subsection (a)(2), a notification of objection must be received by the secured party:

(1) in the case of a person to which the proposal was sent pursuant to Section 9-621, within 20 days after notification was sent to that person; and

(2) in other cases:

(A) within 20 days after the last notification was sent pursuant to Section 9-621; or

(B) if a notification was not sent, before the debtor consents to the acceptance under subsection (c).

(e) A secured party that has taken possession of collateral shall dispose of the collateral pursuant to Section 9-610 within the time specified in subsection (f) if:

(1) 60 percent of the cash price has been paid in the case of a purchase-money security interest in consumer goods; or

(2) 60 percent of the principal amount of the obligation secured has been paid in the case of a non-purchase-money security interest in consumer goods.

(f) To comply with subsection (e), the secured party shall dispose of the collateral:

(1) within 90 days after taking possession; or

(2) within any longer period to which the debtor and all secondary obligors have agreed in an agreement to that effect entered into and authenticated after default.

(g) In a consumer transaction, a secured party may not accept collateral in partial satisfaction of the obligation it secures.

Section 9-621. Notification of Proposal to Accept Collateral.

(a) A secured party that desires to accept collateral in full or partial satisfaction of the obligation it secures shall send its proposal to:

(1) any person from which the secured party has received, before the debtor consented to the acceptance, an authenticated notification of a claim of an interest in the collateral;

(2) any other secured party or lienholder that, 10 days before the debtor consented to the acceptance, held a security interest in or other lien on the collateral perfected by the filing of a financing statement that:

(A) identified the collateral;

(B) was indexed under the debtor's name as of that date; and

(C) was filed in the office or offices in which to file a financing statement against the debtor covering the collateral as of that date; and

(3) any other secured party that, 10 days before the debtor consented to the acceptance, held a security interest in the collateral perfected by compliance with a statute, regulation, or treaty de scribed in Section 9-311(a).

(b) A secured party that desires to accept collateral in partial satisfaction of the obligation it secures shall send its proposal to any secondary obligor in addition to the persons described in subsection (a).

Section 9-622. Effect of Acceptance of Collateral.

(a) A secured party's acceptance of collateral in full or partial satisfaction of the obligation it secures:

(1) discharges the obligation to the extent consented to by the debtor;

(2) transfers to the secured party all of a debtor's rights in the collateral;

(3) discharges the security interest or agricultural lien that is the subject of the debtor's consent and any subordinate security interest or other subordinate lien; and

(4) terminates any other subordinate interest.

(b) A subordinate interest is discharged or terminated under subsection (a), even if the secured party fails to comply with this article.

Section 9-623. Right to Redeem Collateral.

(a) A debtor, any secondary obligor, or any other secured party or lienholder may redeem collateral.

(b) To redeem collateral, a person shall tender:

(1) fulfillment of all obligations secured by the collateral; and

(2) the reasonable expenses and attorney's fees described in Section 9-615(a)(1).

(c) A redemption may occur at any time before a secured party:

(1) has collected collateral under Section 9-607;

(2) has disposed of collateral or entered into a contract for its disposition under Section 9-610; or

(3) has accepted collateral in full or partial satisfaction of the obligation it secures under Section 9-622.

Section 9-624. Waiver.

(a) A debtor or secondary obligor may waive the right to notification of disposition of collateral under Section 9-611 only by an agreement to that effect entered into and authenticated after default.

(b) A debtor may waive the right to require disposition of collateral under Section 9-620(e) only by an agreement to that effect entered into and authenticated after default.

(c) Except in a consumer-goods transaction, a debtor or secondary obligor may waive the right to redeem collateral under Section 9-623 only by an agreement to that effect entered into and authenticated after default.

[Subpart 2. Noncompliance with Article]

Section 9-625. Remedies for Secured Party's Failure to Comply with Article.

(a) If it is established that a secured party is not proceeding in accordance with this article, a court may order or restrain collection, enforcement, or disposition of collateral on appropriate terms and conditions.

(b) Subject to subsections (c), (d), and (f), a person is liable for damages in the amount of any loss caused by a failure to comply with this article. Loss caused by a failure to comply may include loss resulting from the debtor's inability to obtain, or increased costs of, alternative financing.

(c) Except as otherwise provided in Section 9-628:

(1) a person that, at the time of the failure, was a debtor, was an obligor, or held a security interest in or other lien on the collateral may recover damages under subsection (b) for its loss; and

(2) if the collateral is consumer goods, a person that was a debtor or a secondary obligor at the time a secured party failed to comply with this part may recover for that failure in any event an amount not less than the credit service charge plus 10 percent of the principal amount of the obligation or the time-price differential plus 10 percent of the cash price.

(d) A debtor whose deficiency is eliminated under Section 9-626 may recover damages for the loss of any surplus. However, a debtor or secondary obligor whose deficiency is eliminated or reduced under Section 9-626 may not otherwise recover under subsection (b) for noncompliance with the provisions of this part relating to collection, enforcement, disposition, or acceptance.

(e) In addition to any damages recoverable under subsection (b), the debtor, consumer obligor, or person named as a debtor in a filed record, as applicable, may recover $500 in each case from a person that:

(1) fails to comply with Section 9-208;

(2) fails to comply with Section 9-209;

(3) files a record that the person is not entitled to file under Section 9-509(a);

(4) fails to cause the secured party of record to file or send a termination statement as required by Section 9-513(a) or (c);

(5) fails to comply with Section 9-616(b)(1) and whose failure is part of a pattern, or consistent with a practice, of noncompliance; or

(6) fails to comply with Section 9-616(b)(2).

(f) A debtor or consumer obligor may recover damages under subsection (b) and, in addition, $500 in each case from a person that, without reasonable cause, fails to comply with a request under Section 9-210. A recipient of a request under Section 9-210 which never claimed an interest in the collateral or obligations that are the subject of a request under that section has a reasonable excuse for failure to comply with the request within the meaning of this subsection.

(g) If a secured party fails to comply with a request regarding a list of collateral or a statement of account under Section 9-210, the secured party may claim a security interest only as shown in the list or statement included in the request as against a person that is reasonably misled by the failure.

As amended in 2000.

Section 9-626. Action in Which Deficiency or Surplus Is in Issue.

(a) In an action arising from a transaction, other than a consumer transaction, in which the amount of a deficiency or surplus is in issue, the following rules apply:

(1) A secured party need not prove compliance with the provisions of this part relating to collection, enforcement, disposition, or acceptance unless the debtor or a secondary obligor places the secured party's compliance in issue.

(2) If the secured party's compliance is placed in issue, the secured party has the burden of establishing that the collection, enforcement, disposition, or acceptance was conducted in accordance with this part.

(3) Except as otherwise provided in Section 9-628, if a secured party fails to prove that the collection, enforcement, disposition, or acceptance was conducted in accordance with the provisions of this part relating to collection, enforcement, disposition, or acceptance, the liability of a debtor or a secondary obligor for a deficiency is limited to an amount by which the sum of the secured obligation, expenses, and attorney's fees exceeds the greater of:

(A) the proceeds of the collection, enforcement, disposition, or acceptance; or

(B) the amount of proceeds that would have been realized had the noncomplying secured party proceeded in accordance with the provisions of this part relating to collection, enforcement, disposition, or acceptance.

(4) For purposes of paragraph (3)(B), the amount of proceeds that would have been realized is equal to the sum of the secured obligation, expenses, and attorney's fees unless the secured party proves that the amount is less than that sum.

(5) If a deficiency or surplus is calculated under Section 9-615(f), the debtor or obligor has the burden of establishing that the amount of proceeds of the disposition is significantly below the range of prices that a complying disposition to a person other than the secured party, a person related to the secured party, or a secondary obligor would have brought.

(b) The limitation of the rules in subsection (a) to transactions other than consumer transactions is intended to leave to the court the determination of the proper rules in consumer transactions. The court may not infer from that limitation the nature of the proper rule in consumer transactions and may continue to apply established approaches.

Section 9-627. Determination of Whether Conduct Was Commercially Reasonable.

(a) The fact that a greater amount could have been obtained by a collection, enforcement, disposition, or acceptance at a different time or in a different method from that selected by the secured party is not of itself sufficient to preclude the secured party from establishing that the collection, enforcement, disposition, or acceptance was made in a commercially reasonable manner.

(b) A disposition of collateral is made in a commercially reasonable manner if the disposition is made:

(1) in the usual manner on any recognized market;

(2) at the price current in any recognized market at the time of the disposition; or

(3) otherwise in conformity with reasonable commercial practices among dealers in the type of property that was the subject of the disposition.

(c) A collection, enforcement, disposition, or acceptance is commercially reasonable if it has been approved:

(1) in a judicial proceeding;

(2) by a bona fide creditors' committee;

(3) by a representative of creditors; or

(4) by an assignee for the benefit of creditors.

(d) Approval under subsection (c) need not be obtained, and lack of approval does not mean that the collection, enforcement, disposition, or acceptance is not commercially reasonable.

Section 9-628. Nonliability and Limitation on Liability of Secured Party; Liability of Secondary Obligor.

(a) Unless a secured party knows that a person is a debtor or obligor, knows the identity of the person, and knows how to communicate with the person:

(1) the secured party is not liable to the person, or to a secured party or lienholder that has filed a financing statement against the person, for failure to comply with this article; and

(2) the secured party's failure to comply with this article does not affect the liability of the person for a deficiency.

(b) A secured party is not liable because of its status as secured party:

(1) to a person that is a debtor or obligor, unless the secured party knows:

(A) that the person is a debtor or obligor;

(B) the identity of the person; and

(C) how to communicate with the person; or

(2) to a secured party or lienholder that has filed a financing statement against a person, unless the secured party knows:

(A) that the person is a debtor; and

(B) the identity of the person.

(c) A secured party is not liable to any person, and a person's liability for a deficiency is not affected, because of any act or omission arising out of the secured party's reasonable belief that a transaction is not a consumer-goods transaction or a consumer transaction or that goods are not consumer goods, if the secured party's belief is based on its reasonable reliance on:

(1) a debtor's representation concerning the purpose for which collateral was to be used, acquired, or held; or

(2) an obligor's representation concerning the purpose for which a secured obligation was incurred.

(d) A secured party is not liable to any person under Section 9-625(c)(2) for its failure to comply with Section 9-616.

(e) A secured party is not liable under Section 9-625(c)(2) more than once with respect to any one secured obligation.

Part 7. Transition.

Section 9-701. Effective Date.

This [Act] takes effect on July 1, 2001.

Section 9-702. Savings Clause.

(a) Except as otherwise provided in this part, this [Act] applies to a transaction or lien within its scope, even if the transaction or lien was entered into or created before this [Act] takes effect.

(b) Except as otherwise provided in subsection (c) and Sections 9-703 through 9-709:

(1) transactions and liens that were not governed by [former Article 9], were validly entered into or created before this [Act] takes effect, and would be subject to this [Act] if they had been entered into or created after this [Act] takes effect, and the rights, duties, and interests flowing from those transactions and liens remain valid after this [Act] takes effect; and

(2) the transactions and liens may be terminated, completed, consummated, and enforced as required or permitted by this [Act] or by the law that otherwise would apply if this [Act] had not taken effect.

(c) This [Act] does not affect an action, case, or proceeding commenced before this [Act] takes effect.

As amended in 2000.

Section 9-703. Security Interest Perfected before Effective Date.

(a) A security interest that is enforceable immediately before this [Act] takes effect and would have priority over the rights of a person that becomes a lien creditor at that time is a perfected security interest under this [Act] if, when this [Act] takes effect, the applicable requirements for enforceability and perfection under this [Act] are satisfied without further action.

(b) Except as otherwise provided in Section 9-705, if, immediately before this [Act] takes effect, a security interest is enforceable and would have priority over the rights of a person that becomes a lien creditor at that time, but the applicable requirements for enforceability or perfection under this [Act] are not satisfied when this [Act] takes effect, the security interest:

(1) is a perfected security interest for one year after this [Act] takes effect;

(2) remains enforceable thereafter only if the security interest becomes enforceable under Section 9-203 before the year expires; and

(3) remains perfected thereafter only if the applicable requirements for perfection under this [Act] are satisfied before the year expires.

Section 9-704. Security Interest Unperfected before Effective Date.

A security interest that is enforceable immediately before this [Act] takes effect but which would be subordinate to the rights of a person that becomes a lien creditor at that time:

(1) remains an enforceable security interest for one year after this [Act] takes effect;

(2) remains enforceable thereafter if the security interest becomes enforceable under Section 9-203 when this [Act] takes effect or within one year thereafter; and

(3) becomes perfected:

(A) without further action, when this [Act] takes effect if the applicable requirements for perfection under this [Act] are satisfied before or at that time; or

(B) when the applicable requirements for perfection are satisfied if the requirements are satisfied after that time.

Section 9-705. Effectiveness of Action Taken before Effective Date.

(a) If action, other than the filing of a financing statement, is taken before this [Act] takes effect and the action would have resulted in priority of a security interest over the rights of a person that becomes a lien creditor had the security interest become enforceable before this [Act] takes effect, the action is effective to perfect a security interest that attaches under this [Act] within one year after this [Act] takes effect. An attached security interest becomes unperfected one year after this [Act] takes effect unless the security interest becomes a perfected security interest under this [Act] before the expiration of that period.

(b) The filing of a financing statement before this [Act] takes effect is effective to perfect a security interest to the extent the filing would satisfy the applicable requirements for perfection under this [Act].

(c) This [Act] does not render ineffective an effective financing statement that, before this [Act] takes effect, is filed and satisfies the applicable requirements for perfection under the law of the jurisdiction governing perfection as provided in [former Section 9-103]. However, except as otherwise provided in subsections (d) and (e) and Section 9-706, the financing statement ceases to be effective at the earlier of:

(1) the time the financing statement would have ceased to be effective under the law of the jurisdiction in which it is filed; or

(2) June 30, 2006.

(d) The filing of a continuation statement after this [Act] takes effect does not continue the effectiveness of the financing statement filed before this [Act] takes effect. However, upon the timely filing of a continuation statement after this [Act] takes effect and in accordance with the law of the jurisdiction governing perfection as provided in Part 3, the effectiveness of a financing statement filed in the same office in that jurisdiction before this [Act] takes effect continues for the period provided by the law of that jurisdiction.

(e) Subsection (c)(2) applies to a financing statement that, before this [Act] takes effect, is filed against a transmitting utility and satisfies the applicable requirements for perfection under the law of the jurisdiction governing perfection as provided in [former Section 9-103] only to the extent that Part 3 provides that the law of a jurisdiction other than the jurisdiction in which the financing statement is filed governs perfection of a security interest in collateral covered by the financing statement.

(f) A financing statement that includes a financing statement filed before this [Act] takes effect and a continuation statement filed after this [Act] takes effect is effective only to the extent that it satisfies the requirements of Part 5 for an initial financing statement.

Section 9-706. When Initial Financing Statement Suffices to Continue Effectiveness of Financing Statement.

(a) The filing of an initial financing statement in the office specified in Section 9-501 continues the effectiveness of a financing statement filed before this [Act] takes effect if:

(1) the filing of an initial financing statement in that office would be effective to perfect a security interest under this [Act];

(2) the pre-effective-date financing statement was filed in an office in another State or another office in this State; and

(3) the initial financing statement satisfies subsection (c).

(b) The filing of an initial financing statement under subsection (a) continues the effectiveness of the pre-effective-date financing statement:

(1) if the initial financing statement is filed before this [Act] takes effect, for the period provided in [former Section 9-403] with respect to a financing statement; and

(2) if the initial financing statement is filed after this [Act] takes effect, for the period provided in Section 9-515 with respect to an initial financing statement.

(c) To be effective for purposes of subsection (a), an initial financing statement must:

(1) satisfy the requirements of Part 5 for an initial financing statement;

(2) identify the pre-effective-date financing statement by indicating the office in which the financing statement was filed and providing the dates of filing and file numbers, if any, of the financing statement and of the most recent continuation statement filed with respect to the financing statement; and

(3) indicate that the pre-effective-date financing statement remains effective.

Section 9-707. Amendment of Pre-Effective-Date Financing Statement.

(a) In this section, "Pre-effective-date financing statement" means a financing statement filed before this [Act] takes effect.

(b) After this [Act] takes effect, a person may add or delete collateral covered by, continue or terminate the effectiveness of, or otherwise amend the information provided in, a pre-effective-date financing statement only in accordance with the law of the jurisdiction governing perfection as provided in Part 3. However, the effectiveness of a pre-effective-date financing statement also may be terminated in accordance with the law of the jurisdiction in which the financing statement is filed.

(c) Except as otherwise provided in subsection (d), if the law of this State governs perfection of a security interest, the information in a pre-effective-date financing statement may be amended after this [Act] takes effect only if:

(1) the pre-effective-date financing statement and an amendment are filed in the office specified in Section 9-501;

(2) an amendment is filed in the office specified in Section 9-501 concurrently with, or after the filing in that office of, an initial financing statement that satisfies Section 9-706(c); or

(3) an initial financing statement that provides the information as amended and satisfies Section 9-706(c) is filed in the office specified in Section 9-501.

(d) If the law of this State governs perfection of a security interest, the effectiveness of a pre-effective-date financing statement may be continued only under Section 9-705(d) and (f) or 9-706.

(e) Whether or not the law of this State governs perfection of a security interest, the effectiveness of a pre-effective-date financing statement filed in this State may be terminated after this [Act] takes effect by filing a termination statement in the office in which the pre-effective-date financing statement is filed, unless an initial financing statement that satisfies Section 9-706(c) has been filed in the office specified by the law of the jurisdiction governing perfection as provided in Part 3 as the office in which to file a financing statement.

As amended in 2000.

Section 9-708. Persons Entitled to File Initial Financing Statement or Continuation Statement.

A person may file an initial financing statement or a continuation statement under this part if:

(1) the secured party of record authorizes the filing; and

(2) the filing is necessary under this part:

(A) to continue the effectiveness of a financing statement filed before this [Act] takes effect; or

(B) to perfect or continue the perfection of a security interest.

As amended in 2000.

Section 9-709. Priority.

(a) This [Act] determines the priority of conflicting claims to collateral. However, if the relative priorities of the claims were established before this [Act] takes effect, [former Article 9] determines priority.

(b) For purposes of Section 9-322(a), the priority of a security interest that becomes enforceable under Section 9-203 of this [Act] dates from the time this [Act] takes effect if the security interest is perfected under this [Act] by the filing of a financing statement before this [Act] takes effect which would not have been effective to perfect the security interest under [former Article 9]. This subsection does not apply to conflicting security interests each of which is perfected by the filing of such a financing statement.

As amended in 2000.

1. Additions and new wording are underlined. What follows represents only selected changes made by the proposed amendments. Although the National Conference of Commissioners on Uniform State Laws approved the amendments on August 2, 2002, as of this writing, they have not as yet been approved by the American Law Institute or by any state.

*[Section 3-312 was not adopted as part of the 1990 Official Text of Revised Article 3. It was officially approved and recommended for enactment in all states in August 1991 by the National Conference of Commissioners on Uniform State Laws.]

Authors' Note: *Articles 10 and 11 have been omitted as unnecessary for the purposes of this text.*

United Nations Convention on Contracts for the International Sale of Goods (excerpts)

The States Parties to this Convention,

Bearing in mind the broad objectives in the resolutions adopted by the sixth special session of the General Assembly of the United Nations on the establishment of a New International Economic Order,

Considering that the development of international trade on the basis of equality and mutual benefit is an important element in promoting friendly relations among States,

Being of the opinion that the adoption of uniform rules which govern contracts for the international sale of goods and take into account the different social, economic and legal systems would contribute to the removal of legal barriers in international trade and promote the development of international trade,

Have agreed as follows:

Part 1. Sphere of Application and General Provisions

Chapter I. Sphere of Application

Article 1

(1) This Convention applies to contracts of sale of goods between parties whose places of business are in different States:

(a) when the States are Contracting States; or

(b) when the rules of private international law lead to the application of the law of a Contracting State.

(2) The fact that the parties have their places of business in different States is to be disregarded whenever this fact does not appear either from the contract or from any dealings between, or from information disclosed by, the parties at any time before or at the conclusion of the contract.

(3) Neither the nationality of the parties nor the civil or commercial character of the parties or of the contract is to be taken into consideration in determining the application of this Convention.

Article 2

This Convention does not apply to sales:

(a) of goods bought for personal, family or household use, unless the seller, at any time before or at the conclusion of the contract, neither knew nor ought to have known that the goods were bought for any such use;

(b) by auction;

(c) on execution or otherwise by authority of law;

(d) of stocks, shares, investment securities, negotiable instruments or money;

(e) of ships, vessels, hovercraft or aircraft;

(f) of electricity.

Article 3

(1) Contracts for the supply of goods to be manufactured or produced are to be considered sales unless the party who orders the goods undertakes to supply a substantial part of the materials necessary for such manufacture or production.

(2) This Convention does not apply to contracts in which the preponderant part of the obligations of the party who furnishes the goods consists in the supply of labour or other services.

Article 4

This Convention governs only the formation of the contract of sale and the rights, and obligations of the seller and the buyer arising from such a contract. In particular, except as otherwise expressly provided in this Convention, it is not concerned with:

(a) the validity of the contract or of any of its provisions or of any usage;

(b) the effect which the contract may have on the property in the goods sold.

Article 5

This Convention does not apply to the liability of the seller for death or personal injury caused by the goods to any person.

Article 6

The parties may exclude the application of this Convention or, subject to Article 12, derogate from or vary the effect of any of its provisions.

Chapter II. General Provisions

Article 7

(1) In the interpretation of this Convention, regard is to be had to its international character and to the need to promote uniformity in its application and the observance of good faith in international trade.

(2) Questions concerning matters governed by this Convention which are not expressly settled in it are to be settled in conformity with the general principles on which it is based or, in the absence of such principles, in conformity with the law applicable by virtue of the rules of private international law.

Article 8

(1) For the purposes of this Convention statements made by and other conduct of a party are to be interpreted according to his intent where the other party knew or could not have been unaware what that intent was.

(2) If the preceding paragraph is not applicable, statements made by and other conduct of a party are to be interpreted according to the understanding that a

reasonable person of the same kind as the other party would have had in the same circumstances.

(3) In determining the intent of a party or the understanding a reasonable person would have had, due consideration is to be given to all relevant circumstances of the case including the negotiations, any practices which the parties have established between themselves, usages and any subsequent conduct of the parties.

Article 9

(1) The parties are bound by any usage to which they have agreed and by any practices which they have established between themselves.

(2) The parties are considered, unless otherwise agreed, to have impliedly made applicable to their contract or its formation a usage of which the parties knew or ought to have known and which in international trade is widely known to, and regularly observed by parties to contracts of the type involved in the particular trade concerned.

Article 10

For the purposes of this Convention:

(a) if a party has more than one place of business, the place of business is that which has the closest relationship to the contract and its performance, having regard to the circumstances known to or contemplated by the parties at any time before or at the conclusion of the contract;

(b) if a party does not have a place of business, reference is to be made to his habitual residence.

Article 11

A contract of sale need not be concluded in or evidenced by writing and is not subject to any other requirements as to form. It may be proved by any means, including witnesses.

Article 12

Any provision of Article 11, Article 29 or Part II of this Convention that allows a contract of sale or its modification or termination by agreement of any offer, acceptance or other indication of intention to be made in any form other than in writing does not apply where any party has his place of business in a Contracting State which has made a declaration under Article 96 of this Convention. The parties may not derogate from or vary the effect of this article.

Article 13

For the purposes of this Convention "writing" includes telegram and telex.

Part II. Formation of the Contract

Article 14

(1) A proposal for concluding a contract addressed to one or more specific persons constitutes an offer if it is sufficiently definite and indicates the intention of the offeror to be bound in case of acceptance. A proposal is sufficiently definite if it indicates the goods and expressly or implicitly fixes or makes provision for determining the quantity and the price.

(2) A proposal other than one addressed to one or more specific persons is to be considered merely as an invitation to make offers, unless the contrary is clearly indicated by the person making the proposal.

Article 15

(1) An offer becomes effective when it reaches the offeree.

(2) An offer, even if it is irrevocable, may be withdrawn if the withdrawal reaches the offeree before or at the same time as the offer.

Article 16

(1) Until a contract is concluded an offer may be revoked if the revocation reaches the offeree before he has dispatched an acceptance.

(2) However, an offer cannot be revoked:

(a) if it indicates, whether by stating a fixed time for acceptance or otherwise, that it is irrevocable; or

(b) if it was reasonable for the offeree to rely on the offer as being irrevocable and the offeree has acted in reliance on the offer.

Article 17

An offer, even if it is irrevocable, is terminated when a rejection reaches the offeror.

Article 18

(1) A statement made by or other conduct of the offeree indicating assent to an offer is an acceptance. Silence or inactivity does not in itself amount to acceptance.

(2) An acceptance of an offer becomes effective at the moment the indication of assent reaches the offeror. An acceptance is not effective if the indication of assent does not reach the offeror within the time he has fixed or, if no time is fixed, within a reasonable time, due account being taken of the circumstances of the transaction, including the rapidity of the means of communication employed by the offeror. An oral offer must be accepted immediately unless circumstances indicate otherwise.

(3) However, if, by virtue of the offer or as a result of practices which the parties have established between themselves or of usage, the offeree may indicate assent by performing an act, such as one relating to the dispatch of the goods or payment of the price, without notice to the offeror, the acceptance is effective at the moment the act is performed, provided that the act is performed within the period of time laid down in the preceding paragraph.

Article 19

(1) A reply to an offer which purports to be an acceptance but contains additions, limitations or other modifications is a rejection of the offer and constitutes a counter-offer.

(2) However, a reply to an offer which purports to be an acceptance but contains additional or different terms which do not materially alter the terms of the offer constitutes an acceptance, unless the offeror, without undue delay, objects orally to the discrepancy or dispatches a notice to the effect. If he does not so object, the terms of the contract are the terms of the offer with the modifications contained in the acceptance.

(3) Additional or different terms relating, among other things, to the price, payment, quality and quantity of the goods, place and time of delivery, extent of one party's liability to the other or the settlement of disputes are considered to alter the terms of the offer materially.

Article 20

(1) A period of time for acceptance fixed by the offeror in a telegram or a letter begins to run from the moment the telegram is handed in for dispatch or from the date shown on the letter or, if no such date is shown, from the date shown on the envelope. A period of time for acceptance fixed by the offeror by telephone, telex or other means of instantaneous communication, begins to run from the moment that the offer reaches the offeree.

(2) Official holidays or nonbusiness days occurring during the period for acceptance are included in calculating the period. However, if a notice of acceptance cannot be delivered at the address of the offeror on the last day of the period because that day falls on an official holiday or a nonbusiness day at the place of business of the offeror, the period is extended until the first business day which follows.

Article 21

(1) A late acceptance is nevertheless effective as an acceptance if without delay the offeror orally so informs the offeree or dispatches a notice to that effect.

(2) If a letter or other writing containing a late acceptance shows that it has been sent in such circumstances that if its transmission had been normal it would have reached the offeror in due time, the late acceptance is effective as an acceptance unless, without delay, the offeror orally informs the offeree that he considers his offer as having lapsed or dispatches a notice to that effect.

Article 22

An acceptance may be withdrawn if the withdrawal reaches the offeror before or at the same time as the acceptance would have become effective.

Article 23

A contract is concluded at the moment when an acceptance of an offer becomes effective in accordance with the provisions of this Convention.

Article 24

For the purposes of this Part of the Convention, an offer, declaration of acceptance or any other indication of intention "reaches" the addressee when it is made orally to him or delivered by any other means to him personally, to his place of business or mailing address or if he does not have a place of business or mailing address, to his habitual residence.

Part III. Sale of Goods

Chapter I. General Provisions

Article 25

A breach of contract committed by one of the parties is fundamental if it results in such detriment to the other party as substantially to deprive him of what he is entitled to expect under the contract, unless the party in breach did not foresee and a reasonable person of the same kind in the same circumstances would not have foreseen such a result.

Article 26

A declaration of avoidance of the contract is effective only if made by notice to the other party.

Article 27

Unless otherwise expressly provided in this Part of the Convention, if any notice, request or other communication is given or made by a party in accordance with this Part and by means appropriate in the circumstances, a delay or error in the transmission of the communication or its failure to arrive does not deprive that party of the right to rely on the communication.

Article 28

If, in accordance with the provisions of this Convention, one party is entitled to require performance of any obligation by the other party, a court is not bound to enter a judgment for specific performance similar unless the court would do so under its own law in respect of similar contracts of sale not governed by this Convention.

Article 29

(1) A contract may be modified or terminated by the mere agreement of the parties.

(2) A contract in writing which contains a provision requiring any modification or termination by agreement to be in writing may not be otherwise modified or terminated by agreement. However, a party may be precluded by his conduct from asserting such a provision to the extent that the other party has relied on that conduct.

* * * * *

Chapter II. Obligations of the Seller

* * * * *

Article 35

(1) The seller must deliver goods which are of the quantity, quality and description required by the contract and which are contained or packaged in the manner required by the contract.

(2) Except where the parties have agreed otherwise, the goods do not conform with the contract unless they:

  (a) are fit for the purposes for which goods of the same description would ordinarily be used;

  (b) are fit for any particular purpose expressly or implicitly made known to the seller at the time of the conclusion of the contract, except where the circumstances show that the buyer did not rely, or that it was unreasonable for him to rely, on the seller's skill and judgment;

  (c) possess the qualities of goods which the seller has held out to the buyer as a sample or model;

  (d) are contained or packaged in the manner usual for such goods or, where there is no such manner, in a manner adequate to preserve and protect the goods.

(3) The seller is not liable under Subparagraphs (a) to (d) of the preceding paragraph for any lack of conformity of the goods if at the time of the conclusion of the contract the buyer knew or could not have been unaware of such lack of conformity.

Article 36

(1) The seller is liable in accordance with the contract and this Convention for any lack of conformity which exists at the time when the risk passes to the buyer, even though the lack of conformity becomes apparent only after that time.

(2) The seller is also liable for any lack of conformity which occurs after the time indicated in the preceding paragraph and which is due to a breach of any of his obligations, including a breach of any guarantee that for a period of time the goods will remain fit for their ordinary purpose or for some particular purpose or will retain specified qualities or characteristics.

Article 37

If the seller has delivered goods before the date for delivery, he may, up to that date, deliver any missing part or make up any deficiency in the quantity of the goods delivered, or deliver goods in replacement of any nonconforming goods delivered or remedy any lack of conformity in the goods delivered, provided that the exercise of this right does not cause the buyer unreasonable inconvenience or unreasonable expense. However, the buyer retains any right to claim damages as provided for in this Convention.

* * * * *

Chapter III. Obligations of the Buyer

* * * * *

Chapter IV. Passing of Risk

Article 66

Loss of or damage to the goods after the risk has passed to the buyer does not discharge him from his obligation to pay the price, unless the loss or damage is due to an act or omission of the seller.

Article 67

(1) If the contract of sale involves carriage of the goods and the seller is not bound to hand them over at a particular place, the risk passes to the buyer when the goods are handed over to the first carrier for transmission to the buyer in accordance with the contract of sale. If the seller is bound to hand the goods over to a carrier at a particular place, the risk does not pass to the buyer until the goods are handed over to the carrier at that place. The fact that the seller is authorized to retain documents controlling the disposition of the goods does not affect the passage of risk.

(2) Nevertheless, the risk does not pass to the buyer until the goods are clearly identified to the contract, whether by markings on the goods, by shipping documents, by notice given to the buyer or otherwise.

Article 68

The risk in respect of goods sold in transit passes to the buyer from the time of the conclusion of the contract. However, if the circumstances so indicate, the risk is assumed by the buyer from the time the goods were handed over to the carrier who issued the documents embodying in the contract of carriage. Nevertheless, if at the time of the conclusion of the contract of sale the seller knew or ought to have known that the goods had been lost or damaged and did not disclose this to the buyer, the loss or damage is at risk of the seller.

Article 69

(1) In cases not within Articles 67 and 68, the risk passes to the buyer when he takes over the goods or, if he does not do so in due time, from the time when the goods are placed at his disposal and lie commits a breach of contract by failing to take delivery.

(2) However, if the buyer is bound to take over the goods at a place other than a place of business of the seller, the risk passes when delivery is due and the buyer is aware of the fact that the goods are placed at his disposal at that place.

(3) If the contract relates to goods not then identified, the goods are considered not to be placed at the disposal of the buyer until they are clearly identified to the contract.

Article 70

If the seller has committed a fundamental breach of contract, Articles 67, 68, and 69 do not impair the remedies available to the buyer on account of the breach.

* * * * *

Part IV. Final Provisions

* * * * *

Article 96

A Contracting State whose legislation requires contracts of sale to be concluded in or evidenced by writing may at any time make a declaration in accordance with Article 12 that any provision of Article 11, Article 29, or Part H of this Convention, that allows a contract of sale or its modification or termination by agreement or any offer, acceptance, or other indication of intention to be made in any form other than writing, does not apply where any party has place of business in that State.

* * * *

DONE at Vienna, this day of eleventh day of April, one thousand nine hundred and eighty, in a single original, of which the Arabic, Chinese, English, French, Russian, and Spanish texts are equally authentic.

IN WITNESS WHEREOF the undersigned plenipotentiaries, being duly authorized by their respective Governments, have signed this Convention.

Glossary

A

Ab initio
From the beginning.

Abandonment
An owner's voluntary relinquishment of the possession of an item of personal property, with the owner exercising no further interest or control.

Abstract of title
A historical record of the title to a parcel of land, including all changes in the chain of title and all liens and encumbrances recorded against the parcel.

Acceleration clause
Provision in a contract that shortens the time for the performance of that contract.

Acceptance
An offeree's manifestation of assent to the terms of an offer made to him or her by an offeror. The acceptance is the act, the oral or written assent, or in certain instances the silence that creates contractual liabilities for both the offeror and the offeree.

Accession
The acquisition of title to something because it has been added to the property one owns. For example, a tenant plants shrubs and trees on the owner's land, and the owner thus acquires title by accession.

Accommodation party
A cosigner to a credit transaction who signs without receiving any payment or value, doing so merely to help a person obtain credit.

Accord
A new contract that replaces another contract.

Accord and satisfaction
Two persons agree that one of them has a right of action against the other, but they accept a substitute or different act or value as performance.

Account
Any right to payment for goods sold, leased, or delivered or for services performed. Also referred to as an account receivable.

Accretion
Adding to the boundaries of property naturally by gradual deposits of silt, sand, or other solid material. For example, a river deposits sand and silt and builds up the land on its sides.

Acknowledgment
A formally signed statement (usually before a notary public) denoting the execution of a particular legal document.

Act of God
In civil law, an unforeseen accident or casualty caused strictly by the forces of nature, such as flood, drought, and hurricane.

Action
Something that is done; conduct; behavior; in legal terms, a court proceeding for the enforcement of rights.

Ad valorem
According to value.

Adjudication
The pronouncement of a judgment or a decree; a final court determination. (In bankruptcy cases, the proclaiming that a debtor is a bankrupt.)

Adverse possession
Gaining legal ownership of real property by openly, exclusively, and continuously occupying the land for a required amount of time.

Affiant
A person who subscribes to or makes an affidavit.

Affidavit
A printed or written statement or declaration made under oath before an authorized public official, usually a notary public.

Agency
A relationship whereby the principal authorizes another (the agent) to act for and on behalf of the principal and to bind the principal in contract.

Air rights, airspace
Ascertainment of the ownership of the airspace (sky) above one's land.

Alien
Born in one country and residing in another country without being admitted to citizenship in that country.

Alimony
An allowance granted from the husband or wife to his or her spouse, who is living separately or legally divorced. (Laws regarding alimony differ among the states.)

Allegation
The statement or declaration made in a pleading in which a party points out the facts that the party intends to prove.

Amicus curiae
A Latin phrase that means "a friend of the court." An amicus curiae would be a person with a strong interest in the case and the legal principles involved who requests permission to file a legal brief giving his or her views to the court.

Amnesty
In international law, the act of absolution for past offensive acts ("burying the hatchet").

Answer: plaintiff's
The defendant's response to plaintiffs petition or complaint.

Anticipatory breach
Before the performance time on a contract is due, one party announces that he or she will not perform his or her part of the contract, thus giving the nonbreaching party an opportunity to seek a remedy in the courts.

Apparent authority
The assumed authority or permission, not actually granted, that a principal knowingly permits an agent to possess when dealing with a third person.

Appellant

The party appealing to a higher court to overrule a decision made by a lower court.

Appellee

The party against whom an appeal is made; the respondent.

Arbitration

To settle a dispute, an appointed arbitrator (third person) comes in to help the parties make an out of court decision. This saves the time and expense of litigation.

Arbitrator

A third person chosen to decide a dispute between two other persons.

Articles of incorporation

A legal document submitted to a designated officer of the state for permission to commence business as a corporation. The articles of incorporation or the corporate charter state the purpose, rights, and duties of the corporation and must comply with state corporation laws.

Articles of partnership

An agreement drawn up to govern a business to be operated by a partnership. The agreement need not be filed with any state official.

Artisan's lien

A possessory claim levied on goods owned by another because of improvements made or work done thereon by the artisan. An artisan is a skilled trades person, such as a carpenter or a plumber.

Assignee

The person to whom an assignment is made.

Assignment

A transfer of rights (usually contract rights) from an assignor to an assignee.

Assignor

The person who makes an assignment.

Attachment

The seizure through legal process by proper legal authority, usually the sheriff, of nonexempt property of the defendant, pending a lawsuit for the collection of a debt owed by the defendant to a creditor.

Attestation

The act of witnessing the signing of a legal document.

Attractive nuisance

Any dangerous object or condition on real property that is inviting to young children and tempts them to trespass.

Auction with reserve

A sale whereby the goods sold may be withdrawn before the actual bid is accepted by the owner.

Auction without reserve

An auction sale wherein goods are sold to the highest bidder with no chance of withdrawal by the owner after the goods are placed on the auction block.

B

Bailee

A person who receives personal property under contract of bailment.

Bailment

The temporary transfer of possession of personal property without a change of ownership for a specific purpose and with the intent that possession will revert to the owner at a later date. *Example:* Owner gives his or her car to a mechanic for repairs; owner will get the car back when it has been repaired.

Bailor

A person who entrusts or bails personal property to another under a bailment arrangement.

Bankrupt

An insolvent person; one who has been declared by the court to have more debts than assets.

Bankruptcy

When a person is bankrupt, the court proceeds to have that person's nonexempt assets distributed to his or her creditors and releases him or her from further payment of past debts.

Bearer

A person in possession of a security, instrument, or document of title payable to the bearer or endorsed in blank.

Beneficiary

A person receiving proceeds from a will, insurance policy, trust, or third party beneficiary contract.

Bilateral contract

A contract formed by the mutual exchange of promises between an offeror and an offeree.

Bilateral mistake

Both parties to a contract are in error as to the terms of the contract or the performance expected.

Bill of exchange

A written command ordering the addressee to pay on demand or at a predetermined time, a certain sum of money to the holder of the bill.

Bill of lading

A formal document issued by a carrier of goods to a shipper of goods. This document identifies the goods and states the terms of the shipping agreement.

Bill of sale

A written statement by which a seller acknowledges transfer of personal property to another.

Blue sky laws

State regulatory and supervisory laws governing investment companies to avoid fraudulent sales to investors in get rich quick schemes.

Board of directors

A specific number of persons elected by a corporation's stockholders to manage and govern the corporation on their behalf.

Bona fide

With good faith or in good faith.

Bond

With regard to corporate financing, a legal instrument that is evidence of a corporation's debt to the bondholder. The instrument obligates the corporation to pay the bondholder a fixed rate of interest on the principal amount and to pay the principal to the bondholder at a fixed maturity date.

Broker

In real property law, a person who acts as an agent and representative of others to negotiate the purchase and sale of real estate.

Bulk transfer

A sale or transfer of all or the major portion of the total inventory of materials, supplies, or merchandise or other inventory not in the ordinary course of the transferor's business.

C

C&F

Cost plus freight.

Cause of action

The legal grounds needed to successfully pursue a lawsuit in court.

Caveat emptor

A Latin phrase that means "let the buyer beware."

Certiorari

A Latin term that means "to be informed of." It is a writ or certification by which an appellate court orders a review of a case from a lower court. The lower court must then send a certified record of the case to the appellate court.

Chancellor

The name given in some states to the presiding judge of a court of chancery (also called a court of equity).

Chancery court

A court of equity.

Charter

A grant or certification from a state to a corporation granting the corporation the right to operate its business. In maritime law, the leasing or hiring of a vessel.

Chattel

A term used to describe tangible and movable personal property.

Chattel mortgage

A mortgage showing that another person besides the title holder has an interest (lien) on the personal property.

Chattel paper

A writing that shows that there is both a monetary obligation and a security interest in specific goods.

Check

A signed document by which a depositor to a bank orders payment of a certain sum of money to a named payee.

Chose in action

A right to personal things of which the owner does not have possession but the owner does have a right of action for their possession.

CIF

Cost, insurance, and freight.

COD

Cash on delivery.

Collateral

Something of value, either real or personal property, that a creditor can convert into cash to pay off a debt if the debtor fails to pay the debt. For example, you borrow money from a bank, and the bank has you pledge your household furniture as collateral.

Common carrier

A carrier that holds itself out as being for hire to the general public for the transportation of goods and passengers for compensation.

Common law

Written or unwritten laws that have evolved through custom and usage (from English common law) without written legislation.

Common stock

A class of corporate stock that is usually the voting stock in a corporation. Common stockholders have a right to dividends and assets upon dissolution second only to that of preferred stockholders, if any.

Composition agreement

An agreement whereby an insolvent debtor pays each of the creditors a portion of what he or she owes them in return for a release from them for the whole debt.

Condition

A qualifying or limiting provision or clause in a contract that must be taken into consideration by all of the parties involved.

Conditional sales contract

A contract that covers the sale of goods or real estate wherein the seller retains title until the buyer makes the payment in full; however, the buyer has possession and use while he or she makes the payments.

Consignment

The transfer of personal property from one person to another for the purpose of transportation or sale. The owner retains ownership of the property.

Consumer goods

Products primarily purchased for home or private and family use.

Consumer Product Safety Act

This act established the Consumer Product Safety Commission, which oversees the safety of consumer-oriented products.

Contract carrier

A private carrier that transports goods for an individual but not for the general public.

Conveyance

A written instrument that transfers an interest in real property, ordinarily by the execution and delivery of a deed. Personal property can also be conveyed, and this is ordinarily done by a bill of sale.

Corporate express powers

Powers specifically set out in the corporation's articles of incorporation and in statutes.

Corporate implied powers

Those powers reasonable and necessary to carry out the corporation's express powers.

Corporation

A legal entity created by authority of statutory law upon application to a proper state authority. This legal entity is an artificial person with the right to sue or be sued in its own name and to purchase, own, and sell property, real and personal, tangible and intangible.

Counterclaim: plaintiff's

In a civil suit, the claim the defendant makes in opposition to the plaintiffs claim.

Counteroffer

A counterproposal different from an offer that an offeree makes in response to the offer. In making a counteroffer, the offeree rejects the previous offer.

Course of dealing

When two parties have previously been involved in a contract matter, their past performance may be used as a basis for interpreting ambiguities, if any, in the present contract.

Covenant

A contractual promise contained in a deed, mortgage, lease, or contract.

Creditor

A person to whom money or performance is owed.

D

D/b/a

Doing business as.

Damages

Monetary harm or monetary loss caused by wrongdoing that the injured person may recover in court.

De facto

A Latin phrase that means "in fact." A de facto corporation has not "in fact" complied with the laws of a state, and therefore its existence can be challenged by the state.

De jure corporation

A de jure corporation is one that has been rightfully formed in full compliance with the laws of a state.

De novo

(Latin) Starting anew.

Debtor

One who owes payment or performance.

Deceit

Fraudulent misrepresentation of facts intended to mislead or trick another, which in turn causes financial loss or harm.

Deed

A legal instrument that transfers property ownership.

Defamation

The act of intentionally injuring the character or reputation of another person.

Default

The failure to perform a legal obligation or duty.

Defendant

The person who is being sued in a legal action.

Deficiency judgment

A personal judgment against a debtor in default, where the value of the secured property was not equal to the amount of the indebtedness.

Demurrer

This is a pleading that disputes the legal sufficiency of the other party's pleading. It is also referred to as a motion to dismiss for the failure to state a legal cause of action.

Deposition

Testimony that is taken under oath and subject to cross-examination to discover what the witness is going to say and to ensure the preservation of the witness's testimony should the witness die or disappear or forget before the trial.

Derivative suit

An action filed by one or more stockholders of a corporation under the corporation name to enforce a corporate cause of action.

Devise

To give a gift of property by will.

Directed verdict

A verdict that the jury returns as directed by the judge.

Discharge

The termination of a contractual obligation regarding the payment of money or the performance of an act.

Disclaimer

A repudiation or denial of a claim or obligation.

Dissolution

The process by which a corporation or partnership terminates its existence.

Dividend

The portion of corporate profits that is distributed periodically to stockholders.

Document of title

A warehouse receipt, a bill of lading, or any other paper that is evidence of the holder's right to have the goods it covers.

Domestic corporation

A corporation doing business in the state where its incorporation took place.

Donee

A person who receives a gift.

Donor

A person who gives a gift.

Draft

A legal instrument wherein one person orders another person to pay a third party a sum of money.

Duress

Coercion, threat, or force that causes a person to do something he or she would not have done otherwise.

E

Earnest money

Money advanced on a contract by a buyer to bind a seller to his or her obligations. This money is given as an indication of good faith by the buyer and usually will be forfeited if the buyer does not perform.

Easement

The right to use the land of another for a special purpose (such as an easement to lay power lines).

Emancipation

Setting free; release. This term is used with reference to the release of a child from the care and custody of his or her parents before the child reaches the age of majority.

Eminent domain

The government's right to take over private property for public use with just compensation.

Endorsement

The signing of one's name on a negotiable instrument such as a check or draft for the purpose of passing title to the instrument to another person. Usually the endorsement is on the back of the instrument.

Equity

This was a court system separate from the common law system, originating in England. Fairness and justice in the particular case were the concern of the law and the court.

Estoppel

This is a rule of law that bars, prevents, and precludes a party from alleging or denying certain facts because of a previous allegation or denial or because of his or her previous conduct or admission.

Eviction

The legal process of removing a tenant from a landlord's property.

Ex contractu

A Latin phrase that means a right arising out of a contract.

Ex delicto

A Latin phrase that refers to a right arising out of a tort.

Ex post facto laws: Criminal laws

A law passed to punish wrongdoers, which is alleged to apply to acts committed before its passage. Such laws are unconstitutional. Criminal law may apply only to acts committed after their passage.

Express authority

The authority a principal gives to an agent either in writing or orally.

F

Factor

A person or a legal entity employed as an agent to sell goods for a principal. Usually the factor is given possession of the goods for sale and sells them in his or her own name. The factor then receives a commission on the sale.

Fair market value

The price that a willing buyer is willing to pay and that a willing seller will accept for real or personal property.

FAS

An abbreviation of the phrase "free alongside" (a boat).

Fee simple

Absolute ownership of a specific tract of real estate. This gives the owner the unconditional power to dispose of the property during his or her lifetime and to pass the absolute ownership on to his or her heirs at death.

Felony

A statutory criminal offense that is more serious than a misdemeanor. Felonies are punishable by fine or imprisonment or both, and in some situations, by death.

Fiduciary

A person who handles another person's money or property in a capacity that involves a confidence or trust. Examples of fiduciaries are executors or guardians of the estates of minors or deceased persons.

Fixture

An article of personal property that has been affixed to real property with the intent that it become a permanent part of the real property.

FOB

An abbreviation of the phrase "free on board." This phrase means that the seller or consignor of goods will place them on board a carrier such as a train or truck at a designated place with instructions to ship them through to a designated destination. The expense of the shipping and insurance for the trip are to be paid by the buyer or consignee, and thus the shipping and insurance are free to the seller or consignor.

Foreclosure

The legal process used to enforce the payment of a debt secured by a mortgage whereby the secured property is sold to satisfy the debt.

Foreign corporation

A corporation doing business in a state other than the state in which it was incorporated. *Foreign* does not mean from outside the country, only from outside the particular state.

Forensic medicine

Medical jurisprudence; the science of applying medical knowledge to the law.

Forgery

Falsely making or materially altering with criminal intent a legal document such as a check, power of attorney, or deed.

Franchise

In the public sector, a franchise is a right to operate a certain essential business that a city, county, state, or national authority grants to a private entity. For example, a city grants a bus company a franchise to be the sole bus company that can operate within the city, or it grants an electric company a franchise to be the exclusive supplier of electricity to the city. In the private sector, a franchise is a means by which one person can grant another person the right to use his or her name and business expertise on a contract basis. Examples include the various fast food franchises.

Fraud

An intentional concealment or misrepresentation of a material fact with the intent of deceiving another person and that causes damage to the deceived person. Such deceived persons may then sue for their damages, provided they can show that they justifiably relied upon such misrepresentation or concealment and that such reliance caused the damage.

Fungible goods

Goods that if mixed cannot be individually identified, one unit of which is equivalent to any other unit. For example, the milk from five dairy farms is pumped into a storage tank. Each farmer owns the number of gallons taken from him or her but cannot identify the specific milk that he or she contributed once it is mixed with the rest.

Future advances clause

A clause found in security agreements that permits the collateral of the debtor, if sufficiently valuable, to be used to secure future loans.

G

Garnishment

A legal proceeding whereby a creditor can secure the payment of a judgment against a debtor by securing a court order that requires an employer or other person having funds belonging to the debtor to pay such funds directly to the creditor.

Gift causa mortis

(Latin) A gift that is given in contemplation of death, usually with the understanding that the gift will be returned if the donor survives.

Gift inter vivos

(Latin) An irrevocable gift that is given during the donor's lifetime.

Grantee

The person to whom a conveyance of real property is made.

Grantor

The person by whom a conveyance of real property is made.

Guaranty

A promise by one person to pay some or all of the debts of another person or to answer for the performance of some act or acts by another person.

H

Holder in due course

As defined by the Uniform Commercial Code, a holder who takes the instrument for value, in good faith and without notice that it is overdue or has been dishonored or of any defense against or any claim to it.

I

Illusory

Like an illusion; something that seems to be so but really isn't so. An illusory promise appears to be a binding promise but actually promises nothing, as the choice of performance or nonperformance is really left up to the promiser.

Independent contractor

A person who contracts to do a specific piece of work under his own direction and control for an employer.

Indictment

A formal accusation of a crime by a grand jury.

Indorsement

The signing of one's name on a negotiable instrument such as a check or draft for the purpose of passing title to the instrument to another person. Usually the indorsement is on the back of the instrument.

Infant

A person who has not reached the legal age of majority.

Injunction

An order of a court of equity that tells a person to do or refrain from doing some act or acts.

In pari delicto

Equally at fault, equally guilty.

In re

A Latin phrase that means "in the matter of." The phrase precedes the name of the party involved in estate and guardian's matters and other nonadversary judicial proceedings, for example, In re Estate of John Jones, Deceased.

In rem

A Latin phrase that means "against the thing."

Insolvency

A party's inability to pay his or her debts as they come due.

Inter alia

A Latin phrase that means "among other things."

Ipso facto

A Latin phrase that means "by the fact itself."

J

Joint tenancy

An estate owned by two or more persons recognizing the right of survivorship.

Judgment

The final determination of a court in an action or proceeding instituted in that court.

Judgment n.o.v

Judgment notwithstanding the verdict.

Jurisdiction

The power of a specific court to hear and decide certain cases.

L

Lease

A contract whereby an owner of real property, the landlord, agrees to give possession to the tenant, the person requesting possession, for a specific period of time in return for the payment of money or service.

Legacy

A gift made by will.

Legal entity

Also referred to as an artificial person. Legal entities include corporations, which exist by legal creation and have the right to contract and the right to own and dispose of property as well as other rights and duties of natural persons.

Levy

To seize, assess, or collect property or money.

Libel

Written or visual defamation intentionally made to injure the reputation of another.

License

Formal personal authorization to perform some act.

Lien

A claim against property. A lien can be agreed upon under contract, or it can be imposed by law. A carpenter who works on your home will have a right to a lien on your home if you do not pay the reasonable cost of his or her services.

Life estate

An interest in property only for the duration of someone's life, not transferable to an heir.

Liquidated damages

The amount of money that, according to the contract, is to be forfeited or paid as a remedy for breach of the contract.

Long-arm statute

A state enactment allowing service of process on out-of-state residents who own property in the state, had an automobile accident in the state, or do business in the state.

M

Malpractice

Failure of a professional person such as an accountant, physician, or lawyer to provide reasonably competent services.

Mandamus

A Latin term that means "we command." A mandamus is an order issued by a court to an inferior court, a person, or a corporation commanding that a specific act be completed.

Mechanic's lien

A worker's claim by law against property (including the land upon which a building rests) until services and materials provided are paid for.

Mens rea

Guilty mind or wrongful intent.

Minor

A person who has not yet reached the age of majority. The common law age of majority was 21. Most states now set the age of majority for contracts at 18 but still make 21 the age of majority with regard to the drinking of intoxicating beverages.

Misdemeanors

Minor criminal offenses that usually encompass all crimes not classified as felonies or treason.

Mortgage

An interest in property, given to another as security for payment of a debt.

N

Necessaries

This term refers to the needs of minors, such as food, reasonable clothing, reasonable lodging, and medical attention. The reasonableness of such items as food, clothing, and lodging depends on the minor's earning level and the mode of living of the minor's parents.

Negligence

The failure to exercise reasonable care, thereby causing harm to another or to property.

No par stock

Corporate stock to which no par value is assigned. Before stock is issued, the directors fix a sale price per share, but that price is not stated on the stock certificate.

Nominal damages

An award given to a party whose rights have been violated but where no actual loss or damages have occurred.

Non obstante veredicto

A Latin phrase that means "notwithstanding the verdict." It is used to indicate that the court has entered a judgment contrary to the verdict of the jury. In essence, the judge has vetoed the jury's verdict.

Notary public

An appointed public officer who has the authority to administer oaths; to attest to and certify certain legal documents; and to take and certify acknowledgments of deeds, mortgages, and other such legal documents. A notary public is limited in jurisdiction to the state where he or she is appointed and in some instances to the county where he or she resides.

Novation

The substitution of a new obligation for a previous one with the understanding that the previous obligation has been discharged and terminated.

Nuisance

Any activity or use of land that is offensive, obstructs use of property, or is harmful to others.

O

Obiter dictum

Remarks by the court said in passing that are unrelated to the decision of that case.

Obligee

A person to whom an obligor owes an obligation.

Obligor

A person who owes an obligation to an obligee.

Offer

A proposal to make a contract. It is made orally, in writing, or by other conduct, and it must contain the terms legally necessary to create a contract. Acceptance of the proposal creates the contract.

Offeree

A person to whom an offer is made.

Offeror

A person who makes an offer.

Option contract

A contract to hold open an offer to buy or sell something for a certain price within a specified period of time.

Ordinances

The term used to identify the legislative enactments of a city or municipality.

P

Par stock

Shares of corporate stock that have been assigned a fixed "par value" by the articles of incorporation. The par value of one share is printed on each stock certificate.

Pari delicto

A Latin term that means "the parties are equally at fault."

Patent

A title of land given to an individual by the government, or an exclusive right given to an inventor to manufacture and sell an invention for a certain period of time.

Pawn

To pledge tangible personal property as a guarantee for payment of a debt within a certain period of time or the property will be sold.

Pecuniary

Relating to money or financial matters.

Penal damages

A monetary penalty agreed upon in a contractual clause not as compensation for actual losses but as punishment for possible nonperformance or late performance. If in fact the agreed damage amount is a penalty and not a reasonable compensation for loss, the court will not enforce the clause.

Per curiam

A Latin term that means "by the court." The entire court wrote the opinion, not just one justice.

Per se

A Latin term that means "in itself; taken alone; unconnected with other matters."

Plaintiff

A person who files a lawsuit in court.

Pledge

Pawning or giving up the possession of an item of personal property as security for a loan. For example, a person may borrow $100 from the pawnshop and leave his or her gold pocket watch as security.

Possession

Occupancy or control of personal property, land, or buildings.

Power of attorney

A writing whereby one person appoints and authorizes another person to act on his or her behalf. This power can be limited or unlimited and can be for a specified time or for life.

Preferred stock

A class of corporate stock, usually nonvoting stock, that has rights to dividends superior to those of common stock and in case of dissolution also has rights to the assets of the corporation superior to those of common stock.

Prima facie

A Latin phrase that means "on the face of it." For example, a valid driver's license in a person's possession is prima facie evidence that that person has a valid right to drive; however, this evidence could be disproved by evidence that there was a court judgment to pick up and suspend that person's license that had not yet been served upon the person.

Principal

A person who has given an agent authority to do some act or acts for him or her.

Privity

A close mutual relationship, such as that between parties to a contract.

Pro rata

A Latin phrase that means "proportionately"; in other words, to share equally.

Pro tem

A Latin phrase that means "temporarily." For example, a judge pro tem might be a judge who is sitting in temporarily for the regular judge while the regular judge is on vacation.

Probate

The term describing the legal procedure followed in the administration of the estate of deceased persons and persons under guardianship.

Promisee

A person to whom a contractual promise is made.

Promisor

A person who makes a contractual promise.

Promissory estoppel: promisee

A rule of law that is often called justifiable reliance. When the promisor makes a promise and the promise justifiably relies on that promise to his or her detriment, the promisor is estopped from denying liability on the promise.

Promoters

Person or persons who form and organize a corporation.

Proximate cause

The act or omission to act that, in a natural and continuous sequence, unbroken by an intervening cause, produces damage or injury.

Proxy

A document that authorizes another to vote for you. Stockholders who will be absent from stockholders' meetings often give their proxy to persons who will attend the meetings.

Punitive damages

Damages awarded against a person to punish him or her. These damages are in addition to compensatory damages, which pay the plaintiff for his or her actual losses. Punitive damages are often also referred to as exemplary damages because they are awarded not only to punish but to set an example for similar wrongdoers.

Q

Qualified acceptance

A conditional acceptance that modifies the terms of an offer; it is usually a counteroffer.

Quantum meruit

"As much as he deserved." When seeking compensation under common law for services rendered, this term will be used; it also can be interpreted as meaning the reasonable value of the services rendered.

Quasi-contract

The word "quasi" means resembling or somewhat like; thus, a quasi-contract is not a true contract. It resembles a contract but does not possess all the elements of a legally binding contract. The law does not allow unjust enrichment, and it provides a restitutory remedy (quasi-contract) that allows the person with a claim for damages to recover the reasonable value of the goods or services that he or she provided to the other party. Quasi-contract is often referred to as a contract implied in law.

Quit-claim deed

A deed that is intended to pass any title or interest that the grantor has in a certain tract of real estate, but does not warrant, profess, or guarantee that the grantor had any title or interest in the real estate or that his or her title was free and clear of liens.

Quo warranto

A Latin phrase that means "by what authority." It is a legal action that a government may commence to remove a person from a public office or to dissolve a corporation.

Quorum

Both incorporated and unincorporated organizations have a governing body, and a quorum is the minimum number of persons in the governing body that have to be present at a meeting to lawfully conduct the business of an organization. The usual requirement for a quorum is a majority of the persons who are eligible to vote, but a lesser number may be agreed upon in the organization's charter or bylaws.

R

Ratification

The present confirmation of a previous promise or act. In the case of a former minor, ratification is the confirmation by that person once he or she has reached the age of majority of the intention to be bound by a contract that he or she had entered into as a minor. In agency law, ratification is the confirmation by a principal of a promise or act made by his or her agent that was unauthorized at the time it was made. The ratification legalizes the previously unauthorized promise or act and creates a binding contract.

Receiver

A person or a bank or other fiduciary institution appointed by the court to receive and preserve property or funds in litigation. The receiver must have no interest in the litigation and will simply hold and manage the property or funds until directed to hand them over to whomever the court awards them.

Redemption

The repurchasing or buying back of property legally taken from a person and sold. In a mortgage foreclosure, a person's land is taken and sold by the sheriff to secure money to pay the person's debt. After the sale the owner has a limited time during which he or she can redeem the property.

Referee

In bankruptcy, this is the person who is in charge of the administration of the bankrupt's estate until the bankrupt has been discharged and the estate has been distributed among the bankrupt's creditors.

Reformation

The rewriting of a contract by the court to correct ambiguities and errors so that the contract reflects the agreement of the parties.

Release

The voluntary giving up of a claim for money or property from another person, usually for consideration.

Remedy

Action taken to enforce a right or to compensate a violation of rights.

Replevin

A legal action whereby the owner of goods can legally recover them from someone who is holding them unlawfully.

Res

A Latin word that means "the thing."

Res ipsa loquitur

A Latin phrase that means "the thing speaks for itself." For example, an airplane may explode in midair. In tort law, the heirs of the deceased passengers would normally have the burden of proving negligence on the defendant. However, it is obvious that planes do not explode unless there was negligence on someone's part. Thus, the plaintiff sues and pleads res ipsa loquitur, and the defendants must prove that they were not negligent.

Res judicata

A Latin phrase that means "the thing is settled"; that is, the case is finished.

Respondeat superior

A Latin phrase that means "let the master answer." In other words, let the employer be liable for the acts of his or her employees for damages that the employees have caused to others.

Riparian

A term that refers to the bank of a river. A riparian owner is a person who owns land on the bank of a river.

S

Scienter

The knowledge of a person making a representation that the representation he or she is making is false. In a tort action for deceit, scienter must be proved.

Seal

Under common law, an identification mark impressed in wax. Today the letters "l.s." or the word "seal" itself is used and accepted.

Security agreement

An agreement that gives a security interest in certain property to a creditor. Such an agreement must be in writing to be enforced.

Security interest

An interest in a specific item of personal property that a creditor retains to secure the payment of a debt.

Setoff

A claim that a defendant has against a plaintiff; similar to a counterclaim. For example, if the plaintiff sued the defendant for $100 but owed the defendant $50, the plaintiff's $50 debt to the defendant would be a set off and the balance owed by the defendant to the plaintiff would be only $50.

Severable contract

A contract divisible into separate parts; a default of one section does not invalidate the whole contract.

Shareholder

A person who owns a portion of the capital stock of a corporation. The shareholder's interest in the corporation is evidenced by a stock certificate.

Shop right

The employer's right to use, without paying royalties, any invention that an employee developed while using the employer's facilities or any invention that the employee conceived in the course of the employee's employment with the employer. An employee who is hired to do research and development agrees by contract that the employer will own the employee's inventions and discoveries as that is what such an employee would be getting paid for.

Situs

The location of a thing. All tangible property has a situs.

Slander

Defamatory statements orally made by one person that injure the reputation of another person.

Specific performance

A remedy by which a court of equity orders a person to perform in accordance with the terms of his or her contract.

Stare decisis

A Latin phrase that means "to abide by." This phrase is also defined as "let the decision stand." Once a case has set a precedent, courts will follow that precedent wherever it is feasible to do so. However, law must change as technology and mores change; thus, no precedent is cast in concrete.

Status quo

A Latin phrase that means "the state of things at any given time."

Statute of limitations

A statute that sets limits to the time in which a lawsuit may be filed in certain causes of action. For example, a tort lawsuit must be filed within 2 years from the day the wrongful act was committed, and if it was not filed by that time, the action is forever barred.

Subpoena

A legal process from a court ordering a witness to appear and testify or ordering a witness to produce certain documents for the court's inspection.

Subrogation

The act of substituting one person for another to prosecute a lawful claim. In insurance, the insurance company pays the collision loss to your automobile, and you give the company subrogation rights to sue and collect from the person who negligently damaged your automobile.

Substantive law

The law that is concerned with the rights and duties of the parties, as contrasted with procedural law, which is concerned with the procedure to be followed in the litigation.

Sui generis

One of a kind, unique.

Summons

A writ to appear in court in defense of a civil action.

Surety

A person who binds himself or herself with another person, called the principal, for the payment of money or the performance of some obligation. However, the principal is already bound to that payment or obligation and the surety serves as a backup person who is available in case the principal does not pay or perform properly.

T

Tangible property: touched—a tract

Property that can be touched, for example, a tract of land, a chair, a table, etc. Intangible property, on the other hand, is property that cannot be touched, such as the ownership of a patent right or of corporate stock and other such ownerships of rights, not things.

Tenancy

The leasing or renting of land or property, giving certain ownership rights to the tenant.

Tender

An offer to settle or perform an obligation in contract. If a party offers to perform his or her obligation under a contract, such an offer is called a tender. If the other party unjustifiably refuses to accept the performance offered, that party would be guilty of breach of contract.

Testimony

Witnesses' answers given under oath as evidence.

Third-party beneficiary

A person who was not a party to a contract but a party to whom the contracting parties intended benefits to be given.

Torrens system

A system of land registration developed by Sir Robert Torrens in Australia in 1858. This system has been adopted in some jurisdictions in the United States.

Tort

A civil wrong for which civil damages may be awarded, as contrasted with a criminal wrong for which punishment may be given. A wrongful act may be both a tort and a crime.

Trade fixtures

Personal property that has been attached to land or a building and is necessary for conducting a trade.

Trade name

A name under which a particular business operates.

Trademark

A distinctive mark or emblem that a manufacturer prints on or affixes to goods so that consumers can identify the manufacturer's goods in the marketplace.

Trespass

Although most commonly used to refer to a person's unauthorized entry onto another person's real property, in its broadest sense this term refers to any intentional injury or damage caused by force to either the person or the property of another.

Trover

A common law "form of action" to recover damages for the wrongful withholding of personal property, which had been "lost," and is in the possession of the defendant, who refuses to return it.

Trust

A transfer of property or money to one party to be held for the benefit of another.

U

Ultra vires

A Latin phrase that means "beyond the powers of," or beyond the scope of authority. An ultra vires act is an act that is not within the powers of the person who does it.

Unconscionability

Conduct by a party to a contract that cannot be shown to be fraud and is not duress but is unjust and unfair and because of which the court will not enforce performance of the contract.

Undue influence

A condition that results from the use of unfair persuasion by one person to overcome the free will of another person and to influence that person to act in the manner in which he or she is directed to act.

Usury

The charging of an unlawful rate of interest.

V

Valid

Legally sufficient and binding.

Verdict

A jury's decision given to the court.

Vest

To take effect. To vest a right is to give a right to a present or future benefit. The term "vest" is used in pension law. One's rights in a pension plan will be vested after certain minimum requirements have been met.

Void

No legal effect; not binding. If an agreement is void, it is legally unenforceable.

Voidable

A term that means a contract is not void but can be avoided by one or both of the parties at their will. A contract between a minor and an adult is voidable by the minor only; a contract between two minors can be avoided by either minor.

W

Waiver

The voluntary relinquishment by a person of a right that person has.

Warehouse receipt

A written acknowledgment of the receipt of goods by a person engaged in the business of storing goods for hire.

Warranty

In the sale of goods, a promise or guarantee by the seller that goods have certain qualities or that the seller has title to the goods. A warranty may be offered by the seller as a contractual term, or a warranty not stated in the contract may be imposed by law. The warranties imposed by law are the warranty of merchantability and the warranty of fitness for purpose. The warranty of merchantability warrants that the goods are of at least fair or average quality. The warranty of fitness for purpose warrants that the goods are fit for the particular purpose of the buyer.

Watered stock

Par value stock that is issued by a corporation as fully paid up stock when in fact the whole amount of the par value has not been paid in.

Writ

A written document issued by a court, directed to a sheriff or some other officer of the law, and ordering that person to carry out a command of the court. For example, a writ of attachment orders a sheriff to attach certain property and hold it for disposition by the court.

X-Y-Z

Zoning

The process of separating the areas of a city or county by confining them to particular uses, such as residential use, industrial use, or business use.

Index of Cases

H

I

J

K

L

M

N

O

P

R

S

T

U

W

Z

Index

E

F

G

H

I

J

K

L

M

N

O

P

Q

R

S

T

Z